706

MEDIEVAL ISLAMIC CIVILIZATION

AN ENCYCLOPEDIA

Volume 1
A – K
INDEX

MEDIEVAL ISLAMIC CIVILIZATION

AN ENCYCLOPEDIA

Volume 1

A – K

INDEX

Josef W. Meri

Editor

Routledge
Taylor & Francis Group
New York   London

Published in 2006 by
Routledge
Taylor & Francis Group
270 Madison Avenue
New York, NY 10016

Published in Great Britain by
Routledge
Taylor & Francis Group
2 Park Square
Milton Park, Abingdon
Oxon OX14 4RN

Printed in the United States of America on acid-free paper
10 9 8 7 6 5 4 3 2 1

International Standard Book Number-10: 0-415-96691-4 (Vol 1), 0-415-96692-2 (Vol 2), 0-415-96690-6 (Set)
International Standard Book Number-13: 978-0-415-96691-7 (Vol 1), 978-0-415-96692-4 (Vol 2), 978-0-415-96690-0 (Set)
Library of Congress Card Number 2005044229

Library of Congress Cataloging-in-Publication Data

Medieval Islamic civilization : an encyclopedia / Josef W. Meri, editor ; advisory board, Jere L. Bacharach ... [et al.].
    p. cm.
    Includes bibliographical references and index.
    ISBN 0-415-96691-4 (v. 1 : alk. paper) -- ISBN 0-415-96692-2 (v. 2 : alk. paper) -- ISBN 0-415-96690-6 (set : alk. paper)
    1. Civilization, Islamic--Encyclopedias. 2. Islamic Empire--Civilization--Encyclopedias. I. Meri, Josef W. II. Bacharach, Jere L., 1938-

DS36.85.M434 2005
909'.09767'003--dc22   2005044229

Taylor & Francis Group is the Academic Division of T&F Informa plc.

Visit the Taylor & Francis Web site at
http://www.taylorandfrancis.com

and the Routledge Web site at
http://www.routledge-ny.com

CONTENTS

MAPS

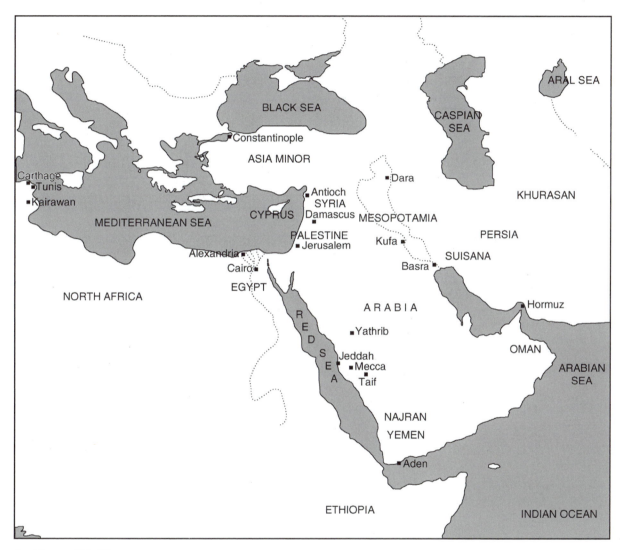

Arabia, ca. 600 CE

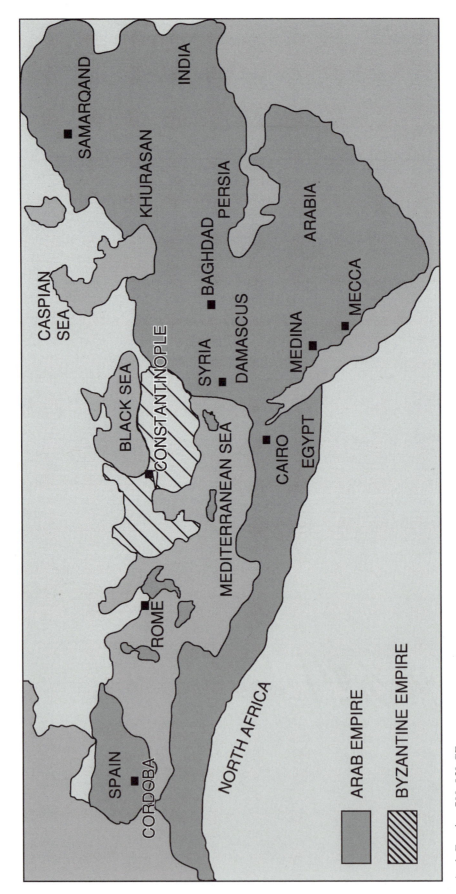

Arab Empire, 700–850 CE

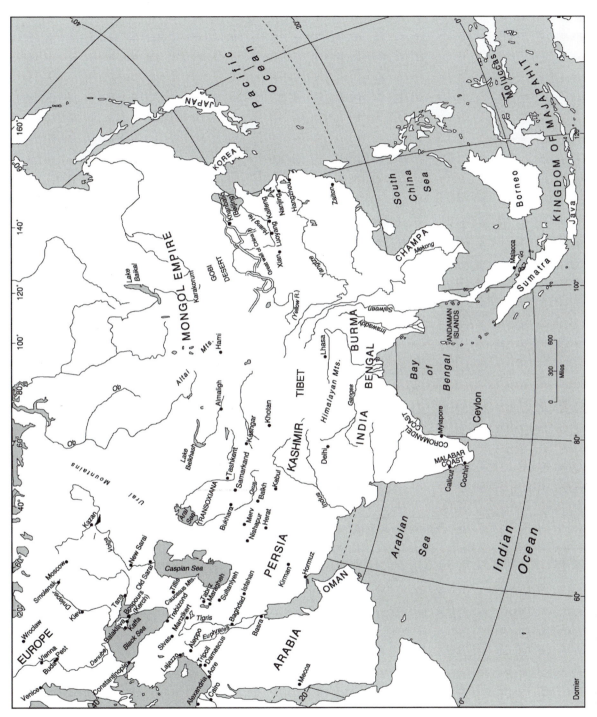

Asia, 1211–1239 CE

INTRODUCTION

The study of Islam as a religion and the languages of the Middle East, especially Arabic and Persian, has gained in prominence. In the West, a common misperception exists that there is something intrinsic in Islam as a religion that engenders acts of violence and terrorism and that Islamics history is replete with instances of pogroms against non-Muslims. On the contrary, the origin of violent acts lies not in the ontology of any given religion whether Islam, Judaism, or Christianity, in any given Scripture whether the Qur'an, Torah, or Bible, or in any given civilization whether Islamic, Greek, or Roman, but rather in a number of factors, including the psychology of human behavior and the often desperate and trying human conditions that compel humans to carry out desperate acts in times of war and peace, sometimes in the name of religion. The historian of any civilization or historical epoch is keenly aware that no premodern (medieval) society was left unscathed by warfare and political conflicts. Lamentably, until now the paucity of easily accessible English language reference sources about the medieval Islamic world has led to a situation in which some discourses concerning the clash of civilizations, current affairs, and modern ideologies and nationalisms have become synonymous with the whole of Islamic civilization. By contrast, the scholar is able to communicate the defining characteristics of a civilization and is moreover, able to critically understand and engage the Islamic world on its own terms—as heir to one of the world's greatest civilizations, not simply as heir to a world religion whose adherents have historically been in conflict with adherents of other faiths.

Despite increased and indeed, highly successful efforts in the academy to teach about Islam as a religion and the Arabic language, the larger civilizational contextual framework of which both are a part is often ignored and marginalized. Medieval Islamic civilization left an indelible mark on Europe in the transmission of knowledge and ideas in such diverse fields as science, medicine, mathematics, literature, and philosophy.

Medieval Islamic Civilization: An Encyclopedia represents a collaborative effort at bridging the gap between that which we perceive Islam and Islamic civilization to be about and what it really is by providing the reader with an easily accessible reference work presented in a concise language.

Such fundamental questions as to what Islamic civilization is and what Muslims did to contribute to European understanding of the sciences, mathematics, arts, literature, philosophy, and government remain largely unanswered. What was the nature of "interfaith" relations in the Islamic world, and what roles did Jews and Christians play in medieval Islamic societies? As a number of the entries highlight, Jews and Christians attained prominent government posts under various Islamic dynasties from Andalusia and Egypt to Iraq and contributed to the preservation and translation of philosophical and theological texts from Greek, Syriac, and Hebrew into Arabic and other Islamic languages, as well as to the creation of new literary and cultural syntheses borne of a common Islamic cultural milieu. These are among the themes that the entries in this work seek to explore. It is our hope that this work will go a long way toward filling the gaps in knowledge.

Audience

The English-speaking world lacks a single reference work that presents Islamic civilization in a manner intelligible to the nonspecialist. Specialist reference works are numerous and offer more detailed and technical articles about various aspects of Islam from pre-Islamic times to the present. The nonspecialist who desires to understand Islamic civilization is left with few choices except to consult general reference works or works devoted to the European Middle Ages, which only give a fragmented picture of medieval Islamic civilization.

It is to be hoped that the nonspecialist reader, as well as university and secondary school students and teachers, will benefit from this work.

Conception and Genesis

Medieval Islamic Civilization was conceived to share our knowledge as experts in the field of Islamic history and civilization and to correct the misconceptions and misinformation that exist. This impetus encouraged me to take up the challenge of helping to produce a unique reference work. However, it must be emphasized that this is very much an international collaborative effort that includes contributions by leading experts in their fields from North America, Europe, and Asia. Contributors come from various academic backgrounds and employ a diversity of approaches. Each of the entries adopts a unique approach to a given topic and is written dispassionately without regard to current political exigencies or political considerations. *Medieval Islamic Civilization* presents cutting-edge research into such pivotal themes relating to daily life, the ethnic and religious communities of the Islamic world, their beliefs and practices, interfaith relations, popular culture and religion, cultural, economic, and political contacts and exchanges with Europe and Asia, learning and universities, and travel and exploration. It provides a comprehensive portrait of the artistic, intellectual, literary, medical, and scientific achievements of Muslims, Jews, Christians, and others who contributed to the flourishing of one of the greatest civilizations known to humankind. Most of the authors are the leading international experts in their field. Yet all the contributions represent the highest standards in scholarship on the Islamic world.

Choice of Entries

While it is impossible to discuss every facet of Islamic civilization in a two-volume reference—nonspecialist encyclopedias are selective by nature—the choice of entries reflects the diversity of the subjects that are covered herein. The editorial board discussed the entries extensively, and certain additions and emendations were made to compensate for underrepresented themes. Unlike other volumes in this highly acclaimed Routledge series on the Middle Ages that are more geographically specific and are focused on the European Middle Ages from the fifth through sixteenth centuries CE, *Medieval Islamic Civilization* posed a considerable challenge given the geographical expanse of the Islamic world, from the Iberian Peninsula and North Africa to the Middle East, South and Southeast Asia from roughly the sixth through seventeenth centuries. Unlike other reference works, *Medieval Islamic Civilization* has de-emphasized historical themes in favor of an original synthesis that gives greater prominence to aspects of daily life and to the non-Arab elements of Islamic civilization.

The Islamic Middle Ages is taken to represent the period from 622 CE, or the first year of the Hijra of the Prophet Muhammad to Medina, which also marks the first year of the Islamic calendar, though we have also included entries that deal with pre-Islamic themes, peoples, and societies down until the seventeenth century in the case of Southeast Asia, where no significant written records exist for earlier periods.

Indeed, the seventeenth and early eighteenth centuries represent the most significant period for written records in Southeast Asia. However, this demarcation is somewhat arbitrary. Indeed, it may be argued that certain continuities existed in Islamic civilization down until the advent of modern secular and national ideologies in the nineteenth century CE.

Acknowledgments

The Board is pleased that so many of our colleagues from around the world recognized the value of *Medieval Islamic Civilization* as not simply another reference work and so enthusiastically answered the call to contribute. We are especially grateful for their inspiring level of commitment and dedication to this initiative and their high-quality contributions.

I would also like to thank the advisory board members for their unstinting dedication, the associate editors Julia Bray and Lutz Richter-Bernburg for expending considerable efforts in commenting on and suggesting revisions to various entries, and to Jere Bacharach for his overall invaluable contributions to *Medieval Islamic Civilization*. I am also grateful to Asma Afsaruddin and Donald Whitcomb for their recommendations. I am especially grateful to the former for agreeing to write a number of significant entries.

This work would not have been possible without the indefatigable efforts and abiding enthusiasm of the editors and publishers at Routledge, in particular Marie-Claire Antoine and Jamie Ehrlich. Also, thanks to the various Routledge staff members who were involved in the early stages of the project.

Finally, it is only fitting that I should pen these words from the Middle East after last having lived here nearly eight years ago.

Josef (Yousef) Waleed Meri
Amman, Jordan

MEDIEVAL SERIES NOTE

The Routledge Encyclopedias of the Middle Ages

Formerly the Garland Encyclopedias of the Middle Ages, this comprehensive series began in 1993 with the publication of *Medieval Scandinavia*. A major enterprise in medieval scholarship, the series brings the expertise of scholars specializing in myriad aspects of the medieval world together in a reference source accessible to students and the general public, as well as to historians and scholars in related fields. Each volume focuses on a geographical area or theme important to medieval studies and is edited by a specialist in that field, who has called upon a board of consulting editors to establish the article list and review the articles. Each article is contributed by a scholar and followed by a bibliography and cross-references to guide further research.

Routledge is proud to carry on the tradition established by the first volumes in this important series. As the series continues to grow, we hope that it will provide the most comprehensive and detailed view of the medieval world in all its aspects ever presented in encyclopedia form.

The present volume, *Medieval Islamic Civilization: An Encyclopedia*, edited by Josef W. Meri, is Volume 13 in the series.

EDITOR

CONTRIBUTORS

Rachid Aadnani
Wellesley College

Asma Afsaruddin
University of Notre Dame

Roger Allen
University of Pennsylvania

Adel Allouche
Yale University

Ilai Alon
Tel Aviv University and University of Chicago

Suat Alp
Hacettepe University

Zumrut Alp
Istanbul Bilgi University

Joseph P. Amar
University of Notre Dame

Mohammad Ali Amir-Moezzi
Université de Paris-Sorbonne

Reuven Amitai
Hebrew University of Jerusalem

Glaire D. Anderson
Massachusetts Institute of Technology

Ali Asani
Harvard University

Mahmut Ay
Ankara University

Sussan Babaie
University of Michigan

Patricia L. Baker
Independent Scholar

Anne K. Bang
University of Bergen

Meir M. Bar-Asher
Hebrew University of Jerusalem

Carol Bargeron
Texas State University

Cedric Barnes
University of London

Doris Behrens-Abouseif
University of London

Persis Berlekamp
University of Texas, Austin

Lutz Richter-Bernburg
University of Tubingen

Zvi Aziz Ben-Dor
New York University

Thierry Bianquis
University of Lyon

Hans Hinrich Biesterfeldt
Ruhr-Universität Bochum

Michal Biran
Hebrew University of Jerusalem

Nader El-Bizri
Institute of Ismaili Studies

Khalid Yahya Blankinship
Temple University

Jonathan M. Bloom
Boston College

Michel Boivin
EHESS/CNRS, Paris

CONTRIBUTORS

Stuart J. Borsch
Assumption College

Ross Brann
Cornell University

Julia Bray
University of Paris, St. Denis

William M. Brinner
University of California, Berkeley

Sebastian Brock
University of Oxford

Rainer Brunner
Universität Freiburg

Richard W. Bulliet
Columbia University

Birsen Bulmus
Georgetown University

Charles E. Butterworth
University of Maryland

Amila Buturovic
York University

Carmen Caballero-Navas
University College London

Pierre J. Cachia
Columbia University

Giovanni Canova
Universita di Napoli

Stefano Carboni
Metropolitan Museum of Art

Michael G. Carter
University of Oslo

Paola Carusi
Università degli Studi di Roma

Brian A. Catlos
University of California, Santa Cruz

Driss Cherkaoui
College of William and Mary

Jamsheed Choksy
Indiana University

Aboubakr Chraibi
Institut National des Langues et Civilisations, Paris

Niall Christie
University of British Columbia

Paul M. Cobb
University of Notre Dame

Mark R. Cohen
Princeton University

David Cook
Rice University

Michael Cooperson
University of California, Los Angeles

Farhad Daftary
Institute of Ismaili Studies

Touraj Daryaee
California State University, Fullerton

Olga M. Davidson
Harvard University

Richard Davis
Ohio State University

Cristina de la Puente
Institute of Philology, CSIC, Madrid

Jesus De Prado Plumed
Universidad Complutense, Madrid

Jonathan P. Decter
Brandeis University

Khalid Dhorat
Dar-al Salam Islamic Center

Eerik Dickinson
Hebrew University of Jerusalem

Amikam Elad
Hebrew University of Jerusalem

Alexander E. Elinson
Queens College, City University of New York

Amira El-Zein
Tufts University

Gerhard Endress
Ruhr-Universität Bochum

Daphna Ephrat
Open University of Israel

Muhammad H. Fadel
Independent Scholar

Rizwi Faizer
Independent Scholar

Sunni M. Fass
Indiana University

Paul B. Fenton
Université de Paris-Sorbonne

Maribel Fierro
Institute of Philology, CSIC, Madrid

Reuven Firestone
Hebrew Union College

Finbarr Barry Flood
New York University

Daniel Frank
Ohio State University

Yehoshua Frenkel
University of Haifa

Bruce Fudge
New York University

Adam Gacek
McGill University

Roland-Pierre Gayraud
Le Laboratoire d'Archéologie Médiévale Méditerranéenne

Eric Geoffroy
Université Marc Bloch

Kambiz GhaneaBassiri
Reed College

Antonella Ghersetti
Università Ca' Foscari

Claude Gilliot
University of Aix-en-Provence

Robert Gleave
University of Bristol

Valerie Gonzalez
Clark University

Matthew S. Gordon
Miami University

William Granara
Harvard University

Frank Griffel
Yale University

Christiane Gruber
University of Pennsylvania

Beatrice Gruendler
Yale University

Li Guo
University of Notre Dame

Kim Haines-Eitzen
Cornell University

Leor Halevi
Texas A&M University

Philip Halldén
Lund University

Abbas Hamdani
University of Wisconsin, Milwaukee

Marlé Hammond
University of Oxford

Andras Hamori
Princeton University

Eric Hanne
Florida Atlantic University

Tilman Hannemann
Universität Bremen

Gerald R. Hawting
University of London

CONTRIBUTORS

Bernard Haykel
New York University

Gisela Helmecke
Staatliche Museem zu Berlin

Konrad Hirschler
Universität Kiel

Jan P. Hogendijk
University of Utrecht

Livnat Holtzman
Bar-Ilan University

Th. Emil Homerin
University of Rochester

James Howard-Johnston
University of Oxford

Rachel T. Howes
*California State University,
Northridge*

Qamar-ul Huda
Boston College

Colin Imber
University of Manchester

Tariq al-Jamil
North Carolina State University

Jan Jansen
Universiteit Leiden

Steven C. Judd
Southern Connecticut State University

Yuka Kadoi
University of Edinburgh

Hossein Kamaly
Columbia University

Ahmad Karimi-Hakkak
University of Maryland

Hassan Khalilieh
University of Haifa

Nurten Kilic-Schubel
Kenyon College

Hilary Kilpatrick
University of Zurich

Leah Kinberg
Tel Aviv University

David A. King
Johann Wolfgang Goethe University

Verena Klemm
University of Leipzig

Alexander Knysh
University of Michigan

Philip G. Kreyenbroek
University of Göttingen

Kathryn Kueny
Lawrence University

Scott A. Kugle
Swarthmore College

Michael Laffan
Princeton University

Arzina R. Lalani
Institute of Ismaili Studies

Ruth Lamdan
Tel Aviv University

Hermann Landolt
Institute of Ismaili Studies

George Lane
University of London

Margaret Larkin
University of California, Berkeley

Gary Leiser
Independent Scholar

Judith Lerner
Independent Art Historian

P. Lettinck
*International Institute for Islamic Thought and
Civilization, Kuala Lumpur*

Yaacov Lev
Bar-Ilon University

Keith Lewinstein
Bridgewater State College

Joseph E. Lowry
University of Pennsylvania

Scott C. Lucas
University of Arizona

Al-Husein N. Madhany
University of Chicago

Roxani Eleni Margariti
Emory University

Louise Marlow
Wellesley College

Andrew Marsham
University of Cambridge

Ulrich Marzolph
Enzyklopädie des Märchens

Christopher Melchert
University of Cambridge

John L. Meloy
American University of Beirut

Charles P. Melville
University of Cambridge

Josef W. Meri
Aal al-Bayt Foundation for Islamic Thought

Alan Mikhail
University of California, Berkeley

Isabel Miller
Institute of Ismaili Studies

Colin Paul Mitchell
Dalhousie University

Jawid Mojaddedi
Rutgers University

James E. Montgomery
University of Cambridge

Shmuel Moreh
Hebrew University of Jerusalem

Michael G. Morony
University of California, Los Angeles

David Morray
University College, Dublin

Robert Morrison
Whitman College

Suleiman A. Mourad
Middlebury College

Hasan M. al-Naboodah
United Arab Emirates University

Azim Nanji
Institute of Ismaili Studies

John A. Nawas
Katholieke Universiteit Leuven

Angelika Neuwirth
Freie Universität Berlin

Andrew J. Newman
University of Edinburgh

Mehri Niknam
The Maimonides Foundation

York Allan Norman
Georgetown University

Alastair Northedge
Université de Paris-Sorbonne

Erik S. Ohlander
Indiana University/Purdue University, Fort Wayne

Mehmet Sait Özervarli
Center for Islamic Studies, Istanbul

Oya Pancaroglu
University of Oxford

Irmeli Perho
Finnish Institute in the Middle East

Andrew Petersen
United Arab Emirates University

Daniel C. Peterson
Brigham Young University

CONTRIBUTORS

Karen Pinto
American University of Beirut

Peter E. Pormann
University of London

Venetia Porter
The British Museum

David Stephan Powers
Cornell University

Tahera Qutbuddin
University of Chicago

Intisar Rabb
Yale University

Babak Rahimi
University of California, San Diego

Leonhard E. Reis
Österreichische Akademie der Wissenschaften

Gabriel Said Reynolds
University of Notre Dame

Lutz Richter-Bernburg
Universität Tübingen

Sajjad H. Rizvi
University of Exeter

Cynthia Robinson
Cornell University

James I. Robinson
University of Chicago

Michael J. Rogers
The Nour Foundation

Leyla Rouhi
Williams College

David J. Roxburgh
Harvard University

D. Fairchild Ruggles
University of Ilinois, Urbana-Champaign

Adam Sabra
Western Michigan University

Noha Sadek
Institut Francais du Proche Orient

Marlis J. Saleh
University of Chicago

Walid Saleh
University of Toronto

Paula Sanders
Rice University

Nil Sari
Istanbul Universitesi

Huseyin Sarioglu
Istanbul Universitesi

Mufit Selim Saruhan
University of Ankara

Tsugitaka Sato
University of Tokyo

Sara Scalenghe
Georgetown University

Sabine Schmidtke
Freie Universität Berlin

Fred Scholz
Freie Universität Berlin

Warren C. Schultz
DePaul University

Stuart D. Sears
Roger Williams University

Recep Senturk
Center for Islamic Studies, Istanbul

Delfina Serrano Ruano
Institute of Philology, CSIC, Madrid

Mustafa Shah
University of London

Reza Shah-Kazemi
Institute of Ismaili Studies

Ayman Shihadeh
University of Glasgow

Boaz Shoshan
Ben-Gurion University of the Nagrev

Kemal Silay
Indiana University

Adam Silverstein
University of Cambridge

John Masson Smith
University of California, Berkeley

Pieter Smoor
Universiteit van Amsterdam

Manu P. Sobti
*Georgia Institute of Technology and Southern
Polytechnic State University*

Jochen Sokoly
*Virginia Commonwealth University School of
the Arts, Qatar*

Bruna Soravia
Luiss University

Denise A. Spellberg
University of Texas, Austin

Peter Starr
Living Human Heritage, Zurich

Devin J. Stewart
Emory University

Paula R. Stiles
University of St. Andrews

Norman A. Stillman
University of Oklahoma

Ian B. Straughn
University of Chicago

Gotthard Strohmaier
Freie Universität Berlin

Sarah Stroumsa
Hebrew University of Jerusalem

Fahmida Suleman
Institute of Ismaili Studies

Mark N. Swanson
Luther Seminary

Samy Swayd
San Diego State University

Richard C. Taylor
Marquette University

Baki Tezcan
University of California, Davis

Marina A. Tolmacheva
Washington State University

Shawkat M. Toorawa
Cornell University

Houari Touati
EHESS, Paris

Alain Touwaide
Smithsonian National Museum of History

William F. Tucker
University of Arkansas

Richard Turnbull
Fashion Institute of Technology

John P. Turner
Kennesaw State University

Geert Jan van Gelder
University of Oxford

Maria Jesus Viguera-Molins
*Universidad Complutense,
Madrid*

Knut S. Vikør
University of Bergen

Paul E. Walker
University of Chicago

Seth Ward
University of Wyoming

Rachel Ward
The British Museum

Anthony Welch
*University of Victoria,
British Columbia*

Brannon Wheeler
University of Washington

CONTRIBUTORS

Clare E. Wilde
Georgetown University

Stéfan Winter
Université du Québec à Montréal

Jonathan David Wyrtzen
Georgetown University

Huseyin Yazici
Istanbul Universitesi

Yetkin Yildirim
University of Texas, Austin

Netice Yildiz
Eastern Mediterranean University

Douglas Young
Stanford University

Hayrettin Yucesoy
Saint Louis University

Homayra Ziad
Yale University

LIST OF ENTRIES A TO Z

THEMATIC LIST OF ENTRIES

Agriculture, Animal Husbandry, and Hunting

Agriculture
Animal Husbandry
Aqueducts
Camels
Horticulture
Hunting
Nomadism and Pastoralism
Sedentarism

Arts and Architecture

Agra Red Fort
Alhambra
Aqsa Mosque
Architecture, Secular—Military
Architecture, Secular—Palaces
Aya Sophia
Badshahi Mosque, Lahore
Baths and Bathing
Beauty and Aesthetics
Books
Carpets
Ceramics
Dome of the Rock
Furniture and Furnishings
Gardens and Gardening
Glassware
Houses
Jewelry
Madrasa
Metalwork
Mosaics
Mosque of Ibn Tulun, Cairo
Mosques
Music
Musical Instruments
Painting, Miniature
Painting, Monumental and Frescoes

Paper Manufacture
Performing Artists
Poetry
Qutb Minar
Sculpture
Selimiye Mosque, Edirne
Shadow Plays
Shahnama
Sinan
Singing
Süleymaniye Mosque
Sunni Revival
Taj Mahal
Talismans and Talismanic Objects
Textiles
Theater
Umayyad Mosque, Damascus
Urbanism
Women, Patrons
Ziryab

Commerce and Economy

Cartography
Chess
Credit
Land Tenure and Ownership, or Iqta‘
Markets
Merchants, Jewish
Merchants, Muslim
Minerals
Mining
Money Changers
Navigation
Road Networks
Ships and Shipbuilding
Silk Roads
Slaves and Slave Trade, Eastern Islamic World
Slaves and Slave Trade, Western Islamic World
Spices
Technology, Mills, Water, and Wind

Geography

History and Historical Concepts

Language

Sibawayh
Syriac
Turkish and Turkic Languages
Urdu

Law and Jurisprudence

Abu Hanifa
Adultery
Apostasy
Bukhari, al-
Commanding Good and Forbidding Evil
Constitution of Medina
Consultation, or Shura
Crime and Punishment
Customary Law
Disability
Divorce
Ethics
Heresy and Heretics
Idolatry
Ibn Hanbal
Inheritance
Ja'far al-Sadiq
Judges
Land Tenure and Ownership
Law and Jurisprudence
Maimonides
Malik ibn Anas
Marriage, Islamic
Marriage, Jewish
Mawardi, al-
Muhammad al-Baqir
Muslim ibn al-Hajjaj
Prisons
Reform, or Islah
Renewal (Tajdid)
Schools of Jurisprudence
Sa'adyah Gaon
Schools of Jurisprudence
Shafi'i, al-
Shari'a
Shawkani, al-
Shi'ism
Usury and Interest
Waqf
Zaydis

Learning

Azhar, al-
Degrees, or Ijaza

Education, Islamic
Education, Jewish
Humanism
Libraries
Madrasa
Manuscripts
Primary Schools, or Kuttab
Scholarship
Seeking Knowledge
Translation, Arabic to Hebrew
Translation, Arabic to Persian
Translation, Pre-Islamic Learning into Arabic

Literature

Adab
Amir Khusraw
'Antara ibn Shaddad
'Attar, Farid al-Din
Autobiographical Writings
Biography and Biographical Works
Decadence
Elegy
Epic Poetry
Epics, Arabic
Epics, Persian
Epics, Turkish
European Literature, Perception of Islam
Excellences Literature
Ferdowsi
Folk Literature, Arabic
Folk Literature, Persian
Folk Literature, Turkish
Foreigners
Hafsa bint al-Hajj al-Rukuniyya
   (Andalusian Poetess)
Harizi, Judah, al-
Humor
Ibn Gabirol
Ibn Hamdis
Ibn al-Muqaffa
Ibn Naghrela, Samuel
Ibn Qutayba
Ibn Quzman
Ibn Sa'd
Ibn Shahin, Nissim ben Jacob
Jahiz, al-
Jami
Judah ha-Levi
Jurjani, Al-
Kalila wa Dimna
Love poetry
Maqama

Razi, al-, or Rhazes
Razia Sultana
Sa'adyah Gaon
Saladin, or Salah al-Din
Salman al-Farisi
Shafi'i, al-
Shah Abbas
Shajar al-Durr
Shawkani, al-
Shirazi, al-, Sadr al-Din
Sibawayh
Sibt ibn al-Jawzi
Sinan
Sirhindi, Ahmad
Suhrawardi, al-, Shihab al-Din 'Umar
Sunni 'Ali
Tabari, al-
Tamerlane, or Timur
Tawhidi, al-, Abu 'l-Hayyan
Tusi, al-, Nasir al-Din
'Umar ibn 'Abd al-'Aziz
'Umar ibn al-Farid
'Umar ibn al-Khattab
Usama ibn Munqidh
'Uthman ibn 'Affan
Waqidi, al-
Ya'qub ibn Killis
Yaqut
Zayd ibn Thabit
Ziryab

Peoples

Arabs
Aramaeans
Berbers
Circassians
Copts
Jews
Kurds
Mongols
Persians
Turks

Philosophy and Thought

Amuli, al-
Aristotle and Aristotelianism
Brethren of Purity
Freethinkers
Gnosis
Kirmani, al-, Hamid al-Din

Ibn al-Rawandi
Ibn Rushd
Ibn Sina
Ibn Tufayl
Ibn Zur'a
Illuminationism
Farabi, al- (Alfarabius or Avennasar)
Kindi, al-
Maimonides
Mu'ayyad fi al-Din, Al-
Mulla Sadra
Plato, Platonism, and Neoplatonism
Philosophy
Razi, al-, or Rhazes
Shirazi, al-, Sadr al-Din
Tawhidi, al-, Abu Hayyan
Tusi, al-, Muhammad ibn Hasan
Time, Notions of

Places and Place Study

Abyssinia
Aden
Aleppo
Alexandria
Andalus
Arabia
Baghdad
Bahrain
Balkans
Basra
Bijapur
Brunei
Bukhara
Cairo
Central Asia, History
China
Cordoba
Cyprus
Damascus
Egypt
Fez
Fustat
Ghana
Gibraltar
Granada
Hebron
Herat
India
Isfahan
Istanbul
Java
Jerusalem

Professions, Groups, and Societies

Religion and Theology

A

'ABBASIDS

The 'Abbasid Dynasty (r. 750–1258) came to power after a revolution (747–750) that resulted in the over-throwing of the Syrian-based Umayyad dynasty (r. 661–750). Scholars have divided the period of 'Abbasid rule into two main eras: (1) 750–945, the "Golden Age" of 'Abbasid rule and the beginning of its decline; and (2) 945–1258, the period after the 'Abbasids' loss of autonomy to regional warlord dynasties and ending with the Mongol execution of the last 'Abbasid caliph in 1258. This division, which is largely artificial in nature, has affected the nature of the modern study of the 'Abbasids, with the majority of work being done on the earlier period of 'Abbasid rule.

Taking their name from an uncle of the Prophet (i.e., al-'Abbas), the 'Abbasids sought legitimacy for both the revolution and their subsequent rule by emphasizing their family lineage to the Prophet and the alleged transference of authority to their family line by a descendant of 'Ali b. Abi Talib. Supporters of the 'Abbasid dynasty argued that the 'Abbasids were part of a literal revolution (dawla) in the sense that the 'Abbasid Caliphate would bring the Islamic community back full circle to its earlier mores as found during the time of the Prophet and the four Rightly Guided Caliphs. Rather than ruling as an elitist Arab dynasty (a crime of which they accused the Umayyads), the 'Abbasids sought to govern in a more universal fashion as symbols of a unified Sunni community. To that end, the 'Abbasid caliphs used honorific titles (laqab/pl. alqab) such as *al-Mahdi,*

al-Ma'mun, and *al-Qadir* to denote their links to Allah, and they adopted the title *al-Imam* in addition to the traditional titles of *Caliph* and *Commander of the Faithful.* Another change from the Umayyad period was that Persian culture (i.e., political, literary, and personnel) was more fully integrated into 'Abbasid society; a key example was the central role played by the Persian Barmakid family of viziers during the early 'Abbasid government. Modern scholars continue to debate the nature of the 'Abbasid revolution and the later 'Abbasid rule, focusing on such issues as the ethnolinguistic and regional backgrounds of those that fought for the 'Abbasid cause (the abna' al-dawla); later disputes about the role of the caliphs in determining correct belief; and the nature of the Islamic polity in light of the loss of 'Abbasid autonomy to regional powers starting in the tenth century.

During the decades after the revolution, the 'Abbasids successfully consolidated and strengthened their control over their lands. Al-Mansur (r. 754–775) was instrumental during these early years in two distinct ways: (1) he removed any potential/actual rivals to 'Abbasid rule through direct assassination and/or putting down localized revolts; and (2) he founded Baghdad as the new capital city for the 'Abbasids in central Iraq. Baghdad soon became the economic, cultural, and intellectual locus of the Muslim world, with the caliphs and their viziers patronizing scholars and promoting the vast translation efforts that integrated works from the ancient world and surrounding cultures into the larger Islamic consciousness. This cultural flowering built upon earlier developments in Islamic theology and law, and it laid the foundation for developments in Islamic philosophy and mysticism as well as advances in the natural sciences (e.g., optics, medicine, chemistry). Over time, Baghdad would become a conduit for scholarship and the exchange of ideas throughout Muslim lands.

In the ninth century, the 'Abbasids began to face problems on a variety of fronts, all of which hampered their ability to rule effectively. A disastrous civil war between two brothers, al-Amin (r. 809–813) and al-Ma'mun (r. 813–833), over the succession to the Caliphate highlighted the weaknesses inherent in the 'Abbasid support base. The 'Abbasid caliphs began acquiring new troop support in the form of slave-soldiers (ghulam/pl. ghilman) from the Turkish population on their eastern borders. To maintain the loyalty of these slave-soldiers, al-Mu'tasim (r. 833–842) established a new capital city, Samarra, to the north of Baghdad. The slave-soldiers would eventually turn against their caliphal masters in 861, precipitating the Samarran captivity (861–870), wherein 'Abbasid caliphs were placed on the throne and removed by competing troop factions.

Throughout the rest of the ninth century and into the tenth century, the 'Abbasids were faced with dwindling resources (e.g., financial, troop support) and increased pressure from newly independent dynasties in formerly 'Abbasid-controlled lands. Most notable were the Samanids (819–1005) in eastern Iran, the Fatimids (909–1171) in Egypt, and the Buyids (945–1055) in Iraq and Iran. It was the Shi'is Buyid amirs who would bring the 'Abbasids to their lowest point in 945, deposing the 'Abbasid caliph al-Mustakfi and replacing him with another of Buyid choosing. Within a century, Buyid control was replaced by that of the Seljuks, a dynasty of Turkish Sunni Muslims (1055–1194). Although the 'Abbasids began to regain some independence of action during the late eleventh century, they would never regain their former glory. The Mongol sacking of Baghdad in 1258 put an end to the 'Abbasid presence in Iraq. Although a scion of the 'Abbasid family would establish a Shadow Caliphate in Egypt that would last until 1517, these 'Abbasids were merely titular figureheads that were far removed from their ancestors with regard to power and authority.

ERIC HANNE

See also Baghdad; Buyids; Caliphate and Imamate; Fatimids; Historical Writing; Intellectual History; Al-Ma'mun; Political Theory; Samanids; Seljuks; Slavery, Military; Slaves and Slave Trade: Eastern Islamic World; Sunni Revival; Translation, Pre-Islamic Learning into Arabic; Umayyads; Viziers

Further Reading

Crone, Patricia. *Slaves on Horses: The Evolution of the Islamic Polity*. London and New York: Cambridge University Press, 1980.

El-Hibri, Tayeb. *Reinterpreting Islamic Historiography: Harun al-Rashid and the Narrative of the Abbasid Caliphate (Cambridge Studies in Islamic Civilization)*. Cambridge: Cambridge University Press, 1999.

Kennedy, Hugh. *The Early Abbasid Caliphate: A Political History*. London: Croom Helm, 1981.

Lassner, Jacob. *The Shaping of Abbasid Rule*. Princeton, NJ: Princeton University Press, 1980.

———. *Islamic Revolution and Historical Memory: Abbasid Apologetics and the Art of Historical Writing*. New Haven, CT: American Oriental Society, 1986.

Shaban, M.A. *The 'Abbasid Revolution*. Cambridge: Cambridge University Press, 1970.

———. *Islamic History. A New Interpretation. Vol. II: A.D. 750–1055*. Cambridge: Cambridge University Press, 1971–1976.

Sharon, Moshe. *Black Banners from the East: The Establishment of the 'Abbasid State—Incubation of a Revolt*. Leiden: E.J. Brill, 1983.

'ABD AL-LATIF IBN YUSUF AL-BAGHDADI, MUWAFFAQ AL-DIN ABU MUHAMMAD (557/1162–623/1231)

'Abd al-Latif was a broadly educated scholar from Baghdad whose studies in grammar, law, tradition, medicine, alchemy, and philosophy are documented in his autobiography, which also vividly depicts contemporary methods of study. Having first followed Ibn Sina as his philosophical mentor, 'Abd al-Latif later devoted himself exclusively to the works of the ancients, particularly Aristotle, only admitting al-Farabi as interpreter. After extensive travels with periods of residence in Mosul (585/1189), Damascus (586/1190), the camp of Saladin outside Acre (587/1191) (where he met Baha' al-Din Ibn Shaddad and 'Imad al-Din al-Isfahani and acquired the patronage of al-Qadi al-Fadil), he settled in Cairo. It was here that he met Maimonides and, most importantly, Abu 'l-Qasim al-Shari'I, who introduced him to the works of al-Farabi, Alexander of Aphrodisias, and Themistius, which turned him away from Ibn Sina and alchemy. After shorter stays in Jerusalem (588/1192) (where he met Saladin) and Damascus, 'Abd al-Latif returned to Cairo only to set off a short time later for the East again. He spent some years at the court of 'Ala'-al-Din Da'ud of Erzindjan, until the city was conquered by the Seljuqid Kayqubadh. Having returned in 621/1229 to Baghdad, 'Abd al-Latif died there two years later.

'Abd al-Latif is an encyclopedic author whose work covers almost the whole domain of the knowledge of his time. Most widely known is his *Kitab al-ifada wa-l-I'tibar*, which is a short description of Egypt that was translated into Latin, German, and French. His intellectual autobiography is preserved by Ibn Abi Usaybi'a; it was originally embedded in an extensive historiographical narrative (al-Sira) that has partly survived in al-Dhahabi's *Ta'rikh al-Islam*. 'Abd al-Latif composed a compendium of Aristotelian metaphysics, *Kitab ma ba'd al-tabi'a*, which was based on the exegesis of Alexander of Aphrodisias and Themistius. The latter's otherwise lost paraphrasal of *Book Lambda*—known to English speakers, however, through a Hebrew translation—has survived in Arabic only through 'Abd al-Latif.

ANGELIKA NEUWIRTH

See also Maimonides; Intellectual History; Philosophy; Ibn Shaddad

Primary Sources

Cahen, Claude, ed. and comm. "'Abdallatif al-Baghdadi, Portraitiste et Historien de Son Temps" (*Al-Sira*, partial). *Bulletin d'Etudes Orientales* 23 (1970): 101–28.

Neuwirth, Angelika, ed. and trans. *'Abd al-Latif al-Bagdadi's Bearbeitung von Buch Lambda der Aristotelischen Metaphysik (Kitab ma ba'd al-Tabi'a, Maqalat Lam)*. Wiesbaden, 1976.

———, ed and comm. "Neue Materialien zur Arabischen Tradition der Beiden Ersten Metaphysik-Buecher" (*Kitab ma ba'd al-tabi'a, maqalat alif*). *Welt des Islams* XVIII (1978): 84–100.

Thies, H.J., ed. and trans. *Der Diabetestraktat*. Bonn, 1971.

Zand, K.H., and J.A. and I.E. Videan, eds. and trans. *The Eastern Key (Kitab al-Ifada wa-l-i'Tibar)*. London, 1965.

Further Reading

Richter-Bernburg, Lutz. *Der Syrische Blitz. Saladins Sekretaer Zwischen Selbstdarstellung und Geschichtsschreibung*. Beirut/Stuttgart, 1998.

Toorawa, Shawkat M. "Language and Male Homosocial Desire in the Autobiography of 'Abd al/Latif al-Baghdadi." *Edebiyat* 7 (1996): 251–65.

'ABD AL-MALIK IBN MARWAN

'Abd al-Malik ibn Marwan was the Umayyad caliph who ruled from 65/685 until 86/705. He inherited a fractured polity from his father, who was apparently murdered in his sleep by one of his wives. The rebel Ibn al-Zubayr controlled the holy sites in the Hijaz, along with significant areas of Iraq, where both he and 'Abd al-Malik confronted 'Alid and Kharijite rebels. Only Syria remained firmly in Umayyad hands, and even there 'Abd al-Malik faced a revolt led by 'Amr b. Sa'id al-Asdaq, a family rival, in 69/688–689. These internal threats forced 'Abd al-Malik to sign a treaty with the Byzantines, paying them tribute in 70/689–690. He was able to restore order and consolidate his power by 73/692. 'Abd al-Malik continued to face occasional revolts in Iraq and farther east in Khurasan, but his viceroy Hajjaj ibn Yusuf contained these threats ably (and sometimes viciously).

'Abd al-Malik devoted the remainder of his reign to centralizing power in the capital at Damascus. He depended on his own family for sensitive positions, which was in contrast with his predecessors' reliance on local elites. He used his powerful Syrian army to crush any provincial resistance. 'Abd al-Malik introduced the first distinctly Islamic coinage. In contrast with older Muslim coins, which were based on Byzantine models, 'Abd al-Malik's coins were devoid of pictorial images and included Qur'anic phrases instead. The remarkable uniformity of these coins demonstrates the degree to which 'Abd al-Malik centralized the control of minting money. His coins remained the model for coins throughout the Umayyad and 'Abbasid periods. In addition, 'Abd al-Malik began the long process of establishing Arabic as the standard administrative language of the realm and invested heavily in agricultural development, particularly in Iraq and the Hijaz. At his death in 86/705 at the age of 60, he was succeeded by al-Walid, the first of four of his sons to ascend to the caliphate.

STEVEN C. JUDD

Primary Sources

al-Baladhuri, Ahmad b. Yahya. *Ansab al-Ashraf*. Damascus, 1996.

al-Tabari, Muhammad b. Jarir. *Ta'rikh al-Rusul Wa-l-muluk*, ed. M.J. de Goeje. Leiden, 1879–1901.

Further Reading

Hawting, G.R. *The First Dynasty of Islam*. London: Croom Helm, 1987.

Kennedy, Hugh. *The Prophet and the Age of the Caliphates*. London: Longman, 1986.

Wellhausen, Julius. *The Arab Kingdom and its Fall*, trans. Margaret Weir. Calcutta, 1927.

'ABD AL-RAHMAN III AL-NASIR

'Abd al-Rahman b. Muhammad b. 'Abd Allah, the first and the greatest of the short-lived line of Marwanid caliphs of al-Andalus, was born in Cordova in AH 277/891 CE, the grandson of the ruling emir 'Abd Allah. In AH 300/912 CE, as the emir 'Abd al-Rahman III, he took on his grandfather's war-ridden and deeply divided reign, during which local strongmen of Iberian or Arabic descent had successfully revolted against the emiral authority and established themselves as independent rulers in most of the territory. Although the fiercest and most well known of 'Abd al-Rahman's triumphs was the defeat inflicted on Ibn Hafsun, the muwallad (Iberian Muslim) lord of Bobastro, in the southeastern part of the country, 'Abd al-Rahman was also able—in less than ten years—to restore the emiral authority to the rest of al-Andalus. Most notably, he achieved this aim not only by way of militarily crushing the revolted warlords but also, in many cases, by making peace deals with them or by having them join his ruling elite. At the same time, 'Abd al-Rahman kept facing the Christian Iberian armies on the northern border, trying to contain the antagonism of the kings of Leon and Asturia, with uneven results. The defeat of Simancas (also known as "The Battle of the Ditch," or Alhandega) in AH 327/939 CE ended 'Abd al-Rahman's campaigns against the Christian kings and provoked a brutal purge in the army, starting a fateful trend toward a more pronounced role being assigned to mercenary troops. Nonetheless, it did not significantly alter the balance of power; this was still favorable to the Muslim side, because the Christian kings remained subject to an annual tribute to the Marwanide ruler.

In AH 316/929 CE, 'Abd al-Rahman proclaimed himself caliph (amir al-mu'minin) of al-Andalus, adopting the honorific title of al-Nasir li-din Allah ("the winner for the religion of God"). This act has been widely interpreted as not only celebrating the reunification of al-Andalus under the Marwanid rule but also challenging the concomitant rise of the Fatimid power in North Africa. From this time on, most of the new caliph's military and diplomatic efforts were directed at contrasting the Fatimid influence in North Africa by supporting the local rulers and tribal leaders who were opposed to the new Shi'is dynasty and establishing military alliances with them. This policy, although not leading to any significant territorial gain aside from the peaceful capture of Ceuta in AH 319/931 CE, would eventually result in the increased influence of the Berber element on the Andalusian army until the end of the Caliphate.

On a more internal plan, 'Abd al-Rahman's action was directed at contrasting the influence of the Marwanid traditional clients (the mawali) over the governmental bureaucracy. To enforce his absolute authority and will over the wheels of the administration, he increased—among other things—the influence and scope of his personal retinue and guard, which comprised many former slaves and depended strictly on his command. He also distanced himself from the view of the general population and created a stricter set of rules for the court protocol and administration. In AH 325/936 CE, al-Nasir started the construction of an entirely new caliphal city, Madinat al-Zahra' (the "City of al-Zahra," after his favorite concubine), which was about five kilometers northwest of Cordova. He eventually retired there with his court, thereby truncating the link between the Marwanid house and its turbulent capital. The construction of Madinat al-Zahra' was supervised by 'Abd al-Rahman's son and heir al-Hakam. The process lasted for about ten years and absorbed most of the caliph's concerns and financial resources: sources describe his endless search for precious materials and skilled craftsmen, which were found in North Africa, the East, and Byzantium. It was also at this new caliphal residence that 'Abd al-Rahman al-Nasir received the ambassadors of many Islamic and Christian kings and potentates, especially the ones sent by the Byzantine emperors, who were actively pursuing an alliance against the Fatimid expansion in the eastern Mediterranean and acknowledged 'Abd al-Rahman's influential role and power.

'Abd al-Rahman III's very long reign, which lasted for half a century until his death in AH 350/961 CE, is unanimously described as the golden age of the Muslim civilization in the Iberian Peninsula. Conversions to Islam started to peak thanks to his politics of integrating religious and social minorities into the mainstream Ibero-Muslim society, the cohesion and vitality of which were greatly increased. At the same time, his patronage of scientific and literary excellence allowed for a fuller expansion of the Andalusian intellectual elite's potential. Although the contributions of Jewish and Christian scholars brought about a remarkable enhancement of philosophical and scientific knowledge, the introduction of many contemporary Eastern literary texts and the imposition of more cogent rules on official court writing resulted in the birth of a full-blown Andalusian literature, which was to reclaim its legitimate place within the overall Arabic literary heritage. On the other hand, 'Abd al-Rahman III's legacy of unchecked authority, in combination with his increased reliance on the mercenary element in the military, was partly responsible for the confiscation of power by the Amirid regency under his feebly determined and less-gifted successors.

BRUNA SORAVIA

Further Reading

Soravia, Bruna. Rome (850 words; actual main body of text, ca. 860).

Lévi-Provençal, E. *Histoire de l'Espagne Musulmane*, vol. III: *Le Siècle du Califat de Cordoue*. Paris, 1950.

ABU BAKR

Abu Bakr b. Abi Quhafa, as his full name is usually given, was from the clan of Taym of the prominent tribe of Quraysh. He is said to have been born two to three years after Muhammad, so he was probably born around 572 CE in Mecca. Sources report that he was a wealthy merchant before his conversion to Islam and that he had expert knowledge of the genealogies of the Arab tribes. He married four times and had six children, the most famous of whom was 'A'isha, who became the Prophet's youngest wife.

Sunni sources eulogize Abu Bakr's position as one of Muhammad's most preeminent Companions as a result of his early conversion to Islam (some sources report that he was the first male to do so) and his subsequent devotion to the Prophet and the cause of Islam. Abu Bakr is said to have spent 40,000 dirhams (or dinars) in charity before his emigration (hijra) to Mecca in 622, much of which went toward the manumission of slaves. Among his best-known sobriquets are al-'Atiq (this generally means "freed slave," but in this case it was explicated by Muhammad himself to refer to Abu Bakr as "freed from hell-fire") and al-Siddiq ("the truthful," "one who believes"; this particularly applied to his having believed the Prophet's account of his nocturnal journey to Jerusalem, which is known as isra'). In Medina, Abu Bakr took part in all of the major expeditions that were led by the Prophet, and he was frequently the Prophet's advisor.

After Muhammad's death in 632, Abu Bakr was selected as the first caliph at the portico (Saqifa) of the Banu Sa'ida, after some contentious debate. Many were convinced that he was the obvious successor to Muhammad as a result of the fact that he had been appointed to lead the pilgrimage during the ninth year of the hijra and because he had been designated as the prayer leader during the Prophet's illness; he also had a positive general record of service to the nascent community. He ruled for only two years, until his death in 634, and he decisively quelled the uprising of some of the Arab tribes against the Medinan government in what have come to be known as the ridda (so-called apostasy) wars. He is the first of the Rightly Guided Caliphs (al-Khulafa' al-Rashidun), and the Sunni literature of excellences (fada'il/manaqib) generously records his many virtues and his loyalty to Islam.

ASMA AFSARUDDIN

See also Caliphate and Imamate

Further Reading

Afsaruddin, Asma. *Excellence and Precedence: Medieval Islamic Discourse on Legitimate Leadership.* Leiden, 2002.

Watt, W. Montgomery. Art. "Abu Bakr." *The Encyclopaedia of Islam*, New Edition, ed. H. Gibb et al. Leiden and London, 1960. Vol. 1, 109–11.

ABU HANIFA AL-NU'MAN

Abu Hanifa al-Nu'man b. Thabit b. Zuta, theologian and jurist, is the eponymous founder of the Hanafi legal school. He was born in Kufa circa AH 80/699 CE and died in 150/767 in a prison in Baghdad at the age of 70. His grandfather Zuta is said to have been brought over from Kabul to Kufa, where he settled after being set free.

There are not many details available about Abu Hanifa's life in Kufa. Sources report that he worked there as a silk merchant and also that he acquired scholarly training in the religious law and hadith. He attended the lecture sessions of Hammad b. Abi Sulayman (d. 120/738) in Kufa and possibly of 'Ata' b. Abi Rabah (d. AH 114 or 115) in Mecca. After Hammad died, Abu Hanifa gained fame as the foremost scholar of religious law in Kufa, but he never served as qadi (judge); however, he was offered judgeships by various rulers, such as Yazid b. 'Amr, the governor of Iraq during the time of Marwan ibn Muhammad, who was the last Umayyad caliph. When Abu Hanifa declined, Yazid had him whipped, and the former escaped to Mecca, where he stayed for five or six years. Abu Hanifa is counted among the most illustrious of the Tabi'un (literally "the successors," which refers to the second generation of Muslims), and some sources relate that he met at least four Companions of the Prophet, including Anas b. Malik. In the eyes of the pious in particular, this distinction conferred on him and his scholarly activities great merit. His usual honorific is al-Imam al-A'zam ("the Greatest Leader"), from which the neighborhood around his mausoleum in Baghdad derives the name al-A'zamiyya.

There is frequent mention of Abu Hanifa's great scrupulousness (wara'), abstemiousness (zuhd), and charity. He is said to have spent generously for the members of his household and given away an equal amount as alms for the poor, and he would also meet the needs of his indigent students. Like other pious scholars, his day was given over to teaching and prayer. His daily routine began with the morning prayer in a mosque, after which he would answer his students' questions until about noon. After the noon prayer, he would teach again until the night prayer. Then he would return home and, after a short rest, later go back to the mosque and worship until morning prayer. He is said to have recited prodigious amounts of the Qur'an regularly, and, according to some sources, he performed the hajj fifty-five times.

Abu Hanifa himself did not leave behind substantial works on religious law, but his legal thought may be reconstructed from the writings of his students. His best-known students were al-Shaybani (d. 189/749–750) and Abu Yusuf (d. 192/798), who have preserved Abu Hanifa's doctrines and opinions in their works. From these works it becomes apparent that Abu Hanifa's legal thought was based to a considerable degree on his personal opinions (ra'y) and that his conclusions were derived through legal reasoning (qiyas). In his theology, Abu Hanifa showed concern for maintaining the unity and harmony of the Muslim community; his time was racked with communal strife, and so he sought a middle ground between extremes. In this propensity Abu Hanifa shows the influence of the Murji'a ("those who defer"), a group that came into existence during the last third of the Umayyad era. The central concern of the Murji'a was the issue of the early caliphate; in an attempt to contain the dissension that had erupted after the murder of 'Uthman, they expressed unequivocal support for Abu Bakr and 'Umar but deferred judgment on the respective merits of 'Uthman and 'Ali. The Murji'a also believed that an individual's faith did not increase or decrease and that it did not include works such as the daily prayers. This Hanafi-Murji'i attitude seminally shaped the political and theological attitudes of the later fully formed Ahl al-Sunna. In Abu Hanifa's letter to the Basran jurisprudent 'Uthman al-Batti, which scholars regard as authentic, the former defends his adherence to Murji'i principles. In the creedal statement known as Fiqh al-Akbar I, Abu Hanifa articulates ten articles of faith that take issue with the positions of the Kharijites, the Shi'is, the Qadariyya, and the Jahmiyya. Abu Hanifa probably did not compose this statement himself, but the Fiqh al-Akbar is deemed to be an accurate summation of his theological views.

The detractors of Abu Hanifa during the later period attributed to him certain unpopular doctrines that were derived not only from the Murji'a but also from the Jahmiyya (the predecessors of the later Mu'tazila); for example, he is described as having subscribed to the position that the Qur'an was created and that hell was not eternal. The rijal works regularly included Abu Hanifa among the weak transmitters of hadith, and the traditionalists in general attacked his perceived excessive reliance on personal opinion and legal reasoning. His staunch supporters from among the later Hanafi jurists attempted to exculpate him of these accusations; his student Abu Yusuf stressed that Abu Hanifa was profoundly learned in hadith, and the Hanafi jurist Ahmad b. al-Salt (d. ca. 308/921) denied that Abu Hanifa had maintained that the Qur'an was created. The Hanafi jurisprudent Abu Ja'far al-Tahawi (d. 321/933) wrote the *Manaqib Abi Hanifa*, which recorded and praised the virtues of the school's eponym.

There are conflicting reports about why Abu Hanifa was imprisoned late in life. Some say it was as a result of his having refused to serve as a qadi under the 'Abbasid caliph al-Mansur, whereas al-Khatib al-Baghdadi relates that it was his rather open criticism of al-Mansur during an 'Alid revolt that landed him in jail, where he eventually died in 767. Under the Saljuqi sultan Malikshah (AH 485), one of Malikshah's viziers had an elaborate dome built over Abu Hanifa's grave, and his mausoleum was restored several times during the Ottoman period.

ASMA AFSARUDDIN

Further Reading

Dickinson, Eerik. "Ahmad b. al-Salt and his Biography of Abu Hanifa." *JAOS* 116 (1996): 408–20.

Hallaq, Wael B. "From Regional to Personal Schools of Law? A Reevaluation." *Islamic Law & Society* 8 (2001): 1–26.

Melchert, Christopher. *The Formation of the Sunni Schools of Law, Ninth–Tenth Centuries.* Leiden, 1997.

Schacht, Joseph. *The Origins of Muhammadan Jurisprudence.* Oxford, 1950.

ABU 'L-'ALA' AHMAD IBN ABD ALLAH, AL-MA'ARRI

Abû l-'Ala' Ahmad ibn Abd Allâh al-Ma'arri, born in 973 CE in Ma'arrat al-Nu'mân in northern Syria, traveled for his education to Aleppo and Baghdad and returned to Ma'arra, where he died in 1058 CE. Ma'arri was the blind author (by dictation) of prose and poetry. He composed poems during his younger years, and these are compiled in *The Spark of the Tinderbox (Saqt al-zand)*, a collection of poems that praised the Hamdanid King Sa'd al-Dawla, the notables of Aleppo, and a few librarians in Baghdad.

Later, in *The Self-Imposed Compulsion (Luzûm mâ lâ yalzam)*, he uses a nonobligatory double rhyme, but these poems are chiefly characterized by their ironic and even cynical descriptions. They are unconventional as compared with the poetic form that is usually found in the odes of this time, because they contain many a thought on religion, death, destiny, the sinful world, the afterlife, resurrection (the question of whether it really shall occur), and the fate of slaughtered animals and their compensation in the afterlife.

Ma'arri's prose is not only found in his short, flowery-styled letters but also in at least two very extensive Epistles *(Risâlas)*. The first letter, which was written in 1021 CE, was always thought to have been lost. However, its manuscript was discovered in 1975 CE by the Egyptian scholar 'A'isha 'Abd al-Rahmân; she became the editor of this work, which is entitled *Epistle of the Neighing and the Braying (Risâlat al-sahil wa l-Shâhij)*. In this text, various animals are described, and they symbolize certain personages from Ma'arri's time. A mule suffering from arduous labor that consists of drawing up water from a deep well symbolizes the author himself. The mule wants to send a petition of complaint to someone, who, in reality, would have been the Fatimid Governor of Aleppo, Abu Shujâ' Fâtik 'Azîz al-Dawla. Several animals are asked to convey this petition—a horse, a camel, and others—but all of them refuse to do so, for different reasons. Finally, a fox comes along and becomes involved in the sudden imminent danger of a Byzantine attack, which had occurred also in reality and which threatened the territory around Aleppo. This attack was organized by the conjoint rulers of the Byzantine Empire: Basil Bulgaroctonus II and his brother Constantine VIII. The mule and other animals, although frightened and panicking, nevertheless discuss the conditions prevailing in the empire.

In this manner the *Risâla* renders information about the ideas prevailing in Ma'arri's time in Syria. *The Epistle of the Neighing and the Braying* is considered by its editor 'A'isha 'Abd al-Rahmân to be a preliminary exercise for Ma'arri's subsequent Letter.

The second prose work composed by Ma'arri in the year 1033 CE is his *Epistle of Forgiveness (Risâlat al-Ghufrân)*. This work consists not only of a description of the gardens of Paradise and the tortures of Hell but also of a discussion about and a criticism of many poetical fragments by Muslims and non-Muslims, ranging from pre-Islamic poets to heretics from Persia and polytheists from India. Some of these poets and also grammarians and scholars enjoy a comfortable afterlife in Paradise; although not expected by them, their sins have been forgiven by Allah the Merciful One.

In 2002, the first half of this work was translated into German by Gregor Schoeler and entitled *Paradies und Hölle*. In this part, an old correspondent of Ma'arri called Ibn al-Qârih 'Alî ibn Mansûr ("Dawkhala") is ironically described as having died and then entered (but not without great difficulties) through the Gates of Paradise. After this, he visits many places of interest, like the regions of Hell, where Satan (Iblîs) dwells and where a few poets are shown being tortured by avenging angels.

The second half of the piece deals with questions pertaining to aspects of religion. A discussion of ideas is forwarded by the author with, it would seem, cynical relish; these ideas are ascribed to Arabs who, by the general public, were considered heretics who should be executed.

Of the other books by Ma'arri, another is worth mentioning here. Its incomplete manuscript version was found in 1918 CE, and it was considered by some scholars to be an imitation of the Qur'an, because of its rhymed prose and typical Qur'anic oaths. It was entitled *Chapters and Endings, Glorifying Allah and Offering Words of Warning (al-Fusûl wa l-Ghâyât fî Tamjîd Allâh wa l-Mawa'iz)*.

As for the author's social relations with personages of the Ismâ'îlî persuasion, a short description of him is found in the traveler Nâsiri Khosraw's book, *Safar Nâmah*, in which the author himself claims to have kept some correspondence with a high Fatimid dignitary called Abû Nasr Mûsâ ibn Abî 'Imrân.

For more information on al-Mu'ayyad fî al-Dîn al-Shîrâzî, see *Margoliouth*, Abu l-'Ala' al-Ma'arri's correspondence on vegetarianism.

PIETER SMOOR

Primary Sources

'Abd al-Rahman, 'A'isha. *Risâlat al-sâhil wa l-Shâhij*, critical edition. Cairo, 1975.
———. *Risâlat al-Ghufrân*. Cairo, 1954.
———. *Risâlat al-Ghufrân wa-ma'a-hâ Risâlat Ibn al-Qârih Miftâh Fahmi-hâ*, 3rd critical edition. Cairo, 1963.
Blachère, R. "Ibn al-Qarih et la Genèse de l'Epitre du Pardon d' Al-Ma'arri." In *Revue des Études Islamiques*, 1–15, 1941–1946.
Nicholson, R.A., ed. and trans. "Risâlat al-Ghufrân." *Journal of the Royal Asiatic Society* (1900): 637–720; (1902): 75–101, 337–62, 813–947.
Saleh, Moustapha. "Abu 'l-'Ala' al-Ma'arri, Bibliographie Critique." *Bulletin des Études Orientales* XII (1969): 141–204; XXIII (1970): 199–309.

Historical Studies

'Abd al-Rahman, 'A'ishah. ("Bint al-Shâti'") "Abu l-'Ala' al-Ma'arri." In *'Abbasid Belles-Lettres*, ed. Julia Ashtiany, 328–38. Cambridge: Cambridge University Press, 1990.
Filshtinsky, I.M. *Arabic Literature*. Moscow: USSR Academy of Sciences, Institute of the Peoples of Asia, Nauka Publishing, 1966, 146–60.
Smoor, Pieter. "Kings and Bedouins in the Palace of Aleppo as reflected in Ma'arri's Works." *Journal of Semitic Studies*, Monograph 8. Manchester, England: University of Manchester, 1985.

Further Reading

Monteil, Vincent-Mansour, trans. *Abu l-'Ala' al-Ma'arri L'Épitre du Pardon Traduction, Introduction et Notes.* Paris: Connaissance d'Orient Collection UNESCO, Gallimard, 1984.

Schoeler, Gregor, trans. *Abu l-'Ala' al-Ma'arri Paradies und Hölle Die Jenseitsreise aus dem «Sendschreiben über die Vergebung.»* Munich: C.H. Beck, 2002. [This offers the translation of the first half.]

Smoor, Pieter. "The Delirious Sword of Ma'arri: An Annotated Translation of his *Luzûmiyya Nûniyya* in the Rhyme-Form 'Nûn Maksûra Mushaddada'." In *Festschrift Ewald Wagner zum 65. Geburtstag*, eds. Wolfhart Heinrichs and Gregor Schoeler, Band 2 *Studien zur Arabischen Dichtung*, 381–424. Beirut: Franz Steiner Verlag Stuttgart, 1994.

Studies concerning The Spark of the Tinderbox

Cachia, P.J. "The Dramatic Monologues of al-Ma'arri." *Journal of Arabic Studies* I (1970): 129–36.

Smoor, Pieter. "Armour description as an independent theme in the work of al-Ma'arri." In *Actes du 8me Congrès de l'Union Européenne des Arabisants et Islamisants*, 289–303. Aix-en-Provence, 1978.

——. "The theme of travel in Ma'arri's early poems." In *The Challenge of the Middle East, Middle Eastern Studies at the University of Amsterdam*, eds. A. El-Sheikh, C.A. van de Koppel, and R. Peters, 133–39, 209–11. University of Amsterdam, 1982.

Studies concerning The Self-Imposed Compulsion

Nicholson, R.A. "The Meditations of Ma'arri." In *Studies in Islamic Poetry*, ed. R.A. Nicholson, 43–289. Cambridge, England: Cambridge University Press, 1969.

Smoor, Pieter. "The Weeping Wax Candle and Ma'arri's Wisdom-Tooth: Night Thoughts and Riddles from the Gâmi' al-Awzân." In *Zeitschrift der Deutschen Morgenländischen Gesellschaft*, Band 138-Heft 2, 283–312. Wiesbaden: Franz Steiner Verlag, 1988.

Studies concerning Chapters and Endings, Glorifying Allah and Offering Words of Warning

Fischer, August. "Der Koran des Abu 'l-'Ala' al-Ma'arri." *Verhandlungen der Sächsischen Akademie der Wissenschaften, Phil.-hist. Klasse* XCIV (1942), no. 2.

Hartmann, Richard. *Zu dem Kitab al-Fusul wa l-Ghâyât des Abu 'l-'Ala' al-Ma'arri*, Abhandlungen Pr. Ak. W., Phil.-hist. Berlin: Klasse, 1944.

Studies concerning The Neighing and the Braying

Smoor, Pieter. "Enigmatic Allusion and Double Meaning in Ma'arri's Newly-Discovered Letter of a Horse and a Mule." *Journal of Arabic Literature* XII (1981) and XIII (1982).

Studies on the short letters of Ma'arri

Margoliouth, D.S. "Abu l-'Ala' al-Ma'arri's Correspondence on Vegetarianism." *Journal of the Royal Asiatic Society* (1902): 289–312.

ABU 'L-FADL AL-BAYHAQI

Al-Bayhaqi, Abu 'l-Fadl (995–1077) was a secretary and historian and the author of the monumental Persian history of the Ghaznavid dynasty generally referred to as the *Tarikh-i Bayhaqi*. Of an original thirty-odd volumes, only six have survived, and this surviving portion, which deals with the reign of Mas'ud I (r. 1030–1041), is known accordingly as the *Tarikh-i Mas'udi*. Bayhaqi, who was born in the district of Bayhaq (modern Sabzavar) in Khurasan, studied in Nishapur. In about 1021, he found employment in the Ghaznavid chancellery, where he first served Mahmud of Ghazna (r. 999–1030) and then several of Mahmud's successors, including Mas'ud I. In his many years of service, Bayhaqi assisted the head of the chancellery, Abu Nasr Mishkan (d. 1039), and then (although less happily) Abu Nasr's successor in office, Abu Sahl Zawzani; under 'Abd al-Rashid (r. 1049–1052), Bayhaqi himself briefly directed the chancellery, but he fell from favor and was imprisoned until the accession of Sultan Farrukhzad (r. 1052–1059), whom Bayhaqi also served, although possibly not at the Ghaznavid court (see Yusofi and Meisami).

Bayhaqi's *History* is a highly individual work in which the author articulates and demonstrates a distinctive approach to historiography, providing a wealth of detailed and carefully documented information about the Ghaznavid court and administration, integrating religious and philosophical perspectives in his descriptions and commentary, and displaying both erudition and subtlety in his masterful use of the Persian language. His long term of administrative service permitted Bayhaqi to observe directly—and on occasion even to participate in—the events he records. When he did not have personal experience to draw from, Bayhaqi handled his sources with much discernment, clearly identifying them and assessing them with regard to their reliability. Furthermore, during the course of his secretarial work, Bayhaqi assembled not only his own detailed notes but also a considerable number of documents, some of which he reproduced in full in his narrative. His *History* thus furnishes thorough accounts of military campaigns, official correspondence, negotiations, and agreements, and it sheds much light on local conditions and customs, the culture of the elites, the lives of the men and women of the Ghaznavid court, and many other topics. The strikingly vivid quality of Bayhaqi's writing derives in part from his proximity to the events and persons he describes, and it is enhanced by his extensive use of direct speech. Although Bayhaqi's high standards of accuracy and his wide-ranging subject matter have rendered his work a particularly valuable source for the study of Ghaznavid history (see especially Bosworth), it is also clear that his personal outlook and literary style are inseparable from his recounting of events (see Waldman and Meisami). Bayhaqi gives distinctive meaning to the events he describes, both in a moral sense and in terms of the recurrent patterns he discerns in the unfolding of history. To communicate these meanings, he employs a variety of rhetorical techniques, including suggestion by analogy, copious quotations from Arabic and Persian poetry, digressions, and flashbacks to episodes drawn from earlier Islamic history (references to Sasanian and other pre-Islamic Iranian traditions are notably sparse). (For an example of Bayhaqi's methods, see Meisami's analysis of his account of the trial and execution under Mas'ud of Mahmud's former vizier Hasanak, pp. 88–94.) Bayhaqi's *History* is, then, amply documented, replete with specific information, and exemplary.

Many titles for Bayhaqi's *History*—or portions of it—are preserved in the sources, and the secretary probably composed other works as well (see Yusofi). Sa'id Nafisi has collected two volumes' worth of passages from lost sections of Bayhaqi's *History* that were cited in later works, together with quotations from other lost works of Bayhaqi.

LOUISE MARLOW

Primary Sources

Bayhaqi, Abu l-Fadl. *Tarikh-i Bayhaqi*, 3 vols., ed. Kh. Khatib Rahbar. Tehran: Sa'di, 1989.
Nafisi, Sa'id. *Dar piramun-i Tarikh-i Bayhaqi*, 2 vols. Tehran: Kitabfurushi-yi Furughi, 1973.

Secondary Sources

Bosworth, C.E. *The Ghaznavids: Their Empire in Afghanistan and Eastern Iran 994–1040*. Edinburgh: Edinburgh University Press, 1963.
Meisami, Julie S. *Persian Historiography to the End of the Twelfth Century*. Edinburgh: Edinburgh University Press, 1999.
Waldman, Marilyn R. *Toward a Theory of Historical Narrative. A Case Study in Perso-Islamicate Historiography*. Columbus: Ohio State University Press, 1980.
Yusofi, G.-H. "Bayhaqi, Abu'l-Fazl," *Encyclopaedia Iranica* III: 889–94.

Further Reading

The literature on Bayhaqi is extensive. His *History* has been printed in many editions and supplemented by glossaries and lexicographical studies of the Persian text; the work has also been translated (see Yusofi 1989). The above bibliography is necessarily limited to the titles referred to in the article.

ABU 'L-FADL 'ALLAMI (1551–1602)

Historian, courtier, ideologue, and intellectual alter ego of the Mughal Emperor Akbar, Abu 'l-Fadl was born in 1551 in Agra. He was the son of Shaykh Mubarak, a scholar from Nagawr in Rajasthan. A precocious talent who had mastered Arabic, the religious sciences, and philosophy, and who was inclined towards Sufism, Abu 'l-Fadl followed his brother Fayzi, Akbar's poet laureate, into service, appearing at court in 1571. A forceful disputant and independent thinker, Abu 'l-Fadl was constantly at odds with the Sunni ulema, and he held their bigotry to be responsible for the persecution and exile of his father, a Shi'is notable and a supporter of the Mahdawiyya. He was thus quite happy to support Akbar in his formation of a new religion, and he provided the intellectual justification for Akbar as the Perfect Man, the philosopher-prophet-king in the *Akbarnama*.

Abu 'l-Fadl formulated the ideology of Akbar's reign, placing the monarch above the petty political and religious squabbles of the court. Consistent with the Iranian tradition, he considered the king to be an emanation of God's pure light, possessing the divine power of sovereignty in his person and the wisdom to deploy it as the Perfect Man of Sufism and the perfect sage of the Illuminationist philosophical tradition. The king as the benevolent face of God on earth would treat all of his subjects—both Muslims and non-Muslims—equally, thereby promulgating an established Sufi ethic of universal peace (sulh-i kull). This theory proposed that all religions are equal representations of a single divine truth and that all express a pure monotheism that lies at the heart of each one of them.

His other major literary achievement was the *A'in-i Akbari*, which was a major gazetteer, a comprehensive history, and a tax register of India.

As Akbar's main spokesman, Abu 'l-Fadl was responsible for the development of the Mughal art of epistolography (insha'); his letters became templates and exemplars for later secretaries. Abu 'l-Fadl headed the chancellery and organized the cultural program of translating major Sanskrit works into Persian. Because of his outspoken advocacy of Akbar's cause and his closeness to the king, Abu 'l-Fadl aroused the jealousy of other courtiers and the suspicion of the heir, Salim, who conspired along with others to have him murdered in August 1602. With Abu 'l-Fadl's death, Akbar lost a close friend and supporter.

SAJJAD H. RIZVI

See also Akbar; Illuminationism; Mughals; Sufism; Shi'ism

Further Reading

Haider, Mansura, trans. *Mukatabat-i 'Allam, (Insha'-i Abu'l-Fazl)*, 2 vols. New Delhi: Munshira Manoharlal, 1998–2000.

Jinarajadasa, C. *Abul-Fazl and Akbar*. Madras: Theosophical Publishing House, 1934.

Nizami, K.A. *The Socio-Religious Outlook of Abu'l-Fazl*. Aligarh: University Press, 1972.

Rizvi, S.A.A. *Religious and Intellectual History of the Muslims in Akbar's Reign*. New Delhi: Munshiram Manoharlal, 1975.

ABU NUWAS

Abu Nuwas Abu 'Ali al-Hasan ibn Hani' al-Hakami (d. ca. 814) was one of the major Arabic poets of the 'Abbasid age. He is known for his poems about wine, love, and unbridled debauchery, but he was also the foremost representative of the "modern" (muhdath) poetry that developed during the late eighth century.

Abu Nuwas was born in the mid-eighth century to an Arab father and Persian mother in al-Ahwaz in Iran, but he moved with his mother to Basra and Kufa, where he received a thorough philological and religious education, studying with a number of poetic authorities, most notably the poet and transmitter Khalaf al-Ahmar (d. 796). He then traveled to Baghdad, where he initially struggled to gain the favor of the notable families of the day. Eventually he became the drinking companion of the caliph al-Amin (d. 813) and enjoyed great notoriety and popularity until his death in Baghdad at some time between 813 and 815. There are countless anecdotes of Abu Nuwas and his scandalous behavior in which the personage corresponds with the libertine spirit of the poetry, and the name has retained associations that are quite independent of the poetry itself. (For example, a completely unhistorical Abu Nuwas appears in some of the tales in *The 1001 Nights*.)

With the wine poem (khamriyya), Abu Nuwas refined a genre that had previously been an occasional element in the polythematic classical Arabic ode (qasida). Wine drinking provides the setting for a number of thematic possibilities: a description of the wine, the seeking of drink, the joys of drunkenness, anecdotes of drinking bouts and their aftermaths, sexual escapades, and episodes of heartbroken or crapulent remorse. The celebration of hedonism and the flaunting of the norms of polite and pious society are seen in the following famous lines:

> Ho! a cup, and fill it up, and tell me it is wine,
>   For I will never drink in shade if I can drink in shine!
>   Curst and poor is every hour that sober I must go,
>   But rich am I whene'er well drunk I stagger to and fro.
>   Speak, for shame, the loved one's name, let vain disguise alone:

> No good there is in pleasures o'er which a veil is thrown.
>   (trans. R.A. Nicholson)

In such verses Abu Nuwas was rebelling not only against contemporary society but against the heroic model of the pre-Islamic poet. The "modern" poetry of his time was in part a reaction against the conventions of the classical, pre-Islamic odes. Although he demonstrates a deep knowledge and appreciation of the older poetry, he is better known for mocking its elements, most famously the prelude, which expresses sorrow at traces of long-abandoned encampments in the desert and the disappearance of those who once dwelt there. Abu Nuwas laments instead the vanished taverns or urges wine in place of nostalgia.

Although best known for his bacchanalia, Abu Nuwas applied his talents to other genres as well, such as panegyric, satire, and, notably, the hunting poem. This latter type, like the wine song, had been a single element in the classical qasida, but Abu Nuwas gave it its own genre (in which he followed the ancients' use of a highly specialized vocabulary and detailed descriptions of nature scenes). The majority of his verses display a simplicity and elegance that matches well his wit and lightheartedness; however, the joys of wine and sex with boys were not his only topics, and he was capable of various shades of sorrow, regret, and awe and of giving voice to these shades with fine poetic precision.

BRUCE FUDGE

Further Reading

Hamori, Andras. *On the Art of Medieval Arabic Literature*. Princeton, NJ: Princeton University Press, 1974.

Kennedy, Philip F. *Abu Nuwas*. Oxford: Oneworld Publications, 2005.

———. *The Wine Song in Classical Arabic Poetry: Abu Nuwas and the Classical Tradition*. New York: Oxford University Press, 1997.

Montgomery, James E. "Revelry and Remorse: A Poem of Abu Nuwas." *Journal of Arabic Literature* 25 (1994): 116–34.

Nicholson, R.A. *A Literary History of the Arabs*. Cambridge: Cambridge University Press, 1930.

Smith, G. Rex. "Hunting Poetry." In *The Cambridge History of Arabic Literature: 'Abbasid Belles-Lettres*, ed. Julia Ashtiany. Cambridge: Cambridge University Press, 1990: 167–84.

ABU SHAMA, 'ABD AL-RAHMAN IBN ISMA'IL ABU MUHAMMAD SHIHAB AL-DIN

Abu Shama was a religious scholar (1203–1268) who spent his entire life in Damascus; he was most renowned for his chronicle *Kitab al-Rawdatayn fi Akhbar al-Dawlatayn al-Nuriyya wa-l-Salahiyya (The Book of the Two Gardens on the Reports of the Two Reigns [of Nur al-Din and Saladin])*. This chronicle treats the main events, including the Crusades, that occurred during the rules of the Zankid ruler Nur al-Din (d. 1174) and the Ayyubid ruler Saladin (Salah al-Din, d. 1193) during the twelfth century. Although written more than fifty years after the death of Saladin, the chronicle has enjoyed wide popularity, because it integrates a number of previous sources into a coherent narrative. Abu Shama's principal aim in composing his chronicle was to present the two rulers as examples of ideal Muslim rulers to be emulated by later rulers.

Abu Shama came from a modest family that did not belong to the civilian elite of Damascus, and he himself was closely linked to its rather marginal immigrant Maghribian community. Throughout his career he held a number of minor teaching posts in madrasas (colleges for higher studies), and it was only toward the end of his life that he was able to briefly attain a more prestigious post. This marginal position in the town's social texture was paralleled by his controversial stances, which tended to criticize his contemporaries in sharp terms. Here he focused on the issue of innovations (i.e., practices that he considered contrary to the teachings of Islam). He finally died by the hands of attackers who beat him to death.

Besides history, Abu Shama's oeuvre was focused on religious sciences such as the variant readings of the Qur'an, law/jurisprudence, hadith, and poems praising the Prophet. It was in the first of these fields that he gained a certain prominence among his contemporaries, especially by commenting on a didactic poem written for students.

From a modern perspective, it is his continuation (Dhayl) of the main chronicle that represents considerable interest, because he included in his poems (such as the poems about one of his wives and about his moods of distress) as well as in his autobiographical sections an unusual array of events that were linked to his inner life.

KONRAD HIRSCHLER

See also Historical Writing

Primary Sources

Abu Shama. *Kitab al-rawdatayn fi akhbar al-dawlatayn al-Nuriyya wa-al-Salahiyya*, 5 vols, ed. Ibrahim al-Zibaq. Beirut: Mu'assasat al-Risala, 1997.

Further Reading

Hillenbrand, Carole. *The Crusades: Islamic Perspectives.* New York: Routledge, 1999.
Pouzet, Louis. "Abu Shama (599–665/1203–1268) et la Société Damascaine de son Temps." *Bulletin d'Etudes Orientales* 37/38 (1985/1986): 115–26.
Reynolds, Dwight F., ed. *Interpreting the Self: Autobiography in the Arabic Literary Tradition.* Berkeley and Los Angeles: University of California Press, 2001.
Robinson, Chase F. *Islamic Historiography.* Cambridge: Cambridge University Press, 2003.

ABU TAMMAM

Abu Tammam was an Arab poet (ca. AH 189–232/805–845 CE), allegedly the son of a Christian wine seller, who rose from his provincial background in Syria to become a panegyrist of the 'Abbasid caliphs al-Ma'mun, al-Mu'tasim, and al-Wathiq and of their great officers of state. He celebrated caliphal campaigns and victories (most notably over the Byzantines at Amorium in 223/838) in qasidas marked by the bloodiness of their battle scenes and the stridency of their religious propaganda. Nevertheless, he was above all an intellectual poet of Mu'tazili leanings who changed the course of Arabic literature by charging the sinewy and concrete pre-Islamic Bedouin qasida with philosophical conceits and with the sophisticated wordplay and metaphors, known as *badi'*, that are typical of "modern" poetry. His originality served as a focus for the Arabic "quarrel of the ancients and moderns." The issue was less whether modern, urban Arabic poetry could stand in worthy succession to its pre-Islamic, Bedouin precursors—this was broadly conceded—than whether poetic truth was a closed system or one that should evolve with social and intellectual change and, if so, at what pace. If poetry outstripped educated conservative taste, would not the concepts of poetry and poetic truth be reduced to playthings of fashion? Abu Tammam's experiments stimulated poetic criticism as a systematic and scholarly discipline, particularly from the century or so after his death; his example took root within his own lifetime and was pervasive. His diwan (collected verse) attracted commentaries as voluminous as those devoted to pre-Islamic poets. Al-Mutanabbi (d. 354/965) was his greatest poetic heir.

Abu Tammam was also an anthologist; his most famous compilation, *al-Hamasa (Valor),* proved no less influential than his own poetry. Carefully crafted from the tribal poetry of all periods to afford an image of timeless Bedouinity, it chimed in with an increasingly romanticized conception of Arab tradition.

JULIA BRAY

See also Poetry: Arabic; al-Ma'mun; Rhetoric; Al-Muntanabbi

Further Reading

'Abbas, Ihsan. *Ta'rikh al-Naqd al-Adab 'Inda al-'Arab*. Beirut: Dar al-Amana, 1971.

Abu Tammam. *Diwan*, with the commentary of al-Tibrizi, ed. M.'A. 'Azzam. Cairo: Dar al-Ma'arif, 1951–1965.

Abu Tammam. *al-Hamasa*, with the commentary of al-Tibrizi, eds. G. al-Shaykh and A. Shams al-Din. Beirut: Dar al-Kutub al-'Ilmiyya, 2000.

al-Amidi. *al-Muwazana Bayna Shi'r al-fia'Iyyayn Abu Tammam wa al-Buhturi*, eds. A. saqr and 'A. Muharib, vols. 1 and 2. Cairo: Dar al-Ma'arif, 1961–1965; vols. 3 and 4, Cairo, 1990.

al-Bahbiti, Najib M. *Abu Tammam al-fia'i, hayatuh wa ayat shi'rih*. Cairo: Dar al-Kutub al-Misriyya, 1945.

Bray, Julia. " 'Al-Mu'tasim's 'Bridge of Toil' and Abu Tammam's Amorium *qasida*." In *Studies in Islamic and Middle Eastern Texts and Traditions in Memory of Norman Calder*, eds. G.R. Hawting et al, 31–73. Oxford: Oxford University Press, 2000. (*Journal of Semitic Studies* Supplement 12.)

Gamal, A.S. "The basis of selection in the *Hamasa* collections." *Journal of Arabic Literature* 7 (1976): 28–44.

Hamori, Andras. *On the Art of Medieval Arabic Literature*. Princeton: Princeton University Press (1974): 125–34.

Klein-Franke, Felix. "The *Hamasa* of Abu Tammam," I and II. *Journal of Arabic Literature* 2 (1971): 13–36; 3 (1972): 142–78.

Stetkevych, Suzanne Pinckney. *Abu Tammam and the Poetics of the 'Abbasid Age*. Leiden: Brill, 1991.

al-Suli. *Akhbar Abu Tammam*, eds. K.M. 'Asakir et al. Cairo: Lajnat al-Ta'lif wa al-Tarjama wa al-Nashr, 1356/1937.

ABYSSINIA

The appearance of Islam in Abyssinia (historical Ethiopia) coincided with the first recognizable polity in the Ethiopian region: Aksum. There are various traditions of contact between ancient Ethiopia and early Islam: the Prophet Muhammad is reported to have written to the Aksumite king (Negus) inviting "People of the Book" to reconsider the teachings of Jesus; the emigration of Muhammad's cousin Ja'far ibn Abi Talib to Ethiopia to escape the Qurayshite persecution and his claimed conversion of the Ethiopian Negus; or indeed the tradition that the second male convert to Islam was Bilal, a slave of Ethiopian origin, whom the Prophet Muhammad appointed the first mu'adhdhin to call the faithful to prayer.

The emergence of the nascent caliphal state coincided with the apogee of Aksumite power when the Ethiopian fleet dominated the Red Sea. In retaliation for an Aksumite attack on the Hijaz, Arab forces occupied the Dahlak islands, which are opposite the Aksumite port of Adulis (in modern-day Eritrea), and Aksumite control of Red Sea trade ended, which precipitated the kingdom's decline. An independent Islamic sultanate emerged on the Dahlak islands, and friendly trade relations were established with Aksum's successor *Habasha*—the term Arab geographers gave the people of the Ethiopian interiors—states in the north of Ethiopia.

However, after the decline of Aksum, the successor states of the Zagwe and Solomonic dynasties began their historic antipathy to the emerging network of Islamic peoples and polities to the southeast. The political—rather than the religious—rivalry between the Habasha Christian polity in Ethiopia and a succession of Islamic sultanates centered on the control of trade. The most important trade route began at the coastal Islamic settlement of Zayla, and the Islamic faith had also traveled along this route. The network of Islamic sultanates known to Arab geographers as the "country of Zayla" consists of ethnically mixed populations of Semitic- and Cushitic-language-speaking traders, agriculturalists, and pastoralists.

At the end of the Zagwe dynasty (c. 1269), an Islamic sultanate of Shawa is documented as being founded by the Makhzumite dynasty (a Meccan clan), dating back to AH 283 or 896/897 CE. Shawa was later eclipsed by the sultanate of Yifat, which was founded by 'Umar Walashama (who traced his origin from the Arabian Quraysh but who was probably of local origin). Yifat intervened in Shawa in 1280 (AH 678) or 1285, apparently with the compliance of a Solomonic Christian emperor. The great Islamic historian Ibn Khaldun mentions Yifat and its Walashama sultans, such as Hakk Al Din I and Sabr/Sa'd al-Din. Both Hakk Al Din I and Sabr Al Din fought with the Habasha king (negus) Amda Seyon, who occupied Yifat. It was not until 1376 that their successor Haqq al-Din II successfully challenged the Christian Solomonic dominance over Yifat, but the Ethiopian ruler Dawit I later reasserted his authority and killed Haqq al-Din II. Another Walashama, Sa'd al-Din II continued to resist, but he fled to Zayla, where he was killed by the Habasha forces of Yeshaq. Scions of the Walashama dynasty took refuge with the King of Yemen, but some returned and ruled further east of Yifat, founding the Sultanate of Adal around 1420.

The new Walashama dynasty in Adal grew larger, expanding into Somali areas (the "black Berbers" of the Arab geographers). The expansion of the power of Adal culminated in the Sultan Ahmad Badlay's attempted reconquest of Muslim areas, which ended in defeat at the hands of Negus Zara Yaqob. The Sultanate of Adal then retreated to Dakar and then

Harar, which was founded in 1520 by Sultan Abu Bakr Muhammad, where a reversal of fortunes culminated in the defeat and destruction of the Christian Solomonic empire (from 1529–1543) by a later military leader of the Adal sultanate, Ahmad ibn Ibrahim al-Ghazi, who was nicknamed *Gran* (the left handed).

CEDRIC BARNES

Further Reading

Braukamper, Ulrich. *Islamic History and Culture in Southern Ethiopia*. Münster and London, 2003.

Cerulli, Enrico. "Ethiopia's Relations With the Muslim World." In *Unesco History of Africa from the Seventh to the Eleventh Century*, ed. M. Elfasi, 575–85. Berkeley, 1998.

Kapteijns, Lidwien. "Ethiopia and the Horn of Africa." In *The History of Islam in Africa*, eds. N. Levtzion and R.L. Pouwels. London, 2000.

Tamrat, Taddese. "Ethiopia, the Red Sea and the Horn." In *The Cambridge History of Africa*, ed. Roland Oliver. Cambridge, 1977.

Trimingham, J.S. *Islam in Ethiopia*. London, 1952.

ADAB

Adab is an Arabic term (pl. adab [pronounced with long a]) for a key concept in medieval Islamic culture. In the culture's self-description, adab is both polite learning and its uses: the improvement of one's understanding by instruction and experience, it results in civility and becomes a means of achieving social goals. Adab requires a knowledge of history, poetry, ideas, proverbs, parallels, precedents, and the correct and pleasing use of language. It is the social and intellectual currency of the elite and of those who aspire to be part of it. Courtiers and politicians should use adab in their dealings with the ruler. Rulers and grandees should be patrons of learning and adab. Adab can be displayed to them as a product (the treatise or compendium); as a performance (the disputation or reading); or simply the apt repartee in the majlis (salon, social gathering; see Socializing and al-Tawhidi). Anyone who practices adab is an *adib* (pl. udaba'); udaba' see themselves as architects of civilization and guarantors of its survival in the teeth of political upheavals.

Under the 'Abbasids and their successor dynasties, adab was a route into office holding and sometimes to the vizierate; see numerous examples in al-Tanukhi's (AH 329–384/940–994 CE) *Table-Talk of a Mesopotamian Judge* and Yaqut's (d. 626/1229) *Dictionary of Men of Adab (Mu'jam al-Udaba')*, among others. The concept of adab as mannerliness could be narrowed to apply to particular groups, such as Sufis (e.g., 'Abd al-Qahir al-Suhrawardi, 490–563/1097–1168, *Adab*

al-Muridin, A Sufi Rule for Novices), or to a given profession or situation (e.g., Ibn Qutayba, d. 276/889, *Adab al-Katib [Skills of the Bureaucrat]*; al-Ghazali, d. 505/1111, *Adab al-Akl [Table Manners]*), not least that of ruler (hence the numerous mirrors for princes in Arabic, Persian, and Turkish).

Historically, adab evolved through several phases from the end of Umayyad rule and over the first two centuries of 'Abbasid rule (mid-eighth to tenth centuries CE). During all of these phases, the written page took the place of the traditional oral study circle (see Books). During a first phase, senior bureaucrats wrote epistles that were designed to imbue caliphs with Sasanian ideas of statecraft and to help them manage the increasingly complex problems of empire (see Ibn al-Muqaffa'). A second phase addressed the senior or junior bureaucracy; thus al-Jahiz (d. ca. 255/869) welcomed the rationalist trends arising from the translation movement (see Translation: Pre-Islamic Learning into Arabic) and championed the intellectual leadership of an enlightened minority. Ibn Qutayba, however, stressed the duty of even the moderately literate to educate themselves through reading and highlighted the imaginative appeal of the huge body of exemplary stories made available by Arab antiquarian scholarship and translations. In Muslim Spain (Andalus), Ibn 'Abd Rabbih (246–328/860–940) synthesized these conceptions of adab in an anthology, *al-'Iqd (The Necklace)*, which lauds rulership (sultan) and reason as given by God, adab, and books as the vehicles of reason.

Meanwhile, a further type of adab had emerged in which political or didactic messages are absent. Instead, poets, musicians, and udaba' are foregrounded as cultural heroes and exemplars of the human condition. The greatest exponent of this type of adab is Abu al-Faraj al-Isfahani (284–ca. 363/897–ca. 972), whose compilations include the monumental *Kitab al-Aghani (The Book of Songs)*, which records the careers and loves of the great men and women musicians and the lives and legends of Arab poets and poetesses down the ages; the slim *al-Ima' al-Shawa'ir (Slave Poetesses)*; and (perhaps) *The Book of Strangers (Kitab al-Ghuraba')*, which contains miniature anecdotes and poems of loss and longing, mostly by obscure or anonymous contemporaries. Both thematic anthologies and the commemoration of contemporary udaba'—obscure as well as famous—continued throughout the medieval period, as did the tradition of providing the common reader with syntheses of the literary heritage (e.g., al-Baghdadi, 1030–1093/1621–1682, *Khizanat al-Adab [The Treasury of Adab]*) and handbooks of general knowledge (al-Tha'alibi, 350–429/961–1038, *The Book of Curious and Entertaining Information*; al-'§mili, 953–1030/

1547–1621, *al-Kashkul [The Beggar's Bowl]*). The patterns of human experience—especially love—held up by adab also enriched religious thought, particularly that of the Sunni Revival.

In modern scholarship, adab is sometimes taken to represent the secular dimension of Islamic culture or Islamic humanism, and the term *adab literature* has been coined as a catch-all to denote any work (e.g., al-Mas'udi's *Meadows of Gold*) or literary form (e.g., the maqama) that is both instructive and pleasurable.

JULIA BRAY

See also Courtiers; Socializing; al-Tawhidi; Yaqut; Ibn Qutayba' al-Ghazali; Mirrors for Princes; Ibn al-Muqaffa'; Bureaucracy; al-Jahiz

Further Reading

Abu al-Faraj al-Isfahani. *al-Ima' al-Shawa'ir*, ed. Jalal al-'Afliyya. Beirut: Dar al-Nidal, 1404/1984.
———. *Kitab al-aghani*. For editions, *see* Kilpatrick, Hilary. *Musiques sur le Fleuve: Les Plus Belles Pages du Kitab al-Aghani*, trans. Jacques Berque. Paris: Albin Michel, 1995.
——— (attrib.). *Kitab al-Ghuraba'*, trans. Patricia Crone and Shmuel Moreh In *The Book of Strangers: Medieval Arabic Graffiti on the Theme of Nostalgia*. Princeton, NJ: Markus Wiener, 2000.
al-Baghdadi, 'Abd al-Qahir ibn 'Umar. *Khizanat al-Adab*, ed. 'Abd al-Salam M. Harun. Cairo: Dar al-Katib al-'Arab, 1967–1986.
———. *Khizanat al-Adab*, eds. M.N. Tarifi and I. Ya'qub. Beirut: Dar al-Kutub al-'Ilmiyya, 1998.
Bell, Joseph Norment. *Love Theory in Later Hanbalite Islam*. Albany: SUNY Press, 1979.
Bosworth, C.E. *Baha' al-Din al-'Amili and His Literary Anthologies*. Manchester: Manchester University Press, 1989.
Bray, Julia. "Lists and Memory: Ibn Qutayba and Muhammad ibn Habib." In *Culture and Memory in Medieval Islam: Essays in Honour of Wilferd Madelung*, eds. F. Daftary and J.W. Meri, 210–31. London: I.B. Tauris, 2003.
———. "Myth and *Adab*: Ibn 'Abd Rabbih and Others." In *On Fiction and Adab in Medieval Arabic Literature*, eds. Philip Kennedy and Sasson Somekh, 1–54. Leiden: Brill, forthcoming.
Encyclopaedia Iranica, ed. Ehsan Yarshater. London: Routledge & Kegan Paul, 1985. "Adab in Iran," vol. I, 341–349, Dj. Khalegi-Motlagh; "Andarz," vol. II, 11–22, S. Shaked and Z. Safa.
al-Ghazali. "Al-Ghazali on the Manners Relating to Eating." Kitab adab al-akl. *Book XI of the Revival of the Religious Sciences*, Ihya' 'ulum al-din, trans. D. Johnson-Davies. Cambridge: Islamic Texts Society, 2000.
Ibn 'Abd Rabbih. *al-'Iqd al-Farid*, eds. A. Amin et al. Cairo: Matba'at Lajnat al-Ta'lif wa-l-Tarjama wa-l-Nashr, 1359–1372/1940–1952.
———. *al-'Iqd al-Farid*, ed. M. QumayΩa. Beirut: Dar al-Kutub al-'Ilmiyya, 1404 (1983).
Ibn Qutayba. *Adab al-Katib*, ed. Muhammad al-Dali. Beirut: Mu'assasat al-Risala, 1982.
———. *'Uyun al-akhbar*. Cairo, Dar al-Kutub al-Misriyya, 1343–1349/1925–1930. Preface trans. Josef Horovitz, "Ibn Quteyba's *'Uyun al-Akhbar.'"* Islamic Culture* 4 (1930): 171–84.
Kilpatrick, Hilary. *Making the Great Book of Songs: Compilation and the Author's Craft in Abu l-Faraj al-Isbahani's Kitab al-Aghani*. London and New York: Routledge-Curzon, 2003.
al-Suhrawardi. *Kitab Adab al-Muridin*, ed. Menahem Milson. Jerusalem: The Hebrew University, 1978.
———. *A Sufi Rule for Novices. Kitab Adab al-Muridin of Abu al-Najib al-Suhrawardi*, introd. and abridged trans., Menahem Milson. Cambridge, Mass., and London: Harvard University Press, 1975.
al-Tanukhi. *Nishwar al-muhadara*, ed. 'Abbud al-Shalji. Beirut: Dar Sadir, 1971–1973.
———. *The Table-Talk of a Mesopotamian Judge*, trans. D.S. Margoliouth. Part I: London: Royal Asiatic Society, 1922; Parts VIII and II: *Islamic Culture* (1929–1932): 3–6.
al-Tha'alibi. *Lata'if al-ma'arif*, eds. I. al-Abyari and H.K. al-Sayrafi. Cairo: Dar Ihya' al-Kutub al-'Arabiyya, 1960, trans. C.E. Bosworth.
———. *The Book of Curious and Entertaining Information*. Edinburgh: Edinburgh University Press, 1968.
Toorawa, Shawkat M. *Ibn Abi Tahir Tayfur and Arabic Writerly Culture: A Ninth Century Bookman in Baghdad*. London: Routledge-Curzon, 2003.
Yaqut. *Mu'jam al-Udaba' (Irshad al-Arib ila Na'rifat al-Adib)*, ed. Ihsan 'Abbas. Beirut: Dar al-Gharb al-Islami, 1993.

ADEN

The Indian Ocean port city of Aden, Yemen, is located in the southwestern corner of Arabia and about ninety-five nautical miles east of the Bab al-Mandab, which is the entrance to the Red Sea. The medieval city stood on the eastern side of the homonymous peninsula in an area that has been known since British times as "the Crater." The modern toponym reflects local geology and topography; the site of the medieval city is nestled in the crater of a defunct volcano, the walls of which surround it on all but the seaward side. Thanks to its general geographical location, defensible topography, and ample and easily accessible anchorages (and despite its arid climate and shortage of potable water), Aden has been the chief port in the region for extended periods during its long history.

The political history of the city can be reconstructed in detail only from the fifth/eleventh century onward. The Sulayhid rulers of Yemen conquered Aden in AH 454/1062 CE and eventually ceded the administration of the port to the Zuray'ids. The latter initially remitted a portion of the lucrative port taxes as tribute to their Sulayhid overlords. As Sulayhid power waned, however, Zuray'id Aden became an autonomous state, with the port at its center and substantial hinterlands under its jurisdiction. In 530/1135, in an episode that highlights both the nature and the rivalries of Indian Ocean maritime principalities, the ruler of the Arabian Gulf island of Kish/Qais attacked Aden and laid siege to the port unsuccessfully. After the 569/1173 conquest of Yemen by the Ayyubids, Aden lost its autonomy but maintained its prominence as the country's main port. The Ayyubids developed the physical and institutional infrastructure of the port, as did their successors the Rasulids (626–858/1229–1454). State-sponsored development included the building of fortifications, harbor works, warehouses, markets, and customs facilities that marked the urban landscape, and the institution of naval patrols that secured the maritime approaches to the port. The Tahirids (858–923/1454–1517) wrested power from the Rasulids when they captured Aden in 858/1454. Although the Portuguese failed to take Aden during the early tenth/sixteenth century, the Ottomans succeeded in 945/1538.

The commercial importance of medieval Aden cannot be overstated. The fourth-/tenth-century Arab geographer al-Muqaddasi described the port as "the vestibule of China, entrepôt of Yemen, treasury of the West, and mother lode of all trade wares." Several travelers, including Marco Polo and Ibn Battuta, passed through Aden and commented on its bustling port. The most extensive account of commercial life and the organization of trade in Aden appears in Ibn al-Mujawir's *Tarikh al-Mustabsir,* a seventh/thirteenth-century work that was quoted and supplemented by Adeni historian Abu Makhrama (870–947/1465–1540). The *Daftar al-Muzaffari,* an administrative document composed for the Rasulid sultan al-Muzaffar (647–694/1249–1295), highlights the significance of the port as a global market and a source of commercial tax revenues. In letters, legal papers, accounts, and lists dating primarily from the fifth/eleventh to seventh/thirteenth centuries and preserved in the document repository of the Cairo Geniza, Aden emerges as the major Indian Ocean hub for the network of Jewish merchants that operated across the Islamic world from Spain to India and beyond. These and other sources testify to the cosmopolitan nature of the city and the ethnic, linguistic, and sectarian plurality of its port society, which included Arabs, Persians, Indians, Africans, Muslims, Jews, Hindus, and Christians.

The urban growth of Aden in modern times, which began with the British capture of the place in 1839, appears to have erased most physical vestiges of the medieval port. Among the scanty remains is an impressive system of interconnected cisterns that served the city's water supply throughout the medieval period; their construction may date to pre-Islamic times. Also impressive is a tall tower structure of disputed function and date, which appears to have stood near the shoreline of the medieval harbor. Alternatively, a number of archaeological sites on the mainland opposite Aden testify to the manufacturing and agricultural activity connected with the port during its heyday.

ROXANI ELENI MARGARITI

See also Arabia; Geniza; al-Muqaddasi; Yemen

Primary Sources

Abu Makhrama. "Tarikh thaghr 'adan." In *Arabische Texte zur Kenntnis der Stadt Aden im Mittelalter,* ed. Oscar Löfgren. Uppsala: Almqvist & Wiksells Boktryckeri, 1936–1950.
Ibn al-Mujawir. "Tarikh al-Mustabsir." In *Arabische Texte zur Kenntnis der Stadt Aden im Mittelalter*, ed. Oscar Löfgren. Uppsala: Almqvist & Wiksells Boktryckeri, 1936–1950.
Jazim, Abd al-Rahim Muhammad. *Lumière de la Connaissance: Règles, Lois et Coutume du Yémen sous le Règne du Sultan Rasoulide al-Muzaffar.* Sanaa: Centre Français d'Archaeologie et de Sciences Sociales de Sanaa, 2003.

Further Reading

Goitein, S.D. "From Aden to India: Specimens of the Correspondence of India Traders of the Twelfth Century." *Journal of Economic and Social History of the Orient* 23 (1980): 43–66.
———. *Letters of Medieval Jewish Traders.* Princeton, NJ: Princeton University Press, 1973.
———. "Two Eyewitness Reports on an Expedition of the King of Kish (Qais) against Aden." *Bulletin of the School of Oriental and African Studies* 16 (1954): 247–57.
Hunter, Frederick M. *An Account of the British Settlement of Aden.* London: Trübner, 1877.
Kay, Henry C. *Yaman, its Early Mediaeval History.* London: E. Arnold, 1892
King, Geoffrey, and Cristina Tonghini. *A Survey of the Islamic Sites near Aden and in the Abyan District of Yemen.* London: School of Oriental and African Studies, 1996.
Margariti, Roxani E. "Like the Place of Congregation on Judgment Day: Maritime Trade and Urban Organization in Medieval Aden (ca. 1083–1229)." Ph.D. dissertation. Princeton, NJ: Princeton University, 2002.
Prados, Edward. "An Archaeological Investigation of Sira Bay, Aden, Republic of Yemen." *International Journal of Nautical Archaeology* 23.4 (1994): 297–307.
Rex Smith, Gerald. "More on the Port Practices and Taxes of Medieval Aden." *Arabian Studies* 3 (1996): 208–18.
———. "Have You Anything to Declare? Maritime Trade and Commerce in Ayyubid Aden: Practices and Taxes." *Proceedings of the Seminar for Arabian Studies* 25 (1995): 127–40.
Shamrookh, N. "The Commerce and Trade of the Rasulids in the Yemen, 650–858/1231–1454." Ph.D. dissertation. Manchester: University of Manchester, 1993.
Whitcomb, D.S. "Islamic Archaeology in Aden and the Hadhramaut." In *Araby the Blest: Studies in Arabian*

Archaeology, ed. D.T. Potts. Copenhagen: Museum Tusculanum Press, 1988.

'ADUD AL-DAWLA

Abu Shuja' Fanna Khusraw (936–983) is usually known by the honorific 'Adud al-Dawla, which was granted by the Caliph al-Muti' in 962. 'Adud al-Dawla ("Aid of the Dynasty") was the Buyid amir who ruled in Baghdad from 977 until his death. The son of Rukn al-Dawla, he was given control of Fars in 949 at the tender age of 13 or 14. It was there that he spent the majority of his career learning statecraft while focusing on expanding and entrenching his own and his family's power. In these endeavors, like most rulers of the time, he was constantly in need of funds. He took the unusual step of improving agricultural infrastructure with the hope of increased productivity and revenue; this largely worked. Consequently, he was always able to muster greater resources than his opponents. In 975, with his father's blessing, he moved his army into Baghdad to quell the disorder that his cousin 'Izz al-Dawla (also called Bakhtiyar) was unable to control. It provided a convenient excuse to fulfill his ambition of unifying and centralizing his hold on the Buyid domains.

Shortly after his arrival, he forced his cousin to abdicate. However, family power dynamics took precedence. Rukn al-Dawla, as head of the family, was none too pleased by this turn of events and ordered his son to restore 'Izz al-Dawla and withdraw. 'Adud al-Dawla complied, but the respite did not last long. When his father died the next year, 'Adud al-Dawla restarted the machinations against his cousin. The lack of clear lines of succession encouraged him in his endeavor to become the dominant member of the family. In 977, he defeated 'Izz al-Dawla, entered Baghdad, and was given the title *Amir al-Umara'* ("Commander of the Commanders"). 'Adud al-Dawla worked with his brother Mu'ayyid al-Dawla to fight and exile a third brother, Fakhr al-Dawla, who had allied with 'Izz al-Dawla. In the process, 'Adud al-Dawla firmly established his control over the Buyid family holdings and himself as their head. His rule marks the high point of the dynasty. He had diplomatic contacts with the Fatimids and the Byzantines, he exerted real political control, and he even had pretensions of using the title *Shahanshah* ("King of Kings"). He behaved as if he were an independent king, but he recognized the limits on the exercise of power. Therefore, he maintained the fiction of his subservience to the caliph as a useful tool for legitimizing his authority.

In the end, as he was dying, 'Adud al-Dawla attempted to formalize arrangements for his son to succeed him. However, for three months, his advisors had to hide his death to allow them time to transfer the reins to Samsam al-Dawla; this highlights the fact that his arrangements could not have been all that secure or formalized if his advisors had to pretend that he was still alive to make for a successful handover. For all of his power and success in reforming the government, he failed to solve many of the outstanding problems of the dynasty, particularly the question of succession and familial power-sharing.

JOHN P. TURNER

See also Buyids

Primary Sources

Ibn al-Athir. *al-Kamil fi'l-Ta'rikh*, ed. 'Abd al-Wahhab al-Najar. Cairo: Idarat al-Tiba'a al-Muniriya, 1929.
Ibn al-Jawzi. *al-Muntazam fi Ta'rikh al-Muluk wa'l-Umam*. Beirut: Dar al-Kutub al-'Ilmiyah, 1992.
Ibn Khallikan. *Ibn Khallikan's Biographical Dictionary*, ed. William Mac Guckin de Slane. Paris: Printed for the Oriental translation fund of Great Britain and Ireland, 1843.
Ibn Miskawayh. *The Eclipse of the Abbasid Caliphate*, eds. H.F. Amedroz and D.S. Margoliouth. Oxford: B. Blackwell, 1920.
Yaqut. *Irshad al-Arib ila Ma'rifat al-Adib*, ed. D.S. Margoliouth, 7 vols. Leiden: E.J. Brill, 1907.

Further Reading

Donohue, John J. *The Buwayhid Dynasty in Iraq 334H./945 to 403H./1012*. Leiden: Brill, 2003.
Kabir, Mafizullah. *The Buwayhid Dynasty of Baghdad*. Calcutta: Iran Society, 1964.
Mottahedeh, R.P. *Loyalty and Leadership in an Early Islamic Society*. New York: I.B. Tauris, 2001.

ADULTERY

The legal notion of adultery in medieval Islam differs in several respects from contemporary ideas. Muslim jurists would not distinguish between forbidden sexual relations of a married person and other forms of intercourse prohibited by the *Shari'a*. On the one hand, these acts were considered in accordance with the judgments on zina (fornication; unlawful intercourse) in the Qur'an and the hadith. On the other hand, not all extramarital affairs necessarily establish the charge of committing zina. Adultery constitutes, on that ground, a subsidiary part inside of a broader legal category that combines moral, religious, and social values.

The noun *zina* and its grammatical derivations (e.g., *al-zani* [the fornicator])—without counting numerous paraphrases—appear in five verses of the *Qur'an*. Three of these verses list zina together with other sins, namely murder (17:32; 25:68; 60:12), infanticide (17:32 and 60:12), theft, and false accusation (60:12). They do not pronounce specific punishments; however, 25:68 refers to the sufferings of fornicators and murderers in the hereafter. The other two verses imply more significant juridical consequences. Sura 24:2 states the Qur'anic penalty of one hundred lashes for each fornicator, both male and female, and the next verse (24:3) sets an impediment to marriage between fornicators and believers. However, this latter stipulation has been either considered abrogated or taken as but a recommendation by most legal scholars. Instead of following the Qur'anic prescription, later jurisprudence sets the norm for the punishment of zina with the example of the Prophet Muhammad and of 'Ali ibn Abi Talib, who pronounced the sentence of stoning in five cases. The application of the punishment relies on the testimony of four witnesses in explicit terms or on the confession of the perpetrator, which is to be repeated four times.

Committing zina figures prominently among the most serious sins imaginable in Islamic ethics and puts into question the actual belief of the perpetrator. More than that, zina imposes one of the five "limit penalties" (hudud, sing. hadd) specified in the Qur'an, the only one that had been sharpened by the more severe precedents in the hadith. Zina constitutes not just a personal sin but a criminal offense against the community to be judged by worldly legal authorities. Accounting the properties of the crime, the Andalusian jurist Ibn Rushd defines zina as "all sexual intercourse that occurs outside of a valid marriage, the semblance *(shubha)* of marriage, or lawful ownership" (1996, vol. 2, 521). To appreciate the significance of this statement, we shall briefly discuss those sexual acts that give rise to uncertainty with respect to their nature as zina.

First, there are a number of practices that are not immediately conceived of as sexual intercourse. Some jurists count masturbation among the manifest forms of zina, but their position is contrasted, for example, by a statement of Ahmad Ibn Hanbal comparing masturbation to a mere phlebotomy. There is also no consensus about whether copulation with animals should be punished with the hadd penalty. Opinions differ not less on homosexual intercourse: some jurists impose stoning in any case, some distinguish between the active and the passive partner, and others leave the decision to the discretion of the judge (Bousquet 1990, 83–4; Musallam 1983, 33–4; Peters 2002, 509). Lesbian activities are rarely introduced in legal manuals; they are generally passed over in silence (see Murray 2005).

Second, a nontrivial topic of legal reasoning on zina consists of the attempt to circumscribe the proper meaning of "lawful ownership." Sexual intercourse with one's own slave is permitted. The category of possession, however, raises economic issues that collide with moral concerns. Typical conflicts are cases in which parental and economical notions intermingle (e.g., the father who has intercourse with his son's slave). Opinions vary widely between the application of the hadd penalty and the requirement of a possession transfer with restitution of the slave's value to the former owner (Ibn Rushd 1996, vol. 2, 522).

Third (and this is related to the second point), an important legal instrument with respect to zina concerns the possible erroneous belief of the perpetrator of having acted within the state of actually being married (i.e., to have intercourse with somebody mistaken to be one's wife or without fulfilling the legal prerequisites of marriage). The avoidance of the hadd penalty for errors resulting from resemblance (shubha) follows from a noncanonical hadith (see Powers 2002, 62–3, n. 40, for references).

The contradictions between the rigorousness of the legal norm and the procedural as well as doctrinal formulations against its strict application allow for different conclusions about the function of the law. One position advances that the entire criminal legislation on zina serves the sole aim of avoiding the "divulgence of scandale" (Bousquet 1990, 89–90). However, because the matrimonial relationship is crucial to the whole fabric of family law in early Islam, this legislation appears also as a "protective wall" that ensures the maintenance of social and economic rights and duties (Coulson 1979, 65–8).

TILMAN HANNEMANN

See also Concubinage; Crime and Punishment; Family; Gender and Sexuality

Further Reading

Bousquet, Georges-Henri. *L'Éthique Sexuelle de l'Islam.* Paris: de Brouwer, 1990.
Coulson, Noel J. "Regulation of Sexual Behavior under Traditional Islamic Law." In *Society and the Sexes in Medieval Islam,* ed. Alaf Lutfi Al-Sayyid-Marsot. Malibu, Calif: Undena Publications, 1979.
Ibn Rushd. *The Distinguished Jurist's Primer: A Translation of Bidayat Al-Mujtahid,* ed. Imran Ahsan Khan Nyazee, 2 vols. Reading: Garnet, 1996.
Murray, Stephen O. "Woman-Woman Love in Islamic Societies." In *Women and Islam: Critical Concepts in Sociology,* ed. Haideh Moghissi, vol. 2. London and New York: Routledge, 2005.
Musallam, Basim F. *Sex and Society in Islam: Birth Control before the Nineteenth Century.* Cambridge: Cambridge University Press, 1983.

Peters, Ruud. "Art. Zina." In *The Encyclopaedia of Islam, New Edition*, vol. XII, 510–11. Leiden: Brill, 2002.

Powers, David S. *Law, Society, and Culture in the Maghrib, 1300–1500*. Cambridge: Cambridge University Press, 2002.

Schacht, Joseph. "Adultery as an Impediment to Marriage in Islamic and in Canon Law." *Archives d'Histoire du Droit Oriental*, NS 1 (1952): 105–23.

AFTERLIFE

"Think not of those who are slain in Allah's Way as dead. Nay, they live, finding their sustenance in the Presence of their Lord" (Qur'an 3:169). Medieval Qur'an commentators usually connect this verse to the battle of Uhud (AH 3/625 CE), during which the Muslims had been defeated and had suffered many casualties. They further explain that the verse had been revealed to console the bereaved. In trying to be more specific as to the bliss bestowed upon "those slain in Allah's Way," these commentators adduce a prophetic tradition (hadith, q.v.) that states that the souls of the shuhada' (those killed in Allah's Way) wander in Paradise, in the bodies of green birds. So wonderful is their bliss that, when God asks them for their wish, their only desire is to return to the present world so that they may be killed again. With this notion in mind, it is not surprising that this particular verse has become one of the most frequently cited verses in the last few years, mainly in relation to suicide bombings.

It is not only the fate of the shuhada' that has created the eagerness to explore the world beyond ours; this yearning is deeply rooted in religious anxieties and aspirations of every pious person. Medieval Islam was very much aware of this need and supplied the "essential information" in various ways: Qur'an commentaries, hadith, and theological and mystical works, as well as more popular treatises. The latter constitute an especially colorful and descriptive genre that consists of hundreds or maybe thousands of tales that provide meticulous details about the world beyond the present one: the encounter with the angels Munkar and Nakir, the Barzakh, the delights of Paradise, the torments of Hell, and so on (see the relevant entries in *The Encyclopaedia of Islam* and *The Encyclopaedia of the Qur'an*). Although these details answer the curiosity of the believers and deliver some comfort, their main purpose is to illuminate the enigma of the Divine Providence. As a counsel to pious Muslims who might wonder about the reason for the scrupulous life they have to lead, this literature elaborates on the ongoing communication between the dead and the living, assuming a direct proportion between the performance of duties in the present world and the rewards granted in the next.

Ibn Abi al-Dunya (d. AH 281/894 CE) may be considered one of the earliest and most prolific writers who developed this popular afterlife genre. He covered the different stages of the hereafter and presented descriptions of the upper worlds in short treatises. His works draw attention to three main ways by which the living can learn about the dead:

1. Tales of people who woke up a few seconds after their death, described their experiences, and died again *(Man 'Asha Ba'da al-Mawt [Those Who Lived After Death])*.
2. Tales of people who stayed in the vicinity of a graveyard and encountered the dead, either inside their graves or nearby, in forms that indicate the taste of death *(Kitab al-Qubur [The Book of Graves])*.
3. Tales of people who appeared in dreams after passing away and portrayed their new abode; dream narrations make the richest source of information about death and the next world *(Kitab al-Manam [The Book of Dreams])*.

Regardless of the method chosen, each anecdote in this genre creates the feeling of a physical contact between the two worlds and alludes to the fact that death is not the final stage of life. The dead in these anecdotes are considered "living dead." They meet with each other and discuss occurrences of the present world; they have doubts and desires; they are capable of building relationships with the living; and they always deliver reliable information. This makes the living believe that they can learn from the experience of the dead, which is accumulated in the dead's new vicinity. The dead are perceived as those who understand the value of duties but who are incapable of performing any, whereas living people can carry out deeds but are not aware of their consequences in the next world. Thus, the living choose to follow the dead's instructions about how to behave to guarantee their own comfortable existence when their turn comes. A large portion of these anecdotes focuses on the fact that the dead's sepulchral sufferings are mitigated through good deeds performed by the living. These tales also illustrate how praying for the dead, visiting their graves, and accomplishing their duties are likely to reduce the agonies of the living after their own deaths.

In accordance with this, the edifying nature of this genre in general and the heritage of Ibn Abi al-Dunya in particular become apparent. Although never straightforward, this genre constantly encourages the dwellers of the present abode to perform certain deeds and refrain from others. Its picturesque and tangible descriptions expressed in simple daily language and phrased in an unequivocal way answer human uncertainties and ease the fears of death. These tales penetrate the heart and become a reliable authority according to which pious life is conducted.

LEAH KINBERG

See also Death and Dying; Dream and Dream Interpretation; Hadith; Jihad; Mecca; Qur'an

Primary Sources

Ibn Abi al-Dunya's treatises. *K. Man 'Asha ba'da al-Mawt*. Beirut, 1986.
———. *K. al-'Uqubat*. Beirut, 1996.
Kinberg, L. *The Book of Death and the Book of Graves by Ibn Abi al-Dunya*. Haifa, Al-Karmil Publication Series, 1983.
———. *Morality in the Guise of Dreams: Ibn Abi al-Dunya's K. al-Manam*. Leiden: Brill, 1994.

Further Reading

Eklund, R. *Life between Death and Resurrection According to Islam*. Uppsala, 1941.
Kinberg, L. "Interaction between This World and the Afterworld in Early Islamic Tradition." *Oriens* 29–30 (1986): 285–308.
———. "The Individual's Experience as it Appears to the Community: An Examination of Six Dream Narrations Dealing with the Islamic Understanding of Death." *Al-Qantara* 21 (2000): 425–44.
O'Shaughnessy. *Muhammad's Thought on Death: A Thematic Study of the Qur'anic Data*. Leiden: Brill, 1969.
Smith, Jane I., and Y.Y. Haddad. *The Islamic Understanding of Death*. New York, 1981.
The Encyclopaedia of Islam. Leiden: Brill, 1960–2004. Barzakh, Djanna, Hurriyya, Ibn Abi 'L-Dunya, Munkar wa-Nakir, Nar.
The Encyclopaedia of the Qur'an, ed. J.D. McOuliffe. Leiden: Brill, 2003. Barzakh, Death and the Dead, Eschatology, Hell and Hellfire, Houris, Paradise.

AGHLABIDS

The Aghlabid dynasty ruled the emirate of Ifriqiyya (modern-day Tunisia) from 800–909 CE. During that century, they consolidated the economic and military position of the province, exercising considerable control over the Mediterranean after the conquest of Sicily. A failure to overcome critical internal divisions, however, weakened the Aghlabids and led to their collapse before the Fatimid army of Kutama Berbers.

Ibrahim b. al-Aghlab (800–812), governor of the Zab region on the western border of the 'Abbasid empire, founded the dynasty after putting down a revolt by the jund (Arab military class) in Qayrawan, the capital of Ifriqiyya. He then negotiated his reward with the 'Abbasid caliph, Harun Al-Rashid. The caliph appointed him emir (prince) and gave him virtual autonomy after Ibrahim pledged forty thousand dinars to the imperial treasury and agreed to forego a one hundred thousand dinar subsidy normally received by the province.

The revolt that brought the Aghlabids to power was a portent of a perennial problem of the Aghlabid rulers: the propensity of the volatile jund to rebel. After two further revolts, Ibrahim I constructed a fortified palace complex, the Qsar al-Qadim, which was three miles south of Qayrawan and protected by a special guard of black slaves. Although the third Aghlabid emir, Ziyadat Allah (817–838), channeled much of the revolutionary potential of the jund toward a jihad (holy war) against Sicily, the Aghlabids never successfully counterbalanced this force.

Another source of tension was the ulama, the influential class of religious scholars whose piety and learning commanded the respect of urban and rural society. The ulama critiqued excesses and injustices they identified in the Aghlabid regime, including usury, un-Islamic taxation (applying a land tax to Muslim subjects and demanding payment of tithes in money not in kind), and the production and sale of wine. The ulama also censured the pleasure-seeking lifestyle of the Aghlabid court as excessive and illicit. In addition, tensions between the rival Hanafite and Malikite schools of Islamic law were compounded by controversy over mu'tazilism (a rationalist approach to Islam), which the caliph Ma'mun (813–833) made the official doctrine of the empire. In Ifriqiyya, the literalist Malikite approach (which was propagated at Qayrawan by the eminent jurist Asad b. al-Furat [d. 828]) took root and became the dominant school. It was under the Aghlabids that Al-Furat's student Sahnun (d. 854) penned the authoritative digest of Malikite doctrine, *Al-Mudawanna*. The emirs, who were sensitive to public opinion, consistently selected Maliki jurists for positions in their administration. As prolific builders, the Aghlabids also attempted to shore up religious legitimacy through the extensive construction of religious buildings. Ziyadat Allah I rebuilt the Great Mosque of Qayrawan in 836, and the Zaytuna Mosque of Tunis was built by Abu Ibrahim Ahmad (856–863). Great resources were also invested in public works, particularly water projects, including aqueducts and the famous circular cisterns at Qayrawan.

These last projects increased the region's agricultural productivity, contributing to economic expansion as Ifriqiyya regained prominence as a grain exporter. Qayrawan also became an important terminus for trans-Saharan trade, primarily of slaves and gold. This rise in east-west and north–south trade proved a significant factor in the Aghlabids' external policies.

With its land borders relatively quiet, the emirate was most vulnerable on its coasts, and a series of ribats (fortified monasteries) were built to guard against Christian raids. Although they had diplomatic exchanges with Charlemagne's Christian empire (which posed no naval threat), the Byzantines posed a recurrent economic and military threat. In 827 C.E., a rebel Byzantine naval commander approached Ziyadat Allah III to help invade Sicily. For the emir, the invasion presented an opportunity to take over a Byzantine base across from Ifriqiyya, to control east-west Mediterranean traffic, and, not insignificantly, to channel the domestic discontent of the ulama and jund into a campaign against an external enemy. The emir placed the jurist Al-Furat, who had argued for jihad against Christian Sicily, in charge of the invasion force, which left from the garrison port of Susa with ten thousand men. They made early gains in the west by taking Palermo in 842, but they took seventy-five years to oust the final Byzantine forces. However, while securing Sicily, the Aghlabids extended their power considerably on the Italian peninsula, sending repeated expeditions to Calabria and Campania, raiding Rome in 846 C.E., and establishing a presence on the Adriatic coast in Brindisi and Bari. By 902 C.E., they were well established in Sicily and dominated the mainland through trade and military power.

Despite these external successes, the policies of Ibrahim II (875–902 C.E.), who tried to consolidate Aghlabid authority by slaughtering the Arab aristocracy and the jund, undermined the Aghlabid position in Ifriqiyya. His repression weakened the military and provoked widespread resentment, thus paving the way for the downfall of the dynasty. In 909 C.E., the last Aghlabid amir, Ziyadat Allah III, fled before the Ismaili armies that helped establish the Fatimids.

JONATHAN DAVID WYRTZEN

See also Kharijis; Berber Revolt; Qayrawan; Al Ma'mun; Tax and Taxation; Slaves and Slave Trade; Western Islamic World; Trade, Mediterranean; Muslim–Byzantine Relations; Sicily; Ismailis; Fatimids; North Africa

Primary Sources

Ibn Al-Athir. *Kamil fi al-Ta'rikh*. Beirut: Dar Sadir, 1965–1967.
Ibn 'Idhari, al-Marrakushi. *Al-Bayan al Mugrib*. Paris: P. Geuthner, 1930.
Al-Bakri. Abi 'Ubayd. *Kitab al-Masalik wa al Mamalik*. Qartaj: Al Dar Al-Arabiyah lil-Kitab, 1992.

Further Reading

Abun-Nasr, Jamil M. *A History of the Maghrib in the Islamic Period.* Cambridge: Cambridge University Press, 1987.
Ahmad, Aziz. *A History of Islamic Sicily.* Edinburgh: Edinburgh University Press, 1975.
Ibn Khaldun. *The Muqaddimah*, trans. Franz Rosenthal. Princeton, NJ: Princeton University Press, 1967.
Julien, Charles André. *History of North Africa: Tunisia, Algeria, Morocco, from the Arab Conquest to 1830*, trans. John Petrie. London: Routledge & K. Paul, 1970.
Kreutz, Barbara M. *Before the Normans: Southern Italy in the Ninth and Tenth Centuries*. Philadelphia: University of Pennsylvania Press, 1991.
Marcais, George. *L'Architecture; Tunisie, Algérie, Maroc, Espagne, Sicile.* Paris: A. Picard, 1926–1927.
Talbi, Mohamed. *L'Émirat Aghlabide*, 184–296, 800–909, *Histoire Politique.* Paris: Librairie d'Amérique et d'Orient, 1966.

AGRA RED FORT

After his victory over the last ruler of the Lodi dynasty, Sultan Ibrahim (1517–1526), the first Mughal emperor Babur (r. 1526–1530) installed himself in the Lodi mud-brick fort at Agra and ordered the construction of a large, three-story stepwell that was completed in March 1527. It was only under his grandson Akbar (r. 1556–1605), however, that imperial patronage seriously focused on Agra and made its fort into an immensely strong fortified palace city to rival Delhi and Lahore. Akbar's chronicler, Abu'l-Fazl, referred to the emperor's five hundred buildings in Agra, an exaggeration that nevertheless suggests the massive transformation Akbar and his architect Qasim Khan Mir Barr u Bahr oversaw between 1565 and 1573. Although very few Akbar-period buildings still stand, the early semicircular ground plan of the Agra Fort is evident, with its 22-meter high walls stretching over 2.5 kilometers.

Faced with red sandstone and white marble, the Hathi (Elephant) Gate on the west was the main public entrance. Built in the same materials is the so-called Jahangiri Mahal, the best-preserved Akbari building inside the walls. Adjacent to and overlooking the Jumna River, its open architecture lets those inside the palace view the hectic river traffic and catch cooling breezes off the water. Its several inner courtyards, its overall layout, and its decorative stonework are influenced by the non-Islamic palace traditions of Gujarat and Rajasthan and of the massive fort at Gwalior, an Akbari synthesis that is most strikingly revealed in the imperial city of Fatehpur Sikri only 42 kilometers to the west, where the emperor resided from 1569–1585.

Additions to the Agra Fort by Akbar's son and successor Jahangir (1605–1627) are also known

View of exterior. Moghul style, 1565. Built by Akbar. Credit: SEF/Art Resource, NY. Jahangiri Mahal, Red Fort, Agra, Uttar Pradesh, India.

largely from texts. They included a small palace and a public audience hall. Contemporary paintings also show the Shah Burj (King's Tower), from which Jahangir suspended a belled Chain of Justice, purportedly designed so that petitioners could ring it and get his attention.

However, it was during the reign of Shah Jahan (1627–1658) that the Agra Fort was transformed through lavish and astute patronage. His regnal name means "King of the World," an image that came to dominate almost all aspects of the arts under his patronage. Between 1627 and 1637, most of the fort's structures were replaced with buildings clothed in white marble or stucco. Materials reflected rank, as did the order of structures. On the east side of a large rectangular courtyard, the pillared public audience hall was built of red sandstone that was covered with white stucco. The hall's east side, however, was lined with white marble and inlaid with precious stones, for it presented a jharoka or balcony window where the emperor made regular formal appearances to his closest adherents, who were assembled according to rank. On the east side of the courtyard was a pillared hall with a throne room containing baluster

columns, a form that was explicitly derived from European prints and used only in an imperial context. To the north was a chahar bagh, a cruciform garden with a central fountain that was particularly favored by Mughal patrons, for whom it recalled their descent from Timur and their origins in Samarqand. On its east side was a private audience hall that contained a Persian inscription likening the emperor to the sun, a conceit that was reinforced by solar medallions in the marble stone. The emperor's private residence was located next to an open court and looked out over the river. His bedroom was so richly gilded that there appeared to be a gold aura around his head during his ritual jharoka appearances.

Within the fort is also a large white marble mosque that was completed in 1653. In keeping with well-established Mughal precedent, it has three white marble domes that rise above its qiblah wall. Stunning black marble inscriptions convey images of paradise and laud Shah Jahan as a world ruler.

Materials, imagery, and inscriptions weave a common theme. Interior gardens and their fountains evoke the desirable order and pure water of paradise. Forms like the baluster column are reserved only for the environment in which the emperor lives. Other forms appropriated from European prints include the scales of justice and the solar orb; in the circumscribed environment of the Mughal court and the Agra Fort, these forms were well understood, although it is unlikely that they would have conveyed much meaning to those outside of the purview of court refinements. Likewise, the intense, concentrated symmetry of architectural space is an expression of social order that is remarkable for its consistency and forcefulness. The ruler and his family were located on an exalted plane. The Agra Fort presented not just symmetry but also precise definition and regulation of movement from courtyard to chamber to courtyard. The temporal world was firmly set in place as well: time was ritualized, and the emperor's set appearances guaranteed that the elaborate system continued to function. It is no wonder that European visitors so admired the Mughal court and that European rulers saw court ceremonies and imagery worth imitating. The Mughals had mastered the political art of fabricating a monarch who was also the empire's indispensable hero.

ANTHONY WELCH

See also Akbar; Alhambra; Architecture, Secular: Civil; Architecture, Secular: Military; Architecture, Secular: Palaces; Architecture, Religious; Babar; Bureaucrats; Delhi; Gardens and Gardening; Hindus; Humayun; India; Mosques; Lahore; Mughals; Nur Jahan; Painting, Miniature; Persian; Persians; Qur'an; Timurids; Turks; Water

Further Reading

Asher, Catherine B. "Architecture of Mughal India." In *The New Cambridge History of India,* I:4. Cambridge: Cambridge University Press, 1992.
Brand, Michael, and Glenn D. Lowry. *Fatehpur-Sikri.* Bombay: Marg Publications, 1987.
Gascoigne, Bamber. *The Great Moghuls.* New York: Harper & Row, 1971.
Koch, Ebba M. *Mughal Architecture.* Munich: Prestel-Verlag, 1992.
———. *Mughal Art and Imperial Ideology: Collected Essays.* Oxford: Oxford University Press, 2001.
Nath, R. *History of Mughal Architecture.* New Jersey: Humanities Press, 1982.
Rizvi, S.A.A. *Fathpur-Sikri.* Bombay: D.B. Taraporevala Sons, 1975.

AGRICULTURE

The history of Islamic agriculture *(filāḥa)* goes back to very ancient times, to the time of the conquests (seventh and eighth centuries). When the Muslims as conquerors came to the different regions—and where the inhabitants of the different regions became Muslims—attention to the land became a concrete and nondeferable matter. The decaying structure of the landed estates of late antiquity, where they still existed, was eliminated; the land was divided up among the warriors and their families; land left neglected and uncultivated for a long time started to be tilled again. This was the start in the Islamic countries of what some scholars have very aptly called the "green revolution": this revolution would later form the basis of countless and advantageous exchanges between the East—including the Far East—and the West, and it points to the Muslims as the pioneers of a new way of farming. Confirmation of what took place can first be found in the many texts and archaeological data concerning the development of technology related to agriculture; several dams and barrage systems that had already existed in pre-Islamic times were restored, and other new ones were built. Systems for transporting water (canals, aqueducts), raising water [šādūf, sāqiya, nā'ūra (noria)], and storing water (tanks with settling apparatus) spread until they became commonplace in the countryside and in towns; various types of water mills and windmills and complex distillation equipment enabled a series of processes related to agriculture (grinding cereals, pressing olives, refining cane sugar, distilling rose water/oil) to be at least partly automated.

In many different parts of the Iranian Plateau and from Mesopotamia to Spain, the digging of a thick network of canals (which made it possible to irrigate the fields regularly) led, on the one hand, to the introduction of crops that needed a lot of water all year round into regions with an unfavourable climate (i.e., the migration of plants from the Far East, acclimation in India, and movements over sea and land to the coasts of Africa and Arabia). On the other hand, it laid the foundations for another important aspect of Islamic agriculture: the growing of flowers and ornamental plants and, essentially, the development of that marvel of art and thought that would continue for centuries to be the art of the Islamic garden. The written "scientific" tradition of the subject also stresses its excellence. Among the many sources in Greek—although there are also many contributions from other cultures—some writings are outstanding:

1. *The Georgika,* which was attributed to Democritus (the author, who is obviously not the pre-Socratic Greek philosopher, may be the same person as second century BC writer Bolos of Mendes).
2. *The Synagogue* by Vindanios Anatolios of Berytos (in Arabic texts he was called Anatolios

or Junius; his work occurred during the fourth and fifth centuries CE).

3. *The Georgika* by Kassianos Bassos Scholasticos (sixth century CE), which was referred to by Muslims as Qusṭus or Kassianos (this work was translated from Greek into Arabic around the year 827 with the title *al-Filāḥa al-rumīya*, but there is also another translation, not from Greek but from Pahlavi, which was entitled *Kitāb al-zar'*).

A special case in the most ancient Arabic literature is the monumental work *al-Filāḥa al-nabaṭīya (Nabatean Agriculture)*. The study of plants accounts for more than half of the work, but it also says a lot about agricultural techniques like grafting, soil improvement, and so on. This work, which introduces itself as being of pre-Islamic origin and being rearranged and translated into Arabic (possibly during the tenth century) by Ibn Waḥšiya—but which may have been written in Arabic between the eighth and ninth centuries—contains many very old contributions of various origins. The fact that, unlike other treatises from the first centuries of Islam, it has come down to us in its entirety makes it a tremendously important point of reference.

In the truly Islamic textual tradition, there are many treatises from different periods and regions. The earliest works, written by grammarians and lexicographers, were concerned with defining the scientific Arabic terminology of the subject; problems arose from the fact that many plants were often called by different names in different (although nearby) places. The works were soon joined by other books that show how the subject evolved. These include the following: in Egypt, the *Qawānīn al-dawāwīn* by Ibn Mammātī (d. 1209); in Spain, the *Kitāb al-mugnī fī'l-filāḥa* (1073) by Ibn Ḥaǧǧāǧ al-Išbīlī (the Sevillian) and, later, the *Kitāb al-filāḥa* by Ibn al-'Awwām al-Išbīlī (twelfth–thirteenth century); in modern times, in Syria, the *'Alam al-malāḥa fī 'ilm al-filāḥa* (1725) by 'Abd al-Ġanī al-Nābulusī, summed up an earlier great work, which has not come down to us, by Riyāḍ al-Dīn al-'Āmirī (d. 1529).

From the fourteenth century onward, Islamic agriculture began a slow but inexorable process of decline (see, for example, the case of Egypt during the Mameluke period; however, but the crisis period started much earlier in several regions). The causes identified include the increasing rigidity of Islamic culture, which was accompanied by less attention to scientific developments and technology; the depopulation of the countryside as a result of wars, invasions, epidemics, and policies that were not favorable to agriculture; and the progressive economic and commercial growth of Europe, which became more

and more competitive as time went on. By the eve of the modern age, no traces would remain of the Islamic "green revolution" of the first centuries; however, the valuable contribution of the Muslims is still universally recognised today in the history of agriculture in both the East and the West.

PAOLA CARUSI

See also Aqueducts; Technology, Mills: Water and Wind

Further Reading

Ashtor, Eliyahu. *A Social and Economic History of the Near East in the Middle Ages*. Berkeley: University of California Press, 1976.

Fahd, T. "Botany and Agriculture." In *Encyclopedia of the History of Arabic Science*, eds. R. Rashed and R. Morelon, 3 vols, vol. 3. London, New York: Routledge, 1996.

al-Hassan, Ahmad Y. and Donald R. Hill. *Islamic Technology: An Illustrated History*. Cambridge: Cambridge University Press; Paris: UNESCO, 1986 (reprinted 1992).

Hill, D.R. "Engineering." In *Encyclopedia of the History of Arabic Science*, eds. R. Rashed and R. Morelon, 3 vols, vol. 3, 751–95. London, New York: Routledge, 1996.

Udovitch, Abraham L., ed. *The Islamic Middle East, 700–1900. Studies in Economic and Social History*. Princeton, NJ: The Darwin Press, 1981.

Watson, Andrew M. *Agricultural Innovation in the Early Islamic world: The Diffusion of Crops and Farming Techniques, 700–1100*. Cambridge: Cambridge University Press, 1983.

'A'ISHA BINT ABI BAKR

'A'isha bint Abi Bakr (d. 678 CE), the second wife of the Prophet Muhammad (d. 632), attained both a revered and reviled status in medieval Islamic civilization. Controversies abounded in the depiction of her life within both Sunni and Shi'is Muslim sources. 'A'isha's remembrance, which was recorded exclusively by men, defined her central role in debates about female sexuality, politics, and sectarianism.

'A'isha was the wife of the most important man in Islamic history and the daughter of Abu Bakr (d. 634), a staunch companion of the Prophet and the first political leader after his death. 'A'isha's marriage to the Prophet at the age of nine was an extension of the close bond between her famous husband and father. 'A'isha, along with the other wives of the Prophet, became a member of a special female elite in Muslim society that is defined in the Qur'an by the phrase "Mothers of the Believers" (33:6). The Qur'an also specifically directed these women to "stay behind a curtain" (hijab) (this is currently defined as a veil) and to "stay in their houses" (33:33), an injunction that was eventually used in the medieval period to separate all women from the public sphere.

'A'isha attained the status of Muhammad's favorite wife after the death of his first wife, Khadija (d. 619), but her reputation was threatened at the age of fourteen by an accusation of adultery. Her innocence was revealed by the Qur'an (24:11–20), but the incident was interpreted differently by the Shi'i Muslim minority, who claimed that the revelation was not directed at 'A'isha, whose name does not appear explicitly in these verses. The accusation of adultery thus became a cause of Sunni-Shi'is Muslim friction during the medieval period.

After the Prophet's death, 'A'isha opposed the fourth caliph, 'Ali ibn Abi Talib (d. 661), the first Shi'is Muslim leader, at the Battle of the Camel (656). Her defeat and the deaths of so many Muslims on both sides of the conflict made 'A'isha an object of shared Sunni and Shi'i Muslim censure. Both groups used this political disaster as a lesson to all medieval Muslim women about the dangers of their participation in politics.

The role of 'A'isha as a source of the Prophet Muhammad's words and deeds as recorded in medieval collections of hadith (traditions) became central to Sunni legal thought during the medieval period. By contrast, Shi'is Muslims rejected 'A'isha as a deeply flawed and unreliable source for their interpretation of Islamic history and law. Sunni Muslims, however, continue to revere her as an object of revelation and the source of much of their faith.

DENISE A. SPELLBERG

See also Abu Bakr; Muhammad, the Prophet

Primary Sources

Spellberg, D.A. *Politics, Gender, and the Islamic Past: The Legacy of 'A'isha bint Abi Bakr*. New York: Columbia University Press, 1994.
Stowasser, Barbara F. *Women in the Qur'an: Tradition and Interpretations*. New York: Oxford University Press, 1994.

AKBAR (R. 1556–1605)

Abu'l-Fath Jalal al-Din Muhammad Akbar was the most celebrated, powerful, and controversial Mughal emperor of India. Succeeding to the throne at the death of his father Humayun in 1556 when he was thirteen years old, he transformed a weak dynasty and administration into a Mughal Empire that controlled most of India from the capital at Agra and that established patterns of administration and rule (eloquently laid out in *A'in-i Akbar*) that would persist for a couple of centuries after him. The first Indian-born Mughal, with a Central Asian father and a Persian mother, Akbar embodied the cultural synthesis that marked out his reign, during which Persianate cultural interaction with Indian vernacular cultures was at its apogee.

In 1560, Akbar brought the regency of Bayram Khan to an end and set out to consolidate his power by a mixed policy of conquest and marriage alliances. He established his power in the Gangeatic plain by conquering Bihar (1574) and Bengal (1576) and extended his power into Malwa and Rajasthan through marriage alliances that brought capable non-Muslim notables (e.g., the organizational genius Raja Todar Mal and his companion Birbal) to court. Akbar perpetuated the Mughal policy of importing talented Persian warriors, bureaucrats, poets, and scholars into India. At the height of his power, his empire included Kashmir (taken in 1587) and parts of the Deccan plateau (taken in campaigns in the 1590s). His incorporation of northern India into the empire meant that, for the first time since Asoka, the ruling dynasty controlled most of the subcontinent. In the *Akbarnama*, his friend Abu 'l-Fadl 'Allami (d. 1602) celebrated him as the shadow of God on earth, whose authority and wisdom was supreme in matters temporal and spiritual. From the 1570s, Akbar began hosting religious dispute in his new 'Ibadatkhana in his retreat of Fatehpur Sikri; in 1579, he declared himself to be the ultimate religious authority in the land, which angered most of the Sunni ulema at court. He created his own religion, which he named the divine faith (din-i ilahi). This was a unique synthesis of Islamic and Indian forms of religiosity. His patronage of fine arts and projects to translate and depict Vedic epics such as the *Mahabharata* (rendered as the *Razmnama*), his encouragement of philosophers, free thinkers, and Shi'is notables at court, and his bibliophilia despite his illiteracy further alienated the ulema. Discontent and the failure of the Deccan campaigns toward the end of his reign led to the rebellion of his son Salim, the future Jahangir. When Akbar died in 1605, his religious innovations had failed to make a lasting impression, but the Mughal Empire was arguably at the height of its power.

SAJJAD H. RIZVI

See also Abu 'l-Fadl 'Allami; Dara Shikuh; Humayun; Mughals

Primary Sources

Abu 'l-Fadl 'Allami. *Akbarnama*, tr. H. Beveridge, 3 vols. Calcutta: Asiatic Society, 1897–1921.
———. *A'in-i Akbar*, tr. H. Blochmann & Jarret, 3 vols.
Habib, Irfan, ed. *Akbar and His India*. New Delhi: Oxford University Press, 2000.

Hottinger, Arnold. *Akbar der Grosse (1542–1605): Herrscher über Indien Durch Verschnung der Religionen.* Munich: W-Fink, 1998.

Moosvi, Shireen, ed. *Episodes in the Life of Akbar: Contemporary Records and Reminiscences.* New Delhi: National Book Trust, 1989.

Nizami, K.A. *Akbar and Religion.* Delhi: Idara-i-Adabiyat-i-Dilli, 1989.

Rizvi, S.A.A. *Religious and Intellectual History of the Muslims in Akbar's Reign.* New Delhi: Munshiram Manoharlal, 1975.

Streusand, D. *The Formation of the Mughal Empire.* New Delhi: Oxford University Press, 1989.

ALCHEMY

The term *kīmiyā'*, which means "alchemy" in Arabic, apparently derives from the Greek *chymeia/chēmeia*, a term that was already used to indicate the science of alchemy in late antiquity in Alexandria, Egypt (see also *cheō* [to pour] and *chyma* [fused metal, particularly gold]).

According to a tradition found in the *Fihrist* of Ibn al-Nadim (tenth century), the Muslims may have acquired their very first knowledge of alchemy at the beginning of the eighth century, when the Umayyad prince Khalid ibn Yazid (d. 705), desiring to know and study the science of the Greeks, brought philosophers from an Egyptian city (presumably Alexandria) and commissioned them to translate a number of scientific texts, including early treatises in alchemy. The texts reached Syria, thus becoming available to Muslim scholars.

Very little is known about which texts were translated into Arabic in the Umayyad period, both alchemic and others. However, it was probably from this time onward—during the earliest years of the 'Abbasid caliphate and certainly more intensively later—that a substantial number of alchemical writers in Greek gradually came to be taught in Arabic in Baghdad: from the pseudo-Democritus, Pythagorus, Hermes, the pseudo-Apollonius of Tyan, Zosimos of Panopolis, Mary the Jewess, and Theodorus to Cleopatra. These figures were considered by Muslim alchemists at every stage of their history as the undisputed masters of an ancient tradition. Over time, other authors of various origin were added to the Greeks—Syrians, Persians, Indians, and perhaps Chinese—so that, between the end of the eighth century and the beginning of the ninth, the time was ripe to start producing new treatises in Arabic. Just a few famous names suffice to recall the importance and continuity of the Islamic alchemical tradition: Jabir ibn Hayyan, who was credited with a corpus of some three thousand titles (eighth/ninth centuries); Muhammad ibn Zakariyya al-Razi (Rhazes); Ibn Umayl al-Tamimi and Maslama al-Majriti (tenth century); and al-'Iraqi, al-Jildaki, and al-Izniqi (thirteenth–fifteenth centuries). In accordance with the most ancient customs of the discipline, the treatises were soon followed by their respective commentaries: from the tenth century on, many alchemical treatises took the form of commentaries on preceding authors, either pre-Islamic or—in the case of the later alchemists—Muslim. Textual materials were thus gradually layered and sedimented to form a palimpsest that became ever more difficult to read.

In Islam, as in ancient times, alchemy revolves around a mysterious central nucleus that is its innermost heart. A very high level of craftsmanship embraces firstly the arts of fire (metallurgy, particularly the working of precious metals, ceramics, and glass [colored glasses, precious synthetic stones, and ceramic enamels]) and then extends to the preparation of various types of coloring (from fabric dyes to artistic materials for book production). Around this nucleus is arranged the chemical knowledge of the alchemists, and from this precious core of objects the less esoteric chemistry probably grew and prospered (i.e., Islamic society's skills in the extraction of cane sugar, the industrial preparation of rose water and various essences, and the perfecting of relatively sophisticated chemical apparatuses).

The link with art probably lies at the origin of the most mysterious and incomprehensible features of alchemy. This link is suggested by the universally accepted need to maintain a secret (in this case, production secrets); the prime role played by the relationship between nature and the human creator (nature, which produces, and the creator, who then perfects the work of nature), and above all the particular interpretation placed by the alchemist on alchemical operations. For the alchemist, who observes his work in the process of formation, what he performs in his laboratory is a real act of creation (cosmogony): his product is the cosmos, and the alchemist its creator. The whole process is then narrated through allegories that are drawn, with no distinction made with regard to genre, from scientific and literary texts, poems, and mythological tales, thereby testifying simultaneously to both the author's learning and his desire to exalt his discipline.

The philosophy on which the alchemist constructs his theory of transmutation, which embraces the findings of other sciences that study physical bodies (e.g., mineralogy, medicine), is Pythagorean in origin (albeit a Pythagorism that knows its Aristotle). Every composite body can be decomposed into four simple bodies (the elements: water, air, fire, and earth), and the elements in their turn can be decomposed into incorporeal "natures," which relate to each other in particular numerical ratios. Operating a chemical transformation—or transmutation—means decomposing a body into its elements; going beyond its material texture into its natures; correcting or modifying the mathematical ratios between these incorporeal natures; and then, by degrees, recomposing a new, "modified" body. In the conceptual framework of alchemy, which always strives towards perfection, the most sought-after composition is that of a fifth nature, the perfect nature, which is able not only to produce a perfect body but also to change all other natures into itself; this is the elixir (Arab. *iksīr*, Gr. *xērion*) that the alchemists recognize as the supreme aim of alchemy.

PAOLA CARUSI

See also Abbasid; Aristotle; Ceramics; Medicine; Precious Metals; al-Razi; Umayyad

Further Reading

Carusi, Paola. "Il Trattato di Filosofia Alchemica «Miftāḥ al-ḥikma» ed i suoi Testimoni Presso la Biblioteca Apostolica." In *Miscellanea Bibliothecae Apostolicae Vaticanae* IX. Città del Vaticano: Biblioteca Apostolica Vaticana, 2002.

Holmyard, Eric J. "Alchemical Equipment." In *A History of Technology*, ed. Ch. Singer et al, 8 vols., vol. 2. Oxford: Clarendon Press, 1954–1984.

———. *Alchemy*. New York: Dover, 1990. (First edition: Harmondsworth: Penguin Books, 1957.)

Kraus, Paul. *Jābir ibn Ḥayyān. Contribution à l'Histoire des Idées Scientifiques dans l'Islām. Jābir et la Science Grecque.* Paris: Les Belles Lettres, 1986. (First edition: Le Caire: Imprimerie de l'Institut Français d'Archeologie Orientale, 1942.)

Sezgin, Fuat. *Geschichte des Arabischen Schrifttums*, 9 vols., vol. 4. Leiden: E.J. Brill, 1967–1984.

Ullmann, Manfred. *Die Natur- und Geheimwissenschaften im Islam* (*Handbuch der Orientalistik*, Ergänzungsband VI, 2 Abschnitt). Leiden Köln: E.J. Brill, 1972.

ALCHOHOL

ALCOHOL

The English word *alcohol* originates from the Arabic *al-kuúl* (English, *kohl*), an antimony which, when pulverized finely, is used for darkening the edges of the eyelids. The meaning of the English is said to derive from an analogy between alcohol's highly refined spirits and the fineness of the pulverized black powder.

The oldest recipe or instruction on human record is for the creation of an alcoholic beverage. Its origin is Sumerian Mesopotamia; not surprisingly, this is also one of the earliest locations in which crop agriculture was practiced. Beer and wine are thus ancient products of human invention, almost certainly discovered by accident from the natural fermentation of grains and fruits. Their utility extended beyond that of their effect on consciousness and the human nervous system, for they also likely preserved the nutrients in juices that might otherwise spoil. They were also invented and developed in Western Asia, which is the same general location out of which emerged the three great monotheistic scriptural religions.

Alcoholic beverages were invented and developed in agricultural economies, and the communities or polities of these areas naturally benefited from control over the production and distribution of these products. Members of pastoral and nomadic economies—not unsurprisingly—have tended to outlaw or distrust the use of alcohol, probably for this reason.

There are two main groups of alcoholic beverages: those that are obtained through fermentation, such as beer and wine, and those that are obtained through distillation, such as whiskey, vodka, and brandy. Because there is no historical evidence of distilled beverages before approximately 1000, Islamic rulings forbidding the use of alcohol referred to wine and beer.

References to the consumption of alcoholic beverages in the Qur'an are not consistent. Verse 16:67 celebrates strong drink from the fruit of palm trees and grapes, associating its inebriating quality (sakar) with good nourishment (rizq hasan). Verse 2:219 associates wine (al-khamr) with games of chance and finds some benefit in both, in addition to greater sin. Verse 4:43 suggests only the prohibition against intoxication while engaged in prayer (wa'antum sukaraa), but only until sober ("until you know what you are saying") (Cf. Lev. 10:8–10). Verse 5:90 associates wine (al-khamr) with games of chance, idolatry, and divination, considering them all to be the work of Satan. These verses are understood by most Muslim commentators and jurists as having been revealed in sequence. In the earliest period of Muhammad's prophetic career, the consumption of alcohol was not forbidden. Wine became forbidden only after the excessive drunken behaviors of Muhammad's generation seemed to get out of control.

Much discussion in the medieval Islamic juridical literature treated the definition of wine, because a number of drinks were prepared from dates, grapes or raisins, figs, and other fruits, and Arabic words other than *khamr* referred to beverages that were or were not fermented. Moreover, some beverages were not intentionally fermented but would become so after being preserved for a long time in storage. Despite the religious prohibition, medieval Muslim anthologists list the ingredients of a wide variety of fermented beverages that were made and consumed by Muslims as well as Jews and Christians.

Because wine was used in both Jewish and Christian religious ritual, it was always permitted for those communities living among Muslims in Islamic lands. This sometimes caused tension and even violence because of the cognitive dissonance between Islam's legal support for the consumption of alcohol by the otherwise socially restricted religious minorities while maintaining its strict prohibition for Muslims. Therefore, although they were legally forbidden for Muslims, alcoholic beverages were always accessible through Christians and Jews, if not directly from Muslims themselves.

Notwithstanding the strict prohibition against imbibing actual alcohol, spiritual or poetic drunkenness through the bacchic wine poem (labeled technically as the "wine poem" or hamriyya only during the modern period) was a regular theme in the repertoire of the Arabic poets. Beginning even before the emergence of Islam, it reached its poetic heights during the second Islamic century with Abu Nuwas (Al-Hasan b. Hani' al-Hakami, d. 813–815), and it continued in various forms into modernity. Perhaps the best-known forms in the West include the spiritual intoxication that epitomizes the medieval mystics, who are spiritually drunk with their love for God.

A different expression is found in the poetry of medieval Islamic Spain, where the bacchic poem is associated with the pleasure of life, the quest for love, and a deep and profound communion with nature. The Andalusian wine poem became so much a part of shared medieval culture that Christians and Jews wrote them in Arabic as well. Jews also wrote wine poems in their own unique genre of poetry in the Hebrew language, which developed along the same lines as the Arabic poetry of their day.

> Pour me a drink, and another,
>   of the wine of Isfahan
>   or the wine of old Chosroes
>   or the wine of Qayrawan.
>   There is musk in the wine cup
>   or in the hand of the one who pours it;
>   or perhaps it was left in the wine
>   when they drew it from the jar.
>   Deck me with crown and diadem,
>   and sing me my own poems.
>   The wine cup is a springtime
>   you can touch with your fingers,
>   and the heat of the wine seeps slowly
>   from my tongue all the way to my feet.
>
> Abu Nuwas

REUVEN FIRESTONE

Further Reading

Bencheikh, J.E. "Khamriyya." In EI2 4 (998–1009).

Hussaini, Mohammad Mazhar, and Ahmad Hussein Sakr. *Islamic Dietary Laws and Practices*. Chicago: Islamic Food and Nutrition Counsel of America, 1983.

Klein, Ernest. *A Comprehensive Etymological Dictionary of the English Language*. Amsterdam: Elsevier, 1966.

Kueny, Kathryn. *The Rhetoric of Sobriety: Wine in Early Islam*. Albany: State University of New York, 2001.

Lewis, Bernard. *Music of a Different Drum: Classical Arabic, Persian, Turkish and Hebrew Poets*. Princeton, NJ: Princeton University Press, 2001.

Al-Qaradawi, Yusuf. *The Lawful and the Prohibited in Islam (Al-Halal Wal-Haram Fil Islam)*. (Translation of *Al-Halal Wal-Haram Fil Islam*. Beirut: Dar al-Qur'an al-Karim, 1978.) Indianapolis: American Trust Foundation, undated.

ALEPPO

Aleppo (in Arabic, Halab) is a city in northern Syria, and it is second in size and importance to Damascus, which is the capital of the modern republic. The site has been continuously inhabited since at least the twentieth century BCE. The large, centrally situated fortified mound that still dominates the city dates from this period.

The mostly Christian population of Aleppo surrendered to the conquering Muslim armies in AH 16/636 CE. After relative obscurity during the time of the Umayyads and early 'Abbasids, the city enjoyed a brief but splendid prominence as capital of the Hamdanid ruler Sayf al-Dawla, who captured Aleppo from its Ikshidid governors in 333/944. Among the literary figures whom Sayf al-Dawla (see Hamdanids) patronized at his court was the Syrian poet al-Mutanabbi.

The interlude came to an end in the winter of 351/962, when the Byzantine general (later emperor) Nicephorus Phocas stormed and sacked the city. Then followed half a century of disorder during which Hamdanid rule over Aleppo was repeatedly challenged by the Fatimids, the Byzantines, and neighboring Arab statelets. After a brief period of Fatimid rule at the beginning of the eleventh century, the Bedouin Arab Mirdasid dynasty took control of the city under the nominal suzerainty of the Fatimids; fifty years of progressively weakening Mirdasid rule followed. An end was put to Arab rule over Aleppo in 479/1086, when the Seljuk sultan Malikshah captured the city and installed a governor.

Turkish rule was to continue in one form or another until Saladin took Aleppo in 579/1183. After the death of Malikshah, a small Seljuk dynasty was founded in Aleppo by Malikshah's brother, Tutush.

Aleppo. Detail of the entrance. Captured during the second crusade. Ayyubid and Mamluk periods, thirteenth to sixteenth c. Credit: Werner Forman/Art Resource, NY. Citadel, Aleppo, Syria.

However, the state was too small and weak to offer meaningful resistance to the Crusaders, to whom Aleppo had to pay tribute in an effort to forestall attack. Seljuk rule gave way to a short-lived period under the ineffective control of the Ortoqid dynasty of Mardin. The weakened and disordered city was only saved from Crusader occupation in 518/1124 as a result of the enterprise of the city's qadi (Islamic judge), Ibn al-Khashshab.

Aleppo's fortunes began to change when, in 523/1129, it was taken by 'Imad al-Din Zanki, governor of Mosul and atabak (guardian) of two sons of the Seljuk Sultan Mas'ud. Zanki's military successes took Frankish pressure off the city. After Zanki's death in 541/1146, his son Nur al-Din Mahmud not only continued his father's struggle against the Crusaders but also restored Aleppo's administrative order and material fabric. Nur al-Din rebuilt the city's fortified walls, the citadel atop the central mound, and the Great Mosque. To assert the orthodox Sunni nature of Zankid rule in a city with a long history of Shi'is activity, he founded six madrasas (Islamic schools) in which an orthodox curriculum was taught.

Medieval Aleppo attained its greatest prosperity under the next ruling dynasty, the Ayyubids. In 579/1183, Saladin took the city from Nur al-Din's successors. Three years later he gave it to his fourth son Ghazi, who was first governor and then, after Saladin's death, ruler, with the title of al-Malik al-Zahir. Under al-Zahir and his two successors, Aleppo became the capital of a strong and prosperous state, the city itself benefiting especially from trade with the Venetians, who established a permanent factory there. As part of an extensive reconstruction program, al-Zahir rebuilt the citadel, thereby creating one of the most impressive military installations in the Near East. Madrasas continued to be built, and there developed a remarkable intellectual life that nurtured people like the traveler and teacher 'Ali ibn Abi Bakr al-Harawi and the chronicler and encyclopedist Ibn al-'Adim.

But it was not to last. In 658/1260, Aleppo was taken by the Mongols under Hulagu and sacked. The last Ayyubid ruler of the city, al-Zahir's grandson al-Malik al-Nasir Yusuf II, who had abandoned Aleppo to its fate, was later captured and killed. The city was occupied by the Mamluks after their victory over the

Mongols at 'Ayn Jalut in the same year, but it was lost to the Mongols several more times before being finally recovered by the Mamluks at the beginning of the following century.

Aleppo took years to recover from the depredations of the Mongols. The situation was made worse by the continuing threat of further Mongol attack and by political instability. Another setback occurred in 803/1400, when Tamerlane sacked the city.

This notwithstanding, the century before the Ottoman occupation of Aleppo after the Ottoman victory over the Mamluks at the battle of Marj Dabiq in 522/1516 saw another revival in the fortunes of the city. Aleppo benefited from disruption of the existing commercial routes to the north and grew rich on the trade that came its way. The suqs (markets) expanded, khans (enclosed warehouses) proliferated, and the walls of the city had to be extended to accommodate the increased population.

DAVID MORRAY

See also Architecture, Secular: Military; Excellences Literature; Madrasa; Merchants, Christian; Muslim–Byzantine Relations; Muslim–Mongol Diplomacy; Silk Roads; Sunni Revival; Trade, Mediterranean

Primary Sources

Ibn al-'Adim. *Zubdat al-Halab fi ta'Rikh Halab*, ed. Sami al-Dahhan, 3 vols. Damascus: Institut Français de Damas, 1951–1968.

Further Reading

Eddé, Anne-Marie. *La Principauté Ayyoubide d'Alep (579/1183–658/1260)*. Stuttgart: Franz Steiner Verlag, 1999.
Ibn al-Shihna al-Saghir. *al-Durr al-Muntakhab fi Ta'rikh Mamlakat Halab*. (Translated by J. Sauvaget as *Les Perles Choisies d'Ibn ach-Chihna. Matériaux pour Servir à l'histoire de la Ville d'Alep.*) Beirut, 1933.
Morray, David W. *An Ayyubid Notable and his World: Ibn al-'Adim and Aleppo as Portrayed in his Biographical Dictionary of People Associated with the City*. Leiden: E.J. Brill, 1994.

ALEXANDER

During the medieval Islamic period, Alexander the Great was most closely associated with the figure Dhu al-Qarnayn, who was mentioned in 18:83–101. Many of the literary motifs and themes developed in the Greek Alexander Romance, which in turn appears to be based on the Epic of Gilgamesh, can be found in Muslim exegeses, histories, and related genres.

Early Muslim exegetes identify the figure Dhu al-Qarnayn with various historical and mythical figures, including Moses, an angel, and different South Arabian kings, although the identification with Alexander predominates in later literature. Other medieval recensions of the Alexander Romance, including the Ethiopic and Persian, likewise identify Alexander with Dhu al-Qarnayn. The figure of Khidr, which was alluded to in 18:60–82 just before the account of Dhu al-Qarnayn, also appears in many of the Islamic recensions of the Alexander Romance, and he may be associated with figures mentioned in Syriac, Greek, and Armenian recensions.

Other sources associate Dhu al-Qarnayn and Khidr with the prophet Abraham. In his history, Tabari relates that there were two Dhu al-Qarnayns: one living in the time of Abraham and another being Alexander. Muslim exegetes conflate Dhu al-Qarnayn with Abimelech, the king who presides over Abraham's claim to the well of Beersheba in Genesis 21:22–34 in the Bible. Ibn Kathir preserves a number of sources that report Dhu al-Qarnayn's visit to Abraham at Mecca during his building of the Ka'bah.

Dhu al-Qarnayn is also conflated with Moses and the Prophet Muhammad. The epithet "Dhu al-Qarnayn" is usually understood to denote a person with two horns or a person who traveled to the two ends of the earth. Moses is portrayed as horned in the Vulgate and in medieval Christian texts, and in his encounter with Khidr in 18:60–82 is said to have traveled to the ends of the earth. The Prophet Muhammad's night journey to the ends of the earth appears to be modeled on the journeys of Dhu al-Qarnayn and Alexander in the different recensions of the Alexander Romance. The journeys of both the Prophet Muhammad and Dhu al-Qarnayn to the two cities at the ends of the earth, where a remnant of the Israelites is living, may also be compared to the exegesis in 7:159, Rabbinic traditions of the "Lost Tribes," and the pseudoepigraphical *History of the Rechabites*.

Dhu al-Qarnayn's world travels in 18:83–101 are interpreted in the light of Alexander's world conquests, and his building of the wall against Gog and Magog is a motif that is found in a wide variety of texts from Josephus to the medieval Jewish and Christian apocalypses.

BRANNON WHEELER

Further Reading

Anderson, A.R. *Alexander's Gate, Gog and Magog and Enclosed Nations*. Medieval Academy of American Publications 12. Cambridge: Harvard University Press, 1932.
Clay, George. *The Medieval Alexander*, ed. D.J.A. Ross. Cambridge: Cambridge University Press, 1956; reprint, 1967.

Ethé, C. Herman. "Alexanders Zug zum Lebensquell im Land der Finsterniss." *Sitzungsberichte der Bayerischen Akademie der wissenschaften. Philosophisch-Historische Klasse.* München, 1871: 343–405.

Friedländer, Israel. *Die Chadhirlegende und der Alexanderroman.* Leipzig: B.G. Teubner, 1913.

Kroll, W. *Historia Alexandri Magni.* Berlin: Weidmannsche Buchhandlung, 1926.

'Ukasha, 'Abd al-Mannan. *Ya'juj wa Ma'juj: Sifatuhum wa 'Adaduhum wa Makanuhum wa Qissat Dhi al-Qarnyan ma'Ahum.* Cairo: Maktabat al-Turath al-Islami, 1989.

Wheeler, Brannon. *Moses in the Quran and Islamic Exegesis.* Curzon Studies in the Quran. London: Curzon, 2002.

ALEXANDRIA

Alexandria, which is presently known as the shining pearl of the Mediterranean, is the second-largest city and the main port of Egypt. Situated northwest of the Nile delta, it stretches along a narrow land strip between the Mediterranean Sea and Lake Mariut.

Founding

When Alexander the Great reached Memphis (Egypt) on his expedition of conquest, he was welcomed by the people who supported him in overthrowing Persian rule. In 331 BCE, Alexander then ordered a city to be founded there to serve as a regional capital. He was later buried there.

The Roman City (30 BC–AD 641)

By the time the Romans conquered Egypt, there was an Egyptian community centered around the old site of Rhakotis, a Greek community downtown, and a Jewish community occupying the eastern districts. Octavian, the new Roman Emperor, founded a new town, Nicopolis, just east of Alexandria (it is now part of the greater city, known as El-Raml). Higher taxes were imposed, but Octavian's successors were less harsh. Matters improved when the Red Sea Canal was cut to link the Nile to the Red Sea, serving as a forerunner to the modern Suez Canal.

During the early rule of the Romans in Egypt, Christianity was introduced into Alexandria by St. Mark, who was martyred in AD 62 for protesting against the worship of Serapis. As Christianity took root, leading ecclesiastical centers such as the oratory of Saint Mark and later the Catechetical School were established as the first of their kind in the world.

However, as the Christian population grew, so did the Roman emperors intensify their persecution against those who resisted it. Persecution reached unprecedented levels during the "Era of the Martyrs" around AD 284, when an estimated 144,000 martyrs—including St. Menas, St. Catherine, and St. Peter of Alexandria—were killed. When, in October 312, Emperor Constantine announced Christianity as the official religion of the Empire, Alexandria was ready for the change.

During the next two centuries, the spiritual power of the Coptic Church in Alexandria grew among Egyptians. However, the power of the "Royal" Patriarchs, appointed by the Roman emperor, was more political than religious. The Coptic Patriarchs, on the other hand, had no political interests.

During the early seventh century, both the Persian Empire and the Roman Empire started to fall apart. In 617, the Persians peacefully captured Alexandria for a short period of five years. By the time the Roman Emperor Heraclius regained his forces and recaptured the lost provinces, the world was ready to witness the birth of a new power. From the desolate Arabian Peninsula came the Arab forces that swept both the Romans and the Persians; they were spiritually powered by the new religion of Islam, and they established an empire that would last for over a thousand years. After negotiating with the Roman Patriarch, Cyrus, who was also serving as the Roman ruler of Egypt, Alexandria was peacefully captured by the Arab commander 'Amr ibn al-'As on November 8, 642 CE and 'Amr and his soldiers entered a city which "contained 4000 palaces, 4000 baths, and 400 theatres".

The Arab–Islamic City

The Caliph 'Umar ibn al-Khattab, who ruled from Medina, appointed 'Amr ibn al-'As governor of Egypt, and he promptly relocated the capital to Fustat, which was the nucleus of modern Cairo. For the next thousand years or so, the glamour of Alexandria declined. However, the Arabs greatly admired the city, and the most descriptive accounts of the Pharos Lighthouse and the pre-Islamic monuments come from Arab historical, geographical, and travel accounts such as those from Ibn Khurradadhbih, Ibn Jubayr, al-Harawi, and Ibn Battuta. Medieval accounts also locate the tombs of Alexander and Aristotle in the city.

When significant parts of the lighthouse collapsed during the 956 and 1323 earthquakes, it was not repaired. In 1498, the medieval fort of the Mamluk sultan Qaytbay was eventually constructed on the foundation of the Pharos. However, this failed to bring Alexandria back to prominence after the discovery of the new route around Africa to the Far East.

Alexandria was also an important port center for Arab and foreign merchants down to the early fourteenth century. European consulates and traveler hostels such as those of the Venetians were established in the city. Alexandria also served as a port of transit for goods to and from India and the Far East. Likewise, it was an important center for the manufacture of textiles.

During the Middle Ages, a number of famous scholars and Sufis hailed from or came to be associated with Alexandria, such as the famous *hadith* scholar Abu Tahir al-Silafi (d. 1180); the Shadhili Sufi Ibn 'Ata' Allah (d. 1309), the author, an important work of Sufi biography; and al-Busiri (d. 1294), the author of the famous *Ode of the Mantle (burda)* of the Prophet Muhammad.

Today, greater Alexandria stretches nearly seventy kilometers along the Mediterranean coast, with urban areas covering more than one hundred square kilometers. Her rich population of more than four million still reflects her ancient history and close ties to the Mediterranean. With ethnic minorities including Armenians, Greeks, Italians, Lebanese, Maltese, and Syrians, among others, Alexandria is considered the most culturally diverse of all Egyptian cities.

KHALID DHORAT AND JOSEF W. MERI

Further Reading

Davidson, Basil. *The African Past*. London: Penguin, 1966.
Doi, 'Abdur Rahman. *Islam in a Multi-Religious Society: Nigeria: A Case Study*. Kuala Lumpur: A.S. Noordeen, 1992.
Fage, J. (ed.). *Cambridge History of Africa*. Cambridge, 1978.

ALGEBRA

The word *algebra* is a Latinized form of the Arabic word *al-jabr,* which means restoration. The word appears in the title *Book on al-Jabr and al-Muqabala;* this is the introductory treatise in Arabic on the solution of linear and quadratic equations, which Muhammad ibn Musa al-Khwarizmi wrote around 830 CE in Baghdad. During the twelfth century, after Spain had been conquered by the Christians, the work was translated as the *Book on Algebra and Almucabala,* from which the field of algebra got its name. During the nineteenth and twentieth centuries, the meaning of the word *algebra* has changed from the science of the solution of equations to the science of a particular class of mathematical structures.

Because al-Khwarizmi's work in algebra is fundamental, a brief summary is presented here. Al-Khwarizmi discusses linear and quadratic equations without algebraic symbolism, and he even writes all numbers out as words. For example, one of his equations is called *capital,* and ten *roots* are the unknown amounts of money. Because the product of the root times itself is supposed to be equal to the capital, the equation can be expressed in modern symbols as $x^2 + 10x = 39$.

Al-Khwarizmi does not use zero and negative numbers, so he has to distinguish three different types of mixed quadratic equations; in modern notation these would be the following: $x^2 + bx = c$, $x^2 = bx + c$, and $x^2 + c = bx$, with $b, c > 0$. He also discusses the two simple quadratic equations $x^2 = bx$ and $x^2 = c$ and the linear equation $x = c$. For each of these six standard forms, he explains a general method of solution in words, using numerical examples. The solutions of $x^2 + bx = c$, $x^2 = bx + c$, and $x^2 + c = bx$ are equivalent to the modern algebraic formula, but al-Khwarizmi only gives positive roots. He correctly states that $x^2 + c = bx$ only has a solution of $b^2 \geq 4c$, but he does not clearly explain that the equation has two different roots if $b^2 > 4c$.

Al-Khwarizmi illustrates the solutions of the three mixed quadratic equations using geometrical figures. He then shows how any quadratic equation can be reduced to one of the standard forms. *Al-jabr* (restoration) is the operation of removing defective terms in the equation. For example, if our equation is one capital except two roots is equal to 10 dirhams, we "restore" the missing two roots to both sides of the equation, and we conclude that one capital is equal to two roots and 10 dirhams. This equation is in the standard form $x^2 = bx + c$, with $b = 2$ and $c = 10$.

Al-Khwarizmi then presents a long series of examples of problems that can be reduced to equations, and he explains how each equation can be solved according to the preceding theory. He adds a brief section on surveying, which has no relation to algebra. His work was a great didactical success, and he is rightly regarded as the founder of Islamic algebra.

In his preface, al-Khwarizmi says that his work contains a certain amount of material that people constantly use in computations. It is true that the contents of his work were indeed known in 1000 B.C. in ancient Babylonia, which is the same area in which he wrote his work. Al-Khwarizmi's statement has been uncritically interpreted by modern historians in the sense that Arabic algebra was "practical" and that the quadratic equations were motivated by practical applications. Al-Khwarizmi presents "applications" of algebra in Islamic inheritance problems, but his examples are very artificial and only lead to linear equations in which $bx = c$. As a matter of fact, there were few if any applications of quadratic equations in the medieval Islamic tradition; the motivation for algebra seems to have been primarily recreational.

Al-Khwarizmi's work was translated into Latin because it was available in Islamic Spain during the eleventh century CE, just before Spain was reconquered by the Christians. In the meantime, algebra developed in the Eastern Islamic world beyond the level reached by al-Khwarizmi. During the late ninth century, Abu Kamil started to solve equations that had irrational coefficients such as *root two*. He also studied systems of linear equations involving several unknowns. Meanwhile, mathematicians were also beginning to look at equations of higher degree. The Iranian mathematician al-Mahani (ca. 860) studied a problem that Archimedes mentioned but did not solve in his work *On the Sphere and Cylinder*. The problem was a preliminary to the division of a sphere by a plane into two parts such that their volumes have a given ratio. Al-Mahani showed that a problem that Archimedes had left unsolved was equivalent to a cubic equation (of the form $ax^2 = x^3 + c$). Unfortunately, the formula for the solution of cubic equations (discovered in Italy during the sixteenth century) produces x as the sum of two complex numbers. Such numbers were meaningless to ancient and medieval mathematicians, and therefore al-Mahani could not solve the equation.

During the mid-tenth century, Abu Ja'far al-Khazin constructed a line segment of length x in a geometrical way by means of a hyperbola. After this breakthrough, other Islamic mathematicians also started to work on geometrical solutions of cubic equations. The famous Iranian mathematician and poet 'Umar al-Khayyam wrote a treatise on algebra that contained geometrical solutions of all types of cubic equations by means of parabolas, hyperbolas, and circles. Just like al-Khwarizmi, al-Khayyam only worked with positive coefficients, and therefore he had to distinguish many types of cubic equations, which were equivalent to the modern $x^3 = ax^2 + c$, $x^2 + ax^2 = c$, $x^3 + c = ax^2$, $x^3 + c = ax^2$, $x^3 + ax^2 = bc + c$, and so on, with $a, b, c > 0$. 'Umar al-Khayyam did not use modern symbolism. His work was not complete according to medieval mathematical standards, because he did not use the precise conditions for the existence of the solutions.

Other algebraic advances were also made. During the tenth century CE, the Iranian mathematician al-Karaji explained how one can draw the square roots of a polynomial such as (in modern symbolism) $x^4 + 6x^3 + 13x^2 = 12x + 4$. He did this by generalizing the way in which square roots of decimal and sexagesimal numbers were extracted. He only discussed cases in which the result comes out nicely (in the above example, $x^2 + 3x + 2$). During the twelfth century, al-Samaw'al explained the same for negative coefficients, and he showed how polynomials can be divided by the same method as decimal and sexagesimal numbers. Also during the twelfth century, Saraf al-Din al-Tusi (who is not the same as Nasir al-Din) discussed rather complicated methods for the numerical approximation of the (positive) root of a cubic equation. He also showed at what points the exact roots of cubic equations exist, and thus he solved one of the problems that al-Khayyam had left open. Neither al-Khayyam nor Sharaf al-Din realized that the cubic equation $x^3 + bx = ax^2 + c$ can have three (positive) roots.

It is perhaps surprising that the Islamic advances in algebra were made without algebraic symbolism. During the fourteenth century, Western Arabic mathematicians used abbreviations of words in equations in much the same way as Diophantus (c. 250) did in his *Arithmetica* and as the mathematicians did in sixteenth-century Europe.

JAN P. HOGENDIJK

See also Mathematics; Geometry; Numbers

Further Reading

Hogendijk, Jan P. "Sharaf al-Din al-Tusi on the Number of Positive Roots of Cubic Equations." *Historica Mathematica* 16 (1989): 69–85.

Kasir, D.S. *The Algebra of Omar Khayyam*. New York: Columbia University, 1931.

Rashad, R. *Sharaf al-Din al-Tusi: Oeuvres Mathematiques*, 2 vols. Paris: Les Belles Lettres, 1986.

Rosen, Fr., ed. *The Algebra of Mohammed ben Musa*. London: 1831; reprints: Hildesheim: Olms, 1986; and Frankfurt: Institute for the History of Arabic-Islamic Sciences, 1997.

Winter, H.K.K., and W. Arafat. "The Algebra of 'Umar Khayyam." *Journal of the Royal Asiatic Society of Bengal Science* 16 (1950): 27–78.

ALHAMBRA/AL-QASR AL-HAMRA'

Alhambra/al-Qasr al-Hamra' derives its name from the Arabic *hamra'* (red), which is probably a reference to the color of the dirt that makes up the high hill (the Sabika) beside the Darro river from which the Alhambra commands panoramic views of Granada and the surrounding countryside. The complex dates largely to the middle- to late-fourteenth century and to the reigns of Nasrid sovereigns Yusuf III and Muhammad V; only the Tower of the Infantas and Christian alterations and additions are known to have been added later. Somewhat removed from the city, its placement follows traditions that began with the 'Abbasids and that are also reflected in the ruling and dwelling spaces built by the Ayyubids and Mamluks in Syria and Egypt as well as Madinat al-Zahra', the earlier Andalusian palace built by the Umayyads outside of Córdoba during the tenth century. The high walls and towers present a forbidding façade to the visitor, who today approaches the palace through a gate (known as the Puerta del Vino) some distance down the hill; he or she is then confronted with the Renaissance-style facade of the Palace of Charles V, which was placed by Spanish architect Antonio Machuca directly against the eastern side of the Palace of the Lions and over the walkway that led through the royal cemetery.

The earliest known architectural activity on the site dates to the eleventh century CE, when Granada was ruled by the Berber Taifa dynasty of the Banu Ziri. This is perhaps connected to the patronage of the Jewish vizier Samuel ha-Levi ben Nagrila; remains from the Arabic al-Qasba (fortress) were found in the southern tip of the complex, which is known as the Alcazaba. These structures were largely functional, and their relationship to the putative vizier's palace has never been determined with certainty. It is also believed that the fountain from which the Palace of the Lions derives its modern name is owed to the Jewish vizier's patronage. It is with the Nasrids, however (the dynasty began in 1238 under Muhammad I Ibn Ahmar, with Granada as its capital), that spaces clearly planned for royal use were designed and built. The earliest of these structures, the Palace of the Generalife, was probably begun under Isma'il in 1314 and destined for relaxation and pleasure in a tradition that is often deemed a quintessentially "Islamic" one, although it was also adopted by medieval Christian sovereigns in Castile, Aragon, and Sicily. The palace's salons and miradors (related to the Arabic *manzara*, or belvedere—a place from which to enjoy a view) open onto a long, rectangular–pool-and-garden complex that is now considerably restored. Interiors are adorned with panels of vegetal and geometric ornamentation; their similarities to Nasrid textiles have often been noticed, but the true object of contemplation is the constructed landscape and gardens.

The Palaces of the Myrtles and the Lions (built between 1333 and 1391) are the best preserved and the most altered, whether during the adaptations of the palace to Christian use carried out under Ferdinand and Isabel (as well as their son, Charles V) or during modern restoration; these two spaces have also fostered the most contention among scholars. Earlier schools of interpretation viewed the complex composed by these two palaces as imbued with a single plan and conception; recent studies have given greater attention to the differences between the two palaces and to the fact that each possessed its own bath complex, orientation, and possibly even entrance, thereby stressing the particular architectural, ornamental, and even poetic coherence of each. The Palace of the Myrtles (in Spanish, *arrayánes*), which is also referred to as the Palace of Comares, is the earliest of the two; it was possibly begun by Isma'il and substantially developed under Yûsuf, but it also owes much to the patronage of Muhammad V. It is preceded by a still poorly understood area referred to as the Mexuar (from the Arabic *mashwar*), which probably served administrative purposes (petitions and other matters of civic import), although disagreements exist regarding the specific function to be attributed to each area. Corridors then lead past a small oratory and into the throne room proper, which is often referred to as the *Sala de Comares*. It looks out onto a central patio and pool complex, and it is separated from the latter by a long, narrow space known as the *Sala de la Barca* (probably from the Arabic *baraka*, or blessing); it is mirrored on the opposite side of the pool by a similar complex of rooms. The stunning effects produced by reflections of the architecture in the still rectangular pool have been commented on by numerous poets and modern scholars; they contribute to a sense of stasis that is echoed in the throne room (and, according to specialists, in the panegyric and battle-centered subject matter of the poetic compositions that adorn the walls), for which a cosmological reading based in what most read as a representation or evocation of the seven heavens in the ceiling. The poetic inscriptions—verses throughout the palace—were taken from longer compositions by three principal poets: Ibn al-Jayyan, Ibn Zamrak, and Ibn al-Khatib, although those authored by the latter would have been effaced after his fall from grace serve to support this interpretation. Again, the throne room participates in a particularly Andalusi tradition of royal spaces; however, Christian sovereigns such as Alfonso X and Muhammad V's contemporary Pedro I ("el Cruel") did not hesitate to adapt them to their own purposes, perhaps even contributing to the development of the Islamic prototype.

During the fourteenth century, it is possible that the two doorways that punctuate the impressive facade of the Palace of the Myrtles were originally located on the southern extreme of the Patio of the Myrtles, which constitutes the palaces' most formal and elaborate entrance, and which led directly into the throne room. Entrance would have been effected through a small space topped by a dome and followed by the *Salon of the Suras;* this mirrors the Sala de la Barca, which precedes the throne room. This debate has awakened considerable controversy, and much work remains to be done before the hypothesis can be fully substantiated; however, such an arrangement would be in keeping with the tradition of Hispano-Islamic palaces, and it would help to explain Charles V's decision to place his palace where he did.

From the Palace of the Myrtles, one passes into the Palace of the Lions. Here, with the exception of the verses in the Mirador of Lindaraja (probably the privileged position occupied by the sovereign when this palace was in use), inscriptions concentrate more on the themes of beauty—specifically those of architecture and gardens—than did those of the Salon of Comares. This fact gives rise to an interpretation that is now believed by many scholars to overemphasize the pleasurable (and even paradisiacal) aspects of the palace and to give short shrift to what was possibly an official or judiciary function. The patio, which is oriented in the opposite direction of that of the Myrtles and punctuated in the center by the famous Fountain of the Lions, is flanked on all four sides by rooms that are covered with spectacular muqarnas vaults and embellished with small fountains that are channeled from the central one. The east and west rooms are preceded by porch-like structures that evoke pavilions, and columns are grouped so as to suggest movement and invite perambulation. Interpretations of the Court of the Lions vary, as noted earlier, from that of a pleasure palace with no other purpose to a new Mexuar to a Sufi madrasa and tomb complex.

Although scholars of the nineteenth century viewed the Nasrid palace through a Romantic lens that emphasized its uniqueness and quintessentially Islamic qualities, the Alhambra in fact gives ample evidence of interactions with contemporary cultures, both Christian and Muslim. Relationships to Marinid Morocco have been suggested on the basis of both shared ornamental tastes and the particular plan of the Palace of the Lions, which the structure in turn shares with the original state of the cloister of a convent of Poor Claires that was established in the Castilian villa of Tordesillas by Pedro I "el Cruel" of Castile in 1373 (the building was previously a palace built under his and his father's patronage). Numerous and as yet incompletely studied interchanges are documented in the corpus of fourteenth- and fifteenth-century architecture and ornament built or adapted by Christian or Jewish patrons according to Islamic models known as *mudéjar*. The textiles that ornamented the Alhambra's salons and walls evidence intriguing similarities to those produced throughout the Mediterranean, including Italy. The painted leather ceilings, moreover, that adorn the so-called Sala de Justicia at the eastern end of the Patio of the Lions are clearly related to European models, although their program has yet to be fully deciphered. Finally, it is known that Isabel I spent a considerable amount of time in the palace before her death and was in fact buried (in the habit of the Poor Claires) for a time in one of the miradors of one of the complex's older palaces that she had donated to the Franciscan order so that a convent might be founded on the palace grounds, which now belonged to her.

CYNTHIA ROBINSON

See also Architecture, Religious; Architecture, Secular; Civil Architecture, Secular; Palaces; Baths and Bathing; Beauty and Aesthetics; Gardens and Gardening; Painting, Monumental and Frescoes; Poetry, Arabic; Poet; Water

Further Reading

Al-Andalus: The Islamic Art of Spain, ed. Jerrilynn D. Dodds New York: The Metropolitan Museum of Art; Harry N. Abrams, 1992.

Arié, Rachel, and Luis A. García Moreno. *España Musulmana: (Siglos VIII-XV)*, 1st ed., 16th printing. Barcelona: Labor, 1994.

———. *El Reino Nasrí de Granada, 1232–1492*. Madrid: Editorial MAPFRE, 1992.

Bargebuhr, Frederick P. *The Alhambra Palace of the Eleventh Century*. Worcester, England: 1956.

Cabanelas, Darío. *El Techo del Salón de Comares en la Alhambra: Decoración, Policromía, Simbolismo y Etimología*. Granada: Patronato de la Alhambra y Generalife, 1988.

———. *Literatura, Arte y Religión en los Palacios de la Alhambra*. (Discurso de apertura del curso Académico 1984–1985.) Granada: Universo de Granada, 1984.

Cabanelas, Darío, and Antonio Fernández-Puertas, "Inscripciones Poéticas del Generalife." *Cuadernos de la Alhambra* 14 (1978): 3–86.

———. "Inscripciones Poéticas del Partal y del Palacio de Comares." *Cuadernos de la Alhambra* 10–11 (1974–1975): 117–99.

———. "El Poema de la Fuente de los Leones." *Cuadernos de la Alhambra* 15–17 (1979–1981): 4–88.

———. "Los Poemas de las Tacas del Arco de Aceso a la Sala de la Barca." *Cuadernos de la Alhambra* 19–20 (1983–1984): 61–152.

Díez Jorge, María Elena. *El Palacio Islámico de la Alhambra: Propuestas para una Lectura Multicultural*. Granada: Universidad de Granada, 1998.

Dodds, Jerrilynn D. "The Paintings in the Sala de Justicia of the Alhambra: Iconography and Iconology." *Art Bulletin* (1978): 186–97.

Fairchild Ruggles, D. *Gardens, Landscape, and Vision in the Palaces of Islamic Spain.* University Park: Pennsylvania State University Press, 2000.

———. "The Eye of Sovereignty: Poetry and Vision in the Alhambra's Lindaraja Mirador." *Gesta* 36, no. 2 (1997): 180–89.

Fernández-Puertas, Antonio. *The Alhambra*, 2 vols. London: Saqi Press, 1997.

———. *La Fachada del Palacio de Comares (The Facade of the Palace of Comares).* Granada: Patronato de la Alhambra, 1980.

García Gomez, Emilio. *Poemas Árabes en los Muros y Fuentes de La Alhambra*, 2nd ed. Madrid: Instituto Egipcio de Estudios Islámicos en Madrid, 1996.

———. *Ibn Zamrak, el Poeta de la Alhambra.* Granada: Patronato de la Alhambra, 1975.

———. *Foco de Antigua Luz Sobre la Alhambra.* Madrid: Instituto Egipcio de Estudios Islámicos en Madrid, 1988.

Gonzalez, Valérie. *Beauty and Islam: Aesthetics in Islamic Art and Architecture.* London: Saqi Press, 2001.

Grabar, Oleg. *The Alhambra*, 2nd ed., revised. Sebastopol, Calif: Solipsist Press, 1992.

Jesús Bermúdez y Pareja. *El Palacio de Carlos V y la Alhambra Cristiana.* Granada: Albaícin, 1971.

———. "El Baño del Palacio de Comares, en la Alhambra de Granada. Disposición Primitiva y Alteraciones." *Cuadernos de la Alhambra* 10–11 (1974–1975): 99–116.

———. "Identificación del Palacio de Comares y del Palacio de los Leones en la Alhambra de Granada." In *Actas del XXIII Congreso Internacional de Historia del Arte,* 55–6. Granada, 1976.

———. *Palacios de Comares y Leones.* Granada: Caja de Ahorros de Granada, 1972.

López, Jesús Bermúdez, and Pedro A. Galera Andreu. *The Alhambra and Generalife: Official Guide.* Granada: Editorial Comares, 1999.

Muhammad ibn Yusuf Ibn Zumruk, Yusuf, King of Granada. *Diwan Ibn Zumruk al-Andalusi,* ed. Muhammad Tawfiq Nayfar. Beirut: Dar al-Gharb al-Islami, 1997.

Puerta Vílchez, José Miguel. *Los Códigos de Utopía de la Alhambra de Granada.* Granada: Diputación Provincial de Granada, 1990.

———. *Historia del Pensamiento Estético Árabe: al-Andalus y la Estética Árabe Clásica.* Madrid: Ediciones Akal, 1997.

———. In *Historia del Reino de Granada,* ed. Rafael G. Penado Santaella. Granada: Universidad de Granada: Legado Andalusí, 2000.

Rubiera Mata, María Jesús. *Ibn al-Jayyâb, el Otro Poeta de la Alhambra.* Granada: Junta de Andalucía, Consejería de Cultura y Medio Ambiente: Patronato de la Alhambra y Generalife, 1984.

———. "Los Poemas Epigráficos en Ibn Yayyâb en la Alhambra." *Al-Andalus* XXV (1970): 453–73.

———. "De Nuevo Sobre los Poemas Epigráficos de la Alhambra." *Al-Andalus* XLI (1976): 207–11.

Ruiz Sousa, Juan Carlos. "El Palacio de los Leones de la Alhambra: Madrasa, Zawiya y Tumba de Muhammad V?" *Al-Qantara* 22, no. 1 (2001): 77–120.

Santiago Simón, Emilio. *El Polígrafo Granadino Ibn al-Jatib y el Sufismo: Aportaciones para su Estudio.* Granada: Excma. Diputación Provincial, Instituto Provincial de Estudios y Promoción Cultural: Departamento de Historia del Islam de la Universidad, 1983.

Seco de Lucena, Luis. *La Alhambra de Granada,* 8th ed. León: Editorial Everest, 1986.

'ALI AL-RIDA

Eighth Imam of the Twelver Shi'is and heir to the 'Abbasid caliph al-Ma'mun, Abu 'l-Hasan 'Ali ibn Musa ibn Ja'far al-Sadiq was born sometime during the late 760s in Medina, the son of the seventh Imam Musa al-Kazim and a Nubian slave wife. His father designated him as his successor before he died in prison in 799. None of his brothers claimed the imamate, although some of them—along with his uncle Muhammad ibn Ja'far—revolted against the 'Abbasids. The real split in the Twelver community took place between al-Rida's supporters and those who insisted that al-Kazim was the messianic Mahdi of the last days and that he had not died but merely gone into occultation. The Waqifiyya, as they became known (particularly in the heresiographies), were prominent in Iraq and withheld the payment of the khums from al-Rida. In Medina, al-Rida narrated hadith from his forefathers, but it seems that he was not received well by Sunni traditionists (or, rather, by the later constructors of hadith criticism), because few Sunnis transmitted from him; however, at the same time, when al-Rida went to Khurasan, famous Sunni traditionists such as Ibn Rahawayh and Yahya ibn Yahya were said to have met him in Nishapur.

In 816, the 'Abbasid caliph al-Ma'mun invited al-Rida to Khurasan and, in a radical policy shift, designated al-Rida, an 'Alid, as his successor and married his daughter Umm Habib to him. Some of the sources, especially the Twelver accounts, make much of al-Rida's "royal progress" to Marv, although it is unclear whether he had even accepted al-Ma'mun's proposal at the time. In an official ceremony in March 817, al-Rida was formally designated an heir apparent. Historians have debated the intentions of all the protagonists; recent research suggests that al-Ma'mun had decided that the best candidates for the caliphate ought to come from the wider pool of Hashimites and that 'Ali ibn Musa was the best candidate. He even gave him the title *al-Rida,* no doubt as a preemptive move against Shi'i rebels who often raised the banner of al-Rida min Al Muhammad, the chosen (messianic) candidate from the family of Muhammad. Al-Rida was given a high status at the court of al-Ma'mun, where he often took part in religious disputations; accounts of this were recorded later in Ibn Babuwayh's *'Uyun akhbar al-Rida,* the main collection of reports about him. Twelver sources categorically state that al-Rida accepted the post reluctantly; he had little taste for political power, and he suspected bad faith on the part of al-Ma'mun. Certainly there is a sense in which the disputations were designed as set pieces to embarrass al-Rida, and it seems unlikely that he would ever have succeeded the much younger al-Ma'mun. Suspicions were further raised by the sudden death of al-Rida at Tus in September 818. Most accounts allege that he was poisoned; most Twelvers historians blamed al-Ma'mun. The sudden change in al-Ma'mun's policy and the attempt to eradicate his memory (despite the immediate signs of grief and funeral arrangements that placed al-Rida's body in the tomb of Harun al-Rashid) seemed to confirm these suspicions. According to Twelver tradition, al-Rida was succeeded by his son Muhammad al-Jawad, whose minority raised issues about the ontological status of the Imam and his knowledge. The tomb near Tus became a major pilgrimage site for the Imam martyred in foreign lands. Pilgrimage to his shrine city, which was renamed Mashhad (place of martyrdom) in his honor, was commended in Shi'i pilgrimage manuals. Miracles ascribed to him in his life multiplied after his death; pilgrims were cured, dilemmas solved, and spiritual guidance found.

Three works are attributed to al-Rida. *Al-Risala al-Dhahabiyya fi 'l-Tibb* is a treatise on Prophetic medicine that is said to have been commissioned by al-Ma'mun and copied in golden ink. Despite questions concerning its provenance, it remains popular in Twelver circles. *Sahifat al-Rida* is a collection of 240 hadith mentioned in some early Imami sources. *Fiqh al-Rida*, which is a work that purports to record al-Rida's legal pronouncements, was unknown until the Safavid period; it is in fact the legal work, *Kitab al-taklif*, of the Imami heresiarch Muhammad ibn 'Ali al-Shalmaghani (d. 934).

SAJJAD H. RIZVI

See also al-Ma'mun; Messianism; Nishapur; Shi'ism; Shi'i imams

Primary Sources

al-Mufid. *Kitab al-Irshad: The Book of Guidance*, trans. I.K.A. Howard. London: The Muhammadi Trust, 1981, 461–79.

Further Reading

Bayhom Daou, T. *The Imami Shi'i Conception of the Knowledge of the Imam and the Sources of Religious Doctrine in the Formative Period from Hisham ibn al-Hakam to al-Kulini*. Ph.D. dissertation. London: School of Oriental and African Studies, University of London, 1996.

Buyukkara, M.A. *The Imami-Shi'i Movement in the Time of Musa al-Kazim and 'Ali al-Rida*. Ph.D. dissertation. Edinburgh: Edinburgh University, 1997.

Cooperson, M. *Classical Arabic Biography: The Heirs of the Prophet in the Age of al-Ma'mun*. Cambridge: Cambridge University Press, 2000.

Gabrieli, F. *al-Ma'mun e gli 'Alidi*. Leigzig: Pfeiffer, 1929.

Hakami, N. *Pèlerinage de l'Emâm Rezâ: Etude Socio-économique*. Tokyo: Institute for the Study of Languages and Cultures of Asia and Africa, 1989.

Madelung, W. "New Documents Concerning al-Ma'mun, al-Fadl b. Sahl and 'Ali al-Rida." In *Studia Arabica et Islamica: Festschrift for Ihsan 'Abbas*, ed. W. al-Qadi, 333–46. Beirut: American University of Beirut, 1981.

Modarressi, H. *Crisis and Consolidation in the Formative Period of Shi'ite Islam*. Princeton: The Darwin Press, 1993.

'ALI IBN ABI TALIB

'Ali ibn Abi Talib (c. 599–661) was the first cousin and son-in-law of the Prophet Muhammad; the fourth of the four Rightly Guided Caliphs (al-khulafa' al-rashidun); and the first of the Imams deemed by all Shi'is Muslims to be appointed by divine mandate. The word *Shi'is* itself is derived from the term *shi'at' 'Ali*, which means "partisans of 'Ali."

Few figures of nascent Islam had as pervasive and enduring an influence—both symbolic and actual—on the unfolding of Islamic thought, culture, and spirituality as 'Ali. Referred to by the Prophet as the "gate" to the city of prophetic science, one of the most noticeable features of his legacy for medieval Islam is indeed the range of disciplines—from theology and exegesis to calligraphy and numerology, from law and mysticism to grammar and rhetoric—that are regarded as having been first adumbrated by 'Ali.

As Companion of the Prophet

'Ali was about five years old when he was taken into the household of Muhammad, and, from this time until the death of the Prophet, was his constant companion. He was one of the first to accept the mission of the Prophet, although he was still but a youth. After the migration *(al-hijra)* to Medina (622), 'Ali distinguished himself principally as the most outstanding warrior in the early battles fought by the Muslims, his valor and strength assuming legendary dimensions through the reports of the battle of Khaybar in 629. He was also one of the scribes of the verses of the continuing revelation of the Qur'an.

In Medina, the Prophet instituted a pact of brotherhood between the emigrants from Mecca and the "helpers" (the Muslims of Medina), and he adopted 'Ali as his brother. The Prophet married 'Ali to his daughter, Fatima, who was considered (along with her mother, Muhammad's first wife, Khadija) to be a paragon of feminine sanctity in Islam. The Prophet's *ahl al-bayt* ("people of the House")—the members of which the Qur'an refers to in 33:33 as being purified of all defilement—was indicated by the Prophet as consisting of himself, 'Ali, Fatima, and their two sons, Hasan and Husayn.

In one of the most famous and controversial sayings of the Prophet, known as the Hadith al-Ghadir, 'Ali is referred to as the *mawla* (guide/master/nearest) of all those who regard the Prophet as their mawla. For Shi'is, this implied a clear designation *(nass)* by the Prophet of 'Ali as his successor. It was belief in 'Ali as the true, divinely appointed successor *(khalifa)* and heir *(wasi)* of the Prophet that formed the theological basis of the distinctive political philosophy of Shi'ism. Such Shi'ite dynasties as the (Isma'ili) Fatimids (q.v.) and the (Ithna'ashari) Safawids (q.v.) were founded on this political philosophy.

As Caliph

The short caliphate of 'Ali (656–661) was marked principally by the first civil wars within Islam. He fought three major battles: that of Jamal (656) against the forces of Talha, Zubayr (two leading companions), and 'A'isha (one of the Prophet's wives); that of Siffin against Mu'awiya (657); and that of Nahrawan (658) against the "Seceders" (Kharijites [q.v.]; those who seceded from his own ranks). Although victorious in the first and last of these battles, the second resulted in a stalemate and an attempt at arbitration. When this attempt collapsed, 'Ali roused his forces for a resumption of the war against Mu'awiya but was attacked by a Kharijite during morning prayers at the congregational mosque in Kufa on 28 January 661; he died from his wounds two days later.

Intellectual and Spiritual Legacy

The chief vehicle of 'Ali's intellectual legacy is the *Nahj al-Balagha*, a text of sermons, letters, and aphorisms that was compiled by al-Sharif al-Radi (d. 1016), a renowned Shi'i scholar of 'Abbasid Baghdad. Few texts have exerted a greater influence on the field of Arabic literature and rhetoric than the *Nahj*. Despite ongoing questions about the authenticity of the text,

recent scholarship suggests that most of the material in it can in fact be attributed to 'Ali (Djebli, 56). The numerous commentaries on this text—the most important being that of the Mu'tazilite, Ibn Abi l-Hadid (d. 655)—greatly amplified its influence on theological speculation, philosophical thought, and literary discourse.

With regard to 'Ali's spiritual legacy, this was transmitted in the Sunni world principally through the widespread Sufi brotherhoods (turuq, s. tariqa, q.v.), all of which trace their spiritual genealogy back to him through an unbroken chain of initiatic masters. In the Shi'i context, his spiritual influence is discerned in the tradition of what came to be called *'irfan* (gnosis; q.v.), which partly overlaps with Sufism but is distinct from it in certain respects.

'Ali's shrine in Najaf, near Baghdad, remains one of the most important places of pilgrimage in the Muslim world.

REZA SHAH-KAZEMI

Further Reading

Chirri, Mohammad Jawad. *The Brother of the Prophet Mohammad*, 2 vols. Detroit: 1979, 1982.
Djebli, Moktar. "Encore à Propos de l'Authenticité du Nahj al-Balagha!" *Studia Islamica* LXXV (1992): 33–56.
Ibn Ishaq. *The Life of Muhammad*, trans. A. Guillaume. London: 1968.
Madelung, Wilferd. *The Succession to Muhammad—A Study of the Early Caliphate*. Cambridge: 1997.
Poonawala, I.K. "'Ali b. Abi Taleb." In *Encyclopedia Iranica*, Part i, 838–43.
al-Radi, al-Sharif. *Nahjul Balaghah (The Peak of Eloquence)*, trans. Sayed Ali Reza. New York: 1996.
al-Tabari, Abu Ja'far Muhammad ibn Jarir. *The History of al-Tabari*, trans. Adrian Brockett. New York: 7. See in particular vol. XVI, "The Community Divided—The Caliphate of 'Ali I, A.D. 656–657/ A.H. 35–36" and vol. XVII, "The First Civil War—From the Battle of Siffin to the Death of 'Ali, A.D. 656–661/ A.H. 36–40."

ALMOHADS

The Almohads were the Berber dynasty that ruled the Islamic West (Morocco, Algeria, Tunis) and al-Andalus (Muslim Spain) from the sixth/twelfth century to the first half of the seventh/thirteenth century.

The name *Almohads* derives from the Arabic *al-muwahhidun* (the Unitarians), which was adopted by the followers of an Islamic reformist movement originating with the teachings of the Masmuda Berber Ibn Tumart, who led a doctrinal opposition against what he saw as the religious and moral corruption of Almoravid times. The sources of Ibn Tumart's thought, which are to be understood within the theological and legal debates about the acquisition of certainty in the interpretation of God's revelation, are still open to discussion.

Ibn Tumart's life in Almohad sources follows the paradigm of the Prophet Muhammad's biography, which makes the disentangling of legend from history difficult. Ibn Tumart performed an emigration (517/1123) with his disciples to the village of Tinmallal (Atlas mountains) to escape Almoravid persecution. There, having gained the allegiance of neighboring Berber tribes, the religious movement transformed itself into a revolutionary army that engaged in military fighting against the Almoravids. Purges of dissidents were carried out, and Ibn Tumart proclaimed himself (or was proclaimed) Mahdi (rightly guided one), a title with Messianic overtones.

After Ibn Tumart's death, his disciple 'Abd al-Mu'min (Zanata Berber) proclaimed himself caliph (r. 524/1130–558/1163), eventually adopting an Arab (Qaysi) genealogy. 'Abd al-Mu'min was the founder of the Almohad empire, managing to conquer Marrakech (the Almoravid capital) in the year 542/1147. He introduced changes in the composition of the Almohad Berber army, incorporating the Arab tribes (Sulaym, Hilal) that had been moving westward in North Africa since the fifth/eleventh century. 'Abd al-Mu'min was also responsible for the creation of the religious elites known as *talaba*. Al-Andalus was partly occupied during 'Abd al-Mu'min's times, and so was Tunis, where he defeated the Normans of Sicily. His successors Abu Ya'qub Yusuf (r. 558–580/1163–1184) and Abu Yusuf Ya'qub al-Mansur (r. 580–595/1184–1199) had to face the Almoravid Banu Ghaniya and internal opponents as well as continue the struggle in the Iberian Peninsula against both local Andalusi independent rulers and the Christians. These groups were defeated at the battle of Alarcos (591/1195), although some years later the Almohads would prove unable to stop them; and by the third decade of the seventh/thirteenth century, major towns such as Seville and Cordoba were lost to the King of Castile. The ruling dynasty was weakened by internal splits, some of which were associated with the maintenance or abandonment of the original Almohad ideology. The empire disintegrated during the first half of the seventh/thirteenth century, and former Almohad territory was divided among the Marinids in Morocco, the Hafsids in Tunis, and the 'Abd al-Wadids in Algeria.

The Almohad movement had aimed at a complete religious renewal that was conceived as a return to the situation of the early Muslim community, when the Prophet ensured the correct understanding and implementation of God's design for the believers. By this, they were proclaiming a break with the existing society, because it represented the degradation of the original community. This break showed itself in certain Almohad peculiarities that aimed at proving the beginning of a new era: the qibla of the mosques was changed; changes were introduced in the public call to prayer; in the Almohad coins, the square shape predominated over the round; and the study of the fundamentals of belief and law was promoted. The Almohad period also witnessed the flourishing of Sufism in the Islamic West and also of philosophy; the main representative of this was Ibn Rushd al-Hafid (d. 595/1198), known in the Latin West as Averroes. The effort for propagating Almohad doctrine among the population led to the use of the Berber language in ritual and writings, while at the same time the penetration of Arab tribes in Morocco would eventually help the process of linguistic Arabization.

MARIBEL FIERRO

See also Ibn Tumart; Almoravids

Further Reading

Overviews

EI2, s.v. al-muwahhidun [M. Shatzmiller], Leiden, 1960.

Guichard, P. "Les Almohades." In *Etats, Sociétés et Cultures du Monde Musulman Médiéval: Xème-XVème Siècle*, 3 vols., vol. 1, 205–31. ed. Jean-Claude Garcin et al. Paris: 1995.

Huici Miranda, A. *Historia Política del Imperio Almohade*, 2 vols. Tetuan: 1956–1957. (Reprinted in Granada: 2000).

Viguera, M.J., ed. "El Retroceso Territorial de al-Andalus. Almorávides y Almohades." In *Historia de España*, ed. R. Menéndez Pidal, siglos XI al XIII, vol. VIII/2. Madrid: 1997.

Partial Studies (Published in the Last Twenty Years)

Conrad, L.L., ed. The World of Ibn Tufayl. Interdisciplinary Perspectives on "Hayy ibn Yaqzan." Leiden: 1996.

Cornell, V. *Realm of the Saint. Power and Authority in Moroccan Sufism*. Austin: 1998.

Ferhat, H. *Le Maghreb aux XIIème et XIIIème Siècles: Les Siècles de la Foi*. Casablanca: 1993.

Fierro, M. "The Legal Policies of the Almohad Caliphs and Ibn Rushd's Bidayat al-mujtahid." *Journal of Islamic Studies* 10/3 (1999): 226–48.

Fricaud, E. "Les Talaba dans la Société Almohade (le Temps d'Averroés)." *Al-Qantara* XVIII (1997): 331–88.

Karmi, M. *La Chute de l'Empire Almohade. Analyse Doctrinale, Politique et Économique*. Lille: Atelier National de Reproduction des Thèses, 1998.

Nagel, T. *Im Offenkundigen das Verborgene. Die Heilszusage des Sunnitischen Islams*. Göttingen: 2002.

Sabbane, A. *Le Gouvernement et l'Administration de la Dynastie Almohade (XIIe-XIIIe Siècles)*. Lille: Atelier National de Reproduction des Thèses, 1999.

Urvoy, D. Pensers d'al-Andalus. *La Vie Intellectuelle à Cordoue et Sevilla au Temps des Empires Berberes (Fin XIe Siècle–Début XIIIe Siècle)*. Toulouse: 1990.

Vega Martín, M., S. Peña Martín, and M. C. Feria García. El Mensaje de las Monedas Almohades: Numismática, Traducción y Pensamiento. Castilla-La Mancha: Servicio de Publicaciones de Castilla-La Mancha, 2002.

ALMORAVIDS

The Almoravids were the dynasty that ruled Morocco and al-Andalus (Muslim Spain) from the fifth/eleventh century to the first half of the sixth/twelfth century.

The Almoravids were recruited from among Berber Sanhaja nomads who inhabited southern Morocco and the Sahara and who were involved in the salt, gold, and slave trades. They were known in Arabic as *al-murabitun*, which means those who engage in *ribat* (this term refers to a fortified convent on the frontiers of Islam but also metaphorically to a spiritual discipline that could be directed to military aims). The origins of the Almoravid movement are connected by sources to the desire of a leader of the Gudala tribe to improve the religious life of his tribesmen (and their relatives, the Lamtuna), convincing a Maliki scholar, Ibn Yasin, to settle with them in what is now Mauritania. Ibn Yasin, while keeping for himself the political and religious leadership, appointed Yahya ibn 'Umar al-Lamtuni leader of the army after the Sanhaja had been organized into a raiding force. They conquered the Sahara and southern Morocco. Ibn Yasin died in 450/1058 while fighting the heretic Barghawata Berbers; although mention is made of some spiritual successors, the movement eventually united under a single religious, political, and military leadership. Yahya ibn 'Umar died in 447–448/1055–1057 and was succeeded by his brother Abu Bakr, who left for the Sahara to put order there and who appointed as commander of the army in Morocco his cousin Yusuf ibn Tashufin (d. 500/1107). The latter became the supreme authority of the Almoravid movement, which he led to the conquests of Morocco, part of Ifriqiya (see North Africa), and al-Andalus. The capital of the empire was established in Marrakech. Ibn Tashufin and his successors, who claimed a Himyari (Southern Arab) genealogy, adopted the title *Prince of the Muslims (amir al-muslimin)* and are said to have acknowledged the 'Abbasid caliphate.

The Andalusi Taifa kings (see Party Kings [Iberian Peninsula]), unable to stop Christian military advance in the Iberian Peninsula, asked for Ibn Tashufin's help; he crossed the Strait of Gibraltar, obtaining a resounding victory at Zallaqa (479/1086). This and later military interventions eventually led to the dethronement of those same Taifa kings, and al-Andalus became part of the Almoravid empire.

The Almoravid dynasty was supported by the Sanhaja murabitun, who constituted a military and political elite, and by the employment of Christian mercenaries and black slaves in the army.

In the religious and legal spheres, the Maliki jurists had great influence, because the Almoravid rulers usually tried to back their political and religious decisions with fatwas (see Law and Jurisprudence). Although the Almoravid movement has usually been portrayed as fanatical and conservative, supporting those Malikis who opposed theology and Sufism (with the episode of the burning of al-Ghazali's *Ihya'* 'ulum al-din [Revivification of the Religious Sciences] figuring prominently in this regard), recent scholarship indicates a more complex situation. The Almoravid program of religious reform, which centered on jihad and the abolition of illegal taxes, went in fact together with an increasing interest in theology, the fundamentals of religion (usul al-din), and the rational sciences, as well as with the flourishing of Sufism, thus prefiguring in many ways the subsequent Almohad intellectual and religious revolution.

The Almoravids, who were weakened by their fight against the Christians of al-Andalus, lost their power at the hands of the Almohads, who accused them of heterodoxy for their un-Islamic dressing (the men were veiled and the women were not) and for their anthropomorphism. In al-Andalus, the disintegration of Almoravid power was the result of the formation of independent polities led by charismatic leaders (e.g., the Sufi Ibn Qasi), military men, or urban notables (mostly judges). Almost all of these autonomous political entities disappeared with the Almohad intervention in the Iberian Peninsula. Only the branch of the Massufa Banu Ghaniya managed to survive, ruling first in the Balearic Islands and then in Ifriqiyya.

MARIBEL FIERRO

See also Jihad; Gibraltar

Further Reading

Overviews

EI2, s.v. al-murabitun [H.T. Norris and P. Chalmeta]. Leiden, 1960.

Bel, A. *Les Benou Ghaniya*. Paris: 1903.

Bosch Vila, J. *Los Almorávides*. Tetuan: 1956. (Reprinted with an introduction by E. Molina; Granada: 1990.)

Codera, F. *Decadencia y Desaparición de los Almorávides en España*. Zaragoza: 1899. (Reprinted with an introduction by M.J. Viguera; Zaragoza: 2004.)

Dandash, I.A.L. Al-Andalus fi Nihayat al-Murabitin wa-Mustahall al-Muwahhidin. _Asr al-Tawa_if al-Thani

(510–546 H./1116–1151 M.). Beirut: Ta'rikh Siyasi wa-Hadara, 1988.

Guichard, P. "Les Almoravides." In *Etats, Sociétés et Cultures du Monde Musulman Médiéval: Xème-XVème Siècle,* ed. Jean-Claude Garcin et al, 3 vols. Paris: 1995.

Lagardére, V. *Les Almoravides Jusqu'au Règne de Yusuf b. Tashfin (1039–1106).* Paris: 1989.

———. *Le Vendredi de Zallaqa (23 Octobre 1086).* Paris: 1989.

———. *Les Almoravides. Le Djihad Andalou (1106–1143).* Paris: 1998.

Viguera, M.J., ed. "El Retroceso Territorial de al-Andalus. Almorávides y Almohades." In *Historia de España,* ed. R. Menéndez Pidal, Siglos XI al XIII, vol. VIII/2. Madrid: 1997.

Partial Studies

al-Q. Butshish, I. *al-Maghrib wa-l-Andalus fi asr al-Murabitin: al-Mujtama', al-Dhihniyyat, al-Awliya'.* Beirut: 1993.

Dandash, I.A.L. *Adwa' Jadida 'ala al-Murabitin.* Beirut: 1990.

Dreher, J. "L'Imamat d'Ibn Qasi à Mértola (Automne 1144–Été 1145): Légitimité d'Une Domination Soufie?" *MIDEO* 18 (1988): 195–210.

Fierro, M. "The qadi as ruler." In *Saber Religioso y Poder Político,* 71–116. Actas del Simposio Internacional, Granada, 15–18 October 1991. Madrid: 1994.

Messier, R. "The Almoravids, West-Africa Gold and the Gold Currency of the Mediterranean Basin." *Journal of the Economic and Social History of the Orient* 17 (1974): 31–47.

———. "Re-thinking the Almoravids, Re-thinking Ibn Khaldun." In *North Africa, Islam and the Mediterranean World. From The Almoravids to the Algerian World,* ed. J. Clancy-Smith, 58–80. London: 2001.

Serrano, D. "Los Almorávides y la Teología as'arí: ¿Contestación o Legitimación de una Disciplina Marginal?" In *Estudios Onomástico-Biográficos de al-Andalus,* ed. C. de la Puente, XIII. Identidades Marginales, 461–516. Madrid: 2003.

Urvoy, D. Pensers d'al-Andalus. La Vie Intellectuelle à Cordoue et Sevilla au Temps des Empires Berberes (Fin XIe Siècle–Début XIIIe Siècle). Toulouse: 1990.

Viguera, M.J. "Las Cartas de al-Gazali y al-Turtusi al Soberano Almorávid Yusuf b. Tasufin." *Al-Andalus* XLII (1977): 341–74.

ALP ARSLAN

Alp Arslan (r. 1063–1073 CE) was the second sultan of the Great Seljuk Empire. Born in 1029, he was a son of Chaghri Beg, a grandson of Seljuk ibn Duqaq (the eponymous founder of the Seljuk dynasty), and a nephew of Toghril Beg, the first sultan of the Great Seljuk Empire (of which Chaghri and Toghril were cofounders). Soon after their conquest of the Middle East began in 1040, Chaghri became ruler of Khurasan, using Merv as his capital. Other regions of the empire were subsequently parceled out to other members of the family. Alp Arslan was close to his father, who, as early as 1043, sent him as the head of forces against the Ghaznavids. In 1050, he plundered Fasa far to the west, in Fars. He fought the Ghaznavids again, successfully, in 1053–1054. When Chaghri died around 1059, Alp Arslan succeeded him as ruler of Khurasan and placed Nizam al-Mulk, who had previously entered his service, in charge of its administration. At about the same time, he marched to Rayy, the capital of the Seljuk Empire, to help Toghril crush a revolt by his cousin Ibrahim Yinal.

Toghril died childless in 1063. Before he died, he married one of Chaghri's wives, whose son he designated his heir. With the support of powerful amirs, Alp Arslan rid himself of his half-brother, overcame rebellious family members (the most formidable of whom was his brother Qavurt, the ruler of Kirman), and took the throne at Rayy, placing Nizam al-Mulk in charge of running the empire. Shortly thereafter, the 'Abbasid caliph al-Qa'im recognized him as sultan; he then concentrated on continuing the Seljuk conquests. In 1064, Alp Arslan marched to Azerbaijan. From there he invaded Georgia and conquered the Armenian cities of Kars and Ani, and afterward he returned to Rayy. In 1065, he consolidated his hold on Transoxania and campaigned beyond the Jaxartes (Syr Darya). In 1067, he turned south to crush a revolt by Qavurt and then returned to the western frontier where, in the meantime, Turkmen raiders had been penetrating ever more deeply into Byzantine territory. In 1068, he again invaded Georgia, and, in 1070, he moved into northern Syria, besieging Edessa and Aleppo. In 1071, while in Syria, he made plans to overthrow the Fatimid caliphate in Egypt. His attention was diverted, however, when he learned that the Byzantine emperor Romanus IV Diogenes was marching into eastern Anatolia. The emperor had decided to put an end to the growing Turkish menace by taking the fortresses of Manzikert and Akhlat, thus sealing off major immigration routes into Anatolia. At Manzikert, Alp Arslan defeated the Byzantine army and captured the emperor. Byzantine defenses in Anatolia collapsed, and Turkish immigration began on a large scale, driven by a desire for booty and pastures. There is no evidence that Alp Arslan ordered a systematic conquest of Anatolia. Indeed, he immediately returned east to face hostilities with the Qarakhanids in Transoxania. In 1073, in the midst of this campaign, a captive Castellan managed to stab him to death; his son Malikshah succeeded him.

GARY LEISER

See also 'Abbasids; Armenia, Byzantine Empire; Fatimids; Muslim–Byzantine Relations; Raids; Seljuks; Seljuk Warfare; Turks

Primary Sources

Ibn al-Athir. *The Annals of the Saljuq Turks*, trans. D.S. Richards. London: Routledge-Curzon, 2002.

Further Reading

Bosworth, C.E. "The Political and Dynastic History of the Iranian World (A.D. 1000–1217)." In *The Cambridge History of Iran*, vol. 5, *The Saljuq and Mongol Periods*, ed. J.A. Boyle. Cambridge: Cambridge University Press, 1968.

Luther, K.A. "Alp Arslan." In *Encyclopaedia Iranica*.

ALPHABETS

The Arabic alphabet (abjad, abajad, or abu jad) consists, in its present state (which has been attested to since the end of the seventh century) of twenty-eight graphemes that are consonantal phonemes. They are as follows (here with a simplified transliteration and numerical value): alif (', 1), ba' (b, 2), ta' (t, 400), tha' (voiceless gingival or interdental: th, 500), jim (j, 3), ha' (h, 8), kha' (voiceless spirant fricative: kh, 600), dal (d, 4), dhal (voiced gingival: dh, 700), ra' (lingual vibrant: r, 200), zay (z, 7), sin (s, 60), shin (voiceless cacuminal spirant, hushing sound, 300), sad (voiceless velar postdental, 90), dad (voiced velar occlusive, 800), za' (voiced velar interdental spirant, 900), 'ayn (voiceless fricative spirant: ', 70), ghayn (voiced fricative spirant: gh, 70), fa' (f, 80), qaf (voiceless back-velar occlusive, together with occlusion of the larynx, 100), kaf (k, 20), lam (l, 30), mim (m, 40), nun (n, 50), ha' (voiceless breath: h, 5), waw (w and long u, 6), and ya' (y and long i, 10).

Like other Proto-Sinaitic–derived scripts, Arabic does not have letters for vowels (haraka [motion]). However, at a later period, diacritical signs were invented to mark the vowels of Arabic and other phenomens of pronunciation. The marks for the short vowels are as follows: fatha (a), kasra (i), and damma (u). The marks of the short vowels, when doubled, are pronounced with the addition of the sound *n* (an, in, un); this is called *tanwin* (*nunation*, from the name of the letter *nun*). The long vowels and diphthongs are indicated by *alif* (long a), *ya'* (for long i and ay), and *waw* (for long u and aw).

When *alif* is not a mere letter of prolongation (i.e., a long *a*) but rather a consonant, pronounced like the *spiritus lenis*, it is distinguished by the mark *hamza*, which means compression, and is shown as follows: '. With the vowels u and a, it is written over the alif; with the vowel i, it is written under. In special conditions, it is put over a ya' or a waw; in others, it is

directly on the line, without a support. The alif maqsura (the alif that can be abbreviated) and the ta' marbuta (the tied ya') are in their forms, respectively, variants of the ya' and the ha'.

The *sukun* (rest) corresponds to the sheva quiescens of the Hebrew: it indicates the absence of vowel or a consonant. A consonant that is to be doubled without the interposition of a vowel is marked by a *shadda* (strengthening mark). When the vowels with hamza ('a, 'i, 'u) at the beginning of a word are absorbed by the final vowel of the preceding word, the elision of the *spiritus lenis* is marked by the sign wasla (union).

There are at least two positions among Western scholars regarding the origin of the Arabic alphabet and writing: the Nabatean Aramaic one and the Syriac one (via the towns of Anbar and Hira). It should be noted that, for most of the ancient Muslim scholars, the Arabic script came from these towns to Mecca. There are also several legends surrounding the origin of the Arabic script. According to the Kufian Ibn al-Kalbi (d. AH 204/819 CE or 206/821), the first to form it was a group of Bedouin Arabs, whose names were Abu Jad (Abdjad), Hawwaz (or Hawwiz), Hutti, Kalamun (or Kaliman), Safas (or Safad), and Qurusa'at (or Qarishat, Qarashat). These legendary persons are supposed to have been kings of Midian (Madian). These names are actually combinations of the letters of the alphabet in the traditional order of the Semitic alphabet that have been combined in groups of four, three, four, and four, from aleph to taw.

Other languages are written in Arabic script: Hausa, Kashmiri, Kazak, Kurdish, Kyrghyz, Malay, Morisco, Pashto, Persian/Farsi, Sindhi, Tatar, Turkish (before the reform of Ata Turk), Uyghur (in the Xinjiang Uyghur autonomous region of China and also in Afghanistan), and Urdu.

Also present are the following consonant alphabets: ancient Berber, Divehi Akuru (Maldivian Indo-Aryan language—"island letters" that were replaced, after the conversion of the Maldives to Islam in 1153, by a new Arabic-influenced alphabet known as *Thaana*), Hebrew, Mandaic, Middle Persian, Nabatean, Parthian, Phoenician, Proto-Hebrew, Psalter (a variant of Persian script), Sabean, Samaritan, South Arabian, Syriac, Tifinagh, and Ugaritic. Tifinagh is thought to have derived from ancient Berber script; it could mean "Phoenician letters," or it may come from the Greek *pinaks* (writing tablets). Since September 2003, the Tifinagh alphabet has been taught in primary schools in Morocco; it is also used by the Tuaregs, particularly the women, for private notes and decoration.

CLAUDE GILLIOT

Primary Sources

Ibn Khaldun. The Muqaddimah. In *An Introduction to History*, trans. Franz Rosenthal, 3 vols., vol. III, 111–70. New York: Bollingen Foundation; Princeton, NJ; Princeton University Press, 1967.

Ibn al-Nadim. "The Fihrist of Ibn al-Nadim." In *A Tenth-Century Survey of Muslim Culture,* ed. and trans. Bayard Dodge, 2 vols., vol. I, 5–10. New York: Columbia University Press, 1970.

Further Reading

Czapkiewicz, Andrzej. *The Views of the Medieval Arab Philologists on Language and its Origin in the Light of as-Suyûtî's "al-Muzhir."* Cracovia: Universitas Iagellonica (Acta Scientiarum Litterarumque, CMIX, «Schedae Grammaticae», Fasciculus XCI), 1988.

Drucker, Johanna. *The Alphabetic Labyrinth. The Letters in History and Imagination.* London: Thames and Hudson, 1995.

Endress, Gerhard. "Herkunft und Entwicklung der Arabischen Schrift." In *Grundriss der Arabischen Philologie,* ed. Wolfdietrich Fischer, 165–97. Wiesbaden: Ludwig Reichert, 1982.

Gruendler, Beatrice. "The Development of the Arabic Scripts. From the Nabatean Aea to the First Islamic Century According to Dated Texts." *Harvard Semitic Studies* 63 (1993).

Naveh, Joseph. *Early History of the Alphabet. An Introduction to West Semitic Epigraphy and Paleography.* Leiden: E.J. Brill, 1982.

Silvestre de Sacy, Antoine-Isaac. "Mémoire sur l'Origine et les Anciens Monuments de la Littérature Parmi les Arabes," *Mémoires Tirés des Registres de l'Académie Royale des Inscriptions et Belles Lettres* L (1785): 247–441.

Troupeau, Gérard. "Réflexions sur l'Origine Syriaque de l'Écriture Arabe." In *Semitic Studies in Honor of Wolf Leslau,* ed. Alan S. Kaye, vol. II, 1562–1570. Wiesbaden: Otto Harrassowitz, 1991.

AMIR KHUSRAW (1253–1325)

Nasir al-Din Abu 'l-Hasan, the son of a Turkish soldier and Indian mother, was born in Patiala in the Punjab in 1253. Perhaps the greatest Persian poet of pre-Mughal India, he took great pride in his Indian origins and was recognized as being the "Parrot of India" for singing its praises. As a boy, his grandfather encouraged his poetic talents; once in Delhi, he found patronage with Sultan Balban and his son Boghra Khan. Amir Khusraw joined the prince on campaign to Multan, which was promptly sacked by the invading Mongols in 1284. The prince was killed, and Amir Khusraw was taken prisoner. Once released, he found favor with the Khalji sultans of Delhi, especially 'Ala' al-Din (d. 1315), under whose patronage he wrote most of his compositions. Like other medieval poets, he moved from one royal patron to another; this occurred quite often given the vicissitudes of political life in the Delhi sultanate.

Amir Khusraw wrote a cycle of five epic poems (khamsa) in imitation of Nizami, odes to the conquests of his patrons, and Hindi love poems and riddles; he is credited with the invention of Hindustani music. He was also a close disciple of the great Chishti Sufi of Delhi Nizam al-Din Awliya'. Throughout his work, Amir Khusraw stressed his Indianness and even wrote a poetic work in nine meters entitled *Nuh Sipihr* that was about nine spheres of existence, with India elevated above all others. Amir Khusraw died in 1325, shortly after his beloved Sufi master and was buried next to him.

SAJJAD H. RIZVI

See also Delhi; Chishti; Epics, Persian; Poetry, Persian; Sufism

Further Reading

Amir Khusraw: Seventh Century Celebrations. Hyderabad: Abul-Kalam Azad Research Institute, 1972.

Brend, B. *Perspectives on Persian Painting: Illustrations on Amir Khusrau's Khamsah.* London: Routledge-Curzon, 2003.

Mirza, W.A. *The Life and Works of Amir Khusrau.* Calcutta: Baptist Mission Press, 1935.

Rizvi, S.A.A. *A History of Sufism in India.* New Delhi: Munshiram Manoharlal, 1983.

AMULI, Al-

Al-Amuli, Al-Sayyid Haydar al-Husayn (d. after AH 787/1385 CE) was an early proponent of the close association between Sufism and Imami Shi'ism and of the notion that the Imams had been guides for their own followers but also for travelers along the mystical path. He was also one of the earliest Imami thinkers to have incorporated the thought of Ibn al-'Arabi (d. 638/1240) into his writings.

Al-Sayyid Haydar initially studied in his hometown of Amul, in Mazandiran, which was long known for its Shi'i proclivities, and then later in Astarabad and Isfahan. Having returned to Amul, he became close to and served the local ruler, whose assassination in 750/1349 coincided with Haydar's abandonment of life at court for Sufism. He visited different Shi'i shrines and also traveled to Jerusalem and the Hijaz, and thereafter he settled in Iraq. In Baghdad he studied with such prominent Shi'i figures as Fakhr al-Din Muhammad ibn al-Hasan al-Hilli (d. 771/1370) (son of the famous Twelver scholar al-Hasan ibn Yusuf, al-'Allama) and Ibn al-Mutahhar al-Hilli (d. 726/1325). He later resided in the Shi'i shrine city of Najaf.

Of the more than forty works authored by Amuli, seven have survived, and some have been published. Perhaps the most famous is *Jami' al-Asrar (A Compendium of Secrets)*, which was completed in 752/1351. His *Asrar al-Shari'a*, which was mentioned in the *Jami'*, has been translated into English as *Inner Secrets of the Path* (1989) and includes Muhammad Khajavi's 1982 essay about Amuli and his thought.

Amuli insisted on the common origins of Shi'ism and Sufism, understanding all knowledge as having derived from the Imams. His project involved an effort to transcend both the normal literal/juridical approach to Islam, especially Shi'i Islam, and those dimensions of Sufism that rejected the grounding of its doctrine and practices in those of the Imams.

The *Compendium* is especially noteworthy for Amuli's efforts to reconcile aspects of Ibn al-'Arabi's thought with Twelver Shi'ism, particularly his reference to pure monotheism and inner/ontological monotheism; in addition, he postulated that the former was taught by the prophets and the secrets of the latter by the awliya' (sing. wali). 'Ali was the seal of the universal walaya, and the Mahdi—who, for Amuli, is the twelfth Imam—was the seal of the Muhammadan walaya. By contrast, for Ibn al-'Arabi, Jesus was the seal of the former.

Amuli's efforts to establish a synthesis between Sufism and Shi'ism were continued by Mir Damad (d. 1630), Mulla Sadra (d. 1640), Hadi Sabzavari (d. 1873), and the Ayatollah Khomayni (d. 1989).

Khajavi's contribution and Corbin's recently translated 1981 lecture remain the only English-language essay-length studies of Amuli's legacy. Kohlberg offers a list of non-English editions of Amuli's published works.

ANDREW J. NEWMAN

Further Reading

Corbin (1986); Kohlberg, E. (1985); J. van Ess (1982) [AJN].

Corbin, H. "The Science of the Balance and the Correspondences Between Worlds in Islamic Gnosis, According to the Work of Haydar Amuli, eighth/fourteenth century." In *Temple and Contemplation*, trans. Philip Sherrard. London: 1986.

van Ess, J. "Haydar-i Amuli." *EI²* Suppl. 5–6 (1982): 363–65.

Kohlberg, E. "Amoli, Sayyed Baha'-al-Din Haydar." *EIr* I (1985): 983–85.

AMULETS

See Talismans and Talismanic Objects

AL-ANDALUS

Al-Andalus is the name used to refer to the Iberian peninsula territories that were ruled by Islamic regimes between 711 and 1492; scholars have yet to reach agreement about the origin of this name. For some, the meaning of al-Andalus is "the land of the Vandals"; others suggest "the Island of the Atlantis," whereas some believe that it comes from the German expression *Landahlauts,* which means "land allotment."

The expressions *Muslim Spain* and *Andalusia* are inaccurate renditions of al-Andalus and should therefore be rejected, because they reflect neither the historical nor the geographical reality of al-Andalus. The territorial limits of al-Andalus varied over time, although they diminished steadily from the eleventh century onward. The political control of the territory also varied significantly from urban centers to rural areas and to the territories on the border with the Christian kingdoms. However, certain elements were constant, including the following:

1. Al-Andalus constituted an Islamic Mediterranean society (which meant a disruption with the previous Hispano-Roman and Visigoth society), and it was distinct from the feudal societies of Christian Medieval Europe. Another important characteristic was its "frontier society" character.

2. Al-Andalus has to be set in the wider context of the premodern Islamic West. The discontinuity with the previous historical reality is evident in the new forms of government, territory organization, production, fiscal system, legal system, religious life, and generational and patrimonial transmission within the family. In addition, a significant aspect of Andalusi collective identity was its majority ascription to the Maliki juridical school.

From the second half of the eighth century (after the arrival of the Umayyad prince 'Abd al-Rahman ibn Mu'awiya), al-Andalus became an Umayyad emirate. During this period, all kinds of exchanges with the rest of the Islamic world occurred. At the beginning of the tenth century, one of 'Abd al-Rahman's descendants, 'Abd al-Rahman III, proclaimed himself caliph. When the caliphate collapsed at the beginning of the eleventh century, al-Andalus was fragmented into a series of independent kingdoms (ta'ifas) that were unable to face the growing strength of the Christians of the North. At the end of the eleventh century, al-Andalus was under the ruling of the North African dynasties of the Almoravids and Almohads. Lastly, Andalusi political power was limited to the kingdom of Granada (thirteenth–fifteenth centuries), which continued in a precarious fashion until 1492.

Political power fluctuated between the two sides of the Strait of Gibraltar, being marked by the supremacy of al-Andalus during the first stage, whereas the Maghrib had priority over al-Andalus after the end of the eleventh century.

The Romance language was preserved in al-Andalus. The Andalusi population spoke Romance along with Arabic, although it is impossible to determine the actual scope of its use. However, the written production that has been preserved had Arabic as its main language of use. Andalusis' input into the development of Islamic culture was derived from Eastern influences, sometimes advancing their Oriental sources. Al-Andalus also played a significant role in the transmission of classical thought and Islamic science to the medieval Christian West. The end of the Islamic state did not put an end to the presence of Islam in the peninsula. Muslim communities, known as *mudejars*, continued to be present in some of the territories conquered by the Christians until the sixteenth century. After the conquest of Granada, their inhabitants were obliged to convert to Christianity. Many of these neoconverts, known as *moriscos*, secretly kept their faith until they were finally expelled from the peninsula at the beginning of the seventeenth century. By this time, some of these moriscos (mainly the elite classes) had already migrated, with the Maghrib as their main destination. To this date, an Andalusi origin in the Maghrib is an important identity mark of their descendants.

DELFINA SERRANO RUANO

Further Reading

Arié, R. *España Musulmana, Siglos VIII-XV*. Barcelona: Labor, 1993.

Chalmeta, P., et al. "Al-Andalus: Musulmanes y cristianos (VIII-XIII)." In *Historia de España Dirigida por Antonio Domínguez Ortiz*, vol. 3. Barcelona: Planeta, 1997.

Corriente, F. "Andaluz y andalús y Andaluz." In *Diccionario de Arabismos y Voces Afines en Iberorromance*. Madrid: 1999.

Fierro, M. *Al-Andalus: Saberes e Intercambios Culturales*. Barcelona: Icaria, 2001.

Fierro, M., and Samsó, J., eds. *The Formation of al-Andalus. Part 2: Language, Religion, Culture and the Sciences*. Aldershot, Hampshire, UK, and Brookfield, Vt: Ashgate, 1998.

García-Arenal, M. *Los Moriscos*. Granada: Universidad, 1996.

García Sanjuán, A. "El Significado Geográfico del Topónimo al-Andalus en las Fuentes Árabes." *Anuario de Estudios Medievales* 33/1 (2003): 3–36.

Glick, T. *Islamic and Christian Spain in the Early Middle Ages*. Princeton, NJ: Princeton University Press, 1979.

Guichard, P. *Al-Andalus. Estructura Antropológica de una Sociedad Islámica en Occidente*. Granada: Universidad, 1995.

Halm, H. "Al-Andalus and Gothica Sors." In *The Formation of al-Andalus. Part 1: History and Society*, ed. M. Marín, 27–50.

Jayyusi, S. Kh., ed. *The Legacy of Muslim Spain*. Leiden–New York–Cologne: Brill, 1992.

Lévi-Provençal, E. "España Musulmana Hasta la Caída del Califato de Córdoba," trans. E. García Gómez. In *Historia de España Dirigida por Ramón Menéndez Pidal*, vols. IV and V. Madrid: Espasa Calpe, 1950 and 1957.

Lévi-Provençal, E., L. Torres Balbás, and G.S. Colins. "Al-Andalus" In *EI²*.

Makki, M.'A. *Ensayo Sobre las Aportaciones Orientales en la España Musulmana y su Influencia en la Formación de la Cultura Hispano-Árabe*. Madrid: Instituto de Estudios Islámicos, 1968.

Marín, M. *Individuo y Sociedad en al-Andalus*. Madrid: Mapfre, 1992.

———. *Al-Andalus y los Andalusíes*. Barcelona: Icaria, 2000.

———, ed. *The Formation of al-Andalus. Part 1: History and Society*. Aldershot, Hampshire, UK, and Brookfield, Vt: Ashgate, 1998.

———, coord. *¿Cómo Entender al-Andalus? Reflexiones Sobre su Estudio y Enseñanza*. Madrid: Anaya, 1999.

Samsó, J. *Las Ciencias de los Antiguos en al-Andalus*. Madrid: Mapfre, 1992.

Vallvé, J. "El Nombre de al-Andalus." *Al-Qantara* 4 (1983): 301–55.

Vernet, J. *La Cultura Hispano-Árabe en Oriente y Occidente*. Barcelona: Akal, 1978.

———. *El Islam en España*. Madrid: Mapfre, 1993.

Viguera, M.J. "De las Taifas al Reino de Granada. Al-Andalus, Siglos XI a XV." In *Historia de España (Historia 16)*, vol. 9. Madrid: 1995.

———. "Planteamientos Sobre la historia de al-Andalus." In *El Saber en al-Andalus. Textos y Estudios*, 2nd ed., ed. J.M. Carabaza Bravo and A.T.M. Essawy, 121–32. Sevilla: 1999.

———, coord. "Los Reinos de Taifas. Al-Andalus en el Siglo XI and El Retroceso Territorial de al-Andalus. Almorávides y Almohades. In *Historia de España Menéndez Pidal*, vols. VIII-1 and VIII-2. Madrid: Espasa Calpe, 1994 and 1997.

Viguera, M.J., and Castillo, C., eds. *Al-Andalus y el Mediterráneo*. Barcelona: Lunwerg, 1995.

Watt, W.M. *Historia de España Islámica*. Madrid: Alianza, 1970.

Wycichl, W. "'Al-Andalus' (Sobre la Historia de un Nombre)." *Al-Andalus* 17 (1952): 449–50.

ANGELS

The Arabic word for angel is *malak* (pl. *mala'ika*; Persian, *firishta*). The Arab lexicographers and exegetes consider it original to Arabic, but in fact it dates back to early north–west Semitic. In Ugaritic, *ml'k* means "messenger" (Hebrew, *malak*; Aramaic, *mal'ak*). Some Western scholars believe that the approximate source of the word in Arabic was the Ethiopian *mal'ak* (pl. *mal'eket*), which is presumably a loanword into Ethiopic from Aramaic or Hebrew. According to some scholars, it is more likely that the word *mal'ak* had already crept from Abyssinia and was known to the people of Mecca before Muhammad used it.

To believe in angels is an article of Muslim creed. The following is from the first article of one of the Creeds that is attributed to Abu Hanifa:

> "The heart of the confession of the unity of God and the true foundation of faith consist in this obligatory creed: I believe in God, His Angels, His Books, His Apotels, the resurrection after death, the decree of God the good and the evil thereof, computation of sins, the balance, Paradise and Hell; and that all these are real."

The angels play a role in three major themes of the Qur'an (creation, revelation, and eschatology), and they play a still greater role in hadith and Qur'anic commentary and in special books about them and about eschatology. The imagination of Muslim scholars with regard to angels seems to have no limit. In the Qur'an, the angels are called the "heavenly host" or "multitude" (al-mala' al-a'la) (37:8; 38:69). They are supposed to guard the walls of heaven against the "listening" of the jinns. The Qur'an stresses the absolute submission of the angels to God (21:19–20).

Some of the angels are named in the Qur'an. The Meccan Qur'an mentions the spirit Gabriel that was sent to Mary to announce the conception of Jesus (19:17). Later in Medina, however, Muhammad gave the name Gabriel (Jibril) as that of the messenger by whom the Qur'an was communicated to him (2:97). Muhammad possibly learned this name from the Jews of Mecca, among whom was his secretary Zayd b. Thabit (who knew Aramaic and/or Hebrew before Muhammad came to this town, according to al-Ka'bi [Abu l-Qasim al-Balkhi, d. 319/931]). *Mika'il* (or *Mikal*; i.e., *Michael*), which is a word that may have come directly from the Hebrew or the Syriac, is mentioned together with Gabriel, also in the Medina Qur'an (2:98). Commentators claim that the two are contrasted: Gabriel is the opponent of the Jews, and Michael is their protector.

In the same sura (2:102), Harut and Marut meet. Muhammad probably became acquainted with the names of these mythical figures in the form in which they are found in the *Avesta* (i.e., Harvotat and Amurtat—Perfection and Deathlessness). In the Slavonic Book of Enoch, they appear as Orioch and Marioch. The Syriac (Aramaic) Marut (Mastery, Lordship) may have been known by the Jews of Medina, and especially by Zayd b. Thabit, the "Secretary of Revelation" and one of the redactors of the Qur'an.

In sura 32:11, the mythical Angel of Death (malak al-mawt) appears, but not by name; he is identified in traditional Muslim literature as *'Izra'il ('Azra'il)*.

Special books were written about the angels, including *al-Haba'ik fi Akhbar al-Mala'ik (The Orbits of the Stars: On the Stories of the Angels)*, by Suyuti (d. 911/1505). This is a collection of legendary and mythical stories taken from Prophetic hadith or from early Muslim scholars.

CLAUDE GILLIOT

See also Al-Suyuti

Primary Sources

Abu Hanifa (attributed to). *Creeds*.
Al-Ghazali. "Kitab Dhikr al-Mawt wa-ma ba'Dahu." ("The Remembrance of Death and the Afterlife.") In *Ihya' 'Ulum al-Din (Book XL of The Revival of the Religious Sciences)*, trans. and intro. by T.J. Winter. Cambridge, UK: Islamic Texts Society, 1989.
Al-Taftazani. *Sharh al-'Aqa'id al-Nasafiyya (Commentary of the Creed of Abu Hafs al-Nasafi)*, ed. Claude Salamé. Damascus: Ministery of Culture, 1974.
Elder, Earl Edgar, trans. and intro. *A Commentary on the Creed of Islam*. New York: Columbia University Press, 1960.

Further Reading

Amir-Moezzi, Mohammad Ali. *Le Guide Divin dans le Shi'isme Originel. Aux Sources de l'Ésotérisme en Islam (The Divine Guide in Early Shi'ism. The Sources of Esoterism in Islam)*, trans. David Streight, Éditions Verdier, 1992. Albany: SUNY, 1994.
Eichler, Paul Arno. *Die Dschinn, Teufel und Engel im Koran*. Inaugural dissertation. Leipzig: Université de Leipzig, Lucka in Thüringen, 1928.
Eickmann, Walther. *Die Angelologie und Dämonologie des Korans im Vergleich zu der Engel-un Geisterlehre der Heiligen Schrift*. New York and Leipzig: 1908.
Gilliot, Claude. "Le Coran, Fruit d'un Travail Collectif?" In *al-Kitab*, ed. Daniel De Smet. La acralité du texte dans le monde de l'Islam, Actes du Symposium international tenu à Leuven et Louvain-la-Neuve du 29 mai au 1 juin 2002. Brussels: Louvain-la-Neuve, Leuven: Acta Orientalia Belgica. Subsidia III, 2004, 185–231.
Jeffery, Arthur. *The Foreign Vocabulary of the Qur'an*. Baroda: Oriental Institute, 1938.
———. *Jewish Proper Names and Derivatives in the Koran*. Hildesheim: Georg Olms, 1964.
Niekrens, Wilhelm. *Die Engel- und Geistervorstellungen des Korans*. Inaugural dissertation. Rohstock: University of Rohstock, 1906.
O'Shaughnessy, Thomas. *The Development of the Meaning of Spirit in the Koran. Pontificium Institutum Orientalium Studiorum (Orientalia Christiana Analecta)* 189 (1953): 51–7.
Sweetman, James Windrow. *Islam and Christian Theology*, 2 parts, 3 vols. London: Lutterworth Press, 1945–1967.

Vorgrimler, Herbert, et al. *Engel. Erfahrungen Göttlicher Nähe*. Freiburg: Herder, 2001.

Wensinck, Arent Jan. *The Muslim Creed. Its Genesis and Historical Development*. Cambridge: Cambridge University Press, 1932.

ANIMAL HUSBANDRY

Animal husbandry was critical to medieval Islam because of Islamic dietary laws. Some animals, such as pigs, for example, were forbidden (haram) to eat because they were scavengers. However, shellfish and most animals that lived underwater were lawful (halal) and could be eaten, save for those that breathed both air and water (i.e., amphibians and crocodiles). This exception allowed for industries like the ancient pearl fisheries in the south of the Persian Gulf. Although what an animal ate determined its appropriateness for consumption, some animals were set outside of food purposes regardless. Dogs were considered unclean, although not so much as pigs. Other animals, such as cats, were favored by the Prophet and therefore forbidden as food.

Aside from the statutes in the Qur'an, some early Islamic sources discussed the subject, showing a keen, scientific interest in the raising of camels, horses, and sheep. Ya'qub ibn akhi Hizam wrote about veterinary matters in his book on horsemanship in 785 CE. 'Abd al-Malik ibn Quraib al-Asmai (740–828), a philologist from Basra, wrote about zoology, human anatomy, and animal husbandry. His books *Kitab al-Ibil (The Book of the Camel)*, *Kitab al-Khail (The Book of the Horse)*, *Kitaba al-Sha (The Book of the Sheep)*, and *Kitab al-Wuhush (The Book of Wild Animals)* had great influence in the field through the ninth and tenth centuries. During the same period, Jabril Ibn Bakhtyshu (d. 828–829), a Christian physician, wrote a book about animal husbandry called *Manaeh al-Hiwan (The Uses of Animals)*. Their contemporary, Abu 'Uthman Al-Jahiz (776–868), wrote a book about zoology called *Kitab al-Hawayan (The Book of Animals)*, which discussed the effects of diet on animals.

The early Islamic Meccan economy prized herd animals like camels, horses, cattle, sheep, and goats. In a dry environment in which agriculture was not possible in many places, raising herd animals could maximize the use of marginal land. Even then, pasture land needed to be close to sources of good water. The Qur'an stated that animals had as much right to life as humans and that humans were only more important than animals because of humans' role as stewards of the earth. According to Islamic law, animals should not be deprived of water where it is available (an important consideration in a desert environment), nor should an animal be forced to witness another animal being slaughtered before it or to see the knife used to kill it sharpened before it. In Islam, animals should be slaughtered as painlessly as possible, with a single cut to the throat that would bleed out most of the blood. Blood, carrion meat from dead animals not slaughtered properly, and meat taken from live animals were also forbidden; this derived from the pre-Islamic Arabian practice of cutting the humps off of camels or the tails off of sheep so that the animals could be eaten yet kept alive for further use. Muhammad condemned the practice and forbade meat taken from living animals as carrion.

Islamic law also forbade the unnecessary caging of birds and animals. The Qur'an frowned on the unnecessary killing of animals (i.e., for sport rather than food) and favored kindness toward them, especially cats. One early story states that a man who killed a bird would answer to the creature at the Last Judgment; another story put a woman who starved a cat to death in Hell.

However, hunting was popular enough to make hawk raising an important part of animal husbandry. Hawks were used to hunt other birds, but only for sport. Pigeons had the more useful function of carrying messages. These usages, like the keeping of zoos, indicate that practice could differ widely from law.

Camels were especially important for use in transportation in addition to the production of milk, meat, and hides, with early Meccan caravans including up to 2,500 camels. Cattle also appeared repeatedly in the Qur'an as an important commodity, providing—like camels—milk, meat, and hides. Oxen also pulled plows and provided the power for other agricultural machinery. Sheep and goats provided milk, meat, wool, and hides. Horses were prized and carefully bred for racing, war, and transportation. By 1285, Muslims were practicing artificial insemination on these animals.

Animal husbandry was sufficiently lucrative to be one of the commodities covered under the zakat (alms) tax, specifically herds of camels, cattle, sheep, and goats (but only over a certain number). This tax was paid in kind. Animal husbandry represented the management of a critical source of movable wealth, especially among the more nomadic elements of Islamic society.

PAULA R. STILES

See also Ayyubids; Camels; Hunting; Tulunids; Zoological Parks

Further Reading

Jayakar, A.S.G. *Ad-damiri's Hayat Al-Hayawan: A Zoological Lexicon*. Bombay: D.B. Taraporevala Sons & Co., 1908.

Lemu, B. Aisha. *Animals in Islam*. East Lansing, Mich: Spectrum Books Ltd., 1993.

Stein, Gil J. "Medieval Pastoral Production Systems at Gritille." In *The Archaeology of the Frontier in the Medieval Near East: Excavations at Gritille, Turkey,* ed. Scott Redford, 181–209. Philadelphia: University Museum Publications (Archaeological Institute of America Monographs, N.S.3), 1998.

'ANTARA IBN SHADDAD

'Antara Ibn Shaddad, the Historical Character

'Antar ("the valiant one"), also known as 'Antara ("courage in war"), was a member of the 'Abs tribe who lived in Arabia shortly before Islam (c. 525–615 CE). 'Antar composed one of the seven famous "suspended odes," which were known individually as mu'allaqa. 'Antar's factual and fictional exploits are recorded in the *Sirat 'Antar*, the most important romance of chivalry in Arabic literature; it is for his exploits as recounted in this epic that he is best known today.

Verifiable historic facts about 'Antar are sketchy. Classical Arab scholars such as al-Tibrizi (d. 1109) and Ibn Qutayba (826–889) agree that 'Antar was the son of Shaddad, born a slave of a black African mother. He is portrayed as a great knight and pre-Islamic poet. Both literary and historical sources mention that 'Antar participated in the battle known as *Dahis wa al-Ghabra'* between the 'Abs and Fazara tribes. The most widely accepted account of 'Antar's death is that he was killed by al-Asad al-Rahis, a knight from the Tayyi' tribe, with a poisoned arrow.

'Antara Ibn Shaddad, the Poet

Ibn Qutayba recounts how 'Antar composed his mu'allaqa in response to an insult about his skin color. Respected scholars attribute various numbers of verses to this poem; al-Tibrizi says it consists of 74 verses. The poem's tripartite structure is common to the highly stylized form of classical Arabic poetry: the nasib (opening section) describes the poet's beloved 'Abla and the ruins of her nomad camp; the second section, known as the journey section, describes 'Antar on his horse and then describes a camel, the pre-Islamic Arabs' most important animal; the third section is the poet's "warrior's boast," which praises his own nobility and generosity, his prowess in battle, and his heroic deeds. 'Antar's mu'allaqa is his most famous poem.

The *Sirat 'Antar*

Many other poems are also attributed to 'Antar in the *Sirat 'Antar,* the epic story of his life. This work was discovered by Europeans in 1801, when the Austrian Joseph Von Hammer-Purgstall came across a manuscript of it in Cairo. In 1820, Terrick Hamilton partially translated the work into English. No European-language translation of the 5,300-page work exists.

The *Sirat 'Antar* paints a striking portrait of the Arabs before Islam and the qualities that the Bedouins admired. Some of the epic's highlights are Shaddad's capture of the beautiful Abyssinian slave Zabiba; his later recognition of 'Antar as the legitimate son of this union; 'Antar's rise in importance in the 'Abs tribe; his adventures while seeking a dowry to marry 'Abla; his voyages to far-flung kingdoms; and the hero's death. The last volume of the *Sirat 'Antar* touches on Islam and Muhammad's miracles. Thanks to the *Sirat 'Antar,* 'Antar remains alive as an eternal hero in the popular mind throughout the Arabic-speaking world.

DRISS CHERKAOUI

See also Abyssinia; Adab; Folk Literature, Arab; Heroes and Heroism; Historical Writing; Ibn Qutayba; Ibn Shaddad; Ka'ba (Kaaba); Names; Poets; Popular Literature; Sira; Slaves and Slave Trade, Western Islamic World; Women Warriors

Primary Sources

Anonymous. *Sirat 'Antar*, 8 vols. Beirut: Al-Maktaba Thaqafiyya, 1979.

Ibn Manzur, Muḥammad Ibn Mukarram. *Lisan al-'Arab*, Beirut: Dar Sadir.

Ibn Qutayba, Abu Muhammad Abdullah. *Al-Shi'r wa l-Shu'ara'*. Beirut: Dār al-Kutub al-'Ilmiyya, 1985.

al-Tibrizi, Yahhya Ibn 'Ali. *Sharh al-Tibrizi 'ala Hamasat Abi Tammam*. Cairo: Bulaq, 1888.

Further Reading

Cherkaoui, Driss. *Le Roman de 'Antar: Perspective Littéraire et Historique*. Paris: Présence Africaine, 2001.

———. "Kings and Heroes as Friends and Foes: the Example of *Sīrat 'Antar*." *Al-Arabiyyah: Journal of the American Association of Teachers of Arabic* 34 (2001): 1–21.

———. "The Pyramidal Structure in the Arabic Siyar, the Example of *Sīrat 'Antar.*" *Al-'Usūr al-Wustā, the Bulletin of Middle East Medievalists, Oriental Institute of the University of Chicago* (2001): 6–9.

Heath, Peter. *The Thirsty Sword.* Salt Lake City: University of Utah Press, 1996.

Norris, H.T. *The Adventures of Antar.* Wilts, England: Aris & Phillips Ltd., 1980.

Richmond, Diana. *'Antar and 'Abla, A Bedouin Romance.* London: Quartet Books, 1978.

APOSTASY

Apostasy (irtidad) is the abandonment of Islam by either a declared desertion of Islam in favor of another religion or a clandestine rejection of Islam that is often combined with secretly practicing another religion. From the earliest time of Muslim law in the seventh century, Muslim jurists agreed that apostasy from Islam bears the death penalty. During the early period, jurists also developed institutions to circumvent this harsh punishment; these institutions set the standard for what counts as apostasy from Islam so high that before the eleventh century, practically no judgment of apostasy could have been passed. This changed during the eleventh century, when jurists lowered the criteria that prevented the death penalty from being executed. During the following centuries, judges could interpret the law in various ways, setting either high or low criteria for apostasy from Islam.

The Qur'an does not mention the case of explicit rejection of Islam after conversion. However, it does address the assumed clandestine apostasy of a group of people at Medina called the hypocrites (al-munafiqun). No worldly penalty is ordained for them so long as they refrain from rebellion, but harsh punishments are proclaimed for them in the afterlife. In Qur'an 49:14, a group of Bedouins is described as Muslims but not believers. This led to heated discussions of the criteria for being a Muslim, understood in terms of legal membership in the Islamic community, versus being a believer (Mu'min), understood as someone deserving otherworldly salvation.

The dispute about the meanings of *Muslim* and *Mu'min* is one of the subjects that led to the First Civil War (656–662). One party, the Kharijs, claimed that committing a capital sin (kabira) constitutes unbelief (kufr). A group of radical Kharijis felt justified to kill grave sinners as unbelievers and thus legitimized the killing of the second caliph, 'Uthman (644–656). At about the same time, Muslims agreed on the death penalty for apostasy from Islam; this judgment is based on the authority of a report (hadith) of the Prophet that said, "whoever changes his religion has his head cut off." After the Kharijis lost the First Civil War, the various groups of their enemies, who dominated the early development of Muslim law, were terrified by the prospect of Muslims killing each other over accusations of apostasy and worked to abate the harsh punishment the Prophetical hadith provides.

Muslim jurists agreed that actions other than the explicit rejection of belief in Islam could not constitute apostasy. In other words, committing a sin could not be an act of apostasy. Apostasy was regarded as the declared rejection of Islam and could only be sufficiently established after a person accused of apostasy had been invited three times to repent and return to Islam. The legal institution of the invitation to repent (istitaba) is mentioned neither in the Qur'an nor in the Prophetical hadith; in early Muslim law, it nevertheless became a necessary condition for convicting an apostate. It safeguarded the ability of an accused apostate to have a chance to return to Islam, fully avert punishment, and be reinstated in all rights as a Muslim. Subsequently, only those Muslim apostates could be punished who openly declared their breaking away from Islam and who maintained their rejection in the face of capital punishment.

Most early jurists understood that the general application of the invitation to repent effectively ruled out any penalty for apostasy. They allowed persons accused of apostasy to declare their return to Islam, even when it was understood to be nominal; this became the accepted position in the early Hanafi and Shafi'i schools of law. Their views fit well into a situation during the eighth and ninth centuries, when conversion to Islam happened collectively and often only nominally. Malik ibn Anas (715–795), the founder of the Maliki school of law, ruled differently, saying that zanadiqa should not be given the right to repent and could thus be killed straightaway. *Zanadiqa* here means clandestine apostates, but later jurists interpreted the term more widely. This ruling meant that the Maliki school of jurisprudence was, in practice, less tolerant toward heterodox Muslim views than the others, and it allowed Maliki jurists to apply the death penalty to accused apostates who had never explicitly broken with Islam. In these cases, heterodox views were regarded as evidence of clandestine apostasy.

During the eleventh century, the consensus of the Hanafi and Shafi'i jurists regarding the general application of the invitation to repent broke down. Hanbali jurists had already argued that some points of religious doctrine were so central to the Muslim creed that a violation should be regarded as apostasy from Islam and punished by death. During the middle of the eleventh century, scholars from all schools argued that, in the case of the political agents of the

Isma'ili counter-Caliphate, no invitation to repent should be granted, and the agents could be killed as apostates. This view was shared by the influential Shafi'i jurist al-Ghazali (1058–1111), who wrote systematically about the criteria of apostasy. Whoever held the views that the world was not created at one point in time, that God is not omniscient, or that the resurrection in the afterlife does not extend to the body was, according to al-Ghazali, an apostate and could be killed.

FRANK GRIFFEL

See also Hadith; Heresy and Heretics; Fatimids; Ibn Hanbal; Kharijs; Malikism; Schools of Jurisprudence

Further Reading

Griffel, Frank. "Toleration and Exclusion: al-Shafifii and al-Ghazali on the Treatment of Apostates." *Bulletin of the School of Oriental and African Studies* 64 (2001): 339–54.

———. *Apostasie und Toleranz im Islam. Die Entwicklung zu al-Gazalis Urteil Gegen die Philosophie und die Reaktionen der Philosophen.* Leiden: Brill, 2000.

Peters, Rudolph, and Gert J. J. de Vries. "Apostasy in Islam." *Welt des Islam* 17 (1976/1977): 1–25.

Jackson, Sherman A.. *On the Boundaries of Theological Tolerance in Islam: Abu Hamid al-Ghazali's Faysal al-Tafriqa.* Oxford: Oxford University Press, 2002.

APPRENTICESHIP

Defined by a variety of terms (mubtadi, terbiye, nazil, yiğit, şagird), an apprentice was the lowest member of a guild in the medieval Islamic world. He was always initiated into a guild along with others who would work under a master teacher (üstad, usta) and the founder of the individual guild (pir). The apprentice's place in the hierarchy was indeed small; his master and the guild founder were themselves part of a greater hierarchy in which masters would form their own councils to select a founder, and the founders of a city's individual guilds played a prominent part in representing the urban social order. At the top of the order were a series of local judicial officials (naib, muhtesib, kadi) who were in charge of keeping the social and moral order of the town.

Although the apprentice was at the bottom step of this urban social order, he immediately gained important privileges. As a member of the guilds, he was likely to live in the town or city itself, and he had much less of a fiscal burden than many peasants in the countryside. Peasants were often tied to the land and forced to deliver a variety of customs and dues. The apprentice was particularly privileged if he was a Muslim urban resident, because only non-Muslims were subject to a special poll tax (haraç, cizye).

The apprentice also had the chance to work his way up the social ladder, changing from a novice to journeyman and, if fortunate, becoming a master of a craft. He could likewise participate in the various social councils, and he might be able to represent his trade, city quarter or even his whole town, if the situation occurred. The role of guildsmen as manufacturers was confused at times with both religious and military hierarchies. Beginning in the tenth century, apprentices—like all guildsmen—tended to be associated with Sufi orders, and they could play a role in the formation of these institutions; sometimes they could even rise to the level of sheikh (a head of a Sufi organization and/or an urban district). During the sixteenth-century Ottoman Empire, guildsmen were often associated with the janissaries (the slave elite that had dominated the sultan's army until the seventeenth century). Association with the military meant that guildsmen were even more autonomous from central control, having the theoretical right to practice arms, if need be.

These opportunities for an apprentice's advancement and social privileges created tensions within the guilds. On the one hand, most apprentices were themselves sons of guild members who wished to carry on the trade of their fathers. The urban hierarchy typically favored this succession and often created legal measures to ensure it. For instance, there are a variety of injunctions in the rules and regulations of guilds that were drawn up in elaborate regulatory documents (fütüvvet-name). Eventually, by the sixteenth century, the Ottomans gave many guildsmen the right to pass on their place in the guild to their sons (gedik). Nevertheless, many had ambitions to enter the guilds despite all obstacles. Indeed, it is interesting that the first mention of guilds after the Arabic conquest refers to apprentices as *fityun*, a term that also meant "young ruffians." Such apprentices were allowed by authorities in towns that were starved for working populations; this was particularly true in frontier societies, where the rulers themselves felt threatened and needed a subject population that would support their cause. The clearest examples of this phenomenon can be seen in fifteenth-century Andalusia and in the Ottoman outposts in the Magreb and the Balkans during the mid-sixteenth century.

Scholars have also tended to see apprentices as part of the stagnant urban order that characterized the Islamic city. Apprentices were supposedly new generations of Muslims who carried the ideal of a noncompetitive social order, who promoted public welfare, and who contended with one's place at the expense of competition, profit, and commercial authority. Although it is true that religious orders played a prominent role in the guilds, there were also times when the guilds would act according to the needs of the market and the society around them. This was demonstrated by the participation of apprentices and guildsmen in the military-item market and pious foundations in the emerging market town of Sarajevo during the late fifteenth and early sixteenth centuries. The guild members played a critical role not only in supplying the empire's military needs but also in helping establish cash-credit institutions that could give credit to parties independently of the will of the central government. Thus, at least in some cases, apprentices appeared to be the youngest members of emerging Islamic civil societies.

YORK ALLAN NORMAN

Further Reading

Faroqhi, Suraiya. *Towns and Townsmen of Ottoman Anatolia, Trade, Crafts and Food Production in an Urban Setting.* Cambridge: Cambridge University Press, 1984.

İnalcik, Halil. Capital Formation in the Ottoman Empire. *The Journal of Economic History* 29; No.1, The Tasks of Economic History (1969): 97–140.

Lewis, Bernard. The Islamic Guilds. *The Economic History Review* 8 (1937): 20–37.

Norman, York A. "Urban Development in Sarajevo." In *Islamization in Bosnia, 1463–1604.* Forthcoming Ph.D. dissertation. Washington, DC: Georgetown University.

Raymond, A., W. Floor, and Özdemir Nutku. "Sınıf." In *Encyclopedia of Islam*, online edition, 2001.

Yi, Euonjeong. *Guild Dynamics in Seventeenth-Century Istanbul: Fluidity and Leverage.* Leiden: Brill, 2004.

AQSA MOSQUE

The Aqsa mosque (al-Masjid al-Aqsa) and the Dome of the Rock in Jerusalem constitute the area known as al-Haram al-Sharif (the Noble Sanctuary), which corresponds to the Temple Mount area and which is regarded by large numbers of Muslims as the third Islamic sacred sanctuary after Mecca and Medina. The Aqsa mosque is located on the southern side of al-Haram al-Sharif, and it has been identified in medieval and modern Islamic scholarship as the place referred to in the chapter of the Qur'an known as "Al-Isra'" ("The Night Journey") (17:1): "Praise be to Him who made His servant journey in the night from the sacred sanctuary (al-masjid al-haram) to the remotest sanctuary (al-masjid al-aqsa) which we have surrounded with blessings to show him of our signs." It is primarily this identification of the Aqsa mosque as the location of the Prophet Muhammad's night journey that has bestowed on the site its most significant

religious importance in Islam; the legend describes how the Prophet Muhammad rode the heavenly creature al-Buraq and was transported by night from Mecca to Jerusalem, where he led the prophets in prayers on the spot of the Aqsa mosque. It is not clear when the association between the Qur'anic reference and the Aqsa mosque in Jerusalem was first established, but it is almost certain that it was made some time after the building was erected. Early Qur'an commentators were in disagreement about the location of the Qur'anic al-masjid al-aqsa; some located it near the town of Mecca, whereas others associated it with the Temple in Jerusalem. Gradually the association with the Temple became cemented in Islamic scholarship and popular imagination.

Another equally fundamental religious belief that Muslims in later centuries have employed in explaining the sanctity of the Aqsa mosque is that it was erected by Caliph 'Umar ibn al-Khattab (r. AH 13–23/634–644 CE) when he visited Jerusalem. This tradition is questionable as well, being another likely case of later projection; the mosque built by Caliph 'Umar, if he actually made it to Jerusalem, was adjacent to or part of the Church of the Holy Sepulchre. One can ascertain, however, that a small mosque built by the Umayyad Caliph Mu'awiya ibn Abi Sufyan (r. 41–60/661–680) stood on the site, and it was destroyed to make room for the Aqsa mosque, which was built by orders from the Umayyad Caliph al-Walid ibn 'Abd al-Malik (r. 86–96/705–715), the son of Caliph 'Abd al-Malik b. Marwan (r. 65–86/685–705), who had ordered the erection of the Dome of the Rock a few decades earlier.

The structure has been subjected to a number of major renovations and even reconstructions over the years, largely because of devastating earthquakes. For instance, it is very likely that the dome was added to the mosque in one of the reconstructions undertaken by orders from the 'Abbasids. The form of the current structure, however, dates to the middle of the eleventh century, because the Aqsa mosque was rebuilt by the Fatimids after a devastating earthquake that leveled most of the city of Jerusalem.

During the early Crusader period, the Aqsa mosque was occupied by the Knights of the Templar order, who used it as a residence and transformed part of it into a chapel. Usama ibn Munqidh (d. 584/1188) reports how his close friendship with some of the Templars earned him permission to pray in the Aqsa mosque, which was otherwise inaccessible to Muslims.

The centrality of Jerusalem and the significance of the Aqsa during the Crusader period are also attested to by the efforts of Sultan Nur al-Din (d. 569/1174) to employ them in his ideological and religious propaganda to rally the Muslims of Syria around him when fighting the Christian invaders. In preparation for the liberation of Jerusalem, he ordered a masterpiece minbar to be built in the hope that he would transport it himself to the mosque. However, it was left for his successor Sultan Saladin (r. 569–589/1174–1193) to bring the minbar, when he reconquered Jerusalem in 1187 and ordered minor renovations to the Aqsa mosque; the minbar in question was unfortunately destroyed in the fire of 1967, which destroyed parts of the mosque.

SULEIMAN A. MOURAD

See also Jerusalem; Muhammad, the Prophet; 'Umar ibn al-Khattab; al-Walid ibn 'Abd al-Malik; Usama ibn Munqidh; Nur al-Din; Saladin

Further Reading

Busse, Heribert. "Jerusalem in the Story of Muhammad's Night Journey and Ascension." *Jerusalem Studies in Arabic and Islam* 14 (1991): 1–40.
Elad, Amikam. *Medieval Jerusalem and Islamic Worship: Holy Places, Ceremonies, Pilgrimage.* Leiden: Brill, 1995.
Grabar, Oleg. *The Shape of the Holy: Early Islamic Jerusalem.* Princeton: Princeton University Press, 1996.
Johns, Jeremy, ed. *Bayt al-Maqdis: Jerusalem and Early Islam* (Oxford Studies in Islamic Art IX.2). Oxford: Oxford University Press, 1999.

AQUEDUCTS

An aqueduct (L. *aquaeductus*) is a structure for artificially conveying a constant supply of water; it consists of a channel that passes underground, that continues on the surface (where topographical conditions are not suitable), that is usually covered to prevent evaporation and/or pollution, and that is supported on piers over valleys, roads, and so on and cut through hills. Numerous remains of aqueducts from the medieval Islamic civilization survived, with the most impressive ones being in Istanbul.

Knowledge of water supply to the urban settlements and irrigation of agricultural areas was based on the ancient civilization. The shadouf, noria (na'ura), quanat, saqiya, and hafirs are the inventions of the Middle East. Besides these, available water sources were utilized by transporting water under pressure and over long distances with aqueducts during the Roman period to supply the heavily populated cities, which were one of the features that shaped the urban landscape during the Roman times in the Middle East; this was continued in some areas during medieval times. Traces of these aqueducts exist in almost all areas that were once under Roman rule.

These pre-Islamic aqueducts did in fact need maintenance, and soon after most of them collapsed. Two aqueducts in Ceasarea built during the reign of Herod were such examples. The more monumental of the two was renovated under Hadrian, and it is now partially freed from the sand that buried it for so long. Several other aqueducts were constructed during the early Islamic period in the Middle East and Europe. One notable example is the system that was built for the holy city of Mecca by Princess Zubaida, wife of the 'Abbasid Caliph Harun al-Rashid (786–809 CE). This aqueduct was later repaired with the addition of cisterns and bends (reservoirs/dams) and extended into the city by Mihrimah Sultana (br. 1522), daughter of Süleyman the Magnificent. The king Al-Mansur Ya'qub Ibn Yusuf also built an aqueduct to supply the capital city Marrakech in Morocco in 1190. The Magra–El-Oyon Aqueduct is another important Islamic monument in Cairo, and it extends between El-Saida Zeineb and Misr–El Kadima. Many quanat (underground canals) discovered in Jordan, Syria, and Iran are also connected to or built in connection with the aqueducts. Noria (paddle wheels) that were powered by either wind or animals, or water-driven ones mounted vertically in front of an aqueduct, were also commonly used in medieval Islamic countries. Aqueducts were also used to supply power to the wheels of wheat or olive-oil mills in the rural areas.

Istanbul is one of the most important cities in the world, and aqueducts from both Roman and Ottoman times can be encountered there. There were four main systems built during Roman times: (1) the aqueduct built by Hadrian (117–138), although there is no sign of a definite route it followed; (2) another major line that came from the Stranca Mountains (Yıldız Dağlari) in Thrace and that was most probably begun by Constantine between 324 and 357; (3) one built by Valens (364–378) that is thought to cross over the Mazul Kemer Aqueduct; and (4) one built by Theodosius I that runs through Belgrade Forest to the north of the city.

When the Ottoman Turks conquered Istanbul, they stopped using the Byzantine cisterns, for both religious and hygienic reasons. Therefore, Mehmet the Conqueror immediately ordered the restoration of the old and damaged water-supply systems; this was done, and new ones were also built to supply water to the city. Monumental aqueducts, as well as smaller ones, were used commonly throughout the empire, with the most imposing ones being those that supplied water to Istanbul. Uzun Kemer (710 m), which had two tiers with fifty upper arches and forty-seven lower arches, and Maglova Aqueduct (258 m in length and 25.30 m in height) are the two aqueducts of the Kirkçesme water-supply system that were built during the reign of Süleyman II (Süleyman the Magnificent) by Sinan, the great architect.

The main sources of water in Istanbul were the bends (reservoirs) that were fed by the springs of the Belgrade Forest. These waters were conducted to the city by aqueducts; the grandest, which was two tiered, was built by Justinian. This aqueduct and others carried water to the taksim (distribution point) at Egrikapı, where the main flow reached the Aqueduct of Valens in the middle of the old city between the mosques of Fatih and Shehzade. These aqueducts were repaired by the Ottomans and properly maintained. However, the Valens Aqueduct was considerably rebuilt by Sinan, the great architect, during the reign of Süleyman the Magnificent in the 1560s, which resulted in the increasing number of fountains. It is easy to distinguish the Turkish stonework, but it is difficult to date some sections of the work, because Mustafa II also ordered extensive repairs to the same aqueduct. The Uzun Kemer (Long Aqueduct) on the Belgrade Forest follows the Byzantine pattern of tiers of tall arches that are pointed but not rounded, and these may have been built in accordance with Sinan's plan; however, the short Kavas Aqueduct, which has only eleven arches, is likely to date from soon after the conquest.

The aqueducts of both Roman and Byzantine origin were usually of equal widths at both the bottom and the top. For this reason, only very thick ones survived, Valens being one of these. The aqueducts built by Sinan demonstrate more engineering calculations. Unlike a normal aqueduct, over which water is transported via an enclosed conduit that consists of a series of arches supported on massive piers, the system used in the Maglova Aqueduct shows further technical solutions. Sinan designed the width of the arches to be even smaller, and he enlarged the piers perpendicular to the arches and extended them in pyramidal shape, like buttresses, toward the ground, thereby forming three-dimensional rather than two-dimensional forms. For this reason, these aqueducts are more durable against the horizontal friction forces, and they retain the equilibrium force to remain at a 1:3 ratio. In addition, on each of these piers Sinan constructed three discharging arches to prevent any damage during flooding; these, when incorporated into the main piers, gave a sense of streamlined unity. The structure is uniquely successful and almost expressionist in nature; vertical, horizontal, and diagonal stresses are uniformly absorbed. The expressionist effect is most obvious in the way in which the static forces are distributed throughout the structure and visibly expressed on that structure. This work of Sinan represents the most important departure from the traditional form of the aqueduct, which had shown little change up to that point since classical Rome.

There are several aqueducts in Balkan and African countries that were under the Ottoman sovereignty, some of which are attributed to the Roman times. There is an aqueduct that is located two kilometers northwest of Skopje (Yugoslavia) that is built of stone and bricks and that has fifty-five arches supported on massive pillars; this structure used to be attributed to Romans or Byzantines, but it was recently discovered that it had in fact been built by İsa Bey during the sixteenth century. Several aqueducts were built in Cyprus during the Ottoman period, the most notable being the Bekir Pasha Aqueduct in Larnaca, the harbor town in which the holy shrine of Hala Sultan (Umm ul Haram bint Sultan) is also located.

It has become clear through written records inherited from medieval times and through manuscripts and inscribed stone tablets that water systems of the Islamic societies were built by local people as charitable works of waqf. Three important sources about the aqueducts constructed by Sinan during the reign of Süleyman the Magnificent and others are the books *Tezkiretü'l Bünyan* (1583–1584), *Tezkiretü'l Ebniye* (1586–87), and *Tuhfetü'l Mimarin* (1590). Several inscription tablets still attached to the monuments, in addition to manuscripts about deeds performed by pious foundations, mention the aqueducts.

NETICE YILDIZ

See also Irrigation; Mehmet, the Conqueror; Sinan; Water

Further Reading

Aslanapa, Oktay. *Turkish Art and Architecture.* London: Faber, 1971.

Ateş, İbrahim, ed. "Deed of Trust for Free Water Supply Endowed by Sultan Süleiman the Magnificent." In *Kanuni Sultan Süleyman'in Su Vakfiyesi.* Ankara: Publications of Ministry of Culture and Tourism, 1987.

Aytöre, A. Turkish Water Architecture. *1st International Congress of Turkish Art Proceedings, 1959.* Ankara, 1962.

Binst, Olivier, ed. *The Levant, History and Archaeology in the Eastern Mediterranean.* France: Könemann, 2000.

Çeçen, Kâzim. *Mimar Sinan ve Kirkçeşme Tesisleri (Sinan, the Architect and the Water System of Kirkçeşme).* Istanbul: İSKİ, 1988.

Çeçen, Kâzim. *İstanbul'un Osmanlı Dönemi Su Yolları (Water Supplying Systems in Istanbul),* ed. Celâl Kolay. Istanbul: İSKİ, 1999.

Curl, James Stevens. *Oxford Dictionary of Architecture.* Oxford: Oxford University Press, 1999.

Dalman, Olof Knut. *Der Valens Aquäduktin Konstantinopel.* Bamberg, 1933.

Goodwin, Godfrey. *Sinan.* London, 1993.

———. *A History of Ottoman Architecture*. London: Thames and Hudson, 1997.

Harris, Cyril M., ed. *Illustrated Dictionary of Historic Architecture*. New York: Dover Publications, 1977.

http://www.WaterHistory_org.htm

Lightfoot, Dale R. "Qanats in the Levant: Hydraulic Technology at the Periphery of Early Empires." *Technology and Culture* 38/2 (1997): 432–51.

Oliver, Paul, ed. *Encyclopedia of Vernacular Architecture of the World*, vol. I, Theories and Principles. Cambridge: Cambridge University Press, 1997.

Sâî Mustafa Çelebi. *Yapılar Kitabi: Tezkiretü'l-Bünyan ve Tezkiretü'l-Ebniye (Mimar Sinanin Anıları) (Memoirs of Sinan, the Architect)*, eds. Hayati Develi and Samih Rifat, transcribed by Hayati Develi, preface by Doğan Kuban. Istanbul: Koçbank, 2002.

Sözen, Metin. *Sinan, Architect of Ages*. Ankara: Ministry of Culture and Tourism of the Turkish Republic, 1988.

Yıldız, Netice. "Turkish Aqueducts in Cyprus." *Turkish Art, 10th International Congress of Turkish Art Proceedings, Géneve 17–23 Sept 1995, Fondation Max Berchem, Genevé* 1999: 775–84.

ARABIA

The Arabian peninsula lies in southwest Asia, with Syria to the north, the Indian Ocean to the south, the Persian Gulf to the east, and the Red Sea to the west. Its highest elevations stand in the west, with the peninsula sloping downward to the east, except for the Hajar Mountains of Oman. Most of Arabia is desert, although there is ample vegetation in mountainous areas.

Arabs of the peninsula are traditionally said to be descendants of the tribes of 'Adnan and Qahtan, originating, respectively, from the north and the southwest of the peninsula. The most important groupings were as follows:

In the 'Adnan group:

1. Rabi'a: Bakr, Taghlib, 'Abd al-Qays
2. Mudar: Tamim, Huthayl, Asad, Quraysh, Qays Aylan

In the Qahtan group:

1. Kahlan: Tayyi', Hamdan, Kinda, Azd
2. Himyar: Quda'a(?), Tannukh, Kalb, Juhayna

Enmity existed between the Rabi'a and the Mudar, which often led the former to forge alliances with Arabs of the southwest against the latter. Tribes emerged on the basis of what was believed to be genealogical origin, and tribalism ('asabiyya) became an essential factor in social life. This tendency facilitates understanding of many historical events before and after the rise of Islam, along with much of Arabia's poetry and literature.

Two important commercial routes crossed the peninsula. One ran between Syria and Yemen; the other linked Yemen to Bahrain, crossing through Yamama and terminating in Iraq and Persia. Urban settlements were established along these routes and thrived when commerce flourished. This contributed to the diffusion of foreign cultures and of Judaism and Christianity during the pre-Islamic era.

Competition for leadership was common, and, during the early history of the Arabs, a number of powerful figures emerged; this was accompanied by numerous wars. The people were known for their courage and generosity and for their close attachment to their tribal affiliations. The character of the Arabs was shaped by their physical environment. The influence of the desert was evident in their lifestyle and their means of expressing themselves. This can be seen in early Arab poetry, with its frequent reference to the sands and to the flora and fauna of the desert, and in the ethics, traditions, and beliefs that governed all aspects of life. Poetry was an important aspect of Arab culture in both the pre-Islamic and Islamic eras, together with the oral stories ("ayyam al-'Arab") that people shared in social gatherings.

People ate simple food and wore simple clothes, and medical knowledge was limited to herbal remedies. The lunar calendar was observed, and it was adapted to approximate the solar year to fix dates for the religious and trading seasons.

The Rise of Islam

Islam had a powerful impact on the Arabs of the peninsula, uniting them for the first time and enabling them to conquer vast areas. The new religion helped to eradicate tribal fanaticism, because it classed all Muslims as equal, regardless of race. In addition, the Arabs rallied in the belief that it was their duty to spread the religion throughout the world, because Islam was the last of the divinely revealed faiths. This conviction inspired them to venture to the lands of older civilizations, as far away as China and Spain.

The conquests stimulated massive migrations out of Arabia. This weakened the peninsula itself, dissipating the unity that had been established during the early years of Islam. Spectacular victories by the Muslims in the Ridda wars, together with the initial confrontations against the Byzantine and Sasanian Empires, led Arabs to flock to take part in battle and then migrate to the newly acquired territories.

Once there, the ideas and beliefs of the immigrants were influenced by the culture of the local populace. Persian converts to Islam, for example, did not abandon their traditions, and over time the melding of cultures affected the doctrines and practices of

Islam, along with Arabic language and literature. The Arabs also built on the heritage of the Greco–Roman past, particularly in the domains of philosophy and the sciences. All of these influences were transmitted back to the peninsula. As a result, the people of Arabia came to be intimately connected with a wider Islamic world. The most tangible link was the annual pilgrimage (hajj), which drew thousands of Muslims to Mecca and Medina.

During medieval times, the most important provinces of Arabia were Hijaz, Yamama (or Najd), Yemen, Oman, and Bahrain.

The Hijaz

With the emergence of Islam, the Hijaz became the center of the new community and the destination of the hajj. During the lifetimes of Muhammad the Prophet and the Rashidun Caliphs (622–660 CE), Medina was the capital of the Islamic state, and it was from there that the first armies of conquest set out.

Even after the seat of government moved outside of Arabia, Mecca and Medina remained the loci of the conflicts that raged throughout the Umayyad and 'Abbasid periods. These included activities by sects whose ideas contravened the policies of the Umayyad and 'Abbasid authorities as well as violent rebellions that depleted the economic and military capacities of both states.

The Hijaz during the Umayyads (661–749 CE)

During 680–692 CE, 'Abd Allah ibn al-Zubayr rose against the Umayyad government in Damascus and, from Mecca, gained control over most of the territory of the Islamic state. He was killed in Mecca in 692 CE. Traces of his movement continued to influence the Muslim community in Mecca, which became the symbol of Sunni opposition to the central authority.

In 746, Abu Hamza al-Khariji, a member of the Yemeni movement led by Talib al-Haqq, was briefly able to take control of Mecca and Medina.

Leading figures among the sons of the Companions of the Prophet, such as Ibn 'Abbas and Ibn 'Umar, concentrated on religious matters and set up, in two mosques of Mecca and Medina, religious groups that laid down the basis of the schools of Fiqh (Islamic jurisprudence) that later emerged, becoming the well-known Sunni schools of law.

During the Umayyad era, poetry, song, and literature flourished in the Hijaz, with the salon of Sakina bint al-Husain being the best-known gathering. Intermingling among men and women was commonplace in such salons, and strict rules regarding women's apparel had not yet emerged.

The Umayyads rebuilt the two grand mosques of Mecca and Medina and introduced a number of new facilities for residents and pilgrims alike.

Hijaz during the Abbasid Period (741–1258 CE)

When the 'Abbasids assumed power, the leaders of the 'Alawites refused to pledge allegiance to them. In 762 CE, Muhammad al-Nafs al-Zakiyya rose in rebellion in the Hijaz, which became a major center of 'Alawite opposition. Al-Husain ibn al-Hasan rebelled in 785, followed by Ibrahim ibn Musa al-Kazim in 817, Isma'il ibn Yusuf in 865, and Muhammad ibn Sulayman in 913. Although these rebellions were suppressed, the 'Abbasids failed to eradicate 'Alawite political and religious influence in the region.

In 929, the Qarmathians invaded Mecca under the leadership of Abu Tahir al-Qurmuti, carrying the Black Stone to Bahrain, where it remained for twenty-two years. From 942 to 968, the Ikhshidids of Egypt controlled the Hijaz.

During the 'Abbasid period, the Hijaz attracted religious students and collectors of the traditions of Muhammad the Prophet (hadith), the most renowned of whom was Imam Malik. The influx of scholars generated a tendency toward asceticism in local society. At the same time, many of the region's singers, poets, writers, and merchants migrated to the more congenial atmospheres of Baghdad and Egypt.

By the end of the 'Abbasid era, the Shafi'i school of law replaced the Maliki school as the dominant body of legal interpretation in the Hijaz.

The Hijaz during the Fatimids (909–1171 CE)

The coming of the Fatimids to Egypt in 969 CE opened the door for the 'Alawite Sharifs of the Hijaz (969–1924 CE), who declared their own state during the same year that the Fatimids founded Cairo. 'Abbasids and Fatimids competed to win the loyalty of the Sharifs, hoping thereby to enhance the legitimacy of their respective caliphates. This competition, however, prompted power to shift from one 'Alawite family to another.

Fatimid influence affected religious and social life more profoundly, and Shi'ism spread widely during the years of Fatimid dominance. Meanwhile, trade with Egypt became more active, and Jeddah's harbor thrived.

The Hijaz during the Ayyubids of Egypt (1171–1250 CE)

Sharifian rule over the Hijaz persisted despite the fall of their Fatimid allies and renewed efforts by the 'Abbasids to destroy them. Competition for hegemony over the Hijaz continued until the end of the 'Abbasid state in 1258. Throughout these years, education was restricted to the study of religious doctrine and jurisprudence. The influence of Shi'ism was reduced, and the Shafi'i school of law prevailed once again. Ibn Jubayr, who visited Mecca in 1183, left lively descriptions of social life and economic affairs.

The Hijaz during the Mamluks (1250–1517 CE)

During their long rule in Egypt, the Mamluks intervened in the Hijaz, forcing the Sharifs to recognize their spiritual authority over Mecca and Medina. Persistent tension marked the relationship, and this was accompanied by many wars. In addition, the rulers of Yemen moved in at the end of the thirteenth century.

Mamluk influence peaked during the fifteenth century, when the authorities in Cairo appointed and removed the Sharifs at will. They paid great attention to the pilgrimage and the ritual covering of the Ka'aba, which was sent from Cairo each year. Widespread cultural and social exchange cemented relations between the Hijaz and the rest of the Muslim world.

Religious teaching remained the area's most salient activity, and the Hanbali school of law began to spread.

Yamama

Yamama, which is now a term used for central Najd, was applied during the medieval period to the whole area between Bahrain and the Hijaz. It was a center for Arab migration both northward and eastward. In pre-Islamic times, Yamama's capital was Hajr, and the area was known for its abundant water and fertile soil.

During the sixth century, the Hanifa tribe replaced the Kinda as the dominant power, deriving its strength from commerce and wheat cultivation. The Hanifa chief, Huda ibn 'Ali, was closely allied with the Sasanians. Other tribes included the Tamim, the Amir ibn Sa'sa'a, the Bahila, the Dabba, the Numair, and the Quda'a. In struggles for pasture and water sources, weaker tribes generally allied with stronger ones.

Although Nestorian Christianity was strong in central and eastern Arabia at that time, pagan elements were also present. Yamama was one of three important religious centers, the others being Mecca and Ta'if.

Huda ibn 'Ali died before the death of Muhammad the Prophet in 632, and he was succeeded by Musaylima ibn Habib, who claimed to have received revelations from God. Musaylima resisted Islam and defeated two armies sent against him by Caliph Abu Bakr. His army of forty thousand men was eventually defeated at the decisive battle of 'Aqraba in 634 by an army led by Khalid ibn al-Walid. This was the most ferocious war yet fought by the Muslims, with many people killed on both sides.

After the war, the Qur'an was collected and written down for the first time. Yamama then lost its political importance, instead becoming a center for amassing armies to send against Iraq. During the Umayyad period (660–749), the only event of importance in Yamama was the rise of the Khariji movement.

'Abbasid influence in Yamama weakened from the middle of the ninth century, and the area fell to the tribes and their neighbors in Bahrain.

During the ninth and tenth centuries, the tribes of 'Amir ibn Sa'sa'a increased their power in central and eastern Arabia. This coincided with the rise of the Qarmathians (c. 900–1076), with whom they shared political interests. Together they defeated the Yamama rulers and the Banu al-Ukhaydir in 928; the Banu 'Amir supported the Qarmathians in their wars in the peninsula, Iraq, and Syria.

The trans-Arabian land route declined with the growth of Red Sea navigation during the Fatimid period. When Nasir-i Khusraw visited Yamama in 1051, he found it to be of minor importance.

From the twelfth century C.E. onward, Yamama was intimately connected to Hasa (Bahrain).

HASAN M. AL-NABOODAH

See also Arabs; Islam; Bahrain; Oman; Yemen; Mecca; Medina; Poetry, Arabic; Hajj; 'Abbasids; Umayyads; Fatimids; Kharijis; School of Jurisprudence; Tribes and Tribal Customs

Further Reading

Al-Askar, Abdullah. *Al-Yamama in the Early Islamic Era.* Reading, UK: Ithaca Press, 2002.

Ashtor, E. *A Social Economic History of the Near East In the Middle Ages.* London: Collins, 1976.

Brockelmann, C. *History of the Islamic People.* London: Routledge & Kegan Paul, 1982.

Browne, E.G. "Some Account of the Arabic Work Entitled: Nihayatu'l-irab fi Akhbar'l-Furs wa'l-Arab." *Journal of the Royal Asiatic Society* (1900): 195–260.

Crone, P. "Were the Qays and Yemen of the Umayyad Period Political Parties." *Der Islam* 71 (1994): 1–57.

Donner, F.M. "Mecca's Food Supplies and Muhammad's Boycott." *Journal of the Economic and Social History of the Orient* 20–3 (1983): 249–66.

———. *The Early Islamic Conquests.* Princeton, NJ: Princeton University Press, 1981.

Hill, D.R. *The Termination of Hostilities in the Early Arab Conquests: A.D.634–656.* London: Luzac & Company, 1971.

Hitti, P. *History of the Arab.* London: The Macmillan Press Ltd., 1982.

Kister, M.J. *Studies in Jahiliyya and Early Islam.* London: Variorum Reprints, 1980.

Krenkow, F. "The Annual Fairs of the Pagan Arabs." *Islamic Culture* 21 (1947): 111–13.

Lane, E.W. *Arabian Society in the Middle Ages.* London: Curzon Press, 1987.

Lecker, M. *Muslims, Jews & Pagans: Studies on Early Islamic Medina.* Leiden: E.J. Brill, 1995.

Nicholson, R. *A Literary History of the Arabs.* Cambridge: Cambridge University Press, 1985.

Nobiron, L. "Notes on the Arab Calendar Before Islam." *Islamic Culture* 21 (1947): 135–53.

O'Leary and D.D. De Lacy. *Arabia Before Muhammad.* London: Kegan Paul, 1927.

Shaban, M.A. *Islamic History: A New Interpretation*, 2 vols. Cambridge: Cambridge University Press, 1981.

Shoufani, E. *AI-Riddah and the Muslim Conquest of Arabia.* Toronto: University of Toronto Press, 1973.

Stillman, Y.K. *Arab Dress From the Dawn of Islam to Modern Times: A Short History.* Leiden: E.J. Brill, 2000.

Teitelbaum, Joshua. *The Rise and Fall of the Hashemite Kingdom of Arabia.* New York: New York University Press, 2001.

Van Grunebaum, G.E. "The Nature of the Arab Unity Before Islam." *Arabica* 10 (1963): 5–25.

ARABIC

Arabic language includes the formal medieval and modern written idioms (al-'arabiyya al-fusha; Classical Arabic, Modern Standard Arabic), past and present dialects (Neo-Arabic), and varying degrees of mixture between these two levels during the premodern period (Middle Arabic).

Following Akkadian and Aramaic, Arabic became the third Semitic lingua franca along the Eastern rim of the Mediterranean as a result of the Islamic conquests, and it extended its linguistic reach to Central Asia, North Africa, and the Iberian Peninsula, coinciding with most of the areas formerly served by Latin in classical antiquity. As the language of Islam, it was further used in liturgy and, in epigraphic form, in architecture by Muslim communities in Middle Africa, Central Asia, Western China, Northern India, and the Southeast Asian archipelago.

The basic grammar of Classical Arabic has remained stable over thirteen centuries. A language of prestige, it developed a rich intertextuality, conferred status on those who mastered it (irrespective of their ethnic background), and retained a unique bimodal transmission in which oral and written media complemented each other.

Successor to both the Byzantine and the Sasanian territories, Arabic–Islamic culture selectively incorporated part of its lexicon and written heritage, especially through the 'Abbasid translation movement from the eighth to the tenth century CE. Inversely, Arabic terms and genres played an important role in the flourishing of Medieval Hebrew, Old Spanish (Castilian), and New Persian (Farsi) literature.

A Semitic Language

Arabic belongs to the Semitic language family, itself forming part of the Afro-Asiatic phylum. Arabic exhibits the typical Semitic features of emphatic (velarized) sounds; a morpheme structure based on a triliteral root that conveys a basic meaning; a highly integrated system of inflection, derivation of word structures (internal flexion), and apophony, which adds semantic nuances to the root; a verbal system with prefix and suffix conjugation; a paratactic syntax; and a list of vocabulary cognates. Nevertheless, the specific place of Arabic within the Semitic family remains unresolved. Advocates of a genetic-tree model place it within the Central Semitic group, together with Canaanite and Aramaic, whereas proponents of natural language change and linguistic drift assign it to the Southwest Semitic group, together with the Ethiopian and South Arabian languages, the latter model being perhaps better suited to the close coexistence and succession of related tongues within the same geographical area, which characterize the Semitic family.

Proto-Arabic

Beginning with the ninth century BCE, Arabic names and terms are seen in Akkadian, Biblical, Greek, Coptic, and late Aramaic sources, whereas, from the sixth century BCE. to the fourth century CE, short epigraphic texts in Old North Arabian (recorded in a derivative of the South Arabian alphabet) survive in the Arabian Peninsula and Syro-Palestine. Their language differs from later Classical Arabic in many ways; for example, the article *ha-* is seen, as opposed to later Classical Arabic *al-*.

Between the third and sixth centuries, five short inscriptions in Syro-Palestine show the adoption of a late Aramean (Nabatean) cursive by writers of Arabic. From Nabatean, the Arabic script inherits salient traits, such as the nondenotation of short vowels (abgad type) and inflectional endings and the lam-alif ligature. Sporadic positional variants and connections and the mergers of letters (e.g., *r* and *z*) in late Nabatean were fully systematized in Arabic, and merged letters were distinguished by diacritic markers.

Pre-Classical and Classical Arabic

The Arabian Peninsula was home to numerous Arabic dialects that were sporadically recorded by later medieval Arabic grammarians, which permits a rough subdivision into a western (e.g., Hudhayl, Tayyi'), an eastern (e.g., Tamim), and a southern group of tribes (e.g., Kinda, Hamdan). Highly complex heroic poetry was composed from the sixth century CE in a supratribal idiom and was notably characterized by inflectional endings (i'rab; literally "making Arabic"), which were absent in many dialects. Scholars still debate whether inflectional endings in the early dialects disappeared long before the onset of Islam or whether they were lost only during the early conquests and the massive adoption of Arabic by foreigners, with the former option being the more likely one. The most influential Arabic text was the Qur'an, which was revealed in 610–632 in a language that was close to the poetic idiom but that displayed certain Western traits.

The codification of Islam's holy book as well as communication within the rapidly expanding Arabic–Islamic state required a unified official tongue, which Arabic came to fulfill under the Umayyad caliph 'Abd al-Malik around 700. It then became the task of grammarians during the mid-eighth century to synthesize prestige literature (the Qur'an, prophetic tradition [hadith], and pre-Islamic poetry and prose) with data gleaned from qualified Bedouins, who were considered experts in the pure Arabic language ('Arabiyya). Grammarians selected core languages (e.g., those of the tribes of Tamim and Hudhayl), and, when these diverged, they chose features according to their prestige (e.g., the hamza [glottal stop]), frequency, or analogical derivation (qiyas). The result was a reduction and systematization of morphology, syntax, and lexicon, and this was completed with the works of al-Khalil (d. 793) and Sibawayhi (d. 791), the respective founders of Arabic lexicography and grammar. The grammarians, however, did not create Classical Arabic; however, through established principles and fieldwork, they homogenized and systematized its disparate and redundant ingredients into a codified common tongue. They then proceeded to link the varied phenomena of language (furu') to a few underlying principles (usul) to demonstrate the perfection of the language that God had chosen for His revelation.

Classical Arabic sounds consist of twenty-eight consonants and three short or long vowels. The noun (ism) is modified by genus (male or female), number (singular, dual, or plural), state (indeterminate, determinate, or construct), and inflection (subject, possessive, or object cases). The verb (fi'l) has both a prefix and a suffix conjugation and expresses time or aspect (perfect or imperfect), mood (indicative, subjunctive, or jussive), voice (active or passive), person, gender, and number. A third and indeclinable word type is the particle (harf); its syntax includes both nominal clause (topic or comment) and verbal clause (verb, subject, or object), which may be built into compound sentences, although the older language tends toward parataxis.

During the same period, Arabic script was made to more accurately reflect spoken Classical Arabic by the addition of (mainly) supralinear symbols for short vowels, hamza, long alif (madda), the doubling of letters (tashdid), and the elision of the initial vowel (wasla).

From contact with preceding civilizations on its territory and in particular the 'Abbasid translation movement, Arabic incorporated vocabulary from Aramaic, Greek, and Middle Persian (Pahlavi), among others. The foreign words entered the language as simple borrowings, or they were likened to Arabic morphological patterns (jins; "species" from the Greek *genos*), recreated by derivation (ishtiqaq; e.g., *kayfiyya,* which means "quality" or, literally, "how-ness"), or again reproduced as Arabic calques. A further method was to extend an existing Arabic root with a meaning it had in another Semitic language; for example, *darasa,* meaning "to be effaced," was thus acquired in addition to the root's Aramaic meaning of "to study" (e.g., *madrasa,* meaning "school; religious college").

Neo-Arabic

The inflective, synthetic language represented by Classical Arabic coexists with a noninflecting analytical type called Neo-Arabic, thereby forming a situation of diglossia. No agreement has been reached about the date of the inception of Neo-Arabic, whether it was extant long before Islam or brought about by the Islamic conquests. Neo-Arabic has many regional dialects, although they share a number of features. Most of these may be subsumed under the analytical trend (fixed word order, expression of the verbal mood by prefixes and of the possessive and object cases by the particle *l-* rather than by inflection) and reduction of the paradigm (the loss of hamza and of the interdentals *dh* and *th*, the merger of the emphatic *d* and *z*, the loss of the dual and feminine plural forms, the merger of different types of defective verbs, and the loss of inflection of the relative pronoun), although some (e.g., the *i*-vowel in the imperfect verb) may derive from ancient Arabic dialects or contact with other Semitic languages. The common traits of Neo-Arabic are attributed to convergence, drift, and parallel developments and are no longer motivated by a koinè that supposedly evolved in the Islamic army camps, although the conquests undoubtedly propelled the development of Neo-Arabic. One medieval dialect that, although extinct (unlike most Arabic dialects, which survive today), has been preserved in written documents is Andalusi Arabic.

Middle Arabic

This label covers all texts whose writers strayed from the rules of Classical Arabic (thus denoting not a chronological period but a level of language). Middle Arabic is characterized by a mixture of dialectal and Classical Arabic forms and pseudocorrections (i.e., instances in which the writer aimed for and missed the more prestigious register and created a form that existed neither in Classical Arabic nor in his native [Neo-Arabic] dialect). Accordingly, Middle Arabic offers a wide spectrum, ranging from the informal level of the uneducated scribe to the grammatical nonchalance or dramatic purpose of the literary author. Middle Arabic is generally divided into three groups of Muslim texts (early papyri, scientific texts, and historiographical and popular literature since the thirteenth century CE), Jewish texts (or Judeo-Arabic, written in Hebrew characters), and Christian texts (occasionally written in Syriac script), although the evidence for the last group is limited.

Today Arabic is the official language of approximately two hundred million speakers in twenty sovereign nations, of the Arab citizens of Israel and the Palestinians, and of communities in Central Asia and East Africa; it is the liturgical language of approximately one billion Muslims.

BEATRICE GRUENDLER

See also Arabs; Arameans; Books; Bureaucrats; Education; Libraries; Folk Literature, Arabic; Greeks; Linguistics, Arabic; Persians; Qur'an and Arabic Literature; Qur'an and Manuscripts; Scribes

Primary Sources

Bateson, Mary Catherine. *Arabic Language Handbook.* Washington: 1967. Reprint: Leiden: Brill, 2003.

Bennet, Patrick R. *Comparative Semitic Linguistics: A Manual.* Winona Lake, Indiana: Eisenbrauns, 1998.

Blau, Joshua. *A Handbook of Early Middle Arabic.* Jerusalem: Max Schloessinger Memorial Foundation, 2002.

Corriente, Federico. *A Grammatical Sketch of the Spanish Arabic Dialect Bundle.* Madrid: Instituto Hispano-Arabe de Cultura, 1977.

Ferrando, Ignacio. *Introducción a la Historia de la Lingua Árabe: Nuevas Perspectivas.* Zaragoza: Navarro & Navarro, 2001.

Fischer, Wolfdietrich, ed. *Grundriß der Arabischen Philologie, vol. 1: Sprachwissenschaft.* Wiesbaden: Reichert, 1982.

Holes, Clive. *Modern Arabic. Structures, Functions and Varieties.* London & New York: Longman, 1955.

Khalil, Hilmi. *al-Muwallad fi l-'Arabiyya: Dirasa fi Numuww al-Lugha al-'Arabiyya wa-Tatawwuriha ba'd al-Islam (Innovation in the 'Arabiyya: A Study of the Evolution of the Arabic Language and Its Development in Islamic Times").* Beirut: Dar al-Nahda al-'Arabiyya, 1985.

Versteegh, Kees. *The Arabic Language.* Edinburgh: Edinburgh University Press, 1997.

Al-Zaydi, G.Y. *Fiqh al-Lugha al-'Arabiyya ("Arabic Linguistics").* Mosul: 1987.

Zwettler, Michael. *The Oral Tradition of Classical Arabic Poetry: Its Character and Implications.* Columbus: Ohio State University Press, 1978.

Further Reading

Arabica 48 (2001). (Contains articles reviewing the state of research in various subfields such as Epigraphic South Arabian, Middle Arabic, linguistic contacts between Arabic and other languages, and Arabic sociolinguistics).

Bergsträsser, Gotthelf. *Introduction to the Semitic Languages*, transl. Peter T. Daniels. Winona Lake, Indiana: Eisenbrauns, 1983.

Blau, Joshua. *Studies in Middle Arabic and Its Judaeo-Arabic Variety.* Jerusalem: Magnes, 1988.

Chejne, Anwar. *The Arabic Language: Its Role in History.* Minneapolis, 1969.

Fleisch, Henri. *Traité de Philologie Arabe*, 2 vols. Beirut, 1961–1979.

Hetzron, Robert, ed. *The Semitic Languages.* London: Routledge, 1997.

al-Rajihi, 'Abduh. *al-Lahajat al-'Arabiyya fi l-Qira'at al-Qur'aniyya (Arabic Dialects in the Readings of the Qur'an).* Cairo, 1968. Reprint: Riyadh: Maktabat al-Ma'arif lil-Nashr wa-l-Tawzi', 1999.

Robin, Christian. "L'Arabie Antique de Karib'il à Mahomet: Nouvelles Données sur l'Histoire des Arabes Grâce aux Inscriptions" *Revue du Monde Musulman et de la Méditerranée*, 61 (1991–1993). Aix-en-Provence: Edisud.

Versteegh, Kees. *Landmarks in Linguistic Thought III: The Arabic Linguistic Tradition*. London & New York: Routledge, 1997.

ARABS

Arabs, who are considered to belong to Semitic tribes, are the biggest community of these tribes. Aside from where they may reside as a result of different unions, it is accepted that their homeland is Arabia. The word *Arab* came after Semite nations established various states with different names in Yemen and Mesopotamia. The oldest information we have about the Arab Peninsula and the communities that lived there is found in the tenth chapter of Genesis in the Old Testament of the Bible. *Arab,* which also means "desert" and which has an origin that is still not clarified, was first seen in an Assyrian document dating back to 853 BCE.

There had been a long period of contact between Arabs and Assyrians in the fields of politics and the military. Both Assyrians and north Arabian tribes were ruled by the Babylonian King Nabonidus. It is possible that, when Alexander the Great conquered Syria and Egypt, he also took north Arabia during his Asian expedition. Meanwhile, The Arab peoples, then a tribal society, and Persians had friendly relations.

Arab historians divide Arabs into two groups, Arab Ba'idah and Arab Baqiyyah. Ba'idah Arabs lived in ancient times and then disappeared. 'Ad, Thamoud, Madyan, 'Ubayl, Jasim, Tasm, Jadis, and Amaliqa are among the important branches of the Ba'idah. Information related to these groups is only found in the Holy Books and in Arab poetry. Arab Baqiyyah refers to still extant Arabic groups. These are divided into two groups: Arab 'Aribah and Arab Musta'ribah, which are mentioned in the Old Testament. Arab genealogists assume that all Arabs are descendants of Abraham; the Old Testament is the basis of this belief, and the Qur'an also states that Arabs are descendants of sons of Abraham. Again, according to the same genealogists, people of north Arabia are descendants of Samuel, and the inhabitants of south Arabia, who have a settled life, are descendants of Qahtan. The people of both regions were always migrating for economic reasons.

Arab 'Aribah, whose homeland is Yemen, are also called Qahtanis. The most famous tribes are Jurhum and Ya'roub. Ya'roub also has two branches, Kahlan and Himyar, and many tribes and branches descend from these.

Arab Musta'ribah (or Arab Muta'arribah) were comprised of tribes that were Arabized afterwards. These were the majority of nomadic Arabs who settled in the area in the central regions of Arabia extending from Hijaz to Badiyah al-Sham; Adnanis, Isma'ilis, Ma'addis, and Nizaris are included in these tribes. Among the main tribes belonging to Adnan, there are Adnan, Ma'ad, Nizar, Rabi'ah, Muzar, Qays, 'Aylan, Ghatafan, Ilyas, Kinanah, Quraysh, Qusayy, and Abd Manaf. The tribes called Adnanis are descendants of Adnan's son Ma'ad. Some tribes of Adnanis settled in the south, where they united with the Qahtanis and became the ancestors of today's Arabs. The states such as the Ma'in, Saba', and Himyari Kingdoms were found in Yemen, and the Nabati, Tadmur, Ghassani Hira, and Kindah Kingdoms were founded in northern Arabia during the tribal period.

The Arab Golden Age, during which a system based on the principles of freedom and equality (especially in the tribes during the Jahiliyyah period) was seen, started with Islam. During Caliph Abu Bakr's period, Damascus was conquered in 635 and Jerusalem was conquered in 638. Iraq was conquered after the Nihawand war in 642, opening the doors of Iran to Islam. In addition, two important encampment cities were founded in Iraq (Basra and Kufah), and these played an important role in the conquest of Iran. Meanwhile, Khalid Ibn Walid's victory in the war of Ajnadayn on July 30, 634, opened the doors of Byzantium to the armies of Islam. Actually, this war opened the doors of the Syrian and Palestinian states to the Arabs and ended the Ghassani state, which was founded as a buffer state of Byzantium.

In the Ajnadayn war, the Arabs defeated the Byzantines soundly; after this war, they started conquering the fortresses and cities in Jordan, Syria, and Palestine, and they finally conquered all of Syria during the period of Caliph Umar. Amr Ibn As conquered Egypt in 641 and Babylon in 641. Alexandria was conquered on September 17, 642. During this period, Arabs progressed from a small state to a major power. During this expansion period, Amr Ibn As controlled the general policies himself, and he determined policy for the conquered lands.

Caliph Othman also continued the expansion period that was begun by Caliph Umar, and conquered Tripoli, Cyprus, Rhodes, Malta, and Crete. During this time, important events such as the Jamal event and the Siffin war took place, and control of Egypt and Hijaz was lost. Afterwards he sent an army commanded by Abd al-Malik Hassan Ibn Nu'man to North Africa, and North Africa was completely conquered between the years of 697 and 703. During this period, the Berbers of Moroccan tribes accepted Islam.

Islamic conquests, which came to an end as a result of caliphate fights, began again after Mu'awiyah dominated events in the country. In 647, Arab armies passed the Ceyhun river and reached Na Wara' al-Nahr. There was a temporary decrease in the conquests, but they accelerated again during the years 705 to 715, after Walid became the caliph.

The most important periods for Arabs were during the reigns of the Umayyids and the 'Abbasids, which enlarged their borders considerably. They faced a new page in their history after the 'Abbasids took over the caliphate. There were separations from the Islamic State during this era, and new states were formed. In the ninth and tenth centuries, new Islamic states were founded in Egypt, Syria, Yemen, and Palestine, and this breakdown continued until the reign of the Ottomans.

In 945, the occupation of Baghdad by Buwayhis resulted in power being transferred to Iranians; afterward, the caliphs did not have any power. In 1258, the occupation of Baghdad by the Mongols ended Arab domination in Iraq, and, beginning in the thirteenth century, Arabs withdrew from the political stage. The conquests that began in 1517 with Yavuz and that were continued by Kanuni resulted in the dominance of the Ottomans in all the regions except the inner regions of Arabia.

HÜSEYIN YAZICI

See also Arabia

Further Reading

Abu 'Ubaydah Mu'mar al-Muthanna al-Taymi. *Kitab Ayyam al-Arab qabla al-Islam.* Beirut, 1987.
Ali, Jawad. *al-Mufassal, I–IX.*
Caetani, L. *İslam Tarihi,* transl. Hüseyin Cahid. Istanbul, 1924.
Çağatay, Neşet. *İslâm Öncesi Arap Târihi ve Câhiliye Çağı.* Ankara: 1982.
———. *İslâm Târihi.* Ankara, 1993.
Caskel, W. *Das Altarabische Königreich Lihjan.* Krefeld, 1951.
Dayf, Shawqi. *al-'Asr al-Jahili.* Cairo, 1986.
Fayda, Mustafa. *İslâmiyet'in Güney Arabistan'a Yayılışı.* Ankara, 1982.
Furat, Ahmet Suphi. *Arap Edebiyati Tarihi.* Istanbul, 1996.
Grohmann, A., and others. "al-Arab." In *EI* (Englih), vol. I, 524–33.
Hasan, Hasan Ibrahim. *İslâm Târihi VI,* transl. İsmail Yiğit et al. Istanbul, 1986–1988.
Hitti, Philip K. *İslâm Târihi, I–II,* transl. Salih Tuğ. Istanbul, 1989.
Ibn Sa'id al-Andalusi. *Nashwah al-Tarab fi Tarikh Jahiliyyah al-Arab, I–II,* ed. Nusret Abdurrahmân. Jordan, 1982.
İslam Dönemine Dek Arap Târihi. Ankara, 1989.
Jabbour, Jabra'il S. *Tarikh al-Arab.* Beirut, 1986.
Lewis, B. *Tarihte Araplar,* transl. Hakkı Dursun Yıldız. Istanbul, 1979.
Mantran, R. *İslam'in Yayılış Tarihi,* transl. İsmet Kayaoğlu. Ankara, 1981.
Sa'd Zaghloul Abd al-Hamid, *Fi tarikh al-Arab Qabla al-Islam (Adil Jasim al-Bayati).* Beirut, 1986.
Von Kremer, A. *Culturgeschichte des Orients, Vienna 1875–1877.* Paris: Cl. Huart, Histoire des Arabes, 1912.
Wellhausen, J. *Arap Devleti ve Sukutu,* transl. Fikret Işıltan. Ankara, 1963.
Wüstenfeld, F. *Genealogische Tabellen der Arabischen Stamme und Familien.* Göttingen, 1852.
Yıldız, Hakkı Dursun. "Arap." In *DİA,* vol. III, 272–76.

ARAMAEANS

Aramaeans are first mentioned in Akkadian texts of the late twelfth century BCE as dangerous enemies to the west of the Assyrian empire. Their territories were organized into independent city states that eventually fell under Assyrian domination, the last being Damascus in 732 BCE. Hostilities between these states and ancient Israel are recorded in the historical books of the Bible and in a fragmentary Aramaic inscription from Tell Dan. The Aramaeans were probably nomads who had settled along the Fertile Crescent and who also spread to the southeast to southern Iraq (Beth Aramaye in Syriac sources). Certain strands of the biblical traditions that concern Jacob point to Aramaean connections, most notably the following profession: "My Father was a wandering Aramaean..." (Deuteronomy 26:5; the passage has subsequently been given many different interpretations).

By the time of the Achaemenid Empire, "Aramaean" had largely lost its ethnic sense and was used instead to denote speakers of Aramaic. In the Hellenistic and Roman periods, "Aramaean" was understood as being synonymous with "Syrian" (i.e., an inhabitant of the general area of Syria). In both Jewish Aramaic and Christian Syriac sources, "Aramaean" also took on a new meaning of "gentile, pagan." In later vocalized texts in both languages, a distinction is made between *Aramaye* (Aramaeans) and *Armaye* (gentiles, pagans). The appearance of the personal name Aram in two different genealogies in the Bible (Genesis 10:22 and 22:21) gave rise in late antiquity to many different mythographic views of the origin and relationship of the Aramaeans to other ethnic groups. According to Strabo (*Geography*, I.2.34; XVI.4.27), the Aramaeans were also identified by Posidonius (early first century BC) as being featured in the works of Homer.

In the Middle Ages, Syriac writers continued to equate *Aramaye* and *Suryaye.* Muslim authors appear to have shown little interest in identifying the ancient Aramaeans, but they used the term *Nabat* to describe the Aramaic speakers of the conquered territories, especially the farmers and peasantry of Iraq.

The *Nabataean Agriculture (al-Filaha al-Nabatiyya)*, which was translated into Arabic from the ancient Syriac by Ibn Wahshiyya in the tenth century, is now thought to be based on reworked late antiquity writings that reflect local traditions. Besides agricultural lore, it contains much about pagan religion and magic. The latter materials were taken up by the Andalusian pseudo-Majriti (dates uncertain) in his *Ghayat al-Hakim (The Aim of the Sage)*. Translated into Latin as *Picatrix* (1256), this work greatly influenced Western magic.

During the late twentieth century, Aramaean has been taken up as an ethnic identity by parts of the Syrian Orthodox Diaspora.

SEBASTIAN BROCK

See also Aramaic; Syriac

Further Reading

Fahd, Toufic. "Nabat, II." In *Encyclopaedia of Islam,* 2nd ed. 7 (1993): 835–838.
Ibn Wahshiyya. *al-Filaha al-Nabatiyya*, ed. T. Fahd. Damascus: 1993–1995.
Lipinski, Edward. *The Aramaeans: Their Ancient History, Culture, Religion*. Orientalia Lovaniensia Analecta 100. Leuven: Peeters, 2000.
Pseudo-Majriti. *Das Ziel der Weisen*, ed. Hellmut Ritter. Leipzig and Berlin: B.G. Teubner, 1933.
Pingree, David, ed. *Picatrix: The Latin Version of the Ghâyat al-Hakîm*. London: Warburg Institute, 1986.

ARAMAIC

Aramaic, like Arabic, belongs to the central group of West Semitic languages and is within the Syro-Palestinian subgroup (with Ugaritic, Phoenician, Hebrew, and others). Its closest affinities are with Arabic. First seen in inscriptions of tenth/ninth century BCE, Aramaic still continues to be used in several modern dialects some three millennia later. The earliest evidence of Aramaic comes from inscriptions and documents on papyrus and skin, but, especially during the first millennium CE, it became an important literary language for three religious communities (Jewish, Christian, and Mandaean), and extensive bodies of literature survive. For well over a millennium, Aramaic (in different dialects) served as the main language of the Middle East, situated between Akkadian and Arabic.

Aramaic is known through many different dialects and scripts, several of which have their own designations (e.g., Palmyrene, Syriac, Mandaic). Different classifications of these dialects have been suggested, but the following seems to be the most satisfactory:

1. Old Aramaic (tenth/ninth–eighth century BCE): This is seen in inscriptions ranging from southeast Turkey to northern Iran.
2. Official Aramaic (seventh–fourth century BCE): Aramaic was already replacing Akkadian in the Neo-Assyrian and Neo-Babylonian empires; under Achaemenid rule, it became the official language of communication. Besides inscriptions, there are archives of documents from Egypt and Afghanistan; those from Egypt include the oldest fragments of a literary text in Aramaic, the story of Ahiqar, which is a political fable followed by a series of wise sayings that subsequently enjoyed great popularity in many different languages.
3. Middle Aramaic (third century BCE–second century CE): Many dialects had by now developed their own scripts (Nabataean, Palestinian Aramaic, Palmyrene, Hatran, Old Syriac), and a fairly standard form of literary Aramaic was emerging. In addition to the Aramaic portions of the biblical books of Ezra and Daniel (which preserve older features), further fragmentary literary texts have come to light among the Qumran manuscripts.
4. Late Aramaic (third century CE onward): Several dialects were used for literary texts; of the western dialects, Jewish Palestinian Aramaic has the most extensive texts, whereas those surviving in Samaritan Aramaic and Christian Palestinian Aramaic are much fewer in number. By contrast, the eastern dialects have proved much more influential. Jewish Babylonian Aramaic features most importantly in the Babylonian Talmud, but many additional texts survive; Mandaic is the vehicle for the corpus of Mandaean religious texts, whereas Syriac provides by far the largest corpus of literary texts in Aramaic.
5. Modern Aramaic (seen in written form from the seventeenth century onward in both Jewish and Christian texts): The modern spoken dialects fall into three groups: (1) Western dialects, which are spoken only in a few villages in the Anti-Lebanon; (2) Central Aramaic, which consists of the dialects of Tur 'Abdin in southeast Turkey (collectively known as Turoyo); and (3) the much more numerous Eastern dialects (Jewish, Christian, and Mandaean).

Aramaic has had a certain influence on Arabic, and some Aramaic loan words are found in the Qur'an.

SEBASTIAN BROCK

See also Aramaeans; Syriac

Further Reading

Conybeare, F.C., Harris, J.R. and Lewis, A.S. *The Story of Ahikar*. Cambridge: Cambridge University Press, 1913.

Jeffery, Arthur. *The Foreign Vocabulary of the Quran*. Baroda: 1938.

Kaufman, Stephen A. "Languages (Aramaic)." In *Anchor Dictionary of the Bible*, ed. David N. Freedman. 4 (1992): 173–178.

Luxenberg, Christoph. *Die Syro-Aramäische Lesart des Korans*. Ein Beitrag zur Entschlüsselung der Koransprache. Berlin: Das Arabische Buch, 2000.

ARCHITECTURE, SECULAR: MILITARY

Islamic military architecture assumed a variety of forms—fortified city walls, citadels, castles, and palaces—that in general did not diverge significantly from the Roman and Byzantine fortifications that Muslim armies encountered in the eastern Mediterranean world or those in Sasanian Iran or Soghdian Central Asia. Many of the standard features of Islamic fortifications (towers, bent entrances, portcullises, machicolation, barbicans, and donjons or keeps) were found not only in pre-Islamic military architecture but in that of medieval Christendom as well. Evidence of early purely Islamic fortifications is scarce, perhaps because many preexisting fortified structures were simply occupied and reused by Muslim armies as a byproduct of conquest. As the Islamic world expanded, the need for new fortifications (especially on the frontiers) became paramount.

The earliest Islamic structures that might properly be considered fortifications are the isolated walled enclosures that were erected as rural or desert retreats by the Umayyad dynasty of Syria (r. 661–750 CE) in the eighth century. These structures (Qasr al-Hayr East and Qasr al-Hayr West in Syria and Mshatta and Qusayr Amra in Jordan) usually featured outer walls with half-round solid towers that are descended in form rather than function from pre-Islamic Roman, Byzantine, and local architectural traditions.

Among the earliest fortified cities in the Islamic world were Raqqa in Syria and the Round City at Baghdad, both dating to the eighth century and both largely the creation of the 'Abbasid Caliph al-Mansur (r. 754–775). The surviving walls at Raqqa are mud-brick rather than stone, and there are remnants of numerous towers on the inner wall of the city. The Round City is today known only through literary evidence, but it seems also to have had mud-brick outer and inner walls punctuated by towers and a moat between the two walls. One notable feature of the Round City was the use of bent entrances in the exterior gates, which forced anyone entering the city to make a series of repeated turns in close quarters that thus minimized the impact of frontal assaults. The bent entrance was later used in monumental gateways in many citadels and palaces (e.g., the Alhambra in Granada, Spain), although its origin is pre-Islamic.

More tangible evidence of military architecture survives from a later date in the walls and gates of Cairo and the remarkable citadel at Aleppo. Cairo was founded in 969 north of the old city of Fustat, and it was originally surrounded by mud-brick walls that were subsequently replaced with stone by the Fatimid vizier Badr al-Jamali between 1087 and 1092. From this same period survive three monumental stone gates (each more than twenty meters high): Bab al-Nasr (Gate of Victory), Bab al-Futuh (Gate of Conquest), and Bab Zuwayla. The masonry techniques here are thought to derive from northern Syria. These gates have straight rather than bent entrances and in general more closely resemble earlier Roman gates than, for example, the aforementioned Islamic examples at Raqqa and Baghdad.

The Ayyubid dynasty (r. 1169–1260) constructed fortified citadels at Cairo, Damascus, and Aleppo, the last of which is the most impressive and best preserved. The Aleppo citadel, which was built on an enormous, partly artificial mound, was established in 1209 and repaired in 1292 and again during the early sixteenth century. It stands nearly forty meters above street level and was preceded by a fortified gate, a bridge, a moat, and a massive barbican. Inside the enclosed citadel was a somewhat random arrangement of baths, living quarters, a mosque, and a royal audience hall—in essence a small city within the city.

One area in which Islamic fortifications differ from their European or pre-Islamic counterparts is the relative lack of isolated castles in the Muslim world. To be sure, these do exist in some areas (e.g., the mountainous regions of northern Iran), but castles in general functioned as adjunct structures to fortified (or soon-to-be conquered) cities. An example of the latter is the well-known Rumeli Hisar on the Bosphorus north of Istanbul, which was built in 1451–1452 by the Ottoman sultan Mehmed II (also known as Mehmed the Conqueror; r. 1445 and 1451–1481) on the site of an earlier Byzantine fortress. It was used (along with its earlier sister fortress Anadolu Hısar on the opposite Asian shore, which was begun by Bayazid I [r. 1389–1402]) to control water traffic and communication between Constantinople (as Istanbul was then known) and the Black Sea before the Ottoman conquest of the city in 1453. The changing nature of siege warfare during Ottoman times is marked by the provisions for gun ports in both the barbican and the easternmost tower of Rumeli Hısar.

RICHARD TURNBULL

See also 'Abbasids; Agra Red Fort; Alhambra; Architecture, Secular: Ayyubids; Bayazid, Yıldırım; Conquest; Mehmet II, the Conqueror; Ottoman Empire; Palaces; Umayyads; Urbanism; Warfare and Techniques

Further Reading

Creswell, K.A.C. *Early Muslim Architecture*, 2 vols. Oxford: Oxford University Press, 1932–1940; reprinted, New York, 1979.
———. "Fortifications in Islam Before A.D. 1250." *Proceedings of the British Academy* (1952): 89–125.
———. *The Muslim Architecture of Egypt*, 2 vols. Oxford: Oxford University Press, 1952–1959; reprinted, New York, 1979.
Grabar, Oleg. "The Architecture of Power: Palaces, Citadels and Fortifications." In *Architecture of the Islamic World*, ed. George Michell. New York: Thames and Hudson, 1984.
King, D.J. "The Defences of the Citadel of Damascus," *Archaeologia*, XCIV (1951): 57–96.
Toy, Sidney. "The Castles of the Bosphorus." *Archaeologia* LXXX (1930): 215–28.

ARCHITECTURE, SECULAR: PALACES

Except for famous complexes—like the Topkapı Saray in Istanbul, the Alhambra in Granada, Fatehpur Sikri near Agra, the Fort at Lahore, and the Red Forts at Agra (all built c. 1565–1573 CE) and Delhi—extant palaces in Islam are few. Essentially used as settings for the ceremonial of princely magnificence, they were often as flimsy as stage scenery. The lack of information about this ceremonial (see "Marasim" and "Mawakib" in *Encyclopaedia of Islam,* 2nd ed.) and its relation to neighboring cultures (this information is enshrined in the *Liber de Ceremoniis* of the Byzantine Emperor Constantine Porphyrogenitus [Stern 1950; Canard 1951; Sourdel 1960]) complicates the interpretation of excavated remains; literary descriptions, which are frequently lacunary and misleadingly hyperbolic, are limited to the public areas.

Islamic palace architecture is often vernacular or domestic architecture writ large, but many palaces exhibit features that are derived from Western Asiatic cultures: a regular layout on built-up terraces, along an axis of symmetry, and a deep axial iwan, fronting, as in palaces of the first Sasanian ruler, Ardashir I (?–242 CE) at Firuzabad (Huff, *Encyclopaedia Iranica*), a central domed throne room, while the great iwan of the Taq (or Iwan)-i Kisra at Ctesiphon on the Tigris south of Baghdad (Kröger, *Encyclopaedia Iranica*), probably built by Khusraw I Anushiravan (r. 531–579 CE), became a topos for palace architecture throughout the Islamic world.

The Umayyad Caliphs in Syria and Palestine favored the villa rustica of late antiquity (a large-scale agricultural enterprise with baths, audience halls, and other amenities), and they progressed seasonally from one to another. More elaborate is Khirbat al-Mafjar, north of Jericho (Baer, *Encyclopaedia of Islam*), a winter residence with a rectangular arcaded courtyard fronting sets of apartments, a bath with rich mosaics, and a porch with a standing figure in Caliphal robes. Later Islamic rulers also made seasonal progresses, and the stations on their route (e.g., the early twelfth-century Seljuk Ribat-i Sharaf, between Tus or Meshhed and Sarakhs) were built like major caravansarays, with inner and outer courtyards. Residences like Madinat al-Zahra outside Córdova and the Seljuk palaces Kubdabad (c. 1220–1230 CE) on Lake Beyşehir (Arık 2000) in Anatolian Pisidia also spawned local satellites (i.e., hunting lodges, garden refuges from the heat of summer, race courses, and grandstands [Northedge 1991]). In addition, the palace of Topkapı (Eldem 1969–1973; Necipolğu 1991) expanded both seasonally and over time to include pavilions, gardens, and summer houses (yalı) all the way up the shores of the Bosphorus.

In palaces, space was ordered hierarchically, from the public to the private domain. The outermost areas included the King's Musick (tabl-khana, naqqara-khana), government offices, the archives, the mint, the armory and stables, and the kitchens, with the hall of public audience beyond. The private areas included halls of private audience, the women's quarters, libraries, treasuries for heirlooms or relics, an observatory, a menagerie, some luxury workshops, and architectural follies, often with glamorous names: Firdaws (The Paradise), Thurayya (The Pleiades), and Chihil Sutun (The Forty Columns, which is the traditional name for the ruins of Persepolis). These might also include belvederes, like those surmounting the towers of the Alhambra (Fernandez-Puertas 1977–1978), or apartments that were artificially cooled, employing running water with weirs and runnels to decorative effect (Rabbat, *Encyclopaedia of Islam*).

Palaces, as seen in Cairo and Aleppo, are often fortified, both for the ruler's security and for prestige (Behrens-Abouseif 1988; Rabbat 1995). Tamerlane's most famous palace, the Aksaray at Shahr-i Sabz (c. 1380 CE), had a colossal tiled entrance but no protective walls. At Samarqand (Clavijo/Sreznevskj, p. 244–45), he entertained in garden pavilions such as the Dilkusha and the Bagh-i Naw, which were set on artificial mounds that were approached by steps.

These were wooden, with tiled dadoes and lavishly painted and gilded ceilings that, as seen in Mughal India, may be transportable. For receptions and feasts, the pavilions were expanded by tents with hangings of cloth of gold and silver (O'Kane 1993). A typical Timurid pavilion is the Çinili Köşk in Istanbul, a two-story structure of brick and stone that was built for Mehmed II in AH 877/1472–1473 CE below the walls of the Topkapı Saray, with a tiled entrance iwan on a columned terrace. Its plan is cruciform, with rectangular rooms in each corner and a domed crossing on plaster fan pendentives, an axial apse providing a view of the palace gardens below. Under Tamerlane's descendants, the formal settings often included picture galleries (suratkhana).

In the Sasanian and Byzantine traditions, rulers presented themselves as magnificent collectors. The 'Abbasids' marble halls, magnificent thrones, lion fountains (e.g., the Patio de los Leones in the Alhambra [Fernandez-Puertas 1997–1998]), golden trees with mechanical singing birds and other automata, pools of mercury or polished tin, displays of arms and armor, and rich wall hangings were described in al-Khatib al-Baghdadi's account of the marvels (see Qaddumi 1996, paragraphs 161–64) encountered by an embassy from the Byzantine Emperor Constantine Porphyrogenitus that was received at Baghdad in 917 CE; these set a norm for palace decoration (Gabrieli 1959).

Audience halls in the Jawsaq al-Khaqabi at Samarra (after 836 CE), the palace of the Ghaznavid Mas'ud III at Lashkari Bazar in Afghanistan (Bombaci 1960), the Qarasaray built at Mosul by the Atabeg Badr al-Din Lu'lu' (d. 1259 CE), and the contemporary Qasr al-Dhahab of Baybars I in the Citadel of Cairo (Rabbat 1995) bore monumental painted friezes of the ruler's amirs. Sometimes inscriptional programs were also seen, as in the palace of Mas'ud III at Ghazni, where there are panels of verse from the *Shahnama* of Firdawsi (Bombaci 1960), and on the palace walls of 'Ala al-Din Kayqubad I's citadel (c. 1220 CE) at Konya in Turkey (Laborde 1836; Bombaci 1969). The elaborately displayed poetical inscriptions of the Court of the Lions in the Alhambra (Fernández-Puertas 1997–1998) paralleled those of the main iwan (Melikian-Chirvani, 1991) at Takht-i Sulayman in the mountains of northwest Persia, which was built around 1270 CE by the Ilkhanid ruler Abaqa and that included verses of Sufi poets as well as more extracts from the *Shahnama* (although there is no indication that his mastery of Persian was such that he could read it). Later palaces, like the Chihil Sutun at Isfahan (Luschey-Schmeisser, *Encyclopaedia Iranica*), which was begun under Shah 'Abbas I (996–1038/1588–1629 CE) and remodeled by Shah 'Abbas II in 1057/1647 CE, bore less

intellectually taxing but more splendid paintings of victories and triumphal celebrations.

The Islamic palaces the Topkapı Saray in Istanbul, which were built in the later 1460s C.E. for Mehmed II, were inhabited for four hundred years, despite the discomfort caused by the heat of summer and the scanty protection against the savage winter climate (Davies 1970; Eldem and Akozan 1982; Necipoğlu 1991). To European visitors, the imposing view of it from a distance did not bear closer inspection; however, the interior plan exhibits a certain cumulative effect in a processional sequence and, with its intimate pavilions and belvederes that are named after conquered kingdoms (thus evoking the imperial pretensions of the Ottoman sultanate), it perhaps reproduces the effect of the great Byzantine palace of Constantinople.

Its three courtyards, each with a grand entrance, were progressively less accessible. The outermost housed the arsenal (the church of St. Irene) and the mint, the second held the Council of State (the Divan) and a large block of kitchens, and the third, with the private audience chamber (Arz Odası), was the sole preserve of the Sultan and his attendants, including the private treasury and a shrine complex, where the Mantle of the Prophet was preserved. On three sides there were landscaped gardens with fountains and splendid views that stretched down to the old Byzantine sea walls; in the late spring on a fine warm day, these views might—according to the praise of Ottoman chroniclers—be a reflection of paradise.

The Topkapı Saray is the only Islamic palace in which the history of the harem quarters—virtually a palace within a palace—is documented (Peirce 1993). Under Murad III, these quarters were reorganized and rebuilt (1578–1579 CE), with additional quarters for the Queen Mother and the eunuch guards and with permanent apartments for the Sultan, including a bedchamber in a two-story domed pavilion, a domed reception hall, two baths, and, from the late sixteenth century onward, schoolrooms and apartments for the princes.

MICHAEL J. ROGERS

See also Agra Red Fort; Alhambra; Gardens and Gardening; Painting, Monumental and Frescoes; Furniture and Furnishings; Ilkhanids; Mahmud of Ghazna; Sasanians; al-Khatib al-Baghdadi; Shahnama; Tamerlane (Timur); Timurids

Primary Sources

Andrews, P.A. "Mahall." In *Encyclopaedia of Islam*, 2nd ed.
Arik, R. *Kubadabad. Selçuklu Saray ve Çinileri.* Istanbul, 2000.

Badeau, J.S. "They Lived Once Thus in Baghdad." In *Medieval and Middle Eastern Studies in Honor of Aziz Suryal Atiya*, ed. Sami A. Hanna, 38–49. Leiden, 1972.

Baer, Eva. "*Kh*irbat al-Maf*dj*ar." *Encyclopaedia of Islam*, 2nd ed.

Bombaci, A. *The Kufic Inscription in Persian Verses in the Palace of Mas'ud III at Ghazni*. Rome, 1960.

———. "Die Mauerinschriften von Konya." In *Forschungen zur Kunst Asiens. In Memoriam Kurt Erdmann*, ed. O. Aslanapa and R. Naumann, 67–73. Istanbul, 1969.

M. Canard. "Le Cérémonial Fatimite et le Cérémonial Byzantin. Essai de Comparaison." *Byzantion* XXI (1951): 355–420.

Caronia, G. *La Zisa di Palermo: Storia e Restauro*. Rome, 1982.

de Laborde, Léon. *Voyage de l'Asie Mineure*. Paris, 1836.

Echragh, E. "Description Contemporaine des Peintures Murales Disparues des Palais de Sâh Tahmâsp à Qazvin." In *Art et Société Dans le Monde Iranien*, ed. Ch. Adle, 117–26. Paris, 1982.

Farmer, H.G. "Tabl-khana." In *Encyclopaedia of Islam*, 2nd ed.

Gabrieli, F. "Il Palazzo Hammadita di Bigaya Descritta da Ibn Пamdis." In *Aus der Welt der islamischen Kunst. Festschrift Ernst Kühnel*, ed. Richard Ettinghausen, 54–8. Berlin, 1959.

Galdieri, Eugenio. "Les Palais d'Isfahan." In *Iranian Studies*, VII/3–4, Studies on Isfahan, vol. II, ed. Renata Holod, 380–405. 1974.

Golombek, Lisa. "The Draped Universe of Islam." In *Content and Context of Visual Arts in the Islamic World*, ed. Priscilla P. Soucek, 25–49. State College, PA: Penn State University Press, 1988.

Gonzales de Clavijo, Ruy. *The Spanish Embassy to Samarkand 1403–1406*. London: Variorum Reprints, 1971.

Goodwin, Godfrey. "Topkapı Sarayı." In *Encyclopaedia of Islam*, 2nd ed.

Hakkı Eldem, Sedat. *Köşkler ve Kasırlar*, I–II. Istanbul, 1969–1973.

Hakkı Eldem, Sedat, and Feridun Akozan. *Topkapı Sarayı. Bir Mimarî Araştırma*. Istanbul, 1982.

Huff, D. "Architecture. III. Sasanian." *Encyclopaedia Iranica*.

al-Íabi, Hilal. *Rusim Dar al-Khilafa: The Rules and Regulations of the 'Abbasid Court*, transl. E.A. Salem. Beirut, 1977.

Keall, E.J. "Ayvan-e Kesra." *Encyclopaedia Iranica*.

Kröger, Jens. "Ctesiphon." *Encyclopaedia Iranica*.

Koch, Ebba. "Diwan-i 'Amm and Chihil Sutun: The Audience Halls of Shah Jahan." In *Mughal Art and Imperial Ideology. Collected Essays*, 229–54. New Delhi: Oxford University Press, 2001.

Lambton, A.K.S. "Nakkara-*kh*ana." In *Encyclopaedia of Islam*, 2nd ed.

Luschey-Schmeisser, Ingeborg. "Cehel Sotin." *Encyclopaedia Iranica*.

Melikian-Chirvani, A.S. "Le Livre des Rois, Miroir du Destin. II. Takht-é Soleyman et la Symbolique du Shah-Name." *Studia Iranica* 20/1 (1991): 33–148.

Northedge, Alastair. "The Racecourses at Samarra." *Bulletin SOAS* 53 (1990): 31–56.

O'Kane, Bernard. "From Tents to Pavilions: Royal Mobility and Persian Palace Design." *Ars Orientalis* 23 (1993): 249–68.

Pinder-Wilson, Ralph. "The Persian Garden: *Bagh* and *Chahar Bagh*." In *The Islamic Garden, Dumbarton Oaks Colloquium on the History of Landscape Architecture*, vol. 4, 69–86. Washington, DC, 1976.

Rabbat, Nasser. "*Sh*adirwan." In *Encyclopaedia of Islam*, 2nd ed.

Reuther, O. *Indische Paläste und Wohnhäuser*. Berlin: 1925.

Rogers, J.M. "Costantinopoli." *Enciclopedia Archeologica Italiana*.

Sanders, P. "Marasim. Under the Caliphate and the Fatimids." In *Encyclopaedia of Islam*, 2nd ed.

———. "Mawakib. Under the 'Abbasids and the Fatimids." In *Encyclopaedia of Islam*, 2nd ed.

Sourdel, D. "Questions de Cérémonial 'Abbaside." *Revue des Etudes Islamiques* (1960): 121–48.

Stern, S.M. "An Embassy from the Byzantine Emperor to the Fatimid Caliph al-Mu'izz." *Byzantion* X (1950): 425.

Thackston, Wheeler M. *A Century of Princes. Sources on Timurid History and Art*. Cambridge, MA, 1989.

van Berchem, Max. "Monuments et Inscriptions de l'Atabek Lu'lu' de Mossoul." In *Opera Minora II*, 659–72. Geneva, 1978.

Further Reading

Ars Orientalis 23 (1992), ed. Gülru Necipoğlu. Special issue on pre-modern Islamic palaces.

Davis, Fanny. *The Palace of Topkapı in Istanbul*. New York: 1970.

Behrens-Abouseif, Doris. "The Citadel of Cairo: Stage for Mamluk Ceremonial." *Annales Islamologiques* 24 (1988): 25–79.

Brand, Michael, and Glenn S. Lowry. *Akbar's India. Art from the Mughal City of Victory*. Exhibition catalog. New York: The Asia Society, 1985.

Fernández-Puertas, Antonio. *The Alhambra*, I–II. London: Saqi, 1997.

Necipo Necipoğlu, Gülru. *Architecture, Ceremonial and Power. The Topkapı Palace in the Fifteenth and Sixteenth Centuries*. Cambridge, Mass, 1991.

al-Qaddumi, Ghada. *The Book of Gifts and Rarities (Kitab al-Hadaya wa'l-Tuhaf)*, transl. Ghada al-Qaddumi. Cambridge, Mass: Harvard University, 1996.

Peirce, Leslie P. *The Imperial Harem. Women and Sovereignty in the Ottoman Empire*. London and New York: OUP, 1993.

Rabbat, Nasser O. *The Citadel of Cairo. A New Interpretation of Mamluk Royal Architecture*. Leiden and New York: Brill, 1995.

Wilber, D.N. *Persian Gardens and Garden Pavilions*. Tokyo, 1962.

ARCHIVES AND CHANCERIES

Muslim tradition has it that the Prophet Muhammad used scribes for record-keeping and that the caliph 'Umar set up the divisions of diwan al-jaysh (bureau of revenues) and diwan al-insha' (chancery) in the central bureaucracy of the state. The ensuing Umayyad period saw the rise of professional writers *(katib,* pl. *kuttab)* serving as confidants of the caliphs and playing a major role in shaping the institution of chancery. Under the 'Abbasids, the growing influence of the vizier resulted in the consolidation of the chancery under his direct supervision. The chancery also became one of the few institutions in the Muslim empire that provided career opportunities for non-Arab and non-Muslim civic professionals. It is from Egypt, however, that original archival materials emerged, shedding light on the organization, protocols, and activities of the chanceries. At the Fatimid court, the centrality of the chancery within the state bureaucracy was firmly established. The Ayyubids inherited many of the traditions. Of the preeminent chancery writers, some had honed their skills at the Persianate Sasanid court, whereas others had flourishing careers in the Fatimid chancery before serving the Ayyubid sultans. The Mamluk time witnessed the final phase of the evolution of the chancery, which was by now a complex of central bureaus and provincial branches. It was also during the Mamluk time that relatively comprehensive documentation of the chanceries was produced, in both archival and literary sources.

Very few Arabic Islamic archives of the pre-Ottoman era have survived (see Appendix). The ample evidence afforded by literary sources, on the other hand, attests to the sophisticated efficiency of the chanceries throughout Islamic history. Chief among these literary sources are chancery manuals, such as al-Qurashi's (c. twelfth century CE) *Kitab ma'Alim al-Kitaba*, al-Nuwayri's *Nihayat al-Arab*, and Ibn Nazir al-Jaysh's *Tathqif al-Ta'rif*. Particularly significant is al-Qalqashandi's *Subh al-a'Sha*, an encyclopedic work that offers detailed descriptions of the history of the chancery, the training of the katib, procedures and protocols, and the formulas and guidelines, along with samples of chancery writings.

Chronicles and royal biographies also form a significant source of chancery writings. By the Mamluk time, nearly all of the chronicles and royal biographies contained some chancery documents; however, many of these were edited later. Of these, some Mamluk treaties with the Ottomans may be collated with the originals that are preserved in the Ottoman archives.

According to al-Qalqashandi, two tasks were to be performed at the chancery: (1) diplomatics (al-mukatabat): communiqués, treaties, and decrees; and (2) personnel management (al-wilayat): certificates of hiring, firing, and promotion. Preparing legal briefings for the civil criminal court (al-mazalim) also fell into the responsibilities of the chancery. Guidelines and rules were developed to standardize the technical aspects of paperwork preparation and processing, and they ranged from the terminology of ranks, titles, and honorifics to the size of the paper

used, the writing style, and the formulas of treaties, royal decrees (al-mukatabat al-sultaniyya), and personal correspondence (al-mukatabat al-ikhwaniyya). Administrative documents under the rubric of al-wilayat are further categorized into subtypes: appointment, dismissal, pledge of allegiance, leases and contracts regarding the iqta' land revenues, advisory memos regarding religious and public affairs (al-wasaya), and so forth.

The qualifications of a chancery writer were commonly defined as al-balagha wa-husn al-kitaba ("rhetoric eloquence and excellent writing skills"). Some chancery writers were among the finest in classical Arabic literature, such as 'Abd al-Hamid al-Katib, Ibn al-Muqaffa', and Ibn Zaydun. Accordingly, the adab al-katib ("the art and craft of chancery writers") developed into an academic discipline that encompassed such pursuits as languages (Arabic and Persian); calligraphy and penmanship; rhetoric; phraseology and stylistics; poetry and proverbs; history; geography; architecture; and knowledge of commerce, weights, and measures.

Appendix: Medieval Arabic Archives

The Mount Sinai documents. This is the only extant archive of chancery documents from medieval Egypt, and it is made up mostly of decrees issued by sultans as edicts of protection and privilege to the Greek Orthodox Monastery of St. Catherine's.

The waqf deeds in Cairo. This collection includes some nine hundred deeds of waqf (religious endowments drawn up on behalf of the sultan and other officials); these are the only Egyptian "state" documents from before the Ottoman conquest.

Arabic documents from European archives. Certain European archives (Venice, Genoa, the crown archives of Aragon, Palermo) house a number of Arabic documents, mainly treaties and diplomatic correspondence of the Mamluk sultanates.

Arabic documents from Jerusalem. These are Mamluk chancery writings preserved in the Franciscan Custodia Terrae Sanctae in Jerusalem.

In addition, some non-archival collections—the Cairo Geniza, "the Vienna papers," and the Haram al-Sharif documents in Jerusalem—contain random chancery documents (see Further Reading).

LI GUO

Primary Sources

Ibn Nazir al-Jaysh, 'Abd al-Rahman. *Kitab Tathqif al-Ta'rif bi-l-Mustalah al-Sharif*, ed. Rodulf Vesely. Cairo: Institut Français d'Archéologie Orientale, 1987.

al-Nuwayri, Ahmad ibn 'Abd al-Wahhab. *Nihayat al-Arab fi Funun al-Adab*, 33 vols., in progress. Cairo: al-Mu'assasa al-Misriyya al-'Amma lil-Ta'lif wa-l-Tarjama wa-l-Tiba'a wa-l-Nashr, 1964 to present.

al-Qalqashandi, Ahmad ibn 'Ali. *Subh al-a'Sha fi Sina'at al-Insha'*, 14 vols. Cairo: al-Mu'assasa al-Misriyya al-'Amma lil-Ta'lif wa-l-Tarjama wa-l-Tiba'a wa-l-Nashr, 1964.

al-Qurashi, Ibn Shith. *Kitab Ma'alim al-Kitaba wa-Maghanim al-Isaba*. Beirut: al-Matba'a al-Adabiya, 1913.

Further Reading

Alarcón y Santón, M.A., and de Linares, R.G. *Los Documentos Arabes Diplomaticos del Archivio de la Corona de Aragon*. Madrid: Impr. de E. Maestre, 1940.

Amari, Michele. *I Diplomi Arabi del R. Archivio Fiorentino*. Firenze: F. Le Monnier, 1863.

Amin, M. *Catalogue des Documents d'Archives du Caire, de 239/853 à 922/1516*. Cairo: Institut Français d'Archéologie Orientale, 1981.

Atiya, A.S. *The Arabic Manuscripts of Mount Sinai: A Hand-list of the Arabic Manuscripts and Scrolls Microfilmed at the Library of the Monastery of St. Catherine, Mount Sinai*. Baltimore: Johns Hopkins Press, 1955.

Diem, Werner. *Arabische Amtliche Briefe des 10. bis 16. Jahrhunderts aus der Österreichischen Nationalbibliothek in Wien*, 2 vols. Wiesbaden: Harrassowitz, 1996.

Ernst, Hans. *Die Mamlukischen Sultansurkunden des Sinai-Klosters: Herausgegeben, Übersetzt und Erläutert*. Wiesbaden: Otto Harrassowitz, 1960.

Khan, Geoffrey. *Arabic Legal and Administrative Documents in the Cambridge Genizah Collections*. Cambridge: Cambridge University Press, 1993.

Hein, Horst-Adolf. *Beiträge zur Ayyubidischen Diplomatik*. Freiburg im Breisgau: Klaus Schwarz Verlag, 1971.

Holt, P.M. *Early Mamluk Diplomacy (1260–1290): Treatises of Baybars and Qalawun with Christian Rulers*. Leiden: Brill, 1995.

Jamil, Nadia, and Jeremy Johns. "An Original Arabic Document from Crusader Antioch (1213 AD)." In *Texts, Documents and Artefacts: Islamic Studies in Honour of D.S. Richards*, ed. Chase Robinson. Leiden: Brill, 2003.

Little, Donald P. *A Catalogue of the Islamic Documents from al-Haram as-Sarif in Jerusalem*. Beirut: In Kommission bei Franz Steiner Verlag. Wiesbaden, 1984.

Richards, D.S. "A Fatimid Petition and 'Small Decree' from Sinai." *Israel Oriental Studies* 3 (1973): 140–58.

———. "The Mamluk Chancery Manual, *Tathqif al-ta'rif*: Its Author's Identity and Manuscripts." *Cahiers d'Onomastique Arabe 1985–1987* (Paris, 1989): 97–101.

———. "A Mamluk Emir's 'Square' Decree." *Bulletin of the School of Oriental and African Studies* 54 (1991): 63–7.

Risciani, Noberto, and Eutimio Castellani, eds. *Documenti e Firmani dei Sultano che Occuparono il Trono d'Egitto, dal 1363–1496*. Jerusalem: Press of the Franciscan Fathers, 1936.

Al-Samarrai, Q. "A Unique Mamluk Document of al-Malik al-Mu'izz Aybak al-Turkumani al-Salihi." *Orientalia Lovaniensia Periodica* 21 (1990): 195–211.

Stern, S.M. *Fatimid Decrees: Original Documents from the Fatimid Chancery*. London: Faber and Faber, 1964.

———, ed. *Documents from Islamic Chanceries*. Oxford: Bruno Cassirer, 1965.

———. "An Original Document from the Fatimid Chancery Concerning Italian Merchants." *Studi Orientalistic in Onore di Giorgio Levi Della Vida*, vol. II (Rome, 1956), 529–38.

———. "Three Petitions of the Fatimid Period." *Oriens* 15 (1962): 172–209.

———. "Petitions from the Ayyubid Period." *Bulletin of the School of Oriental and African Studies* 27 (1964): 1–32.

———. "Petitions from the Mamluk Period (Notes on the Mamluk Documents from Sinai)." *Bulletin of the School of Oriental and African Studies* 29 (1966): 233–76.

———. "A Petition to the Fatimid Caliph al-Mustansir Concerning a Conflict Within the Jewish Community." *Revue des Études Juives* 127 (1969): 203–22.

Wansbrough, John. "A Mamluk Letter of 877/1473." *Bulletin of the School of Oriental and African Studies* 24 (1961): 200–13.

———. "A Moroccan Amir's Commercial Treaty with Venice of the Year 913/1508." *Bulletin of the School of Oriental and African Studies* 25 (1962): 449–71.

———. "A Mamluk Ambassador to Venice in 913/1507." *Bulletin of the School of Oriental and African Studies* 26 (1963): 503–30.

———. "Venice and Florence in the Mamluk Commercial Privileges." *Bulletin of the School of Oriental and African Studies* 28 (1965): 483–523.

———. "The Self-conduct in Muslim Chancery Practice." *Bulletin of the School of Oriental and African Studies* 34 (1971): 20–35.

ARISTOTLE AND ARISTOTELIANISM

The rise of philosophy and theology in Arabic Islamic civilization was accompanied by the reception of the Aristotelian canon of the rational sciences. Developing in close contact with Near Eastern Hellenism—at home in Syria and Mesopotamia—the urban culture of Islam not only received the practical arts and sciences of the Greeks from a continuous tradition of teaching and learned transmission but also adopted Greek concepts and methods of reasoning into the disciplines of theology and the law.

Early reports from Umayyad Damascus (seventh–eighth centuries CE) bear witness to the first exchanges of the arts, crafts, and practical knowledge and also a few translations in the fields of popular wisdom and political ethics (e.g., the correspondence of Aristotle with Alexander the Great). After the shift of power to Iraq and the Iranian East under the 'Abbasid caliphate (from 750), the reception of the practical sciences and the progressive Arabization of the Near East under Islamic rule led to a massive translation movement from Persian, Greek, and Syriac–Aramaic sources into Arabic, first in Baghdad and the Eastern provinces and soon in all of the urban centers of the Near East. Initially, Iranian traditions in astrology, medicine, and popular ethics were predominant. From the turn of the ninth century began the triumphant advance of the Greek authorities and their basic manuals, particularly the mathematics of Euclid, the astronomy and astrology of Ptolemy, and the medicine of Hippocrates and Galen and their schools. From the beginning, Aristotle accompanied the professional disciplines as a teacher of the encyclopedia of the sciences, the principles of rational deduction, and the scientific conception of the world. Foremost in the center of interest—and first translated—were Aristotle's writings about physics and natural science: *Physics,* about the principles of natural processes; *On the Heavens,* about the celestial cosmos; *On Generation and Corruption,* about composition and change of the elements; *Meteorology,* about sublunar phenomena, and the *Books on Animals*, about the natural history of the animate creatures.

In the milieu of rationalist theologians supported by the early 'Abbasid court and its administration, interreligious debate fostered a growing interest in hermeneutics and logic. Methods of syllogistic reasoning entered legal and dogmatic deduction. What is more, monotheistic theology sought solutions of its aporias—the antinomy between the absolute One and the multiple phenomena of created being, the chasm between the transcendent, ineffable First Cause and the possibility of knowledge via the sensible world—in the Aristotelian books about the principles of being and movement and of the soul. Aristotle's authentic *Metaphysics*—his exposition of a science of being *qua* being, and his philosophical theology (i.e., the doctrine of the First Unmoved Mover)—was read in Arabic from the first half of the ninth century. The book *On the Immortality of the Soul* was first read in a paraphrase that stressed the immortality of the rational soul, which was regarded as a substantial, intelligible form. On the other hand, the authentic writings of Aristotle, which were transmitted by the Neoplatonic schools of Athens and Alexandria and their Christian continuators, were accompanied by and harmonized with Neoplatonic texts, which were interpreted excerpts from Plotinus and Proclus published under Aristotle's name: the so-called *Theology of Aristotle* and the Proclean sources of the *Book of the Pure Good*, which was translated into medieval Latin under the title *Liber de Causis*. These connected the doctrine of the First Mover with the model of emanation: creation as an eternal pouring forth from the One, passed on by the Intelligences of the celestial spheres. The interpretation of the Arabic Aristotle identified First Cause, first being, and first intelligence and made this the efficient cause of creation: a creation from nothing.

In this understanding—and applied to the questions discussed in earlier Islamic theology—Arabic Aristotelianism served the philosopher–scientists of the early 'Abbasid society to legitimate rational science as a superior way to establish the true creed of monotheism. On this basis, the versatile al-Kindī (d. after 868) demonstrated the harmony between Islamic monotheism and philosophical principles. From al-Kindī to the branches of his school in Transoxania, from the natural sciences in Jābir ibn Hayyān's alchemy to the Gnostic cosmology of the *Book of the Sincere Brethren* (→ *Ikhwān al-Safā'* → Ismā'īliyya), the sciences of proportions, arithmology, and musical harmony led the rational soul on its way to a vision of the absolute: to the World of Intellect. The cosmic blueprint of this world, as depicted by the progression (creation) and regression (knowledge) of intellect through a cosmic hierarchy of ensouled spheres, was found in the teachings of late Neoplatonism, which harmonized with the Aristotelian and Ptolemaic models of celestial mechanics. Still in the same tradition, the Platonic ethics of knowledge was supplemented with Aristotelian catalogs of virtues and vices in tenth-century ethical handbooks by the Christian Yahyā ibn 'Adī (d. AH 363/974 CE) and by the Iranian Muslim → Miskawayh (d. 421/1030).

In a further phase of reception, Aristotle came to be the authority of an autonomous philosophy that was seen as a universal demonstrative science. The rise of Aristotelian metaphysics and epistemology among the scientific and administrative elite of Islam introduced a more strictly Aristotelian paradigm. Carried by the competitors of al-Kindī's circle inside and outside the 'Abbasid court and its administration—above all by the activity of Qustā ibn Lūqā, Thābit ibn Qurra, and those around Ishāq, the son of Hunayn, as translators and original authors encompassing all of the scientific encyclopedia—science was raised from empeiria to apodeixis. Until the middle of the tenth century, the *Organon* of logic was translated in its entirety, including the *Analytica Posteriora (Book of Demonstration)*, which was regarded as the crown of logic and the basis of epistemology. Finally, all commentaries on the *Corpus Aristotelicum*—from Alexander of Aphrodisias [c. 200 CE]) to the lecture courses of the late Alexandrian school (fifth–sixth centuries)—that could be traced in Syriac versions from the Greek were made accessible by the Christian translators of Baghdad, who taught logic as the leading art of all rational activity (most notably Abū Bishr Mattā and Yahyā ibn 'Adī).

On this basis, al-Fārābī (d. 345/950) founded the philosophy of Islam by integrating prophecy, revelation, and religious language into the Aristotelian theory of the cosmos and of intellect. Aristotle's Active Intellect—the active momentum in the acquisition of knowledge by the rational soul—is seen as a cosmic entity in a Neoplatonic model, and it serves as a mediator conveying the universal forms in the process of abstraction from the sensible particulars and translating the universals—in the superior mind of the Prophet—into the representations of positive religion. Here the concepts of Aristotelian poetic and rhetoric are employed to build a theory of religious language: the symbols of revealed religion imitate the absolute. From the perspective of metaphysics as the ruling science of being *qua* being, the theoretical and practical sciences and the *Organon* of logic (interpretation and deduction) are integrated into a unified system of the rational sciences, together with their corollaries in the particular disciplines of the religious–linguistic community, theology, jurisprudence, and grammar.

Aristotle is, from this point forward, regarded by his Arabic followers (the falāsifa) as the guarantor of the way toward demonstrable truth, for both the rational sciences and the religious disciplines: the First Teacher, so called by Ibn Sīnā (Avicenna, d. 428/1037). Ibn Sīnā set out to rewrite the *Peripatetic* canon of readings according to the order and under the titles of the Aristotelian works: *Logica, Physica,* and *Metaphysica,* supplemented by the mathematical quadrivium and by the *Canon* of theoretical and practical medicine. His *Summa* of philosophy was based on a new metaphysics that was to supersede Aristotle's. It is Aristotelian in that the universals are bound up with real substances, but they can be abstracted by intellectual analysis, relying on self-evident principles and on demonstrative reasoning; it is Platonic in that the divine mind is given the role of the Active Intellect, conferring the divine illumination necessary for all true and necessary knowledge. Departing from the concepts of substance and accident, essence and existence, matter and form, potentiality and actuality, Ibn Sīnā specified the concept and proof of the divine cause under the terms of Kalām theology. He established the First Cause as the necessary existent that alone has being essentially and that is necessary by itself and not composite of essence and existence. All contingent, temporal being needs a first cause, which is necessary and eternal and confers being upon the creation; together with its eternal cause, the whole of the world coexists eternally. The hierarchy of creation is modeled in a Neoplatonic cosmology: descending from the First Cause over the celestial spheres to the sublunar world of form in matter. The emanation of the forms from the Giver of Forms, the Agent

Intellect, into the genera and species of the material substances, corresponds with the Plotinian model of the return of the soul to its origin: to the vision of the intelligible cosmos.

For the religious community, however, this Aristotelian/Neoplatonic cosmology—which implied the eternity of the world—remained a stumbling block, even for those theologians who adopted Aristotelian logic as a basis of rational discourse. The refutation written by the jurist and theologian → al-Ghazālī (d. 505/1111), who was well versed in philosophy, contested the philosophers' claim that human reason was consistent with God's wisdom, but he nevertheless placed Aristotelian logic and hermeneutic into the service of the religious disciplines. Through al-Ghazālī's adoption of Aristotelian concepts and systematized by the schools of Sunnī Kalām that developed in his wake (→ Fakhr-al-Dīn al-Rāzī), Avicenna's new interpretation of Aristotelian metaphysics shaped the scholarship of later Islamic theology.

Meanwhile, the Aristotelians of the Muslim West (Andalusia and North Africa) took up the challenge of al-Ghazālī: Ibn Bājja (d. 533/1139) in the spirit of al-Fārābī; Ibn Tufayl (d. 581/1185) in an attempt to mediate between Avicenna and al-Ghazālī; and, finally, Ibn Rushd (Averroes, d. 595/1198) in his large-scale defense of the authentic Aristotle, based on extensive commentaries of his works and summaries of his doctrine. Against Avicenna, Averroes purged Aristotle from the elements of Neoplatonism and re-established metaphysics on the basis of Aristotle's physics of real substances, providing the demonstration of being that must precede the demonstration of the cause. The Latin and Hebrew translations of his commentaries became the main sources of Jewish and Christian Aristotelianism during the Middle Ages, lasting until the early Renaissance.

Syntheses of rationalist and religious discourse in the religious community created complex systems of legal demonstration, of speculative theology, and of mystical philosophy. The philosophy of illumination (ishrāq)—as established by Shihāb-al-Dīn al-Suhrawardī (d. 587/1198)—employed the formal epistemology of the *Peripatetics* (i.e., Avicenna) as a metaphor for the process of illumination, going forth from the First Cause, which is first light and highest reality (Avicenna's Necessary Being). Although the "divine Plato" is invoked as an authority, the concepts result from a chain of re-interpretations of Aristotle. For the vision of the cosmic hierarchy, mediating through monads of light between the First and the inner eye of contemplation, the spiritual metaphysics of the Arabic Plotinus provided a proven paradigm that was read by Avicenna as well as his successors until the theosophy of Safavid Iran (Sadr-al-Dīn al-Shīrāzī, d. 1050/1640).

GERHARD ENDRESS

Further Reading

Daiber, H. *Bibliography of Islamic Philosophy*. Leiden: 1999.

Endress, G. "Die Wissenschaftliche Literatur." *Grundriss der Arabischen Philologie* 2 (Wiesbaden 1987): 400–506; 3 (1991): 3–152.

———. *Aristotle and the Arabs: The Aristotelian Tradition in Islam*. New York, 1968.

Endress, G., et al, eds. *Averroes and the Aristotelian Tradition*. Leiden, 1999.

Gutas, D. *Avicenna and the Aristotelian Tradition*. Leiden, 1986.

Peters, F.E. *Aristoteles Arabus: The Oriental Translations and Commentaries on the Aristotelian Corpus*. Leiden, 1968.

ARWA

Daughter of Ahmad ibn Muhammad ibn Qasim al-Sulayhi and a celebrated Queen of Yemen of the Sulayhid dynasty, Arwa was de facto co-ruler with her husband, Sultan Ahmad al-Mukarram, from 467 AH/1074 CE and sole ruler from 477/1084 until her death in 532/1138, which marked the end of the Sulayhid dynasty. She exercised both political and religious leadership in Yemen on behalf of the Fatimid Isma'ili Caliphs of Egypt for almost sixty years. She became the founder of the Tayyibi Da'wa, independent of Egypt, in 526/1132 after the death of the eleventh Fatimid Caliph al-Amir in 524/1130. She is alternately known as Arwa and Sayyida in many sources and by the popular designation *hurra* (an independent lady) or, as Leila al-Imad would describe her, a "liberated woman."

Arwa was born in 440/1048 and was brought up by her mother-in-law, Asma' bint Shihab, herself a cultured lady known to people as *hurra*. She was married to al-Mukarram ibn 'Ali al-Sulayhi in 458/1066. Many sources, Isma'ili and otherwise, praise Arwa's knowledge of the Qur'anic exegesis, Prophetic hadith, history, and poetry, and her personality and prowess are widely admired. No doubt, they would dare not refer to her by her first name Arwa.

When her husband died, Arwa's minor son 'Ali 'Abd al-Mustansir was named as ruler; however, Arwa exercised complete authority. She was served by several prominent leaders and army commanders. The Qadi 'Imran ibn al-Fadl, who had been 'Ali al-Sulayhi's envoy to the Fatimid Caliph and the Commander of the Sulayhid army but had later fallen out of grace, nevertheless fought for her against the

Najahids and was killed in battle in 479/1086. Two Amirs, Abu Himyar Saba' ibn Ahmad al-Sulayhi and Abu 'l-Rabi' 'Amir ibn Sulayman al-Zawahi (both bitter rivals who fought several battles against each other), served Arwa nevertheless and carried out her bidding. Saba' contrived to get the Fatimid Caliph's permission to marry her. She obeyed; the marriage was contracted but never consummated. Saba' remained loyal to her in any case. Both Amirs died around 492/1098. Arwa's two sons, 'Ali and al-Muzaffar, also died near this time. In her sorrow, the Queen turned to yet another, 'Amir al-Mufaddal ibn Abi 'l-Barakat ibn al-Walid al-Himyari, to whom she entrusted her treasury at Mount Ta'kar near Dhu Jibla. He was not able to withstand the inroads made in her realm by the Zuray'ids of Aden, who owed tribute to her but were now falsely claiming to be da is.

The affairs of the Da'wa occupied Arwa. Imam al-Mustansir had appointed her as the Hujja of Yemen, which was the highest rank in the region; in a letter to her in 481/1088, he asked her to supervise the Da'wa in India. Lamak b. Malik al-Hammadi was the Da'i Balagh under her. On his death, also around 492/1098, his son Yahya took charge of the Da'wa. On Yahya's death in 520/1126, the scholar Dhu'ayb ibn Musa al-Wadi'i was entrusted with the affairs of the Da'wa.

In the meantime, Al-Afdal, son of Badr al-Jamali and the dictator in Egypt under the Fatimid Caliph al-Must ali (487–495/1094–1101), had sent, in 513/1119, Ibn Najib al-Dawla as an administrator and Da'i of Yemen, sensing the power vacuum that prevailed after 'Amir al-Mufaddal's death in 504/1110. His conflict with Queen Arwa's Da'wa and the local Amirs prompted the Queen to contrive to get him drowned in the Red Sea. However, she patched up the problem by giving a member of her own Sulayhid family, 'Ali ibn 'Abd Allah, the title of Fakhr al-Khilafa to please the Fatimid Caliph, who now was al-Amir (495–524/1101–1130). By now Arwa had tired of the Fatimid connection. The opportunity for independence came when, on al-Amir's death in Egypt in 524/1130, his minor son al-Tayyib's right to succeed was usurped by his uncle al-Hafiz li-din Allah.

The Queen and her Da'wa under Dhu'ayb declared for Tayyib and severed their relationship with the last Fatimid Caliphs in 526/1132. Dhu'ayb al-Wadi'i was declared the first Da'i Mutlaq of the new Tayyibi Da'wa of Yemen and India, and he was assisted by a valiant Sultan of Jurayb, al-Khattab ibn al-Hasan ibn Abi 'l-Haffaz al-Hamdani, a warrior and a poet. When the enemies pointed out that a woman could not have religious leadership, al-Khattab defended

Arwa's position with the argument that her womanly form is only an outward cover. He stated that one had to look to her inner essence, and he compared her to Maryam, the mother of Jesus; Khadija, the wife of the Prophet Muhammad; and Fatima, the wife of 'Ali.

The power options of the old Queen had now run out. The last Fatimids were supporting the Zuray'ids of Aden and the Hamdanids of San'a'. There were other rivals, such as the Najahids and Mahdids of Zabid, the Sulaymani Sharifs, and the Banu Akk. Arwa realized that the end of her dynasty had come. She died in 532/1138, leaving a long list of her treasures in a will and bequeathing them to the absent Imam Tayyib (i.e., the Da'wa that now continued to exist in Yemen, not as a state but as a community, and which proliferated in India).

Arwa's last supporter, 'Amir al-Khattab, died the next year, in 533/1139, and Yemen was soon inundated by the Ayyubid invasion and conquest in 569/1173.

ABBAS HAMDANI

See also Sulayhids; Women Rulers

Primary Sources

ibn 'Ali al-Hakami, Umara. *Nuzhat al-Afkar*, vol. I (Ms. Hamdani coll.). *Ta'rikh al-Yaman*, ed. Hasan Sulayman Mahmud. Cairo: Maktabat Misr, 1957. (See Kay for English translation).
Imad al-Din, Idris (b. Hasan al-Anf). *Uyun al-Akhbar (The Fatimids and Their Successors in Yemen)*, vol. VII, ed. Ayman Fu'ad Sayyid, English summary by Paul Walker. London: I.B. Tauris, 2001.
Al-Janadi Baha' al-Din. *Al-Suluk*.
Al-Khazraji. *Al-Kifaya Wa-l-i'lam*. (See Kay for copious English notes.)

Further Reading

Daftary, Farhad. "Sayyida Hurra: The Isma'ili Sulayhid Queen of Yemen." In *Women in the Medieval Islamic World: Power, Patronage and Piety*, 117–29, ed. Gavin R.G. Hambly. New York: St. Martin's Press, 1998.
Al-Hamdani, Husayn F. "The Life and Times of Queen Saiyidah Arwa, the Sulaihid of Yemen." *Journal of the Royal Central Asian Society* 18 (1931): 505–17.
Al-Imad, Leila. "Women and Religion in the Fatimid Caliphate: The Case of al-Sayyidah al-Hurra, Queen of Yemen." In *Intellectual Studies on Islam in Honor of Martin B. Dickson*, 137–44, ed. Michel M. Mazzaoui and Vera B. Moreen. Salt Lake City: University of Utah Press, 1990.
Kahhala, 'Umar R. *A'lam al-nisa'*, 3rd ed., 253–4. Beirut: Mu'assasat al-Risala, 1977.
Mernissi, Fatima. *The Forgotten Queens of Islam*, 139–58, transl. M.J. Lakeland. Cambridge: Polity Press, 1993.
Traboulsi, Samer. "The Queen was Actually a Man—Arwa Bint Ahmad and the Politics of Religion." *Arabica* 50 (2003): 96–108.

ASCETICS AND ASCETICISM

The terms *ascetics* and *asceticism* refer first to deliberate austerity as part of a life of devotion. This discussion will chiefly address the ascetics (zuhhad, nussak) of the eighth century CE, who are widely regarded as the forerunners of the Sufis of the later ninth century and after. Some did wear wool (suf), which was scratchy, smelly when wet, and liable to become ragged. However, the term *Sufi* did not appear until the later eighth century, and few of the ascetics whom later Sufi writers regarded as their forebears were expressly called "Sufis" during their lifetimes.

As for austerity, many early exemplars of piety were notable for their poverty. When some Basrans went to visit al-Hasan al-Basri (d. 728) on his sickbed, they found that "there was nothing in the house: no bed, no carpet, no pillow, and no mat except a bed of palm fronds that he was on." His fellow Basran Malik ibn Dinar (d. late 740s) thought the only necessary furniture for one's house was "a prayer mat, a copy of the Qur'an, and a stand for ritual ablutions." The Kufan Dawud al-Ta'i (d. ca. early 780s) would move from room to room of his house as it gradually fell into ruin.

More than particular austerities, early Muslim ascetics had in common their devotion of extraordinary amounts of time to Qur'anic recitation and prayer. *Qari'* ("reciter") became another term for *ascetic*. The Basran Thabit al-Bunani (d. ca. 744–745) recited the whole Qur'an daily and fasted throughout the year (i.e., he abstained from food and drink during daylight hours). The Kufan al-Hasan ibn Salih ibn Hayy (d. 814–815), his brother 'Ali (d. ca. 768–769), and their mother used to recite the Qur'an nightly in shifts; the two brothers continued to do this in shifts after their mother died, and finally al-Hasan performed this task alone after his brother died. 'Amr ibn Dinar, a Meccan jurisprudent (d. 743–744), divided his nights into a third each for sleeping, studying hadith, and performing the ritual prayer. Nighttime devotions had the advantage of taking place outside of most people's observation, and hence they were less likely to be performed merely to impress others. Makhul of Damascus (d. 730s) asserted, "There are two eyes that will not be touched by Hellfire: an eye that has wept for fear of God and an eye that has stayed awake out of sight of the Muslims."

Morally, the early ascetics cultivated sadness and fear—sadness especially over past sins and fear of judgment to come. They interpreted the Qur'an as enjoining such sadness and fear. The chief point of austerity was to keep one's attention on the important things, mainly God and future judgment. When someone suggested to al-Hasan al-Basri that he wash his shirt, he replied, "I cannot but see that the matter is more pressing than that." Malik ibn Dinar gave away a pot because it made him fear its being stolen. Practically, it was probably difficult to make a good living if one stayed up every night to recite and pray.

Disparagement of outward austerity seems to have arisen during about the last third of the eighth century. Ascetics such as al-Hasan al-Basri had called for inward dispositions to match the outward ones, but Sufyan ibn 'Uyayna, a Kufan, who was active mainly in Mecca (d. 814), went further, calling for inward detachment alone: "Renunciation means shortness of hope, not eating poorly." Al-Shafi'i (d. 820) and Ibn Hanbal (d. 855) likewise considered poverty no necessary part of an ideally righteous lifestyle. At the same time, there arose more extreme forms of asceticism. Shaqiq al-Balkhi (d. 809–810) rejected all deliberate pursuit of gain, teaching that the pious should live on alms alone. Tawakkul (dependence [on God]) came to be practiced with such recklessness that ascetics would set off on journeys across the desert without carrying food or water, expecting to be sustained accidentally; that is, by divine provision alone. As it crystallized around al-Junayd (d. ca. 911), Sufism repudiated the most extreme forms of austerity in favor of inward dependence on God. Moderate asceticism remained an important part of ideal religious deportment among Sufis and non-Sufis alike until modern times.

Sociologists have used the term *asceticism* to refer to the piety that stresses obedience to the transcendent deity. They contrast it with *mysticism,* which is defined as the piety that stresses communion with the immanent deity. Islamic law is a major expression of Islamic asceticism in this sense (i.e., Sufism or Islamic mysticism). A predominantly mystical piety seems to emerge in the literary record during the mid-ninth century, in the generation before al-Junayd.

CHRISTOPHER MELCHERT

See also Al-Hasan al-Basri; Hadith; Sufis

Further Reading

Andrae, Tor. *In the Garden of Myrtles,* transl. Birgitta Sharpe. New York: State University of New York Press, 1987.

Livne-Kafri, Ofer. "Early Muslim Ascetics and the World of Christian Monasticism." *Jerusalem Studies in Arabic and Islam* 20 (1996): 105–29.

Massignon, Louis. *Essay on the Origins of the Technical Language of Islamic Mysticism,* transl. Benjamin Clark. Notre Dame, Ind: University Press, 1997.

Melchert, Christopher. "The Transition from Asceticism to Mysticism at the Middle of the Ninth Century C.E." *Studia Islamica* 83 (1996): 51–70.

Reinert, Benedikt. *Die Lehre vom Tawakkul in der Klassischen Sufik. Studien zur Sprache, Geschichte u. Kultur des Islamischen Orients, n.s. 3.* Berlin: W. de Gruyter, 1968.

Al-Sulami. *Early Sufi Women,* transl. Rkia E. Cornell. Louisville, Ky: Fons Vitae, 1999.

ASKIYA MUHAMMAD TOUARE

After the death of Sunni Ali in 1492, his son Abu Bakr succeeded him as the ruler of the Songhay Empire, for which Sunni Ali's father had laid the foundations. However, Abu Bakr was soon overthrown by one of Sunni Ali's generals, a person of mixed Soninke/Songhay origin. This ruler took the title of Askiya, and he ruled from 1493 until 1529. Under his rule, the Songhay Empire gained territory and increased its hegemony throughout its territory as well as its vassal states; the empire's influence stretched from Hausa-land (present-day northern Nigeria) to present-day Senegal. Several of Askiya Muhammad's conquests were, however, temporary, and debate surrounds which areas were dominated and to what extent. Askiya Mohammad is said to have gone on a pilgrimage to Mecca, launched a series of military campaigns to expand the empire, and spread the word of Islam throughout the region; he was deposed by his son Askiya Musa, who exiled him.

Currently Askiya Muhammad and his empire are considered to be the historical predecessors of the Republic of Niger, and they are extensively celebrated in oral tradition. These oral accounts, which suggest his downfall resulted from his policy of following both Islam and pagan tradition, appear to be modeled on modern themes of interest, and they do not provide information about the historical figure of Askiya Muhammad.

JAN JANSEN

See also Sunni Ali; Songhay Empire

Further Reading

Hale, Thomas A. *Scribe, Griot, & Novelist—Narrative Interpreters of the Songhay Empire.* Gainesville, Fla: University of Florida Press/Center for African Studies, 1990.

ASSASSINS: ISMAILI

Assassin is a name that was applied originally by the Crusader circles in the Near East and other medieval Europeans to the Nizari Ismailis of Syria. From the opening decade of the twelfth century, the Crusaders had numerous encounters with the Syrian Nizaris, who reached the peak of their power under the leadership of Rashid al-Din Sinan (d. 1193 CE), their most famous dai and the original "Old Man of the Mountain" of the Crusaders. It was, indeed, in Sinan's time (1163–1193) that the Crusaders and their European observers became particularly impressed by the highly exaggerated reports and rumors about the daring behavior of the Nizari *fidais,* who were devotees who selectively targeted and removed their community's prominent enemies in specific localities. As a result, the Nizari Ismailis became famous in Europe as the Assassins, the followers of the mysterious "Old Man of the Mountain."

The term *assassin,* which appeared in European languages in a variety of forms (e.g., assassini, assissini, and heyssisini), was evidently based on variants of the Arabic word *hashishi* (pl. *hashishiyya, hashishin*). The latter was applied by other Muslims to Nizaris in the pejorative senses of "low-class rabble" or "people of lax morality," without any derivative explanation reflecting any special connection between the Nizaris and hashish, a product of hemp. This term of abuse was picked up locally in Syria by the Crusaders and European travelers and adopted as the designation of the Nizari Ismailis. Subsequently, after the etymology of the term had been forgotten, it came to be used in Europe as a noun meaning "murderer." Thus, a misnomer rooted in abuse eventually resulted in a new word, *assassin,* in European languages.

Medieval Europeans—and especially the Crusaders—who remained ignorant of Islam as a religion and of its internal divisions were also responsible for fabricating and disseminating (in the Latin Orient as well as in Europe) a number of interconnected legends about the secret practices of the Nizaris, the so-called "assassin legends." In particular, the legends sought to provide a rational explanation for the seemingly irrational self-sacrificing behavior of the Nizari fidais; as such, they revolved around the recruitment and training of the youthful devotees. The legends developed in stages from the time of Sinan and throughout the thirteenth century. Soon, the seemingly blind obedience of the fidais to their leader was attributed, by their occidental observers, to the influence of an intoxicating drug like hashish. There is no evidence that suggests that hashish or any other drug was used in any systematic fashion to motivate the fidais; contemporary non-Ismaili Muslim sources that are generally hostile toward the Ismailis remain silent on this subject. In all probability, it was the abusive name *hashishi* that gave rise to the imaginative tales disseminated by the Crusaders.

The assassin legends culminated in a synthesized version that was popularized by Marco Polo, who combined the hashish legend with a number of other legends and also added his own contribution in the form of a secret "garden of paradise," where the fidais supposedly received part of their training. By the fourteenth century, the assassin legends had acquired wide currency in Europe and the Latin Orient, and they were accepted as reliable descriptions of the secret practices of the Nizari Ismailis, who were generally portrayed in European sources as a sinister order of drugged assassins. Subsequently, Westerners retained the name *assassins* as a general reference to the Nizari Ismailis, although the term had now become a new common noun in European languages meaning "murderer." It was A.I. Silvestre de Sacy (1758–1838) who succeeded in solving the mystery of the name and its etymology, although he and the other orientalists continued to endorse various aspects of the assassin legends. Modern scholarship in Ismaili studies, which is based on authentic Ismaili sources, has now begun to deconstruct the Assassin legends that surround the Nizari Ismailis and their fidais—legends rooted in hostility and imaginative ignorance.

FARHAD DAFTARY

Further Reading

Daftary, F. *The Assassin Legends: Myths of the Ismailis,* 88–127. London: I.B. Tauris, 1994.

Hodgson, Marshall G.S. *The Order of Assassins,* 82–84, 110–115, 133–137. The Hague: Mouton, 1955.

Lewis, B. *The Assassins,* 1–12, 124–40. London: Weidenfeld and Nicolson, 1967.

Polo, Marco. *The Book of Ser Marco Polo,* 3rd revised ed. by H. Cordier, ed. and transl. H. Yule, vol. 1, 139–146. London: J. Murray, 1929.

Silvestre de Sacy, A.I. "Mémoir sur la Dyanastie des Assassins, et sur l'Étymologie de leur Nom." *Mémoires de l'Institut Royal de France* 4 (1818): 1–84. (English translation in F. Daftary, *The Assassin Legends,* 136–188.)

ASTROLABES

The astrolabe is a two-dimensional representation of the three-dimensional celestial sphere, a model of the universe that one can hold in one's hand. The representation is achieved by a mathematical procedure known as stereographic projection. There is a "celestial" part called the *rete,* which is a cutout frame with star pointers for various bright stars and a ring for the ecliptic (the path of the sun against the background of the stars). Next, there is a "terrestrial" part that consists of a set of plates for different latitudes, with markings for the local horizon and altitude circles up to the zenith and azimuth circles around the horizon. The rete is placed on top of the appropriate plate, and the ensemble fits in a hollowed-out frame called the *mater.* On the back of the mater is a

Astrolabe. From Cordoba. Moorish, 1154. Engraved with the Latin Julian calendar in Italy during the fourteenth century c. Credit: Bridgeman-Giraudon/Art Resource, NY. Jagellon Library Museum, Cracow, Poland.

viewer called the *alidade* that is used for measuring the altitude of any celestial body, and there are also scales for finding the position of the sun using the date, for measuring shadows, and often for obtaining additional information. If one rotates the rete over one of the plates, one can simulate the apparent daily rotation of the sun or the starry heavens above the horizon of the observer. The passage of time is measured by the rotation of the rete (360 degrees corresponds to 24 hours). In addition, one can investigate the position of the ecliptic relative to the local horizon and meridian; these are configurations of prime importance in astrology.

The astrolabe is a Greek invention that was inherited by the Muslims during the eighth century and much developed by them thereafter. It was the favorite instrument of the Muslim astronomers, and hundreds survive, although only about 150 of them are from before 1500. Below are some of the most historically important examples.

- An astrolabe that was preserved until recently in the Archaeological Museum in Baghdad can be

dated to the late eighth century. It has a Hellenistic design for the rete and plates for each of the climates of antiquity. The star positions are wrong (they are based on Greek coordinates updated with the incorrect Greek value of precession), proving that the instrument predates the Baghdad observations of the early ninth century.

- One of a dozen astrolabes surviving from 'Abbasid Baghdad and Buwayhid Isfahan was made by the astronomer al-Khujandî in 984. Already the astrolabe is a scientific work of art; it is richly decorated with a quatrefoil and zoomorphic star pointers, and it has highly accurate markings. (The so-called Astrolabe of Pope Sylvester II, which has featured in several exhibitions, is nothing more than an unsigned, undated astrolabe from 'Abbasid Baghdad with some dubious nineteenth-century Italian additions on the back.)

- Of some dozen and a half astrolabes from al-Andalus, all from the eleventh century, one made in Cordova in 1054 bears later additional markings in Hebrew on the plates for Cordova and Toledo, and another bears later medieval Catalan additions. The study of the second and further layers of inscriptions is particularly rewarding for investigating the later fate of individual instruments.

- Some two dozen astrolabes survive from Ayyubid and Mamluk Egypt and Syria, and their variety reflects the colorful tradition of astronomy there. Of these, the remarkable universal astrolabe of Ibn al-Sarrâj (made in Aleppo in 1328) is the most sophisticated astrolabe ever made. It can be used for any latitude in five different ways. An astrolabe with numbers in Coptic alphanumerical notation has been dated to 1282 and comes from Cairo.

- An astrolabe signed by the Yemeni Prince al-Ashraf in 1291 was deemed suspicious until (1) it was established that there was a vibrant tradition of astronomy in Yemen from the tenth to the nineteenth century (which was confirmed by the finding of many Yemeni manuscripts about astronomy) and (2) that there is a manuscript in Cairo of a treatise on the construction of the astrolabe authored by and penned by the prince himself. Appended to this are some notes of approval (ijâzas) in the handwriting of the prince's teachers describing six astrolabes that he made under their supervision and authorizing him to continue making the instruments.

- Alas, none of the instruments made for the fourteenth-century Delhi Sultan Fîrûz Shâh

Tughluq [q.v.], which are described in a historical work, survive. Some were made in silver and others in gold and silver; others were very large. The earliest surviving astrolabe from Muslim India, which is half a meter in diameter, can be associated with Maqsûd Hirawî in Lahore (c. 1550). He is known from a contemporaneous chronicle to have made astrolabes and globes for Humâyûn "in such a manner that the observers of his work were wonderstruck."

- On an astrolabe signed by Jalâl al-Kirmânî and dated 1426, the name on the dedication to the throne has been eradicated, although the person it was made for was obviously a prince of some importance. Special plates serve Samarqand and Herat; Jalâl al-Asturlâbî is named as the instrument maker at the observatory of Ulugh Beg in Samarqand, and that ruler commuted between the two cities. A solitary unsigned rete obviously by the same maker is fitted to a magnificent thirteenth-century Syrian astrolabe (damaged booty from the Mongol attack on Damascus, perhaps) and is dated a few years earlier. Of the dedication to a sultan on the new rete, only the letter's title remains intact; the name of Shâhrukh has been broken off.

- An astrolabe now in Cairo is dedicated to the Ottoman Sultan Bayazid II, who was particularly interested in astronomy. The maker is named as Mukhlis al-Shirwânî, so it is not surprising that the instrument is in the Iranian tradition.

- Perhaps the most colorful example is a quatrefoil astrolabe that has inscriptions in Hebrew, Latin, and Arabic. It was made around 1300, probably in Toledo, and the bare instrument was made by a Jewish craftsman, who left scratches in Hebrew alphanumerical script for the latitudes on each of the plates. The design of the rete is European, with strong mudéjar influence. The inscriptions on the rete and the plates are in a scholastic Latin, with very distorted Arabic names for the stars and some regional peculiarities that could eventually localize the engraver. However, the back was never completed by the scholar, and the piece fell into the hands of a Muslim Arab, who put his name, Mas'ûd, on the shackle of the throne. He also had plans to emigrate to more hospitable climes: he replaced one of the plates with one of his own that served Algiers and Mecca. He seems to have been at least partly successful, because there is an Ibn Mas'ûd who was born in Tlemcen at the right time who later wrote on instruments. In any case, the creator's father's

astrolabe ended up in Northern France by the sixteenth century, according to a fourth layer of markings.

Arabic treatises about the construction and use of the astrolabe abound. The earliest surviving one was written by al-Khwârizmî (now published), but those by al-Farghânî and al-Bîrûnî (still unpublished) are the most important.

The second most popular astronomical instrument of the Muslims was the quadrant, of which several varieties were available. Below three types of quadrants are considered: (1) horary quadrants; (2) trigonometric quadrants; and (3) astrolabic quadrants.

The horary quadrant is essentially a device for keeping time using the sun. It bears a set of markings that are graphical representations of the altitude of the sun at the hours throughout the year. The user holds the quadrant vertically with one axis toward the sun, and a movable bead on a thread with plummet, set to the appropriate solar longitude, falls on the appropriate markings to determine the hour of the day. The horary markings are either for a specific latitude or for all latitudes, with markings of the latter variety being necessarily approximate. Both types of quadrants were invented in Baghdad during the ninth century. Quadrants for a fixed latitude are known to exist for Rayy and Cairo (both from the thirteenth century), and they are also found on the backs of two astrolabes from Baghdad (tenth century). However, tables displaying the altitude of the sun as a function of the time of day for, say, each sign of the ecliptic (which one needs to construct the markings on such a quadrant) are known to be from ninth-century Baghdad. Quadrants for all latitudes are much more common, not least because they were often included on the backs of astrolabes. They provide a quick means of finding the time in seasonal hours for any latitude, whereas, with the front of the astrolabe, one can—with more effort—find the time in equatorial hours or seasonal hours for any latitude represented by the plates.

Another Islamic invention was the trigonometric quadrant, with which one can solve trigonometric formulae without any calculation. The simplest kind was developed for timekeeping in ninth-century Baghdad, and the most sophisticated kind, with markings resembling modern graph paper, was known already in the tenth century. Quadrants with such markings were often included on the backs of astrolabes or on the backs of astrolabic quadrants. This last type, which was developed in Cairo around 1200, essentially consists of half of the markings on a standard astrolabe plate (necessarily serving a single latitude), with an ecliptic scale and a thread with a movable bead. With such a handy device, one can perform most of the standard operations that are possible with an astrolabe. It replaced the astrolabe as the most popular instrument in the Ottoman world.

DAVID A. KING

Further Reading

Brieux, Alain, and Francis R. Maddison. *Répertoire des Facteurs d'Astrolabes et de Leurs Œuvres.* Paris: C.N.R.S., in press.

Charette, François, and Petra Schmidl. "Al-Khwârizmî and Practical Astronomy in Ninth-Century Baghdad. The Earliest Corpus of Texts in Arabic on the Astrolabe and Other Portable Instruments." *SCIAMVS* 5 (2004): 101–98.

Gunther, Robert T. *The Astrolabes of the World*, 2 vols. Oxford: Oxford University Press, 1932. Reprint in 1 vol.: London: The Holland Press, 1976.

King, David A. "Astronomical Instruments between East and West." In *Kommunikation Zwischen Orient und Okzident—Alltag und Sachkultur,* ed. Harry Kühnel, 143–98. Vienna: Österreichische Akademie der Wissenschaften, 1994.

King, David A. *In Synchrony with the Heavens...,* vol. 2: *Instruments of Mass Calculation.* Leiden: Brill, 2005.

Mayer, Leo A. *Islamic Astrolabists and Their Works.* Geneva: A. Kundig, 1956.

ASTROLOGY

Astrology as it was practiced in the Muslim world is divided into two types: judicial astrology (ahkam al-nujum) and popular astrology. The former type seeks to use the Ptolemaic understanding of the cosmos and to find patterns in it that can be helpful for prognosticating the future of a given individual or group. Although judicial astrology as such is a pseudoscience, the tables used by Muslim astrologers—who were often undifferentiated from astronomers (both being referred to as *munajjim*) until approximately the twelfth to fifteenth centuries—were remarkable achievements of mathematics and gematria. Popular astrology combined the lore of judicial astrology with Sufi teachings and continues to this day to be part of mystic literature.

The Muslim attitude toward astrology is somewhat ambiguous. One statement concerning the subject reads: "The [pre-Islamic] Arabs specialized in (several) faculties: in soothsaying, in prognostication *(qiyafa)*, augury by the flight of birds *('ayafa)*, astronomy–astrology, and gematrical calculations; Islam destroyed soothsaying and confirmed the rest of them." (al-Zubayr ibn al-Bakkar. *Akhbar al-Muwaffaqiyyat,* 300 [no. 213].) Most of the paradigmatic astrologers, such as Abu Ma'shar (d. AH 273/ 886 CE), held prominent positions in society and were frequently advisors to rulers and elites. Many of the most famous astrologers were non-Muslims, such as the Jewish figure Masha'allah (c. third/ninth centuries). In addition to this proximity to power, many famous scientists and astronomers, such as Abu Rayhan al-Biruni (d. 440/1048–1049), either practiced astrology on the side or at least wrote books on the subject. However, starting in the tenth century, Muslim religious scholars began to cast doubt on the religious acceptability of astrology. Their task was a difficult one, because astrologers seemed to have access to genuine knowledge. Al-Sharif al-Murtada (the famous Shi'i theologian of Baghdad, d. 436/ 1044–1045), stated the following:

...how can we say that the astrologers are guessing [about their predictions] when their dictions are almost invariably right? They predict solar eclipses—their time and extent—and it happens exactly as they say it will. What is the difference between their prediction of the happening with this effect up that body [the sun] and their prediction of the happening with its effect upon our bodies?

(*Rasa'il,* vol. 2, pp. 301–2.)

This dilemma and the fact that astrologers commanded a good deal of social prestige during the Umayyad and 'Abbasid periods made it more difficult for religious leaders to deal with the subject of astrology.

The most successful method of polemicizing with the astrologers was ridicule. Because most of Muslim history was written by religious leaders, there are abundant examples of their attempts to discredit the astrologers. Occasionally astrologers made verifiably incorrect predictions, the most famous of which was a deluge of fire and water that was supposed to occur on August 17, 1186. The Ghaznavid historian al-'Utbi writes the following:

In the year 582 [1186–1187] the sign Libra had assembled within itself the seven planets; and it had been for a long time reported in men's mouths and in their books, that the astrologers had averred their judgment that at this time there would be a deluge of wind three *kos* [about two miles] long, and as some said ten *kos* wide, which would extend over twenty *kos* of ground, which would carry off high mountains, so that neither men nor beasts would remain, and at this time would be the season of the judgment, which according to the glorious Qur'an, to histories and by investigation is to come.

(al-'Utbi, *Ta'rikh-i Yamini,* transl. James Reynolds, p. 489)

This prediction was recorded all over the Muslim world from Ghazna in the east to Spain, and it reached Europe as well. The disconfirmation of their prediction was cause for the appearance of a large number of treatises attacking astrology, including that of the Jewish philosopher and community leader Maimonides.

However, astrology continued to be important for the Sufi mystical systems, especially those that were based on the thought of Muhyi al-Din Ibn al-'Arabi (d. 638/1240). This construction of astrological spirituality promoted the idea that there was a close correlation between the seen cosmos and the unseen spiritual cosmos. On the basis of this idea, one could ascend spiritually to the upper realms and experience them while still bodily upon the earth. These ideas continue to be influential in Sufi circles, although astrologers as a whole suffered from diminishing prestige after the Mamluk period. However, it was rare to find a court without an astrologer before modern times.

DAVID COOK

Further Reading

Burckhardt, Titus. *Mystical Astrology According to Ibn 'Arabi*, transl. Bulent Rauf. Oxford: Beshara Publications, 1989 (reprint).

Kennedy, E.S., and Pingree, David, transl. *The Astrological History of Masha'allah*. Cambridge, Mass.: Harvard University Press, 1971.

Langermann, Y. Tzvi. "Maimonides' Repudiation of Astrology." In *Maimonidean Studies*, vol. 2, 123–58. New York: Michael Sharf Publication Trust, 1991.

Michot, Yahya. "Ibn Taymiyya on Astrology: Annotated Translation of Three Fatwas." *Journal of Islamic Studies* 11:2 (2000): 147–208.

Saliba, George. "The Role of the Astrologer in Medieval Islamic Society." *Bulletin d'Études Orientales* 44 (1992): 45–67.

Al-Sharif al-Murtada. *Rasa'il*, 3 vol., ed. Ahmad al-Husayni. Beirut: Mu'assasat al-Nur li-l-Matbu'at.

Al-'Utbi. *Ta'rikh-i Yamini*, ed. Ihsan Dhanun al-Thamiri. Beirut: Dar al-Tali'a, 2004. (Translation by James Reynolds. London: Oriental Translation Fund, 1888.)

ASTRONOMY

Islamic astronomy grew out of conditions in the Umayyad and 'Abbasid Caliphates. The Umayyads had initially preserved the preexisting administrative apparatus of the lands they conquered. However, when the caliph 'Abd al-Malik ibn Marwan (d. 705 CE) decided to translate the administrative apparatus of the Empire into Arabic, information about surveying and calendar calculation also had to be translated into Arabic for the benefit of ministers and scribes who could not read Persian or Greek. The 'Abbasids, after coming to power in 750, invoked the pre-Islamic Sasanian cultural heritage to stabilize

their rule. Original research in astronomy was part of an ongoing dialectic with translation, not merely its subsequent effect.

Although the Hellenistic influence would eventually predominate in Islamic astronomy, the earliest translations, under the Umayyads and 'Abbasids, involved ephemerides (zij, pl. azyaj) of Indian and Persian provenance. An ephemeris contained tables of planetary positions and the necessary theoretical explanations of how to use the tables. A zij was designed for applications such as calendar calculations and astrological forecasting, and the caliph al-Mansur consulted astrologers to great public effect when he commenced the construction of the new 'Abbasid capital at Baghdad. Al-Khwarizmi's (d. 833) original Zij al-Sindhind was the first complete text of Islamic astronomy to survive, although only in a Latin version of the original Arabic. Although most of the parameters in the zij were of Indian origin, the text was influenced by Ptolemy's (fl. 125–150) *Handy Tables*. First, al-Khwarizmi's *Zij al-Sindhind*, the source of which was the Sanskrit work of Brahmagupta, demonstrated that, although Islamic astronomers knew of Ptolemy's work, they would never accept it uncritically. Second, little time elapsed between Islamic astronomers' awareness of Ptolemy's parameters and the ninth-century translations of Ptolemy's *opus magnum, Almagest*.

Astronomers translated *Almagest* into Arabic during the beginning of the ninth century, and it would prove to be the most influential Greek text for Islamic astronomers. Two different Arabic translations survive, and reports exist of two others. As these translations were occurring, astronomers reassessed important parameters, and they found, notably, that the aphelion (the point of the sun's greatest distance from the earth) moved. In addition, Islamic astronomers criticized Ptolemy's views about how orbs could move. Specifically, during the ninth century, Muhammad ibn Musa argued that one orb could not move another with which it is concentric. By the eleventh century, Islamic astronomers detected the most famous physical inconsistency of *Almagest*: the equant problem. In the models for Mercury, Venus, Mars, Jupiter, and Saturn, Ptolemy's mathematical analysis showed that the planet's mean motion, which he attributed to a single orb, was not uniform about the center of that sphere. Nor was that motion uniform about the center of the universe: instead it was uniform about another point, called the *equant*. The discovery of the equant posed a problem from a physical standpoint, because spheres had to move about axes passing through their centers. Ibn al-Haytham's (d. c. 1040) *al-Shukuk 'ala Batlamiyus (Doubts Concerning Ptolemy)* enumerated the problems associated with the equant.

In addition, by the eleventh century, religious scholars and philosophers questioned the metaphysical assumptions of astrology, in part because of their threat to God's absolute unity and in part because astrological predictions could be wrong. As a result, a new field of astronomical study was generated, known as 'ilm al-hay'a ("science of the configuration"), whereas astrology came to be known most frequently as 'ilm ahkam al-nujum ("science of the judgments of the stars"). The genre of 'ilm al-hay'a became the locus for most of Islamic astronomy's subsequent achievements. Beginning during the mid-thirteenth century, Islamic astronomers proposed new models that preserved Ptolemy's models' correspondence with observations and that yet did not suffer from the physical inconsistencies of the equant. In other words, these astronomers all retained the equant, because it was the point about which the planet's mean motion was uniform; however, they no longer posited that the axis of any orb's uniform motion would pass through the equant. The early figures in this line of research who wrote 'ilm al-hay'a texts—such as Mu'ayyad al-Din al-'Urdi (d. 1259), Nasir al-Din al-Tusi (d. 1274), and Qutb al-Din al-Shirazi (d. 1311)—were associated with the Maragha observatory in Azerbayjan. Later figures, such as Sadr al-Shari'a (d. 1347) and Ibn al-Shatir (d. 1375), are said to belong to the Maragha school of thought. Recent research has shown that the construction of non-Ptolemaic models continued at least into the sixteenth century, when Shams al-Din al-Khafri (d. 1525) proposed multiple mathematically equivalent models for the complicated motions of the planet Mercury.

Astronomers in Andalusia, too, produced works of significance. Before the twelfth century, widely circulated contributions of theirs were the Toledan Tables and models for variations in the precession and retrocession of the equinoxes, known as *trepidation*. During the twelfth century, philosophers such as Ibn Bajja (d. 1138) and Ibn Rushd (d. 1198) advocated a reading of Aristotle's *Physics* that led one astronomer, al-Bitruji (fl. ca. 1217), to propose astronomical models based solely on homocentric orbs. That constraint meant that al-Bitruji's models could not approach the predictive accuracy of the Maragha astronomers' models or of those of Ptolemy. A fourteenth-century attempt to improve on al-Bitruji departed from his strict insistence on homocentric spheres. 'Ilm al-hay'a texts were also distinctly Islamic inasmuch as they contained sections about locating the qibla (the direction of prayer). Back in the ninth century, the need to determine the qibla spurred new developments in spherical trigonometry. During the eleventh century, al-Biruni's (d. 1048) *Exhaustive Treatise on Shadows* explained the calculation of prayer times according to the shadow cast by a gnomon. The relationship between astronomy and religious scholarship became closer during the thirteenth century, when information about astronomy began to appear in texts of *kalam* (speculative investigations about God) and in Qur'an commentaries. Besides the famous example of Ibn al-Shatir being employed as a timekeeper in the Great Mosque of Damascus, Qutb al-Din al-Shirazi, Sadr al-Shari'a, and Shams al-Din al-Khafri were all religious scholars of note. The research of David King, in particular, has shown that not only did astronomers develop highly sophisticated applications of astronomy to religious problems but that there was also a parallel popular literature that answered the same questions in a less exacting—but no less complex—manner.

ROBERT MORRISON

See also Mathematical Geography; Astrology; Intellectual History; Translation, Pre-Islamic Learning into Arabic

Further Reading

Kennedy, E.S. *Studies in the Islamic Exact Sciences*, eds. David A. King and Mary Helen Kennedy. Beirut: American University in Beirut, 1983.

King, David A. *Astronomy in the Service of Islam*. Aldershot, UK: Variorum, 1993.

Ragep, F. Jamil, ed. and transl. *Nasir al-Din al-Tusi's Memoir on Astronomy (al-Tadhkira fi 'ilm al hay'a)*. New York and Berlin: Springer Verlag, 1993.

Saliba, George. *A History of Arabic Astronomy: Planetary Theories During the Golden Age of Islam*. New York and London: New York University Press, 1994.

Sezgin, Fuat. *Geschichte des Arabischen Schrifttums, Band VI*. Leiden: E.J. Brill, 1978.

'ATTAR, FARID AL-DIN

A celebrated Persian poet and Sufi hagiographer, 'Attar lived during the second half of the twelfth century CE and the first two or three decades of the thirteenth century in or near Nishapur. According to the most commonly received scholarly opinion, he died during the Mongol sack of Nishapur in April 1221, but 1230 also remains a possibility. Reliable biographical information about him is scarce, and many supposed autobiographical indications derive from works that have turned out to be spurious. It is nevertheless clear that he was known as an expert pharmacist. He appears to have had close ties with the well-known Sufi of Khwarazm, Majd al-Din Baghdadi (d. 1209 or later) or with one of his disciples, Ahmad Khwari, in Nishapur. However, 'Attar generally had very little to say about the Sufis of his own time, and he never mentioned anyone as his own Sufi master, whereas he obviously admired the great Sufi saints (awliya') of the past. Unlike his famous counterpart among the Sufi poets, Mawlana Rumi (d. 1273), he does not seem to have played any active role in organized Sufism. The oft-repeated story of 'Attar meeting young Rumi in Nishapur belongs to the realm of succession myths (F.D. Lewis, 2000). The literary historian Muhammad 'Awfi, who visited Nishapur around 1200, describes 'Attar as a pious, withdrawn Sufi and a fine mystical poet. 'Awfi cites examples from 'Attar's lyrical poetry but does not comment on his mathnawis (narrative poems). Another early account comes from the Shi'i scholar and philosopher Nasir al-Din al-Tusi (1201–1274), who visited 'Attar personally when he was a student in Nishapur. Tusi was impressed with the old poet's "eloquence" and his way of interpreting the "discourse of the [Sufi] masters, the knowers [of God] and the spiritual guides," as he later put it to his student Ibn al-Fuwati (d. 1323). The latter, in his report, adds a reference to 'Attar's complete collection of lyrical poetry (his "great *Diwan*") and to one of his mathnawis, the "Mantiq al-Tayr."

A number of works attributed to 'Attar were in fact written by a later poet using the same pen name or have otherwise turned out to be falsely attributed to the famous 'Attar. This applies not only to those works portraying him as a fervent Shi'i but also to the so-called *Khusraw-Nama* (also known as *Gul-u-Hurmuz*), a romance that was regarded as authentic until recently, and the spuriousness of which has been convincingly demonstrated by contemporary Iranian scholarship (M.R. Shafi'i-Kadkani, 1996 and 1999). 'Attar's authentic works include, in addition to the *Diwan* and a selection of quatrains titled *Mukhtar-Nama*, four great mathnawis that are mentioned in the introduction to the latter work in the following order: "Ilahi-Nama" (properly called "Khusraw-Nama"), "Asrar-Nama," "Mantiq al-Tayr" (or "Maqamat al-Tuyur"), and "Musibat-Nama." It is not clear whether this sequence also reflects their relative chronological order; references to the poet's advanced age in the first two would rather speak against such an assumption. 'Attar's prose work about the saints, *Tadhkirat al-Awliya'*, is nowhere mentioned by the poet himself, but there is no good reason to question the authenticity of its first part (i.e., the part ending with the entry about al-Hallaj).

The most famous among the mathnawis is the "Mantiq al-Tayr." This is the tale of the mystical journey of the birds through seven valleys in search of their mythical king, Simurgh, a cosmic bird of ancient Iranian lore, who turns out to be their real Self. The theme of the journey of the birds had been used long before 'Attar as a symbol for the soul's attempt to approach God in philosophical (Ibn Sina) and Sufi (Ghazali) literature; however, 'Attar's adaptation is by far the most poetic and mystical. The main theme of the "Musibat-Nama" is also a mystical journey, but this time the wayfarer is thought itself (fikrat), guided by a master who is not of this world, although he must be found in this world. This journey leads the wayfarer through forty encounters with fantastic angelic, human, and purely physical beings to the recognition that he has to submerge himself in the Ocean of the Soul: only then can the "journey *in* God" begin. In the "Ilahi-Nama", a king/caliph teaches his six sons how to transform their worldly desires into related spiritual aims. The "Asrar-Nama" is, despite its mathnawi form, not really a tale but rather a meditation on the themes of death and resurrection.

HERMANN LANDOLT

See also Rumi; Saints; Nishapur; Mystical Poetry; Nasir al-Din al-Tusi; Ghazeli; Al-Hallaj

Primary Sources

'Attar, Farid al-Din. *Asrar-Nama*, ed. S. Gawharin. Tehran: Chap-i Sharq, 1338 (AHS/1959). (French translation by C. Tortel. *Le Livre des Secrets*. Paris: Les Deux Océans, 1985.)

———. *Diwan-i Ghazaliyat-u Qasayid*, ed. T. Tafazzuli. Tehran: Chap-i Bahman, 1341 (AHS/1962). (Second edition by M. Darwish, ed. Tehran: Jawidan, 1359. [AHS/1980]).

———. *Ilahi-Nama*, ed. H. Ritter. Leipzig and Istanbul: F.A. Brockhaus and Ma'arif, 1940. (Translation by J. A. Boyle. *The Ilahi-Nama or Book of God of Farid al-Din 'Attar*. Manchester: Manchester University Press, 1976.)

———. *Mantiq al-Tayr*, 3rd ed., ed. M.J. Mashkur. Tehran and Tabriz: 1347 (AHS/1968). (English verse translation (incomplete) by C.S. Nott. *The Conference of the Birds*. London: Penguin Books, 1984. Complete prose translation by P. Avery. *The Speech of the Birds: Concerning Migration to the Real*. Cambridge, UK: Islamic Texts Society, 1998.)

———. *Mukhtar-Nama*, 2nd ed., ed. M.R. Shafi'i-Kadkani. Tehran: Intisharat-i Sukhan, 1375 (AHS/1996).

———. *Musibat-Nama*, 3rd ed., ed. Nürani-Wisal. Tehran: Zawwar, 1364 (AHS/1985). (French translation by I. de Gastines. *Le Livre de l'Epreuve*. Paris: Fayard, 1981.)

———. *Tadhkirat al-Awliya'*, part I, ed. R.A. Nicholson. London and Leiden: Luzac & Co. and E.J. Brill, 1905; part II, London and Leiden: Luzac & Co. and E.J. Brill, 1907. (Partial translation by A.J. Arberry. *Muslim Saints and Mystics: Episodes from the Tadhkirat al-Auliya' ("Memorial of the Saints")*. London: Routledge & K. Paul, 1966.)

Further Reading

Handbook of Oriental Studies I, The Near and Middle East, 69, 1st ed. Leiden: Brill, 1955.

Lewis, F.D. *Rumi—Past and Present, East and West: The Life, Teaching and Poetry of Jalâlal-Din Rumi.* Oxford: Oneworld, 2000.

Lewisohn, L., and C. Shackle, eds. *Farid al-Din 'Attar and the Persian Sufi Tradition.* London: I.B. Tauris and Institute of Ismaili Studies, forthcoming.

Reinert, B. "'Attar, Shaikh Farid-al-Din." In *Encyclopedia Iranica I*, 20–5.

Ritter, H. *The Ocean of the Soul: Men, the World and God in the Stories of Farid al-Din 'Attar*, transl. J. O'Kane. Leiden: Brill, 2003.

Shafi'i-Kadkani, M.R. *Zabür-i Parsi: Nigahi bi Zindagi wa Ghazalha-yi 'Attar.* Tehran: Agah, 1378 (AHS/1999).

AUTOBIOGRAPHICAL WRITINGS

Extended first-person narrative was a recognized and frequently practiced form of writing in premodern Arabic, Persian, and Turkish. The earliest known example in Arabic is the autobiography of the physician Burzoe, translated from Sanskrit into Pahlavi in Sasanian times and later from Pahlavi into Arabic by Ibn al-Muqaffa' (d. ca. 759 CE). The author describes his search for a satisfactory belief system, his rejection of formal religion, and his adoption of asceticism. More directly influential, however, were translations from Greek. The self-bibliographies of the Roman physician Galen inspired the Nestorian translator Hunayn ibn Ishaq (d. 873 or 877) to write a similar catalog of his own works and possibly to also write— or have written for him—a defense against the accusations of iconoclasm brought against him by his co-religionists. Similarly, the life of Socrates served as a model for al-Razi (also known as Rhazes, d. 925 or 935), who wrote a defense of his own pursuit of the philosophical life. The tradition of philosophical autobiography was later followed by Ibn Sina (also known as Avicenna, d. 1036) and Ibn al-Haytham (also known as Alhazen, d. ca. 1039). The related genre of autobiographies by physicians is exemplified by the work of Ibn Ridwan (d. 1061), who includes details about his humble birth, his struggle for recognition, and his unhappy family life, along with a description of a typical workday.

Another productive strand of first-person narrative was that of the mystics. The first such texts to have survived are those of al-Muhasibi (d. c. 857) and al-Hakim al-Tirmidhi (d. between 905 and 910). The former is a brief account of the author's conversion experience, whereas the latter begins with the author's birth and ends with the revelation of the sublime Name of God—not to the author but to his wife. The most famous example in this genre, the autobiography of al-Ghazali (d. 1111), combines the philosophical and mystical modes of self-presentation. The author describes the crisis of faith brought on by his study of philosophy, his subsequent search for truth among representatives of different Muslim traditions, and his final decision to join the Sufi mystics. Later Sufi biographies include those of Ruzbihan al-Baqli (d. 1209), who describes the mystical visions that he received beginning at the age of fifteen; Rukn al-Dawla al-Simnani (d. 1336), who served as a companion to a Buddhist prince before undergoing a conversion experience on the battlefield; and 'Abd al-Wahhab al-Sha'rani (d. 1565), whose extensive autobiography offers a detailed account of his personal and professional life. There are also autobiographical accounts of conversion to Islam, including that of the Jew Samaw'al al-Maghribi (d. 1174) and the Christian Anselmo Turmeda (d. 1432?).

To be included among works of an autobiographical character are memoirs, which combine descriptions of the author's own experience with accounts of contemporary events. Examples include the works of Ja'far al-Hajib (d. ca. 954), a partisan of the first Fatimid caliph; al-Mu'ayyad al-Shirazi (d. 1077), a Fatimid missionary and holy warrior; Ibn Buluqqin (d. ca. 1090), the last Zirid ruler of Granada; Abu Bakr al-Baydhaq (d. after 1164), a companion of Ibn Tumart, the founder of the Almohad dynasty; Umara al-Yamani (d. 1175), a poet executed by Saladin for his Fatimid sympathies; Usama ibn Munqidh (d. 1188), who provides a description of the European crusaders; and 'Imad al-Din al-Isfahani (d. 1201), whose account of Saladin's reign emphasizes his own role in the events he describes. Works of this type are sometimes difficult to separate from the autobiographies of historians, such as those by Abu Shama (d. 1268), a historian of Damascus, and Ibn Khaldun (d. 1406), whose autobiography—originally an appendix to his work on history—records his meeting with Tamerlane.

Aside from autobiographies that appear as more or less independent works, there are many examples that take the form of entries in biographical dictionaries. In some cases, biographers interviewed their subjects and produced entries of an autobiographical character. In other cases, subjects prepared accounts of themselves to be used by their biographers. An example of both cases is the entry about Ibn al-'Adim (d. 1262) by Yaqut al-Hamawi (d. 1229), which combines extracts from the subject's autobiography with oral testimony taken during the course of an interview with the author. Biographers and historians commonly included an entry about themselves in their works. Many of these entries are concise accounts of the author's education, but some—such as that of the Shi'i jurist Yusuf al-Bahrani (d. 1772)— contain information of a more personal character. Occasionally a religious scholar would abandon the convention of self-restraint and write an extended account of his career. The best-known example is the autobiography of the Hadith scholar, linguist, exegete, jurist, and historian al-Suyuti (d. 1505), which is organized thematically rather than chronologically.

The convention of writing autobiographies was carried from Arabic into Persian and Turkish. Persian examples include the autobiography of Shah Tahmasp (d. 1576) and the poet Mir Muhammad Taqi (d. 1810). The most famous example in the Turkic languages is the lively autobiography of Babur (d. 1530), the founder of the Mughal dynasty. There are also many examples of first-person narratives in Ottoman Turkish, including the autobiography of the historian Mustafa Ali (d. 1600).

Premodern Muslim scholars came to recognize self-narrative as a distinct genre. In the preface to his autobiography, al-Suyuti lists eight predecessors who had written similar accounts of themselves. For al-Suyuti and many of his predecessors, the pretext for writing such an account was "to speak of the bounty of God" (an allusion to Qur'an 93:11). Authors freely list their honors and achievements, because doing otherwise would be a sign of ingratitude. They were also willing to admit their failures and shortcomings, because doing so only emphasizes God's mercy in having guided them to the right path. However, their works differ from those written in the confessional mode that is common in the Christian tradition, where the author exposes his transgressions in the hope of gaining absolution for himself and providing a lesson for others. Muslim autobiographers are often forthcoming about themselves, albeit in different ways. Personal characteristics commonly appear in anecdotes about childhood, in stories of dreams, in reflections about the onset of old age, and, above all, in poetry.

Until the late twentieth century, Western scholarship tended to assume that there were relatively few premodern first-person narratives in Arabic, Persian, and Turkish. Until recently, Western scholarship has argued that these texts—with certain exceptions, such as the self-narratives of al-Ghazali or Babur—were not genuine autobiographies, because they were insufficiently personal in character. The assumption of relative paucity is now being revised: a recent study of the genre has found more than eighty pre–twentieth century examples in Arabic alone. Similarly, growing familiarity with non-Western traditions has led scholars away from the search for "genuine autobiography" and toward a reexamination of the strategies of self-presentation in different times and cultures.

MICHAEL COOPERSON

See also Babur; Ibn al-Muqaffa; Hunayn ibn Ishaq; al-Razi, or Rhazes; Ibn Sina; Mystics; Samaw'al al-Maghribi; Anselmo Turmeda; Usama ibn Munqidh; Ibn Khaldun; Yusuf al-Bahrani; al-Suyuti

Further Reading

Reynolds, Dwight F., ed. *Interpreting the Self: Autobiography in the Arabic Literary Tradition.* Berkeley: University of California Press, 2001. Available at: http://www.ucpress.edu/books/pages/8736.html.

AYA SOPHIA

The first Aya Sophia was built in 326 CE and was an aisled basilica linked to its palace by corridors and stairs. It was destroyed and rebuilt twice, and it finally acquired its present form during the Justinian period. The first church was begun during the reign of Constantine (324–337), and it was completed by Constantinus (337–361). It was set on fire during the banishment of St. John Chrysostom. However, the rededication of the second church took place in 415, under Theodosius II (408–450). The earlier church on the site was destroyed by fire during the Nika riot of 532; unfortunately, no description of either of the pre-Justinian churches has survived. Justinian ordered a new church to be built, and five years later it was solemnly inaugurated. Justinian's church, which was designed by the architects Anthemus and Isidore, was dedicated in 537.

The general plan of the building is a near square that is divided into a large central nave and two side aisles. The central nave is covered by a colossal dome that is supported on the east and west by half domes. However, the ground plan of the building is not of prime importance; the essential features of this architecture are the great central dome and the piers, arches, and subsidiary vaults that hold it up. The central nave is flanked by side aisles and preceded by a narthex and atrium on the west side, providing a gradual transition from the street to the interior of the church. The side aisles and narthex were surmounted by a U-shaped gallery. The longitudinal axis of the nave terminated in an apse, which formed the visual focus of the interior. The sanctuary, containing the altar, lay just before the apse and extended into the nave. The great dome, which is the dominant theme of the building's design, rises above the nave. To place a dome above a rectilinear plan of a basilica required some transition. A square central bay is defined by four great piers, and, above, the pendentives (spherical triangles) appear at the corners to bridge the transition from square to circle. It is actually the four great arches that are most significant in the structural system, and, along with the pendentives, they adjust the weight of the dome to the four piers. The present dome rises about fifty-five meters above the floor.

When seen from the outside, the great church seems to rise up harmoniously from level to level to the very top of the central dome; however, its soaring lines are by no means free from a somewhat excessive ponderousness. Inside, on the other hand, everything conspires to produce the impression of an immense space that is ideally organized. From the main door to the nave, looking along the axis of the church toward the apse, the beholder can appreciate the noble sweep and majestic proportions of the vast interior, with its supporting columns and walls covered with polychromatic marble.

Much damage has been inflicted on the building by several earthquakes. The dome collapsed in 557, and it was partially repaired in 989. In 1346, another earthquake damaged the dome, and this time it was restored by Astras and the Italian Giovanni Peralta. The present dome thus represents these three periods of reconstruction.

The church of St. Sophia was converted into a mosque soon after the conquest of Constantinople. What makes the monument an Islamic building (a mosque) are the additions to the interior and exterior from all periods of the Ottoman Empire. A marble mihrab has been erected, and several mahfils were built during different periods. Of the four minarets, that at the southeast corner represents an original construction of Mehmed II. The northeast minaret was then erected by Bayezid II, and the one at the southwest corner was begun during the reign of Selim II, but it was unfinished at his death in 1574; it was completed by Murad III on his accession to the throne. The latter minaret at the northwest corner had the architect Sinan as its designer. Other structures of significance outside of the main building are the sultans' tombs to the south of the building.

Significant restorations and repairs were carried out during the Ottoman period. In 1573, the entire building underwent a thorough renovation, because various buttresses were in need of repair. In 1847, another extensive restoration was undertaken with the supervision of the Fossati brothers. Between these major phases there were various minor repairs and consolidations, both within and outside of the mosque. In November 1934, the Turkish Ministry of Education, acting on the proposal of Atatürk, converted the monument into a museum.

SUAT ALP

See also Istanbul; Ottoman Empire

Further Reading

Emerson, W., and R.L. Van Nice. "Hagia Sophia and the First Minaret Erected After The Conquest of Constantinople." *American Journal of Archaeology* LIV: 28–40.

Grabar, André. *The Golden Age of Justinian.* New York: Odyssey Press, 1967.

Kırımtayıf, Süleyman. *Converted Byzantine Churches in Istanbul. Their Transformation into Mosques and Masjids.* Istanbul: Ege Yayınları, 2001.

Krautheimer, R. *Early Christian and Byzantine Architecture.* Baltimore, Md, and Victoria, BC, Canada: Penguin Books, 1960.

Mainstone, R.J. *Hagia Sophia. Architecture, Structure and Liturgy of Justinian's Great Church.* London: Thames and Hudson, 1988.

Mango, C. *Byzantine Architecture.* New York: Harry N. Abrams Inc., 1976.

Mathews Thomas, F. *The Early Churches of Constantinople: Architecture and Liturgy.* State College, Penn: The Pennsylvania State University Press, 1971.

Müller-Wiener, W. *Bildlexikon zur Topographie Istanbuls: Byzantion—Konstantinopolis—Istanbul bis zum Beginn des 17. Jahrhunderts.* Tubingen: Archäologisches Institut, 1977.

Rice, D.T. *Constantinople from Byzantium to İstanbul.* New York: Stein and Day Publishers, 1965.

'AYN JALUT

'Ayn Jalut ("The Spring of Goliath"), located in the Jezreel Valley in northern Palestine at the foothills of the Gilboa range, is the site of an indecisive encounter between Saladin and the Franks (September 1183 CE) and, more importantly, of a crucial battle between the Mamluks and Mongols on September 3, 1260.

The Mongols under Hülegü, the grandson of Genghis Khan, had taken Baghdad at the beginning of 1258 and put Caliph al-Musta'sim to death, thereby effectively ending the 'Abbasid dynasty. From there, Hülegü, who was also known by the title *ilkhan*, moved to Azerbaijan. After desultory negotiations with the Ayyubid sultan of Syria, al-Nasir Yusuf, the Ilkhan advanced with a large army into Syria at the end of 1259 and put Aleppo under siege at the beginning of the following year. It was taken within a week (although its citadel held out for another month before it capitulated). Hülegü himself first remained in the northern part of the country, but he sent south a forward division numbering some ten thousand horsemen under his trusted general Kitbuqa. The latter gained control of Damascus without opposition and set about subjugating the surrounding area. Mongol raiders advanced as far as Gaza and Hebron, entering Jerusalem and the area north of Karak in trans-Jordan. Hülegü, meanwhile, had withdrawn from Syria, and he returned to Azerbaijan with the remainder of his army, perhaps as a result of news about the death of his brother, the Great Khan Möngke, and the resulting political disorders, or perhaps as a result of logistical reasons (i.e., a lack of pastureland and water for his cavalry-based army in Syria during the dry summer months).

The Mamluk Sultan Qutuz, who had acceded to the throne only at the end of 1259, decided during the summer of 1260 not only to reject Hülegü's demands for unconditional surrender but to set out for Syria to take advantage of the presence of a now relatively small Mongol force. In this he was supported by Baybars, his hitherto bitter opponent. The Sultan succeeded in cajoling the recalcitrant Mamluk officers (as a result of fear of the Mongols) out of Cairo, and on July 15, 1260, the Mamluk army set out for Syria. After crossing the Sinai Peninsula, the Mamluk advanced guard, under Baybars, encountered a small Mongol force at Gaza, which withdrew and alerted Kitbuqa to the unexpected appearance of the Mamluks. Qutuz and his army advanced northward, bypassing Crusader-held cities, until they reached Acre. The Franks wisely decided to maintain neutrality in the upcoming battle, but they did give supplies to the nearby Mamluks. From Acre, the Mamluk advance guard (again under Baybars) entered the Jezreel Valley. Meanwhile, Qutuz gathered his officers and gave them an inspiring pep talk, emphasizing the need to defend Islam, their families, and their position in Egypt.

The Mongols, however, had not been idle. When they received word of the Mamluk advance, Kitbuqa—still in Damascus—moved south to meet the enemy. He took up a position at 'Ayn Jalut, some fifteen kilometers northwest of Baysan (Beth Shean), which was well watered and provided with pasturage. Kitbuqa also sent out scouts, who encountered the Mamluk advance force. Skirmishing commenced, and it seems to have been fairly wide ranging. In the end, Baybars came upon the Kitbuqa's force near 'Ayn Jalut. He withdrew a bit and was soon joined by Qutuz with the main Mamluk army. Final preparations were thereupon made for the battle by both sides.

The battle commenced on the morning of Friday, September 3, 1260 (AH 25 Ramadan 658). The Mamluks, who appear to have had a certain numerical advantage, advanced first, but they were preempted by a Mongol attack. Both armies were composed mainly—if not exclusively—of mounted archers, and the battle settled into a series of attacks and counterattacks of waves of these troops. The leadership and pluck of Qutuz, who was found at the head of his troops, is mentioned in the Mamluk sources. He did not lose his head when the left wing of the Mamluk army began to waver, but rather organized his troops

and led a counterattack that supposedly won the day. No less important was the death in battle of Kitbuqa, whose bravery is lauded in the pro-Mongol sources. He was shot down during the fighting, and this probably led to a disintegration of the Mongol army. Also important was the sudden withdrawal of a group of Muslim Syrian troopers who had been pressed into the Mongol army, thereby leaving a gap in the Mongol line. The relative numerical superiority of the Mamluks (whose exact numbers are not clear) also had its effect as the battle wore on. The Mongols fled the battle, and the Mamluk squadrons under Baybars—as well as local farmers and nomads—killed many in the confusion. The remaining Mongols and their supporters withdrew from Syria across the Euphrates River.

The Mamluk sources note the importance of the similarity between the two forces: only soldiers of similar provenance, fighting with comparable methods (masses of mounted archers), had a chance of beating the Mongols. The effects of the battle were significant: Syria became an integral part of the centralized Mamluk Sultanate based in Cairo; the fledging Mamluk state (founded in 1250) was given an important basis for its legitimization; and the myth of the invincible Mongols was weakened, if not shattered. The Mamluks were aware that they had defeated only a small part of the Mongol army, and they soon began preparations for meeting a more serious threat. In any event, Qutuz was not to enjoy his victory for long: he was soon assassinated by Baybars, who assumed the throne and inaugurated one of the longest and most successful reigns in the history of the Mamluk Sultanate.

REUVEN AMITAI

See also Baybars I; Genghis Khan; Ilkhanids; Mamluks; Mongol Warfare; Mongols; Slavery, Military

Further Reading

Amitai-Preiss, Reuven. *Mongols and Mamluks: The Mamluk-Ilkhanid War, 126-1281*, Cambridge: Cambridge University Press, 1995.

Jackson, Peter. "The Crisis in the Holy Land in 1260." *English Historical Review* 95 (1980): 481–513.

Lewis, Bernard. "'Ayn Djalut." In *Encyclopaedia of Islam*, 2nd ed. 1:786.

Morgan, David O. "The Mongols in Syria, 1260–1300." In *Crusade and Settlement*, ed. Peter Edbury. Cardiff: University College Cardiff Press, 1985.

Smith, John Masson, Jr. "'Ayn Jalut: Mamluk Success or Mongol Failure?" *Harvard Journal of Asiatic Studies* 44 (1984): 307–45.

Thorau, Peter. "The Battle of 'Ayn Jalut: A Re-examination." In *Crusade and Settlement*, ed. Peter Edbury. Cardiff: University College Cardiff Press, 1985.

AYYUBIDS

The Ayyubid confederation was established by al-Malik al-Nasir Salah al-Din Yusuf b. Ayyub (Saladin), a Kurdish military commander in the service of Nur al-Din b. Zangi. Saladin took control of Egypt in 1171 CE, and, from this Egyptian base, brought much of Bilad al-Sham (Syria) and the Jazira (upper Mesopotamia) under his rule. After his death in 1193, control of the many cities and provinces of Saladin's empire was divided between his sons, his brother, his nephews, and their respective descendants. Although these princes owed allegiance to whomever was recognized as the Ayyubid Sultan, within their own territories they were autonomous. Ayyubid history after Saladin is thus characterized by complex and shifting webs of alliances and rivalries between these various Ayyubid princes, and these webs were complicated by the presence of the Crusader states, whose forces were occasionally drawn into intra-Ayyubid conflicts. (As R.S. Humphreys recently put it, the Ayyubids were "reluctant warriors" against the Franks.) Nevertheless, the political history of the post-Saladin era was usually dominated by the Ayyubid who ruled Egypt. For most of the first half of the thirteenth century, this role was filled by Saladin's brother al-Malik al-'Adil Sayf al-Din Abu Bakr Muhammad and his descendants.

Al-'Adil (d. 1218), who was known to the Crusaders as Sephadin, was supreme within the Ayyubid dominions from 1200 to 1218. He was in Egypt when the armies of the Fifth Crusade arrived in the Nile delta in May 1218. After al-'Adil died in August 1218, his son al-Malik al-Kamil Muhammad (d. 1238) assumed the sultanate, although not all of the other Ayyubids acquiesced. Al-Kamil's dealings with the Crusaders over the course of his reign were tightly interwoven with his relations with his relatives. Al-Kamil's lifting of the Crusader occupation of Damietta (1219–1221), for example, was accomplished with the assistance of his brothers al-Malik al-Ashraf Musa in the Jazira and al-Malik al-Mu'azzam 'Isa in Syria. However, in 1227, when the armies of Emperor Frederick II threatened Egypt, al-Kamil was engaged in a power struggle with al-Mu'azzam, and he therefore offered Jerusalem to Frederick to avoid an invasion of Egypt. The emperor refused. Al-Kamil's position was subsequently strengthened by Al-Mu'azzam's death in late 1227, but al-Kamil continued negotiations with Frederick after he arrived in Acre in 1228. These negotiations led to the establishment of a limited truce, signed in February 1129, that restored an unfortified Jerusalem to the Franks for ten years, five months, and forty days. Both the emperor and the sultan were severely criticized by their respective co-religionists for this agreement.

Al-Kamil died in 1238, and two years later his son al-Malik al-Salih Ayyub assumed control of Egypt. Al-Salih was schooled in the ways of Ayyubid rivalry. To strengthen his position, he purchased and trained a corps of military slaves (mamluks). Called the Bahri Mamluks because their barracks were on an island in the Nile (bahr al-nil), this 800- to 1,000-man force was the core of al-Salih's military forces. The Bahri Mamluks played a significant role in fighting and eventually defeating the forces of King Louis IX of France when the Fifth Crusade invaded the Egyptian Delta (1249–1250). Al-Salih died in November 1249 in the midst of that invasion, and control of Egypt soon passed to his son, al-Malik al-Mu'azzam Turanshah. Turanshah quickly alienated his father's mamluks, who, fearing loss of position or even life, revolted against Turanshah and murdered him in April 1250.

The events of the ten years after the murder of Turanshah are complex, but they resulted in a complete Mamluk takeover of Egypt by 1260. The Ayyubids in Syria and the Jazira subsequently fell to either the Mamluks or the Mongols, although the Ayyubid principality in Hamah was maintained until 1341 by the Mamluk Sultanate.

WARREN C. SCHULTZ

See also Fatimids; Mamluks; Mongols; Saladin or Salah al-Din; Sultan

Primary Sources

Abu'l-Fida'. *The Memoirs of a Syrian Prince*, transl. P.M. Holt. Wiesbaden: Franz Steiner Verlag, 1983.
Al-Maqrizi. *A History of the Ayyubid Sultans of Egypt*, transl. R.J.C. Broadhurst. Boston: Twayne Publishers, 1980.

Further Reading

Balog, Paul. *The Coinage of the Ayyubids*. London: Royal Numismatic Society, 1980.
Hillenbrand, Carole. *The Crusades: Islamic Perspectives*. Chicago: Fitzroy Dearborn, 1999.
Humphreys, R. Stephen. *From Saladin to the Mongols: The Ayyubids of Damascus, 1193–1260*. Albany: State University of New York Press, 1977.
———. "Ayyubids, Mamluks and the Latin East in the Thirteenth Century." *Mamluk Studies Review* II (1998): 1–17.

AZHAR, AL-

Located in Cairo, Al-Azhar is one of the earliest Jami' (mosque/university) complexes in the Muslim world. It was founded by the Fatimid Ismaili dynasty; the dynasty's Caliph, Imam Muizz li-Din Allah, established Cairo as his capital in 969–970 CE. The complex is so named in memory of the title *al-zahra* ("the luminous"), which is associated with Fatima, the daughter of the Prophet and the wife of the first Shia Imam, Ali, from whom the Fatimids claimed direct descent.

Although it served initially as a congregational mosque for Friday prayers, it soon developed into a seat of learning. It has continued to exercise this role throughout Muslim history, attaining recognition first as the foremost center for Shi'i Ismaili learning and then, after the twelfth century, as a major Sunni educational institution.

During the Fatimid period, it developed into a center for higher learning and was richly endowed to support students, teachers, and one of the largest libraries of the time in the Muslim world. The curriculum was diverse; among the sessions offered were dedicated classes for women on topics including law and Qur'anic studies, and there were special sessions devoted to advanced hermeneutics and religious interpretations in Ismaili intellectual contexts.

After a period of neglect under the Ayyubids, who supplanted the Fatimids and ruled Egypt from 1171 to 1252, Al-Azhar was revived by the Sunni Mamluks (1252–1517) and became a center of Qur'anic teaching and Shafi'i jurisprudence. The subjects traditionally associated with the Sunni madrasas of the time came to predominate, although Al-Azhar remained open to influences, including Sufism. During the Ottoman period (1517–1805), Al-Azhar continued to be a major center, attracting Sunni ulama and students from across the Muslim world. Theology and law remained the main foci of study and research.

With the end of Ottoman rule and the onset of European occupation and influence, Al-Azhar's role began to change. Under French occupation, it became a seat of resistance and was bombarded by the French army. With the rise to power of Muhammad Ali in 1811 and his policies of centralized state control, Al-Azhar was forced to accept changes to its traditional autonomy, and it responded by bringing about internal changes in its organization, requirements, and regulations. It also developed a network of preparatory schools all over Egypt from which it could recruit students as well as extend its influence on religious education in the state.

During the early part of the twentieth century, Al-Azhar became the locus for reformist views of Islam, mainly under the influence of Muhammad Abduh (1849–1905), who taught there. Although some of his views did not gain acceptance, a change in the intellectual climate had begun to take hold. During the 1930s, Al-Azhar was granted university status and reorganized into academic units. It started to publish a journal, added new disciplines to its curriculum, and established women's colleges. Its influence in the wider Sunni Muslim world expanded, and many future international religious leaders and teachers received their training there. During the 1990s, there were approximately six thousand international students enrolled at Al-Azhar, and they represented seventy-five countries. From time to time, the institution has taken controversial positions on issues that affect Muslims and Muslim societies, as well as on international affairs. With the rise of other religious institutions and centers of Muslim learning in the Middle East and the Sunni world, Al-Azhar lost many of its best faculty members to these institutions. Having recently entered the world of the Internet, Al-Azhar continues its influential role as a place of learning and leader of opinion on Muslim issues and affairs in a more globalized environment.

AZIM NANJI

Further Reading

Dodge, B. *Al-Azhar. A Millennium of Muslim Learning*. Washington: Middle East Institute, 1961.

Halm, Heinz. "The Fatimids." In *Institutions of Learning*. London: The Institute of Ismaili Studies and I.B. Tauris, 1998.

B

BABAR [BABUR]

Born in 1483 CE in the Farghana region of Central Asia, Babar, the founder of the renowned Mughal dynasty in India, claimed an illustrious pedigree by virtue of descent from two important rulers—Timur (Timurlane) (through his father, Umar Shaikh Mirza) and Chingiz Khan (through his mother, Qutluq Nigar Khanum). His father was one of several princes, all descendants of Timur, who engaged in constant rivalry and battles for control over territory in fifteenth-century Central Asia. In 1494, as a result of a fall from a collapsing wall, Babar's father died, leaving the eleven-year-old boy to succeed him to rule the kingdom of Farghana. Like his father, Babar, too, spent much of his early political career engaged in endless wars and intrigues contending with his Timurid cousins for suzerainty over territory in Transoxiana and Khurasan, particularly the cities of Samarqand, Bukhara, and Herat. In these internecine Timurid struggles, his fortunes were mixed. He found it difficult to assert his authority over any city in the region for a sustained length of time. For example, by age 30, he had won and lost Samarqand three times. Particularly intense were his conflicts with Shaibani Khan, an Uzbeg prince, whose armies managed to drive Babar and his followers out of Transoxiana to territories farther to the south. There, Babar was eventually successful in establishing control over Kabul, Ghazni, and Badakshan.

It was in Kabul, conquered in 1504, that Babar established a home base, away from the turmoil of Transoxiana. The relatively stable life there allowed him to establish a cultured court on the Timurid model and pursue his hobbies, particularly gardening. However, because Kabul was rather poor in terms of its economic resources, the wealth of India tempted Babar to look eastward. He organized several raiding expeditions into the region, bringing back with him much booty. Success encouraged him to penetrate even deeper into Indian territory, eventually threatening the Lodis, an Afghan dynasty that ruled from Agra. In 1526, in the course of his fifth expedition into India, he defeated Sultan Ibrahim Lodi at the battle of Panipat; in the following year, he defeated a coalition of Rajput forces led by Rana Sanga. Although these victories marked the beginning of his control over substantial territory in India, the task of consolidating and strengthening what eventually came to be called the Mughal empire was not to be completed until the reign of his grandson, Akbar (ruled 1556–1605).

In India, although military expeditions continued to make considerable demands on his time and energy, Babar found more opportunity to take up leisurely pursuits. He commissioned several beautiful Timurid-style gardens in North India, personally supervising their development. These gardens were intended to remind him of Kabul, providing a respite from the heat of the summer months. Babar also had literary talents, being a particularly gifted poet in Turkish. Once, during an illness, he occupied himself by reorganizing the words of a couplet in 504 ways. He is particularly renowned for his remarkable autobiography, *The Baburnama*. Written in Chagatay

Turkish, these memoirs not only record his early struggles for power in Central Asia but also contain detailed descriptions of his newly acquired Indian territory and various aspects of the social, cultural, and economic life of its inhabitants. The memoirs reveal his passion for nature through his keen observations of India's fauna and flora, which he describes with the precision of a naturalist, obviously delighting in attention to minor details. Aside from his horticultural and literary pursuits, Babar was also interested in mysticism and spirituality, as evidenced by his translation into Turkish verse of *Risala-i walidiyya*, a treatise by the venerated Naqshbandi sufi teacher, Ubaidullah Ahrar, whom Babar admired greatly. Victory in Hindustan did not, however, mean that Babar, and later his descendants, gave up hope of one day conquering their ancestral homeland of Farghana, and the city of Samarqand. Babar disapproved of much of what he saw and experienced in India and, notwithstanding the power and wealth he enjoyed there, he always longed for Kabul. The climate of India, the hardships he had experienced in his youth, and the heavy use of alcohol and drugs all took their toll on Babar's health, for he was frequently sick as he grew older. He died December 26, 1530, after a short illness, and was temporarily buried in Agra. His longing for Kabul was fulfilled posthumously when, several years after his death, his body was returned to that city for burial in his favorite garden.

ALI ASANI

Further Reading

Gascoigne, Bamber. *The Great Moghuls*. London: Constable, 1998.
Thackston, Wheeler. Trans and Ed. *The Baburnama. The Memoirs of Babur, Prince and Emperor*. Washington and New York: The Smithsonian Institution and Oxford University Press, 1996.

BACKGAMMON

The game of backgammon is first mentioned in Bhartṛhari's *Vairāgyaśataka* (p. 39), composed around the late sixth or early seventh century CE. The use of dice for the game is another indication of its Indic origin, since dice and gambling were a favorite pastime in ancient India. The rules of the game, however, first appeared in the Middle Persian text *Wīzāriśn ī Čatrang ud Nihišn ī Nēw-Ardaxšīr* (*Explanation of Chess and Invention of Backgammon*), composed in the sixth century during the rule of the Sasanian king Khousro I (530–571). The text assigns its invention to the Persian sage Wuzurgmihr (Arabic/Persian) Buzarjumihr/Buzorgmihr, who was the minister of King Khousro I, as a challenge for the Indian sages. According to the Middle Persian text, the name that Wuzurgmihr gives the game of backgammon is *Nēw-Ardaxšīr*, ("Noble is Ardaxšīr"), in memory of Ardaxšīr I (224–240), the founder of the Sasanian dynasty. *Nēw-ardaxšīr* (Middle Persian) > *nard* or *nardašīr* (Persian and Arabic), also found in *nrdšyr* (Babylonian Talmud), has had popular etymologies among Arab lexicographers, composed of *nard* and *šīr*.

According to the *al-Fihrist* of Ibn Nadim, Wuzurgmihr is also said to have written a commentary on astronomy, the *Anthologiae* of Vettius Valens, which is lost, but fragments of the Arabic translation of the Middle Persian version exist. The reason for mentioning the preoccupation of Wuzurgmihr with astronomy and astrology is the cosmological explanation of the game of backgammon in the Middle Persian text. Wuzurgmihr's explanation of the game is analogous to the processes of the cosmos and human life. He makes fate the primary reason for what happens to mankind, and the roll of the dice in the game performs the function of fate.

Wuzurgmihr explains that the pieces of the game represent humans and their function in the universe, which is governed by the seven planets and the twelve zodiac signs. The shape of the game board is likened to *spandarmad zamīg* (the goddess of the earth). The pieces represent the thirty nights and days. The die represents the *axtarān* and *spihr* (constellations and firmament), which by their turn and position (number) decide one's movement and predict human life. The "one" on the die, according to the text, represents Ohrmazd's omnipotence and his oneness. The "two" on the die represents *mēnōg* and *gētīg*, the spiritual and the material world. The three represents the three stages of heaven in Zoroastrianism, *humat and hūxt and huwaršt,* preceding paradise. The four represents another cosmological expression, *čahār sōg ī gētīg,* "the four corners of the world." The five represents the five luminaries according to the text, which are the divisions of the heavens. According to the *Avesta*, the heavens had four stations, which were the stars, the moon, the sun, and the eternal light. Here we have in a disorderly fashion the divisions of the heavens into the following stations: the sun, the moon, the stars, fire, and, finally, the heavenly brightness (Pananio 1995, 205–226). Finally, the six represents the *šaš gāhānbar,* or the six seasonal feasts, according to the Zoroastrian religion. The hitting of pieces is likened to killing, and when the pieces come back to the game it signifies the act of resurrection according to Zoroastrian cosmology.

A silver-gilded hemispherical bowl housed at the Arthur M. Sackler Gallery depicts several important scenes from the Sasanian period. They include a scene of marriage, a wrestling scene, and several other scenes, including a scene of two people playing backgammon. One can conclude that this bowl represents the things that mattered in the courtly life (Harper 1978, 75). One can suggest that the bowl represents the activities in which a noble should engage or have knowledge of. These include wrestling, being informed in religious precepts and ritual, marrying and having offspring, playing instruments, and being able to play board games, that is, backgammon (Daryaee 2002, 292). The other pictorial evidence for the game of backgammon comes from Central Asia, from the city of Panjikent. Among the wall paintings from Panjikent, which are now housed in the Hermitage museum in St. Petersburg, Russia, there is a scene of what can be called court activity. The painting shows two people playing a board game, which in all probability is a backgammon game, along with several other personages beside them (Bussagli 1963, 46–47). A nimbus appears to encircle the head of one of the players, who has his right hand raised as a gesture of victory. The man seated on the left has his left hand raised, showing the bent forefinger. A figure behind the victorious person also appears to be pointing to the loser with the bent forefinger. A fourteenth-century manuscript of the Šāhnāme contains two scenes, one at the court of King Khousro I and the second at the court of the Indian ruler Dēwišarm. In one of the scenes, Wuzurgmihr is seated on the floor with three other Persians, all with white turbans. In front of the Persian sage is a backgammon board. The Indian king is seated on his throne and is surrounded by Indian sages who are painted darker and have darker turbans. Wuzurgmihr has his right hand pointing to the backgammon board, which probably means that he is either challenging the Indian sages or explaining the rules of the game after the Indian sages have been dumbfounded (Wilkinson 1968, xii). It is particularly interesting to note that one of the two older Indian sages, who have white beards, has his hand by his mouth, symbolizing his amazement or perplexity.

The Arabs were familiar with backgammon as early as the time of the Prophet Muhammad and know that the game was popular (Rosenthal 1975, 88). Thaʿālibī relates a popular story that when the Arab Muslims conquered the Sasanian capital of Ctesiphon, they found a set of backgammon pieces belonging to Khousro II (CE 590–628), pieces of which were made of coral and turquoise. There were those opposed to the game, especially the companions of the prophet, such as Abu Ḥurayra (d. 676), who refused to meet Muslims who had played backgammon. He is also thought to have said, "One who plays *nard* with stakes is like one who eats pork; one who plays without stakes is like one who puts his hand in pig's blood; and one who watches the game is like one who looks at pork meat" (Al-Bukhārī 1375, 326–328). By the eighth century C.E., the four schools of Islamic jurisprudence considered the game of backgammon *ḥarām* (illicit). We, however, have many textual references to the game being played at the court in many regions of the Islamic Near East, which means that the game may have been played by the masses as well, and, in fact, its popularity confirms this suggestion.

During the early 'Abbasid period (750–900), the game of backgammon was popular both at the court of Harun al-Rashid and that of his son, al-Ma'mun. It is said that Ma'mun liked to play backgammon, because if he lost, he could place the blame on the dice, meaning fate (Falkner 1892, 115). The same may be said of the game of chess, which was seen by many Muslims as a form of gambling. Medieval authors justified the game by stating that as long as it was played for mental exercise it would be beneficial. The *Qābūs-nāme* dedicates a chapter to the games of chess and backgammon, where the proper etiquette of playing and when and to whom one should lose or win is discussed. It is strictly stated that one should not make bets on the games, and only then does playing the game become a proper activity (Yusefī 1375, 77). During the Seljuk period, it is reported that Alp Arsalan was also fond of backgammon (Gazvini 1331, 68–69).

In Persian poetry there are many references to the game by Anwarī, Asadī, Ferdowsī, Khāghānī, Manūčehrī, Mas'ūd Sa'd, Mokhtārī, Mowlavī, Sa'dī, and Sanā'ī (Mo'īn 1972:421–422). Several of the poets place the game in its original cosmological function, which means they have stayed faithful to Wuzurgmihr's description of the game. Manūčehrī gives the following couplet in regard to human fate and the cosmos: "The firmament is like the victorious looking backgammon (game), Its pieces from coral, and the quality of pearl."

TOURAJ DARYAEE

Further Reading

Al-Bukhārī. *al-Adab al-mufrad*, ed. M.F. 'Abd al-Bākī, Cairo, 1375.

Bussagli, M. *Painting of Central Asia*. The World Publishing Company, Ohio, 1963.

Henry Corbin. *Spiritual Body and Celestial Earth, from Mazdean Iran to Shī'ite Iran*. Bollingen Series XCI: 2, Princeton, NJ: Princeton University Press, 1977.

Daryaee, T. "Mind, Body and the Cosmos: The Game of Chess and Backgammon in Ancient Persia." *Iranian Studies* 35, 4 (2002): 281–312.

Falkner, E. *Games of Ancient and Oriental and How to Play Them: Being the Games of the Ancient Egyptians, the*

Hiera Gramme of the Greeks, the Ludus Latrunculorum of the Romans and the Oriental Games of Chess, Draughts, Backgammon and Magic Squares. New York: Dover Publications, 1892.

Ghazvini, M. (ed.). *Čahār maghāle.* Tehran: Armaghān Publishers, 1331.

Harper, P.O. *The Royal Hunter, Art of the Sasanian Empire.* New York: The Asia Society, 1978.

Loghat Nāme Dehkhodā, ed. M. Mo'īn and Dj. Shahidī, Letter N, Fas. 10, Tehran, 1972.

Pananio, A. "Uranographia Iranica I: The Three Heavens in the Zoroastrian Tradition and the Mesopotamian Background," *Au carrefourdes religions, Mélanges offerts à Philippe Gignoux,* ed. R. Gyselen, Groupe pour l'Étude de la Civilisation du Moyen-Orient, Bures-sur-Yvette (1995): 205–226.

Rosenthal, F. *Gambling in Islam.* Leiden: E.J. Brill, 1975.

Qābūs nāme (ed. Q.-H. Yusefī). Tehran: Scientific and Cultural Publishers, 1375.

Wilkinson, C.K. *Chess: East and West, Past and Present, A Selection from the Gustavus A. Pfeiffer Collection.* New York: The Metropolitan Museum of Art, 1968.

BADR AL-JAMALI

Badr al-Jamali was wazir and virtual dictator of Fatimid Egypt for more than twenty years, from 1074 to 1094 CE. Once in that position, he ruled with an iron fist, controlling all aspects of government save only the caliphal throne itself. Ethnically an Armenian, Badr was originally purchased in his youth for a relatively small sum, becoming thereafter a *mamluk* (slave) of the Syrian amir Jamal al-Dawla, hence his name al-Jamali, which indicates that he once belonged to this Jamal. When he arrived in Egypt, he was nearly sixty years old; he was over age eighty at his death in 1094. The date of his birth must accordingly be around the year 1015.

Prior to his arrival in Egypt, Badr had risen in military service over a long career to twice become governor of Damascus on behalf of the Fatimids. Over much of the same period Egypt suffered a series of internal disorders and revolts, leading to the near-total breakdown of the central government. The caliph al-Mustansir steadily lost ground against the encroaching chaos; by 1074, many parts of the country were run independently by tribal forces and renegade troops. Finally, al-Mustansir asked Badr to come to his rescue. Then the governor of Acre, Badr insisted that he bring with him his own army. In the winter of 1074, he crossed to Egypt by sea with that same army and began to rid the country of all opposition, both to the caliph and to himself. In rapid succession, he conducted a purge in the capital and a campaign in the Delta against Bedouin and various other rebels there, then marched through Upper Egypt for a similar purpose, and finally returned to the Delta to face an invading force of Seljuks intent on occupation and the overthrow of the Fatimids. In each of these separate conflicts he was victorious. In the process he restored the power of the caliph, resurrected the caliphate, and gave it new life in place of almost certain imminent death. Thanks almost solely to these decisive actions by Badr, it was to last yet another century.

As ruler, Badr brought calm and prosperity and, though noted at the time for harsh repression of all dissent, he is best known for numerous buildings, including the memorial shrine *(mashhad)*—the Juyushi—now visible on the plateau above the modern city of Cairo. He was also responsible for expanding the size of the medieval city enclosure and fortifying its walls, putting in place in the process a number of monumental gates—four of them survive—three of which, the Bab al-Futuh, Bab al-Nasr, and Bab al-Zuwayla, are easily recognized today.

At his death, just months before that of the caliph al-Mustansir, his favored son, al-Afdal Shahinshah, successfully claimed his legacy and control of the private militia that had sustained him. The son was therefore in a position to ensure that the new caliph would be approved by him, a transition he appears to have engineered to his liking, although it set in motion a major schism among the Isma'ilis, both in Egypt and elsewhere. Even so, the Fatimids survived and al-Afdal himself ruled Egypt as its military wazir (Amir al-Juyush) for almost three decades.

PAUL E. WALKER

Further Reading

Becker, C.H. "Badr al-Djamali." *Encyclopaedia of Islam,* new edition.

BADSHAHI MOSQUE, LAHORE

The late-twelfth-century Qutb mosque in Delhi was based on a well-established pillared model widely used in Islam to the west. The fourteenth-century Tughluq sultans were patrons of a variety of mosque types, including mosques built around a single courtyard with a single- or multi-aisled qiblah prayer chamber covered by three domes. It was this latter type, seen in mosques in Delhi, Jaunpur, and Gujarat, that formed the basis for the classic Mughal mosque from the sixteenth through eighteenth centuries.

The most striking early example is the 1571–1574 mosque in Fatehpur Sikri, the emperor Akbar's citadel. Built of red sandstone with marble accenting structural elements, the mosque consists of single-aisled trabeate arcades on the north, south, and east sides that frame a great open courtyard. A four-aisled prayer hall crowned with three domes marks the

Badshani Mosque (Imperial Mosque). Exterior. Built by Aurangzeb. Moghul dynasty. 1673–74. Red sandstone and marble. Credit: Bridgeman-Giraudon/Art Resource, NY. Lahore, Pakistan.

qiblah on the west. The central dome is the largest and is preceded by a massive arched niche (pishtaq) that projects into the courtyard. The mosque's aesthetics are characterized by clarity, order, and the grandeur of its controlled interior space.

In the great imperial cities of Lahore, Agra, and Delhi, the Mughals oversaw the construction of mosques of this type adjacent to the central citadel. These giant houses of worship accommodated huge numbers of the faithful and emphasized the power of Islam and the Mughal state. Where the Delhi sultans had experimented with a wide array of types, the Mughal rulers eschewed eclecticism and focused on a single, classic form.

The largest of the great imperial mosques, the Badshahi mosque in Lahore, is also the last. It was constructed under the aegis of the emperor Awrangzeb (1658–1707). Much of his reign was spent in military campaigns to suppress revolts and conquer southern India, and his attention to architecture was much more limited than that of his father, Shah Jahan (1627–1658), who had spent vast sums of money building forts, palaces, tombs, and mosques. The son was neither a great patron of palace construction

nor a ruler inclined toward the royal rituals to which Shah Jahan had paid so much attention.

The strategically important city of Lahore in the northwest was an ancient center of commerce and culture and was strategically vital because it protected the Mughal empire from potential invaders to the west. Akbar had established it as one of the Mughal capitals, and the massive citadel he built there, like the forts in Agra and Delhi, was substantially embellished by Shah Jahan. Lahore had a marked regional tradition of architecture, and the surfaces of the 1634 Mosque of Wazir Khan are decorated in colorful glazed tiles reflecting strong Iranian influence.

The supreme achievement of Awrangzeb's architectural patronage is Lahore's Badshahi Mosque (Imperial Mosque). It commemorated military campaigns to the south, particularly against the Hindu insurgent Shivaji in Maharashtra. However, Awrangzeb's efforts weakened the state and exhausted the treasury. When he died in 1707, he left to his successor a truncated and bankrupt empire. Built between 1673 and 1674 under the direction of Fidai Khan Koka, Awrangzeb's master of ordinance, the Badshahi Mosque combined the functions of mosque and idgah (a building for the celebration of the religious festival of the Id). On its east side is an imposing entrance stairway that leads through a great vaulted entrance made of red sandstone. The single-aisled arcades enclose an enormous central space open to the sky, and this courtyard can accommodate sixty thousand worshippers. At each corner of the mosque is a three-story, octagonal, red sandstone minar topped with an open, marble-covered canopy. Framed by four smaller minars and projecting from the west side into the courtyard, the prayer chamber is dominated by a central arched niche flanked on each side by five arches, each one-third the size of the central niche. Three bulbous marble domes on high drums divide the roofline, and the largest dome is directly behind the central arch.

On the exterior, floral and geometric decoration is inlaid in white marble; the interior is ornamented in polychromed stucco. Formerly appearing only in imperial palaces, stucco baluster columns appear like tall slender vases holding ornate, delicate floral decorations. Still one of the largest mosques in the Islamic world, the Badshahi Mosque projects great size with balanced proportions and clarity.

ANTHONY WELCH

See also Agra Red Fort; Akbar; Architecture, Religious; Babar; Beauty and Aesthetics; Dara Shikoh; Delhi; God; Hadith; Hindus; Imam; India; Islam; Lahore; Mosques; Mughals; Persians; Prayer; Qur'an; Qur'an: Reciters and Recitation; Taj Mahal

Further Reading

Asher, Catherine B. *Architecture of Mughal India: The New Cambridge History of India I:4.* Cambridge: Cambridge University Press, 1992.
Chughtai, M.A. *Badshahi Mosque.* Lahore: Lahore, 1972.
Gascoigne, Bamber. *The Great Moghuls.* New York: Harper & Row, 1971.
Koch, Ebba M. *Mughal Architecture.* Munich: Prestel-Verlag, 1992.

BAGHDAD

The origin of the name Baghdad, clearly pre-Islamic, is undetermined. Few physical traces remain of the original Arab–Islamic site founded (c. 762 CE) by the 'Abbasid caliph Abu Ja'far al-Mansur (r. 754–775). The written accounts by geographers and historians—these include al-Ya'qubi, al-Tabari, al-Muqaddasi, and al-Khatib al-Baghdadi—are thus essential to any reconstruction of the city's early history. Designated officially *Madinat al-Salam* ("the City of Peace"), al-Mansur's project was built in the round, hence its nickname *al-Mudawwara* ("the Round City"). Completed (c. 777) at great expense, it surrounded the caliph's massive domed residence and a congregational mosque. The Khurasani regiments—the forces that had brought the 'Abbasids to power—were quartered in al-Harbiyya to the northwest.

Designed initially as an administrative center—it became, in this sense, the prototype for later Near Eastern dynasts—it was soon transformed, through population growth, private construction initiatives, and other factors, into a dynamic and sprawling urban hub. By the mid-tenth century, the markets and residential neighborhoods of Baghdad were vast, both in number and in variety of population. Security demands played no less a part. Al-Mansur and his immediate successors, faced with threats in outlying districts, particularly from Shi'i and Khariji opponents, along with restive elements within Baghdad itself, completed large-scale projects, including the palace complexes of al-Khuld and al-Rusafa in the 770s. The Round City ceased to function as the official caliphal residence by the early ninth century. Its large mosque retained its congregational function into the premodern period.

The city's subsequent political history was often troubled. A civil war (809–819) between the designated heirs of Harun al-Rashid (r. 786–809)—his sons Muhammad al-Amin and 'Abd Allah al-Ma'mun—led to years of war in and around Baghdad, a collapse of central authority in most provinces, and the demise of the Khurasani army as the imperial mainstay. Al-Ma'mun, as governor of Khurasan, waged a successful campaign against al-Amin (r. 809–813). Only partly through his own reign (813–833) did al-Ma'mun take up residence in Baghdad (819). His brother and successor, Abu Ishaq al-Mu'tasim (r. 833–842), largely in an effort to accommodate a complex Turkish, Iranian, and Central Asian military, created a new center at Samarra, located north on the Tigris River. Samarra replaced Baghdad as the imperial hub for some sixty years (836–892). Developments in Samarra over ensuing decades, particularly the political interference of the Turkish high command, exacted a grim toll upon the caliphate. In Baghdad, the Tahirid family wielded considerable influence, highlighted during a brief but costly siege by Samarran forces in 865–866. The return of the 'Abbasids to Baghdad in the 890s did little to restore their early authority.

Entry into Baghdad by Ahmad ibn Buya, who reigned as Mu'izz al-Dawla (945–967), initiated roughly a century-long period of Buyid suzerainty over the city and the Iraqi hinterlands. The Buyids, a north Iranian clan, established a base of power in Fars, from which they controlled Iraq into the mid-eleventh century. The city's fortunes in the tenth century were mixed. The flow of tax revenue slowed

Mosque, Baghdad, Baghdad was the seat of the 'Abbasid caliphate and the center of the Islamic world of its time. Credit: Werner Forman/Art Resource, NY. Kadiomin mosque, Baghdad, Iraq.

markedly due to the degradation of the Iraqi agrarian infrastructure; the autonomy of most provinces, notably Egypt and Khurasan; and the shift of much political and economic energy to Fars. Ordinary crime increased, as did religious and military factional violence. In addition, by the end of the century, the new Fatimid capital of Cairo began to overshadow Baghdad on the political and economic fronts. The Buyids, however, devoted themselves to urban renovation and large-scale construction (palaces, congregational mosques, and markets). Baghdad retained its highly "decentered" character in this period: It remained a city of disparate quarters and neighborhoods with little municipal integration or centralized authority. Patterns of sectarian and social tension from the ninth century on are understood largely in these terms (see below).

The city's internal sociopolitical and physical divisions sharpened with the arrival of the Seljuks in the mid-eleventh century. A Turkish clan of the Oghuz (or Ghuzz) people, the Seljuks had overrun the Ghaznavids and thus established authority over Khurasan and Iran before seizing Baghdad from the Buyids. The Seljuk leader Toghril Beg (d. 1063) formed diplomatic ties with the 'Abbasid caliph al-Qa'im (r. 1031–1075) in 1050. He led forces into Baghdad, initially in 1055, then again in 1058, at which point the caliph granted permission for his use of the title "Sultan." The Seljuks spent relatively little time in Baghdad, preferring to govern from afar through local officials. Relations with the Abbasid caliphate remained uneasy throughout. However, their deep impact on the history of Baghdad had much to do with their promotion of Sunni Islam, a position the Seljuks largely defined in terms of anti-Shi'ism. In this sense they found a willing ally in the 'Abbasids, already engaged against their various Shi'i detractors. For both the Seljuks and the 'Abbasids, it was especially important to resist the authority and military ambitions of the Fatimid/Isma'ili caliphate in Egypt.

Baghdad's significance in Islamic history as a nexus of intellectual and religious activity is difficult to exaggerate. Scholarship (literary, religious, and scientific) was tied, though by no means exclusively, to shifting political currents. Due in part to 'Abbasid patronage, particularly that of a dynamic administrative elite (the *kuttab*), ninth-century Baghdadi literary culture flourished. 'Amr ibn Bahr al-Jahiz (d. 869), a towering figure, contributed key works of *adab* (belles-lettres) and Mu'tazili theology. Ninth-century religious scholarship, including Qur'anic exegesis, *hadith*, law, and theology, was no less dynamic, as shown by the work of Abu Ja'far al-Tabari (d. 923) (see al-Tabari). The work of Arab/Muslim scientists benefited considerably from the translation movement of works from Persian, Greek, Syriac, and Sanskrit into Arabic, which began under al-Mansur and then flourished under al-Ma'mun.

Subsequent developments in the city's religiopolitical history proved critical to the formation of the two foremost branches of Islam. The maturation of "Twelver" (Imami) (see Shi'ism) scholarship and devotional life is dated to the Buyid period. Due in part to the foundational work of such scholars as al-Kulayni (d. 941) and al-Shaykh al-Mufid (d. 1022), and in part the patronage of the Buyid court, Twelver doctrines on the occultation of the Imam and related ideas emerged. So too did Twelver ritual, notably that associated with Ghadir Khumm and mourning rites for al-Husayn ibn 'Ali. It is also to the Buyid period that one must date the crystallization of Sunnism, this in good measure a response to the assertion of Shi'ism. A hardening of Sunni-Shi'i loyalties, often played out violently over subsequent centuries, divided the city physically as well. The Seljuk period, as previously noted, was critical to Sunni history. Of particular note were the careers of Nizam al-Mulk (d. 1092), chief vizier and Seljuk regent, and Abu Hamid al-Ghazali (d. 1111), theologian, jurist, and Sufi (see Sufis and Sufism); both men associated with the Nizamiyya *madrasa* in Baghdad. This was among the first such institutions founded in Iraq and a significant facet in the spread of Sunni thought and practice.

Baghdad's history as a commercial hub was no less significant. As a critical link in a complex trade network connecting the Indian Ocean, eastern Europe, the Asian steppe, and the Mediterranean, the city housed a large multiethnic and religious merchant community. Evidence for the tenth century indicates important strides in the development of banking and related areas within the city. In good part, the activity of Baghdadi merchants was driven by the needs of the court and elite society. The caliphs and, in time, Buwayhid and Seljuk interlocutors, after all, required all appropriate displays of luxury. Written sources indicate the availability of fabrics (silks, brocades, linens); jewelry of gold, silver, and gems; carpets; intricate metalwork; weaponry; fine musical instruments; and an array of exotic foodstuffs. Baghdad was also home to a busy commerce in slave trade.

The wealth of the Iraqi merchant class was tied as well to trade in manufactured goods, such as textiles and paper. Papermaking had spread into the Islamic world, from China through Central Asia, in the eighth century and rapidly became an important industry. The Suq al-Warraqin ("the Stationer's Market") is said to have included, at its height, more than one hundred shops. Trade in more ordinary goods flourished as well. To feed a large population, Baghdad drew on the agricultural production of the Sawad, the highly fertile lands located between the Tigris and Euphrates rivers, as well as regions farther afield that produced rice and sugar, among other widely consumed products. New types of fruits and vegetables, produced in the Near East from at least the early Islamic period on, also came available in the markets of Baghdad. It follows, of course, that the relationship between the large urban centers and the countryside was crucial to the 'Abbasid economy. The 'Abbasids, like the Umayyads before them, were fortunate in having inherited from the Sasanians a long-established and well-functioning irrigation system. High levels of agricultural production were maintained in the early 'Abbasid period. As 'Abbasid authority waned (by the late ninth century), however, maintenance of the agricultural infrastructure suffered as well.

MATTHEW S. GORDON

Further Reading

Duri, A.A. "Baghdad." *The Encyclopedia of Islam*, Second Edition.

Kennedy, Hugh. *The Prophet and the Age of the Caliphates*. Harlow, U.K.: Pearson Education Ltd., 2004.

Kraemer, Joel L. *Humanism in the Renaissance of Islam*. Leiden: E.J. Brill, 1992.

Lassner, Jacob. *The Topography of Baghdad in the Early Middle Ages*. Detroit: Wayne State University Press, 1970.

al-Muqaddasi. *The Best Divisions for Knowledge of the Regions*. Edited and translated by Basil Collins. Reading, U.K.: Garnet Publishing, 2001.

Wheatley, Paul. *The Places Where Men Pray Together: Cities in Islamic Lands, Seventh through the Tenth Centuries*. Chicago: The University of Chicago Press, 2001.

BAHRAIN

The term *Bahrain* was used during medieval times to describe the coastal area extending from Kuwait down to Abu Dhabi on the southern shore of the Gulf. Its population centers included Hajar (in Islamic times, Hasa), Qatif, and Awal (Bahrain Island). Before Islam, Bahrain was inhabited by Arab tribes, mainly the 'Abd al-Qays and groups from the Banu Tamim and Bakr ibn Wa'il. These tribes shared common interests with the Sasanians, although tensions were common. Small Persian and Indian communities also lived along the coast.

Due to its geographical position and its links with Persia and Iraq, Bahrain was prosperous. Nestorian Christianity was strong in the area, while Bahraini poets such as al-Mutalammis and al-Muthaqqab used to attend the court of the Mundhir dynasty in Iraq.

After the emergence of Islam in the seventh century CE, Bahraini tribes played an important role in the Arab conquests and also in political events in Iraq during the Umayyad era (660–749). The spread of war damaged commerce, and many Bahraini tribes migrated to the newly founded Iraqi cities of Basra and Kufa. As a result, Bahrain declined in importance and was ruled by the governor of Basra, creating an important vacuum that led the area to become one of the centers of opposition to the Umayyad caliphate, in which the Kharijis played a prominent part.

During the 'Abbasid period (749–1258), the rise of Basra as a commercial center, along with Siraf, Qays, and Hormuz, led to the further decline of Bahrain. Groups opposed to the 'Abbasids, such as the Zanj (c. 868–883) and the Qarmathians (c. 900–1076), gained strength. These movements eventually subsided, while Shi'ism spread in Hasa and Awal.

New migrants from Central Arabia arrived, and an independent state was founded by Abd Allah bin Ali. The dynasty that followed, the 'Uyunids, lasted from c. 1076 to 1228. Supported by the Seljuk rulers of Iraq, this dynasty relied on the power of the Banu 'Amir tribes who had migrated from Najd.

The Banu 'Amir were initially allies of the Qarmathians and then of the 'Uyunids, but they eventually overthrew the latter and established a dynasty of their own. Founded by 'Usfur ibn Rashid and known as the 'Usfurids, the dynasty dominated Bahrain from c. 1228 to 1383, but finally came to an end with the rise of the Kingdom of Hormuz in fourteenth century.

Another branch of the Banu 'Amir, led by Zamil ibn Jabir, then managed to gain control of Bahrain, founding the dynasty of the Jubur (c. 1446–1519). This dynasty adopted the Maliki school of Islamic jurisprudence, but little is known of the cultural and social life of its people. Although their influence spread throughout the Gulf, the Jubur were swiftly overwhelmed by the technologically superior Portuguese, who arrived in the Gulf at the beginning of the sixteenth century.

Throughout the medieval period, the coastal economy of the extensive area known as Bahrain was based on commerce, pearling, and date cultivation.

HASAN M. AL-NABOODAH

See also Arabia; Trade, African; Trade, Indian Ocean; Tribes and Tribal Customs

Further Reading

Al-Khalifa, Shaikh Abdullah, K., and Michael Rice, Editors. *Bahrain through the Ages: The History*. London and New York: Kegan Paul International, 1993.
Hasan, N. *The Role of the Arab Tribes in the East during the Period of the Umayyad (40–132/660–749)*. Baghdad: Baghdad University, 1976.
Miles, S. B. *The Countries and Tribes of the Persian Gulf*. London: Frank Cass, 1966.
Morony, Michael. "The Arabisation of the Gulf." In *The Arab Gulf and the Arab World*. Edited by B.R. Pridham. London, New York, and Sydney: Croom Helm, 1988.
Naboodah, H. *Eastern Arabia in the Sixth and Seventh Centuries A.D.*, Ph.D. dissertation, University of Exeter, UK, 1989.
———. "The Commercial Activity of Bahrain and Oman in the Early Middle Ages." *Proceedings of the Seminar for Arabian Studies* 22 (1992): 81–96.
Potts, D.T. *The Arabian Gulf in Antiquity*. 2 vols. New York: Oxford University Press, 1990 (reprinted 1992).

BAKRI, AL-, GEOGRAPHER

Abu 'Ubayd 'Abd Allah, b. 'Abd al-'Aziz al-Bakri (d. 487/1094), was the greatest geographer of Muslim Spain. Little is known about his life. He was a native of Cordova, where he died. His father was the only one, or else the second, ruler of the small principality of Huelva and Saltes, founded in 402/1012, at the time of the fall of the Umayyad caliphate in Cordova. In 443/1051, when his father, 'Izz al-Dawla, was obliged to give up his power, Abu 'Ubayd, who was at that time approximately thirty years old, accompanied him to Cordova. He was the the pupil of the historian Abu Marwan Ibn Hayyan (d. 469/1076) and of other masters, and moved in various court circles, especially Almeria. He quickly became a distinguished writer. Several books are attributed to him, in the religious sphere, in philology, on the correct names of the Arabic tribes, and one in botany, none of which has come to us.

In geography, the work on which Abu 'Ubayd's renown is mainly based is his *Book of the Itineraries and Kingdoms (al-Masalik wa l-mamalik)*. He appears never to have traveled in the east, or even in North Africa. He composed this book in 461/1068 assisted by literary and oral information. For North Africa and some parts of Northern Black Africa (such as Sudan), his main source is *Book of the Itineraries and Kingdoms* of Muhammad b. Yusuf al-Warraq (d. 363/973 in Cordova), which has not come to us. Not all of the book has been published or translated. The following sections are edited and/or translated separately: Northern Africa, fragments on the Russians and Slavs, parts related to Muslim Spain, the Arabian Peninsula, Egypt, and Europe.

Following the usual practice of the geographers of his time and before him, Abu 'Ubayd gave to this work the form of a roadbook, including distances between towns and staging posts. Most of his descriptions of towns are remarkably precise. His toponymic material for Muslim Spain, the Maghrib, Northern Africa, and so on is no less worthy of interest. Many of his historical notices and remarks are also invaluable. He was also interested in social and religious matters, for instance, about the Berber Moroccan tribe of the Banu Lamas, who were Shi'i; or his statement on Yunus of the Barghawati Berber tribe of Morocco, who made a journey in the first half of the third/ninth century to the East of the Islamic empire, together with other North Africans and Andalusis, of whom three claimed to be prophets upon their return, including Yunus himself. Abu 'Ubayd also gives social and economic information, such as on the presence of Andalusi traders in al-Mahdiyya (Tunisia), providing detailed and varied itineraries for their maritime crossings of the channel between North Africa and al-Andalus.

Abu 'Ubayd's *Dictionary* on the toponyms, mostly referring to the Arabic Peninsula, which occur in pre-Islamic poetry and in the literature of the Islamic traditional reports, the spelling of which has given rise to discussions among the philologists and traditionists, has been edited. It includes a long and interesting introduction on the geographical setting of ancient Arabia and the habitats of the most important tribes.

CLAUDE GILLIOT

See also Geography

Primary Sources

Works of al-Bakri:

Das Geographische Buch des Abu 'Obeid 'Abdallah ben 'Abd el-'Aziz el-Bekri. 2 vols. Ed. Ferdinand Wüstenfeld. Paris: Göttingen, 18761877; reprint Osnabrück: Biblio-Verlag, 1976; reprint Frankfurt: Publications of the Institute for the History of Arabic-Islamic Sciences, 1994 Islamic Geography, vols. 206–207).

Description de l'Afrique septentrionale, par Abou-Obeïd-el-Bekri, I, Texte arabe, ed. Mac Guckin de Slane, Alger and Paris, 1910.

II, *Description de l'Arique septentrionale* [. . .], translated by Mac Guckin de Slane, Alger and Paris, 1913; reprint together, Paris: Adrien-Maisonneuve, 1965; reprint Frankfurt: Publications of the Institute for the History of Arabic-Islamic Sciences, 1993 (Islamic Geography, vols. 134–135).

Geografia de España, Introduction. Translation and notes by Eliseo Vidal Beltrán. Zaragosa: Anubar, 1982.

Kitab al-Masalik wa l-mamalik, 2 vols. Ed. André Ferré and Adrian van Leeuwen. Carthage: Beit al-Hikma, 1992; reprint Beirut, Dar al-Gharb al-islami, between 1992 and 1995.

Mu'jam ma sta'jam min asma' al-bilad wa l-mawadi', 4 vol. in 2. Ed. Mustafa al-Saqqa. Cairo, 1945; reprint Beirut: 'Alam al-kutub, 1983 (is only a copy of the ed. of Wüstenfeld).

The Arab geographer Abu 'Ubayd al-Bakri, 2nd part: *The Arabic Peninsula* (in Arabic). Ed. 'Abd Allah Yusuf al-Ghunaym. Kuwait: Dhat al-Salasil, 1977.

The Geography of al-Andalus and Europe (in Arabic). Ed. 'Abd al-Rahman 'Ali al-Hajj. Beirut: Dar al-Irshad, 1968.

The Geography of Egypt (in Arabic). Ed. 'Abd Allah Yusuf al-Ghunaym. Kuwayt: Dar al-'Uruba, 1980.

Further Reading

Gilliot, Claude. "Al-Warrak, Muhammad b. Yusuf," *EI*, XI, 151.

Lévi-Provençal, E. "Abu 'Ubayd al-Bakri," *EI*, I, 155–157: Miquel, André. *La géographie humaine du monde musulman jusqu'au milieu du 11e siècle*. 4 vols. Paris: La Haye: Mouton, 1967 (1973²), 1975, 1980, 1988.

BALKANS

Although interactions between the Balkan Slavs and Greeks with Arab Muslims can be traced back to the medieval Arab-Byzantine relations, Islam spread through the Balkans with the Ottoman invasion that commenced in the mid-fourteenth century. No medieval Balkan state was strong enough to halt the advancing Ottoman army, especially given that the Ottomans had acted several times as mercenary allies in the internecine wars, which had led to political divisions, deteriorating living conditions, and general economic instability. After capturing Adrianople (Edirne) in 1365, the Ottomans pushed farther into the Balkans in several waves: Serbia fell by 1389 (the Battle of Kosovo); Bulgaria and Wallachia by 1402; Bosnia by 1463; Greece, including a number of Aegean islands, and Albania by 1481. The apex of Ottoman expansion was reached by the mid-sixteenth century with the acquisition of Transylvania, large parts of Hungary, and Slavonia.

Organized into the millet system of religious grouping, the Balkan people remained predominantly Orthodox Christian. However, the presence of Islam intensified through two main processes: (1) the controlled movement of Muslim populations from other parts of the Empire, and (2) conversions to Islam that took place among local populations in uneven waves and over several centuries. In such diverse religious space, some pockets of the Balkans continued being predominantly Christian, whereas others became mainly Muslim. The largest Muslim communities were found in Bosnia, Albania, Bulgaria, and Western Thrace. Furthermore, after the Spanish Reconquista, many Sephardic Jews settled in the Balkans on the invitation of the Ottoman sultan.

Because Islam was spread by the Ottomans, Muslims of the Balkans became predominantly Sunni, of Hanafi legal orientation, though Shi'i teachings were introduced by, and confined to, the Bektashi and the associated Kizilbashi Sufi orders. The denominational and legal uniformity among Balkan Muslims did not lead to their integration or unification otherwise. On the contrary, because of the lack of assimilationist policies by the Ottoman government, most Muslims retained their cultural and linguistic distinctiveness and separate ethnic identities.

Excluding the elite population, the majority of the Balkan people were peasants and shepherds whose religious beliefs revealed many syncretic practices adapted from pagan, Christian, and now Islamic beliefs. Whether Muslim, Christian, or Jewish, they placed the main emphasis on local praxis rather than official teachings. This was reflected in their customs and rituals, funerary architecture, festivals, and folk literature.

The situation was somewhat different in the cities that were erected or invigorated through Ottoman state policies and pious endowments (waqfs), generating lively economic, intellectual, architectural, and social activities. Here, Ottoman Islamic values flourished in a way that reflected a clearer connection with the larger imperial system, though local sensibilities remained palpable and important. The urban elite, made up of literary figures, historiographers, theologians, philosophers, jurists, merchants, and others, reveals a polyglot culture in which the Ottoman languages (Turkish, Arabic, and Persian) were used along with local languages in intellectual production and exchange. Among the most prominent scholars worthy of mention are Ali Dede Bosnevi (d. 1598), who wrote comprehensive commentaries on Sa'di, Rumi, and Hafiz; Hasan Kafi of Prusac (d. 1616), a judge whose treatise on the qualities of good governance became widely known and cited throughout the Empire; the prolific scholar Mustafa b. Yusuf of Mostar, known as Sheyh Yuyo (d. 1707), who wrote multidisciplinary commentaries on medieval Islamic thought; and Yahya Bey of Taslidja (d. 1575), a prolific poet of lyrical and mystical odes and couplets that drew inspiration from popular legends as well as great Sufi masters.

The Balkans also provided a receptive ground for the dissemination of Sufi ideas and practices, as evidenced by the diversity and number of Sufi orders. Among the most important orders were the Khalwati, Naqshbandi, and Bektashi, while less prevalent ones included the Qadiri, Rifa'i, Mawlawi, Bayrami, Malami, and Badawi orders. Overall, Sufi orders invigorated Balkan Islam in both belief and practice. In fact, many conversions to Islam happened through Sufi activities. Their presence in cities and villages across the Balkans, as testified to by the number of tekkes (convents) and türbes (mausoleums), shows their ubiquitous presence in different spheres of life. While some were more attractive to intellectual and literary circles (such as the Khalwati), others were highly syncretic and enjoyed popular appeal. Most syncretic was the Bektashi order. Long associated with the Ottoman military establishment, Bektashis spread throughout the Balkans, as evidenced by the remains of their tekkes and turbes in Greece, Macedonia, Bosnia, Bulgaria, and Albania. Shi'i in orientation and organized around a sheikh referred to as *baba*, the Bektashis intertwined Islamic teachings with local customs and folklore, making the order popular, especially in rural areas, and involving equal participation by both men and women.

AMILA BUTUROVIC

Further Reading

Birnbaum, Henrik and Speros Vryonis. *Aspects of the Balkans: Continuity and Change.* Hague: Mouton, 1972.
Brown, L. Carl. *Imperial Legacy: The Ottoman Imprint on the Balkans and the Middle East.* New York: Columbia University Press, 1996.
Fine, John V. A. *The Late Medieval Balkans: A Critical Survey from the Late Twelfth Century to the Ottoman Conquest.* Ann Arbor: University of Michigan Press, 1987.
Jelavich, Barbara. *History of the Balkans.* Joint Committee on Eastern Europe Publication Series. No. 12. 2 vols. Cambridge: Cambridge University Press, 1983.
Kiel, Machiel. *Art and Society of Bulgaria in the Turkish Period: A Sketch of the Economic, Juridical, and Artistic Preconditions of Bulgarian Post-Byzantine Art and Its Place in the Development of the Art of the Christian Balkans, 1360/70–1700: A New Interpretation.* Assen, The Netherlands: Van Gorcum, 1985.
Norris, H.T. *Islam in the Balkans: Religion and Society between Europe and the Arab World.* London: Hurst & Co., 1993.
Poulton, Hugh and Suha Taji-Farouki (eds.). *Muslim Identity and the Balkan State.* New York: New York University Press, 1997.
Rexhebi, Baba. *The Mysticism of Islam and Bektashism.* Naples: Dragotti, 1984.
Skendi, Stavro. "Crypto-Christians in the Balkan Area under the Ottomans." *Slavic Review* 26:2 (1967): 227–246.
Stavrianos, Leften Stavros. *The Balkans since 1453.* New York: Rinehart, 1958.

BARAKA

Baraka, which means "blessing," is a divinely inspired quality or force of presence that is often associated with prophets, saints, and other holy persons, and more generally with pious and learned individuals, as well as with sacred places and objects. The Jews and Christians of the Islamic world held similar beliefs concerning baraka. Muslims regard God as the ultimate source of baraka and the Qur'an as embodying it. The Prophet Muhammad, his family, and the Shi'i imams possessed baraka in life and posthumously, as did certain rulers such as Saladin and Nur al-Din. Baraka was also associated with individuals who possessed exemplary learning, including theologians such as al-Ghazali and Sufis such as Ibn 'Arabi and 'Abd al-Qadir al-Jilani. Rulers sought the baraka of saints, especially before waging war and at times of illness. Baraka could be transmitted simply by touching a person and their clothing or by embracing them. Baraka was also manifest in articles of clothing and other personal effects of pious persons, such as the mantle of the Prophet Muhammad and Dhu 'l-Fiqar, the famed sword of the Prophet's cousin and fourth caliph 'Ali b. Abi Talib. Certain mosques, tombs, and shrines, wells, and natural formations, such as springs and trees, were particularly renowned for their baraka to the extent that they became pilgrimage places. The earliest codices of the Qur'an attributed to the third Rightly Guided Caliph 'Uthman b. 'Affan and to his successor, 'Ali b. Abi Talib, were objects of pious visitation. Visitors sought to obtain baraka by touching and kissing them.

JOSEF W. MERI

See also Saints

Further Reading

Meri, Josef W. *The Cult of Saints Among Muslims and Jews in Medieval Syria.* Oxford: 2002.

Meri, Josef W. "Aspects of *Baraka* (Blessings) and Ritual Devotion among Medieval Muslims and Jews." *Medieval Encounters: Jewish, Christian and Muslim Culture in Confluence and Dialogue* 5 (1999) 46–49.

Westermarck, Edward. *Ritual and Belief in Morocco.* 2 vols. London: 1926.

BARANI, ZIA' AL-DIN, HISTORIAN OF PRE-MUGHAL INDIA

A prominent theorist on Islamic political thought in fourteenth-century India, Barani was born (circa 1285) in an aristocratic family with excellent connections to the ruling elite of the Delhi sultanate. His grandfather, father, and uncle held important governmental positions. Barani himself had the opportunity to serve at the court of Sultan Muhammad ibn Tughluq (r. 1325–1350) as companion to the ruler. At the beginning of the reign of Firuz Shah Tughluq, Muhammad ibn Tughluq's successor, Barani fell out of royal favor, apparently because he had been involved in a conspiracy to overthrow the new ruler. After a brief imprisonment, he spent several years in banishment from the court. Until his death in 1357, he continued writing in the futile hope that he would one day regain his position at the court.

In his major works, *Fatawa-yi jahandari* and *Tarikh-i Firuz Shahi,* Barani expounds his conceptions about the norms that Muslim rulers should observe while exercising their authority, specifically in the Indian context. In *Fatawa-yi Jahandari,* written as a guidebook for princes, he conceives of God having delegated authority over human societies to prophets and kings. Because authority to rule is God-given, the ideal ruler should manifest divine virtues of mercy and wrath, which are essential ingredients for a successful reign. He declares that it is the basic duty of a pious Muslim ruler to repudiate all that is non-Islamic and promote the propagation of proper "Islamic" values. To preserve these values, it is incumbent on the ruler to severely limit the role of non-Muslims in the administration of the state. Using a Sunni yardstick to determine what was correctly Islamic, and upholding the *Shari'ah* as interpreted by Sunni theologians to be normative, he considered the Shi'is and the *falsafa* (philosophers) to be heretics who should be exterminated. In this regard, he extols Mahmud of Ghazna as the ideal Sunni Muslim ruler for his determination to exterminate idolatry and all forms of infidelity. Barani's writings show intolerance toward not only non-Muslims but also Muslims of indigenous Indian origin whom he thought of as low-born and not worthy of anything but a basic education about Islamic rites and practices. His class- and race-based notions, which run contrary to Islamic ideals of equality, extolled only those of pure Perso-Turkish origin to be "true" Muslims. In this he reflected the views of many of the *ashraf,* or the aristocracy, of his time.

As is evident in *Fatawa-yi Jahandari* and *Tarikh-i Firuz Shahi,* Barani's conception of historiography was primarily didactic and not meant to chronicle events. As a result, he only includes information that validates his religiopolitical theories. His works should, therefore, be read from this perspective. He often conceives his heroes as being motivated by solely religious concerns, without paying attention to historical and political realities of the time. Of particular interest is *Tarikh-i Firuz Shahi,* in which he writes an account of the rulers of the Delhi Sultanate from Sultan Balban (r. 1266–1287) to Muhammad ibn

Tughluq with the goal of demonstrating how rulers prospered when they adhered to his ideals and suffered failure and disgrace when they deviated from them. When a ruler such as Ala A.D.-Din Khalji (r. 1296–1316), who clearly did not live up to Barani's standards for a good Muslim ruler, seems to have enjoyed a prosperous reign, Barani attributes this success to the presence in his realm of Nizam ad-Din Awliya, the preeminent Shaykh of the Chishti Sufi order. However, since Ala ad-Din Khalji was blind to the power and virtues of Nizam ad-Din Awliya, he and his family suffered terrible personal fates.

ALI ASANI

Further Reading

Hardy, Peter. *Historians of Medieval India.* London: Luzac and Co., 1960.

BARTER

See Trade, African; Trade, Indian Ocean; Trade, Mediterranean

BASRA

The medieval city of Basra was located just west of the Shatt al-Arab, the confluence of the Tigris and Euphrates rivers in what is now Iraq. Basra was first settled between AH 14/635 CE and 17/638 by Arab tribesmen who participated in the Muslim conquest of the Sasanian Empire. Most likely it was little more than a military camp during the first years of its existence. Basra's strategic location allowed it to dominate both the Tigris and Euphrates rivers and important overland trade routes. Consequently, it grew into a thriving military city. By the time of the Battle of the Camel in 36/657, Basra is estimated to have had some fifty thousand residents.

Topographically, the city was divided into five tribal zones, each under the leadership of the tribal ashraf (notables). Tribal relations in the garrison towns were complex, but Basra was generally dominated by the Tamim tribe. The city originally served as a garrison town from which to control newly conquered territory in Iraq and to launch further expeditions into Fars. Thanks to extensive irrigation works, Basra eventually became an agricultural center as well. It was particularly famous for the quality of its date orchards. Its strategic location also made it a trading center of some importance. During the Umayyad period, Basra did not join the neighboring garrison town of Kufa in supporting various 'Alid movements. It was not, however, immune to

rebellion, becoming the center for Ibn al-Ash'ath's rebellion in 81/701 and Ibn al-Muhallab's revolt in 101/719. The 'Abbasid revolution of 132/750, which came in the wake of a plague in Basra, brought a slow decline in the city's status, as the newly established capital city of Baghdad overshadowed the older garrison towns. Basra was not initially a focus for opposition to the 'Abbasids, but as the town shrank in size (from a peak of at least two hundred thousand residents) and influence, it became susceptible to revolts, the most notable of which was the Zanj rebellion of 257/871. The fact that this was a rebellion of agricultural slaves and not of disgruntled soldiers (who fomented earlier rebellions) underlines Basra's transition from a garrison town to an agricultural center. As the 'Abbasids lost their grip on power, Basra suffered a variety of invasions and pillages, particularly during the sixth/twelfth century.

In addition to its strategic importance, Basra was also a significant center for scholarly activity, a status that the rise of Baghdad did not diminish. During the Umayyad period, a variety of important theological thinkers called Basra home, including al-Hasan al-Basri (d. 110/728) and the early Mu'tazilite leaders Wasil ibn 'Ata' (d. 131/748) and 'Amr ibn 'Ubayd (d. 144/761). Basra was the focus of the theological debate over human free will and the birthplace of the Mu'tazilite movement. In addition, Basra was the earliest center for the study of Arabic grammar. Unlike Kufa, Basra did not, however, become an important venue in the debates that shaped early Islamic jurisprudence.

STEVEN C. JUDD

Primary Sources

al-Tabari, Muhammad ibn Jarir. *Ta'rikh al-rusul wa-l-muluk.* ed. M.J. de Goeje. Leiden, 1879–1901.
Yaqut ibn 'Abdallah al-Hamawi. *Mu'jam al-buldan.* ed. F. Wüstenfeld as Jacut's Geographisches Wörterbuch. Leipzig, 1866–1873.

Further Reading

Pelat, Charles. *Le Milieu Basrien et la Formation de Gahiz.* Paris: Libraire d'amérique et d'orient, 1953.
van Ess, Josef. *Theologie und Gesellschaft im 2. und 3. Jahrhundert Hidschra.* Band II. Berlin: Walter de Gruyter, 1992.

BATHS AND BATHING

Baths in the Islamic world have almost always focused on the institution of the bathhouse, known as the *hamam*. Having its roots in the Roman and Byzantium bathhouse tradition, the hamam was

The Royal Baths in the harem. The Star-shaped roof lights were once covered in red glass. Tiles line the walls. Credit: Werner Forman/Art Resource, NY. Alhambra, Granada, Spain.

built and functioned in a similar manner over its thirteen-and-a-half centuries of existence. The hamam as a building was often distinguished by several large brick domes that were interspersed with a great number of bulbous pieces of glass that would let light shine into the building without letting the furnace heat escape. The bathhouse typically had three main chambers. The customers, segregated by gender, and often by religious community, would first enter an unheeded resting area where they would take off their clothes, dresses, towels, and/or loincloths. They would then enter a warmer antechamber where they would be exposed to a moderate amount of the furnace's moist heat. They would then enter the main sweating room, a large chamber where the steam of the hamam's furnaces would bring about an intense sweat. Once the customer had properly sweated, he or she would have their body rubbed and lathered, which would clean the pores and remove any dirt. After this, a customer would rinse himself or herself with warm water and/or take a bath in the water basins of the room. After the customer had done this, he or she would return to the initial rest area to relax and prepare for leaving the bathhouse.

Hamams were typically staffed by at least eight to ten attendants. These included one who would maintain the resting area and the linens and two to three people who would help the clients with washing, scrubbing, or even massages in the main sweating chamber. Two to three others would work to heat the large cauldrons of water in the furnace area. They would either bring in fuel (in the form of coal or dried dung) from a nearby depot area or be building the fire with the fuel.

Hamams played a role in a great number of social functions in the urban neighborhoods where they were established. Indeed, they were considered to be vital for the establishment of each new Muslim city quarter, as they helped maintain God's will for all to be cleanly. The sweating and cleansing processes in various degrees of heat and humidity also were vital to maintaining the body's humoral balance, a key Galenic concept that predominated in medieval medicine throughout the Mediterranean and Middle East. Muslim travelers from the ninth century onward have remarked on the great number of hamams in the cities of the Muslim world, including Cordoba, Tunis, Cairo, Baghdad, and Istanbul. The loss of a hamam, like that of a mosque, was considered tantamount to the destruction of the city itself. Local authorities would often go to great lengths to reestablish the hamam and enhance normal social life.

People also used the hamam as a place where one could relax and interact with one's neighbors. It is no coincidence that baths were taken in groups, since this would allow numbers of people to enjoy the baths as they escaped from the trials and tribulations of everyday life. People would typically gossip with each other as they sipped a hot drink in the rest chamber. As noted earlier, hamams would be segregated by gender and religious community to maintain social mores. For example, hamams would allow Muslims and non-Muslims on specific days of the week, and might allow women in during the day and men during the night. There was a particular concern about protecting female patrons from moral and physical danger, leading the hamams to establish separate staffs for male and female clients. The penalties for theft and nude activity were extremely high if the victim was a recognized female client.

However, if a woman entered a bath at the wrong time, she lost all legal rights for her own protection. She was often regarded as a mere prostitute who could be abused by men with impunity. Beyond potentially being raped or sexually harassed was the loss of social station among her neighbors.

Despite these social restrictions, hamams on occasions would be used for illicit relations. We know, for instance, from sixteenth-century Ottoman court records, that some hamams were shut down after the local authorities found out that men and women were using the same facilities with the collusion of the hamam's staff. In later centuries, the abuse of questionable substances such as heroin, tobacco, and coffee were also duly noted.

BIRSEN BULMUŞ

See also Personal Hygiene

Further Reading

Burns, Robert Ignatius. "Baths and Caravanserais in Crusader Valencia." *Speculum* 46, no. 3 (July 1971): 443–458.

Powers, James F. "Frontier Municipal Baths and Social Interaction in Thirteenth-Century Spain." *The American Historical Review* 84, no. 3 (June 1979): 649–667.

Reeves, Mary Barbara. *The Roman Bath-House in Humeima in Its Architectural and Social Context.* Master of Arts. University of Victoria, 1996.

Semerdjian, Vivian Elyse. "Off the Straight Path: Gender, Public Morality and Legal Administration in Ottoman Haleppo, Syria." Unpublished dissertation. Georgetown University, October 2002.

Sourdel-Thomine, J. and Louis, A. "Hamam." *IE* Online Edition, 2001.

BAYBARS I, MAMLUK SULTAN

Baybars I, fifth ruler (r. 1260–1277) of the Mamluk Sultanate of Egypt and Syria, was in many ways the most important leader in its history.

Baybars was born around 1220 CE among the Qipchaq Turks, who lived in the steppe region north of the Black Sea. Fleeing from the Mongol invasions in the area in 1241–1242, Baybars and his family moved to Anatolia. There, Baybars was captured and ended up in the slave market of Damascus. Eventually he ended up in the service of the great Ayyubid sultan, al-Salih Ayyub (1238–1249), founder of the famous Bahriyya regiment, of which Baybars was a member. Baybars first came to prominence in the fighting in Mansura (1250) in the eastern Nile Delta during the Fifth Crusade; his bravery and leadership helped turn the tables against the Franks. Baybars was one of the conspirators who killed the new sultan, Turanshah, son of al-Salih, an event that led to the establishment of the Mamluk rule in Egypt. The Bahriyya, led by Aqtai and seconded by Baybars, was one of the main factions in the fledging Mamluk state, but it was soon bested in the internal power struggles by Sultan Aybak. Aqtai was killed in 1254, and Baybars fled with seven hundred Bahris to Syria, where they remained as mercenaries serving various Ayyubid princes until the approach of the Mongols at the beginning of 1260. Baybars realized that there was no chance of resistance to the Mongols in Ayyubid Syria, so he was reconciled with the new Mamluk sultan, Qutuz (a Mamluk of Aybak and therefore an enemy). The Bahriyya under Baybars returned to Egypt in March 1260. Baybars became a trusted subordinate in the campaign against the Mongols in the summer of 1260. He led the advance guard that came across the first Mongols at Gaza, and then again in the skirmishing in the Jezreel Valley before the battle of 'Ayn Jalut, where his courage is also noted by various sources; he also led the subsequent mopping-up operations. Relations with Qutuz soon soured, however, particularly when Baybars was not awarded the governorship of Aleppo as he had hoped. On their way back to Cairo, both men were on their guard. Baybars, however, struck first. With a group of conspirators, he fell upon the sultan while hunting and killed him. This was the second time that Baybars was deeply involved in a regicide. He was recognized as ruler in late October 1260.

The reign of Baybars was in many ways the formative years of the Mamluk Sultanate. Emerging from a decade of political disorder on the one hand, and having just gained control over most of Syria up to the Euphrates River on the other hand, the Sultanate was put on a firm footing militarily, politically, and economically. Baybars was surely aware that it was only a matter of time until the Mongols attempted another large-scale invasion of Syria. Any doubts that he might have harbored on this matter were removed by the many Mongol raids, as well as truculent letters that he received from the Ilkhans, as the Mongol rulers of Iran and the surrounding countries were known. He set about enlarging and strengthening his army. An efficient foreign espionage service was established, as was a communication network connecting the capital, Cairo, with the main cities of Syria and the far-flung frontier along the Euphrates, through the use of horse relays, pigeon post, and bonfires. Fortifications were set in order along the frontier and inside the country, although those captured from the Franks along the coast were destroyed. Diplomatic relations were established and maintained with various non-Muslim rulers, including the Byzantine emperor Michael VIII Palaeologus. The most significant diplomatic *démarche* was the relations established with Berke Khan, the Muslim Mongol ruler of the Golden Horde in the southern Russian steppe. Baybars encouraged him to continue fighting his cousin the Ilkhan, which meant that the Mongols of Iran were often fighting on a second front and could not devote themselves to the war against the Mamluks. Although there were no major Mongol campaigns into Syria during Baybars's reign, the frontier was a scene of frequent warfare, with raiders going both ways. In this border war, the Mamluks were usually more successful, perhaps due to the greater importance they attached to this front compared with their Ilkhanid enemies. In 1277, Baybars launched his one major campaign into Mongol-controlled territory, Anatolia. This resulted in a Mamluk victory at Abulustayn (which later became Elbistan), but Baybars—after sweeping through the country—withdrew because of supply difficulties and the prospect of a major Mongol counterattack. Throughout his reign, Baybars also launched several large-scale raids on the Kingdom of Lesser Armenia in Cilicia, a loyal ally of the Mongols.

In the years after gaining power, Baybars consolidated Mamluk rule in Syria. A number of minor rulers, including Ayyubid princes, were either eliminated or brought under control. His legitimacy was strengthened by the welcome of a scion of the 'Abbasid family. After ascertaining his genealogy, Baybars had him declared caliph with the title al-Mustansir. In a well-directed spectacle, the new caliph promptly handed over all functions to Baybars, who was officially declared sultan. Baybars also significantly reduced the Frankish presence in Syria and Palestine. There is no indication that Baybars had planned an

aggressive anti-Frankish policy from the beginning of his reign, and he may well have thought to continue the modus vivendi that characterized Muslim–Crusader relations during the Ayyubid period. Perhaps his growing awareness of the Ilkhans' attempts to achieve an alliance with the Pope and rulers of Latin Europe in order to launch a joint campaign against the Mamluks led the sultan to adopt a more truculent strategy *vis-à-vis* the Franks in Syria. In a series of campaigns, Baybars captured a large number of Crusader cities and forts (some notable examples include Caesarea and Arsuf in 1265; Safad in 1266; Jaffa, Beaufort, and Antioch in 1268; and Crac des Chevaliers in 1271). Baybars left his successors a much-reduced Crusader entity that was finally eliminated in 1291 by the sultan al-Ashraf Khalil ibn Qalawun.

Baybars was responsible for the greater institutionalization of the army, the *iqta'* (land allocation) system, and provincial and central administration, as well as a reform of the judiciary system, which led to the placing of all four Sunni schools of law on an equal footing (albeit with a slight preference for the Shafi'i school). He was also a great builder of fortifications and religious buildings. Although not the first ruler of the Sultanate, he was in many ways its real founder. He was succeeded by his son al-Sa'id Berke Khan, who was, however, removed after two years. After a short interlude in which another son, Sulamish, served as a puppet ruler, Baybars's colleague and associate Qalawun (r. 1279–1290) ascended to the throne.

REUVEN AMITAI

See also 'Ayn Jalut; Land-Tenure; Mamluks; Mongols

Further Reading

Amitai, Reuven. "The Mamluk Officer Class during the Reign of Sultan Baybars." In *War and Society in the Eastern Mediterranean, 7th–15th Centuries.* Edited by Yaakov Lev. Leiden: Brill, 1997, 267–300.

Amitai-Preiss, Reuven. "Mamluk Perceptions of the Mongol–Frankish Rapprochement." *Mediterranean Historical Review* 7 (1992): 50–65.

———. *Mongols and Mamluks: The Mamluk–Ilkhanid War, 1260–1281.* Cambridge: Cambridge University Press, 1995.

Holt, Peter M. *The Age of the Crusades: The Near East from the Eleventh Century to 1517.* London and New York: Longman, 1986.

———, *Early Mamluk Diplomacy, 1260–1290: Treaties of Baybars and Qalawun with Christian Rulers.* Leiden: Brill, 1995.

Irwin, Robert. *The Middle East in the Middle Ages: The Early Mamluk Sultanate, 1250–1382.* London: Routledge, 1986.

Khowaiter, Abdul-Aziz. *Baibars the First: His Endeavours and Achievements*. London, 1978.

Northrup, Linda. "The Bahri Mamluk Sultanate, 1250–1390." In *The Cambridge History of Egypt*. 2 vols. Vol. 1. Edited by Carl Petry. Cambridge: Cambridge University Press, 1998, 242–289.

Thorau, Peter. *The Lion of Egypt: Sultan Baybars I and the Near East in the Thirteenth Century*. Trans. P.M. Holt. London and New York: Longman, 1992.

Wiet, Gaston. "Baybars I." *Encyclopaedia of Islam*, Second Edition. 1:1124–1126.

BEAUTY AND AESTHETICS

Muslim medieval culture, like contemporary European culture, did not articulate a philosophical concept of art. It dealt, however, with various concepts of beauty and aesthetics.

Islam can be considered to take an aesthetic approach to faith: The unique beauty of the Qur'anic text, whether read or recited, and hence its inimitability, are believed to be the evidence for its divine nature. Tradition tells about people being converted through the fascination with the beauty of the recited Qur'an.

The Qur'an neither refers explicitly to issues of artistic relevance nor prescribes the shape of the mosque or the use of liturgical objects, Islam being rather a religion without complex liturgy, which allows the worshipper direct communication with God. However, it uses a dozen terms that refer to moral rather than aesthetic beauty. Muslim theologians and, in particular, the Sufis, have often dealt with the beauty of God; however, this approach is spiritual, with no artistic or aesthetic associations. Al-Ghazali, in his book *Ihya' 'ulum al-din (Revivification of the Religious Sciences)*, discusses the subject of divine beauty, as well as the issues of ethics and behavior, such as the permissibility of music. Al-Ghazali's book includes some interesting statements with relevance to material culture and art.

Muslim theologians were not involved in shaping the architecture of the mosque; rather, this was shaped by the patrons (that is, the rulers), whose duty it was to establish and oversee religious institutions. Alongside its religious meaning, it acquired a political significance. The decorative arts, including objects related to religious monuments, were shaped by the secular patronage of the court and a sophisticated urban society. Although calligraphy has the status of a sacral art, because of its association with the Qur'an, designers from the chancellery created it as a discipline. It was the only visual art in medieval Islam to have a written canon based on precisely established rules of proportions and to be considered a truly scholarly discipline. No other discipline in the visual arts is known to have had such a scholarly status. Whereas medieval Islamic culture did not conceptualize the visual arts and include them in the discourse on beauty, Arabic literary criticism has elaborated highly sophisticated aesthetic concepts for the belles-lettres. Although the origins of Arabic literary criticism are rooted in the religious tradition of Qur'anic exegesis, it expanded to play a significant role in poetry. Because poetry had a rather controversial status from the orthodox viewpoint, it remained, like the visual arts, in the secular domain. The mainstream of Arab literary criticism, following the Aristotelian principle, which distinguishes between content and form, considered good poetry as uncongenial with moral or religious intentions. The view that the form was the decisive factor in the artistic assessment reveals an aesthetic rather than moral approach. Implicitly, a corresponding principle ruled the visual arts, which used the same artistic and decorative vocabulary for the secular and religious domains.

Arabic classical literature deals with human beauty and love, the prevailing view being that beauty is a matter of subjective appreciation.

DORIS BEHRENS-ABOUSEIF

Further Reading

Behrens-Abouseif, D. *Beauty in Arabic Culture*. Princeton, 1999.

Giese, A., A and Ch Bürgel (eds). *Gott ist schön und Er liebt die Schönheit. Festschrift für Annemarie Schimmel*. Bern, 1994.

Kirmani, N. *Gott ist Schön*. München, 1999.

Puerta Vilchez, José Miguel. *Historia del Pensamiento Estético Árabe. Al-Andalus y la Estética Árabe Clásica*. Madrid, 1997.

'Usfur, Jamal J. *Qira'at al-turath al-naqdi*. Kuwait, 1992.

'Usfur, J. *al-Sura al-fanniyya fi l-turath al-naqdi wa-l-balaghi*. Cairo, 1992.

Von Grünebaum, G. *Kritik und Dichtkunst. Studien zur arabischen Literaturgeschichte*. Wiesbaden, 1955.

Ward Gwyne, R. "Beauty." In *Encyclopaedia of the Qur'an*. Vol. 1. (Brill) Leiden and Boston: Köln, 2001.

BERBER, OR TAMAZIGHT

Tamazight (Berber) is a language of the Afro-Asiatic family and comprises a number of related dialects spoken by the indigenous populations of North Africa. The geographical expanse covered by these dialects once included virtually all of Africa north of the great Sahara Desert. Variations of it are still used from the Canary Islands off the Moroccan Atlantic coast in the West to the oasis of Siwa, in the western desert of Egypt to the east, and from the Mediterranean shores of Africa in the north to the Saharan villages of Niger and Mali in the south. Although the different spoken varieties of Tamazight are related closely enough to be viewed as dialects of the same language, the degree of intelligibility among speakers of different varieties is subject to a great deal of variation depending on distance, the amount of interaction among different communities, and the level of awareness interlocutors have, whether or not they belong to the same language family.

The name *tamazight* is used in the Middle Atlas region of Morocco and is the same term used to refer to a singular feminine member of the community (*amazigh* for the singular masculine and *imazighen* for the plural). Northern speakers in the Rif Mountains use the terms *tarifit (arifi, irifiyn)* or *trifsht*; in the High Atlas and Lower Atlas and southern Morocco the name used is *tashelhit (ashelhi, ishelhiyen)*. In Algeria the names frequently used are *taqbaylit* n the mountainous areas of Kabylia, *tashawit* in the Aures Mountains, and *tamzabit* in the south. Among the populations of Siwa in Egypt the appellation used is *tasiwit*. In the vast expanses of the great Sahara Desert some of the names used are *tamasheq*, *tamajeq*, and *tamahar*.

There are no reliable sources as to the numbers of Tamazight speakers in North Africa today, as official population counts generally do not address the language issue. The available information usually presents the number of Tamazight speakers in Tunisia as being around 1 percent of the population, 20 percent in Algeria, and as high as 40 percent in Morocco, but the accuracy of these numbers will only be verified when reliable scientific surveys are carried out.

According to the *al-moheet* dictionary, the Arabic name *barbari* used to refer to speakers of this language is derived from the verb *barbara*, meaning to speak loudly in an agitated manner and unintelligibly. The same verb is used to refer to sounds made by agitated or overexcited animals. The French historian and ethnographer Gabriel Camps traces the histories of the different names used throughout history to name the 'Berbers.' With regard to the *amazigh* appellation, he notes the existence of a name based on a three-letter root, composed of [M, Z, G] or [M, Z, K], that has been used by North Africa, as well as by early historians, notably Greek and Roman. Possible ancient renditions of the word *amazigh* include Roman *mazices*, Greek *maxyces* or *mazyes*, and *meshwesh*, which appears in ancient Egyptian inscriptions. Camps cites the existence of differences in pronunciation and

spelling of modern names, for example *imusagh* or *imajighen* of the great Sahara Desert and the *imazighens* of the Aurès and Middle and High Atlas, as being comparable (p. 66). Many researchers in the field, including Muslim scholars, concede that the Arabic name 'barbar' and its 'berber' descendant in Western languages have never been used by the populations in question to refer to themselves.

Based largely on information provided by writers including Al-Qayrawani, Al-Bekri, Ibn Hayyan, Al-Qurtubi, Al-Warraq, Ibn Khaldun, and many other Muslim historians who wrote between the ninth and fifteenth centuries, it is understood that varieties of Tamazight were spoken all over North Africa and that Arabic was limited to the larger urban centers. Tamazight-speaking populations gave rise to some of the most powerful empires that North Africa has ever known: the Al-Moravids (eleventh and twelfth centuries), followed by the Al-Mohades (twelfth and thirteenth centuries). The Barghwata tribes who controlled the Atlantic plains of Morocco for almost four centuries (ending in the twelfth century) became notorious in Muslim and Arab sources because they composed what was said to be a heretical Qur'an in their own language and attempted to replace mainstream Islam.

The status of Tamazight in the postcolonial states of North Africa has never been fully recognized. Indeed, writing or publishing in Tamazight was discouraged and often repressed. Thanks to recent political and cultural changes in the area, Tamazight is making a spectacular comeback into the world of media and even the school systems. Indeed, both Algeria and Morocco have started introducing Tamazight into their elementary-school curricula.

RACHID AADNANI

Further Reading

Abun-nasr, Jamil M. *A History of the Maghrib in the Islamic Period.* Cambridge: Cambridge University Press, 1987.

Azaykou, Ali Sidqi. *Histoire du Maroc Ou les interprétations possibles.* Rabat: Centre Tariq In Zyad, 2002.

Brett, Michael, and Elizabeth Fentress. *The Berbers.* Malden, MA: Blackwell Publishers, 1996.

Camps, Gabriel. *Les Berberes: Mémoires et identité.* Paris: Editions Errance, 1987.

Chaker, Salem. *Textes en Linguistique Berbère: Introduction au domaine berbère.* Paris: CNRS, 1984.

Ibn Khaldun. *The Muqaddimah: An Introduction to History.* Trans. Franz Rosenthal. London: Routledge, Kegan and Paul, 1967.

Laroui, Abdallah. *The History of the Maghrib: An Interpretative Essay.* Trans. Ralph Manheim. Princeton: Princeton University Press, 1970.

Norris, H.T. *The Berbers in Arabic Literature.* Essex: Longman, 1982.

BERBERS

"Berbers" is the generic name given to various people native to North Africa, also called "Berberia" for the pre-Islamic and early medieval period, or "Maghrib," an Arabic term meaning "the land of the sunset." The Berbers, who settled in African lands in the first millennium BCE, primarily belonged to the same linguistic community based on the nonwritten language called Tamazight. Although they shared common cultural features, Berbers distinguished one another through different modes of living—sedentary, seminomadic, and nomadic (for those from the Sahara Desert, which were called "Targis" or "Touaregs"). The Berbers had embraced Christianity and Judaism before they became Muslim, following the Arab conquest in the seventh-century CE. Divided into families, groups of descendants, and tribes, they settled in territories stretching from the Atlantic Ocean to Cyrenaica and some locations of Western Egypt. These territories cover three main areas: Occidental, Central, and Oriental Berberia, also called "Ifriqiyya." The Tunisian historian Ibn Khaldun (1332–1406) was the first to study the history, culture, and sociology of Berbers in his seven-volume treatise *Al-Kitab al-Ibar (The Book of Historical Examples)*. His distinction between Arabs and Berbers, their lifestyle, economies, and power relationships, illustrates the sociopolitical situation of medieval Maghrib. In particular, the rivalries between the two ethnic groups have marked the history of Muslim North Africa and Al-Andalus (Islamic Spain) as well, because Spain was invaded by an Islamic Berber–Arab army in 711 and constituted a part of the Muslim Empire for about eight centuries.

The advent of Islam in North Africa led to a phenomenon of Arabization of the Berbers, although they have never lost entirely their cultural identity. However, the Arab occupation in the seventh and eighth centuries, following the Byzantine domination, was not accomplished without a fierce resistance. Accordingly, the Islamization of Berberia was relatively slow and completed only in the twelfth century. Always rebellious, Berbers were in favor of heterodox religious trends and sectarian movements, such as Kharijism and Shi'ism, opposing the Sunni Caliphate and local governing class before the generalized adoption of the Malikism School in Maghrib in the dawn of modern times. The complex relationships of Berber clans with these various Islamic trends superimposed on the sociological phenomena of family alliances or dissensions and tribal confederations underlies the troubled dynastic history of medieval Maghrib. Following the period of dependence on the Umayyads of Damascus (660–749), the first dissident states from the Caliphate in the East appeared in Maghrib, supported by local Berbers: the Shi'i kingdom of the Idrisids (789–974) in Occidental Berberia and the Kharijid kingdom of the Rostamids (777–909) in Central Berberia. The Zanata on the one hand and the Masmouda, Kotama, and Sanhaja on the other hand are to be associated with the division of Berberia, in the tenth and eleventh centuries, into two zones of political and religious influence of the rival Caliphates in the West of the Sunni Umeyyads in Cordoba and the Shi'i Fatimids in Cairo. Besides, before it was transferred to Egypt, the schismatic Fatimid State initially took place in Ifriqiyya, thanks again to the Berber support. The second half of the eleventh century saw the rise of the first great Sunni Berber Empire of the Almoravids (1056–1147), Al-Murabitun, "people of the *ribat*" (Islamic fortress). Founded by the nomadic tribe of the Lamtuna, the Almoravids developed a bright civilization called "Hispano-Berber" or "Hispano-Maghrebi" in Occidental and Central Berberia and Al-Andalus. In Spain, they had progressively reunified the Islamic land that, after the fall of the Umeyyad Caliphate in 1031, was partitioned into multiple kingdoms governed by either Arab or Berber dynasties called "Reyes de Taifas" (Party Kings). The Almoravids also had temporarily stopped the "*Reconquista*" (eleventh century to 1492), the ongoing Christian conquest of Al-Andalus. The direct contact with the Andalusi urban culture greatly contributed to the development of the Almoravid civilization in North Africa. However, soon the refined courtly life of the Almoravids came up against the rigorous religious feelings of the society. In the twelfth century a reformative movement founded by the *mahdi* ("the well-guided") Ibn Tumart, based on an absolute respect of divine uniqueness, allowed a new Berber dynasty to take over all Maghribi regions. The Almoravids (1130–1269) or Al-Muwahhidun ("the partisans of divine uniqueness") established a second Hispano-Berber Empire more powerful than the previous one. An economical prosperity relying on exchanges between Black Africa, Berberia, and Mediterranean Europe, and an active cultural life enlightened by great philosophers such as Ibn Rushd and Ibn Tufayl, built the grandeur of the Almohad Empire, the most glorious episode of Berber history. The subsequent dynasty of the Marinids (1258–1465), from the Zanata tribe, was the last Berber reign in Maghrib in the Middle Ages.

VALERIE GONZALEZ

Primary Sources

Ibn Khaldun. *Kitab al-Ibar wa diwan al-mubtada' wa l-khabar fi ayyami l-Arab wa l-Agam wa l-Barbar*. Bulaq

Editions, 1867–1868, translation of Vol. I by Rosenthal, F. *The Muqqadimah, An Introduction to History*. New York, 1958, 3 vol.

See also Almohads; Almoravids; Andalus; Berber (Tamazight); Caliphate and Imamate; Conquest; Family; Fatimids; Free Thinkers; Heresy and Heretics; Ibn Khaldun; Ibn Rushd (Averroes); Ibn Tufayl; Ibn Tumart; Idrisids; Kharijis; Malikism; Marinids; Nomadism and Pastoralism; Party Kings; Reform; Schools of Jurisprudence; Sedentarism; Shi'ism; Trade, African; Trade, Mediterranean; Umayyads

Further Reading

Abun-Nasr, J.M. *A History of the Maghrib in the Islamic Period*. Cambridge, MA, 1987.

Brett, Michael. "The Spread of Islam in Egypt and North Africa." In *Northern Africa: Islam and Modernization*. Ed. Brett. London, 1973.

The Further Islamic Lands, *The Cambridge History of Islam*. Vol. II. Cambridge University Press, 1970, 211–237 and 406–440.

Chejne, A.G. *Muslim Spain: Its History and Culture*. Minneapolis, 1974.

Encyclopédie Berbère, sous la direction de Gabriel Camps. Aix-en-Provence, 1985.

Johnson, D.L. *The Nature of Nomadism: A Comparative Study of Pastoral Migrations in Southwestern Asia and North Africa*. Chicago, 1969.

Marçais, Georges. *La Berbérie Musulmane et l'Orient au Moyen Age*. Paris, 1946.

BEVERAGES

After water, the most essential beverage is milk, whether human or animal. Mothers' milk is not merely nutritional but produces, in the case of suckling by a foster mother, a bond considered in Islam nearly as strong as a blood relationship and similarly causes a series of marriage impediments. Animal milk may be from cow, camel, sheep, or goat. The Qur'an (47:15) promises to the god-fearing "rivers of water unstaling, rivers of milk unchanging in flavour, and rivers of wine–a delight to the drinkers, rivers, too, of honey purified" (tr. Arberry). These four drinks were popular on earth, too, even the one forbidden to Muslims, which is celebrated far more often and more fervently in poetry than any other drink. Milk and milk products are typical in Bedouin life; urban society has added a large number of other drinks. Many of these were mildly alcoholic, being fermented infusions of cereals or fruits; the word *fuqqa'* stands for a range of sparkling drinks, many of which could be considered kinds of beer, ale, or shandy. Others were soft drinks, being fruit juices made of lemon, apple, pomegranate, tamarind, jujube, and so on, often flavored with honey, sugar, sumac, musk, mint, and other ingredients, and cooled with snow or ice, if one could afford it. The great variety in methods of preparation and in the appellations used (which differ through time and according to local traditions and languages) gave much work to the religious scholars who attempted to distinguish the forbidden from the permissible. Recipes for drinks are found in culinary, as well as medical, works: There is no clear boundary between, on the one hand, drinks for nutrition and pleasure and, on the other hand, tonics or medicinal beverages. The Arabic word *sharab* is ambiguous: It means "beverage" in general, but in many contexts it is obviously used as a euphemism for wine or other alcoholic drinks. It is also used for any kind of syrup or cordial. That the word syrup, together with its English and European cognates (including sherbet and sorbet), derives from *sharab* illustrates the importance and appeal of medieval Middle Eastern beverages.

Coffee and tea, so popular in the modern Middle East, are relatively recent innovations: The latter is postmedieval and only the former can be called a (late) medieval drink. The Arabic word *qahwa* (from which "cafe" and "coffee" are derived) is found in much older periods as a rather rare word for "wine." It was used for coffee when this drink spread in the fourteenth and fifteenth centuries from Ethiopia via Yemen and Arabia to the rest of the Middle East, reaching Cairo in the early sixteenth century. Initially, many puritan scholars regarded it as suspect or even forbidden, not merely because of its name and its being an innovation, but because it was thought to be associated with sin (listening to music, drinking wine, eating hashish) and mysticism and was seen to affect the mind. In the end it was acknowledged that its effects could not be compared to those of alcohol or drugs.

GEERT JAN VAN GELDER

See also Alcohol; Rosewater; Water; Wine

Further Reading

Hattox, Ralph S. *Coffee and Coffeehouses: The Origins of a Social Beverage in the Medieval Near East*. Seattle and London: University of Washington Press, 1988.

Rodinson, Maxime, A. J. Arberry, and Charles Perry. *Medieval Arab Cookery*. Totnes, Devon: Prospect Books, 2001; see general index s.v. drinks, milk, syrup, verjuice.

Sadan, J. "Mashrubat." *Encyclopaedia of Islam*, New edition. Vol. 6. Leiden: Brill, 1991, 720–723.

BIBLE

The question of whether or not the Bible was translated into Arabic before the rise of Islam was debated in the early twentieth century by two German scholars: Anton Baumstark and Georg Graf. Their debate centered on biblical references in Arabic poetry traditionally held to be pre-Islamic and in later Arabic works, references that according to Baumstark proved the existence of such a translation. The debate was never settled. Today, scholars such as Irfan Shahid uphold the position of Baumstark, while others, among them Sidney Griffith, support the position of Graf, by reminding us that although there is still no convincing material evidence of a pre-Islamic Arabic Bible, there is evidence that Arabic-speaking Christians of the time used a Syriac Bible.

Nevertheless, the Qur'an is replete with references to, and even quotations of, biblical material. Indeed, the Qur'an might be considered under the category of biblical literature, which is broadly understood. As the scholars A. Geiger, M. Grünbaum, H. Speyer, and A. Jeffery have shown, the Qur'anic worldview, from the seven days of creation through the apocalyptic Day of Judgment, is articulated through biblical terminology, narratives, characters, and symbolism. Although apologetic arguments maintaining the absolute independence of the Qur'an have gained popularity, readers familiar with biblical (including Mishnaic/Talmudic and apocryphal texts) writings will find the Qur'anic narratives of biblical figures—from Adam to Jesus—familiar. Meanwhile, many other narratives in the Qur'an, including the three separate stories of *sūra* 18 (companions of the cave, Moses and the servant of God, and the two-horned one), prove to be connected to biblical or parabiblical works (Seven Sleepers of Ephesus, Legend of Joshua ben Levi, Syriac Romance of Alexander, respectively).

However, the Qur'an itself refers neither to the Bible nor to an Old or New Testament but rather to the Torah (*tawrāt*; 3:3, 3:48, 61:6, passim), the Gospel (*injīl*, cf. Gk. εὐαγγέλιον; 3:3, 3:48, 5:47, passim), and the Psalter (*zabūr*, cf. Syriac *mazmūrā*; 4:163, 17:55, 21:105), in addition to the sheets *(suḥuf)* of Moses and Abraham (20:133, 53:50, 87:18, passim). These references have fueled the development of an Islamic scriptural theology, by which Muslim scholars argue that God brought down scriptures to various messengers, scriptures akin to the Qur'an in both form and substance, but in the language of the people for whom they were intended (cf. 14:4). In a more abstract fashion, Muslim scholars, influenced by Qur'anic references to the "mother of the Book" (13:39, 43:4) and a "preserved tablet" (85:22), depict the Qur'an as only part of a greater scripture preserved from eternity in heaven, from which the Torah, the Gospel, and the Psalter were also sent down. At one point (10:94), in fact, the Qur'an counsels the reader to consult those who read "the Book" before.

This scriptural theology raised a dilemma, however, as Muslim scholars were confronted with the fact that the Bible agrees with the Qur'an neither in form nor substance and could not therefore be understood as part of the heavenly book sent down to earth. The dilemma was generally settled, with help from a reference in the Qur'an to Jews "altering *(yuḥarrifūna)* the meaning of speech" (2:75, 4:46, 5:13, 41), by accusing Jews and Christians, the "People of the Book," of scriptural alteration *(taḥrīf)*. In a tradition attributed by later authors to Muhammad himself, the Prophet argues that "the People of the Book altered that which God wrote, altering the book with their hands" (Bukhārī *Ṣaḥīḥ* [Beirut 1999] 2:182). Yet while the early commentators generally agree that the Jews and Christians altered scripture, few are willing or able to speculate on how they did so.

In the late tenth century, however, 'Abd al-Jabbār (d. 1025) developed a detailed explanation of part of this matter in *Confirmation of the Proofs of Prophecy*, arguing that a group of hypocritical disciples of Christ agreed to adopt pagan practices in order to win the support of the Romans against the Jews. Those disciples who refused this pernicious maneuver then fled with the true Gospel. The hypocrites, with the help of Paul, decided to write their own gospels on the model of Old Testament narratives. This polemical vision of biblical origins—particularly the depiction of Paul therein—would later shape the development of modern Muslim apology.

Meanwhile, this rejection of the Bible's validity did not prevent Muslim scholars from drawing on the biblical text to find proof *(dalā'il)* of Islamic doctrine and accusing the "People of the Book" of misunderstanding their own scriptures. Employing this accusation, sometimes referred to as "semantic alteration" *(taḥrīf al-ma'nā)*, scholars including 'Alī al-Ṭabarī (d. 855), al-Qāsim b. Ibrāhim (d. 860), Ibn azm (d. 1064), and Aḥmad al-Qarāfī (d. 1285) cite biblical passages, such as John 14:16 (arguing that the paraclete is not the Holy Spirit but Muhammad) and John 20:17 (concluding from his reference to "my God" that Christ is not divine). This apologetical strategy has likewise been embraced by modern Muslim apologists. At the same time, Christian scholars, both medieval (Paul of Antioch [d. 1180]) and modern (G. Basetti-Sani), have used a similar strategy by developing a Christian reading of the Qur'an, which, they argue, was missed by Muslims' "semantic alteration."

Finally, it should be noted that certain Muslim scholars of the medieval period pursued alternative, constructive readings of the Bible. On the one hand, certain scientifically minded historians, most notably Ya'qūbī (d. 897) but also Mas'ūdī (d. 956), relied on Jewish and Christian sources for their writings of biblical figures. Thus Ya'qūbī's biography of Paul, quite unlike the standard hostile Islamic depiction of him, closely resembles the Acts of the Apostles narrative. On the other hand, a number of philosophically minded Shi'ite Muslim scholars, mostly from the Ismā'īlī or Sevener movement (among whom are Abū Ḥātim al-Rāzī [d. 934] and Aḥmad al-Kirmānī [d. 1020]), cited and even defended the biblical text, as they sought to describe a harmony of prophetic religions, according to which Judaism, Christianity, and Islam are three rays from the one divine light of wisdom.

GABRIEL SAID REYNOLDS

Further Reading

Accad, Martin. "The Gospels in the Muslim Discourse of the Ninth to the Fourteenth Centuries: An Exegetical Inventorial Table." In *Islam and Christian-Muslim Relations* 14, no. 1 (Jan 2003): 67–91; 14, no. 2 (Apr 2003): 205–220; 14, no. 3 (July 2003): 337–352; 14, no. 4 (Oct 2003): 459–479.

al-Ṭabarī, 'Alī. *The Book of Religion and Empire.* Trans. A. Mingana. Manchester: Manchester University Press, 1922.

Basetti-Sani, Giulio. *The Koran in the Light of Christ.* Chicago: Franciscan Herald Press, 1977.

Cragg, Kenneth. *A Certain Sympathy of Scriptures.* Brighton: Sussex Academic Press, 2004.

Goddard, Hugh. *Muslim Perceptions of Christianity.* London: Grey Seal, 1996.

Griffith, Sidney. *The Beginnings of Christian Theology in Arabic.* Burlington, VT: Ashgate, 2002.

Jeffery, Arthur. *The Qur'ān as Scripture.* New York: Books for Libraries, 1980.

Lazarus-Yafeh, Hava. *Intertwined Worlds: Medieval Islam and Bible Criticism.* Princeton: Princeton University Press, 1992.

Reynolds, Gabriel Said. *A Muslim Theologian in the Sectarian Milieu: 'Abd al-Jabbār and the "Critique of Christian Origins".* Leiden: E. J. Brill, 2004.

Shahid, Irfan. *Byzantium and the Semitic Orient before the Rise of Islam.* London: Variorum, 1988.

Thomas, David. "The Bible in Early Muslim Anti-Christian Polemic." In *Islam and Christian-Muslim Relations* 7, no. 1 (March 1996): 29–38.

BIJAPUR

A province of the Persianate Bahmanid Kingdom of the Deccan, Bijapur became the center of the domain of one of the key successor states to the Bahmanids, namely the 'Adil Shahi dynasty (1489–1686). Located in the Deccan on the edge of the Western Ghats, south of the Bahmanid capital of Bidar, Bijapur was founded as Vijayapura by the Calukyas in the eleventh century. It was incorporated into the Bahmanid realm in 1347 and made one of the five provinces of that empire by Khwaja Mahmud Gawan (d. 1481), the powerful Persian vizier of Muhammad Shah II (d. 1482).

In 1481, Yusuf 'Adil Khan, a Persian slave who claimed to descend from the Ottoman sultan Murad III, became the governor of Bijapur. Taking advantage of his position and consolidating it, he declared independence in 1489, establishing the 'Adil Shahi dynasty that was to rule Bijapur for another two centuries. In 1502, he declared Twelver Shi'ism to be the religion of the realm and established close ties with the Safavids, further encouraging the influx of talented Persians into the Deccan, a policy initiated by Mahmud Gawan. In imitation of the Safavids, he promoted the wearing of the red twelve-pointed cap of the Qizilbash at court. The height of Persian and Shi'i influence was during the reign of 'Ali 'Adil Shah (r. 1558–1580), who had the Shi'i *khutba* read in mosques. A brief Sunni restoration, coupled with a move away from Persian influence, took place under his grandson Ibrahim 'Adil Shah II (d. 1618). But the Persianate culture of the kingdom was never in doubt and its Shi'ism was one of the *casi belli* cited by Awrangzeb when he conquered it in 1686.

Bijapur was perhaps more culturally influential than politically. Most of the monarchs were keen Persian poets and encouraged courtiers to take up poetry. The two most famous poets of Bijapur, Nur al-Din Muhammad Zuhuri (d. 1618) and his father-in-law Mulla Malik Qummi (d. 1618) were both Persian immigrants. Persians also penned the the two main histories of the dynasty, which provide important accounts of the Deccan as a whole and are invaluable sources for north India: *Tadhkira-yi Ibrahimi,* or the *Ta'rikh-i Firishta,* by Muhammad Qasim Firishta, written in 1611 for Ibrahim 'Adil Shah II, and *Tadhkirat al-muluk* by Rafi' al-Din Ibrahim Shirazi for the same patron in 1609. Bijapur was the center of Perso-Deccan cultural synthesis. The new chancellery language of Perso-Marathi was created in its administration, and the exquisite tombs of the kings were exemplars of a Persianate-Deccan style. The tomb of Ibrahim 'Adil Shah, the *Ibrahim Rawza,* was built in 1627 and is said to have influenced the construction of the Taj Mahal, and the tomb of Muhammad 'Adil Shah (d. 1656) has the second-largest dome in the world and is celebrated as the *Golgumbaz* because of it. The Sufis of the city became significant power brokers in their own right, defending Sunni orthodoxy and extending the influence of the orders into the Deccan.

SAJJAD H. RIZVI

See also Mughals; Sufism

Primary Source

Muhammad Qasim Firishta. *Ta'rikh-i Firishta (The Rise of Muhammadan Power in India)*. Tr. J. Briggs, Calcutta: Susil Gupta, 1958 [1829].

Further Reading

Cousens, H. *Bijapur and Its Architectural Remains*. Bombay: Govt. Central Press, 1916.
Eaton, R. M. *Sufis of Bijapur, 1300–1700: Social Role of Sufis in Medieval India*. Princeton, NJ: Princeton University Press, 1978.
Ghauri, I. A. "Central Structure of the Kingdom of Bijapur." *Islamic Culture* 44 (1970).
Nayeem, M. A. *External Relations of the Bijapur Kingdom (1489–1686 A.D.)*. Hyderabad: Bright Publishers, 1974.
Sherwani, H. K. *Mahmud Gawan: The Great Bahmani Wazir*. Allahabad: Kitabistan, 1942.
Subramanyam, S. "Iranians Abroad: Intra-Asian Elite Migration and Early Modern State Formation." *Journal of Asian Studies* 51 (1992): 430–463.
Verma, D. C. *History of Bijapur*. New Delhi: Kumar Bros, 1974.
www.bijapur.net

BILĀL AL-ḤABĀSHĪ

Bilāl al-Ḥabāshī (d. AH 17–21/638–642 CE) a major Companion (*ṣaḥābī*), was best known as Prophet Muḥammad's special appointee for delivering the call to prayer (*adhān*) and was often regarded as a representative of disenfranchised groups (*al-mustaḍ'afūn*) who were drawn to Islam, and as the icon of racial and social equality advocated by this religion. He is sometimes referred to as Bilāl ibn Rabāḥ (son of Rabāḥ), after his father, or alternatively as Bilāl ibn Ḥamāma, after his mother. The patronymic title (*kunya*) of Abū 'Abd-Allāh has been recorded for him, but he had no known children.

Bilāl was born to a black slave-girl named Hamāma in the Arab clan of Banū Jumaḥ in Hijāz. His full name indicates that he had roots in Abyssinia (Ar. Ḥabasha, roughly identifiable with present-day Ethiopia). Sources describe him as dark-skinned, thick-haired, tall, and thin. He was one of the earliest converts (*al-sābiqūn*) to Islam, and when the clansmen of Banū Jumaḥ found out the news about their slave, they subjected him to heavy corporal punishment and brutal torture. Bilāl's main tormentor was Umayya ibn Khalaf ibn Wahb ibn Ḥudhāfa al-Jumaḥī, chief of the clan of Banū Jumaḥ, who showed the utmost animosity toward Prophet Muḥammad and his followers. Bilāl persevered steadfastly in the face of pressure until, finally, Abū Bakr ibn Abī Quḥāfa (d. 13/634), an affluent close Companion of the Prophet, bought his freedom from the clan of Banū Jumaḥ.

Bilāl exhibited exemplary loyalty to the Prophet throughout his life after conversion. He was among the pioneering group of Meccans who emigrated to Medīna in the year 622. In Medina, he briefly stayed with a number of other poverty-stricken Muslims known as "men of the vestibule" (*ahl al-ṣuffa*), who, having no other place of their own, shared part of the entrance to the mosque of Medina as a dwelling. Shortly after initial settlement in Medina, in the process of establishing ties of brotherhood (*ukhuwwa*) between Meccan emigrants (*al-muhājirūn*) and their hosts in Medina (*al-anṣār*), the Prophet declared the Meccan Bilāl and the Medinan Abū Ruwayḥa al-Khath'amī as brothers. Years later, under caliph 'Umar ibn Khaṭṭāb (r. 13–23/634–644), this tie of brotherhood between Bilāl and an Arab man of the clan of Khath'am provided the precedent for considering other black and African warriors as belonging to that tribe as well.

In his first year in Medina, the Prophet Muḥammad initiated the practice of vocally calling his followers to prayer (*adhān*), and from the beginning he charged Bilāl with performing the task as muezzin (*mu'adhdhin*). The most momentous occasion when he delivered the *adhān* was when Muḥammad and his followers victoriously entered Mecca (8/629) and cleansed the House of Ka'ba and its environs of all idols. Bilāl also performed personal tasks for the Prophet, such as acquiring incense for the wedding of his daughter Fāṭima (1/623), and he was trusted as the Prophet's treasurer (*khāzin*). He always accompanied the Prophet on military expeditions (*ghazwas*), and in the Battle of Badr his former tormenter was killed by Muslim troops.

After the Prophet's death, Bilāl was reluctant to deliver the call to prayer, as he may have felt dissatisfied with succession arrangements. Reportedly, he declined to pledge allegiance (*bay'a*) to Abū Bakr (r. 11–13/632–634) as caliph, and he eventually emigrated and settled in Shām. On at least one moving occasion, Bilāl is known to have delivered the *adhan* after the Prophet, and that was upon the request of Muḥammad's beloved daughter Fāṭima (d. 11/632) and her two sons, al-Ḥasan (d. 50/669) and al-Ḥusayn (d. 61/680).

As a close Companion of the Prophet, Bilāl enjoyed high esteem during his lifetime. He died in Shām, and his tomb is most commonly believed to be in Damascus.

HOSSEIN KAMALY

Further Reading

Craig, H.A.L. *Bilal* (a screenplay). London and New York: Quartet Books, 1977.
Landau-Tasseron, Ella (translation and annotation). *Biographies of the Prophet's Companions and Their*

Successors. Vol. 39 of the translation of selected passages from *Ta'rīkh al-rusul wa al-mulūk* originally by Muḥammad b. Jarīr al-Ṭabarī (d. 923). Albany: State University of New York Press, 1998.

Qasi, M. A. *Bilal, the First Muadhdhin of the Prophet of Islam*. Chicago: Kazi Publications, 1976.

BIOGRAPHY AND BIOGRAPHICAL WORKS

No direct Arabic equivalents exist for the English "biography" and "biographical works." Arabic words associated with biography include *tarjama* and *sira*; with biographical works, *tabaqat* or *rijal*. This may in part be due to the fact that the literary genre of Arabic biographical works is an original contribution of medieval Islamic civilization, having no real precursor. While information contained in medieval Arabic biographical dictionaries resembles contemporary *Who's Who* works or a modern-day *curriculum vitae* rather than the introspection of the self found in (auto)biographies, they do contain more social data than any other preindustrial society for a large segment of the population. This entry includes the origin of this literary genre within Islamic civilization, the four categories of medieval Arabic biographical dictionaries that exist, the overall arrangement of a biographical notice and, finally, the five rubrics of information encountered in these works.

Origin of the Genre

The first biographical dictionaries date back to the ninth century CE, some two hundred years after the death of the Prophet Muhammad. They came into being as Islam was embarking on the last phase of self-definition as a fully crystallized and coherent system of faith. The contemporaneity is no coincidence. Indeed, the two features of biographical data collection and integral doctrinal crystallization went hand in hand. The oldest extant biographical dictionary, written by Ibn Sa'd (d. 845) and titled *al-Tabaqat al-kubra*, concretely illustrates this union. Ibn Sa'd, together with six other prominent religious scholars, had been ordered to appear before the 'Abbasid caliph al-Ma'mun (r. 813–833), a summons that marked the beginning of this caliph's inquisition *(mihna)*. The aim of this inquisition was to impose caliphal will in religious matters above that of the group to which Ibn Sa'd belonged, the religious scholars. Ultimately, some fifteen years later, the caliphs had to give in, and from that day onward, religious scholars and not caliphs exacted religious authority in Islam. It

is this "religious authority" that motivated the first compilers of the first biographical dictionaries.

The connection between religious authority on the one hand and biographical data on the other hand goes back to the inception of Islam. From the very beginning, Islam had a very strong oral tradition in the transmission of knowledge because the Qur'an, being God's literal word, had itself been orally transmitted through the angel Gabriel to the Prophet Muhammad. Soon the Prophet's Companions *(sahaba)* and their successors, in time *(tabi'un)*, started to pass on stories about the words and/or deeds of the Prophet to help understand the meaning of God's Message to humankind (the *hadith*). The chain of transmission continued from one generation to the next; a continuous line of oral transmission came into being, ultimately going back to the Prophet, who was closest to the Sacred. Contemporaries of Ibn Sa'd had introduced as criterion of validity for the truth of the stories about the Prophet that the chain of transmission *(isnad)* only contain individuals who were morally sound and hence beyond any reproach. The first biographical dictionaries, including the aforementioned one by Ibn Sa'd, contained necessary information to evaluate the moral qualifications of individuals, alongside detailed information about the Prophet's life, his Companions, and their Successors up to the author's own time. Ibn Sa'd's work was not only chronologically arranged (that is, per generation) but also geographically distributed across the most important settlements of the early Islamic empire. This tradition of data collection about individuals continued and was elaborated upon throughout the Middle Ages, again and again, which led to the emergence of an entire genre in Arabic literature, that of the biographical dictionaries. The literary genre of biographical dictionaries is large in scope and quantity, a subject to which we now turn.

Categories and Organizational Forms of Biographical Dictionaries

Hundreds of separate titles of medieval Arabic biographical dictionaries exist. Both format and contents vary among these works. Some works limit themselves to a single volume, whereas others can run into more than eighty (printed) volumes. The quality of information also vacillates among the various works. Nonetheless, four different categories of biographical dictionaries can be identified and among these, combinations of the following four categories are encountered: (1) General biographical dictionaries. A good example of this category is al-Dhahabi's (d. 1374) *Siyar a'lam al-nubala'*, the published edition of which totals twenty-five volumes (two are index volumes), and there is a supplement of one volume written by another author. Such a supplement or appendix is called a *dhayl* and is a continuation of an existing work written by another person to complement what that author thought was missing from the original. The *dhayl* constitutes a subcategory of biographical dictionaries because it was often written after the volume. (2) Chronological biographical dictionaries, such as Ibn al-Jawzi's (d. 1200) *al-Muntazam fi ta'rikh al-umam wa al-nuluk*. These eighteen printed volumes are an example of how combinations were made, because this author first lists per year the most important events, then gives obituaries of those who died in that same year. These obituaries were written as more or less curricula vitae of the generation involved, one presented after the other. (3) Geographical biographical dictionaries. Some were limited to a particular city (such as al-Khatib al-Baghdadi's [d. 1071] *Ta'rikh Baghdad*, which includes 15 volumes proper with five extra *dhayl* volumes) or a specific region (such as Abu Hayyan al-Qurtubi's [d. 1076] *al-Muqtabas min abna' ahl al-Andalus,* with one volume). (4) Thematic biographical dictionaries. These biographical dictionaries could include any group ranging from Sufis to philosophers, both groups considered in the Middle Ages as slightly outcast, to mainstream branches of one of the Islamic sciences, such as law, or a particular law school (for example, all Hanbalite law scholars or earlier scholars whom the compiler wanted included among them), and even to collections of individuals who were explicitly considered to be unreliable and thus untrustworthy transmitters of *hadith (rijal)*. The great scholar Ibn Hajar al-'Asqalani (d. 1449), for instance, wrote a nine-volume work on unreliable *hadith* narrators (his *Lisan al-mizan*) and another, a twelve volumes, on reliable transmitters of (Sunnite canonical) *hadith (Tahdhib al-tahdhib)*. As an aside, the latter work provides us with another characteristic of biographical dictionaries. The *Tahdhib al-tahdhib* constitutes a reworking of an earlier and larger dictionary on the same subject by al-Mizzi (d. 1341), *Tahdhib al-kamal fi asma' al-rijal*, itself drawing from an earlier *rijal* work. Despite being a summary of a summary, and to the delight often felt by researchers working with biographical dictionaries, Ibn Hajar either adds information culled from other sources than his main one (some now lost) or explains obscure passages found in the earlier work or works. In other words, one may not simply rely on one single work to uncover details about a scholar's life, since even a revision of an earlier work can include new information. Practically any intellectual field broadly relevant to Islamic civilization received, at one time or another, the attention of a compiler, even if the group was considered negative or marginal.

The arrangements of biographical dictionaries differ. If the compiler of a biographical dictionary opted for an alphabetical arrangement, it could also be his or her choice to put all men whose name starts with "Muhammad" at the very beginning of the dictionary out of respect for the Prophet. Then, the order of the Arabic alphabet dealt with men whose names were known. Women were then listed, followed by men who were only known by their agnomen ("Abu"), then those whose identity was not fully known *(majhulun)*—though the ordering of the last categories can alternate.

Structure and Information

Biographical entries generally tend to have a uniform character, with the focus of attention, as previously mentioned, being more of a summing up of dry facts or anecdotes in the fashion of today's *curriculum vitae* rather than offering psychological insights about the person dealt with, let alone dealing with inner motive. The first part of an entry starts with an enumeration of the name of the person. Included, here, is the genealogy (on average, five generations are listed). Other elements included in the onomastic section are adjectives of relation *(nisba)* referring either to one's tribal or geographical affiliation. If someone had a nickname *(shuhra)* or honorific title *(laqab),* these are included, too. After the onomastic part of the entry, sometimes the names of teachers and pupils the person at hand narrated from or studied under, and to whom this information was in turn passed on to, are provided (more so in collections about *hadith* transmitters, and some collections, such al-Mizzi's *Tahdhib al-kamal fi asma' al-rijal*, additionally included—in abbreviated form indicating the line of transmission of the person involved is found—the letter *"mim"* standing for Muslim's collection or the letter *kha'* for al-Bukhari's compilation, to mention the two most important Sunnite *hadith* works). Anecdotes about the person's life are then given, the gist of which can vary greatly. The year of death, if known, usually closes the entry.

Unsurprisingly, information contained in biographical dictionaries enjoys much variety. Taken as a whole, however, the literary genre of medieval Arabic biographical dictionaries contains five main rubrics of information. As already noted, onomastic data are given, which by nature include the person's genealogy and tribal or geographical circumstances (though care must be taken that the *nisba* encountered in the listing of names sometimes refers to an ancestor who had that *nisba* rather than the person at hand). Secondly, demographic information includes ethnicity, tribal affiliation, occupation, years of birth and death, and occasionally the cause of death. Intellectual direction and standing constitute a third rubric of information, telling the reader which fields of learning a person was involved in, who his (or very rarely her) teachers and/or pupils were, if knowledge was committed to writing, or if the savant had a particular ideological position that differed from the main aim of the biographical dictionary being composed. Third, it was often noted if the person narrated *hadith*, together with (moral) qualifications about that person (incidentally, we do not know what, if any, nuance existed between qualifications like "trustworthy" [*thiqa*] or "pious" [*salih*]). Fourth, one comes across various distinctive features like someone's tendency to pray or to fast beyond the call of duty, or dyeing one's beard, sometimes noting the color; if someone became sick toward the end of his or her life (blindness and senility being the leading two diseases noted for this preindustrial society), or if the person belonged to a special group (for example, participated in a famous battle or was one of those who became exceptionally old and so forth). At times one reads that the person was *awwalu man* ("the first to have done ..."), in itself another original literary genre of Islamic civilization that led to separate compilations listing as many "first to's" as possible. Finally, biographical dictionaries are rich in geographical information, ranging from place of birth to that of death and all in between, such as place of first residence, any places they moved, and place of occupation or of study and/or teaching. It should immediately be reiterated that this is a total picture of what kind of information is found in the biographical dictionaries and that not all the people listed have by extension all of this information about them individually; some dictionaries give information for some of these characteristics while other dictionaries give the researcher other data about the same person.

In summary, Arabic biographies and biographical dictionaries offer a relatively large range of data for a preindustrial society, because no other preindustrial society can claim such an abundance of information about various segments of the population. Unfortunately, medieval Arabic biographical dictionaries have hardly been utilized by researchers outside Islamic Studies proper, like historical demographers who tend to be thrilled if they uncover data that date back to the sixteenth century CE; finding medieval social data about Islamic civilization still requires much mining.

JOHN A. NAWAS

See also 'Abbasid Caliph; Al-Bukhari; Al-Khatib al-Baghdadi; Al-Ma'mun; Companions of the Prophet; Hadith; Ibn Al-Jawzi; Ibn Sa'd; Sira; Sufis

Further Reading

Bulliet, Richard. "A Quantitative Approach to Medieval Muslim Biographical Dictionaries." *Journal of the Economic and Social History of the Orient.* 13 (1970): 195–211.

Gibb, H.A.R. "Islamic Biographical Literature." In *Historians of the Middle East*, eds. Bernard Lewis and P.M. Holt. London: Oxford University Press, 1962, 54–58.

Gilliot, Cl. "*Tabakat*." In *The Encyclopaedia of Islam. Second Edition*. Volume X: 7–10.

Hafsi, Ibrahim. "Recherches sur le genre 'Tabaqat' dans la literature arabe," *Arabica*, xxiii (1976): 227–265; and xxiv (1977): 1–41, 150–186.

Makdisi, George. "*Tabaqat*–Biography: Law and Orthodoxy in Classical Islam." *Islamic Studies* 32 (1993): 371–396.

Qadi, al-, Wadad. "Biographical Dictionaries: Inner Structure and Cultural Significance." In *The Book in the Islamic World. The Written Word and Communication in the Middle East*, ed. George N. Atiyeh. Albany: State University of New York, 1995, 93–122.

Young, M. J. L. "Arabic Biographical Writing." In *The Cambridge History of Arabic Literature 3: Religion, Learning and Science in the 'Abbasid Period*, eds. M. J. L. Young, J. D. Latham, and R. B. Serjeant. Cambridge: Cambridge University Press, 1990, 168–187.

BIRUNI

Al-Biruni, Abu Rayhan Muhammad Ibn Ahmad, was one of the greatest scholars of Medieval Islam, not merely of encyclopedic range, but perhaps the most original among them. Unlike his famous contemporaries Ibn Sina and Ibn al-Haytham, who influenced Latin scholasticism, Biruni became known in Europe only in the later nineteenth century, mainly by way of the editions by Eduard Sachau. Biruni was born September 4, 973, in Kath, the capital of Khwarezm, on the river Amu Darya (classical Oxus). Although his native Khwarezmian was also an Iranian language, he rejected the emerging neo-Persian literature of his time (Firdawsi), preferring Arabic instead as the only adequate medium of the sciences. Although probably of humble origin, he was, for unknown reasons, educated at the court of the Khwarezm-Shahs, where he received a solid training in mathematics, astronomy, and mathematical geography. In his early years he constructed a model, with a diameter of five meters, of the northern hemisphere of the earth. In collaboration with a colleague in Baghdad he determined the difference in longitude between this city and Kath by determining the difference in time between the observations of a lunar eclipse in the two places. He discussed the theory of the earth's rotation and found that from a purely mathematical standpoint it was unobjectionable but not sustainable on physical grounds. In a contentious correspondence with Ibn Sina, he even doubted some basic tenets of Aristotelian cosmology, the eternity and unicity of this world. In this respect he was closer to Muslim orthodoxy than his philosophical counterpart. In later works he stressed that there are no contradictions between science and the Koran. Although he condemned the heretical opinions of al-Razi, he nevertheless compiled a bibliography of his writings. During a sojourn in Gurgan on the southern coast of the Caspian Sea, he wrote his *Chronology of Ancient Nations,* a description of the calendar systems of various peoples and religious communities including critical examinations of popular traditions, for example, about Alexander the Great, as well as some historical data on the Bible. When Khwarezm was invaded by Mahmud of Ghazna, Biruni, together with other scholars, was taken to Ghazna (known today as Afghanistan). There, at Mahmud's court, he obtained acceptable working conditions. From a mountain overlooking the Indus Plain, near the fortress of Nandana, he measured the earth's circumference by a method previously used by the caliph Al-Ma'mun's astronomers. Mahmud's repeated incursions into northwest India gave him the opportunity to study the customs, folklore, literature, and sciences of the Hindus. He even learned some Sanskrit and translated, probably with indigenous help, from Arabic into this language and from Sanskrit into Arabic. Observing similarities between pagan Greek and Hindu mythologies, he censured the Hindus' idolatry, as well as their scholars' deferral to popular superstitions. He compared their mathematical and astronomical doctrines with those of the Greeks, which he always found superior, and he observed that India did not have such heroes as Socrates who were willing to die for the sake of truth. His wish that by their conversion to Islam the Hindus might be saved from their totally alien mindset tallied with Mahmud's imperial ambitions. To Mahmud's successor, Mas'ud, Biruni dedicated the "Mas'udic Canon," a huge reference work of astronomy, and for Mawdud, the next ruler of the dynasty, he wrote the "Mineralogy," a sometimes amusing description of various metals and gemstones. With the help of a vessel constructed for the purpose, meticulous research was carried out on the specific weight of some eighteen substances. He even resorted to experiments, not, as customary with ancient and contemporaneous scholars, in order to prove a previously formulated idea, but instead to check a commonly accepted opinion, largely with negative results. He was skeptical about alchemy and astrology, although he dedicated a concise introduction to the latter, in the form of questions and answers, to a fellow Khwarezmian, a woman named Rayhana. Almost until his death on December 11, 1048, Biruni worked on his "Pharmacology"; it contained the names of 1116 items of materia medica in Greek, as well as in Iranian, Indian, and Semitic languages, arranged alphabetically by their Arabic names.

GOTTHARD STROHMAIER

See also 'Abbasid Caliph; Al-Ma'mun, Al-Razi; Alexander the Great; Aristotle and Aristotelianism; Firdawzi; Ibn al-Haytham, or Alhazen; Ibn Sina, or Avicenna; Idolatry; Mahmud of Ghazna; Materia Medica

Further Reading

Alberuni's India. Trans. Eduard Sachau. London, 1888.
Kennedy, Edward S. "Al-Biruni." In *Dictionary of Scientific Biography*. 18 vols. Edited by Charles C. Gillispie and Frederic L. Holmes. New York.
Strohmaier, Gotthard. *Al–Biruni. In den Gärten der Wissenschaft*. 3rd revised ed. Leipzig, 2002.
The Chronology of Ancient Nations. Trans. Eduard Sachau. London, 1879.

BLACK DEATH

The Black Death was a pandemic that swept through almost every part of the Old World, beginning in the 1330s with repeated waves of infection continuing into the fifteenth century. The bacteria that spreads the plague is *Yersinia pestis,* a small, rod-shaped bacillus that lives in the gut of certain fleas, particularly the rat flea, *Xenopsylla cheopis.* The spreading bacteria block the infected flea's esophagus, and the flea is no longer able to feed itself; it simply regurgitates the bacteria into its host as it attempts to feed. It is at this point that the flea will typically move from its usual host, the black rat *(Rattus rattus),* and bite and infect humans.

In the case of the bubonic form of the plague, the lymph glands filter the bacilli out of the bloodstream. The glands, typically those in the neck or groin area, subsequently become engorged with bacilli. This causes agonizing pain at the site of the lymph nodes as they first appear as dark accretions and then swell to form a "bubo" (hence "bubonic" plague) ranging in size from an almond to an orange. The victim then develops flu-like symptoms, including a high fever. The bacilli subsequently cause widespread damage throughout the victim's body, attacking the lungs, heart, and kidneys. The bacilli also attack the nervous system, sometimes leading to a wild hysteria that gave rise to the phrase "the dance of death." In most cases the victim then hemorrhages massive amounts of blood, which causes dark blotches to appear before the victim slips into a coma and dies. The total time from infection to death is typically about two weeks.

Pneumonic plague, a more deadly and infectious form of the disease, appears in cases where the bacteria multiply in the lungs of the victim. This form of the plague is highly contagious because it is transmitted when an infected person coughs up droplets of the bacilli. The pneumonic plague is 100 percent fatal. A third form of the plague (septicemia) bypasses the lymph glands altogether and concentrates bacilli in the body at such a rate that the victim usually dies in just a few hours.

The Black Death struck the Middle East with as much ferocity as it did Europe. The disease originated in Central Asia, where it had been endemic to an isolated species of rodent for hundreds of years. Evidence seems to indicate that this isolated strain of *Yersinia pestis* mutated over the course of centuries of isolation. Its isolation and mutation account for its particularly rapid spread and exceptional lethality. It spread both east and west along Mongol trade routes, attacking China, India, Europe, and the Middle East. From Central Asia it spread to Kaffa on the Black Sea and then to Constantinople, where it spread throughout the Mediterranean. It first arrived at the port of Alexandria in the fall of 1347. From there it spread throughout Egypt and wiped out nearly 50 percent of the population.

It was equally devastating in North Africa, Palestine, and Greater Syria. Medieval medicine was unable to cope with or understand this virulent disease. It was known as either "*ta'un*" or "*al-waba' al-iswid*" in Arabic. Many people believed that it was caused by earthquakes that had released a deadly air (miasma) into the environment. Some attempted to flee to isolated places, although this did not occur as much in the Middle East as in Europe.

The socioeconomic consequences were such that it left Egypt's irrigation system in ruins. It seems to have had an equally devastating economic and social impact on North Africa. Less is known about its socioeconomic impact in Iran, Iraq, Palestine, and Greater Syria, although reports from contemporary observers attest to its equal lethality in these areas.

STUART J. BORSCH

See also Death and Dying; Folk Medicine; Physicians

Further Reading

Conrad, Lawrence. *The Plague in the Early Medieval Near East*. Ph.D. dissertation. Princeton, NJ: Princeton University, 1981.
Dols, Michael W. *The Black Death in the Middle East*. Princeton, NJ: Princeton University Press, 1977.

BOOKS

Books (sing. *kitab*; pl. *kutub*) count among the chief objects of artistic expression throughout the Islamic lands, beginning with Islam's most formative historical phases. The early prestige accorded to the book by Islamic society is generally considered to derive from the Qur'an *(mushaf)*. Notwithstanding the status of the divine revelation itself, copying the Qur'an provided a strong impetus for formal and aesthetic exploration. The materials of the Qur'an—writing supports and inks—were produced with care; numerous scripts were developed over time to write out the text; illuminations were created to mark internal divisions of the text, count verses, frame the text, and introduce the book through elaborate frontispieces; and the finished, stitched textblock of folios was placed inside a protective binding. From the earliest period, the codex emerged as the chief structural form of the book, though this single form was subject to a host of permutations and adaptations over time. It was perhaps the Qur'an more than any other text that lent cultural importance to the book as a physical object and that motivated its artistic elaboration.

By the tenth and eleventh centuries, a corpus of traditions had developed around the book that stressed its eminence and importance. These sayings record cultural notions that additionally explain the high status of the book in Islam. The book was heralded as the means by which human thought could be preserved over time—a permanent and reproducible trace of thought—the most effective vehicle for recording achievements of various sorts, whether broadly intellectual, literary, or political. One of the most complete corpuses of aphorisms appears in a treatise on the technique and art of calligraphy composed by Abu'l-Hayyan al-Tawhidi (d. after 1009 CE). The sayings cited by al-Tawhidi are mainly concerned with the merits of calligraphy, a skill sought out and acquired by people of high culture. Calligraphy not only recorded the thoughts of mankind but could also embody the person's morality as ideas—the proper content of the text—as well as in the physical form of writing. Fine writing—and the labor that preceded accomplishment in writing—offered a trace, like a footprint, of the person for posterity. Calligraphy was an impressed presence. Sayings in al-Tawhidi's treatise include one attributed to Ja'far b. Yahya al-Barmaki (d. 803), "Handwriting is the necklace of wisdom. It serves to sort the pearls of wisdom, to bring its dispersed pieces into good order, to put its stray bits together, and to fix its setting." Another saying attributed to a certain 'Abbas reads: "Handwriting is the tongue of the hand. Style is the tongue of the intellect. The intellect is the tongue of good actions and qualities. And good actions and qualities are the perfection of man" (Rosenthal 1947, 1–20). Given that books are primarily vehicles of texts, it is not difficult to comprehend the logic of other sayings cited by another writer, Ibn al-Nadim (fl. 987), in his *Fihrist*, a virtual encyclopedia of the culture of books in the tenth century. The sayings given by Ibn al-Nadim include al-'Attabi's remark, "Books smile as pens shed tears," and Buzurgmihr's saying, "Books are the shells of wisdom, which are split open for the pearls of character" (Ibn al-Nadim 1970). Such sayings continued to have currency over time and were amplified by notions that the first thing created by God was the pen and that He had written out creation on the preserved tablet *(lawh al-mahfuz)*. The synergy of these cultural notions and values secured the preeminence of the written word and the book across a wide spectrum of texts and resulted in the formation of personal, institutional, and royal libraries of often-massive scope. Although books were always adjuncts to processes of learning based on oral transmission and audition, the physical text permitted the transport of knowledge through space and time and "independently of their human transmitters," as Bloom notes (Bloom 2001, 123).

The principal materials used in the early production of books were parchment, vellum, and papyrus. These materials were quickly supplanted by paper, an inherently cheaper medium that had a profound impact on book culture. This new medium made books more readily available and permitted the widespread dissemination of knowledge on an unprecedented scale (see Bloom). It also provided an inherently more coherent surface for writing, illumination, and painting while matching the pliancy of other supports. By the year 1000, paper had even supplanted papyrus in Egypt. It had also been accepted as a suitable medium for the production of the Qur'an, though the use of materials such as parchment continued in some regions of the Islamic world, especially in North Africa, perhaps as a way of marking the separate status of the Qur'an. Various primary sources record the different formats of paper sheets.

A rich technical literature similarly records recipes for black and colored inks and pigments prepared from vegetable and mineral sources, methods of preparing and decorating papers through dyes, tints, and gold flecking, and the manufacture of book bindings. The earliest known text to devote itself wholly to the techniques and materials of the art of the book is Ibn Badis's *'Umdat al-kuttab* (ca. 1025). The transmission of technical lore became a subject for many later writers, and there is a rich literature on this topic (see 'Abd al-Hayy Habibi and Porter). Over time, many additional techniques were used to augment the visual dimensions of the book. Papers could be decorated with marbling or stenciling, text blocks framed inside multiple rulings that formed a border to divide the text field *(matn)* from margin *(hashiya)*, and calligraphy could be executed in black or colored inks—sometimes spotted with flecks of crushed mother-of-pearl—or assembled from cut paper (decoupage) of differing colors. Leather bindings were equally inventive: Beginning with the relatively simple use of tanned leather over pasteboard covers, bindings came to be decorated with blind-tooled designs (punched or stamped into the leather and often augmented by the selective application of gold) organized into lines, clusters of motifs, or geometric compositions. More complex stamped ornament was developed through the use of engraved metal plates in various shapes arranged on book covers as medallions and corner pieces. The binding's inner surfaces, the doublures, could either be fashioned from sheets of leather or cut leather (filigree) laid over colored paper grounds. The binding's interior and exterior were also embellished in some contexts through patterned textiles or lacquer. By the middle years of the 1400s, the artistry of the bookbinder had reached a staggering level.

Despite the development of many different techniques and decorative effects, however, the structure of the binding remained constant. It was assembled from upper and lower covers connected to the book's spine, with a board attached along the outer edge of the lower cover—as wide as the depth of the textblock—that in turn supported an envelope flap. When the book was closed, the envelope flap was placed underneath the upper cover, thereby protecting the outer edge of the textblock. Although elegant and alluring, the binding offered a robust protection for the text that it contained.

Because the Islamic book lacked pagination and an index, other means were required to enhance the clarity of the book's organization and thus facilitate its use. These challenges were solved by several means. Illumination was developed to mark the beginnings and endings of chapters or book sections, as full-page designs, double pages, or rectangular panels *('unwan, sarlawh)*. Books may also have opened with a table of contents *(fihrist)* or an illuminated panel carrying the name of the text. An additional form of illumination was composed as a roundel *(shamsa)* that might contain the owner's ex libris. The calligraphy proper was also manipulated to enhance the clarity of the work. Prose was usually arranged as running text, whereas poetry was divided into columnar formats of either four or six; colophons marking the end of chapters or books were generally arranged as an inverted triangle of text and conformed to established textual protocols. Variations in the color of ink or in the type and size of script were also used to announce subdivisions of the text, which are transitions from one subject to another on a single page. In the case of illustrated manuscripts, an encapsulation of the image's content could appear in the form of a brief explanatory text enclosed in a small panel. These organizational challenges were even more severe in the anthology, books assembled from different texts that might treat various topics and that might unite works of prose and poetry in a single volume.

The many processes associated with the production of the textblock could be undertaken in several sequences, though the copying of the text was usually completed first. After the folios had been cut to the appropriate size, the page was marked with a grid as a guide for the calligrapher. This was done either through the use of a sharp instrument that scored lines into the folio, or by pressing a cardboard with threads arranged across it *(mastar)* into the folio. Catchwords written in the lower-left margin of each folio guaranteed the correct collation of the manuscript at the time of its stitching to form a fixed textblock. In the course of writing the text, the copyist left spaces for illumination or for illustrations, which would generally be completed after the text was copied. Other processes, such as ruling, were generally accomplished last.

Throughout the period between the seventh and sixteenth centuries, books were made under various circumstances and in different contexts. Some were made by copyists *(warraq, nassakh)*, who were also booksellers in the market, under direct commission or speculatively. Some were made in the context of mosques or madrasas and provided for by the endowment of the *waqf*. Other book production occurred under caliphal or princely support, the best-known early medieval example being al-Ma'mun's *Bayt al-hikma* in Baghdad. Degrees of specialization in the production of books always varied in each context and were not subject to a linear development over time. For example, in a volume of the Qur'an signed by Ibn al-Bawwab (d. 1022), the colophon notes that Ibn al-Bawwab copied the text and executed the illuminations. In an illustrated copy of al-Hariri's

Maqamat, dated 1237, the copyist (al-Wasiti) was also responsible for executing the many paintings. In the later 1500s, such dual expertise was also applied to the production of books.

Book production under royal patronage, whenever or wherever it occurred, was generally more specialized. Two documents from the early 1400s, for example, describe the highly specialized bookmaking procedures in the Timurid workshops *(kitabkhana)* of Herat and Shiraz. One document is a progress report about projects in the Herat workshop presumably addressed to the Timurid prince, Baysunghur (d. 1433); the other is a letter inviting an illuminator to become the chief of the Shiraz workshop and lists the workers under his direction by their specialization. These workshops were institutions, devoted in large part to the creation of books, that assembled skilled calligraphers, painters, draftsmen, illuminators, outliners, rulers and binders, and artists who were not only in command of the requisite skills of their particular medium but who also knew how to prepare materials. Additional evidence also suggests that some practitioners worked across different media. Some of the more stunning developments in the art of the Islamic book occurred under royal patronage because it alone was capable of sustaining specialized production—gathering the requisite human talent and procuring the necessary materials—and coordinating numerous practices into coherent, unified books. By the late 1400s, artists associated with the production of books were being recorded in histories; in the 1500s, authors such as the Ottoman man of letters, Mustafa Ali, composed texts devoted entirely to the history of artistic practice. These texts, prefaces to album collections and treatises, are yet another testament to the high status of books in Islam, but they express an appreciation for skill and artistic accomplishment in the terms of a history of art.

DAVID J. ROXBURGH

See also Abu'l-Hayyan al-Tawhidi; Adab; Alphabets; Al-Ma'mun; Arabic; Archives and Chanceries; Cultural Exchange; Humanism; Knowledge ('Ilm); Libraries; Madrasa; Manuscripts; Painting, Miniature; Paper Manufacture; Persian; Qur'an, Manuscripts; Scribes; Turkish and Turkic Languages; Waqf

Primary Sources

'Abd al-Hayy Habibi. "Literary Sources for the History of the Arts of the Book in Central Asia." In *Arts of the Book in Central Asia, 14th–16th Centuries*, ed. Basil Gray, appendix 1. Boulder, CO: Shambhala Press, 1979.

Al-Mu'izz b, Badis. *Mediaeval Arabic Bookmaking and its Relation to Early Chemistry and Pharmacology*, [by] Martin Levey. Philadelphia, 1962.

Ibn al-Nadim. *The Fihrist of al-Nadim: A Tenth-Century Survey of Muslim Culture*. Trans. and ed. Bayard Dodge. 2 vols. New York and London: Columbia University Press, 1970.

Mustafa Ali. *Menakib-i hunervaran*. Tehran: Surush, 1991.

Sadiqi Beg Afshar. "Qanun al-suwar." In Martin Dickson and Stuart Cary Welch, *The Houghton Shahnamah*. 2 vols., vol. 1, appendix 1. Cambridge, MA: Harvard University Press, 1981.

Further Reading

Atiyeh, George N., ed. *The Book in the Islamic World: The Written Word and Communication in the Middle East*. Albany: State University of New York Press, 1995.

Bloom, Jonathan M. *Paper Before Print: The History and Impact of Paper in the Islamic World*. New Haven and London: Yale University Press, 2001.

Bosch, Gulnar K. "The Staff of the Scribes and the Implements of the Discerning: An Excerpt." *Ars Orientalis* 4 (1961): 1–13.

Bosch, Gulnar, John Carswell, and Guy Petherbridge. *Islamic Bindings and Bookmaking*. Chicago: Chicago University Press, 1981.

Cagman, Filiz, and Zeren Tanindi. *The Topkapi Museum: The Albums and Illustrated Manuscripts*. Boston: Little, Brown, 1986.

Déroche, François. *Manuel de Codicologie des Manuscrits en Écriture Arabe*. Paris: Bibliothèque Nationale de France, 2000.

Déroche, François, ed. *Les Manusrits du Moyen-Orient: Essais de Codicologie et de Paléographie*. Paris: Institut français d'études anatoliennes, 1989.

Dutton, Yasin, ed. *The Codicology of Islamic Manuscripts*. London: Al-Furqan, 1995.

Eche, Youssef. *Les Bibliothèques Arabes Publiques et Semi-Publiques en Mésopotamie, en Syrie et en Égypte au Moyen-Age*. Damascus: Institut français de Damas, 1967.

Ettinghausen, Richard. *Arab Painting*. Geneva: Skira, 1962.

Gacek, Adam. *The Arabic Manuscript Tradition: A Glossary of Technical Terms and Bibliography*. Leiden: Brill, 2001.

Gray, Basil. *Persian Painting*. Geneva: Skira, 1977.

Gray, Basil, ed. *The Arts of the Book in Central Asia, 14th–16th Centuries*. Boulder, CO: Shambhala Press, 1979.

Haldane, D. *Islamic Bookbindings in the Victoria and Albert Museum*. London: World of Islam Festival Trust, 1983.

Pedersen, Johannes. *The Arabic Book*. Princeton: Princeton University Press, 1984.

Porter, Yves. *Peinture et Arts du Livre: Essai sur la Littérature Technique Indo-Persane*. Paris and Tehran: Institut français de recherche en Iran, 1992.

Raby, Julian, and Zeren Tanindi. *Turkish Bookbinding in the 15th Century: The Foundation of an Ottoman Court Style*. London: Azimuth Editions, 1993.

Rosenthal, Franz. "Abu Haiyan al-Tawhidi on Penmanship." *Ars Islamica* 13–14 (1947): 1–20.

Roxburgh, David J. *Prefacing the Image: The Writing of Art History in Sixteenth-Century Iran*. Leiden: Brill, 2001.

Touati, Houari. *L'Armoire à Sagesse: Bibliothèques et Collections en Islam*. Paris: Aubier, 2003.

Weitzmann, Kurt. *Studies in Classical and Byzantine Manuscript Illumination*. Edited by Herbert L. Kessler. Chicago: University of Chicago Press, 1971.

Welch, Anthony. *Arts of the Islamic Book: The Collection of the Prince Sadruddin Aga Khan*. Ithaca, NY: Cornell University Press, 1982.

BOTANY

Arabic botanical knowledge was mainly practical and descriptive. It was contained principally in pharmacological literature and secondarily in agricultural literature. Theoretical botany was a matter of philosophical speculation.

Early Arabic plant knowledge relied on agricultural literature of Greece and Byzantium, with the *Geôrgika* by Demokritos (in fact, Bolos of Mendes, ca. 200 BCE), Anatolios of Berytos (possibly Vindonius Anatolius, d. AD 360), and Kassianos Bassos (sixth century. CE), as well as on literature from the Syriac world, with the so-called *Nabatean agriculture* encyclopedia. Ninth-century CE translation activity in Baghdâd introduced Greek material: (1) theoretical botany (genesis, reproduction, and growing of plants, their parts and physiology, plant classification, the nature and origin of their qualities and peculiarities) with *De plantis* by Aristotle (384–322 BCE), not known in the original but in the commented version by Nikolaos of Damas (first century BCE/CE), and *De historia plantarum* or *De causis plantarum* by Theophrastus (372/70–288/86 BCE) (the text is lost; hence the uncertainty of the translated work); (2) pharmacobotany (plants used as medicines), with *De materia medica* by Dioscorides (first century CE), an encyclopedia on the natural products used for therapeutic purposes.

As in the Greek world, Dioscorides's treatise dominated the field. It was repeatedly translated, first into Syriac by Hunayn ibn Ishaq, and then into Arabic by the same working in collaboration with Istifan ibn Basil. The Arabic text was further revised during the tenth century CE in the East and the West (Cordova), and the Syriac treatise was translated twice into Arabic in the East during the twelfth century CE. Each translation seems to have been widely circulated, and Dioscorides's treatise was abundantly commented on—particularly by such North African and Western scientists as ibn al-Gazzâr, abû al-Qâsim al-Zahrâwî, al Ghâfiqî, and ibn al-Baytâr—in order to equate Dioscorides's Mediterranean species with local ones.

In Dioscorides's model of botany, each plant is dealt with in a monographic chapter, which proceeds both synthetically (plant type) and analytically (plant description, neither systematic nor complete, but limited to the major characteristics from the top to the roots). Classification is based on the therapeutic properties of plants. The text is completed in several manuscripts with color representations of the plants, the authenticity and origin of which is still debated. Such a model was reproduced in the Arabic world but with two major modifications: (1) plants were no longer classified according to their properties, but according to the alphabetical sequence of their names, a fact that provoked the loss of plant classification; and (2) plant representations, which originally resembled those in Greek manuscripts, increasingly tended toward symmetrical and stylized pictures and also introduced elements that suggested the natural environment of the plants.

Greek pharmacobotany in the Arabic world agglutinated data of different provenances (Mesopotamian, Persian, Indian), and new works were produced, best represented in the East by al-Bîrûnî's *Kitâb al-Saydalah* and ibn Sînâ's *Qanûn*, and in the West by ibn al-Gazzâr, abû al-Qâsim al-Zahrâwî, al Ghâfiqî, and ibn al-Baytâr, the last two of whom are credited with the most achieved works of descriptive botany in the Arabic world. Special aspects were dealt with in other works, as, for example, plant nomenclature in lexica, phytogeography, and plant distribution in geographical descriptions and travel books, plant physiology in philosophical and metaphysical treatises such as ibn Sînâ's *Kitâb al-shifâ*, and plant production in agricultural manuals, as ibn Bâjja's *Kitâb al-nabât*.

ALAIN TOUWAIDE

Further Reading

Ben Mrad, Ibrahim. *Ibn al-Baytâr. Commentaire de la «Materia Medica» de Dioscoride.* Carthage: Beït al-Hikma, 1990.

Brandenburg, Dietrich. *Islamic Miniature Painting in Medical Manuscripts.* Basel: Roche, 1982.

Die Dioskurides-Erklärung des Ibn al-Baitâr. Ein Beitrag zur arabischen Pflanzensynonymik des Mittelalters. Göttingen: Vandenhoeck & Ruprecht, 1991.

Die Ergänzungen Ibn_ul_ul's zur Materia Medica des Dioskurides. Arabischer Text nebst kommentierter detuscher Übersetzung. Göttingen: Vandenhoeck & Ruprecht, 1993.

Dietrich, Albert. *Dioscurides Triumphans. Ein anonymer arabischer Kommentar (Ende 12. Jahrh. n. Chr.) zur Materia Medica,* 2 vols. Göttingen: Vandenhoeck & Ruprecht, 1988.

Drossaart Lulofs H.J., and E.L.J. Poortman. *Nicolaus Damascenus de Plantis.* Five translations. Amsterdam, Oxford, and New York: North-Holland Publishing Company, 1989.

Dubler, Cesar. *La Materia Médica de Dioscórides.* Barcelona and Tetuan: Tipografía Emporium, 1953–1959.

Le Dictionnaire Botanique d'Abû Hanîfa ad-Dînawari, compiled according to the citations of later works. Cairo: Institut Français d'Archéologie Orientale, 1973.

Levey, Martin. *Early Arabic Pharmacology.* Leiden: E.J. Brill, 1973.

Lewin, Bernhard. *Abû Hanîfa ad-Dînawari, Kitâb al-nabât. Fifth part.* Uppsala University, Wiesbaden: Harrassowits, 1953.

Sadek, M. *The Arabic Materia Medica of Dioscorides.* Québec: Les Editions du Sphinx, 1983.

Said, Hakim Mohammed, and Sami Khalaf Hamarneh. *Al-Biruni's Book on Pharmacy and Materia Medica.* 2 vols. Karachi: Hamdard National Foundation.

Sezgin, Fuat. *Geschichte des arabischen Schrifttums. 4. Alchimie, Chemie, Botanik, Agrikultur bis ca. 430 H.* Leiden: E.J. Brill, 1971.

Ullmann, Manfred. *Die Natur- und Gegeimwissenschaften in Islam.* Leiden & Cologne: E.J. Brill, 1972.

BRETHREN OF PURITY

Ikhwan al-Safa' (the Brethren of Purity) were the affiliates of an esoteric coterie that was based in Basra and Baghdad around the last quarter of the tenth century CE. The learned adepts of this fraternity authored a compendium, *Rasa'il Ikhwan al-Safa' (The Epistles of the Brethren of Purity),* which was structured in the form of an encyclopedia. This voluminous work grouped fifty-two tracts that treated themes in mathematics, music, logic, astronomy, and the physical cum natural sciences, as well as exploring the nature of the soul and investigating associated matters in ethics, revelation, and spirituality. This series offered synoptic elucidations of the classical traditions in philosophy and science of the ancients and the moderns of the age. It was also accompanied by a dense treatise titled *al-Risala al-jami'a (The Comprehensive Epistle)* and further complemented by an appendage known as *Risalat jami'at al-jami'a (The Condensed Comprehensive Epistle).* The precise identity of the authors of this monumental corpus, and the exact chronology of its composition, remain unsettled matters of scholarly debate in the field of Islamic studies. Although the Ikhwan's writings have been described as being affiliated to Sufi, Sunni, or Mu'tazilite teachings, it is more generally accepted that their line in literature belonged to a Shi'ite legacy that had strong connections with the Ismaili tradition. While some scholars assert that the Rasa'il Ikhwan al-Safa' are attributable to early Fatimid sources, others maintain that this textual legacy transcended sectarian divisions in Islam and, in its spirit of openness, should consequently lead us to treat its authors as freethinkers who were not bound within the doctrinal confines of a specific creed. Moreover, besides founding their views on the Qur'an and the teachings of Islam, the Ikhwan did not hesitate to appeal in their Rasa'il to the other scriptures of Abrahamic monotheism, such as the Torah of Judaism and the Canonical Gospels of Christianity. The Ikhwan were also implicitly influenced by Ancient Indian and Persian classics, and they were enthusiastically inspired by the Greek legacies of the likes of Pythagoras, Socrates, Plato, Aristotle, Plotinus, Euclid, Ptolemy, Porphyry, and Iamblichus. Finding "truth in every religion" and seeing knowledge as the pure "nourishment for the soul," the Ikhwan associated the pursuit of happiness and the hope of salvation with the scrupulous unfolding of rational and intellectual quests. They furthermore promoted a friendship of virtue among their companions and gave a venerable expression to the liberal spirit in Islam. Their syncretism, which is not reducible to a mere form of eclecticism that may have been partly influenced by Mesopotamian Sabaean practices and beliefs, did ultimately ground their eschatological aspiration to found a spiritual sanctuary that would prudently assist their co-religionists in overcoming the sectarian discords that plagued their era. Oriented by a literal interpretation of the classical microcosm and macrocosm analogy, as it was primarily noted in their conception of the human being as a microcosm and of the universe as a macroanthropon, the Ikhwan did avidly attempt to restore the sense of harmony and equipoise between the psychical order and its correlative cosmological shaping forces. Their analogical thinking was furthermore inspired by a Pythagorean arithmetic grasp of the structuring orderliness of the visible universe, and they moreover adopted a Neoplatonist explication of creation by way of emanation in a creditable attempt to reconcile philosophy with religion. Drafted in an eloquent classical Arabic style, the Ikhwan's epistles displayed a remarkable lexical adaptability that elegantly covered the language of mathematics, logic, and natural philosophy, as well as encompassing the intricacies of theological deliberation and occultist speculation, while also giving expression to a poetic taste that was ingeniously embodied in resourceful fables and edifying parables. In terms of the scholarly significance of the *Rasa'il,* and the cognitive merits of the Ikhwan's views, it must be stated that, despite being supplemented by oral teachings in seminaries, their textual heritage was not representative of the most decisive of achievements made in the domains of mathematics, and the natural and psychical sciences of their epoch. Nonetheless, the Ikhwan's intellectual acumen becomes most evident in their original and sophisticated reflections on matters related to spirituality and revelation, which did compensate the ostensible scholarly limitations that may have resulted from the diluted nature of their investigations in classical philosophy and science. However, in spite of these traceable shortcomings, their corpus remains exemplary of medieval masterpieces that represented erudite popular adaptations of protoscientific knowledge. Assimilated by many scholars across a variety of Muslim schools and doctrines, the Ikhwan's textual heritage acted as an important intellectual catalyst in the course of development of the history of ideas in Islam, rightfully deserving the station that it has been assigned amid the Arabic classics that constituted the high literature of the medieval Islamic civilization.

NADER EL-BIZRI

See also Aristotle and Aristotelianism; Eschatology; Fatimids; Gnosis; Ismailis; Knowledge (*'ilm*); Mysticism; Plato and Neoplatonism; Shi'i Thought; Theology

Primary Sources

Ikwan al-Safa'. *Rasa'il ikhwan al-Safa' wa Khullan al-Wafa'.* Beirut: Dar Sadir, 1957.

Further Reading

'Awa, Adel. *L'esprit Critique des "Frères de la Pureté": Encyclopédistes Arabes du IVe/Xe siècle.* Beirut: Imprimerie Catholique, 1948.
De Callatay, Godefroid. *Ikwan al-Safa'. Les révolutions et les Cycles (Épîtres des Frères de la Pureté, XXXVI).* Beirut: al-Buraq, 1996.
Farrukh, "Umar. 'Ikhwan al-Safa'." In *A History of Muslim Philosophy.* 3 vols. Edited by M. M. Sharif. Wiesbaden: O. Harrassowitz, 1963–1966.
Goodman, Lenn E. *The Case of the Animals versus Man before the King of the Jinn: A Tenth-Century Ecological Fable of the Pure Brethren of Basra.* Boston: Twayne Publishers, 1978.
Hamdani, Abbas. "A Critique of Paul Casanova's Dating of the Rasa'il Ikhwan al-Safa'." In *Mediaeval Isma'ili History and Thought.* Edited by Farhad Daftary. Cambridge: Cambridge University Press, 1996.
Marquet, Yves. *La Philosophie des Ihwan al-Safa'.* Algiers: Société Nationale d'Édition et de Diffusion, 1975.
Marquet, Yves. "Ikhwan al-Safa'." In *The Encyclopaedia of Islam, Volume III.* Leiden: E.J. Brill, 1960.
Netton, Ian Richard. *Muslim Neoplatonists: An Introduction to the Thought of the Brethren of Purity.* London: Allen and Unwin, 1982.
Tibawi, Abdul-Latif. "Ikhwan as-Safa' and their *Rasa'il:* A Critical Review of a Century and a Half of Research." *Islamic Quarterly* 2 (1955): 28–46.

BUDDHISM AND ISLAM

The infamous destruction of the giant Buddha images at Bamyan, Afghanistan, by the radical Islamic Taliban regime serves as a potent symbol of the culmination of the centuries-long coexistence and contact between Islam and Buddhism. The destruction of the statues not only eclipses that history but also underscores a tone of intolerance toward Buddhism on the part of some Muslim thinkers today. A new book bearing the title *Islam and Buddhism* by Harun Yahya, perhaps the only contemporary work specifically dedicated to the question of the Islamic-Buddhist relationship, provides a characteristically hostile depiction of Buddhism as an idolatrous religion and the quintessential example of "falsehood," as it is defined by the Qur'an and Islamic thought more generally. Thus, Buddhism, with its "deification" of human beings, a cult of idols, a massive iconography, and its pessimism toward the material world and consequent extreme asceticism, seems to be worlds apart from Islam.

However, the mere fact that an important Buddhist monument might exist in what is now known as an Islamic country indicates that Buddhism, in its varieties, existed in territories to which Islam also extended its reach during its advent to East and Southeast Asia. Many of the people who converted to Islam in these territories were originally Buddhists, and for long periods there was in these regions some sort of coexistence between the two realms, one far more varied and peaceful than certain events and publications might lead us to believe.

The encounter between Islam and Buddhism can be documented from as early as the late seventh century (or first Islamic century). Buddhist converts, like many other converts to Islam, enriched Islam with troves of cultural expression of all sorts, and imported into the religion their own distinctive practices and theological interpretations. Perhaps the best concrete example of such Buddhist converts is the Barmaki lineage during the early days of the 'Abbasid caliphate. The father of the family was a Persian-Buddhist priest from Balkh, whose descendants rose to power and glory as grand viziers and are often associated with the golden age of the 'Abbasid caliphate. It was probably during that period, when the 'Abbasid caliphs sponsored huge translation projects of Eastern and Western texts, that the most fruitful connections between Islam and Buddhism occurred. However, we must be very cautious before attributing any *specific* practice or idea in Islam to Buddhism, even when we find similarities between the two religions, since in most cases one cannot really pinpoint any direct influence. It is more plausible to speak of general Central Asian or Indian practices and ideas in relation to Islam rather then specifically Buddhist ideas or practices and to conceive of this syncretism in generally cultural terms rather than specific one-to-one correlative ones.

The most well-known attempt to draw a direct connection between Buddhist practices and Islam was undertaken by the great Hungarian–Jewish Orientalist Ignaz Goldziher. In a study titled *A Buddhizmus Hatása az Iszlámra (On the Impact of Buddhism on Islam)*, published in 1903, Goldziher demonstrated similarities between Sufism and Buddhism and claimed that the former sprung forth when Islam came in contact with the latter in India (he repeated a version of this claim in his *Lectures on Islam*.)

While Goldziher was basically right in drawing the attention of the debate toward the Indian connection to Sufism, one is hard-pressed to say that it was Buddhism per se rather than Indian practices such as *Bhakti* (devotionalism, in this context) that had some generalized impact on the early Sufi practitioners. (Of all dimensions of Islam, Sufism today is most readily compared to Buddhism, but then again, Sufism is indeed most inclusive and eclectic and thus most easily compared to strains within all religions). On the ideational level we find the unique case of a Chinese Sufi scholar, Wu Zixian, who translated the *Mirsad al-'ibad*, a major Sufi compendium, into Chinese and stated freely in his preface to the book that he had consulted Buddhist texts to come up with the suitable Chinese vocabulary for Sufi terms. Wu is unique not because he was an East Asian Muslim inspired by Buddhism but rather because he was one who openly admitted this influence.

Buddhists and Muslims today coexist in significant numbers in virtually all Southeast and East Asian countries (and also Korea and Japan). There have been some serious scholarly and religious attempts to renew and open the dialogue between the two faiths. One such attempt worthy of mentioning is by the major Japanese Buddhist thinker and educator Daisaku Ikeda. For the most part, however, this remains an undeveloped field, and what has been written on the topic is largely polemical.

ZVI AZIZ BEN-DOR

Further Reading

Azuma, Ryushin. *Nihon no Bukkyo to Isuramu (Japanese Buddhism and Islam)*. Tokyo: Shunjusha, 2002.

Ben-Dor Benite, Zvi. *The Dao of Muhammad: A Cultural History of Muslims in Late Imperial China*. Cambridge: Harvard University Asia Center, forthcoming.

Goldziher, Ignác. *A Buddhizmus Hatása az Iszlámra*. Budapest: Kiadja a Magyar Tudományos Akadémia, 1903.

Harun, Yahya. *Islam and Buddhism*. New Delhi: Islamic Book Service, 2003.

Ikeda, Daisaku. *Global Civilization: A Buddhist–Islamic Dialogue* (with Majid Tehranian). London and New York: British Academic Press, 2003.

Murata, Sachiko. *Chinese Gleams of Sufi Light*. Albany: State University of New York Press, 2001.

Zu'bi, Muhammad 'Ali. *al-Budhiya wa-ta'thiruha fi l-fikr wa-l-firaq al-Islamiya al-mutatarrifa*. Beirut: Matba'at al-Insaf, 1964.

BUKHARA

Bukhara is an oasis city in central Asia in the Zaraf-shan River Valley (in present-day Uzbekistan). According to traditions preserved in the partly legendary Islamic conquest literature, the first Arab forces reached Bukhara during the early Umayyad period. Ubayd Allah b. Ziyad concluded an agreement with the *khatun* (a Sogdanian title for the ruler's wife) who governed the great and rich oasis (in AH 54/674 CE). Yet the actual capture of the region started a generation later during the governorship of Qutayba Ibn Muslim (89/708), and it was not secured until the days of Nasr Ibn Sayyar (738–748), when the armies of the caliphate succeeded in repelling the Western Turks (Turgish /Türgiş).

According to Islamic historiography, the victorious Muslim commanders constructed a mosque and recruited local clients to the armies of the caliphate, though it is difficult to gauge the number of converts and their percentage among the indigenous population. Judging by their participation in heretical movements, however, it can be assumed that in Bukhara during the eighth and ninth centuries, a considerable number of people were giving up local beliefs and joining Islam. Already during the early 'Abbasid period, contacts between the core land of the caliphate and the periphery became more firmly established. A governor was sent from Baghdad to collect taxes and command the army.

The rank of Bukhara in the administrative machinery of the caliphate was upgraded during the years of the Tahirids (207–278/822–891). The new importance of the city resulted from developments in Khurasan. The coming of Isma'il b. Ahmad to Bukhara (in 262/875), whose position was confirmed by the caliph al-Mu'tadid (279–89/892–902), opened a new chapter in the history of the oasis. Bukhara became the capital city of the Samanids, a local Iranian dynasty that became integrated into the 'Abbasid system.

After the fall of the Samanids (395/1005) and the emergence in present-day Afghanistan of new centers, that of Ghazna, who for a short period the Ghaznawids (367–583/977–1187) played a role in the history of Central Asia, Bukhara lost its political and administrative importance. Yet, due to cultural and economic reasons it did not disappear from chronicles that narrate the history of power struggles in medieval Central Asia. With the help of the Saljuqid sultan Sanjar, a Qarakhanid (Ilig/Ilek Khans) prince named Arslan Khan Muhammad occupied Bukhara (495/1102). The city remained in the hands of the Qarakhanids while it was governed by the Ilig Nasr b. 'Ali the. After a few decades the Kara Khitay captured the town (536/1141). The Kara Khitay people did not rule Bukhara directly but rather installed a local family as head of tax collection and bureaucracy *(sadr)*.

Mongol invasions (616/1220) brought havoc to Bukhara. Nevertheless, the city soon recovered. A revolt led by a pseudoprophet (636/1238) began the re-emergence of a local community. Yet after a few years, Bukhara once again was destroyed, first by the Il-Kahn Abaka of Iran (671/1278) and then by a Chaghtayid rebel (716/1316). Later, Bukhara was taken over by Timur Leng (Tamerlane, d. 1405). It remained in the hands of the Timurid Turkish–Mongol dynasty until the advance of Shibani Khan the Uzbek (905/1500). It seems that during these years the city had no political importance. The topographical history of Bukhara in the seventh to ninth centuries is shrouded in obscurity. On more solid ground is the information from the 'Abbasid period. Arab and Persian geographers provide information on the structure and topography of Bukhara. They describe a large city *(shahristan)* protected by double walls with several gates (the sources name seven to eleven), a citadel *(quhunduz; ark)*, water canals *(arik)*, and suburbs *(rabd)*. The Samanids built a royal palace that accommodated the administration *(divan)*. Arslan Khan became noted as a great builder. He rebuilt the walls and citadel of Bukhara and constructed a mosque. A dozen monuments have survived as evidence of the architectural achievements of the years described in the previous paragraph.

Being populated by Arabs, Iranians, and Turks, Bukhara served as a center to spread the new culture that developed within the boundaries of the caliphate. This deduction is supported by biographical dictionaries that use new nomenclature to name renowned Muslim scholars. In biographical entries these writers use genealogy based on geography *(nisba)* to name the personas. Money among them bore the *nisba* al-Bukhari. The lists of the numerous scholars named al-Bukhari are long. Abu al-Fadl Bal'ami and his son Abu 'Ali Muhammad (d. 363/973) are further examples. Both served as viziers of the Samanids. Translating into New Persian, the chronicles of al-Tabari, Muhammad gained fame as one of the first Persian authors.

Bukhara functioned as an axis of Islamic culture and innovation and a hub of the Hanafi School of Islamic law, which molded the Islam of recently converted Turks. Patronized by the Samanids, the Persian language, which served as the lingua franca between the Muslim governors and the population of Transoxiana, developed into a pivot of the new Islamic civilization. From Bukhara it spread to the central parts of Iran and advanced into Central Asia. The city's role as the heart of Islamic learning was not eclipsed even under the Mongols. Moreover, Baha al-Din Naqshaband (791/1389) started his brotherhood of dervishes *(al-tariqa al-Naqshabandiyya)* during the years of the Chaghatayid dynasty.

YEHOSHUA FRENKEL

Further Reading

Collins, B. A. *Al-Muqaddasi—The Best Divisions for Knowledge of the Regions.* Reading, MA, 1994.

Frye, Richard Nelson (Trans). *The History of Bukhara* [being a translation of Narshakhi]. Cambridge, MA: Mediaeval Academy of America, 1954.

Frye, Richard Nelson. *Bukhara: The Medieval Achievement.* Norman: University of Oklahoma Press, 1965.

Le Strange, Guy. *The Lands of the Eastern Caliphate.* London, 1905.

Vambery, Armin. *History of Bokhara from the Earliest Period Down to the Present, Composed for the First Time after Oriental Known and Unknown Historical Manuscripts.* London: H.S. King, 1873.

BUKHARI

Al-Bukhari, Abu Ja'far Muhammad b. Isma'il was an expert in hadith. Muslims consider his work, *al-Jami' al-Sahih,* or more commonly, *Sahih al-Bukhari,* to be the foremost collection of the accounts of the words, deeds, and opinions of the Prophet Muhammad.

The purview of the collection is indicated by the title which al-Bukhari apparently gave his work, translated as: *The Comprehensive Collection of Supported Sound Hadith Summarized from the Actions, Practices, and Battles of the Messenger of God.* The hadith are arranged topically. The emphasis is on Islamic religious law, although there is much material that can be more narrowly defined as theology and religious history.

According to the traditional estimate, it consists of roughly 7275 hadith. Many of the hadith are mentioned more than once, and it is said that without the duplicates the total is 4000 separate hadith. Both figures include hadith lacking a chain of transmission *(isnad)*, hadith repeated with more than one chain of transmission, and those ascribed to religious authorities other than Muhammad. Unfortunately, nowhere does al-Bukhari explain the criteria he applied in selecting hadith for inclusion, although tales assert that only a small fraction of what he knew he found worthy. For the most part, later scholars held that al-Bukhari's mere mention of a transmitter in this work was sufficient proof that the transmitter was reliable. We may take the estimate of the esteemed scholar

al-Safadi (AH 696/1297–764/1363 CE) of the work as representative: "[Al-Bukhari]'s collection is the most exalted book on hadith in Islam; and the best of them after [the Qur'an]." Considering al-Bukhari's later fame, the sources give us very little information about his life, and what we are told is largely hagiography mixed in with tidbits of information that, in most cases, could well have been derived from the examination of his works. He was born in Bukhara in 194/810 to non-Arab parents. He took up the study of hadith at an early age and traveled throughout Persia, Iraq, the Hejaz, Syria, and Egypt. In 256/870, he died in Khartank, a village near Samarqand, and was buried in the latter. The most serious blemish on his reputation was the allegation leveled by some of his contemporaries that he asserted that one's recitation of the Qur'an is "created," and therefore not pre-eternal. During his lifetime, issues surrounding the nature of the Qur'an were bitterly disputed, and later generations of scholars have generally held this particular doctrine to be heretical. In the traditional biographical accounts of the life of al-Bukhari, we find him unequivocally denying that he ever subscribed to such an odious view.

Al-Bukhari wrote other works on subjects concerning hadith, but they are, considering his fame, unimpressive. Of these, his *al-Ta'rikh al-kabir* (ed. 'Abd al-Rahman b. Yahya al-Mu'allimi al-Yamani, 4 vols. in 8 parts, Hyderabad, 1361–1365), a more or less alphabetically arranged biographical dictionary of hadith transmitters, is probably the most notable. Despite its immense size, it was quickly eclipsed as a practical reference by even larger and more informative books covering the same ground.

EERIK DICKINSON

Primary Sources

Al-Khatib al-Baghdadi. *Ta'rikh Baghdad.* 14 vols. Cairo: Maktabat al-Khanji, 1349/1931, 2: 4–34.

Al-Safadi, Khalil b. Aybak. *al-Wafi bi-'l-wafayat.* Edited by Hellmut Ritter et al. Istanbul/Wiesbaden: Franz Steiner Verlag, 1931 ff., 2: 206–209.

Further Reading

Encyclopaedia of Islam. Second ed. Leiden: E.J. Brill, 1953 ff., 1:1296–1297.

Sezgin, Fuat. *Geschichte des arabischen Schrifttums.* Leiden: E.J. Brill, 1967 ff., 1:115–134.

BURIAL CUSTOMS

See Funerary Practices, Muslim

BURIDS

The Burids, or Börids, were a Turkish dynasty that ruled Damascus and much of its hinterland from 1104 to 1154 CE. Its founder was Zahir al-Din Tughtigin, the *atabeg* (a kind of "guardian and tutor") of Shams al-Mulk Duqaq, the son of the Seljuk sultan in Syria, Tutush (r. 1078–1095), who was the son of Alp Arslan and the brother of Malikshah (r. 1073–1092). Tutush took Damascus from Atsiz ibn Uvaz, who had conquered southern Syria and Palestine from the Fatimids. On Tutush's death, his sons divided his territory, Duqaq taking Damascus while placing his affairs in the hands of Tughtigin. When Duqaq died in 1104, Tughtigin became the de facto ruler of Damascus.

Tughtigin (r. 1104–1128) was the most remarkable member of the dynasty that he had founded. He maintained his independence with great dexterity while contending with the Fatimids in Egypt and Palestine, the newly arrived Franks of the First Crusade, also in Palestine, the 'Abbasid caliph and Seljuk sultan in Baghdad, and other members of the Seljuk family in Syria and Iraq. Sometimes allied with, or against, one or another of these parties, he skillfully played them against each other. In the course of this, he established his authority in the region between the Hawran south of Damascus and Hamah to the north. He played an important role in the struggle against the Franks, who threatened his grain supply in the Biqa'a Valley, and launched several expeditions against them. He made valiant but unsuccessful attempts to save Tripoli from them in 1109 and Tyre in 1124. He lacked the forces to drive the Crusaders from Palestine yet was distrustful of his disunited Muslim neighbors. In 1115, when the Seljuk sultan Muhammad sent an army to bring him under control and then attack the Franks, Tughtigin sided with the latter. Later, however, he traveled to Baghdad to seek the sultan's pardon.

On his death, Tughtigin was succeeded by his son Taj al-Muluk Böri (r. 1128–1132). He captured Hamah in 1129 and then blunted a Frankish campaign against Damascus. He almost immediately faced a major challenge with the rise of the Zankids in Mosul. The founder of this dynasty, Zanki, took Aleppo in 1128 and Hamah in 1130 while demanding the cooperation of Damascus against the Crusaders. He reached Homs before returning to Mosul. Meanwhile, in Damascus, Böri was threatened by the growing power of the Batinis, or Ismailis, who had been supported by his father. In 1129, Böri broke their power and exterminated a large number of them. In 1132, however, they assassinated him.

Böri was succeeded by his son, Shams al-Muluk Isma'il (r. 1132–1135). He captured Banyas from the Franks in 1132, took Hamah back from Zanki in 1133, and forced back a Frankish invasion of the Hawran in 1134. Despite these actions, he was considered so corrupt and tyrannical that his mother ordered his assassination in 1135. His brother Shihab al-Din Mahmud (r. 1135–1139) then took the throne. Zanki attempted to take advantage of this turmoil by marching on Damascus, but the people of the city stoutly resisted him and he withdrew. Mahmud and Zanki contracted a marriage alliance in 1138 that appeared to resolve their differences. Shortly thereafter, however, Mahmud was murdered by two of his slaves.

After Mahmud's murder, the city's military leaders first placed his brother Muhammad on the throne, but he died shortly thereafter. They then replaced him with Mahmud's young son, Mujir al-Din Abaq (r. 1140–1154), while placing actual control of Damascus in the hands of his *atabeg*, Mu'in al-Din Unur. Zanki again attacked the city, and again it resisted. Unur formed an alliance with the Franks to keep him at bay. Relations with the Franks were stabilized for the next few years. Zanki's preoccupation with Edessa in 1144 and his death in 1146 relieved the pressure from the north and allowed Unur to expand his territory. However, Zanki's son and successor, Nur al-Din Mahmud, proved to be equally determined to capture Damascus. In early 1147, Nur al-Din married Unur's daughter and the two leaders carried out joint operations against the Franks. A few months later, when the Second Crusade attempted to conquer Damascus, Nur al-Din provided some relief. When Unur died in 1149, Abaq was incapable of retaining control of the city. Nur al-Din forced him to accept his guardianship and finally drove him out in 1154.

On the whole, Damascus prospered under the Burids, enjoying a long period of relative security after several centuries of anarchy. The city expanded and new institutions, notably *madrasas* (colleges of law), took root.

GARY LEISER

See also 'Abbasids; Assassins; Jihad; Madrasa; Muslim–Crusader Relations; Seljuks

Primary Sources

Ibn al-Qalanisi. *The Damascus Chronicle of the Crusades.* Trans. H.A.R. Gibb. London: Luzac, 1932.

Further Reading

Baldwin, Marshall. ed. *A History of the Crusades.* Vol. 1. Madison: University of Wisconsin Press, 1969–1989.

Mouton, J.-M. *Damas et sa Principauté sous les Saljoukides et les Bourides 468–549/1076–1154.* Cairo: Institut Français d'Archéologie Orientale, 1994.

BUYIDS

The Buyid (Buwayhid) dynasty lasted from AH 334/945 CE until 449/1057. This family originated from the hills of Dailam near the Caspian Sea. 'Ali ibn Buya, in close collaboration with his two brothers, Ahmad and al-Hasan, led them to power at the head of a predominantly infantry army recruited in Dailam. Their first major success came when they took Shiraz in 322/934. Shortly thereafter they began adding Turkish cavalry to the army. The province of Fars served as one of their three centers of power. Al-Hasan took and ruled from Rayy. Ahmad marched on Baghdad, taking it in 334/945.

The Buyid family ruled as a confederation, with the eldest member having precedence. They did not depose or eliminate the caliph but acted as his "deputies." In reality they acted as kings while maintaining the legal fiction of subservience. All signs indicate that they were Shi'i, but pragmatically they made no effort to replace the 'Abbasid caliph with a Shi'i imam or to rule in his name. However, they did remove uncooperative caliphs. Immediately following the conquest of Baghdad, the caliph al-Mustakfi granted the three brothers the titles by which they are typically known: Ahmad became Mu'izz al-Dawla, al-Hasan became Rukn al-Dawla, and 'Ali became 'Imad al-Dawla. The caliph was then promptly removed from the throne, with al-Muti' taking his place. 'Imad al-Dawla, as the dominant member of the family, ruled from Shiraz until his death in 338/949. When he died, he had no sons and his role in Shiraz was assumed by 'Adud al-Dawla, the son of Rukn al-Dawla. Rukn al-Dawla then became head of the confederation. Mu'izz al-Dawla died in 356/967 having never attained headship.

'Adud al-Dawla represents the pinnacle of Buyid power and authority. As long as his father was alive, he maintained obedience to the familial structure of precedence. However, once his father died in 366/977, he seized Baghdad from his cousin and from there dominated the family. He was able to centralize rule and enforce unity.

After 'Adud al-Dawla's death in 372/983, the unity that he had created crumbled and the Buyids reverted once more to their previous pattern of family rule from their three main capitals of Baghdad, Shiraz, and Rayy. The position of senior amir was almost continually under dispute after 'Adud al-Dawla's death, and each prince usually ruled his capital independently. Only Baha' al-Dawla (r. 398/1007–403/1012) and Abu Kalijar (r. 435/1044–440/1048) can be said to have held the position of senior amir.

In addition to familial squabbles, the composite nature of the Buyid army meant that there were constant quarrels between Dailamite and Turkish troops. The later Buyids also faced considerable outside challenges. There were small challenges from Arab and Kurdish tribes and attempts by other dynasties, such as those of Oman and Isfahan, to break free from Buyid control. In the East there were major invasions by the Ghaznavids and Seljuks. The beginning of the end was the Ghaznavid conquest of Rayy in 1029. The demise of arguably the most active of the later Buyids, Abu Kalijar 'Imad al-Din, in 440/1048 left no clear ruler for the whole of Buyid territory and no established princes in the major cities. The Seljuks under Tughril Bek took this opportunity to take control of Buyid territories, and the last independent Buyid, Khusraw Firuz al-Malik al-Rahim, was captured outside of Baghdad in 449/1057.

Although politically chaotic, the Buyid courts provided havens for intellectuals, artists, and scientists from a variety of ethnic and religious persuasions. One can point to such luminaries as the philosopher Ibn Sina as examples of the breadth of intellectual achievement of this period.

JOHN P. TURNER AND RACHEL T. HOWES

See also 'Abbasids; 'Adud al-Dawla; Baghdad; Ghaznavids; Ibn Sina; Imam; Iran; Iraq; Isfahan; Kurds; Mahmud of Ghazna; Oman; Seljuks; Shi'ism; Turks

Further Reading

Bowen, H. "The Last Buyids." *Journal of the Royal Asiatic Society* (1929).

Busse, H. *Chalif, und Grosskonig Die Buyuden in Iraq (945–1055).* Beiruter Texte und Studien, bd 6. Beirut: In Kommission bei F. Steiner, Wiesbaden, 1969.

Busse, Heribert. "Iran Under the Buyids." *Cambridge History of Iran, vol. 4. From the Arab Invasion to the Saljuqs.* Cambridge: Cambridge University Press, 1975.

Donohue, J.J. *The Buwayhid Dynasty in Iraq 334H./945 to 403H./1012.* Leiden: Brill, 2003.

Kabir, M. *The Buwayhid Dynasty of Baghdad.* Calcutta: Iran Society, 1964.

Mottahedeh, R.P. *Loyalty and Leadership in an Early Islamic Society.* New York: I.B. Tauris, 2001.

Primary Sources

Ibn al-Athir. *al-Kamil fi l-ta'rikh.* Edited by 'Abd al-Wahhab al-Najjar. Cairo: Idarat al-Tiba'a al-Muniriyya, 1929.

Ibn al-Jawzi. *al-Muntazam fi ta'rikh al-muluk wa-l-umam.* Beirut: Dar al-Kutub al-'Ilmiyya, 1992.

Ibn Khallikan. *Ibn Khallikan's Biographical Dictionary.* Edited by W.M. de Slane. Paris: Oriental translation fund of Great Britain and Ireland, 1843.

Ibn Miskawayh. *The Eclipse of the Abbasid Caliphate.* Edited by H.F. Amedroz and D. S. Margoliouth. Oxford: B. Blackwell, 1920.

Al-Shirazi, Al-Mu'ayyad fi l-Din. *Sirat al-Mu'ayyad fi l-Din Da'i al-Du'at.* Edited by Muhammad Kamil Hussain. Cairo: Dar al-Katib al-Misri, 1949.

Yaqut. *Irshad al-arib ila ma'rifat al-adib.* Edited by D.S. Margoliouth. 7 vols. Leiden: E.J. Brill, 1907.

BYZANTINE EMPIRE

Byzantium was that part of the Roman Empire that retained its independence after the first ultradynamic phase of Islamic expansion (634–652 CE). Its principal components were (1) the islands of the Aegean, (2) the fertile coastal plains that fringe Asia Minor, (3) the mountain ranges that back onto those plains and the rolling plateau that they encircle, (4) those parts of the southern Balkans (Thrace, a coastal strip running west to Thessalonike, eastern Greece), which had not been colonized by Slavs in the late sixth and early seventh centuries, (5) a cluster of substantial territories in the central Mediterranean (central and southern Italy, Sicily, Carthage and its large hinterland), and (6) far to the northeast, enclaves on the Black Sea (the Crimea and Lazica). The capital, the ancient Greek colony of Byzantium (renamed Constantinople), had been developed into one of the three great cities of the East Mediterranean by Constantine the Great (324–337 CE) and his immediate successors. It was endowed with impressive public buildings, grand processional ways, and a spectacular domed cathedral. This late-antique armature provided visible proof to Byzantines, as well as to outsiders, that theirs was indeed a latter-day Roman Empire. Much changed in the Middle Ages, but the importance of Byzantium's Roman heritage should not be underestimated. The people were Romans, ruled by an uninterrupted sequence of emperors from successive dynasties. The Senate continued to exist in its Late Antique guise of a court at the apex of an aristocracy of service. The modification of inherited institutions was a gradual, long, drawn-out process. Law, language, and coinage remained Roman. Most important of all was continuity in the spheres of secular culture, religion, and ideology. Byzantium retained imperial status, in its own eyes as well as those of others. Its identity was defined ultimately by Greco-Roman culture and Christian faith, deepened by the harrowing experiences through which the people at large and the governing elites lived.

Struggle for Survival (Seventh to Ninth Centuries CE)

Initially, Byzantium's history was shaped by the threat from Islam. Constantinople itself came under attack in 654, for several years in the 670s, and again in 717–718. Territory was lost—Cilicia in the southeast in the 690s, North Africa in 698, and Sicily gradually from 827. Asia Minor suffered severe damage from repeated invasions. It was only in interludes of civil war within the Caliphate that the Byzantine army could be reorganized properly for defense and the administrative system adapted to ensure efficient, effective support for the war effort. The cumulative effect of a multitude of ad hoc responses and more methodical reforms was to transform state and society by the end of the eighth century.

First, the imperial center tightened its grip over the localities. The tax system inherited from antiquity was used to suck up an unprecedentedly high percentage of surplus resources. Second, the empire was militarized. Army commands and their subdivisions replaced provinces and cities as the units of regional and local government in Asia Minor. The burden of supporting the troops was distributed over the countryside. The peasantry enlisted in large numbers. The army adopted guerrilla tactics, relying on urban fortifications (usually much reduced in size) and strategically placed castles to secure the civilian population and their moveable wealth. Third, a quiet social revolution occurred. The urban-based land-owning aristocracy did not survive the era of extensive war damage and urban decline. The peasant and the peasant village gained unprecedented recognition as the basis of society and the state.

The reforms were mainly the work of Constans II (641–668), grandson and successor of Heraclius (610–641) and the first two Isaurian emperors, Leo III (717–741) and Constantine V (741–775). What emerged was a state with a high military gearing and a resilient social and ideological base, able to project power far beyond its borders by a variety of means (naval, military, diplomatic, and propaganda). After defense in the East, the highest priority was reassertion of authority in the Balkans. When Islam turned in on itself, offensives were launched against the hybrid nomad–sedentary state established in the 670s by Bulgars south of the Danube by Constantine IV in 681, by Constantine V, who sustained the pressure from 759 to 775, and (disastrously) by Nicephorus I in 811. Transalpine Europe and Italy tended to slip beyond the horizon of vision, unless there was an acute threat, and action was usually limited to the diplomatic sphere (as when the Franks occupied Venice in 812).

Foreign policy was reactive until the 860s, when the initiative in the Near East passed to Byzantium. The same was true in the domestic sphere. The catalyst for the drive to decontaminate Christianity of icon veneration, formally initiated by Leo III in 730, was undoubtedly the explosive eruption of Thera in the Aegean core of the empire. There could have been no plainer sign of divine displeasure at the flouting of the Second Commandment, at this accretion to the faith, which was conspicuous for its absence in Islam. Much political and intellectual effort was subsequently expended before the final restoration of icons in 843. Similarly, a renewed interest in classical Greek literature, mathematics, science, and philosophy in the reign of Theophilus (829–842) was triggered by the 'Abbasid-sponsored program of translation and commentary.

Political Acme (Tenth to Eleventh Centuries CE) and Subsequent Decline

With the accession of Basil I (867–886), founder of the Macedonian dynasty, Byzantium entered its heyday. A cautious, carefully targeted aggressive policy was adopted against Islam, which resulted, by 976, in annexation of a broad swath of land in the southeast and western Armenia. By the time of Basil II's death in 1025, Bulgaria was conquered, the whole Balkans reintegrated into the empire, and Byzantine prestige raised to new heights in the West. In the East, Christian Armenian princes were yielding to blandishment and ceding sovereignty to the emperor. By the middle of the eleventh century, Byzantium achieved something close to hegemony in the East Mediterranean. At home, emperors from Romanos I Lekapenos (920–944) to Basil II (976–1025) asserted their authority over the aristocracy (now solidifying its wealth and status by investing in land) in a series of legal enactments, charged with emotive appeals to Christian moral standards. Their prime concern was to conserve the old social order and its peasant base. Modifications were introduced into provincial administration (notably allocation of executive authority to judges). Minor adjustments were made in the central apparatus. The army was concentrated behind the frontiers, but the main structures put in place in the age of crisis were retained.

It is open to debate whether or not the agrarian legislation of the tenth century succeeded in stemming the long-term growth of aristocratic power and the concomitant subordination of peasants to lay, clerical, and monastic landowners. It is known, however, that there was steady demographic growth to the eve of the Black Death, increasing commercial activity, and a reemergence of urban notables as a significant political force. More is learned about the church and monasticism in the last centuries, but their essential characteristics were unchanged: (1) an otherworldliness, long manifest in church decoration (which transformed the interior into a microcosm of heaven) and in the striving for seclusion of monks, nuns, and holy men and women; (2) a faith made live by regular reenactment of the salvation story; and (3) an episcopate of greater intellectual than political weight. Art and learning flourished more than hitherto. From the middle of the eleventh century Byzantium declined swiftly as a political power. The causes of a first collapse were primarily external: the swift westward advance of the Turks, which spilled over into Asia Minor from 1058, depredations by Norman adventurers in southern Italy and the Balkans, and the growing commercial ambitions and naval power of the Italian city-states, including Byzantium's long-standing client, Venice. Among them, these three forces drove Byzantium to the brink of destruction by 1081. All the resources of Byzantine statecraft, eventually harnessed to the cause of the Crusade, were required for the reconstitution of an empire, now centered on the Balkans, by Alexius Comnenus (1081–1118).

The triggers for a second collapse, culminating in the capture of Constantinople by the Fourth Crusade (1204), were defeat at the hands of the Turks in 1176, the massacre of Latins at Constantinople in 1182, and successful rebellions by Serbs and Bulgarians in the Balkans from the mid-1180s. The final phase of revival, initiated by the Lascarid rulers of a rump state in northwest Asia Minor, peaked with the recapture of Constantinople by Michael VIII Palaeologus in 1261. Thereafter, decline resumed, exacerbated by civil war and social conflict. Repeated attempts to secure western help were thwarted by popular opposition to the doctrinal concessions required by the Papacy. The establishment of a secure Ottoman bridgehead across the Dardanelles in 1354 marked the beginning of the end. It was only deferred by the crushing Mongol victory over the Ottomans at Ankara in 1402. Constantinople, by then a small island in an Ottoman sea, was finally captured, after heroic resistance by an outnumbered garrison, on May 29, 1453.

JAMES HOWARD-JOHNSTON

Further Reading

Angold, Michael. *The Byzantine Empire 1025–1204: A Political History*. London and New York: Longman, 1984.

Haldon, John F. *Byzantium in the Seventh Century: The Transformation of a Culture*. Cambridge: Cambridge University Press, 1990.

Harris, Jonathan. *Byzantium and the Crusades*. London and New York: Hambledon and London, 2003.

Hussey, Joan M. *The Orthodox Church in the Byzantine Empire*. Oxford: Clarendon Press, 1986.

Laiou-Thomadakis, Angeliki E. *Peasant Society in the Late Byzantine Empire: A Social and Demographic Study*. Princeton, NJ: Princeton University Press, 1977.

Laiou, Angeliki E., ed. *The Economic History of Byzantium from the Seventh through the Fifteenth Century*. 3 vols. Washington: Dumbarton Oaks, 2002.

Lemerle, Paul. *The Agrarian History of Byzantium from the Origins to the Twelfth Century: The Sources and the Problems*. Galway: Galway University Press, 1979.

Mango, Cyril. *Byzantium: The Empire of New Rome*. London: Weidenfeld and Nicolson, 1980.

Mathews, Thomas F. *The Art of Byzantium: Between Antiquity and the Renaissance*. London: Weidenfeld and Nicolson, 1998.

Nicol, Donald. *The Last Centuries of Byzantium, 1261–1453*. London: Rupert Hart-Davis, 1972.

Obolensky, Dimitri. *The Byzantine Commonwealth: Eastern Europe, 500–1453*. London: Weidenfeld and Nicolson, 1971.

Whittow, Mark. *The Making of Orthodox Byzantium, 600–1025*. London: Macmillan, 1996.

Wilson, Nigel G. *Scholars of Byzantium*. London: Duckworth, 1983.

C

CAIRO

Cairo is the best documented and best preserved of the medieval Islamic capitals and, for most of this period, its largest city.

Originally, Cairo (Ar. *Al-Qahira*) referred only to a small part of the Egyptian capital, although it later developed into a term for the whole medieval city. In 641 CE, soon after the conquest of Egypt, the Arabs established a new garrison city known as al-Fustat next to the old Roman city of Babylon at the southern tip of the Nile Delta. The new settlement resembled other early Islamic cities, such as Basra and Kufa, with a congregational mosque and Dar al-'Imara at its center. In 750, the 'Abbasids built a new administrative center to the north called al-'Askar ("the soldier") in reference to the troops stationed there. More than one hundred years later, in 870, the semi-independent Tulunids established another city on higher ground to the northeast, which was called al-Qata'i' ("the wards"). The last of the four cities that comprised medieval Cairo was established one hundred years later by the Fatimids to mark the completion of their conquest of North Africa. The city, which was completed in 971, was originally named al-Mansuriyya by the caliph al-Mu'izz after his father al-Mansur, though it was later changed to al-Qahira ("the victorious") both as a signal that the Fatimids had achieved their objective and because the planet Mars *(al-Qahir)* was in the ascendant when work started on the construction of the city.

The first three early Islamic cities were located on the west bank of the Nile and merged into each other to form a single city. However, al-Qahira (Cairo) was farther to the northeast and for some time remained separate from the other cities, which were known by the collective name of al-Fustat. Under the early Fatimids, al-Qahira remained a palatial city closed to the general public, housing the caliph, royal officials, and the administration. Both al-Qahira and Fustat each had their own port on the Nile and functioned as separate cities. In the twelfth century, this situation changed when Fustat entered into a period of decline caused by famines, earthquakes, and other natural and manmade disasters. One of the most significant factors was that the Nile was gradually moving westward, leaving the port facilities of Fustat high and dry. The decisive change came when the Fatimid vizier Badr al-Jamali allowed the transfer of some markets from Fustat and also permitted inhabitants of Fustat to build houses within al-Qahira. In order to accommodate the increasing population, the walls of the Fatimid were expanded, first by Badr al-Jamali between 1087 and 1091 and later (1176–1193) by Salah al-Din. From this point on, al-Qahira became the main focus of activity and the heart of the later medieval metropolis.

The transfer of power to the Ayyubids consolidated these changes, although it is notable that Salah al-Din attempted to enclose both Fustat and al-Qahira within one massive defensive wall, with the citadel occupying the area in between. Under the Mamluks, al-Qahira continued to develop outside the old walls mainly in the area to the south of the old city and to the west of the Ayyubid citadel. There was also some expansion to the north of the city chiefly around the Mosque of Baybars (1266–1269), which was built on the site of the former royal polo ground. After the Ottoman conquest in the sixteenth century the direction of expansion was toward the west, following the westward deflection of the Nile. The nucleus of the Ottoman expansion was the mosque of Sinan Pasha built in 1571.

The early expansion of Cairo (including Fustat) was characterized by the construction of congregational mosques, which became nuclei for settlement. The principal monuments of Fatimid Cairo are the mosques of al-Azhar and al-Hakim. Soon after its construction in 970–972, the al-Azhar mosque became a teaching institution propagating the Fatimid *da'wa* (propaganda). The increasing educational importance of al-Azhar may have been the impetus for the construction of al-Hakim's mosque in 990–991 (completed under al-Hakim by 1012). Under the Ayyubids a new factor was introduced in the form of small religious foundations such as madrasas and zawiyas, which formed the focal points of smaller local communities. This process continued under the Mamluks and, with the exception of the Mosque of Baybars, all of the Mamluk mosques appear to have formed part of a religious complex, which may have included a tomb, madrasas, or khanqah. Under the Ottomans the situation was reversed and mosques once again became the principal type of religious architecture.

ANDREW PETERSEN

Further Reading

Behrens-Abuseif, D. *Supplement to Muqarnas.* Leiden: E.J. Brill.
Creswell, K.A.C. *Muslim Architecture of Egypt* 2 Vols. Oxford, 1952–1960.
Rogers, M. "Al-Khaira." in *Encyclopaedia of Islam,* 424–441.

CALIPHATE AND IMAMATE

The caliphate is arguably the most central issue associated with the Muslim polity and its administration. In the political realm, *khilafa* (anglicized as "caliphate") refers to the "succession" of an individual as leader of the polity after the Prophet Muhammad's death in AD 11/632 CE. The etymologically related word *khalifa* (pl. *khulafa'*; anglicized as "caliph") occurs in the Qur'an in which its context is understood mainly as referring to humans as God's "vicegerent" or "representative" on Earth (2:30; 38:26). *Khalifa* in Qur'anic usage does not evidence explicit political meaning. Early Qur'an exegetes through the second/eighth century, in fact, understood the term to refer broadly to the basic function of humans as custodians and cultivators of the earth. Later exegetes increasingly came to understand this term in highly political terms, reflecting the historical and theological developments of the formative period.

The Rightly Guided Caliphate

Sunni sources almost unanimously inform us that when Abu Bakr was selected as the leader of the polity after the Prophet's death in Medina, after what appears to have been a contentious debate, the title applied to him was *Khalifat Rasul Allah*, meaning "the Successor of the Messenger of God." Abu Bakr is said to have recoiled from adopting another suggested title, *Khalifat Allah*, meaning "God's deputy" or "vicegerent," because he regarded himself as someone merely following in the footsteps of Muhammad, not as someone entrusted with political and religious authority by God himself, as this title would imply. The latter title, however, was adopted by both the Umayyad and 'Abbasid caliphs to signal an enhanced status for themselves.

Abu Bakr ruled for a mere two years (632–634), but within this period he subdued those tribes in Arabia that rose in revolt against the Medinan government and refused to pay *zakat*, the obligatory alms tax. The wars that were waged against these fractious tribes are known as the *ridda* wars, the so-called wars of apostasy, which decisively aborted this uprising and restored unity to the polity, at least for a while. Before he died in 13/634, Abu Bakr took the precaution of naming Umar as his successor, so as to prevent the kind of confusion and heated debate that had arisen during the process of his selection as the first caliph. The choice of 'Umar as the second caliph seems to have won general ratification, except in the case of the faction who consistently advocated 'Ali's candidacy. This faction was consequently dubbed *Shi'at 'Ali* ("the partisans of 'Ali"), *Shi'is* for short. Shi'i conceptions of the caliphate–imamate are presented separately in the following paragraphs.

'Umar's ten-year rule was decisive and critical for the still-nascent Muslim community. Among the titles applied to 'Umar were *Khalifat Abi Bakr* ("the Successor of Abu Bakr") and *Khalifat khalifat Rasul Allah* ("the successor of the Successor of the Messenger of God"). The clumsiness of the second title would partially explain why 'Umar preferred the title *Amir al-Mu'minin* ("Commander of the Faithful"). According to the sources, 'Umar was an energetic, even abrasive ruler, gifted interpreter, stern enforcer of the law, and shrewd political administrator. He instituted the famous *diwan*, the register of pensions, which awarded stipends to Muslims on the basis of their priority in conversion and extent of service to Islam, and established garrison towns in the newly conquered realms. Under his reign, the Islamic realm expanded to include Syria–Palestine, Egypt, Mesopotamia, and Persia, a project already underway under his predecessor. 'Umar's shaping of certain Islamic practices at this early stage is regarded as critical by later historians, for which he is praised by Sunnis but denounced by the Shi'is.

'Umar's reign was followed by 'Uthman ibn 'Affan, elected by the six-man electoral council called the *shura*, which was appointed by the former as he lay on his deathbed, mortally wounded by a Persian assailant. 'Uthman's reign, which was the longest (644–656), was marred by continuous strife and factionalism. His perceived nepotism—many of his relatives and fellow clan members from the Banu Umayya had been appointed to high offices—caused widespread disgruntlement, particularly in the garrisons of Kufa, Basra, and Egypt. In 656, as 'Uthman sat in the mosque at Medina reading the Qur'an, a cabal of some of these garrison dwellers attacked and killed him.

'Ali ibn Abi Talib, the Prophet's cousin and son-in-law, next assumed the caliphate to lead a highly fractious polity. 'A'isha, the Prophet's widow, instigated what became known as the Battle of the Camel when 'Ali refused to accede to her demands to avenge the death of 'Uthman and punish his assailants. 'A'isha and her cohorts were roundly defeated, but civil war (*fitna*) soon broke out between 'Ali and Mu'awiya, a kinsman of 'Uthman's who similarly wanted the third caliph's assassins punished. The two sides met at the Battle of Siffin in 657, which came to a halt when Mu'awiya sued for arbitration, to which 'Ali agreed. This angered a number of 'Ali's troops, who seceded from his army and became known as the Khawarij ("the seceders"). Negotiations with Mu'awiya dragged on indecisively until 'Ali was murdered by a Khariji assassin, bringing what became known as "the Age of the Rightly Guided Caliphs" to a close. Mu'awiya, who was the governor of Syria, declared himself caliph and initiated dynastic rule in the Islamic world.

The Umayyads, the 'Abbasids, and the Later Caliphate

The Umayyads ruled between 661 and 750 with their capital in Damascus, Syria. Although later 'Abbasid sources regularly vilify them as godless usurpers of power, some Umayyad rulers took an interest in matters of religious law and ritual. 'Umar ibn 'Abd al-'Aziz (r. 717–720) is distinguished from practically all other Umayyad rulers by later historians for his exceptional piety and religious scholarship, a standing indicated by the fact that he is frequently referred to as the fifth Rightly Guided Caliph. In the late first/seventh century, 'Abd al-Malik ibn Marwan made Arabic the official language of the empire, instituted a sophisticated postal system, and commissioned the building of the Dome of the Rock in Jerusalem. Increasing unrest and dissension marked the latter part of Umayyad rule. The Shi'is and the Khawarij had sporadically kept up their rebellion against the government. Unfair taxation practices against the *mawali*, Muslim converts from non-Arab backgrounds, and other instances of preferential treatment for Arabs over non-Arabs were among the significant factors that fomented widespread resentment and hostility toward the Umayyads. This culminated in the outbreak of the 'Abbasid revolution of 749 and the Umayyad assumption of the caliphate in 750. An Umayyad scion escaped to Spain and established the Andalusian Umayyad dynasty in Cordoba.

The 'Abbasids

In 762, the second 'Abbasid caliph, al-Mansur, founded Baghdad, which soon became the capital of the new dynasty, inaugurating a new era (Ar. *dawla*). The 'Abbasid period (750–1258) has been described as the golden age of Islamic civilization, and with good justification. The efflorescence of learning, culture, the arts, architecture, and the natural sciences is associated with this period, triggered to a great extent by the great translation activity of the second/eighth and third/ninth centuries, which made a considerable part of the scholarship of antiquity available to Muslims. Major schools of Sunni and Shi'i law were established during the first two centuries of 'Abbasid rule, and the authoritative Sunni *hadith* compilations were made. Persian notions of political administration gained much influence, reflected in a more hierarchical division of society, in the creation of the chancelleries and their largely Persian coterie of secretaries, and in the conception of the 'Abbasid caliph as "God's shadow on Earth." The Mongol sacking of Baghdad in 1258 effectively put an end to the active 'Abbasid caliphate, with the murder of the caliph, al-Musta'sim. The Mamluks, who defeated the Mongols at 'Ayn Jalut in 1260 and also put an end to the Fatimid dynasty (r. 969–1171), installed a series of nominal 'Abbasid caliphs in whose name the actual holder of power, called the *sultan*, ruled. This state of affairs would last until the advent of the Ottomans in 1517, who eventually assumed the caliphate themselves.

The Caliphate in Classical Sunni Political Thought

The classical conception of the Sunni caliphate is formulated by the Shafi'i jurist al-Mawardi (d. 1058) in his famous work *al-Ahkam al-Sultaniyya ("The Governmental Ordinances")*. According to him, the caliph discharges ten functions, which include enforcement of the Shari'a, defense and expansion of the boundaries of Islam, proper administration of the government, and disbursement of revenues. Al-Mawardi maintained that the title *Khalifat Allah* was illegal and impious. He also upheld the general Ash'ari position that the caliphate–imamate was obligatory by revelation and not by reason, as the Mu'tazila had maintained. There cannot be two Imams at one and the same time, he affirmed, and a duly elected Imam could not be displaced by a worthier candidate, as maintained by the Mu'tazila. Election was mandatory, however, even if there was only a single qualified candidate.

The Imamate in Classical Shi'i Political Thought

Both Sunni and Shi'i sources report that a small group of people, later termed the *Shi'at 'Ali*, were vocal in their opposition to the election of Abu Bakr as the first caliph–imam. Although it is generally assumed that they based their opposition on the belief that a blood member of the Prophet's family should assume the caliphate, the early sources also suggest that their position was based on their conviction that 'Ali was more morally excellent *(afdal)* than Abu Bakr and therefore more qualified for the office. Classic Shi'i views, however, emphasize the legitimist position and restrict the office to the direct descendants of 'Ali and Fatima. In Imami Shi'ism, the largest Shi'i denomination, there are twelve such infallible Imams, the twelfth Imam having gone into Occultation (Ar. *al-ghayba*) in 874 and being expected to return at the end of time. In the absence of the rightful Imam, the duty of holding Friday congregational prayers and the waging of *jihad*, for example, remain in abeyance. The Imamiyya reject the first three caliphs and hold a poor opinion of most of the Companions, since they are assumed to have wrongfully usurped 'Ali's exclusive right to the caliphate–imamate after the Prophet's death.

The next major Shi'i faction, the Isma'iliyya, believe in seven Imams; hence, they are called the Seveners. The Isma'iliyya developed further subfactions over time, such as the Nizaris and the Musta'lis; the former has living Imams. The Zaydis believe in five Imams and are regarded as the closest in their political thought to the Sunnis, since they, unlike the Imamiyya and the Isma'iliyya, accept the first three caliphs as legitimate, even though they were less excellent than 'Ali.

ASMA AFSARUDDIN

Further Reading

Afsaruddin, Asma. *Excellence and Precedence: Medieval Islamic Discourse on Legitimate Leadership*. Leiden, 2002.

Arnold, Thomas Walker. *The Caliphate*. New York, 1966.

Crone, Patricia, and Martin Hinds. *God's Caliph: Religious Authority in the First Centuries of Islam*. Cambridge, 1986.

Kennedy, Hugh. *The Prophet and the Age of the Caliphates: The Islamic Near East from the Sixth to the Eleventh Century*. Longman, 1991.

Madelung, Wilferd. *The Succession to Muhammad: A Study of the Early Caliphate*. Cambridge, 1997.

Al-Tabari, Muhammad b. Jarir. *The Crisis of the Early Caliphate*. Trans. R. Stephen Humphreys. Albany, NY, 1990.

CALLIGRAPHY

The art of writing Arabic in an aesthetically pleasing manner appears to have been cultivated from the earliest years of Islam. As the Arabic script came to be adopted for such other (and unrelated) languages as Persian, Turkish, and Urdu, it remained a constant feature of Islamic civilization. Beautiful writing is considered to be the pre-eminent form of visual art throughout the Islamic lands.

The earliest Arabic inscriptions were written in a South Arabian script, but by the fourth century CE, Arabic speakers had adopted a variant of the Aramaic alphabet used by the Nabateans. Within two centuries the essential features of the modern Arabic script had been developed, so that Arabic script has remained remarkably consistent over the fourteen centuries since the revelation of Islam. Like Hebrew and Syriac, Arabic is a Semitic language. Like them, but unlike Greek and Latin, it is always written from right to left. The Arabic script, like that used for most Semitic languages, is based on an *abjad,* or consonantary, rather than a true alphabet, for it uses one symbol per consonantal phoneme, or distinctive sound. Nabatean Aramaic had only eighteen letterforms, but because Arabic had twenty-eight phonemes, most of the Aramaic letters were pressed to represent more than one Arabic consonant. By the seventh century, diacritical marks had been added

Making lead. Manuscript from Baghdad, Iraq. 'Abbasid caliphate, 1222. Gouache on paper. Credit: Bridgeman-Giraudon/ Art Resource, NY. Louvre, Paris, France.

over or under some letters to distinguish them from those with a similar shape, such as *ba', ta', tha'* or *ha', jim,* and *kha'.* Like other abjads, Arabic lacks symbols for vowels: The morphemic structure of the language usually allows the reader to supply them from the context. Eventually, however, Arabic, like other

Semitic abjads, came to use 'helping' consonants to represent the long vowels, and ultimately other signs were developed to represent short vowels, doubled consonants, and pauses in fully vocalized texts.

Many of the world's writing systems have developed two or more forms of writing, including a "monumental" form in which the letters are written separately for legibility and a "cursive" form in which they are connected together for speed in writing. Although Arabic eventually developed many different *styles* of script, it has only one form of writing: in all styles some of the letters may sometimes connect to neighboring ones. Consequently, individual letters may change shape depending on their position in a word: The same letter can have one form when it stands alone, another at the beginning of a word, another in the middle of a word, and yet another at the end of a word. All of these features made Arabic relatively difficult to read and indicate that only readers who already had a good idea of what a given text would say were expected to be able to read it; therefore, writing was not normally intended to convey new information to the uninitiated.

The preferred tool for writing Arabic has always been a reed pen, and ink was prepared from carbon black or gallnuts, depending on the intended support. Parchment (and to a lesser degree papyrus) eventually gave way to paper, which was introduced after the conquest of Central Asia in the eighth century and quickly became popular throughout the Muslim world. Although connoisseurs always appreciated the subtle beauty of the script alone, fine writing was often embellished with decorative designs worked in color and gold, particularly in the later periods.

The earliest surviving examples of Arabic calligraphy are written in an angular script commonly but incorrectly known as "kufic" after the city of Kufa in Iraq. Although manuscripts of the Qur'an were surely produced by the latter part of the seventh century, no examples have been dated convincingly before the ninth. Most early manuscripts of the Qur'an are written on horizontal-format ("landscape") parchment sheets with an odd number of lines per page. Letterforms are based on relatively simple but harmoniously proportioned geometrical shapes that can often be elongated. Some texts have diacritical marks to distinguish one letter from another having a similar shape, and colored dots or marks are sometimes used to indicate vowels. The individual letters, as well as groups of connected letters forming word fragments or entire words, are always separated by spaces of equal width. This uniform spacing makes it difficult for a reader to tell where one word ends and another begins and reveals how these texts must have been "read" by people who already knew what they had to say.

New, more "cursive" scripts began to appear in secular manuscripts copied on paper in the ninth century. Commonly, but quite confusingly, known by such names as "Qarmatian [or Karmathian] Kufic," "broken Kufic," "eastern Kufic," "Kufic-naskhi," "New Style," "*warraq* [stationer's] script," or "broken cursive," these scripts were usually written in carbon black ink on paper. They have an accentuated angular character and a deliberate contrast between thick and thin strokes; in some examples the script is quite vertical and elongated. Spaces between words are always wider than the spaces between the nonconnecting letters of a word, and diacritical marks distinguish the different letters sharing the same shape. Most scholars have seen these new scripts as logical outgrowths of earlier "Kufic" scripts used for copying the Qur'an. However, as these scripts first appear in secular contexts, it seems much more likely that they were developed by professional secretaries and copyists who regularized the cursive handwriting they had previously used for transcribing paper documents into a new and more legible script appropriate for copying books.

In the tenth century, calligraphers, particularly in Iran, began to use these new scripts to copy the Qur'an, and at the same time they began to replace parchment with paper as a support for copying the holy text. Although these secretarial hands continued to be used for several centuries in special situations, their success paved the way for the development of rounded styles of Arabic handwriting in the tenth century. Normally known as *naskh*, this group of related scripts remains common to the present day, being the type of script most familiar and legible to ordinary readers. In the Maghrib, or western Islamic lands, however, the secretarial hands were transformed into a distinctive script often known as *maghribi*; it is characterized by an evenness and flatness of line and looped descenders.

As with the broken cursive script, the origins of the rounded hands popular in the eastern and central Islamic lands are obscure, but tradition reports that the 'Abbasid secretary (and later vizier) Ibn Muqla (885–940) introduced a new method of writing known as "proportioned script" *(al-khatt al-mansub)*. Although no genuine examples of his writing are known to survive, Ibn Muqla is known to have developed a system for calculating the size of letters based on the rhombic dot formed when the nib of a reed pen is applied to the surface of the paper. Ibn Muqla calculated the height of an *alif*, the first letter of the Arabic alphabet, in terms of these dots and then calculated the size of all other letters in relation to the *alif*. Ibn Muqla's skill in writing passed on to the next generation in the person of 'Ali ibn Hilal, known as Ibn al-Bawwab (d. 1030), who began his career as a house painter but soon turned to calligraphy, where he added elegance to the system developed by his predecessor.

Calligraphers in thirteenth-century Iraq and Iran eventually codified the various hands used during the lifetime of Ibn Muqla into six round hands, comprising three pairs of large and small scripts *(thuluth–naskh, muhaqqaq–rayhan, and tawqi'–riqa')*, which were known collectively as the "Six Pens." The most famous master was the calligrapher Yaqut al-Musta'simi (1242–1298), who served the last 'Abbasid caliph al-Musta'sim (r. 1242–1258) as secretary. These six scripts, disseminated through his many pupils and disciples, have remained the core of the calligrapher's art until the present day, although Iranian calligraphers beginning in the fourteenth century developed an even more fluid script known as *nastaliq*, or "hanging naskh," which became the principal hand for copying secular manuscripts in Persian.

JONATHAN M. BLOOM

Further Reading

Blair, Sheila S. *Islamic Calligraphy*. Edinburgh: Edinburgh University Press, 2006.
Bloom, Jonathan M. *Paper Before Print: The History and Impact of Paper in the Islamic Lands*. New Haven: Yale University Press, 2001.

CAMELS

Belonging to the *Camelidae* family of even-toed mammals, camels are generally classified into two species: *Camelus bactrianus*, the Bactrian or two-humped camel; and *Camelus dromedarius*, the Dromedary or one-humped (also known as the Arabian camel). The Dromedary occupies the warmer regions of the Middle East and Northern and West Africa. The habitat of the Bactrian camel is in the colder regions of East-Central Asia and China. The hybrid camel, a crossbreed between these two species, has been known to exist in Anatolia, Turkey, northern Iran, and Afghanistan.

The humps of the camel are repositories of fat, which the animal uses as a source of food at times of scarcity, thus allowing it to survive for long periods without sustenance. Contrary to common belief, camels do not store water but, rather, efficiently conserve water by distributing it throughout their bodies within forty-eight hours of consuming it. Camels are also able to take in heat, allowing their blood temperature to rise without causing them to perspire and dehydrate.

Besides its two humps, the main physical feature of the Bactrian camel is its shaggy coat, which enables the animal to withstand the cold temperature of southern Russia, east-central Asia, and western China. The Dromedary single-humped camel, however is short-haired, allowing it to conserve body moisture in a variety of ways, and hence to easily adapt to regions with high temperatures.

Most likely, original camel domestication occurred in southern Arabia, with its remote valleys and dry climate, between 3000 and 2500 BCE. In the first stage of domestication, Dromedary camels served as a source of meat, milk, and hair; later they were used as mounts and a means of transport—though not for hauling. The first domestication process appears to not only have been connected with trade, but also with sacrificial religious purposes in regard to the animal's association with both benevolent and demonic spirits that were believed to inhabit the desert.

The supernatural quality of the camel in the pre-Islamic era has continued into the present day, as the animal continues to be used as a sacrificial beast during major religious processions, such as the Feast of Sacrifice (*'id-i qurban*) on the tenth of *Zu'l-Hajja*, across the Islamic world. The sacrifice ritual of the camel is an occasion for Muslims to celebrate the day when Abraham was ordered by God to offer his son, Isma'il, for slaughter instead of an animal, recalling the dramatic trial that the prophet experienced as a sign of faith in God.

In the course of their spread throughout Asia, single-humped camels began to gradually supplant the Bactrian species, with the former becoming widely used in Persia, southern Afghanistan, and the Indus valley. Although bred throughout northern Iran to East-Central Asia in the first centuries of the Islamic period, Bactrian camels were primarily kept to produce hybrids. The hybrid camels then began to emerge as an ideal breed because of their body size, strength, and longevity. The hybrid camel, a stronger pack animal than either of the other two species, played a central role in the transportation of goods in the caravan trade that developed after the opening of the Silk Road, which linked Central Asia and Mesopotamia under Parthian rule (247–228 BCE).

The evolution of the camel in its two species and hybrid types is inextricably tied to the history of transportation. As Richard W. Bulliet has described it, since pack camels were cheap and efficient transporters over long distances, they progressively replaced wagons and wheeled transports. Accordingly, the proliferation of the caravan trade across Asia led to the spread in the breeding of camels and, in turn, reinforced the decline of wheeled vehicles and the disappearance of wagon roads.

The advent of Islam in the seventh century led to the greatest distribution of the camel, as the expansion of the new faith allowed the Arabs to reinforce the status of the animal as a source of labor and a means of caravan transportation across Asia, in particular, eastward in northeastern Iran and westward along the Mediterranean shores of North Africa. The camel's impact on transportation reached its height in the medieval Islamic world, during which time no evidence of the use of wheeled vehicles from Morocco to Afghanistan can be found. However, with the rise of the European-dominated maritime trade after 1600 CE, the camel caravan began its initial stages of decline, a process that eventually led to the disappearance of the camel as a central means of transportation.

BABAK RAHIMI

See also Animal Husbandry; Festivals and Celebrations; Nomadism and Pastoralism; Processions, Religious; Road Networks; Silk Road; Trade, African; Trade, Mediterranean

Further Reading

Bulliet, Richard W. "Camel." *Encyclopaedia Iranica*. Vol. 4, ed. Ihsan Yarshatir. Costa Mesa, CA: Mazda, 1991.
———. *The Camel and the Wheel*. New York: Columbia University Press, 1990.
———. "Why They Lost the Wheel" *ARAMCO World*, 24 (1973): 22–25.
———. "Le Chameau et la Roue au Moyen-Orient." *Annales: Économies, Sociétés, Civilizations* 24 (1969): 1092–1103.
Calmard, Jean. "Shi'i Rituals and Power II. The Consolidation of Safavid Shi'ism: Folklore and Popular Religion." In *Safavid Persia*, ed. Charles Melville. Cambridge: Cambridge University Press, 1996.
Gauthier-Pilters, Hilde, and Dagg, Anne Innis. *The Camel: Its Evolution, Ecology, Behavior, and Relationship to Man*. Chicago: Chicago University Press, 1981.
Goitein, Shelomo Dov. *A Mediterranean Society. Vol. I. Economic Foundations*. Berkeley: California University Press, 1967.
Omidsalar, M. "Šotor-qorbani." *Encyclopaedia Iranica*. Vol. 4, ed. Ihsan Yarshatir. Costa Mesa, CA: Mazda, 1991.
Pellat, Charles. "Ibil." In *Encyclopaedia of Islam*, new ed. Vol. 3, ed. H. A. R. Gibb. Leiden: Brill, 1971.
Rahimi, Babak. "The Rebound Theater State: The Politics of the Safavid Camel Sacrifice Rituals, 1598–1695 C.E." *Iranian Studies*, 37 (2004): 451–478.
Rodinson, M. "'Adjala." *Encyclopaedia of Islam*, new ed. Vol. 1, ed. H. A. R. Gibb. Leiden: E. J. Brill, 1960.
Roux, J.-P. "Le Chameau en Asie Centrale." *Central Asiatic Journal* 5 (1959–1960): 35–76.
Siddiqi, Muhammad Iqbal. *Animal Sacrifice in Islam*. Lahour: Kazi, 1978.
Tapper, Richard. "One Hump or Two? Hybrid Camels and Pastoral Cultures." *Production Pastorale et Société* 16 (1985): 67.

CARPETS

The manufacture of heavy textiles of felted or woven wool to serve as floor coverings, cushion facings, room dividers, and other furnishings is a very old and important technique throughout the region stretching from the Atlantic coasts of Spain and Morocco across North Africa to West and Central Asia. The relative warmth and aridity of the climate throughout most of the region encouraged people to live and work on or close to the ground, without the wooden furniture used in colder and damper regions, and the tribal or nomadic way of life followed by many inhabitants of the region was further encouragement of the production and use of heavy woolen textiles for furnishing. Indeed, the region is sometimes referred to as the "Rug Belt." The introduction of Islam encouraged the use of carpets, for Muslims are required to prostrate themselves in worship five times a day, an act customarily accomplished privately on a small carpet or mat or collectively in a mosque on large carpets often bearing geometric designs that allow worshippers to arrange themselves in lines facing Mecca.

Apart from felted rugs, in which the fibers are simply matted together through pressure and moisture, carpets are either flat-woven (a technique usually known as *kilim* or *gelim*) or given a pile surface by knotting short lengths of yarn around one or more warp threads. Sheep's wool is the most common fiber, but extremely fine carpets are knotted from such fibers as goat hair and silk on wool, silk, or cotton warps. From the earliest times, different colors of fiber were used to create beautiful and intricate patterns that have made these carpets universally admired.

As most carpets were literally worn into the ground, it is difficult to reconstruct the history of the medium. The oldest known knotted example, discovered in a frozen burial mound at Pazyryk in southern Siberia, is conventionally dated to the fifth century BCE. The carpet, which measures 1.8×2.0 m (6×7 ft), is knotted of wool; it has a central field of stylized flowers surrounded by several borders with animal friezes, a type of design that would continue to be popular over the millennia. The high technical quality of this carpet, which has more than 1.2 million knots, indicates that it must have been the product of a long tradition of carpet weaving, although the actual place of production is unknown. Apart from scattered references to carpets in medieval Arabic texts and a few fragmentary finds, the oldest significant group of knotted carpets to survive comes from thirteenth- and fourteenth-century Anatolia and Iran. Nearly twenty large carpets with geometric designs were discovered in the early twentieth century on the floor

Carpet showing the fight between the dragon and a phoenix. Ca. 1400. Turkey. Wook, 172 × 90 cm. Inv. I. 4. Photo: Georg Niedermeiser. Credit: Bildarchiv Preussischer Kulturbesitz/Art Resource, NY. Museum fuer Islamische Kunnst, Staatliche Museen zu Berlin, Berlin, Germany.

in the mosques of Konya and Beysehir; a much smaller number of small carpets bearing designs of stylized animals, mostly discovered in Europe, have been attributed to Iran. The generous size of the Anatolian carpets suggests they were made commercially but not exported; the European provenance of the animal carpets, as well as their appearance in European paintings, indicates they were precious goods exported to Europe by merchants such as Marco Polo.

Increased numbers of carpets survive from the period after 1450, not only because more were produced but also because many of them were exported to Europe, where they were either preserved intact in churches and royal treasuries or portrayed in contemporary representations by such painters as Bellini, Crivelli, and Holbein, who have given several types of Anatolian carpets their conventional modern names. Court carpet workshops were established under the patronage of the Ottoman, Safavid, and Mughal dynasties to supply the needs of the courts and to produce carpets for export. At the same time, particularly in factory production, the traditional process of designing carpets by combining units retrieved from the weavers' memories began to be replaced by a new process in which a designer, often the employee of the court or of a merchant, prepared designs on paper for the artisans to execute in wool. By the mid-nineteenth century, a huge demand for "Oriental" carpets had developed in Europe, popularized by international exhibitions and the arts and crafts movement. While Anatolian production remained largely village based, in Iran, local entrepreneurs were increasingly supplanted by Europeans, who organized production in factories and cottages, supplying not only the designs but also the European yarns to produce carpets in standard sizes for the export market.

JONATHAN M. BLOOM

See also Textiles

Further Reading

Denny, Walter B. *Sotheby's Guide to Oriental Carpets*. New York: Simon & Schuster, 1994.

CARTOGRAPHY

Contrary to the impression that one receives from scholarship on the history of cartography, the richest, largest, and among the earliest extant collections of maps hails from the medieval Muslim world, *neither* from ancient Greece nor medieval Europe. It is generally held that Ptolemy and the Greeks were the earliest constructors of cartographic images. However, the earliest surviving "Ptolemaic" manuscript incorporating maps dates back *only* to the thirteenth century. This glaring discrepancy in the extant record has been the subject of heated debates in the history of cartography circles, yet the master narrative remains unaltered.

At a time when Europe was producing rudimentary T-O maps of the world, the geographical scholars of the Muslim world, drawing upon knowledge acquired during conquests and extensive travel and trade, naturally influenced by the ancient Greek, Babylonian, Egyptian, Sasanian, Indian, Chinese, and Turkish learning traditions, among others, were producing detailed images of the world and various regions in the Islamic world. There exist thousands of traditional Islamic cartographic images scattered throughout the medieval and early modern Arabic, Persian, and Turkish manuscript collections worldwide. Yet, until recently, most of these maps have lain virtually untouched and have often been deliberately ignored on the grounds that they are not

"mimetically" accurate representations of the world. What many failed to see is that these schematic, geometric, and often perfectly symmetrical images of the world are iconographic representations of the way in which the medieval Muslims perceived their world. Granted, these are stylized *amimetic* visions restricted to the literati—the readers, collectors, commissioners, writers, and copyists of the geographical texts within which these maps are found. Yet the plethora of extant copies produced all over the Islamic world, including India, testifies to the enduring and widespread popularity of these medieval Islamic cartographic visions for not less than eight centuries.

Fons Et Origo

What is the source of this rich and widespread medieval Islamic propensity to map? Some scholars believe that the answers lie in the earliest Arabic textual references to maps. For instance, consider the incredible silver globe *(al-Sura[h] al-Ma'muniyya[h])* that the 'Abbasid caliph al-Ma'mun (r. 813–833) is said to have commissioned from the scientists working in his *Bayt al-hikma (House of Knowledge)*, or the maps of the eastern part of the Muslim empire, specifically of the region of Daylam, as well as the city of Bukhara, that the Umayyad governor, al-Hallaj ibn Yusuf, commissioned toward the end of the first century *hijra* (ca. 702 CE). In *Kitab al-Buldan (Book of Countries)*, Ahmad ibn Abi Ya'qub al-Ya'qubi (d. ca. late ninth century) reports that a plan of the round city of Baghdad was drawn up in 758 for the 'Abbasid caliph al-Mansur (r. 754–775). The Egyptian chronicler al-Maqrizi mentions that a "magnificent" map on "fine blue" silk with "gold lettering" upon which were pictured "parts of the earth with all the cities and mountains, seas and rivers" was prepared for the Fatimid caliph al-Mu'izz (r. 953–975) and entombed with him in his mausoleum in Cairo.

A few scholars assert that versions of the mid-ninth-century al-Ma'munid world map can be found in later works, such as Ibn Fadl Allah al-'Umari's (d. 1349) *Masalik al-absar fi mamalik al-amsar (Ways of Perception Concerning the Most Populous/Civilized Provinces)*, or the recently discovered thirteenth-century Fatimid geographical manuscript, *Kitab ghara'ib al-funun wa mulah al-'uyun (Book of Curiosities)*.

The problem with the al-Ma'munid silver globe is that it is probably mythical. Other than an extremely vague passage cited in Abu al-Hasan 'Ali ibn al-Husayn al-Mas'udi's (d. 956) *Kitab al-tanbih wa-l-ishraf (Book of Instruction and Revision)*, we have no other descriptions of it. Al-Mas'udi's description is very confused. It suggests an impossibly complicated celestial map superimposed on a globe—that is, an extremely sophisticated armillary sphere of which we have no extant example until the fourteenth century. David King provides the most likely explanation when he reads al-Mas'udi's description as an astrolabe with world map markings superimposed on it.

In fact, to date, the earliest extant medieval Islamic source containing maps is a ninth-century copy of Abu Ja'far Muhammad ibn Musa al-Khwarazmi's (d. 847 CE) *Kitab Surat al-Ard (Picture of the Earth)*. Composed primarily of a series of *zij* tables (that is, tables containing longitudinal and latitudinal coordinates), it also includes four maps. Of these, two have been identified: one as a map of the Sea of Azov and the other as a map of the Nile.

Islamic Atlas Series

The four maps of al-Khwarazmi's manuscript copy appear to be related to the earliest cartogeographical atlas tradition, best known by the title of its most prolifically copied version: al-Istakhri's *Kitab al-Masalik wa al-Mamalik (Book of Roads and Kingdoms)*. Most of the maps in this earliest-known atlas-like mapping tradition occur in the context of geographical treatises devoted to an explication of the world, in general, and the lands of the Muslim world, in particular. These map-manuscripts are sometimes called *Surat al-Ard (Picture of the Earth)* or *Suwar al-Aqalim (Pictures of the Climes/Climates)*. They emanate from an early tradition of creating lists of pilgrim and post stages that were compiled for administrative purposes. They read like armchair travelogues of the Muslim world, with one author copying from another.

Beginning with a brief description of the world and theories about it—such as the inhabited versus the uninhabited parts, the reasons why people are darker in the south than in the north, and so on—these geographies methodically discuss details about the Muslim world, its cities, its people, its roads, its topography, and more. Sometimes the descriptions are interspersed with tales of personal adventures, discussions with local inhabitants, debates with sailors as to the exact shape of the earth and the number of seas, and so forth. They have a rigid format that rarely varies: first, the whole world, then the Arabian peninsula, then the Persian Gulf, then the Maghrib (North Africa and Andalusia), Egypt, Syria, the Mediterranean, upper and lower Iraq, and twelve maps devoted to the Iranian provinces, beginning with Khuzistan

and ending in Khurasan, including maps of Sind and Transoxiana. The maps, which usually number precisely twenty-one—one world map and twenty regional maps—follow exactly the same format as the text and are thus an integral part of the work.

The earliest extant Islamic cartogeographical map atlas comes from an Ibn Hawqal manuscript housed at the Topkapi Saray Museum Library (Ahmet 3346) firmly dated to AH 479/1086 CE by an accurate colophon. Counterintuitively, this earliest extant manuscript also contains *the most mimetic* maps of all the existing copies. The striking mimesis of the maps in the earliest extant copy stands in stark contrast to the maps of the later copies, which abandon any pretense of mimesis. As the maps of the later copies become more and more stylized, they move further into the realm of *objects d'art* and away from direct empirical inquiry. By the nineteenth century some of these maps became so stylized that, were it not for the earlier examples, they would be unrecognizable as maps.

Popularization of the *Book of Roads and Kingdoms* Mapping Tradition

This form of geographical text became extremely popular in the twelfth and thirteenth centuries, and the original tenth-century geographical texts, along with enhanced and more colorful versions of the maps, were copied prolifically right up until the late seventeenth century. The Ottomans, Safavids, and Mughals were all interested in commissioning copies, and many famous scholars, such as the Ilkhanid scholar Nasiruddin Tusi, used versions of these earlier map forms in their work.

The popularization of illustrated geographical manuscripts also influenced the works of late medieval Islamic scholars, such as al-Qazwini (d. 1283) and Ibn al-Wardi (d. 861), authors of '*Aja'ib al-Makhluqat wa ghara'ib al-mawjudat (The Wonders of Creatures and the Marvels of Creation)* and *Kharidat al-'aja'ib wa faridat al-ghara'ib (The Unbored Pearl of Wonders and the Precious Gem of Marvels)*, respectively. Judging by the plethora of pocketbook-size copies that still abound in every Oriental manuscript collection, the *Kharidat al-'Aja'ib* must have been a bestseller in the late medieval and early-modern Islamic world. It is therefore significant that copies always incorporated, within the first four or five folios, a classical Islamic world map.

Eventually the classical Islamic world maps also crept into general geographical encyclopedias, such as Shihab al-Din Abu 'Abdallah Yaqut's (d. 1229) thirteenth-century *Kitab Mu 'jam al-Bldan (Dictionary of Countries).* The earliest prototype of the Yaqut world map is found in a copy of Abu al-Rayhan Muhammad ibn Ahmad al-Biruni's (ca. d. after 1250 CE) *Kitab al-tafhim (Book of Instruction).* World maps were also used to open some of the classic histories. Copies of such well-known works as Ibn Khaldun's (d. 1406) *al-Muqaddimah (The Prologue)* often begin with an al-Idrisi type of world map, whereas copies of the historian Abu Ja'far Muhammad ibn Jarir al-Tabari's (d. 923) *Ta'rikh al-rusul wa-l-muluk (History of Prophets and Kings)* sometimes include a Ptolemaic "clime-type" map of the world as a frontispiece. Similarly, classical Islamic maps of the world find their way into sixteenth-century Ottoman histories, such as the scroll containing Seyyid Lokman's *Zübdetü't-tevarih (Cream of Histories)* produced in the reign of Suleyman I (1520–1566).

Other Mapping Traditions

There are other more mimetic and better-known Islamic mapping traditions, such as the work of the well-known twelfth-century North African geographical scholar al-Sharif al-Idrisi (d. 1165). The Norman King, Roger II (1097–1154 CE) commissioned al-Idrisi to produce an illustrated geography of the world: *Nuzhat al-Mushtaq fi Ikhtiraq al-Afaq (The Book of Pleasant Journeys into Faraway Lands),* also known as the *Book of Roger.* Al-Idrisi divided the world according to the Ptolemaic system of seven climes, with each clime broken down into ten sections. The most complete manuscript (Istanbul, Köprülü Kütüphanesi, Ms. 955, 1469 CE) contains one world map and seventy detailed sectional maps.

The sixteenth-century Ottoman naval captain, Muhyiddin Piri Re'is (d. 1554) is another Muslim cartographer who is world famous. Renowned for the earliest extant map of the New World, Piri Re'is and his incredibly accurate early-sixteenth-century map of South America and Antarctica has been the subject of many a controversial study. Piri Re'is also produced detailed sectional maps but—like the Italian *isolarii*—he restricted himself to the coastal areas of the Mediterranean. The second version of his *Kitab-i bahriye (Book of Maritime Matters)* contains 210 unique topocartographic maps of important Mediterranean cities and islands.

This is but a brief summary of the incredible depth and variety of the rich medieval Islamic mapping traditions. Those interested in learning more should consult the "Further Reading" section.

What all these extant maps say is that—at least from the thirteenth century onward, when copies of

Islamic map-manuscripts began to proliferate—the world was a very depicted place. It loomed large in the medieval Muslim imagination. It was pondered, discussed, and copied with minor and major variations again and again.

KAREN PINTO

Further Reading

Edson, Evelyn, and E. Savage-Smith. *Medieval Views of the Cosmos.* Oxford: Bodleian Library, 2004.

Harley, J.B., and David Woodward, eds. "Cartography in Traditional Islamic and South Asian Societies." In *History of Cartography.* Vol. 2, Book. 1. Chicago: University of Chicago Press, 1992.

King, David A. *World-Maps for Finding the Direction and Distance to Mecca: Innovation and Tradition in Islamic Science.* Leiden: E.J. Brill, 1999.

Pinto, Karen. "Ways of Seeing. 3 Scenarios of the World in the Medieval Islamic Cartographic Imagination." Doctoral Dissertation. New York: Columbia University, 2002.

Sezgin, Fuat: *Geschichte des arabischen Schrifttums.* Vol. XII: *Mathematische Geographie und Kartographie im Islam und ihr Fortleben im Abendland. Kartenband* Frankfurt: Institut für Geschichte der Arabisch-Islamischen Wissenschaften, 2000.

CENTRAL ASIA, HISTORY (750–1500 CE)

Modern Central Asia comprises the territories that are occupied by Asiatic Russia and the republics of the former Soviet Union: Uzbekistan, Kazakhstan, Turkmenistan, Tajikistan, Kyrgyzstan, and Uighuristan (Xingjian in China), countries that are predominantly populated by Iranian and Turkic Muslims. In premodern times, Arab and Persian authors used various terms to refer to this continent.

Some 'Abbasid period sources combine it with the province of Khurasan (East, or Land of the Rising Sun) and refer to "the eastern region" *(iqlim al-mashriq).* However, the great majority of Muslim authors distinguish between Cisoxiana and Transoxiana. They regarded the Oxus River *(Jayhun* in Arabic; *Amuya* or *Amu Darya* in modern Persian) as the border between the Iranian plateau and the vast land that they called (in Arabic) *ma-wara-al-nahr* (the land beyond the Oxus river), namely Sogdiana *(Sughd* in Arabic) in the Hellenistic sources. They divided it into five major zones: Khwarazm (modern Khiva) around the Oxus delta and the shores of the Aral Sea; the upper Oxus region; Sughd along the Zarafshan valley, where the major cities Bukhara and Samarqand are located; Fraghana; and Shash (Tashqent).

The relationships between Eurasia (including Central Asia) and the Fertile Crescent were established immediately after the emergence of the Islamic caliphate. An important source of goods and manpower, Central Asia attracted the attention of Muslim authors. The bonds that connected the urban hubs in the Central Islamic lands with Eurasia are clearly reflected in the 'Abbasid-age literature. Several writers report the chronicles of Muslim conquests and chapters on the history of ma wara al-nahar down to the sixteenth century. 'Abbasid administrative and geographical volumes contain information on locations, population, commerce, and goods. Various accounts, including mythological narratives, linked the landscape and people of Central Asia with those of the Central Islamic lands. Some commentators related the mysterious Gog and Magog with the Turks and other Steppe peoples.

Following the flight of the last Sasanid king (in 651), the Arab forces reached Turkmenistan. A settlement was probably reached early on with Mahoye, the ruler of Marv (Merv), who bore the title *marzaban* (*marzuban*; the warden of the march). However, the actual conquest of the lands beyond the Oxus River started during the governorship of al-Hajjaj b. Yusuf (d. 95/714). This energetic vice-royal dispatched Qutayba b. Muslim to capture the Zarafshan basin (87–90/706–709). Yet the Umayyads' grip was not firm. Turkic forces inflicted a heavy defeat on the Islamic armies (106/724). Under the command of Nasr b. Sayyar (d. 131/748), the tide was reversed. Heading the Muslim fighters, he was able to infiltrate the ethnic mosaic of Central Asia and succeeded in embedding Islam deeply in *ma-wara-al-nahr*'s soil. The Arabs were the backbone of a bureaucratic empire and adherents of a new universal religion, while the success of their competitors, the Steppes peoples, was limited to a short-lived nomadic empire.

Several religious uprisings led by radical rebels *(ghulat)* are recorded in the Arabic and Persian sources during the late Umayyad and early 'Abbasid periods. Although these revolts were directed against the caliphate and as such voiced social discontent with the government and taxation, nevertheless, the rebels did not attack the very idea of an Islamic world order but rather adopted heterodox views. Syncretism enabled the forging of alliances between Zoroastrians, Mazdakites, and Shi'is.

Iranians had played an important role in the army and administration of the new 'Abbasid order. With time, some of the local Iranian forces accumulated strength. The first significant force was the Tahirid dynasty. They boasted a double-noble lineage, claiming to be the descendants of Rustam b. Dustan (*al-shadid*, "the Strong Man"), the ancient Iranian hero, as well as of the Arab tribe Khuza`a. Tahir changed the residence of Khurasan's governors from Merv to Nishapur (in 821), and this seems to have been a turning point in the administrative history of the oasis of Bukhara. Following this alteration, the city acquired a new importance and became a governmental center at the edge of the caliphate, which affected developments all over Transoxiana.

This facilitated the rise to prominence of a local force in Transoxania that came under the rule of the Samanids (203–395/819–1005). Although the Samanids claimed to be the offspring *(farzand)* of Bahram Jubin (Chubin, Chobin), the great mythological Iranian hero, the Samanid family probably had a more humble background. In 204/819, four sons of Asad b. Saman were appointed governors of various districts in Central Asia: Nuh (d. 227/842) governor of Samarqand, Ahmad (d. 846) of Fraghana, Yahya of Shash (Tashqent), and Ilyas (d. in 856) of Herat. The country under their rule was known as the Turk Barrier *(sadd al-ghuzz)*, a name that referred to their role in fighting against the polytheistic nomads of Eurasia.

The Saman family reached the zenith of its power during the governorship of Isma'il b. Ahmad, who had conquered Bukhara (in 262/875). The caliphs al-Mu'tadid (279–289/892–902) and al-Muktafi (289–295/902–908) further rewarded him with the governorship of Khurasan. This development opened a new chapter in the history of Transoxiana and the neighboring Eurasian steppes. The Samanids conducted an offensive policy toward the steppes people, as a result of which Islam spread among the population of Central Asia.

At the zenith of their power the Samanids had command of a large professional army. They recruited Turkic slaves outside the Abode of Islam, and these recent converts made up the fighting battalions of the Samanids. This was in line with steps taken by the caliphs from the days of al-Ma'mun (d. 833), if not earlier. The historical contribution of the Saman house was the establishment of an Islamic and Iranian presence in Transoxiana and Inner Asia. Their achievements did not save the Samanids from breakdown. The deep demographic and cultural changes that swept across the Eurasian steppes cast a shadow over the history of *ma-wara-al-nahr*. This Iranian-speaking land underwent a process of Turkification.

With the collapse of the Samanids a cultural chapter in the history of Central Asia came to an end. The Qarakhanid state (the Ilek or Ilig-khan Khanate) was active in Central Asia from the ninth to the thirteenth centuries. The nucleus of the state was the Qara-luq Turk tribal confederation. Following clashes with the Samanids of Bukhara, Sabuq (or Satuq) Bugha (Boğra) Khan converted to Islam and even assumed the Arab–Islamic name 'Abd al-Karim (d. 344/955).

Led by Shihab al-Dawla Harun b. Sulayman b. Bughra Khan Ilek, the Qarakhanids attacked (in 382/992) Nuh b. Mansur, the Samanid ruler of the Syr Darya valley (366–387/976–997). If the fragmented information is accurate, it was during these years (probably in 382/992) that the Qarakhanids gained control over Fraghana and Bukhara. Like other steppes empires, the Qarakhanid armies consist of two kinds of soldiers: a small troop of retinues and a large body of nomadic Turk tribesmen (turkmen). The Qarakhanids accepted the authority of Baghdad inasmuch as the 'Abbasid caliph was the only source of legitimacy. The historical importance of this Turk dynasty stems from their role in leading the way for the conversion of Turkic people in the Eurasian steppes. In addition to this, they were patrons of Islamic institutions.

Corresponding to the disintegration of the Samanid regime and the emergence of the free Qarakhanid power in Central Asia, another Turkic dynasty played an important role in shaping the history of this vast territory. An ex-slave of the Samanids, the Turkish commander Alp-Takin (tegin), who was their commander in chief, left Khurasan and established himself in Ghazna near Kabul (in present-day Afghanistan, in 350/961). He was succeeded by Nasir al-Dawla Sebuk-Takin, another slave-soldier of Turkic origin, whose son, Yamin al-Dawla Mahmud (388–421/999–1031), was the founder of the Ghaznawid dynasty and bore the title Sayf al-Dawla (Sword of the State; r 388(421/998–1030). For a short period the Ghaznawids played a role in the history of Central Asia.

The lofty position of the Ghaznawids suffered a deadly blow from a new power that arose in Central Asia during the last quarter of the tenth century. Various Turk (Turkmaniyyah) tribes, among them the Ghuzz (Oghuz) nomads, crossed into the districts of Transoxiana and Khwarazm. At this stage in their history the Ghuzz were led by the house of Saljuq (Seljuk), at least according to late Saljuq sources. The Saljuqs, almost from the very beginning of their presence in the land south of the Oxus River, clashed with the Ghaznawids (about 416/1025). When Yamin al-Dawla Mahmud died (in 421/1031), the Turks constituted a threat that his heirs found difficult to ignore. The crucial clash took place in Dandanqan (near Merv in 431/1040), where the Ghaznawid forces were routed.

The Saljuqs reduced the Qarakhanid rulers of Transoxiana and Sinkiang to vassalage. Sanjar, the great Saljuq, took Merv as his capital city, and it flourished as a center of art and commerce. However, the Qarakhitay, a force that emerged in northern China, advanced westward and near Samarqand were able to defeat the great Saljuqs in 1141. The success of these steppe nomads did not last long, however. 'Ala al-Dim Muhammad (1200–1220), the Khwarazm-Shah, advanced from Urgench, his capital city (Chorasmia, in the delta oasis of Khiva, where the Amu Darya and the Shavat canal flow into the Aral Sea in contemporary Uzbekistan), eastward and defeated the Qarakhanids. He then turned his attention southward to the Iranian plateau.

After conquering northern China (Beijing, 1215), Genghis (Temujin) Khan turned his attention westward to the territories controlled by the Khwarazms. The Mongols did not stop at the Aral Sea (1219–1225) but swept on to Anatolia, Iran, Baghdad, and Syria (1234–1258). Following the death of Genghis Khan (in 1227), Central Asia became the territory of his son Chaghatay. With the conversion to Islam of the Mongol Chaghatay people (ulus), a new Mongol–Islamic culture developed in the land between the Oxus and Sinkiang.

After their disintegration, a new force emerged in Central Asia. Timur Lenk (Tamerlane, 1335–1405) succeeded in establishing a new nomad empire. He became the de facto ruler of ma-wara-al-nahr, leaving the Chaghatay dynasty as the nominal rulers and the source of his legitimacy. Tamerlane proceeded to conquer all of western Central Asia, Iran, and Asia Minor. In his capital of Samarqand, Timur gathered numerous artisans and scholars from the lands he had conquered and imbued his empire with a very rich culture.

After the death of Timur, the Timurid state quickly broke in two. His youngest son and successor, Shah Rukh (1407–1447), crossed the Oxus southward to the Iranian area and established his headquarters in Herat. Babur, the last representative of the Timurid dynasty, was driven out by the Uzbek Shibanid dynasty (in 1501) to seek his fortune in India.

YEHOSHUA FRENKEL

Further Reading

Bartold, Vasilii Vladimirovich. (W. Barthold). *Turkestan Down to the Mongol Invasion*. London: Luzac, 1968/1977.

Dankoff, Robert, trans. *Compendium of the Turkic Dialects (Diwan lugat At-Turk by Mahmud ibn al-Husain al-Kashgari)*. Harvard University Print Office, 1982–1984.

Darke, R., trans. *Nizam al-Mulk: The Book of Government*. London, 1960.

Hamada, M. "Le Mausolee et le cults de Satuq Bughara Khan." *Journal of the History of Sufism* 3 (2001): 63–87.

Hamilton A. R. Gibb. *The Arab Conquests in Central Asia*. London, 1923. (Reprint New York, 1970.)

Khadr, M., and Cahen, Cl. "Deux actes de waqf d'un Qarahanide d'Asie centrale," *JA* 255 (1967): 305–334. Bosworth, C. E. "A propos de l'article de Mohamed Khadr—Deux actes de waqf d'un Qarahanide d'Asie centrale." *JA* 256 (1968): 449–453. [Reprinted in his *The Medieval History of Iran, Afghanistan and Central Asia.* London: Variorum Reprints, 1977, art. 21.]

Le Strange, Guy. *The Lands of the Eastern Caliphate.* London, 1905.

Manz, Beatrice Forbes. *The Rise and Rule of Tamerlane.* Cambridge: Cambridge University Press, 1989.

Minorsky, V., trans. *Hudud al-Alam: The Regions of the World—A Persian Geography 372 AH/982 AD.* London: Luzac, 1970.

Richards, D.S., trans. *The Annals of the Saljuq Turks: Selections from al-Kamil fi'l-Ta'rikh of 'Izz al-Din Ibn al-Athir [1160–1233].* London: Routledge Curzon, 2002.

Thackston Jr., W. M., trans. *Baburname*, Vol 1. Harvard University, 1993.

CERAMICS

Around the year 1135 CE, a merchant from Aden wrote the following letter to his counterpart in Egypt: "Please buy me six painted platters, made in *Misr* [Old Cairo]. They should be of middle size, neither very large nor very small; and twenty regular bowls and forty small ones. All should be painted, and their figures and colors should be different." The history of ceramic production in the medieval Muslim world, from the period of the Umayyads in the seventh century to the Ottomans and Safavids in the seventeenth century, attests to the superior creativity and experimentation of Islamic potters, demonstrated through their innovations in shape and design, clay recipes, glazes, and techniques of decoration. Glazed ceramics represent a very small percentage of the total ceramic assemblage produced in the medieval Muslim world. The majority of domestic earthenwares comprised unglazed storage and transport jars—for items such as grain, oil, and water—and unglazed bowls, platters, and receptacles, which were made for the kitchen, pharmacy, or market shop. However, as the letter from the Adenese merchant indicates, glazed and painted ceramics were highly sought commodities in urban, as well as courtly, contexts. This entry highlights several types of glazed ceramics produced in the medieval Islamic period, although it is in no way comprehensive, and readers are referred to the bibliography for more detailed studies on the subject.

Medieval sources refer to pottery or ceramics as *khazaf, fakhkhar,* and *ghadar,* although we often find the generic term *sini* used particularly for fine glazed ceramics. The term *sini* is derived from the Arabic word for China—*al-Sin*—since both potters and consumers of the medieval Muslim world considered Chinese ceramics the pottery *par excellence.* Chinese wares were imported into the Islamic world by the early ninth century and have been discovered in archaeological sites across Muslim Spain to India. Their influence on Islamic ceramics was immediately felt within the ninth-century 'Abbasid pottery-making industry and their impact persisted as late as the nineteenth century. Potters of the Islamic lands, wanting to imitate the whiteness of the elegantly shaped Chinese wares, experimented with specially made tin and alkaline glazes that fired to an opaque creamy-white finish. Around the twelfth century, medieval potters also developed alternative clay recipes by adding large quantities of crushed quartz to produce a hard, white ceramic body, which when thinly potted resembled the translucency of Chinese porcelain. This new ceramic body, known as "fritware" or "stone-paste," was used for all fine ceramics of the Islamic world from the twelfth century onward until the European discovery of the secret of high-firing Chinese porcelain clays in the eighteenth century.

With the invention of white ceramic bodies and opaque glazes, Islamic potters were free to experiment with various techniques of ceramic decoration. An exciting decorative scheme introduced by the potters of Samarra and Basra in the ninth century was the use of cobalt blue pigments, which they painted as stark epigraphic and vegetal designs onto opaque-white wares, creating the very first "blue-and-white wares." The Iraqi potters appear to have held a monopoly on cobalt at this time until its appearance on fritware ceramics of the twelfth century, and it was later exported outside the Islamic lands to China in the fourteenth century. Soon after, cobalt-painted Chinese blue-and-white porcelain arrived in the Middle East and caused a fashion craze in the Islamic markets. By the middle of the fifteenth century, potters from Egypt to Central Asia were producing their own varieties of blue-and-white ceramics based on both Chinese and Islamic models.

Slip-painted pottery, another major type of Islamic glazed ware, did not require special opaque glazes or a fritware body and was produced throughout the Muslim world from the tenth century onward. Slip is essentially semifluid clay, and white slip was often used by the Islamic potter to coat the entire surface of an earthenware vessel in order to create a blank canvas for further decoration. Floral, geometric, animal, and figural designs were often incised through the slip coating before the bowl was covered in a transparent clear or colored glaze and fired. For added drama, copper-green and iron-brown splashes of colored glazes were also incorporated on slip-covered bowls, with or without incised decoration. Another variety of slip-painted pottery, using primarily black, white, and red slips, achieved great heights of sophistication in the tenth and eleventh centuries in the Samanid territories of Eastern Iran and Central Asia. These types of dishes were normally covered in a white slip, and benedictory phrases or proverbs such as, "May everything eaten from this [bowl] be wholesome," or "Generosity is a quality of the people of paradise," were painted in sharp, angular scripts along the rims with a black slip. Another type of slip-painted pottery centered at Samanid Nishapur offered a livelier aesthetic by using a riot of colors including green, acid yellow, black, and red to depict stylized figural subjects, such as seated figures, dancers, horses, and other animals, which were surrounded by various floral and epigraphic motifs.

One of the truly great inventions of potters of the medieval Islamic world is lustre-painted ceramics. The technique of lustre decoration on glass was already practiced in Egypt and Syria as early as the fifth century; however, Iraqi potters appear to have been the first to experiment with lustre decoration on opaque-glazed ceramics in the ninth century. Lustre pigments made of silver and copper oxides were painted in a variety of figural and vegetal designs onto the surface of a glazed vessel, which was then refired under special conditions. The results of a successful refiring created a ceramic ware with painted decorations that gleamed like gold or silver. The highly sought 'Abbasid lustre wares were exported across the Muslim world and as far away as India and Thailand. This complex technique of pottery decoration was probably transferred to Egypt in the tenth century through the migration of Iraqi potters to Fatimid-governed domains. As lustre pigments were better controlled on a paintbrush, this enabled Egyptian potters to expand their iconographic repertoire of images using more precise line-drawn figures. During the twelfth century the technique seems to have spread to Spain, Syria, and Iran, leading to greater variations in styles of painting and the transfer of the technique to Europe.

During the Seljuk period between the twelfth and thirteenth centuries in Iran, a new type of glazed pottery was developed, later coined as *mina'i,* or enameled ware, typified by its wide-ranging color scheme and intricate narrative compositions. The paintings on *mina'i* ceramics attest to the existence of a vibrant tradition of Persian illustrated manuscripts from this period, now lost. Indeed, both *mina'i* and Persian lustre portray visual and poetic themes derived from Persian literature, such as the *Shahnama* epic or the romance of *Varqa va Gulshah,* depicting warriors, heroes, lovers, and fantastical beasts. The *mina'i* technique of applying colored pigments over an already glazed fritware vessel allowed the potter to expand his color palette to include blue, green, red, purple, brown, black, pink, and gold, which were then fixed by a second low-temperature firing. As with Persian lustre, Kashan appears to have been the main center of production for *mina'i,* with vessel shapes ranging from bowls, pilgrims' flasks, ewers, cups, and in rare instances, tiles.

The Turkish city of Iznik in western Anatolia became the preeminent center of a court-sponsored pottery-making industry during the Ottoman period between the fifteenth and seventeenth centuries. "Iznik" has come to refer to the distinctive pure-white frit-bodied ceramic vessels and tiles that were covered in a brilliant white slip and then decorated, over the course of time, with various combinations of colored slips beginning with cobalt blue and turquoise, followed by the introduction of a subtle palette of sage green, manganese purple, black, and finally the use of a more vibrant color scheme in blue, green, black, and "sealing-wax red." Art historians have discerned several chronological and stylistic groups of Iznik wares based on color and design patterns, and the ceramics are best understood in the context of a larger production program of Ottoman courtly arts including architectural decoration, textiles, and manuscript illumination.

FAHMIDA SULEMAN

See also 'Abbasids; Andalus; Architecture, Religious; Architecture, Secular: Palaces; Artisans; Baghdad; Baraka; Basra; Cairo; Cairo Geniza; Central Asia; China; Damascus; Dome of the Rock; Egypt; Epic Poetry; Epics, Persian; Fatimids; Firdawsi; Food and Diet; Fustat; Gifts and Gift Giving; Glassware; Heroes and Heroism; Iran; Iraq; Isfahan; Istanbul; Khurasan; Love Poetry; Mamluks; Manuscripts; Markets; Merchants, Christian; Merchants, Jewish; Merchants, Muslim; Minerals; Mining; Mosaics; Mosques; Mythology and Mythical Beings; Nishapur; Ottoman Empire; Painting, Miniature; Poetry, Persian; Proverbs; Precious Metals; Safavids; Samanids; Samarqand; Samarra; Seljuks; *Shahnama*; Silk Road; Sinan; Stories and Storytelling; Süleymaniye Mosque (Istanbul); Syria, Greater; Textiles; Timurids; Trade: Indian Ocean; Trade: Mediterranean; Transoxania; Transport; Travel

Further Reading

Allan, James W. *Islamic Ceramics.* Oxford: Ashmolean Museum, 1991.

Atasoy, Nurhan, and Julian Raby. *Iznik: The Pottery of Ottoman Turkey.* London: Alexandria Press, 1989.

Atil, Esin. *Ceramics from the World of Islam (Freer Gallery of Art Fiftieth Anniversary Exhibition).* Washington: Smithsonian Institution, 1973.

Fehérvári, Géza. *Ceramics of the Islamic World in the Tareq Rajab Museum.* London and New York: I.B. Tauris, 2000.

Ghouchani, Abdallah. *Inscriptions on Nishabur Pottery.* Tehran: Reza Abbasi Museum, 1986.

Goitein, S.D. *A Mediterranean Society: The Jewish Communities of the Arab World as Portrayed in the Documents of the Cairo Geniza.* Vol. 4: Daily Life. Berkeley, CA: University of California Press, 1983.

Golombek, Lisa, Robert Mason, and Gauvin Bailey. *Tamerlane's Tableware: A New Approach to the Chinoiserie Ceramics of Fifteenth- and Sixteenth-Century Iran.* Costa Mesa, CA: Mazda Publishers, 1996.

Grube, Ernst. *Cobalt and Lustre: The First Centuries of Islamic Pottery.* Nasser D. Khalili Collection of Islamic Art. Vol. IX. London: Nour Foundation, 1994.

Melikian-Chirvani, Assadullah Souren. "Le Roman de Varqe et Golsah," *Arts Asiatiques*, 22 (1970): 1–262.

Porter, Venetia. *Islamic Tiles.* London: British Museum, 1995.

Watson, Oliver. *Ceramics from Islamic Lands.* London: Thames & Hudson, 2004.

CHARITY, ISLAMIC

Charity, the obligation to help those less fortunate than oneself, was a fundamental concept for medieval Muslim ethics. Muslim authors did not have a word that can be translated as "charity," and the use of the Arabic word *khayri* to mean charitable is a modern invention. Nonetheless, medieval Muslims were familiar with a number of practices that might be characterized as charitable. The most prominent of these were *zakat* (the alms tax), *sadaqa* (alms, most often voluntary), and *waqf* (the pious endowment that sometimes served a charitable purpose).

Zakat is one of the five pillars of Islam and as such can be regarded as an article of faith. Muslim jurists characterized it as one of the *huquq Allah* (duties owed to God), and failure to pay it could result in one's being regarded as an apostate. The obligation to pay *zakat* is mentioned throughout the Qur'an and collections of Hadith, but the most important proof text is Surat al-Tawba, verse sixty, "Alms *(sadaqat)* are only for the poor, the indigent, those who collect them, those who reconcile people's hearts, for slaves, debtors, for the path of God, and for the traveler, an obligation imposed by God. God is all-knowing and most wise." This verse established the proper recipients of *zakat*. In addition to the expected recipients, such as indigent people, indentured slaves, debtors, and travelers, the verse also provides for alms to be distributed to holy warriors (those on the path of God) and to persons who reconciled non-Muslims and Muslims. In addition, the verse makes it clear that the original intention was for the state to collect alms and distribute them.

In subsequent Muslim practice, however, *zakat* was usually left to the conscience of the individual. People identified worthy recipients, such as beggars, and paid them alms. Since *zakat* was due every Islamic year, many people paid their alms tax in the month of Muharram, the first of the Islamic calendar. *Zakat* was due on a number of commodities, including herd animals, grains and fruit, gold and silver, commerce, and precious metals. The rate varied by item but was most commonly paid as a 2.5 percent tax on gold, silver, and commerce. At the end of Ramadan, fasting Muslims would pay an additional *zakat al-fitr* (alms for the feast) to celebrate the upcoming feast. This obligation consisted of a sum sufficient to feed one individual for one day.

In addition to these obligatory alms, Muslims also paid voluntary alms when and where they wished. These voluntary alms were usually called *sadaqa*, although this term was sometimes also applied to *zakat*. There was a considerable debate in Muslim ethical writings over whether it was appropriate to publicize one's good deeds. Most authors agreed that it was better to give alms in private, since to do so in public would suggest that one was more interested in achieving social status than in pleasing God. Others, however, pointed out that public almsgiving would encourage others to follow one's example. Beggars congregated outside mosques, especially after Friday prayers, in markets, and at funerals. The fourteenth-century author Ibn al-Hajj noted that it was common to give alms at a funeral, in the hope that this final good deed would ease the deceased's passage into paradise. Funeral processions in medieval Cairo, for example, often included a *kaffara* (expiatory gift) that would be turned over to the poor people who followed the procession.

Begging posed a number of problems for medieval Muslims and their rulers. A considerable literature grew up describing the proper etiquette of the beggar and his benefactor when giving alms. Al-Ghazali (d. 1111 CE) argued that begging was forbidden unless necessary for one's survival and worried that the beggar was in danger of replacing his divine benefactor with a human one. Taj al-Din al-Subki (d. 1370) was outraged by some of the more theatrical techniques used by beggars to solicit alms and worried that the sight of Muslims begging would humiliate the Muslim community in the eyes of Christians and Jews. Some of the rulers of Mamluk Egypt found the presence of lepers and beggars in public places and tried to remove them from the capital. In 1264 or 1265, Sultan al-Zahir Baybars tried to remove Cairo's beggars to al-Fayyum, and similar attempts were made by other sultans in 1330, 1392, and 1438. Such efforts do not seem to have been effective, because begging continued in public places and the professional beggar was a standard character in medieval Arabic literature.

The third major charitable practice in medieval Islamic society was *waqf*. Endowments of this type served many different purposes, including benefiting family, religious institutions, hospitals, and even family tombs. In the medieval period, especially from the early fifteenth century on, it was impossible to distinguish family *waqf*s from charitable *waqf*s, as was done in modern times. Many *waqf*s provided income to a wide range of beneficiaries. Still, it is possible for the modern researcher to isolate those functions that were charitable, in the sense of aiding the poor or infirm.

Some of the wealthiest endowments of the Islamic Middle Ages were hospitals. Although these institutions were not always founded with *waqf*s, many Muslim rulers followed the example of Nur al-Din ibn al-Zanki (d. 1174), who founded a hospital in Damascus. A similar institution established by Sultan al-Mansur Qalawun in 1284 in Cairo provided food, shelter, and medicine to patients. Since the wealthy preferred to be treated at home, the inmates of the hospital were largely poor people or travelers. There were separate sections for men and women, as well as a ward for the insane. Another popular type of *waqf* was the *maktab*, or Qur'an school for orphans. These schools provided orphaned boys with small stipends and some food, as well as teaching them the Qur'an, some basic literacy, and arithmetic. Some waqf supported *ribat*s, which were homes for widowed or divorced women. These institutions were usually founded by wealthy women and were frequently presided over by female administrators. Some endowments provided food and water to pilgrims and residents of the holy cities of Mecca and Medina. There were also many smaller *waqf*s, many of them associated with family tombs, that provided food and water to the poor on a weekly basis, in exchange for the poor saying prayers for their deceased benefactors. These tomb *waqf*s became quite popular in Cairo in the second half of the fifteenth century. The practice of building kitchens to feed the employees of large endowments gave rise in the Ottoman Empire to the foundation of separate soup kitchens (sing. *'imaret*), such as the one established by Hasseki Hurrem Sultan in Jerusalem in the 1550s. Finally, some endowments provided for the washing and burial of the dead. This service was of particular importance in the late Middle Ages, when outbreaks of plague repeatedly struck the Middle East.

ADAM SABRA

See also Black Death; Burial Customs; Death and Dying; Egypt; Epidemics; Ethics; Funerary Practices, Muslim; Gifts and Gift Giving; Hospitality; Hospitals; Mamluks; Mecca; Medina; Mental Illness; Mosques; Nur al-Din ibn al-Zanki; Ottoman Empire; Pilgrimage; Poverty; Public Works; Syria; Waqf

Further Reading

Amin, Muhammad Muhammad. *Al-Awqaf wa-l-hayat al-ijtima 'iyya fi Misr 648–923 H./1250–1517 M*. Cairo: Dar al-Nahda al- 'Arabiyya, 1980.

Bonner, Michael, Mine Ener, and Amy Singer, eds. *Poverty and Charity in Middle Eastern Contexts*. Albany: State University of New York Press, 2003.

Hoexter, Miriam. "*Waqf* Studies in the Twentieth Century: The State of the Art." *JESHO* 41 (1998): 133–156.

McChesney, Robert D. *Charity and Philanthropy in Islam: Institutionalizing the Call to Do Good*. Indianapolis: Indiana University Center on Philanthropy, 1995.

Sabra, Adam. *Poverty and Charity in Medieval Islam, Mamluk Egypt, 1250–1517*. Cambridge: Cambridge University Press, 2000.

Singer, Amy. *Constructing Ottoman Beneficence: An Imperial Soup Kitchen in Jerusalem*. Albany: State University of New York Press, 2002.

Stillman, Norman. "Charity and Social Service in Medieval Islam." *Societas* 5 (1975): 105–115.

Tolmacheva, M. "Female Piety and Patronage in the Medieval 'Hajj'." In *Women in the Medieval Islamic World*, ed. Gavin R. G. Hambly. New York: St. Martin's Press, 1998, 161–179.

CHARITY, JEWISH

In the absence of taxation—a significant resource for poor relief in European Jewish communities—we find a "mixed economy" of charity in Fustat. Private charity was one major source. By nature usually hidden from the historian's gaze, it is well documented in the Geniza through letters of appeal from the poor or on their behalf (see Poverty, Jewish). Family charity, the most private of private charities, existed, too, although it is usually documented only when people complain that it is not forthcoming. People often gave charity in their wills. However, confraternities, a favored vehicle for delivering poor relief in European Jewish communities as of the thirteenth century in Spain (copying Catholic confraternities in this endeavor), do not appear in the Geniza evidence (nor in the Islamic surroundings). The purposes served by European Jewish charitable confraternities, such as teaching poor children and orphans, clothing the needy, burying the indigent, and dowering orphan girls, were, as far as the evidence permits us to conclude, provided by bequests, private gifts, revenues of pious foundations, and communal poor relief.

Public charity—the charity provided through the community—is richly documented in the Geniza, though it was not as well differentiated from private philanthropy, as was the case with Christian poor relief in early modern Europe. Most of the structures of communal charity had been established long before the advent of Islam. One of them, the *heqdesh,* or pious endowment, is abundantly present in medieval Fustat. Often established or supported by deathbed declarations but also, in the manner of its Islamic counterpart, the *waqf,* by healthy benefactors, the Jewish pious endowment consisted mainly in houses donated to the community. Like the original *heqdesh,* which supported the needs of the sacrificial temple *(beit ha-miqdash)* in Jerusalem, revenues from the rent of *heqdesh* properties in the Geniza mainly supported communal institutions, such as the upkeep of the synagogue, salaries of communal officials, and teachers' fees. Only a small percentage went for direct charity to the poor. Like the Islamic *waqf,* however, the institution was conceived of as a form of charity and so was referred to by the moniker "for the poor."

Shelter for the poor, especially foreigners lacking means of livelihood or suffering from illness, was provided, as in late antiquity, both in the synagogue and in the Jewish *funduq,* or inn (*see* Hospitality). The Fustat community maintained at least two *funduqs* as *heqdesh* properties lodging foreign travelers. Public funds were also sometimes used to subsidize rents of needy persons residing in regular apartments. Pledge drives throughout Egypt to ransom captives were coordinated out of Fustat. In the Talmud, ransom of captives was designated a "great mitzva," and in the medieval Mediterranean lands it became an even more urgent necessity.

Medical charity expressed itself when physicians provided care for the ill without charge, in bequests for the sick poor in wills, or in collections to pay the medical and other expenses of a visiting sick scholar. The community had no hospital, differing again from European Jewish communities, where in the late Middle Ages the word *heqdesh* became synonymous with hospital, and from the Ottoman communities, which also ran their own hospitals.

The most visible form of public charity consisted in direct donations of money or in kind to provide either bread, wheat, clothing, or cash for the poor. Bread was distributed twice a week (Tuesday and Friday) in rations of four one-pound (450 grams) loaves per adult per week. Since this did not provide adequate nutrition, it was supplemented on an irregular basis by wheat and cash. The money went to buy other food necessities or to help the poor pay their annual poll tax to the government. Clothing was also disseminated.

Hundreds of Geniza alms lists and donor registers illustrate the administration of public charity. People donated money, or sometimes wheat in kind. Revenues were collected by officials called *jabi* (like Hebrew *gabbai*) or by the administrators of the social services, the *parnasim.* Detailed accounts itemize income and expenditures—direct charity and salary subsidies for communal officials together. Though controversial,

the latter was considered a legitimate use of monies collected for the poor. The collections themselves were done, usually in the synagogue, through pledges, called *pesiqa,* a term also used for ad hoc pledges for specific uses, including private charity solicited by individuals and money for ransom of captives. *Parnasim* collected the pledges, sometimes making the rounds of businesses in the marketplace. The *pesiqa* illustrates a characteristic of the "mixed economy" of charity in medieval Fustat and doubtless other locales in the medieval Islamic world, as well as the blurred boundaries between public and private charity.

Sometimes a whole week's distribution of bread would be paid for by one person (for example, a donation of three dinars in 1107 by the Nagid and head of Egyptian Jewry to purchase 600 loaves of bread). Bakers brought their loaves to the pickup point in the synagogue compound. Scribes kept careful records of each person and the number of loaves per head of household. These numbers were revised with changes in need, and names were crossed out when the indigents no longer were present. A large number of lists contain items of clothing, because the poor usually possessed not much more than the proverbial "shirts on their backs." Many letters seeking private charity request an item of clothing to replace what was lacking.

In the Talmud, alms for the poor were provided through the weekly *quppa* (the "basket" containing bread or money for the local poor) and the daily *tamhui* (mostly, food for wayfarers). These terms do not appear in medieval Fustat. Rather, the alms system there was unified and called *mezonot,* an old rabbinic term for maintenance for wives, children, orphans, widows, and others, here enlisted in a charitable context for food for the poor. The unified system may have been in force much earlier. It was still the custom in the Egyptian capital at the beginning of the sixteenth century, when the new chief Rabbi, an exile from Spain, found it unusual and commented to that effect when glossing Maimonides' astonishing statement in his Code of Jewish Law that some communities no longer employ the *tamhui.*

MARK R. COHEN

Further Reading

Ashtor, Eliyahu. "Some Features of the Jewish Communities in Medieval Egypt" (Hebrew). *Zion* 30 (1965): 61–78, 128–157.

Ben-Naeh, Yaron. "Poverty, Paupers and Poor Relief in Ottoman Jewish Society" (Hebrew). *Sefunot* 23 (2003): 195–238.

Cohen, Mark R. *Poverty and Charity in the Jewish Community of Medieval Egypt.* Princeton, NJ: Princeton University Press, 2005.

Gil, Moshe. *Documents of the Jewish Pious Foundations from the Cairo Geniza.* Leiden: E.J. Brill, 1976.

Goitein, S.D. *A Mediterranean Society: The Jewish Communities of the Arab World As Portrayed in the Documents of the Cairo Geniza.* 5 vols plus index volume by Paula Sanders. Berkeley, CA, and Los Angeles: University of California Press, 1967–1993, esp. Vol. 2.

Idem. *The Voice of the Poor in the Middle Ages: An Anthology of Documents from the Cairo Geniza.* Princeton: Princeton University Press, 2005.

Sabra, Adam. *Poverty and Charity in Medieval Islam: Mamluk Egypt 1250–1517.* New York: Cambridge University Press, 2000.

Shefer, Miri. "Charity and Hospitality: Hospitals in the Ottoman Empire in the Early Modern Period." In *Poverty and Charity in Middle Eastern Contexts*, eds. Michael Bonner, Mina Ener, and Amy Singer. Albany: SUNY Press, 2003, 121–143.

Vaza, Ora. "The Jewish Pious Foundations According to the Cairo Geniza Documents: Appendix to Prof. M. Gil's Study" (Hebrew). M.A. thesis, Tel Aviv University, 1991.

CHESS

The words for the game of chess in Middle Persian *(čatrang)* and in Persian and Arabic *(šatrang/ šaṭranj)* are derived from (Sanskrit) *caturanga,* meaning army consisting of four divisions (Falkner 1892, 125). This is because the Indian army consisted of four groups: *hasty-aśva-nauka-padāta,* which translates as "elephant, horse, ship, foot soldiers." Thus the game was meant to be a simulation for battle. The game entered the Near East, specifically to Persia in the sixth century CE during the rule of the Sasanian king, Khosrow I (Arabic Kisra) (530–571). The game was meant to be part of princely or courtly education in acquiring (Middle Persian) *frahang* or (Persian) *farhang,* which means culture. The playing of the game as part of princely education continued in the Medieval Islamic period, as is attested in such works as the *Qābūs-nameh* of Ibn Wašmgir (Yusefī 1375, 77), and *Chahār maqāla* by Samarqandi (Qazvini 1331, 68–69).

The games of chess and backgammon, along with a variety of literary works, were introduced to Persia from India, including the *Pañcatantra,* which, according to tradition, was translated into Middle Persian by a physician named Burzoe. The Middle Persian version is lost, but a Syriac translation of it was made in 570 under the name *Kalīlag wa Damnag.* These stories were taken from another Indian text called the *Hitopadeśa (Book of Good Counsel).* This book was part of the Indian genre known as *nītiśāstra* ("mirror for princes"), which also existed in Persia, and in Middle Persian was known as *ēwēn-nāmag* (Persian) *āyīn-nāme (Book of Manners)*, which is mentioned in the earliest text on the games of chess and backgammon. These books were also commonly known as "Mirror for Princes" or *Siyār al-mulūk* or *Naṣīhat 'al-mulūk* in the Medieval Islamic period (Daryaee 2002, 285–286).

The earliest text on the games of chess and backgammon is found in Persia in Middle Persian, and it is known as *Wizārišn ī Čatrang ud Nihišn ī Nēw-Ardaxšīr (The Explanation of Chess and the Invention of Backgammon).* According to *Wizārišn ī Čatrang ud Nihišn ī Nēw-Ardaxšīr*, there are four major personages involved in making the game; Dēwišarm/Sačidarm, the Indian king and his minister, Taxtrītos, sent the game to Persia. On the Persian side, Khusrow I and his minister, Wuzurgmihr/(Arabic and Persian) Buzarjumihr/Bozorgmihr were to decipher the game. The wise Persian minister Wuzurgmihr gives an explanation of the game, making an analogy to war or battle between two armies: "He made the king like the two overlords, the rook (on) the left and right flank, the minister like the commander of the warriors, the elephant is like the commander of the bodyguards, and the horse is like the commander of the cavalry, the foot-soldier like the same pawn, that is at front of the battle(field)" (Daryaee 2002, 304).

The earliest surviving chess pieces are also from Persia. These include an elephant carved from black stone (2 7/8 inches). The piece is from the late sixth or seventh century, which corresponds to the time when the Middle Persian text was composed (Dennis and Wilkinson 1968, xxxvii). A fourteenth-century manuscript of the *Šāhnāme* contains two scenes, one at the court of Khusrow I and the second at the court of Dēwišarm. In the scene Wuzurgmihr is seated on the floor with three other Persians, all with white turbans. In front of the Persian sage is a board game where by taking into account the story, we can see that the board game is a backgammon board. The Indian king is seated on his throne and is surrounded by the Indian sages who are painted darker and have darker turbans. Wuzurgmihr has his right hand pointing on the backgammon board, which probably means that he is either challenging the Indian sages or explaining the rules of the game after the Indian sages have been dumbfounded. It is particularly interesting to note that one of the two older Indian sages with a white beard has his hand by his mouth, symbolizing his amazement or perplexity (Dennis and Wilkinson 1968, xii). What can be concluded from these representations and our text is that board games such as chess were likened to battle and the struggle in life. These board games were sports that were meant to train the mind in order to be a well-rounded person, namely someone who has acquired *frahang/farhang* (culture).

During the early 'Abbasid period, the game of chess was seen as a form of gambling by some Muslim scholars. This argument was put forth based on two reasons: first, there was betting placed on the game, and so it was considered to be a form of gambling,

Tournament scene. Chess pawn. Spain, twelfth century ivory carving, 6.4 × 6.8 cm. Inv: OA 3297. Photo: J.G. Berizzi. Credit: Réunion des Musées Nationaux/Art Resource, NY. Louvre, Paris, France.

which made it *harām* (illicit). Second, enthusiasts would spend so much of their time playing chess that they forgot to pray and participate in the religious life (Rosenthal 1975, 37–40). Some authors justified the game by stating that as long as it was played for mental exercise it would be beneficial. The *Qābūs-nāme* dedicates a chapter to the games of chess and backgammon, detailing the proper etiquette of playing and when one should win and to whom one should lose. It is strictly stated that one should not make bets on the games, and only then does playing the game become a proper activity (Yusefī 1375, 77). The game of chess entered Europe, specifically Andalusia, with the Muslim conquest of the region. When the Christian Spaniards were able to beat back the Muslims, the game had already become popular (in Spanish, *aje-drez*), except that one piece of the game was changed, that of the Queen for the Wazīr.

TOURAJ DARYAEE

Further Reading

Daryaee, T. "Mind, Body and the Cosmos: The Game of Chess and Backgammon in Ancient Persia." *Iranian Studies* 35, 4 (2002): 281–312.

Falkner, E. *Games of Ancient and Oriental and How to Play them Being the Games of the Ancient Egyptians, the Hiera Gramme of the Greeks, the Ludus Latrunculorum of the Romans and the Oriental Games of Chess, Draughts, Backgammon and Magic Squares.* New York: Dover Publications, 1892.

Rosenthal, F. *Gambling in Islam.* Leiden: E.J. Brill, 1975.

'Umar b. 'Alī Nizami Samarqandi. *Chahār maqāla.* Edited by M. Qzvini. Tehran, 1331.

'Unsur al-ma 'ālī Kai-Kāwūs b. Iskadar b. Qabūs b. Wašmgīr b. Ziyār. *Qābūs nāme.* Edited by Q.-H. Yusefī. Tehran: Scientific and Cultural Publishers, 1375.

Wilkinson, C. K. *Chess: East and West, Past and Present, A Selection from the Gustavus A. Pfeiffer Collection.* New York: The Metropolitan Museum of Art, 1968.

CHILDREN AND CHILDHOOD

In Islam, children are viewed as precious gifts from God. Islam teaches that children are born sinless and are certain to gain paradise if they pass away before reaching puberty. Children need to be loved, taken care of, and protected with compassion and tenderness by their parents and their surrounding communities to ensure their healthy physical and psychological growth (Yildirim 2005).

In medieval medical writings on infancy, feeding of children and, breast-feeding in particular constitute a central theme. Additional topics include how to treat infants immediately after birth, how to prepare their cradles, how to wash and swaddle them, how to calm weeping children, teething, how to treat children when they start walking and talking, and recommendations regarding entertainment and the company of other children.

Because childhood is considered to be a time of weakness and vulnerability, ignorance and absence of intellectual grasp, and a lack of willpower, Islam not only gives parents the responsibility for the spiritual and physical well-being of children and a correct religious upbringing but also makes them accountable. Viewing children as vulnerable and dependent, Islamic law supplies various rules for the protection of not only themselves but also their property. A special legal status was given to children; they did not owe full obedience to criminal law and therefore could not be punished as Muslims who are sane and of age. More attention is given to the child's benefit than to the interest of his or her parents. Fathers retained guardianship over the child, which involved guardianship over property and over the person, including overall responsibility for physical care, socialization, and education. Mothers were entrusted with the care and control of their children for the first few years of their lives (al-Ghazali 1967).

Following the example of the Prophet Muhammad, the Islamic scholar Said Nursi states that children need kindness and compassion. Medieval Islamic sources abound in accounts of loving, tender relationships between parents and children, including close physical contact (al-Ghazali 1967). Because children are weak and powerless, their spirits can flourish best in knowing and experiencing a compassionate and powerful Creator. Only in an environment where mercy exists can children feel secure. The best way to give them this sentiment completely is to teach them that God is The Most Merciful and The Most Compassionate and that He is the one who is protecting them from all evil and bad things. They will be able to deal with facing fears in later years through trust in God and surrender to God's guidance (Nursi 1997).

In medieval times, spiritual and moral education in childhood and adolescence was crucial for raising physically and psychologically healthy people, because a balanced moral character was seen to be essential in maintaining psychological and physical health (Giladi 1992). Education in childhood was especially important owing to the view that in its pristine state, the child's soul is pure and impressionable. The main purpose of education was to ensure the future of the believer in the next world. As stated by Said Nursi, if a child was not exposed to belief in God, spirituality, and correct morals at an early age, it would be much more difficult to settle belief and spirituality in their hearts in later years, establish good habits, or change bad ones. Good habits were generosity, honesty, diligence, and restraint of one's desires. The more a child was exposed to a community observing religion the easier it would be to understand religion and spirituality later in life (Nursi 2002). Writings also addressed the principles and methods of correcting bad conduct, conduct that might result in the immortal loss of the believer.

In medieval times, childhood was divided into two stages from a religious point of view: (1) before puberty, when a child begins to distinguish between good and evil, and (2) after puberty. Adolescence was generally considered to be around the age of fifteen. Entrusting a boy or a girl with respective adult functions was the accepted way to determine mental maturity (Bosworth et al. 1995). Age and maturity were taken into account when considering a child's education. Education at a young age, when the pupil's mind is open and free from adult cares, was emphasized.

YETKIN YILDIRIM

See also Education; Family; Toys

Further Reading

Bosworth, E., E. van Donzel, W.P. Heinrichs, and G. Lecomte, eds. *The Encyclopedia of Islam.* Leiden: E.J. Brill, 1995.
Al-Ghazali, A. *Iha' 'ulum al-din.* Cairo, 1967.
Giladi, A. *Children of Islam, Concept of Childhood in Medieval Muslim Society.* New York: St. Martin's Press, 1992.
Nursi, S. *Letters.* Istanbul: Sozler Publication, 1997.
Yildirim, Y. "Islamic Perspectives on Spirituality in Childhood and Adolescence." In *Religious Perspectives on Spirituality in Childhood and Adolescence.* Lanham, MD: Rowman and Littlefield, 2005.

CHINA

The history of Islam in China is, naturally, intertwined with the historical development of a Muslim presence there. It is also connected, albeit to a much lesser extent, to the history of relations between China and the Muslim world. A Muslim presence has been recorded in China as early as the seventh century, when Muslim envoys visited Chang'an, then the capital of the Tang dynasty. As early as the eighth century there is evidence of a more permanent Muslim presence, as merchants settled in China's larger cities and established communities there. Both Chinese and Muslim records speak of these communities, which maintained regular contacts with the Muslim world. Al-Sirafi, the tenth-century author of *Akhbar al-Sin wa'l-Hind*, mentions a community of more than one hundred thousand Muslims in Khanfu (Canton). While it is clear that this number is quite exaggerated, it indicates that the community must have been fairly significant in size. Over the years, Muslim quarters were established elsewhere in the major Chinese cities and in the northwestern and southwestern regions of China, which were closer to the Muslim territories of Central Asia. The highlight of these settlements was "Zaitoon" (Quanzhou), a city on China's southeastern coast where large numbers of Muslim merchants resided during the times of such travelers as Marco Polo and Ibn Battuta (both of whom wrote extensively about the city).

The main bulk of Muslims, however, came to China along with the occupying Mongols, for whom Muslims served as soldiers, administrators, tax collectors, and scientists. The brief integration of China with the rest of the world during the days of the Mongol empire intensified the trade with Muslim regions even further. When the Mongols left China and the Chinese Ming dynasty was founded in 1368, these Muslims remained in China and settled in different parts of the empire, creating an array of forms of Muslim presence in the country—from Muslim villages in the rural northwest to Muslim quarters within the large Chinese urbanities of the east. The early years of the Ming period (roughly from the fourteenth through sixteenth century) saw also the transformation of these people from "Muslims in China" to "Chinese Muslims," a new and diverse social entity that used Chinese as its language and had some form of Islam as its religion.

This wide range of forms of Muslim life in China gave rise to an equally diverse range of forms of Chinese Islam in the following centuries. The Northwest saw the appearance of *menhuan* (saintly lineage), devout Sufi orders organized around the cult of Sufi saints and the practice of Sufi rituals such as the vocal and the silent *dhikr* (remembrance). The urban communities of eastern China gave rise to a textual canon known as the *Han Kitab* (Chinese book), a sophisticated amalgamation of Islamic thought and neo-Confucian philosophy. In both of these forms we can see a distinctive form of Islam, which can be termed "Chinese Islam." The emergence of these distinctive forms of Chinese Islam is traced back to roughly the end of the sixteenth century, although they reached their peak during the eighteenth century.

Of the numerous Sufi orders of northwestern China the most influential was the *Naqshbandiyya*, whose masters moved their activities from Central Asia into China during the seventeenth century. Shortly thereafter, local Chinese forms of these grew up around northwestern Chinese leaders such Ma Laichi (1673–1753), founder of the first indigenous Chinese order, and Ma Mingxin (1719–1781), who formed a rival order with different practices. Ma Mingxin's career led him and his followers to serious clashes with the Chinese authorities that in turn resulted in a series of violent outbreaks in the Northwest that lasted, off and on, for more than a century and devastated the Muslim communities of the region.

The *Han Kitab* scholars of eastern China emerged from an education system that was in structure very much like the Confucian education system and which espoused similar values, such as textual learning and scholarly perfection. The first *Han Kitab* texts appeared in the early seventeenth century and were mainly translations into Chinese of Sufi texts such as the *Mirsad al-'Ibad*. Shortly thereafter, original works appeared. This tradition reached its peak with the career of Liu Zhi (ca. 1755–1730), whose work created a coherent philosophical system that combined key neo-Confucian and Sufi concepts. The cornerstone of Liu's thought was the identification he made between Ibn-'Arabi's concept of *Insan Kamil* (Ar., perfect man), with the Confucian concept of *Shengren* (Ch., sage). The Prophet Muhammad, according to this formulation, was the ultimate Confucian sage.

Both of these distinct forms of Chinese Islam disappeared, or were radically transformed, during the twentieth century. However, their legacies—of the Sufi orders in particular—still persist in China.

ZVI BEN-DOR BENITE

Further Reading

Benite (Ben-Dor), Zvi. *The Dao of Muhammad: A Cultural History of Muslims in Late Imperial China*. Cambridge: Harvard University Asia Center, forthcoming.

Broomhall, Marshall. *Islam in China: A Neglected Problem*. London: Morgan and Scott, 1910.

Chu, Wen-djang. *The Moslem Rebellion in Northwest China: A Study of Government Minority Policy*. The Hague: Mouton, 1966.

Fletcher, Joseph. *Studies on Chinese and Islamic Inner Asia*. London: Variorum, 1995.

Gladney, Dru. *Muslim Chinese: Ethnic Nationalism in the People's Republic*. Cambridge: Harvard University Press, 1991.

Israeli, Raphael. *Islam in China: A Critical Bibliography*. London: Greenwood Press, 1994.

———. *Muslims in China: A Study in Cultural Confrontation*. London: Curzon, 1978.

———. Canberra: Canberra College of Advanced Education, 1981.

Leslie, Donald. *Islam in Traditional China: A Short History*. Canberra: Canberra College of Advanced Education, 1986.

Lipman, Jonathan. *Familiar Strangers: A History of Muslims in Northwest China*. Seattle: Washington University Press, 1998.

CHISHTI, MU'IN AL-DIN
(C. 1141/2–1236)

One of the eponymous founders of the Chishti Sufi order in India, Khwaja Mu'in al-Din Hasan Sijzi was born in Sistan around 1141 or 1142. Following political upheavals in Sistan and his father's death, Mu'in al-Din Chishti set out on his travels, linking up in Nishapur with the wandering circle of Khwaja 'Uthman, a Sufi master from Chisht near Herat. We know little about his travels before he moved to India; certainly, hagiographies that describe his meetings with other founders of famous Sufi orders, such as 'Abd al-Qadir al-Jilani (d. 1166), Najib al-Din Suhrawardi (d. 1168), and Najm al-Din Kubra (d. 1221), have little basis in history. Our earliest sources for the life of Mu'in al-Din are Amir Khwurd's *Siyar al-awliya'*, a collection of Chishti hagiographies, and *Surur al-sudur*, conversations *(malfuzat)* of Hamid al-Din Nagawri penned posthumously some two hundred years later. Contemporary accounts such as Minhaj's and Fakhr-i Mudabbir's do not mention him, nor do the earliest Chishti works, namely the *Fawa'id al-fu'ad*, the conversations of Nizam al-Din Awliya' penned by Amir Hasan Sijzi (d. 1336), and the *Khayr al-majalis*, the conversations of Nasir al-Din Chiragh-i Dihlavi (d. 1356) compiled by Hamid Qalandar. It is thus unclear when exactly he moved to Delhi and then Ajmer. The hagiographies often stress that he settled in Ajmer when it was still non-Muslim territory (and the center of the Rajput Chauhan realm, as well as a religious place of significance), and through his spiritual power and example brought the natives into the fold of Islam; the date given is usually before 1192. In other accounts, he moved to Ajmer after the Muslim conquest of Rajasthan in the 1190s and settled after the death of the Ghurid sultan Mu'izz al-Din in 1206. He is said to have married locally and been revered as a holy man, gathering around him disciples such that when he died in 1236, his tomb became a place of pilgrimage.

Although Mu'in al-Din Chishti left no writings, some of his key doctrines are recorded by Amir Khwurd. First, he stressed that seekers should be like lovers and when they gain insight and experience, they realize that love, lover, and beloved are all one. This monism may account for the later successful spread of the influence of Ibn 'Arabi's ideas among the Chishtis. Second, serving humanity and, in particular, the poor was actually true service to God and defined the very essence of religion. Chishti centers became known for their open-door policy and their doctrine of universal peace. Third, generosity, love, and hospitality were the key virtues to be inculcated. Religious parochialism and exclusivism were to be avoided. Chishti shrines embodied this ethos in their daily functions and provided shelter and sustenance for the poor and destitute, encouraging non-Muslims and Muslims to benefit from the spiritual power of the Sufis.

We know much about the development of the cult of Khwaja Mu'in al-Din, who became known as the stranger who is generous *(gharib navaz)*, through the patronage of the later Delhi sultans and the Mughals, especially Akbar. The spread of the Chishti order throughout India is credited to his disciples and the Sufis in the two generations after him, in particular Farid al-Din Ganj Shakar (d. 1265), whose shrine is at Ajodhan, Nizam al-Din Awliya' of Delhi (d. 1325), Qutb al-Din Bakhtiyar of Mehrauli (d. 1235), and Hamid al-Din of Nagawr (d. 1274). The cult of the shrines of the famous Chishti Sufis, encouraged by the Mughals through endowments and bequests, established the Chishti order as the most widespread, wealthy, and influential Indian Sufi order.

SAJJAD H. RIZVI

See also Delhi; Farid al-Din Ganj Shakar; Herat; Nishapur; Sufism

Further Reading

Currie, P.M. *The Shrine and Cult of Mu'in al-Din Chishti of Ajmer*. New Delhi: Oxford University Press, 1989.

Ernst, C., and B. Lawrence. *Sufi Martyrs of Love*. London: Palgrave, 2002.

Farooqi, N.R. "The early Chishti Sufis of India I and II." *Islamic Culture* 77.1 (2003): 1–29, 77.2 (2003): 1–33.

Haeri, M.. *The Chishtis*. Karachi: Oxford University Press, 2001.

Nizami, K.A. *Religion and Politics in India during the Thirteenth Century*. New Delhi: Oxford University Press, 2002 [1961].

CHIVALRY

Celebrated in numerous medieval romances, such as that of the legendary pre-Islamic Arab knight 'Antar (*Sirat 'Antar*), the figure of the gallant horseman (*faris*) had a distinguished history in pre-Islamic Arab and early Islamic Arab tradition. Rooted in the hard realities of Bedouin tribal life, the motif of the valiant cavalier celebrated for his matchless courage and prowess on the battlefield is captured most directly in the pre-Islamic Arab concept of manliness (*muruwwa*), an ideal that embraced the virtues of courage, forbearance, generosity, fidelity to kin, and magnanimity toward enemies. This motif was easily accommodated in Islamic military culture, and descriptions of the chivalric exploits of gallant warriors for the faith abound in accounts of the early Arab conquests. In the 'Abbasid era, epics recounting the heroism of figures such as Hatim al-Ta'i, 'Antar, Hamza, or the Persian hero Rustam captured the imagination of the masses, being retold, recorded, and eventually versified in a literary testament to a collective celebration of chivalric virtues.

In the increasingly cosmopolitan atmosphere of the major urban centers of medieval Islamdom, the ideal of manliness soon came to include the religiously inspired virtues of love of truth and justice, reverence for women, protection of the poor and indigent, piety, altruism, and indefatigable devotion to the faith. Beginning in the eighth century CE, this expanded chivalric ideal began to be referred to by the term *futuwwa* (valorous young manliness; Persian, *javanmardi*), and it is no accident that the figure of the Prophet's cousin and son-in-law 'Ali (d. 661 CE) came to represent the paragonal "valiant young man" (*fata*), something well evinced in the oft-quoted saying: "There is no *fata* save 'Ali, and no sword save Dhu 'l-Faqar." At the same time, however, the term *futuwwa* began to be used in contexts oftentimes quite unconnected with mastery of the martial arts. It was within Sufism, in particular, where *futuwwa* took on explicitly religious connotations, Sufi scholars such as al-Sulami (d. 1021) devoting entire treatises to the subject. For them, the *futuwwa* was above all a moral and ethical ideal, a tradition of chivalric behavior stripped of its martial connotations and then refashioned in light of the Sufi spiritual universe. Here, the ideals of the gallant warrior were applied not to the military battlefield but rather to the spiritual struggle against the malicious armies of those lower drives and passions that estrange the soul from God.

At the same time, however, the military connotations of the pre-Islamic ideal of manliness and chivalric virtue never lost its vitality or importance, and there is ample evidence to suggest its continued persistence in medieval Islamic martial culture. Although never fully transformed into the aristocratic type of social and military organization characteristic of chivalric knighthood in medieval Europe, the presence of chivalric brotherhoods in the form of various self-styled *futuwwa* organizations was a prominent feature of urban landscapes across the central and eastern regions of the medieval Islamic world. Generally speaking, members of such groups were unmarried young men bound together by oaths of fidelity, special costume, and a shared allegiance to chivalric virtues. Although the details vary considerably, such *futuwwa* or *futuwwa*-inspired groups often appeared on the public stage during times of disorder and civil strife, playing roles as varied as neighborhood militias and police auxiliaries to trouble-making urban gangs bent on rabble-rousing, banditry, and extortion in the marketplace. Perhaps in response to the anarchic potential of such groups, in the early thirteenth century, the 'Abbasid caliph al-Nasir (r. 1180–1225) set out to promulgate a courtly form of the *futuwwa*, sponsoring the dissemination of manuals outlining its principles and practices and sending out specially designated agents to initiate various sultans, princes, and governors into its fold.

As organizations devoted to the ideals of manliness and chivalry, membership in a medieval *futuwwa* group often brought with it an expectation to participate in various sports, normally games stressing martial skills such as pigeon breeding, archery, birding, riding, and wrestling. In Iran and Anatolia between the thirteenth and sixteenth centuries, the *futuwwa* tradition made its way into urban craft guilds, becoming so prevalent that in the Ottoman and Safavid domains most guilds were distinguished by their own chivalric rules, initiatory rites, hierarchies, and ceremonials. Scholars have long noted the similarity between certain aspects of Islamic chivalry and the chivalric organizations of medieval Europe, normally understood in the context of mutual influence in Islamic Spain, as well as a result of Muslim–European encounters and interchange in the eastern Mediterranean during the period of the Crusades.

ERIK S. OHLANDER

See also **Gangs; Guilds, Professional; Heroes and Heroism; Hippology; Pigeons; Police; Sports; Sufism and Sufis; Thieves and Brigands; Urban Gangs**

Primary Sources

Al-Sulami. *The Book of Sufi Chivalry (Futuwwah): Lessons to a Son of the Moment*. Translated by Sheikh Tosun Bayrak al-Jerrahi al-Halveti. New York: Inner Traditions, 1983.

Kashifi. *The Royal Book of Spiritual Chivalry*. Translated by Jay R. Crook. Chicago: Great Books of the Islamic World, 2000.

Further Reading

Arnakis, G.G. "Futuwwa Traditions in the Ottoman Empire: Akhis, Bektashis, Dervishes and Craftsman." *Journal of Near Eastern Studies* 12.4 (1953): 232–247.

Cahen, Claude, and Franz Taeschner. "Futuwwa." In *The Encyclopaedia of Islam*. 2 ed, ed. H.A.R. Gibb et al. Leiden: E.J. Brill, 1954–2003.

Renard, John. *Islam and the Heroic Image: Themes in Literature and the Visual Arts*. Columbia, SC: University of South Carolina Press, 1993.

Riaz, Muhammad. "A Study of the 'Javanmardi' Movement in the World of Islam." *Journal of the Pakistan Historical Society* 29.1 (1981): 3–17.

Salinger, Gerard. "Was the Futuwwa an Oriental Form of Chivalry?" *Proceedings of the American Philosophical Society* 94.5 (1950): 481–493.

CHRISTIANS AND CHRISTIANITY

Until at least 1000 CE, Christians of various denominations were the majority of the population in the Islamic world.

While Christian Arabs such as the Banu Taghlib fared poorly under Islam (Tritton 1930:89–92), the post-Qur'anic caliphate developed a profitable relationship with its non-Muslim subjects: the Arab conquests of Antioch, Jerusalem, and Alexandria had brought three ancient Christian centers under Islamic rule (Griffith 2001) and were followed by the incorporation of Persian (Le Coz 1995) and Iberian Christians. One of the Qur'anic "People of the Book" (see Q 3:65 f.; 5:18–19), Christians were among the communities to whom the Islamic state pledged its protection *(dhimma)* in exchange for their payment of a poll tax *(jizya*; cf. the sole Qur'anic attestation of this term at Q 9:29). Although the status of these "protected persons" has come under attack (Ye'or 2002), Christians did participate in, and contribute to, classical Islamic civilization (Friedman 2003).

The Qur'an itself distinguishes those who acknowledge the Prophet Muhammad from their monotheistic counterparts (for example, Q 2:142–147; 5:51)—although Christian (and Jewish) women and food are lawful for Muslims (cf. Q 5:5). Similarly, while inscriptions on the Dome of the Rock and the earliest Islamic coinage explicitly refute the Trinity, claims of a clear separation of Muslims and non-Muslims—as indicated in the terms of Christian acceptance of Muslim rule contained in the Covenant of 'Umar (Tritton 1930)—are at variance with the pre-Crusade historical record: early 'Abbasid caliphs

held interreligious debates (Griffith 1999); classical Qur'an commentators extrapolated from the Christians in their own milieus when commenting on those Qur'anic passages alluding to Christians (McAuliffe 1991); and the Qur'anic charge of scriptural corruption leveled against the Children of Israel—Jews and Christians (for example, Q 5:12–14)—prompted Muslim scholars such as Ibn Hazm (d. 1064 CE) to engage in biblical exegesis. Finally, some of the most detailed sources about Christians in the classical Islamic world come from Muslim authors such as 'Abd al-Jabbar (d. 1025; cf. Reynolds, 2004).

In the East, all the denominations came to express themselves in Arabic while retaining their ancient liturgical languages and patristic heritage. The emergence of the new genre of inter-Christian theological debates in Arabic is contemporaneous with the development of Islamic "dialectical theology" (*'ilm al-kalam*; cf. Griffith 2002), with parallels between, respectively, Christian Trinitarian and Christological debates, and Muslim "divine attribute" *(al-asma' al-husna)* and "createdness of the Qur'an" discussions. Christians who spoke Syriac were particular vehicles for cultural exchange: Employed by the caliph in the translation of Greek texts into Arabic, scholars such as Yahya b. 'Adi (d. 974) were active participants in the philosophical movement at Baghdad (Gutas 1998; Yahya b. 'Adi 2002). In addition to their scholarly contributions, Christians were employed as doctors and scribes. On the Iberian Peninsula, the Mozarabs profited from and added to the works of their eastern counterparts (Burman 1994).

Already culturally and linguistically (and, for most, theologically) distanced from their Latin and Greek counterparts before the Arab conquests, a common experience and language under Islamic rule united the Christians in the eastern Islamic lands (Melkites, Maronites, Jacobites—both Syrians and Copts—and Nestorians); evidence of this unity—despite theological differences—is that the Nestorian Catholicos became the chief representative of Christian interests at the caliph's court in Baghdad.

The end of the demographic dominance of Christians in the Islamic world coincided with the Crusades and the Mongol invasion. With the accession of the Ottomans, the chief Christian was no longer the Nestorian Catholicos of Baghdad; rather, the head of the Christian *millet* (organized religious minority, from Ar. *milla* [religion]) became the (Greek Orthodox) Patriarch of Constantinople (Armenians, however, formed their own *millet*).

Despite Christian martyrdoms at the hands of Muslims (Gaudeul 1984; although some—such as those at Cordoba in 850—may have been self induced), apocalyptic denunciation of Islamic rule (Martinez

2003) and policies such as the Ottoman *devshirme* (levy of Christian youths), the Islamic state's promise of "protection" of both the persons and practices of its Christian subjects, assured Christians the ability to practice their religion (within limits: Tritton 1930; cf. Q 5:82). Particularly in the period after the Crusades, when Islamic thought increasingly made a distinction between Muslim and non-Muslim (which also included "bad" Muslims; cf. Michel 1984), conversions to Islam, from conviction, coercion, or socioeconomic aspirations (as well as the interventions of foreign "Christian" powers; Frazee 1982), undermined the position of Christians within the Islamic world.

CLARE E. WILDE

See also 'Abbasids; Abyssinia; Alexandria; Aramaeans; Ascetics and Asceticism; Churches; Coptic; Copts; Interfaith Relations; Al-Jahiz; Jerusalem; Al-Ma'mun; Merchants, Christian; Mirrors for Princes; Muslim–Byzantine Relations; Muslim–Crusader Relations; Ottoman Empire; Qur'an and Christianity; Romance, Iberian; Scholars; Scribes; Syria, Greater; Syriac; Theology; Trade, Mediterranean; Umayyads; Women, Christian

Further Reading

Bulliet, Richard W. *Conversion to Islam in the Medieval Period: An Essay in Quantitative History.* Cambridge, MA: Harvard University Press, 1979.

Burman, Thomas E. *Religious Polemic and the Intellectual History of the Mozarabs, c. 1050–1200.* Leiden: Brill, 1994.

Ducellier, Alain. *Chrétiens d'Orient et Islam au Moyen Age: VIIe-XVe siècle.* Paris: Armand Colin/Masson, 1996.

Ebied, Rifaat, and Herman Teule. *Studies on the Christian Arabic Heritage in Honour of Father Prof. Dr. Samir Khalil Samir S.I. at the Occasion of his Sixty-Fifth Birthday* [Eastern Christian Studies, 5]. Leuven: Peeters, 2004.

Frazee, Ch. *Catholics and Sultans: The Church and the Ottoman Empire 1453–1923.* London: Cambridge University Press, 1982.

Friedman, Yohanan. *Tolerance and Coercion in Islam: Interfaith Relations in the Muslim Tradition.* Cambridge, MA: Cambridge University Press, 2003.

Gaudeul, Jean-Marie. *Encounters & Clashes: Islam and Christianity in History.* 2 vols. Rome: Pontificio Istituto di Studi Arabi e Islamici, 1984.

Griffith, Sidney H. "The Monk in the Emir's *majlis*: Reflections on a Popular Genre of Christian Literary Apologetics in Arabic in the Early Islamic Period." In *The Majlis: Interreligious Encounters in Medieval Islam* [Studies in Arabic Language and Literature, 4], ed. Hava Lazarus Yafeh et al, 13–65. Wiesbaden: Otto Harrassowitz, 1999.

———. "Melkites, Jacobites and the Christological Controversies in Arabic in Third/Ninth-Century Syria." In *Syrian Christians under Islam: The First Thousand Years,* ed. David Thomas, 9–55. Leiden: Brill, 2001.

———. *The Beginnings of Christian Theology in Arabic: Muslim-Christian Encounters in the Early Islamic Period* [Collected Studies Series, 746]. Aldershot, Hamp: Variorum/Ashgate, 2002.

Gutas, Dimitri. *Greek Thought, Arabic Culture: The Graeco-Arabic Translation Movement in Baghdad and Early 'Abbāsid Society (2nd–4th/8th–10th centuries).* London and New York: Routledge, 1998.

Khoury, Paul. *Matériaux pour Servir à l'Étude de la Controverse Théologique Islamo-Chrétienne de Langue Arabe du VIIIe au XII Siècle* [Religionswissenschaftliche Studien, 11:1–4]. 4 vols. Würzburg and Altenberge: Echter & Oros Verlag, 1989–1999.

Le Coz, R. *L'Eglise d'Orient: Chrétiens d'Irak, d'Iran et de Turqie.* Paris: Editions du Cerf, 1995.

Martínez, F.J. "La literatura apocalíptica y las primeras reacciones cristianas a la conquista islámica en Oriente." In *Europa y el Islam,* edited by Gonzalo Anes and Álvarez de Castrillón, 143–222. Madrid: Real Academia de la Historia, 2003.

McAuliffe, J. *Qur'ānic Christians: An Analysis of Classical and Modern Exegesis.* Cambridge, MA: Cambridge University Press, 1991.

Michel, Thomas F. *A Muslim Theologian's Response to Christianity: Ibn Taymiyya's al-Jawāb al-⊂a ī .* Delmar, NY: Caravan Books, 1984.

Reynolds, Gabriel Said. *A Muslim Theologian in the Sectarian Milieu: 'Abd al-Jabbar (415/1025) and the 'Critique of Christian Origins.'* Leiden: Brill, 2004.

Tritton, A.S. *The Caliphs and Their Non-Muslim Subjects: A Critical Study of the Covenant of 'Umar.* London: Oxford University Press, 1930.

Yahyā ibn 'Adī. *The Reformation of Morals* [Eastern Christian Texts, 1], ed. Samir Khalil Samir, trans. Sidney H. Griffith. Provo, UT: Brigham Young University Press, 2002.

Ye'or, Bat. *Islam and Dhimmitude: Where Civilizations Collide.* Teaneck, NJ: Fairleigh Dickinson University Press, 2002.

CIRCASSIANS

Circassians is the general name for the group of peoples in the northwestern Caucasus region who speak a language of the Abazgo–Circassian branch of the Caucasian languages. In Arabic, they are usually referred to as Jarkash (pl. Jarakish); in Turkish, Čerkes; and in their own language, Adygei. The Circassians were renowned for their military skills and played an important role in the history of the Mamluk Sultanate in Egypt and Syria, and to a certain degree later in the Ottoman Empire and the Safawid Empire. The territories inhabited by the Circassians are today part of the Russian Federation, and people of Circassian descent also live in Turkey, Jordan, and Israel.

Circassians and their lands were known to the early Arab geographers but were generally off the main path of early Muslim history. Their territory was ruled by the Khazars in the seventh to eleventh centuries, and the Mongol Golden Horde in the thirteenth through fifteenth centuries. Throughout this period, the Circassians followed their indigenous pagan traditions, although Christianity made some inroads among them. The Circassians began adopting Islam starting around the sixteenth century. The fact that they were pagans, along with their prowess, made them ideal candidates for military slavery (*see* Slavery, Military), not the least since at times it was difficult to procure Mamluks from the traditional Qipchaq Turkish areas farther north. Circassians first achieved prominence in the Mamluk Sultanate under Sultan Qalawun (1279–1290), who enrolled them in his Burjiyya regiment, named after the towers *(abraj)* of the Cairo citadel in which they resided. The members of this formation were only part of the large number of Mamluks whom this sultan purchased, and besides their military skills and availability, another reason for their purchase appears to have been a desire to counterbalance the influence of the Turkish Mamluks. The Circassians at that time, as well as later, showed a great degree of ethnic solidarity *(jinsiyya)*, and rallied behind their compatriot Baybars al-Jashnakir (the taster), one of the strongmen of the Sultanate after Qalawun's death who was briefly sultan (r. 1309–1310), known to modern historians as Baybars II. While not disappearing, the power of the Circassians was subsequently weakened in the following generations but was to reemerge after the rise to power of Sultan Barquq (r. 1382–1406), a Circassian who made a special effort to import Mamluks from among his countrymen, at the expense of Turks and other groups. In fact, the second half of the Mamluk Sultanate is known by contemporary sources as the "Circassian State/Dynasty" (dawlat al-jarakisa), reflecting the predominant role of this group. Modern historians and students often mistakenly call this time the Burji period and its rulers Burji sultans, probably unintentionally (but still falsely) seeing a connection between the Circassian Burjiyya regiment of the late thirteenth century and the Circassian rulers, officers, and common Mamluks of a century later.

The Circassian period was generally one of economic decline and political disorder. Certainly there was a growing lack of discipline among the Mamluks. Contemporary writers, sometimes followed by modern historians, have attributed this to the character of the Circassians. It probably has more to do with a declining economy (a legacy of the middle fourteenth century), which in turn generated problems with paying the army, as well as the necessity of importing older Mamluks, meaning less education for the common soldier and future officer; he was therefore less formed than his predecessor and more prone to rioting and other forms of lack of discipline. There was a notable tendency for the Circassians to bring over family members once they were well established, breaking a long-held tradition of the Mamluk system, where the young military slave lost contact with his family, thus becoming dependent on his new patron and fellow Mamluks. Interestingly enough, during the Circassian period there was a certain flowering of Mamluk Turkish literature in the Sultanate, indicating that perhaps Turkish remained the lingua franca of the Mamluk class in spite of demographic changes. Circassians remained among the Mamluks of Egypt in the Ottoman period and were settled in Palestine and Jordan in the nineteenth century by the Ottoman authorities as part of the effort to increase control in the area, as well as to provide a solution to the thousands of Circassians who fled their homeland after the Russian conquest.

REUVEN AMITAI

See also Mamluks

Further Reading

Ayalon, David. "The Circassians in the Mamlūk Kingdom." *Journal of the American Oriental Society*. 69 (1949): 135–147. (Reprinted in D. Ayalon. *Studies on the Mamlūk of Egypt [1250–1517]*. London: Variorum Reprints, 1977.)

Flemming, Barbara. "Literary Activities in the Mamluk Halls and Barracks." In *Studies in Memory of Gaston Wiet*, ed. Myriam Rosen-Ayalon. Jerusalem: Institute of Asian and African Studies, Hebrew University of Jerusalem, 1977.

Manz, Beatrice. "Čarkas." *Encyclopaedia Iranica*. 4: 816–818.

Quelquejay, Ch et al. "Čerkes." *Encyclopaedia of Islam*, new edition. 2: 21–26.

CIRCUMCISION (*KHITAN*)

The Arabic word for circumcision (*khitan*) is used interchangeably with both the male and the female versions, although the term *khifad* often appears in specific reference to female excision. Nowhere mentioned in the Qur'an, and only briefly discussed in legal materials, circumcision has become inextricably tied to one's identity as a Muslim in popular piety and practice. In fact, many Muslims recognize it as a necessary step in conversion to Islam. From a religious studies perspective, the manipulation of the genitalia ultimately epitomizes a believer's submission to divine control over human, procreative instincts and base passions.

Circumcision was a common practice in pre-Islamic Arabia that was later absorbed into the Islamic tradition. Both Philo (ca. 40 CE) and Josephus (ca. 100 CE) note its presence in Egypt, Ethiopia, and Arabia prior to the coming of Islam. They suggest circumcision was tied to certain rites of passage, like puberty or marriage, in these regions. Philo observes that Egyptian males and females were circumcised after the fourteenth year before marriage, whereas Josephus claims the Arabs performed it on males just after the thirteenth year, at the time Ishmael was circumcised. In one of the earliest biographies of the Prophet Muhammad, Ibn Ishaq (d. 767 CE) records that in pre-Islamic times the Quraysh would slaughter a camel to Hubal, the central idol of the Ka'ba, before their sons were circumcised. Ibn Ishaq mentions girls were also circumcised, but in less celebratory fashion. Oddly, these early biographical materials do not mention the Prophet Muhammad's circumcision. The explanations for how the Prophet was circumcised only appear in later works. For example, some fourteenth- and fifteenth-century documents suggest 'Abdu'l Muttalib circumcised Muhammad; others insist that the prophet was, in fact, born circumcised.

The justifications for circumcision vary dramatically in early Sunni sources and practices. The majority of Sunni *hadith* associate circumcision with rites of purification *(tahara)*. Cutting the foreskin often appears in lists that include other acts of general hygiene, including the clipping of nails, the use of the tooth-stick, the trimming of mustaches, and the depilation of both the armpits and the pubic region. Adherence to these purity practices, which call for the removal of excess bodily materials, allows the true believer to realize the *fitra*, which the *hadith* define as the originary religion reflected in one's true nature as God created it.

Some Sunni *hadith* also link the practice of foreskin removal back to Abraham, who circumcised himself at the age of eighty with a pickax. Unlike Judaism, Islam does not view circumcision as the sole signifier of the covenant between God and his people. Circumcision stands as just one of many tests Abraham performed to demonstrate his unflinching adherence to the true faith. Just as Abraham was willing to sacrifice his son, so too was he willing to sacrifice a part of himself to fulfill God's command. Like many other Muslim ritual practices, circumcision is significant only insofar as it reflects a deeper intent to submit fully to God's will.

In early Sunni legal circles, Islamic scholars debate whether the practice of circumcision is *wajib* (obligatory) or *sunna* (customary), or whether its obligations extend solely to males, or to males and females. Al-Shafi'i considers the practice mandatory for both sexes, whereas Malik and others consider it *sunna* only for males. Those who consider the practice mandatory for males and females look to those *hadith* that combine circumcision with non–gender specific purificatory rituals, such as the removal of armpit hair and the shaving of the pubic region. Female circumcision is supported by relatively few numbers of *hadith*, many of which are attached with some sort of disclaimer. In those that do support female circumcision, the command is to cut, but not to cut too severely for the sake of the woman and her husband. These *hadith*, which stem back to the Prophet himself, condemn practices of excessive mutilation or radical infibulation. In addition to debates about to whom the practice should apply, many legal schools also deliberate the time a circumcision should be performed. Some recommend the seventh day following the birth of a male child (as distinct from Jewish law), while others propose its performance after a child reaches his tenth birthday.

Like their Sunni counterparts, Shi'i jurists support the practice of circumcision. Not insignificantly, the Shi'is do insist that all major prophets, including Abraham and Muhammad, were born purified and circumcised, along with every Shi'i *imam*. The Shi'i view that foreskin, or any other body part that requires cutting, clipping, shaving, or plucking, would somehow mar the flawlessness of a prophet or *imam*, may be what informs this doctrine.

KATHRYN KUENY

See also Birth; Customary Law; Festivals and Celebration; Gender and Sexuality; Hadith; Ibn Ishaq; Law and Jurisprudence; Malik ibn Anas; Muhammad the Prophet; Personal Hygiene; Purity, Ritual; Qur'an; al-Shafi'i; Shi'ism; Sira

Further Reading

Hoffman, Lawrence A. *Covenant of Blood: Circumcision and Gender in Rabbinic Judaism.* Chicago: The University of Chicago Press, 1996.

Kister, M.J. *Concepts and Ideas at the Dawn of Islam.* Aldershot, Great Britain and Brookfield, VT: Ashgate/Varioram, 1997.

Kueny, Kathryn. "Abraham's Test: Islamic Male Circumcision as Anti/Ante-Covenantal Practice." In *Bible and Qur'an: Essays in Scriptural Intertextuality*, ed. John C. Reeves, 161–182. Atlanta: Society of Biblical Literature, 2003.

Waugh, Earl. "Circumcision." In *The Oxford Encyclopedia of the Modern Islamic World,* edited by John L. Esposito. Oxford: Oxford University Press, 1995.

Wensinck, A.J. "Khitan." In *The Encyclopedia of Islam,* 2d ed, ed. H.A.R. Gibb et al. 9 vols. New York: Macmillan, 1987.

CLIMATE, THEORIES OF

There are two interconnected understandings of climate that developed in medieval Islamic society. The first derives from the rich Arabic geographical literature that variously divided the world into different "climates" as a framework for topographical description and cartography. These geographical climates were referred to by the Arabic term *iqlim* (pl. *aqalim*), which derived originally from the Greek *klima* (inclination), the basis of the Ptolemaic cartographic system. The use of *aqalim* in Arabic geography is considerably varied and does not simply follow the patterns of the Greek tradition as it was translated through Syriac authors. Several individual geographical treatises, such as that of al-Khuwarizmi, as well as more encyclopedic works, such as Yaqut, tended to reproduce the original seven climates of Ptolemy. These consisted of horizontal bands that began at the equator and progressively moved northward to cover the whole of the northern hemisphere. The width of each band was determined by the length of the day at the summer solstice and therefore did not represent any topographical or anthropological reality. Nevertheless, as discussed in the work of the Ikwan al-Safa' and others, residence in a particular *iqlim* was considered to affect the health of its inhabitants, their capabilities, both mental and physical, and even their body types and skin color. For most medieval authors there was a distinctly marked preference for the middle latitudes, which represented regions of climatic balance, in both temperature and seasonality. One of the chief advantages of this theory was that Baghdad, the official capital of the Caliphate for much of the 'Abbasid dynasty, was located squarely in the fourth/middle climate, thus advantageously placed to represent the essence of *ta'adil* (equilibrium/moderation in all things).

This latitudinal division of the world was largely rejected, or at least significantly reworked, by many medieval geographers who preferred to categorize the world in more civilizational or administrative terms. In maintaining the number seven as definitional to a theory of *aqalim*, certain authors were influenced by the Persian notion of *kishvar* regions, each of which comprised a large empire/civilization. Al-Biruni provided a diagram of the world based on the *kishvar*, such that his climates are represented by circles, not latitudinal bands, with Baghdad's *iqlim* in the center and the other six arranged around it. Within the tradition of descriptive geography that was championed by authors of the so-called Balki school of the tenth century, a more administrative logic would define these regions and also increase their number. In probably the most sophisticated geographical treatise of the medieval period, al-Muqaddasi's *Ahsan al-Taqasim fi Ma'rifat al-Aqalim (The Best Division for Knowledge of the Regions)*, the author describes fourteen regions (six Arab, eight non-Arab) that were described not only using the administrative boundaries but also numerous other cultural and environmental factors, such as ethnicity and cultivation.

In virtually all of the works that used the notion of *iqlim* as part of a theory of geographical classification, the intent was to provide a framework for presenting information on the cities, settlements, populations, and topographical features located in these regions. This geographical literature tended not to prioritize the description of climate in a more meteorological sense, although this was addressed peripherally in many works, particularly compendia of knowledge such as the epistles of the Ikhwan al-Safā'. Rather, this second understanding of climate, distinguished in Arabic by the term *manakh* (climate, atmosphere), which encompasses notions such as weather and seasonality, was often dealt with in other sources. Medieval Arabic texts, particularly those that dealt with the question of the *'aja'ib* (miracles, natural wonders), such as al-Qazwini, have provided extensive information about issues such as the division of the seasons, the influence of weather on the body and culture, and general understandings of ecology and health. Two realms of knowledge have contributed to theories surrounding these questions: (1) Islamic cosmological/theological understandings of the four elements, the three kingdoms, the nature of the physical world, and the role of humanity as steward of God's creation; and (2) "folk" understandings based on practical experience and knowledge of the environment, which are often correlated with economic lifeways (such as agriculture, pastoralism, craft production) or landscapes (such as desert, irrigated agricultural plain, cities). Despite the distinctions between the geographical and meteorological senses of climate, there have been moments of convergence between the understanding of *manakh* and *iqlam*, particularly in connection with the understanding of what constituted the ideal climate for the development of civilizational and spiritual achievements. Ibn Khaldun noted in his seminal work of social history, *al-Muqaddimah,* that the middle three *aqalim* were the most suitable for civilization, particularly the proliferation of great monuments and advanced urban centers, because of the moderation of their meteorological climate. Moreover, these more temperate regions were envisioned as the place of prophets and righteous people, a testament to the link made in medieval Islamic society not only between climate and civilization, but also between climate and morality.

IAN B. STRAUGHN

See also Agriculture; Cartography; Geography; Human Geography; Ibn Khaldun; Meteorology; Nomadism and Pastoralism, al-Qazwini; Yaqut

Further Reading

Ahmad, Sayyid Maqbul. *A History of Arab-Islamic Geography*. Amman: Ahl al-Bayt University Press, 1995.

al-Muqaddasi, Muhammad ibn Ahmad. *The Best Division for Knowledge of the Regions.* Translated by Basil A. Collins. Reading, UK: Garnet Publishing, 1994.

Al-Qazwīnī. *'Ajā'ib al-Makhlūqāt wa gharā'ib al-Mawjudāt.* Cairo, 1957.

Harley, J.B., and D. Woodward, eds. *The History of Cartography: Cartography in the Traditional Islamic and South Asian Societies.* Vol. 2.1. Chicago: The University of Chicago Press, 1987.

Hopkins, J. F. P. "Geographical and Navigational Literature." In *Religion, Learning and Science in the Abbasid Period,* edited by M.J.L. Young, J. D. Latham, and R. B. Serjeant, 301–327. Cambridge, MA: Cambridge University Press, 1990.

Ibn Khaldun. *The Muquaddimah.* 2 vols. Translated by Franz Rosenthal. Princeton: Princeton University Press, 1967.

Ikhwān al-Safā'. *Rāsa'il Ikhwān al-Safā' wa-khullān al-wafā'.* Egypt: al-Maktaba al-Tijārīya al-Kubrā, 1928.

Miquel, Andre. "*Iklīm.*" In *The Encyclopedia of Islam.* 2d ed. Leiden: E.J. Brill.

———. *La Géographie Humaine du Monde Musulman jusqu'ua Milieu de 11e Siècle.* 4 vols. Paris: Mouton & Co, 1967–1988.

Musā, 'Alī Hassan. *Al-Manākh fī al-Turāth al- 'Arabī (Climate in Arab Heritage).* Damascus: Dār al-Fiqh, 2001.

Yāqut ibn 'Abd Allah al-Hamawī. *Mu 'jam al-Buldān.* Beirut: Dār Sādir, 1955–1957.

CLOTHING AND COSTUME

Although there were regional and temporal variations in clothing styles throughout the medieval Muslim world, there was a distinct civilization-wide mode of dress that Yedida Kalfon Stillman has dubbed "the Islamic vestimentary system." This vestimentary system, which remained remarkably constant throughout the Middle Ages, developed from the gradual fusion of three different fashion systems that existed in the lands, rather cultural zones, that became the caliphate: the Arabian Peninsula, the Hellenistic Mediterranean, and Iranian and Turkish Central Asia. The pre-Islamic Arabian mode of dress was characterized by loose, flowing, untailored garments; the Hellenistic Mediterranean by tunics and wraps; and the Central Asian by fitted or tailored garments such as coats, jackets, and trousers. The process of fusion had already begun in the Arab kingdoms of Hira and Ghassan in northern Arabia that bordered the Byzantine and Sasanian empires and were zones of cultural osmosis just prior to the advent of Islam.

Early Islamic Clothing: Style and Religious Ideology

The general mode of dress of the Muslim community at the time of the Prophet was generally that of pre-Islamic Arabia with some modifications in accordance with new moral sensibilities. The new Islamic notions of corporal modesty were not unlike those of Near Eastern Judaism and Christianity. The Qur'an declares that God revealed *libas* (clothing) to humanity "to conceal your shame" (Sura VII, 26). The medieval Arabic lexicographers even defined *libas* as "that which conceals or covers the sexual organs." (It is noteworthy that in many modern Arabic dialects the word is used to denote underwear, not merely as a euphemism, but in recognition of clothing's essential nature.) Like Jews and Christians, the early Muslims were prudish about pagan society's easygoing attitude toward nudity, and the *hadith* literature stresses the importance of underwear. The basic Arab undergarment going back to Antiquity was the *izar*. This loincloth is already mentioned by Herodotus and still constitutes the lower half of the ritual *ihram* attire worn by male pilgrims to Mecca. During the formative period when Muhammad led the community in Medina (622–632), a new undergarment of Persian origin, *sirwal* (drawers), also came into use. Because not everyone in the early *umma* could afford a separate undergarment, there are numerous traditions warning against exposing one's private parts when sitting, squatting, or trussing up one's garment while working.

The principal article of clothing at the time of the Prophet was one of a variety of body shirts, such as the *qamis*, or tunics, such as the *thawb*. The latter was so basic that the word also simply means "cloth" or, in the plural, "items of clothing." Depending on weather, occasion, or wealth and status, a person might wear over the body-covering a mantle *(rida')*, a wrap *(burd, milhafa, shamla, or izar)*, a coat *(qaba')*, or a sleeveless robe *('aba'a)*. Many of the same garment names are used for male and female attire, although there probably were often some gender differences of style.

Following norms going back to the ancient Near East, covering the head was considered a mark of modesty for both men and women. Exposing one's hair was a sign of arrogance, and the Qur'an threatens the sinner with being dragged down to hell by his "lying, sinful forelock" (Sura 104, 15–16). Early Muslims covered the head with a variety of caps, such as the *qalansuwa* (considered so distinctively Arab that it was specifically forbidden to non-Muslim subjects by the Pact of 'Umar after the conquests), a headcloth, such as the *mandil*, or a turban *('imama)*. The early turban was probably a simple strip of fabric wound about the head and not the composite head-gear of later medieval and early modern times, which consists of one or more caps and a winding cloth. It certainly did not have the significance that it came to have in the later Middle Ages as "the crown of the Arabs," "the badge of Islam," and "the divider between unbelief and belief." Because of the turban's later significance, pious legends about the Prophet's turban abounded, and one of his epithets came to be *sahib al-'imama* (the wearer of the turban). Early *hadiths*, however, mention him appearing publicly with his mantle pulled over his head and held in place with a headband (*'isaba*).

With the exception of Muhammad's wives, whose special status set them apart, strict veiling for women does not seem to have been the norm in the early Muslim community. Around 626–627, the Prophet received a revelation that in public his and the Believers' wives should draw their *jilbab*, an enveloping outer wrap, "close about them. . . .so they be recognized and not molested" (Sura XXXIII, 59). Another Medinese verse (Sura XXIV, 31) enjoins Muslim women to be modest and cover their bosoms with a *khimar*, another female veil-cum-wrap, but makes no mention of covering the face. It would appear that strict veiling practices, together with the seclusion of women, only evolved among the bourgeoisie over the first two centuries of Islam in emulation of the Prophet's personal *sunna* (practice).

Since many of the most stirring prophetic utterances seemed to imply that Judgment Day was nigh, the early Islamic community tended toward sartorial austerity. According to the Qur'an (Sura XXII:23), the Believers will be clothed with raiment of silk and bracelets of gold and pearls in Paradise, but according to the *hadith*, Muhammad forbade men to indulge in such luxuries in this world. He did, however, make exceptions for men with pruritic skin conditions or body lice, as well as for women. During the century following the Islamic conquests, this early austerity in male attire rapidly gave way to greater luxury for the upper classes, and only the poor and the ascetic pietists continued wearing simple garments. Because of their plain wool (*suf*) robes, the ascetics came to be known as Sufis.

Evolution of the Islamic Vestimentary System under the Caliphates

The Islamic vestimentary system evolved in the great caliphate established by the Arab conquests. As noted at the beginning of this entry, the expanded empire included three different cultural zones, each with its own distinctive fashion system. At first, the Arabs, who were a minority in their own empire, tried to maintain identifiable differences of attire between themselves and their subjects. This led to the *ghiyar* (differentiation) regulations, which required the *dhimmi*s, or tolerated non-Muslim population, to be visibly dissimilar in dress from Muslims. These sumptuary laws evolved over a long period but were ascribed by later tradition to the so-called Pact of 'Umar, which was attributed to Caliph 'Umar ibn al-Khattab (r. 634–644). The earliest of these rules probably only date from the time of 'Umar ibn 'Abd al-'Aziz (r. 717–720). The requirement to have distinctly distinguishing clothing also applied to the Arab militia that stood guard over the empire. Arab warriors in the eastern provinces, for example, were forbidden from wearing the Persian *khaftan* (cuirass) and *ran* (leggings). However, by the end of the Umayyad period, the Arabs living in Khurasan had become increasingly assimilated into the local culture, and this certainly included their style of dress.

The fusion of vestimentary styles and a movement away from the earlier austerity were already taking place in the highest echelons of Islamic society shortly after the conquests. Both historical sources and artistic representations attest to the fact that some of the Umayyad rulers wore Persian-style coats, pantaloons, and the regal, high, miterlike hat known as the *qalansuwa tawila*. They also adopted, from both the Byzantine and the Sasanian courts, the custom of wearing special royal garments of such luxury fabrics as silk, satin, and brocade. Umayyad official attire was white, while the protocol of their successors, the 'Abbasids, required black. The Umayyads further emulated the Byzantine and Persian rulers by establishing state factories to produce royal fabrics with embroidered bands (*tiraz*) containing written inscriptions. Along with a mention of the caliph's name in the Friday sermon, having his name inscribed on *tiraz* and on coins came to be regarded as the ruler's prerogative. Garments of these regal fabrics were not only worn by the caliphs and their retinues but also were given as gifts. The bestowal of the *khil'a*, or robe of honor, became a standard practice in Islamic courts throughout the Middle Ages and continued until early modern times. Not only did the wearing of luxurious clothing spread down from the elite to the bourgeoisie, but also private ateliers began imitating royal *tiraz*. We know both from actual relics preserved in museums and from the documents of the Cairo Geniza that ordinary people who could afford it copied the practice of bestowing robes of honor on family and friends. Valuable articles of clothing were considered part of personal wealth and were handed down as family heirlooms.

Kaftan. Turkish, late sixteenth-early seventeenth century CE (CT22668). Credit: Victoria & Albert Museum, London/Art Resource. Victoria and Albert Museum, London, Great Britain.

During the ninth and tenth centuries, fashion consciousness reached new heights in Baghdad. Sartorial style and elegance formed part of the polite cultural ideal of *adab*. In his manual for members of refined society, *Kitab al-Muwashsha' aw al-Zarf wa-l-Zurafa' (The Book of Ornamentation on Elegance and Elegant People)*, the aesthete al-Washsha' (d. 936) devotes several chapters to proper attire and the etiquette of dress for members of both sexes. Many

Persian garments were integrated into the Islamic vestimentary system during that time. The 'Abbasids increasingly adopted elements from Sasanian court protocols, such as red leather boots. As a demonstration of their Arabian roots, Islamic legitimacy, and charisma, the 'Abbasid caliphs would on certain ceremonial occasions don the simple woolen *burda* (cloak) that had supposedly belonged to the Prophet Muhammad.

The Fatimid dynasty (909–1171) exceeded both the Umayyads and the 'Abbasids in their use of clothing as part of their pomp and ceremony. A government agency oversaw the production, storage, and distribution of seasonal ceremonial attire for all officials from the caliph down to minor civil servants. A complete outfit might consist of a dozen articles of clothing. Fatimid ceremonial costumes were mostly white and embroidered with gold and silver thread in accordance with the dynasty's official image as bearers of divine light *(nur ilahi)*.

Turkish Military Dynasties and Later Medieval Fashion Trends

Yedida Stillman has noted three significant trends occurring in the Islamic vestimentary system during the late eleventh through thirteenth centuries under the Turkish military dynasties of the Seljuks, the Ayyubids, and the Mamluks, and under the Mongol Ilkhanids. These trends were (1) the introduction of new garments and fashions from Central Asia and the Far East; (2) increasing social stratification reflected by clothing; and (3) ever-stricter interpretation and enforcement of the dress code for *dhimmis*.

The first category included a variety of Asian coats, jackets, and vests *(qaba' turki, qaba' tatari, bughlutaq, sallariyya, malluta)*; caps and hats *(sharbush, kalawta, saraquj, zamt)*; and military belts *(hiyasa, band)* and boots *(khifaf)* emblazoned with heraldic devices. Originally reserved only for the ruling military elite, some variants of these items were in time adopted by the bourgeoisie.

The increased social stratification under the feudalistic military regimes was reflected in the dress of the different classes of society. Not only did the "men of the sword" *(arbab al-suyuf)* have their own distinctive fashions, but so did the bureaucrat "men of the pen" *(arbab al-aqlam)*, the religious scholars *('ulama')*, the urban notables *(al-a'yan)*, the Sufis, the young mens' associations *(al-fityan)*, and the masses *(al-'amma)*. During this period, for example, the Persian shawl known as the *taylasan* was the badge of qadis and jurists, and the miterlike *qalansuwa tawila*, a symbol of royalty under the Umayyads and a fashionable hat under the 'Abbasids, became the mark of a dervish.

The strictness of application of *ghiyar* for the clothing of *dhimmis* was due both to the increased social stratification of the times and to a hardening of attitudes toward non-Muslims. The Mamluks imposed a color code on *dhimmi* women's outdoor clothing. Jewish women were to be identified by a yellow *izar*, Christian women by a blue one, and Samaritans by red. In Sharifan Morocco, Jewish men (the only *dhimmis*) had to wear black, and in Zaydi Yemen, Jewish males and females dark indigo. In Safavid Iran, *dhimmi* men wore an identifying patch, while their womenfolk were forbidden to veil their faces like Muslim women.

Overall, the Islamic vestimentary system remained remarkably constant both in its basic form and in ideology throughout most of the Middle Ages. There was continual evolution, introduction of new garments, and regional stylistic variation, but the fusion in different proportions over time and space of the three basic components—Arabian, Hellenistic, and Irano–Turkic—was the essential hallmark of the fashion system. This system would only begin to experience radical changes during the nineteenth century as a concomitant of modernization and the impact of the West.

NORMAN A. STILLMAN

See also Court Dress

Further Reading

Gordon, Stewart, ed. *Robes and Honor: The Medieval World of Investiture*. New York and Houndsmill, 2001.

Mayer, L.A. *Mamluk Costume: A Survey*. Geneva, Albert Kundig, 1952.

Serjeant, R.B. *Islamic Textiles: Material for a History up to the Mongol Conquest*. Beirut, Librairie du Liban, 1972.

Stillman, Yedida Kalfon. *Arab Dress: A Short History from the Dawn of Islam to Modern Times*. Edited by Norman A. Stillman. Leiden, Boston and Köln, 2000 and 2003.

———. "Costume as Cultural Statement: The Esthetics, Economics, and Politics of Islamic Dress." In *The Jews of Medieval Islam: Community, Society, and Identity*, ed. Daniel Frank. Leiden: Brill, 1995.

———. "The Medieval Islamic Vestimentary System: Evolution and Consolidation." In *Kommunikation zwischen Orient und Okzident: Alltag und Sachkultur*. Vienna, Verlag der Österreichischen Akademie der Wissenschaften, 1994.

———. "The Importance of the Cairo Geniza Manuscripts for the History of Medieval Female Attire." *International Journal of Middle East Studies* 7 (1976): 579–589.

COINS AND CURRENCY

Without any own monetary traditions, the Arabs of Mecca and Medina at first adopted the preexisting coinages in the conquered regions. The result was the development of two currencies: the so called Arab-Byzantine in copper and gold and the Arab-Sasanian coinage almost entirely in silver, both with minor modifications to their prototypes. During the reign of the Umayyad caliph 'Abd al-Malik ibn Marwan, coins of purely Islamic inspiration were struck. In AH 77/696 CE, the caliph issued the first gold *dinars* at weight of one *mithqal* (4.25 g). Silver *dirhams* followed in AH 79/698 CE, at the "canonical" weight of 2.97 g. These coins were entirely anonymous; the inscriptions consisted of religious phrases. Additionally to those phrases, *dinars* also bear the date, *dirhams,* the mint and date. No such uniform design was applied to the copper coins, called *fulus* (sg. *fals*), which were more or less a local affair. During the 'Abbasid caliphate the epigraphic style of coinage continued with minor changes in the used formulas. In the 770s, the caliph's name often appeared on the coins, as did the names of the designated heirs, local governors, and court officials. From this period on *dinars* started to bear the mint, too. During the ninth century, copper coinage was largely abandoned. It is also apparent that Islamic *dirhams* started to be an important trading medium outside the Caliphate.

The various dynasties that took political authority from the 'Abbasids retained the standard design for their precious metal coinage. Sovereignty is expressed by the right of *sikka* (the mention of the ruler's name on the precious metal coinage). In addition to the existent denominations, new ones were introduced, at first in 'Abbasid Yemen.

As the western lands became independent of the 'Abbasids, they began to strike their own coinage. The Umayyads of Spain continued to strike silver coins like those of the Umayyads and later introduced a gold coinage. The coinage of the Almoravides reflected their fervor for the holy war by introducing pugnacious legends. The Idrisids minted silver *dirhams*, lighter than the contemporary 'Abbasid ones. The Sunni Aghlabid gold coinage, on the other hand, was of normal 'Abbasid type and weight.

In the East the Tahirids were the first to issue coins independently. Their Saffarid and Samanid coins were *dirhams* of the normal 'Abbasid type. The main post-'Abbasid coinage in this region was that of the Buyids, which was predominantly in gold. From circa 940, because of the lack of silver in Islam, the Samanids turned to the production of low-grade silver coins of large model, weighing up to twenty grams. Large, billon- or plated-copper coins were first struck by the Qarakhanids. Most dynasties followed and billon coinage came into prominence. By 1010, fine silver coinage had become uncommon in the Muslim world. Umayyad standards of monetary stability were never reached again.

The first to depart from the classical coin type was the Fatimid dynasty. On his accession, al-Mu'izz introduced new coinage bearing militant Shi'i inscriptions in a concentric coin design. Also, a new dinar with the legend "extremely high" to demonstrate the gold fineness was introduced. The twelfth century had some changes in the coinage of the eastern Islamic lands: copper coins reappeared as important money, sometimes in the form of large copper coins. Also, good silver *dirham* coinage was reintroduced by the Ayyubid sultan Saladin. Because of several monetary reforms, the Mamluks minted distinctive precious metal coins and coppers that displayed a variety of heraldic emblems. In 1225, the dominance of the Venetian gold *ducat* forced the introduction of a new Mamluk gold coinage, the *ashrafi*, at the same standard, which was also adopted by the Ottomans. In the Maghreb, the Almohads also used distinctive new coin types to emphasize their dissident beliefs. Their "square in circle" type of gold coinage and their square-shaped silver coins were adopted by all subsequent Western dynasties.

In the late twelfth and the thirteenth centuries, silver coinage spread to Anatolia, Iraq, and Iran. The Rum-Seljuk *dirhams* were minted copiously. Under the Mongol Ilkhan Ghazan Mahmud, the continued local coinages were abandoned. He created a silver coinage with uniform appearance, weight, and fineness. The early fourteenth century started with a series of reductions under his successors, which went along with changes in the coin design. This system was retained at a regional level by the post-Ilkhanid dynasts. The coinage of the Timurids was based on the Ilkhanid tradition but was dominated by a new and larger silver denomination. Timurid style and denomination spread widely through Safavid Iran and northern India. In their time, each of the great empires, Ottoman, Iranian, and Mughal, had their own diverse and complex coinage.

LEONHARD E. REIS

See also 'Abbasids; 'Abd al Malik ibn Marwan; Credit; Markets; Mining; Moneylenders; Precious Metals; Saladin (Salah al-Din); Tax and Taxation; Trade, Mediterranean; Weights and Measurements; Umayyads

Further Reading

Album, Stephan. *Marsden's Numismata Orientalia Illustrata*. New York: Attic Books, 1977.
———. *A Checklist of Islamic Coins*. 2d ed. Santa Rosa: private publishing house, 1998.
Bates, Michael. *Islamic Coins*. ANS Handbook 2. New York: American Numismatic Society, 1982.
Broome, Michael. *A Handbook of Islamic Coins*. London: Seaby, 1985.
Codrington, O. *A Manual of Musulman Numismatics*. London: Royal Asiatic Society, 1904.
Deyell, John. *Living Without Silver: The Monetary History of Early Mediaeval North India*. New Delhi: Oxford University Press India, 1999.

Ilisch, Lutz, ed. *Sylloge Numorum Arabicorum Tübingen.* 6 vols. Tübingen: Wasmuth, 1993.

Lane-Poole, Stanley. *Catalogue of Oriental Coins in the British Museum.* 10 vol. London: British Museum, 1875–1890.

Lavoix, Henri. *Catalogue des Monnaies Musulmanes de la Bibliothèque Nationale.* 3 vol. Paris: Bibliothèque Nationale, 1887–1896.

Mitchener, Michael. *Oriental Coins and Their Values: The World of Islam.* London: Hawkins, 1977.

Plant, Richard. *Arabic Coins and How to Read Them.* London: Seaby, 1973.

Roberts, James. "Early Islamic Coins." http://users.rcn.com/j-roberts/home.htm, 2005.

Treadwell, Luke, ed. *Sylloge of Islamic Coins in the Ashmolean.* 3 vols. Oxford: Oxford University, 1999.

Zambaur, Eduard von. *Die Münzprägungen des Islams, Zeitlich und Örtlich Geordnet. I. Der Westen und Osten bis zum Indus mit Synoptischen Tabellen.* Wiesbaden: Franz Steiner Verlag, 1968.

COMMANDING GOOD AND FORBIDDING EVIL

The principle of commanding the good and forbidding the evil *(al-amr bi al-ma'rūf wa al-nahy 'an al-munkar),* which is applied to any action promoting what is good and prohibiting what is reprehensible, formulates a religious and moral duty based on the Qur'an. The terms *ma'rūf* and *munkar* in the expression occur in the Qur'an sometimes in tandem, as in *al-amr bi al-ma'rūf wa al-nahy 'an al-munkar* (Q 3:110, 114; 7:157; 9:71, 112; 22:41), and at times separately (Q 4:114; 5:79; 16:90; 29:45).

In its basic sense, *ma'rūf* refers to good manners and behaviors that are well known, recognized, and embraced and that are not considered to be strange when seen among people, while *munkar* is the misdeed that is not approved and accepted. Discussions that took place in the Muslim community in political, dogmatic (confessional), and juristical domains and the distinction of reason and tradition *(aql* and *naql)* resulting therefrom, gave way to the reformation of the meanings of *ma'rūf* and *munkar* in accordance with this distinction. Thus, these two terms, in addition to their religious and moral significance, gained political and juristical content. While most Mu'tazilite theologians called *ma'rūf* what reason deems as good and *munkar* what reason deems evil in accordance with their position on the issue of good and bad *(husn* and *qubh),* the Salafis and the Ash'arites defined *ma'rūf* as the deeds and utterances that the law says are good, and *munkar* as what the law says is improper. No matter how they are determined, all political, theological, and jurisprudential schools are in complete agreement that performing this duty is obligatory. However, there is a disagreement on whether this duty must be performed individually or collectively. There is a difference of opinion on such issues as to the way in which this principle should be implemented and the means of this implementation. The principle of commanding the good and forbidding the evil appears to have been enforced in two ways: (1) formally undertaken by the state, or (2) left to the individual responsibility of the Muslims. The former was institutionalized with the name of *hisbah* in such a way as to include the preservation of morality and the public order in society. *Hisbah* was intended to deal with the violation of individual, communal, and state rights and with the *munkar* about which there was no disagreement.

Commenting on the verse *"let there be a community of you, calling to all that is good, commanding what is right and forbidding what is wrong"* (Q 3:104), scholars such as Abū Ya'lā, al-Juwaynī, al-Ghazālī, Fakhr al-Dīn al-Rāzī, Ibn Taymiyya, and Zamakhshari maintained that this duty was to be performed by those who are knowledgeable about *ma'rūf* and *munkar* and the methods of commanding and prohibiting such things and those who possess good qualities.

By citing the prophetic *hadith* that reads *"whoever of you sees wrong being committed, let him rectify it with his hand, if he is unable, then with his tongue, and if he is unable, then with this heart, which is the bare minimum of faith,"* Muslim scholars also held that everyone should carry out this duty with their hands, tongues, and hearts in accordance with their ability. Among the scholars, there are those who, restricting this duty to tongue and heart, disapproved of the use of force, and there are also those who contended that the use of force and coercion should be resorted to when tongue and heart are ineffective.

The Kharijis asserted that this duty must be carried out, regardless of the circumstances, with anyone who goes astray, be it the state, the community, or the individual, and that the use of force and arms is required to do it. The Kharijis, who had as their motto the principle of commanding the good and forbidding the evil, accused anyone who did not agree with them of deviating from God's true path, and hence claimed that these deviants from God's path could only be fought through waging holy war against them. Grounding the legitimacy and the necessity of revolting against the state in this principle, the Kharijis had the lion's share in this principle's gaining a political content. The Ibadis, a Khariji faction, though disapproving of the use of weapon against people, believed that the tyrannical ruler has to be hampered and ousted by any means necessary, with or without arms. Although the Zaydiyyah and the Imāmiyyah of the Shi'i were in favor, like the Kharijis, of the use of force and arms against tyrannical political authority, the Imāmīs in particular suspended this practice until the Imam in occultation appears.

Muslim scholars such as al-Hasan al-Basrī and Abu Hanīfah viewed "the commanding the good and prohibiting the evil" as more of a moral principle and thus did not approve of the use of force against the state and the community on the ground that it would effect mistrust among people, harm the integrity of the community, and cause further social disintegration and unrest.

As against the Khawarij, there was a group who considered *al-amr wa al-nahy* to be subject to the aforementioned conditions, and moreover did not go beyond the confines of the heart and the tongue for its sake. Ahmad b. Hanbal is counted among them. According to this group, a bloody uprising for the sake of struggling against unlawful activities is not permissible. The Salafiyyah, which also includes the people of *hadith,* did not deem it appropriate to resort to the use of force against political authority, even in the event that people are murdered and family members are harmed, in order to preserve social peace, to keep social order unharmed, and to prevent the community from breaking up due to disorder and corruption. Regarding this principle as one of the five fundamentals that complement the faith, the Mu'tazilah held that to make the good prevail in social life and to avoid the evil, gentle language or method should first be used; if it is not effective, then a harsh expression may be employed; and if this does not prevail, then hand or force (sword) are to be used until the goal has been achieved. The Mu'tazilah accepted the conditions for *al-amr wa al-nahy*, but, not limiting to the heart and the tongue, maintained that if the unlawful practices become common, or if the state is oppressive and unjust, it is obligatory for Muslims to rise in armed revolt. The Mu'tazilah perceived this principle as the legitimate source of revolt during the Umayyad period and determined the method and conditions of revolting against the government in accordance with this principle. However, when they rose to power during the reign of the 'Abbasid caliph Ma'mūn, the Mu'tazilah made use of the same principle as a means to coerce others into accepting their views. For them, in order to rise against the authority, certain conditions such as "just imam," "loyal and sincere followers," and "hope of success" must obtain.

In modern times, it is possible to consider within the extension of this principle the activities of the opposition parties in politics and the activities of civil organizations for protecting the rights of the individual in Muslim societies.

MAHMUT AY

Further Reading

Abū Ya'lā al-Farrā'. *Al-Mu'tamad fī Usūl al-Dīn*. Beirut, 1974, 194–199.

Al-Ash'arī. *Maqālāt al-Islāmiyyīn*. Wiesbaden, 1963, ii, 451–452.

Bayjūrī. *Tuhfat al-Murīd*. Beirut, 1983, 202–203.

Cagirici, Mustafa. "Emir bi'l Ma'ruf Nehiy ani'l Munker." *EI* (TDV) xi. (1995): 138–141.

Cook, Michael. *Commanding Right and Forbidding Wrong in Islamic Thought*. Cambridge, MA, 2000.

Fakhr al-Dīn al-Rāzī. *Asās al-Taqdīs*. Cairo, 1328 H, 88–89.

Al-Ghazālī. *Ihyā' 'Ulūm al-Dīn*. Cairo, 1967, ii, 179, 155, 455.

Ibn Manzūr. *Lisān al-'Arab*. Beirut, 1956, ix, 238–240.

Ibn Taymiyyah. *al-Hisbah fi al-Islām*. Cairo, 1318 H, 54–55 ff.

Jalāl al-Dīn al-'Umarī. *al-Amr bi al-Ma'rūf wa al-Nahy 'an al-Munkar*. Kuwait, 1400 H.

Al-Juwaynī. *Kitāb al-Irshād*. Cairo, 1950, 368–370.

Madelung, W. "Amr bi Ma'rūf." *EIR*, i, 92–95.

Mahmut Ay. *Mu'tazilah and Politics*. Istanbul, 2002, 193–203.

Al-Mas'ūdī. *Murūj al-Dhahab*. Beirut, 1965, iii, 154.

Al-Māwardī. *Ahkām al-Sultāniyyah*. Cairo, 1973, 240.

Al-Mukhtasar fī Usūl al-Dīn. In *Rasā'il al-'Adl wa al-Tawhīd*, ed. Muhammad Ammarah, 248–249. Cairo, 1971, i.

Al-Qādī 'Abd al-Jabbār. *Sharh al-Usūl al-Khamsah*. (Cairo, 1988), 741–756.

Rāghib al-Isfahānī. *al-Mufradāt fī Gharīb al-Qur'ān*. Cairo, 1980, entries of "arf" and "nkr."

Tahānawī. *Kashshāf Istilāhāt al-Funūn*. Istanbul, 1984, ii, 994, 997, 1003.

Wensinck, A.J. *The Muslim Creed*. Cambridge, MA, 1932, 106–107.

Al-Zamakhsharī. *al-Kashshāf 'an Haqā'iq Ghawāmid al-Tanzīl wa 'Uyūn al-Aqāwīl fī Wujūh al-Ta'wīl*. Beirut, 1947, i, 396 ff.

COMMENTARY

Commentary is a type of scholarship that attempts to elucidate, complement, correct, or even sophisticate an existing body of literature. Sometimes the underlying assumption is that the body of literature in question requires a commentary because it was produced at such a time in the past that its meanings and/ or historical circumstances are concealed to the current reader or the knowledge in it requires updating. However, in some cases, commentaries are authored precisely to infuse into that body of literature ideas and beliefs that are not there in the first place, and subsequently make it harmonious with those championed by the commentators. Commentaries are extremely important for the proper understanding of the dissemination of knowledge in the medieval Islamic world. Invariably, it was in commentaries that authors embedded their own views and sometimes corrections on earlier knowledge and dogma and opened new venues for the succeeding generations. In medieval Islamic scholarship, hundreds of commentaries were produced on a variety of religious and secular subjects, ranging from the Qur'an (being the most prestigious subject to compile a commentary on), Hadith, Sufism, and theology, to grammar, poetry, adab, and science.

Qur'an

A commentary on the Qur'an usually engages one or more of the following issues: meaning(s) of particular words and expressions, grammar and proper reading, circumstances of revelation, abrogating and abrogated verses, and political or theological implications of particular verses. The earliest Qur'an commentators from the first century of Islam (seventh century CE) seem not to have had a comprehensive approach to interpreting Islam's scripture. Rather, their commentary glosses are fragmentary and tend to represent one particular point of view. Later, in the second/eighth century, more comprehensive commentaries with a variety of opinions started to appear, such as the *Tafsir* of 'Abd al-Razzaq al-San'ani (d. 211/826). Commentaries on the grammar of the Qur'an also started to appear around that time, such as *Ma'ani al-Qur'an* by al-Farra' (d. 207/822). The most notable commentary from the medieval period is that of al-Tabari (d. 310/923), entitled *Jami' al-bayan 'an ta'wil ay al-Qur'an*, which preserves a large number of commentary glosses by scholars from the first two centuries of Islam whose commentaries, if they ever existed as individual compilations, are otherwise lost to us. Other influential commentaries include *Haqa'iq al-tafsir* by al-Sulami (d. 412/1021), which extracts the "hidden" mystical meanings of the verses of the Qur'an; *al-Kashf wa-l-bayan 'an tafsir al-Qur'an* by al-Tha 'labi (d. 425/1037), which incorporates Sunni, Shi'i, and Sufi interpretations but leaves out, intentionally it seems, the Mu'tazila views; *al-Tibyan fi tafsir al-Qur'an* by Abu Ja'far al-Tusi (d. 460/1068), which preserves the traditions of several Twelver Shi'i imams; *al-Kashshaf* by al-Zamakhshari (d. 538/1144), which preserves moderate views of Mu'tazila commentators; and *Tafsir al-Jalalayn,* started by Jalal al-Din al-Mahalli (d. 864/1459) and completed by his student Jalal al-Din al-Suyuti (d. 911/1505), which is the most popular commentary in the Arab world because of its conciseness.

Hadith

The Qur'an was not the only religious text that received the attention of medieval Muslim commentators. The Hadith, perceived by most Muslims as second in importance to the Qur'an, received its share of commentaries. Such works were authored precisely to verify the authenticity of the *hadith*s they contain and their transmission, as well as the circumstances that allegedly led the Prophet Muhammad to utter them. For instance, several commentaries were authored on the famous *Sahih* of al-Bukhari (d. 256/870); the most notable of them is *Fath al-bari bi-sharh sahih al-Bukhari* by Ibn Hajar al-'Asqalani (d. 852/1448). Similarly, commentaries were written on the *Muwatta'* of Malik ibn Anas (d. 179/796), like the one by al-Zurqani (d. 1122/1710), and on the *Sahih* of Muslim (d. 261/875), like the one by al-Nawawi (d. 676/1277). Commentaries on Hadith were also authored by grammarians who were eager to explain away certain grammatical inaccuracies in the words attributed to the Prophet Muhammad, like the one by Ibn Malik (d. 672/1274) on the *Sahih* of al-Bukhari.

Sufism and Theology

Sufi commentaries were written sometimes to "unveil" the mystical treasures hidden in a given text, like those on the Qur'an, but were also authored to clarify and simplify a complicated, difficult-to-comprehend, mystical language for the novice mystics. For instance, Shams al-Din Shahrazuri (fl. seventh/thirteenth century) wrote a commentary on the Sufi gnostic work *Hikmat al-ishraq* of Shihab al-Din al-Suhrawardi (d. 587/1191). *Ihya' 'ulum al-din* of al-Ghazali (d. 505/1111) was the subject of a major commentary by al-Zabidi (d. 1205/1791), entitled *Ithaf al-sada al-muttaqin bi-sharh ihya' 'ulum al-din*. Several commentaries were authored on *al-Futuhat al-makkiyya* by Ibn 'Arabi (d. 638/1240), including *Sharh mushkil al-futuhat al-makiyya* by 'Abd al-Karim al-Jili (d. ca. 832/1428). Similarly, the mystical poem *Qasidat al-Burda* of al-Busiri (d. 694/1294) was the subject of several commentaries. Theological commentaries were also written on topics ranging from the one hundred names of God, such as *Lawami' al-bayyinat sharh asma' Allah ta'ala wa-l-sifat* by Fakhr al-Din al-Razi (d. 606/1210), to other theological compilations, such as the several commentaries written on the *Kitab al-fiqh al-akbar* attributed to Abu Hanifa (d. 150/767).

Grammar, Poetry, and Adab

Besides the several commentaries on the grammar of the Qur'an, one can mention the *Alfiyya* of Ibn Malik (d. 672/1274), a thousand-line poem (a summary of his 2757-line poem) on Arabic grammar, which received more than forty commentaries, the most notable of which is that of Ibn 'Aqil (d. 769/1367), which in turn received minor commentaries, like the one by al-Suyuti (d. 911/1505). The grammar book of Sibawayh (known as *Kitab Sibawayh*) also received several commentaries. Poetry, especially pre-Islamic poetry, received tremendous attention on the part of medieval commentators. For instance, several commentaries were produced on the seven or ten most-celebrated epics *(al-mu'allaqat)*. Other examples include commentaries on the poetry of al-Mutanabbi (d. 354/955), like *Sharh diwan al-Mutanabbi* by al-Wahidi (d. 468/1075), and on the celebrated *Diwan al-Hamasa*, a collection of poems attributed to Abu Tammam (d. 231/845). The belletristic masterpiece *Maqamat* of al-Hariri (d. 516/1122) received several commentaries as well.

Science and Philosophy

Science and philosophy received their share of commentaries, and it is in such commentaries that one is likely to encounter the original contribution of Muslim, Christian, and Jewish scholars from the medieval Islamic World, who corrected or elucidated the knowledge presented in earlier Greek and Arabic books. Because of their significance, some of these commentaries were translated into Latin in the late Middle Ages and during the Renaissance. Several commentaries were written on Ptolemy's *Almagest* on astronomy, and on Euclid's *Elements* on geometry. With respect to medicine, Ibn al-Nafis (d. 687/1288) probably stands out as one of the most prolific medieval commentators. He authored an extensive commentary on the medical encyclopedia *al-Qanun fi l-tibb* of Ibn Sina (d. 428/1037) and another commentary on the *Aphorisms*, the *Prognostics*, and *De natura hominis* of Hippocrates. Logic was also an attractive subject—Ibn Rushd (d. 595/1198) wrote on the *Logic* of Aristotle *(Sharh al-burhan li-Aristu)*; but it was Porphyry's *Isagogep* that received the most attention, like the commentary on it by the Nestorian monk Abu 'l-Faraj ibn al-Tayyib (d. 435/1043). In philosophy, Ibn Sina's two masterpieces, *Kitab al-Shifa'* and *Kitab al-isharat wa-l-tanbihat,* are the most original philosophical compilations ever produced in medieval Islam and feature extensive commentaries on the philosophies of Aristotle, Plotinus, and al-Farabi (d. 339/950).

SULEIMAN MOURAD

See also Scriptural Exegesis

Further Reading

Rippin, Andrew, ed. *The Qur'an: Formative Interpretation.* Aldershot, England: Ashgate, 1999.
Saleh, Walid. *The Formation of the Classical Tafsir Tradition: The Qur'an Commentary of al-Tha 'labi (d. 427/1035).* Leiden: Brill, 2004.

COMPANIONS OF THE PROPHET

The term *Companions* refers to anyone living in the original community of the Prophet, though the precise definition varies greatly. In Arabic sources, it is rendered *sahaba*. Companions are generally held in high esteem due to their close relationship to the Prophet. They are a source of prophetic traditions, as well as heroes and role models for later generations of Muslims.

Khadija, the Prophet's first wife, was the first to convert to the new faith in approximately 612 CE and may be considered the earliest Companion. She was followed by the prophet's nephew, 'Ali b. Abi Tâlib, the Prophet's adopted son Zayd, and Abû Bakr, who would later become the first caliph. The early conversion of influential and respected Quraysh, such as the Prophet's uncle, Hamza b. Abi Tâlib, and 'Umar b. al-Khattâb, helped establish respect for the new faith.

Many Companions faced persecution for their beliefs. At Mecca, most clans in Quraysh allowed the harassment and, in extreme cases, the torture and execution of kinsmen who converted to Islam. These circumstances led a large number to emigrate to Ethiopia in approximately 615. When the Banu Hâshim withdrew its protection of the prophet after the death of Abû Tâlib, the Prophet and most remaining Companions emigrated to Yathrib, to the north of Mecca, in 622.

The sanctuary at Yathrib, later called Medina, allowed the Muslim community to grow. Because belief in Islam rather than loyalty to a tribe or clan formed the basic bond in the new state, the closeness of companionship, often coinciding with priority in conversion, had important implications in deciding social and political rank. Many Medinese converts became close advisors of the Prophet despite their tribal origin. When the Prophet showed favors to later converts from among the Meccan nobility later in his life, many early converts, including those from Mecca, complained bitterly.

The decision, upon the death of the Prophet, to keep the Muslim community united politically ensured for several decades the primacy of Companions in Muslim government. The caliphate was established in the Quraysh. The first four caliphs, however, were all close Companions. The first caliph, Abû Bakr, was one of the earliest converts and had no important clan affiliation to aid his rise to power.

The caliph 'Umar b. al-Khattâb formalized the privileged status of Companions. He created a dîwân, which fixed the stipends of Muslims according to the approximate date of their conversion and service to Islam. Those who joined the community before the battle of Badr in 624 received higher stipends than those who converted before the Pledge of Hudabiyya or the Conquest of Mecca.

Much of the prestige and authority of Companions, nevertheless, remained charismatic. As the Muslim conquests brought large numbers of countries and peoples into the Muslim fold, either as converts or *dhimmis*, Companions provided an important link to the original Muslim community at Mecca and Medina. They held themselves as the guardians of the true Islamic tradition. People turned to them for arbitration much as they once turned to the Prophet. They did not hesitate to criticize even a caliph where they deemed him in error.

These different views of companionship led to open conflict during the reign of the caliph 'Uthmân b. 'Affân and the First Fitna (656–661 C.E.). Although 'Uthmân was himself a Companion, many Companions turned the community against him for his innovations and his favoritism of his clan in dispensing favors and appointments. The Companion and son of the first caliph, Muhammad b. Abi Bakr, led a faction that stormed his house and killed him. In the First Fitna, which followed, Companions led and fought on all major sides. At the Battle of Camel, the celebrated Companions Talha b. 'Ubayd Allâh and al-Zubayr b. 'Awwâm and the Prophet's favorite wife, 'Â'isha bt. Abi Bakr fought against the Prophet's nephew, 'Ali b. Abi Tâlib. In the end, Mu'âwiya b. Abi Sufyân, the son of one of the Prophet's Meccan persecutors, became caliph.

Subsequent years saw the sharp decline in the political influence of Companions, but not in their general esteem. When Mu'âwiya died in 680, his son succeeded him as caliph. Although most Companions would have resisted the innovation of hereditary succession, very few survived. Those who remained had been very young at the time of the Prophet's death and were known mainly for their activities since that time as representatives of one faction or another. Hussayn b. 'Ali, for example, had become the recognized leader of the Banû Hâshim, representing the Prophet's extended family and descendants. He revolted, but his following could not match the resources of the caliphal state. He was quickly massacred.

Nostalgia for an earlier era, nevertheless, kept alive veneration for the memory of Companions. A number of piety-minded individuals and groups emulated their simple austere piety. This piety inspired new forms of popular activism. Individuals such as al-Hasan al-Basrî, Ibn Sîrîn, and Ibrahîm al-Nakha'î became renowned for their modest lifestyles, religious knowledge, and frank judgments. Khârijis, promoting a more radical agenda, disavowed the corrupt centers of caliphal power. They formed small bands in the countryside and waged ceaseless battle against the government.

The development of Islamic law in the eighth, ninth, and tenth centuries greatly elevated the moral status of Companions among Sunni Muslims. As scholars sought to validate traditions of the Prophet upon which much of Sunni law rested, they resolved the character of every Companion to have been unimpeachable. If any report could be reliably traced back to one, then it was presumed to be true. This doctrine became known as the "Rectification of the Companions" *(ta 'dil al-sahaba)*. It eliminated the need to discuss and judge numerous controversies that had divided different groups of Companions and which may have called into question fundamental principles of belief. It led, nevertheless, to disputes over who actually qualified as a Companion, with some insisting a candidate must have attained a mature age or have visited the Prophet before his or her death.

The doctrine had a profound impact on Sunni historiography. Later Sunni historians treat early controversies with great unease. Their descriptions are generally terse. Where they must, they choose reports that are theologically sound and refrain from assigning blame to any known Companion. While they admit something happened, they often claim the reasons for such a thing happening are not known. They criticize earlier historians as indiscriminant in their choice of reports, which ascribe a wide range of motives and calculations to many Companions.

At the same time, while early writers subsumed both Companions and subsequent transmitters of prophetic traditions in their biographical dictionaries, later writers sometimes devoted dictionaries to the lives of Companions exclusively. The later works attempt to decide definitively who was a Companion and to assert their excellent character beyond any doubt. They often add anecdotal information absent from earlier sources without giving documentation. Ibn al-Athir's discussion of Talha b. 'Ubayd Allâh and al-Zubayr b. 'Awwâm illustrates this tendency.

He mentions the great service each provided for Islam, the favors the Prophet bestowed upon them that recognized this service, and the excellent reputations they enjoyed among their peers. However, when he reaches the Battle of Camel, where both opposed the Prophet's nephew and the caliph 'Ali b. Abi Tâlib, he gives only a lengthy account about how each, upon meeting 'Ali on the battlefield, withdrew rather than fight their fellow Companion. Both were later killed against 'Ali's wishes. Despite the detail, Ibn al-Athir never gives the sources of his information.

Shi'is, in contrast, maintained a more critical perspective. Their faith emphasized their loyalty to the Prophet's descendants through 'Ali b. Abi Tâlib and his daughter Fatima. They held most, but not all, Companions to be virtuous. As a group, they failed to support 'Ali's claims to the caliphate. Many were responsible for acts of violence against 'Ali's supporters. The caliph 'Uthmân, for example, exiled the prominent Abû Dharr, thereby bringing about his early death. Talha, al-Zubayr, and Mu'âwiya are also objects of reprobation. Shi'i historical writers, as a result, extol the virtues of 'Ali and his followers but transmit more freely than Sunni sources reports that give more human characterizations, if not impugn the integrity, of many other Companions.

STUART D. SEARS

Primary Sources

Ibn al-Athîr, Usd al-Ghâba fî ma'rafat al-æaìâba. Ibn Sa'd, Tabaqât al-Kubrâ. Ibn al-Ìajar al-'Asqalânî, and al-Iæâba fî tamyîz al-æaìâba. Ibn Hisham. *The Life of Muhammad: A Translation of Ibn Iæiâq's Sîrat rasûl Allâh*, ed. and trans. A. Guillaume. Oxford, [1955] 2001.

Further Reading

Coulson, N. *A History of Islamic Law*. Delhi, [1964] 1997.
Hallaq, W. *The Origins and Evolution of Islamic Law*. Cambridge, UK, 2005.
Hodgson, M.G.S. *The Venture of Islam: Conscience and History in a World Civilization*. Vol I. Chicago, 1974.
Kennedy, H. *The Prophet and the Age of the Caliphates*. London and New York, 1986.
Shoufani, E. *Al-Riddah and the Muslim Conquest of Arabia*. Beirut and Toronto, 1972.

CONCUBINAGE

In the Muslim world, a concubine was a female slave who had a sexual relationship with her Muslim master. According to Islamic law, concubines, like slaves in general, had to be of non-Muslim origin, on the basis that they were legitimate booty from holy war.

There were benefits and drawbacks for both the master and the concubine. For the master, control over the concubine was much greater than that of a wife. He could initiate and terminate the relationship at will and could have as many concubines as he could afford, unlike the limit of four wives. He also did not have to pledge a dowry to his partner, which wives would often use as a bargaining chip for their own well-being. This relationship of a concubine was also widely respected in Islamic law and most often carried no social stigma. The downside for the master included three points: (1) the initial cost of a slave was often greater than a dowry, (2) he had to respect the offspring of a concubine as his own child, and (3) he owed basic obligations to humane treatment for the concubine as a slave. The concubine often had little power, except when she bore her master a child. At this time she held the status of *umm-i veled*, namely, a mother who could advocate the well-being of his child. The concubine faced many more disadvantages, as she had no power to resist the advances of his master and was subject to his mercy for her financial well-being, including inheritance rights, except for any children. If the concubinage was terminated, she had to wait forty-five days before she could enter a relationship with a second party.

Concubinage was common in the Muslim world, beginning with the initial Arab conquests when a massive influx of non-Muslim captives were taken. A booming trade of female slaves continued throughout the medieval period. Umayyads, 'Abbasids, Fatimids, Mamluks, the Crimean Tatars, Seljukids, and Ottomans alike often took the slaves from the Caucasus, the Crimea, western Ukraine, and the Balkans.

Concubinage was practiced at all levels of society. On a popular level, concubines were most often taken on the frontiers, where slaves were taken by armies, raiding forces, or slave traders. Concubines often had a strategic value for Muslim soldiers in a border garrison, as they could help establish a new social group that would help consolidate Muslim power in the region. This can be seen particularly in the Ottoman-area regions such as Tunis, western Anatolia, and the Balkans, where non-Muslim concubines bore a new Muslim generation that identified itself with the interest of the emerging regime. Concubines were commonly sold in market towns and large metropolitan areas. Many urban Muslim subjects saw concubines as an attractive relationship when the single female population was low.

The most famous concubines were those which rulers and high Muslim administrators took as their own. While a number of 'Abbasid and Mamluk rulers had concubine mothers, the Ottoman dynasty was by far the most concubine dominated. Sultans started to have concubines as consorts at least since the mid-fourteenth century, when Sultan Murad I fathered his son, the future Bayezid I, with a concubine. Sultans still occasionally took wives, however, since it could help cement regional alliances with outside dynasties. After the conquest of Constantinople in 1453, the Ottoman Sultans began to only have children from concubines, since having a wife entailed granting significant privileges to someone besides the sultan. Concubines also fit very well within an emerging palace system in Istanbul, which regulated all members as slaves of circumstance. Concubines who inhabited the harem, or female section of the palace, and had relations with the sultan had the right to bear only one male child. Having such a child was a greatly sought honor. Yet their male children competed with all their half-brothers to become the next sovereign. In the late fifteenth and sixteenth centuries, a son who succeeded to the throne regularly murdered all of his half-brothers in the name of a unified sultanic authority. If the son was somehow able to become a successor, the concubine, as the mother of the sultan, could exert enormous privilege, including control over all female members of the court. Even if she did not succeed in this ultimate aim, a concubine held an extremely influential social position that compared with many of the greatest Ottoman military and administrative officials. Many also were eventually married to many of these officials, as they too were originally slaves of the palace.

YORK ALLAN NORMAN

Further Reading

Brockopp, Jonathan E. *Slavery in Islamic Law: An Examination of Early Maliki Jurisprudence.* Unpublished dissertation. Yale University, 1995.

Brunschvig, R. "Abd." In *Encyclopedia of Islam.* Online edition, 2001.

Pierce, Leslie P. *The Imperial Harem Women and Sovereignty in the Ottoman Empire.* New York and Oxford: Oxford University Press, 1993.

Rapoport, Yossef. *Marriage and Divorce in the Muslim Near East, 1250–1517.* Unpublished dissertation. Princeton University, June 2002.

Semerdjian, Vivian Elyse. *"Off the Straight Path": Gender, Public Morality and Legal Administration in Ottoman Haleppo, Syria.* Unpublished dissertation. Georgetown University, October 2002.

THE CONSTITUTION OF MEDINA

The Constitution of Medina is the modern name for an ancient Muslim document embedded in the text of the biography of the Prophet Muhammad by Ibn Ishaq (d. AH 151/768 CE) in the recension of Ibn Hisham (d. 218/833). The document consists of a set of articles that bind the subscribing tribal groupings in the oasis of Medina to a single polity through a strong mutual alliance that is both offensive and defensive. Each clan remains a separate constituent unit of the new polity, with accountability to the whole group and responsibility for the actions of its members. No member clan is to shelter or protect anyone betraying or acting against the Medinan polity, particularly the Qurashi enemies of the Muslims that had recently arrived from Mecca. Nevertheless, the right of protecting other outsiders is accorded to all individual tribal members according to existing custom, except that a woman may only be granted that status with the approval of her own clan.

As a collectivity, the members of the Medinan polity are all identified as believers (*mu'minun*) and one community (*umma*), whether Muslims or Jews, reflecting perhaps the situation shown in Qur'an 2:62, 3:64, and 5:69, among other verses. That is, in opposition to the pagans, all of the members of the Medinan polity believe in God and the Last Day, providing an ideological basis for the polity. Also, the constitution declares the inner part (*jawf*) of Medina an inviolable sanctuary (*haram*) like Mecca. This declaration further emphasizes the establishment of a zone of safety and peace among the parties to the agreement. The constitution authorizes little internal political structure or enforcement mechanism. Such central authority as exists appears limited to the Prophet Muhammad, who is the final arbiter of disputes that may arise, including those concerning the interpretation of the document, and the Prophet alone having the decisive authority to authorize offensive military expeditions in case of war. He lacks, however, the power to conscript troops, as the permissibility of holding back from fighting is clearly stated. Thus, overall the document pictures a federation of tribes more akin to a republic than an autocracy.

Although scholars disagree about whether this document was written all at once or added to from an original base, most likely all of it dates from shortly after the arrival of the Prophet Muhammad in Medina in 1/622, and certainly it was completed by his death in 11/632. This certainty about the earliness of its date arises because in it the Prophet is not given a clearly sovereign or commanding position as he later attained; the Quraysh, who later became honored nobles, are shown only to be the enemy; and the Jews are included in the polity as allies and members, all suggesting the situation at the beginning of the Muslim era. Despite changes as the Prophet's authority grew, the document probably remained in force, for the Medinan polity remained rather rudimentary right up to his death. Thus, as shown by the late verses in Qur'an 9:38–50, 81–96, and 118–122, the Prophet had to use exhortation and lacked the power to actually conscript troops right to the end, exactly as in the constitution.

For modern Muslims, the Constitution of Medina has been hailed as a predecessor to modern constitutionalism and rule of law equivalent to the Magna Carta and is often cited as a key precedent for constitutionalism, rule of law, collective leadership, and democratizing reform.

KHALID YAHYA BLANKINSHIP

Further Reading

Humphreys, R. Stephen. *Islamic History: A Framework for Inquiry*. Revised ed. Princeton, NJ: Princeton University Press, 1991, 92–98.
Ibn Hisham, 'Abd al-Malik. *The Life of Muhammad: A Translation of Ibn Ishâq's Sîrat Rasûl Allâh*. Translated by Alfred Guillaume. Oxford: Oxford University Press, 1955, 231–233.

CONSULTATION, OR *SHURA*

The word *shura* occurs in the Qur'an and means "consultation." Two verses specifically refer to this concept. The first (Q 3:158–159) states, "So pass over [their faults], and ask for [God's] forgiveness and consult them in matters; then, when you have made a decision, put your trust in God." The second verse (Q 42:38) runs, "And [they are] those who answer the call of their Lord and perform prayer, and who conduct their affairs by mutual consultation, and who spend of what We have bestowed upon them."

Consultation (also referred to as *mashwara* and *mashura*) has been regarded as obligatory *(wajib)* or simply recommended *(mandub)*, depending on the circumstances. The predominant sentiment in the literature is that *shura* as mutual consultation in various spheres (political–administrative, communal, military, familial) is the preferred and desirable method of resolving matters. In the political realm, it is often considered a duty incumbent on the ruler to confer with knowledgeable advisors. For example, the Qur'an commentator Muhammad b. Ahmad al-Qurtubi (d. AH 671/1272 CE) states, "It is the obligation of the rulers to consult the scholars on matters unknown to them and in religious matters not clear to them. [They should] consult the leaders of the army in matters having to do with war, and leaders of the people in administrative issues, as well as teachers, ministers, and governors in matters that have to do with the welfare of the country and its development."

Shura was known in the pre-Islamic period as well. Arab tribes before Islam had a loosely formed council of elders called *shura* (also known as *majlis* or *mala'*), which adjudicated intratribal and intertribal matters through consultation. Like a number of other Jahili virtues and customs, the Qur'an endorsed *shura* as an acceptable and normative practice within Islam. This is evidenced in Muhammad's own adherence to this principle in variegated circumstances and the precedent established by the first two caliphs in particular, as documented in *hadith*, biographical, and historical literature.

For example, during the preparations for the battle of Badr, the Prophet is said to have consulted with Habbab al-Mundhir, recognized for his military expertise, and with Salman al-Farisi before the Battle of Khandaq in 627; on the latter's recommendation the Prophet had a ditch dug around Medina, which successfully prevented a potentially disastrous siege by the pagan Meccans. Before concluding the Treaty of Hudaybiyya in 630, Muhammad conferred with his Companions on the provisions of the treaty and the propriety of acceding to them. Numerous other instances of prophetic consultative activities are to be found in these literatures, creating, in fact, a powerful precedent for succeeding generations. The Companion Abu Hurayra is thus said to have remarked, "I did not see anyone more [predisposed] to consultation *(mushawara or mashwara)* with his Companions than the Prophet."

After Muhammad's death in 632, Abu Bakr publicly declared his commitment to the principle of *shura*. The historian al-Tabari (d. 310/923) refers to the Saqifa episode when Abu Bakr got up to address the Ansar, who at first had opposed his nomination as the caliph. Abu Bakr reassured them by saying that he would not fail to consult them with regard to political matters, nor would he adjudicate matters without them.

The most famous *shura* in the sense of a consultative body is the six-man electoral council set up by 'Umar b. al-Khattab in 644, as he lay on his deathbed, to elect a candidate who would succeed him. The deliberations of this council brought 'Uthman, the third caliph, to power.

As dynastic rule became the norm after the death of 'Ali in 661, the last "Rightly Guided Caliph," invocation of *shura* as a mandated social and political practice became a way to register disapproval of a political culture that had progressively grown more authoritarian by the 'Abbasid period (750–1258). Therefore, some political and religious dissident groups, like the Khawarij, made *shura* their clarion call against dynastic government starting in the Umayyad period. Certain genres of ethical and humanistic literature *(adab)* continued to extol the merits of consultation in various spheres, including bureaucratic, military, and, of course, political administration.

To this day, *shura* as a religiopolitical principle resonates strongly with a significant cross-section of Muslims, as it had with a considerable number of medieval Muslims, representing just, consultative government as opposed to arbitrary despotism *(istibdad)*. In the contemporary period, reformist Muslims tend to conflate *shura* with the modern concept of democracy.

ASMA AFSARUDDIN

Further Reading:

Ayalon, A. "Shura." In *The Encyclopaedia of Islam*. New ed. C. E. Bosworth et al., vol. 9, 505–506. Leiden and London, 1997.

Lewis, B. "Mashwara." In *The Encyclopaedia of Islam*. New edition H. Gibb et al. Leiden and London.

Muslih, Muhammad. "Democracy." In *Oxford Encyclopedia of the Modern Islamic World*. Vol. 1, 356–360. New York and Oxford: Oxford University Press, 1995.

COPTIC LANGUAGE

The latest stage of the Egyptian language, Coptic emerged in the second century CE and lasted as a spoken and written language until the eleventh century, after which it remained in use only for liturgical purposes by the Copts of Egypt. From the ninth century onward, Arabic gradually replaced Coptic; today, Arabic is the primary language used in the Coptic Church.

The term *Coptic* is derived from Greek word *Aiguptios* (Egyptian), which was subsequently brought into Arabic as *qibt*. After the conquests of Alexander in 332 BCE, Greek became the administrative language of Egypt and eventually superseded the use of the Egyptian language, which came to exist only in spoken form. Greek language had the advantage of a simple alphabet (the Demotic script had already supplanted the traditional hieroglyphic script); its practical advantage was significant. By the end of the first century CE, in unknown circumstances, the Coptic alphabet had emerged. The Coptic alphabet borrowed the twenty-four letters of the Greek alphabet and added seven letters from Demotic (Egyptian) for sounds found in Egyptian but not in Greek. Although the vocabulary of Coptic was largely Egyptian, many words were borrowed (especially in biblical and liturgical texts) from Greek. Some ten major regional dialects of Coptic have been identified;

among these, the Sahidic Coptic of Upper (that is, southern) Egypt and the Bohairic dialect of Lower (that is, northern) Egypt are most important. Sahidic Coptic was the primary dialect for written literary texts (and documents such as contracts, wills, and letters) until the eleventh century; Bohairic emerged somewhat later, was the only dialect to survive after the ninth century, and continues in limited liturgical use until today.

Of the diverse texts produced in Coptic (including documentary and literary texts), the vast majority pertain to Christianity in Egypt; indeed, many of the earliest extant texts in Coptic are Sahidic translations from Greek of biblical books (from both the New Testament and the Septuagint). In addition, apocryphal works, martyrologies, monastic rules and letters, hagiographical literature, patristic works, and other ecclesiastical texts came to be translated into Coptic during the third century and beyond.

One of the most important discoveries for the study of Coptic and the history of Christianity was a cache of thirteen codices (containing fifty-two individual works) found in 1945 at Nag Hammadi in Upper Egypt. Many of the texts in this collection of fourth-century CE Coptic translations of Greek works (which came to be called the Nag Hammadi Library) have been associated with a form of Christianity loosely identified as gnostic in orientation. In texts such as The Apocryphon of John, the Testimony of Truth, the Gospel of Thomas, and many others, there emerges a privileging of esoteric knowledge necessary for salvation.

Literary works originally composed in Coptic began to appear in the fourth-century Pachomian monastic literature and, more importantly, in the writings of the fifth-century abbot of the White Monastery, Shenoute. Although the large literary corpus of Shenoute has yet to be published in a critical edition, much debate has circled around his pioneering use of Coptic for his theological compositions. Was his decision, for example, influenced by his hostility to classical Greek culture? Or was it motivated by his desire to reach a local population that could not understand Greek? When so much of our knowledge of Coptic is mediated through a bilingual lens (as in the many Greek–Coptic bilingual manuscripts), Shenoute's choice of Coptic over Greek deserves continued study.

After the Arab conquests of the seventh century, the subsequent increased Muslim immigration to Egypt, and the conversion of many Copts to Islam, Coptic gradually gave way to Arabic. The transition is readily apparent in the numerous extant Coptic–Arabic bilingual manuscripts. Such manuscripts have provided an important source for the study of ancient Egyptian and Coptic. Today the academic study of Coptic is particularly vibrant among scholars in the fields of religion (especially the history of early Christianity) and papyrology (the study of ancient papyrus remains). Among the Copts of Egypt today, there have been attempts to revive the use of liturgical Coptic, but Arabic continues to be the primary language of Egypt, even in the Coptic Church.

KIM HAINES-EITZEN

See also Alexander; Arabic; Copts; Greek

Further Reading

Bagnall, Roger S. *Egypt in Late Antiquity*. Princeton, NJ: Princeton University Press, 1993.
Bishai, Wilson B. "The Transition from Coptic to Arabic." *The Muslim World* 53 (1963): 145–150.
Metzger, Bruce M. *The Early Versions of the New Testament: Their Origins, Transmission and Limitations*. Oxford: Clarendon Press, 1977.
Pagels, Elaine. *The Gnostic Gospels*. New York: Random House, 1979.
Watterson, Barbara. *Coptic Egypt*. Edinburgh: Scottish Academic Press, 1988.

COPTS

Origins and Theology

The Coptic Orthodox Church, the native church of Egypt, is one of the oldest Christian churches in the world. The word *Copt* is derived from the Greek word *Aigyptos,* which was in turn derived from "Hikaptah," one of the names for Memphis, the first capital of ancient Egypt.

Tradition holds that the church in Egypt was founded by the evangelist St. Mark in the first or third year of the reign of the Roman emperor Claudius, in 41/42 or 43/44 CE, and Mark is considered the first in an unbroken chain of 117 patriarchs. The new faith spread quickly throughout Egypt, and Alexandria, its capital, soon became a major spiritual center of the Christian church. The Catechetical School in Alexandria, the most important institution of learning in early Christendom, fostered such seminal theological scholars as Clement, Origen, Athanasius, and Cyril of Alexandria. The school worked to prove that reason and revelation, philosophy and theology were not only compatible but also essential for each others' comprehension.

The Egyptian church, like others, suffered intense persecution from its rulers, the Roman government,

prior to the 313 Edict of Milan, which granted freedom of worship to Christians within the Roman Empire. In fact, the Coptic calendar, called the Era of the Martyrs, begins August 29, 284, the beginning of the reign of the great persecutor Diocletian. As a result, the concept and ideal of martyrdom is extremely central to the Church's ethos. When "opportunities" for martyrdom diminished, the Egyptian Christians' energies were channeled toward its symbolic substitutes: asceticism and monasticism.

The monastic movement was the truly outstanding contribution of the Egyptian church to world Christianity. The origins of the movement are traditionally ascribed to St. Anthony, who practiced a rigorous asceticism in the Egyptian desert in the third century. All Christian monasticism stems, either directly or indirectly, from the Egyptian example.

From its position at the center of the world Christian church, the Church of Alexandria became marginalized in the fifth century, when its members ended up on the losing side of the controversies over the nature of Christ, which had been raging for hundreds of years. Cyril of Alexandria, concerned to emphasize the divinity of Jesus Christ, refused to accept the pronunciation of the Council of Chalcedon in 451, which proclaimed that Christ was truly God and truly man, and as such possessed two natures (human and divine). By the sixth century, those who rejected Chalcedon had consolidated into three great monophysite ("one nature") churches: the Coptic Church with its daughter church, the Ethiopian; the Syrian Jacobite Church; and the Armenian Church.

History from the Islamic Conquest through the Mamluk Period

The disaffection felt by the Copts for their Chalcedonian–Byzantine (Roman Empire successor) rulers contributed to their lack of resistance to the Islamic conquest of 642. In return for payment of a special poll tax, the Copts were classified as protected people *(ahl al-dhimma)*. The native patriarch Benjamin I, who had been in hiding from the persecution of the Byzantine-appointed patriarch, was encouraged to emerge and reassume the leadership of his church. There was no attempt to force the Copts to convert to Islam; indeed, conversion was rather discouraged because it decreased the base of those liable for the poll tax and thus state revenue.

The Byzantine system of taxation, combining a land tax with a poll tax (for non-Muslims), was basically maintained, though streamlined and centralized. Copts continued to staff the tax and administrative

Woman and her lover in a garden. Panel of woven Coptic textile. Fatimid period, eleventh century. Credit: Erich Lessing/Art Resource, NY. Museum of Islamic Art, Cairo, Egypt.

bureaus, except at the highest levels, and when the official language of the administration was changed from Greek to Arabic in 705, the Copts learned Arabic and maintained their predominance in that field, increasing the speed of Arabization and the transition of Coptic to a purely liturgical language.

Taxation was heavy, leading to a number of tax rebellions in the eighth and ninth centuries, the most serious being the Bashmuric Rebellion of 829–830.

The harsh suppression of these revolts, combined with the heavier taxes and other social disabilities endured by the Copts, contributed to an increased pace of conversion to Islam. Some believe that by the end of this period the Copts' shift from majority to minority had already occurred, while others place that milestone later, in the Mamluk period.

During the Fatimid period (969–1171), the Copts, if not the majority, were still a substantial minority of the population. While still in the minority, the Copts flourished, participating actively in the social, artistic, and economic life of the country and sporadically even reaching the highest ranks of the government. This era of tolerance was not unmarred, however; the persecution of the caliph al-Hakim (r. 996–1021) is one such example.

The advent of the Crusades led to a deterioration of the position of the Copts, who were suspected of sympathizing with their co-religionists (the Muslims being unfamiliar with the doctrinal differences between the Copts and the Western Christians). In fact, the Crusades were disastrous for the Copts, as the Crusaders scorned them as heretics and forbade them to make their accustomed pilgrimages to Jerusalem.

The thirteenth century, despite its turbulence, turned out to be the great century of Copto-Arabic literature. Led by the four Awlad al-'Assal, brothers theological, linguistic, and historical scholarship, as well as literature, enjoyed a renaissance.

The deterioration of the Copts' situation, however, intensified under the rule of the Mamluks (1250–1517), perhaps due to their perception of themselves as the "defenders of Islam" against outside threats such as the Mongols and the Crusaders. Six hundred years after the conquest, the Copts still filled the ranks of the bureaucracy, for which they were considered to have a natural affinity. Under this regime, most of the bureaucrats had converted to Islam, but their sincerity was doubted and they were still labeled Copts. On numerous occasions the government dismissed the Copts en masse from their bureaucratic posts, only to be forced to reinstate them in the face of the ensuing administrative chaos.

If the Copts were not already a minority before this time, the numerous conversions brought on by the difficult conditions of the Mamluk period assured that they were so by the end of it. The core who remained have clung to their faith and traditions, maintaining their self-awareness as a distinct community that persists to this day.

MARLIS J. SALEH

Further Reading

Atiya, Aziz Suryal. *A History of Eastern Christianity*. London: Methuen, 1968.

——— (Ed). *The Coptic Encyclopedia*. 8 vols. New York: Macmillan, 1991.

Butcher, Edith Louisa. *The Story of the Church of Egypt: Being an Outline of the History of the Egyptians under Their Successive Masters from the Roman Conquest until Now*. 2 vols. London: Smith, Elder & Co., 1897.

Meinardus, Otto Friedrich August. *Christian Egypt: Faith and Life*. Cairo: American University in Cairo Press, 1970.

———. *Christian Egypt: Ancient and Modern*. Cairo: American University in Cairo Press, 1977.

Partrick, Theodore Hall. *Traditional Egyptian Christianity: A History of the Coptic Orthodox Church*. Greensboro, NC: Fisher Park Press, 1996.

Sawirus ibn al-Muqaffa', Bishop of el-Ashmunein [and continuators]. *Tarikh Batarikat al-Kanisah al-Misriyah (History of the Patriarchs of the Egyptian Church)*. Translated from the Arabic by Antoine Khater and O.H.E. KHS-Burmester. Cairo: Publications de la Société d'Archéologie Copte, 1943–1970.

"The Christian Coptic Orthodox Church of Egypt." Online at www.coptic.net (accessed November 19, 2003).

CORDOBA

Cordoba, named *Qurtuba* in Arabic and *Córdoba* in Spanish, was the political capital of al-Andalus during the Umayyad emirate and caliphate periods (AH seventh century first quarter of the eleventh century CE). Today it is the capital of the province of the same name. Cordoba is located in the southwest of the Spanish state, overlooking the medial course of the Guadalquivir River (*Wadi al-kabir* in Arabic) on both banks.

The rural area of the south of the city was called *qanbaniya*, approximately the same rural area known these days as "the Cordoba countryside." The plain known as *Fahs al-Ballut* (field of oaks) was located to the north of the province, where the little town of Pedroche is found (known by the Arabs as *Bitrawj* or *Bitrush.*). Until the thirteenth century, the Cordoban region was known for the wheat produced in its countryside and for the gardens and meadows that flanked the river. Nevertheless, the main areas of farming production of al-Andalus were found far from the capital, in the Seville highlands and the Toledo surroundings. Mining exploitation did not completely disappear with Cordoba's decadence, and there is evidence that still in the thirteenth century, Ovejo (located forty kilometers from the capital) was an important center of extraction of cinnabar, from which mercury is obtained.

The city was occupied by the Muslim armies in AH Shawwal of 92/July–August 711 CE. Leading these armies was the manumitted slave Mughith al-Rumi, deputy of Tariq ibn Ziyad. Governor al-Hurr ibn 'Abd al-Rahman al-Thaqafi (r. 97–100/716–719) transferred the capital of al-Andalus from Seville to Cordoba. His successor, al-Samh ibn Malik al-Jawlani (r. 100–102/719–721), repaired the old Roman bridge and some demolished parts of the protective enceinte. Al-Samh also founded the first Islamic cemetery of the city, the *Maqbarat al-rabad* (cemetery of the suburb), in the north bank of the river. In 133/750, governor Yusuf 'Abd al-Rahman (r. 129–138/ 747–756) bought the church of Saint Vincent to make it the first cathedral mosque *(al-jami')* of Cordoba. In 138/756, the governor was overthrown by the Umayyad prince 'Abd al-Rahman, who had managed to escape from the massacre of his family in Syria. 'Abd al-Rahman made Cordoba the administrative, political, military, religious, and cultural capital of his new emirate.

In this way, Cordoba came to monopolize most of the artistic activities. Its monumental center was composed of the fortress or alcazar (erected on the remains of the old Visigoth palace), the main mosque, and the bridge. The fortress and the mosque were located on the north bank of the Guadalquivir River, separated from the river by a terrace.

Work began on the mosque in 785, under the rule of 'Abd al-Rahman I, and it was enlarged on several occasions, as a parallel process to the city's growth and development, during the governments of 'Abd al-Rahman's successors, Hisham I (r. 172–180/788–796), 'Abd al-Rahman II (r. 206–238/822–852), and Muhammad I (r. 238–273/852–886). During the rule of 'Abd al-Rahman III (300–350/912–961)—the first to adopt the title of caliph—the city enjoyed its apogee. It was this same caliph who ordered the palatine city of Madinat al-Zahra' three to be built, approximately three miles northeast of Cordoba, at the foot of the mountains. The remains of this city were declared a national monument in 1923. Since then, some of its old rooms have been restored, among which the so-called Rich Room is especially significant. In regard to the old fortress of Cordoba, it has to be said that it was assigned to administrative uses when the court was transferred to Madinat al-Zahra'. Later on, when the palatine city was destroyed, the fortress was used again as the residence of the different governors of the city.

The most important enlargement of the main mosque of Cordoba was carried out by al-Hakam II (r. 350–366/961–976), son and successor of 'Abd al-Rahman III. The last big enlargement was commissioned by al-Mansur ibn Abi 'Amir, the mighty *visir* of Hisham II (r. 366–399/976–1009). Al-Mansur built his own palatine city, Madinat al-Zahira, east of Cordoba. This city underwent the same fate of Madinat al-Zahra' and was destroyed during the widespread revolts that took place at the beginning of the fifth/ eleventh century.

After the fall of the caliphate, Cordoba was ruled by the Jahwarids, between 1031 and 1070. It then became a part of the territories governed by the Seville monarch Banu 'Abbad. In 1091, Cordoba was taken by the Almoravids, who built the defensive wall of the eastern part of the city. In 1236, the city passed into Christian hands for good, after its conquest by Ferdinand III of Castile.

After the disappearance of the caliphate and the subsequent loss of Cordoba's political and economic hegemony, the city still kept its intellectual prestige, especially in the area of religious sciences. However, Cordoba was no longer the main representative of Andalusis' cultural life. Rather, it had to share this role with the capitals of the different petty kingdoms into which al-Andalus was fragmented from the eleventh century onward. The city recovered its capital status under the Almoravid rule, but the construction of monuments could never equal the emirate and caliphate periods. Almohads, for their part, clearly showed a preference for the city of Seville.

After the Christian conquests, the process of conversion of churches into mosques, which had taken place during the Islamic invasion of the Iberian Peninsula, was reversed. Cordoba was taken by the Christians in 1236, and its main mosque was converted into a cathedral. The modifications undergone by the mosque did partially alter its original shape. However, contrary to what happened to other mosques that underwent a similar transformation process, the Cordoba temple still keeps a markedly Arabic and Islamic character. This is probably related to the artistic and architectonic singularity of the building, the preferred object of all the descriptions of Islamic Cordoba.

Cordoba was the home of *"ulama"* such as of Ibn Hazm (d. 456/1064), Ibn Rushd (Averroes) (d. 595/ 1198), and Maimonides (d. 601/1204).

MARIBEL FIERRO

See also Andalus; Ibn Hazm; Ibn Rushd (Averroes); Maimonides

Further Reading

Arberry, A.J. "Muslim Cordoba." In *Cities of Destiny*, edited by A. Toynbee, 166–177. London, 1967.

EI², s.v. *Al-Andalus*. [Lévi-Provençal, E.; Torres Balbás, L.; and Colins, G. S.].

EI², *s.v. Kurtuba*. [Seybold, C.F.; [Ocaña Jiménez, M.]

Grabar, O. "Great Mosque of Cordoba." In *The Genius of Arab Civilization. Source of Renaissance*. Cambridge, MA, 1978, 106.

Hillenbrand, R. "The Ornament of the World. Medieval Córdoba As a Cultural Centre." In *The Legacy of Muslim Spain*, ed. S.Kh. Jayyusi, 112–135. Leiden, New York, and Cologne: Brill, 1992.

Lévi-Provençal, E. *España musulmana 711–1031* (tran. García Gómez, E.), *Historia de España*, dirigida por R. Menéndez Pidal. Madrid, 1965, vols. V–VI.

Urvoy, D. *Pensers d'al-Andalus. La vie Intellectuelle a Cordoue et Seville au Temps des Empires Berbères (fin Xie Siècle-Début XIIIe Siècle)*. Toulouse: Presses Universitaires du Mirail, 1990, 52–77.

COSMETICS

In Islamic times both sexes used cosmetics extensively, continuing a long tradition in the pre-Islamic Near East going back in time to the ancient civilizations of Mesopotamia, Ancient Egypt, and Iran. Cosmetics were used for different purposes and can be studied under different aspects: in connection with cleaning and hygiene; as perfumes; for skin protection, especially from the sun; for hair coloring; for medicine; and also for magical purposes. Generally, cosmetics were linked to traditional views about beauty and appearance, carrying especially for women a sexual aspect. The important role cosmetics played in social life was highlighted at wedding ceremonies. Many cosmetics combine different uses and applications. Henna and *kuhl* (as ophthalmic medicine) possess medical properties as well. Even the expensive ointment *ghaliya*, mainly made of musk and ambergris, had a double use as perfume and medication. Generally, women used cosmetics widely, but mainly in the private sphere, and only slave girls, singers, and the like used it more extensively in public. For men and children the usage of decorative cosmetics was restricted to basics such as *kuhl* and henna mentioned in the traditions *(hadith)*, as recommended by the Prophet Muhammad. Cosmetic substances came mainly from plants such as henna, indigo *(nil, wasma)*, saffron, and sandalwood. Others were derived from minerals such as ochre, or metals such as *kuhl;* a few have an animal origin, like musk.

Historical sources give a lot of information: in the works of the medieval Arab and Persian historians and scientists, such as Biruni, Ibn Sina, Nasir ad-Din Tusi, al-Kindi, and others, and also in medical works and in sociocultural writings like those of Ibn al-Washsha'. Some works include hundreds of recipes for cosmetic substances, including their surrogates and falsifications. These existed parallel to innumerable local and individual recipes, transmitted by family tradition and health care professionals.

The traditional ideal of beauty stated that women's skin should be white, soft, smooth, and hairless. Ointments and pastes were used for lightening the skin. For the face, white powders and powdered rouge were used. Often, yellow pastes made of sandalwood, saffron, and similar substances were used to protect the face from sunlight and to soften the skin. A beauty spot made with perfumed crèmes was not unusual. For body hair removal, a large variety of different mixtures were used, based mostly on either sugar or honey. A special technique to remove body hair consists of a twisted thread pulled back and forth by the fingers of both hands.

Coloring the hair was practiced by both sexes. For thick, long, and dark black hair both sexes used mixtures of indigo, oak apple, walnut, and similar materials. Henna could be added for extra shine. Henna was also used to cover gray and white hair, producing shades of orange-red. After cleaning and coloring the hair, perfumed oils and ointments could be added, as mentioned in the traditions of A'isha, the Prophet's favored wife. For the men it was important to have a black beard like the Prophet, and it could be perfumed, as practiced by the Prophet with the precious *ghaliya*.

The primary cosmetic used by men, women, and children for eyes was *kohl (ithmidh, surma)*, a black mixture in use since pre-Islamic times. The best varieties came from Iran. Its main substance was powdered antimony sulphide. Some mixtures contained lead among other metal or mineral substances, and occasionally, organic materials such as nut shells and even soot were used. Other recorded eye cosmetics, equally called *kuhl*, were made from a variety of substances, which produced dark blue, dark red, purple, or even yellow hues.

Henna, partly enriched with indigo (or a substitute such as oak apple ink), was the main body paint used for hands and feet. Medieval Persian and Indian miniature paintings depict ladies and occasionally men with hands and feet dyed in different shades of orange-red. Also, they picture ladies adorned with intricate body paintings in black, blue, or dark brown, or while applying makeup. The important role henna plays in wedding customs all over the Islamic world is especially visible in the "henna night" bearing witness to the magical properties ascribed to cosmetics.

Combs; metal mirrors; mortars; small, narrow-necked vessels for liquid cosmetics and makeup jars for powders and ointments; applicators; makeup palettes; and other small tools and vessels come from all parts of the Islamic world. A variety of materials were used in their production, reflecting local resources, customs and habits, and the user's financial status.

GISELA HELMECKE

See also Baths; Marriage; Medicine; Painting; Perfume; Women

Further Reading

Colin, G.S. "Hinna." In *The Encyclopaedia of Islam*. Vol. 3. Leiden and London, 1971.

"Cosmetics." In *Encyclopaedia Iranica*. Vol. 6. Costa Mesa, 1993.

Dietrich, A. "Sandal." In *The Encyclopaedia of Islam*. Vol. 9. Leiden, 1997.

Wiedemann, Ernst, and James. W. Allan. "Kuhl." In *The Encyclopaedia of Islam*. Vol. 5. Leiden, 1986.

COURT DRESS, 'ABBASID

By the early tenth century CE, Islamic society was perceived as consisting of four classes: (1) the ruling family, (2) the chief ministers (viziers), (3) the wealthy upper classes and educated middle classes, and (4) "The remainder ... a filthy refuse, a torrent of scum" (al-Fadl ibn Yahya, courtier quoted in Levy 1957, 67). It was understood that the individual's social rank and occupation should be visible in dress; to adopt fabric, styles, and colors associated with a higher class displayed dissatisfaction with the God-given order and thus challenged spiritual and temporal authority, whereas wearing clothing associated with a lower social grade displayed proper humility, so pious Muslim rulers were always recorded as being austere in their attire. At the same time, political statesmen such as Nizam al-Mulk (d.1092) argued for the importance of rich, colorful, ostentatious court dress and ceremonial to demonstrate secure political power, economic prosperity, and social well-being. This apparent contradiction was never resolved.

Caliph al-Mansur (r. 754–775) is traditionally credited with the introduction of black robes as the 'Abbasid dynastic color to be worn by all court bureaucrats and theologians at audiences and at public investiture of sultans and governors; failure to do so was seen as a public rejection of the regime, the ruler, and his policies. Black banners had heralded the 'Abbasid uprisings against Umayyad authority, and it was understood that the color signified the need for revenge and mourning for the tragic deaths of the Prophet's grandsons (*see* Hasan and Husayn ibn Ali Talib). (In contrast, the dynastic color of Egypt's Fatimid caliphate [c. 969–1171] was white, reflecting luminous splendor and divine light.) At each caliphal investiture, the legitimacy of 'Abbasid rule was reinforced by donning several relics of the Prophet Muhammad's, including his *burda* (mantle), implying the transference of authority, and blessing.

The 'Abbasid court had two main groupings, the military and the bureaucrats, known by their different

Scene from a picnic of the court of Abbas I. Safavid mural, 1640s. Credit: SEF/Art Resource, NY. Chihil Sutun (Pavilion of Forty Columns), Isfahan, Iran.

modes of dress, as their Arabic names imply: *ashab al-aqbiyya* (men of the *qaba'*: the military garment) and *ashab al-darari'* (men of the *durra'a*: voluminous robe). However, the precise structure of such garments is unclear. A third group, the *'ulama* (*see* Theologians) increasingly adopted a distinctive dress indicating their growing separation from the other court power groups, while in time the 'Abbasid caliphs took to wearing military dress for most ceremonial duties, mirroring their growing dependence on army support. Gifts of clothing and other presents *(khil'a)* became an established court ritual, accompanied by due ceremony. It could consist of one garment, but generally four or more items were presented, in one of three price ranges according to the recipient's status. These could be decorated with a *tiraz* (embroidered band, identifying the donor (and thus the honor bestowed), the date, the place of manufacture, and so on (*see* Tiraz).

While medieval Arabic literature contains a great variety of clothing terms, the exact structure and characteristics of these garments were not detailed, and few items have survived. It appears the wraps and simple garments with minimal seaming (such as the so-called Coptic tunics) of the Umayyad period were replaced by more multiseamed items, perhaps to minimize costly fabric wastage or marking changes in loom technology. Late-ninth-century Baghdadi fashionable citizens were known for their keen knowledge and appreciation of fabrics, obtained from across the Islamic empire (*see* Textiles, 'Abbasid). Graduated coloring and textural compatibility were important considerations. Strident color shades were best avoided, while thick and thin textiles, and linen and cotton were not to be worn together.

Small fragments of 'Abbasid textiles are found in most major museum collections, but few were acquired from controlled archaeological excavations. *Tiraz* pieces have generally had extraneous material removed, so they provide few clues as to their original placing and the clothing items they once decorated. However, a number of Islamic manuscript paintings produced in or around the thirteenth century (such as *Kitab al-Diryaq*, 1199, probably Northern Iraq, ms. Arabe 2964; and *Maqamat al-Hariri*, 1237, probably Iraq, ms. Arabe 5847, Bibliotheque Nationale, Paris) are known, and these, along with figural depictions on contemporary ceramics and metalwork, help the dress historian. However, for the early 'Abbasid period, aside from murals located in the remote eastern regions of the empire, the pictorial evidence is virtually limited to wall paintings from the Samarran palaces (*see* Architecture, 'Abbasid).

PATRICIA L. BAKER

Further Reading

Ahsan, M.M. *Social Life under the Abbasids, 170–289 AH/ 786–902 A.D* London: Longman, 1979.

Ettinghausen, Richard. *Arab Painting*. Cleveland: Skira, 1962.

Golombek, L., and V. Gervers. "Tiraz Fabrics in the Royal Ontario Museum." In *Studies in Textile History in Memory of Harold B. Burham*, edited by L. Golombek and V. Gervers, 82–126. Toronto: Royal Ontario Museum, 1977.

Levy, Reuben. "Notes on Costume from Arabic Sources." *Journal of Royal Asiatic Society* (London). (1935): 319–338.

———. *An Introduction to the Sociology of Islam.* Vol.1. London: Williams & Moorgate, 1957.

Salem, Elie A., trans. *Hilal ibn al-Muhassin al-Sabi 'Rustam dar al-Khilafah'*. Beirut: American University of Beirut, 1977 (use with caution).

Serjeant, R.B. *Islamic Textiles: Materials for a History up to the Mongol Conquests*. Beirut: Librairie du Liban, 1972.

Tyan, Emile. *Histoire de l'Organisation Judicaire en Pays d'Islam*. Vols. 1 and 2. Paris: Librairie du Receuil Sirey, 1938.

COURT DRESS, FATIMID

The Fatimids, who ruled Egypt from 969 to 1171 CE, followed the conventions of other Islamic dynasties in their adoption of an official dynastic color. The Fatimid color was white. Most court costumes were a white luxury fabric (fine linens, silks, or brocades) with inscribed or ornamental bands (tiraz), and embroidered with gold or silver threads. Every member of the court received a ceremonial costume, often for the public celebration of a festival in the Islamic calendar. These costumes often were complete outfits (including underclothes) and consisted of anywhere from five to fifteen separate pieces. The base material, the number of pieces in the costume, and the amount of gold or silver in the costume were tied to rank. Our sources provide almost no information about tailoring of these garments, which is typical of the period, where there were a limited number of styles and most garments were woven in a single piece.

In the sources dating to the early eleventh century, most court garments are described as being woven or embroidered with gold *(muthaqqal, mudhahhab)*, but silk is mentioned rarely. Inventories describing clothing distributed for festivals from the early twelfth century onward, however, mention numerous garments of both silk and gold, often woven into or embroidered onto a linen base. Silk was so readily available in the twelfth century that its presence in an inventory is not necessarily a sign of high rank, but the presence of gold (a more expensive commodity) always indicates high rank. The gold thread used in the production of textiles for the court was produced under the supervision of the director of the caliph's mint. The predominance of linen as a base material for court costumes is a function of the central importance of flax to the Egyptian agricultural economy of the Middle Ages.

Clothing in the Fatimid period was a form of capital, and the luxury materials used in the production of court costumes carried significant economic, as well as symbolic, value. The Fatimids kept large treasuries of fabrics and costumes that were distributed at designated times for use by court personnel. The detailed inventories of the contents of these wardrobe treasuries show that they formed a significant part of the Fatimid dynasty's wealth. In the 1060s, the caliph al-Mustansir was forced to sell the contents of his wardrobe treasuries to raise money to placate his rebellious army. When the economy recovered, his successor replenished the wardrobes and multiplied the number of costumes distributed on ritual occasions. The textiles and garments were produced in government factories. Many of them had inscribed or ornamental borders (tiraz). The caliph did not wear a crown, but rather an elaborately wrapped turban. His eunuch bodyguards also wore specially wrapped turbans, with a "tail" left hanging down to the side or back. His highest-ranking eunuchs were distinguished by wrapping the tail under their chin (called muhannak). Princesses of the royal family received gold robes, while their eunuch guardians received garments of silk. The most luxurious costumes came in wrappers of fine linens or in chests.

In addition to the costumes given to courtiers at festival times, dignitaries received robes of honor (khil'a, pl. khila') as a mark of special favor, to mark important events, and when invested with office. The term literally means "cast-off," and originally a khil'a was a piece of clothing actually worn by the ruler and then given to another. By the tenth century, these honorific robes were only rarely actual cast-offs, and the caliphal textile mills produced robes specifically for this purpose. At the Fatimid court, honorific robes were typically given whenever an official was appointed to an office at court, and the phrase "he was invested with a robe of honor" clearly meant that he was appointed to office. These robes carried both prestige and material value, since they were made of luxury fabrics at a time when clothing was a form of capital and could represent considerable wealth.

The noncourtier middle and upper classes imitated court fashions by wearing luxury fabrics, giving robes of honor as gifts, and wearing inscribed bands (or bands that created the appearance of being inscribed) on their robes. Important officials of the Jewish community, for example, conferred embroidered silk robes of honor upon scholars, and men of higher status conferred robes of honor as gifts upon men of lesser status. Such costumes were extremely expensive, often costing as much as twenty dinars, a sum of money sufficient to support a lower middle class family for nearly a year.

PAULA SANDERS

See also Fatimids; Gifts and Gift Giving

Further Reading

Baker, Patricia Lesley. "A History of Islamic Court Dress in the Middle East." Ph.D. dissertation, School of Oriental Studies. University of London, 1986.
Sanders, Paula. "Robes of Honor in Fatimid Egypt." In *Robes and Honor: The Medieval World of Investiture,* ed. Stewart Gordon. New York: Palgrave, 2001.
Serjeant, R.B. *Islamic Textiles: Material for a History up to the Mongol Conquest.* Beirut: Librairie du Liban, 1972.
Stillman, Yedida Kalfon. *Arab Dress, A Short History.* Leiden: Brill, 2000.
———. "Libas." In *Encyclopaedia of Islam. New ed.* Leiden: Brill.
———, and Paula Sanders. "Tiraz." In *Encyclopaedia of Islam.* New ed. Leiden: Brill, 1999.

COURT DRESS, MAMLUK

As in 'Abbasid times, the two major court groupings were distinguished by dress: the military, calf-length qaba' garment with close-fitting sleeves, which was designed for riding and fighting and worn with breeches tucked into high boots; and the ample, full-length robes of bureaucrats (arbab al-'ama'im, turban wearers), worn with loose trousers. It appears the basic, simple robe and wraps of the early Islamic period had been set aside for more tailored garments, using the fabric loom width to form the front and back with, if required, extra material in the form of triangular inserts or gussets added to the selvage sides of the main panels. Indeed, by the late fourteenth century CE, tailoring was perceived as a mark of civilized urban society (Ibn Khaldun 1967).

The Mamluk sultanate retained the Ayyubid dynastic color (yellow) for battle dress, but for court parades and ceremonials, certain military sections jealously guarded their exclusive right to various dress items and colors; thus, in 1498, the royal Mamluks reacted aggressively to the sultan's honorific presentation (khil'a) of their short-sleeved sallari tunic and special turban form to the black commander of the musketeers, instead of that section's usual red wool cloth (qaba'). The khassikiya (royal bodyguard) was renowned for its meticulous dress, which incorporated a section of *tiraz zarkash* (see Textiles), presumed to be a highly decorative band woven with gold or silver metallic thread, perhaps with an honorific inscription, placed at the (dropped) shoulder-sleeve join. The terminology suggests there were at least five or six types of *qaba'*, and possibly the method of fastening still denoted the ethnic origins of the wearer as in Mongol times (see Mongol Dress); certainly the so-called *qaba' tatari* (diagonal fastening from left shoulder to waist) and the *qaba' turki* (from right shoulder diagonally to left) implied this. There was also a great variety in headgear, with some forms worn by the Bahri Mamluks falling out of favor by the mid-thirteenth century CE, the so-called Burji period. Certain court members were permitted blazons *(rank),* which were displayed on their belongings, their buildings, and their servants' clothing; these could be simple shapes, say of a lozenge form (the royal napkin holder's serviette), or a stylized composite design indicating the various court responsibilities associated with the owner (see Heraldry).

Our knowledge of bureaucratic dress mainly derives from historical descriptions of the *khil'a* awarded by the sultan for loyal service, at least twice a year at the major Muslim festivals, but also given to mark new appointments, honorable dismissals, and so on. As with the military, bureaucrats were presented with robes according to status. Viziers and chief secretaries could expect white *kamkha* (patterned woven silk) robes decorated with embroidery and lined with squirrel and beaver, whereas lower ranks were given cheaper fabrics in other colors, and fur-trimmed only. Similar voluminous robes with long, wide sleeves were presented to members of the *'ulama,* but generally speaking, because of theological antipathy to men wearing silk, theirs were made of wool. The 'Abbasid caliph in exile (see 'Abbasid caliphate) wore black at all court ceremonies and invested each new Mamluk sultan with black robes, thus symbolizing the legitimate transference of authority with his blessing (see *Burda, Khirqa* of Muhammad).

Apart from market regulations *(hisba)* concerning tailors, dyers, cobblers, and so on, sumptuary legislation was regularly issued by the sultan, often at the request of the *'ulama.* Male and female descendants of the Prophet Muhammad were required from 773 AH/1371–1372 C.E. to wear in public a piece of green fabric about their clothing, so that due respect could be paid. However, the chief targets for such legislation were women's attire and that of non-Muslims (see Dress, *dhimmi*). Insisting street patrols policed matters, the *'ulama* bitterly criticized the outrageous sums spent on women's garments, the excessive amounts of fabric used particularly for sleeves, bejewelled hems, and shoes, and railed against ladies wearing headcoverings based on men's styles, and the fashion of wearing *sirwal* (trousers) low on the hips.

Few complete dress items have survived—the occasional shoe (Keir Collection, London; Royal Ontario Museum, Toronto), caps (minus turban cloths) (V&A Museum, London; Ashmolean Museum, Oxford), and embroidered tailored linen shirts (Royal Ontario Museum; Textile Museum, Washington, DC; V&A Museum). Nevertheless, garment fragments in the major collections often possess informative cutting and tailoring details as to buttons, loops, and seams. Mamluk manuscript illustrations provide useful information about certain styles, although artistic license may have impinged on depictions of garment colors and patternings; similarly, the inclusion of Mamluk men and women in European paintings (such as the work of Giovanni Bellini, d. 1516) should be viewed as "Orientalizing" additions rather than accurate records of contemporary fashion.

PATRICIA L. BAKER

Further Reading

Ayalon, David. *Gunpowder & Firearms in the Mamluk Kingdom: A Challenge to a Mediaeval Society.* London: Frank Cass, 1973.

Haldane, Duncan. *Mamluk Painting.* Warminster, UK: Aris & Phillips, 1978.

Ibn Khaldun. *An Introduction to History: The Muqaddimah.* Translated by Franz Rosenthal. Cambridge, MA: Princeton University Press, 1967.

Ibn al-Ukuwwa. *The Ma'alim al-Qurba fi Ahkam al-Hisba.* Translated by Reuben Levy. E.J.W. Gibb Memorial Series. London: Cambridge University Press, 1938.

Mayer, Leo Ary. "Costumes of Mamluk Women." *Islamic Culture* 17 (1943): 298–303.

———. *Mamluk Costume: A Survey.* Geneva: Albert Kundig, 1952.

———. "Some Remarks on the Dress of the Abbasid Caliphs in Egypt." *Islamic Culture* 17 (1943): 36–38.

CREDIT

Many scholars have cited the lack of credit as a reason why Islamic societies were unable to effectively compete with the Western European commercial interests that emerged during the twelfth and thirteenth centuries. This argument is based on the premise that only Western Europeans tolerated the development of financial interest and profit as commercial practice.

It is clear, however, that Islamic notions of profit and interest also developed to a substantial degree during the medieval era.

Both Muslim and non-Muslim merchants who engaged in long-distance trade constantly risked social alienation. Most outsiders viewed the overseas and caravan trade in luxury items such as spices and silk as sinful because the money spent on non-necessities could have been used for the greater social good. Only those who gained a profit—namely the state, which took custom imposts; the merchants; financiers and adventurers who ran the trade; and the patrons and retailers who purchased the items—saw the venture in positive terms. On a number of occasions and places, others sought to prevent "injustices," most often invoking the religious principle that merchants and traders who took financial interest and profit exploited the productive forces in society.

Merchants in the Islamic world sought a number of legal means to protect themselves against such allegations. The first of these constructions were joint-venture contracts for long-distance trade, either in credit (*şirket'ül-vücüh*) or involving both labor and capital (*commenda; mudaraba*). In both cases the merchant and financiers involved would combine their assets before the venture, and later would split the profits. Such arrangements circumvented measures against interest. These merchants also developed a new means of transferring funds (*havale*), which involved one permanently based merchant issuing a deed to another, who would redeem the promise once the traveling merchant brought it to the permanently based merchant. This practice was absolutely critical because coinage was often in very short supply, was bulky, and was very liable to be stolen.

As in most European economies, merchants in the Muslim world faced considerable resistance from local manufacturers and traders. These local urban economies were organized into guilds that continually tried to monopolize economic activity. Guilds wielded considerable power in enforcing "just regulation" among the urban populace. Many historians argue that merchants made little headway in developing commercial capital among these local economies.

However, a number of intriguing recent studies have pointed to commercial development, particularly in the sixteenth-century Ottoman Empire. Commercial activity again established itself through Islamic legal institutions, in particular the pious foundation (*waqf*), a welfare institution that often formed the basis of each city quarter (*mahalle*), a structure arguably as central to urban life as the guilds themselves. Although early *waqfs* were donations of land and immovable property for the good of the Islamic community, donations of cash *waqfs* began to boom in the mid-sixteenth century. Cash from these *waqfs* was lent to merchants and other parties at interest (*rib*). This innovation was justified by Ebu's-suud, the leading Ottoman religious authority, who argued that taking of interest was justified if it served the

public welfare of the Muslim community. While this author has only seen detailed evidence of this in Sarajevo, there are also signs of the practice in other major urban centers of the empire, such as Istanbul, Edirne, and Bursa. Some scholars have commented that the interest this money was lent at was very high, sometimes reaching 25 percent or even 50 percent. Nevertheless, the prevalence of a rate of 8 percent to 10 percent in Sarajevo at least might beg a reconsideration of the issue as a whole.

Finally, merchants were increasingly used as a means for the state to develop their treasuries, particularly when they were to embark on military campaigns, as seen most clearly in the conflicts between Muslim and non-Muslim Mediterranean powers in the late fifteenth and early sixteenth centuries. It was during this time that the Ottoman sultan, like his French and northern European counterparts, came to rely heavily on long-distance merchant families who had just suffered persecution as Jews from the Iberian Peninsula. These merchant families became an attractive asset to the state because they could garner considerable amounts of cash. They additionally could more effectively collect revenues, even though they too made a hefty profit from the transaction. One should not ignore, however, that Muslim merchants made up a majority of the tax farmers, particularly in provincial settings. In time they would work alongside emerging urban elites, such as the money changers and jewelers, and would help break down the barrier between the commercial and local urban economies.

YORK ALLAN NORMAN

Further Reading

Çizakça, Murat. *A Comparative Evolution of Business Partnership, The Islamic World and Europe, with Specific Reference to the Ottoman Archives.* Leiden and New York: E.J. Brill, 1996.

Imber, Colin. *Ebu's-su'ud: The Islamic Legal Tradition.* Stanford: Stanford University Press, 1977.

Inalcik, Halil, "Capital Formation in the Ottoman Empire." *The Journal of Economic History. The Tasks of Economic History.* 29, no. 1 (March 1969): 97–140.

Norman, York A. "Urban Development in Sarajevo." In *Islamization in Bosnia, 1463–1604.* Forthcoming Ph.D. dissertation. Georgetown University.

Schacht, J. "Rıb." In *Encyclopedia of Islam.* Online Ed., 2001.

CRIME AND PUNISHMENT

To appreciate the general concept of crime in Muslim societies requires appreciating very different properties of the legal framework. Due to the composite nature of the *Shari'a*, the assessment of a crime is contingent on multiple types of reasoning—those of religious law rooted in Tribes and Tribal Customs developed and transformed into a legal scholar's law, and finally, legal doctrine often reconciled to new social and cultural conditions. Our discussion will be confined to the most elementary categories of crimes and punishments according to Muslim jurists, to the social meaning of retaliation and collective liability, and to the question of judicial arbitrariness.

Taking the perspective of a legal scholar's law, criminal acts are basically grouped into six categories: (1) interfering with the order of descent, such as by adultery; (2) affecting another's honor by slanderous accusation; (3) detriment to one's own power of reason, such as by intoxication; (4) illegal seizure of wealth as through theft or highway robbery; (5) attacks against life or physical integrity; and (6) perturbation of public order. The first categories, in particular fornication, wrongful accusation, drinking wine, theft, and highway robbery, comprise the *hadd,* or limit penalties. They are rights or claims of God *(huquq Allah)* explicitly stated in the *Qur'an* (Q 24:2 f.; 24:3 f.; 5:33; 5:38; 5:90 f.). The pursuit and the punishment of these crimes are incumbent on the Muslim community—that is, the legal authorities. Such crimes require corporal punishment ranging eighty lashes for slanderous accusation and capital punishment, either by stoning for fornication or, for highway robbery, by crucifixion or decapitation. Apostasy does not fall into the judicial categories of crime. From a religious point of view, the punishment of the apostate belongs to the hereafter; however, in this world he is condemned to death inasmuch as he places himself out of the bounds of the social community.

The fifth category comprising homicide and bodily injury—and occasionally other damages as well—is known as *jinayat* (offenses). Since they belong to the rights of humans *(huquq adami),* prosecution of such crimes only takes place at the request of the offended party. The penalties vary based on either an intentional or an erroneous commitment of the crime (Schacht 1964, 181). In the case of voluntary murder, there follows a threefold penalty: the punishment in the hereafter, the loss of inheritance rights, and retaliation for the damage of the victim's group. The latter can change its claim on the culprit's life into recompensation *(diya)*, which might also be paid, in the case of involuntary homicide, by the "blood-money group" *('aqila).*

The term *'aqila* signifies the agnatic descent in its largest sense and refers to tribal notions of collective liability. However, the importance of the *diya*—a fact of which medieval Muslim jurists were particularly aware—resides in the function of replacing or restricting the circular exchange of violence resulting from blood feuds of the tribal factions (Brunschvig 1960, 338; see, for example, Hart 1996, on the mechanisms of tribal feuds). It has often been aptly stated that the introduction of the *diya* in early Islam marks a major shift in the transition from private revenge to penal law. Furthermore, legal doctrine transcended gradually the tribal notion of collective liability toward a concept of responsibility based on the obligations of property and geographical closeness (Johansen 1999, 370). In a comparable way the scholars elaborated definitions of theft to the effect that they translated divergent variants of economic and social patterns into the legal doctrines of their respective Schools of Jurisprudence. Since progress of law offers a rather tautological explanation for these developments, only detailed studies of relevant social and historical backgrounds could shed more light on the primary agents of legal change (Johansen 1998).

In cases of uncertainty about an offense punishable by a *hadd* penalty, as well as in instances of transgression of the public order, the decision is left to the discretion of the judge. He is authorized to pronounce a wide range of punishments, such as public announcement of the crime, imprisonment, exile, corporal punishment, or monetary fines. However, all these punishments shall not be more severe than the *hadd* penalty. The judge's discretionary power *(ta'zir)* has given rise to the famous Weberian formulation of *Kadijustiz,* which points to a state of legal uncertainty and arbitrary justice. A number of studies criticize this statement on the ground that it lacks the necessary reflection about judicial considerations of social relations or legal doctrine. The ongoing discussion focuses on the importance of the legal sphere (Powers 2002, 23–52; Dakhlia 1993).

TILMAN HANNEMANN

See also Commanding Good and Forbidding Evil; Ethics; Peace and Peacemaking; Police; Prisons; Thieves and Brigands; Usury and Interest; Wine

Further Reading

Brunschvig, Robert. Art. "Akila." In *The Encyclopaedia of Islam. New ed.* Vol I, 337–340. Leiden and London: Brill, 1960.
Dakhlia, Jocelyn. "Sous le vocable de Salomon: L'Exercice de la 'Justice Retenue' au Maghreb." *Annales Islamologiques* 27 (1993): 169–180.
Eigentum. "Familie und Obrigkeit im hanafitischen Strafrecht: Das Verhältnis der privaten Rechte zu den Forderungen der Allgemeinheit in hanafitischen Rechtskommentaren." In *Contingency in a Sacred Law: Legal and Ethical Norms in the Muslim.* Fiqh. Leiden [et al.]: Brill, 1999, 349–420.

Hart, David M. "Murder in the Market: Penal Aspects of Berber Customary Law in the Precolonial Moroccan Rif. *Islamic Law and Society* 3 (1996): 343–371.

Johansen, Baber. "La Mise en Scène du vol par les Juristes Musulmans." In *Vols et Sanctions en Méditerranée*, ed. Maria Pia di Bella, 41–74. Amsterdam: Éd. des Archives Contemporaines, 1998.

Krcsmárik, Johann. "Beiträge zur Beleuchtung des islamitischen Strafrechts mit Rücksicht auf die Theorie und Praxis in der Türkei." *Zeitschrift der Deutschen Morgenländischen Gesellschaft* 58 (1904): 69–113; 316–360; 539–579.

Powers, David S. *Law, Society, and Culture in the Maghrib, 1300–1500.* Cambridge, MA: Cambridge University Press, 2002.

Schacht, Joseph. *An Introduction to Islamic Law.* Oxford: The Clarendon Press, 1964.

CRUSADES

Crusades is the name commonly given to a period of conflict between Roman Catholic Christians and non-Christians that lasted, at its height, from the eleventh to thirteenth centuries CE. It is important to note that this term is a modern label applied to this period retrospectively by historians. The numbering of the major expeditions of the Crusades (First Crusade, Second Crusade, etc.) is also a modern invention used merely for convenience's sake; in reality, the passing of warriors from Europe to the Levant was a much more continuous process.

Although the major targets of the Crusades were the Muslims of the Levant, Crusades were also conducted against a variety of groups in other locations, including non-Christians, heretics, and political opponents of the papacy in various parts of Europe. However, as far as the Muslim world is concerned, it was the Levant that felt the greatest impact from the Crusades.

The First Crusade (1096–1102) was launched by Pope Urban II (d. 1099) in 1095. At the Council of Clermont in France he exhorted his Catholic brethren to march to the aid of the Christians of the East, who were suffering under Muslim rule, in return for which he promised his listeners remission of their sins. The call was answered by both of Urban's intended targets: the knightly classes, and members of the lower classes who were stirred up with religious fervor. Starting in 1096, a number of armies marched to the Levant, the most successful ones fighting their way across Asia Minor and down the Levantine littoral, establishing Catholic Christian states at Antioch, Edessa, and Jerusalem. A fourth Catholic state, based at Tripoli, came into being when Crusaders took the city in 1109. A number of major expeditions to the Levant were launched over the course of the twelfth and thirteenth centuries, one of which, the

Third Crusade (1189–1192), took Cyprus from its Byzantine ruler in 1191, establishing yet another Catholic state there.

After the initial shock of the loss of Jerusalem, the third holy city of Islam, had passed, the Muslim response to the arrival of the First Crusade was largely one of apathy and compromise. While a number of Muslims, particularly preachers and poets, called on their political authorities to respond to the Crusader invasion, and some undoubtedly did, many rulers were preoccupied with struggles with other Muslim rivals and found that it was actually more convenient to ally themselves with the Franks, as the European Crusaders were called by the Muslims; indeed, one finds several cases of Muslim and Frankish leaders joining together to fight against other Muslims, Franks, or even both! Thus the Crusaders became integrated into the political framework of the region. However, over time, and particularly during the reigns of the sultans Zanki (r. 1127–1146), Nur al-Din (r. 1146–1174), Salah al-Din (Saladin, r. 1169–1193), Baybars (r. 1260–1277), and Qalawun (r. 1279–1290), there was a gradual hardening of Muslim hostility to the Franks that led to an increase of the *jihad* (holy war) against them, resulting in the gradual reconquest of territory by the Muslims. The last Frankish stronghold on the coast, Acre, fell to Qalawun's son, al-Ashraf Khalil (r. 1290–93), in 1291, while Cyprus lasted until 1570, when it was conquered by the Ottomans. By this time, despite further attempts that had been made to launch Crusades to the East, the era of Catholic states in the Levant had come to an end.

However, it would be a mistake to see the Crusadeing period as merely one of conflict. During the period there was a vibrant trade of goods between the Levant and Europe that experienced only temporary hiatuses during periods of increased hostility between Muslims and Crusaders. Some features of the Franks, especially military prowess, seem to have been admired by the Muslims, and a number of genuine friendships, transcending the religious barriers, seem to have formed. That said, in the sources, Muslim perceptions of the Franks still tend to be tinged with an air of superiority. While Franks clearly adopted Muslim habits and practices that were more suited to life in the Middle East, the Muslims seem to have felt that the Europeans had little to teach them in return.

NIALL CHRISTIE

See also Abu Shama; Architecture, Secular: Military; Ayyubids; Baybars I; European Literature about Medieval Islam; Fatimids; Franks; Ibn al-'Adim; Ibn al-Athir; Ibn al-Furat; Ibn Shaddad; Ibn Taghribirdi; Ibn Wasil; Interfaith Relations; Jerusalem; Jihad;

Mamluks; Manzikert; Muslim–Crusader Relations; Nur al-Din ibn Zanki; Pacts and Treaties; Saladin (Salah al-Din); Seljuks; Sibt ibn al-Jawzi; Trade, Mediterranean; Warfare and Techniques; Weapons and Weaponry; Zankids

Further Reading

Arab Historians of the Crusades, trans. Francesco Gabrieli and E.J. Costello. Berkeley and Los Angeles: University of California Press, 1984.

Dajani-Shakeel, Hadiah, and R.A. Messier, eds. *The Jihad and Its Times*. Ann Arbor, MI: University of Michigan Center for Near Eastern and North African Studies, 1991.

Gervers, Michael, and James M. Powell, eds. *Tolerance and Intolerance: Social Conflict in the Age of the Crusades*. Syracuse, NY: Syracuse University Press, 2001.

Goss, Vladimir P., and Christine V. Bornstein. *The Meeting of Two Worlds*. Kalamazoo, MI: Medieval Institute Publications, 1986.

Haddad, Yvonne Y., and Wadi' Z. Haddad (Eds). *Christian-Muslim Encounters*. Gainesville and Tallahassee, FL: University Press of Florida, 1995.

Hallam, Elizabeth, ed. *Chronicles of the Crusades*. Godalming, Surrey: Bramley Books, 1996.

Hillenbrand, Carole. *The Crusades: Islamic Perspectives*. Edinburgh: Edinburgh University Press, 1999.

Holt, Peter M. *The Age of the Crusades*. London and New York: Longman, 1986.

Kedar, Benjamin Z. *Crusade and Mission: European Approaches Towards Muslims*. Princeton, NJ: Princeton University Press, 1984.

Laiou, Angeliki E., and Roy P. Mottahedeh, eds. *The Crusades from the Perspective of Byzantium and the Muslim World*. Washington, D.C.: Dumbarton Oaks Research Library and Collection, 2001.

Maalouf, Amin. *The Crusades Through Arab Eyes*, trans. J. Rothschild. London: Al Saqi Books, 1984.

Madden, Thomas F., ed. *The Crusades: The Illustrated History*. Ann Arbor, MI: University of Michigan Press, 2004.

Mayer, Hans Eberhard. *The Crusades*, trans. John Gillingham. London: Oxford University Press, 1972.

Murray, Alan V., ed. *The Crusades: An Encyclopedia*. Santa Barbara, CA: ABC-Clio, 2005.

Richard, Jean. *The Crusades, c. 1071–c. 1291*, trans. Jean Birrell. Cambridge and New York: Cambridge University Press, 1999.

Riley-Smith, Jonathan. *The Crusades: A Short History*. London: Athlone, 1987.

——— (Ed). *The Oxford Illustrated History of the Crusades*. Oxford and New York: Oxford University Press, 1995.

Shatzmiller, Maya, ed. *Crusaders and Muslims in Twelfth Century Syria*. The Medieval Mediterranean Vol. 1. Leiden and New York: E.J. Brill, 1993.

Sivan, Emmanuel. *l'Islam et la Croisade*. Paris: Librairie d'Amérique et d'Orient Adrien Maisonneuve, 1968.

Usamah ibn Munqidh. *An Arab-Syrian Gentleman & Warrior in the Period of the Crusades: Memoirs of Usamah ibn-Munqidh*. Translated by Philip K. Hitti. New York: Columbia University Press, 2000.

CURSING

Although using the name of God in promissory oaths is perfectly acceptable Muslim practice, invoking God's power against fellow Muslims in the form of a curse *(sabb, la'n)* is regularly condemned in the *hadīth* literature. The Prophet is remembered never to have cursed a Muslim (although he is said to have cursed his enemies), and to have included among the rights of a wife that she not be cursed by her husband. In one report, the Prophet is shown to have equated cursing a believer with murdering him, a statement that reflects a widespread belief in the power of curses to do real harm. Oaths were, in fact, sometimes strengthened with self-curses ("May God blacken my face if I fail to do such-and-such"), although swearing in this manner was widely disapproved of by the legal scholars. Even so, exposing oneself to curses was the central feature of the judicial procedure known as *li'ān*, an ordeal used to resolve accusations of adultery in cases where neither confession nor witnesses were on hand. The Prophet is said to have invited a delegation of Christians from Najran to resolve their dispute with him by recourse to reciprocal cursing *(mubāhala)*, an invitation that was not in the end taken up.

Early Muslims commonly expressed their affiliation with a particular faction by dissociating from and cursing its enemies. 'Ali was cursed by the Umayyads soon after the First Civil War ended, and those who supported 'Alid claims likewise cursed 'Uthman and Mu'awiya. Eventually, Imami (and some Zaydi) Shi'is would incorporate cursing of the first three Caliphs into their supererogatory prayers. (The *qunūt*, understood in classical Sunni and Shi'i law as a prayer of supplication, in fact, began as an imprecation against enemies used by Muslims of various sects.) More generally, Muhammad's Companions were cursed by Imamis and some Zaydis; in certain contexts, this "vilification of the Companions" *(sabb al-s.ah.āba)* could take place during public festivities commemorating the Prophet's designation of 'Ali at Ghadīr Khumm.

KEITH LEWINSTEIN

See also Oaths

Further Reading

Encyclopaedia of Islam. 2d ed. s.vv. mubāhala, li'ān.

Kohlberg, E. "Barā'a in Shī'ī Doctrine." *Jerusalem Studies in Arabic and Islam*. 7 (1986): 139–175.

———. "Some Imāmī Shī'ī Views on the S.ah.āba." *Jerusalem Studies in Arabic and Islam*. 5 (1984): 143–175 (E. Kohlberg. *Belief and Law in Imāmī Shī 'ism*. Brookfield, VT: Variorum Reprints, 1991, IX).

Pedersen, J. *Der Eid bei den Semiten*. Strassbourg, 1914, 64–107.

CUSTOMARY LAW

With the establishment of the Islamic sphere of influence in North Africa and Asia, large segments of the rural population, such as Berbers or Kurds, progressively converted to Islam and became, in theory, subjects of Islamic law and jurisprudence. However, sedentary tribes, as well as Arab Bedouins, retained distinctive types of jurisdiction, to such an extent that the fourteenth-century CE historian Ibn Khaldun stated in regard to the notion of common descent, "The only meaning of belonging to one or to another group is that one is subject to its laws and conditions" (Ibn Khaldun 1967, 267). The question of customary law in the Islamic world touches accordingly on the problem of accommodating concurrent normative orders, as well as the negotiation of group identities in the context of state expansion into tribal areas.

Approaches, Sources, and Terminology

In studies of Muslim societies, the term *customary law* usually adopts one of three meanings representing different approaches to the subject. First, customary law might refer to a body of rules or to judgments, enacted either by state agencies or by Muslim jurists, and stating or regulating generally accepted social practices. In this case, the legal character of custom is acknowledged because it has been sanctioned by formal authorities. The research interest then focuses on the particular modes of sanctioning, that is, the conditions under which a specific custom might become integrated, temporarily or permanently, into the normative body of the *Shari'a* (cf. Libson 1997; Johansen 1999). Second, customary rules and judgments were also pronounced by informal authorities, such as tribal assemblies, arbiters, charismatic leaders, and so on. Since the legal character of these customary rulings is not immediately apparent, most studies of tribal jurisdiction are indecisive about whether they deal with "custom" or with "law." Some authors, mostly of Islamic studies, have applied the first approach in classifying any custom not in accordance with Islamic law under "social practice" (cf. Coulson 1959–1961). Colonial legal practitioners and social anthropologists have proposed rather two distinct spheres of Islamic and customary jurisdiction (cf. Milliot 1932; Gellner 1969). The importance given to custom in this latter framework characterizes the third meaning, according to which Islamic law scarcely produced social significance in tribal contexts (cf. Chelhod 1971). The activities and notions considered as "customary law" might then encompass the whole range of social practices. As a result, the legal aspects of custom are determined by the respective research interests and vary considerably; the investigated subjects include such different topics as folklore and ethnology, popular religion, social structure, vengeance and blood money, and arbitration procedures. However, since most of these questions belong to Tribes and Tribal Customs (q. v.) in general, we will limit our discussion to the first two meanings.

A central feature of tribal customary law is the fact that it was only occasionally written down. The sources are therefore unevenly distributed, and most of the material dates back merely as far as the eighteenth century. Throughout the medieval period, no testimonies other than the consideration of custom by formal authorities meet the requirement of sufficient documentation for analytical purposes. However, this author believes that it is relatively safe to further define the characteristics of tribal customary law from more recent material, if some precautions are observed. A number of studies suggest that customary law evolves in close relationship to other normative conceptions within legal pluralistic settings. Therefore, all too factitious presumptions on its immutability—expressed, for example, in the widely accepted evaluation of custom as a pre-Islamic residuum—are sometimes misleading. Another important factor restraining the general value of some assertions about the contents of customary law is the actual diversity of local practices. Both the adaptivity to changing social and cultural conditions and the variability of practice contribute to a multifaceted picture of our subject hardly obtainable within narrowing definitions.

The textual basis for considering custom in Islamic law appears in the *Qur'an* (Q 7:199): "Observe forgiveness, and command what is just" *(khudh al-'afw wa 'amur bil-'urf)*. Despite the fact that the translations of the term *'urf* in this verse differ widely, it refers literally to "what is known." In this sense, *'urf* evoked a local or a general custom and could acquire the legal value of a contractual stipulation. The other main technical term for designating custom, *'ada,* or literally "what is repeated," is not attested in the *Qur'an.* In the vocabulary of the legal sciences, it appeared with the meaning of "common usage" after the tenth century. *'Urf* and *'ada* are often mentioned in law texts as a pair. Some authors tried to arrive at a general definition allowing discrimination between *'urf* and *'ada* (see Libson 1997, 133, n. 4). However, the technical usages of both terms varied according to the contexts of text production and might be best traced in considering the texts of selected discursive fields throughout a certain period.

Customary Law According to the Schools of Jurisprudence

The attitudes of the four Sunni schools of jurisprudence toward 'urf and 'ada show remarkable differences. Social practice among the people of Medina became an important part of nascent Maliki legal doctrine under the precondition that it had been confirmed as judicial practice ('amal) by Malik ibn Anas or his contemporaries (cf. Dutton 1999). From the tenth century onward, the 'amal evolved into a juridic tool enabling judges to pronounce legal solutions founded on local 'urf, even if these solutions differed from the majority doctrine (mashhur). Andalusian and Maghrib cities such as Cordoba, Fez, and Qayrawan established in this way their distinctive, unified judicial practice. The prerequisites for this procedure had been summed up by the Moroccan jurist Miyyara (d. ca. 1662–1663 CE) and included the confirmation of the 'urf by righteous witnesses, a continuous legal precedence of exemplary jurists, and the principal conformity with Islamic law (on Maliki 'amal, see references in Toledano 1981:14 f.; Libson 1997:134, n. 8). Besides the 'amal, there are numerous general statements of renowned Maliki jurists, from Abu 'Imran al-Fasi (d. 1038) to Ahmad al-Dardir (d. 1786), on the necessity of considering 'urf in legal evaluation.

Whether or not custom constituted a formal legal source in early Hanafi law is a question still awaiting further research. The prevailing opinion among Hanafi jurists came to be the preference of textual authority found in Hadith and Qur'an, which would definitively override deviating 'urf. In cases in which the texts were silent, the jurists disagreed whether local 'urf could be taken into consideration. However, when the 'urf in question enjoyed universal acceptance among the Muslims, it possessed the force of legal argument. There are some noteworthy exceptions from the majority opinion, such as the Egyptian scholar Ibn Nujaym (d. 1563), who openly argued against Hanafi doctrine by first acknowledging certain local customs of Usury and Interest not explicitly mentioned in the texts and then trying to establish his judgment as a principle (see Johansen 1999; Libson 1997, 142–154; Hallaq 2001, 215–233).

The positions regarding custom in the Shafi'i and Hanbali schools have not been thoroughly studied. The prolific Shafi'i scholar al-Suyuti (d. 1505) dedicated a full chapter of a treatise to custom, but he could nevertheless entirely avoid the problem of local 'urf in his response to questions emerging in the central Sudanese Tekrur (Libson 1997, 154; Hunwick 1970). Driven by obvious political motives, the Hanbali scholar Ibn Taymiyya (d. 1328) denounced in his condemnation of the Mongol rulers of Baghdad their adherence to Mongol custom despite their previous conversion to Islam, and turned it into a primary reason for declaring them to be unbelievers. Finally, in Shi'i legal literature, 'urf figures merely in the sense of "habit" and no allusion is made to specific tribal custom. However, the particular notion of legal reasoning in Shi'ism might have contributed to its greater flexibility in adjusting custom and legal doctrine.

Tribal Customary Law

The case of Maliki law in North Africa, which recognized custom to a large extent, affords significant insights into the modes of negotiating the concurrent normative orders of tribal groups. Berber customary law differed from Islamic law in several important, and by no means tolerable, aspects; for example, denial of inheriting real estate by females, the dower for a wife's family at marriage, the taking of interest, and the avoidance of bodily punishments. Moreover, state jurisdiction (hukm al-sultan) and officially appointed judges were almost absent in tribal areas. Instead, tribal assemblies (jama'at), as well as arbiters (muhakkamun), delivered legal judgments.

It is possible that most tribal actors conceived customary law in the framework of "their" shari'a, the only semantic reference to law available for them (see Rosen 1995). However, both sides, jurists and tribes, spent considerable effort to adjust conflicting norms of customary and religious law. On the one hand, various legal remedies of Islamic law, from gifts and sales to endowments, were intentionally employed for legalizing inheritance practice (see Powers 2002, chapters 4 and 6). On the other hand, the authors of a tribal resolution from 1749, declaring overtly female disinheritance and laying explicit claim to the equal value of 'ada and state jurisdiction, carefully sought to satisfy the formal requirements for the establishment of a Maliki 'amal (cf. Patorni 1895). Both accommodation and self-authorization, different modes of dealing with the same problem, demonstrate the awareness of distinct legal orders, which nevertheless intersect and interact within the legal process.

Though there are no empirically founded reasons to presume a common language of the 'ada forming the equivalence of legal doctrine, legal and political discourses generated images of tribal 'ada reduced to changing features of unbelief, from disinheritance to highwaymen. A comprehensive study on the selective processes of these contested markers of customary law promises important insights about the transformations of Muslim rural societies.

TILMAN HANNEMANN

See also Agriculture; Irrigation; Muslim Conceptions of Past Civilizations; Pagans and Pagan Customs

Further Reading

Chelhod, Joseph. *Le Droit dans la Société Bédouine: Recherches Ethnologiques sur le 'orf ou Droit Coutumier des Bédouins.* Paris: Rivière et C, 1971.
Coulson, Noël James. "Muslim Custom and Case-Law." *Welt des Islams* 6 (1959–1961): 13–24.
Dutton, Yasin. *The Origins of Islamic Law: The Qur'an, the Muwatta' and Madinan 'Amal.* Richmond: Curzon, 1999.
Gellner, Ernest. *Saints of the Atlas.* Chicago and London: University of Chicago Press/Weidenfeld & Nicholson, 1969.
Hallaq, Wael B. *Authority, Continuity, and Change in Islamic Law.* Cambridge, MA: Cambridge University Press, 2001.
Hunwick, John. "Notes on a Late Fifteenth-Century Document Concerning 'al-Takrur'." In *African Perspectives: Papers in the History, Politics and Economics of Africa,* edited by Christopher Allen and R.W. Johnson, 7–33. Cambridge, MA: Cambridge University Press, 1970.
Ibn Khaldun. *The Muqaddimah: An Introduction to History.* 2 vols. Translated by Franz Rosenthal. Princeton, NJ: Princeton University Press, 1967.
Johansen, Baber. "Coutumes Locales et Coutumes Universelles aux Sources des Règles Juridiques en Droit Musulman Hanéfite." In *Contingency in a Sacred Law: Legal and Ethical Norms in the Muslim Fiqh.* Leiden [et al.]: Brill, 1999, 163–171.
Libson, Gideon. "On the Development of Custom As a Source of Law in Islamic Law: *Alruju'u ila al-'urfi ahadu al-qawa'idi al-khamsi allati yatabanna 'alayha al-fiqhu.*" *Islamic Law and Society* 4 (1997): Nr. 2, 131–155.
Milliot, Louis. "Les Institutions Kabyles." *Revue des Etudes Islamiques* 6 (1932): 127–174.
Patorni, F. "Délibération de l'année 1749 dans la Grande Kabylie." *Revue Africaine* 39 (1895): 315–320.
Powers, David S. *Law, Society, and Culture in the Maghrib, 1300–1500.* Cambridge, MA: Cambridge University Press, 2002, Cambridge Studies in Islamic Civilization.
Rosen, Lawrence. "Law and Custom in the Popular Legal Culture of North Africa." *Islamic Law and Society* 2 (1995): Nr. 2, 194–208.
Toledano, Ehud R. *Judicial Practice and Family Law in Morocco: The Chapter on Marriage from as-Sijilmasi's Al- 'Amal Al-Mutlaq.* Boulder, CO: Social Science Monographs, 1981.

CYPRUS

Cyprus (*Kıbrıs* in modern Turkish, *Kubrus* in old Ottoman or Arabic text, and *Kypros* in Greek) is the largest island in the Eastern Mediterranean. The first encounter of Cyprus with Islam began in 632 CE when the Arab invaders under Abu Bakr, according to the Arab and Greek chronicles, showed themselves in Cyprus capturing the Byzantine city of Salamis (Constantia) and converting the large basilica of St. Epiphanios into a mosque. During another expedition by Mu'awiya, governor of Syria in 649, Umm Haram bint Milhan, wife of Ubada ibn as-Shamit, a close relation of the Prophet, died by a fall from her mule in Larnaca. Hala Sultan Tekke, a *külliye* including her mausoleum erected at the spot of her tomb, marked by a megalithic monument, is the most venerated Islamic monument in the island.

The Arab expeditions continued during the Latin Crusading Kingdom between the eleventh and sixteenth centuries. In one of these, the Memelouk Sultan Emir Tanriverdi al-Mahmoudi from Cairo landed at Limassol with his army in 1426 and proceeded as far as Nicosia, where he enjoyed the luxury of the Lusignan king's palace and demanded a quarter to be allocated to them in the capital city, as well as making an agreement of an annual tribute.

Islamic societies took part sometimes as allied forces beside the Lusignans against the Byzantines or the Genoese. However, there is not much known about the extent of the spreading of the Islamic culture in Cyprus dating back to pre-Ottoman rule, although medieval chronicles referred to mosque building and the presence of the Turcopoles on the island. There are several Ottoman buildings (St. Ömer Tekke, Kirklar Tekke, and Ömerge Mosque) dedicated to the early Islamic martyrs.

The Ottoman conquest during the reign of Selim II in 1570/71, with the consent of the *Sheyh ül Islam*, introduced the permanent Islamic culture on the island. An organized settlement policy by forced migrations from Anatolia, mainly Konya, Karaman, Larende, Niğde, Ichel, Menteshe, Denizli, and Zülkadiriye, created a Turkish Islamic population beside the Orthodox Greek natives. Institutions of the Ottoman administration and the Islamic religion were established, the most significant being the *Evkaf (waqf)* institution, which still functions as the administrator of the religious and philanthropic affairs as the greatest property holder in the island. Trade activities from the Islamic countries also increased during this period.

Cyprus became a chief principality governed by a *Beylerbeyi* in Nicosia and *Sancak Beys* in the *kazas,* including some provinces in Anatolia such as Ichel, Sis, Alaiye (Alanya), and Tarsus until the early decades of the seventeenth century. British rule terminated the Ottoman administration in 1878, although the Turkish Islamic culture continued.

The language of the Turkish Cypriots is in the southeastern dialect deriving from Oghuz Turks.

Büyük Han in Nicosia, c. 1571. © N. Yıldız.

Islamic architectural heritage is of Ottoman character. Büyük Han, Büyük Hamam, Ömeriye complex, Arap Ahmet and Agha Cafer Mosques, Hala Sultan and Mevlevi Tekkes, aqueducts, fountains, and the castles in Paphos, Larnaca, and Limassol are the most notable ones from the sixteenth century. Also, Latin monuments, mainly Selimiye (Ayia Sophia) Mosque in Nicosia, Lala Mustafa Pasha (Ayia Sophia or St. Nicholas) Mosque in Famagusta, the city walls, and citadels and domestic buildings, restored and renovated according to Turkish culture during the last quarter of the sixteenth century, is a sign of the respect of the Ottoman administrators toward the cultural heritage. Several others were constructed during the seventeenth to nineteenth centuries, including Bekir Pasha Aqueduct and Sultan Mahmut Library. Museums located in Mevlevi Tekke, Dervish Pasha Konak, and Canpolat Bastion display art and ethnographical collections of Islamic origin. Islamic manuscripts and Ottoman documents in the possession of the Turkish Cypriot Archive and Documentary Centre and the *Waqf* Administration in North Cyprus and the Prime Ministry Ottoman Archive in Istanbul show the legacy of the Islamic culture in Cyprus.

NETICE YILDIZ

See also Abu Bakr

Further Reading

Boustronios, George. *The Chronicles of George Boustronios 1456–1489*, ed. and trans. R. M. Dawkins. Melbourne: University of Melbourne, Cyprus Expedition Publication, No. 2, 1964.

Cobham, Claude Deleval, ed. and trans. *Excerpta Cypria, Materials for a History of Cyprus.* Cambridge, MA, 1908.

Çuhadiroğlu, Fikret, and Oğuz, Filiz. "Kıbrıs'ta Türk Eserleri [Turkish Historical Monuments in Cyprus]." *Vakiflar, Rölöve ve Restorasyon Dergisi*, Vakiflar Genel Müdürlüğü Yayinlari No. 2 (1975): 1–76.

De Groot, A. H. "Kubros." In *The Encyclopaedia of Islam*, ed. Bosworth, E. van Donzel, Lewis, B., and Pellat, Ch. Vol V. Leiden: E.J. Brill, 1986.

Esin, Emel. *Aspects of Turkish Civilization in Cyprus.* Ankara: Türk Kültürünü Araştıma Enstitüsü, 1965.

Gazioğlu, Ahmet Cemal. *The Turks in Cyprus*. London: Kemal Rustem and Brother, 1990.

Hill, George. *A History of Cyprus*. 4 vols. Cambridge, MA: University Press, 1948–1952.

İnalcik, Halil (Ed). *The First International Congress of Cypriot Studies (14–19 April 1969), Ankara*. Institute for the Study of Turkish Culture, 1971.

Le Januen, C.D. *Histoire Générale Des Roiaumes de Chypre de Jerusalem*. 3 vols. A Leide, 1785.

Jennings, Ronald C. *Christians and Muslims in Ottoman Cyprus and the Mediterranean World, 1571–1640*. New York, 1993.

Latrie, L. de Mas. *Histoire de L'Ile de Chypre Sous le Règne des Princes de la Maison de Lusignan*. Paris, 1862 (Famagouste, Chypre: Les Edition l'Oiseau), 1970.

Makhairas, Leontis. *Recital Concerning the Sweet Land of Cyprus, Entitled 'Chronicle*, ed. and trans., R. M. Dawkins. Oxford: Clarendon Press, 1932 (Famagouste, Chypre: Les Edition l'Oiseau), 2 vols.

Ostrogorsky, George. *History of the Byzantine State*. New Brunswick, NJ: Rutgers University Press, 1969.

Roper, Geoffrey, ed. *World Survey of Islamic Manuscripts*. 2 vols. London: Al-Furqan Islamic Heritage Foundation, 1992.

Runciman, Steven. *History of the Crusades*. 3 vols. Cambridge, MA. 1951–1954.

Setton, Kenneth M., and M. W. Baldwin, eds. *A History of the Crusades*. VI vols. Madison, Milwaukee, and London: University of Wisconsin Press, 1969–1989.

Şeşen, Ramazan, Altan, Mustafa Haşim, and İzgi, Cevat. *Kıbrıs İslam Yazmaları Kataloğu*. İstanbul: İslam Tarih ve Kültürünü Araştırma Vakfı, 1415/1995.

Uluçam, Abdülsellam. "The Architectural Characteristics of Turkish Monuments in Cyprus." *Cyprus International Symposium on Her Past and Present, Gazimağusa, 28 October Ekim–2 November 1991*. Ankara: Eastern Mediterranean University of TRNC and Van Yüzüncü Yıl University of Turkish Republic, No: 9, 1994, 149–181.

Yıldız, Netice. "The Koran of Lala Mustafa Paşa." *New Cyprus* (July 1991): 22–25.

———. "Ottoman Period in Cyprus, A Glance at Turkish Architecture." *New Cyprus* (February–March 1992): 22–27.

———. "Aqueducts in Cyprus." *Journal for Cypriot Studies* 2/2 (1996): 89–112.

———. "Ottoman Houses in Cyprus." *Proceedings on the International Symposium on The Ottoman Houses, Papers from the Amasya Symposium, 24–27 September 1996*, The British Institute of Archaeology at Ankara and the University of Warwick, BIAA Monographs 26, 1998, 79–88, pl. 10.1–8

———. "Ottoman Culture and Art in Cyprus." *Learning and Education in the Ottoman*. World Proceedings, İstanbul 12–15 April 1999, Research Centre for Islamic History, Art and Culture (IRCICA), İstanbul, 2001, 259–276.

———. "Kıbrıs'ta Osmanlı Kültür Mirasına Genel Bir Bakış." In *Türkler*, edited by H. C. Güzel, K. Çiçek, and S. Koca, vol. 19, 966–993. Ankara: Yeni Türkiye Yayınları, 2002.

———. "*Vakfs* in Ottoman Cyprus." CIEPO–15th Symposium, (International pre-Ottoman and Ottoman Studies, The London School of Economics and Political Science, 7–12 July 2002 (in print by TAURIS Publications).

D

DAMASCUS

Damascus (Dimashq) is the current capital of the Arab Republic of Syria. In popular usage, it is widely referred to as *al-Sham,* a term that is also used to refer to greater Syria (i.e., *Bilad al-Sham*).

Damascus owes its existence to the river Barada, which springs from the eastern slopes of the Anti-Lebanon mountain range, and, after crossing Damascus, empties into the eastern and southern desert, forming around the city a fertile agricultural land known as *al-Ghuta.* The abundance of water and agriculture, along with the city's strategic location on the internal highway that connects the south (Egypt and Arabia) and the north (Mesopotamia and Asia Minor), allowed Damascus to play a significant role in Near Eastern trade and communication, and, at times, in politics, too, from antiquity to modern times.

The city plan took its shape inside the surrounding wall and its seven gates during the Roman period. The main east–west street (decumanus) is still partly in existence, and approximately in its middle was the Temple of Jupiter (which was converted during the Byzantine period into the Church of St. John the Baptist) and the market place (agora), the ruins of which still exist just outside the southern gate of the Umayyad Mosque. The town's houses were arranged in quarters on both sides of the main street, with small alleys and paths leading to them.

Damascus fell to the Muslim army in AH 15/636 CE and ever since has been under Islamic rule. It rose to significance under the Umayyads (r. 41–132/661–750), who chose it as their main capital and reorganized it as an imperial city. During that period, the first mosque built on a grand scale in Islam (the Umayyad Mosque) was constructed by orders from Caliph al-Walid b. 'Abd al-Malik (r. 86–96/705–715), who also ordered the construction of the Aqsa Mosque in Jerusalem. The site of the Umayyad Mosque and its courtyard was originally occupied by the Church of St. John, which included a small chapel built to house a casket that was believed to contain St. John's head. After the Islamic conquest, an earlier mosque was built in the southern corner of the Church's courtyard, although some Muslim historians suggest that the Church itself was divided into two sections: one for the Muslims and another for the Christians. Al-Walid ordered the confiscation of the property, and all preexisting buildings, including the Church and the earlier mosque, were razed to the ground to allow for the new mosque. The casket containing St. John's head was incorporated into the main mosque, where it still exists today. In 61/680, the head of al-Husayn b. 'Ali, the grandson of the Prophet Muhammad and the third Shi'i Imam, was buried in the eastern side of the mosque complex; however, it was moved shortly after 359/970 and buried in Cairo, in a mosque built for that purpose by the Fatimids of Egypt (the al-Husayn Mosque). These two figures of tremendous religious and spiritual authority made the Umayyad Mosque a center especially for local pilgrimage and subsequently augmented the religious symbolism (fada'il) of Damascus.

In addition to the two key figures mentioned above, local legends identify Damascus and its surrounding area as the birthplace of Abraham and the burial place of Moses and Mary, the mother of Jesus. Similarly, Jesus is believed to have escaped to Damascus with Mary and Joseph at the time of the Massacre of the Innocents—hence its association with the Qur'anic reference "wa-awaynahuma ila rabwatin dhati qararin wa-ma'ini" (23:50); it is also believed that He will descend into the city to usher in the End Times. The town's main medieval cemetery, Maqbarat al-Bab al-Saghir (this is outside of the southern Small Gate, which is also known as Bab al-Hadid), contains the graves of a large host of significant Muslim public figures and religious scholars, including companions of the Prophet Muhammad. All of this bestowed on Damascus—and, by extension, on Syria—additional holiness.

The city grew outside its walls, but it gradually lost most of its prestige and centrality, especially as compared with towns in Syria like Aleppo (Halab) and Hims after the ousting of the Umayyads. It reclaimed its political, intellectual, economic, and religious supremacy back when Sultan Nur al-Din (d. 569/1174) captured it in 549/1154 and made it his capital city, although its political prominence was lost again with his death. Nur al-Din ordered a major facelift for the city, including major renovations of some of its existing monuments and the addition of new ones, such as a hospice (al-Bimaristan al-Nuri), several schools for religious sciences (e.g., Dar al-Hadith al-Nuriyya), and several mosques. Since the time of Nur al-Din, Damascus has become one of the most prestigious centers for Sunni Islam, and its scholars (both natives and residents) played a significant role in the promotion and diffusion of Sunni Islam in Syria and the Middle East. During the Ottoman period, Damascus rose back to political supremacy, especially with the al-Azm family during the eighteenth century. Many members of the family were governors of the wilayet (province) of Damascus, which extended east to the Bekaa valley in modern-day Lebanon and south to Jordan and northern Palestine. The al-Azm family left their mark on the city, with their splendid palaces and public undertakings, including construction and renovation of the city's markets and caravanserais.

Damascus gave its name to several types of merchandise that were initially produced there and traded widely during the Middle Ages. The two most notable items are *damask*, which is a firm, lustrous fabric that blends linen and silk, and the *damask rose* (ward juri), which is a very fragrant red rose. A special syrup is made from the damask rose and used in desserts and a few other recipes; if diluted in water, the syrup becomes a refreshing drink that is usually served at weddings and on special occasions.

SULEIMAN A. MOURAD

See also Syria; Umayyad Mosque

Further Reading

Elisseéff, Nikita. *La Description de Damas d'Ibn 'Asakir*, 3 vols. Damascus: Institut Français de Damas, 1959.
Hillenbrand, Carole. *The Crusades: Islamic Perspectives*. Edinburgh: Edinburgh University Press, 1999.
Lindsay, James E. *Daily Life in the Medieval Islamic World*. Westport, Conn: Greenwood, 2005.

DANCING

At least from the early 'Abbasid period, Muslim authors were troubled by the active role of female participants in various popular festivals, the mingling of genders, and the sensuality that accompanied some of these rites. They particularly addressed the issue of music and dancing during these ceremonies; hence, the prevalent attitude of Muslim writers toward dancing is concentrated in works that criticize Sufi customs or condemn manifestations of popular Islam.

That these questions alarmed some writers is reflected in an anecdote narrated by Ibn 'Abd al-Hakam: Yazid ibn Abi Habib wrote to 'Umar and asked him about playing music and using tambourines and guitars at weddings. In response, the righteous caliph prohibited the playing of guitars but let the public beat tambourines. According to 'Umar, this denotes the difference between a wedding and fornication (sifah).

The jurists turned their attention mainly to those circles of Sufis that—through tambourine (daff) and flute (shabbaba) playing, hand clapping, and dancing (raqs)—attracted audiences to their public performances. Chanting, playing musical instruments, and dancing were magnets for the populace. Interestingly, the jurisprudents did not dwell on the music and dancing that were performed in the royal palaces.

An examination of hisba manuals and bid'a criticism confirms that dancing and music were not approved of. Condemnation of them is particularly conspicuous in works that criticize the quasi-Sufis (fuqara'). It is not surprising to find that those who wrote against popular culture and expressed disapproval of music and dancing also participated in campaigns against the manners and customs of the fuqara'. It seems that the principal objection of these fuqaha to music and dancing sessions (sama) was the sexuality associated with them, which would also explain their objection to singing (ghina).

A well-known example of such writers is Ibn Hajj al-'Abdari. This famous jurisprudent took a particularly fierce stand against the mingling of men and

Marriage of Akbar's brother at Agra in 1561. Folio from the Akbar-nama. Moghul miniature, c. 1590. (CT3443). Credit: Victoria & Albert Museum, London/NY. Victoria and Albert Museum, London, Great Britain.

women in any social or religious situation, and this was also the attitude of Ibn Taymiyya toward dancing and music playing as expressed in several of his works. In his discussions of the sama', Ibn Taymiyya provides his readers with extensive descriptions of the fuqara's' rituals and performances as well as with information about popular Islam.

Ibn Taymiyya differentiates between two types of spiritual concerts (dhikrs): one is legal (sama' shar'i), but the other one oversteps the bounds of Islamic law (kharij shurut al-masha'ikh). Ibn Taymiyya argues that, during the forbidden dhikrs, music is used to bring the participants to a state of ecstasy. He compares this practice to the consumption of alcohol or the use of drugs, both of which are strictly prohibited. He considers the deeds of the quasi-Sufis' to be a taboo, and he deduces that the shari'a forbids sama' that leads to ecstasy.

Ibn Qayyim al-Jawziyya opens his examination of music and dancing with a pseudo-fatwa (dated 740/ 1339). The question reads as follows: "What is the stand of our learned masters *(al-sada al-'ulama')* regarding *sama'*, which consists of playing musical instruments such as tambourine and flute, hand clapping, singing, and amusement. Men and women mingle and recite Qur'anic verses. Claiming that this ritual brings the participants in these ceremonies closer to Allah, the partakers argue that if a person dance his sins will be forgiven."

The question posed by Ibn Qayyim al-Jawziyya triggered answers by other fuqaha, thereby raising a wide range of issues. Some scholars imposed a total ban on music. They depicted behavior by the Sufi brethren that led some to brand such a group as "a band of disgrace." Moreover, they were incensed by scenes of women and young men dancing and chanting in the presence of mixed audiences. In one case, the heads of the Kilaniyya brotherhood applied to the Hanbali qadi of Cairo (in 852/1448) to ban singing and the playing of musical instruments. They further appealed to the sultan to prohibit the playing of drums and flutes in al-Rifa'i's lodge.

It goes without saying that the fulminations against music and dancing achieved only limited results. Rigorous 'ulama never succeeded in eliminating music from Arab, Turkish, or Persian societies, as can be deduced from chronicles and biographies; proof is to be found in the performances by Sufis that used music as an instrument to attain unity with God, in works by authors favoring music, and in accounts of the activities of professional musicians. The tariqa Mavlawiyya (Mevleviler) are perhaps the best–known examples that support this proposition.

The failure of the puritans might explain the position arrived at by other jurists, who distinguished

between licit and illicit poetry. These fuqaha' regarded loud supplication (awrad) and the reciting of Qur'anic verses as noble, and they permitted the chanting of hymns. An example of this line of argumentation can be seen in the writing of 'Alwan al-Hamawi.

YEHOSHUA FRENKEL

Further Reading

Al-'Abdari, Ibn Hajj. *al-Madkhal.* Cairo.

Al-Din Ahmad Ibn Taymiya, Taqi. *Al-Risala fi al-Sama' wal-Raqs.* In *Musique et Danse Selon Ibn Taymiyya,* ed. J.R. Michot. Paris, 1991.

Memon, Muhammad U. *Ibn Taimaya's Struggle Against Popular Religion: With an Annotated Translation of his Kitab Iqtida Assirat al-Mustaquin Mukhalafat Ashab al-Jahim.* Berlin and New York: Mouton de Gruyter, 1976.

Al-Din Muhammad Ibn Qayyim al-Jawziyya al-Dimashqi, Shams. *Kashf al-Ghita' 'an Hukam Sama 'al-Ghina',* ed. R.A. Khalaf. Cairo, 1991.

Al-Din al-Suyuti, Jalal. *al-Amar bil-Itiba 'wal-Nahi 'an al-Ibtida',* ed. M.H. Salman, 99–113. Cairo, 1990.

Izzi Dien, Mawil. *The Theory and the Practice of Market Law in Medieval Islam: A Study of Kitab Nisab al-Ihtisab of Umar b. Muhammad al-Sunami.* Warminster, UK: Gibb Memorial Trust, 1997.

Al-'Abbas Ahamd Ibn Hajar al-Haythami, Abu. *Kaf al-ra'a' 'an Muharramat al-Lahw wal-Sama'.* Cairo, 1951.

Al-Shadhili al-Tunisi, Muhammad. *Farh al-Asma' bi-Rukhs al-Sima',* ed. M. Sh. al-Rahhamuni. Tripoli/Tunis, 1985.

'Ali b. 'Atiyya b. al-Hasan al-Hiti al-Husayni al-Shafi'i 'Alwan al-Hamawi. *al-Sham a'Rasuha wa-Fada'il Suknaha (A'ras al-Sham),* ed. N. Alwani. Damascus, 1997.

Pouzet, L. "Prises de Position Autour de Sama' en Orient Musulman au VIIe/XIII Siecle." *Studia Islamica* 57 (1983): 119–34.

Gribetz, A. "The *Sama'* Controversy: Sufi vs. Legalist." *Studia Islamica* 74 (1991): 43–62.

Markoff, I. "Music, Saints and Ritual: Sama' and the Alevies of Turkey." In *Manifestations of Sainthood in Islam,* eds. G.M. Smith and C.W. Ernest, 95–110. Istanbul: ISIS Press, 1993.

Hammarlund, A., Tord Olsson, and E. Ozdalga, eds. *Sufism, Music and Society in Turkey and the Middle East.* Richmond, VA: Curzon, 2001.

DARA SHIKOH (1615–1659)

The eldest son and the heir apparent of the Mughal Emperor Shahjahan (d. 1657) and his favorite wife Mumtaz Mahal and himself an Emperor manqué, Dara never showed much interest in political affairs. He took part in one military campaign to Kandahar in 1659, which resulted in failure, and he only accepted the governorship of Allahabad in 1645 so that he could be near the Chishti mystic and philosopher Muhibb Allah Ilahabadi (d. 1648); he never took up his post in Allahabad and merely corresponded with the philosopher. Along with his favorite sister, Jahanara, he spent more time with literati and Sufis, affiliating himself with the Qadiri order. Their political disinterest led to his younger brother Awrangzeb to launch a successful bid to become emperor and outflanking Dara Shikoh. European travelers such as Bernier and Manucci regarded him as an aloof and arrogant man who had no real convictions and was hence interested in syncretism.

Dara was already associated with the Qadiri order at the time of Miyan Mir (d. 1635), but, along with his sister, he only formally joined in 1640, paying allegiance to Mulla Shah Badakhshi (d. 1661), Miyan Mir's successor. This in itself was a significant act: the heir apparent pledging allegiance to a Sufi master was an almost unique step during the Mughal period. Dara wrote two hagiographies of famous Sufis of the past and of the Qadiri order: *Safinat al-Awliya'* in 1640 and *Sakinat al-Awliya'* in 1642. However, his major literary contribution came later. In 1646, he completed his best work, *Risala-yi Haqq-numa*, which was a defense of monism that was steeped in the learning of the school of Ibn 'Arabi. His growing interest in following in the footsteps of his great-grandfather Akbar led to his encounters with Indian thought. In 1653, he met the kabirpanthi ascetic Baba La'l Das and asked him questions about truth, religion, and community, a conversation that was recorded for posterity in an intriguing mix of Persian, Sanskrit, and Hindavi by Dara's secretary, Candrabhan Brahman.

Dara's most obvious expression of syncretism came in 1655 with the completion of *Majma' al-Bahrayn (The Mingling of the Two Oceans)*. Drawing on Qur'an 18:60, he argued that the essences of Indian religions (he meant the Vedanta and Natha paths) and Sufism were the same. A rather mediocre work, its significance lies not in the quality of its composition but rather the identity of its author. It does seem that Dara had a good grasp of Sanskrit and of the technical terminology of the Vedic schools, because he himself translated this work as *Samudrasangama*. He extended this by commissioning a translation of the Upanishads. which was completed in 1657 with the title *Sirr-i Akbar (The Great Secret)*. He claimed that the Upanishads were the "hidden scripture" alluded to in Qur'an 56:78.

A patron of the arts, Dara commissioned paintings and albums that included depictions of himself that still survive. Awrangzeb, who was seen as a heretical aesthete, took advantage of Shahjahan's illness in 1658 and had Dara declared a heretic. During the ensuing trial, Dara was condemned, and he was executed on August 12, 1659. His political failure meant that he could not call on powerful defenders for his cause.

Since then, historians and Indians have debated what might have been. Awrangzeb has been cast as Dara's opposite, associating with Naqshbandis and treating non-Muslims harshly; this was in contrast with Dara's syncretic idea of "universal peace." Dara's real problem was that, by focusing on lofty ideals and transcendental unity, he had little understanding of political realities.

SAJJAD H. RIZVI

See also Akbar; Mughals; Sufism

Primary Sources

Shikoh, Dara. *Majma' al-Bahrayn (The Mingling of the Two Oceans)*, ed. and trans. M. Mahfuz ul-Haq. Calcutta: Biblioteca Indica, 1929.

———. "Mukalama Baba La'l (Entretiens de Lahore)." ed. and trans. C. Huart and L. Massignon, *Journal Asiatique* 209 (1926): 285–334. (English translation in Waseem, M., ed. and trans. *On Becoming an Indian Muslim: French Essays on Aspects of Syncreticism*, 106–30. New Delhi: Oxford University Press, 2003.)

Hasrat, B.J. *Dara Shikuh: Life and Works*. New Delhi: Munshiram Manoharlal, 1979.

Filliozat, J. "Dara Shikoh's *Samudrasangama*'." In *On Becoming an Indian Muslim: French Essays on Aspects of Syncreticism*, Waseem, M., ed. and trans., 131–44. New Delhi: Oxford University Press, 2003.

Göbel-Gross, E. *Sirr-i Akbar. Die Upanishad-Übersetzung Dara Shikohs*. PhD dissertation. Marburg: 1961.

Renard, P. "Historical Bibliography of Upanisads in Translation." *Journal of Indian Philosophy* 23 (1995): 223–46.

Shayegan, D. *Les Relations de 'Hindouisme et du Soufisme*. Paris: Editions de la Difference, 1979.

DATES AND CALENDARS

The Islamic calendar, also known as the Hijra calendar, is based on a lunar cycle that has twelve months of approximately twenty-nine to thirty days each. The term *Hijra* refers to the emigration of the early Muslim community in Mecca to the northern oasis of Yathrib (later known as Medina), a seminal event in Islamic history. 'Umar b. al-Khattab (r. 634–644 CE), the second Rightly Guided Caliph, designated the year that the Emigration (Hijra) took place (622 CE) as Year One of the Islamic calendar in 638. It has become a standard convention of the modern scholarship of Islamic history to provide both dates, with the Hijra year first, followed by the Gregorian calendar-based Common Era (CE) date: for example, 450/1058. Conversion from the Hijra calendar to other calendars is not an exact science, and detailed data (i.e., the day of the week, the month, and the year) are required before one can obtain an accurate conversion. This is due in large part to the methods that have been traditionally used to determine the changeover from one month to the next.

According to traditions that predate the rise of Islam, each new month begins with the sighting of the new crescent moon right after sunset and lasts until the sighting of the next new crescent moon; this system of dating based on the movement of celestial bodies or the moon with the sun is also known as a synodic system. Although this is fraught with potential human error, medieval scholars eventually settled on a more consistent system of giving the odd-numbered months thirty days each and the even-numbered months twenty-nine days each.

The twelve months of the Islamic calendar, in order, are as follows: (1) Muharram; (2) Safar; (3) Rabi' al-Awwal; (4) Rabi' al-Akhir (or al-Thani); (5) Jumada 'l-Ula; (6) Jumada 'l-Akhira; (7) Rajab; (8) Sha'ban; (9) Ramadan; (10) Shawwal; (11) Dhu 'l-Qa'da; and (12) Dhu 'l-Hijja. For administrative and agricultural reasons, medieval Muslims also used derivations of existing solar and/or fixed-month calendars from the region; these include aspects of the Ancient Egyptian seasonal calendar, the Roman Julian calendar, and the Persian calendar. Although the Islamic calendar and dating system was the overarching system used by medieval Muslims (especially with regard to religious holidays [eids]), Muslims from such places as al-Andalusia, Central Asia, and India would retain their traditional calendars and practices at the local level. Some key days in the Muslim calendar are Eid al-Adha (The Feast of the Sacrifice), which commemorates Ibrahim's willingness to sacrifice his son, Isma'il (10 Dhu 'l-Hijja); Eid al-Fitr (Breaking of the Fast), which is celebrated at the end of Ramadan; and Laylat al-Qadr (The Night of Power), which occurs during one of the last ten nights of Ramadan; on this night, the prayers of sincere Muslims are said to be answered. In addition to these days, such local traditions as the Persian Nawruz (Festival of the New Year) are observed, regardless of their non-Islamic origin. It should also be noted that, within Islamic society itself, there are some minor deviations in terms of ritual practice concerning dates and calendars between the Sunni and Shi'i communities. The most famous difference involves the commemoration of Ashura (10 Muharram); within the Sunni community this has some significance, but, within the Shi'i community, it is the commemoration of the martyrdom of Husayn b. Ali, the grandson of the Prophet, in 680 at the hands of Umayyad forces.

The Islamic calendar of twelve lunar months creates a year with 354 days; the result of this is that, over decades, the Islamic months actually travel throughout the solar-based seasonal year. The practical effect of this can be seen with the example of Ramadan, the Islamic month of fasting, during which Muslims refrain from drinking and eating between sunrise and sunset. At one point, Ramadan will fall during the winter season, when the days are shorter; a decade or so later, Ramadan will fall during the summer, when the time between sunrise and sunset is much longer. Medieval scholars of both the religious and natural sciences wrote numerous works about the proper methods for ascertaining the change in months as well as about their astronomical observations. Modern scholars have used these works, in addition to more modern calculation methods, to create reliable conversion tables; students and scholars also have Internet-based conversion tables at their disposal that allow for day-to-day conversions.

ERIC HANNE

See also Astrology; Astronomy; Festivals and Celebrations; Nawruz; Pagans and Pagan Customs

Further Reading

Birashk, Ahmad. *A Comparative Calendar of the Iranian, Muslim Lunar, and Christian Eras for Three Thousand Years: 1260 B.H–200 A.H./639 B.C.–2621 A.D.* Costa Mesa: Mazda in association with Bibliotheca Persica, 1993.

Freeman-Grenville, G.S.P. *The Islamic and Christian Calendars, AD 622-2222 (AH 1–1650): A Complete Guide for Converting Christian and Islamic Dates and Dates of Festivals*, revised edition. Reading, UK: Garnet, 1995.

Ilyas, Mohammad. *A Modern Guide to Astronomical Calculations of Islamic Calendar, Times and Qibla.* Kuala Lumpur: Berita, 1984.

Minai, Hasan Ahmad. "The Hijri Calendar." *Islamic Order* 2i (1980): 64–77.

DEATH AND DYING

Qur'anic Themes

"Every soul shall taste of death," declares the Qur'an in verse 3:185, in an expression suggesting why death ought to be a universal concern. Yet human beings, in the Qur'anic understanding, are not equally preoccupied with their mortality. Their attitudes differ strikingly, depending on whether or not they believe in the afterlife.

According to the Qur'an, infidels enjoy life without giving much thought to the hereafter. They cultivate the vineyards of this world, pay no heed to the Hour of Reckoning, and doubt that God has the power to recreate life from bones and fragmented corpses. A harsh surprise awaits them, for, after passing away from this life, they will suffer a second death, an afterlife of torment in the fire of Hell. Believers, by contrast, live in awe of God's power to create and destroy. They argue against the infidels that, if God can revivify with vegetation a lifeless land, so too can he quicken the dead, and that, on the Day of the Resurrection, they shall be rewarded with eternal life in the Garden.

This polemic dialog, recorded in verses 36:78, 56:47–8, and elsewhere, does not necessarily reflect actual exchanges between incredulous infidels and believing Muslims. However, regardless of its historic truth, the dialogue served to emphasize—if only in believers' minds—the reassuring notion that an omnipotent God would allow life to continue after death. The related belief that God controlled life and death—and that in fact He decreed or predetermined the very moment at which every individual's life should end—also offered consolation. Muslims, unlike early Arabic poets, did not see death as a misfortune striking loved ones unjustly and arbitrarily; rather, death for them was a part of God's wise—if inscrutable—plan.

Such consolation derived special meaning in an environment in which, as a result of tribal warfare and the military struggles of the first Muslims, the way of death was often violent. In fact, the theme of violent death is an essential one in the Qur'an. It recurs most frequently in the so-called Medinan verses, as O'Shaughnessy has pointed out. There are references to the persecution and violent death of several prophets, and one reads about killing by drowning, stoning to death, burning to death, and crucifixion. These ways of dying, although gruesome, need not be feared by those fighting in God's path, for martyrs only *seem* to undergo death: in reality, they continue to live with God.

Upon death, as during sleep, God sends angels to take the souls of women and men. He returns the souls of the sleepers to their bodies so that they will continue to live until their predetermined end, and He keeps with Him the souls of the dead. Deceased wrongdoers plead with God, asking Him to allow them to return to Earth, where they hope to accomplish the good works they had neglected to do during life. However, a barrier that shall be breached only on the Day of the Resurrection, according to verses 23:99–100, prevents the dead from crossing over into the realm of the living. In death, they must live with the consequences of their actions in the physical world.

The Ideal Way of Dying

Throughout early Islamic times, the Qur'anic ideal of suffering a violent death in the name of Islam remained appealing. In biographical works and in the hadith, the bravery of warriors for the faith, who expressed a yearning to die of battle wounds, was celebrated. Thus, Khubayb ibn 'Adiyy (d. 625 CE), who, according to Muslim tradition, inaugurated the custom of offering a special prayer before suffering death in captivity, boasted in a poem that mutilation was in no way a concern to him, convinced as he was that God would bless the limbs of his amputated body. The reward of Paradise was on the minds of holy warriors, according to Muslim tradition, and this belief inspired them to fight bravely even while anticipating the disfiguration of their bodies beyond recognition.

The hadith granted the status of martyr not only to those who died on the battlefield but also to several other categories of Muslims. For instance, those who died of plague, of a stomach ailment, by drowning, or in the destruction of a building were considered martyrs. The logic underlying this formulation seems clear: to undergo a painful, gruesome death counted as a way of meriting in the afterlife the rewards of martyrdom. It was essential, however, for the dying person, in agony, to not succumb to desperation; to reach Paradise alongside the martyrs of the battlefield, one needed to retain until the end a sense of composure and patience supported by trust in God's judgment.

Dying of old age in one's bed was less admirable than dying in battle, but Muslims who anticipated a peaceful death could undertake certain preparations to reach the end of life properly. First, they would need to discharge any unpaid debts. Failure to fulfill this financial obligation would result in suffering in the afterlife, according to the hadith. Second, dying persons were obliged to provide loved ones with instructions about what shrouds they wished to wear to the grave. This was an important specification to make, because burial attire was typically very expensive and often purchased after death. Muslims typically expressed in their last will not only a desire for modest clothes (as noted by Ibn Sa'd in his biographies of famous women and men), but they also often specified that their funeral procession should not be accompanied by candles, which seemed a superfluous expenditure, nor by professional wailers, whose laments seemed to protest God's decree to terminate an individual's life.

These deathbed instructions may not appear particularly Islamic, but Muslims did develop certain idealized, Islamic forms of reaching the end of life. Reiterating the name of Allah and reciting Surat Ya-Sin or another section of the Qur'an dealing with the resurrection of the dead were considered exemplary ways to die. However, the most striking of the Islamic forms of dying involved one's physical orientation. It was associated in the first instance with Muhammad's daughter, Fatima (d. 632). Anticipating death, she asked for her bed to be placed in the middle of the house, and she then lay down on it facing the qibla, the Muslim direction of prayer. This way of dying became an ideal that, according to biographers, pious Muslims such as Caliph 'Umar ibn 'Abd al-'Aziz (d. 720) followed in the moments before death.

Natural and Unnatural Death

Death as a result of illness, old age, or holy war did not require theological explanation. It seemed clear in such cases that the event had been decreed if not predetermined by God. What was harder to explain was death by an unnatural or accidental cause, as in the cases of murder and suicide. A death of this sort seemed, in the eyes of some Mu'tazilites, to cut short the natural span of one's life, of which God knew in his prescience. Murderers and suicide victims, they argued, followed their own wills in terminating life prematurely and acting against God's foreknowledge of the time at which death would have occurred had the divine plan not been interfered with. It was wrong to commit murder or suicide, they reasoned, and therefore unreasonable to believe that God in his justice and goodness predetermined such a way of dying in advance. Orthodox theologians disagreed. In their predestinarian view, the moment of death was always anticipated by God, whether the death seemed just or unjust; divine justice was postponed until after death. Persons who killed others or themselves would be tortured in the afterlife in a retributive scheme, punished in Hell with the same instruments they had used to terminate life.

Natural death was the subject not of theological but of medical explanation. In the view of Ibn Sina (d. 1037) and other exponents of Greco-Muslim medicine, this way of dying appeared to be the endpoint of the process of senescence. With aging, the human body gradually loses the ability to balance its primary qualities and constituent humors. Because, in old age, the innate heat (one of the primary qualities that burns most vigorously in youthful bodies) begins to fail, the body enters a state of disequilibrium. It steadily loses moisture, and it becomes drier and colder; eventually this process results in death. In juxtaposition with this explanation, which follows the Aristotelian view of the etiology of disease, Muslim authors also presented the Galenic–Hippocratic scheme of humoral pathology. According to this scheme, disease was caused by a disturbance of the mixture of essential bodily fluids: blood, phlegm, black bile, and yellow bile—the four humors. A pronounced disorder of humoral composition could also end in death.

To prevent natural death from occurring is not the aim of medicine, Ibn Sina clarified in *The Canon of Medicine*. Natural death occurs by divine decree, whenever a person reaches his or her appointed end, which depends on one's own individual constitution. The purpose of the art of medicine was simply to maintain, through a regimen that took both dietary and environmental factors into account, a person's body in a state of equilibrium. In his treatise about the ailments of the body in Egypt, Ibn Ridwan (d. 1068) lists exposure to overly dry air, an abrupt change in diet, and drinking water contaminated with dead matter as factors leading to epidemic disease and widespread mortality.

This discussion about the natural and unnatural causes of death was of course theoretical: it reveals attitudes toward death, but it does not provide a concrete idea about how Muslims usually died, how long their life spans were, and so on. Such knowledge could come only from archaeological excavations of Muslim cemeteries, accompanied by paleopathological analysis. Unfortunately, the archaeology of death in Islam is still in its infancy, and such analysis is lacking. However, there is one short study of a cemetery in Alexandria, whose burials dating from the thirteenth and fourteenth centuries are worthy of report. Of 489 subjects, 172 were adult males, 193 were adult females, 115 were children, and 9 were of undetermined age or sex. The mean age of the adult males was forty-five years; of the females, it was thirty-five years. Spondylitis, an inflammation of the vertebrae, affected many of the older men and women, who lived beyond the age of sixty and seventy. Neoplastic tumors and skull traumas were not uncommon. These findings provide us with some indication of the high incidence of mortality in children (nearly a quarter of the total deaths) as well as some measure of the average life span of women and men in a late-medieval city.

Status of the Corpse

Collections of hadith and of law and jurisprudence include numerous regulations regarding the care of the dead. Normally they devote an entire volume to the subject under the title *Kitab al-Jana'iz (The Book on Funerals)*; however, occasionally, discussion of the topic is subsumed under the volumes devoted to prayer and purity. In this corpus, the acts of the Prophet Muhammad and of the first generation of Muslims figure prominently. One learns from this literature about the proper way for Muslims to mourn, wash corpses, process toward the cemetery, and bury and pray for the dead. These rituals are discussed elsewhere in this encyclopedia (see also: Burial Customs) and by Halevi in his social history of death. Here it will suffice to mention something about the status of the corpse in relation to notions of purity.

The ability of the deceased to produce impurity in corpse handlers was a key subject of discussion in Islamic law. Jurisprudents debated in particular whether or not corpse washing and pall bearing subjected one to a state of major ritual impurity; positions on these subjects varied. At one extreme, certain Sunni jurisprudents subscribed to a ruling by 'Abdallah ibn 'Abbas (d. 687), according to which deceased Muslims were considered pure and therefore in no way sources of impurity. At the other extreme stood Shi'is jurisprudents, who regarded deceased human beings as generators of major ritual impurity. What did this divergence of opinions entail? For Shi'is, it seemed necessary to perform a major ritual ablution after disposing of a corpse; for Sunnis, this seemed to be optional.

Pondering Death

The most famous medieval authors of books about death—Ibn Abi al-Dunya (d. 894), al-Ghazali (d. 1111), Ibn Qayyim al-Jawziyya (d. 1350), and al-Suyuti (d. 1505)—had moral lessons to impart. They described the process of dying and the afterlife to warn believers to lead a virtuous life, and they encouraged readers to imagine in detail their own deaths—down to the worms feasting on a putrefied corpse—to emphasize the basic notion that death was not an endpoint but rather a point of transition toward an afterlife that could be blessed or horrible.

These authors represented the process of dying as being most painful for the wicked. The spirit of an evil person was violently extracted from the body by terrifying angels. Then, after a brief tour of the hereafter, it was deposited in the grave to dwell in the corpse until the final judgment. During this period of the afterlife between death and the resurrection, sinners suffered tortures. The spirits of Muslims who died a natural death, who had prayed diligently, who had performed good deeds, and who had thought about the hereafter also inhabited the grave between death and the resurrection. However, these spirits—unlike those of sinners—experienced a blessed existence in the grave as a foretaste of Paradise.

Life in the grave was in some ways remarkably similar to life before death. The inhabitants of the grave lacked the ability to move their bodies, but they possessed an intellect. They were able to hear (according to an oral tradition that to some degree contradicted a Qur'anic pronouncement), and they could communicate with the living, mostly by the mediation of dreams. In these dreams, they would sometimes ask the living to perform deeds on their behalf—deeds from which the dead would draw tangible benefit, as Kinberg has shown. The gift of prayer would fill the grave of the deceased with light, and this light would ward off the dark tortures of the grave.

The stories by Ibn Abi al-Dunya and others regarding death and dying suggest a stark contrast between the fate of the blessed and the doomed; in this respect, they echo the sharp Qur'anic division between infidels bound for Hellfire and believers bound for Paradise. However, this similarity in moral outlook should not obscure two significant changes. The original post-Qur'anic stories dwell on the condition of the dead in the grave between death and the resurrection, a period of the afterlife neglected by the Qur'an, which concentrates instead on the fate of souls on the Day of the Resurrection and thereafter. More importantly, the post-Qur'anic stories admit a certain ambiguity in the status of believers after death. The tortures of the grave concern not only infidels but also Muslims who failed to pray earnestly or to pay their debts before dying. These Muslims could still hope to reach Paradise, but only after suffering retribution in the grave.

LEOR HALEVI

See also Afterlife; Black Death; Burial Customs; Disease; Epidemics; Inheritance; Suffering

Further Reading

Abdesselem, Mohammed. *Le Thème de la Mort dans la Poésie Arabe des Origines à la Fin du IIIe/IXe Siècle.* Tunis, 1977.

Abrahamov, Binyamin. "The Appointed Time of Death *(Ajal)* According to 'Abd al-Jabbar: Annotated Translation of al-Mugni, vol. XI, pp. 3-26." *Israel Oriental Studies* 13 (1993): 9–38.

Bauer, Thomas. "Todesdiskurse in Islam." *Asiatische Studien* 53.1 (1999): 5–16.

Eklund, Ragnar. *Life between Death and Resurrection According to Islam.* Uppsala, 1941.

Ghazali, al-. *The Remembrance of Death and the Afterlife (Kitab Dhikr al-Mawt Wa-ma ba'Dahu): Book XL of The Revival of the Religious Sciences (Ihya' 'Ulum al-Din),* trans. T.J. Winter. Cambridge, UK, 1995.

Halevi, Leor. "Muhammad's Grave: Death, Ritual and Society in the Early Islamic World." PhD dissertation. Harvard University, 2002.

Kinberg, Leah. "Interaction between This World and the Afterworld in Early Islamic Tradition." *Oriens* 29–30 (1986): 284–308.

Dols, Michael, transl. *Medieval Islamic Medicine: Ibn Ridwan's Treatise "On the Prevention of Bodily Ills in Egypt."* Berkeley, 1984.

Prominska, Elzbieta. "Paleopathology According to Age at the Moslem Necropoles at Kom el-Dikka in Alexandria (Egypt)." *Africana Bulletin* 14 (1971): 171–3.

Ragib, Yusuf. "Faux Morts et Enterrés Vifs dans l'Espace Musulman." *Studia Islamica* 57 (1983): 5–30.

Rosenthal, Franz. "On Suicide in Islam." *Journal of the American Oriental Society* 66.3 (1946): 239–59.

Simpson, St. John. "Death and Burial in the Late Islamic Near East: Some Insights from Archaeology and Ethnography." In *The Archaeology of Death in the Ancient Near East*, eds. Stuart Campbell and Anthony Green, 240–51. Oxford, 1995.

Smith, Jane, and Yvonne Haddad. *The Islamic Understanding of Death & Resurrection.* Albany, 1981.

Smoor, Pieter. "Elegies and Other Poems on Death by Ibn al-Rumi." *Journal of Arabic Literature* 27.1 (1996): 49–85.

Welch, Alford. "Death and Dying in the Qur'an." In *Religious Encounters with Death*, eds. F. Reynolds and E. Waugh, 183–99. University Park, 1977.

DECADENCE: NOTION OF

In the context of the analysis of cultures and the writing of their histories, the notion of *decadence* (and, by extension, the phrase "age of decadence") is used to describe a process of "falling away" (the literal meaning of the word) and of "decline." By implication, therefore, other phases or periods in accounts of developments within that cultural tradition are portrayed as being on a "higher" level from one or more points of view, that being a necessary prerequisite for the process of decline. The criteria that are involved in making such assessments involve assigning value to certain cultural trends while devaluing others. The entire matrix fits within what may be called the "rise and fall" model of cultural history, a term and title adopted by a variety of composers of narratives, Edward Gibbon and Edgar Allan Poe being two of the better-known examples.

An age of decadence is thus normally seen as a kind of "middle" period, one akin to eras otherwise known as "dark ages" or even "middle ages." The implication is that, although such periods may possess their own particular traits and trends, they are generally less worthy of the ascription of cultural value than those periods that precede and follow them. The precedent period is often regarded as a "classical" era (sometimes also called a "golden age" within the logic of such terminology), that being the time period during which a particular cultural system chooses to find the major bases for its sense of heritage and the system of moral values that are implicit in the construction of such a heritage. Such a classical period is normally seen as being brought to a close by one or more of a series of cataclysmic events, mostly involving invasions by outside forces. At the other end of such a central era, a process of modernity commences with yet another contributor to this model of history, in the form of a renaissance, whereby a movement of ascent out of a "lower" (dark, decadent) level of cultural production (however er determined) leads inexorably toward the contemporary period, from which the concept of modernity and the process of modernization can be assessed.

The application of these ideas to the organization and sequencing of Islamic history has been a complex process. What seems clear is that, although there were indeed several significant invasions of the Islamic world that had profound effects on the cultural history of the regions involved (e.g., the sacking of Baghdad in 1258 CE, the fall of Constantinople in 1453, the fall of Granada in 1492, and the fall of Cairo to the Ottomans in 1516), the way in which these transformations of the balance of power have been applied to the sphere of cultural production has created a set of historical divides that tend to de-emphasize those continuities that provide a more plausible logic for the analysis of creativity and changing trends in esthetics and critical thinking.

The very term *decadence* (inhitat) and its use to describe—or even to create—an historical sub-period in Arab–Islamic history seems to have been, in fact, an import to the region, one based on studies undertaken by both Western specialists on the Middle East region and Islam and also by the large number of Middle Eastern intellectuals who, beginning in the nineteenth century, traveled to Europe to receive their higher education. For example, the great Egyptian scholar Taha Husayn (d. 1973) wrote a dissertation about the historical theories of Ibn Khaldun (d. 1406) and encountered the writings of the French scholar, Gustave Lanson (d. 1934) about the nationalist project of writing literary history. He returned to Egypt after his studies in France to advise his fellow countrymen to return to the great era of the eleventh century and earlier in their quest for inspiration rather than looking into the creativity of the seven or so centuries of the more immediate past and its precedents.

Quite apart from the peculiar kind of logic represented by this attitude, it was to have an enduring effect on the sense of modernity that has been the topic of considerable debate throughout the twentieth century: any assessment of the balance between the indigenous and the imported, the Islamic and Middle Eastern on the one hand and the Western on the other, was heavily tilted in favor of the latter of the two. More recent times have seen attempts at a total reassessment of this balance, involving not only a re-examination of cultural movements during the nine-teenth century but also research into the cultural production of the so-called period of decadence itself to come to some conclusions about not merely the nature of the postclassical and premodern within Arab–Islamic cultural history but also the esthetic bases for the evaluation of the creative production of the time. These bases, to put it mildly, emerge as radically at odds with those of Western critical norms and expectations; these issues, one might suggest, are the origins of the entire problem.

Within the context of the Arab–Islamic heritage, one consequence of this set of scholarly attitudes has been a tendency to downplay and often to ignore some seven centuries of scholarship and creativity. This period is, almost by definition, indeterminate, but it can be seen from a cultural (i.e., nondynastic) perspective as stretching—mostly by default—from roughly 1150 until 1830. This is the period during which a short list of renowned writers would include the following: Ibn al-Farid (d. 1235), Ibn al-'Arabi (d. 1240), Ibn Khaldun, Al-Qalqashandi (d. 1418), Al-Maqrizi (d.1441), Jalal al-din al-Suyuti (d. 1505), Al-Maqqari (d. 1631), and 'Abd al-Ghani al-Nabulusi (d. 1731). However, apart from the relatively limited amount of attention that has been paid to these and a few other notable figures, there is a great deal else that is habitually glossed over as being part of an age of decadence and thus lacking in interest or importance. In more recent times, the earlier half of this lengthy time period—often dubbed the "Mamluk" period (a term, needless to say, that can only be used to refer to the more Eastern segments of the total region)—has been the subject of more concentrated attention. A somewhat more detailed and accurate picture is now beginning to emerge of at least the earlier centuries of the period—a picture that reveals the continuingly elaborate structures of court life, with its hierarchies of bureaucrats and chancellery officials, many of whom were contributors to the preservation and ad-vancement of knowledge. If their predilection for compilation and their tendency to digress and to in-dulge in elaborate wordplay have failed to interest or excite Western scholars who choose to base their evaluations on entirely different criteria than those favored by the indigenous culture, that should be seen as implying a confrontation of approaches but not an ascription (or condemnation) of "decadence."

By contrast, the period from the sixteenth to the eighteenth century remains almost a closed book in many disciplines of Arab–Islamic scholarship. The reasoning that suggests that the diminution of inspi-ration and output in Arabic scholarship and creativity can be attributed to the use of Ottoman Turkish in administrative matters appears on the surface to have only the most limited validity. This period is, above all, the one during which the label of decadence appears to have been the most harmful in that, apart from the efforts of a very few scholars, almost no attention has been paid to the cultural milieu of the times. As noted earlier, any assessment of the nature and process of the nineteenth-century movement known as *al-nahdah* (renaissance) is radically com-promised by this lack of information and scholarly interest.

The notion of decadence as a culturally evaluative term is one that is in need of a complete re-examina-tion within the context of Arabic and Islamic scholar-ship. The (mis-)use of the term as a way to leapfrog from a classical period directly to a purportedly mod-ern one continues to distort current understanding of those continuities whereby today's Arab and Islamic worlds link themselves to their heritage.

ROGER ALLEN

Further Reading

Allen, Roger. "Fikrat al-'Usur al-Wusta wa-Ishkaliyyat Kitabat Tarikh al-Adab" ("The Concept of Middle Ages and the Problematics of Writing Literary Histo-ry"). In *Fi Mihrab al-ma'Rifah (Festschrift for Ihsan Abbas)*, 167–73. Beirut: Dar Sadir, 1997.
———. "Introduction to The Post-Classical Period." In *Cambridge History of Arabic Literature*. Cambridge: Cambridge University Press, forthcoming.
Faysal, Shukri. "'Asr al-Inhitat." In *Al-Adab al-'Arabi fi Athar al-Darisin*, eds. Al-'Ali et al. Beirut: Dar al-'Ilm li-al-Malayin, 1971.
Musa Pasha, 'Umar. *Tarikh al-Adab al-'Arabi: al-'Asr al-Mamluki*. Beirut: Dar al-Fikr al-mu'Asir, 1989.
———. *Tarikh al-Adab al-'Arabi: al-'Asr al-'Uthmani*. Bei-rut: Dar al-Fikr al-mu'Asir, 1989.
———. Sallam, Muhammad Zaghlul.

DEGREES, OR IJAZA

Meaning "permission, license, or authorization," the term *ijazah* refers to several distinct types of academ-ic certificates in common use in medieval Islamic scholarship. The best known of these are the license of transmission (ijazat al-riwayah) and the license of audition (ijazat al-sama', sama'), which originally (or ideally) served as written records of the direct audi-tion of a text on the part of the recipient from the transmitting authority, whether the text was a single hadith report, a work by the transmitting teacher himself, or a work by a third party. The ijazah played an important role in the transmission of texts in all fields, and it was meant to guarantee the accuracy and authenticity of the student's manuscript copy. In an age before printing, the ijazahs recorded in series at the end of a manuscript often provided an accurate codical genealogy that reached back to the original author. In the field of Prophetic hadith, the formal transmission of a report from one authority to the next in the chain of transmission (isnad), authorized by an ijazah, was considered an important indication of its authenticity.

Technical discussions of textual transmission in works about hadith criticism (usul al-hadith or mustalah al-hadith) and in chapters about scriptural reports (akhbar) in manuals of jurisprudence (usul al-fiqh) assign the highest degree of reliability to direct aural contact, in which the student hears the dictation of the transmitting authority or reads the text back to that authority, descending by degrees to munawalah (the "handing over" of a text by the authority to the student) and wijadah (the "finding" of a text in the hand of the author). This scheme reflects a formal stress on the value of oral/aural transmission that early on became archaic, particularly when most of the texts so authorized were standard published works (e.g., the six canonical compilations of Sunni hadith). In practice, the ijazah of transmission was often a formality that did not guarantee that direct audition had taken place. In fact, the sources often report that a scholar transmitted a text ijazatan (by license) to indicate that he had not studied or heard it directly from the transmitting authority, which is in contradistinction with qira'atan (by reading). Teachers granted ijazahs for a book after the recipient had read out a few lines from its opening pages. They granted ijazahs by correspondence to "students" they had never met, or they granted ijazahs for all of their own works to students who could not possibly have studied them all. Young children—even babies—received ijazahs for attending dictations they could not understand. Students often received a general certificate (ijazah 'ammah) that granted them blanket permission to relate all of the works that a given teacher had the authority to transmit. Referring to this practice, Ibn Hazm remarks that the license that is in common use by his contemporaries is invalid, and he insists that the transmitting authority must list the texts for which he is giving authorization completely and exactly.

The acquisition of ijazahs played an important part in establishing scholarly status by documenting links to earlier generations of scholars in the Muslim community. The ijazah granted scholars permission to teach the fundamental works of the Islamic sciences and to cite them authoritatively. In some ways, however, ijazah collection became a symbolic activity. Al-Suyuti, for example, related hadith from more than six hundred authorities, and Ibn Qadi Shuhbah mentions another scholar who received ijazahs from thirteen hundred authorities; it is unlikely that these contacts could have involved any sustained study. Nevertheless, the piles of certificates that such scholars assembled were often collected into volumes, and they represented symbolic academic capital and served the important social function of establishing a scholar's identity and credentials. Shi'is and other minority figures could divert suspicion by collecting ijazahs from prominent scholars whose orthodoxy was unimpeachable. In addition, the exchange of ijazahs became a part of professional academic camaraderie. Certificates were usually expressed in elaborate rhymed and rhythmical prose (saj'), and they provided opportunities for scholars to impress their peers, flattering them with honorific epithets and showing off their skills in artistic prose composition.

There were no set texts for ijazahs, which could vary in length from a single paragraph to a sizable volume, but they did follow a relatively standard outline: (1) an opening prayer, praising God and blessing the Prophet Muhammad; (2) an introduction of the student, with genealogy and flattering epithets that were intended to indicate his academic accomplishments and relative scholarly merits; (3) some description of the circumstances under which contact occurred and under which the ijazah is being granted; (4) permission to transmit or teach, expressed by the term *ajaztuhu* ("I hereby permit him") and followed by the list of works subject to this permission; (5) a summary of the authority's own chains of transmission, establishing his right to transmit said works; (6) the authority's own bibliography, listing the works he has written for which he is granting permission to the student (this was not always included); and (7) a colophon giving the precise date on which the document was granted and often recording the place as well. Ijazahs were often issued in response to an istid'a' (written petition); the scholar so petitioned would record the ijazah on the same sheet of paper. Little is known about payment for ijazahs, but it is likely that payments or gifts were expected in some cases.

Al-Qalqashandi defines three categories of ijazah in common usage in Mamluk Egypt and Syria, including not only the license of transmission but also the 'ard (presentation of books) and the ijazat al-ifta' wa'l-tadris (license for issuing legal opinions and teaching law). Before embarking on advanced study, students would memorize introductory textbooks in various fields and then present them in an oral examination ('ard). The examiner would open the book chosen and ask the student to recite from memory the passages on which he alighted. One generally performed this 'ard in one's teens and repeated the performance before a number of scholars. For example, Muhammad b. Tulun (d. AH 953/1546 CE) received ijazahs for presenting one set of books from eightteachers at the age of fourteen. The certificate was written on a small square piece of paper, and several examiners might write certificates on the same sheet.

The license to teach law and issue legal opinions (ijazat al-ifta' wa 'l-tadris; also ijazat al-tadris wa'l-ifta' or simply ijazat al-ifta') is the type of ijazah that resembles the medieval European university degree most closely, for, rather than authorizing the recipient to transmit or teach a particular text, it attests to his or her mastery of an entire field (in this case, the law) and permits entry into professional categories: law professor (mudarris) and jurisconsult (mufti). The main difference between the two is that the granting authority is an individual professor, in the Islamic case, rather than a corporate institution in the case of the university. Despite this point, Makdisi has likened the ijazat al-ifta' wa'l-tadris to the medieval Latin *licentia docendi* and suggests that it served as a model for that degree. The license to teach law and issue legal opinions was clearly an actual document of official or legal standing. Al-Qalqashandi reports that such licenses were written in the riqa' script on Syrian or Egyptian paper, in folio, with evenly spaced lines a finger's width apart; this is the same format that was used for other important legal documents, such as patents of probity (isjalat al-'adalah), which established the candidate's qualification to serve as a notary or official witness. Al-Qalqashandi himself received a license to teach Shafi'i law and grant legal opinions in 778/1376–1377, at the age of twenty-one, from the leading jurist Ibn al-Mulaqqin (d. 804/1401). He copies the original document, with minor omissions, in Subh al-a'sha. Like the patent of probity, the license was often drawn up before a judge and signed by witnesses in addition to the granting authority. This license shows many similarities to the medieval Rabbinic semekha, although the relationship between the two has not been investigated to date.

The license to issue legal opinions is said to go back to the eighth century. Malik b. Anas (d. 179/795) was supposedly authorized to give legal opinions by seventy teachers. Al-Shafi'i (d. 204/820) was reportedly granted permission by his Meccan teacher Muslim b. Khalid to issue legal opinions when he was either fifteen or eighteen. The Maliki judge Isma'il b. Ishaq (d. 282/896) was authorized to issue legal opinions by Ahmad b. al-Mu'adhdhal (d. ca. 240/854–855). In these instances, it is not clear that a written certificate

was granted. At this point, it is clear that the practice of granting such licenses had become prevalent in Egypt and Syria by the thirteenth and fourteenth centuries, because the sources quote or describe a number of actual licenses, usually restricted to the law of one of the four recognized Sunni legal madh-habs from this period. Research to date does not indicate when the practice first became widespread. Occasionally, women also received the license: 'A'ishah bint Yusuf al-Ba'uniyah (d. 922/1516), scion of the distinguished Ba'uni line of Damascene scholars, studied law in both Cairo and her native Damascus; she obtained the license to teach law and grant legal opinions, and she gained wide recognition as a jurist (al-Ghazzi, 1945–1948, pp. 287–92) In Sunni circles, granting of the ijazat al-ifta' wa'l-tadris seems to have lapsed after it was replaced at al-Azhar by the European-inspired shahadat al-alimiyah (degree of scholarly status) in 1871. Called *ijazat al-ijti-had,* it survives to this day as part of traditional Twelver Shi'i legal education at the centers of learning in Najaf and Qum.

DEVIN J. STEWART

Further Reading

al-Amin, Muhsin. *A'yan al-Shi'ah*, 10 vols. Beirut: Dar al-Ta'aruf li'l-Matbu'at, 1984.

Dodge, Bayard. *Muslim Education in Medieval Times*. Washington DC: The Middle East Institute, 1962.

Fayyad, 'Abd Allah. *al-Ijazat al-'Ilmyah 'ind al-Muslimin*. Baghdad: Matba'at al-Irshad, 1967.

al-Ghazzi, Najm. *al-Matba'ah al-Amirikaniyah, 1945–58*.

Goldziher, Ignaz. *Muhammedanische Studien*, 2 vols. Hildesheim: George Olms, 1961.

———. "Idjaza." In *EI1*.

al-Hazm, Ibn. *al-Ihkam fi Usul al-Ahkam*, 2 vols. Cairo: Dar al-Hadith, 1984.

Tulun, Ibn. *al-Fulk al-Mashhun fi Ahwal Muhammad b. Tulun*. Damascus: Matba'at al-Taraqqi, 1929–1930.

al-Idfuwi, Ja'far b. Tha'lab. *al-Tali' al-Sa'id al-Jami' li-Asma' al-Ruwat bi-a'la al-Sa'id*. Cairo: Matba'at al-Jammaliyah, 1914.

Leder, Stefan, Yasin Muhammad al-Sawwas, and Ma'mun al-Sagharji. *Mu'jam al-Sama'at al-Dimashqiyah al-Muntakhabah min Sanat 550 ila 750 h./1155 ila 1349 m.* Damascus: Institut Français, 1996.

Majlisi, Muhammad Baqir. *Bihar al-Anwar*, vols. 107–10. Tehran: al-Maktabah al-Islamiyah, 1971–1972.

Makdisi, George. *The Rise of Colleges*. Edinburgh: Edinburgh University Press, 1981.

———. *The Rise of Humanism*. Edinburgh: Edinburgh University Press, 1990.

al-Munajjid, Salah al-Din. "Ijazat al-Sama' fi al-Makhtutat al-Qadimah." *Majallat ma'Had al-Makhtutat al-'Arabiyah (Cairo)* 1 (1955): 232–51.

al-Qalqashandi, Ahmad b. 'Ali. *Subh al-a'Sha fi Sina'at al-Insha*, 17 vols. Cairo: al-Mu'assasah al-'Ammah, 1964.

al-Sakhawi, Shams al-Din Muhammad. *al-Daw' al-Lami' li-Ahl al-Qarn al-Tasi'*, 12 vols. Cairo: Dar al-Kitab al-Islami.

Sezgin, Fuat. *GAS*. al-Sha'rani, 'Abd-al-Wahhab. *al-Tabaqat al-Sughra*. Cairo: Maktabat al-Qahirah, 1970.

Stewart, Devin J. "Taqiyyah as Performance: The Travels of Baha' al-Din al-'Amili in the Ottoman Empire (991–93/1583–85)." In *Law and Society in Islam*, eds. D.J. Stewart et al, 1–70. Princeton, NJ: Markus Wiener Publishers, 1996

———. *Islamic Legal Orthodoxy: Twelver Shiite Responses to the Sunni Legal System*. Salt Lake City: Utah University Press, 1998.

———. "Documents and Dissimulation: Notes on the Performance of Taqiyya." In *Identitades Marginales (Estudios Onomástico-Biográficos de al-Andalus XIII)*, ed. Cristina de la Puente. Madrid: Consejo Superior de Investigaciones Científicas, 2003.

———. "The Doctorate of Islamic Law in Mamluk Egypt and Syria." In *Law and Education in Medieval Islam*, eds. Joseph Lowry, Devin Stewart, and Shawkat Toorawa. E.J.W. Gibb Memorial Trust (forthcoming).

Al-Suyuti, Jalal-al-Din 'Abd-al-Rahman. *al-Tahaddoth bi-Ni'mat Allah*, ed. Elizabeth Sartain. Cambridge, 1975.

Tihrani, Agha Buzurg. *al-Dhari'ah ila Tasanif al-Shi'ah*, 26 vols. Beirut: Dar al-adwa', 1983.

Tritton, A.S. *Materials on Muslim Education in the Middle Ages*. London: Luzac, 1957.

Vajda, Georges. *Les Certificats de Lecture et de Transmission dans les Manuscrits Arabes de la Bibliothèque Nationale de Paris*. Paris: Centre National de la Recherche Scientifique, 1957.

———. "Idjaza." In *EI2*.

DESSERTS AND CONFECTIONS

Traditionally, the Arab cardinal virtues of generosity and hospitality are expressed by means of lavishly giving meat; milk, bread, and salt also play their parts in the rituals of hospitality. However, when food is lovingly described for its own sake, it is the sweet rather than the savory that takes pride of place. The pre-Islamic Arabs relished their dates and honey, both of which were beloved by the Prophet and extolled in the Qur'an; they remained important throughout Islamic times. Already, however, in pre-Islamic times, the inhabitants of Mecca had a foretaste of the sweet luxuries that were to become commonplace after the early Islamic conquests: 'Abd Allah ibn Jud'an, who had been at the Sasanid court, introduced the Persian sweetmeat called faludhaj (paludag in Pahlavi), a relatively simple affair made from wheat flour and honey but considered a great delicacy. It was in Persia that the conquering Arabs were to encounter a sophisticated cuisine that boasted numerous kinds of sweetmeats and confections. Its impact is visible in the Arabic culinary vocabulary, in which many names of the most popular confections are derived from Persian. In addition to faludhaj (which remained, in more elaborate forms [usually with almonds and sugar], among the most beloved sweets), one finds judhab (Persian gudab), sanbusak (Persian sanbusa; a kind of pastry or pie), and khushk-nanaj (Persian khoshk-nana, a kind of sweet biscuit), among others. An interesting hybrid is the very popular lawzinaj, which is made of almond paste wrapped in flaky pastry. The first half of its name is the Arabic word for almonds (lawz); the word entered many European languages, through medieval translations of Arabic medical treatises, as *lozenge*. The word *marzipan* (another sweet based on almond paste) has also been said to derive from Persian or Arabic; although this seems likely, none of the conjectures that have been proposed are entirely convincing.

The precise translation or identification of these and other sweetmeats is made difficult by the instability of the dishes: many different recipes are given for the same term throughout the centuries, with a variety of ingredients and methods of preparation, and they may even waver between the sweet and the savory as a result of the common habit of adding sweeteners to meat dishes. Gudab, for instance, is described in a Persian–English dictionary as follows: "Syrup of dates boiled down; a dish of meat, rice, vetches, and walnuts, on which a condiment of vinegar and syrup is poured; food dressed under roast meat." Alternatively, in a poem about a judhaba by the ninth-century poet Ibn al-Rumi, it is called (in Arberry's translation) "sweeter than the sweet...It is more sweet than sudden peace/That brings the quaking heart release." Another meat dish with sweet ingredients (honey, sugar, or molasses of dates or grapes) is sikbaj, a great favorite.

In addition to the Persian terms, however, there are many Arabic ones, such as *khabisa* (for a wide variety of puddings and jellies), *fatira* (a kind of pancake-like bread), *qatifa* (a kind of crêpe or pancake), *kunafa* (a kind of shredded-wheat pastry), *'asida* (a kind of pudding, already known from pre-Islamic times), and *halwa*, in its many forms, a term that itself means "sweet." Colorful names include *asabi' Zaynab* (Zaynab's fingers), a sweet pastry filled with nuts, and *luqaymat al-qadi* (the qadi's tidbits), sweet pastries shaped like dinars (according to a Mamluk cookery book) made with pistachio nuts and flavored with nutmeg, cubeb, clove, saffron, and musk, according to taste.

Although honey remained important as a basic sweetener, it had a serious rival in cane sugar (sukkar), which became known in early Islamic times, the word as well as the substance coming from Persia and ultimately India. The less wealthy would use the cheaper dibs (treacle or molasses). Although the place of sweets and desserts during the course of a formal dinner was by no means as invariably at the end as it is in modern practice, they tended to come toward the conclusion of a meal during medieval times as well. This seems to be reflected in the cookery books, in which the sections on sweet dishes are usually found toward the end. Large quantities of sweets were traditionally consumed at certain festivals, such as the end of Ramadan and the birthday of the Prophet. A "war" between meat dishes led by King Mutton and sweets (aided by vegetables and dairy products) under King Honey, with a wealth of culinary information, is the subject of an amusing literary composition from Mamluk times.

GEERT JAN VAN GELDER

See also Food and Diet

Further Reading

Finkel, J. "King Mutton, A Curious Egyptian Tale of the Mamluk Period." *Zeitschrift für Semitistik und Verwandte Gebiete* 8 (1932): 122–148; 9 (1933–1934): 1–18.

Rodinson, Maxime, A.J. Arberry, and Charles Perry. *Medieval Arab Cookery*. Totnes, Devon: Prospect Books, 2001.

Waines, D. "Sukkar." In *The Encyclopaedia of Islam, New Edition*, vol. 9, 804–5. Leiden: Brill, 1997.

DHIMMA

Dhimma is the term used in Islamic law for the covenant of protection (also called *aman*) that exists between the Islamic state and the tolerated members of the Qur'anically recognized non-Muslim religious communities (Christians, Jews, Zoroastrians, and Sabaeans) who live permanently within its boundaries. The medieval Arab lexicographers explained the word as being derived from the root for "blame," meaning that to violate the covenant was blameworthy. The protégés under this covenant were designated individually as *dhimmis* and collectively as *ahl al-dhimma* (people of the covenant). Although the specifics of dhimma came to be elaborated over the centuries, its essence goes back to two legal precedents: a Qur'anic verse and the theoretical treaty of surrender between the Christian communities of Syria and Palestine and the Muslim armies.

Sura IX, 29 enjoins Muslims: "Fight against those to whom the Scriptures were given...and follow not the true faith, until they pay tribute (*jizya*) out of hand, and are humbled." That is, after the scriptural peoples (*ahl al-kitab*) have surrendered, accepted the suzerainty of the Muslim community, and become humble tribute bearers, they are to be accorded permanent protection. The form of tribute paid for this protection was not regularized during Muhammad's lifetime. The Jews of Khaybar and of the oases of

northern Arabia paid half of their annual date harvest; the Christians and Jews of Yemen paid a poll tax of one dinar that fell upon all adults of both sexes, and they had to furnish certain services to the dominant community.

The second precedent was the so-called Pact of 'Umar, which was supposedly a writ of protection (*dhimma* or *aman*) from the time of Caliph 'Umar ibn al-Khattab (r. 634–644). It was based on several capitulation agreements, most notably the agreement with Sophronios, the patriarch of Jerusalem. The text of the document was probably redacted during the caliphate of 'Umar ibn 'Abd al-'Aziz (717–720), when there was a hardening of attitudes toward dhimmis in Islamic public policy. The Pact of 'Umar stipulates that, in exchange for the guarantee of life, property, and religious freedom, dhimmis accept a host of restrictions that reflect their subject status. Among these are the following: they may never strike a Muslim; they may not bear arms, ride horses, or use normal riding saddles on their mounts; they may not sell alcoholic beverages to Muslims; they may not proselytize, hold public religious processions, build new houses of worship, or repair old ones; and they may not teach the Qur'an (for polemical purposes), prevent kinsmen from embracing Islam, dress like Arabs, cut their hair like Arabs, or adopt Arabic honorific names *(kunyas)*.

Many of the provisions of the pact established a social hierarchy, with Muslims being dominant and dhimmis subordinate. Certain provisions, such as the obligation to provide hospitality to the Arab troops, to supply military intelligence, and to not harbor spies, reflected the first century after the Islamic conquests, when the Arabs were a minority occupying a vast empire; these eventually fell into desuetude. Other provisions, such as the prohibition against dhimmis building their homes higher than those of Muslims, clearly reflected a much later period; during the early years of Islamic rule, Muslims tended to settle in their own fortified camp towns and not in close proximity to the subject population. Other provisions (e.g., prohibitions against building or repairing houses of worship) seem to have been observed only sporadically. Because many of the new cities founded by the Arab conquerors came eventually to have dhimmi inhabitants with their own churches and synagogues, it was clear to all that they were built after the Pact of 'Umar had gone into effect. Sometimes a church or synagogue was found to be in violation of the pact, but usually the payment of a bribe or fine sufficed to avoid demolition or confiscation of the offending building. So, too, the many decrees throughout the Middle Ages renewing the stipulations that dhimmis wear dress that distinguished them from Muslims indicate that there was a lack of consistent enforcement. The fact that the Pact of 'Umar mentions only Christians is immaterial, because the Shari'a makes no juridical distinction among the ahl al-kitab. As a social reality, however, Christians and Zoroastrians were more highly regarded during the early Islamic centuries than were Jews, a fact that is noted by the essayist al-Jahiz (778–868/869) in his polemic against Christians, and that is also reflected in popular lore.

As Islamic law, institutions, and administrative practice evolved, the rules of dhimma became more highly defined and ramified. The tribute paid by the conquered peoples varied greatly from one province to another, depending on the terms of surrender made with the Arab commanders. Eventually, Islamic law required all adult dhimmi males to pay a graduated poll tax (jizya) of five dinars for the wealthy, three for the middle class, and one for the working poor (although not for the totally indigent), as well as a land tax (kharaj) for those who owned real estate. In his treatise on taxation written for Harun al-Rashid, the qadi Abu Yusuf (d. 798) discusses the proper administration of the jizya, kharaj, and percent ushur (literally tithes, but, in this case, tariffs). Dhimmis were required to pay a 5 percent tariff on their merchandise, as opposed to the Muslims, 2.5 percent. This still gave them a distinct advantage over foreign merchants, who paid a ten-percent rate. Abu Yusuf clearly states that dhimmis "are not to be oppressed, mistreated, or taxed beyond their means." He specifically rules out torture as a means of extracting payment of taxes, although he does require imprisonment. Nevertheless, jurists came to view certain repressive and humiliating aspects of dhimma as *de rigueur*. Dhimmis were required to pay the jizya publicly, in broad daylight, with hands turned palm upward, and to receive a smart smack on the forehead or the nape of the neck from the collection officer.

Differentiation (ghiyar) in dress from Muslims, which was probably originally a security measure after the Islamic conquests, came to be interpreted as a mark of humiliation. The Pact of 'Umar mentioned only that dhimmis should wear Arab headgear and that they should wear a distinctive belt (the zunnar). Specially colored garments and patches on outer clothing were added to the distinguishing costume by a decree of Caliph al-Mutawakkil in 850. Although this imposition was probably short-lived, distinguishing garments became the norm for non-Muslims during the later Middle Ages, particularly during the Mamluk Empire (1250–1517) and in the Maghrebi states. The muhtasib (inspector of markets and censor of public morals) was in charge of seeing that dhimmis complied with the dress code and the other restrictions on their mounts, saddles, and general comportment.

From the earliest days of the Islamic conquest, dhimmi officials had not only been left in charge of their own communities but were employed because of their administrative skills in the wider bureaucracy. The imposition of Arabic as the sole language of government records and correspondence under 'Abd al-Malik (r. 685–705) did not change this situation. In the eastern provinces, Nestorian Christians and Zoroastrians were particularly prominent in government offices; in Egypt, the same was true for the Copts, and, in North Africa and Spain, it was so for Jews. The only position not normally open to a dhimmi was that of vizier. Conversion to Islam, however, easily removed this obstacle to advancement, and, in a few instances, even this formality proved unnecessary. Muslim jurists and preachers decried dhimmis holding any positions of authority over Muslims, and pious edicts by rulers, such as the decree of al-Mutawakkil, occasionally purged non-Muslim officials. However, these bans proved only temporary. Islamic law finally came to justify the situation. The constitutional theorist of Islamic government, al-Mawardi (974–1058) ruled that a dhimmi could even hold the vizierate so long as it was a ministerial position of tanfidh (i.e., executing orders from the ruler) rather than one of tafwid (i.e., delegated with fully initiating powers). Public demonstrations of pomp and power by non-Muslim officials were viewed by the pious and by the Muslim masses as violations of the dhimma and at times led to violence not only against the offending official but against his entire community. The uprising and assassination of the Jewish vizier of Granada, Yehosef ibn Naghrela, in 1066, was accompanied by the wholesale destruction of the Jewish quarter of that city. The assassination of the Jewish vizier Aaron ibn Batash in Fez in 1465 not only entailed massacres of Jews throughout Morocco but brought down the Marinid ruler, 'Abd al-Haqq, and his dynasty as well.

There was a marked rise in anti-dhimmi sentiment and increasingly restrictive implementation of the rules of dhimma throughout the Islamic world during the later Middle Ages as a result of profound changes in the spiritual, social, and economic climates. The Reconquista in Iberia, the Crusades, and the Mongol invasions heightened the antipathy toward non-Muslims. Islamic society became more institutionalized around religious brotherhoods, guilds, and state monopolies. Graduates of madrasas (Islamic schools of higher education) increasingly squeezed non-Muslims out of the bureaucracy. The secular and humanistic atmosphere of the Hellenistic renaissance of the ninth through twelfth centuries also waned.

However, the basic notion of the dhimma as a binding compact of protection for the ahl al-kitab was never rescinded, except under heterodox regimes such as that of the Almohads during the twelfth and thirteenth centuries.

NORMAN A. STILLMAN

See also Almohads; Christians; Churches; Clothing and Costume; Copts; Diplomacy; Interfaith Relations; Al-Jahiz; Jews; Al-Mawardi; Synagogues; Zoroastrianism

Further Reading

Bosworth, C.E. "The Concept of *Dhimma* in Early Islam." In *Christians and Jews in the Ottoman Empire: The Functioning of a Plural Society. Volume 2: The Arabic-Speaking Lands*, eds. Benjamin Braude and Bernard Lewis. New York and London: Holmes & Meier, 1982.

Fattal, Antoine. *Le Statut Légal des Non-musulmans en Pays d'Islam*, 2nd ed. Beirut: Dar El-Machreq, 1995.

Lewis, Bernard. *The Jews of Islam*. Princeton: Princeton University Press, 1984.

Stillman, Norman A. *The Jews of Arab Lands: A History and Source Book*. Philadelphia: Jewish Publication Society, 1979.

Tritton, A.S. *The Caliphs and Their Non-Muslim Subjects: A Critical Study of the Covenant of 'Umar*. London: Oxford University Press, 1930.

DIPLOMACY

Diplomacy has been a core feature of Islamic political life since the days of the Prophet Muhammad. The earliest recorded instances of envoys and ambassadors appear when Muhammad dispatched message-bearing representatives to various oasis settlements in the Arabian Peninsula and to a number of political states (e.g. Byzantines, Sasanians) in the Hijaz, North Africa, the Holy Land, and the Iranian Plateau. Likewise, the Prophet was involved in negotiating and establishing a number of treaties, most notably the one of Hudaiba in 628, with non-Muslim communities. This early diplomatic activity was framed by a strong ethical agenda and sense of religious conviction; the Prophet's message to rival communities and empires was clear and unambiguous: submit and accept Islam or suffer the consequences. It is this polarized view of the relationship between the ummah and surrounding states that defined the future mechanics of international diplomacy, whereby the known civilized world was divided into the dar al-Islam (house of Islam) and the dar al-harb (house of war; everywhere that Shari'ah was not practiced). It was the obligation of every Muslim to expand through effort (jihad) the boundaries of the house of Islam at the expense of the house of war. However, during the initial phases of Islamic conquest, well-populated regions in Syria, Egypt, and Iran would capitulate and negotiate settlements whereby an annual tribute (kharaj or jiyya) was remitted in exchange for religious independence and military protection. The jurists were eventually forced to address this dilemma as the frontiers of the Islamic empire continued to expand: Which "house" did these autonomous non-Muslim regions belong to? Some, like Abu Hanifa and Ibn Hanbal, were committed to the traditional polarity, but others, like al-Shafi'i, accepted the existence of a third house: the dar al-'ahd (house of the covenant). It would appear that most medieval Islamic states accepted this schema for reasons of practicality and *realpolitik*. This was especially true for those densely populated peripheral areas of the Islamic world in which frontiers between dar al-Islam and dar al-harb had emerged: the Iberian peninsula, the Balkans, the Caucasus, and the Deccan.

In this context, the dispatching of ambassadors (safirs) by states such as the Cordoba Umayyads, the 'Abbasids, the Fatimids, and the Seljuks to negotiate ceasefires, peace treaties, and tributary arrangements became a regular occurrence in Islamic political activity. By the ninth century, there existed in 'Abbasid Baghdad a special government office entitled divan al-rasa'il wa'l-sirr (office of letters and confidential records). Moreover, as the 'Abbasid empire fragmented and semiautonomous states began appearing in Central Asia and North Africa, envoys (qasids) were sent regularly to Baghdad to secure appointments of investiture ('ahd, manshur) from the caliph. Nizam al-Mulk's eleventh-century *Siyasat Nama (Book of Government)* contains a chapter that describes the prerequisites for an ambassador: piety, diligence, loyalty, gravity, and—above all else—keen eyes. In addition to reporting the events of his mission, an ambassador was also expected to provide detailed information to his king about a rival empire's army, defenses, road networks, public works, and so on. The sending of ambassadors for such purposes became especially common in Spain and the Holy Land during the respective crusading periods, and it would appear that the twelfth and thirteenth centuries were especially formative for medieval Islamic diplomatic sensibilities. This sense of growing importance is attested to by the emergence of 'ilm al-insha (the science of epistolography) in different Islamic administrations and the production of a number of didactic and formulaic texts addressing standards of diplomatic correspondence for chancery officials.

Ambassadorial missions became increasingly elaborate and politically ambitious during the post-Mongol age; indeed, the Mongols themselves considered ambassadors to be sacrosanct representatives of a ruler, and they were shocked and outraged at the

Khvarazmian ruler 'Ala al-Din Muhammad's misguided decision to murder a retinue of Mongol ambassadors (ilchis) at Utrar in 1219. The Mongols used their affinity for diplomacy effectively after their invasions of the Islamic lands, receiving all manner of emissaries at the great tent-court in Qara Qorum and negotiating and concluding diplomatic arrangements with the Christian Crusader states in the Levant. Confessional divisions became less of a consideration during the fifteenth and sixteenth centuries as Ottoman rivals (Aq Qoyunlu, Safavids) approached various Christian powers (Venice, Hapsburgs, Spain) with proposals of Muslim–Christian alliances; indeed, the Ottomans arranged such an agreement with Francis I in the 1530s against Charles V. By the sixteenth century, ostentatious ambassadorial trains—with equally grandiose diplomatic communications and lavish gift-giving ceremonies—were the diplomatic norm in the Ottoman, Safavid, and Mughal empires. In fact, it was diplomacy and gift giving that allowed for the transmission of all manners of cultural artifacts across the central Islamic lands: scientific treatises, literary texts, illustrated manuscripts, *objets d'art*, and innovative craftsmanship and technology.

COLIN PAUL MITCHELL

See also Archives and Chanceries; Cultural Exchange; Espionage; Gifts and Gift Giving; Interfaith Relations; Muslim–Byzantine Relations; Muslim–Crusader Relations; Muslim–Mongol Relations; Nizam al-Mulk; Pacts and Treaties; Peace and Peacemaking; Political Theory

Primary Sources

'Abd al-Husain Nava'i. *Asnad va Mukatabat-i Tarikhi-yi Iran az Timur ta Shah Isma'il.* Tehran, 1963.
Ahmad ibn 'Ali al-Qalqashandi. *Subh al-'Asha*, 14 vols. Cairo, 1914–1922.
Faridun Beg. *Munsha'at al-Salatin*, 2 vols. Istanbul, 1858.
'Imad al-Din Mahmud Gavan Sadr-i Jahan. *Riyaz al-Insha'.* Hyderabad, 1948.

Further Reading

Aubin, Jean. "Les Rélations Diplomatiques entre les Aqqoyunlu et les Bahmanides." In *Iran and Islam*, ed. C.E. Bosworth. Edinburgh, 1971.
Bayerle, Gustav. *Ottoman Diplomacy in Hungary: Letters from the Pashas of Buda, 1590–1593.* Bloomington, IN, 1972.
Farooqi, Naimur Rahman. *Mughal–Ottoman Relations.* Delhi: 1989.
el-Hajji, A.A. *Andalusian Diplomatic Relations with Western Europe during the Umayyad Period.* Beirut, 1970.
Hamidullah, Muhammad. *The Muslim Conduct of State.* Lahore, 1973.
Holt, P.M. *Early Mamluk Diplomacy, 1260–1290: Treaties of Baybars and Qalawun with Christian Rulers.* Leiden, 1995.
Hurewitz. *Diplomacy in the Near and Middle East. A Documentary Record: 1535–1914*, 2 vols. Princeton, NJ, 1956.
———. "Ottoman Diplomacy and the European State System." *Middle East Journal* (1961): 141–52.
Istanbuli, Yasin. *Diplomacy and Diplomatic Practice in the Early Islamic Era.* Oxford, 2001.
Iqbal, Afzal. *The Prophet's Diplomacy: The Art of Negotiation as Conceived and Developed by the Prophet of Islam.* Cape Cod, 1975.
Islam, Riazul. *A Calendar of Documents on Indo-Persian Relations*, 2 vols. Tehran, 1979.
———. *Indo-Persian Relations: A Study of Political and Diplomatic Relations between the Mughal Empire and Iran.* Tehran, 1970.
Khadduri, Majid. *War and Peace in the Law of Islam.* Baltimore, 1962.
Lambton, A.K.S. *State and Government in Medieval Islam.* Oxford, 1981.
al-Hasan Shaybani, Muhammad b. *The Islamic Law of Nations (Shaybani's Siyar)*, transl. M. Khadduri. Baltimore, 1966.
al-Mulk, Nizam. *The Book of Government: The Siyasat Nama*, 2nd ed., trans. H. Darke. London, 1978.
Tolan, John. *Les Relations des Pays d'Islam avec le Monde Latin.* Breal, 2000.

DISABILITY

The study of disability in the medieval Islamic world is still in its infancy. Preliminary evidence indicates that infectious diseases and epidemics were the foremost causes of disabilities; other causes included wars, old age, and heredity. Although primary sources attest to the presence of a variety of disabilities, such as lameness, hemiplegia, and deafness, the extent and significance of such conditions—as well as attitudes toward them—remain largely unexamined. Scholarly studies of blindness, leprosy, and insanity in the medieval Islamic world do exist, however.

Blindness was one of the most common disabilities in the medieval Islamic world. Causes were many and included accidents, aging, and contagious infections like trachoma and smallpox. Glaucoma, cataracts, and ophthalmia also appear to have been widespread. In addition, consanguineous marriages may have resulted in a relatively high incidence of hereditary blindness. Blindness appears in a variety of works composed in the medieval period. Physicians wrote extensively about eye diseases, and they paid special attention to developing surgical treatments for cataracts. Biographical sources abound in descriptions of blind men (and, far more rarely, women). For example, the Mamluk official Khalil ibn Aybak al-Safadi (d. 1363) composed a biographical dictionary devoted exclusively to 313 distinguished blind men who lived between the seventh and fourteenth centuries. These include, among others, poets, scholars, physicians, political figures, muezzins, and those skilled in Qur'anic recitation. In addition, at the other end of the socioeconomic spectrum, sources indicate that blind beggars were a fairly common phenomenon. As for societal attitudes toward the blind, preliminary evidence implies that the blind were not necessarily stigmatized or marginalized and that their condition was not associated with moral, mental, or spiritual deficiencies (Malti-Douglas 1989).

Leprosy (Hansen's disease) appears to have occurred with moderate frequency. Medical, legal, and popular beliefs about the disease were complex and often contradictory, and the attitudes toward the leper were ambivalent. Some sayings of the Prophet Muhammad recorded in the hadith literature, such as "one should run away from the leper as one runs away from the lion" (Al-Bukhari, VII, pp. 408–409), were interpreted by some as an indication that leprosy was a punishment from God and/or contagious (although the Prophet himself denied the transmissibility of diseases in other sayings). Medical writings stressed belief in the contagious and hereditary nature of leprosy, and Islamic law curtailed some of the leper's rights, especially in matters of marriage and divorce. Although lepers were sometimes confined to hospitals or leper houses, they more often had freedom of movement, and, like the blind, many appear to have survived by begging. One historian has concluded that, unlike in contemporaneous Western European societies, "there was no social opprobrium" for leprosy (Dols 1983, 913).

The complex subjects of insanity and mental illnesses in medieval Islamic societies have received the most scholarly attention and are the subject of one monograph (Dols, 1992). A multifaceted picture emerges from a wide range of medical, legal, and literary sources, and from chronicles and travel accounts. There were several different types of conditions that today would be grouped under the categories of "madness" or mental illnesses, such as the following: the *majnun* (madman), who was often believed to be possessed by a jinn (spirit); the *majdhub* (holy fool); the melancholic; and the feeble minded. The legal rights and obligations of those considered feeble minded or insane were considerably curtailed, and a legal guardian was usually entrusted with their welfare. Physicians emphasized the physiological causes of mental illnesses, and they believed that most disturbances could be healed by restoring the correct balance of humors. Healing practices, however, were highly pluralistic: other treatments included religious healing, amulets, incantations, magic, and

exorcisms. Although the family would usually be responsible for its mentally ill members, hospitals usually included a section that was reserved for the insane.

Much more research is required before any meaningful conclusions can be drawn about societal attitudes toward physical and mental disabilities in the various regions of the Islamic world between the seventh and sixteenth centuries. Nevertheless, preliminary evidence suggests that the physically and mentally disabled were not necessarily stigmatized or marginalized.

SARA SCALENGHE

See also Disease; Epidemics; Mental Illness

Further Reading

Al-Bukhari, Muhammad ibn Isma'il. *The Translation of the Meanings of Sahih Al-Bukhari: Arabic-English*, 9 vols., trans. Muhammad Muhsin Khan. New Delhi: Kitab Bhavan, 1984.

Bazna, Maysaa S., and Tarek A. Hatab. "Disability in the Qur'an: The Islamic Alternative to Defining, Viewing and Relating to Disability." 2004. Available at: http://www.lancs.ac.uk/fss/apsocsci/events/dsaconf2004/fullpapers/bazna_hatab.pdf.

Dols, Michael W. "The Leper in Islamic Society." *Speculum: A Journal of Medieval Studies* 54 (1983): 891–916.

———. *Majnun: The Madman in Medieval Islamic Society*. Oxford: Clarendon Press, 1992.

Haj, Fareed. *Disability in Antiquity*. New York: Philosophical Library, 1970.

Malti-Douglas, Fadwa. "Mentalités and Marginality: Blindness and Mamlûk Civilization." In *The Islamic World from Classical to Modern Times: Essays in Honor of Bernard Lewis*, ed. C.E. Bosworth et al., 211–37. Princeton, NJ: 1989.

Miles, M. "Some Historical Texts on Disability in the Classical Muslim World." *Journal of Religion, Disability & Health* 6 (2002): 77–88.

———. "Disability in the Middle East: A Bibliography Comprising Materials with Technical, Cultural and Historical Relevance to Child and Adult Disabilities, Special Needs, Social and Educational Responses and Rehabilitation." 2002. Available at: http://cirrie.buffalo.edu/bibliography/MEasttoc.html.

DIVINATION

Divination in Islamic cultures—known variously as fal, tira, zajr, kihana, and jafr—consists of a wide variety of practices in which predictions about the course of future events are derived from the letters of the alphabet ('ilm al-huruf), numbers (hisab al-jummal), God's Beautiful Names (al-asma' al-husna), the stars ('ilm al-nujum), the reading of the patterns of tea or coffee left at the bottom of a cup (qira'at al-finjan), and the interpreting words and letters in the Qur'an (fal-i Qur'an) or verses composed by poets such as Hafiz (d. AH 792/1390 CE). Many divinatory practices—whether they emerged from the analysis of books (bibliomantic) or the interpretation of visions (oneiromantic)—were related closely to the religious concepts of revelation, prophecy, and the Apocalypse (Fahd 1987; Fahd, "Fa'l").

Falnamas (divination books) were composed for rulers in need of guidance during military campaigns or who were caught in difficult political circumstances. Among many such works were those executed for the Ottoman Sultan Mehmet II (d. 886/1481), who conquered Constantinople/Istanbul in 1453 CE (Ates 1953), and Cem Sultan, who vied for the Ottoman throne and died in 900/1495 while in exile in Naples (Ersoylu 1981; Ertaylan 1951, 38–42). During the sixteenth century, a variety of other apocalyptic–prognosticative (jafr or malahim) texts, some illustrated with paintings of the Mahdi (Messiah), Christ, Dajjal (the Anti-Christ), and so forth (TSK B. 373 and IUK T. 6624), were commissioned by Ottoman rulers and officials as well (Fleischer, 1990). At the same time, Sultan Murad III (d. 1004/1595) commissioned a Turkish translation and illustration of a fal-i anbiya' or fal-i payghambaran (divination by the prophets). At least two manuscripts of the work survive (Morgan 788, 242), both of which draw substantially on the text and iconography of a Jalayrid anthology of astrological and divinatory texts in Arabic that was executed in Baghdad in 801/1399 (Bodleian 133, 163v-169v; Carboni 1988).

Divinatory works (risala-ya fal or falnama) attributed to the last Shi'i imam Ja'far al-Sadiq (d. 148/765) (at times also attributed to the Prophet Muhammad's son-in-law 'Ali) use the verses and letters from the Qur'an for divinatory purposes or for seeking guidance (istikhara) from God (Duvarci 1993:53–116). Such works survive today either as autonomous treatises known as *Divination by the Qur'an (Fal-i Qur'an)* (e.g., BnF Sup Turc, 26; Sup Turc, 49; Turc, 191–192); more often they were inserted at the very end of Qur'an manuscripts and were given the titles *Fal-i Mushaf (Divination by the Codex)* and *Fal-i Kalam Allah (Divination by God's Words)*. Even the famous Mamluk historian Ibn 'Arabshah (d. 901/1495) composed a treatise about divining by the Qur'an (al-tafa'ul min al-kitab al-'aziz), a copy of which was executed in 1080/1670 (Princeton, Yahuda, 4639). Although many sixteenth-century Persian and Ottoman Turkish *Fal-i Qur'an* treatises survive today (*inter alia* Keir VI.42, VII. 48, VII.49, VII.52; Bodleian Or., 793, fs. 334v-336r; Staabi Ms. Or. Oct. 86,

fs. 370v-371r), this divinatory genre has not yet been subject to systematic research.

Scholarly attention has started to focus more carefully on the illustrated falnama genre, which typically combines large-scale paintings and facing texts that provide advice to the augury seeker (sahib-i fal) about when to get married, engage in trade, or set out for battle. The majority of these works were made in Iran, Turkey, and India from approximately 1540 to 1630 and bear the imprint of the earlier Jalayrid illustrated fal-i anbiya' mentioned above (Bodleian Or. 133). The earliest two falnamas were commissioned around 1540 to 1560 by the second Safavid ruler, Shah Tahmasp (r. 1524–1576). One is dispersed, and its paintings are held in a number of libraries, museums, and private collections (e.g., Lowry 1988:120–129; Robinson 1992, cat nos. 89–92; Welch 1985), whereas the other manuscript, although damaged, remains complete (Dresden Eb 445; Rührdanz 1987). These manuscripts combine representations of the prophets, Shi'i legends, folk stories about heroes and rulers, astrological symbols, and apocalyptic events such as the Day of Judgment.

Both Safavid-illustrated falnama manuscripts appear to have served as prototypes for a large illustrated falnama made in Istanbul for Sultan Ahmet I in 1019/1610 (TSK H. 1703) and another illustrated *Book of Divination* made in Golconda around 1610 to 1630 C.E. (Leach 1998, 221–227). A number of Mughal illustrated falnamas were made during the seventeenth century (Falk and Digby, 1979, pp. 13–9), and at least one late-eighteenth-century Persian manuscript survives as well (Robinson 1992, 297).

In general, divinatory procedures arose from folklore, although they flourished under the aegis of rulers. Finding Qur'anic roots to legitimize a number of such practices (in particular dream interpretations [Lamoreaux, 2002, cf. *Dreams and Dream Interpretations*]) or theological opinion toward divination was ambivalent at best and hostile at worst. Many practices thrived in the form of "licit magic," whereby prognosticative customs were seen as seeking guidance from God rather than seeing into the future.

CHRISTIANE GRUBER

See also Amulets; Astrology; Magic; Talismans and Talismanic Objects; Mythical Places; Mythology and Mythical Beings

Institutional Abbreviations

BnF	Bibliothèque Nationale de France, Paris
Bodleian	Bodleian Library, Oxford University
Dresden	Sächsische Landesbibliothek—Staats- und Universitätsbibliothek, Dresden
Keir	Keir Collection, London

IUK	Istanbul Universitesi Kütüphanesi, Istanbul
Morgan	Pierpont Morgan Library, New York
Princeton	Princeton University Library, Rare Books and Manuscripts Collection
Rotterdam	Rotterdam Wereldmuseum, Rotterdam
Sackler	Sackler Gallery of Art, Smithsonian Institution, Washington, DC
Staabi	Staatsbibliothek zu Berlin, Berlin
TSK	Topkapi Sarayi Kütüphanesi, Istanbul

Further Reading

Ates, Ahmet. "Fatih Adina Yazilan Falname Tercümesi." *Tarih Hazinesi* 11 (1953): 539–48.

Carboni, Stefano. *Il Kitab al-Bulhan di Oxford, Eurasiatica—Quaderni del Dipartimento di Studi Eurasiatici, Universita' degli Studi di Venezia*, 6. Torino: Editrice Tirrenia Stampatori, 1988.

Duvarci, Ayse. *Türkiye'de Falcilik Gelenegi ile bu Konuda Iki Eser: "Risâle-i Falnâme lî Ca'fer-i Sâdik" ve "Tefe'ülname*. Ankara: Ersa Matbaasi, 1993.

Ersoylu, Halil. "Fal, Falname ve Fal-i Reyhan-i Cem Sultan." *Islam Medeniyeti Mecmuasi* 5/2 (1981): 69–81.

Ertaylan, Hikmet. *Falnâme*. Istanbul: Sucuo lu Matbaasi, 1951.

Fahd, Toufic. "Fa'l." In *The Encyclopaedia of Islam, New Edition*, vol. 2, 758–60.

Fahd, Toufic. *La Divination Arabe: Études Religieuses, Sociologiques et Folkloriques sur le Milieu Natif de l'Islam*. Paris: Sinbad, 1987.

Falk, Toby, and Simon Digby. *Paintings from Mughal India*. London: Colnaghi, 1979.

Fleischer, Cornell. "The Lawgiver as Messiah: The Making of the Imperial Image in the Reign of Süleymân." In *Süleymân the Magnificent and His Time*, ed. Gilles Veinstein, 159–77. Paris: Documentation Française, 1990.

Shirin, Ibn. *The Interpretation of Dreams*, transl. Aisha Bewley. London: Dar Al Tawqa Ltd., 1994.

Lamoreaux, John. *The Early Muslim Tradition of Dream Interpretation*. Albany: State University of New York Press, 2002.

Lowry, Glenn D., with Susan Nemazee. *A Jeweler's Eye: Islamic Arts of the Book from the Vever Collection*. Washington, DC: Smithsonian Institution, 1988.

Leach, Linda. "Paintings from India." In *The Nasser D. Khalili Collection of Islamic Art*, vol. 8, ed. Julian Raby. London: Nour Foundation in association with Azimuth Editions and Oxford University Press, 1998.

Robinson, Basil, ed. *Islamic Painting and the Arts of the Book*. London: Faber and Faber, 1976.

Robinson, Basil, et al. *Jean Pozzi: L'Orient d'un Collectionneur*. Geneva: Musée d'Art et d'Histoire, 1992.

Rührdanz, Karin. "Die Miniaturen des Dresdener 'Falnameh'." *Persica* 12 (1987): 1–56.

Schimmel, Annemarie. *Die Träume des Kalifen: Träume und Ihre Deutung in der Islamischen Kultur*. Munich: C.H. Beck, 1998.

Welch, Antony. "The *Falnameh* (Book of Divination) of Shah Tahmasp." In *Treasures of Islam,* ed. Toby Falk, 94–9. Secaucus, NJ: Wellfleet Press, 1985.

DIVORCE

The legal dissolution of marriage in Islam includes four basic procedures: (1) the talaq (lit. "release"), which is the divorce of the wife after the triple pronouncing of a legally valid formula by the husband; (2) the tamlik (assignment) of the full power of dissolution to the wife in a contract; (3) the dissolution of the marriage by khul', which is the restitution of the bride dowry by the wife or her relatives; and (4) the divorce in mutual agreement and release of all respective rights (mubara'a). There are several other procedures, mainly different types of oaths and vows, that are provided for by the law but that are shown only limited social relevance.

The talaq is, according to a definition of the Tunisian jurist Ibn 'Arafa (d. 1400 CE), agreed on by most of the schools of jurisprudence as "a legal state that denies the husband the right to enjoy the benefits of his wife, and, if repeated two times by a free man and one time by a slave, renders his wife forbidden to him until after another husband intervenes" (Ibn 'Asim 1958, 318, n. 401). The latter clause pertains to the important judicial distinction between talaq raj'i and talaq ba'in (revocable and definite divorce). After the first and the second utterance of the divorce formula, a marriage is still legally valid and the reestablishment of marital relations a simple matter of revocation. After a triple divorce, remarriage is only possible with the intervening of tahlil: the former wife has to conclude a marriage with another man who subsequently divorces her. Legal proceedings—namely the intervention of a judge or a court session—are not a necessary prerequisite for the validity of talaq; more important are the choice of the right moment by the husband (a divorce should not take place during the wife's menses) and the observance of the waiting period ('idda) of three menstrual cycles of the wife. Another significant consequence of talaq addresses economical considerations: the wife preserves her own possessions, particularly the dowry that the bride received for the conclusion of the marriage.

The husband might assign the right for repudiation to his wife by allowing her choice (takhyir). However, the constitutive element of a tamlik contract is a predefined formula; for example: "Your divorce is in your hands" (talaquki bi-yadiki). The parties often set up conditions that delimit the wife's right to the occurrence of special circumstances (e.g., a prolonged absence of the husband, his marriage to another woman).

The definition of *khul'* by the Egyptian Khalil b. Ishaq (d. ca. 1365) emphasizes the judicial analogy with definite divorce: "The *khul'* is [...] a *talaq* with compensation" (Khalil b. Ishaq 1885, 96). Whereas a khul' divorce has to be initiated by the wife, its success depends on consent by the husband. However, if he is not willing to pronounce the talaq, his acceptance of a khul' divorce is more likely, because he could expect a significant restitution of his prior financial investment.

If both parties agree, divorce is possible with no compensation whatsoever. The opinions differ regarding whether divorce with mutual renunciation (mubara'a) constitutes a special form of khul' or a stand alone procedure of dissolution. Although there are no quantitative studies of this subject, one should not underestimate that, in a tribal context, most divorces seem to involve mutual consent (Layish 1991, 46).

Despite an obvious focus on divorce in the debates about Islamic family law, the state of research has remained rather behind most arguments. The literature is essentially marked by a lack of symmetry between the description of legal foundations and the evaluation of legal and social practice. As a result of this disproportion, most general statements about divorce in the Muslim world assess the provisions laid down in the Qur'an (notably verses 2:228–32 and 65:1–6) and in early Islamic jurisprudence (Schacht 2000). A small selection of more extensive firsthand sources is also available in English editions (Malik ibn Anas 1989, 221–238; Spectorsky 1993; Ibn Rushd 1996(2), 71–120). The evolution of divorce in customary law had been studied in tribal areas, from which one may infer more traditional situations (Layish 1991; Hanoteau and Letourneux 2003(2), 125–133; Schacht 2000, 155). Another approach to the social relevance of family law lies in case studies. For example, they have exemplified that women could acquire and use expert legal knowledge for the pursuit of their personal interests (Powers 2003). The attested-to material is, however, not yet sufficient to establish widely recognized patterns, and there is no doubt that social roles in divorce need further investigation.

TILMAN HANNEMANN

See also Adultery; Family; Gender and Sexuality; Marriage; Love; Tribes and Tribal Customs

Further Reading

Hanoteau, Adolphe, Aristide Letourneux, Alain Mahé, and Hannemann Tilman, eds. *La Kabylie et les Coutumes Kabyles*, 3 vols. Paris: Bouchène, 2003.

Asim, Ibn. *Al-'Açimiyya ou Tuh'fat al-h'Ukkâm fî Nukat al-'Uqoûd wa'l-ah'Lâm: Le Présent fait aux Juges Touchant les Points Délicats des Contrats et des Jugements*, ed. Léon Bercher. Alger: Institut d'Etudes Orientales, 1958.

Rushd, Ibn. *The Distinguished Jurist's Primer: A Translation of Bidayat Al-Mujtahid*, 2 vols., ed. Imran Ahsan Khan Nyazee. Reading, UK: Garnet, 1996.

Ishaq, Khalil b. *Mukhtasar fi l-Fiqh 'ala Madhhab al-Imam Malik ibn Anas li-Khalil ibn Ishaq ibn Ya'qub al-Maliki*, ed. Gustave Richebé. Paris: Imp. Nationale, 1885.

Layish, Aharon. *Divorce in the Lybian Family: A Study Based on the Sijills of the Shari'a Courts of Ajdabiyya and Kufra*. New York and others: New York University Press and The Magnes Press, 1991.

ibn Anas, Malik. *Al-Muwatta of Imam Malik ibn Anas: The First Formulation of Islamic Law*, ed. Aisha Abdurrahman Bewley. London and New York: Kegan Paul, 1989.

Powers, David S. "Women and Divorce in the Islamic West: Three Cases." *Hawwa* 1 (2003): 29–45.

Schacht, Joseph. "Art. Talak (In Classical Islamic Law)." In *The Encyclopaedia of Islam, New Edition*, vol. X, 151–5. Leiden: Brill, 2000.

Spectorsky, Susan A., ed. *Chapters on Marriage and Divorce: Responses of Ibn Hanbal and Ibn Rahwayh*. Austin: University of Texas Press, 1993.

Toledano, Ehud R. *Judicial Practice and Family Law in Morocco: The Chapter on Marriage from Sijilmasi's Al-'Amal Al-Mutlaq*. Boulder, CO: 1981.

DOME OF THE ROCK

The Dome of the Rock (Qubbat al-Sakhra) in Jerusalem is the oldest standing monument of Islamic architecture. It was built on the site of the Jewish Temple by orders from the Umayyad caliph 'Abd al-Malik b. Marwan (d. AH 65–86/685–705 CE), and its construction was completed in 72/691–692. The Dome of the Rock, along with the Aqsa mosque (al-Masjid al-Aqsa) constitute the Haram al-Sharif, which corresponds to Herod's enlarged Temple Mount area.

The Dome of the Rock is a unique monument as compared to other Islamic monuments. It is not a mosque, and it was not intended to function as such. Whatever the reason for its construction might have been, it was and remains the most impressive example of Islamic religious architecture. The shape of the building is octagonal, with a diameter of forty-eight meters, and the structure consists of two ambulatories that surround the Rock, which are believed to be the site of the biblical story of the binding of Isaac (Genesis 22). The building stands on two arcades: an inner circular arcade that supports the dome and comprises twelve columns and four piers, and an outer octagonal arcade that consists of sixteen columns and eight piers. The dome is approximately twenty meters in diameter, and it rises approximately thirty meters above the building floor. In the panel on top of the octagonal arcade, there is the 240-meter-long foundation inscription that is coated in gold. At the beginning of the inscription, one encounters the name of the 'Abbasid caliph al-Ma'mun (r. 196–218/812–833), but this is because, when he authorized the

Exterior View. Completed in 691 CE Umayyad caliphate. Credit: SEF/Art Resource, NY. Dome of the Rock, Jeruselem, Israel.

renovation of the building, he ordered the name of 'Abd al-Malik to be effaced and replaced by his own. Part of the text of the inscription quotes Qur'anic passages (the most obvious cases are the references to Jesus [3:18-19, 4:171–172, and 19:33–36]), making it the earliest dated reference to the Qur'anic text.

The architects and artisans who constructed the building were local Christians, and they were well versed in that particular style of architecture, which is also found in similar monuments—especially *martyriums*—in Jerusalem and Syria. In its decoration, which blends Byzantine and Persian styles, the

creators used marble, painted wood, mosaics, and colored tiles. The outside of the dome was originally covered with gold sheets, which were later removed by the 'Abbasids. The building has undergone several major renovations; the most recent one, made between 1956 and 1964, restored the entire building, including the current gilded dome.

There are many explanations for why 'Abd al-Malik built the Dome of the Rock. The first explanation is that he was eager during the challenging first years as caliph to create a pilgrimage shrine in his domain to which Syrians would journey, for the

Ka'ba in Mecca was under the control of his enemy, Caliph Ibn al-Zubayr (d. 73/692). 'Abd al-Malik, according to this explanation, wanted to prevent any possible influence that Ibn al-Zubayr might exercise on the Syrians during the pilgrimage season. The town of the Jewish temple, Jerusalem, was the most appropriate choice for 'Abd al-Malik, and it was probably the only option. It has been also suggested that the Dome of the Rock was meant as a proclamation of the triumph of the new faith over the other two monotheistic traditions, Judaism and Christianity. With this second explanation, too, Jerusalem was the obvious choice because of its centrality to Jewish and Christian thought. A third explanation, which lacks support in Islamic literature, is that 'Abd al-Malik was rebuilding the Temple. A few contemporary Christian and Jewish accounts attest to this, including a Jewish *midrash* that names 'Abd al-Malik as the one who rebuilds the Temple.

Sometime after the completion of the Dome of the Rock, the site was identified as the place from which the Prophet Muhammad ascended to Heaven (mi'raj). This association, which represents the fourth and most popular explanation for why it was built, bestowed on the Dome of the Rock—and by extension, on Jerusalem—an additional, exclusively Islamic layer of holiness. Muslim legend has it that the Rock lifted itself when the Prophet stood on it to start his ascension; hence the widespread popular Muslim belief that the Rock is hanging up in the air. The inscription from the time of 'Abd al-Malik does not reflect any connection between the building and Muhammad's mi'raj.

Throughout Islamic history, the Dome of the Rock has attracted a cult of minor pilgrimage among the local population of greater Syria, and, to a lesser extant, Egypt, especially as a stop on the way to perform the major pilgrimage to Mecca and Medina. This practice generated protest from theologians like Ibn Taymiyya (d. 728/1328), who wrote against the practice of the minor pilgrimage to Jerusalem. In recent years, the Dome of the Rock has become widely used as the representative symbol for Jerusalem in Palestinian, Arab, Islamic, and even Israeli media.

SULEIMAN A. MOURAD

See also 'Abd al-Malik b. Marwan; Al Ma'mun; Jerusalem; Palestine

Further Reading

Elad, Amikam. *Medieval Jerusalem and Islamic Worship: Holy Places, Ceremonies, Pilgrimage.* Leiden: Brill, 1995.
Grabar, Oleg. *The Shape of the Holy: Early Islamic Jerusalem.* Princeton, NJ: Princeton University Press, 1996.
Raby, Julian, and Jeremy Johns, eds. *Bayt al-Maqdis: 'Abd al-Malik's Jerusalem* (Oxford Studies in Islamic Art IX.1). Oxford: Oxford University Press, 1992.
Johns, Jeremy, ed. *Bayt al-Maqdis: Jerusalem and Early Islam* (Oxford Studies in Islamic Art IX.2). Oxford: Oxford University Press, 1999.
Robinson, Chase. *'Abd al-Malik* (Makers of the Muslim World series). Oxford: Oneworld, 2005.

DREAMS AND DREAM INTERPRETATION

Terminology and Genres

Hulm, manam, and *ru'ya* are the three main terms that the Arabic language uses for "dream" (for Persian dream literature, see Ziai *Encyclopaedia Iranica*: 549–551). All three terms appear in the Qur'an (Kinberg 2001, 546–553) and in different genres of the Islamic Medieval literature (for Sufism, see Corbin in Grunebaum, 1996; for Shi'i Thought, see Ziai *Encyclopaedia Iranica*, 549–551, and Cemal Kafadar and Katz 1996). Hulm and manam occur during sleep, whereas ru'ya can take place either in sleep or in wakefulness (for ru'ya as a vision, see Fahd and Daiber 2002, 645–649). Manam and ru'ya usually indicate reliable and "true" dreams, whereas hulm is mostly associated with "false" dreams or nightmares (adrath ahlam).

Medieval Islamic literature makes a clear distinction between dreams and dream interpretation. As two separate genres, each is characterized by its own goals and styles. Dream interpretation is known in Arabic as *ta'bir* (interpretation of dreams; oneirocriticism), and it exists as an independent genre or as part of the inclusive adab literature. Dreams consist of dream narratives, known as *manamat* (pl. of *manam,* which means dream). Dream narratives have never developed into a separate genre and can be considered part of the hadith literature.

Works that belong to the ta'bir literature and that specialize in the interpretation of dreams often function as reference books. They provide general information about the scientific aspects of oneirocriticism, deal with the necessary qualifications that dream interpreters should acquire, discuss the dreamer's mental and physical conditions that are critical to the right understanding of dreams, and state strict rules for interpretation. These works are often arranged thematically, or they may take the form of a lexicon and deal with the items that appear in the dreams. Prominent representatives of the Muslim oneirocriticism works that have survived out of a much larger number of works (for a list of dream-interpretation works, see Fahd 1966:330–61) include the pseudo Ibn Sirin's *Muntakhab al-Kalam fi Tafsir al-Ahlam*; *'Ibarat al-Ru'ya* (manuscript) by Ibn Qutaybah (d. AH 276/889 CE); *al-Bisharhah wa-al-Nidharah fi Ta'bir al-Ru'ya wa-al-Muraqabah* (manuscript) by Abu Sa'd al-Khargushi (d. AH 406/1015 CE); *al-Isharat fi 'Ilm al-'Ibarat* by Ibn Shahin al-Zahiri (d. AH 873/1468 CE); and *Ta'tīr al-Anam fi Tafsir al-Ahlam* by 'Abd al-Ghani al-Nabulsi (d. AH 1144/1731 CE). Although the pre-Islamic heritage (especially pre-Islamic poetry) and the Islamic spirit (especially Qur'anic verses) inspire large portions of these books, their methodology is based on the old Greek system of dream interpretation. The latter was introduced into Islam during the third/ninth century, mainly by Hunayn Ibn Ishaq's (d. 260/873) translation into Arabic of the book of dreams of Artemidorus (see Mavroudi for the relationships between five medieval Arabic dream books, Artemidorus' work, and the *Oneirocriticon of Achmet*).

Dream narrations (manamat) have nothing in common with ta'bir manuals. The former are not concerned with oneirocriticism, they rarely use symbols, and they belong to works that impart verbal communication and bear self-explanatory messages. As a result of their explicit nature, these dreams naturally release the dreamer from the need to consult a dream interpreter. They are distributed in various genres of the classical Islamic literature, either in separate chapters within general works (each of the canonical hadith collections has a chapter dedicated to dreams) or as separate narrations scattered among traditions that do not use the medium of dreams (mainly biographical dictionaries). The only extant exception is the book of dreams, *Kitab al-Manam*, by Ibn Abi al-Dunya (d. 281/894); this is a collection of more than three hundred dream narratives that are mostly short and that follow a set of basic patterns (Kinberg 1994). The introductory part of the book addresses the relationship between the dead and the living and illuminates the general purpose of the work: to supply the inhabitants of the present world with moral advice that has originated in the other world and been delivered through dreams.

Function

From the earliest days of Islam, dreams have been treated as the bearers of transcendental knowledge, and they have consequently functioned as a reliable source of guidance. A widely circulated prophetic hadith regards dreams as the continuation of the Prophet's preaching, as part of prophecy, and as a compensation for prophetic guidance that has come to an end (Wensinck, 1/181, *b.sh.r.*). This notion is confirmed in another well-known hadith that declares that a vision of the Prophet in a dream is deemed equal to his actual appearance (Wensinck, 7/53, *n.w.m.*). In other words, it is not merely the actual meeting or the physical hearing of the Prophet that instructs people about how to behave; prophetic words heard in dreams may have the same impact. Since the vision of the Prophet in a dream is equal to actually meeting with him, Muslims who lived after the Prophet's death (10/632) may nevertheless "consult" with the Prophet in a dream. The ability to see the Prophet in dreams conveys a comforting notion of guidance that accompanies the righteous Muslims of all generations in their sleep.

It would be a major misunderstanding of the nature of the Islamic dream literature to assume that authorization through dreams was possible only with the Prophet's appearance. A saying ascribed to one of the leading dream interpreters, Muhammad Ibn Sirin (d. 110/728; see http://www.ibnsereen.com), states the following: "Whatever the deceased tells you in sleep is truth, for he stays in the world of truth" (*Ithaf al-Sada al-Muttaqin* 10/431). This saying is not focused on the Prophet's appearance but rather recognizes the authority of any dead person who appears in dreams. Here it is the medium of the dream—and not the presence of the Prophet—that creates authenticity. This idea underlies the hundreds—even thousands—of dreams found in classical Islamic literature in which a dead person appears in a living person's dream advising, instructing, preaching, or just telling about his or her own experience in the afterlife. The dreamer takes the advice or analyzes the implications of the condition of the deceased and acts accordingly. These dreams are based on the idea that the dead know (ya'lamun) but cannot perform, whereas the living can act (ya'malun) but do not know (Kinberg 2000, 425–444). The living are able to carry out deeds, yet they are not aware of their future significance; for this they need the special insight of the dead.

Guiding dreams, in most cases, are good dreams (manamat salihah) sent from God, whereas bad dreams (hulm, pl. ahlam) originate from the Devil (Wensinck, 1/504, *h.l.m.*; 2/205, *r.'.y.*). Having good dreams is considered a divine grace that is bestowed only on pious people; thus, when a righteous Muslim has a dream, it definitely contains trustworthy advice to be adopted and followed in daily life.

The large variety of dream-supporting statements created confidence in dreams and encouraged people to use this medium to promote their ideas. At the same time, however, it may have encouraged the misuse of dreams. It may be assumed that various trends and tendencies in Islamic society were furthered by groups using this medium and making up dreams to legitimize their ideas and goals. This means that, when examining dream material, one should not inquire about its authenticity but rather about the time and place in which it was told (Kinberg 1993, 279–300). Dreams of the manamat kind, therefore, should be evaluated as historical pieces of evidence. Like hadith, they should be treated as products of given circumstances that prevailed at a given time and place, made to answer certain questions or to approve of existing phenomena; like hadith, they should be considered as a mirror of their environment.

LEAH KINBERG

See also Adab; Death and Dying; Greek; Hadith; Hunayn Ibn Ishaq; Ibn Qutayba; Muhammad, the Prophet; Qur'an; Translation; Shi'i Thought; Sufism and Sufis

Primary Sources

Kinberg, L. *The Book of Death and the Book of Graves by Ibn Abi al-Dunya.* Haifa: Al-Karmil Publication Series, 1983.
———. *Morality in the Guise of Dreams: Ibn Abi al-Dunya's K. al-Manam.* Leiden: Brill, 1994.
al-Zabidi, Murtada. *Ithaf al-Sada al-Muttaqin.* Beirut; Reprint: Cairo: Bulaq, 1893.
Wensinck, A.J., and J.P. Mensing, eds. *Concordance et Indices de la Tradition Musulmane.* Leiden: Brill, 1936–1964.

Further Reading

Kafadar, Cemal. "Self and Others: The Diary of a Dervish in Seventeenth Century Istanbul and First-Person Narratives in Ottoman Literature." *Studia Islamica* 69 (1989): 121–50.
Fahd, T., and H. Daiber. "Ru'ya." In *Encyclopaedia of Islam,* 11 vols., vol. 8, 645–9. Leiden: Brill, 2002.
Fahd. "Les Procédés Oniromantiques." In *La Divination Arabe,* 247–367. Leiden: Brill, 1966.
Green, N. "The Religious and Cultural Roles of Dreams and Visions in Islam." *JRAS* 3 (2003): 287–313.
Gruenbaum, G.E., and R. Caillois, eds. *The Dream and Human Societies.* Berkeley and Los Angeles: University of California Press, 1966.
Katz, J. *Dreams, Sufism and Sainthood: The Visionary Career of Muhammad al-Zawawi.* Leiden: Brill, 1996.
Kinberg, L. "Dreams and Sleep." In *Encyclopaedia of the Qur'an,* vol. 1, 546–53, ed. J.D. McAuliffe. Leiden: Brill, 2001.
———. "Literal Dreams and Prophetic Hadith in Classical Islam—A Comparison of Two Ways of Legitimation." *Der Islam* Band 70 Heft 2 (1993): 279–300.
———. "The Individual's Experience as it Appears to the Community: An Examination of Six Dream Narrations Dealing With the Islamic Understanding of Death." *Al-Qantara* 21 (2000): 425–44.
Kister, M.J. "The Interpretation of Dreams, an Unknown Manuscript of Ibn Qutaybah's Ibarat al-Ru'ya." *IOS* 4 (1974), 67–103.
Lamoreaux, J.C. *The Early Muslim Tradition of Dream Interpretation.* Albany: State University of New York Press, 2002.
Mavroudi, M. *A Byzantine Book on Dream Interpretation—The Oneirocriticon of Achmet and Its Arabic Sources.* Leiden: Brill, 2002.
Ziai, H. "Dreams and Dream Interpretation." In *Encyclopaedia Iranica,* vol. 7, 549–51, ed. Ehsan Yarshater. New York: Bibliotheca Persica Press.

DRUZE

Druze historical origins are often traced to eleventh-century Fatimi Egypt, particularly to the year 1017 CE, when the propagation of Druzism began. The term *Druzism* is nearly one hundred years old and refers to the Druze religious doctrine, which advocates a strict form of Unitarianism (tawhid). Like other esoteric traditions, Druzism began covertly, and the Druze manuscripts speak of a twenty-one-year period of secret missionary activities between 996 and 1017. Both the historical accounts and the Druze manuscripts agree that the propagation of Druzism continued until the year 1043. Three leading figures—al-Hakim bi-Amr Allah, Hamza ibn 'Ali al-Zawzani, and Baha' al-Din al-Samuqi—were important during the initial years of the movement (996–1043).

From what little is known about the connection between al-Hakim and Druzes, it can be concluded that, between 996 and 1021, al-Hakim did not ban the Druze missionaries but rather permitted their activities, protected their followers, and approved their epistles. In 1021, al-Hakim left on one of his routine trips to the hills of al-Muqattam east of Cairo and mysteriously never returned. Unlike al-Hakim, his successor, al-Zahir, did not protect members of the Druze movement and instead ordered their persecution, because they recognized him as caliph and not as imam. This instigated a period of hardship that lasted several years.

Hamza Ibn 'Ali, the second leading figure, came to Cairo from eastern Iran in December 1016. A few months later, in May 1017, al-Hakim granted him the title of imam and the freedom to preach his reform doctrine openly. However, public resistance to Hamza's teachings increased as he spoke against corruption, the practice of polygamy, the remarriage of one's divorcee, and other social customs. During this external resistance, an internal rivalry arose between Hamza and one of his subordinates, al-Darazi. Darazi deviated from the essence of the movement's message and falsified the writings and teachings of Hamza to present al-Hakim as divine. He had hoped that al-Hakim would favor him over Hamza, but instead public opposition to Darazi's teachings increased. Darazi then redirected the public's resistance by declaring that he had acted on Hamza's instructions. Consequently, instead of attacking Darazi, the crowd turned against Hamza and his associates, who were in the Ridan Mosque at the time. Although Darazi was eventually killed and his teachings repudiated, many early and later observers, ironically, attribute the Druze doctrine to Darazi and do not mention Hamza at all. To date, Druzes and the Druze manuscripts consider Darazi the most heretical apostate. More importantly, Hamza is considered to be the actual founder of Druzism and the primary author of the Druze manuscripts.

During the same year that al-Hakim disappeared, 1021, Hamza went into retreat and delegated the affairs of the community to the third leading figure, Baha' al-Din al-Samuqi. Baha' al-Din continued public preaching with the approval of Hamza, who was in an undisclosed location known only to Baha' al-Din and a few other missionaries. He wrote epistles to both prospective members in new destinations and to those followers who had seceded from the teachings of the movement. He also sent missionaries to strengthen the believers and to provide further spiritual direction. Baha' al-Din continued his activity until the closing of Druzism in 1043; from that year to the present, no one has been permitted to join the Druze movement. During the same year, Hamza Ibn 'Ali, Baha' al-Din, and the other leading figures left Egypt. Druzes believe that these individuals will return on the Day of Judgment.

After this establishment period of the Druze movement, the Druze princes of the Buhturi (1040s–1507) and then the Ma'ni (1507–1697) families provided leadership to the Druze masses and protected the continuity of the religious reforms issued by Hamza Ibn 'Ali. Prince Fakhr al-Din al-Ma'ni II (r. 1590–1635) is often mentioned by some Lebanese historians as the early founder of Lebanon and as the source of Lebanese nationalism. Druze history itself was not, of course, devoid of both internal and external tribal rivalries. For example, to guarantee their survival, Druzes and their allies often fought against or cooperated with different Muslim regimes, including Mamluks, Ayyubids, and Ottomans.

Today there are approximately one million Druzes in the world, the majority of them living in four Middle Eastern countries: Lebanon, Syria, Israel, and Jordan. In addition to these larger concentrations of Druzes, smaller diaspora communities can be found in Australia, Canada, Europe, the Persian Gulf nations, the Philippines, South America, West Africa, and the United States.

SAMY SWAYD

See also al-Hakim; Isma'ilis; Fatimids

Further Reading

Abu Izzeddin, Nejla M. *The Druzes: A New Study of their History, Faith, and Society*. Leiden: Brill, 1984 and 1993.

Betts, Robert Benton. *The Druze*. New Haven, Conn: Yale University Press, 1988.

Firro, Kais. *A History of the Druzes*. Leiden: Brill, 1992.

Hitti, Philip K. *The Origins of the Druze People and Religion*. New York: Columbia University Press, 1928.

Makarem, Sami Nasib. *The Druze Faith*. Delmar, NY: Caravan Books, 1974.

Swayd, Samy. *The Druzes: An Annotated Bibliography*. Kirkland, Wash: Ises Publications, 1998.

E

EARTHQUAKES

Vast regions of the Islamic world frequently experienced earthquakes during both medieval and modern times. The main zones of high seismicity within the Islamic heartlands have been areas such as the Red Sea, the valley of the Jordan, and the Anatolian fault zone, which are situated on the borders between the Eurasian plates to the north and various plates to the south (most importantly the Arabian, the African, the Anatolian, and the West Iranian Plates). These zones display significant differences in their tectonic evolutions: whereas some are characterized by spreading and the formation of new oceanic crust (Red Sea), others are characterized by collision and subduction (Eastern Mediterranean). However, these regions have in common a long-standing history of active tectonic developments, and these have continued through the present. Alternatively, some regions (e.g., the Arabian Peninsula situated on the Arabian shield) belong, with the exception of Yemen and the Hejaz (incorporating Mecca and Medina), to the most seismically stable areas in the world. Although the inland of North Africa (the modern states of Egypt, Libya, and Sudan) is rather aseismic, it has been subject to infrequent earthquakes of considerable size.

In the self-view of the Muslim community, its history itself started with an earthquake: the birth of the Prophet Muhammad was purportedly accompanied by a violent seism felt throughout the known world. The early awareness of living in a seismically active region was also expressed by the fact that year 5 of the Muslim calendar was named the Year of the Earthquake and that the Qur'an contains an Earthquake Chapter (Sura 99, surat al-zalzala).

Reliable quantitative data about the occurrence of earthquakes during medieval times or even their effects are not available, and one has to rely to a large degree on anecdotal evidence. Furthermore, the sources present a highly biased picture, because earthquakes far from urban centers hardly found entrance into the written record. Consequently, knowledge of the geographical distribution of earthquakes during the medieval period reflects at least as much patterns of population density as the occurrence of earthquakes themselves.

Among the most destructive earthquakes in the medieval period were those in northern Persia, which were centered on the town of Qumis in 856 CE and felt throughout the Middle East, with a reported death toll of two hundred thousand; in northern Syria, which centered on the town of Aleppo in 1138; and again in Syria, in 1202, with the epicenter on the Lebanese coast. The effects of these and other earthquakes were similar: high death tolls, the wide-ranging destruction of fortifications and buildings, and the ensuing economic losses for most sections of the population.

The 1202 earthquake, for example, destroyed several towns situated on the Syrian coast, such as Acre, and it also destroyed large numbers of buildings inland, in towns such as Nablus and Damascus. The effects of the shock were felt in distant regions such as Sicily and Iraq, and they caused destruction as far away as Cyprus and Egypt. Sources quote a death toll of more than one million for the years 1201 and 1202 in Syria and Egypt, the latter also having been ravaged by famine and epidemics. Although such figures were rough estimations with a strong tendency toward exaggeration, they may be used at least as an indicator to show the extent of destruction; the total of thirty thousand casualties for the Nablus region alone for the 1202 earthquake, as quoted by a local source, reinforces this impression.

Such catastrophic events shaped the course of medieval Islamic history in demographic, economic, and military terms. The severe death toll and the material destruction caused by a series of earthquakes that ravaged Syria during the late eleventh century (1050, 1063, 1068, 1069, 1086, and 1091), for example, arguably contributed to the successful Crusader conquests during the following years. Earthquakes (as well as other natural catastrophes) proved to be highly destructive for much medieval building structure, because the traditionally used materials for houses in regions such as Persia—mud walls and adobe bricks—were of very limited stability when it came to withstanding seismic shocks.

For medieval Muslim authors, the occurrence of earthquakes was a phenomenon to be dealt with on many different levels. Chroniclers registered earthquakes and their effects generally quite laconically, without going into too much depth. Nevertheless, some members of the elite wrote about such catastrophes in more detail, such as the twelfth-century military commander and litterateur Usama ibn Munqidh, who composed a lengthy poetic work after he lost most of his relatives in an earthquake that destroyed the clan's stronghold in middle Syria.

A number of scholars wrote treatises that were specifically devoted to this subject, as did medieval scholars about other catastrophes, such as famine and plague. For example, the third-century philosopher al-Kindi dealt with the *Occurrence of Winds under the Earth Which Cause Many Earthquakes and Eclipses,* and Ibn 'Asakir (d. 1176) authored a *Book Of Earthquakes* (both of these have been lost); the Egyptian polymath al-Suyuti (d. 1505) included a detailed list of earthquakes in his treatise about the subject. These authors differed with regard to the explanations that they advanced for earthquakes. Some earlier scholars argued, under the influence of antique pneumatic theories of earthquakes, that they were caused by gases under the surface that could not condensate or escape. According to writers such as al-Kindi, al-Biruni (d. 1050), and Ibn Sina (d. 1037), the increasing pressure led finally to the seismic vibrations of the earth and its crust.

A second group of authors (especially after the eleventh century) ascribed earthquakes to God's immediate will and advanced elaborate cosmological descriptions to explain how He caused them. These descriptions focused either on the Mountain Qaf that, in their view, surrounded the earth and was linked to it by subterranean ramifications, or on the idea that the earth was placed on the horns of a bull that was carried by a fish. According to this group of authors (e.g., al-Suyuti), earthquakes were either the result of deviating behavior (adultery, usury, and consumption of alcohol) or signs of the approaching Last Judgment, an idea that is based on the Qur'anic Earthquake Chapter. In this worldview, God caused the Mountain Qaf or the bull and the fish to move so that the earth was seized by a wave of shocks as a punishment. A third set of explanations was brought forward by chroniclers who treated earthquakes only briefly in their writings; this group of authors suggested that the causes of earthquakes were astrophysical circumstances, such as planetary constellations or comets with long tails.

KONRAD HIRSCHLER

See also Floods, Epidemics

Primary Sources

Al-Suyuti. *Kashf al-Salsala 'an Wasf al-Zalzala*, ed. Muhammad Kamal al-Din 'Izz al-Din. Beirut: 'Alim al-kutub, 1987.

Further Reading

Ambraseys, Nicholas N., and C.P. Melville. *A History of Persian Earthquakes.* Cambridge: Cambridge University Press, 1982.
———. "An Analysis of the Eastern Mediterranean Earthquake of 20 May 1202." In *Historical Seismograms and Earthquakes of the World*, eds. W.H.K. Lee, H. Meyers, and K. Shimazaki, 181–200. San Diego: Academic Press, 1988.
Ambraseys, Nicholas N., C.P. Melville, and R.D. Adams. *The Seismicity of Egypt, Arabia and the Red Sea. A Historical Review.* Cambridge: Cambridge University Press, 1994.
Melville, Charles P. "Zalzala." In *Encyclopaedia of Islam, New Edition*, 11 vols. Leiden: Brill, 1960–2002.
Taher, M. "Les Grandes Zones Sismiques du Monde Musulman à Travers l'Histoire." *Annales Islamologiques* 30 (1996): 79–104.

EDUCATION, ISLAMIC

Education in Islam is understood as nurturing, raising, and teaching knowledge and moral values to improve oneself or somebody else spiritually, intellectually, and morally by following the orders of Allah and learning how to obey His will (Ittihad 1994). In

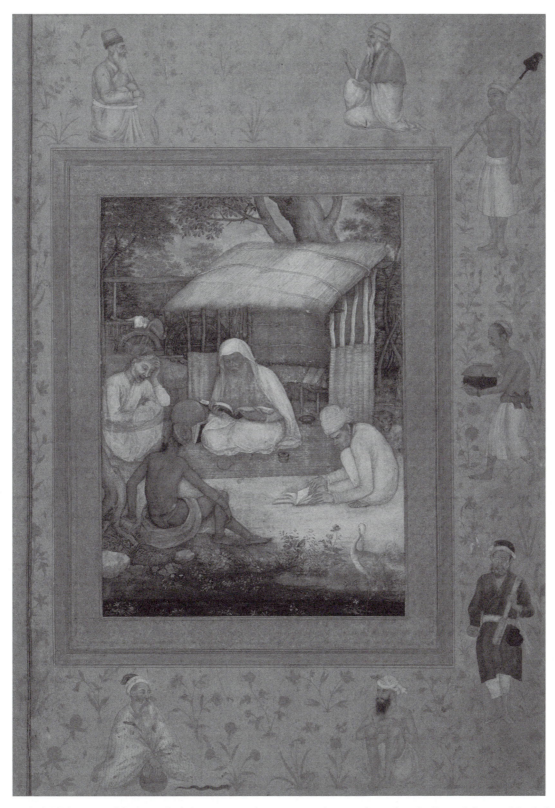

School, Moghul. Holy man with three disciples commenting on a text in a rustic setting. Indian miniature, Mughal school, early thirteenth century. Credit: Réunion des Musées Nationaux/Art Resource, NY. Musee des Arts Asiatiques-Guimet, Paris, France.

the Qur'an, God is referred to as *Rabbul-ul Alemeen*, which includes the meaning "the educator of all the worlds," thus showing the importance that Islam gives to education. Education is one of the most important factors of a healthy society; it is a means for a creature to achieve the purpose for which God created it, and, as such, belief and education cannot be separated from each other (Ittihad 1994; Gülen 2003).

Education in Islam is based on Qur'anic concepts. The Qur'an, according to Islamic teachings, is the literal word of God and contains all of the information that is required to lead a fulfilling life in this world and in the hereafter. The Qur'an states the following in verse 16:89: "And We have sent down to thee the Book explaining all things, a Guide, a Mercy and Glad Tidings to Muslims." The first revealed verse of the Qur'an is "Read," which demonstrates the importance that is placed on knowledge and learning.

An understanding of hadith (the teachings of Prophet Muhammad) is necessary to fully understand the Qur'an. This point is expressed in verse 16:44: "And We have sent down unto thee the Message that thou mayest explain clearly to men what is sent for them, and they may give thought" (Abdul-Rahman Salih Abdullah 1982). Prophet Muhammad said, "He who leaves his home in search of knowledge walks in the path of God" (Himiuddin Khan 1967, 2–3). This search for knowledge was the goal of every Muslim man and woman, whose foremost duty was to learn the Qur'an, the rituals of prayer, and the divine revelation (Ahmed 1968, 30).

In Islam, education covers all aspects of life, including knowledge of the Qur'an and the laws of Islam, as well as the customs, knowledge, and skills that people need to function effectively in daily life. The aim of education is to prepare a person for a moral and religious life, thereby creating sincere, practical people who can win spiritual blessings and God's favor in the hereafter (Himiuddin Khan 1967, 171).Whatever action man performs should be linked to God, indicating that God cannot be restricted to a certain period of life or to certain aspects of a person's actions (Abdul-Rahman Salih Abdullah 1982).

During the Medieval Period, education in the Islamic world achieved great success, with immense respect given to scholars. The encouragement in Islamic teachings for education created an environment in which people could freely exchange ideas. During the European Dark Ages, the Islamic world established a golden age of education. During the ninth century, the library of the monastery of St. Gall was the largest in Europe, containing thirty-six volumes. At the same time, most cities in the Islamic world built public and private libraries, with some cities like Cordoba and Baghdad possessing libraries with more than 400 thousand books. The accumulated knowledge in the Islamic world later became the basis for achievements in the European Renaissance (Horace Mann, WP; Himiuddin Khan 1967, 133).

The education of Muslim children began at home around the age of four, when they began the study of the Qur'an (Himiuddin Khan 1967, 172). There were two levels of education: primary and advanced. Primary education was conducted in schools called Kuttab and Maktab (Ahmed 1968, 41). The purpose of these schools was to teach the Qur'an, basic principles of Islam, and reading, writing, and mathematics. Advanced studies were conducted in the Halka systems before the establishment of the Madrasa system (Ahmed 1968, 52). Subjects studied included philology, grammar, syntax, rhetoric, literature, reading and recitation (of the Qur'an), hadith, jurisprudence, Islamic law, theology, logic, tasawwuf, tafsir, scholastics, medicine, genealogy, and astronomy (Ahmed 1968 32–39; Himiuddin Khan 1967, 134). There was also an emphasis on physical education, because Islam gives importance to the training of the body as well as of the mind (Himiuddin Khan 1967, 179). In Islam, as a rule, everyone could participate in classes, regardless of one's ethnicity, social group, age, or gender (Ahmed 1968, 86).

Universities were also established in many cities, such as Cordoba and Malaga in Spain, Istanbul and Konya in Turkey, Cairo in Egypt, Baghdad in Iraq, and Mansura and Delhi in India. These universities included departments of astronomy, mathematics, medicine, theology, law, jurisprudence, chemistry, and philosophy, where the enrollment ran into the thousands (Alavi 1988).

YETKIN YILDIRIM

See also Madrasa; Primary Schools; Libraries; Childhood

Further Reading

Abdullah, A.S. *Educational Theory: A Qur'anic Outlook*. Umm All-Qura University: Makkah Almukarramah, Faculty of Education, Educational & Psychological Research Center, 1982.

Ahmed, M. *Muslim Education and the Scholars' Social Status up to the 5th Century Muslim Era*. Zurich: Verlag Der Islam, 1968.

Alavi, Z.S.M. *Muslim Education Thought in the Middle Ages*. New Delhi: Atlantic Publishers & Distributors, 1988.

Gülen, F. *Religious Education of the Child*. Somerset, NJ: The Light Publication, 2003.

Himiuddin Khan, M. *History of Muslim Education*. Karachi: Academy of Educational Research, 1967.

Ittihad Research Committee. *Islam Prensipleri Ansiklopedisi*, ed. Ittihad Yayincilik. Istanbul: 1994.

EDUCATION, JEWISH

The Jewish emphasis on education can be traced directly to the Bible, which enjoins constant meditation on the law or Torah (Joshua 1:8). Already during the time of the Second Temple in Jerusalem (515 BCE–70 CE), Scripture was studied according to an authoritative, interpretive tradition. During the first six centuries CE, leading Jewish scholars (rabbis) in Palestine and Babylonia codified these oral teachings, producing canonical works of law (Mishnah, Talmud) and exegesis (Midrash). Together with the Bible, this rabbinic literature has furnished the Jewish core curriculum for the past millennium and a half. It is analogous in terms of sanctity, authority, and function to the Qur'an and hadith in Sunni Islam. In Islamic lands, however, many Jews also studied general subjects, such as Arabic language, mathematics, astronomy, philosophy, and medicine. In this environment, moreover, Jewish subjects were often pursued from a rationalistic perspective.

In his code, *Mishneh Torah*, Moses Maimonides describes the religious obligation of a father to teach his son Torah and the obligation of a community to support a school. From the age of six or seven, children learned the Hebrew alphabet and the Bible, which they were taught to gloss in Aramaic and Arabic. Like a Muslim maktab, the Jewish school house stressed the memorization and proper recitation of Scripture. Girls attended separate schools, which taught these subjects as well; rabbinic literature was introduced later and taught only to boys. Unlike elementary-school teachers, who were remunerated, Talmud instructors were not supposed to receive payment. For advanced Talmudic studies, young men attended a yeshiva (academy). Dating back to antiquity, this institution was dedicated to teaching and promulgating the rabbinic tradition. Similar in purpose to the madrasa, which only developed during the tenth and eleventh centuries, the yeshiva combined the functions of a college and a court. Supported by communal donations, it funded both faculty and students, who were trained as legal experts. The oldest yeshivot were based in the Land of Israel and in Babylonia. Each was headed by a gaon (president) and was organized hierarchically. During the 'Abbasid period, the academies of Sura and Pumbedita moved to Baghdad, where they attained preeminence as centers of Jewish legal scholarship, issuing responses to queries from distant communities and sponsoring month-long terms of study for visitors from abroad. However, with the migration of Jews westward, independent colleges were established in Egypt, North Africa, and Andalusia during the late tenth century. Those in Qayrawan and Lucena (near Cordoba) became quite famous; during the eleventh century, the former was headed by Hananel ben Hushiel and Nissim ben Jacob Ibn Shahin.

Outside the yeshivot, secular subjects formed an important part of the curriculum. The ability to read a Bible also meant literacy in Arabic, whereas Jews customarily read and wrote in Hebrew characters. Letters from the Cairo geniza attest to widespread Jewish literacy in the Mediterranean and also to the effort expended in securing a good education. Geniza documents and letters reveal that some parents engaged Arabic tutors for their children. Although the language and literary quality of Judeo-Arabic documents vary considerably, many Middle Eastern and North African Jews could write effectively and fluently. Some of the leading scholars, such as Sa'adyah Gaon, Samuel ben Hophni Gaon (d. 1113), and the Karaite Ya'qub al-Qirqisani (d. after 938), read widely from non-Jewish sources.

As early as the ninth century, North African and Andalusian Jews cultivated a broad education, which enabled the best scholars to attain influential positions at court. Hasday Ibn Shaprut (c. 915–970) served two Umayyad Caliphs of Cordoba as a physician, translator, and diplomat. Samuel Ibn Naghrela (993–1055/1056), vizier to two Kings of Granada, achieved fame as a Hebrew poet and talmudic scholar; according to the Muslim historian Ibn Hayyan (987–1076), Ibn Naghrela wrote both Arabic and Hebrew with equal facility. Both Hasday and Ibn Naghrela mastered a dual curriculum of sacred and secular subjects that was reminiscent of the one prescribed by the Andalusian Muslim Ibn Hazm (994–1064) in his *Maratib al-'Ulum (Categories of the Sciences)*. The *Tibb al-Nufus (Hygiene of the Souls)* by Joseph ben Judah Ibn 'Aqnin (late thirteenth century) outlines a detailed course of study: reading and writing Hebrew characters precedes the study of the Bible, Mishnah, Hebrew grammar, and Hebrew poetry; at fifteen, boys begin Talmud; subsequently, they learn some speculative theology. Philosophy and the sciences follow: logic, mathematics, arithmetic, geometry, optics, astronomy, music, mechanics, natural sciences, medicine, and, finally, metaphysics. Moses Maimonides dedicated his *Guide to the Perplexed* to a favorite disciple who had been trained in precisely this kind of curriculum. During the twelfth through the fourteenth centuries, Jewish émigrés from Andalusia, such as Judah Ibn Tibbon, championed these education ideals in Christian Spain and Provence, where they were instrumental in maintaining the rationalistic, literate, and cultured outlook of the Greco-Arabic tradition.

DANIEL FRANK

See also Baghdad; Hebrew; Judeo-Arabic; Kalam; Karaites; Scriptural Exegesis, Jewish; Translation, Arabic to Hebrew; Education

Primary Sources

Ben Judah Ibn Aqnin, Joseph. "A Course of Study." In *The Jew in the Medieval World*, ed. Jacob Rader Marcus, rev. Marc Saperstein, section 77/1, 428–32. Cincinnati: Hebrew Union College Press, 1999.

Ibn Tibbon, Judah. "A Father's Admonition." In *Hebrew Ethical Wills*, ed. and transl. Israel Abrahams, vol. 1, 51–92. Philadelphia: JPSA, 1926.

Maimonides, Moses. "Study of the Torah." In *Mishneh Torah: The Book of Knowledge*, transl. Moses Hyamson, fols. 57a–65a. Jerusalem: Feldheim, 1981.

Further Reading

Ashtor, Eliyahu. *The Jews of Moslem Spain*, 3 vols., vol. 3, 91–105. Philadelphia: JPSA, 1973–1984.

Brody, Robert. *The Geonim of Babylonia and the Shaping of Medieval Jewish Culture*. New Haven: Yale University Press, 1998.

Goitein, S.D. *A Mediterranean Society*, vol. 2, 171–211, vol. 5, 415–26. Berkeley and Los Angeles: University of California, 1967–1988.

Sklare, David E. *Samuel ben Hofni Gaon and His Cultural World*. Leiden: Brill, 1996.

EGYPT

From the Arab Conquest until the end of the Umayyad Period, the Arab army commanded by 'Amr ibn al-'As entered Egypt in late 639 or early 640 CE, initially laying siege to the Byzantine fortress at Babylon at the meeting place between Lower and Upper Egypt. The Arabs proceeded to conquer Upper Egypt before marching on Alexandria. Faced with numerous internal problems, the Byzantines eventually surrendered the city by treaty. As was the case elsewhere in the conquered lands, the Arabs did not take up residence among the conquered people—the Egyptian Christians (Copts)—but rather settled in a garrison city (misr) known as al-Fustat. There they established their administration and institutions, including a mosque that was named for 'Amr and a diwan to record the financial and military affairs of the new territory. The Arab tribesmen proved to be difficult to govern, and this task, along with the collection of taxes and the provision of revenues to the Caliph, were the responsibility of the governor (wali).

'Amr took control of the province on behalf of Mu'awiya during the First Civil War (656–661) and was thus on the side of the victor. During the Second Civil War, Marwan ibn al-Hakam seized control of the province to keep it loyal to the Umayyads.

Perhaps the best known governor of Egypt during the Umayyad period is Qurra ibn Sharik (709–715); this is because the survival of numerous documents on papyrus provides more knowledge about his administration than is available for any other governor of early Islamic Egypt. The classical tax system of land tax (kharaj) and poll tax (jizya) was not solidified until the middle of the eighth century, and the Umayyads frequently experimented with their revenue collection system. One attempt to raise taxes in 725 or 726 resulted in a major uprising by Coptic peasants. As the Umayyad Caliphate weakened, the Arab rulers of Egypt fought among themselves for control of this wealthy province.

An 'Abbasid Province

After the 'Abbasid occupation in the summer of 750, Egypt was governed by a series of men who originated in the Khurasani units that had overthrown the Umayyads. From 775 to 785, the governor was the Caliph al-Mansur's son, al-Mahdi (the Umayyad governors had also frequently been members of the ruling family). In 784, attempts to raise taxes led to a major revolt by Arab tribesmen that had to be suppressed. The period from 809 to 826 was characterized by instability, and it must have become clear to the 'Abbasids that the status quo was unworkable. Eventually, the rise of Turkish slave soldiers provided a solution, albeit a disastrous one from the point of view of the Caliphs. In 831, the Turkish general Afshin put down a joint Arab–Coptic rebellion, and the Arab families of Egypt lost power for good.

In 868, Ahmad ibn Tulun, the son of a Turkish slave soldier, was appointed governor of Egypt. His arrival began a process whereby governors of Egypt, although never renouncing their allegiance to the 'Abbasids, nonetheless ruled Egypt in an autonomous manner. In fact, Ibn Tulun ruled on behalf of his stepfather and then of his father-in-law; this aided in the establishment of a mini dynasty. Furthermore, because Ibn Tulun could dispose of the significant resources of Egypt, he was in a position to solidify his control over the province. He raised an army of Turkish, Greek, and Black soldiers, which immediately caused disquiet in Baghdad. Because the 'Abbasids were unable to defend Syria and Cilicia from the Byzantines, they were obliged to delegate this authority to Ibn Tulun, demonstrating the degree to which Baghdad had become dependent on Egypt. A rebellion by his son al-'Abbas forced Ibn Tulun to return to Egypt. In 880, Ibn Tulun founded a new town, al-Qata'i', not far from al-Fustat. Al-Qata'i' later fell into ruin, but Ibn Tulun's mosque was renovated during the thirteenth century by Mamluk Sultan Lajin.

Ibn Tulun died in 884. His descendants lost power in 905, and the Fatimids, who ruled Ifriqya from 909, made several attempts to seize control of Egypt. In 935, Muhammad ibn Tughj, who later received the title "Ikhshid," became governor. He restored some of Egypt's autonomy; this policy was continued by the eunuch Kafur, who seized power after the Ikhshid's death in 946. After Kafur's death in 968, there was little to stop the Fatimid conquest, which occurred the following year.

The Fatimid Caliphate

The Fatimid conquest and the establishment of the city of Cairo as its capital turned Egypt into a regional power, a status it would not surrender until the Ottoman conquest of 1517. Egypt was at its height as an economic power under the Fatimids, producing more food than it could usually consume and boasting a robust textile industry. Thanks to the survival of the Geniza documents, it is known that Fustat's Jewish community had trade relations with co-religionists throughout the Mediterranean and Indian Ocean worlds as well as with rural Egypt. The Fatimid Caliphate employed men of talent of a variety of ethnicities and religious persuasions. In addition to the Fatimids themselves, Ismaili Shi'is who claimed descent from the Prophet Muhammad through his daughter Fatima, Arabs, Berbers, Turks, Armenians, Copts, Jews, and others served in the Fatimid army and administration.

Unlike his predecessors in Egypt, the Fatimid Caliph al-Mu'izz was a determined opponent of the 'Abbasid Caliphate in Baghdad. Egypt now became the base for a campaign to unseat the 'Abbasids and establish Fatimid rule over the Muslim world. Although this campaign was ultimately unsuccessful, the Fatimid state was not merely concerned with consolidating its rule but also with spreading its Ismaili doctrine. To this end, Caliph al-Mu'izz established al-Azhar as the center of the Ismaili mission (da'wa). Fatimid missionaries traveled throughout the Muslim world, enjoying some success in Yemen, Syria, and Iran. They were unable, however, to prevent the fall of Baghdad to the Seljuks, an event that greatly reduced Shi'i influence in the 'Abbasid capital.

In 1094, the Fatimids underwent a fundamental schism, which resulted in the victory of the Caliph al-Musta'li and the death of his rival Nizar. Nizar's supporters fled to the Ismaili communities outside of Fatimid territory and established the "new mission," which survived the dissolution of the Fatimid Caliphate in 1171. As time went, on, however, the influence of the Fatimid caliphs waned. Their army was torn by ethnic divisions, and this led to a major conflict between black and Turkish soldiers in 1060, which was only resolved by the arrival of an Armenian force. Increasingly, it was the wazir who held real power in the Fatimid state, exercising control over an impressive centralized bureaucracy. Many wazirs were also military men. By 1169, when Nur al-Din Mahmud sent his Kurdish retainers—Asad al-Din Shirkuh and his nephew Salah al-Din Yusuf (Saladin)—to Egypt, the Fatimids had been reduced to paying tribute to the Latin Kingdom of Jerusalem.

The Ayyubid Sultanate

After the death of his uncle, Shirkuh, Salah al-Din initially served as the wazir to the Fatimid Caliph. After the latter's death in 1171, Salah al-Din ordered the 'Abbasid Caliph's name to be mentioned in the Friday sermon, thus abolishing the Fatimid Caliphate. For some time, it looked as if relations might break down between Salah al-Din and Nur al-Din, but Nur al-Din's death in 1174 presented a golden opportunity for Salah al-Din to add Syria to his holdings, as well as parts of Iraq, the Hijaz, and Yemen. By 1183, he was in a position to turn against the Kingdom of Jerusalem, and his famous victory at Hittin in 1187 allowed him to recover Jerusalem for Islam.

Salah al-Din and his successors, known as the Ayyubids (after Salah al-Din's father), built on the Fatimid state, but they also made significant changes. The Fatimid chancery and tax administration were quite sophisticated, and the Ayyubids and Mamluks regarded the Fatimid precedent as the basis for their own bureaucracies. At the same time, the Ayyubids introduced some elements of Seljuk bureaucratic practice, including military iqta', whereby amirs were rewarded for their service by being assigned the tax revenues of a certain area or areas. This new system, which was preceded by a cadastral survey of Egypt, gave increased administrative responsibilities to the military, a trend that continued through the Mamluk period. As a result of their concern for gaining support from the religious scholars and promoting Sunnism, the Ayyubids built a series of law schools (madrasas) and Sufi convents (khanqahs).

The Mamluk Sultanate

The Mamluk Sultanate, a government of Turkish (and later Circassian) soldiers of slave origin, was born of crisis. In the wake of the Ayyubid victory over Louis IX at al-Mansura in 1250, a group of Mamluks belonging to the deceased Sultan al-Malik al-Salih Ayyub overthrew and murdered his successor, Turanshah; they apparently feared being marginalized or eliminated in favor of the new Sultan's entourage. A period of instability followed, only coming to an end after the Mamluk defeat of the Mongols at 'Ayn al-Jalut in 1260. After the battle, the amir Baybars assassinated Sultan Qutuz and took control of the state.

Baybars (r. 1260–1277) can be seen as the founder of the Mamluk Sultanate. He waged a series of campaigns against the Crusaders and Mongols that left Cairo the capital of a large empire that included Syria and the Hijaz. To bolster his authority, he installed 'Abbasid survivors of the Mongol sack of Baghdad as "shadow caliphs" in Cairo; he also gave official recognition to all four of the Sunni schools of law, which gave the increasingly centralized Mamluk state greater flexibility.

Although every Mamluk sultan attempted to establish a dynasty, they had very limited success. Baybars's descendants were overthrown by another powerful amir, Qalawun (r. 1279–1290). Qalawun's descendants ruled—although often in name only—until 1382. His son al-Ashraf Khalil (r. 1290–1293) captured Acre, the last Crusader possession in the Levant, in 1291.

Another son, al-Nasir Muhammad (r. 1294–1295, 1299–1309, 1309–1340) presided over what was perhaps the greatest period of prosperity in medieval Egypt. The Mongol threat had receded, commerce between Egypt and Syria and between the Mamluks and the Europeans was booming, and the political system was stable for three decades. Al-Nasir used this opportunity to increase the authority of the sultan by redistributing iqta's in his favor and by becoming increasingly involved with commerce, which provoked accusations of monopolization. He also seized much of the property of the Coptic Church, and the Copts were subjected to a period of persecution that led to large numbers of conversions to Islam.

Unfortunately, if al-Nasir Muhammad's intention was to shore up the position of the sultan, he failed. In 1347, the Black Death arrived in Egypt and brought about a demographic crisis of unprecedented proportions. By the 1370s, famine became increasingly common, leading to the crisis of 1403 through 1405, when famine and disease struck together. The result of these events and of subsequent outbreaks of plague is that Egypt's population remained low until at least the mid-sixteenth century, thus reducing the possibilities for economic recovery. Agricultural production was reduced, and the sultans attempted to compensate for the loss in tax revenues by intervention in commerce and the establishment of monopolies of certain commodities. European merchants who wished to buy goods imported from the Indian Ocean were obliged to purchase them from the sultan in Alexandria.

The collapse of the Qalawunid "dynasty" in 1382 led to the rise of a series of sultans who ruled as strongmen. Increasingly these new rulers were Circassians rather than Turks, and they had little success passing on their powers to their sons. Although al-Nasir Faraj (r. 1399–1405, 1405–1412) succeeded his father al-Zahir Barquq, he failed to respond to the crisis of 1403 through 1405 or to prevent Timur Lenk from seizing Aleppo and Damascus in 1399. Although these cities were recovered in 1402, Faraj was remembered as a Mamluk Nero. The reign of Sultan al-Ashraf Barsbay (1422–1438) was more successful. Barsbay established a monopoly on the trade in spices, reducing the Karimi merchants who had controlled this commerce to his agents. He used his improved financial situation to launch successful raids on Cyprus in 1425 and 1426, avenging the sack of Alexandria by Peter I of Cyprus in 1365.

The longest-reigning sultan of the fifteenth century was al-Ashraf Qaytbay (r. 1468–1496), who has been described as a conservative who was concerned with maintaining the traditions of the sultanate. By the beginning of the sixteenth century, however, change was clearly in order. The Ottoman sultans were a growing threat, and the rise of the Shi'i Safavids in Iran changed the political map of the region. In 1498, Vasco de Gama reached the Indian Ocean, and Portuguese attacks on ships and ports brought about a sudden reduction in the revenues of the Mamluk state. Sultan al-Ashraf Qansuh al-Ghuri (r. 1501–1516) made an alliance with the Ottomans and tried to reorganize his army to face the new threat, but this was in vain. When Ottoman Sultan Selim I turned against the Mamluks, he must have sensed an opportunity. Syria fell to the Ottomans in the summer of 1516, and Egypt fell in January through April of 1517.

With the end of the Mamluk Sultanate, an era came to an end. For much of the Middle Ages, Egypt had been the greatest power of the Middle East; now it became a province in a great empire, with a center of gravity that was elsewhere. In many ways, Mamluk Egypt was the most successful medieval state (excluding the Ottomans, who represented a break with many aspects of medieval Islamic statecraft). The Mamluks reigned for more than 250 years. Despite the competitive character of the sultanate, Mamluk rule was generally peaceful. Egypt was the center of a flowering culture in areas such as historical writing, Islamic legal scholarship, Sufism, and even Arabic literature. A new international style came into being in Mamluk architecture, and Mamluk textiles, glasswork, and metalwork were of a high quality until the late-medieval depression. During the fifteenth century, Egypt became more dependent on European imports, but this dependence was not as total as has sometimes been claimed. Mamluk rule came to an end as the result of the rise of a new power—the Ottomans—and not as the result of any inevitable decline. Indeed, one legacy of the Mamluk Sultanate was the incorporation of some aspects of its administration into the Ottoman state.

ADAM SABRA

See also Alexandria; Assassins (Ismaili); 'Ayn Jalut; Ayyubids; Al-Azhar; Badr al-Jamali; Baybars I; Black Death; Cairo; Cairo Geniza; Caliphate and Imamate; Copts; Coptic; Fatimids; Fustat; Al-Hakim; Ibn Taghribirdi; Ibn Tulun; Ismailis; Mamluks; Al-Maqrizi; Mosque of Ibn Tulun (Cairo); Nur al-Din ibn Zanki; Nile; Qadi Numan; Saladin (Salah al-Din); Shajar al-Durr; Sultan; Tamerlane (Timur); Tulunids

Further Reading

Ashtor, Eliyahu. *The Levant Trade in the Later Middle Ages.* Princeton: Princeton University Press, 1983.

Atiya, Aziz S. *The Coptic Encyclopedia*, 8 vols. New York: MacMillan, 1991.

Berkey, Jonathan P. *The Transmission of Knowledge in Medieval Cairo: A Social History of Islamic Education.* Princeton: Princeton University Press, 1992.

Brett, Michael. *The Rise of the Fatimids: The World of the Mediterranean & the Middle East in the Tenth Century CE.* Leiden: Brill, 2001.

———. "The Way of the Peasant." *Bulletin of the School of Oriental and African Studies* 47 (1984): 44–56.

Cresswell, K.A.C. *The Muslim Architecture of Egypt*, 2 vols. Oxford: Clarendon Press, 1952–1959.

Dols, Michael. *The Black Death in the Middle East.* Princeton: Princeton University Press, 1977.

Fernandez, Leonor. *The Evolution of a Sufi Institution in Mamluk Egypt: The Khanqah.* Berlin: K. Schwarz, 1988.

Garcin, Jean-Claude. *Un Centre Musulman de la Haute-Égypte Médiévale: Qus.* Cairo: Institut Français d'Archéologie Orientale, 1976.

Goitein, S.D. *A Mediterranean Society: The Jewish Communities of the Arab World as Portrayed in the Documents of the Cairo Geniza*, 6 vols. Berkeley: University of California Press, 1967–1994.

Irwin, Robert. *The Middle East in the Middle Ages: The Early Mamluk Sultanate 1250–1382.* London: Croon Helm, 1986.

Lev, Yaacov. *State and Society in Fatimid Egypt.* Leiden: E.J. Brill, 1991.

Lyons, Malcolm Cameron, and D.E.P. Jackson. *Saladin: The Politics of the Holy War.* Cambridge: Cambridge University Press, 1982.

Petry, Carl F., ed. *The Cambridge History of Egypt: Volume 1, Islamic Egypt, 640–1517.* Cambridge: Cambridge University Press, 1998.

Petry, Carl F. *The Civilian Elite of Cairo in the Later Middle Ages.* Princeton: Princeton University Press, 1981.

———. *Protectors or Praetorians? The Last Mamluk Sultans and Egypt's Waning as a Great Power.* Albany: State University of New York Press, 1994.

Rabie, Hassanein. *The Financial System of Egypt AH 564–741/AD 1169–1341.* London: Oxford University Press, 1972.

Raymond, André. *Cairo.* Cambridge and London: Harvard University Press, 2000.

ELEGY

The elegy (*marthiyeh* in Persian) exists in two forms in Persian poetry: as a section of a longer narrative work and as a discrete poem. Because narratives are always in the mathnawi (couplet) form in Persian, elegies of the former kind are invariably in couplets; notable examples are to be found in Ferdowsi's *Shahnameh* and in various medieval romances. The elegies in the *Shahnameh* are very often spoken by women (examples are Gordyeh's elegy for her brother Bahram Chubineh, Roshanak's for her husband Sekandar, and Rudabeh's for her son Rostam), and this corresponds with the relatively public role undertaken by women during mourning ceremonies in many Middle Eastern cultures, including Persian. Ferdowsi's elegiac passages use the ubi sunt topos extensively, and typically many successive lines begin with the evocation "Where now is...?" as the dead subject's virtues and glories are listed. Ferdowsi also inserts into the *Shahnameh* an elegy spoken *in propria persona*; this is a lament on the death of his own son, in which he reproaches his child for leaving him alone in the world; this trope became standard.

As a discrete poem, the elegy usually took the form of a qasideh (a praise poem in monorhyme). One of the earliest and most famous examples of the genre is that by Farrokhi (early eleventh century) for the Ghaznavid King Mahmoud (d. 1030). The poem evokes the monarch's past pleasures and glories and describes the desolate state of the land and its populace now that Mahmoud has departed; its diction and imagery were widely imitated by later writers of elegies for the politically powerful. Court poets were expected to produce elegies after the death of a prominent member of the ruling family, and they were remunerated for doing so. However, not all elegies were written for such practical motives. For example, for Sa'di to write his fine elegy about the last 'Abbasid Caliph, who was murdered by the Mongols in 1258, was a politically risky move that could well have provoked retribution. Although the form was primarily associated with the court and traditionally invoked an atmosphere of formal, public mourning, elegies were also written for dead friends, presumably with little hope of remuneration; an example of a more personal elegy of this kind is that by Atai Razi (early twelfth century) about the death of his fellow poet at the Ghaznavid court, Mas'ud Sa'd. After the triumph of Shi'ism in Iran, with the accession to power of the Safavid dynasty in 1501, elegies for the significant martyrs of Shi'i Islam were widely written. In these poems, the emphasis is generally on the innocence and sufferings of the elegy's subject rather than on past pleasures or glories. Some of these religious elegies have achieved the status of widely-diffused folk poetry, and a number of them have retained great popularity among the more pious sections of Iranian society.

RICHARD DAVIS

Further Reading

Pagliaro, A., and A. Bausani. *Storia della Letteratura Persiana*. Milan, 1960.
Safa, Zabihollah. *Tarikh-e Adabiyat dar Iran (The History of Literature in Iran)*, 5 vols. Tehran, 1366/1987.

EMIGRATION, OR HIJRA

The emigration, or hijra (Latinized as hegira), of Muhammad ibn 'Abdallah (d. 632 CE), the Arab Prophet of Islam, from his place of birth (Mecca) to the town that was to become his adopted home (Yathrib; later renamed Madinat al-Nabi, the city of the Prophet, al-Medina, in short) took place circa September 622 CE. Muhammad had, despite political and social opposition to his teachings, achieved a considerable reputation as fair-minded, wise, and trustworthy, even in Mecca. The people of Yathrib, therefore, invited him to come and live with them and act as a mediator when quarrels arose between the major tribes of the region, the Aws and the Khazraj.

The emigration was seen as an important event for Islam, because it marked the beginning of a new life for Muhammad, who, from then on, was able to live amidst his followers in security. A few years after the death of the Prophet, when the then-leader of the Muslims, 'Umar ibn al-Khattab (d. 642), who succeeded Abu Bakr (d. 634) as "The Commander of the Faithful," was to establish an Islamic calendar, it was this event that he chose to mark as its beginning.

The actual emigration of Muhammad from Mecca to Yathrib was arranged at 'Aqaba several months before it actually occurred. The Prophet's teachings were not welcome to the elite of Mecca, who were mostly polytheists by religion and who did not recognize the possibility of a life after death; their opposition led to aggression against the Muslims. Soon, a group of Muslims was forced to leave Mecca for Abyssinia, where, fortunately, a Christian king saw fit to welcome them. Muhammad himself turned to Hira, a town not far from Mecca, only to be rebuffed. The invitation to Yathrib from its inhabitants was therefore most welcome, but it had to be dealt with secretly, because the hostility toward Muhammad in Mecca was now considerable; his life there was possible only because tribal ties forced his relatives to protect him. However, when both his uncle, Abu Talib, and his wife, Khadija, died around 621, it was clear that he was no longer safe. Indeed, Muhammad barely escaped a plot by the Meccans to jointly murder him. He left 'Ali, his nephew, in his bed, to fool his enemies, and then he quietly departed with the help of his dear friend, Abu Bakr, who was able to provide him with a camel. Some traditions paint his departure as a miracle, describing Muhammad as becoming invisible and then leaving right before the eyes of the Meccan polytheists who had come to attack him. When the Meccans discovered that it was 'Ali who lay in Muhammad's bed, they immediately followed Muhammad's tracks. Again, however, by God's grace, Muhammad and Abu Bakr were saved: they had taken shelter in a cave on Mount Thaur, over the mouth of which a spider had built its web. The Meccans—believing that such a web would have been broken if Muhammad had entered—did not think to look within (Qur'an verse 9:40).

Muhammad's entry into Yathrib is described as a joyful event. The people of Yathrib—mainly Arabs as well as significant Jewish tribes—saw him as a uniting force who would end the divisiveness and the destruction that came with it. Tradition holds that there were many agreements made between the Meccan Muslims (who were known as the *Muhajirun,* or emigrants) and the several new converts to Islam among the residents, who, because of their generosity, came to be known as the *Ansar,* or helpers. Indeed, Ibn Ishaq mentions a "Constitution of Medina" that was designed by Muhammad in which both Arab and Jewish tribes of Yathrib participate, essentially laying down the terms by which Muhammad hoped to achieve a single monotheistic community.

Muhammad's resort to emigration as a means of avoiding hostility to his beliefs is recommended by Islam. According to the Qur'an, "The sins of the emigrants, of those driven from home, are forgiven" (3:195). "He who emigrates, finds a home on this earth, and when he dies, God will reward him" (Q4:101). According to tradition, those who remained in Mecca and feared to migrate—although the earth was large enough to afford them shelter—are censured. Thus, the term *emigrant* became a title of honor among Muslims. In the recent past, it was used in South Asia to encourage those who left modern India for Pakistan.

RIZWI FAIZER

Further Reading

Arberry. *The Koran Interpreted.* Macmillan, 1965.
Lings, Martin. *Muhammad: His Life Based on the Earliest Sources.* George Allen and Unwin Ltd, 1983.
Watt, W.M. *Muhammad: Prophet and Statesman.* Oxford University Press, 1960.

EPIC POETRY

Very few long poems remain of the Jahiliyya and the Umayyad poetry that narrate the deeds of a hero. Selected verses of heroic poems were collected in anthologies during the 'Abbasid period by famous poets such as Abu Tammam (d. 849), al-Buhturi (d. 897), and others (until the thirteenth century). These collections were entitled *Hamasa* (bravery, fervor in war); their first and main chapters contain a short poem about pre-Islamic battles of the Arabs that praises their heroism. The subsequent chapters are selections from other funun al-shi'r (genres of poetry): elegy (ritha'), eulogy (madîÎ), chaste erotic opening line (nasib), morality (adab), description (wasf), and others. In *Rasa'il Ikhwan al-Safa* (tenth-eleventh centuries), some verses that are quoted by Abu Tammam are called al-mushajji' (the favoring or the encouraging verses); they are used during battles and wars and sung with heroic melodies (*Rasa'il Ikhwan al-Ñafa*, Cairo, 1928:132–36).

In his translation of Aristotle's *Poetica* from Syriac into Arabic, Matta b. Yunis used the Greek term *Epi* (in Arabic, *Afi*), whereas the editor 'Abd al-Rahman Badwi himself used, in his modern translation, the term *malhama* (see *Fann al-Shi'r*, ed. 'A.-R. Badawi, 143). Ibn Sina (Avicenna) (980–1037), in his attempt to survey Greek science and philosophy for the benefit of the Muslim culture, also used the term *Afi* (Ibid., 194–5). Although Ibn Sina was aware that Homer, in his epics, used blank (unrhymed) verse, he confirmed that "We [in Arabic culture] almost do not call that which is unrhymed, poetry" (Ibn Sina, *Jawami' 'ilm al-Musiqa*, ed. Z. Yusuf, Cairo, 1956, 122–3). Hazim al-Qartajanni (1211–1285), in his *Minhaj al-Bulagha' wa-Siraj al-Udaba' (The Program of*

Rhetoric and the Lamp of Men of Letters) (Tunis 1966), explained why the Arabs did not translate Greek literature: "The Greek poets would invent things upon which they would set their poetic imagination and they made this an aspect of their speech. They presumed things which did not happen at all and used them as a model for what happens, and they built upon them legends such as those old women relate to their grandchildren at night, fables of things which cannot possibly happen." Al-Qartajanni concluded his argument by saying, "Avicenna condemned this kind of poetry and said: 'There is no need for poetic imagination of the simple fables which are but invented narratives.'" He also said, "...this (type of poetry) does not suit all temperaments." Moreover, even during the thirteenth century, Âiya' al-Din Ibn al-Athir (d. 1239), in his *al-Mathal al-Sa'ir,* noticed that the Arabs—unlike the Persians—like long poetic genres, as the *Shahnama*.

The use of end-stop monorhyme in Arabic poetry limits the length of the heroic ode (qasida). Arab poets used in their narrative poetry a simple form of urjuza muzdawija (a couplet in rajaz meter); this form helped them, during the 'Abbasid period, to get rid of the burden of monorhyme, which dictates the content of the verse. In such couplets, many didactic fables, narrative poems, and chronicles were versified. The most famous work is *Kalila wa-Dimna,* which was versified by Aban al-Lahiqi (d. ca. 815); the work was imitated in *al-Ñadi   Î wa-'l-Baghim (The Singing Birds and the Gazelles)* by Ibn al-Habbariyya (d. ca. 1111). The history of some Islamic dynasties was also versified, mainly in Andalus. However, the talented poet Ibn al-Farid (d. 1235) was able to write his epic about Sufism, *Nazm al-Suluk (Poem of the [Sufi] Way),* known as *al-Ta'iyya al-Kubra,* in about 730 verses rhyming with the letter *ta'.* Such long poems were called *mutwwalat* (long poems).

Arab scholars wrote in classical Arabic, the sacred language of the Qur'an, in religious and serious literature. They expressed their contempt toward popular narrative literature and used colloquial or semi-literary style in their popular oral literature, such as shadow plays (khayal al-zill), popular entertainment, and narrative genres of *Siyar.* This was evident as in the romances *Sirat 'Antar* (thirty-two parts), *Sirat 'Ali al-Zibaq, Qissat Bni Hilal, Qissat al-Zir Salim, Sirat al-Amira Dhat al-Himma* (seventy parts), *Sirat* (or *Qissat*), and *Sayf ibn Dhi Yazan* (nineteen parts). These heroic, romantic, and chivalrous romances were recited in cafés, at assemblies, and during feasts and festivals, and they were accompanied by rababa or rabab esh-sha'er (poet's one string viol) and chanted by the storytellers (hakawati) of the romance of *Aboo-Zeyd.* The chanting narrator of such poetry is called *sha'ir*

(Lane 1954, 370–71, 397, 406.) This term must be an old one, because Pedro de Alcala, in his dictionary *Vocabulista Arabigo en Leta Castellana,* defined the Arabic term *sha'ir* as "representador de comedias/ tragedias." Arab scholars considered these romances, which are composed in rhymed prose (saj') in a semi-literary style that shifts into verse when tense emotional situations are depicted, to be popular epics.

In their attempt to keep pace with European literature from the second half of the nineteenth century onward, Arab critics adopted the Western classification of poetry, based on Plato's theory that poetry is divided into the lyrical, the epic, and the dramatic (see Sulayman al-Bustani 1904, 163–64, 171–72). To their amazement, they found that the bulk of Arabic poetry written throughout its long history was mainly lyrical (ghina'i) and that it did not deal with the narrative (qasasi), dramatic (masrahi), or epic (malhami) genres. They argued that the reason for this phenomenon in Arabic poetry is the rigid tradition of using monorhyme whereas, among other nations, rhyme is not essential, and it can be used to change simple patterns of rhyme schemes.

Among the first Arab scholars who tried to give the Arabs a model of Greek epic poetry and its history in European literature was Sulayman al-Bustani (1856–1925). Unlike Ibn Sina and al-Qartajanni, who based their arguments against Greek literature on taste, al-Bustani argued that it was a religious factor (i.e., the *Iliad* contains pagan elements, whereas Greek philosophy, logic, and medicine were useful to the Arabs [Bustani 1904, 65–7]). He added that the Arabs wrote epics by combining poetry and rhymed prose (Bustani 1904, 171–72). He took the formidable task of versifying the *Iliad* into more than ten thousand Arabic verses using various patterns of rhyme schemes and conventional Arabic meters, such as monorhyme and couplets; Arabic and European stanza forms of quatrain and quintet; and forms of Andalusian muwashshah. His pioneering translation encouraged other poets to write epics (malahim or mutawwalat) in modern Arabic literature.

By introducing dramatic, narrative, and epic poetry, the modernist poets considered the monorhyme in Arabic poetry the main obstacle in their attempts to enrich Arabic literature with the new genres. They were astonished to note that lyric, dramatic, and epic poetry are the main genres in Western poetry. The problems that attracted the attention of Arab poets and critics at the end of the nineteenth century were the questions of why the Arabs translated Greek writing about philosophy, logic, and medicine while ignoring Greek literature and why the Arabs did not write epic poetry. (Other Eastern peoples, such as the Indians, Persians, ancient Egyptians, and Turks, wrote epics, and the Indians, Persians, and Syrians translated the *Iliad* into their own languages [see al-Bustani 1904, 61–3, 165–7, 265]).

Encouraged by al-Bustani's translation of and introduction to the *Iliad,* Arab poets such as al-Zahawi (1864–1946), A.Z. Abu Shadi (1892–1955), Muhammad 'Abd al-Muttalib (1871–1931), and M.F. Abu Hadid (d. 1967) wrote articles about and experimented with epic poetry. Other poets, such as Ahmad Muharram, Bulus Salama, and Fawzi Ma'luf, tried to compose historical and philosophical epics in conventional Arabic meters. However, not all of them were successful. To be able to compose or translate epic poetry, Arab critics and poets defended the use of blank verse (shi'r mursal). Most of their attempts were doomed to failure, because they used connotative diction with end-stop rhyme and were unaware of the technique of enjambment used in European blank verse. However, using *vers irregulier* (which they called *shi'r hurr* [free verse]) with an irregular number of feet and an irregular rhyme scheme with enjambment, they were successful in writing mutawwalat. The Iraqi poet Badr Shakir al-Sayyab (1926–1964) is the leading Arab poet in this modern genre of Arabic poetry; his works include *Haffar al-Qubur* (1952), *al-Muwmis al-'Amya'* (1954), and *al-Asliha wa-'l-Atfal,* (1954), which was later included in his anthology *Unshudat al-Matar.*

SHMUEL MOREH

Further Reading

Bausani, A. "Elementi Epici Nelle Letterature Islamiche." In *La Poesia Epica e la sua Formazione,* 759–69. Rome, 1970.

Al-Bustani, Sulayman. *Le Illiade d'Homere. Traduite en Vers Arabes, Avec une Introduction Historique et Litteraire.* Cairo, 1904.

Canova, G. "Epic Poetry." In *Encyclopedia of Arabic Literature.* London & New York: Routledge, 1998.

Gabrieli, G. "Elementi Epici Nell'Antica Poesia Araba." In *La Poesia Epica e la sua Formazione,* 759–69. Rome, 1970.

Lane. *Manners and Customs.* London, 1954.

Moreh, S. *Modern Arabic Poetry 1800–1970.* Leiden: Brill, 1976.

Pellat, Ch. "Hamasa." In *EI,* 2nd ed.

EPICS, ARABIC

If by the word *epic* is meant a lengthy poetic narration with the aim of exalting a hero or the ancient endeavors of a nation (e.g., Homer's *Iliad*), it must be recognized that classical Arab literature has not cultivated this genre. The medieval translators of Aristotle's *Poetics* found themselves seriously embarrassed at being unable to translate the very term *epic.*

The tales of the tribal wars of the Jahiliyya (pre-Islamic era), the life of the Prophet Muhammad, the heroic deeds of the champions of Islam, and the epos of the Muslim conquests—all the material that could have become the subject matter of Arabic epics—have in fact developed in a specific fashion. These stories, on the one hand, have not undergone any mythic elaboration, having been accepted as historical fact—or presumed to be so—in the great works of historiography, such as al-Tabari's *Annals;* on the other hand, they have taken on the dimension of popular narrative through the work of the storytellers, who have been subject to the censure of the elitist, turban-wearing 'ulema, the jealous custodians of orthodoxy. Thus, the Arab epic tradition has developed in the form of chivalrous romances, and, because of its semi-classical language (middle Arabic) and its unpretentious style, it has not found its place within the restricted canons of Arabic literature.

Popular Arab epics have found their expression in a longstanding oral tradition in which generations of storytellers have operated and in a written tradition that is comparable, in certain respects, with the romances of the European Middle Ages. The epic cycle is called sira (course of life, biography) or, more generically, qissa (story), whereas single episodes can take the name diwan (collection of poems). The most important sources from which this oral-written corpus has spread are Syria and Egypt. A number of ancient cycles—albeit in their primitive form—are part of the repertoire of the storytellers, such as the story of 'Antara ibn Shaddād, the pre-Islamic Black hero of the Banu 'Abs and of his beloved 'Abla, whose adventures are extended right up to the era of the Crusades; the story of al-Zir Salim, which re-evokes in the form of a legend the war of al-Basus; or the heroic deeds of the Banu Hilal warriors. Other narrative cycles are from the Mamluk era (fourteenth and fifteenth centuries, especially), such as the story of the Yemeni prince Sayf ibn Dhi Yazan; of princess Dhat al-Himma and her son 'Abd al-Wahhāb, in the context of the tribal battles between the Banu Kilab and the Sulaym and Arab expeditions against Byzantium; and of al-Malik al-Zāhir Baybars, the Mamluk king of Egypt and Syria whose reign was the backdrop to a whole series of picaresque adventures. These works present an alternation of parts in rhyming prose, in which the singer–narrator describes the scenes and introduces the characters, and parts in poetry, which include the dialogues of the heroes boasting about their achievements and the description of the duel, perhaps the primitive core around which the romances have developed. Their pseudohistorical perspective, however, reveals itself to be fragile, particularly when it

re-evokes the intertribal wars of the Ayyam al-Arab (the pre-Islamic "battle days of the Arabs" [al-Zir Salim]), the campaigns for the expansion of Islam (Antara, Dhat al-Himma) or Sayf's struggle to thwart the Abyssinian plans to control the course of the Nile (whereas the historical Himyarite Sayf liberated the Yemen from the yoke of the Abyssinians in the sixth century). The atmosphere is that of the medieval furusiyya, the chivalrous spirit of the Arab hero exalted by the art of the storyteller into a series of astonishing deeds.

The epic cycles became most widespread during Mamluk rule, but it is important to state that each story has its own particular origin and literary development. Whereas for the *Sirat Bani Hilal,* it is the oral tradition that prevails (even if a later parallel written tradition did exist), for the other epic cycles the problem is a more complex one in that the manuscript tradition would seem to have a more determining importance. One particular concern for scholars is determining whether a textual version is the result of collective creation successively brought together by a rawi (collector–transmitter, possibly the storyteller himself) or whether it is the creation of one or more humble writers interpreting the tastes of the greater public, imitating the art of the storytellers. The circular nature of the relationship between oral and written narrations should not be underestimated, although the multiplicity of versions could be explained by the necessity on the part of the storytellers to invent new plots. This heterogeneous material proves interesting as a documentation of the worldview of the medieval Arab populace. In terms of strictly literary aspects, historians of classical Arabic literature have shown reservations because of the modest tone of these popular narratives, the use of middle Arabic, the continuous repetitions, the disordered accumulation of episodes, and the disarming prolixity (the current printed edition of the story of 'Antara covers 5,600 pages). It should nonetheless be emphasized that these works were intended for public performances rather than to be read.

The *Sirat Bani Hilal,* which was already cited by Ibn Khaldun during the fourteenth century, constitutes the continuation of the ancient Bedouin poetic tradition and is probably the only one to possess the characteristics of a true epic. Unfortunately, only fragments of it remain. It narrates the exploits of the Banu Hilal, a Bedouin tribe that abandoned the Arabian Peninsula and eventually succeeded, after various vicissitudes, in conquering North Africa (tenth and eleventh centuries). There are four cycles: (1) the Sira, the ancient story of the Hilali princes in the Arabian Najd and in Yemen; (2) the Riyada, the mission of exploration after the tribe had been decimated by a long famine; (3) the Taghriba, the emigration toward the Maghreb; and (4) the intense wars after the conquest of North Africa. The main characters are the Black hero Abu Zayd, the fierce Diyab, princess Jaziyya, and the king of Tunis, Zanati Khalifa. Their adventures are narrated by a professional "singer of tales" who, in Egypt, where the oral tradition has been particularly strong (as attested to by nineteenth-century writer E.W. Lane's report), is called sha'ir (poet) par excellence. He is a wandering minstrel who has specialized in the exploits of the Banu Hilal. He is often an outcast of gypsy origin whose craft continues a family tradition, and he sings his verses accompanying himself with a stringed instrument (rababa) or a tambourine. The art of the storyteller, called muhaddit in Egypt and hakawati in Syria, is quite different: he reads the story of 'Antara or of Baybars aloud in the cafés of Cairo or Damascus, from manuscripts. Nonetheless, even in this case, his performance is characterized by a dramatization that aims to captivate the public.

Research on Arabic oral epic poetry (on both its actual performance and its context), on the social position of the storyteller, and on the rhetorical peculiarities of the narrations contained in the handwritten texts (mostly from the seventeenth and eighteenth centuries) has increased considerably after a long period of stagnation. The scholar of comparative literatures will greatly take advantage of the painstaking analysis of M.C. Lyons's *Arabian Epic,* which offers a synthesis of the content of each sira, a survey of their narrative motifs, and a comparison with similar motifs in other medieval epic traditions.

GIOVANNI CANOVA

See also Chivalry; Epic Poetry; Heroes and Heroism; Musical Instruments; Poets; Popular Literature; Stories and Storytelling; Storytellers

Further Reading

Canova, Giovanni. "Twenty Years of Studies on Arabic Epics." In *Studies on Arabic Epics,* ed. G. Canova. Monographic issue of *Oriente Moderno,* Rome, N.S. 12 (2003), no. 2.
Connelly, Bridget. *Arabic Folk Epic and Identity.* Berkeley: University of California Press, 1986.
Galley, Micheline, and Abderrahman Ayoub. *Histoire des Beni Hilal et de ce qui leur Advint dans leur Marche vers l'Ouest.* Paris: Armand Colin, 1983.
Heath, Peter. *The Thirsty Sword: Sīrah 'Antar and the Arabic Popular Epic.* Salt Lake City: University of Utah Press, 1996.
La Guerre de la Chamelle: La Geste de Zîr Sâlim, transl. Marguerite Gavillet Matar. Arles: Actes Sud, 2001.
Lane, Edward W. *An Account of the Manners and Customs of the Modern Egyptians, The Definitive 1860 Edition.*
Cairo and New York: The American University in Cairo Press, 2003.
Lyons, Malcolm C. *The Arabian Epic,* 3 vols. Cambridge: Cambridge University Press, 1995.
Madeyska, Danuta. *Poetics of the Sīrah: A Study of the Arabic Chivalrous Romance.* Warsawa: Academic Publishing House, 2001.
Norris, Harry T. *The Adventures of Antar.* Warminster: Aris & Phillips, 1980.
Ott, Claudia. *Metamorphosen des Epos. Sīrat al-Muğāhidīn (Sīrat al-Amīra Dhāt al-Himma) Zwischen Mündlichkeit und Schriftlichkeit.* Leiden: CNWS, 2003.
Reynolds, Dwight F. *Heroic Poets, Poetic Heroes: An Ethnography of Performance in an Arabic Oral Epic Tradition.* Ithaca and London: Cornell University Press, 1995.
Roman de Baïbars, transl. Georges Bohas and Jean-Patrick Guillaume. Paris: Sindbad, 1985.
Slyomovics, Susan. *The Merchant of Art: An Egyptian Oral Hilali Poet in Performance.* Berkeley, Los Angeles, and London: University of California Press, 1987.
The Adventures of Sayf ben Dhi Yazan: An Arab Folkepic, transl. Lena Jayyusi. Bloomington: Indiana University Press, 1996.

EPICS, PERSIAN

Medieval Persian literature has a long and rich epic tradition, reaching back for its major sources to the pre-Islamic era and continuing in a weakened form into the Safavid (sixteenth through eighteenth centuries) and even early Qajar (nineteenth century) periods. Persian epics may be divided into three kinds, according to their subject matter: (1) those that deal with pre-Islamic material; (2) those that take historical or contemporary rulers as their protagonists and that become essentially panegyrics in narrative form; and (3) religious epics that focus on significant Islamic figures. The epics about pre-Islamic material are the most significant of the three categories; epics in the other two styles were written in imitation of them.

There are strong indications that an oral epic tradition existed in pre-Islamic Iran and that the medieval epics dealing with pre-Islamic narratives are ultimately based on the stories preserved and elaborated on by this tradition. The *Shahnameh (Book of Kings)* of Ferdowsi (940–ca.1020) overshadows all other works in this category; it was preceded by a now-lost (apart from a few fragments) *Shahnameh* by the tenth-century poet Marvazi and also by the incomplete *Goshtaspnameh* of Daqiqi (d. 978). Ferdowsi incorporated approximately one thousand lines of Daqiqi's poem (those dealing with the advent of the prophet Zoroaster) into his *Shahnameh.*

The *Shahnameh* begins with a Zoroastrian cosmogony and ignores the Qur'anic account of the creation of the world and man. The earliest myths treated clearly go back to prehistory; they have parallels with Indo-European myths in other traditions, and they must in origin predate the arrival from central Asia of the Iranians in Iran toward the end of the second millennium BCE. Evil at the poem's opening is the work of malevolent supernatural beings called *divs;* it has been plausibly suggested that these represent the conquered indigenous peoples of the Iranian plateau. Much of the poem is taken up with fairly constant warfare between central Asian Turks and Persians with the River Oxus as their border, although other antagonists are also present, including China (whose people are often treated as Turks by Ferdowsi), Rum (Greece, Rome, Byzantium) and, as the poem draws to a close, the Arabs. The poem is structured as a royal chronicle, and the reigns of fifty monarchs (including three queens) are recorded. Two separate cycles of heroic tales—those dealing with the kings of Iran and those dealing with the house of Nariman, which rules in Sistan (southeastern Iran and western Afghanistan, south of the River Helmand)—are interwoven; the most famous hero of the poem, Rostam, belongs to the Sistani cycle. The common Indo-European epic theme of king–champion rivalry generates a number of the legendary tales, and to this is added a recurrent father-son rivalry, which lies at the heart of the poem's best-known narratives. The *Shahnameh* is notable for its frequent foregrounding of ethical preoccupations, and the moral dilemmas of a good man ruled by an evil or incompetent monarch are explored in a number of its narratives. The work's closing section, which opens with the conquest of Alexander the Great and ends with the mid-seventh-century overthrow of the Sasanian dynasty by Arab invaders, is largely a romanticized history of the Sasanian monarchy.

The rhetoric of Ferdowsi's poem was extensively imitated by other poets, and the motaqareb meter that he and Daqiqi used (Marvazi's *Shahnameh* was in the hazaj meter) became standard for epics. The best-known examples of epics about pre-Islamic material after Ferdowsi's *Shahnameh*—and written within a hundred years of his poem—are the *Garshaspnameh* of Asadi (ca.1010–1073) and the *Faramarznameh,* the *Borzunameh,* the *Azarbarzinnameh,* the *Banugoshaspnameh,* and the *Shahryarnameh,* all of unknown authorship; these poems are concerned, respectively, with an ancestor, a son, a grandson, another grandson, a daughter, and a great-grandson of Rostam. Another epic, the *Bahmannameh,* treats of the son of a prince (Esfandyar) killed by Rostam and ends shortly after a report of Rostam's death. That all these epics relate somehow to Rostam suggests that this hero and his family were at the center of the Persian pre-Islamic tradition of heroic narratives, although some epics (e.g., the *Kushnameh,* the *Bizhannameh*) about pre-Islamic legendary figures unrelated to Rostam also exist. Throughout the medieval period and beyond, in addition to being imitated, Ferdowsi's *Shahnameh* was subject to considerable expansion—from approximately forty thousand lines in the earliest manuscript to more than sixty thousand—and was clearly never regarded as a canonical, fixed text. These later interpolations to Ferdowsi's poem often add magical or bizarre events to the relatively sober original chronicle; these types of changes are also apparent in epics written after the *Shahnameh,* most notably Asadi's *Garshaspnameh.*

The tradition of writing epics about pre-Islamic legendary material lasted until the end of the thirteenth century (the date of the *Samnameh,* which was concerned with Rostam's grandfather), but it was meanwhile gradually replaced by two derivative traditions: historical and religious epics. Nezami's *Sekandarnameh* (ca. 1200) treats the life and conquests of Alexander, considerably expanding on Ferdowsi's account; the *Zafarnameh* by Hamdallah Mowstafi (d. 1349) continues Ferdowsi's *Shahnameh,* which ended with the coming of Islam to Iran, up to the author's own time. Tabrizi's *Shahanshahnameh* picks up where the *Zafarnameh* leaves off; it was written in praise of Jenghiz Khan and his family. Subsequent historical epics tended to praise living rulers or their ancestors and were in effect a form of panegyric.

The first significant religious epic involving a protagonist from Islamic history is the Shi'i-oriented *Khavarannameh* (1427) of Ebn Hesam, which deals with Ali, the central figure of Shi'ism, and his legendary conquests in eastern Iran and central Asia. The Shi'i triumph in Iran, with the establishment of the Safavid dynasty in 1501, meant that epics on approved Shi'i themes received court encouragement; typical of them is Heirati's *Shahnameh* (1546), which was dedicated to Shah Tahmasp and concerned with the battles fought by the Prophet Mohammad. Heirati calls his poem a "Shahnameh of righteousness"; his use of the name of Ferdowsi's poem makes explicit the replacement of pre-Islamic concerns by the values of Shi'i Islam.

RICHARD DAVIS

Further Reading

Hanaway, William L. "Epic Poetry." In *Persian Literature,* ed. E. Yarshater, 96–108. New York, 1988.

Safa, Zabihollah. *Tarikh-e Adabiyat dar Iran (The History of Literature in Iran),* 5 vols. Tehran, 1366/1987.

———. *Hemaseh Sarai dar Iran (Epic in Iran).* Tehran, 1369/1990.

EPICS, TURKISH

The Turkic epic (destan, dessan, dasitan, jir, boy) tradition in its pure epic form (épopée) has not survived in the Oguz Turkish-speaking area. A Turkish epic similar to the Kirgiz *Manas* is yet to be discovered, although scholarship by Mehmet Fuat Köprülü and Pertev Naili Boratav suggests the existence of "pure" Turkish epics that did not survive in either oral tradition or manuscript form. The closest counterpart to this genre would be the *Kitab-ı Dede Korkut*, which includes a prologue and twelve legends (boys), composed predominantly in prose. These legends were passed down through two manuscripts written toward the end of the fifteenth century. It is not easy to come up with definitive conclusions about the historical facts and settings of this text. All of the epic protagonists of these legends demonstrate a mixture of cultural and historical characteristics; elements from shamanism, Islam, and other traditions manifest themselves in a single character. What was important for the epic composer was to turn these characters into die-hard fighters of the Oguz. One cannot speak of single authorship when it comes to a work like this; however, there are strong suggestions that the epic-teller of the book was Dede Korkut, who was the shaman of the Oguz, a Muslim saint, and an epic composer and teller with his musical instrument, the kopuz.

What has been predominant and abundant in the Oguz tradition are those works that derived directly from the pre-Islamic epic form, such as the *Dâstân-ı Tevârîh-i Mülûk-i Âl-i 'Osmân*s (Ottoman chronicles), folk hikâyes (romantic epics told by âşıks (troubadours) with the accompaniment of the musical instrument the saz, which is most likely the replacement of the ancient kopuz), menâkibnâmes (hagiographic legends), and gazavâtnâmes and jihâdnâmes (heroic/religious epics, holy war epics). These works may be classified as transitional genres of the historical development from the ancient epic to the modern novel.

Although the Turkish âşık poetry has gone through tremendous structural and thematic transformations over the centuries, it is still a living part of Turkey's cultural prosperity. Traditionally, there was an indispensable ritual attached to becoming an âşık: a dream was always involved in the birth of a troubadour. A holy man or sometimes a maiden would offer one or three cups of wine to the hero in his dream. İlhan Başgöz mentions that, despite the variety of holy persons in this so-called dream motif, their role was almost always the same: they would (1) act as cup bearers, (2) introduce a beautiful maiden to the âşık, (3) bestow a pseudonym upon the hero to be used in his poetry, and (4) offer their help whenever the hero was in trouble. There were also physical ritualistic effects of the holy wine or love potion upon the hero. After drinking the wine, a flame would consume the body of the hero. He would faint, blood would come out of his mouth, and he would remain in this condition for three to seven days. After that, an old woman would appear to the hero, bringing him the traditional stringed instrument, the saz; the hero would then take the instrument and begin playing it. He would immediately start singing, composing poetry orally, and revealing his newly bestowed poetic name. Başgöz argues that the Turkish dream motif complex containing the above-mentioned characteristics occurs *only* in Turkish romantic epics collected from oral tradition (see Silay 1998). Indeed, such rituals in oral tradition are often seen as acting as a bridge between the pre-Islamic Turkic nomadic cultures and the sedentary Islamic Anatolia. As Başgöz argues, there is little or no doubt that the dream motif complex has strong shamanistic elements (this is one of the religious practices of the Turkic peoples). After accepting the precepts of Islam, which are based on sedentary cultural values, Turkish society began mixing elements from both cultures. In an unconscious and natural manner, numerous pre-Islamic cultural rudiments were carried over to the newly Islamized Anatolia.

After the 1960s, the Turkish romantic epic tradition went through a major transformation and gradually became more urban and highly political. A Marxist–Leninist discourse against the Republican regime became the dominant quality of this once most-celebrated form of literary entertainment in rural Anatolia. Especially during the decade before the 1980 military coup, the Turkish romantic epic poetry became the political weapon of both the Turkish left and the conservative and often ultra-nationalist right. Currently this tradition is going through another fascinating social stage in the overpopulated urban centers of Turkey. It now has a brand new house of performance: the Türkü bars. Usually located next to or near the other bars of these cities, the Türkü bars have become an alternative form of entertainment for the educated population, and the performers are no longer the holy-man–inspired âşıks of Anatolia. Wine, beer, and other alcoholic beverages are served in these places, not in a traditional or religious ceremonial sense but in an effort to compete financially with the more established places of night-life entertainment in the neon-lit cities of modern Turkey.

KEMAL SILAY

Further Reading

Eberhard, Wolfram. *Minstrel Tales from Southeastern Turkey*. Berkeley: University of California Press, 1995.

Silay, Kemal, ed. *Turkish Folklore and Oral Literature: Selected Essays of Ilhan Başgöz*. Bloomington: Indiana University Turkish Studies Series, 1998.

Sümer, Faruk, Ahmet Uysal, and Warren Walker, eds. and transl. *The Book of Dede Korkut: A Turkish Epic*. Austin and London: University of Texas Press, 1972.

EPIDEMICS

Medieval Arabic sources use the term *wabā'* (or its variant *waba'*) to designate pestilence, epidemic, and pandemic; the same term is also applied to epizootic disease. From a linguistic standpoint, Ibn Manzūr (d. 1311 or 1312), in his dictionary *Lisān al-'Arab*, equates *wabā'* with *ta'ūn*, a term that appears in medieval chronicles to specifically denote the plague. This confusion is likely the result of the common perception that the plague was the most visible epidemic endured by the populace. The common view among medieval historians is that *ta'ūn* is a *wabā'* but that the occurrence of *wabā'* does not necessarily mean that of *ta'ūn*. In other words, the plague is an epidemic or a pandemic, but epidemics vary and are not limited to the plague.

The Concept of Contagion

The issue of contagion (*'adwā*) is problematic. On the one hand, diseases such as the plague, leprosy, smallpox, and measles are classified as contagious in early medieval medical works, notably those of Abu Bakr Muhammad ibn Zakariya al-Razi (better known in the West as Rhazes, d. ca. 925) and al-Majūsi (tenth and eleventh centuries). On the other hand, a hadith (saying) of the Prophet Muhammad is often quoted in support of the denial of the concept of contagion. It is found with many variations in several hadith collections, including (but not limited to) the *Muwatta'* of Malik ibn Anas (d. 795), the *Sahih* of Bukhari (d. 870), and the *Sunan* of Ibn Majah (d. 887). This hadith includes, in all its versions, the invariable statement "*lā 'adwa*" (there is no contagion). Here, the denial of contagion is clear. However, of these sayings of the Prophet Muhammad, one version advises to keep the sick away from the healthy, another to run away from the leper "the same way one runs away from a lion," and a third not to worry about mixing healthy camels with scabby ones. The last version is mentioned by Ibn Majah; in the narrative, a Bedouin tries to draw Muhammad's attention to the fact that a scabby camel may infect a whole herd, to which the Prophet responds: "That is all divine providence (*dhālikumu al-qadar*). Who caused the first camel to be scabby in the first place? (*fa-man ajraba al-awwala?*)." Another version of this hadith substitutes sheep for camels.

These examples demonstrate an awareness of the existence of contagious and infectious diseases and an empirical way of avoiding them by taking the precaution of not mixing the sick with the healthy. However, the clear statement "there is no contagion (*la 'adwa*)," which is common to this cluster of hadith, has resulted in a general theological attitude that adheres to the text of the hadith and in turn denies the existence of contagion. This is in opposition to the medical texts, in which the concept of contagion (*i'da'* or *'adwa*) is well stated. Despite this, the historical accounts of the recurrence of the plague and its high morbidity contain an implied acceptance of the principle of contagion in explaining the elevated number of casualties. This has led to the introduction of a divine element in the process of contagion as a way to resolve the hadith with the empirical observation. Such is the position of Ibn Hajar al-Asqalani (d. 1449), who maintains in his *Badhl al-Ma'ūn fi Fadl al-Ta'ūn (Offering Kindness in [Explaining] the Virtue of the Plague)* that accepting the thesis that disease is contagious by its own nature is an expression of unbelief. However, the same author recounts, with regard to the plague of AH 833/1430 CE, a huge jump in the morbidity rate in Cairo (from forty a day to one thousand a day in less than a month) after a large gathering held outside of the city for the purpose of prayer to end the plague.

The Etiology of Pestilence

Drawing on the Greek medical tradition, medieval Arabic texts adhere to the miasmic theory in their etiology of pestilence; this is reflected both in medical treatises and in historical works. Pestilence results from the quality of the air and from the physical disposition of one's body; it is then the "corruption" of the air that affects the lungs and leads to epidemics. In his analysis of the decline of dynasties, Ibn Khaldūn (d. 1406) states that "in the later years of dynasties, famines and pestilences become numerous." On the surface, this statement may refer to the appearance of these phenomena as bad omens that foretell the fall of a given dynasty, but, for this author, bloodshed increases during the final years of a dynasty because of unrest; he then draws a causal link between the bloodshed and the plague. In his view, the decomposed bodies corrupt the air and cause epidemics. He further explains that this is the reason why pestilence is more prevalent in urban areas and less so in rural or less-inhabited areas.

The Plague as Divine Punishment and as Martyrdom

Of all epidemics, the plague has attracted the most attention. Obviously, the concrete and devastating consequences of the recurrence of the plague in the medieval Middle East are the main reason. In general, medieval works give a chronological history of these pandemics together with theological reflections drawn from earlier religious and legal works. This genre has developed mostly after the outbreak of the Black Death, the bubonic plague that swept across the Middle East in 1348 and most of the known world between 1347 and 1349. The devastating demographic and economic effects of the Black Death may have contributed to the rise of this genre of religious and historical literature. Among the religious literature, two assertions tend to be pervasive: (1) the plague is a divine punishment, and (2) death from the plague is martyrdom. The injustice of the rulers, the lack of religiosity, and particularly the spread of adultery are often blamed for the outbreak of the plague. According to Ibn Hajar al-'Asqalāni, a group of theologians agreed that the plague that hit Egypt in 833/1430 was a divine punishment for the oppressive measures taken by the sultan and his subordinates. Likewise, the closing of taverns and houses of ill repute are among the measures often decided upon during a plague epidemic, a prolonged drought, or hard times in general; these measures tend to emphasize the adherence to the text of Islamic law. However, how can the plague equate martyrdom when it is actually considered a divine punishment? A hadith defines ta'ūn (understood to be the plague) as "the stabbing by your enemies the *Jinn*, and in all cases it is martyrdom (or, in some versions, martyrdom for the Muslim)". Another one states that the plague is an act of divine mercy. Islamic tradition clearly states that martyrdom is rewarded with heaven. Therefore, in the case of the plague, God is punishing Muslims by spreading this epidemic and causing martyrdom that will guarantee the victim of the plague a heavenly abode in the afterlife.

The real question, then, is as follows: Is the plague a punishment or a reward? To begin with, this question becomes irrelevant in the case of non-Muslims, because the Islamic concept of martyrdom does not apply to them. Thus, in the case of non-Muslims, the plague is simply a divine punishment. However, for Muslims, this punishment is also a martyrdom that guarantees heaven for the victim of the plague. Medieval Arabic works about the plague strive to resolve this apparent contradiction and offer various explanations.

Modern Scholarship

The historical investigation of epidemics in the medieval Middle East and of their impact is relatively recent and has focused primarily on the plague. To date, the works of the late Michael W. Dols and of Lawrence I. Conrad are viewed as the pioneering efforts in the field. In the case of the medieval Middle East, the historian is faced with the paucity of demographic and economic data and is compelled to rely heavily on chronicles and other general works; this is true even in the cases of the Black Death and later plagues, both bubonic and pneumonic. There are no specific and detailed data about the demographic impact of these pandemics. In the words of David Ayalon, "At the present state of our knowledge attempts at estimates of population sizes in the countries of medieval Islam should be postponed for quite a long time." By the same token, our knowledge of the economic impact of the plague in the medieval Middle East is still fragmentary. Egyptian chronicles belonging to the post–Black Death era show an awareness of the impact of the recurrence of epidemics (particularly of the plague), but the information that one can cull from them is limited. In his doctoral dissertation, Conrad explores the recurrence of the plague in the Middle East from 541 to 749, a period that corresponds with the first occurrence of the Plague of Justinian until the end of the Umayyad dynasty. With regard to the Black Death, the monograph of Dols is the only work devoted to the question. Finally, with respect to the demographic impact of the Black Death, the estimate of a mortality corresponding to one-fourth to one-third of the population is generally accepted in the case of Egypt, but this is not the result of rigorous calculations. It is predicated on the estimates reached in the case of Europe and on the presumed higher degree of urbanization of Egypt. This assumption is in turn built on the narratives of medieval European travelers to the area and particularly to Egypt.

ADEL ALLOUCHE

See also Black Death; Ibn Bakr; Al-Majusi; Malik Ibn Anas; Ibn Khadun

Primary Sources

Al-Bukhāri, Muhammad ibn Ismā'il. *Sahih*, 25 vols. Misr: al-Matba'ah al-Bahiyah al-Misriyah, 1933–1962.

Ibn Ridwān, 'Ali. *Medieval Islamic Medicine. Ibn Ridwān's Treatise "On the Prevention of Bodily Ills in Egypt,"* transl. Michael W. Dols. Berkeley and Los Angeles: University of California Press, 1984.

Ibn Hajar al-'Asqalani, Ahmad ibn 'Ali. *Badhl al-Mā'un fi Fadl al-Ta'ūn*, ed. Ahmad 'Isam 'Abd al-Qādir al-Kātib. Al-Riyād: Dār al-'Asimah, 1991.

Ibn Khaldūn. *The Muqaddimah. An Introduction to History*, 2nd ed., transl. Franz Rosenthal, 3 vols. Princeton: Princeton University Press, 1967.

Ibn Mājah, Muhammad ibn Yazid. *Sunan*, 2 vols., ed. M.F. 'Abd al-Bāqi. Bayrūt, Dār al-Fikr.

Ibn Manzūr, Muhammad ibn Mukarram. *Lisān al-'Arab*, 15 vols. Bayrūt: Dār Sādir, 1955.

Mālik ibn Anas. al-Muwatta'', 2 vols., ed. M.F. 'Abd al-Bāqi. Bayrūt: Dār Ihyā'' al-Turāth al-'Arabi, 1985.

Rāzi, Abū Bakr Muhammad ibn Zakariyā. *Rhazes on the Small-Pox and Measles*. Birmingham, AL: The Classics of Medicine Library, 1987.

Al-Suyūti. *Mā Rawāhu al-Wā'ūn fi Akhbār al-Ta'ūn; wa-Yaiih Maktabat al-Imām al-Suyūti fi al-Tibb al-Nabawi*, ed. Muhammad 'Ali al-Bārr. Dimashq: Dār al-Qalam, 1997.

Further Reading

Allouche, Adel. *Mamluk Economics: A Study and Translation of al-Maqrīzī's Ighāthah*. Salt Lake City: University of Utah Press, 1994.

Ayalon, David. "Regarding Population Estimates in the Countries of Medieval Islam." *Journal of the Economic and Social History of the Orient* 28 (1985): 1–19.

———. "The Plague and its Effects on the Mamluk Army." *Journal of the Royal Asiatic Society* (1946): 67–73.

Conrad, Lawrence I. "Epidemic Disease in Formal and Popular Thought in Early Islamic Society." In *Epidemics and Disease: Essays on the Historical Perception of Pestilence*, eds. Terence Rander and Paul Slack, 77–99. Cambridge: Cambridge University Press, 1995.

——— "Arabic Plague Chronologies and Treatises: Social and Historical Factors in the Formation of a Literary Genre." *Studia Islamica* 55 (1981): 51–93.

——— "Tā'ūn and Wabā": Conception of Plague and Pestilence in Early Islam." *Journal of the Economic and Social History of the Orient* 25 (1982): 268–307.

——— "The Plague in the Early Medieval Near East." PhD Dissertation. Princeton, NJ: Princeton University, 1981.

Dols, Michael W. "The Leper in Medieval Islamic Society." *Speculum* 58 (1983): 891–916.

———. "The Second Plague Pandemic and its Recurrences in the Middle East: 1347–1894." *Journal of the Economic and Social History of the Orient* 22 (1979): 162–89.

——— *The Black Death in the Middle East*. Princeton, NJ: Princeton University Press, 1977.

——— "Ibn al-Wardi's *Risālat al-Naba' 'an al-Waba'*. A Translation of a Major Source for the History of the Black Death in the Middle East." In *Near Eastern Numismatics, Iconography, Epigraphy and History: Studies in Honor of George C. Miles*, ed. Dickran K. Kouymjian, 443–55. Beirut: American University of Beirut, 1974.

——— "Plague in Early Islamic History." *Journal of the American Oriental Society* 94 (1974): 371–83.

Elgood, Cyril. *A Medical History of Persia and the Eastern Caliphate: The Development of Persian and Arabic Medical Sciences from the Earliest Times until the Year AD 1932*. Cambridge: Cambridge University Press, 1951.

McNeill, William H. *Plagues and Peoples*. New York: Doubleday, 1989.

Russell, Josiah C. "The Population of Medieval Egypt." *Journal of the American Research Center in Egypt* 5 (1966): 69–82.

Shoshan, Boaz. "Notes sur les Épidemies de Peste en Egypte." *Annales de Démographie Historique* (1981): 387–404.

Stathakopoulos, Dionysios Ch. *Famine and Pestilence in the Late Roman and Early Byzantine Empire: A Systematic Survey of Subsistence Crises and Epidemics. (Birmingham Byzantine and Ottoman Monographs, Volume 9)*. Aldershot, Hant: Ashgate Publishing Ltd., 2004.

Sublet, Jacqueline. "La Peste Prise aux Rêts de la Jurisprudence: Le Traité d'Ibn \ağar al-'Asqalānī sur la Peste." *Studia Islamica* 33 (1971): 141–9.

Ullman, Manfred. *Islamic Medicine*. Edinburgh: University Press, 1978.

ESCHATOLOGY

In accordance with literary apocalypses present in other monotheistic and dualistic faiths (Judaism, Christianity, Zoroastrianism, and Manichaeism), Muslim apocalyptic narratives are designed to explain the (usually) difficult circumstances of the present and to overcome them by forging a plausible chain of events that entails the establishment of an ideal messianic society and extends to the very day of judgment. Eschatological narratives appear in both Sunni and Shi'i Islam, but they have greater import in Shi'-ism. Like most Muslim religious ideas, eschatology is primarily based on hadith (tradition), which is believed to present sayings and doings of the Prophet Muhammad; a large number of pertinent texts are to be found in the six Sunni canonical hadith collections and in specialized compilations of apocalyptic materials, whereas the Qur'an's eschatology did not have nearly the same impact.

In Sunni Islam, specifically apocalyptic works began to appear from the middle of the eighth century onward and expanded, within a century, into voluminous collections; thus the rich apocalyptic heritage of Syria is known thanks to Nu'aym ibn Hammad al-Marwazi (d. 844). Ibn al-Munadi (d. ca. 947), who probably had pro-'Alid or Shi'i sympathies, collected a substantial number of Iraqi traditions during the following century, and, subsequently, important works such as those of al-Dani (d. 1052) and al-Qurtubi (d. 1272) were produced in Muslim Spain. The apocalyptic heritage was partially accepted into the six canonical collections, whereas, usually, material that concerned the messianic figure of the Mahdi or that was critical of, for example, the 'Abbasids (749–1258), was not. More expressly messianic Shi'i materials are found in books about the ghayba (occultation) of the Twelfth Imam.

Sunni Muslim eschatological scenarios usually begin with a historical base that is taken from one of three optional time frames. The first and earliest relates to the period of the late seventh and early eighth centuries, is based in Syria-Palestine, and envisions the beginning of the end of the world starting from the wars between the Muslims and the Byzantine Empire. The foremost goal of this scenario is the conquest of the Byzantine capital of Constantinople and, in a larger sense, the entire Mediterranean basin. These traditions often begin with an alliance between the Byzantine Christians and the Syrian Muslims against the Iraqi Muslims. This alliance, however, breaks down at the question of spoils and whether the cross or Allah was responsible for the victory. Both groups then return to their homes, and the Byzantines invade the coastal areas of Syria. Eventually the Muslims prevail and conquer Constantinople. However, the entire cycle of historical narratives includes a great many defeats for the Muslims, some of which involve a temporary Byzantine reconquest of the region of Syria–Palestine. After these events have played out, then the more integrally religious events, such as the appearance of the messianic figure and the antichrist (see below), are added to the story line.

The second historical time frame of Sunni apocalyptic literature relates to the events of the middle of the eighth century, when the 'Abbasid revolution began in the region of Khurasan (eastern Iran and western Afghanistan). This scenario portrays the appearance of the messianic figure, the Mahdi (see below), during a time of oppressive rule, when he will rise up in revolt and come from this distant land to the center of the Muslim world in Iraq and liberate the Muslims, thereby ushering in the messianic age. The third time frame is more divorced from history and uses the so-called "signs of the Hour" as a prelude. These signs, which can also be attached to the other two base scenarios, are those events that will warn Muslims and non-Muslims of the gravity of the times. The signs include political events such as those described above, moral and social decay, religious corruption, natural disasters (earthquakes, droughts, plagues), and cosmic phenomena (comets, meteorites, eclipses of the sun and the moon). Any number of these events, when known to occur in close proximity to one another, can trigger apocalyptic anticipation, panic, or speculation, and it is most probable that the Muslim apocalyptic books produced throughout this period were either in response to or because of these signs.

After either the historical setting is given or the "signs of the Hour" are listed, then both Sunni and Shi'i apocalyptic scenarios describe the rise of the Sufyani, a figure who is a descendent of Mu'awiya ibn Abi Sufyan (r. 661–680). In general, he represents the messianic aspirations of the Syrian Muslims, but he is considered to be a negative figure by Sunnis outside of Syria and a malevolently evil one by Shi'is. He is usually said to rise to power after appearing in the region of the Balqa' south of Damascus, after which he will conquer most of the Muslim world. Many of the accounts describing his reign give detailed descriptions of his cruelty toward the people of Iraq and especially toward the descendants of the Prophet Muhammad. In both Sunni and Shi'i accounts of the Sufyani, he is eventually defeated by the Mahdi, who is the universal messianic figure. The Sufyani is a purely Muslim figure who later appears in eastern Christian apocalypses.

The Mahdi in Sunni Islam is a warlike figure who will conquer non-Muslim regions of the world and eventually establish an ideal peaceable state that will fill the world with justice and righteousness. As stated previously, he will appear in either the Hijaz (Medina or Mecca) or Khurasan. Irrespective of his origin, he proceeds to gather an army, march toward the center of the Muslim world (Syria and Iraq), defeat the Sufyani, and establish his messianic kingdom in Jerusalem. Although the conquest of the Byzantine Empire in some scenarios is accomplished during the historical prelude to the messianic future, in others the Mahdi himself is the conqueror. He is usually said to conquer the entire Mediterranean basin and the difficult-to-conquer regions of Afghanistan and Central Asia.

There are differing opinions as to whether the Mahdi will forcibly convert non-Muslims to Islam. Although, according to some texts, he uses force to convert non-Muslims, according to others he governs each non-Muslim community (e.g., Jews, Christians) according to its own holy book and does not compel its members to accept Islam. The dominant feature of the Mahdi's rule is that it is characterized by absolute justice, peace, and plenty, with the evil characteristics of the world during the time of tribulation having passed completely away. However, his rule only lasts for a very short period of time, usually said to be up to nine years.

In contradistinction to the Sunni Mahdi, the Shi'i Mahdi (also known as the Qa'im) is more of an absolutely powerful and dominating figure. Shi'i scenarios usually portray the Mahdi appearing in Medina or Mecca, where he gathers an army of 313 men (the number who fought at the Battle of Badr in 624) to him. These followers, together with the Mahdi, are more interested in vengeance than are their analogous figures in Sunni scenarios, and most of their conquests are directed against the Sunnis. However, eventually the Shi'i Mahdi will establish a messianic kingdom in which he will rule throughout the period of his elongated lifetime (usually more than three hundred years). In some accounts, he establishes a dynasty of the Prophet Muhammad's family to rule this kingdom. Other elements of the Shi'i messianic age are similar to those of the Sunnis.

In many scenarios, the Dajjal—the Muslim antichrist—appears before the time of the Mahdi, whereas in others he follows the Mahdi. In certain scenarios (especially Shi'i ones), there are a series of messianic figures or even dynasties of Mahdis (or other lesser messianic figures) that are punctuated by the appearance of the Dajjal. The latter is said to be Jewish, and he has a defect in one of his eyes (usually the left one) and the word kafir (infidel) written on his forehead. He will appear in the area of Persia or Iraq, and many accounts specify the city of Isfahan. After his appearance, the Dajjal will travel through the entire world with the objective of tempting every single person—whether Muslim or non-Muslim—to deny Allah and worship the Dajjal himself. Although there are a few groups that will be capable of resisting his temptation, most accounts emphasize that he will be successful in seducing large numbers of people. However, he will be unable to enter the holy cities of Mecca and Medina, where true Muslims will take refuge from him. Another place of refuge will be Jerusalem, where a substantial number of Muslims will be besieged by the Dajjal and his followers. Just when the city is about to fall, Jesus will return from heaven (where he was raised, according to Qur'an 3:55) to kill the Dajjal and disperse his followers. It is very probable that substantial parts of the Dajjal story were influenced by eastern Christian apocalyptic beliefs.

In some traditions, as previously noted, this act then opens the messianic age or allows it to continue. Jesus then prays behind the Mahdi, ensuring that his presence on earth does not come into conflict with the doctrine of khatam al-nubuwwa (the finality of Muhammad's prophethood). Many accounts then describe Jesus' actions with regard to the Christians: breaking the crosses, killing swine, and facilitating their conversion to Islam. After this period, Jesus will live out his life as an ordinary Muslim and be buried in the Prophet's Mosque in Medina, together with Muhammad, Abu Bakr, and 'Umar.

Usually the appearance of the nomadic tribes of Gog and Magog (Ezekiel 38–9, Revelation 20:7–10) follows the death of Jesus. Gog and Magog will appear suddenly after the barrier Dhu 'l-Qarnayn built to restrain them (Qur'an 21:96) is allowed to collapse.

These tribes will overcome the entire world and destroy it. They will originate in either the north or to the east of the region of Central Asia and make straight for Jerusalem, which they will not be able to take. God will cause them to die by means of a worm that will invade their bodies. A large part of the Gog and Magog stories owe their provenance to the *Alexander Romance,* which was popular throughout the Middle East. In general, Muslim apocalyptic literature and scenarios do not include a picture of the actual end of the world nor do they bridge between the cataclysmic events of the last days and the resurrection of the dead and the Last Judgment.

After these early apocalyptic scenarios, the genre of the apocalypse continued to be significant for both Sunni and Shi'i Muslims. New works on the subject were written in the wake of the Crusader and Mongol invasions, most notably by Ibn Kathir (d. 1378); his collection is often seen as the most authoritative one by contemporary Sunnis. It is not always easy to find unity in Muslim apocalyptic or eschatological material, because there are few literary apocalypses that could serve to standardize the tradition as a whole, and there are numerous internal contradictions. However, Muslim scholars, especially those working on hadith criticism and commentary (e.g., al-Nawawi [d. 1277], Ibn Hajar al-'Asqalani [d. ca. 1438]), established a more-or-less accepted timetable.

DAVID COOK

See also 'Abbasids; Byzantine Empire; Hadith; Jesus; Messianism; Muhammad, the Prophet; Muslim–Byzantine Relations; Shi'ism

Further Reading

Cook, David. "An Early Muslim Daniel Apocalypse." *Arabica* 49 (2002): 55–96.
———. *Studies in Muslim Apocalyptic*. Princeton: Darwin Press, 2002.
Al-Dani, Abu 'Amr 'Uthman ibn Sa'id. *al-Sunan al-Warida fi al-Fitan wa-Ghawa'iliha wa-l-sa'a wa-Ashratiha*. Riyad: Dar al-'Asima, 1995.
Ibn al-Munadi, Ahmad ibn Ja'far. *al-Malahim*. Qumm: Dar al-Sira, 1997.
Al-Marwazi, Nu'aym ibn Hammad. *Kitab al-Fitan*. Beirut: Dar al-Fikr, 1993.
Madelung, Wilferd. "The Sufyani between History and Legend." *Studia Islamica* 63 (1986): 5–48.

ESPIONAGE

The earliest accounts of spies, known as 'uyun (eyes), refer to individuals in the pre-Islamic period who collected intelligence that could be used by the tribes in their continual skirmishes. During the early Islamic period, the eyes spied on enemies of the state both within and outside of its borders. Under the Rashidun, a system of night watchers ('asas) was introduced; this consisted of a network of guards who were responsible for ensuring security after dark. Later, the watchers were used to observe the whereabouts, activities, and opinions of individuals, developing into a web of secret agents that was associated with the office of "Postmaster," which was responsible for supervising the mail and intelligence services during the Umayyad Caliphate.

Mu'awiyya ibn Abi Sufyan was the first to use intelligence for political goals during his war against Ali ibn Abi Talib. This practice contributed greatly to his eventual victory. After assuming the Caliphate, Mu'awiyya focused his attention on his two archenemies, the Shi'is and the Kharijites.

Spying was used by the Umayyads for a variety of purposes, with each caliph having his own network of spies to gather information about opponents and supporters alike. Others also used spies; for example, the well-known governor Ziyad ibn Abi Sufyan was the first to inflict punishments on the basis of suspicion or intelligence reports. His son 'Ubayd Allah and al-Hajjaj ibn Yusif developed a network of agents to deal with political unrest in Iraq and the eastern provinces of the caliphate. Later, Abd al-Malik ibn Marwan developed the postal system to provide him with regular news, which helped him to outmaneuver his rivals.

The later Umayyads, however, failed to detect the clandestine activities of the 'Abbasid movement, the members of which managed to build an extensive intelligence network that helped them to topple the Umayyads. Suspicious by nature, al-Mansur, the second 'Abbasid caliph, developed the existing eyes into a disciplined corps of spies who reported directly to him. This is attested to by the appearance in Arabic of the term *Sahib al-Khabar* to refer to the caliph's secret agents, whose main tasks were to gather information, protect the caliph and his authority, and defame or liquidate opponents.

During his long struggle (749–762 AD) with al-Nafs al-Zakiyya, al-Mansur developed innovative techniques, such as sending letters in his rival's name to opponents in Khurasan and Hijaz, using spies for a single mission only, and recruiting merchants and women to gather information. He also monitored charity groups in Iraq and spread rumors in Hijaz about planned revolts; this forced al-Nafs al-Zakiyya to rebel prematurely.

The 'Abbasids chose spies for specific missions, selecting only those whose allegiance was unquestioned. Slaves were sometimes used for delicate missions: by al-Mansur, for example, when he had Abi

Muslim killed, and by Harun al-Rashid in his dealings with the Baramkids. The 'Abbasids also used women to compromise high-ranking statesmen, eyes to monitor merchants and strangers in markets, travelers to investigate distant provinces, and beggars to monitor the leaders of religious sects.

Opposition movements, such as the Shi'is and the Ibadis, developed elaborate strategies to deceive the authorities and their spies, most notably by adopting the religious principle of taqiyya (concealing their true religious and political inclinations). They met secretly and dispatched more than one messenger on every mission to guarantee delivery of the message; they also used codes in case messages were intercepted. Their success can be seen in the establishment of states in areas that were remote from the center of caliphal power, such as those of the Idrisids in Morocco, the Fatimids in Egypt, and the Ibadi imams in Oman.

During the later 'Abbasid era, almost everyone fell under suspicion, and spying was frequently used for political purposes, with allegations of treason or atheism used as the pretext to liquidate opponents. As a result, the secret service sharply deteriorated in quality, while plots and conspiracies flourished. The practice of espionage itself became dangerous as a result of the emergence of rival authorities to the 'Abbasid state in Baghdad. If caught, spies faced torture or death. Some became turncoats or double agents.

Many opposition movements emerged, the most important of which was the hashashin (assassins), who relied on a widespread network of spies to assassinate statesmen and other powerful figures. After the fall of Baghdad to the Mongols in 1256 AD, the institutions of the 'Abbasid state collapsed. The Mamluks, who eventually took power in parts of the former 'Abbasid state, had to rebuild the intelligence services from scratch, and they eventually came to rely on these services to consolidate their power.

HASAN M. AL-NABOODAH

See also Police; Post (Barid)

Further Reading

Abd al-Ghani, A. *Nuzum al-Istikhbarat 'ind al-'Arab wa al-Muslimin*. Beirut: Mu'assasat al-Risalah, 1991.

Al-'Araji, M.H. *Jihaz al-Mukhabarat fi al-Hadarah al-Islamiyya*. Beirut: Dar al-Mada, 1998.

Leder, S. "The Literary Use of Khabar." In *The Byzantine and Early Islamic Near East*, ed. A. Cameron and Conrad, 277–315. Princeton, NJ: Princeton University Press, 1992.

Al-Naboodah, H.M. "*Sahib al-Khabar*: Secret Agents and Spies During the First Century of Islam." *Journal of Asian History*, forthcoming.

Sadeue, S.F. "Development of al-Barid or Mail-post during the Reign of Baybars I of Egypt." *Journal of the Asiatic Society of Pakistan* 14 (1969): 167–83.

Sourdel, D. "Barid." In *Encyclopaedia of Islam, New Edition*, vol. I, *The First Century of Islam*, 1045–6.

Wensinck, A.J. "Khabar." In *Encyclopaedia of Islam, New Edition*, vol. IV, 895.

ETHICS

Ethics can be an elusive subject, because the term in English refers to both (1) the variety of moral principles that help define cultures and individual behavior and (2) systematic inquiry into the universal nature and necessity of morality. In the medieval Islamic tradition, the first of these connotations was discussed primarily as adab (proper conduct and manners; also, belles-lettres) and the second as akhlaq (sing. khulq; the innate disposition from which human acts emanate). Although differences between adab and akhlaq were often obscured in practice—because both aimed to cultivate virtue in human beings—this article focuses on akhlaq, or ethics as a discipline.

The akhlaq literature of medieval Islam can be characterized as a synthesis of the scriptural sources of Islam (Qur'an and hadith) with elements from different cultures (particularly pre-Islamic Arabian, Greek, Christian, and Iranian) that came under Muslim rule. A form of eudaemonism, which is prominent in Greek philosophy, provided the framework for this synthesis.

The scripture of Islam, however, is not eudaemonistic. The Qur'an is concerned with moral action and religious duty rather than moral theory or individual happiness. It assumes that the goodness and badness of acts are evident to anyone who simply reflects on the circumstances of the act. The Qur'an considers morality to be binding and thus, rather than justifying moral behavior, exhorts it. Nonetheless, the Qur'anic promise of divine reward and punishment presumes a relationship between individuals' behavior and their well-being.

The appropriation of eudaemonistic philosophy in Muslim ethics was not so much a rejection of the Qur'anic worldview as it was an attempt to resolve apparent moral ambiguities embedded in the monotheism of the Qur'an. According to the Qur'an, God is the sole omnipotent, omniscient Creator. As such, God predestines everything in creation, including human action (57:2–3 and 76:30). The Qur'an, however, also obligates human beings to be righteous and warns that they will be held accountable for their actions on Judgment Day (18:28–29 and 20:84). The Mu'tazilites, who are regarded as the first systematic theologians of Islam, sought to resolve this problem by arguing that it would be unjust for God to punish humans for acts for which they were not responsible.

They developed a deontological ethics in which they maintained human free will and argued that the goodness or badness of acts was innately known by humans to be praiseworthy or blameworthy because of their ontological status as such. This knowledge and ability obligated humans to do good and held them morally accountable to God. Although Mu'tazilism influenced Zaydi, Imami Shi'i, and early Hanafi theology (kalam), it was deemed heretical by Ash'aris, Ma'turidis, and Traditionalists (ahl al-hadith) for limiting God's will and power on the basis of human conceptions of what is just. Ash'aris, whose theoretical defense of Traditionalism eventually dominated Sunni kalam, argued for divine volunteerism, defining goodness and badness solely in terms of divine commands and prohibitions.

Because inquiry into what is commanded and prohibited by God fell under the purview of Muslim jurists, Ash'arism helped remove ethical inquiry in Islamic intellectual history from the realm of theology, which was concerned with theories of goodness, into the realm of fiqh (law and jurisprudence), which was concerned with defining right action on the basis of divine law (shari'a). This move is evidenced in discussions of the Qur'anic duty of commanding good and forbidding evil (3:104). Although this injunction was a major theological concern for Mu'tazilites, Ash'aris and Traditionalists did not discuss it much outside of their jurisprudential works.

The literature about akhlaq, however, was not concerned with morality solely as obedience to divine law. The ethical works of such thinkers as al-Farabi (d. 950 CE), Ibn Sina (d. 1037), and Miskawayh (d. 1030)—whose monumental *Tahdhib al-Akhlaq (Refinement of Character)* heavily influenced the field as evidenced in the works of such Persian authors as Nasir al-Din al-Tusi (d. 1274) and Jalal al-Din al-Dawwani (d. 1501)—aimed to justify the sources and the need for moral principles. Their ethical theories sought to synthesize social customs, revelation, and philosophy by arguing that, when properly understood and practiced, they all worked to fulfill the purpose of human existence and effect real happiness.

Despite the differences in the works of individual moral thinkers, several Neoplatonic (see Plato and [Neo-]Platonism) themes shaped the contours of their discourse. In their anthropology, humans were a composite of base matter and a spiritual soul and as such represented a microcosm of the material and spiritual dimensions of existence; it was claimed that this was the reason for the Qur'an's declaration of humans as viceregents of God on Earth (2:30).

In their psychology, they followed the threefold Platonic division of the soul into a rational, irascible, and concupiscent soul or faculty, which corresponded with the Qur'anic quiescent (mutma'innah), blaming (lawwāmah), and commanding (ammārah) souls, respectively (89:27, 75:2, 12:53). After Aristotle, the telos of humanity was defined by its distinctive ability to reason, and as such the ultimate superiority of the rational soul was asserted. Practical philosophy or ethics aimed to cultivate virtues in humanity that would bring the demands of their bodies and different souls into balance with one another under the rule of the rational soul. To achieve this state was to realize one's divine purpose, eternal bliss, and union with the divine.

With regard to social customs, it was argued that, as inherently social beings, humans could not realize their lofty end alone. Division of labor, contracts, and cultural conventions all helped create the social cohesion necessary for individuals to fulfill their potential and attain happiness. Political rulers were needed to create and maintain a social order aimed at maximizing the potential of individuals in accord with their aptitude; this was also seen as the aim of religious practice. Religion specified moral principles and duties for the vast majority of humans who did not have the acumen to reason for themselves the means by which they could cultivate virtues and attain their divinely ordained purpose.

Although philosophy, as an end in itself, was not central to Islamic education (because of the mystical implications of such concepts as ascending to the divine through self-refinement), many philosophical ethical theories were appropriated by mystics such as al-Ghazali (d. 1111) and popularized through Sufi teachings.

KAMBIZ GHANEABASSIRI

See also Adab; Theology; Laws and Jurisprudence; Commanding Good and Forbidding Evil; Al-Farabi; Ibn Sina; Aristotle; Plato and (Neo-)Platonism; Nasir al-Din al-Tusi; al-Ghazali

Further Reading

Cook, Michael. *Commanding Right and Forbidding Wrong in Islamic Thought.* Cambridge: Cambridge University Press, 2000.

Fakhry, Majid. *Ethical Theories in Islam.* Leiden: E.J. Brill, 1991.

Hourani, George F. *Reason and Tradition in Islamic Ethics.* Cambridge: Cambridge University Press, 1985.

———. *Islamic Rationalism: The Ethics of 'Abd 'Abd al-Jabbār.* Oxford: Clarendon Press, 1971.

Hovannisian, Richard G. *Ethics in Islam.* Malibu, Calif: Undena, 1985.

Izutsu, Toshihiko. *Ethico-Religious Concepts in the Qur'an,* rev. ed. Montreal: McGill University Press, 1966.

Miskawayh, Ahmad b. Muhammad. *The Refinement of Character: A Translation from the Arabic of Ahmad ibn-Muhammad Miskawayh's* Tahdhīb al-Akhlāq, transl. Constantine K. Zurayk. Beirut: American University of Beirut, 1966.

Reinhart, A. Kevin. *Before Revelation: The Boundaries of Muslim Moral Thought.* Albany, NY: State University of New York Press, 1995.

EUNUCHS

Eunuchs were emasculated guardians of political, sacred, and sexual boundaries in the medieval Islamic world. The term *khasi* (eunuch) refers to a man who went through the ablation of testicles, whereas a man deprived of all sexual organs is called a *majbub;* use of the latter term is less frequent in the narrative sources. From the tenth century CE on, the term *khadim* (servant) becomes the term that is most commonly used to refer to eunuchs.

Eunuchs were the (obviously) male servants in the women's quarters in the dwellings of the upper classes and in the royal palaces. In the context of Islamic sexual morality, other than one's husband, only certain adult males are allowed to see a woman unveiled, such as her father and brothers. These males are referred to as *mahrams,* or the forbidden ones, because they are, by virtue of their kinship, forbidden sexually. Eunuchs thus enter the world of the women in the same category as mahrams, not because of a kinship relationship but by virtue of their emasculation. It must be added, however, that few eunuchs had direct contact with their master's wives or concubines; there were female servants who acted as intermediaries between the two parties. Depending on one's wealth, the number of servants and eunuchs could well multiply.

The use of eunuchs at private homes is well attested to in medieval narrative sources. These sources suggest that the role of the eunuchs was not limited to serving the women of the house. The medieval scholar al-Subki describes the duties of the eunuch supervisor employed in the interior part of a dwelling as follows: "He is the one who is concerned with women. It is his duty and his right to cast his eyes upon their affairs and to advise the master of the house [concerning them]. He must inform him [the master] of any suspicion which he himself is unable to clear, and he must prevent agents of debauchery such as old women and others from gaining access to the women [of the household]." A fourteenth-century author places the eunuch in the vestibule of the dwelling and not in the residential quarter, where one would expect to find the women of the household. It seems that the entire home, rather than simply the residential quarters where women live, was considered a sacred, forbidden space, with the vestibule forming its boundary. Even one's closest friend would be expected to ask for permission to enter the inner part of the dwelling (Marmon 1995, 6–7); the vestibule in which the eunuch is located would be the place where this permission would be issued or denied.

When one moves up to the ultimate dwelling—that of the sultan—it is found that the eunuchs were the guardians of spaces that were political as well as sacred. Eunuchs have been employed at the courts of Muslim rulers since the Umayyad era. During the 'Abbasid age, the institution of elite slavery (mamluk) was developed, which creates new functions for eunuchs throughout the remainder of medieval Islamic history. The mamluks, who were enslaved at a relatively young age, had to be educated and introduced to the ways of imperial rule; this important political function came to be played by the eunuchs. There were eunuchs who served both the women and the mamluks, thereby establishing connections between the royal women and the administrators and generals of the future.

During the long reign of the Ottomans, there developed a differentiation within the body of the eunuchs employed at the court that seems to have followed the lines drawn by skin color. That the Ottoman court included eunuchs from the fourteenth century on is well attested to by documents referring to *tawashis* (a Turko-Arabic term denoting a servant) during the early fourteenth century. During the fifteenth century, reference is made to Ottoman eunuchs who were appointed to commanding positions outside of the court, such as a vizierate. During the sixteenth and seventeenth centuries, there are several Ottoman grand viziers and governors of Egypt who had been eunuchs at the palace. Available evidence suggests that these eunuchs and others who had administrative functions at the court were "white," whereas the eunuchs who served the women of the residential quarters were "black." What complicates this neat picture, which is suggestive of a division of labor between the two contingents of eunuchs at the Ottoman palace, is that the chief of all eunuchs was an African one from the late sixteenth century on.

BAKI TEZCAN

Further Reading

Ayalon, David. *Eunuchs, Caliphs and Sultans: A Study in Power Relationships.* Jerusalem: Magnes Press, 1999.
Marmon, S.E. *Eunuchs and Sacred Boundaries in Islamic Society.* New York: Oxford University Press, 1995.
Orhonlu, Cengiz. "Khasi—in Turkey." In *Encyclopaedia of Islam, New Edition,* vol. 4, 1092–3.

EUROPEAN LITERATURE, PERCEPTION OF ISLAM

Faced with the expansion of Islam, the crises of power over Jerusalem, the proximity of a thriving Islamic civilization in parts of Spain and Italy, and the uneasy transmission of knowledge (especially in the realm of science), medieval Christians imagined and recorded Muslim identity in diverse ways. Those who traveled to Muslim lands also provided accounts of their experiences. In the world of non-fiction, Christian Europeans produced propaganda, travel accounts, chronicles, and theological treatises in which they addressed Islam, often from an adversarial stance that aimed at disqualifying Islam's claims to the status of a revealed religion. Christian theologians in particular generated much debate about Islam, challenging it in terms of doctrine in a variety of tones ranging from pacifist invitations to conversion to obvious belligerence.

Fiction, which is the subject to be addressed in this entry, also portrayed Islam and the Muslim, often referring to the religion and its practitioners in terms that in contemporary English would translate as "Mohammedan," "Saracen," "Moor," or "pagan." When Islam and the Muslim were portrayed in medieval European fiction, the representation was not only informed by the contextual concerns outlined above but also by each author's own creativity and engagement with literary tradition.

On the most visible level, throughout the European Middle Ages, the Saracen or Mohammedan fulfilled a basically propagandistic role in both fiction and non-fiction, driven by the spirit of the Crusades. This is particularly true of epic poetry; for example, the French *La Chanson de Roland* (ca. 1100 CE), the English romances of Troy and Alexander (14 CE), and the Italian *Orlando Furioso* (1532 CE) contain references to the Saracen as the enemy, highlighting the courage and faith of the Christian warrior through the deserved defeat or ill-gained success of the Muslims. The long Arthurian tradition highlights the Christian knight's perfection against a vast range of foils, among them the Muslim. *Gerusalemme Liberata (Jerusalem Liberated)* by Torquato Tasso (1544–1595 CE) portrays Muslims as sorcerers and pagans, celebrating the liberation of Jerusalem during the first Crusade circa 1099 CE. The crusading spirit thus permeates much of the literature that features knights and kings.

In his monumental poem the *Inferno*, the Italian poet Dante Alighieri (1265–1321 CE) does not devote much space to Muslims; however, his depictions do merit attention because of his tremendous impact on Western literature. He places Mohammad and Ali in the ninth valley, alongside a number of Christian heretics and sinners, which suggests that he sees the Prophet and his nephew as apostates; indeed, scholars have argued that this shows Dante's and the general medieval European public's notion that Islam was not a religion in and of itself but rather a horrific schism in Christianity and therefore a heresy. Interestingly, Dante places Saladin, Averroes (Ibn Rushd), and Avicenna (Ibn Sina) in limbo, possibly because of the general (although ambivalent) respect with which these men were held by erudite medieval Europeans. Scholarship is divided regarding whether Dante's depiction of Muslims is a calculated propagandistic move or if he is too unaware of the facts about the religion to go beyond a generally vague condemnation of it (the latter is more in line with the common wariness of Islam in Medieval Europe). Saints' lives provided a vehicle for a suspicious portrayal of Islam as well; the basic conviction that Islam is a heresy to be mistrusted is reflected in *The Canterbury Tales* by Geoffrey Chaucer (d. 1400 CE), specifically in the "Man of Law's Tale," in which the King of Syria converts to Christianity to be able to marry a Christian princess. This man's mother, who is depicted as unequivocally evil, thwarts his plans because she is against the conversion. Giovanni Boccaccio's *Decameron* (1353 CE) also contains a few stories about Saracens, often against the backdrop of the Crusades. The French Alexandre du Pont's *Roman de Mahomet* (1258 CE) discusses the life of Mohammad as prophet with apocalyptic and crusading zeal.

The case of Christian Spain is quite different from the rest of Europe. Despite the anti-Muslim spirit of Reconquest, portrayals of Muslims in Spanish literature suggest a more textured and subtle poetics of representation than, say, French *chansons de geste*. Thus, for example, in the epic of El Cid (c. 1100 CE), the Christian hero counts the Muslim Abengalbón among his closest friends; the playful *Libro de Buen Amor*, written around 1330 CE by a Christian archpriest and filled with references to Christian ritual, displays profound sensitivity to its own Islamo-Hispanic context and demonstrates coexistence with Spanish Muslims to have permeated life to the extent that the boundary between enemy and friend is no longer as clear as a zealous theologian would have it be. This complexity is to be expected given that Muslims were not distant and unfamiliar to Iberian Christians but rather were counted for centuries as their own countrymen—albeit uneasily so—because of the Islamic settlements in Spain.

Some caution must be exercised against the temptation to consider all medieval European literature as simply anti-Muslim, with no room left for tolerance. The enduring works of a Dante or a Chaucer, as well as the vibrant traditions of epic poetry and the prose narratives of Boccaccio, are too poetically intricate to allow for the prevalence of obvious moral judgment over all other types of interpretation. Thus, even if the depiction of Muslims displays the largely antagonistic spirit of the times, one could still justify the search for ambiguity and paradox in some of the representations, largely because of the sophisticated narrative strategies employed by the prominent authors of the European Middle Ages.

LEYLA ROUHI

Further Reading

Asín Palacios, Miguel. *Islam and the Divine Comedy*, transl. Harold Sunderland. London: J. Murray, 1926.

Classen, Albrecht, ed. *Meeting the Foreign in the Middle Ages*. New York: Routledge, 2002.

Daniel, Norman. *Heroes and Saracens: An Interpretation of the Chansons de Geste*. Edinburgh: Edinburgh University Press, 1984.

Galmés de Fuentes, Álvaro. *Romania Arabia: Estudios de Literatura Comparada Árabe y Romance*. Madrid: Real Academia de la Historia, 2000.

Hyatte, Reginald. *The Prophet of Islam in Old French: The Romance of Muhammad (1258) and The Book of Muhammad's Ladder (1264)*. Leiden: Brill, 1997.

Linehan, Peter, and Janet L. Nelson, eds. *The Medieval World*. New York: Routledge, 2001.

Russell, Peter. *Dante & Islam: Una Introduzione Generale: Quattro Conferenze*. Arezzo, Italy: Pian de Sco, 1991.

Tolan, John V., ed. *Medieval Christian Perceptions of Islam: A Book of Essays*. New York: Garland, 1994.

———. *Saracens: Islam in the Medieval European Imagination*. New York: Columbia University Press, 2002.

Watt, W. Montgomery. *Muslim–Christian Encounters: Perceptions and Misperceptions*. London: Routledge, 1991.

Wolf, Kenneth Baxter. *Christian Martyrs in Muslim Spain*, Cambridge Iberian and Latin American Studies. Cambridge, Mass: Cambridge University Press, 1988.

EXCELLENCES LITERATURE

During roughly the last quarter of the AH first/ seventh CE century, reports are said to have been circulated that extolled the merits (fada'il or manaqib) of, for example, reciting the Qur'an; of the Companions of the Prophets; of holy cities such as Jerusalem, Mecca, and Medina; and of the performance of particular religious duties such as the hajj and jihad. These fada'il reports were initially a part of the burgeoning hadith corpus, and the fada'il al-Qur'an traditions appear to be the oldest strand in this literature. Discrete treatises about the excellences of the Qur'an, cities, regions, and people began to make their appearance during the eighth century CE. The composition of fada'il works about countries is understood to have preceded that of fada'il compositions about people. An early example of the latter kind is *Fada'il al-Ansar (The Merits of the Helpers [of Madina])* by Wahb ibn Wahb (d. 200/815).

The obvious anachronisms contained in the texts of a number of these reports and their vaunting nature make clear that a significant number of the manaqib/fada'il traditions came into existence well after the death of the Prophet and, as a consequence, encode the doctrinal sympathies of their propagators and the political climate of their times. It is possible, therefore, to suggest with judicial circumspection tentative links between the texts of various manaqib traditions and the sociopolitical milieu that may have instigated their circulation. It should be pointed out that medieval Muslim scholars were fully aware of the tendentious nature of many of the manaqib/fada'il reports. The hadith scholar Ibn al-Jawzi (d. 597/1200), for example, lists many manaqib traditions in his *Kitab al-Mawduʿat (The Book of Spurious Reports)*, which he dismisses as blatant fabrications. Other kinds of adiths, which were traditions that greatly exaggerated the merits of particular cities, such as Jerusalem, of certain Qur'anic chapters, and

of the early caliphs, were regarded with suspicion and often rejected. The qussas (sing. qass; preacher; literally, "storyteller") played a significant role in the dissemination of a significant number of these praise traditions.

The manaqib/fada'il literature is a rich source of sociohistorical information about the Muslim polity that may be regarded as charting the checkered terrain of the growing political and communal consciousness of the early Muslims. As such, they remain a valuable source for reconstructing the formative period of Islam.

ASMA AFSARUDDIN

Further Reading

Afsaruddin, Asma. *Excellence and Precedence: Medieval Islamic Discourse on Legitimate Leadership*. Leiden, 2002.
———. "The Excellences of the Qur'an Textual Sacrality and the Organization of Early Islamic Society." *Journal of the American Oriental Society* 122 (2002): 1–24.
Sellheim, R. Art. "Fadila." In *Encyclopaedia of Islam, New Edition*, Leiden and London, 1965.
Pellat, Ch. Art. "Manakib." In *Encyclopaedia of Islam, New Edition*, Leiden and London, 1991.

F

FARABI, AL- (ALFARABIUS OR AVENNASAR)

Despite uncertainty about Alfarabi's place of birth and the early years of his life, there is general agreement that he was born in approximately 870 CE, beyond the Oxus River—either in Farab, Kazakhstan, or Faryb, Turkestan. In the course of his life, AbuNasr Muchamad Ibn Muhammad Ibn Tarkh n Ibn Awzalagh al-Farabi resided in Bukhara, Marv, Haran, Baghdad, Constantinople, Aleppo, Cairo, and Damascus, where he died in 950. He studied Islamic jurisprudence and music in Bukhara then moved to Marv, where he began to study logic with a Nestorian Christian monk, Yuhanna Ibn Hayln. While in his early 20s, Alfarabi went to Baghdad and continued to study logic and philosophy with Hayln.

At the same time, he improved his grasp of Arabic by studying with the prominent philologist Ibn al-Sarraj, and followed the courses of the famous Nestorian Christian translator and student of Aristotle Matta Ibn Yunus.

Around the year 905 or 910, Alfarabi left Baghdad for Constantinople, where he remained for approximately eight years studying Greek sciences and philosophy. On his return to Baghdad, he busied himself with teaching and writing. In about 942, political upheavals forced him to seek refuge in Damascus. Political turmoil in Damascus drove him to Egypt two or three years later, where he stayed until returning to Damascus in 948 or 949, a little over a year before his death.

Generally known as "the second teacher," that is, second after Aristotle, Alfarabi must be accounted the most important philosopher within the Arabic–Islamic tradition. His writings, charming yet deceptively subtle, use simple language and straightforward sentences. Most often, he expounds what resembles a narrative, a story about natural and conventional things that is simply unobjectionable. As the exposition unfolds, the reader discovers that Alfarabi has accounted for the natural order, political leadership, prophecy, moral virtue, civic order, the order of the sciences, and even the philosophic pursuits of Plato or Aristotle—in short, all the major subjects of interest to humans—in an unprecedented and seemingly unobjectionable manner. Often, it sets forth the reasons that human beings live in civic association, how it can best be ordered to meet the highest human needs, the way most actual regimes differ from this best order, and why philosophy and religion deem this order best.

These writings, extraordinary in their breadth and deep learning, extend through all the sciences and embrace every part of philosophy. Alfarabi's interest in mathematics is evidenced in commentaries on the *Elements* of Euclid and *Almagest* of Ptolemy, as well as in several writings on the history and theory of music. Indeed, his *Large Book on Music* may well be the most significant work in Arabic on that subject. He also wrote numerous commentaries on Aristotle's logical writings, was knowledgeable about the Stagirite's physical writings, and is credited with an extensive commentary in *Nicomachean Ethics,* which has not survived. In addition to accounts of Plato's and Aristotle's philosophy, he composed a commentary on Plato's *Laws*. Alfarabi's distinction as the founder of Arabic–Islamic political philosophy is due to his being the first philosopher within Islam to explore the challenge to traditional philosophy presented by revealed religion, especially in its claims that the Creator provides for human well-being by means of an inspired prophet legislator. Those who now contest that distinction turn a blind eye to the way he sets forth two accounts of the old political science in the last chapter of a popular writing, *Enumeration of the Sciences*. Both presuppose the validity of the traditional separation between practical and theoretical science, but neither is adequate for the radically new situation created by the appearance of revealed religion. The two accounts explain in detail the actions and ways of life needed for sound political rule to flourish but are silent about opinions—especially the kind of theoretical opinions set forth in religion—and thus are unable to point to the kind of rulership needed now that religion holds sway. Nor can either speak about the opinions or actions addressed by the jurisprudence and theology of revealed religion. These tasks require a political science that combines theoretical and practical science, along with prudence, and shows how they are to be ordered in the soul of the ruler.

In other writings—most notably in his *Book of Religion* and *Aphorisms of the Statesman*—Alfarabi outlines this broader political science. It speaks of religious beliefs as opinions and of acts of worship as actions, noting that both are prescribed for a community by a supreme ruler or prophet. The new political science views religion as centered in a political community whose supreme ruler is distinct in no way from the founder of a religion. Indeed, the goals and prescriptions of the supreme ruler are identical to those of the prophet lawgiver. Everything said or done by this supreme ruler finds constant justification in philosophy, and religion thus appears to depend on philosophy—theoretical and practical. Similarly, by presenting the art of jurisprudence as a means to identify particular details the supreme ruler did not regulate before his death, Alfarabi makes it depend on practical philosophy and thus be part of this broader political science. In sum, his new political science offers a comprehensive view of the universe and indicates what kind of practical acumen permits the one who possesses this understanding, either the supreme ruler or a successor endowed with all of his qualities, to rule wisely. Able to explain the various ranks of all the beings, this political science also stresses the importance of religion for uniting the citizens and for helping them attain the virtues that prolong decent political life. Then, in *Political Regime* and *Principles of the Opinions of the Inhabitants of the*

Virtuous City, he illustrates how this new political science might work. A general overview of this whole undertaking is provided in *Attainment of Happiness*—the first part of his famous trilogy *Philosophy of Plato and Aristotle*—where he declares that "the idea of the philosopher, supreme ruler, prince, legislator, and imam is but a single idea."

CHARLES E. BUTTERWORTH

Further Reading

Alfarabi's Philosophy of Plato and Aristotle, trans. Muhsin Mahdi. Ithaca, NY: Cornell University Press, 2002.
Enumeration of the Sciences, trans. Charles E. Butterworth. In *Alfarabi, The Political Writings: "Selected Aphorisms" and Other Texts*, ed. and trans. Charles E. Butterworth, 71–84. Ithaca, NY: Cornell University Press, 2001.
Butterworth, Charles E. "The Rhetorician and His Relationship to the Community: Three Accounts of Aristotle's *Rhetoric*." In *Islamic Theology and Philosophy: Studies in Honor of George F. Hourani*, ed. Michael E. Marmura, 111–136. Albany, NY: SUNY Press, 1984.
Mahdi, Muhsin S. *Alfarabi and the Foundation of Islamic Political Philosophy: Essays in Interpretation*. Chicago: University of Chicago Press, 2001.
———. "Alfarabi." In *History of Political Philosophy*, eds. Leo Strauss and Joseph Cropsey, 160–180. Chicago: Rand McNally and Co., 1963.

FATIMA (AL-ZAHRA') BINT MUHAMMAD (CA. 12 BEFORE HIJRA–11/CA. 610–632)

Fatima was the youngest daughter of the Prophet Muhammad and Khad'ja. She was born in Mecca, probably soon after the beginning of the Prophet's mission in 609–610; according to some sources, a few years earlier. Little is known of her childhood. In the first or second year after the Hijra to Medina in 622, after refusing the suit of Abu Bakr and 'Umar, Muhammad gave her in marriage to his cousin 'Ali ibn Abi Talib; 'Ali was to become the fourth Rightly Guided Sunni Caliph and, according to the Shi'i, Muhammad's divinely appointed successor. Most of the historical reports on Fatima's life are about the details of her marriage. 'Ali did not take another wife in Fatima's lifetime. They had four children, all of whom had important roles in the political and religious life of the first Islamic century: Hasan, the first Shi'i imam; Husayn, the second Shi'i imam and the martyr of Karbala; and Zaynab and Umm Kulthum, who both intrepidly confronted Umayyad authority.

When Muhammad died, Fatima maintained with 'Ali his superior right as the Prophet's successor. She disputed the caliphate of Abu Bakr and had several fierce altercations with him and his supporter and successor-to-be, 'Umar. Alarmed by her forceful opposition, 'Umar threatened to burn her house down, along with its inhabitants, if her husband did not acknowledge Abu Bakr as caliph; under threat of execution, 'Ali eventually capitulated—according to some reports, only after Fatima died. Fatima also argued with Abu Bakr for her own right to inherit the lands of Fadak; Abu Bakr had denied her Fadak, declaring that he had heard Muhammad say prophets have no heirs. On one occasion of dispute, Fatima is reported to have delivered an eloquent oration (text in *Balaghat al-nisa'*, 54–69) to the assembly of Companions gathered around Abu Bakr. She died at the young age of 23, just two and a half months (six, according to some sources) after Muhammad's death in AH 11/632 CE, and was buried in the Baqi' cemetery in Medina.

The sources attribute several verses of poetry to her in grief-filled elegy of her father, which have been collected in modern times in a slim *Diwan*. Some hadith are also related on her authority, many of which were collected by the historian al-Suyuti in a book titled *Musnad Fatima al-Zahra'*.

Muhammad's line continued solely through Fatima and her children. In particular, the Hasanid and Husaynid lines were religiously and politically important. Shi'i imams of all denominations trace their lineage to the Prophet through Fatima, mostly through her son Husayn, and several ruling dynasties have claimed special status because of ancestry from her. Among them is the Fatimid dynasty of Isma'li caliph-imams who ruled North Africa and Egypt from the ninth through the twelfth centuries; their genealogy was a key factor in legitimizing their claim to the caliphate and the imamate.

Although Sunnis honor Fatima as the beloved daughter of the Prophet and the ideal of gentle Muslim womanhood, the Shi'is venerate her further as one of the "Five Pure Ones" (*Panj-tan Pak* in Persian and Urdu; *al-Khamsat al-Athar* in Arabic), namely, Muhammad, 'Ali, Fatima, Hasan, and Husayn. The Shi'is consider her one of the *ahl al-bayt* (people of the Prophet's house) from whom God "removed all impurity" (Q 33:33). They believe that Fatima, although not an Imam, possessed the infallibility (*'isma*) and the power of intercession (*shafa'a*) of the Imams. They attribute several miracles to her, such as the miracle of her divinely luminous veil, which caused an entire Jewish clan to convert to Islam.

Fatima is known by several titles, the best known of which is "al-Zahra'" (the luminous one); the Fatimids named their famed Al-Azhar University after her. She is also known as "Batul" (the virgin),

referring to purity and piety rather than celibacy. Enigmatically, she is also called "Umm abiha" (the mother of her father), a title interpreted in various historical or esoteric ways. Finally, both Shi'is and Sunnis believe—the latter following hadith considered sound by authors of their canonical collections, Bukhari and Muslim—that Muhammad designated her "mistress of the women of Paradise" (*sayyidat nisa' al-janna*) and "mistress of all the women in the world" (*sayyidat nisa' al-'alamin*).

TAHERA QUTBUDDIN

See also Shi'ism

Primary Sources

Fatima al-Zahra'. *Diwan*, ed. Kamil Salman al-Juburi. Beirut: Mu'assasat al-Mawahib, 1999.

Al-Khurasani, Ahmad ibn Abi Tayfur. *Balaghat al-nisa.'* ed. 'Abd al-Hamid Hindawi. Cairo: Dar al-Fadila, 1998.

Al-Suyuti, Jalal al-Din. *Musnad Fatima al-Zahra.'* Beirut: Mu'assasat al-Kutub al-Thaqafiyya, 1992 (Hadith related on Fatima's authority).

Al-Tuwaysirkani, Husayn. *Musnad Fatima al-Zahra.'* Beirut: Dar al-Safwa, 1992 (speeches and words—*aqwal*—attributed to Fatima).

Further Reading

Al-Amin, Muhsin. *A'lam al-Shi'a*. Vol. 1. Beirut: Dar al-Ta'aruf, 1983, 306–326.

Beinhauer-Köhler, Bärbel. *Fatima bint Muhammad: Metamorphosen einer frühislamischen Frauengestalt*. Wiesbaden: Harrosowitz Verlag, 2002.

Darwish, Linda. "Images of Muslim Women: 'A'sha, Fatima, and Zaynab Bint 'Ali in Contemporary Gender Discourse." *McGill Journal of Middle Eastern Studies (Revue d'études du moyen-orient de McGill)* 4 (1996): 93–132.

Al-Fadili, Husayn Muhammad 'Ali. *Ummu Abiha fi Sihah al-Muslimin wa Masanidihim*. Beirut: Dar al-Murshid, 2001.

Ibn Sa'd. *Al-Tabaqat al-Kubra*. Vol. 8. Beirut: Dar Sadir, 1958, 19–30.

Kahhala, 'Umar Rida. "Fatima bint Muhammad ibn 'Abd Allah ibn 'Abd al-Muttalib." *A'lam al-Nisa' fi 'Alamay al-'Arab wa al-Islam*. Damascus: al-Matba'a al-Hashimiyya, 1940, 1199–1223.

Madelung, Wilferd. *The Succession to Muhammad*. Cambridge, MA: Cambridge University Press, 1997, 3–63.

Massignon, Louis. "Der Gnostische Kult der Fatima im Schiitischen Islam." *Eranos Jahrbuch* 6 (1938): 161–173.

———. "La Mubahala: Etude sur la Proposition d'Ordalie Faite par le Prophète Muhammad aux Chrétiens Balharith du Nejran en l'an 10/631 à Médine." *École pratique des hautes études* (1943): 5–36.

———. "La Notion du Voeu et la Dévotion Musalmane à Fatima." In *Studi Orientalistici in Onori Di Giorgio Levi Della Vida*, 102–126. Rome: Instituto per l'Oriente, 1956.

McAuliffe, Jane Dammen. "Chosen of All Women: Mary and Fatima in Qur'anic Exegesis." *Islamochristiana* 7 (1981): 19–28.

———."Fatimah bint Muhammad." *The Encyclopedia of Religion*, ed. Mircea Eliade. New York: Macmillan, 1987, 298–299.

Al-Nu'man, al-Qadi. *Sharh al-Akhbar fi Fada'il al-a'Imma al-Athar*. Vol 2. Beirut: Dar al-Thaqalayn, 1994, 355–360 (Fatima's marriage to 'Ali).

Öhrnberg, Kaj. *The Offspring of Fatima: Dispersal and Ramification*, Vol. 54. Ed. Finnish Oriental Society. *Studia Orientalia*. Helsinki, 1983.

Shari'ati, 'Ali, *Fatima is Fatima*, trans. Laleh Bakhtiar. Tehran: Shariati Foundation, 1981.

Vaglieri, Laura Veccia. "Fatima." In *Encyclopaedia of Islam*. Vol 2. ed. H.A.R. Gibb et al. Leiden: Brill, 1960–2003, 841–850.

FATIMIDS

The Fatimids were a major Isma'ili Shi'i dynasty that ruled over different parts of the Islamic world, originally from Ifriqiyya and later Egypt, from AH 297/909 CE until 567/1171. Comprised of the following fourteen caliphs, the Fatimids were also acknowledged as Isma'ili imams:

1. al-Mahdi (297–322/909–934)
2. al-Qa'im (322–334/934–946)
3. al-Mansur (334–341/946–953)
4. al-Mu'izz (341–365/953–975)
5. al-'Aziz (365–386/975–996)
6. al-Hakim (386–411/996–1021)
7. al-Zahir (411–427/1021–1036)
8. al-Mustansir (427–487/1036–1094)
9. al-Musta'li (487–495/1094–1101)
10. al-Amir (495–524/1101–1130)
11. al-Hafiz

   As regent (524–526/1130–1132)
   As caliph (526–544/1132–1149)

12. al-Zafir (544–549/1149–1154)
13. al-Fa'iz (549–555/1154–1160)
14. al-'Adid (555–567/1160–1171)

The Fatimids traced their ancestry, through the early Shi'i imam Ja'far al-Sadiq (d. 148/765), to 'Ali ibn Abi Talib and his wife Fatima, the Prophet Muhammad's daughter and the eponym of the dynasty.

Foundation and North African Phase

By the middle of the third/ninth century, the Isma'ilis had organized a dynamic, revolutionary movement, designated as *al-da'wa al-hadiya*, the rightly guiding mission, or simply as *al-da'wa*. The aim of this movement, led secretly from Salamiyya in Syria, was to install the Isma'ili imam to a new caliphate, in rivalry with the 'Abbasids. The Isma'ili imams claimed to possess sole legitimate religious authority as the divinely appointed and infallible spiritual guides of Muslims; hence they regarded the 'Abbasids, like the Umayyads before them, as usurpers who had deprived the rightful 'Alid imams of their claims to leadership. The message of the Isma'ili *da'wa* was spread in different parts of the Muslim world, from Transoxiana and Sind to North Africa, by a network of *da'is*, religiopolitical propagandists.

The early Isma'ili *da'wa* achieved particular success in North Africa due to the efforts of Abu 'Abdullah al-Shi'i, who was active as a *da'i* among the Kutama Berbers of the Lesser Kabylia, in present-day eastern Algeria, since 280/893. He converted the bulk of the Kutama Berbers and transformed them into a disciplined army, which later served as the backbone of the Fatimid forces. By 290/903, Abu 'Abdullah had commenced his conquest of Ifriqiyya, covering today's Tunisia and eastern Algeria. The Sunni Aghlabids had ruled over this part of the Maghrib, and Sicily, since 184/800 as vassals of the 'Abbasids. By Rajab 296/March 909, when Abu 'Abdullah entered Qayrawan, the Aghlabid capital, Aghlabid rule was ended. Meanwhile, the Isma'ili imam, 'Abdullah al-Mahdi, had embarked on a long and historic journey. He left Salamiyya in 289/902, avoiding capture by the 'Abbasids, and after brief stays in Palestine and Egypt, he had been living in Sijilmasa, today's Rissani in southeastern Morocco, since 292/905. 'Abdullah continued to hide his identity while maintaining contact with the *da'i* Abu 'Abdullah. In Ramadan 296/June 909, Abu 'Abdullah set off at the head of his army to Sijilmasa, to hand over the reins of power to 'Abdullah al-Mahdi. 'Abdullah al-Mahdi entered Qayrawan on 20 Rabi' II 297/4 January 910, and was immediately acclaimed as caliph. This represented a great achievement for the Isma'ilis whose *da'wa* had finally led to the establishment of a *dawla*, or state, headed by the Isma'ili imam.

In line with their universal claims, the Fatimid caliph–imams did not abandon their *da'wa* activities on assuming power. Aiming to extend their authority and rule over the entire Muslim community (*umma*) and others, they retained their network of *da'is*, operating both within and outside Fatimid dominions. However, the *da'wa* was reinvigorated only after the Fatimids transferred the seat of their state to Egypt. The first four Fatimid caliph–imams, ruling from Ifriqiyya, encountered numerous difficulties while consolidating their power. In addition to the continued hostility of the 'Abbasids, and the Umayyads of

Spain, who as rival claimants to the caliphate had their own designs for North Africa, the early Fatimids had numerous military encounters with the Byzantines in Sicily and elsewhere. The Fatimids were also obliged to devote much of their energy during their North African period to subduing the rebellions of the Khariji Berbers, especially those belonging to the Zanata confederation, and the hostilities of the Sunni inhabitants of Qayrawan and other cities of Ifriqiyya led by their Maliki jurists. As a result, the Fatimids could not control any region of the Maghrib, beyond Ifriqiyya, for any extended period. The Fatimids were city builders and founded Mahdiyya and Mansuriyya, which served as their new capitals in Ifriqiya. As successors to the Aghlabids, the Fatimids inherited their fleet and the island of Sicily (Siqilliyya). Thus, from early on, the Fatimid state was also a sea power with Mahdiyya serving as a naval base.

Fatimid rule was firmly established in north Africa only during the reign of al-Mu'izz, who was able to pursue successful policies of war and diplomacy, resulting in territorial expansion. He contributed significantly to the development of the state's political, administrative, and financial institutions, in addition to concerning himself with the *da'wa* activities. Indeed, al-Mu'izz succeeded in transforming the Fatimid caliphate from a regional power into a great empire. He made detailed plans for the conquest of Egypt, then ruled by the Ikhshidids on behalf of the 'Abbasids, a hitherto perennial objective of the Fatimids as the first phase in their eastern strategy of conquest. Jawhar, a commander of long services to the dynasty, led the Fatimid expedition to Egypt in 358/969. Jawhar's campsite outside of Fustat rapidly developed into a city, Cairo (al-Qahira). Al-Mu'izz had supervised the plan of the new royal city, with its palaces, gates, and the mosque of al-Azhar and special buildings for government departments and the Fatimid armies. Al-Mu'izz arrived in his new capital in 362/973, marking the end of the North African phase of the Fatimid caliphate (292–362/909–973).

Egyptian Phase

The rule of al-Mu'izz in Egypt lasted just more than two years, during which he entrusted Ibn Killis with the task of reorganizing the state's finances. The consolidation and extension of Fatimid power in Syria, at the expense of the 'Abbasids and the Byzantines, was the primary foreign policy objective of al-Mu'izz's son and successor, al-'Aziz, the first Fatimid caliph–imam to begin his rule in Egypt in 365/975. In spite of al-'Aziz's hard-won victory in Syria, however, Damascus remained only nominally in Fatimid hands for some time and the Fatimids failed to seize Aleppo in northern Syria. In North Africa, the Zirids who ruled on behalf of the Fatimids had already begun to detach themselves from the Fatimid state. Despite these setbacks, by the end of al-'Aziz's reign in 386/996 the Fatimid empire attained its greatest extent, at least nominally, with the Fatimid sovereignty recognized from the Atlantic and the western Mediterranean to the Red Sea, the Hijaz, Syria, and Palestine. At the same time, *da'i*s acting as secret agents of the Fatimid state had continued to preach the Isma'ili *da'wa* in many eastern regions, notably Persia and Iraq. Al-'Aziz was the first member of his dynasty to use the Turks in the Fatimid armies, to the strong dissatisfaction of the Berber officers, and with catastrophic consequences. Al-'Aziz adopted a tolerant policy toward non-Muslims, also utilizing the services of capable men irrespective of their ethnicities or religious persuasions. The assignment of numerous high administrative and juridical positions to Sunni Muslims, as well as Christians and Jews, in a Shi'i state, in fact, was a distinctive practice of the Fatimids. Ibn Killis (d. 380/991), a convert from Judaism, became the first Fatimid vizier under al-'Aziz in 367/977. The credit for utilizing al-Azhar as a university also belongs to Ibn Killis. The last of al-'Aziz's viziers was a coptic Christian, 'Isa ibn Nasturus (385–386/995–996).

Al-'Aziz's son and successor, al-Hakim, faced numerous difficulties during his long and controversial reign, including factional conflicts within the Fatimid armies and confrontations with different religious groups. One of his most important acts was, however, the foundation of the Dar al-'Ilm (the House of Knowledge) in 395/1005. This became an institution of learning with a fine library, where Shi'is and Sunnis studied a variety of sciences. The Isma'ili *da'i*s also received part of their training there. In al-Hakim's time, the Isma'ili *da'wa* spread successfully in Iraq and Persia through the efforts of Hamid al-Din al-Kirmani and other learned *da'i*s. It was also in his reign that certain *da'i*s began to preach extremist ideas, culminating in the proclamation of al-Hakim's divinity and the formation of the Druze movement, which met with the opposition of the Fatimid state and the *da'wa* organization in Cairo.

Fueled by factional fighting within the Fatimid armies, the Fatimid caliphate embarked on its decline during the long reign of al-Mustansir, who was eventually obliged to call on Badr al-Jamali for help. In 466/1074, Badr arrived in Cairo with his Armenian troops and quickly succeeded in subduing the unruly

Turkish troops and restoring relative peace and stability to the Fatimid state. Badr became the commander of the armies *(amir al-juyush)*, also acquiring all the highest positions of the Fatimid state. Badr (d. 487/1094) ensured that his son, al-Afdal (d. 515/1121), would succeed him in due course as the real master of the Fatimid state. Hence, the viziers, rather than caliphs, exercised effective power in the Fatimid state. Territorially, too, the overall extent of the Fatimid empire began to decline in al-Mustansir's reign. The Fatimids lost parts of Syria and, in North Africa their dominions were practically reduced to Egypt. On the other hand, the Isma'ili *da'wa* activities outside of Fatimid dominions reached their peak in al-Mustansir's time, with much success in Yaman, Persia, and Transoxiana. The *da'wa* was organized hierarchically, with the Fatimid caliph–imam as its supreme leader. A chief *da'i (da'i al-du'at)* acted as the executive head of the *da'wa* organization centered in Cairo. The regions outside the Fatimid state were divided into twelve islands *(jaziras)* for *da'wa* purposes, each one placed under the charge of a high-ranking officer, called *hujja* (proof, guarantor), who headed a hierarchy of subordinate *da'i*s and assistants.

The organization of the Fatimid state remained rather simple during its North African phase, when the caliph–imams acted as the supreme heads of the government administration and commanders of the armies, and the highly centralized administration was normally situated at the Fatimid palace. From the early years in Egypt, the organizational structure of administration and finance introduced by Jawhar and Ibn Killis provided the basis of a complex system of institutions. The Fatimid system of administration in Egypt remained centralized, with the caliph and his vizier at its head, while the provincial organs of government were under the strict control of central authorities in Cairo. The central administration of the Fatimids was carried on through various ministries and departments, known as *diwan*s. Foremost among these units were the *diwan al-insha*, or chancery of state, responsible for issuing and handling various types of official documents; the *diwan al-jaysh*, the department of the army; and the *diwan al-amwal*, the ministry of finance. The officials of the Fatimid state, both civil and military, were organized in terms of strict hierarchies. The Fatimids also developed an elaborate system of rituals and ceremonials. They established a vast network of trade and commerce after settling down in Egypt, providing the state with a significant economic base. In Egypt, the Fatimids patronized intellectual activities, transforming Cairo into a flourishing center of Islamic scholarship, sciences, art, and culture.

On the death of al-Mustansir in 487/1094, the Isma'ilis permanently subdivided into Nizari and Musta'li factions, named after al-Mustansir's sons who claimed his heritage. Hence, the Nizari and Musta'li Isma'ilis recognized different lines of imams. The Musta'lis of Egypt and elsewhere acknowledged al-Musta'li, al-Mustansir's son and successor to the Fatimid throne, as their imam. By 526/1132, in the aftermath of al-Amir's assassination and the irregular succession of his cousin al-Hafiz, the Musta'li Isma'ilis were split into the Tayyibi and Hafizi branches. Only the Hafizi Musta'lis, situated mainly in Fatimid Egypt, recognized al-Hafiz and the later Fatimids as their imams.

The final phase of the Fatimid caliphate, 487–567/1094–1171, was a turbulent one. Reduced to Egypt proper, the Fatimid state was now almost continuously beset by political and economic crises worsened by intense disorders within the Fatimid armies and the arrival of the invading Crusaders. The later Fatimids all died prematurely, and they remained puppets in the hands of their powerful viziers, who controlled the armies. The last Fatimid caliph–imam, al-'Adid, was only nine years old at the time of his succession and his nominal reign represented the most confusing period in Fatimid history. Power remained in the hands of several short-lived viziers, who continuously intrigued against one another. The crusading Franks also had almost succeeded in establishing a virtual protectorate over Fatimid Egypt, while the Zangids of Syria had resumed their own invasions. Ironically, it was left to the last Fatimid vizier, Salah al-Din (Saladin) to terminate Fatimid rule on 7 Muharram 567/10 September 1171, when he had the *khutba* read in Cairo in the name of the reigning 'Abbasid caliph, symbolizing the return of Egypt to the fold of Sunni Islam. A few days later, al-'Adid, the fourteenth and final Fatimid caliph–imam, died after a brief illness while the Isma'ilis, who had always remained a minority in Egypt, began to be severely persecuted. The Fatimid state had thus come to a close after 262 years. Subsequently, Egypt was incorporated into the Sunni Ayyubid state founded in 569/1174 by Salah al-Din.

FARHAD DAFTARY

Primary Sources

Ibn al-Haytham. *Kitab al-Munazarat*, ed. and trans. W. Madelung and P. E. Walker (as *The Advent of the Fatimids.*) London, 2000.

Al-Maqrizi, Taqi al-Din Ahmad. *Itti'az al-Hunafa,'* ed. J. al-Shayyal and M.H.M. Ahmad. 3 vols. Cairo, 1967–1973.

Al-Nu'man ibn al-Muhammad, al-Qadi Abu Hanifa. *Iftitah al-Da'wa*, ed. W. al-Qadi. Beirut, 1970.

Further Reading

Barrucand, Marianne, ed. *L'Egypte Fatimide, son art et son histoire*. Paris, 1999.

Brett, Michael. *The Rise of the Fatimids*. Leiden, 2001.

Daftary, Farhad. *The Isma'ilis: Their History and Doctrines*. Cambridge, MA, 1990.

Halm, Heinz. *The Empire of the Mahdi: The Rise of the Fatimids*. Translated by M. Bonner. Leiden, 1996.

———. *Die Kalifen von Kairo. Die Fatimiden in Ägypten 973-1074*. Munich, 2003.

Sanders, Paula. *Ritual, Politics and the City in Fatimid Cairo*. Albany, NY, 1994.

Sayyid, Ayman Fu'ad. *Al-Dawla al-Fatimiyya fi Misr*. 2nd ed. Cairo, 2000.

Walker, Paul E. *Exploring an Islamic Empire: Fatimid History and Its Sources*. London, 2002.

FERDOWSI

Ferdowsi, the major epic poet of Persian civilization, was born in 940 CE near the town of Tus in Khorasan, where he apparently spent most of his life. The date of his death is unknown, but it is traditionally given as ca. 1020. His epic *Shahnameh*, a retelling of the pre-Islamic myths, legends, and history of Iran, is one of Persian literature's most significant works.

Ferdowsi began *Shahnameh* when Khorasan was still ruled by the Samanids, who fostered an interest in Iran's pre-Islamic past and were the first significant patrons, after the Islamic conquest, of literature in Persian. The Samanid domains were overrun by the Ghaznavid Turks under Mahmud of Ghazni during Ferdowsi's lifetime—a number of anecdotes recounted by medieval writers concerning Ferdowsi's bad relations with Mahmud are probably apocryphal.

The epic *Shahnameh* is in the *masnavi* (couplet) form and uses the *motaqareb* meter (one of only two medieval Persian meters that do not derive from an Arabic model; *motaqareb* may derive from a pre-Islamic Persian meter). Manuscripts of the poem differ widely in length, with the longest containing up to sixty thousand couplets; earlier and more reliable manuscripts tend to have approximately forty thousand couplets. After relatively conventional introductory matter, the poem divides into three unequal sections: a short mythical section, a legendary section, and a quasihistorical section. Ferdowsi cites both written and oral sources; it is clear that he relied heavily on written sources for the quasihistorical section, but the earlier sections seem to owe much to oral tradition.

In contrast to other contemporary authors concerned with Iran's pre-Islamic past, Ferdowsi's cosmogony is wholly Persian, and he makes no attempt to integrate Persian creation myths, or Persian legendary material, with Qur'anic accounts of the world's early history. Evil is present at the opening of the poem in the form of supernatural beings *(div)*; the first evil person in the poem is the demon king Zahhak, identified as an Arab, and at the poem's end a commander who has foreseen Persia's defeat in the seventh-century Arab invasion prophesies the moral and political disasters that will come to Iran at the Arabs' hands. The poem is thus framed by a fairly overt hostility to Arab culture.

Shahnameh is structured as a king list, and the reigns of fifty monarchs are described, some very briefly, others at considerable length (for example, the reign of the legendary king Kavus covers three of the nine volumes of the standard edition). The earliest stories of the mythical and legendary sections go back to a prehistoric Indo-European past and have some parallels in other Indo-European mythologies (such as Hindu and Greek). The legendary section incorporates into the narrative a separate cycle of tales concerned with the rulers of Sistan (southeastern Iran, Afghanistan south of the River Helmand), the most famous of whom is Rostam, who was in all probability a Parthian hero whose tales of exploits had survived in oral form. The prophet Zoroaster enters the narrative (in the one section of the poem not written by Ferdowsi, but by his predecessor Daqiqi) during the reign of the legendary king, Goshtasp (possibly to be identified with the Achaemenid Hystaspes), and the religious milieu of the poem is generally Zoroastrian, although Ferdowsi shows little detailed knowledge of Zoroastrian beliefs and makes frequent anachronistic references to the religion. The emphatically ethical orientation of many of the tales of the legendary section (such as those of Kaveh, Iraj, Seyavash, and Kay Khosrow) may be considered in part as a legacy of pre-Islamic Zoroastrianism.

The quasihistorical section begins approximately with Alexander the Great's conquest of Iran. From this point on, rulers mentioned in the poem correspond with historical personages, but often in a romanticized or garbled way (for example, Alexander is given a Persian father; Ferdowsi confuses the reigns of the Sasanian kings Shapur I and Shapur II). This section is much less smoothly constructed than the poem's earlier portions, and the narrative contains frequent self-contradictions (for example, the founder of the Sasanian dynasty is given two differing genealogies). The Parthians, who in reality ruled Iran longer than any other dynasty, are very summarily dealt with (their almost five hundred-year reign is compressed into a couple of generations), and this is certainly due to the Sasanian attempt to obliterate the Parthians from the historical record. The legendary grandeur of the poem's opening half gives way to tales of royal hedonism (such as during the reign of

Bahram Gur) and detailed accounts of court intrigues, rebellions, and palace revolutions.

RICHARD DAVIS

Further Reading

Banani, Amin. "Ferdowsi and the Art of Tragic Epic." In *Persian Literature*, ed. E. Yarshater. New York, 1988.

Davidson, Olga M. *Poet and Hero in the Persian Book of Kings*. Ithaca, 1994.

Davis, Dick. *Epic and Sedition*. Fayetteville, 1992.

Safa, Zabihollah. *Hemaseh Sarai dar Iran (Epic in Iran)*. Tehran, 1369/1990.

FESTIVALS AND CELEBRATIONS

The 'Id al-Fitr (Festival of Breaking the Fast) and the 'Id al-Adha (Festival of Sacrifice), although not mentioned in the Qur'an and hadith and usually referred to by legal literature only marginally, have been considered the only two canonical festivals that the Prophet prescribed. This meagerness of religious feasts in Islam is difficult to explain, although it may be connected with the constant struggle against pagan phenomena and remnants of the past. Thus, festivals were relegated to the background, at least by theologians and jurists. Not surprisingly, however, the ordinary folk satisfied their need for celebration by adopting and reviving alien and pre-Islamic festivals, such as Nawruz, Nile festivals, and the Night of the Middle of Sha'ban. In the following paragraphs, only a few of the better-documented festivals and celebrations will be discussed.

Calendaric Festivals

Also called the Minor Feast *(al-'Id al-Saghir)* to distinguish it from the "major" Festival of Sacrifice, 'Id al-Fitr occurs immediately after the Ramadan fast, on the first day of Shawwal. A special prayer led by an imam is mandatory, and one is enjoined to give alms known as *zakat al-fitr*. It was the custom of 'Abbasid viziers and the military commanders to march in processions through Baghdad at dawn, dressed in gorgeous attire, with hundreds of torchbearers, as well as a large number of naphtha throwers. The caliph used to attend the prayer at Baghdad's main mosque. The palaces were illuminated, and dining places were laid out. Decorated boats of the caliph and dignitaries were displayed on the Tigris and lit with lamps. The festival usually lasted three days. In Fatimid Egypt the main celebrations took place at the open praying ground outside Cairo. The caliph went there in a splendid procession to perform prayers and to deliver a sermon. On his return to the palace, a meal was served, which members of the ruling elite attended. Around AH 437/1045 CE, the traveler Nasir-i Khusraw was dazzled by dishes in the form of trees and palaces made of sugar that were prepared for the occasion. In Mamluk times, a special procession of the vizier from the citadel to his residence concluded the day. A detailed description dating from 1515 CE tells, among other details, of a stage erected by the mansion of the Mamluk sultan's son, with trees and bushes of leather, and fountains spraying water.

The celebration of the Muslim New Year at the beginning of Muharram is best known from Fatimid Egypt. It was largely an exclusive court ceremony, which, besides the caliphal display of pomp, included banquets and the presentation of annual reports by officials. We first learn of a caliphal procession in 517/1123. Following ceremonies in the palace, the Fatimid ruler went riding with his insignia (parasol, sword, and inkstand), accompanied by the vizier and his own insignia, emirs and their sons, and mixed units of elite soldiers wearing their distinctive uniforms and carrying parade arms. As soon as the procession became visible to the inhabitants, trumpets were sounded and the caliphal parasol was opened. The procession left Cairo from one of its main gates and re-entered through another one. Merchants decorated the route with their goods, and the gates of the quarters next to the city wall were decorated with drapes and curtains. Alms to the poor and pensions to the high-ranking officials were distributed.

A supererogatory fast on the tenth of Muharram, which had been replaced by Ramadan in order to efface Jewish influence, 'Ashura' has been mainly associated with the Shi'i commemoration of the martyrdom of Husayn in Karbala' in 60/680. However, the Sunnis, possibly the Ayyubid dynasty, reintroduced it as a joyous festival to counteract the Shi'is. Popular practices seem to have developed especially in Egypt and North Africa. Special dishes, rites of fire, visiting of graves, application of henna by women, and almsgiving and spending are customs mentioned by medieval scholars, who largely condemned these innovations.

The night of the fifteenth of Sha'ban was one of the *Layali al-wuqud* (Nights of Bonfires) celebrated in the 'Abbasid and Fatimid states. It was believed that on that night, deeds were examined and destinies determined. The tree of life, on which the name of every human being is written, was believed to be shaken, with the leaves of those divinely sentenced to die in the course of the year thus to fall off. Inhabitants of Baghdad used to flock to the banks of the Tigris

River, illuminate boats, dance and sing, and put up banquets. The barges of the caliphs and the elite were decorated and illuminated. Dressed in their best attire, the rulers were drawn in the barges along the river, a splendid procession of boats, followed by ordinary people. Many spent the whole night rejoicing and playing around bonfires. Customs included fumigating houses to ward off misfortune, and driving wild animals into fire. A special report is of the festival at the time of the Daylamite Mirdawij, who celebrated it in 323/935 with unusual splendor. He collected faggots, set up large candles, and stationed a number of naphtha throwers near the Persian town of Isfahan. Near each elevated place in the town a "castle" made of tree trunks was erected. Wax figures were made to increase the effect of illumination. Lit birds were released into the dark night to create a spectacle.

Islamicized Festivals

Of festivals adopted from pre-Islamic cultures, one should mention Mihrjan, after the Persian Mihragan, an originally Mazdean festival dedicated to the Vedic divinity Mithra/Mihr and celebrated around the autumn equinox. Together with Nawruz, it assumed great importance with the rise of local dynasties in medieval Iran in the latter part of the ninth century to the time of the Mongol invasion. It was the custom to change dress, add extra coverings to beds, and prepare for the cold season. There was an exchange of gifts, and people sent perfumed cards of congratulations.

Shi'i Festivals

Celebrated on the eighteenth of Dhu 'l-Hijja to mark the designation of 'Ali as the Prophet's successor, Ghadir Khum was initiated in Baghdad by the Buyid Mu'izz al-Dawla in 352/963. In Egypt it was institutionalized under the Fatimids approximately 10 years later. Initially it was primarily a popular celebration. However, under the Fatimid al-'Amir (495–524/1101–1130), it was orchestrated by the regime and modeled on the Festival of Sacrifice that immediately preceded it, hence deemphasizing the Shi'i aspects and attempting a universal Muslim appeal. Under al-Hafiz (525–544/1131–1149), due to political inner struggles, Ghadir Khum once again became a thoroughly Shi'i-Isma'ili affair. In a detailed description from ca. 549/1154, we find its high point in the

reading of the supposed text of 'Ali's investiture (nass) before a royal assembly.

Celebrations

Festive occasions in Baghdad were the installation of a new caliph or a birth of a caliph's son, royal circumcision, and marriage. In the circumcision festival of Mu'tazz, son of al-Mutawakkil (232–247/847–861), a thousand robes of honor were distributed to the guests, and the same number of mounts to depart on, each clad in gold and silver trappings. Also, a thousand slaves were manumitted. It was the custom of 'Abbasid caliphs to invite orphans and boys of poor families into the palace to be circumcised with the royal prince. Gifts were bestowed on their parents and alms were distributed. The wedding of al-Ma'mun to Buran, daughter of his vizier, was celebrated in 210/825–826 in Wasit for more than forty days. Thousands of pearls of unique size were showered from a golden tray upon the couple, sitting on a golden mat. Balls of musk, each containing the name of an estate, slave-girls, or other gifts, fell on the guests, who thereafter received the promised gifts.

Mawlid

Perhaps the most significant development in the history of medieval Islamic festivals is the emergence of the *mawlid al-nabi*, namely, the celebration of the birthday of the Prophet Muhammad on the twelfth Rabi' al-Awwal. It possibly was first celebrated in Fatimid Egypt in the eleventh century. During the celebration in Cairo in 517/1123, the earliest for which a description is available, the Fatimid caliph distributed alms, bread, and dishes and held a reception. From descriptions derived from the Fatimid period, we learn of the participation of the Chief Judge (qadi al-qudat) and other high officials, who rode in a procession to the major square known as Bayn al-Qasrayn. Sermons were given and the Qur'an was recited. The oldest celebrations among the Sunnis were under Nur al-Din ibn Zanki (511–569/1118–1174). The mawlid was celebrated at night, fires were lit, a banquet was held, and poems were recited. Ibn Khallikan's description of the mawlid in his hometown of Irbil, southeast of Mosul, at the beginning of the thirteenth century is probably an eyewitness account and emphasizes the large number of participants who came from Mosul, Baghdad, and other large cities. Due to differences of opinion regarding the Prophet's date of birth, the festival was celebrated alternately on the eighth and twelfth of Rabi' al-Awwal. In another report of the Irbil festival, we learn of the banquet, the robes distributed by the ruler to scholars and Sufis, a concert (sama') given to the Sufis, and alms donated. Twenty wooden decorated pavilions were erected along the road leading from the citadel to the Sufi lodge (khanqah), to accommodate visitors, musical bands, and shadow-players. Masses of sheep, camels, and cows were slaughtered. On the Night of the Nativity, a candle-light procession, each candle fastened to the back of a mule and supported by an attendant, moved from the citadel to the khanqah. Next morning, notables and others assembled around a wooden tower, where the ruler watched a military parade in the hippodrome (maydan) and listened to the preachers clustered around the pulpit, all the while summoning guests to him to present them with robes of honor. Two elements in the Irbil festival are noteworthy: the prominent role of the Sufis and the candlelight procession.

In Mamluk Egypt, Sufi shaykhs performed nocturnal celebrations of the mawlid at their zawiyas in the presence of large crowds. On occasion, and not without criticism, wine was consumed and women were present, making one wonder how much of the religious aspect remained. The mawlid was introduced to the Maghrib via Ceuta sometime in the thirteenth century, possibly as a countermeasure to Muslims' participation in Christmas. It was not before 690/1291, however, that the Marinid sultan made it official in Morocco. By the beginning of the sixteenth century, at the latest, the observance of certain mawlid rites seems to have become the concern of the Moroccan commoners as well. Leo Africanus reports that schoolchildren in Fez were expected to present their teachers with colored and decorated candles, some of which were exceptionally heavy, with assorted fruit and flowers in wax. In the second half of the fourteenth century, Abu Hammu Musa of the 'Abd al-Wadid dynasty at Tlemsen bestowed special splendor on the mawlid celebration. The central feature was the nightly recital of poems in praise of the Prophet, followed by pious exhortations. People of all ranks were admitted to the ceremony at the palace's decorated courtyard. Celebration lasted till daybreak and was concluded by a banquet. In Andalus, the mawlid was introduced around the mid-thirteenth century. As for Mecca, early detailed descriptions derive from the mid-sixteenth century, yet celebrations probably antedate them. We learn of processions of the qadis to the Prophet's birthplace, the illumination of streets, musical performances and large crowds.

Not proscribed by law, the mawlid was opposed by certain Orthodox theologians, such as the Hanbali Ibn Taymiyya and the Maliki Ibn al-Hajj al-'Abdari and their supporters. However, a legal opinion (fatwa) written ca. 890/1485 by al-Suyuti, the Egyptian scholar, considers the mawlid a "good innovation" (bid'a hasana) as long as it just consisted of a gathering, Qur'an recitation, the recounting of the Prophet's biography, and the miracles associated with his birth, and a banquet.

In Fatimid times there were five other mawlid celebrations of 'Ali, Fatima, Hasan, Husayn, and the reigning caliph. In later periods in Egypt, mawlids emerged to honor various Sufi saints. Such was the commemoration at Tanta of Ahmad al-Badawi, the most popular Egyptian saint. In late Mamluk and early Ottoman times it is reported to have attracted more people than the Prophet's mawlid or even the Pilgrimage. Another famous mawlid was in honor of Shaykh Isma'il (d. 790/1388) at Inbaba, west of Cairo, which possibly absorbed elements of the ancient festival of Isis. Also, in historical accounts of these sorts of mawlids, "scandalous" behavior is occasionally condemned, as is the replacement of Qur'an recitals by songs and music, and even the performance of shadow plays.

In conclusion, one should note that despite objections to the participation of Muslims in non-Muslim festivals, reality was different. In Egypt, for example, there appears to have been significant participation by Muslims in the Festival of Immersion and in Epiphany.

BOAZ SHOSHAN

See also Nawruz; Nile

Further Reading

Ahsan, Muhammad Mnazir. *Social Life under the Abbasids*. London: Longman, 1979.

Ferhat, Halima. "Le Culte du Prophete au Maroc au XIIIe siècle: Organisation du Pelerinage et Celebration du Mawlid." In *La religion civique a l'epoque medievale et moderne*, ed. Andre Vauchez, 89–97. Palais Farnese: Ecole française de Rome, 1995.

Fierro, Maribel. "The Celebration of 'Ashura' in Sunni Islam." In *Proceedings of the 14th Congress of the Union Europeenne des Arabisants et Islamisants*, Pt. 1, ed. A. Fodor, 193–208. Budapest, 1995.

Grunebaum, G. E. von. *Muhammadan Festivals*. London: Curzon Press, 1976.

Kaptein, N. J. G. *Muhammad's Birthday Festival*. Leiden: E. J. Brill, 1993.

———. "Materials for the History of the Prophet Muhammad's Birthday Celebration in Mecca." *Islam* 69 (1992): 193–203.

Langner, Barbara. *Untersuchungen zur Historischen Volkskunde Agyptens nach Mamlukischen Quellen*. Berlin: Klaus Schwarz, 1983.

Lazarus-Yaffeh, Hava. "Muslim Festivals." In *Some Religious Aspects of Islam*. Leiden: Brill, 1981, 38–47.

Lev, Yaacov. *State and Society in Fatimid Egypt*. Leiden: E.J. Brill, 1991.

"Mihragan." *Encyclopaedia of Islam*. New ed. Leiden: E.J. Brill.

Sanders, Paula. *Ritual, Politics, and the City in Fatimid Cairo*. Albany, NY: SUNY Press, 1994.

Shinar, P. "Traditional and Reformist Mawlid Celebrations in the Maghrib." In *Studies in Memory of Gaston Wiet*, ed. Myriam Rosen-Ayalon, 371–413. Jerusalem: The Hebrew University, 1977.

Shoshan, Boaz. *Popular Culture in Medieval Cairo*. Cambridge, MA: Cambridge University Press, 1993.

FEZ

The city of Fez (Fas in Arabic) was founded by the Idrisid dynasty at the end of the AH second/eighth CE century, in the north of Morocco. It was composed of two cities separated by the Wadi Fas. It had considerable strategic significance in the fight between the Umayyads of al-Andalus and the Fatimids of Ifriqiyya. At the beginning of the eleventh century, Fez was taken by the Berber tribe of the Zanata, and at the end of the same century, it fell into the hands of the Almoravids. Fez then became the Almoravids' main military base in Morocco. It is also in this period that the Qarawiyyin mosque began to acquire increasing significance as a center of learning. Many of the *'ulama'* representatives of Western Malikism were trained in this center. During the Almohad period, the old city of Fez grew to its present proportions. In the thirteenth century, Fez became part of the Marinids' territories, who made it their capital and under whose government it reached its highest economic development. The Marinids built a new urban center, Fas al-Jadid, to the west of the old city. Fas al-Jadid came to be the administrative and military center, whereas Fas al-Bali (old Fez), also known as *al-Madina*, remained the center for commercial activities. In the aftermath of the Christians' conquest of Cordova and Seville, important Andalusi, families learned men and landowners migrated to Fez and other cities in Morocco. When the Sa'dids took Fez in 955/1459, the city became the center of Sharifism, radiating its influence out to the rest of Morocco. The success of this movement is linked to the personality of Idris II (d. 828), considered to be a direct descendant of the Prophet Muhammad. He was the founder of the city and "sultan" of its saints. What was principally indicative of the beginning of the veneration of Idris was the discovery of his tomb in 1438, in the Shurafa' mosque. By the middle of the sixteenth

Mosque of Qarawyin, Fez, Morocco. View from the main entrance into the courtyard with ablution basin. Last enlargement under Almoravid sultans (1062–1147 CE). Credit: Erich Lessing/Art Resource, NY.

century the situation in Fez had deteriorated while retaining certain prosperity. Many Hispanic Jews found refuge in Fez after the expulsion of 1492.

DELFINA SERRANO RUANO

Further Reading

Beck, H.L. *L'Image d'Idris II, ses Descendants de Fas et la Politique Sharifienne des Sultans Marinides (656-869/ 1258-1465)*. Leiden: E.J. Brill, 1989.

Bennassar, B. "La Vida de los Renegados Españoles y Portugueses en Fez (hacia 1580-1615)." En *Relaciones entre la Península Ibérica con el Norte de África (siglos XIII-XVI)*, ed. M. Garcia Arenal and M. J. Viguera, 665–678. *Actas del Coloquio, Madrid, 17–18 Diciembre 1987*. Madrid, 1988.

Berque, J. "Ville et université. Aperçu sur l'histoire de l'école de Fès." *Revue Historique du Droit Français et Etranger* (1949): 64–116.

Blachère, R. "Fèz chez les géographes Arabes du Moyen-Age." *Hespéris* 18 (1934): 41–48.

———. "Fès, ou le destin d'une médina." *De l'Euphrate à l'Atlas*. París, 1978.

Burckhardt, T. "Fez." En *La Ciudad islámica*, ed. R. B. Serjeant, 209–221. Barcelona, 1982.

———. *Fez, City of Islam*, trans. W. Stoddardt. Cambridge, MA: The Islamic Texts Society, 1992.

Calasso, G. "Genelogie e Miti di Fondazione: Note sulle Origini di Fas secondo le Fonti Merinide." In *La Bisaccia dello Sheikh. Omaggio ad Alessandro Bausani Islamista nel sessantesimo compleanno*. Venecia, 1981, 17–27.

Cigar, N. "Societé et Vie politique à Fès dans les premiers 'Alawites (ca. 1660/1830)." *Hespéris-Tamuda* 18 (1978–1979): 93–172.

The Encyclopaedia of Islam s.v."Fas" [R. Le Tourneau] and [H. Terrase].

The Encyclopaedia of Islam s.v. "al-Karawiyyin" [G. Deverdun].

Gaillard, H., *Une Ville de l'Islam: Fez*. París, 1905.

García-Arenal, M. "The Revolution of Fas in 869/1465 and the Death of Sultan 'Abd al-Haqq al-Marini." *Bulletin of the School of Oriental and African Studies* 41 (1978): 43–66.

———. "Les Bildiyyin de Fès, un Groupe de Nèomusulmans d'origine Juive." *Studia Islamica* 66 (1987): 113–143.

———. "Mahdi, murabit, sharif: L'avènement de la dynastie Sa'dienne." *Studia Islamica* 71 (1990): 74–114.

———. Sainteté et Pouvoir Dynastique au Maroc: la résistance de Fès aux Sa'diens." *Annales ESC* (1990–1994): 1019–1042.

García-Arenal, M., y Wiegers, G. *Entre el Islam y Occidente. Vida de Samuel Pallache, judío de Fez*. Madrid: Siglo Veintinuno, 1999.

Gerbert, J.S. *Jewish Society in Fez (1450–1700): Studies in Communal and Economic Life*. Leiden, 1980.

Ibn Suda, 'A.S. "Buyutat Fas qadiman wa hadithan." *Al-Bahth al-'ilmi* 22 (1973): 23(1974) y 25(1976).

Kably, M. *Société, pouvoir et religion au Maroc à la fin du Moyen Age*. Paris, 1986.

Le Tourneau, R. *Fès avant le Protectorat: Étude Économique et Sociale d'une Ville de l'Occident Musulman*. París, 1949.

Mezzine, M. *Fas wa Badiyatuha. Musahama fi ta'rikh al-Maghrib al-Sa'di*. Rabat, 1986.

———. "Les rélations Entre les Places Occupées et les Localités de la Région de Fès aux XVème et XVIème siècles a partir des Documents Locaux Inédits: les Nawazil." En *Relaciones entre la Península Ibérica con el Norte de África (siglos XIII-XVI)*, ed. M. García-Arenal and M. J. Viguera, 539–560. *Actas del Coloquio, Madrid, 17–18 diciembre 1987*. Madrid, 1988.

Naciri, M. "La Mèdina de Fès: Trame Urbaine en Impasses et Impasse de la Planification Urbaine," in *Present et avenir des mèdinas (de Marrakech à Alep)*, ed. J. Bisson and J.-F. Troin. Tours, 1982, 237–254.

Nwya, P. *Un Mystique Prédicateur à la Qarawiyyin de Fès: Ibn 'Abbad de Ronda (1332-1390)*. Beirut, 1961.

Peretie, M. A. "Les médrasas de Fès." *Archives Marocaines* 18 (1912): 257–372.

Powers, D. *Law, Society and Culture in the Maghrib, 1300–1500*. Cambridge: Cambridge University Press, 2002.

Revault, J. L. Golvin, and A. Amahan. *Palais et demeures de Fès. Epoques Mérinide et Saadienne (XIV–XVII siècles)*. París, 1985.

Rodríguez Mediano, F. *Familias de Fez (ss. XV–XVII)*. Madrid: CSIC, 1995.

Shatzmiller, M. "Les Premiers Mérinides et le Milieux Religieux de Fès: l'Introduction des Médersas." *Studia Islamica* 43 (1976): 109–118.

Al-Tazi, M. *L'Université Qarawiyyin*. Mohammedia, 1980.

FLOODS

Any assessment of economic life in the Islamic world in the Middle Ages, whether rural or urban, is incomplete without considering numerous natural disasters occurring throughout the region and the period. With the exception of work on plague epidemics and the writings of professors N.N. Ambraseys and Charles Melville about earthquakes in the Middle East, there is a dearth of literature about disasters in Islamic/ Middle East history. This article is a modest attempt to fill at least one gap in the historiography of the Near East and Islamic Spain in the era prior to 1700. The purpose of the present study is to indicate the nature and impact of floods in Muslim lands between 600 and ca. 1600 CE, to address the consequences, both direct and indirect, of these floods, and to assess their role in the lives of the affected areas. The focus will be on floods as disasters rather than, for example, the benign effects of the annual Nile flood, with its attendant benefits of water for irrigation and alluvial soil.

The first and obvious point is that floods occurred primarily in the two great river valley systems of the Near East. Hence, most floods were associated with the areas of the Tigris and Euphrates and with the Nile Valley. It should be understood, however, that floods were not confined to these regions. Damaging floods occurred in other places, such as Arabia and Iran. An overwhelming number, however, were centered in Iraq and Syria. When unusually heavy rain came, the result was often devastation for cities or villages on or near rivers or streams.

Floods were an equal menace to people and property. In 960, Egyptian pilgrims drowned in a flood. In the city of Samarra (Iraq), many people perished in the terrible flood of 841. A flood in Jubba, Khuzistan in 902 also killed many people. Examples could be multiplied. Suffice it to say that, like famines, epidemics, and earthquakes, floods were lethal. Again, that one is dealing with a life-threatening event must be recalled when analyzing demographic trends or patterns in the early Islamic period. The sources provide virtually no mortality statistics for floods, but it is evident that losses could be severe and, as a result, flood mortality must be factored into systematic discussions of mortality patterns.

The economic historian must also consider the destruction of property and animals occasioned by especially severe floods. One reads of numerous examples of destroyed shops and houses, livestock killed, and crops devastated. In 43/742, shops were ruined and houses damaged along the Tigris in northern Iraq. In 46/845, similarly, Mosul experienced a terrible flood that ravaged market areas and residences. Sources also record instances of destruction of goods in the shops, for example, in Hamah, Syria, in 44/1343. Frequently, cultivation was disrupted or wiped out by floods. Destruction might result from the inundation of fields or demolition of irrigation works or dams. In 1104, the Tigris flooded, with crops, houses, and other property damaged. A flood hit Andalusia in Islamic Spain in 848–849, devastating dams, barrages, and mills. Frequently, animals perished, confronting affected societies with a loss of power, food, and transportation. Also, populations were deprived of revenues from the sale of the animals.

Communications systems were disrupted at times with the inundation of roads and destruction or damaging of bridges. This impeded the movement of travelers and negatively affected the movement of goods to market. Coupled with the actual loss of crops, this no doubt had an impact on supplies and prices in contiguous market areas, as reflected, for example, in the price rises associated with the Baghdad flood of 1325.

Floods also disrupted normal educational and religious life. On any number of occasions, mosques and madrasas were damaged or demolished. The Baghdad flood of 1159 damaged mosques, whereas a flood of 1242–1243, in the same city, damaged the Nizamiyya Madrasa, a main center of learning in the Islamic East. Madrasas in Damascus were destroyed in the flood of 1316. Obviously, the normal functioning of religious and educational institutions was hampered or nullified by these events.

Ultimately the worst damage was personal loss suffered by citizens of various regions. Chronicles are replete with statements of private dwellings being destroyed or damaged. One reads of the destruction of gardens or trees and other personal property that could be used to supplement diet or, at the very least, to make life more pleasant. Furthermore, survivors of floods were prey to fears and stress associated with the catastrophe. In the Tigris flood of 1207–1208, one reads of the fright experienced by the people affected. When the Nile flooded in 1371–1372 people went to the Mosque of 'Amr and prayed that God would cause the waters to recede. Floods caused trauma and disease. Cemeteries were inundated and damaged. Floods overwhelmed sewers and plumbing in Baghdad, with serious disease outbreaks or epidemics ensuing. The Baghdad flood of 1495 caused the spread of throat disease, fever, and even typhoid fever. In this way, floods sparked another major disaster touching the Muslim world: epidemic disease. Here, again, one sees evidence that one catastrophe could contribute to or reinforce others.

In the final analysis, floods served as another source of disruption and loss for those living in the medieval Islamic regions. Earthquakes, epidemics, famines, and other disasters caused a great deal of suffering and trauma between 600 and 1500. Floods, although not as devastating as outbreaks of bubonic plague or particularly powerful earthquakes, took their share of lives and destroyed property in a serious fashion. Revenues for private individuals, landlords, governments, and military establishments fell prey to this catastrophe, as they did to others. Suffering exceeded a simple loss of revenue. Floods, like other disasters, affected lives in the most fundamental emotional and psychological ways. Chronicles cannot help us quantify this, if such a thing was possible, but they show us the existence of deeper effects.

WILLIAM F. TUCKER

Primary Sources:

Arib ibn Sa'd Katib al-Qurtubi. *Silat ta'rikh al-Tabari.* Leiden, 1965.
Al-'Ayni. *Ta'rikh al-Badr.* British Library Ms. Or. Add. 22: 368.
Al-Bayhaqi. *Tarikh-i Masud*, trans. as *Istorija Masuda*, by A. K. Arends. Tashkent, 1962.
Al-Dhahabi. *Kitab al-'ibar fi khabar man ghabara.* Bibliotheque Nationale Ms. Arabes, 5819.
Dionysus of Tell-Mahre. *Chronique.* Trans. J. B. Chabot. Paris, 1895.
Ibn al-Athir, 'Izz al-Din. *Al-Kamil fi al-Ta'rikh.* Vols VII–VIII. Beirut, 1965–1966.
Ibn al-Dawadari. *Kanz al-Durar wa Jami' al-Ghurar.* Part 8. Freiburg, 1971.
Ibn al-Fuwati. *Hawadith al-Jami'a.* Baghdad, 1932.
Ibn Idhari. *Bayan Al-mughrib.* Vol II. Beirut, 1967.
Ibn al-Jawzi. *Al-Muntazam fi Ta'rikh al-Muluk wa al-Umam.* Vol. IX. Beirut, 1967.

Ibn Kathir. *Al-Bidaya wa al-Nihaya.* Vol. XII. Cairo, no date.

Ibn Qadi Shuhbah. *Dhayl 'ala Ta'rikh al-Islam.* Bibliotheque Nationale Ms. Arabes 1598.

Michel le Syrien. *Chronique.* Trans. J. B. Chabot. Beirut, 1963.

Sibt ibn al-'Ajami. *"Les Tresors d'Or" de Sibt ibn al-Ajami.* Vol. II. Trans. Jean Sauvaget. Beirut, 1950.

Further Reading

Ambraseys, N.N. and C.P. Melville. *A History of Persian Earthquakes.* Cambridge, MA, 1982.

Ambraseys, N.N., C.P. Melville, and R.D. Adams. *The Seismicity of Egypt, Arabia and the Red Sea: A Historical Review.* Cambridge, MA, 1994.

Borsch, Stuart. "Nile Floods and the Irrigation System in Fifteenth-Century Egypt." *Mamluk Studies Review.* IV (2000): 131–145.

Sousa, Ahmad. *Fayadanat Baghdad fi al-ta'rikh.* Vols. I and II. Baghdad, 1963–1965.

Tucker, William F. "Natural Disasters and the Peasantry in Mamluk Egypt." *J.E.S.H.O.* XXIV, ii (1981): 215–224.

———. "Environmental Hazards, Natural Disasters, Economic Loss, and Mortality in Mamluk Syria." *Mamluk Studies Review* III (1999): 109–128.

FOLK LITERATURE, ARABIC

Muslim Arabs revered the language that enshrined their poetic heritage, and in which the Qur'an had been revealed. This conservativeness gave their high culture remarkable continuity, but it also almost eclipsed their folk literature.

Regional uninflected vernaculars soon replaced classical Arabic as the medium of everyday spoken communication, yet most of the learned saw no merit in any text that did not conform to classical grammar, and they resisted its preservation. It may, however, be assumed that the masses had some stake in the belief-system of the elite, and with it in much that is found in early standard texts. Some pre-Islamic notions, such as that each poet had an identifiable demon inspiring him, were used fancifully by established writers, but close to folk perceptions were accounts of encounters with such creatures metamorphosed into animals in Abu Zayd al-Qurash's (late ninth/early tenth century) *Jamharat Ash'ar al-'Arab (The Gathering of Arabs' Verses')* and in *Kitab al-Hayawan ('The Book of Animals')* by 'Amr ibn Bahr al-Jahiz (ca. 775–868/869 CE). Fables were also embedded in such books by al-Jahiz.

As still happens, the Qur'an gave scope for embroideries on its narratives and on the interventions of jinns and sorcerers. Heroic exploits by early defenders of the faith were no doubt inspiring, as were later the deeds of holy men recorded in Sufi literature. A less conjectural picture of what Arab folk literature was may be sought in the genres shunned by the learned. These were the "idle" tale (that is, the one serving no purpose other than entertainment), the epic, and the theatrical representation.

The richest treasury of Arab folk narratives is *The Thousand and One Nights,* bringing together fables, fairy tales, romances, and humorous anecdotes whose folk origin is unquestioned. Some spontaneity was lost when the material went through the hands of scribes who found it necessary to bring the language into conformity with classical grammar, but the marks of oral delivery are there, not least in the artful nesting of stories that served the performer well by enticing his audience to attend yet another session.

Ironically, scholars once debated why there was no Arab epic, although at the folk level, they could have found a dozen extensive cycles of stories full of martial deeds, which some call epics but others call romances (see Epics, Arabic).

The record of premodern dramatic literature consists solely of three shadow plays by Shams al-Din Ibn Daniyal (1248–1310). These are only partly in the vernacular, so their status in the literary canon is uncertain; but testimonies abound to the popularity of shadow plays and of puppet shows and peep shows both before and after Ibn Daniyal. Live performers appeared in the passion play performed in Kerbela every year, commemorating the martyrdom of the Prophet's grandson al-Husayn. Dressed-up characters also took part in religious processions. But actors of reliably professional status are mentioned only in the later centuries, performing in a kind of monologue or dialogue, usually characterizing some trade or occupation. None of these activities, however, appears to have involved the unfolding of a play with a many-sided self-consistent plot.

Echoes of other forms of folk literary activity may be discerned in the work of Abu 'l-Hasan Ibn Sudun (1407–1464), a learned man who nevertheless made a name for himself, mainly as an entertainer, using both the classical and vernacular idioms in prose and in verse.

It is in Islamic Spain, where Arabized Muslims and Romance speakers interacted extensively, that folk literature made its clearest mark in literary history. Here narratives, which must have been popular elsewhere, survived in Romance translation, if not in their Arabic originals. One example is the *Legend of Alexander,* which was widely disseminated from the third century on, and in its Arabic version was tenuously linked with the Qur'anic Dhu 'l-Qarnayn. Here also, stanzaic verse in the vernacular, known as *zajal,* had its first celebrated exponent by Abu Bakr Ibn Quzman (ca. 1086–1160), who mentions several forerunners. Once this door had been opened, a number of learned treatises on nonclassical verse forms appeared in many Arab lands, beginning with *Safiyy al-Din al-Hilli's* work (ca. 1278–1349), in which he described the so-called Seven Arts, including meters used in folk compositions. Al-Hilli's illustrations are mostly compositions of his own, but some that he quotes as belonging to different regions may be close to genuine folk items. Thereafter it became common for established poets to use these forms, but only for occasional witticisms. Worthy of closer attention is 'Abd Allah al-Ghubari (second half of fourteenth century), whose compositions in the vernacular are extensive and varied. Like Ibn Sudun, he may yield clues to the tastes and practices of folk poets. Yet the record of genuine premodern folk poems and songs remains scanty.

PIERRE CACHIA

See also Epics

Further Reading

Arabian Nights, trans. Husain Haddawy. New York and London: W.W. Norton & Co, 1990.

El-Shamy, Hasan. *Folk Traditions of the Arab World: A Guide to Motif Classification*. Bloomington, IN: Indiana University Press, 1995.

Lyons, Malcolm C. *The Arabian Epic*. 3 vols. Cambridge, MA: Cambridge University Press, 1995.

Moreh, Shmuel. *Live Theatre and Dramatic Literature in the Arab World*. Edinburgh University Press, 1992.

FOLK LITERATURE, PERSIAN

The folk literature in Persia is rich and varied; its interactions with the polite literature, commonly considered canonical, have historically been complex and more intimate than has been recognized. In form and style, as well as in ideas and worldview, this tradition generally reveals the urge on the part of the common people to compensate and complement, reiterate, and respond to writings produced and supported by the intellectual elites and the ruling classes. At its inception in the early centuries of the Islamic period, the polite literature, born and bred in Eastern Iranian courts, drew heavily on the extant oral materials and changed their language and style, as well as their basic ideological thrust, to make them suitable for courtly presentations articulating the vision and aspirations of its makers and supporters. This tendency becomes most visible when we examine the portrayal of heroes in the two aesthetic systems. Whereas in the early folk tradition strong preference is given to social mobility through native intelligence, cunning conduct, or good fortune, the polite literature tends to emphasize an illustrious lineage and nobility of spirit as determinants of success.

In matters of language, style, and substance, interactions between folk and polite literature reveal important differences from European literary traditions. In the Persian tradition, the wall between the two parallel developments is far more porous, with folk materials providing the basic matter of much polite literature and the latter being recast in diction, in presentation style, as well as in ideology, to satisfy the tastes of the lower classes. Thus the great tenth-century Persian epic known as *Shahnameh (Book of Kings)*, undoubtedly inspired at least in part by oral narratives related to Persian mythical and pre-Islamic Iranian history, in turn gives rise to countless retellings and dramatic coffeehouse performances in subsequent centuries, at times intermingled with Islamic tales designed to ensure the cohabitation of the national and religious components of Iranian identity.

Ethnic, cultural, and religious considerations have added new dimensions to the interactions—and the difference—between the two. By and large, while polite literature, insofar as it reflects official ideologies advanced by the Persian elites facing and fighting Arab and Turkic domination, have aimed at registering a Persian sense of identity distinct from that of the Arabs and the Turks, with whom the Persians have been mixed over the centuries, the folk literature presents little evidence of ethnic pride, sense of separateness or superiority, or much resistance to Arabization and Turkicization. In recent centuries, this is exemplified most vividly by the immense popularity of the Ashiq traditions and the Hikayas they present in the regions of Iran inhabited by Turkish-speaking Iranians.

Historically, Persian folk literature thrived in times when royal courts or Sufi lodges proved less capable of supporting the production and dissemination of popular ideas through literature. Thus, while the tenth through thirteenth centuries were dominated by courtly works of diverse generic divisions, inclusive of epics, romances, and lyrical expressions, with the Mongol and Tartar invasions of the early thirteenth and late fourteenth centuries, folk traditions began to dominate, particularly in prose narratives. These were not only sanctioned but also taken over and strengthened by official efforts in the sixteenth and seventeenth centuries to propagate the religious ideology of Shi'i Islam through various religious epics. Such developments are seldom reflected in either the premodern Tazkerehs or the official histories of Persian literature; they have begun to come to light only in the nineteenth and twentieth centuries, first through the works of Soviet and Eastern European scholars such as Aleksander Chodzko and Jiri Cejpek and later by amateur native folklorists such as Hedayat and Enjavi. Most recently, fieldwork by Iranian anthropologists and ethnographers has shed additional light on this dark corner of the Persian literary past.

With the advent of modernity and the cultural realignment that it gave rise to, old and established categorizations that favored polite literature over folk literature began slowly to be moderated. Modern scholars, particularly in Central Asia, continue to unearth new storehouses of Persian folktales in Central Asia, Afghanistan, and Iran, much of which still awaits scholarly attention.

AHMAD KARIMI-HAKKAK

See also Epics

Further Reading

Adams, I. *Persia by a Persian: Personal Experiences, Manners, Customs, Habits, Religious and Social Life in Persia.* Chicago, 1900.
Chodzko, Aleksander. *Specimens of the Popular Poetry of Persia, As Found in the Adventures and Improvisations of Kurroglou.* London, 1842.
Enjavi-Shirazi, Abolqasem. *Qessheha-ye Irani.* 3 vols. Tehran, 1973–1975.
———. *Mardom va Shahnameh.* Tehran, 1975.
Hedayat, Sadeq. *Nayrangestan.* Tehran, 1963.
Ra'isnia, Rahim. *Koroghlu dar Afsaneh va Tarikh.* Tabriz, 1987.
Ravandi, Morteza. *Tarikh-e Ejtema'i-ye Iran.* 3 vols. Tehran, 1977.
Rypka, Jan et al. *History of Iranian Literature.* Dordrecht, Holland, 1968.
Shahri, Ja'far. *Tarikh-e Ejtema'i-ye Terhan-e Qadim.* 6 vols. Tehran, 1990.

FOLK LITERATURE, TURKISH

Turkish folk (or oral) literature includes, but is not limited, to folk poetry (*'halk şiiri', 'âşik şiiri'*), tales (*'masal'*), jokes (*'fikra'*), legends (*'efsane'*), hagiographic legends (*'menakibnames'*), riddles (*'bilmece'*), proverbs (*'atalarsözü'*), epics (*'destan'*) and romantic epics (*'hikâye'*), and folk theater (*'seyirlik oyunlar'*). The most significant aspect of all these genres is the fact that they are produced predominately in the oral mode and have survived and been (re)created through oral transmission for centuries.

Riddles constitute a significant portion of Turkish folk literature. Riddling has indispensable social and cultural functions, especially in the rural communities of Anatolia. In Turkish, generally the term *bilmece* is used for riddle. However, in some local dialects, we observe the usage of *tapmaca* for the same concept. In addition, in many areas of Anatolia, the term *matal* (or *metel, metal, masal, mesel*) is commonly employed

(see Başgöz and Tietze 1973). Başgöz and Tietze have provided us with more than twelve thousand Turkish riddles in a single volume.

Turkish *menakibname*s are composed of hagiographic folk legends surrounding the lives of famous religious figures. In these legends, we find the representation of the extraordinary powers and events associated with Islamic saints and their miracles. Such common motifs as "resuscitation," "killing a dragon," "curing the sick," "transformation," "foreseeing the future," "total control over natural forces," "feeding the entire population of a community with a single fruit tree," "praying on a rug on the water," "communicating with animals," "incarnation," and the like constitute the basic thematic content of these stories. Even though the corpus of surviving Turkish *menakibname* literature seems to have been produced in written form, different levels of orality can be observed in almost all of them. The figures and geographical settings of these manuscripts can be local and culture–specific, but their motifs and structure show similarities to other traditions.

If we were to illustrate only one representative form of folk theater from the Ottoman Empire to the Republic of Turkey, it would be the Turkish shadow theater called *Karagöz*. The name of this performance comes from one of the two main characters: Karagöz (the other being Hajivat). It is a comedy form performed by a single puppeteer using entirely handmade, two-dimensional colorful puppets, reflecting their shadows through a transparent screen. Continuously changing his voice from one character to another, the puppeteer becomes the voice and life of many social, cultural, and political entities of the Ottoman state. He mimics, for instance, the voice, appearance, and manners of an Arab, an Albanian, an Armenian, a Greek, an Iranian, a drunk, an opium addict, or sometimes even an animal such as a dog or a cat, in order to make his audience laugh. Usually what creates the comical element for the audience is the stereotypical representation of the many different peoples of the Ottoman Empire, and this includes a Turkish character as well, called Baba Himmet, undoubtedly one of the most idiotic characters of the play. Legend has it that the *Karagöz* theater was born in the city of Bursa during the time of Orhan Gazi (1326–1362 CE). Two men, Hajivat (a mason) and Karagöz (a blacksmith), were workers in the construction of a mosque in Bursa. They were so funny that the other workers would listen to them and laugh all day, thus delaying the construction process of the mosque. Informed about this serious problem, the Ottoman Sultan gave the order for their execution. According to Ilhan Basgoz, this performance art appeared in Istanbul right after the 1517

Egypt campaign of Sultan Selim I (1512–1520), who had watched a similar shadow theater performance in Egypt, seeing an Arab puppeteer making fun of the enemy of the victorious sultan. Pleased with this mockery, the Ottoman sultan invited the puppeteer to Istanbul to repeat the same performance to his sons (Silay 1998). Karagöz performances remained one of the major sources of entertainment for the people until the introduction of Western-style theater and modern Turkish cinema later in the nineteenth century. Obviously, the birth of the modern performing arts and media, such as radio and television, contributed greatly to the demise of this traditional performance, although numerous fruitless attempts were made to give it a new lease on life during the Republican period.

The two most fundamental Turkish folk poetry forms are: (1) *mâni*, and (2) *türkü*. *Mâni* is the shortest poetic form and is composed of four seven-syllable lines. Its rhyme scheme is the following: a a x a. *Türkü* is an orally composed and generally speaking an anonymous poetic form, even though a significant number of *türkü*s were composed by known individuals. The themes of *türkü*s can vary from love to natural disasters to everyday life events. There seems to be no limit as to what can constitute the "appropriate" theme of a *türkü*. From this point of view alone, *türkü*s make up the most important and perhaps richest literary form of Turkish folk literature. *Türkü*s are usually composed either in three-line stanzas, four-line stanzas, or in couplets, and some of the most widely used *türkü* rhyme schemes are the following: a a x a/b b x b/c c x c/d d x d...; b b b a/c c c a/d d d a/e e e a...; a a a/b b b/c c c/d d d...; and a a/b b/c c/d d....

Kemal Silay

Further Reading

Başgöz, İlhan, and Tietze, Andreas. *Bilmece: A Corpus of Turkish Riddles.* Los Angeles: University of California Press, 1973.
Silay, Kemal, ed. *Turkish Folklore and Oral Literature: Selected Essays of İlhan Başgöz.* Bloomington: Indiana University Turkish Studies Series, 1998.

FOLK MEDICINE

Various types of medical practices, none of which had absolute authority over the others, were recognized in society. Doctors and apothecaries well versed in the Greek–Islamic medical theories mixed their potions and treated people in accordance with humoral principles. Greek–Islamic medicine was at its best in advising healthy diets and moderate habits and stressing the prevention of illnesses. However, the humoral theory was not sufficient to detect the actual causes of illnesses, and when it came to treating a disease, therapies did not necessarily cure the patient. Thus at times, alternative views prevailed and people chose not to ask a doctor's advice but trusted well-tested household remedies, bought protective amulets, or sought the help of the spiritual world by visiting tombs of saints or other holy places.

One of the available medical systems was the so-called medicine of the Prophet, which was derived from alleged sayings of the Prophet Muhammad. Some of these sayings reflect medical practices and beliefs popular among pre-Islamic Arabs: "There is health in three things: drinking of honey, incision made by the cupper's knife and cautery with fire; I forbid my people to cauterize," and, "Fever is of fire, cool it with cold water." These types of sayings were included in the major hadith collections, and some scholars subjected them to closer analysis with reference to the Greek–Islamic medical system.

Humoral physiology and pathology were widely accepted by the authors of "prophetic medicine"; they did not question that illness, caused by humoral imbalance, was to be cured by correcting such imbalance. Scholars in this field accepted dietary cures administered by medical practitioners, and in many cases they just repeated the physicians' recommendations; in some instances, however, they were able to point out shortcomings of medical theory and to introduce their own healing methods.

Although the Prophet's medicine in many ways reflected popular views on disease and cures, it did not approve of all aspects of folk medicine. The authors accepted some traditional cures and etiological concepts, but they considered folk medicine in many ways inefficient. In the hierarchy of medical systems, the authors ranked the Prophet's medicine at the top and folk medicine at the bottom, asserting that the Prophet's medicine related to Greek–Islamic medicine as the latter did to the medicine of roadside practitioners and old women.

The ordinary people did not necessarily agree with this view but considered the various forms of therapy as more or less equal alternatives. The choices people made in deciding how to cure a particular illness varied according to their understanding of the causes of the illness and their experience in the effects of the various treatments offered. The choice of therapy depended also on social and financial status. Those who could afford the fees called a doctor to treat their ailments, whereas others resorted to the services of apothecaries and herbalists and bought the ingredients for traditional household remedies. Medicaments could be chosen on the basis of their temperamental qualities, but they might also be herbs known by experience to be efficient against ordinary aches and pains.

Popular views on the etiology of illnesses sometimes differed from the views of the physicians. They held that the plague was caused by putrid air (miasma) and that in turn, miasma was caused by agents such as stagnant water, drought, or rotting cadavers. The theory did not explain why putrid air did not always make people ill and when it did, why not everybody was affected. Many people rejected the medical opinion and instead considered spirits (jinn) the cause of plague. The spirits pierced the victims with poisonous arrows, which explained why they could afflict a person with the disease and leave the neighbor healthy. The way to avoid plague was not to purify the air by incense, as the doctors recommended, but to protect oneself from the spirits by wearing amulets.

The authors of the Prophet's medicine disapproved of the widespread use of amulets as a protection against illnesses, considering them a form of idolatry. The scholars accepted that spirits caused illnesses, but the evil influence had to be combated with carefully chosen means that were compatible with Islam. It was far better to strengthen one's own faith and turn to God for protection against evil. Amulets as such were not forbidden as long as they did not contain magic symbols, but consisted of Qur'anic verses or other pious words. The scholars also stressed that the amulet did not in itself protect, but it was God who protected and who cured or prevented illness.

Epilepsy was another serious disease in which medical and popular etiologies differed decisively. According to Greek–Islamic theory, epilepsy was caused by either phlegm or black bile and could be treated by a dietary regimen aided by herbal drugs. In many instances the treatment proved inefficient, which lessened the credibility of the humoral explanation. In popular opinion, epilepsy was caused by demonic possession and the only cure was to exorcise the spirit. The Prophet's medicine offered a compromise, accepting the popular idea of spirits as a mere alternative to the humoral etiology. If a patient did not respond to the doctor's therapy, his or her epilepsy was obviously not caused by an imbalance of humors but by spirits that had to be exorcised.

None of the various medical systems could put an end to suffering and cure all illness. If no cure was found for a disease, the Prophet's medicine gave people the consolation that an illness, if endured patiently, strengthened the patient's faith and brought him closer to God. This gave meaning to the suffering and made it bearable.

IRMELI PERHO

See also Baraka; Disease; Epidemics; Food and Diet; Health and Hygiene; Saints and Sainthood

Further Reading

Dols, Michael W. *The Black Death in the Middle East.* Princeton: Princeton University Press, 1977.

Dols, Michael W., and Adil S. Gamal. *Medieval Islamic Medicine, Ibn Ridwan's Treatise 'On the Prevention of Bodily Ills in Egypt.'* Berkeley: University of California Press, 1984.

Ibn Qayyim al-Jawziyya. *Medicine of the Prophet.* Trans. Penelope Johnstone. Cambridge: Islamic Texts Society, 1998.

Perho, Irmeli. *The Prophet's Medicine: A Creation of the Muslim Traditionalist Scholars. Studia Orientalia,* vol. 74. The Finnish Oriental Society: Helsinki, 1995.

———. "Medicine and the Qur'an." In *Encyclopaedia of the Qur'an, vol. III J-O.* Ed. Jane D. McAuliffe, 349–367. Leiden: Brill, 2003.

Rahman, Fazlur. *Health and Medicine in the Islamic Tradition: Change and Identity.* New York: Crossroad, 1987.

FOOD AND DIET

Medieval Islamic culinary culture mirrored the territorial expansion of the Islamic empire. Before AH 132/750 CE, the diet of the peoples of the Arabian Peninsula generally consisted of local, simply prepared foods. Pastoral staples such as dates, milk and dairy products, and some meats (particularly mutton, but also camel, goat, rabbit) predominated, along with grains and vegetables cultivated by the sedentary populations in the southern part of the Peninsula.

After 132/750, the sociopolitical unification of a vast geographical territory led to the dissemination of crops across the Islamic lands whose consumption had formerly been confined to limited areas. Rice and sugar cane, originally cultivated in India, are two examples of a variety of food crops that moved westward across the empire as far as the western Mediterranean.

With the expansion of the Islamic empire after the mid-eighth century, a variety of regional cooking traditions were absorbed, notably that of the pre-Islamic Sasanian empire of Persia. The combination of traditional Arab dishes with the refined Persian culinary tradition and many other regional cooking practices characterized the "high" cuisine of courts and urban centers. This cuisine is reflected in surviving works of medieval Islamic culinary literature: cookbooks, treatises on dietetics, agriculture, handbooks of etiquette, and other literary works that celebrated food as one of life's pleasures.

Food was prepared both in private households and in public markets. Rulers and other wealthy elites

Sufavid mural, 1640s. Female courtier of Abbas I during a picnic. Chihil Sutun (Pavilion of Forty Columns), Isfahan, Iran. Credit: SEF/Art Resource.

enjoyed specialized kitchens furnished with ovens, fireplaces, a variety of cooking implements, and a dedicated kitchen staff, whereas others made do with simple areas for food preparation in the home, supplemented by the services of public ovens and the offerings of public food markets.

The main grains consumed were wheat, barley, and rice, as well as chickpeas, lentils, and mungo beans. Wheat was a major commodity, and bread was a staple throughout the Islamic lands, though the wealthy enjoyed loaves made from fine wheat flour while the poor made do with loaves made from coarser flours. Mutton and lamb were the most favored types of meat, but goat, fowl, fish, and a variety of game animals were also eaten. The great variety of fruits, nuts, vegetables, and herbs available to consumers is reflected in cookbooks and in agricultural treatises, particularly those of the Islamic Iberian Peninsula.

Food served as a luxury product for the wealthy, and status was displayed at feasts. Culinary manuals created by and for the wealthy reflect a concern that food appeal to all the senses. Dishes were served with a variety of condiments and were often decorated with other foodstuffs arranged in decorative patterns

or chosen to lend color to the dish. Saffron was especially favored for the golden color (and the implication of wealth) that it provided finished dishes. In addition to their appearance, medieval Islamic cooks and diners were also attuned to the fragrance of dishes. Finished dishes and drinks were often perfumed with fragrant substances like rosewater, or for the very wealthy, musk and camphor, which were also believed to function medicinally.

Drinks were generally consumed after meals, and were made from a variety of fruits. A tenth-century 'Abbasid text mentions wine made from grapes, raisins, honey, and dates, while an Andalusi agricultural calendar of the same period refers to the juices of green grapes, blackberries, and pomegranates. The consumption of intoxicating beverages was generally frowned upon for religious reasons. Despite injunctions against it, however, members of all social classes throughout the Islamic lands consumed wine. Toleration of the consumption of intoxicating substances varied according to specific segments of the population, as well as with time and place, and jurists devoted a great deal of attention to the subject.

Food was popularly believed to affect the human body and temperament, and opinions on the relationship between substances consumed and the one who consumed them circulated in popular culture, as well as in scientific literature. For example, eating the heart or liver of a sheep was popularly believed to strengthen one's heart and liver, whereas consuming the sheep's brain was believed to lead to the mental weakness associated with the animal. Dietetics was considered a branch of medicine, and medical treatises approached food from a scientific standpoint, detailing the positive and negative effects of specific foods on the physical, mental, and spiritual health of the consumer.

GLAIRE D. ANDERSON

See also Agriculture; Animal Husbandry; Beverages; Cash Crops; Desserts and Confections; Medicine, Diet and Dietetics; Nomadism and Pastoralism; Sedentarism; Spices; Wine

Further Reading

Encyclopedia of Islam, 2nd ed. Leiden: Brill, 1960 (s.v. "Ghidha'," "Tabkh," "Tabbakh," "Matbakh").
Medieval Arab Cookery: Essays and Translations by Maxime Rodinson, A. J. Arberry, and Charles Perry. Devon: Prospect Books, 2001.

FOREIGNERS

Unlike Greco–Roman civilization, Islam did not see the use or the need to confer legal status to the foreigner. Even if we were to comb through all Muslim law texts, we would not find a single judicial definition of the foreigner. This person, however, does appear in Muslim historico-literary sources. Foreigners even led to the creation in the tenth century of a unique literary genre practiced by both religious and profane scholars. In one exemplary tale, a few witty words, or a graffiti, this genre restored the otherness experienced by all who embarked on the adventure of faraway countries and who left vestiges worth saving in books. The *Book of Foreigners* from Pseudo-Abû'l-Faraj of Isfahan is a good representative of the genre, presenting itself as a collection of graffiti with nostalgia as a theme.

Close and remote at the same time, the figure of the foreigner fascinated Muslims of the Middle Ages with its fundamental ambiguity, probably because medieval Muslim societies used voluntary exile as one of their great social initiation rites. They expected one who returned home, after having been away for a more or less long time, to be radically, but also positively, transformed by his search. Under such conditions, the ideal was to return basking in the attributes of glory, such as those earned through the conquest of knowledge and of riches—unless one returned with narrative results noteworthy enough to make a successful book. It is understandable then that the foreigners most often depicted in the sources were young peoples from all social backgrounds who found in the experience of becoming someone else a way to extend, under socially and culturally acceptable conditions, one stage of their lives: that of youth. An entire generation had to cut their social ties to lead, for many years, a life at times lofty but often economically fruitless and socially risky.

Ghârib is the word used by the medieval Arabic language to signify the foreigner. One of the many anecdotes found in the literary genre of the "books of foreigners" can help reveal its meanings. The mystical theologian Qushayrî (d. AH 465/1073 CE) was invited to a session of religious exhortation upon his arrival in Baghdad, where he was greeted by a compact mass of listeners who were for the most part foreigners like him, a fact he did not know beforehand. No doubt suffering from the pains of exile, he began his exhortation session with a famous *hadith* in which the founder of Islam said, "Travel is a part of suffering." An audience member interrupted him, wanting to know why the prophet would say such a thing, to which the master answered, "Because of the separation from loved ones!" This answer so strongly moved the many foreign listeners that no one in the audience could repress their pain. Tears flowed and emotions rose. The exhortation session became a psychodrama. The scholar, who could not go on, stopped it amid cries and emotional confusion. This touching anecdote explains one of the conditions of the foreigner. Another one, noted since the ninth century, was the emphasis on the distance from one's homeland. In either case, moving away from relations and country was made to be seen as an individual motion (even when done collectively, it was assumed individually), socially disassociating and psychologically and emotionally destabilizing. Upon leaving his or her familiar space, the foreigner entered another world. This break with what was known caused in him or her a psycho-affective instability that often led to comparing him or her with a sick man. Thus a medieval treatise on the art of traveling stated that, according to Galen, the foreigner who became ill would be cured upon seeing his or her homeland: his or her heart would then be freed from pain "as the earth is relieved from drought by an abounding rainfall." That is why, the same source also revealed, Hippocrates—the other great name in Greek medicine—recommended that a sick person be healed only by using plants indigenous to his or her homeland. This explains why those who were to be absent too long from their country, far from their nearest and dearest ones, were advised to carry some clay from their country, to purify the water they would drink and perhaps also heal the burns from the nostalgia that would consume them.

Yet one did not need to leave one's land or to separate from one's relations to become a stranger. Individuals, in their own country and amidst their compatriots, were "foreign," in fact, and right to any lineage that was not their own. In this case, *ajnabî* was the term used; it might belong more specifically to the judicial vocabulary. When used less technically, it referred to any foreigner to a country, a community, or a language. In this latter sense, it was synonymous to *ajnab*, which seemed to have first been used to indicate the "intractable," the "disobedient," and the "recalcitrant" before referring to the "one who does not belong to a community or a company." The figure of the foreigner took on a new consistence with these two terms, compared with that of the *gharîb*, which medieval Arabic seems to have used exclusively for Arabs and Muslims. The terms designated indistinctively all foreigners, no matter their ethnic, cultural, or religious origins.

What about foreigners from non-Muslim countries? Oddly, they did not have the status of foreigner, at least not from a legal point of view. Otherwise, the image of neutrality would have been projected on them, neutrality that the Muslim law did not grant them because it subdivided the oikoumene in two distinct and irreconcilable categories: one Islamic, the other non-Islamic. The first was called "territory of peace"; the second, "enemy territory." As a result of this antagonistic opposition, foreigners coming from infidel countries were "belligerents" even when they were not professional soldiers nor felt any particular hostility toward Islam and Muslims. Since they were considered enemies, however, they had to be pacified when they traveled through Muslim land. How? By obtaining a safe-conduct *(amân)* from the legal authorities, who thus temporarily eliminated their status of enemy, replacing it with the one—no less temporary—of *musta'min.*

It is different from a sociological point of view. Any person far from his country or community was foreign. Thus, in his *History of India,* Biruni used the plural *ajânib* to refer to those whom the Indians saw as foreigners. The obstacle was first of all religious: Indians, who called all foreigners "impure," were forbidden to have any contact with them, such as getting married, sitting beside them, or eating or drinking with them. They went as far as to refuse the company of those who wished to convert to the faith. Biruni, who noted that "this is what hinders any closeness, what builds a fence between them and us" (p. 47), added "political reasons" to the "obstacles between Hindus and (Muslim) foreigners" who came to conquer their country and eradicate their religion.

This plural word, *ajânib,* linked to the singular *ajnabî* that defined the condition of one who was foreign to the lineage, would be ultimately used in the nineteenth century to designate the non-Arabs, before encompassing all foreigners. Thus the Egyptian became the foreigner of the Syrian, who became the one of the Algerian or the Moroccan. The word *ajnabî/ajânib* would suffer another semantic surgery dictated to the Arabs—under the rule of colonization in particular and of westernization in general—when they restructured their living together within a new European political frame: that of the nation.

HOUARI TOUATI

Further Reading

Azari, A. "Al-Hanîn ilâ'l-Awtân entre Ğâhiliyya et l'Islam. Le bédouin et le Citadin Réconciliés." *Zeitschrif der Deutschen Morgenländischn Gesellschaft* 143 (1993): 287–327.

Crone, P., and S. El Moreh. *The Book of Stangers: Medieval Arabic Graffiti on the Theme of Nostalgia,* attr. to Abû'l-Faraj al-Isfahânî, trad. Princeton, 2000.

Kilpatrick, H. "The *Kitâb adab al-Gurabâ'* of Abû'l-Faraj al-Isfahânî." In *Actes du 8me Congrès de l'Union Européenne des Arabisants et Islamisants.* Aix-en-Provence, 1978, 127–135.

Lewis, B. "The Other and the Enemy." In *Religionsgespräche im Mittelalter,* ed. B. Lewis and F. Niewöhner. 372, 1992 (Wiesbaden: *Wolfenbütteler Mittelalter-Studien* 4).

Rosenthal, F. "The Stranger in Medieval Islam." *Arabica* 44 (1997): 34–75.

Sachau, E. *Alberuni's India,* trad. anglaise en 2 vol., Lahore, 1888, 1962 (voir aussi trad. partielle en français: Monteil [V.-M.], *Bîrûnî, Le Livre de l'Inde,* Paris, 1996).

FRANKS, OR IFRANJ

Frank is a term used by the Muslim Middle East to denote the inhabitants of Western Europe generally, rather than specifically, the people of the Holy Roman Empire: Christian descendants of barbarian tribes. However, the term was not normally used of Spanish Christians, who were referred to by Muslim writers as Rum, a name also used for the Byzantines.

The looseness of the designation would seem to reflect the low level of Muslim interest in western Christendom, except on the part of Arab writers in the Iberian Peninsula. Elsewhere in the Muslim world, eastern Christendom commanded more immediate attention, at least at the start of the Islamic era. The victory of the Franks, under their leader Charles Martel at the Battle of Poitiers in western France in AH 114/732 CE, seems to have mattered much less to the defeated Arabs than the latter's failure to take Constantinople from the Byzantines. The Balat al-Shuhada' (Thoroughfare of the Martyrs), as the Arabs call the setback at Poitiers, is first mentioned in the eleventh century, and then only in Spanish-Arab chronicles.

There are remarkably few reported encounters between Muslims and western Europeans before the Reconquista and the Crusades. The Frankish chronicles mention an exchange of envoys that may have taken place at the beginning of the ninth century between Martel's grandson Charlemagne, king of the Franks and Holy Roman emperor, and the fifth 'Abbasid caliph Harun al-Rashid. More certainly, one hundred years later, the seventeenth 'Abbasid caliph al-Muktafi received in Baghdad an embassy from the daughter of the Frankish ruler of Lorraine.

For much of this period, any precise knowledge the Arabs had of the peoples, languages, geography, and history of Europe mostly concerned Muslim Andalusia. Information about the rest of Europe is largely fable, with the exception of some geographical data, based largely on Greek sources. The first Arab writer to touch on the history of Western Europe was al-Mas'udi in the middle of the tenth century. In his historical and geographical survey, *Muruj al-dhahab (The Meadows of Gold)*, al-Mas'udi gives a list of Frankish kings from Clovis to Louis IV, based apparently on a Frankish source.

Reinforcing the lack of Muslim interest in medieval Europe was the reluctance of Muslims to travel in Christian lands. It was left to a Spanish Jew, Ibrahim b. Ya'qub, from Tortosa near Barcelona in Arab Spain, to provide the Muslim world with the first detailed eyewitness information about Western Europe. In the middle of the tenth century, Ibrahim travelled, perhaps on official business for the ruler of Andalusia, through France, Holland, northern Germany, Bohemia, Poland, and northern Italy. The account of his travels, which he wrote in Arabic, survives only in fragments that were incorporated into the work of later writers. Ibrahim b. Ya'qub was the source for many subsequent Islamic descriptions of Western Europe.

Toward the end of the eleventh century, there began a period of more direct encounters, beginning with the Reconquista of the Iberian Peninsula and culminating in the Crusades, as a result of which western Europeans occupied parts of the Muslim Near East. Muslim personal impressions of the intruders were added to the written record, notably those of the Syrian belle-lettrist Usama Ibn Munqidh, and the Andalusian traveler Ibn Jubayr. However, the Muslims evinced little interest in the polities of the Crusader states, the differences between the various nationalities, and the places in Europe from which the Crusaders had come. By contrast, the thriving mercantile relationship between East and West, established as a result of the European settlement of the Levant, would continue even after the Muslims had regained the sovereignty of the region.

There is a section on Frankish history in the early fourteenth-century Persian chronicle of Rashid al-Din Tabib, the *Jami' al-tawarikh (The Universal History)*, based on written and oral European sources. Otherwise, the level of Muslim intellectual interest in the West would remain the same until the sixteenth century, when the Ottoman Turks embarked on their pragmatic engagement with Europe.

DAVID MORRAY

See also Andalus; Crusades; Cultural Exchange; Diplomacy; Interfaith Relations; Muslim–Byzantine Relations; Muslim Conceptions of Past Civilizations; Muslim–Crusader Relations; Syria; Greater Syria

Primary Sources

Ibn 'Abd al-Mun'im al-Himyari. *Kitab al-rawd al-Mi'tar fi khabar al-aqtar*, ed. Ihsan 'Abbas. Beirut: Librarie du Liban, 1975.

Further Reading

Hillenbrand, Carole. *The Crusades: Islamic Perspectives*. Edinburgh: Edinburgh University Press, 1999.
Ibn Munqidh, Usama. *Kitab al-i'Tibar*. Translated by P. K. Hitti, as *Memoirs of an Arab-Syrian Gentleman*. Beirut, 1964.
Lewis, Bernard. *The Muslim Discovery of Europe*. London: Weidenfeld and Nicolson, 1982.

FREETHINKERS

The term *freethinker* was originally coined in early modern Europe, where it denoted diverse, independent thinkers who shared in a rejection of ecclesiastic authority. According to some modern scholars of Islam, the term has been used to describe various rationalist currents of thought, such as the Mu'tazilites (see Theology) or Aristotelian philosophy. In this entry, it is used to denote those individuals in medieval Islamic society who rejected the belief in divine revelation through prophecy, in the validity of revealed scriptures, and in the authority of the prophets, or indeed in any religious authority.

Among those individuals, the most famous are the ninth-century theologian Ibn al-Rawandi, the tenth-century physician and neoplatonist philosopher Al-Razi (Rhazes), and the eleventh-century ascetic poet Abu 'l-'Ala' al-Ma'arri. In particular, Ibn al-Rawandi and al-Razi are credited with books that explicitly reject both the notion of prophecy as such and the authenticity of specific prophets. Although none of these books is extant, extensive quotations in subsequent refutations by Muslim authors allow us to appreciate the radical contents and ferocious tone of the freethinkers' works. They depict the prophets as impostors, charlatans who exploit their knowledge of natural phenomena in order to deceive, delude, and manipulate simple people. In its less biting form, the criticism was formulated as a skeptic argument for the equivalence of all religions, but their criticism of Islam was particularly passionate.

People who were suspected of harboring such views ran the risk of persecution; thus they but rarely expressed them in prose. After the tenth century, dissenting intellectuals sought other venues to disseminate their ideas. Poets, however, enjoyed a modicum of license.

In their attempts to free themselves of their own monotheistic tradition, the freethinkers sometimes relied on a real or fictitious nonmonotheistic legacy. Indeed, some pre-Islamic sources, such as the pagan philosophers of late antiquity, argued a rejection of revealed religion. However, such notions gained unprecedented importance in the Islamic world. Because Muhammad's prophethood is a cornerstone of the Muslim faith, the belief in prophecy in general has also acquired a place of honor. The insistence of nonconformist intellectuals on a rejection of prophecy developed as a counterreaction to the importance of this dogma in Islam. It can thus be seen as a typically Islamic disbelief, which mirrors a specifically Islamic creed.

Despite the freethinkers' radical views, their criticism of religion should not be construed as atheism. They never denied God's existence, and only rarely did their opponents impute such a denial to them. Even when they did, it was the scriptural image of God that the freethinkers were said to deny: a personal God who interferes in the course of history through revelation, and who takes people to task for their acts. To some extent, the freethinkers' perception of God can be described (again borrowing a term from European intellectual history) as that of deists. They believed in natural reason as sufficient to guide humanity to truth; and some of them (like al-Razi) also believed in benevolent divine providence.

Also typical of the freethinkers is the preoccupation with questions of theodicy: they rebel against the existence of evil and suffering in the world, and they reject the justification of these sufferings as divine punishment.

The place accorded to freethinking in Islamic literature far exceeds the meager number of these individuals. The role of responding to the freethinkers' challenge was taken up by Muslim intellectuals of practically all persuasions—orthodox Sunni Muslims, Mu'talizilites (see Theology), and Ismailis. However, the impact of the freethinkers was not limited to polemical literature. For example, in the political thought of Aristotelian philosophers, prophecy played a vital role. This may be partly explained as a reaction to the freethinkers, reflecting the philosophers' attempts to dissociate themselves from unacceptable ideas like those expressed by al-Razi and Ibn al-Rawandi.

The impact of freethinking can be best appraised through its reflections in non-Muslim authors. Jewish writers of Arabic, like Maimonides, presented freethinking—a disbelief in prophecy thought typical of arrogant intellectuals—as the worst kind of disbelief. In European Christianity, its impact made itself felt more slowly. *The Book of Three Impostors* most likely owed its existence to this particular variety of Islamic disbelief, transmitted to Christian Europe via Sicily or Spain.

SARAH STROUMSA

See also Abu 'l-Ala' al-Ma'arri; Aristole and Aristotelianism; Heresy and Heretics; Ibn al-Rawandi: Ismailis; Al-Razi (Rhazes)

Further Reading

Kraemer, Joel. L. "Heresy versus the State in Medieval Islam." In *Studies in Judaica, Karaitica and Islamica Presented to Leon Nemoy on his Eightieth Birthday*, ed. S.R. Brunswick, 167–180. Ramat Gan, 1982.

Niewohner, Friedrich. "Are the Founders of Religions Impostors?" In *Maimonides and Philosophy—Papers Presented at the Sixth Jerusalem Philosophical Encounter,* May 1985. Ed. S. Pines and Y. Yovel. Dodrecht, 1986, 233–245.

Stroumsa, Sarah. *Freethinkers of Medieval Islam: Ibn al-Rawandi, Abu Baker al-Razi, and Their Impact on Islamic Thought*. Leiden: Brill, 1999.

FUNERARY PRACTICES, JEWISH

Islamic tradition reports that Muhammad stood up when the funeral bier of a Jewish woman passed by; he remarked that "Death is a terrible thing" and ordered his followers to stand when any cortege passed by. However, another report tells us that his practice had been to follow funerals and remain standing until the body was interred. This practice was changed, however, after a rabbi approached him and said, "We do likewise O Muhammad!" at which point he "took his seat, exclaiming, 'Oppose them.'"

The Jewish funeral procession predates Islam, of course; it is known from Flavius Josephus (*Against Apion* 2, 205) and Talmudic sources, but it remained an important practice among Jews living in Islamic lands, even if some of the other funerary practices known from those times had fallen into disuse. Those who could afford it had cantors to provide accompaniment; for example, the wealthy Jewess known as Wuhsha the Broker allocated the princely sum of fifty dinars to make sure professional singers followed her bier. Musical accompaniment was rare. Elaborate funeral processions, however, could be a provocation to Muslims, as happened in Egypt in 1011–1012, when Muslims attacked a funeral procession and denounced the Jews to the authorities; some two dozen were arrested on their way home from the cemetery. This may well have been the reason the Ben Ezra synagogue discontinued the practice of bringing unused sacred documents to the cemetery and began to discard them into the attic, forming the Cairo Geniza. Presumably, this is also why some wills specify that the Muslim wailers should be used.

The wills and financial receipts found in the Geniza detail the allocations for burial preparations: the washing and purification of the body, preparing the grave, expenses for pallbearers, food for mourners, and other expenses. Coffins were used, even though the dead were not buried in them. Geniza sources suggest they were not reused either, at least if the deceased could afford a new one. Wealthy Jews—men and women—often allocated large sums for sumptuous final vestments, perhaps because some Jews assumed that the resurrection of the dead would include the restoration of their funeral vestments, a view associated with Sa'adia Gaon (d. 942), and, according to Maimonides, unfortunately much discussed by Jews (introduction to the commentary on Sanhedrin, chapter 10). In some locations, graves were built with brick and elaborate preparations were made; in Spain, Samuel Ha-Nagid of Granada (d. 1056) reports that he descended into the grave to prepare the final resting place for his brother's body. Elaborate eulogies were given at the funeral, cantors sang the prayers movingly, and there was much wailing. Women had special gowns they wore in mourning.

An important part of the preparations for the funeral included community judges making sure financial considerations were put in order, including making sure the poll tax was paid off. There are reports that authorities prevented burial if this was not done. The deceased will often also have made arrangements to give charitable contributions to the poor and the synagogue, and to provide for education of children, maintenance of widows, and marriage of girls.

In Jewish tradition, seven days of mourning were observed, starting with the day of burial. Traditional observances included ripping the clothing, not wearing shoes, sitting on low benches rather than regular couches, not shaving or cutting the hair, and not going outside the house, and accepting condolence calls from extended family, friends, and the general community. As was noted by a question put to Taqi al-Din al-Subki in the fourteenth century, some of these practices diverged from those of Islamic society, particularly in the number of days in which a woman mourned for her husband, and the limitation of mourning to 3 days for everyone else.

SETH WARD

Further Reading

Goitein, S.D. *A Mediterranean Society*. Vol. 5. Los Angeles: University of California Press, 1988, 127–128.

Maghen, Ze'ev. "The Interaction Between Islamic Law and Non-Muslims: Lakum Dinukum Wa-li Dini." *Islamic Law and Society* 10, no. 3 (2003): 267.

Ward, Seth. "Dhimmi Women and Mourning." In *Islamic Legal Interpretation: Muftis and Their Fatwas*, ed. Masud, Messick and Powers, 87–97. Cambridge and London: Harvard University Press, 1996.

FUNERARY PRACTICES, MUSLIM

Before burying the dead in the earth, Muslims typically performed a number of death rituals to express their grief and to prepare the corpse for its sojourn in the grave. Immediately after hearing the news of the death, bereft women would lament and wail. Pious men might then protest that wailing for the dead is wrong. A Muslim, they would argue, should be able to bear the loss of a loved one's life with stoic forbearance, submitting to God's judgment. As soon as possible after the moment of death, before the onset of *rigor mortis*, family members or professional corpse washers would begin to clean the corpse with the aim of burying it in a state of ritual purity. The corpse would then be wrapped in shrouds, hoisted on a bier, and hastily transported by pallbearers to the cemetery. Women were, in some places, forced to stay behind, at home, while men would leave for the cemetery, joining the funeral procession. At the cemetery, by the empty grave, the men would line up in rows and follow the imam in a prayer seeking God's mercy on behalf of the deceased. The corpse would then be deposited in the grave, laid on the right side facing in the Muslim direction of prayer. After the burial, the neighbors would approach the family of the deceased to offer food and consolation.

The Qur'an includes only a handful of statements regarding burial and associated ritual practices. It refers to the mythical origins of burial in a story about Cain, Abel, and the raven (Q 5:31), yet it does not provide any specific instructions on how to bury the dead. In one instance, the Qur'an alludes to prayer for the dead and standing over the grave. However, its interest lies not in describing these rituals so as to provide Muslims with directions on how to carry them out. It refers to these rituals simply in order to prohibit Muslims from honoring with last rites those who had denied God and his Messenger and remained as sinners until the moment of death (Q 9:84).

In contrast to the Qur'an, collections of hadith, or oral tradition, and books of law and jurisprudence would pay close attention to funeral practices. Many of these works include a book or chapter devoted exclusively to the subject, the *Kitab al-Jana'iz*. Others discuss certain funeral practices—in particular, the washing of corpses and the prayer for the dead—in the books or chapters concerning the rituals of purity and prayer. These works cover a number of different funerary practices, beginning with the recitation of Qur'anic verses in the moments before imminent death and ending with the pattering of sandals over the fresh grave mound. Traditionists and jurisprudents considered in depth common and mundane practices, such as ritual laments, the preparation of corpses for burial, the procession toward the cemetery, the funeral prayer, and the construction of the tomb. Yet they also pondered rare and unusual cases; for instance, how to dispose of a corpse at sea, where interment was impossible.

The status of funerary practices in Islamic law depends on the practice in question. Burial was considered a Muslim's right, yet the duty to bury a Muslim was not incumbent on each and every individual. It was sufficient for part of the Muslim community to take it upon itself to bury the dead. To follow a funeral procession toward the cemetery was deemed a good deed, for which Muslims might earn the reward of forgiveness for their sins. Jurisprudents tended to recommend certain practices, such as burial in white shrouds, without making them obligatory. Certain other practices, such as wailing for the dead or inscribing tombstones, they decried as odious. Yet the performance of acts of this kind, however repugnant, would lead neither to criminal prosecution nor to the grave charge of apostasy. In fact, violators would suffer not so much in this world as in the next. Perhaps the greatest criminal violation of funerary law consisted of exhuming the dead with the intent of despoiling them of their shrouds—a robbery, which according to some jurisprudents should be punished by the amputation of the hand. Generally, however, the law of funerals concerned ethical standards rather than criminal matters. It concentrated on defining proper and improper behavior.

In Islamic funerary law there are frequent and extensive references to the acts and sayings of Muhammad and early converts to Islam, as these were remembered by traditionists. There are, by contrast, few explicit references to the funerary practices of Jews and Christians, even though Islamic funerary law developed in part in relation to non-Muslim customs and laws. Nowhere does Islamic law decree that Muslims should imitate the customs of non-Muslims, as of Muhammad. The opposite is true. Thus, for instance, jurisprudents decreed that the Jewish custom of rising in honor of a funeral procession passing by was abrogated, for Muhammad had declared it was essential for Muslims to diverge in their ritual practices from the Jews. This advocacy of communal distinction could not be adhered to uniformly, however, for in certain cases Muslim and non-Muslim practices were, at a basic level, obviously the same. So it was, for example, with the ritual of inhumation. Jews and Christians buried their dead in the earth, as did Muslims. Hence it was impossible, in this case, for Muslims to represent the ritual as if it originated with Muhammad and to view it as a departure from Judeo-Christian ways. Instead, jurisprudents referred to burial as part of the "custom of the sons of Adam."

Having considered the relation of Muslim to non-Muslim funerary practices, the question arises whether there was a similar attempt at communal distinction within Islam. Internal boundaries were certainly manifest in the orthodox boycotting of heretics' funerals or in the sectarian tendency toward violent lament in the commemoration of the deaths of Shi'i martyrs. Yet did Sunni and Shi'i jurisprudents try to develop distinctive death rituals that would serve one sect to differentiate it from the others? By and large, they did not. One does find Sunnis and Shi'is subtly divided on certain topics, such as the permissibility of lamenting for the dead, preparing funerary repasts, and using tombstone inscriptions. However, with few exceptions, differences of opinion about funerary practice tended not to correspond in any straightforward way to sectarian divisions. An obvious example is the debate about whether it is best in the funerary procession to walk in front of or behind the bier. Tradition holds that the first three caliphs, whose right to rule was celebrated by Sunnis but not by Shi'is, walked in front of the bier, whereas the fourth caliph, whom Shi'is supported, walked behind the bier. Correspondingly, one would expect Sunni and Shi'i law to be neatly divided into two camps, with each supporting a different position. However, one of the Sunni schools of jurisprudence, which followed the teachings of Abu Hanifa, subscribed to the same position as did the Shi'is.

Our knowledge of funerary practices in medieval Islamic civilization derives not only from the corpus of Muslim tradition and law, but also from the archaeological record. So far, archaeologists have not excavated early Islamic cemeteries, yet there are a handful of reports on late-medieval necropoles. These studies show that burial practices varied from one location to another and diverged, sometimes in surprising ways, from the ideals of Islamic law. An example may be cited, by way of conclusion, from the excavations at Málaga and Murcia in al-Andalus. It seems that in these places Muslim scholars were sometimes buried in mosques, much as Christian monks in churches, despite the fact that Islamic law prohibited the practice.

LEOR HALEVI

See also Death and Dying

Further Reading

Fierro, Maribel. "El espacio de los muertos: fetuas andalusíes sobre tumbas y cementerios." In *L'urbanisme dans l'Occident musulman au Moyen Âge: Aspects juridiques*, eds. Patrice Cressier, Maribel Fierro, and Jean-Pierre Van Staëvel, 153–189. Madrid: Casa De Velázquez, Consejo Superior de Investigaciones Científicas, 2000.

Halevi, Leor. "The Paradox of Islamization: Tombstone Inscriptions, Qur'anic Recitations, and the Problem of Religious Change." *History of Religions* 44, no. 2 (2004).

———. "Wailing for the Dead: The Role of Women in Early Islamic Funerals." *Past & Present* 183 (2004): 3–39.

———. *Muhammad's Grave: Death Rites and the Making of Islamic Society*. Forthcoming book.

Leisten, Thomas. "Between Orthodoxy and Exegesis: Some Aspects of Attitudes in the Shari'a toward Funerary Architecture." *Muqarnas*, 7 (1990): 12–22.

Simpson, St. John. "Death and Burial in the Late Islamic Near East: Some Insights from Archaeology and Ethnography." In *The Archaeology of Death in the Ancient Near East*, eds. Stuart Campbell and Anthony Green, 240–251. Oxford: Oxbow Books, 1995.

Sokoly, Jochen. "Between Life and Death: The Funerary Context of Tiraz Textiles." In *Islamische Textilkunst des Mittelalters*, eds. K. Otavsky et al., 71–78. Riggisberg, 1997.

Tritton, A. S. "Muslim Funeral Customs." *Bulletin of the School of Oriental and African Studies* 9 (1937–1939): 653–661.

Zaman, Muhammad Qasim. "Death, Funeral Processions, and the Articulation of Religious Authority in Early Islam." *Studia Islamica* 93 (2001): 27–58.

FURNITURE AND FURNISHINGS

Traditionally, life in the Middle East is lived not with furniture—chairs, tables, beds, wardrobes, and the like—but with woven materials designed for life on the ground, such as carpets, flat-woven textiles, and cushions and bed mattresses, reflecting nomadic customs. By European standards, the interior space in the Middle East remained empty till modern times.

Neither archaeological nor literary sources help to pin down the development of domestic furniture in the Islamic world of the Middle Ages. But it is assumed that the house interior was empty of furniture and essentially consisted of matting laid on the floor and low tables at meals. Seating levels, which were presumably suggested by the number of cushions and the range and quality of fabrics, may have been major indicators of social rank.

Nevertheless, furniture played a key role on ceremonial occasions in the medieval Islamic lands. Certain types of portable wooden furniture, such as *minbar*s (pulpits), *maqsūra*s (screened enclosures for the ruler), Qur'an stands, and bookcases were incorporated into mosques and other religious settings. Most of the earliest surviving examples of such furnishings came from the western Islamic lands and some of them are still extant.

Information about furniture provided by visual sources (for example, fresco painting, miniature painting, ceramics, metalwork) is rich enough to demonstrate the significance of furnishings in court life in the medieval Islamic world. A type of throne differs from dynasty to dynasty: frescoes discovered from the Umayyad (661–750 CE) sites, for example, those from Qasr al-Hayr West and Qusayr 'Amra, have often been cited as evidence for the use of chairlike thrones in the Umayyad court. It seems that a low throne suitable for the cross-legged posture was introduced during the early 'Abbasid period (749–1258) and became increasingly popular in the Saljuq (1040–1194) political and cultural sphere. The ubiquity of folding stools in the medieval Islamic world, which were derived from classical models, can be attested to by those depicted in the court scenes in pre-Mongol miniature painting, such as a frontispiece of the *Kitāb al-aghānī (Book of Songs)*, probably executed in Mosul in 1216–1220 (Istanbul, Millet Yazma Eser Kütüphanesi, Feyzullah Efendi 1566), and they continued to be represented in later miniature painting of the Middle East. As often seen in the enthronement scenes in early fourteenth-century copies of *Jāmi' al-Tawārīkh* of Rashid al-Din *(Compendium of Chronicles)* and the *Shāhnāma (Book of Kings)* by Ferdowsi, the Mongol invasion facilitated the introduction of a new type of royal furniture into the Eastern Islamic lands—namely, a high-backed throne with decorative side panels based on the Chinese prototype. Although it remains unclear whether actual examples of such furniture were imported westward into the Middle East, this kind of elaborate throne, together with a low footstool become an important component of royal iconography in Persian miniature painting. Another important royal furnishing of the period is a tent hanging woven in brocade under the inspiration of Mongol customs. The depiction of furnishings became more detailed in miniature painting under the Timurids (1370–1505) and the Safavids (1501–1722), and several kinds of throne, seat, and low table function as pictorial devices and, moreover, visualize the rich material culture of the pre-modern Islamic world.

YUKA KADOI

Further Reading

Kurz, Otto. "Folding Chairs and Koran Stands." In *Islamic Art in the Metropolitan Museum of Art*, ed. R. Ettinghausen, 299–314. New York: Metropolitan Museum of Art, 1972.

Sadan, Joseph. *Le Mobilier au Proche-Orient Médiéval.* Leiden: Brill, 1976.

———. "Furniture, Islamic." In *Dictionary of the Middle Ages*, vol. 5. Ed. J. R. Strayer. New York: Scribner, 1985, 313–316.

Upton, Joseph M., and Phyllis Ackerman. "Furniture." In *A Survey of Persian Art from Prehistoric Times to the Present*, vol. 3. Eds. A. U. Pope and P. Ackerman. London and New York: Oxford University Press, 1939, 2628–2658.

FUSTÂT

The city of Fustât *(Misr al-Fustât)*, capital of Islamic Egypt, was founded in 642 CE by 'Amr ibn al-'As when the Arabs conquered Byzantine Egypt during the reign of the caliph 'Umar. The city was located on the eastern shore of the Nile, just below the Delta, close to the ancient Roman fortress of Babylone *(Qasr al Sham'* for the Arabs). It controlled the passageway south of the Delta. To the east of the city stands the Muqattam, a tabular mountain of white limestone stretching from the north to the south; some of its lower protuberances have allowed an urban occupation, such as the Citadel *(al-Qal'a,* or *Qal'at al-Gabal)*, the plateau of Istabl 'Antar *('Amal Fawq)*. At its foundation the city was divided into plots *(khitta, khitat)*, which the emir 'Amr shared out to the tribes and clans. The center of the city was allotted to the People of the Banner *(ahl al-râya)*: This is where the first mosque on African ground was erected, known still today as the mosque of 'Amr.

The real extent and density of the city founded by 'Amr ibn al-'As are but imperfectly known, and therefore one cannot appreciate its true importance. At the time of its foundation, the territory of Fustât extended between the vast lake known as *Birkat al-Habash*

in the south to the *khittat al-Hamrâ al-quswâ* where the Yashkur were settled in the north, that is, from the present area of Basâtîne to that of Sayyida Zaynab. This would represent a north-south extension of slightly more than 4.5 km. Fustât soon turned into a metropolis. The excavations of the Istabl 'Antar plateau have revealed that the southern quarters of the town were densely built during the first centuries after its foundation. However, the city went through many variations throughout its history, with important territorial changes, such as extensions, recesses, and changes of location, in an area now completely absorbed by the modern metropolis.

Throughout the twentieth century, the site of Fustât was excavated by various archaeological missions. The first excavations, carried out by Aly Bahgat, were published in collaboration with Albert Gabriel in 1921. In the same area, important excavations were also carried out by George T. Scanlon and Wladyslaw Kubiak (1964–1980), and later by Mutsuo Kawatoko. These investigations have revealed living quarters of the first Fatimid century, some belonging to a well-to-do class (Bahgat), others to a humbler part of the population (Scanlon). The excavations of the French Institute located in the southern part of the town were the first to reveal layers pertaining to the foundation of the Arab city, as well as a vast necropolis of the eighth and tenth centuries.

Few of the Fustât monuments have survived. The most ancient one is the 'Amr mosque, but it has been widened and transformed many a time, making its original state hardly discernible. The latest restorations have probably disfigured it permanently. The Istabl 'Antar excavations revealed the most ancient plan of a mosque in Egypt, as well as many mausolea belonging to the same period (that is, between ad 750 and 765). The Nilometer *(Miqyas)* at the southern tip of the Roda island *(Rawda)* is a particular kind of monument, reconstructed in 861 and used for measuring the high waters of the Nile. The mosque of Ibn Tûlûn is probably the most impressive monument of Fustât that can still be admired. It was inaugurated in 879 and witnesses the importation of the Mesopotamian Samarra art to Egypt. Two aqueducts have partially survived: parts of the aqueduct supplying Ibn Tûlûn's palatial residence on Gabal Yashkur, with water coming from the lake of Birkat al-Habash, can still be seen, as well as its *sâqîya*. The other one, known as "the Saladin wall," crossed the ruins of Fustât and reached the foot of the citadel northeast of the city. One may also add five aqueducts dating from the eighth to eleventh centuries, found in the excavations of Istabl 'Antar.

Most of the monuments of Fustât still to be seen are funeral constructions, their position in the cemetery, as well as their function, having spared them from destruction. One may mention the mausolea of Sab' Banât and that of Hadrâ al-Sharîfa in the southern part of the city, built in the beginning of the eleventh century, Ikhwât Yûsuf (1125–1150), the Imâm Shâfi'î reconstructed in 1211 in the cemetery of Qarâfa. One may add numerous other mausolea to the list, many of which have been altered during their history, such as Sayyida 'Atîka and Muhammad al-Ga'farî (1122); Sayyida Ruqayya (1133); Umm Kulthum (1122); Yahyâ al-Shâbihî (1150); al-Hasawâtî (1150); and Fâtima Khatûn (1283). Various churches, as well as the synagogue of Old Cairo, have a complex architectural history and also suffered from poor restoration. They should be added to this list.

Today, unlike the medieval city of Cairo, Fustât offers a scattered architectural heritage, difficult to preserve, a situation that does not reflect the grandeur of its history.

ROLAND-PIERRE GAYRAUD

Further Reading

Bahgat, A., and A. Gabriel. *Fouilles d'al-Foustât*. Paris, 1921.

Casanova, P. *Essai de Reconstitution Topographique de la Ville d'al-Foustât, MIFAO*, 35, Le Caire, 1919.

Creswell, K.A.C. *The Muslim Architecture of Egypt*. 2 vols., Oxford UP, 1952–1959.

Denoix, S. *Décrire Le Caire. Fustât-Misr d'après Ibn Duqmâq et Maqrîzî*. IFAO, 1992.

———. "Les premiers siècles arabes." In *Le Caire*, ed. A. Raymond, 57–145. Paris: Citadelles & Mazenod, 2000.

Fuad Sayyed, A., and R.-P. Gayraud. "Fustât-Le Caire à l'époque fatimide." In *Grandes Villes Méditerranéennes du Monde Musulman Médiéval*, ed. J-Cl. Garcin, 135–156. Rome: EFR, 2000.

Gayraud, R-P. *Fustât aux Origines du Caire: Les Fouilles d'Istabl 'Antar*, IFAO, Le Caire (à paraître).

Kubiak, W. *Al-Fustat: Its Foundation and Early Urban Development*. Cairo: AUC Press, 1987.

Kubiak, W., and G. T. Scanlon. *Fustât Expedition Final Report. Vol. 2: Fustât-C.*, ARCE, 1989.

Raymond, A. *Le Caire*. Paris: Fayard, 1993.

Williams, C. *Islamic Monuments in Cairo: A Practical Guide*, 4th ed. AUC Press, 1993.

G

GAMBLING

Gambling *(qimar)* is strictly forbidden by Islamic law on the basis that it represents an exchange of property that is neither productive nor sanctioned and is thus a frivolous and useless business transaction. Moreover, gambling also prevents Muslims from performing their obligations of prayer and worship and has the potential to lead to arguments and violence. Despite legal injunctions against the practice, gambling did occur throughout the medieval Islamic world at all levels of society. It may be divided into two broad categories. The first sort of gambling consisted of board games such as *nard* (backgammon), chess, throwing dice, casting lots, cards, guessing games, and *manqalah* (the game of fourteen). The other kind of gambling was the placing of stakes on sports. The most common sports involving stakes were horse and camel racing, swimming, archery, wrestling, foot racing, pigeon flying, and polo. Gambling on sporting events usually took place in large open spaces, whereas game playing with stakes generally occurred in private. Large cities often housed gambling establishments or casinos, and some even offered gamblers the allure of on-site loans to continue their play. Legal authorities tended to ignore gambling unless it caused a disturbance to neighboring residents or businesses in the form of noise, crime, or disorder.

The roots of gambling in the medieval Islamic world and the debates surrounding it go back to pre-Islamic Arabia, where a game known as *maysir* was widely played. In this game, a maximum of seven players each purchased an arrow with differing numbers of notches representing shares (one through seven) of a camel divided into 10 parts. These seven arrows, along with three blank ones, were placed in an empty drum and then chosen at random one at a time. The winners were those whose arrow was drawn out of the drum first. They received shares of the camel commensurate to the number of shares purchased and represented by the notches on their arrow. The losers paid for the camel and its slaughter. In the Qur'an, *maysir* is likened to wine and explicitly forbidden as a sin. Many later Muslim jurists based their judgments of gambling on the example of the treatment of *maysir* in the Qur'an.

As debates among Muslim jurists progressed, the relative legality of various sorts of gambling changed. For instance, while some jurists argued against the legality of chess because the game's pieces bore what they took to be idolatrous images, others pointed to what they viewed as the utility of the game in teaching foresight and military strategy. Similarly, even if backgammon was played without stakes, some still deemed it illegal because the game involved the throwing of dice. What is more, the flexible nature of Islamic law allowed technically illegal forms of gambling to become legalized through the mechanism of a *muhallil* (a legalizer). This individual participated in the gaming or sport but did not contribute to the stakes. Because gambling in which all the participants added to the stakes was strictly forbidden by Muslim jurists, the presence of an individual who did not contribute to the stakes made the activity in question a legal form of gambling.

As the most common forms of gambling, backgammon and chess were at the center of most debates on the subject. One of the most important challenges these games raised struck at a core concept in the metaphysics of Islamic monotheism: the nature of fate. Specifically, backgammon came to be seen as the epitome of the orthodox belief in predetermination and trust in God because the roll of the dice was beyond the control of human will and desire. Chess, on the other hand, symbolized all that was wrong with humanity because it encouraged players to rely on their own capacities and gave them a false sense of freedom of choice.

ALAN MIKHAIL

See also Backgammon; Camels; Chess; Divination; Numbers; Pigeons; Pre-Destination; Sports; Toys; Usury and Interest

Further Reading

Mayer, Leo Ary. *Mamluk Playing Cards.* Eds. R. Ettinghausen and O. Kurz. Leiden: E. J. Brill, 1971.
Rosenthal, Franz. *Gambling in Islam.* Leiden: E. J. Brill, 1975.

GANJ-I SHAKAR, FARID AD-DIN

A prominent Sufi master of the Chishti order in India, Farid ad-Din was born in Kahtwal, a village close to Multan (Punjab) around 1175 CE, to a family that had immigrated to the region from Kabul. Receiving his early religious education (particularly in mysticism) from his mother, Farid ad-Din also attended a *madrasa* attached to a mosque in Multan. It was there that he is believed to have met Qutb ad-Din Bakhtiyar Khaki, a prominent Sufi master from Delhi who initiated him into the Chishti order, an order that was rapidly becoming one of the most powerful Sufi fraternities in northern India. According to hagiographic accounts of his life, Farid ad-Din quickly became renowned in Chishti circles for his ascetic practices, such as hanging upside in a well for 45 while meditating and praying. He also became famous for his fasts through which he is believed to have attained the power of turning stones into sugar; hence, his epithet Ganj-i Shakar (the treasure house of sugar). His asceticism was so extreme that even his own wives and children had to endure severe austerities and restrictions on his account.

In keeping with early Chishti tradition, Farid ad-Din considered association with rulers to be detrimental to a life devoted to inculcating spiritual values. Hence he rejected land grants or gifts from rulers, preferring to rely on gifts from devotees as a means of maintaining himself and his disciples. His mistrust of government and politics was so intense that he eventually decided to abandon Delhi and the political turmoil of a capital city to settle in Ajodhan, a small, remote settlement on the Sutlej River in the Punjab. As Farid ad-Din's fame spread throughout the region and pilgrims flocked to Ajodhan, it was eventually renamed Pakpattan (the ferry of the pure), presumably because devotees could board the metaphorical ferry of salvation, piloted by Farid ad-Din, at this location. On Farid ad-Din's death in 1265, a shrine complex developed around his tomb in Pakpattan. As an important north Indian pilgrimage center, Pakpattan continues to attract devotees of all religious faiths, who come here to seek Farid ad-Din's blessings and his intercession so that their prayers may be answered.

Farid ad-Din played an instrumental role in the expansion of the Chishti order in north India by training several prominent disciples who eventually were responsible for consolidating the order's authority in important cities and towns. Most prominent among them was Nizam ad-Din Awliya, the famous Chishti master of Delhi, whom he met in 1257, only a few years before his death. Shaykh Salim Chishti of Fatehpur Sikri, on account of whom the Chishti order attained great influence in the Mughal court in the sixteenth and seventeenth centuries, was also one of his spiritual descendants. Although Farid ad-Din taught his disciples classical Sufi texts, he himself is not believed to have left behind any important treatise. Oral tradition attributes to Farid ad-Din numerous poems and verses in local north Indian vernaculars, such as Panjabi and Hindawi (the earliest form of Urdu-Hindi), suggesting that he attempted to spread Sufi ideas among ordinary people by composing mystical folk poetry. A few scholars also believe that the poems ascribed to a Shaykh Farid ad-Din and incorporated into the *Adigranth,* the scripture of the Sikh community may also have been composed by Farid ad-Din (Ganj-i Shakar), although there is no consensus on this issue.

ALI ASANI

Further reading

Nizami, K.A. *The Life and Times of Shaikh Farid ad-Din Ganj-i Shakar.* Aligarh, 1955.

GARDENS AND GARDENING

The pleasurable aspects of medieval Islamic gardens—the sensory delights of sight, scent, sound, and refreshing spray—were balanced with their ability to yield

Gardens. Islamic, fourteenth century. Nasrid period. Alhambra, Granada, Spain. Credit: Werner Forman/Art Resource, NY.

useful fruit and to display the process by which fertility was transformed into profit. Agriculture and trade in agricultural products were the economic foundation of medieval Islam, and gardens were an aesthetic expression of how that spatial economy and ecological system operated. For example, at Khirbat al-Mafjar in Jordan (724–743 CE), an enormous roofed fountain in the outer courtyard provided water and drew attention to water's power to transform the surrounding desert into a habitable landscape of orchards and crops. At Qasr al-Hayr al-Sharqi in Syria (728–729), a seasonal stream controlled by low walls and sluices irrigated an extensive olive orchard that was probably interplanted with spring crops needing shade. This was a working farm that produced olives and oil to be traded between nomadic country dwellers and merchants from the city of Palmyra; yet the estate must also have been enjoyed as a green oasis in the midst of harsh desert.

The human fulfillment of the Qur'an's command to serve as stewards of the earth and to care for the plants and animals was expressed in gardens where the agricultural landscape of irrigation, plants, architectural structures, and planning was reproduced in microcosm for display. The most powerful example of landscape planning occurs in the *chahar bagh*

(four-garden) plan, the earliest known example of which is the Umayyad palace at Rusafa in Syria (724–742), where a raised pavilion stood at the intersection of walkways in an irregular garden enclosure. Although a quadripartite organization was implicit in Roman and Achaemenid gardens, in Islamic Syria it appeared as a formal plan with paved walkways axially dividing the garden into quadrants with a pavilion or fountain at the center. The *chahar bagh* plan next appeared at Madinat al-Zahra' in Cordoba (936), although there have been many other examples that left no archaeological trace. Thereafter the quadripartite plan spread across the Islamic world from Spain (Castillejo of Monteagudo and the Alhambra) and Morocco (the garden excavated beneath the Kutubiyya Mosque, Marrakesh) to Afghanistan (Lashkari Bazar), culminating in the great gardens of Timurid and Safavid Iran and Mughal India.

Irrigation was essential for gardening in the dry climate of north Africa and the Middle East. Except during brief rainy seasons, it was drawn from catchment basins (particularly along the Nile), rivers, canals (particularly in Mesopotamia), rainwater cisterns, and even from the water table itself. Ideally, the source of water was above the destination point: at Qasr al-Hayr al-Gharbi in Syria (724–727), a surface canal led to a basin on high ground near the palace, where it could be released as needed, flowing by gravity into the palace and gardens. When the source of water was lower than the field, garden, or residence where it was to be used, either a noria (waterwheel) or *shaduf* (pole and lever) was used to lift the water in buckets. Alternatively, in some landscapes a *qanat* (subterranean canal) could tap the elevated water table at the base of a mountain and carry it underground for many miles to a human-made oasis of farms and gardens. The mutual reliance on irrigation is but one indication of the close connection between gardening and farming.

Due to the ephemeral nature of plant life, no gardens survive from the medieval era, but historical descriptions, botanical treatises, agricultural manuals, and even poetry reflect the importance of gardening. Manuscript paintings (such as the "Bayad wa Riyad" and Mongol copies of the "Shanameh") that depict gardens are equally important, although these are scarce prior to the thirteenth century. Although they are untrustworthy as literal representations, they do show that gardens and landscapes provided the setting for public ceremonies, private colloquia, amorous trysts, hunts, outdoor banquets, and other social gatherings.

Few medieval Islamic gardens have been excavated because of the high cost and the specialized expertise necessary for soil archaeology. Consequently, we know very little about the specific botanical contents of early gardens, gardening tools, planting pots, or even correct soil surface levels. One exception is the Alhambra, where the original soil level in the Court of the Lions was observed .80 meters below the present pavement surface. Similarly, at the Generalife's Patio del Acequia, emergency excavations following a fire revealed an original soil level .70 meters lower than the present surface and pits for large shrubs in the corners of the garden. At Rusafa (Syria), the existence of a garden was inferred merely from the walkways and the lack of other built fabric. However, such excavations are rare and usually occur as an unanticipated archaeological by-product. Generally, site directors respect architectural authenticity more than the accurate design or horticultural contents of historic gardens. The unfortunate result is that medieval Islamic garden sites are today routinely planted with botanical matter from the Western hemisphere and modern hybrids that lack the intoxicating perfume of their medieval ancestors, or simply left as bare earth.

D. FAIRCHILD RUGGLES

See also Agriculture; Horticulture; Irrigation; Technology; Mills, Water, and Wind

Further Reading

Brookes, John. *Gardens of Paradise*. New York: New Amsterdam, 1982.

Macdougall, Elizabeth, and Richard Ettinghausen, eds. *The Islamic Garden*. Washington, D.C.: Dumbarton Oaks, 1976.

Ruggles, D. Fairchild. *Gardens, Landscape, and Vision in the Palaces of Islamic Spain*. University Park, PA: Pennsylvania State University Press, 2000.

———. "Il giardini con pianta a croce nel Mediterraneo islamico." In *Il Giardino Islamico: Architettura, Natura, Paesaggio*, ed. Attilio Petruccioli, 143–154. Milan: Electa, 1993. German edition in *Der islamische Garten: Architektur. Natur. Landschaft*. Stuttgart: Deutsche Verlag-Anstalt, 1994, 143–154.

GENDER AND SEXUALITY

Compared to its contemporaries in the Middle Ages, Islamic society significantly promoted equality between the sexes and improved the social status and rights of women. Yet, judged from the perspective of modern conceptions of women's rights, some of the practices associated with Islam in the Middle Ages may appear discriminatory, owing to continually changing conceptions about women's identity and role in society and family. Islam emerged in a patriarchal society where fathers felt deeply ashamed for having a female child, often culminating in the common practice of pre-Islamic Arabia of burying her alive. There was no limit to the number of wives a man could have. Suppression of women and inequality between the sexes were apparent in all types of interaction.

With the emergence of Islam, the Qur'an reframed gender difference as part of God's creation and will (Q 49:13). The Qur'an is explicit in calling for the elimination of practices and customs that discriminate against women, with the purpose of establishing equality between the sexes, and it curses those who kill their daughters out of shame (Q 81:8–9). The interpretation and implementation of these reforms has varied across the considerable historical and geographical spans encompassed by Islamic societies. Some of the local customs of pre-Islamic times survived by concealing themselves behind a veneer of religious sanction. Consequently, the Prophet Muhammad's ideals concerning equality between the sexes have seldom been realized in a full and consistent manner.

The Prophet Muhammad demonstrated through his life and actions the special importance of equality, proper etiquette, and the mutual expression of love and kindness between the sexes. He strictly prohibited the beating of women, which was a common practice before his time. He also successfully campaigned against killing newborn daughters out of shame. He firmly established women's rights to property, inheritance, and equality before the law. With the purpose of promoting personal modesty and preventing sexual corruption, he enjoined men and women not to expose their bodies in public, except in the company of their spouses and family members. He also commanded both men and women to lower their gaze in public places. He prohibited celibacy and strongly encouraged marriage, stating: "Marriage is my practice; whoever turns away from my practice is not from me." The Prophet first married at age twenty-five, to his wife Khadija, a forty-year-old widow. They lived together for about 25 years and had six children. After her death, he contracted other marriages with elderly and widowed women, mostly to support them and keep them from destitution. The one exception to this was Aisha, the only virgin among his wives.

The Qur'an declares that God created man and woman from one soul in a perfect manner: "O people! Take shelter in your Lord, Who created you from a single self and created from it its mate, and spread, from these two, men and women in abundance. And guard yourselves [for Allah] in Whom you claim [your rights with one another], and do not cut the ties [of kinship] to the wombs [that bore you]. Truly Allah is ever watchful over you." (Q 4:1). It is significant that the wording of the previous verse is explicit in ruling out that the first woman was derived or created from the first man. Instead, both are created simultaneously from a single primordial self.

Love and affection between men and women likewise comes from God: "And among His Signs is that He created for you mates from among yourselves, that you may find tranquility in them, and He has put love and mercy between you. Surely in this are Signs for a people who reflect" (Q 30:21). God's purpose in creating differences between the sexes is not only to facilitate reproduction but also to play a role in God's self-disclosure through human diversity at other levels: "O people, surely We have created you female and male and made you peoples and tribes, so that you might come to know one another. Truly the most honorable among you in the sight of Allah is the one who is most conscious of Allah, warding off evil [within and without]" (Q 49:13).

According to the Qur'an, the duties and the rights of both sexes are the same, except that man is elevated one degree above woman because particular financial responsibilities are imposed upon him as the head of the household (see Q 2:221; 3:195; 4:32; 4:124; 6:139; 9:67–68; 9:71–72; 16:58–59; 16:97; 24:30–31; 33:35; 33:58; 33:73; 40:40; 42:49–50; 47:19; 48:5–6; 57:12; 57:18; 60:10). Expressed metaphorically, man and woman are "garments" for each other (Q 2:187), providing protection, pleasure, adornment, and beauty to one other.

The Qur'an tells us that the first marriage was conducted in Paradise between Adam and Eve before their fall from Paradise (the Qur'an does not blame Eve [*Hawwa* in Arabic] for the first sin committed in Paradise; see Q 7:20–23, and many similar passages, where it is made clear that the fall from this original state of grace is a responsibility shared equally between Eve and Adam). The act of marriage in this world must be undertaken in the intention and expectation of permanence, as the righteous married couple who love each other has the choice to continue their marriage, even after death, in Paradise (Q 36:56; 40:8; 43:70). The Qur'an strongly recommends a man to have only one wife based on the reason that it would be almost impossible to maintain justice among multiple wives (Q 4:129). However, it also allows a man to have up to four wives provided that he treats each one of them equally.

The only woman whose proper name is openly mentioned in the Qur'an is the Virgin Mary, in Arabic *Maryam,* to whom chapter nineteen is devoted. Chapter four in the Qur'an is titled "Women" and presents some, but by no means all, of the issues in relations between the sexes. Another chapter ("The Woman Who Pleads") describes the struggle of one woman for the rights of all women. Following a dispute with the Prophet Muhammad, she pleaded to God for the abolition of an unjust pre-Islamic custom, and God accepts her prayers by prohibiting that custom (Q 58:1–3).

In Islamic law the members of both sexes are treated equally at the level of basic rights: inviolability of life, property, religion, consciousness, family, and honor. Islamic law granted women the right to work, to own property, and to inherit it, which were rather exceptional rights in the seventh century compared with other legal systems where women could not own property independent of their husbands up until recently.

Islamic law took special measures to protect women from false accusations by male members of the community for unchaste behavior. If such a claim is not proved with certainty by the testimony of four direct witnesses, the person who makes the false accusation is severely punished (Q 24:4, 24:19, 24:23). Furthermore, because he has been shown to be dishonest, he loses his right to testify before a court from that point forward. In Islamic law, differences between the sexes emerge in such issues as each parent's necessary role in the family, testimony in court, and inheritance.

Unlike many religions, sexuality is not stigmatized in Islam. On the contrary, moral and moderate sexuality is sanctified within the boundaries clearly set by the Qur'an and the example and teachings of the Prophet Muhammad. Adultery and fornication are strongly prohibited (Q 4:24–27; 5:5; 17:32; 25:68). The sexual attraction between members of the opposite sex is a creation of God which functions as a crucial drive for reproduction, but complete surrender to lust is considered destructive. Moderation and morality in sexual life are enforced by laws and moral guidelines; while the jurists dealt with the legal rules, the Sufis concentrated in their writings on moral education by cleansing the heart to protect a person from the danger of enslavement by lust. The Sufis saw human love as a stepping-stone to divine love. An important means of protecting self-restraint against overwhelming lust is the lowering of the gaze and not looking at members of the opposite sex, particularly at the eyes. A lustful gaze is condemned as a sin and as "adultery by the eyes," which is very much in line with the biblical judgment on the same issue (Matthew 5:27–29).

In a marriage, both parties have the right to sexual satisfaction, which in its absence may constitute a legal ground for divorce. Lawful sex and sexual satisfaction are praised as aids to the concentration of the mind and heart and a means of protection for both wife and husband from sin and corruption. Above all, a lawful and moderate outlet for sexual expression protects the gaze of the eyes from unlawful and immoral looks. Husband and wife are required to love and respect each other and to be responsive to each other's sexual needs. It is the duty of both partners to offer their best in the relationship.

The medieval Islamic literature does not recognize a conflict between *agape* (divine love) and *eros* (human love); instead, sexuality and love were not seen to be mutually exclusive. In place of conflict the relationship between them was characterized as complementary, similar to the relationship between *ying* and *yang* in Taoism. In contrast with medieval Christianity, which maintained a high level of tension between *agape* and *eros* (see John 2:15–17), a Muslim is encouraged both to marry and to love his or her spouse. Human feelings of love in marriage are reinforced by divine command, as conjugal love is required to be for the sake of God and with the intention of following His command and the tradition of the Prophet Muhammad. This positive approach to sexuality and love between the sexes drew criticism from some Christian theologians during the Middle Ages as evidence of depraved sensuality.

RECEP SENTURK

Further Reading

Barlas, Asma. *"Believing Women" in Islam: Unreading Patriarchal Interpretations of the Quran.* Austin: University of Texas Press, 2002.

Bell, Norment Joseph. *Love Theory in Later Hanbalite Islam.* Albany, NY: State University of New York Press, 1979.

Mernissi, Fatima. *The Veil and the Male Elite: A Feminist Interpretation of Women's Rights in Islam.* Philadelphia: Perseus, 1992.

Murata, Sachiko. *The Tao of Islam: A Sourcebook on Gender Relationships in Islamic Thought.* Albany, NY: SUNY Press, 1992.

Schimmel, Annemarie. *My Soul Is a Woman: The Feminine in Islam.* New York: Continuum, 2003.

Stowasser, Barbara Freyer. *Women in the Qur'an, Traditions, and Interpretation.* Oxford: Oxford University Press, 1994.

Wadud, Amina. *Qur'an and Woman: Rereading the Sacred Text from a Woman's Perspective.* Oxford: Oxford University Press, 1999.

GENGHIS KHAN

Genghis Khan (Mongolian: Chinggis; 1167–1227 CE) was the founder of the Mongolian world empire. Most of the information about his life is derived from the anonymous and partly mythical Mongolian source known as *The Secret History of the Mongols,* compiled probably around 1228. Born as Temüjin to a minor chieftain in northeastern Mongolia, the future Genghis Khan went through hard times as a youth. When Temüjin was just nine, his father Yesugei was poisoned by an enemy tribe. Yesugei's supporters abandoned Temüjin's family to its fate. Gradually, Temüjin managed to attract supporters from other clans and tribes, who became his *nökörs* (followers, comrades) and began to assert his authority over his clan and over the neighboring Turco-Mongol tribes. He advanced by forging alliances with influential leaders, then discarding them after they had served their turns. During his rise to power he attacked and executed his "sworn brother," Jamuqa, and his first patron, Ong Khan. In 1184, Temüjin was enthroned the khan of his tribe, the Mongols, and in 1206, an assembly of the Mongol tribes *(quriltai)* proclaimed him as Genghis Khan, the harsh or universal khan, ruler of all the Mongols. Soon after the *quriltai,* Genghis Khan began his conquests. First, he turned to China, starting by attacking the Xi Xia dynasty in northwestern China in 1207 and reducing it into a tributary state in 1209. In 1211, Genghis Khan turned against the Jin dynasty that had ruled in Manchuria and northern China, and in 1215, he conquered its capital in present-day Beijing. Then his attention was drawn westward. In 1218, he overran the Central Asian empire of the Qara Khitai, which had been briefly ruled by one of his old enemies in Mongolia, Küchlüg (Güchülüg). This conquest brought Genghis Khan face to face with the empire of the Khwarazm Shah, the strongest ruler in the eastern Islamic world. Khwarazm's massacre of a group of merchants who

Detail of Genghis Khan and his sons by Rashid al-Din (d. 1318). Persian manuscript. 19157, Sup Pers 113, f.44. Credit: Art Resource, NY. Bibliotheque Nationale, Paris, France.

served as Genghis Khan's messengers in 1218 furnished a pretext for a long and bloody campaign against the Khwarazm Shah (1219–1224), in which the great Transoxianan cities of Bukhara and Samarqand were fiercely sacked, Khurasanian cities were razed to the ground, and millions of Muslims were slaughtered. Moreover, the neglect and ruin of Iran's irrigation system during the Mongol invasion inflicted long-term damages on Iranian agriculture. The Mongol troops chased the fleeing Khwarazm Shah to the Caspian Sea, and his son to the Indus. Returning to Mongolia on the road to the north of the Caspian Sea, Genghis Khan's generals also conquered vast tracts of Russia. Genghis Khan's last campaign was the final subjugation of the Xi Xia dynasty in 1227, during which the great conqueror died.

Genghis Khan died ruling over the territory between northern China and the Caspian Sea. Yet apart from this spectacular military success, he also laid institutional foundations for an empire that continued to expand for several generations. One of his main achievements was the reorganization of the army: he retained the traditional decimal units (of ten, one hundred, one thousand, and ten thousand men) but eliminated its connection to the tribal system. Tribes (or their remnants) were divided among the different units, which were headed by Genghis Khan's loyal nökers. They replaced the former tribal elite and became a focus of loyalty and identification. This disciplined and mobile army was also armed with an ideology, according to which Heaven entrusted Genghis Khan with the mission of world dominion, their blessing demonstrated by his spectacular success.

Genghis Khan also created a law system for his people, known as the Yasa (jasaq), the exact form and contents of which are still debated among scholars. He also established a juridical system, which benefited from his former decision to adopt the Uighur script for writing the Mongolian language. Genghis Khan borrowed administrators and administrative techniques from the states that came under his control, making use of different ethnic groups, such as Khitans, Uighurs, Khwarazmians, and Chinese. The combination of the newly organized army, the unprecedented amount of devastation it created, and Mongol willingness to learn from their subjects were among the main reasons for Genghis Khan's success.

Despite his tolerant attitude toward Islam and religions in general, Genghis Khan's violent invasion into the Muslim world, and his heirs' extermination of the 'Abbasid caliphate, earned him the reputation of an archenemy of Islam. However, with the Islamization of the Mongols in Iran and later in southern Russia and Central Asia in the late thirteenth to mid-fourteenth centuries, Genghis Khan became the revered father of and a source of political legitimacy to several Muslim dynasties in the Turco-Iranian world. The Genghisid principle, according to which only descendants of Genghis can bear the title of khan, remained valid in Muslim Central Asia until the nineteenth century, and the Yasa ascribed to him influenced the legal and political systems of the Uzbeks, Mughals, and Ottomans. While in the modern Arab world Genghis Khan is usually portrayed as a villain, the Turco-Iranian world gives more credit to his heroic achievements.

MICHAL BIRAN

See also Bukhara; Central Asia; China; India; Khurasan; Mongol Warfare; Mongols; Mughals; Nomadism and Pastoralism; Samarqand; Silk Road; Tamerlane; Transoxiana

Further Reading

Anonymous. Shengwu qingzheng lu [Record of the Personal Campaigns of the Holy Warrior], ed. Wang Guowei. In *Wang Guowei yi shu.* Shanghai 1983. Vol. 13; translation of part 1 in *Histoire des Campagnes de Gengis Khan.* Ed. and trans. P. Pelliot and L. Hambis. Leiden, 1951, vol. 1.

Ibn al-Athīr, ʿIzz al-Dīn ʿAlī. *Al-Kāmil fī al-taʾrīkh.* 13 vols. Beirut, 1966,.

Juwaynī, ʿAlāʾ al-Dīn ʿAÔāʾ-malik. *Taʾrīkh-i Jahān-Gushā.* Ed. M. M. Qazwīnī. 3 vols. London, 1912–1937; *History of World Conqueror.* Trans. J.A. Boyle. Rpt. Manchester, 1997.

Jūzjānī, Minhāj al-Dīn. *Ṭabaqāt-i NāÔirī.* Ed. W. Nassau Lees. Calcutta, 1864.

———, ed. A. Habibi. Kabul, 1342–1344/1963–1964. 2 vols; *Tabakāt-i NāÔirī.* Trans. H. G. Raverty. 2 vols. London, 1881–1899.

De Rachewiltz, I., transl. and annot. *The Secret History of the Mongols: A Mongolian Epic Chronicle of the Thirteenth Century.* 2 vols. Brill, 2004.

Rashīd al-Dīn, FaÄlallāh Abū al-Khayr. *Jāmiʿ al-tawārīkh.* Ed. B. Karīmī. 2 vols. Tehran, 1338/1959.

Jamiʾuʾt-tawarikh [sic] *Compendium of Chronicles.* 3 vols. Trans. W.M. Thackston. Cambridge, MA, 1998–1999.

Studies

Allsen, Thomas T. "The Rise of the Mongolian Empire and Mongolian Rule in North China." In *The Cambridge History of China, Vol. 6.* Eds. H. Franke and D. Twitchett, 321–413. Cambridge: Cambridge University Press, 1994.

De Rachewiltz, Igor. "The Title Ÿinggis Qan/Qaʾan Reconsidered." In *Gedanke und Wirkung. Festschrift zum 90. Geburstag von Nikolaus Poppe.* Wiesbaden: Harrasowich, 1989, 281–298.

McChesney, Robert D. *Central Asia: Foundations of Change.* Princeton, 1996.

Morgan, David O. *The Mongols.* Oxford: Blackwell, 1986.

———. *Medieval Persia.* London: Longman, 1988.

Ratchnevsky, Paul. *Genghis Khan—His Life and Legacy.* Trans. T.N. Haining. Oxford: Blackwell, 1991.

GENIZA

Definition, Collection, and Contents

Jews in the lands of Islam deposited damaged sacred books in repositories called *geniza* or *genizah* prior to giving them a proper ritual burial in their cemeteries. Sacred books—primarily those with the name of God written upon them—were treated with the same respect as the human body and were never simply thrown away. In time, this respect accorded to sacred books was extended to written documents in general, nearly all of which contained the name of God due to the numerous blessings, invocations, and eulogies that were a part of epistolary convention. We know of genizas only in the lands of the Arabic-speaking world. In Cairo, genizas have been found at a Karaite synagogue, in the Basatine cemetery, and at the Ben Ezra synagogue in Old Cairo (called Fustat in the Middle Ages). The largest of these repositories, which is commonly referred to as the "Cairo Geniza," was the one at the Ben Ezra synagogue. The contents of the Cairo Geniza were transferred to European and American libraries in the late nineteenth century. The only geniza documents remaining in Egypt are those excavated in the 1980s by the Egyptian Department of Antiquities from three sites in the Basatine cemetery.

Genizas As a Source for Jewish History and Culture

The contents of the Cairo Geniza, which date largely to the years 1000–1300 CE, are of central importance for the information they provide about the history of the local Jewish communities of medieval Egypt, the Jewish communities of Palestine and North Africa, and their relations with communities elsewhere in the Near East. Marriage contracts between Rabbanite and Karaite couples (with special provisions relating to religious practice), charity lists containing the names of both Rabbanite and Karaite contributors and recipients, and business documents all provide evidence for extensive social and economic relations between Rabbanite and Karaite communities, in spite of their doctrinal and ritual differences. The Cairo Geniza also yields materials to write the social and institutional history of major Jewish institutions of law and higher learning in Mesopotamia. Our knowledge of the actual workings of the Babylonian academies has been expanded greatly by the materials available in the Geniza.

Geniza fragments allow us to contextualize previously known Jewish philosophical works in Judeo-Arabic (a form of Arabic written in Hebrew characters) and Hebrew, providing information about the circumstances of their composition, their distribution and readership, and their reception. In the case of the *Kuzari* of Judah ha-Levi (ca. 1071–1141), letters from a merchant friend of his reveal that the first version of the book was written as a response to a Karaite who lived in a Christian country. In addition, the Geniza has provided important finds for the historical reconstruction of religious texts and their variants. For example, the importance and specific content of the Palestinian Talmud is now known in some detail. Similarly, original Hebrew versions of books such as the *Ecclesiasticus* of Ben Sira, once thought lost forever, were in circulation in the Islamic world in the Middle Ages and are now available to us. In addition, the existence of a rich post-Talmudic exegetical literature is known from the answers of legal authorities to questions addressed to them *(responsa)*, many of which were deposited in the Geniza.

While most genizas were repositories for prayer books and other sacred writings, the Jews of medieval Egypt deposited a variety of different documents, including business accounts, wills, inventories of various kinds, marriage contracts, trousseau lists, wills, and commercial and private correspondence. Based largely on these documents, S.D. Goitein (1900–1985) produced his five-volume magnum opus, *A Mediterranean Society*, which provides a comprehensive picture of the social, economic, communal, family, and religious history of the Jewish communities of medieval Egypt.

Geniza documents reveal that Jews were integrated into economic and social life in Islamic lands to a very high degree. There were no legal restrictions on the economic activities of Jews and Christians, and the Geniza makes it clear that no social or cultural impediments to full participation in economic life existed. Unlike Christian Europe, where Jews were restricted to a small number of occupations and could not own property, the Geniza reveals Jews working in hundreds of occupations and owning property. The documents of Jewish pious foundations reveal that the poll tax was not merely a symbolic payment, but was a significant financial burden for Jewish communities and a major expenditure for Jewish charities. The documents of the Geniza show clearly that some provisions of the Pact of Umar were often ignored and became an issue largely at times of economic and political stress. Family life, particularly social and economic aspects of marriage, is richly documented. From the Geniza we learn, in some detail, that Jews in the lands of Islam practiced polygyny. We learn also about the daily lives of women, including their extensive economic activities. The Geniza provides ample evidence of Jewish use of the Muslim courts even to adjudicate disputes between Jews, who had the right under Islamic law to appeal intracommunal disputes to the rabbinic courts.

The predominant language of the documentary material of the Cairo Geniza is Judeo-Arabic. The Judeo-Arabic of the Geniza documents is characterized by the use of quotations in Hebrew and Aramaic from the Bible and the Talmud, and by the assimilation of Hebrew vocabulary into Arabic. The use of Judeo-Arabic in writing, as well as in speech, reflects the fact that, by the tenth century, Arabic had displaced Aramaic as the lingua franca of Jews (and other communities) in the lands of Islam. The use of an Arabic vernacular had a noticeable impact on the development of religious and philosophical thought among Jewish thinkers. One major effect of this exposure to the so-called secular branches of learning that were widespread among Muslim intellectuals in the ninth and tenth centuries was the adoption of rationalist thinking as a method of studying Jewish texts. Arabophone Jewish rationalists embraced the exegetical culture of the classical Islamic world and began to write commentaries on Torah and other parts of the Hebrew Bible in Arabic. Later commentators used the same rationalist methods to produce commentaries in Hebrew. The study of Hebrew grammar came to be considered fundamental to the exegetical enterprise and was developed along the model of Arabic grammar.

Genizas As a Source of Information on Islamic History and Culture

The Geniza contributes to many aspects of broader Islamic history and is particularly rich in many areas that are otherwise sparsely documented. Arabic scribal encyclopedias and historical works, often written at a much later period, describe administrative structures and transmit caliphal and administrative decrees from the eleventh through the thirteenth centuries, but they are often described in anachronistic terms. Legal documents of various kinds and administrative documents emanating from the government chanceries are rare, and they are known largely from the Geniza. A number of these legal documents are contracts concerning the sale of properties. These documents are written in Arabic script, and many are contracts between Muslim parties that made their way into the Geniza because they concerned a property that eventually came into the hands of Jews, at which time the contracts documenting the property's history came into the possession of these later owners. Other documents no doubt made their way into the Geniza because they were registered in a court archive, an act that gave the written document a probative value that it would not otherwise have had in the Islamic legal system, in which oral testimony was ordinarily required as legal proof. Arabic Geniza documents reveal the frequent use of petitions to rulers, judges, and other dignitaries to appeal for assistance or redress grievances. The information in literary historical sources about petitions is more than verified by the petitions in the Geniza, many of them from the Fatimid (969–1171) and Ayyubid (1171–1250) periods.

The Geniza provides extensive material on commerce. It contains hundreds of trade letters, many between Jewish merchants but a significant number involving Muslims and Christians. These letters, as well as inventories, accounts, and court cases, demonstrate the extensive use of informal cooperation and partnerships that characterized commerce in the medieval Islamic world. They also document the range of techniques used to provide credit, given Islamic law's prohibition on interest, particularly the use of the *commenda*. Commercial documents and letters from the Geniza provide impressive detail on industries, manufacturing processes, local and regional market conditions and prices, and business practices. We also learn from these documents that the government's involvement in commerce was expressed primarily in exercising its rights as first buyer and in the collection of taxes. One of the richest contributions of the Geniza is to the history of material culture. The trousseau lists, inventories, accounts, and business letters provide voluminous information about textiles and clothing, including details about color, fabric, ornamentation, and value. Collectively, the Geniza provides extensive lexical material, allowing us to understand vocabulary in Arabic historical texts that would otherwise remain obscure. Similar information is available about housing, furnishings, food, and jewelry.

PAULA SANDERS

See also Family; Grammar and Grammarians; Hebrew and Judeo–Arabic; Interfaith Relations; Jewish Languages; Jews; Marriage, Jewish; Textiles; Trade, Mediterranean; Translation, Arabic to Hebrew; Usury and Interest

Further Reading

Ben-Shammai, Haggai. "Medieval History and Religious Thought." In *The Cambridge Genizah Collections: Their Contents and Significance*, ed. Stefan C. Reif. Cambridge: Cambridge University Press, 2002.

Brody, Robert. *The Geonim of Babylonia and the Shaping of Medieval Jewish Culture*. New Haven and London: Yale University Press, 1998.

Cohen, Mark. *Jewish Self-Government in Medieval Egypt*. Princeton: Princeton University Press, 1980.

———. "Goitein, the Geniza, and Muslim History." Available on line at *www.dayan.org/mel/cohen.htm* (2001).

Friedman, M.A. *Jewish Marriage in Palestine: A Cairo Geniza Study*. Tel Aviv: Tel-Aviv University, Chaim Rosenberg School of Jewish Studies; New York: Jewish Theological Seminary of America, 1980–1981.

Gil, Moshe. *Documents of the Jewish Pious Foundations from the Cairo Genizah*. Leiden: E. J. Brill, 1976.

Goitein, S.D. *Letters of Medieval Jewish Traders*. Princeton: Princeton University Press, 1973.

———. *A Mediterranean Society: The Jewish Communities of the Arab World As Portrayed in the Documents of the Cairo Geniza*. 6 vols. Berkeley and Los Angeles: University of California Press, 1967–1993.

Kahle, Paul. *The Cairo Geniza*. Oxford: Blackwell Press, 1959.

Khan, Geoffrey. *Arabic Legal and Administrative Documents in the Cambridge Genizah Collections*. Cambridge: Cambridge University Press, 1993.

Lambert, Phyllis, ed. *Fortifications and the Synagogue: The Fortress of Babylon and the Ben Ezra Synagogue, Cairo*. London: Weidenfeld & Nicolson, 1994.

Olszowy-Schlanger, Judith. *Karaite Marriage Documents from the Cairo Geniza: Legal Tradition and Community Life in Mediaeval Egypt and Palestine*. Leiden: E. J. Brill, 1998.

Rabi', Hasanayn Muhammad. *Dalil watha'iq wa-awraq al-Jiniza al-jadidah (Catalogue of latest Geniza Documents and Papers)*. Al-Qahirah: Jami'at al-Qahirah, Markaz al-Dirasat al-Sharqiyah, 1993.

Reif, Stefan C. "A Centennial Assessment of Genizah Studies." In *The Cambridge Genizah Collections: Their Contents and Significance*, ed. Stefan C. Reif. Cambridge: Cambridge University Press, 2002.

———. *A Jewish Archive from Old Cairo: The History of Cambridge University's Genizah Collection*. Richmond, Surrey: Curzon Press, 2000.

Stillman, Yedida. "Female Attire of Medieval Egypt: According to the Trousseau Lists and Cognate Material from the Cairo Geniza." Ph.D. dissertation, University of Pennsylvania, 1972.

Udovitch, Abraham L. *Partnership and Profit in Medieval Islam*. Princeton: Princeton University Press, 1970.

GEOGRAPHY

The science of geography in Islam developed on a foundation of previous civilizations and was strongly impacted by the expansion of the Islamic state and the spread of the Islamic faith. The rise of the Islamic empire entailed four major developments in regard to scientific geography and travel: (1) the rise of a need for geography as an auxiliary discipline to government and administration; (2) access to the academic and cultural heritage of the Hellenic, Mesopotamian, Iranian, Indian, and other civilizations conquered by Islam; (3) a new impetus and opportunities for travel, exploration, and long-distance trade; and (4) a specifically Islamic branch of cartography and astronomical geography focused on Mecca and the direction of prayer (*qibla*, q.v.). The great majority of geographical works combined aspects of science and literature and were composed in Arabic, although non-Arabs and even non-Muslims made important contributions. Some scholars treated geography as part of history; it was also customary to discuss other sciences in the introductions to geographical works. For some parts of the world, or certain periods of their history, medieval Islamic geographers provide major, if not the only, sources of information. Their works are thus invaluable and often indispensable to the study of history and historical ethnography, as well as historical geography and the history of science.

The cosmographic views of early Muslims absorbed the pre-Islamic vision of the world registered in the Qur'an and some *hadiths*, or the pre-Islamic traditions recorded in the second and third centuries of Islam by authors such as the historian al-Dinawari (d. AH 281 or 282/894–895 CE) and geographers such as al-Ya'qubi (259–292/872–873 to 905), al-Hamdani (d. 334/945), al-Mas'udi (d. 345/956). According to one view recorded by al-Ya'qubi, the earth has the shape of a bird with spread wings whose head is in the East (China), tail in the West, and the breast encompasses Mecca, Hijaz, Syria, Iraq, and Egypt, that is, the core of the early Islamic empire. The Umayyad postal service drove the development of precise itineraries and distance measurements. The Roman mile, *mil* (pronounced "meel"), became the common unit of distance in the western parts of the empire. Another measure of distance was the Iranian *farsakh*, equal to three *mil*s (six kilometers). Itineraries also used "marches" *(marhal)* or "days of journey" (approximately twenty kilometers). Degrees of longitude and latitude were long confined to works of mathematical geography and only gradually made their way into geographical narratives. They are not found on extant maps predating the fourteenth century, even those using grids.

Among the earliest geographical compositions are travel records of the Umayyad period and the early genre of *fada'il*, descriptions of "advantages" of places sacred to Muslims in some ways, which later acquired an increasingly secular nature. Scientific Islamic geography began in Baghdad in the early 'Abbasid period and was particularly encouraged by the caliph al-Ma'mun (r. 198–218/813–833). The first steps included the measurement of the degree of latitude, construction of observatories, production of maps and instruments, and especially the translation and adaptation of Indian, Iranian, and Greek geographical and astronomical treatises. Among the Indian borrowings were the imaginary Mount Meru, the highest point on dry land directly under the North Pole, the division of the inhabited regions of the earth into nine sections, and the calculation of the longitude from the meridian of Sri Lanka, drawn from Mount Meru through the Cupola of the Earth (Ar. *Arin*, from Ujjain—modern Avanti—site of an ancient Indian observatory). From the Greeks were borrowed

the limitations of the inhabited world to a quarter of the globe, the concept of the continents (Europe, Libya, Ethiopia, Scythia), the idea of the Indian Ocean landlocked between Asia and Africa, and the word *jughrafiya* for the discipline. In mathematical geography Arabic scholars accepted the system of seven latitudinal climates, or climes (Ar. *aqalim*; sing. *iqlim*), from the equator to the polar circle. Ptolemy's *Geography* was translated repeatedly (as was his *Almagest*); particularly influential was the version of al-Khwarizmi (also Khorezmi, fl. ca. 205/820). Iranian influences were the strongest in descriptive geography and in cartography, including the method of describing the world following the four cardinal directions (beginning in the East) and the division of the earth into seven *kishvarha* (equal geometric circles), the central one representing Iran (with Mesopotamia). The lost map of al-Ma'mun supposedly followed this pattern, though it was also supposed to use the projection of Marinus.

Other notable early advances in Islamic geography came when the administrators of the vast, newly reordered empire composed or commissioned geographical reference books in the genre of *Masalik wa al-Mamalik* (Routes and Kingdoms), from the title of the first extant composition of this nature, by Ibn Khurdadhbih (ca. 205–300/820–912). Other authors include al-Balkhi (235–322/849–850 to 934), al-Istakhri (ca. 340/951), and Ibn al-Faqih al-Hamadhani (ca. 290/903), all of whom functioned in the eastern parts of the empire. These treatises concentrate on such practical needs of government as topography, administrative information, commercial and postal routes, and descriptions of boundaries. A separate branch of mathematical geography, shaped by Ptolemaic influence, was developed by al-Khwarizmi, al-Farghani (Alfraganus, fl. 247/861), and al-Battani (Albategnius, d. AH929). To begin with, their works contained the tables of astronomical coordinates of locations and geographical features, and descriptions of maps with coordinates (very few of the maps survive).

During the classical period of Islamic geography (ninth to eleventh centuries), two schools of descriptive geography developed. The first was the Iraqi school, so called because it often followed the Iranian system of *kishvars*, but substituted Iraq (the center of the 'Abbasid caliphate) for Iran as the center of the Islamic empire. This school included Ibn Khurdadhbih, al-Ya'qubi, Ibn Rusta (fl. ca. 290–300/903–913), Ibn al-Faqih, and al-Mas'udi, all of whom wrote world geographies. Al-Ya'qubi and al-Mas'udi traveled extensively, but their personal experiences seem to have had little effect on their geographical concepts. The second school was that of al-Balkhi, whose own work does not survive. Among his followers were al-Istakhri, Ibn Hawqal (ca. 366/977), and al-Muqaddasi (al-Maqdisi, ca. 335–390/946–947 to 1000). These geographers focused on the world of Islam and attached central importance to Mecca. They introduced the concept of a country as a geographical unit and enlarged the scope of their science with elements of "human geography," discussing the languages and races of people, their occupations, customs, and religions. Firsthand observation during their travels was an important source of information for these authors, though they also borrowed heavily from their predecessors. Al-Muqaddasi, the last and most original representative of this school, created the systematic foundation of Arab geography by discussing its uses and scopes, the geographical terminology, the various methods of division of the earth, and the value of empirical observation. A distinctive characteristic of this school is its attention to cartography. Texts often seem to follow the map and were usually accompanied by a set of twenty-one maps: one of each of the twenty climes or regions into which they divided Islamic lands, and one world map. These maps are very similar to each other in character and are composed of peculiarly simplified geometric shapes. They show roads and towns but give no indication of coordinates or distances; collectively, they are known today as the "Atlas of Islam."

The physical geography of Muslim scholars in part depended on their Greek precursors and in part contributed new thinking on the nature of physical phenomena. They saw the earth as a sphere, resembling the yoke within the white of the egg. They understood that the changing positioning of the sun resulted in differences between climatic zones: hot, temperate, and cold. They agreed that climate, topography, and soils conditioned the spatial distribution of life and water. They discussed the causes of wind, clouds, rain, tides, and earthquakes. Many geographers who adopted the Greek notion of the Inhabited Quarter assumed that the parts of the earth south of the equator were uninhabitable due to excessive heat. Unique among the geographers of the late classical period of Islam is al-Biruni (*c.* 442/1050). Apart from his important contribution to regional geography (he described India in detail), he compared and critically evaluated the contributions to geography of the Arabs, Greeks, Indians, and Iranians. An advanced theoretician of geography and astronomy, he was also a bold and undogmatic thinker. For example, he discussed the difference in seasons between the northern and southern hemispheres and argued that, contrary to the prevailing views, life was possible south of the equator; he, alone, among Muslim geographers conjectured that the Indian Ocean communicated with the Atlantic (the earliest maps showing the Indian Ocean somewhat realistically are considerably older, found in manuscripts ascribed to Ibn Sa'id al-Maghribi [610–673 or 685/1214–1274 or 1286] and the encyclopedist Ibn Fadlallah al-'Umari [700–749/1301–1349]).

The spirit of exploration and inquiry generated both active travel beyond the better-known areas of the Middle East, India, and Africa and demand among the reading public for travel accounts. Some of these accounts were reports of authentic journeys, such as Ibn Fadlan's diplomatic mission to the Volga region (ca. 921) and Ibrahim ibn Ya'qub's journey from Spain to Germany (ca. 354/965). Others belong to the genre of *'aja'ib* (marvels): surviving compositions by Abu Zayd al-Sirafi (ca. 306/916) and Buzurg ibn Shahriyar (ca. 342/953) contain, together with factual information, semilegendary stories, including maritime tales; a few found their way into the *One Thousand and One Nights* as the stories of Sinbad the Sailor and may have been heard by Marco Polo. Yet, although Muslim seafarers knew the Indian Ocean well enough to sail from Malacca to Southeast Africa, the formal geographical works say disappointingly little about distant areas. Moreover, the new facts were often overlooked or stubbornly fitted into the old theoretically devised patterns. This conservative attitude forced practical geography to yield to theory and gradually led to scientific stagnation.

In the area of world geography the highest achievement was attained by al-Idrisi (493–560/1098–1165), who worked at the Norman court in Sicily and used data produced by the Islamic and European geographers and travelers. His *Nuzhat al-Mushtaq fi Ikhtiraq al-Afaq* (Entertainment for One Who Wants to Travel the World) was conceived as a description of a large map, each chapter detailing itineraries within one of seventy sections illustrated by a regional map. The innovation was to subdivide each of the seven Greek climes into ten longitudinal sections, starting from the west. Although some of the information was incorrect or outdated even at the time, as a universal geography his work remained unsurpassed in the Islamic world, and among mapmakers al-Idrisi's cartographic tradition survived as late as the sixteenth century. His system influenced Ibn Sa'id al-Maghribi, who supplemented his description with the coordinates of many locations, and Ibn Khaldun.

The twelfth to sixteenth centuries produced little conceptual development, but they are marked by the emergence of new specialized genres: geographical dictionaries, cosmographies, travel narratives *(rihla)* and pilgrimage guides *(ziyarat)*, and the works of marine geography. The largest and most famous geographical dictionary is that of Yaqut (ca. 575–626/1179–1229), who presents a great number of place-names, listed alphabetically and accompanied by a wealth of geographical and historical information. His method and much of his information were borrowed by the most prominent cosmographer, Zakariya al-Qazwini (d. 682/1283), whose works remain popular even with modern Arab readers. Specifically Islamic variations of the dictionary genre were the guides to religious places or pilgrimage centers, the *ziyarat* (see pilgrimage); the most famous of these is by al-Harawi (d. 611/1215). Among the travel narratives, of particular significance for Arabia was the work of Ibn al-Mujawir (ca. 626/1229); for the Near East, that of Ibn Jubayr (540–614/1145–1217); and for Europe, Abu Hamid al-Andalusi (473–565/1080–1170). The most outstanding traveler, Ibn Battuta, whose journeys took him from his native Maghrib to Arabia, Europe, Central Asia, India, Indonesia, China, and sub-Saharan Africa, was not famous in his own time.

Outside the Arabic tradition of Islamic geography, Persian scholarship, represented by the anonymous *Hudud al-ʿAlam* (Regions of the World, ca. 372/982), was influenced by the work of al-Istakhri, which had been translated into Persian. Some of al-Biruni's works were originally written in, or later translated into, Persian. His contemporary, Nasir-i Khusraw (394–481/1003–1060), wrote in Persian, describing the travels in Egypt and Arabia. Generally derivative of Arabic authorities, the works in Persian were produced mainly in Iran, Central Asia, and India. The development of Ottoman geography began in the fourteenth century. At first it popularized translations of Arab cosmographies; later translations were also made from Persian and Greek. From the early sixteenth century, Ottoman geography was continuously influenced by European scholarship, especially in cartography. A specifically Ottoman genre was represented by the campaign itineraries of the Turkish sultans.

All the main genres of Islamic geographical literature had been set by the fourteenth century. Although travel accounts and regional studies produced new data, systematic innovation ceased. The new cosmographies, often of inferior quality, simply rehashed outdated information. Use of others' material without credit and indiscriminate compilation prevailed, and pre-Islamic concepts and mythological motifs continued to fascinate the reader. Especially popular among these were the Encircling Ocean surrounding the landmass, and Mount Qaf in turn surrounding the ocean; the Fortunate Isles and the Pillars of Hercules as the western boundary of the inhabited earth; the Wall of Alexander separating the civilized world from Gog and Magog; the Isles of Waq-Waq where trees allegedly bore fruit of human heads; and the number seven (seven *climata*, seven *kishvarha*, seven seas). Marine geography for the most part remained outside the mainstream of Islamic scholarship. Only works of Ahmad ibn Majid (second half of the fifteenth century) and Sulayman al-Mahri (first half of the sixteenth century) survive. Among them are sailing manuals and nautical instructions, often in verse (for better memorization by navigators), for the Mediterranean and the Red Seas, but particularly for the Indian Ocean.

The majority of extant Islamic maps are found in copies dating from the thirteenth and later centuries, though the first Islamic reference to mapmaking dates to 83/702. A few authors give instructions for map production, and some texts describe maps, but extant maps cannot be used as exact guides to locations and the projections used are still not fully understood. In form, Arabic maps typically included round world maps and rectangular regional maps. There were also separate maps of seas, small maps of astronomically determined zones, and special Islamic maps of the Kaʿba for orienting the viewer to the *qibla* (sacred direction of prayer) from any location. City plans must have existed, but those extant are from the sixteenth century and later. There are no topographical maps, though there may be some color coding of geographical features such as rivers, cities, mountains, and roads. Ethnic divisions and major features such as deserts are marked in writing. Sailing charts reportedly existed, but none survives.

The round maps show the continents of Europe, Asia, and Africa surrounded by the Encircling Ocean *(al-Bahr al-Muhit)*, which is sometimes surrounded in turn by Mount Qaf, a concept of Qurʾanic cosmogony. Round maps were usually centered on Mesopotamia (in the "Iraqi" school) or Mecca (in the tradition of the "Atlas of Islam"). The oldest Turkish world map, found in the encyclopedia of Mahmud al-Kashghari (ca. 466/1074), is centered on Balasaghun, the capital of the then Uighur state in the mountains of Tien Shan. Round maps were usually oriented to the south or east, rectangular maps almost always to the south. Some round maps mark the seven *climata* of the Inhabited Quarter as latitudinal bands, numbered from the equator to the Polar Circle. The Greco-Muslim tradition of cartography is best represented by al-Idrisi, who adopted Ptolemy's map of the world and, abandoning Ptolemy's outdated content and tables, superimposed on it an enormous amount of new information gathered from books and travelers. Al-Idrisi is also one of the few Arabic scholars who provided instructions for map production and discussed distance measures. His works contain 70 detailed sectional rectangular maps and a round world map; he reportedly created a silver planisphere based on the so-called al-Ma'mun map, which does not survive.

MARINA A. TOLMACHEVA

See also Human Geography

Further Reading

Ahmad, S. Maqbul. *A History of Arab-Islamic Geography (9th–16th century AD)*. Amman: al-Bayit University, 1995.
———. "Djughrafiya." In *The Encyclopaedia of Islam*. New ed. 2:575–587.
———. "Kharita." In *The Encyclopaedia of Islam*. New ed. 4:1077–1083.
Donini, Pier Giovanni. *Arab Travelers and Geographers.* London: IMMEL, 1991.
The History of Cartography, vol. 2, book 1: Cartography in the Traditional Islamic and South Asian Societies. Eds. J.B. Harley and David Woodward. Chicago and London: The University of Chicago Press, 1992.
Ibn Battuta. *The Travels of Ibn Battuta, AD 1325–1354.* Trans. with revisions and notes from the Arabic text C. Defrémery and B.R. Sanguinetti by H.A.R. Gibb. 5 vols. Cambridge: Hakluyt Society, 1971–2000.
Ferrand, Gabriel. *Relations de Voyages et Texts Géographiques Arabes, Persans et Turks, Relatifs à l'Extrême-Orient du VIIIe au XVIIIe siècles.* 2 vols. Paris: Leroux, 1913–1914. Reprint, 2 vols. in one. Frankfurt: Institut für Geschichte der Arabisch-Islamischen Wissenschaften, 1986.
———. *Studies by Gabriel Ferrand on Arab-Muslim Geography, Cartography and Navigation.* Reprint in 3 vols. Ed. Fuat Sezgin. Frankfurt: Institut für Geschichte der Arabisch-Islamischen Wissenschaften, 1994.
Kennedy, Edward S., and Mary Helen Kennedy. *Geographical Coordinates of Localities from Islamic Sources.* Frankfurt: Institut für Geschichte der Arabisch-Islamischen Wissenschaften, 1987.
King, David A. *World-Maps for Finding the Direction and Distance to Mecca: Innovation and Tradition in Islamic Science.* London: Al-Furqan Islamic Heritage Foundation, 1999.
Krachkovskii, I. Iu. *Arabskaia geograficheskaia literatura.* Moscow, Lenigrad: Izdatel'stvo Akademii Nauk SSSR, 1957. Trans. into Arabic Salah al-Din 'Uthman Hashim. *Ta'rikh al-Adab al-Jughrafi al-'Arabi.* 2 vols. Cairo, 1963–1965.
Mappae Arabicae: Arabische Welt- und Länderkarten des 9.-13. Jahrhunderts, ed. Konrad Miller. 5 vols. Stuttgart, 1927–1931. Reprint in 2 vols.: Frankfurt: Institut für Geschichte der Arabisch-Islamischen Wissenschaften, 1994.
Miquel, André. *La Géographie Humaine du Monde Musulman Jusqu'au Milieu du 11e siècle.* 4 vols. Paris, La Haye: Mouton, 1967–1988.
Reinaud, Joseph Toussaint. *Géographie d'Abou 'l-Féda.* Vol. 1: *Introduction Générale á la Géographie des Orientaux.* Paris: Imperimérie Nationale, 1848. Reprint: Frankfurt: Institut für Geschichte der Arabisch-Islamischen Wissenschaften, 1998.
Sezgin, Fuat. *The Contribution of the Arabic-Islamic Geographers to the Formation of the World Map.* Frankfurt: Institut für Geschichte der Arabisch-Islamischen Wissenschaften, 1987.
Sezgin, Fuat. *Mathematische Geographie und Kartographie im Islam und ihr Fortleben im Abendland.* 3 vols. Geschichte des arabischen Schrifttums, vols. X–XII. Frankfurt: Institut für Geschichte der Arabisch-Islamischen Wissenschaften, 2000.
Tolmacheva, Marina. "The Medieval Arabic Geographers and the Beginnings of Modern Orientalism." *International Journal of Middle East Studies* 27 (1995): 141–156.
Youssouf Kamal. *Monumenta Cartographica Africae et Aegypti.* 5 vols. In 16 parts. Cairo, 1926–1951. Reprint in 6 vols. Frankfurt: Institut für Geschichte der Arabisch-Islamischen Wissenschaften, 1987.

GEOMETRY

At the beginning of Islam, some knowledge of geometry was available in Syria and Iran, and in the eighth century CE, practical geometrical rules were transmitted from India into Islamic lands. However, the history of geometry in Islamic civilization really started when the basic textbook of Greek geometry, the *Elements* of Euclid (ca. 300 BCE), was translated into Arabic in Baghdad in the early ninth century CE. Euclid begins with definitions and axioms (fundamental assumptions), but he then proves by logical reasoning a series of more than three hundred geometrical propositions and constructions. Initially, the Islamic scholars of the ninth century CE studied the *Elements* to understand Greek astronomy, but some of them fell in love with Greek geometry for its own sake and searched for Greek manuscripts of the works of Archimedes (ca. 250 BCE) and Appollonius (ca. 200 BCE). In the mid-ninth century CE, the three sons of Musa (Banu Musa)—Ahmad, Muhammad, and Hasan—were interested in the *Conics* on the basis of two very corrupted Greek manuscripts of Books 1–4 and Books 5–7. After they had succeeded, they hired two translators—Hilal ibn Abi Halal al-Himsi and Thabit ibn Qurra—and had them translate Books 1–4 and Books 5–7, respectively. Books 5–7 are now lost in Greek, and thus the Banu Musa sons and Thabit ibn Qurra saved one of the most profound works of Greek geometry for posterity. Book 8 of the *Conics* was entirely lost but reconstructed by Ibn al-Haytham in the early eleventh century.

Already in the mid-tenth century, some Islamic mathematicians embarked on deep investigations of the definitions and basic assumptions made by Euclid in *Elements*. In Book 5 of *Elements*, Euclid presented a complicated definition of proportional magnitudes *(a : b = c : d)* in order to deal with rational and irrational ratios at the same time. In European mathematics the motivation of this definition was understood only after the discovery of the modern concept of real numbers around the year 1860. A thousand years earlier, around 860, the Iranian mathematician al-Mahani had replaced Euclid's definition by an alternative definition related to the modern mathematical theory of continued fractions. He also proved that the two definitions are equivalent. A number of Islamic mathematicians studied Euclid's parallel postulate, to the effect that if two straight lines *m* and *n* are intersected by a straight line *l* in such a way that the sum of the two adjacent angles between *l* and *m* and between *l* and *n* is less than two right angles, the two lines *m* and *n* must intersect. Many mathematicians found it inappropriate that Euclid assumed such a complicated postulate right at the beginning of his work *Elements*. Unfortunately, the postulate is necessary in the proofs of the theorem of Pythagoras and the theorem that the sum of the angles in a triangle is equal to two right angles. Several mathematicians, including Ibn al-Haytham (eleventh century) and Nasir al-Din al-Tusi (thirteenth century), tried to prove Euclid's parallel postulate on the basis of other assumptions that they found more natural or simpler. In the nineteenth century, it turned out that the parallel postulate could not be proved from the other postulates of Euclidean geometry. If we assume the negation of the parallel postulate, we obtain the modern non-Euclidean geometry, which was never studied in medieval Islamic civilization.

In the tenth century, the Islamic geometers in Iraq and Iran started to work on conic sections. They used parabolas and hyperbolas to solve problems such as the construction of the regular heptagon, the trisection of the angle, and cubic equations. By means of conic sections, Ibn al-Haytham solved the following problem in optics, which was later named the "problem of Alhazen" after the Latinized version of his first name al-Hasan: Given a convex or concave circular spherical, cylindrical, or conical mirror, and the positions of the eye and the object, construct the places in the mirror where the eye sees the object. Conic sections were also used for the theoretical construction of some mosaic patterns.

Another theoretical field of study was the determination of surface areas, volumes, and centers of gravity of curvilinear figures. Archimedes' work on the surface area and volume of a sphere had been translated into Arabic, and in the preface to this work, Archimedes says that he had found the area of a parabolic segment as four-thirds of its inscribed

triangle. His work on the parabolic segment, as well as most of his other investigations, were not transmitted into Arabic, and thus the Islamic mathematicians did not know Archimedes' famous work, *Method of Mechanical Theorems*. (This work was discovered around 1900 in a Greek palimpsest manuscript, which was stolen but has since resurfaced.) Thabit ibn Qurra (d. 901), Ibrihim ibn Sinan (d. 946), and Abu Sahl al-Kuhi (ca. 970) succeeded in proving that the area of a parabolic segment is four-thirds of its inscribed triangle. They then went on to study other curved figures and solids. Most of their achievements are independent rediscoveries of results in Archimedes' *Method of Mechanical Theorems*. Ibn al-Haytham determined the volume of a solid not studied by Archimedes, namely the solid of revolution of a parabola around a segment perpendicular to the axis. To solve this difficult problem, Ibn al-Haytham had to find a formula for the sum of the first *n* and fourth powers.

In modern mathematics the surface areas, volumes, and centers of gravity of curved figures and solids are computed by means of the integral calculus, which was discovered in the late seventeenth century by Leibniz and Newton. It does not follow that the Islamic mathematicians possessed anything like the integral calculus, because the methods of Leibniz and Newton were generally applicable, whereas Archimedes and the Islamic mathematicians had to design for every solid a new procedure. It should also be noted that Leibniz and Newton did not prove their methods in ways that are now considered to be rigorous, but Archimedes and the Islamic mathematicians gave rigorous proofs.

Abu Sahl al-Kuhl determined the centers of gravities of various curvilinear solids. He thought that he had found a regularity, and derived $\pi = 3\ 1/9$, in contradiction to the fact that Archimedes had proved that $\pi > 3\ 10/71$. Around 1420, the first sixteen decimals of π were determined correctly by Al-Kashi in Samarkand.

Spherical trigonometry was important in late Greek and medieval Indian and Islamic mathematics because astronomy depends on the accurate computation of arcs on the celestial sphere. In the tenth century, three Iranian mathematicians introduced the concept of a spherical triangle consisting of six elements: three arcs of great circles and three angles contained by these arcs. A little later, the methods are analogous to, but more complicated than, the formulas for a plane triangle. The solution of spherical triangles was studied systematically by al-Biruni around 1030 and by Nasir al-Din al-Tusi around 1260. The Islamic mathematicians computed trigonometrical tables that were much more accurate than the tables known in Greek and Indian mathematics. A difficult problem is the computation of sines (without computers), especially the computation of the sine of one degree. No exact methods for the computation were known until Al-Kashi (ca. 1420) discovered a method by which the sine of one degree can be easily computed with any desired accuracy. He expressed the unknown sine as the root of a cubic equation with known coefficients. He then presented an easy iterative algorithm for the numerical solution of the cubic equation.

Various projections of the sphere on a plane were applied in geographical maps, and stereographic projection was used in the construction of astrolabes.

It is clear that the designers of Islamic mosaics makers and architects employed complicated geometry in their designs, but very little information on their methods has been preserved in medieval Arabic and Persian sources. Perhaps they transmitted their methods orally.

JAN P. HOGENDIJK

See also Algebra; Astronomy; Al-Biruni; Ibn al-Haytham; Nasir al-Din al-Tusi; Numbers; Mathematics

Further Reading

Berggren, J. Len. "Mathematics and Her Sisters in Medieval Islam: A Selective Review of Work Done from 1985 to 1995." *Historica Mathematica* 24 (1997), no. 4, 407–440.
———. "The Correspondence of Abu Sahl al-Kuhi and Abu Ishaq al-Sabi: A Translation with Commentaries:" *Journal for the History of Arabic Science* 7 (1983): 39–124.
Ozdural, Alpay. "Mathematics and Arts: Connections between Theory and Practice in the Medieval Islamic World." *Historica Mathematica* 27 (2000): 171–201.
Rosenfeld, B.A., and Jan P. Hogendijk. "A Mathematical Treatise Written in the Samarqand Observatory of Ulugh Beg." *Zeitschrift fur Geschichet der arabisch-islamishcn Wissenschaften.* 15 (2003): 25–65.
Vahabzadeh, B. "Al-Mahani's Commentary on the Concept of Ratio." *Arabic Sciences and Philosophy* 12 (2002): 9–52.

GESUDARAZ

Sayyid Muhammad Husayni, popularly known as Gesudaraz ("He With the Long Tresses") and Bandanawaz ("The One Who is Kind to His Servants"), was a prominent Sufi teacher responsible for the establishment of the Chishti Sufi order in the Deccan province of southern India. Born in 1321 CE into a family tracing its ancestry to Khurasan (Iran), Gesudaraz received his early education in Delhi studying various religious sciences, including Qur'anic exegesis, theology, and jurisprudence. In 1336, he was formally initiated into the Chishti order by becoming a

disciple of the renowned Chishti master Nasir ad-Din Chiragh-i Dihli ("The Lamp of Delhi"). Gesudaraz so distinguished himself on the Sufi path that upon the death of his teacher he assumed leadership of the order. As a consequence of rumors concerning Timur's (Tamerlane's) invasion of northern India in 1398, Gesudaraz left Delhi and traveled south. At the invitation of the Bahmanid ruler Firuz Shah, Gesudaraz eventually settled in Gulbarga, the capital of the Bahmanids. Gesudaraz's initial association with Firuz Shah, as well as his later involvement with intrigues in the Bahmanid court over the succession to the throne, in which he supported the cause of Firuz Shah's brother Ahmad Shah (r. 1422–1436), indicate that he had moved away from the ideals of previous Chishti masters who considered contact with royalty to be detrimental to spiritual well-being. Apparently, Gesudaraz saw nothing wrong in accepting tax-free land from his royal patrons.

In terms of his teachings, Gesudaraz was more conservative than his Chishti predecessors, such as Nizam ad-Din Awliya, who were strong proponents of *wahdat al-wujud* (unity of existence), a philosophical doctrine traditionally associated with the Andalusian Sufi Ibn Arabi (d. 1240) and interpreted as *hama ust* (everything is He). Gesudaraz felt that this doctrine went against the legal and theological precepts of Islam because it blurred the distinction between created and Creator. Instead, he supported the theory of *wahdat ash-shuhud* (unity of witnessing) which, when interpreted as *hama az ust* (everything is from Him), emphasized the distance between creation and a transcendent God. Gesudaraz was also a strong upholder of the law *(shari'ah)*. As a result, he was critical not only of Ibn Arabi but also considered Sufis such as Jalal ad-Din Rumi to be enemies of the faith because of their liberal pantheistic/monistic teachings. Notwithstanding his conservatism on doctrinal issues, Gesudaraz upheld the Chishti tradition of *sama'* (musical concerts), because he was a firm believer in the power of music as an aid to spiritual transformation and ecstasy. Not surprisingly, he was also a strong supporter of love mysticism, for he saw passionate love as the basis of the relationship between creation and the Divine.

Gesudaraz was such a prolific scholar and writer that he has been called the Chishti *sultan al-qalam* ("King of the Pen"). Although the exact number of his works is not known—estimates range from thirty-six to one hundred and fifty—he is believed to have been multilingual, being competent in Arabic, Persian, and several Indian languages. Through his commentaries, he popularized the works of classical Sufi thinkers such as Qushayri and Suhrawardi in the Indian subcontinent. In using Dakhani, a local Indian vernacular, to compose the *Mi'raj al-'ashiqin (The Celestial Ascent of Lovers)*, a book on the Prophet Muhammad, Gesudaraz played a pioneering role in promoting the use of local languages in religious literature, a trend that became increasingly important in subsequent centuries.

Gesudaraz died November 1, 1422, and is buried at Gulbarga in a vast tomb–shrine complex, the upkeep of which has been generously patronized by various rulers. His tomb, which is one of the most important centers of religious pilgrimage in southern India, attracts thousands of devotees, Muslim and non-Muslim, who come here to seek his blessing and intercession.

ALI ASANI

Further Reading

Eaton, Richard. *The Sufis of Bijapur 1300–1700*. Princeton: Princeton University Press, 1978.

Hussaini, S.S.K. *The Life, Works, and Teachings of Khwajah Bandahnawaz Gisudaraz*. Gulbarga, 1986.

GHANA

Drawing on both written sources and oral sources (the so-called Epic of Wagadu), Levtzion (1980) dates the origins of Ghana to the first millennium CE: "By the end of the eighth century, Ghana was known in the Muslim world as 'the land of Gold'. Al-Ya'qubi, a widely-traveled official in the service of the 'Abbasid caliphs during the ninth century described the Kingdom of Ghana 'whose king is also powerful. In his country are the gold mines, and under his authority are a number of kings. Among them are the kingdom of 'Am and the kingdom of Sama. Gold is found in the whole of the country'" (Hopkins and Levtzion 1981, 21).

According to the written sources, in the second half of the ninth century, *Kawkaw* (an early version of the modern term for Gao, and a predecessor of the Songhay Empire) and Ghana were the two most powerful kingdoms of western Sudan, each with vassal chiefdoms under its dominion (Levtzion 1980, 22). In 1067–1068, the Arab geographer al-Bakri, drawing on accounts by travelers and other written sources, wrote an oft-cited description of the capital of Ghana. The city was divided into two towns, one for the Moslems, the other, ten kilometers away, for the ruler and his entourage. Archaeological work points toward the remains of Ghana at Kumbi Saleh in southeastern Mauretania. Note that there is no historical or cultural connection between medieval Ghana and the present-day Republic of Ghana.

Medieval Ghana lay far inland from the west coast of West Africa; its main cities were Awdaghost,

situated almost five hundred kilometers from the ocean, and Kumbi Saleh, the capital, three hundred kilometers farther east. It sat astride the trade routes for gold shipped from the sources of the Senegal and Niger rivers northward via Walata to the Maghreb, and for salt from the city of Teghazza (six hundred kilometers to the north), which was transported throughout the region. It is to be noted that present-day archaeologists hesitate to point to Kumbi Saleh as the capital of an empire, since it has no hinterland; archaeologists have increasingly had more difficulty in finding proof of "empires" in the Sahel, because excavations give increasingly more and diverse data. (A revision of Levtzion 1980 is in process.) Current scholarship pictures in this part of West Africa, in the Middle Ages, a trend toward the creation of state organizations with central agencies of redistribution possessing a majority or monopoly of power and authority, at least episodically, for the duration of one or more regimes. Rulers accomplished centralization by absorbing, first politically (through conquest or vassalage) then culturally, regions into the empire.

Probably because of its location and its powerful army, Ghana seems to have been able to remain unaffected by the wars and social dislocation caused by the migrants and influence of the Almoravids until the middle of the eleventh century. By controlling trade in the region, the empire developed a reputation for prosperity throughout the Sahel and the larger Islamic world. The rulers of Ghana maintained their own belief system while allowing that of Islam to develop in their cities; al-Bakri underscores the freedom allowed to believers of Islam and those of the local religion. The degree of Islamization probably remained low until the nineteenth century. Ghana's decline can be dated by the late twelfth century, and in the thirteenth century Mali developed as the second great empire of the Sahel.

JAN JANSEN

Further Reading

Hopkins, John F.P., and Nehemiah Levtzion. *Corpus of Early Arabic Sources for West African History*. Cambridge: Cambridge University Press, 1981.

Levtzion, Nehemia. *Ancient Ghana and Mali*. 2nd ed. New York: Africana, 1980.

Masonen, Pekka. *The Negroland Revisited: Discovery and Invention of the Sudanese Middle Ages*. Helsinki: The Finnish Academy of Science and Letters, 2000.

GHASSANIDS

A branch of the Azd tribal group, the Ghassanids (or Banu Ghassaan) migrated into northern Arabia at the end of the fifth century. They quickly superseded the dominant Banu Salih as the principal local tributary of the Byzantine Empire. Thus Ghassanid history is to be situated against the backdrop of competing efforts by the Byzantine and Sasanian empires to win supremacy over southern Syria/northern Arabia. By the turn of the fourth century, a new policy of direct ties to nomadic powers of the region involved the distribution of treaties, subsidies, and formal titles. In the case of Byzantium, the rewards included security along the southern Syrian frontier from nomadic forces; protection of imperial commercial and political interests, particularly those related to trade in spices, aromatics, and other luxury goods; and auxiliary military strength against the Sasanians.

The Ghassanids played their part ably. Their alliance with Byzantium was formalized around 502 CE by Jabala, the first Ghassanid *phylarch* (Greek, tribal chief). From their principal residence, al-Jabiya, located in al-Jawlan, a district of southern Syria (modern-day Golan), the Ghassanids are reported to have conducted regular campaigns as far south as the Hijaz and central Najd. The principal phase of their history involved the career of al-Harith ibn Jabala (d. 569), known in Roman sources as "Arethas" and head of the Jafna, chief clan of the Ghassanid confederation. He is reported to have fought with distinction against the Sassanids during Justinian's reign (527–565) and, at a later point, against forces led by Mundhir ibn Nu'man (d. 554), head of the Lakhmid state, the principal Sassanid client in the region. His son, Mundhir ibn al-Harith, later sacked the Lakhmid capital of al-Hira (570), a near-fatal blow to the standing of the Lakhmids. At an early point in his career, al-Harith was rewarded for his efforts on behalf of Byzantium, with the rank of king *(basileus)* and various titles, including *patrikios* and *gloriosissimus*.

Historians part ways in explaining subsequent strains in Ghassanid–Byzantine relations. The arrest of Mundhir ibn al-Harith in 580, and of his son, Nu'man ibn Mundhir, in 583, clearly signaled imperial displeasure. One explanation holds that the Byzantines deeply resented the Ghassanid embrace of the Monophysite form of Christianity. Efforts by al-Harith proved vital to the survival of the Syrian Monophysite (Jacobite) church in its confrontation, in the mid-sixth century, with Byzantine orthodoxy. These efforts were pursued, in particular, by Mundhir ibn al-Harith as described in a long biographical notice by John of Ephesus (d. ca. 589), a leading sixth-century Monophysite historian. A second explanation is that the Byzantines sought to curtail the ambitions of an emerging regional power. The Ghassanids, routed by Sassanid forces during the invasion of Syria (613–614), took part in the Byzantine counter-invasion under Heraclius (r. 622–628). As Byzantine allies, they then confronted the initial Arab–Islamic campaigns. In 634, at Marj Rahit outside Damascus, Ghassanid forces were overrun by a force led by Khalid ibn al-Walid (d. 642). The remaining Ghassanids either dispersed to Anatolia or settled in Syria, many of them as converts to Islam.

MATTHEW S. GORDON

Further Reading

Hoyland, Robert G. *Arabia and the Arabs from the Bronze Age to the Coming of Islam*. London: Routledge, 2001.
Muraviev, Alexei. "Ghassanids." In *Late Antiquity: A Guide to the Postclassical World*, ed. G. W. Bowersock et al., 468–469. Cambridge, MA: The Belknap Press, 1999.

GHAZALI

Abu Hamid Muhammad al-Ghazali was one of the most prominent theologians, jurists, and mystics of Sunni Islam. He was born in 1058 CE in Tabaran-Tus (fifteen miles north of modern Mashhad in northeastern Iran), where he received his early education with his brother Ahmad (1061–1123 or 1126), who later became a famous preacher and Sufi scholar. Muhammad went on to study with the influential Ash'ari theologian al-Juwayni (1028–1085) at the Nizamiyya Madrasa (q.v.) in nearby Nishapur. This brought him in close contact with the court of the Grand Seljuk Sultan Malikshah (r. 1071–1092) and his grand vizier Nizam al-Mulk (1018–1092) (q.v.). In 1091, al-Ghazali was appointed professor at the prestigious Nizamiyya Madrasa in Baghdad. In addition to being a confidante of the Sultan in Isfahan, he became closely connected to the caliphal court in Baghdad. He was undoubtedly the most influential intellectual of his time, when in 1095 he suddenly gave up his posts in Baghdad and left the city. Despite the information al-Ghazali gives in his autobiography *The Deliverer from Error (al-Munqidh min al-dalal)*, it is still not known what led al-Ghazali to leave his posts. This decision has become the subject of wide-ranging speculations about a drastic change in his intellectual outlook. Al-Ghazali went on to teach in Damascus and Jerusalem. At the tomb of Abraham in Hebron, he vowed never to return to the services of political authorities. After performing the pilgrimage in 1096, al-Ghazali returned via Baghdad to his hometown of Tus, where he founded a small private school. In 1106, al-Ghazali broke his vow and returned to teach at the Nizamiyya Madrasa, apparently succumbing to pressure from the authorities at the Seljuk court. After teaching for a couple of years in Nishapur he again retired to Tus, where he died in 1111.

Al-Ghazali is a towering figure in Sunni Islam, active at a time when Sunni theology had just passed through its consolidation and entered a period of intense challenges from Shi'i Ismaili theology (see Shi'i thought) and the tradition of Peripatetic philosophy (see Aristotle and Aristotelianism). Al-Ghazali understood the severity of the confrontation with these two movements and devoted his early works to addressing the challenges presented by these schools of thought. He closely studied the works of the Peripatetic philosophers Ibn Sina (d. 1037) (q.v.) and al-Farabi (d. 950) (q.v.) and wrote *The Incoherence of the Philosophers (Tahafut al-falasifa)*, a book he later described as a "refutation" *(radd 'ala)* of the philosophical movement. His critique is focused on epistemology. The scholars versed in the philosophical sciences are convinced, al-Ghazali complains, that their way of knowing by "demonstrative proof" *(burhan)* is superior to the kind of knowledge drawn from revelation and its interpretation. Discussing 20 positions from the teachings of the philosophers, al-Ghazali attempts to show that their conclusions are not based on demonstration but often rely on unproven premises concealed within their arguments. The philosophers therefore have no more certain knowledge than the theologians. Both groups' convictions rely on unproven premises that are accepted only within that group. However, while the unproved premises of the philosophers are based on no more than their school tradition, those of the theologians are rooted in divine revelation and must be given preference. *Incoherence of the Philosophers* ends with the legal condemnation of three teachings of the philosophers as apostasy from Islam, punishable by death.

Al-Ghazali argues similarly against the Ismaili Shi'is, criticizing the fact that they base their faith on the teachings of the living imam rather than on accepted interpretations of revelation. In this instance, his attacks have a distinctly political component, since the Ismaili Shi'is, whom al-Ghazali called "Batinites" (meaning those who arbitrarily follow inner meaning), challenged the authority of the 'Abbasid Sunni caliphate. Their movement undermined the credibility of Sunni theology, claiming its interpretation of scripture is arbitrary. The Sunni theologians submit God's word to seemingly reasonable judgments, the Ismailis said, that are purely capricious. Subsequently, al-Ghazali found himself criticizing one kind of reliance on reason, practiced by the philosophers, while defending another kind in the Muslim theologians' reliance on reason against Ismaili attacks.

Al-Ghazali's departure from his academic and political career in 1095 led him to focus on ethical subjects, a topic barely touched upon in earlier works. It is at this point that he starts to write his most influential book, the voluminous *Revivication of the Religious Sciences (Ihya' 'ulum al-din)*, a comprehensive guide to ethical behavior in the everyday life of Muslims. He severely criticizes the coveting of worldly matters and reminds his readers that human life is a path toward Judgment Day and the reward or punishment gained through it. He vigorously attacks his colleagues in Muslim scholarship, questioning their intellectual capacities and independence, as well as their commitment to gaining reward in the world to come. This increased moral consciousness brings al-Ghazali in close connection to Sufi attitudes (Sufism), which have a profound influence on his subsequent writing, most notably on his autobiography and on *The Niche of Lights (Mishkat al-anwar)*, a commentary on the Light-Verse (Q 24:35) in the Qur'an.

FRANK GRIFFEL

See also Ismailis

Further Reading

Frank, Richard M. *Al-Ghazali and the Ashfiarite School*. Durham/London: Duke University Press, 1994.
Al-Ghazali. *Freedom and Fulfillment: An Annotated Translation of al-Ghazali's al-Munqidh min al-dalal and Other Relevant Works of al-Ghazali*. Transl. Richard J. McCarthy. Boston: Twayne, 1980. Reprinted: *Deliverance from Error: Five Key Texts Including His Spiritual Autobiography al-Munqidh min al-Dalal*. Louisville, KY: Fons Vitae, 2000.
―――. *The Incoherence of the Philosophers/Tahafut al-falasifa, a Parallel English-Arabic Text*. Transl. Michael E. Marmura. Provo, UT: Brigham Young University Press, 1997.
―――. *Faith in Divine Unity and Trust in Divine Providence* [Book 35 of *Revivication of Religious Sciences*]. Transl. David Burrell. Louisville, KY: Fons Vitae, 2001.
―――. *The Niche of Lights: A Parallel English-Arabic Text*. Transl. David Buchman. Provo, UT: Brigham Young University Press, 1998.
"Gazali." *Encyclopeadia Iranica*. Ed. Ehsan Yarshater. Vol. 10. New York: Bibliotheca Persia Press, 2001, 358–377.
Watt, William M. *Muslim Intellectual: A Study of al-Ghazali*. Edinburgh: University Press, 1963.

GHAZNAVIDS

The Ghaznavids (r. 977–1186 CE) established the largest empire in the eastern Muslim world since the 'Abbasids. The dynasty was of Turkish slave origin, first ruling on behalf of the disintegrating Samanid Empire of Transoxiana and Khurasan, later as independent sovereigns. In 962, the rebel slave commander Alptigin established himself at Ghazna. His slave Sebuktigin (r. 977–997) lay the foundations of the empire; he was awarded governorship of much of present-day Afghanistan (including Ghazna) by the Samanids in 977, annexed Khurasan, Sistan, and Lamghan, and, crushing offensives by the Hindushahi *raja* Jaipal (979 and 988), conquered territory up to Peshawar.

Sebuktigin's son Mahmud (r. 998–1030) declared independence, with nominal loyalty to the 'Abbasid caliph al-Qadir. He extended the empire from western Persia to the Ganges valley, financing his army and sophisticated bureaucracy by campaigns against wealthy Hindu religious centers and excessive taxation of Khurasan and Afghanistan. The religious impetus of Mahmud's Indian forays was minimal; he fought equally tenaciously against rival Muslim rulers and established permanent dominion in India only up to Lahore.

Mas'ud (r. 1030–1041) had to contend with the rise of the Seljuks in the eastern Muslim world, losing much of Iran and his Central Asian territories in 1040 and shifting the dynasty's orientation toward India. Fleeing to Lahore, he was overthrown by mutinous palace guards. Though Mawdud (r. 1041–1050) stabilized the Ghaznavid position, chaos reigned until 1059, with power contested by various governors, the loss of some Hindu centers, and the siege of Lahore by the *raja* of Delhi.

Ibrahim (r. 1059–1099) ushered in a golden era marked by treaties and cultural interaction with the Seljuks. His army crossed the southern border of Punjab, and Lahore became a major cultural center. By Bahram's reign (1118–ca. 1152), however, the Ghaznavids were little more than Seljuk vassals. Furthermore, long-standing trouble with Ghur, near Herat, came to the forefront. Bahram's injudicious poisoning of a Ghuri chief led to the destruction of Ghazna around the year 1150 and its occupation by the Oghuz in the early 1160s. Khusrau Shah (r. ca. 1152–1160) most likely escaped to the Punjab, the sole remaining Ghaznavid possession. After Khusrau Malik's rule (r. 1160–1186) in Lahore, the city was annexed and Khusrau captured by Muhammad Ghuri, bringing the end of the Ghaznavid dynasty.

The Ghaznavids inherited Samanid administrative, political, and cultural traditions and laid the foundations for a Persianate state in northern India. Under Mahmud, Ghazna approached Baghdad in importance, hosting luminaries such as al-Biruni and Ferdowsi. Though the Ghaznavids initially spoke Turkish, Persian literature was promoted at both Ghazna and Lahore, encouraging poets such as Unsuri, Farrukhi, Manuchihri, Runi, Sana'i, Masud Sa'd Salman, and the Sufi al-Hujwiri. The dynasty presided over new developments in Persian literature, notably in lyrical romances and romantic epics, as well as a budding Turkish literature. Art and architecture also flourished. In jurisprudence, the early Ghaznavids were Shafi'i, but Hanafism gained ascendancy by Mas'ud's time. Though their campaigns against the Ismailis, Shi'i Buyids, and Hindus were driven by material considerations and imperial ambition, the early rulers often styled themselves as Sunni champions of the faith.

Successful Ghaznavid military strategy involved small forces, mounted archers, and lightning raids, and the army's most important components were the Turkish slave elite and Hindu Indians. In India, Hindu chiefs usually became tributaries in a system of indirect rule. There was no significant loss of population through conquest and negligible conversion to Islam. Some scholars maintain that the large transfer of wealth under the Ghaznavids facilitated trade between India and the Muslim world. Much of this was later passed to the Seljuks as tribute payments, expanding circulation of precious metals to the Levant and Asia Minor.

HOMAYRA ZIAD

See also 'Abbasids; Abu Hanifa; Al-Biruni; Al-Shafi'i; Buyids; Epics, Persian; Ferdowsi; India; Iran; Khurasan; Lahore; Mahmud of Ghazna; Persian; Poetry, Indian; Poetry, Persian; Samanids; Seljuks; Shahnama; Sindh; Slavery, Military; Turkish and Turkic Languages; Turks; Warfare and Techniques

Further Reading

Bosworth, Clifford E. *The Ghaznavids*. Edinburgh: Edinburgh University Press, 1963.
———. "The Development of Persian Culture Under the Early Ghaznavids." *Iran* 6 (1968): 33–44.
———. *The Later Ghaznavids: Splendour and Decay*. Edinburgh: Edinburgh University Press, 1977.
———. *Medieval History of Iran, Afghanistan, and Central Asia*. London: Variorum Reprints, 1977.
Wink, Andre. *Al-Hind: The Making of the Indo-Islamic World, Vol. 2, The Slave Kings and the Islamic Conquest, 11th–13th Centuries*. Leiden: Brill, 2002.

GIBRALTAR

The city of Gibraltrar is located to the southeast of the Spanish province of Cadiz and to the east of the Algeciras Bay. It dominates the Strait of Gibraltar, the necessary gateway from Europe to Africa, from which stems its strategic value. Gibraltar has been under British sovereignty since 1704. The Arabs called it Jabal Tariq after Tariq ibn Ziyad, who disembarked there in AH 92/711 CE, starting the conquest of al-Andalus from this spot (see Andalus).

Although Gibraltar was used as a naval base for the armies that crossed the Strait in one direction or the other, it was Algeciras, on the other side of the bay, that became the most prosperous center of the southern extreme of al-Andalus. Almohads built a new city in Gibraltar, named Jabal al-Fatih, with a congregational mosque, a palace (some remains of its fortifications remain), and vast dwellings for taking in high government officials. In 709/1309, Gibraltar fell into the hands of the Castilians, but it was recaptured by the Marinids of Morocco (see North Africa) in 733/1333, and later on by the sultan of Granada, in 813/1410. The Marinids, well aware of the importance of their bases on both sides of the Straits, reinforced the defensive installations of Gibraltar and built another congregational mosque and some dockyards. In 866/1462, Gibraltar definitively passed into Christian hands.

DELFINA SERRANO RUANO

See also Andulus; Almohads; Mosques; Marinids; North Africa

Further Reading

Castillo, C. "La Conquista de Gibraltar en el *Diwan* de 'Abd al-Kariim al-Qaysi." *Miscelánea de Estudios Árabes y Hebraicos* 42–43/1 (1993–1994): 73–80.

EI², s.v. "*Djabal Tarik*" (Seybold, C.F.- [Huici Miranda, A.]).

Gozalbes Busto, G. "Gibraltar y el Estrecho en las Fuentes Árabes." *Almoraima* 21 (1999): 397–410.

Manzano Rodríguez, M.A. *La Intervención de los Benimerines en la Península Ibérica*. Madrid: CSIC, 1992, 223–232 y 305–307.

———. "Abu Malik 'Abd al-Wahid, Conquistador de Gibraltar, Rey de Algeciras y Ronda." In *Actas XVI Congreso UEAI*. Ed. C. Vázquez de Benito and MA. Manzano Rodríguez, 309–322. Salamanca, AECI-CSIC-UEAI, 1995.

Norris, H.T. "The Early Islamic Settlement in Gibraltar." *Journal of the Royal Anthropological Institute* 91 (1961): 39–51.

Rosenberger, B. "Le Contrôle du Détroit de Gibraltar aux XII–XIII Siècles." In *L'Occident Musulman et l'Occident Chretien au Moyen Age*, Rabat, Faculté des Lettres et des Sciences Humaines, Serie: Colloques et seminaires, no. 48.

Vallvé Bermejo, J. "Las Relaciones entre Al-Andalus y el norte de Africa a Través del Estrecho de Gibraltar: (siglos VIII–XV)." In *Actas del Congreso internacional El Estrecho de Gibraltar, Ceuta noviembre 1987*, ed. E. Ripoll Perelló, 9–36. Madrid, 1998.

GIFTS AND GIFT GIVING

There are many Arabic terms to express the concept of gift, including *hadiyya, nihla, tuhfa, in'am,* and *hiba,* the latter being the preferred legal term. This terminology was also adopted in medieval Turkish and Persian contexts in addition to the Persian term *pishkash* (royal tribute). According to the French sociologist Marcel Mauss, gift giving is the means by which value can be taught and understood in society, and the size of a gift is often linked to the giver's status in the community. This analysis holds true in the Islamic context and, in addition, gift giving in the form of charitable efforts raises one's spiritual status, as the rewards for those who dispense of their wealth for the good of humankind are doubled (Q. 64:15–18). The Prophet Muhammad is said to have encouraged the exchange of gifts with friends and family to maintain good relations or remove existing grudges, and he maintained that the recipient of a present should reciprocate with another gift of equal value, unless he or she is unable to do so, in which case the offering of thanks and a prayer on behalf of the giver would suffice.

Gift giving in the medieval Islamic context functioned in the social and political spheres of society, and the literature of this period offers us substantial examples of the contents of gifts that were presented or exchanged within the royal and urban milieus. Gifts played a major part in joyous occasions such as weddings, childbirth, circumcision ceremonies, when a child displayed a proficiency in reading the Qur'an, and during important festivals such as the *'Id al-Fitr* (Feast of Ramadan) or *Nawruz* (New Year). According to the medieval historian al-Tha'alibi (d. 1037 CE), the marriage celebration of the 'Abbasid caliph al-Ma'mun, hosted by his father-in-law al-Hasan b. Sahl, was one of the most lavish events to have ever been held. Following a 40-day feast for al-Ma'mun's military commanders and courtiers, al-Hasan scribbled the names of various estates on small pieces of paper and whoever got hold of one of these was transferred ownership of the named estate as a parting gift. For the caliph's womenfolk, al-Hasan ordered large, unpierced pearls to be scattered among them, and each of them chose one to show their respect to their host.

We can glean from the documents of the Cairo Geniza that the medieval Mediterranean Jewish, Christian, and Muslim urban communities of the eleventh and twelfth centuries also held elaborate parties on such occasions. Although the magnitude of these events was scaled down in comparison to the banquets held at court, they were, nevertheless, full of pomp and excitement and involved the generous distribution of gifts. On the occasion of a circumcision ceremony, held eight days after the birth of the child, the family organized a grand affair that was described as "second [only] to a wedding" celebration. Poems proffering good wishes upon the child and his family were recited and ample rewards were dispensed to the poets. Official court histories recount the elaborate social gatherings *(majalis)* held by caliphs and sultans during which panegyrists were awarded with fistfuls of gold, silver, and precious gems for their poetic performances. The gifts or rewards presented to poets, artists, and calligraphers in this way were deemed as necessary forms of artistic patronage.

Another form of official gift giving at court was the bestowal of robes of honor (khil'a) to esteemed individuals, a custom with pre-Islamic origins that was institutionalized in the 'Abbasid period and spread across Muslim Spain to Central Asia well into the premodern period. These costly garments were woven in state-owned factories (dar al-tiraz) and embellished with epigraphic bands often including the name of the ruler, the date, and pious phrases. The 'Abbasid court historian, Hilal al-Sabi', described the investiture ceremony of the Buyid prince, 'Adud al-Dawla, during which the caliph presented him a 'Kufi robe' embroidered with gold threads and jewels, a golden tiara, gold and crystal vessels, and a gold-embroidered "seat of honor" with leather cushions. Interestingly, we have evidence from the Fatimid period that members of the urban population also adopted the custom of presenting robes of honor to friends and family members.

There is a great deal of literature devoted to the content and context of diplomatic gifts exchanged between Muslim rulers and between Muslim and non-Muslim rulers. An excellent source for the period up to the eleventh century is the *Book of Gifts and Rarities (Kitab al-Hadaya wa'l-Tuhaf)*. The value and rarity of the gifts presented were not only incisive indicators of the political power and stability of the giver, but they also set the standard for the recipient to reciprocate in equal measure. The Byzantines were one of the most important players in Muslim diplomatic affairs, and the choice of gifts arriving from either side was always carefully selected and often imbued with symbolic value. According to the *Book of Gifts and Rarities*, on one occasion the Byzantine emperor presented the Fatimid caliph of Egypt with three heavy saddles, once belonging to Alexander the Great, made of cloisonné enamel and inlaid with gold. Apart from gifts made of rare and precious materials, rulers presented giraffes, elephants, and other exotic beasts as symbolic expressions of their power and largesse. This is particularly the case for rulers from Egypt (Fatimids, Mamluks, and Ottomans) and India (Mughals) who owned extensive animal menageries, because they could source such magnificent wild creatures from lands under their jurisdiction.

From the sixteenth century onward the diplomatic activities of the three great Muslim empires, the Safavids, Mughals, and Ottomans, maintained the tradition of exchanging manmade rarities of precious materials, Chinese porcelain, textiles, robes of honor, thoroughbred horses, and exotic birds and animals. Furthermore, with the increase in European and Russian contacts, Muslim rulers began to desire items such as surgical and optical instruments, chandeliers, mirrors, clocks, and firearms. A hitherto unmentioned commodity that was always greatly valued by rulers and was presented as tribute from the earliest periods of Muslim civilization was the trafficking of human slaves, for the military, court administration, or harem.

FAHMIDA SULEMAN

See also 'Abbasids; 'Adud al-Dawla; Alexander; Birth; Byzantine Empire; Cairo Geniza; Ceramics; Circumcision; Charity; Court Dress; Cultural Exchange; Diplomacy; Egypt; Fatimids; Festivals and Celebrations; Historical Writing; Mamluks; Al-Ma'mun; Marriage, Islamic; Marriage, Jewish; Muhammad, the Prophet; Mughals; Muslim–Byzantine Relations; Nawruz; Ottoman Empire; Poets; Precious Metals; Safavids; Slaves and Slave Trade; Textiles; Zoological Parks

Further Reading

El-Aswad, El-Sayed. "The Gift and the Image of the Self and the Other Among Rural Egyptians." In *The Gift in Culture*, ed. R. Godula, 35–49. Krakow: Jagiellonian University Press, 1993.

Book of Gifts and Rarities (Kitab al-Hadaya wa al-Tuhaf). Selections Compiled in the Fifteenth Century from an Eleventh-Century Manuscript on Gifts and Treasures. Transl. Ghada al-Hijjawi al-Qaddumi. Cambridge, MA: Harvard University Press, 1996.

Brookshaw, D.P. "Palaces, Pavilions and Pleasure-Gardens: The Context and Setting of the Medieval *Majlis*." *Middle Eastern Literatures* 6 (July 2003): 199–223.

Goitein, S.D. *A Mediterranean Society: The Jewish Communities of the Arab World As Portrayed in the Documents of the Cairo Geniza*. 6 vols. Berkeley and Los Angeles: University of California Press, 1967–1993.

Mauss, Marcel. *The Gift: Forms and Functions of Exchange in Archaic Societies*. Transl. Ian Cunnison. London: Cohen & West, 1954.

Rosenthal, F., C.E. Bosworth et al. *"Hiba," Encyclopaedia of Islam*. New ed. Vol. 3, Leiden: E. J. Brill, 342–351.

Al-Sabi', Hilal. *Rusum Dar al-Khilafah (The Rules and Regulations of the 'Abbasid Court)*. Transl. Elie A. Salem. Beirut: American University of Beirut Press, 1977.

Stillman, N.A. "Khil'a." *Encyclopaedia of Islam*. New ed. Vol. 5, Leiden: E.J. Brill, 6–7, plate 1.

Al-Tha'alibi, Abu Mansur. *The Book of Curious and Entertaining Information. The Lata'if al-Ma'arif of al-Tha'alibi*. Transl. C.E. Bosworth. Edinburgh: Edinburgh University Press, 1968.

White, C.S.J. "Gift Giving." In *The Enclopedia of Religion*, ed. Mircea Eliade, vol. 5, 552–557. New York: Macmillan.

GLASSWARE

Glass in medieval Islam was widely produced from Egypt to Central Asia, drawing on the basic recipes of earlier traditions (a silica–soda–lime composition in which the soda was provided by natural natron as in Roman times and was then slowly supplanted by plant ashes in the ninth and tenth centuries CE) and finding inspiration in shapes, decorative patterns, and colors that were popular in the former Roman/Byzantine lands and in Sasanian Iran and Iraq. Muslim and non-Muslim glassmakers working in the Islamic areas, however, were extraordinarily creative and, in tune with the general evolution of Islamic art, brought this craft to new technical, technological, and artistic heights. In the Islamic world, glass, commonly known in Arabic as *zujāj* and in Persian as *ābgīneh*, had a significant role both as an artistic medium, known and appreciated as far as China and Japan, and as an economically viable material widely used to make windows and containers for commercial goods (mainly liquids such as perfumes, wine, and chemicals). An awareness of its commercial importance is highlighted by the evidence that there were factories, mostly on the Eastern Mediterranean coast, specializing in producing large slabs of glass that were shipped far from the shores to glassmaking areas where the raw material was not readily available, in order to remelt it at a lower temperature, thus simplifying the technology and making it less expensive. Glass was also widely recycled for the same reason, the most important archaeological evidence for which is provided by the shipwreck of Serçe Limanı off the coast of Bodrum in Turkey: The ship, sailing from the shores of the eastern Mediterranean, carried hundreds of baskets full of broken glass that were meant to be used for remelting in factories along the Black Sea or possibly in southern Europe.

Much work still needs to be done by art historians in this relatively neglected field. Broadly speaking, however, the development of Islamic glass is reasonably comprehensible both within the context of the evolution of Islamic art and of glassmaking in the medieval period. Shortly after the beginning of the Islamic era, forms, decorative patterns, and colors continued to resemble closely those glass objects that were created in blown and hot-worked glass by the late Roman and Byzantine glassmakers along the eastern Mediterranean coasts and Egypt. Among them are small flasks enveloped in a trailed cage supported by a quadruped and bottles with fancifully applied decorations. Bold and contrasting colors and textured surfaces are characteristic traits

Goblet of luster-painted glass, made in honor of Abd al-Sammad bin Ali. Fatimid caliphate, eleventh century CE. 10.5 cm. Credit: Erich Lessing/Art Resource, NY. Museum of Islamic Art, Cairo, Egypt.

of glass produced in this area, as well as in Iraq, in the first centuries of Islam: "Stained" or lustre-painted vessels, *millefiori* (thousand flowers) tiles and small vessels, and needle-point incised objects are the most representative of this trend.

In the formerly Sasanian regions of Iran, almost colorless wheel-cut glass continued to be fashionable through the creation of mirrorlike surfaces by means of contiguous facets making up honeycomb patterns; forms changed with time, but this pattern remained a favorite until the tenth century. In the same areas the glasscutters developed sophisticated yet stylized figural and vegetal patterns in relief, sometimes using two layers of glass of contrasting colors (the so-called cameo technique), which can be regarded as among the best artistic achievements in the arts of the early Islamic period.

The transmission of the craft from father to son for generations (a common trait of glassmaking worldwide) favored the perpetuation of traditional techniques of decoration and colors into the medieval and late medieval periods. A large variety of shapes and details in the decoration, however, allows for a better understanding of both chronology and place of origin of many types. Objects with "marvered" (or "pushed-into") threads of a paler color, applied trails, a variety of impressed or molded patterns, and often combinations thereof provide the widest range of artistic glass vessels created from the tenth through thirteenth centuries in the Islamic world. Marvered and applied glass was more popular in the central lands and in Egypt, whereas impressed and molded glass was favored in the Eastern Islamic areas.

The most celebrated and best-known type of Islamic glassware has a polychrome and gilded surface decoration. Probably originating in Syria in the twelfth century, it was produced in Syria and Egypt until at least the middle of the fifteenth century. Certainly patronized by all layers of the wealthy society, there is evidence under the Mamluks (1250–1517) that the court and its entourage were eager sponsors of this type of glass. Large lamps hanging from mosques, madrasas, and mausoleums, as well as an abundance of secular drinking vessels, bottles, basins, and bowls include the names of sultans and emirs, making a chronology of enameled and gilded glass possible.

The fifteenth century marks the decline of glass production in Egypt and Syria—a decline that had started earlier in Iran with the advent of the Mongols in the thirteenth century—due both to economic and political crises and to the fast rise of the glass industry and trade in Europe. Therefore, little is known of glassmaking in Iran in the Timurid and early Safavid periods and in the former Mamluk, now Ottoman, regions and in Anatolia. In Iran the industry was

revived with the help of European, mostly Venetian, craftsmen in Isfahan and Shiraz from the seventeenth century. Western shapes and technology also influenced products manufactured in the Mughal territories of the Indian subcontinent, but their glassmaking quickly gained inventive independence and can be regarded as the best artistic output of the later period.

STEFANO CARBONI

Further Reading

Brill, Robert. *Chemical Analyses of Early Glasses*. 2 vols. Corning, 1999.

Carboni, Stefano. *Glass from Islamic Lands: The Al-Sabah Collection, Kuwait National Museum*. New York: Thames & Hudson, 2001.

Carboni, Stefano, and David Whitehouse. *Glass of the Sultans*. Exhibition catalogue. New York: The Metropolitan Museum of Art, 2001.

Charleston, Robert J. "Glass in Persia in the Safavid Period and Later." *AARP—Art and Archaeology Research Papers* 5 (1974): 12–27.

Clairmont, Christoph. *Benaki Museum. Catalogue of Ancient and Islamic Glass* (Based on the notes of C. J. Lamm). Athens, 1977.

Dikshit, Moreshwar. *History of Indian Glass*. Bombay, 1969.

Fukai, Shinji. *Persian Glass*. Tokyo, 1977.

Goldstein, Sidney M. "Islamic Cameo Glass." In *Cameo Glass: Masterpieces from 2000 Years of Glassmaking*, ed. S. Goldstein, L.S. Rakow and J.K. Rakow. Corning, 1982.

Hasson, Rachel. *Early Islamic Glass*. L.A. Mayer Memorial Institute for Islamic Art. Jerusalem, 1979.

Kröger, Jens. *Glas. Islamische Kunst. Loseblattkatalog unpubliziert Werke aus deutschen Museen. Band 1: Berlin Staatliche Museen Preussischer Kulturbesitz, Museum für Islamische Kunst*. Mainz/Rhein, 1984.

——— *Nishapur: Glass of the Early Islamic Period*. New York: The Metropolitan Museum of Art, 1995.

Lamm, Carl Johan. *Das Glas von Samarra*. Berlin, 1928.

Oliver (Harper), Prudence. "Islamic Relief Cut Glass: A Suggested Chronology." *Journal of Glass Studies* 3 (1961): 9–29.

Schmoranz, Gustav. *Altorientalische Glas-gefässe*. Vienna, 1898.

Smith, Ray Winfield. *Glass from the Ancient World: The Ray Winfield Smith Collection*. Exhibition catalogue. Corning, 1957.

Van Doorninck, Frederick H. "The Serçe Limani Shipwreck: An 11th Century Cargo of Fatimid Glassware Cullet for Byzantine Glassmakers." In *I. Uluslarasi Anadolu Cam Sanati Sempozyumu 26–27 Nisan 1988 / 1st International Anatolian Glass Symposium, April 26–27, 1988*. Istanbul, 1990, 58–63.

Ward, Rachel, ed. *Gilded and Enamelled Glass from the Middle East*. London: British Museum Press, 1998.

Whitehouse, David. "The Corning Ewer: A Masterpiece of Islamic Cameo Glass." *Journal of Glass Studies* 35 (1993): 48–56.

Wiet, Gaston. *Catalogue Général du Musée Arabe du Caire. Lampes et Bouteilles en Verre Émaillé*. Cairo, 1929.

GNOSIS

Gnosis is a Greek term meaning knowledge. When used in a theological discourse, its meaning becomes synonymous with knowledge of the deity and the spiritual realm. Therefore, a gnostic system aspires to define the composition of the realm of the divine and the agents that communicate between the spiritual realm and the physical world. In Islamic religious thought, gnosis corresponds to the Arabic *ma'rifa*, specifically the knowledge of (1) the nature and attributes of God and (2) the ways He communicates with this world. The association of gnosis with *ma'rifa* is largely championed in Sufism and Shi'ism, but one has to be careful here for there are certain differences in the way gnosis is conceptualized by these groups. However, in a strictly traditional Sunni context, there is no such thing as gnosis: neither the concept nor its theological implication is recognized.

In Sufism the entire mystical experience starts as a quest through several stages of spiritual progression to attain gnosis, and from there to the spiritual unity with God. However, gnosis is not achieved by the power of reason alone, which can barely touch the surface. It is God who plants gnosis in the heart of the Sufi. For that matter, what the Sufi has to do is to be completely obedient and turn himself entirely to God *(tawakkul)* and be patient *(sabr)*. According to the celebrated Sufi Ibn 'Arabi (d. 638/1240), it is the force of obedience *(al-ta'a)* that prepares the Sufi to receive the seed of gnosis where God becomes his raison d'être; for then he knows God and all other things through God. The light of gnosis illuminates for the Sufi the various aspects of the nature and attributes of the deity and allows him to witness the divine through the senses. Once gnosis is entrenched in the Sufi's heart, he becomes one of God's hands in this world: He will be entirely consumed with the divine and has no concern for his own self any longer. Those who attain that stage are usually referred to as "the ones who witnessed Him" *(ashab al-mushahada)*. The miracles that a Sufi saint performs are proofs that he attained that stage. In this respect, the following *hadith* attributed to the Prophet Muhammad is especially praised by the Sufis: "If you truly know God you can say to the mountains move and they will move at your command." One of the notable Sufi movements that formulated a gnostic system is the Ishraqi school—founded by the mystic Shihab al-Din 'Umar al-Suhrawardi (d. 587/1191). For the Ishraqis, gnosis is a light revealed by the Angel Gabriel, the same angel who revealed the Qur'an to the Prophet Muhammad.

Gnosis is equally celebrated within Shi'ism, precisely by the Ismailis and the Twelvers. For both of these sects, the world cannot exist without an imam to lead in matters of life and religion. Like prophets, imams are infallible *(ma'sum)*. In Twelver theology, the imam is the proof *(hujja)* that God exists, and hence it is the divinely revealed gnosis that empowers the imam to know God, interpret God's revealed scripture, and do God's work in this world, even if the imam is a minor. Thus the imams are the lights of God, and, subsequently, the references in the Qur'an to the light of/from God (see Q 4:174; 5:15; 9:32) are understood as references to the Twelvers' imams.

In an Ismaili context, gnosis is a much more sophisticated system. It comprises a cosmological order of Intellects and Emanations, along with a cyclical vision of sacred history that revolves around seven prophets, each of whom brings a revelation. The first six prophets are Adam, Noah, Abraham, Moses, Jesus, and Muhammad, and the *qa'im* or *mahdi* is Muhammad ibn Isma'il (grandson of Ja'far al-Sadiq), who is in a stage of occultation. Each prophet ushers in an era that features several imams who assume his role and function until the coming of the following prophet. But in an Ismaili context, the prophet is also the *Logos*: an emanation from the Active Intellect (one of the Intellects that form the Islamili cosmological system). Hence, with the power of gnosis, the prophet or imam defines the exoteric meaning of the revealed scriptures for his era (which is assumed to change over time) but maintains the fixed esoteric meaning (which is assumed to be unchangeable). Generally, three angels mediate between the physical world and the spiritual world until the completion of the seventh and last cycle of human history, when the last prophet returns to bring an end to human history. These angels are Gabriel (Jibra'il), Michael (Mika'il), and Raphael (Israfil).

SULEIMAN A. MOURAD

See also Ibn 'Arabi; Shihab al-Din 'Umar al-Suhrawardi; Shi'ism

Further Reading

Corbin, Henry. *Cyclical Time and Ismaili Gnosis*. London: Kegan Paul, 1983.
———. *Histoire de la Philosophie Islamique*. Paris: Gallimard, 1986.
Knysh, Alexander. *Islamic Mysticism: A Short History*. Leiden: Brill, 2000.

GRAMMAR AND GRAMMARIANS

The science of grammar is intimately bound up with the Islamic religion on the one hand and the predominant Arabic culture of medieval Muslims on the other. As the language of revelation, Arabic became the principal medium of discourse for all theology, the Traditions of the Prophet, and jurisprudence, not to mention the secular disciplines and belles lettres. It is no coincidence that the word for grammar, *nahw*, means literally "way," synonymous with several other key terms such as *sunna*, *shari'a*, *tariqa*, *madhhab*, all denoting a "way" or "path" taken by Muslims. Eventually, when Islamic learning had been institutionalized in the colleges (see Education, Madrasa), the grammarian was simply one of a community of scholars united in the function of expounding, preserving, and implementing the beliefs of Islam.

Although the beginnings of grammar are obscure, by the end of the eighth century we have the first complete description of Arabic by Sibawayhi, a Muslim of Persian descent who died in approximately 795 CE. His untitled work, known only as *Kitab Sibawayhi Sibawayhi's Book,* has never been surpassed and remains the final authority in grammar. Significantly, he approached language as a social activity in which the participants (speaker and listener) are under an obligation to produce utterances that are both "good" (*hasan,* that is, structurally well-formed) and "right" (*mustaqim,* that is, conveying the intended meaning), with failed utterances being termed *muhal* (absurd, perverted). The ethical origin of these concepts is unmistakable, and they reflect the notion that correct speech and correct religious behavior are analogous.

Before becoming institutionalized, however, grammar passed through a number of stages. Sibawayhi's grammar was primarily descriptive, and it first had to be processed into a form suitable for prescriptive grammar, with which the name of al-Mubarrad (d. 898) is associated. It was not long before the appropriation of Greek scientific concepts led to a questioning of basic theoretical principles as the grammarians strove to establish their professional autonomy: here the outstanding figures are Ibn al-Sarraj (d. 928) and al-Zajjaji (d. 949). During this period the leading grammarians polarized themselves into Basrans and Kufans (named after the two great intellectual centers of the eighth to tenth centuries). The core of the dispute was the validity of induction in deriving grammatical rules: The Basrans argued that such rules could not be authoritative unless the corpus on which they were based was closed, while the Kufans maintained that new data could always be admitted. Needless to say, the Basran position was the only one that would guarantee the integrity of Islam against change and the Kufans were effectively sidelined. It is important to observe that the legal system went through a similar process at

much the same time, resulting in what was called "the closing the gate of *ijtihad*," meaning that the corpus of the Qur'an and the Sayings of the Prophet, the textual basis of all legal reasoning, were now fixed and immutable.

The ideological conflict between the Basrans and Kufans is recorded in some detail, but the grammarians soon turned to a new problem, the development of efficient pedagogical methods. Teaching manuals (such as those by Ibn al-Sarraj and al-Zajjaji) appear as early as the tenth century, and by the eleventh century, Ibn Babashadh (d. 1077), al-Jurjani (d. 1078), and al-Zamakhshari (d. 1134) created rigidly schematic textbooks designed to serve the new scholasticism of the Madrasa; we also find a serious interest in the history of grammar and its place among the Islamic sciences, notably in Ibn al-Anbari (d. 1181). After this there is little to do but refine and rearrange the material, culminating in the works of the great masters Ibn al-Hajib (d. 1249), Ibn Malik (d. 1274), and Ibn Hisham (d. 1360). Ibn Malik is renowned for his enthusiastic use of verse as a pedagogical medium, while Ibn Hisham was praised as "an even better grammarian than Sibawayhi" for his expository talents, though the most widely used primer in the whole history of Arabic grammar is the *Ajurrumiyya* of Ibn Ajurrum (d. 1327).

It should not be imagined that the grammarians were all mere pedagogues with no concern for the abstractions and subtleties of their art. There was scope for every kind of speculation and controversy, manifested, for example, in the occasional public debates between grammarians and philosophers, the latter perhaps entertaining the hope that language control could be exercised through a universal Greek logic rather than a specifically Islamic social theory, which is certainly what the philosopher al-Farabi (d. 950) believed. Ibn Faris (d. 1004), by contrast, strongly asserted the uniqueness of Arabic and the necessity of grammar for the maintenance of Islamic law and values, while his contemporary, Ibn Jinni (d. 1002), displayed a remarkably open-minded curiosity about the workings of human speech, posing, among others, the question of whether language operates on theological principles (that is, is essentially arbitrary and nonrational) or on logical principles (he inclines to the former). This reminds us that medieval Islam accommodated a broad range of intellectual freedom and could tolerate at one extreme a hyperrationalist grammarian such as al-Rummani (d. 994), who was committed to the view that language was entirely rational, and at the other extreme the Andalusian fundamentalist Ibn Mada' al-Qurtubi (d. 1196), who not only denied the existence of figurative, nonliteral meaning but also the concept of linguistic causality altogether.

As long as Islam remains anchored in its Qur'anic textual base, there will always be a normative role for grammar, and the classical form of the Arabic language, which it was the achievement of the medieval grammarians to define and preserve, will continue to act as a restraining force.

MICHAEL G. CARTER

See also Arabic; Basra; Education; Hadith, Kufa; Law and Jurisprudence; Madrasa; Mu'tazilites; Sibawayhi

Further Reading

Auroux, Sylvain et al, eds. *History of the Language Sciences: An International Handbook on the Evolution of the Study of Language from the Beginnings to the Present*. Handbücher zur Sprach- und Kommunikationswissenschaft. Bd. 18. Berlin: de Gruyter, 2000.

Bakalla, Muhammad H. *Arabic Linguistics, and Introduction and Bibliography*. London: Mansell, 1983.

Bohas, Georges, Jean-Patrick Guillaume, and Djemal E. Kouloughli. *The Arabic Linguistic Tradition*. London/ New York: Routledge, 1990.

Carter, Michael G., ed. *Arab Linguistics: An Introductory Classical Text with Translation and Notes*. Amsterdam: John Benjamins, 1981.

———. "Arab Linguistics and Arabic Linguistics." *Zeitschrift für Geschichte der Arabisch–Islamischen Wissenschaften* 4 (1989): 205–218.

———. "Grammar." In *Religion, Learning and Science in the Abbasid Period*, ed. Michael J.L. Young et al, 118–138. Cambridge: Cambridge University Press, 1991; additional bibliography 531–533.

———. "Writing the History of Arabic Grammar." *Historiographia Linguistica* 21 (1994): 387–416.

———. *Sibawayhi (Makers of Islam)*. Oxford: Oxford University Press/I. B. Tauris, 2004.

Diem, Werner. "Bibliographie/Bibliography, Sekundärliteratur zur einheimischen arabischen Grammatikschreibung." In *The History of Linguistics in the Middle East*, ed. C.H.M. Versteegh, K. Koerner, H. -J. Niederehe, 195–250. Amsterdam: John Benjamins, 1983; *Historiographia Linguistica*, 8 (1981): 431–486.

Goldziher, Ignaz. *On the History of Grammar among the Arabs, an Essay in Literary History*, trans. and ed. Kinga Dévényi, Tamas Ivanyi. Amsterdam/Philadelphia: John Benjamins, 1994.

Gully, Adrian. *Grammar and Semantics in Medieval Arabic*. Richmond: Curzon Press 1995.

Owens, Jonathan. *Early Arabic Grammatical Theory: Heterogeneity and Standardization*. Amsterdam/Philadelphia: John Benjamins, 1990.

Sezgin, Fuat. *Geschichte des arabischen Schrifttums*. Vol. ix, Grammatik bis c. 430 H., Leiden: E. J. Brill, 1984.

Talmon, Rafael. *Eighth-Century Iraqi Grammar: A Critical Exploration of Pre-Halilian Arabic Linguistics*. Winona Lake, IN: Eisenbrauns, 2003.

Versteegh, Cornelis H. M. [Kees]. "Die arabische Sprachwissenschaft." In *Grundriß der arabischen Philologie*, ed. H. Gäthe, vol. ii, 148–176. Wiesbaden: Reichert, 1987; additional bibliog. vol. iii, *Supplement*. Ed. W. Fischer, Wiesbaden: Reichert, 1992, 269–274.

———. *The Explanation of Linguistic Causes: az-Zaggaga's Theory of Grammar, Introduction, Translation and Commentary*. Amsterdam/Philadelphia: John Benjamins, 1995.

———. *Landmarks in Linguistic Thought III: The Arabic Linguistic Tradition*. London/New York: Routledge, 1997.

GRAMMAR AND GRAMMARIANS, HEBREW AND JUDEO-ARABIC

Hebrew grammar and philology did not exist as disciplines or even as systematic activities until the classical age of Islam. For the Jews, these intellectual ventures first arose in the Muslim East in the late ninth century as a result of their encounter with Arabo-Islamic culture in general and their adoption of Arabic as a spoken and literary language in particular. Hebrew grammatical works in Judeo-Arabic and Hebrew follow Arabic models and terminology and represent some of the earliest literary manifestations and the most critical components of the Jewish subcultural minority's efforts to adapt Jewish culture to the intellectual regimen established by Islam. Just as Arabic grammar and philology were essential tools for Qur'anic exegesis, Hebrew linguistic study became the cornerstone for biblical exegesis and the revival of Hebrew as a literary language.

The first major figure associated with this cultural program was Sa'adia ben Joseph al-Fayyumi (882–942 CE), the communal leader and august head of one of the rabbinical academies in Iraq. Sa'adia, who wrote poetry in Hebrew but virtually everything else (including Hebrew languages studies) in Judeo-Arabic, was critical in legitimizing Hebrew grammatical research because of his authority as a scholar of Jewish law. His writings, which include *Kitab fasih lughat al-'ibraniyyin (Book on the Eloquence of the Language of the Hebrews)* and *Kitab usul al-shi'r al-'ibrani: ha-Egron (The Essentials of Hebrew Poetry: The Compilation)*, have been considered unique and foundational efforts in establishing Hebrew grammar and philology. However, fragmentary materials discovered in the Firkovitch *genizah* collection demonstrate that Qaraite Jewish intellectuals in the Muslim East contemporary with Sa'adia were equally immersed in the systematic study of biblical Hebrew. Several tenth-century North African scholars appeared in the generation after Sa'adia, including Judah ibn Quraysh, who authored an epistle *(Risala)* on comparative philology addressed to the community of Fez, and David ben Abraham al-Fasi, who composed a Hebrew–Arabic biblical lexicon, *Jami'l-alfaz*.

Al-Andalus emerged as a significant center of Jewish cultural activity during the mid-tenth century. Menahem ibn Saruq (b. 910–920), a court secretary of the Umayyad Jewish official Hasdai b. Shaprut, composed a Hebrew dictionary of biblical Hebrew roots (*Mahberet*) that would be the last effort to eschew the comparative method. Shortly thereafter Judah Hayyuj (ca. 970 to ca. 1010) first applied the principle of the tri-literal root and its derived forms to Hebrew in *Kitab al-af'al dhawat huruf al-lin* (*Weak and Geminate Verbs*) and another work. His student, Jonah ibn Janah (eleventh century), took this insight further still in his companion studies, *Kitab al-usul* (*The Book of Hebrew Roots*), a Hebrew Arabic lexicon, and *Kitab al-luma'* (*Book of Variegated Flower Beds*), a comprehensive grammar of biblical Hebrew. At the end of the eleventh century, Isaac ibn Barun's *Kitab al-muwazana bayn al-lugha al-'ibraniyya wal-'arabiyya* (*The Book of Comparison between the Hebrew Language and Arabic*) represents the fullest systematic application of the comparative method to the study of Hebrew grammar and philology.

Hebrew and Judeo-Arabic grammar and philology survived in Christian lands following the dispersal of the Jews of al-Andalus under al-Muwahhid rule. Some Arabic works of the previous centuries were translated into Hebrew, while newer Hebrew studies by the Iberian exile Abraham ibn 'Ezra (1092–1167) and the Provençal scholar David Qimhi (ca. 1160–1235) synthesized the results of earlier grammarians and achieved new insights into the behavior of classical Hebrew. Several important grammarians and lexicographers are known from twelfth-century Yemen, thirteenth-century Egypt, and fourteenth-century Catalonia, while Sa'adia ibn Danan was a Hebrew linguist writing in Judeo-Arabic at the fall of Nasrid Granada and the expulsion of the Jews from Spain.

Ross Brann

Further Reading

Eldar, Ilan. "Hebrew Philology Between the East and Spain: The Concept of Derivation as a Case Study." *Journal of Jewish Studies* XLIII (1998): 49–61.

Khan, Geoffrey. *The Early Karaite Tradition of Hebrew Grammatical Thought.* Leiden: Brill, 2002.

Téné, David. "Linguistic Literature, Hebrew." *Encyclopedia Judaica.* Vol 16. Jerusalem: Keter, 1972, 1354–1390.

GRANADA

Granada (Arabic, Gharnata) is the capital of the homonymous district (*kura*) and kingdom, situated on the banks of the Darro River, near its confluence with the Genil.

The first Muslim governors of the area lived in the Roman settlement of Illiberris, which they Arabicized into Ilbira or Elvira, until they moved to a new foundation in its neighborhood, Granada. The district continued to be named *kura* of Elvira, until the name was replaced by that of Granada. The administrative and military territory of the *kura* of Elvira corresponds roughly to the present Spanish province of Granada, to the southeast of the Iberian Peninsula. At the beginning of the eleventh century, after the fall of the Umayyad caliphate of Cordoba, Granada gained prominence at the cost of Elvira. During that time, it became the capital of an independent kingdom ruled by the Zirids, a branch of the Berber Sanhaja tribe. Until then, mainly Jews and Christians had occupied the city. When the Zirids consolidated their power, Granada was the scene of a pogrom against the Jewish community, some of whose members had managed to exert political influence with the *amirs* Habus and Badis ibn Ziri. Of the Zirid palace, situated on the side of a hill sloping down toward the Darro, only a cistern and several pieces of wall remain. The site is known today as the Alcazaba qadima.

In AH 483/1090 CE, 'Abd Allah, the last Zirid king of Granada, was dethroned by the Almoravids. They governed in the city until 551/1156, when it was surrendered to the new lords of al-Andalus, the Almohads. In the interval between 557/1162 and 561/1166, Granada was under the control of the Andalusian rebel Ibn Hamushk, who had taken the city with the help of the Jewish and Christian population. Subsequently, the city fell in the hands of Ibn Hud al-Judhami, under whose leadership a general insurrection against the Almohads took place. In 635/1237, Ibn Hud was assassinated and a year later, his former enemy and founder of the Nasrid dynasty, Muhammad Ibn al-Ahmar, took possession of Granada.

The Nasrid kingdom of Granada included the old provinces of Elvira-Granada, Almería, Malaga, Ronda, and part of Algeciras. The Nasrids maintained constant economic relations with their Christian neighbors, with whom they managed to keep a precarious political balance until 897/1492, when the city was conquered by the Catholic monarchs. The fall of Granada put an end to Muslim political power in the Iberian Peninsula.

Representative of the high level reached by the Arabo-Islamic civilization of Granada are the Maliki jurist al-Shatibi, who in the fourteenth century elaborated a new legal methodology that has been a source of inspiration for reformist thinkers of the contemporary Islamic world, and the polymath Ibn al-Khatib.

The Court of the Lions. The fountain and water course. Credit: Werner Forman/Art Resource, NY. Alhambra, Granada, Spain.

The most remarkable example of Nasrid architecture, the famous palace of the Alhambra, has been defined as the final outcome and the supreme flowering of Andalusi art.

DELFINA SERRANO RUANO

See also Alhambra; Almohads; Cordoba

Further Reading

Arié, R. *España Musulmana, Siglos VIII-XV*. Barcelona: Labor, 1993.

————. *L'Espagne Musulmane au Temps des Nasrides (1232–1492)*, reimpression suivie d'une postface et d'une mise à jour par l'auteur. Paris: De Boccard, 1990.

El Siglo XI en 1ª Persona: Las "Memorias" de 'Abd Allah, Último Rey Zirí de Granada Destronado por los Almorávides (1090). Traducidos, con introducción y notas por E. Lévi-Provençal y Emilio García Gómez. Madrid: Alianza, 1982.

EI², *s.v.* "Gharnatta." [A. Huici Miranda]. Monuments [H. Terrace].

Hoenerbach, W. "Was bleibt uns vom arabischen Granada?" *Die Welt des Islams* 23–24 (1984): 388–423.

'Inan, M.A.A. *Lisan al-Din Ibn al-Khatib: Hayatuhu wa-Turathu-hu al-Fikri*. Cairo: Maktabat al-Khanyi, 1968.

Masud, M. Kh. *Shatibi's Philosophy of Islamic Law*. Islamabad, 1995.

Molina López, E. *Ibn al-Jatib*. Granada: Comares, 2001.

Orihuela Uzal, A. "Granada, Capital del Reino Nazarí." In *La Arquitectura del Islam Occidental*, R. López Guzmán (coord), 195–209. Barcelona: Lunwerg, 1995.

De Santiago Simón, E. *El Polígrafo Granadino Ibn al-Jatib y el Sufismo: Aportaciones Para su Estudio*. Granada: Diputación Provincial, 1983.

Viguera, M.J., coord. *El Reino Nazarí de Granada (1232–1492)*. Historia de España Musulmana Menéndez Pidal, vols. VIII-3 and VIII-4, Madrid, 2000.

GREEK

After Alexander the Great, Greek language and culture began to spread over large sections of the previously non-Greek conquered regions in the Levant and southwest Asia. Centers where Greek science and philosophy came to be studied and further developed were established and continued to exist even after those areas of the world had become part of the Roman—later Byzantine—and Sasanian empires, and eventually, the caliphate. Such centers included Alexandria, Antioch, Qinnesrin, Harran, Edessa, Nisibis, al-Hira, Jundaysabur, and Marw. In addition to Greek works on theology, books on medicine, logic, and astrology were translated into Syriac and Persian (Pahlavi). Farther east, in India, Pataliputra, the capital of the Gupta kingdom, and the port of Ujjain were centers where Greek mathematics and astronomy were studied and developed from the fifth to seventh centuries.

When the Arabs had conquered Damascus and the caliphate of the Umayyads had been established, they were confronted with the existing Greek–Christian culture. Muslims became acquainted with Greek philosophy and Christian theology. The cities al-Basra and al-Kufa became centers of study of disciplines such as Arabic grammar and lexicography, jurisprudence, and theology, and there is evidence of the influence of Greek philosophy on Muslim theology. However, only scant evidence of any translation activity of Greek scientific or philosophical works during the Umayyad caliphate has come down to us.

This changed with the establishment of the 'Abbasid caliphate and especially after the foundation of Baghdad as the capital in 762; until around 1000, a majority of Greek scientific and philosophical works were translated into Arabic, either via Syriac or Pahlavi, or directly. The translators were, for a large part, Syriac-speaking Christians who also knew Greek and Arabic. This translation movement was supported and funded by the elite of 'Abbasid society: caliphs, viziers, merchants, and scholars. Caliphal support was initially motivated by interest in astrology, a legacy of Sasanian culture. Another motivation was the obvious need for knowledge of medicine and the knowledge of accounting and surveying for the secretaries that administered the empire. Indeed, works on astrology and medicine were among the first Arabic translations, soon to be followed by books on arithmetic, geometry, and astronomy. Translations were patronized by the Bukhtishū' family, who had been heads of the hospital of Jundaysabur and were called to Baghdad as physicians at the caliphal court. The Barmakid family, originally from Balkh (Bactria), later living in Marw, came to Baghdad as caliphal viziers. They took an interest in Greek science with which they had become acquainted in Marw. The three Banu Musa brothers also patronized the translation of Greek works; they built an observatory in Baghdad and wrote several works on geometry.

Among the most important translated works were Euclid's *Elements*, Ptolemy's *Almagest*, nearly the entire collections of Aristotle and Galen, and major *Hippocratica*. Arabic translations from Greek science and philosophy formed the basis for the further elaboration of these disciplines in the Arabic–Muslim world.

P. LETTINCK

See also Hunayn ibn Ishaq; Translation, Pre-Islamic Learning into Arabic

Further Reading

Gutas, Dimitri. *Greek Thought, Arabic Culture*. London: Routledge, 1998.

O'Leary, De Lacy. *How Greek Science Passed to the Arabs*. London, Boston, and Henley: Routledge & Kegan Paul, 1979 (first edition 1949).

Rosenthal, Franz. *The Classical Heritage in Islam*. London and New York: Routledge, 1992; reissue of the first English edition, 1975 (translation of the German edition, Zürich, 1965).

GUILDS, PROFESSIONAL

The study of the origins and the development of guilds (*sinf*, pl. *asnaf*) in the Islamic world has been a difficult task for scholars because such organizations have assumed diverse manifestations with respect to economic, political, and religious terms, which has caused difficulty in knowing their exact characteristics. For the most part, however, the origins of guilds in the Islamic history can be traced to the pre-Islamic marketplace in the Arabian peninsula and the Sasanian-controlled territories in eastern Mesopotamia and Central Asia, where most professional organizations formed the basic cadre for the control of the urban economic, political, and social sectors.

In the Caliphate period of Islamic history, from the seventh to the mid-tenth centuries CE, the members of professional organizations primarily consisted of craftsmen and merchants in cities and towns of the eastern Islamic world. These organizations were also comprised of professional groups such as performers, orators, porters, blacksmiths, coppersmiths, braziers, goldsmiths, silversmiths, tailors, and butchers. With the decentralization of the 'Abbasid caliphal empire after 945, in what can be regarded as the collapse of the classical caliphate, guild institutions also underwent major changes. From the tenth to the mid-thirteenth centuries, prior to the Mongol conquest of Baghdad in 1258, the guild associations became increasingly autonomous with the trade guilds, acquiring an effective strength in the cities.

In this period, many of the guilds appear to have also been organized in the form of *futuvvat* organizations, although as Willem Floor has argued, there is lack of evidence for a strong link between the two. The *futuvvat,* the plural of an Arabic term literally meaning "young manhood," identified chivalric and religious brotherhoods that were widespread throughout all urban communities in the medieval Islamic world. The *futuvvat* circles fused the dual ethos of manliness and ethics with spirituality, emphasizing both worldly and otherworldly strength and knowledge. These chivalric circles were built around notions of comradeship, celibacy, equality, and justice, stressing the ties of mutual loyalty among members. In this regard the Islamic guilds, increasingly known as *futuvvat* circles, were autonomous urban institutions that maintained a strong sense of egalitarian and religious spirit, while at times expressing the interests of their associates against the official power and, at other times, serving as a liaison between the state and the workers. This fraternal expression of mutual loyalty mainly involved rigorous examination of a potential's character and initiation ceremonies rather than training in the trades. Under the forty-five year reign of Caliph al-Nasir in the late twelfth and early thirteenth centuries in Baghdad, the *futuvvat* clubs were revived and expanded as a consequence of the growth of trade and revival of towns under the Seljuk rule.

By the time of the Mongol invasion, a major development occurred in the professional groupings with the merging of the *futuvvat* circles and Sufism. With the exception of Syria and Egypt, where the *futuvvat* maintained aristocratic features, by the end of the fifteenth century the *futuvvat* had become, especially in Anatolia and northwestern Iran, essentially the Sufi component of guild associations. In the post-Mongol era of Islamic history, the *futuvvat* associations increasingly began to merge with the Anatolian Sufi orders. This led to the creation of *Akhiyat al-Fityan* or *Akhi* movements, which tended to fuse the horseback warrior culture of inner Asia, embedded in a culture of reverence for the spiritual sacred person *(baba)*, with the urbanite *futuvvat* traditions of Irano-Mesopotamian regions.

Such development set the cultural and political landscape for the emergence of an important dynastic empire in Islamic history, namely the Safavids, at the start of the sixteenth century. As a Sufi brotherhood revolutionary movement, the Safavids were the most militant political manifestation of the *futuvvat* in the form of spiritual warriors in consolidating political authority in Anatolia and the Irano-Mesopotamian regions. The development of guilds in the late fifteenth century also played an important role in the expansion of the Ottoman Empire in the fifteenth and sixteenth centuries: They supplied armies for imperial military campaigns and organized guild ceremonies that provided a channel through which the sultan could reach the whole population of the empire, especially during the imperial circumcision rituals. The Ottoman guilds were autonomous institutions that identified a corporate, economic, and religious community in the cities.

BABAK RAHIMI

See also Artisans; Chivalry; Festivals and Celebrations; Merchants, Muslim; Performing Artists; Religious Movements; Sufism and Sufis; Textiles; Trade, African; Trade, Indian Ocean; Trade, Mediterranean; Urbanism

Primary Sources

Kashifi, Husayn Va'iz. *Futuvvatname-yi Sultani.* Ed. Muhammad Ja'far Mahjub. Tehran: Buhyad-I Farhang-I Iran, 1971.

Further Reading

Babayan, Kathyrn. *Mystics, Monarchs, and Messiahs: Cultural Landscapes of Early Modern Iran.* Harvard: Harvard University Press, 2002.

Bulliet, Richard. *Islam: The View from the Edge.* New York: Columbia University Press, 1994, 164–165.

Cahen, Claude. "Futuwwa." *Encyclopedia of Islam,* new ed. Vol 2. Ed. H.A.R. Gibb. Leiden: Brill, 1965.

Cohen, Amnon. *The Guilds of Ottoman Jerusalem.* Leiden and Boston: Brill, 2001.

Floor, Willem. "The Guilds in Iran: An Overview from the Earliest Beginnings to 1972." *Zeitschrift des Deutschen Morgenlädischen Gesellschaft.* 125 (1975) 99–116.

Levtzion, Nehemia. "The Dynamics of Sufi Brotherhoods." In *The Public Sphere in Muslim Societies,* ed. Miriam Hoexter, Shmuel N. Eisenstadt, and Nehemia Levtzion. New York, 2002.

Massignon, Louis. "La 'Futuwwa' ou 'Pacte d'Honneiur Artisanal' entre les Travailleiurs Musulmans au Moyen Age." In *Opera Minora,* ed. Youakim Moubarac. 3 vols. Beirut, 1963.

H

HADITH

The word *hadith* refers to "speech," meaning, in this case, both collective and individual reports of what the Prophet said and did. Through these words is known the Sunna, which is the model of behavior that all Muslims should imitate. The earliest written collections of hadith date to the last third of the eighth century CE. The Six Books, which make up the most highly respected Sunni collections, are those of al-Bukhari (d. 870), Muslim (d. 875), Abu Dawud (d. 889), al-Tirmidhi (d. 892), al-Nasa'i (d. c. 915), and Ibn Maja (d. c. 887). Four collections enjoy almost as much prestige among the Twelver Shi'is, mainly those of al-Kulayni (d. c. 940) and Ibn Babawayh (d. 991) and two books by al-Tusi (d. c. 1067). Other sects have their own collections of hadith.

An individual hadith always has two parts. First is a list of its transmitters called the *isnad* (support); second is the actual text, called the *matn* (main part). For example, al-Bukhari reports this: < Muhammad ibn Bashshar < Ghundar < Shu'ba < Qatada < Anas ibn Malik < Qatada ibn al-Samit < Prophet: "The believer's dream is one forty-sixth part of prophecy." The isnad protects against forgery. Bukhari goes on to name another isnad that is completely different but in support of the same matn to show that there is no need to rely on the veracity of any one of these men; in addition, four persons related the same matn from Anas directly from the Prophet, without Qatada ibn Samit matn between them. Muslim offers eight isnads to support the same matn.

If a hadith was supported by only a single isnad or if only one person was known to have transmitted it during a generation, it was called *khabar al-wahid* ("the report of one") and considered sound only if that one person's transmission was usually corroborated by others. For example, "The servant's dream is one forty-sixth part of prophecy" appears in a collection of suspect hadith with the isnad < Ishaq ibn Abi Isra'il < 'Abd Allah ibn Yahya ibn Abi Kathir < his father < Abu Salama < Abu Hurayra < the Messenger of God. It is suspect, because the link between Ibn Abi Kathir and his father has few parallels. It was a matter of dispute how much corroboration was enough.

Transmission of hadith by paraphrase was evidently once common. Accordingly, the tradition claims only that it reliably contains the gist of what the Prophet said and not his exact words; this is one reason that philologists continually quote the Qur'an and old poetry to establish correct Arabic usage and rarely quote hadith.

Most of the rules of Islamic law are based on hadith. Disagreements about the rules are usually associated with contradictory hadith. Muslim jurisprudents held that hadith afforded probable knowledge rather than certain. In case of contradiction between hadith and the Qur'an, most jurisprudents held that hadith explained the Qur'an; hence, in practice, hadith took precedence. Only Mu'tazili and Khariji jurisprudents argued for dismissing hadith that seemed to contradict the Qur'an.

The ninth and tenth centuries were the great age of hadith criticism, when the sound was sorted from the unsound. Hadith remained the most popular of the Islamic sciences throughout the Middle Ages, and lectures in hadith attracted great numbers. Even if they could look up the reliable hadith in respected collections, Muslims enjoyed reenacting the experience of the Companions listening to the Prophet.

CHRISTOPHER MELCHERT

See also al-Bukhari; Muslim; al-Kulayni; Ibn Babawayh; al-Tusi

Further Reading

Dickinson, Eerik. *The Development of Early Sunnite Hadith Criticism. Islamic History and Civilization, Studies and Texts,* 38. Leiden: Brill, 2001.

Siddiqi, Muhammad Zubayr. *Hadith Literature: Its Origin, Development and Special Features,* ed. Abdal Hakim Murad. Cambridge, UK: Islamic Texts Society, 1993.

HAFSA BINT AL-HAJJ AL-RUKUNIYYA

Hafsa Bint al-Hajj al-Rukuniyya was a Granadan Arabic poet who died in AH 586/1190–1191 CE. Louis di Giacomo suggests that she was perhaps the most celebrated Andalusian woman poet of her time. In his view, only two others warrant comparison: her eleventh-century Cordoban predecessor Wallada Bint al-Mustakfi and her twelfth-century Granadan contemporary Nazhun Bint al-Qila'i. Indeed, this supposition has some merit. Hafsa's love affair and dialogue with fellow poet Abu Ja'far Ibn Sa'id may be less legendary than Wallada's romantic liaison with the poet Ibn Zaydun, but Hafsa seems to have been more prolific. Only Nazhun's extant corpus, which includes an oft-overlooked strophic poem *(muwashshaha)*, can quantitatively compare to that of Hafsa, which contains about sixty lines of verse set among nineteen compositions. Furthermore, her biography is somewhat less sketchy than those of many female poets of her era, although the details of her childhood (e.g., her date and place of birth) are elusive, and little is known about her family other than that her father was Berber. However, once she establishes her relationship with Abu Ja'far at about the time that the Almohads come to power in 1154 CE, her historical personage becomes more defined, and she begins to be linked to specific people, places, and dates. The figure of Abu Sa'id 'Uthman, an Almohad prince, patron of poets, and rival of Abu Ja'far for Hafsa's affections, is particularly significant in this regard. The rivalry between prince and poet turned deadly when Abu Ja'far joined his extended family, the Banu Sa'id, in their political opposition to the reign of Abu Sa'id's father 'Abd al-Mu'min Bin 'Ali. For this infraction, Abu Ja'far was imprisoned and eventually executed in 1163 CE. At some point after this, Hafsa seems to have made a career change, establishing herself primarily as a pedagogue rather than a poet. In later life, she was hired by the Caliph Ya'qub al-Mansur to educate his daughters in Marrakech, where she died.

One of the most famous poems attributed to Hafsa—perhaps incorrectly—is a succinct panegyric addressing 'Abd al-Mu'min in which she cleverly alludes to her patron's official insignia. Another is her response to a poem by Abu Ja'far. In his piece, Abu Ja'far personifies a garden where the lovers met and implies that its scents and sounds were expressions of its delight in their rendezvous. In her reply, Hafsa accuses her beloved of misinterpreting the garden's motives, asserting that it acted not out of admiration but rather out of envy and spite. Her corpus also features a rather intriguing scatological invective that she is said to have co-composed with Abu Ja'far, each poet extemporizing alternate lines. Although many Andalusian women poets composed amatory, satirical, and obscene verse, Hafsa is additionally remembered for her elegies devoted to Abu Ja'far; hence her poetic output had a thematic variety and depth that make her a distinctive figure in the history of women's writing.

MARLÉ HAMMOND

See also 'A'isha Bint Ahmad al-Qurtubiyya; Almohads; Wallada Bint al-Mustakfi; Women Poets

Primary Sources

Al-Maqqari, Ahmad Ibn Muhammad. *Nafh al-Tib min Ghusn al-Andalus al-Ratib,* 8 vols., vol. 4, 172–8, ed. Ihsan Abbas. Beirut: Dar Sadir, 1968.

Al-Suyuti, Jalal al-Din. *Nuzhat al-Julasa' fi Ash'ar al-Nisa',* ed. Salah al-Din al-Munajjid, 32–7. Beirut: Dar al-Kitab al-Jadid, 1978.

Further Reading

Arberry, A.J. *Moorish Poetry: A Translation of* The Pennants, *an Anthology Compiled in 1243 by the Andalusian Ibn Sa'id,* 94–5. Cambridge, UK: Cambridge University Press, 1953.

Di Giacomo, Louis. *Une Poétesse Grenadine du Temps des Almohades: Hafsa Bint al-Hajj.* Collection Hespéris. Paris: Larose, 1949.

Gruendler, Beatrice. "Lightning and Memory in Poetic Fragments from the Muslim West: Hafsah Bint al-Hajj (d. 1191) and Sarah al-Halabiyyah (d.c.1300)." In *Crisis and Memory: Dimensions of Their Relationship in Islam and Adjacent Cultures,* eds. A. Neuwirth and A. Pflitsch, 435–52. Beirut/Stuttgart: Steiner BTS, 2001.

Pellat, Ch. "Hafsa Bint al-Hadjdj al-Rukuniyya (al-Rakuniyya)." *Encyclopaedia of Islam.* CD-ROM Edition, vol. 1.1. Leiden: Brill, 2001.

HAFSIDS

The Hafsids were a Berber dynasty of governors of Ifriqiyya that stopped paying allegiance to the Almohad caliph and that started to rule independently from AH 627/1229 CE. Together with the Banu 'Abd al-Wad of Tlemcen and the Marinids of Morocco, they exerted control over the African part of the former Almohad empire, whose unity they all tried to restore, the Hafsids with the argument that they were the legitimate heirs of the Almohad caliphs. The civil and military administration of the Hafsids and their official ideology was based on the Almohad model, without this fact having interfered with the spread of Malikism and mysticism (see Sufism). They made Tunis their religious, political, and economical capital—a situation that has prevailed to the present day—and filled it with monuments.

At the beginning of the thirteenth century, Hafsid Tunis received a wave of Andalusi Muslims who fled the lands conquered by the Christians. Among them the writer Ibn al-Abbar (d. 658/1260) and the ancestors of the historian Ibn Khaldun are to be counted. A second wave of Andalusi immigrants arrived by the end of the fifteenth century, after the fall of Granada to the Catholic monarchs. In their new destination, Andalusis made up a powerful social group whose influence is visible in Tunisian architecture.

The Hafsids kept commercial relationships with Provence, Languedoc, the Italian republics, Sicily, and Aragon. These relationships experienced occasional setbacks (e.g., in 668/1270, when the crusade of St. Louis attacked Tunis). Despite its short duration, the presence of the crusaders gave a serious blow to Hafsid prestige and opened a period of disturbance and secession that culminated in 693/1294. In this year, Abu Zakariyya', a nephew of the amir Abu Hafs (683–694/1284–1295), gained control over the Western part of the territory, including Bougie and Constantine (and later over Gabes). The Hafsid emirate enjoyed a period of relative peace and prosperity with Abu 'l-Abbas (772–796/1369–1370) and his successors. However, by the end of the fifteenth century, internal division allowed first the Spaniards and, subsequently, the Turks to take hold of the land. In 982/1574, Tunis became part of the Ottoman Empire.

DELFINA SERRANO RUANO

See also Almohad; Malikism

Further Reading

Annabi, H., M. Chapoutot-Remadi, and Samia Kamarti, eds. *Itineraire du Savoir en Tunisie: Les Temps Forts de l'Histoire Tunisienne*. Paris, CNRS, 1995.
Brunschvig, R. *La Berbérie Orientale sous les Hafsides: Des Origines à la Fin du XVème Siècle*, 2 vols. Paris, Adrien Maisonneuve, 1940–1947.
Daoulatli, A. *Tunis Sous les Hafsides: Évolution Urbaine et Activité Architecturale*. Tunis: Institut National d'Archéologie et d'Art, 1976.
Idris, H.R. "Hafsids." In *EI²*
Julien, Ch.A. *Histoire de l'Afrique du Nord: Tunisie, Algérie, Maroc: De la Conquête Arabe a 1830*. Paris, Payot, 1969.
———. *Histoire de l'Afrique du Nord: Des Origines à 1830*. Paris, Payot, 1994.
Van Staevel, J.P. "Savoir Voir et le Faire Savoir: L'Expertise Judiciaire en Matière de Construction, D'Après un Auteur Tunisois du viiie/xive Siècle." *Annales Islamologiques* 35 (2001).
Le Tourneau, R. "North Africa to the Sixteenth Century." In *The Cambridge History of Islam, Vol. 2., The Further Islamic Lands, Islamic Society and Civilization*, eds. P.M. Holt, A.K.S. Lambton, and B. Lewis, 211–37. Cambridge, UK: Cambridge University Press, 1970.

HAJJ

The Semitic root from which the Arabic term *hajj* derives is associated with the visitation of sacred shrines. It is an old word that is found in the northwest Semitic languages of Hebrew, Phoenician, Syriac, and Aramaic and South Semitic Sabaean, as well as Arabic. In the Hebrew Bible, it references the three Pilgrimage Festivals: "Three times in the year all your males shall appear before the Lord God" (Exodus 23:14–18). The core meaning likely includes circumambulation (Hebrew *hug*: Proverbs 8:7, Job 26:10) and perhaps even leaping or reeling from excessive consumption and celebration (1 Samuel 30:16, Psalm 107:27). Indeed, depictions of pre-Islamic hajj practice mention members of the Meccan tribe of Quraysh dancing around the Ka'ba—even naked—as part of the encircling ritual.

Hajj visitations were a core part of pre-Islamic religious practice in the area around Mecca. They included a spring visitation called 'Umra to the Meccan Ka'ba during the month of Rajab, a circumambulation between two low nearby hills named Safa and Marwa, and a regular visitation to 'Arafat some eleven miles away from the Ka'ba. According to the Qur'an (2:196–200), these appear to have been separate rituals that were united under the leadership of Muhammad to form the complex Islamic pilgrimage ritual of today.

The Islamic pilgrimage became a sober time for personal reflection and collective association with the multiethnic and multiracial community of Muslims, culminating in an animal sacrifice to be eaten and distributed to the poor (22:28). The Qur'an associates the Hajj with Abraham. After coming to Mecca to (re) build the Ka'ba, God tells him (22:27), "Call humanity to the Hajj!" The traditional commentaries mention how Abraham's voice carried not only to all corners of the world but even into the wombs of mothers; all humanity heard the call.

Hajj is therefore a duty that is incumbent upon those who are able (3:97), but the Qur'an was silent regarding most of the ritual details. These were filled in and authorized through commentaries on the Qur'an and through the Sunna, the tradition literature that articulates the acts and discourse of the Prophet Muhammad.

Muhammad inherited visitation activities that had been practiced as pagan ritual for generations. Traditions therefore emerged that associated the ritual stations (manasik) with Abraham, the indigenous monotheist forbear of Islam (3:67). According to these traditions, the originally monotheistic pilgrimage rituals established by Abraham were corrupted over the ages; Muhammad therefore restored them to their original and pristine status of worship and adoration of the one great God.

The Islamic hajj ritual is too complex to describe here in any detail, but it includes the circumambulation (tawaf) of the Meccan Ka'ba, "running" (sa'i) between Safa and Marwa, "standing" (wuquf) at 'Arafat, and animal sacrifice. These and more ritual acts take place during the first ten days of the month called *dhul-hijja*, culminating in the Feast of Sacrifice ('id al-adha), which is associated by some with the divine command of Abraham to sacrifice his son Ishmael at the site of the Ka'ba (although early Muslim scholars differed strongly over who was the intended sacrifice and where it would have taken place).

Medieval pilgrimage routes criss-crossed the Islamic world and beyond, bringing all kinds of Muslims together to share the common pilgrimage experience. Official caravans departed from key points such as Syria, Egypt, Persia, and Iraq for the protection of pilgrims who were sometimes attacked by Arab marauders—even during the ten ritual days themselves—if left unprotected. The "protection" of pilgrims and control of pilgrimage routes signified political power, so opportunists from Ibn Zubayr in 692 to the followers of Ibn 'Abd al-Wahhab (wahhabis) in the late eighteenth and early nineteenth centuries preyed upon and "protected" pilgrims in a manner that made the journey precarious into the modern period. Many pious believers would remain in Mecca after their hajj, where they learned, taught, and shared knowledge, creating a cosmopolitan center in the middle of the Arabian desert that remains one of the more broadminded cities of Saudi Arabia to this day.

REUVEN FIRESTONE

Further Reading

Asad, Muhammad. *The Road to Mecca*. New York: Simon and Schuster, 1954.

Al-Azraqi, Abu al-Walid Muhammad b. 'Abdallah. *Akhbar Makka*, 2 vols., ed. F. Wustenfeld. 1858.

Firestone, Reuven. *Journeys in Holy Lands*. Albany, NY: State University of New York, 1990.

Kamal, Abdul Aziz. *Every Man's Guide to Hajj and Umra*. Lahore, 1978.

Kamal, Ahmad. *The Sacred Journey*. New York: Duell, Sloan and Pearce, 1961.

Peters, F.E. *The Hajj: The Muslim Pilgrimage to Mecca and the Holy Places*. Princeton, NJ: Princeton University Press, 1994.

———. *Mecca: A Literary History of the Muslim Holy Land*. Princeton, NJ: Princeton University Press, 1994.

Sargent-Aure, Barbara, ed. *Journeys Toward God: Pilgrimage and Crusade*. Kalamazoo, Mich, 1992.

HAKIM, AL-, FATIMID CALIPH

Al-Hakim bi-amr Allah, Abu 'Ali Mansur, was the sixth of the Fatimid caliphs, whose quite unusual reign featured a range of odd—even bizarre—acts that have left a strange enigmatic historical record not easily explained or fairly judged. As imam of the Ismaili Muslims, he was the divinely ordained successor of the Prophet Muhammad, with full and exclusive authority over his followers. Accordingly, his word was law; Islam would be defined by his words and actions. In practice, his various attempts at reform through legal restrictions on, among other things, the consumption of certain foodstuffs and alcoholic beverages, games of chance, religious rites he did not approve of, the public movements of women, the appearance of Jews and Christians without markers to identify them as such, and public expressions of veneration for the Companions of the Prophet were never accepted by the majority in his realm and were anathema to most. To enforce his order, he had many killed, especially from the higher elite of his government; he commanded the destruction of a large number of churches and synagogues, the most famous of which was the Church of the Holy Sepulchre in Jerusalem (destroyed in 1009 CE). However, he was well known for his generosity and beneficence and his support of the sciences and learning. Above all, after he reached maturity, he conducted the affairs of government personally and circulated at will among the populace both by night and by day, riding a donkey with little or no escort.

Born in Egypt in 985, al-Hakim assumed the caliphate upon the unexpected early death of his father, al-'Aziz, in 996 at the age of eleven. Initially he was under the constraint of the powerful commander of his Berber troops, Ibn 'Ammar, and his tutor, the eunuch Barjawan. One by one he rid himself of these men and emerged on his own, when he began the series of legal enactments for which he is famous. Many of these acts both came into effect and were later rescinded. Cursing of the Prophet's Companions because they had failed to uphold the right of ‘Ali to succeed ended with an order to remember them for the good they had done before that fateful betrayal. In 1005, al-Hakim created a public academy and library, the Dar al-‘Ilm, which was staffed with Sunni professors. The Isma‘ilis had their own teaching institution, the Majlis al-Hikma. Churches and synagogues once looted and torn down were given permission to reopen; Christians formerly oppressed were allowed to emigrate, and those who had converted to Islam could return to their original faith.

At least twice al-Hakim faced quite serious revolts on the fringes of his domain. In 1005, an Umayyad pretender, Abu Rakwa, rallied tribal forces in the Libyan desert and marched into the Delta. At first he succeeded in defeating the Fatimid armies sent against him, although eventually he fell himself and was executed in Cairo two years later. In 1011 and 1012, previously loyal tribesmen in southern Palestine rose to establish, in conjunction with the amir of Mecca, a counter-caliphate. Skillful negotiations and the payment of bribes by al-Hakim to the leading men involved eliminated this threat. Despite these signs of resistance, in general, al-Hakim's rule prevailed; the Fatimids lost no territory during his reign, preserving their hold on much of Syria and the Hijaz and the titular overlordship of North Africa and Sicily. On one occasion in 1010, al-Hakim was even acknowledged—albeit briefly—as caliph throughout northern Mesopotamia.

During the final seven years of his life, al-Hakim adopted a style of rule that was increasingly more ascetic and less regal. He began to ride in public exclusively on a donkey, he let his hair and nails grow, he wore rough black clothing, and he tried to delegate official functions to a cousin that he appointed as his heir apparent. His most ardent supporters confirm that many became perplexed as a result, so unaccustomed were they to such behavior by a supreme leader and imam. By 1017 or possibly even earlier, others turned more enthusiastic, declaring that al-Hakim was in fact divine, a god whose actions were not to be judged by human standards. That same year, Hamza ibn ‘Ali, the eventual founder of the Druze, and al-Darazi, the man whose name provided the word Druze itself, both began to preach openly that al-Hakim was God Himself, appearing in human form. Whether the caliph actually encouraged these men is doubtful; those who held official positions under al-Hakim fought as forcefully as they could against such tendencies. However, in 1021, al-Hakim disappeared mysteriously during the course of one of his nightly excursions, leaving those who considered him to be God even more convinced of that fact and the rest of his followers scrambling to arrange for the succession of his son, al-Zahir; this feat was engineered under these unusual circumstances by the absent caliph's powerful sister, Sitt al-Mulk.

PAUL E. WALKER

Further Reading

Canard, M. "Al-Hakim bi-Amr Allah." In *Encyclopaedia of Islam, New Edition.*

Halm, Hainz. *Die Kalifen von Kairo: Die Fatimiden in Ägypten, 973–1074*, 167–304. Munich: C.H. Beck, 2003.

Walker, Paul E. "The Ismaili *Da'wa* in the Reign of the Fatimid Caliph al-Hakim." *Journal of the American Research Center in Egypt* 30 (1993): 161–82.

———. "Fatimid Institutions of Learning." *Journal of the American Research Center in Egypt* 34 (1997): 179–200.

———. *Hamid al-Din al-Kirmani: Ismaili Thought in the Age of al-Hakim.* London: I.B. Tauris, 1999.

HAMADHANI, BADI‘ AL-ZAMAN

Abu al-Fadl Ahmad ibn al-Husayn al-Hamadhani (968–1008 CE) was given the nickname "Badi‘ al-Zaman" ("The Wonder of the Age") in recognition of his mastery of Arabic prose writing in the high style. Among his teachers was the illustrious grammarian Ibn Faris (d. 1004), and he spent the earlier part of his career as a littérateur in Rayy at the renowned court of al-Sahib ibn ‘Abbad (d. 995) before moving further East.

Al-Hamadhani was, it appears, a complete master of the Arabic and Persian languages, able to translate instantaneously between the two and to improvise elaborate exercises in verbal virtuosity. Although he wrote a number of works, including a set of rasa'il (epistles), he is remembered chiefly as the writer who managed to combine different narrative features into an entirely new genre: the *maqamah* (the name of the genre being derived from the idea of "standing," and thus perhaps contrasted with the institution of *majlis,* a name that implies an "evening session"). The primary element involved in the emergence of this new genre was the ancient style known as *saj‘,* a form of rhyming and cadenced prose that finds its most notable place of expression in the text of the Qur'an itself. The revival (and elaboration) of this style of writing in al-Hamadhani's time was one of the consequences of a conscious decision on the part of those udaba' (littérateurs) in the chancelleries (diwan al-rasa'il) of the Islamic courts to develop a more elaborate form of prose style. Al-Hamadhani's invocation of this style was coupled with another element: anecdotes concerning the daily life of the inhabitants of the cities and regions of the Arab–Islamic world and in particular the underworld inhabited by beggars and tricksters. These elements were combined into a set of fifty maqamat in which two principal characters, a narrator named 'Isa ibn Hisham and a perpetually shifting rogue figure named Abu al-Fath al-Iskandari, are placed into a variety of venues throughout the Islamic regions of West Asia and ply their routines of trickery. The denouement of each episode involves the disclosure of the true identity of Abu al-Fath who, up to that point, has been playing any one of a wide variety of roles, thus allowing for a good deal of pastiche of different genres—critical debate, sermon, will and testament, and so on—before the truth is revealed.

Although the above description covers a good percentage of the maqamat included in al-Hamadhani's collection, there is nevertheless considerable diversity in narrative approach and content. Some examples have 'Isa ibn Hisham, the narrator, acting as his own trickster (the Baghdad maqamah, for example), whereas, in the famous *al-Maqamah al-Madiriyyah* (a masterly and insightful commentary on middle-class values reminiscent of Petronius's "Cena Trimalchionis" in the *Satyricon*), the narrator does not appear at all. The Saymari maqamah is an elaborate morality tale that points out the dangers of excessive luxury and indulgence. The maqamah of Hulwan consists of two separate sections (as do several other examples): in the first, a truly farcical situation in a barber's shop emerges as a parody of judicial practice, whereas, in the second, the reader/listener is treated to a wonderful exercise in malapropism.

The pioneer status of al-Hamadhani's set of maqamat was to be acknowledged many years later by his successor, Abu Muhammad Qasim al-Hariri (d. 1122). However, it is this latter figure who is still one of the most celebrated figures in the history of Arabic prose writing; his own stylistic virtuosity exceeded even that of al-Hamadhani and took the maqamah genre to even greater linguistic and rhetorical heights.

ROGER ALLEN

Further Reading

The Maqamat of Badi' al-Zaman al-Hamadhani, transl. W.J. Prenderghast. London: Curzon Press, 1973.
Makamat or Rhetorical Anecdotes of Al-Hariri of Basra, transl. Theodore Preston. London: Gregg International Publishers, 1971.
Bosworth, C. Edmund. *The Mediaeval Islamic Underworld*. Leiden: E.J. Brill, 1976.
Hameen-Anttila, Jaako. *Maqama: A History of a Genre*. Wiesbaden: Harrassowitz, 2002.
Kilito, Abdelfattah. *Les Séances*. Paris: Sindbad, 1983.
Monroe, James. *The Art of Badi' az-Zaman al-Hamadhani*. Beirut: American University in Beirut Press, 1983.

HAMDANIDS

The Hamdanids are an Arab (i.e., Bedouin but not nomadic) family from the Banu Taghlib tribe that has been recorded in the Djazira since pre-Islamic times. Although initially Bedouin, the Hamdanids established an urban regime. Their headquarters were located in the ancient cities of Mesopotamia and Northern Syria, and they replaced their tribal armies with slave soldiers.

The first member of the family—and the person after whom the family was named—was Hamdan ibn Hamdun, who played a minor role in 'Abbasid politics during the second half of the AH third/ninth CE century. His descendants established two minor dynasties in Mesopotamia and Aleppo that survived until the second half of the fourth/tenth century. In addition, they gained fame for their cultural role, particularly in Arabic poetry.

Three stages can be differentiated in the history of the Hamdanids. The first took place in northern Iraq and Baghdad during the final decades of the third/ninth century. Hamdan b. Hamdun and his son Husayn were involved in fighting against the Khawaridjs as well as battling the armies of the 'Abbasid caliphate. This stage ended with the incorporation of the Hamdanids into the coalition that converged around the 'Abbasid family.

Abu Muhammad al-Hasan, who succeeded his father (317/929), became the head of the Hamdanid family. At that junction, he served as the governor of Mawsil (Mosul) in northern Mesopotamia. Taking advantage of the violent struggle within the 'Abbasid court (which led to the murder of the caliph by his Turkish guards and the emergence of a military regime headed by the commander in chief (amir al-umaraa') in 324/936), al-Hasan was able not only to maintain his position in Mawsil but also to extend his influence southward, along the Tigris River. During these troubled years, his achievements peaked. Al-Hasan had Muhammad ibn Ra'iq assassinated and forced the caliph al-Muttaqi to bestow on him the royal title (laqb) Nasir al-Dawla (defender of the 'Abbasid dynasty). Later, in 330/942, he married the caliph's granddaughter.

The second chapter in the history of the Hamdanids began after their withdrawal from Baghdad, which was taken over by the Buwayhids. During this period, they failed to hold onto their possessions in the Djazira, and the emirate of Mosul was seized by the Buwayhids (367/978). They were more successful in the land west of the Euphrates, extending their rule to new territories.

This development is related to Abu al-Hasan 'Ali Sayf al-Dawla (the sword of the 'Abbasid dynasty). Taking advantage of the complicated political conditions in Northern Syria, a land that was out of reach of the three major forces in the Middle East (the fragile 'Abbasids in Baghdad and the Ikhshids in Egypt and Byzantine [who were gaining new lands in Asia Minor]), he was able to become the master of Aleppo (333/944). The fighting against the Byzantines served one of Sayf al-Dawla's legitimacy claims. However, his delicate position was clearly demonstrated when the Byzantine armies succeeded in temporarily conquering Aleppo (351/962).

The emirate that Sayf al-Dawla established gained fame primarily because of its role in the history of Arabic literature. The circle of poets that congregated in Sayf al-Dawla's palace spread his name. Among the prominent intellectuals in his court were his cousin Abu Firas, al-Mutannabi, Abu al-Faradj al-Isfahani, and al-Farabi.

After Sayf al-Dawla's death (356/967), Aleppo became the seat of his son Sa'd al-Dawla Abu al-Ma'ali, who was challenged by his uncle Abu Firas and who, because of inner opposition, had to fight his way into the city. This marked the beginning of the third stage of the history of the Hamdanids. It ended with the advance of the Fatimid armies (406/1015) and the emergence of a new Bedouin dynasty, Banu Kilab (414/1023).

YEHOSHUA FRENKEL

Further Reading

Canard, Marius. *Histoire de la Dynastie des Hamdanides de Jazira et de Syrie*. Algiers, 1951.

Smoor, Peter. *Kings and Bedouins in the Palace of Aleppo as Reflected in Ma'arri's Works*. Manchester, UK: University of Manchester Press, 1985.

HARAWI, AL-, 'ALI B. ABI BAKR

Al-Harawi (d. 1215 CE) was an ascetic, a Sufi, a scholar, a preacher, a poet, a pilgrim, an emissary, and a counselor to rulers. He was born in Mosul, Iraq, possibly to a family from Herat, in present-day Afghanistan, and he later settled in Baghdad, where he was a protégé of the 'Abbasid Caliph al-Nasir li-Din Allah, who appointed him to the post of preacher in the congregational mosque of Baghdad. Al-Harawi was among a number of prominent Sufis and ascetics who were intimates of the Caliph, who was instrumental in consolidating his spiritual authority over the Sufi orders of Baghdad and facilitating rapprochement between the Sunnis and the Shi'is. It is alleged that al-Nasir gave al-Harawi charge over regulating the moral conduct of the markets in all of Greater Syria, reviving the uncultivated lands, and serving as preacher in the congregational mosque of Aleppo.

Although an ascetic, al-Harawi was very much involved in diplomacy and warfare by serving as an emissary during the reign of Saladin, and he most likely joined the ruler on military campaigns. In this role, al-Harawi met with the Muslim ruler of Sicily and, in 1179 or 1180, with the Byzantine Emperor Emmanuel Comnenos. From 1173, he even visited Jerusalem and other cities in Palestine that were under Crusader rule and the Muslim and Christian holy sites therein. In 1192, King Richard the Lionheart requested an audience with al-Harawi to return to him his stolen writings and recompense him after his troops set upon al-Harawi's convoy at the outskirts of Palestine near Gaza. Circumstances did not permit al-Harawi to meet him.

Al-Harawi eventually came to reside in Aleppo, where he served as an advisor to Saladin's son al-Malik al-Zahir Ghazi, who endowed a madrasa (teaching college) for him. His detractors falsely accused al-Harawi of being a Shi'i, and he was also accused of being a conjurer and magician who exercised undue influence over his patron, al-Malik al-Zahir Ghazi.

Al-Harawi is the author of the only pilgrimage guide to the shrines, holy places, and antiquities of the entire medieval Islamic world: *Kitab al-Isharat ila Ma'rifat al-Ziyarat (Guide to Pilgrimage Places)*. Al-Harawi's guide is a testament to the diversity of Muslim—and, to a lesser extent, Christian and Jewish—holy places and to the antiquities of ancient civilizations. Al-Harawi also authored a manual on warfare entitled *al-Tadhkira al-Harawiyya fi 'l-Hiyal al-Harbiyya (Memoirs of al-Harawi on the Stratagems of War)*, which he wrote for the ruler of Aleppo and which focused on the etiquette of waging war.

The inscriptions on his Aleppo mausoleum that al-Harawi built during his lifetime attest to his longing for the hereafter and meeting the Creator and his lack of faith in his fellow man.

JOSEF W. MERI

See also Ascetics and Asceticism

Further Reading

Guide de Lieux des Pèlerinage, transl. Janine Sourdel-Thomine. Damascus, 1957.

A Lonely Wayfarer's Guide to Pilgrimage: 'Ali b. Abi Bakr al-Harawi's Kitab al-Isharat ila Ma'rifat al-Ziyarat, transl. Josef W. Meri. Princeton, NJ, 2004.

HARIZI, AL-, JUDAH

An eight-page entry from the Arabic biographical dictionary of Ibn al-Sha'ar al-Mawsili (1197–1256) contains an entry about Judah al-Harizi (b. ca. 1166 in Toledo, d. 1225 in Aleppo):

> Yahya Ibn Suleiman Ibn Sha'ul Abu Zakariyya al-Harizi the Jew from the people of Toledo. He was a poet of great talent and prolific creation who composed poems in the area of panegyric and invective... He composed numerous works in the Hebrew language such as the "Book of *Maqamat;*" [he also composed] a single *maqama* in the Arabic language that he titled "The Elegant Garden."

The entry preserves Arabic poems by al-Harizi and reveals details such as the author's uncommon height, his inability to grow a beard, and his Maghrebi accent. Al-Harizi was born in Toledo, which was then part of the Iberian Christian kingdom of Castile, and he later migrated to the Islamic east, traveling as far as Baghdad and ultimately settling in Aleppo. Al-Harizi's earliest Hebrew compositions are translations from Arabic and Judeo-Arabic, including Maimonides' *Guide of the Perplexed;* Ali Ibn Rudhwan's (d. ca. 1068) *Epistle on Morals;* a book about poetics and exegesis by Moses Ibn Ezra; and the famous maqama collection of al-Hariri of Basra. Al-Harizi's translation method preserves the sense of the original, often through paraphrase, while striving to produce a Hebrew text that is clear and elegant. His translation of al-Hariri's maqamat entitled *Mahbarot 'Itti'el ('Itti'el's Compositions)* is executed in a pure biblical Hebrew and replaces Arabic and Islamic references with Hebrew and Jewish ones. Al-Harizi strives to preserve literary conceits (e.g., the composition of palindromes) around which he structures maqamat.

Al-Harizi composed his original Hebrew maqama collection, *The Book of Tahkemoni*, after leaving Iberia for the east. Following a trend toward Hebrew rhymed-prose composition and modeling structure after the maqamat of al-Hamadhani and al-Hariri, al-Harizi produced fifty tales in rhymed prose with poems interspersed. As in the classical maqamat, episodes revolve around the encounters of a narrator and a protagonist rogue. The rhetoric-hungry narrator travels throughout the world and repeatedly encounters an itinerant rhetorician who makes a living through eloquence and petty scams. Episodes often incorporate a ruse motif, denouement through anagnorisis (recognition), and witty speech mediated through biblical allusions. Al-Harizi undertakes literary feats, including a trilingual poem (Hebrew, Aramaic, and Arabic) in a single rhyme and meter and a letter that, read forward, is panegyric but that, read backward, is invective. Numerous plots are borrowed from al-Hamadhani, al-Hariri, and other Arabic authors.

The six surviving Arabic poems by al-Harizi include panegyrics to the Ayyubid ruler Al-Malik al-Ashraf Ibn Abu Bakr Ayyub (d. 1237). Al-Harizi's *al-Rawda al-Aniqa (The Elegant Garden)* is an Arabic maqama that details the author's journeys through the lands of the Islamic east (paralleling chapter forty-six of the *Tahkemoni*). He describes Damascus as a "garden for souls... the torrent beds of its elevated places are like those of *Najd*." Since Najd is a place the author never visited, the author's association with the nostalgia-laden locus of the Arabian Peninsula demonstrates his intimacy with the Arabic literary tradition.

JONATHAN P. DECTER

See also Al-Hamadhani; al-Hariri; Maqama; Poetry, Hebrew

Further Reading

Al-Harizi, Judah Ben Solomon. *The Book of Tahkemoni: Jewish Tales from Medieval Spain*, transl. David Simha Segal. London and Portland, Oregon: The Littman Library of Jewish Civilization, 2001.

Drory, Rina. "Al-Harizi's *Maqamat*: A Tricultural Literary Product?" *Medieval Translator* 4 (1994): 66–85.

Sadan, Joseph. "Rabi Yehudah al-Harizi ke-Tzomet Tarbuti." *Pe'amim* 68 (1996): 52–61.

Yahalom, Joseph, and Joshua Blau. *Mas'ei Yehudah*. Jerusalem: Ben-Zvi Institute, 2002.

HARUN AL-RASHID

Harun, the son of al-Mahdi, became the fifth 'Abbasid caliph in the fall of 786 CE. He ruled until 809. His succession to rule was a result of a factional power struggle within the court. In short order after the death of Harun's older brother al-Hadi, the Barmakid faction—in collusion with Harun's mother, al-Khayzuran—was able to outmaneuver the supporters of al-Hadi's son Ja'far. Harun's reign is often described as a golden age or, at the very least, as the apex of 'Abbasid stability and culture. Although this is not necessarily true, his reign does represent a period of tremendous wealth and the furthest extent of the 'Abbasid realm.

The empire was prosperous. Baghdad was a thriving, cultured metropolis to which poets, artists, and litterateurs flocked. In the west, Harun's court is known as the one that presided over the tales of the *One Thousand and One Nights*. However, it is in comparison with the civil war between Harun's two sons and the steady decline thereafter that Harun's reign shines so brightly. For the first decade of his reign, Harun was under the tutelage of the Barmakids. They endeavored to more aggressively assert central control, which left Harun in a much stronger financial position. However, they were never quite able to garner the military support that they needed. In addition, in trying to soften the policy towards the Alids, they made many enemies within the court.

The beginning of the end for the Barmakids came with the succession arrangement established in Mecca in 802. It was there that Harun declared that his son Muhammad al-Amin would succeed him and following him would be Abdallah al-Ma'mun; he made all parties swear publicly to uphold this. Also, when Muhammad came to the throne, his brother would be autonomous in Khurasan. This elaborate succession arrangement appears to be intended to short-circuit factional rivalries and to channel them in productive ways. Muhammad's support base was among the non-Barmakid elite of Baghdad, whereas Abdallah's was among the Barmakids and consequently the bureaucracy. It was upon return from a pilgrimage in 803 that the fall of the Barmakids occurred. As a result of its shockingly precipitous nature, this episode stands out and has been the object of much commentary.

It seems that, fundamentally, Harun was no longer willing to accept so powerful a faction within the court. Kennedy suggests that perhaps the family resisted an arrangement that clearly subordinated them, and this was the trigger for their fall. In the wake of this action, Harun began a campaign of strengthening his legitimacy by participating in raids against the Byzantines. These raids did not bring new lands under control, but they did serve to highlight his role as Commander of the Faithful. For the rest of his reign, he spent very little time in Baghdad and based himself on the Byzantine frontier. A series of rebellions broke out in the east, and, in 808, Harun went to deal with them. It was on this campaign that he died in 809 in Tus, near present-day Mashhad.

JOHN P. TURNER

See also 'Abbasids; Baghdad; Khurasan; Tus

Primary Sources

Dinawari, Abu Hanifa Ahmad b. Dawud. *Kitab al-Akhbar al-Tiwal*, eds. V.F. Guirgass and I.I.U. Kratchkovsky. Leiden: E.J. Brill, 1888.
Ibn al-Athir, Izz al-Din. *al-Kamil fi'l-Ta'rikh*, ed. K.J. Tornberg. Beirut: Dar Sadir, 1965.

Tabari, Abu Ja'far. *The Abbasid Caliphate in Equilibrium*, vol. 30, transl. C.E. Bosworth. Albany: State University of New York Press, 1989.
Ya'qubi, Ahmad b. Abi Ya'qub. *al-Ta'rikh*, 2 vols., ed. M.T. Houtsma. Leiden: E.J. Brill, 1883.

Further Reading

Bonner, M. "Al-Khalifa al-Mardi: The Accession of Harun al-Rashid." *Journal of the American Oriental Society* 108 (1988): 79–91.
El-Hibri, T. "Harun al-Rashid and the Mecca Protocol of 802." *International Journal of Middle East Studies* 24 (1992): 461–80.
Kennedy, H. *The Prophet and the Age of the Caliphates: The Islamic Near East from the Sixth to the Eleventh Century*, 2nd ed. London: Longman, 2004.
———. *The Early Abbasid Caliphate*. London: Croom Helm, 1981.
Kimber, R.A. "Harun al-Rashid's Meccan Settlement of AH 186/AD 802." *Occasional Papers of the School of Abbasid Studies* 1 (1986): 55–79.

HASAN AL-BASRI, AL-

Al-Hasan ibn Abi al-Hasan al-Basri was born in AH 21/624 CE and probably grew up in or around Medina. He resided most of his life in Basra (Iraq), where he died on Rajab 1, 110/October 10, 728.

Al-Hasan's legacy must have originated from his charisma as a storyteller and from his piety; it was then spread by a number of disciples who played a significant role in the development of several religious and theological trends. The corpus of anecdotes attributed to him is often contradictory and irreconcilable. Al-Hasan's significance, therefore, is not to be measured with respect to his historical role in the formulation of particular trends. It is rather the ongoing expansion of his posthumous legacy as one of the founding fathers of Islam that has been used for legitimization by competing religious movements and sects.

Al-Hasan likely believed in part to Free Will theology (Qadar): sins are made by humans and cannot be attributed to God. The advocates of that doctrine, including Mu'tazilites and Shi'is, claimed al-Hasan and attributed to him a significant number of anecdotes and letters supporting their theology. They also ascertained that he was involved in uprisings against the Umayyads, especially the revolt of Ibn al-Ash'ath (killed AH 85/704 CE). However, one has to be cautious with what these groups attributed to al-Hasan, for two reasons: (1) they had a theological and political anti-Umayyad agenda, and (2) they reclaimed al-Hasan after the proto-Sunnites and then Sunnites were on a crusade to dissociate him from the Free Will doctrine and from political activism. The *Epistle against the Pre-Destinarians* to Caliph

'Abd al-Malik ibn Marwan that has been ascribed to al-Hasan is the most elaborate example of false attribution. The text reflects theological debates of the third/ninth and fourth/tenth centuries, and it includes anachronistic cases that cannot be dated to 'Abd al-Malik's reign.

The proto-Sunnites and later Sunnites who advocated predestination ascertained that al-Hasan upheld their creed and similarly attributed to him anecdotes and correspondences, which include the inauthentic *Treatise against the Believers in Free Will* to Caliph 'Umar ibn 'Abd al-'Aziz. They also ascertained that al-Hasan, as a notable predecessor, could not have participated in intra-Muslim civil wars. This concerted effort on their part leaves many obvious clues that they were "changing" the historical al-Hasan to fit Sunni expectations.

As for piety, medieval literature overwhelmingly presents al-Hasan as a model, but they disagree as to whether he enjoined moderation in life or complete renunciation of worldly pleasures and preoccupations. In this respect, the largest body of material transmitted about his authority are piety-related sermons and letters, including the inauthentic *Treatise on Asceticism* to Caliph 'Umar ibn 'Abd al-'Aziz, which ridicules this world and warns against its deception. The claim that al-Hasan was the inceptor of Mysticism (Sufism) was initially made in Basra by groups like that of Abu Talib al-Makki (d. 386/996), and al-Hasan's name gradually became a major feature in mystical silsilas (chains of teachers/disciples) going back to Muhammad. The mystic 'Attar produced fabricated hadiths in which the child al-Hasan is said to have met the prophet of Islam.

Al-Hasan was a qadi (judge) of Basra for a short time, but only a small number of legal opinions attributed to him survived. That none of his disciples went on to become prominent scholars of law probably helps explain why his legal legacy did not form. However, he is famous for clashing with a few of his students, who established the Mu'tazilite movement over the judgment of a Muslim committing a grave sin; al-Hasan's position was that the grave sinner is a hypocrite.

Al-Hasan was also believed to have authored a commentary of the Qur'an (Tafsir). However, the glosses attributed to him in a number of Tafsirs do not constitute a complete work. Al-Hasan was a reciter of the Qur'an, and in that capacity it is likely that he offered commentary glosses that were later recorded by his disciples, giving the impression that he authored a Tafsir. It is in this context as well that his famed Qur'an recitation and occasions of revelation (asbab al-nuzul) glosses were likely taught.

SULEIMAN MOURAD

See also Qur'an, Reciters and Recitations

Primary Sources

Al-Dhahabi, Muhammad ibn Ahmad. *Siyar a'Lam al-Nubala'*, 25 vols., vol. 4, 563–88, eds. Shu'ayb Arna'ut and Ma'mun al-Saghirji. Beirut: Mu'assasat al-Risala, 1990–1992.
Al-Isfahani, Abu Ny'aym. *Hilyat al-Awliya' wa-Tabaqat al-Asfiya'*, 10 vols., vol. 2, 131–61. Beirut: Dar al-Kitab al-'Arabi, 1967–1968.
Ibn al-Jawzi. *Adab al-Shaykh al-Hasan ibn Abi al-Hasan al-Basri*, ed. Sulayman M. al-Harash. Riyad: Dar al-Mi'raj, 1993.
Ibn Hanbal. *Kitab al-Zuhd*, ed. Muhammad Zaghlul, 367–406. Beirut: Dar al-Kitab al-'Arabi, 1994.
Ibn Sa'd. *Al-Tabaqat al-Kubra*, 8 vols., vol. 7, 156–78. Beirut: Dar Sadir, 1958.

Further Reading

Cook, Michael A. *Early Muslim Dogma: A Source-Critical Study*, 112–23. Cambridge, UK: Cambridge University Press, 1981.
Knysh, Alexander D. *Islamic Mysticism: A Short History*, 10–3. Leiden: Brill, 2000.
Mourad, Suleiman A. "Between Myth and History: al-Hasan al-Basri in Medieval and Modern Scholarship." PhD dissertation. New Haven, CT: Yale University, 2004.
"The Letter of al-Hasan al-Basri." In *Textual Sources for the Study of Islam*, eds. Andrew Rippin and Jan Knappert, 115–21. Chicago: The University of Chicago Press, 1986.
Van Ess, Josef. *Theologie und Gesellschaft im 2. und 3. Jahrhundert Hidschra*, 6 vols., vol. 2, 41–50. Berlin: Walter de Gruyter, 1991–1997.

HASAN-I SABBAH

Hasan-i Sabbah was a prominent Isma'ili da'i (religiopolitical missionary) and founder of the Nizari Isma'ili state in Persia. The events of Hasan's life and career as the first ruler of the Nizari state, centered at the fortress of Alamut, were recorded in a chronicle, *Sargudhasht-i Sayyidna,* which has not survived. However, this work was available to a number of Persian historians of the Mongol Ilkhanid period, most notably Juwayni and Rashid al-Din, who remain the chief authorities on Hasan-i Sabbah.

Hasan-i Sabbah was born in the mid-1050s CE in Qum, Persia, into a Twelver Shi'i family. His father, 'Ali ibn Muhammad b. Ja'far al-Sabbah, a Kufan claiming Yamani origins, had migrated from Kufa to Qum. Subsequently, the Sabbah family settled in the nearby city of Ray, another center of Shi'i learning as well as Isma'ili activities in Persia. There, Hasan was introduced to Isma'ili teachings and converted to the Isma'ili form of Shi'ism around the age of seventeen, taking the oath of allegiance to the Isma'ili imam of the time, the Fatimid Caliph al-Mustansir.

Soon afterward, in 1072, Hasan was appointed to a position in the da'wa (missionary organization) by Abd al-Malik ibn 'Attash, the chief Isma'ili da'i in Persia, who had been impressed by the talents of the newly initiated youth. In 1076, Hasan left for Fatimid Egypt to further his Isma'ili education, and he spent three years in Cairo and Alexandria. In 1081, he returned to Isfahan, the secret headquarters of the Isma'ili da'wa in central Persia. Subsequently, Hasan traveled for nine years to different parts of Persia in the service of the da'wa while also formulating his own revolutionary strategy against the Seljuk Turks, whose alien and oppressive rule was detested by the Persians. Hasan's seizure of the fortress of Alamut in northern Persia in 1090 by a clever plan of infiltration marked the beginning of the open revolt of the Persian Isma'ilis against the Seljuks as well as the foundation of the Nizari Isma'ili state of Persia, which later acquired a subsidiary in Syria. In the dispute over the succession to the Fatimid Caliph/imam al-Mustansir (d. 1094), Hasan supported Nizar, the original heir-designate, against his brother al-Musta'li, who was installed to the Fatimid caliphate. Hasan now recognized Nizar as al-Mustansir's successor to the Isma'ili imamate, effectively founding the Nizari Isma'ili da'wa independently of Fatimid Cairo, henceforth the seat of the rival Musta'li da'wa. After Nizar, who was murdered in Egypt in 1095 in the aftermath of his abortive revolt, the Nizari imams remained in hiding for three generations, while Hasan and his next two successors at Alamut led the Nizari da'wa and state with the rank of hujja (chief representative) of the hidden Nizari imam.

Outsiders from early on had the impression that the movement of the Persian Isma'ilis under the leadership of Hasan-i Sabbah represented a new preaching (al-da'wa al-jadida) that was in contradistinction with the old preaching (al-da'wa al-qadima) of the Fatimid times. However, the new preaching was no more than the reformulation by Hasan of the established Shi'i doctrine of ta'lim (authoritative instruction). In his reformulation, which contained a treatise entitled "The Four Chapters" that has been preserved only fragmentarily, Hasan argued for the inadequacy of human reason for knowing God and for the necessity of an authoritative teacher as the spiritual guide of humankind: a teacher who would be none other than the Isma'ili imam of the time. The anti-Isma'ili literary campaign of the contemporary Sunni establishment, led by Muhammad al-Ghazali, was directed against this doctrine, which served as the central teaching of the early Nizaris and was also designated as the Ta'limiyya.

An organizer and a strategist of the highest caliber, Hasan-i Sabbah was also a learned theologian. He led an austere life, and he observed the shari'a very strictly. He died on June 12, 1124, and was buried near Alamut. Although Hasan failed to uproot the Seljuks, he did succeed in founding both a territorial state and the independent Nizari Ismai'ili da'wa, which survived the downfall of the Nizari state in 1256.

FARHAD DAFTARY

See also Ghazali, Ismailis

Primary Sources

Al-Din Fadl Allah, Rashid. *Jami' al-Tawarikh: Qismat-i Isma'iliyan*, eds. M.T. Danishpazhuh and M. Mudarrisi-Zanjani, 97–137. Tehran: Bungah-i Tarjuma va Nashr-i Kitab, 1959.
Juwayni, Ata Malik. *Tarikh-i Jahan-Gusha*, ed. M. Qazwini, vol. 3, 186–216. Leiden: E.J. Brill, 1937. (Translated as *The History of the World-Conqueror*, transl. J.A. Boyle, vol. 2, 666–83. Manchester, UK: Manchester University Press, 1958.)

Further Reading

Daftary, F. *The Isma'ilis: Their History and Doctrines,* 324–371. Cambridge, UK: Cambridge University Press, 1990.
———. "Hasan-i Sabbah and the Origins of the Nizari Isma'ili Movement." In *Mediaeval Isma'ili History and Thought*, ed. F. Daftary, 181–204. Cambridge, UK: Cambridge University Press, 1996.
Hodgson, Marshall G.S. *The Order of Assassins*, 41–98. The Hague: Mouton, 1955.
Lewis, Bernard. *The Assassins*, 38–63, 145–52. London: Weidenfeld and Nicolson, 1967.

HEBREW

A member of the Semitic language family, like Arabic and Aramaic, Hebrew *('ivrit)* is the language of the Jewish Bible (Old Testament). In the Bible, the adjective *'ivri* connotes a specific ethnic origin or affiliation (e.g., Genesis 14:13, 39:14; Exodus 1:15, 21:2). Rabbinic sources dating to the first centuries CE (e.g., Mishnah Gittin 9:8; Yadayim 4:5) refer to the Hebrew language as *'ivrit,* which they also call "the sacred tongue" *(leshon ha-qodesh)*. Although it probably was no longer spoken during this period, Hebrew retained its special place in Judaism as the language of the Torah, the Mishnah, and the liturgy. According to Midrashic texts, Hebrew is the primordial language with which God created the world.

With the rise of Islam, the Jewish belief in Hebrew's primacy was challenged by Muslim claims for the purity, perfection, and inimitability *(i'jaz)* of Qur'anic Arabic. Prompted by the development of

Arabic grammar and lexicography, Jews in Islamic lands founded the field of biblical Hebrew philology. Sa'adyah Gaon (d. 942) compiled the first Hebrew dictionary and composed grammatical treatises; Karaite grammarians in Jerusalem were not far behind. The greatest Hebraists, however, were Andalusians, most notably Judah Hayyuj (d. ca. 1010) and Abu'l-Walid Ibn Janah (fl. 1050), whose works have shaped virtually all subsequent Hebrew philology. These authors all wrote in Arabic, which served as the primary language of scholarship among the Jews of Islam during the Middle Ages. In general, they reserved Hebrew for poetry and belles-lettres. According to the Andalusian poets, in fact, only pure biblical Hebrew would do. The verse they wrote was intended, in part, as a statement of cultural independence from the Arabic aesthetic espoused by contemporary Muslims. By contrast, prose works, such as Judah Halevi's *Kuzari* and Moses Maimonides' *Guide,* were composed in Judeo-Arabic for purely utilitarian reasons. When a new readership for them emerged in Provence, they were quickly translated into Hebrew.

The Muslim encounter with Hebrew dates back to the Prophet's lifetime. Indeed, the Qur'an itself contains words of obvious Hebrew origin for which traditional Muslim scholarship has sought Arabic etymologies in an attempt to demonstrate the purity of the Qur'anic idiom. Examples include the following: *sakina,* meaning "divine presence" (2:248, 9:26; cf. Hebrew *shekhinah*); *taurat,* meaning "law"; "Torah" (48:29); *jahannam,* meaning "hell" (3:12; cf. Gehenna); and *al-rahman,* meaning "the Merciful" (1:1,3; cf. *ha-rahaman*). However, although Muslims and Jews have long lived in close proximity, there has never been a concerted Muslim effort to learn Hebrew that is comparable with the European phenomenon of Christian Hebraism. In large measure this is the result of the lack of a shared scripture, but it has meant that Muslim access to Hebrew writings has always been limited. A few medieval Muslim scholars, such as al-Kirmani, al-Biruni, and Ibn Hazm, cite the Bible in polemic contexts but without evincing real familiarity with the Hebrew language. A few converts, such as Samau'al al-Maghribi (d. 1175), learned Hebrew when they were still Jewish. However, these were exceptions. Mastery of Arabic could open many doors in the world of medieval Islam; by and large, basic Hebrew literacy helped bind most Jews to their ancestral faith.

DANIEL FRANK

See also Poetry, Hebrew; Scriptural Exegesis, Jews; Translation, Arabic to Hebrew; Judah ha-Levi; Judeo-Arabic

Further Reading

Adang, Camilla. *Muslim Writers on Judaism & the Hebrew Bible.* Leiden: E.J. Brill, 1996.

Halkin, A.S. "The Medieval Jewish Attitude Toward Hebrew." In *Biblical and Other Studies,* ed. Alexander Altmann, 233–48. Cambridge, Mass: Harvard University Press, 1963.

Jeffery, Arthur. *The Foreign Vocabulary of the Quran.* Baroda: Oriental Institute, 1938.

Khan, Geoffrey. "The Karaite Tradition of Hebrew Grammatical Thought." In *Hebrew Study from Ezra to Ben-Yehuda,* ed. William Horbury, 186–203. Edinburgh: T & T Clark, 1999.

Maman, Aharon. "The Linguistic School." In *Hebrew Bible/Old Testament,* vol. 1/2, ed. Magne Sæbø, 261–281. Göttingen: Vandenhoeck & Ruprecht, 2000.

Sáenz-Badillos, Angel. *A History of the Hebrew Language.* Cambridge, UK: Cambridge University Press, 1993.

Wechter, Pinchas. *Ibn Barûn's Arabic Works on Hebrew Grammar and Lexicography.* Philadelphia: Dropsie College, 1964.

HEBRON (AL-KHALĪL AL-RAHMĀN; AL-KHALĪL)

Known in Arabic as *al-Khalīl al-Rahmān* (the Friend of God; Abraham) or simply as *al-Khalīl,* Hebron's name reflects its long past in pre-Islamic and Islamic history as well as emphasizing the perdurance of the sacred character of the city within the monotheistic tradition that Islam continues. Located in al-ard al-muqaddas (the Holy Land), Hebron lies in a mountainous region roughly twenty miles south of al-Quds (Jerusalem) at approximately three thousand feet above sea level. Associated with Abraham, al-Khalīl constitutes sacred space to Muslims, Christians, and Jews. These religious communities all revere the Tomb of the Prophets (al-Anbiyā'), and each recounts the story of Abraham's resting place under an oak in Hebron's plain of Mamre as well as his subsequent purchase from Ephron the Hittite of the burial cave at Hebron. Muslims also believe that the prophet Muhammad visited the city on his isrā' (nocturnal journey) from Mecca to Medina.

Hebron's Islamic history begins with the peaceful surrender of the city to 'Umar ibn al-Khattāb in 638 CE. The ninth-/fifteenth-century Jerusalem-born historian of al-Quds and al-Khalīl, Mujir al-Dīn al-'Ulaymī al-Hanbalī records fully the Prophet Muhammad's gift in 630 or 631 of Hebron and its surrounding territory to Tamīm al-Dārī and his brothers. Muslim patronage of al-Khalīl revived its fortunes; the city had suffered Byzantine neglect.

The Haram al-Ibrāhīmī (Sanctuary of Abraham) sits atop the cave and the ruins of a Byzantine church. The foundation and the walls of the structure are Herodian. Added to by the Crusaders who captured the city in 1099, the Haram also benefited from Ayyūbid and Mamlūk constructive energies. Although Salāh al-dīn ibn Ayyūb (Saladin) donated its intricately carved wooden minbar in 1191 and 1192, internally and externally, much of the present mosque reflects Mamlūk (1259/1260–1516) efforts to preserve and embellish this important Muslim religious site. Baybars I restored the Tomb of Abraham, while Mamlūk amīrs, serving either as nā'ib al-sultāna, nāzir al-Haramayn al-Sharīfayn, or both continued to beautify and maintain al-Khalīl. Notably, the seventh-/thirteenth-century nāzir al-Haramayn 'Ala' al-dīn al-Aydughdī personally oversaw the distribution of the weekly meal of lentils, barley, and bread that the Khalīlī waqf (endowment) provided to the poor of the city and to travelers. Generosity to pilgrims of all nations marked the pious endowment at al-Khalīl and drew extensive favorable comment. Mamlūk attention to the city was consistent, and it aimed toward good government, especially in terms of the management of the waqf funds that supported worthy religious and charitable purposes.

Selim I's victory at Marj Dābiq in August 1516 brought new rulers to Palestine; the Ottoman sultan entered al-Quds in December. Under Selīm's successor, his son Suleiman al-Qānūnī (1520–1566), prosperity reigned in al-Quds, al-Khalīl, and the entire region. Late in the sixteenth century, as a result of the marked decline in public security (especially along the shrine routes where Bedouin tribesmen attacked pilgrim caravans en route to al-Haram al-Ibrāhīmī), Hebron's socioeconomic position deteriorated during the early modern era. Al-Khalīl, however, retained its status as the fourth-holiest city within the Muslim world.

CAROL L. BARGERON

See also Baybars I; Jerusalem; Mamluks; Muhammad, the Prophet; Ottoman Empire; Palestine; Saladin (Salah al-Din); Suleiman the Magnificent; Waqf

Primary Source

Al-'Ulaymī, Mujir al-dīn 'Abd al-Rahmān ibn Muhammad. *al-Uns al-Jalīl bi-Tārīkh al-Quds wa-al-Khalīl*, 2 vols. Amman: Maktabat al-Muhtasib, 1973.

Further Reading

Gil, Moshe. *A History of Palestine, 634 to 1099*. Cambridge, UK: Cambridge University Press, 1992.
Le Strange, Guy, transl. *Palestine Under the Moslems: A Description of Syria and the Holy Land from A.D. 650 to 1500*. Oriental Repr. no. 14. Beirut: Khayats, 1965.
Little, Donald. "Mujir al-Dīn al-'Ulaymī's Vision of Jerusalem in the Ninth/Fifteenth Century." *Journal of the American Oriental Society* 115 (1995): 237–47.

HERAT

Herat was a city of considerable prominence during the medieval period that was located on the Hari Rud river in eastern Khurasan (now Afghanistan).

The origins of Herat date back to the Achaemenian age (c. 550–330 BCE), and its name in Old Persian (Haraiva) reflects its proximity to the vigorous Hari Rud river. The river valley and plains, which are bordered by the Ghur and Safid Kuh mountain ranges, made Herat an optimal oasis area and caravan way station for the web of trade routes connecting East Asia with the Indian Ocean and the Irano-Mediterranean frontier. Historical evidence suggests that Alexander the Great made this city a provincial capital of Areia after his campaign of 330 BCE, and subsequent records indicate that Herat grew in strategic and administrative importance during the Sasanian period (226–652 CE). With the seventh-century Arab Muslim invasions and the subsuming of this region into the Umayyad and 'Abbasid empires, Herat attained a greater profile; its agricultural prosperity and commercial potential encouraged Arab tribal settlement, and, by the tenth century, the city was noted by geographers such as Ibn Hawqul and Istakhri for its urban infrastructure, markets, and mosque complexes. Herat would change hands innumerably during the ninth through eleventh centuries as various eastern Iranian dynasties (Tahirids, Saffarids, Samanids, Ghaznavids) vied with one another for control of eastern Khurasan. Political continuity and substantial economic growth (Herat was especially coveted for its currency mint) were achieved under the Ghurids during the twelfth century, but not without numerous invasions and sieges by the Khvarazmian dynasty to the northwest.

In 1221, the history of Herat was changed inexorably with the arrival of the Mongol invasions in Khurasan. The response to the Heratis' decision to kill some Mongol representatives was swift and brutal: the city was pulverized, and every single citizen was massacred. The demographic and agricultural impact of the Mongol invasion and their subsequent policies in Khurasan was profound: numbers vary considerably, but it would not be ambitious to put the number of regional casualties in the millions. After a brief period of governing on behalf of the Mongols, the Kartid dynasty (1245–1389) attained independence; they rebuilt the city, restored the surrounding qanat (canal) systems, and developed a comprehensive administration. The Kartids were subjugated by Timur in 1380, and, by the time of Timur's death in 1405, Herat had been fully subsumed into the expansive Timurid empire. Because of the public works programs and systems of patronage developed by the Timurid ruler Shah Rukh (1405–1447), Herat recaptured much of its cultural and economic appeal. This, in turn, laid the foundation for the architectural, intellectual, artistic, and agricultural flourishing of Herat under Sultan-Husain Baiqara (1470–1506). As a result of the efforts of courtly litterateurs like Mir 'Ali Shir Nava'i and 'Abd al-Rahman Jami and artists and calligraphers like Kamal al-Din Behzad, Herat materialized as the preeminent center of Perso-Islamic culture during the fifteenth century. The Shibani Uzbek invasions of the early sixteenth century terminated the Timurid dynasty in Khurasan, and the remainder of the sixteenth and seventeenth centuries saw the vitality of Herat depreciate considerably as the rival Safavid and Uzbek dynasties fought numerous wars in the region.

COLIN PAUL MITCHELL

See also Jami; Kabul; Khurasan; Road Networks; Safavids; Tamerlane; Timurids

Primary Sources

Amir Mahmud ibn Khvandamir. *Tarikh-i Shah Isma'il va Shah Tahmasp*, ed. Muhammad Ali Jarahi. Tehran, 1994.
'Ata Malik Juvaini. *Tarikh-i Jahan Gusha*, 3 vols., ed. M. Qazvini. Leiden, 1912–1937.
Ghiyas al-Di ibn Humam al-Din Khvandamir. *Habib al-Siyar*, 3 vols., ed. Muhammad Dabir Siyaqi. Tehran, 1983.
Hamd-Allah Mustaufi. *Nuzhat al-Qulub*, 2 vols., ed. and transl. G. LeStrange. London, 1916–1919.
Kamal al-Din 'Abd al-Razzaq Samarqandi. *Matla'-i Sadain wa Majma'-i Bahrain*, ed. A. Nava'i. Tehran, 1978.
Mu'in al-Din Muhammad Zamchi Isfizari. *Rauzat al-Jannat fi Ausaf Madinat Herat*, 2 vols., ed. S.M.K. Imam. Tehran, 1959.
Rashid al-Din Fadl Allah Hamadani. *Jami' al-Tavarikh*, 3 vols., ed. B. Karimi. Tehran, 1959.
Saif b. Muhammad b. Ya'qub Haravi. *Tarikh-i Nama-i Harat*, ed. M.Z. Siddiqi. Calcutta, 1944.
Shihab al-Din 'Abd Allah Hafiz-i Abru. *Zail-i Jami' al-Tavarikh-i Rashidi*, ed. K. Bayani. Tehran, 1938.
Zain al-Din Muhammad Vasifi. *Badayi'-i al-Vaqayi'*, ed. A.N. Boldyrev. Moscow, 1961.

Further Reading

Allen, Terry. *Timurid Herat*. Wiesbaden, 1983.
Bartold, W. *Four Studies in the History of Central Asia*, 3 vols., ed. and transl. T. Minorsky. Leiden, 1956–1962.
———. *Herat Unter Husein Baiqara*, ed. and transl. W. Hinz. Nendeln Kraus, 1966.
Daniel, E. *The Political and Social History of Khurasan under Abbasid Rule, 747–820*. Chicago, 1979.
Dickson, Martin. *The Duel for Khurasan: Shah Tahmasp and the Özbeks*. Unpublished PhD dissertation. Princeton, NJ: Princeton, 1958.
Gaube, Heinz. "Herat: An Indo-Iranian City?" In *Iranian Cities*, 31–63. New York, 1979.
McChesney, Robert. "The Conquest of Herat 995–6/1587–8: Sources for the Study of Safavid/Qizilbash-Shibanid/Uzbak Relations." In *Études Safavides*, ed. J. Calmard, 69–107. Paris, 1993.
Paul, Jürgen. *Herrscher, Gemeinwesen, Vermittler: Ost Iran und Transoxanian in Vormongolischer Zeit*. Stuttgart, 1996.
———. "The Local Histories of Herat." *Iranian Studies* 33 (2000): 93–115.
Subtelny, Maria. "A Medieval Persian Agricultural Manual in Context: The *Irshad al-zira'a* in Late Timurid and Early Safavid Khorasan." *Studia Iranica* 22 (1993): 167–217.
———. "A Timurid Educational and Charitable Foundation: The Ikhlasiyya Complex of 'Ali Shir Nava'I in 15th-century Herat and its Endowment." *Journal of the American Oriental Society* 111 (1991): 38–61.
———. "The Timurid Legacy: A Reaffirmation and a Reassessment." *Cahiers d'Asie Centrale* 3–4 (1997): 9–19.
Szuppe, Maria. *Entre Timourides, Uzbeks et Safavides: Questions d'Histoire Politique et Sociale de Hérat dans la Première Moitie du XVIe Siècle*. Paris, 1992.
———. "Herat: iii. History, Medieval Period." In *Encyclopedia Iranica*, vol. 11, ed. E. Yarshater.
———. "Les Résidences Princières de Herat: Problèmes de Continuité Fonctionnelle Entre les Époques Timouride et Safavide (1 Ère Moitié du XVIe Siècle)." In *Études Safavides*, ed. J. Calmard. 267–86. Paris, 1993.
Tumanovich, Nataliya. "The Bazaar and Urban Life of Herat in the Middle Ages." In *Matériaux pour l'Histoire Économique du Monde Iranien*, eds. R. Gyselen and M. Szuppe, 277–85. Paris, 1999.

HERESY AND HERETICS

Deviation from proper Islamic norms and beliefs is rendered in Arabic with different terms, many of which precisely imply the idea of going astray from the right path that believers must follow. That path was laid out by God through His revelation contained in the Qur'an and the Prophetic example compiled in the hadith literature; after the prophetic/revelatory event, the right direction and margins of the path were explained to the Muslim community by experts engaged in authoritative legal and theological reasoning. A widely used term to refer to deviations from the path established by Revelation and Tradition is *bid'a* (pl. *bida'*), which means "innovation" and is used to refer to those religious beliefs and practices that, regardless of their historical antiquity, were condemned by some religious authorities as novelties introduced in the Islamic tradition ("Every novelty is an innovation, every innovation is an error, and every error leads to Hell," says a well-known hadith).

Although the term *bid'a* was often applied to theological doctrines, it came to be used mostly to refer to the *'ibadat* (the ritual practices pertaining to the relationship between God and the believers). Examples of these are local pilgrimages seen as rivaling the pilgrimage to Mecca, worship of local saints feared as detrimental to the veneration due to the Prophet Muhammad, the celebration of non-Islamic festivals and of festivals of contested Islamic soundness (e.g., a mid-sha'ban), and funerary ceremonies in which forbidden practices were acted upon. Some scholars labeled such practices "innovations," whereas others defended them as traditional and correct practices and beliefs or as "good innovations" that did not go against God's law. The latter possibility was introduced by the Shafi'is, who deemed all bida' to be bad but not all novelties to be bida'. This differentiation opened the road to the application to bid'a of the five legal categories so that an innovation could be labeled as forbidden, reprehensible, indifferent, commendable, or even obligatory (e.g., hospitals, madrasas).

Throughout history, Muslim scholars have engaged in debates involving different understandings of the Revelation and the Prophetic tradition as well as the relationship between universal norms and local practices. Diversity of opinion *(ikhtilaf)* was, in itself, not considered to be negative but rather a necessary outcome of the hermeneutical process (ikhtilaf ummati rahma; "difference of opinion in my community is a concession [rahma] on the part of Allah," as a Prophetic tradition states). Because of this, a plurality of interpretations was accepted insofar as these were contained within the framework of the four legal schools (Hanafis, Malikis, Shafi'is, and Hanbalis) and the accepted theological doctrines (Ash'arism and Maturidism).

Disagreement with regard to legal and religious matters in the fields of worship *('ibadat)* and mu'amalat (the relationships inter vivos et mortis causa) as well as on theological issues would sometimes provoke bitter exchanges among scholars, who could even attack their opponents with accusations of infidelity *(kufr)*, apostasy *(irtidad, radd)*, hidden apostasy, and heresy *(zandaqa, ilhad, zaygh, dalal)*. Those accusations did not usually have much effect (unless a faction of scholars could secure support from the ruler) apart from trying to influence the formation of a consensus *(ijma')* in favor of one's opinion against the other's view, always with the risk of provoking the opposite effect by appearing too radical and extremist in the attack against a fellow scholar who was just doing his job in trying to understand God's will. The doctrine "every interpreter (of that will) is correct" *(kull mujtahid musib)* was meant to counteract any attempt at disqualifying as deviants or heretics those opponents who had the required training and abilities and who followed adequate methodologies in their interpretative effort (Hallaq, 2001). The famous jurist and theologian al-Ghazali, in his work *Faysal*

al-Tafriqa Bayna l-Islam wa-l-Zandaqa, aimed as well at putting restrictions on the accusation of infidelity in theological disputes (Jackson, 2002).

This does not mean, of course, that there were no limits to what was deemed to be acceptable both in practices and beliefs, and al-Ghazali's work points to some of these limits, condemning, for example, the belief in the eternity of the world. Islam had its own share of free thinkers, sectarians, and heretics. The early history of the community witnessed the appearance of internal divisions centered on different theological issues, such as who the legitimate political and religious imam should be (the salvation of the community was at stake) and determinism and free will.

The hadith predicting that the Muslim community would divide into seventy-three sects reflects this early split among sectarian lines. Heresiographical treatises were written to identify those sects. Although seventy-two of them were said to be destined to Hell and only one to salvation, in fact there was reluctance to allow an indiscriminate use of the accusation of unbelief *(takfir)* against sectarians. The abuse of declaring one's opponents infidels had precisely been a distinguishing feature of one of the early sects, the Kharijites, among whom the most radical branches even allowed the killing of those who did not partake in their beliefs. Shi'is (especially the Imamis) and Sunnites found ways of accommodating themselves to living together (Stewart, 1998). Only extremist groups like the zindiqs (Manicheists) of the early 'Abbasid times and the Shi'i ghulat (those who denied the finality of prophecy or those who supported antinomianism) were clearly excluded from the Muslim community. However, other religious thinkers who were subject to continued suspicion concerning the correctness of their beliefs were never completely marginalized or excluded from the Islamic community, as shown in the case of the famous Sufi Muhyi al-din Ibn 'Arabi (Knysh, 1993).

Islam has often been defined as an orthopraxis more than an orthodoxy, so, according to this view, it would be the area of religious practices in which Muslims had to prove themselves. However, to drink wine was to commit a forbidden act that involved a specified penalty without the sinner ceasing to be a Muslim, whereas to maintain that drinking wine was a licit act meant departing from correct belief (i.e., heterodoxy). Now, in Sunni Islam, no institutionalized religious hierarchy was put in charge of identifying and persecuting dissenters by labeling them heretics, which has led some Western scholars to point out the difficulties of finding a term equivalent to the Christian notion of heresy (an opinion chosen by human perception contrary to holy scripture, publicly avowed and obstinately defended).

However, this does not mean that Muslims lacked the concept of orthodoxy and heterodoxy. T. Asad (with his insistence on Islam as a "discursive tradition") and S. Jackson, among others, have reminded us that orthodoxy can be established and sustained not only by an institution backed by formal authority but by authority that may be formal or informal. Religious scholars such as the ulama, whose (mostly) informal authority was based on reputation without any formal investiture, can succeed in establishing and sustaining orthodoxy in their religious communities, even in the absence of a formal ecclesiastical hierarchy. The pedagogical process is of fundamental importance here, involving the transmission of knowledge, the debates among scholars, the social practices of the scholars themselves, and their ability to influence the community through the acknowledgment and acceptance of their authority.

The fact that suspects of heretical ideas were often never persecuted has been pointed by almost every scholar dealing with the subject of heresy in Islam. J. Kraemer explains that the Mu'tazilis or the philosophers were not persecuted as such, because, although they upheld the supremacy of reason over revelation, they expounded a system that kept the revealed law of Islam intact, and they remained relatively free from harm provided they maintained a low profile and did not openly attempt to convert others to their views. Alternatively, the heretics who were truly heretics (e.g., Ibn al-Rawandi) were considered to be the enemies of religion, because their rationalism attacked the revealed religions in general and Islam in particular; they were also considered to be a danger to the state and social order, thereby provoking persecution and suppression on the part of the state authorities.

The legal rationale for punishing religious and ideological dissent was that the views and beliefs of those accused would cause upheaval if allowed to be propagated. The punishment inflicted upon deviants, apostates, and heretics was the same as the retribution meted out to ordinary brigands, highwaymen, and rebels. However, persecution usually took place only during times of stress and upheaval, when revolutionary movements posed a military and political threat against the state. Official persecution on the part of the state was rare, the most famous case being the mihna (inquisition) in the times of al-Ma'mun, and even then the point at issue was not so much a particular theological doctrine but rather the authority of the caliph versus the authority of those men who saw themselves—rather than the caliph—as the legitimate repository and authentic transmitters of religious knowledge and tradition (Nawas, 1994). Apart from this mihna and other similar episodes, there were no state or corporate bodies with jurisdiction over heresy, no specialized agencies for determining truth from error, and no specialized procedures such as trials or inquisitions (although there were trends toward the latter) (Chamberlain, 1994; Fierro, 1992).

Generally, the identification and suppression of error took the form of debates among scholars before the elites, with or without the presence of the ruler. When the latter took part in these struggles, it was usually at the instigation of an outside group; in any case, his interest was usually in maintaining a balance between social peace and the satisfaction of the scholarly factions that supported him (Chamberlain, 1994). This attitude on the part of the rulers may have helped the trend toward moderation and homogenization.

A. Knysh has insisted upon the need to recreate the wide variety of conflicting visions and understandings of Islamic religion that existed in the Islamic societies, a variety that has been well depicted by some Muslim Medieval scholars (e.g., the well-known heresiographer al-Shahrastani) and that has found an excellent treatment in the historical and social study of early Muslim theology by the German scholar J. van Ess. What this reveals, to borrow A. Knysh's expression, is "orthodoxy-in-the-making": "a perpetual collision of individual opinions over an invariant set of theological problems that eventually leads to a transient consensus that already contains the seeds of future disagreement."

For his part, N. Calder, in a very perceptive study, put the emphasis on the discursive process (the ongoing process of interpreting their tradition) in which Muslims are embroiled. He added that, if it is accepted that a religious belief can be categorized under the five headings of "scripture, community, gnosis, reason, and charisma," Sunni Islam would lie somewhere between scripture and community, the latter being of paramount importance, because the major understanding of God is expressed through the acknowledgment of what happens inside the community. This means that each succeeding generation has to take into consideration the work of the preceding generations and that those thinkers who go back to the original sources of revelation without taking into account the accumulated experience of the community are liable to be met with rejection and exclusion.

MARIBEL FIERRO

Further Reading

Asad, T. "Medieval Heresy: An Anthropological View." *Social History* 11/3 (1986): 345–62.
Ayoub, M. "Religious Freedom and the Law of Apostasy in Islam." *IslamoChristiana* 20 (1994): 75–91.

Calder, N. "The Limits of Islamic Orthodoxy." In *Intellectual Traditions in Islam*, ed. F. Daftary, 66–86. London, 2000.

Chamberlain, M. *Knowledge and Social Practice in Medieval Damascus, 1190–1350*. Cambridge, UK, 1994.

Chokr, M. *Zandaqa et Zindiqs en Islam au Second Siècle de l'Hégire*. Damascus, 1993.

Cook, M. "Weber and Islamic Sects." In *Max Weber and Islam*, eds. Toby E. Huff and Wolfgang Schluchter, 273–9. New Brunswick and London, 1999.

Eddé, A.-M. "Hérésie et Pouvoir Politique en Syrie au XIIe Siècle: L'Exécution d'al-Suhrawardi en 1191." *La Religion Civique à l'Epoque Médiévale et Moderne (Chrétienté et Islam)*, 235–44. Rome, 1995.

van Ess, J. *Theologie und Gesellschaft im 2. und 3. Jahrhundert Hidschra. Eine Geschichte des Religiösen Denkens im Frühen Islam*, 6 vols. Berlin, 1991–1998;

Fierro, M. "The Treatises Against Innovations (*Kutub al-Bida,*)." *Der Islam* 69 (1992): 204–46.

Fierro, M. "Religious Dissension in al-Andalus: Ways of Exclusion and Inclusion." *Al-Qantara* XXII (2001): 463–87.

Gaborieau, M. "*Tariqa* et Orthodoxie." In *Les Voies d'Allah. Les Ordres Mystiques dans l'Islam des Origines à Aujourd'hui*, eds. G. Veinstein and A. Popovic, 195–202. Paris, 1996.

Griffel, F. *Apostasie und Toleranz im Islam: Die Entwicklung zu al-Gazalis Urteil Gegen die Philosophie und die Reaktionen der Philosophen*. Leiden, 2000.

Hallaq, W.B. *Authority, Continuity and Change in Islamic Law*. Cambridge, UK, 2001.

Masud, M. Kh., B. Messick, and D. Powers, eds. *Islamic Legal Interpretation. Muftis and Their Fatwas*. Cambridge, Mass, and London, 1996.

de Jong, F., and B. Radtke. *Islamic Mysticism Contested. Thirteen Centuries of Controversies and Polemics*. Leiden, 1999.

Jackson, Sh. *On the Boundaries of Theological Acceptance in Islam. Abu Hamid al-Ghazali's Faysal al-Tafriqa Bayna l-Islam wa-l-Zandaqa*. Princeton, NJ, 2002.

Knysh, A. "Orthodoxy and Heresy in Medieval Islam: An Essay in Reassessment." *The Muslim World* LXXXIII (1993): 48–67.

———. *Ibn 'Arabi in the Later Islamic Tradition: The Making of a Polemical Image in Medieval Islam*. New York, 1999.

Kraemer, J. "Heresy Versus the State in Medieval Islam." In *Studies in Judaica, Karaitica and Islamica Presented to Leon Nemoy on his Eightieth Birthday*, ed. Sh. R. Brunswick, 167–80. Bar-Ilan, 1982.

Laoust, H. *Les Schismes dans l'Islam*. Paris, 1977.

Lapidus, I.M. "State and Religion in Islamic Societies." *Past and Present* 151 (1996): 3–27.

Lewis, B. "Some Observations on the Significance of Heresy in the History of Islam." *Studia Islamica* I (1953): 43–64.

Makdisi, G. "*Tabaqat*-biography: Law and Orthodoxy in Classical Islam." *Islamic Studies* 32 (1993): 371–96.

Melchert, Ch. "Sectaries in the Six Books: Evidence for Their Exclusion from the Sunni Community." *The Muslim World* LXXXII/3–4 (1992): 287–95.

Memon, M.U. *Ibn Taymiya's Struggle against Popular Religion*. The Hague: Mouton, 1976.

Nawas, J. "A Reexamination of Three Current Explanations for al-Ma'mun's Introduction of the *Mihna*." *IJMES* 26 (1994): 615–29.

Rispler-Chaim, V. "Toward a New Understanding of the Term *Bid'a*." *Der Islam* 68 (1992): 320–8.

Stewart, D. *Islamic Legal Orthodoxy: Twelver Shiite Responses to the Sunni Legal System*. Salt Lake City, Utah, 1998.

Stroumsa, S. *Freethinkers of Medieval Islam. Ibn al-Rawandi, Abu Bakr al-Razi and Their Impact on Islamic Thought*. Leiden, 1999.

Urvoy, D. *Les Penseurs Libres dans l'Islam Classique*. Paris, 1996.

Watt, W.M. "Conditions of Membership of the Islamic Community." *Studia Islamica* XXI (1964): 5–12.

HEROES AND HEROISM

The terms *hero* and *heroism* have lost the cultural grounding of their ancient Greek provenance. In modern usage, they refer simply to the protagonist in any narrative or drama. In ancient Greek epic and drama, on the other hand, the heroism of the hero was clearly defined in terms of the interaction between character and plot in these genres, as Aristotle indicates in his *Poetics*. To the extent that the genres of literary traditions in medieval Islamic civilization are comparable to what we find in classical traditions stemming directly from ancient Greek civilization, the terms *hero* and *heroism* are also applicable for comparison.

Older modern scholarship on heroes and heroism in medieval Islamic civilization applied the classical models in negative ways, holding Islamic values up to the standards of Greek values in a mismatch between supposedly inferior and superior systems. The empiricism that is required for typological comparison was wanting. A case in point is the work of Ignaz Goldziher, who saw a sharp division between the Islamic notion of dîn (the faith-based code of Islam) and the pre-Islamic Arab system of conduct exemplified in the word *murûwwa*, which was defined in Greco-Roman terms as "virtus." Goldziher (1967) concedes, however, that this word *murûwwa* was still in use after the rise of Islam: hence the famous Islamic saying "there is no religion [dîn] without manly virtue [murûwwa]." More recent modern scholarship (Bravmann, 1972; Fares Izutsu, 1966) elaborates on the convergences as well as divergences between murûwwa and dîn, emphasizing the subtle changes and shifting associations in the meanings of these concepts over time.

Both pre-Islamic Arabia [Jahiliya] and the pre-Islamic Iran of the Sasanian dynasty have been regarded in the popular imagination as "heroic ages," providing fecund sources for the portrayal of heroes and heroism. Such foregrounding has led modern scholars to exaggerate a sense of rupture between the pre-Islamic and the Islamic eras. The exaggeration is less pronounced in the case of Iranian traditions, which preserve genres that closely parallel what is known as epic in Greek terms. The *Shâhnnâma* of Ferdowsi is a case in point: greater in length than the Homeric *Iliad* and *Odyssey* combined, this monumental composition highlights the Iranian heroic ideal of *javânmardi* (youngmanliness), the meaning of which is roughly the equivalent of chivalry.

The exaggeration of differences between the pre-Islamic and the Islamic eras is far more pronounced in the case of Arab traditions. For example, von Grunebaum (1975) implies that the Arabs essentially lacked the concept of a hero because they did not produce any long epic poems. Even the Persians do not escape the negative comparison. Although von Grunebaum concedes that they had heroes like Rostam, Sohrab, Esfandiyâr, and so on, he insists that such characters were not tragic heroes; rather, the overriding fatalism inherent in the Persian epic precludes any possibility of tragedy. However, the heroism of Persian epic figures like Iraj or Siyâvosh derives precisely from the fact that, despite their foreknowledge, they do not swerve from righteous conduct.

In ongoing modern research on heroism and the hero, scholars have moved away from applying ethnocentric criteria and have gravitated toward the goal of finding ethical and esthetic norms from within Islamic civilization itself, which has its own critical vocabulary. The range of study needs to extend to genres that are quite different from epic and drama: examples include the *Maqamat* and popular prose narratives (Arabic) as well as the popular oral poetry of Central Asia, among many others.

OLGA M. DAVIDSON

See also Alexander; Biography and Biographical Works; Death and Dying; Epic Poetry; Epics, Arabic; Epics, Persian; Epics, Turkish; Folk Literature, Arabic; Folk Literature, Persian; Folk Literature, Turkish; Mahmud of Ghazna; Maqama; Mirrors for Princes; Nizami; Popular Literature; Saints and Sainthood; Sasanians: Islamic Tradition; Shahnama; Sira, Stories and Storytelling; Sufism and Sufis; Supernatural Beings; Women Warriors

Further Reading

Bravmann, M.M. *The Spiritual Background of Early Islam*. Leiden: E.J. Brill, 1972.
Encyclopaedia of Islam, 2nd ed.
"Hamâsa." Ch. Pellat, Arabic; H. Massé, Persian; I. Mélik-off, Turkish; A. T. Hatto, Central Asia; Aziz Ahmad, Urdu, vol. III, 110–9.
"Manâkib." Ch. Pellat, vol. VI, 349–57.
"Marthiya." Ch. Pellat, Arabic; W. L. Hanaway, Jr. Persian; B. Flemming, Turkish; J. A. Haywood, Urdu; J. Knappert, Swahili, vol. VI, 602–13.
"Murû'a." B. Farès, vol. VII, 636–38.
"Sira."
Davidson, O.M. *Poet and Hero in the Persian Book of Kings*. Ithaca: Cornell University Press, 1994.
Davis, D. *Epic and Sedition: The Case of Ferdowsi's Shâhnâmeh*. Fayetteville, AK, 1992.
Goldziher, I. "Introductory: 'Muruwwa and Dîn.'" In *Muslim Studies (Muhammedanische Studien)*, 2 vols., ed. S.M. Stern, vol. 1, 11–44. London: Gerge Allen & Unwin, 1967.
Von Grunebaum, G.E. "The Hero in Medieval Arabic Prose." In *Concepts of the Hero in the Middle Ages and the Renaissance*, eds. N.T. Burns and C.J. Regan, 83–100. Albany: State University of New York Press, 1975.
Izutsu, T. *Ethico-Religious Concepts in the Qur'an*. Montreal: McGill University Press, 1966.
Lyons, M.C. *The Arabian Epic*, 3 vols. Cambridge, UK: Cambridge University Press, 1995.
Renard, J. *Islam and the Heroic Image*. Columbia, SC: University of South Carolina Press, 1993.
Reynolds, D.F. *Heroic Poets, Poetic Heroes: An Ethnography of Performance in an Arabic Oral Epic Tradition*. Ithaca: Cornell University Press, 1995.

HILLI, AL-, AL-ALLAMA, HASAN IBN YUSUF IBNAL-MUTAHHAR

Al-Hilli was a prominent Twelver Shi'i theologian and jurist from a well-established family of Imami scholars who was born in al-Hilla on 27 or 29 Ramadan AH 648/23 CE or 25 December 1250 and died there on 20 or 21 Muharram 726/27 or 28 December 1325. Among his first teachers in al-Hilla were his father Sadid al-Din Yusuf al-Mutahhar al-Hilli (d. c. 665/1267) and his maternal uncle, al-Muhaqqiq al-Hilli (d. 676/1277). He subsequently spent some time at the Maragha observatory founded by Nasir al-Din al-Tusi (d. 672/1274), where he studied primarily philosophy and logic with al-Tusi and al-Katibi al-Qazwini (d. 675/1277). Presumably after the death of al-Tusi, al-Hilli left Maragha for Baghdad, where he studied with the Sunni scholars Shams al-Din Muhammad ibn Muhammad ibn Ahmad al-Kishi (d. 695/1296), Burhan al-Din Muhammad ibn Muhammad al-Nasafi (d. 687/1288), Jamal al-Din Husayn ibn Ayaz al-Baghdadi al-Nahwi (d. 681/1282–1283), and 'Izz al-Din Abu al-'Abbas ibn Ibrahim ibn 'Umar al-Faruthi al-Wasiti (d. 694/1294–1295). For a short time, al-Hilli studied in Kufa with the Hanafi scholar Taqi al-Din 'Abd Allah ibn al-Sabbagh Kufi. From around 709/1309–1310 to 714/1314–1315 or perhaps 716/1316–1317, al-Hilli, together with his son Fakhr al-Muhaqqiqin (d. 771/1369), stayed at the court of the Ilkhan Öljeitü (r. 703/1304–716/1316). Some biographical accounts attribute Öljeitü's conversion to Shi'ism in Sha'ban 709/January–February 1310 to the influence of al-Hilli, although the historical sources of the period do not confirm these reports. During his stay at court, al-Hilli frequently engaged in theological discussions with other scholars. He was on good terms with the vizier Rashid al-Din (d. 718/1312–1313), and he was highly regarded by Öljeitü, who appointed al-Hilli as teacher in the madrasa sayyara that accompanied the Ilkhan wherever he went. Al-Hilli also authored several works of Shi'i apologetics dedicated to Öljeitü. It is not clear when al-Hilli departed from court; the last years of his life were spent in al-Hilla.

Al-Hilli was a prolific writer on a wide range of religious topics. He composed more than a hundred works, of which nearly sixty are extant. The number of extant manuscripts as well as the amount of commentaries written about his works indicate the popularity of most of his writings. Of his works about theology, mention should be made in particular of his popular commentary on Nasir al-Din al-Tusi's *Tajrid al-i'Tiqad, Kashf al-Murad fi Sharh al-i'Tiqad.* His most extensive work in this discipline was *Nihayat al-Maram fi 'ilm al-Kalam.* One of his most popular works was his short creed *al-Bab al-Hadi Ashar;* this is indicated by numerous commentaries and translations. Of his philosophical works, only a few are extant, among them his commentary of al-Katibi al-Qazwini's *Hikmat al-'Ayn, Idah al-Maqasid fi Sharh Hikmat al-'Ayn.* In the field of legal methodology, his most extensive work is *Nihayat al-Wusul Ila 'Ilm al-Usul,* which was completed in 704/1305. Al-Hilli played a formative part in the development of Shi'i law; he composed numerous legal works, the most important of which are extant. His first work in the field, as well as his most extensive, was *Muntaha al-Matlab fi Tahqiq al-Madhhab,* although it only covers the field of acts of devotion ('ibadat). *Mukhtalaf al-Shi'a fi Ahkam al-Shari'a,* another extensive work of al-Hilli about jurisprudence, covers all fields of law; however, it merely describes various legal questions about which there was disagreement among the Shi'i jurists. His more concise legal writings, *Qawa'id al-Ahkam* and *Irshad al-Adhhan fi Ahkam al-Iman,* were extremely popular among later scholars as is indicated by the large number of commentaries on both. Among his last and very extensive works about fiqh were *Tadhkirat al-Fuqaha' 'ala Talkhis Fatawi al-'Ulama'* and *Nihayat al-Ihkam fi ma'Rifat al-Ahkam.* Among al-Hilli's biographical works, mention should be made in particular of his *Khulasat al-Aqwal fi ma'Rifat al-Rijal,* which lists reliable transmitters in the first part and unreliable ones in the second. None of al-Hilli's writings about grammar and tafsir are extant. Of his works about traditions, only *al-Durr wa-l-Marjan fi l-Ahadith al-Sihah wa-l-Hisan* is partly extant in manuscript form.

SABINE SCHMIDTKE

Primary Sources

Al-Hilli, Hasan ibn Yusuf. *Idah al-Maqasid Min Hikmat 'Ayn al-Qawa'id,* ed. 'A. Khaqani Najafi. Najaf, 1354/1935.

———. *Kashf al-Murad fi Sharh Tajrid al-I'tiqad.* Qum.

———. [*Khulasat al-Aqwal*] *Kitab al-Rijal,* ed. M.S. Bahr Al-'Ulum. Najaf, 1381/1961.

———. *Mukhtalaf al-Shi'a fi Ahkam al-Shari'a.* Tehran, 1323–1324/1905–1906.

———. *Muntaha al-Matlab fi Tahqiq al-Madhhab.* Tehran, 1333/1915.

———. *Nihayat al-Maram fi 'Ilm al-Kalam,* ed. Fadil al-'Irfan. Qum, 1412/1992.

———. *Qawa'id al-Ahkam fi ma'Rifat al-Halal wa l-Haram.* Qum, 1984. (Reprint of the 1315/1898 edition.

———. *Tadhkirat al-Fuqaha' 'Ala Talkhis Fatawi al-Fuqaha'.* Tehran, 1984. (Reprint of the 1388/1968 edition.)

Further Reading

Laoust, H. "La Critique du Sunnisme dans la Doctrine d'al-Hilli." *Revue des Études Islamiques* 34 (1966): 35–60.

———. "Les Fondaments de l'Imamat dans le Minhaj d'al-Hilli." *Revue des Études Islamiques* 46 (1978): 3–55.

Miller, W.M., transl. *Al-Babu 'l-Hadi 'Ashar. A Treatise on the Principles of Shi'ite Theology.* London, 1928.

Modarressi Tabataba'i, Hossein. *An Introduction to Shi'i Law: A Bibliographical Study,* 8, 23, 47–49, 70–76, 103, 152, 204. London, 1984.

Pfeiffer, Judith. *Twelver Shi'ism in Mongol Iran.* Istanbul, 1999.

Schmidtke, Sabine. *The Theology of al-'Allama al-Hilli (d. 726/1325).* Berlin: Klaus Schwarz Verlag, 1991.

Stewart, Devin J. *Islamic Legal Orthodoxy: Twelver Shiite Responses to the Sunni Legal System,* 72ff, 191ff, 205ff. Salt Lake City, UT: The University of Utah Press, 1998.

Al-Tabataba'i, 'Abd al-'Aziz. *Maktabat al-'Allama al-Hilli.* Qom, 1348/1416.

HIPPOLOGY

Numerous Arabic texts deal with horse knowledge from either a theoretical or practical point of view. This knowledge *(furusiyya)* refers to hippological matters or to the nature of horses *(khalq al-khayl),* such as their different illnesses and cures *(baytara)* and equestrianism or horsemanship *(siyasa al-khayl).* Among these Arabic texts are the following:

1. Religious works: The Qur'an exalts the horse. For example, it refers to "pure-bred horses" among the things of which man is fond (3:14); it mentions horses' efficacy during combat (8:60), and horses are also mentioned as divine favors (16:8). Religious tradition (hadith) praises horses for their usefulness, for the honor they produce, and also for their strength and speed, which distinguish them from other animals.

2. Juridical works: These include chapters or even entire treatises on warfare based on faith (Jihad) and horses' role in it, with praises for their fundamental intervention. For example, Ibn Abi Zamanin (d. 399/1009) describes "the model fighter" in his book *(Kitab qidwat al-gazi)*.

3. Military technical works: These deal with the horse with regard to its fighting strategies.

4. Lexicons: These are collections of terminology such as "books of horses" *(Kitab al-Khayl)*, like the famous one by Ibn al-Kalbi (d. 204/819 or 206/821). The numerous works about "horses' characteristics" (khalq al-faras/sifat al-khayl) are placed between lexicography and literature.

5. Adab: The adab encyclopedia gathers technical and scientific data, religious traditions, verses, and heroic anecdotes about horses within a cared-for literary framework. Examples of this styles are *The Book of Animals (Kitab al-hayawan)* by al-Jahiz (d. 255/868) and various works by Ibn al-Hudhayl al-Garnati (eighth/fourteenth century), especially his work *Kitab Hilyat al-Fursan wa-Shi'ar al-Shuj'an,* which includes fourteen chapters about horses that deal with, for example, their creation and taming; good habits and vices; management and care; colors; hair; and riding. In Arabic poetry, horses are seen with an outstanding frequency that shapes their characteristics and activities.

6. Scientific works: These deal with the physiology of the horse, in such works as veterinary (bay-tara) books, in which Fuat Sezgin and other authors bring forward abundant information. Arabic zoological and veterinary knowledge has incorporated elements from Greek and Latin science; later on it had its own contributions, which were handed down to Europe. Arabic agricultural treatises contain, at times, animal references, such as Ibn al-'Awwam's (fifth/twelfth century) *Kitab al-Filaha*, of which Chapters 31 and 33 clearly state many matters that are relevant to the horse.

All of these kinds of works form a large whole that contains an impressive quantity and diversity of data about horses, showing not only their real dimensions but also their symbolic ones, because they have been an indispensable element of Islam's defense and expansion. This high appreciation for horses imbues all kinds of Arabic sources, even the iconographic ones; there are numerous references to cared-for horse representations in various types of pieces of Islamic and Arabic art.

M.J. VIGUERA AND T. SOBREDO

Primary Sources

Ibn Abi Zamanin. *Kitab Qidwat al-Gazi*, ed. 'A. al-Sulaymani. Beirut: Dar al-Garb al-Islami, 1989.
Ibn al-'Awwam. *Le Livre de l'Agriculture (Kitab al-Filaha)*, transl. J.J. Clément-Mullet. Arles: Actes Sud, 2000.
Ibn Hudhayl. *La Parure des Cavaliers et L'Insigne des Preux*, transl. L. Mercier. Paris, 1924.
M.J. Viguera, transl. *Gala de Caballeros, Blasón de Paladines.* Madrid: Editora Nacional, 1977.
Al-Jahiz. *Kitab al-Hayawan*, 7 vols., ed. 'A. al-S.M. Harun. Cairo: Dar al-ma'Arifa, 1378/1958. (Reprint, Beirut: Dar ihya' al-Turath al-'Arabi, 1388/1969.)
Les "Livres des Chevaux" de Hisham ibn al-Kalbi et Muhammad ibn al-A'rabi, Publiés D'Après le Manuscrit de l'Escorial Ar. 1705, ed. G. Levi della Vida. Leiden: E.J. Brill, 1928.

Further Reading

Al-Andalus y el Caballo. Granada: El Legado Andalusí, 1995.
Álvarez de Morales, C., ed. *Ciencias de la Naturaleza en al-Andalus.* Granada: Consejo Superior de Investigaciones Científicas, 1996.
Araber, Asil. *Arabians Edle Pferde/The Noble Arabian Horses*, 5 vols. Hildesheim: Georg Olms, 1985–2000.
Brockelmann, C. *Geschichte der Arabischen Litteratur*, 5 vols. Leiden: E.J. Brill, 1937–1949.
Encyclopaedia of Islam, CD-ROM Edition. Leiden: E.J. Brill, 2001.
Guintard, Claude, and Christine Mazzoli-Guintard, eds. *Élevage D'Hier, Elevage D'Auhourdhui. Mélanges d'Ethnozootechnie Offerts à Bernard Denis.* Presses Universitaires de Rennes, 2004.
Gutas, Dimitri. *Greek Thought, Arabic Culture: The Graeco-Arabic Translation Movement in Baghdad and Early 'Abbasid Society (2nd–4th/8th–10th centuries).* London and New York: Routledge, 1998.
Pinon, Laurent. *Les Livres de Zoologie à la Renaissance.* Genève: Droz, 2004.
Sánchez Gallego, R., and M. Espinar. "Arqueología y Cultura Material de Lorca (Murcia): El Caballo y Otros Amuletos." *Estudios Sobre Patrimonio, Cultura y Ciencia Medievales*, 5–6 (2003–2004): 121–44.
Sezgin, Fuat. *Geschichte des Arabischen Schrifttums, Vol. 3, Medizin, Pharmazie, Zoologie, Tierheilkunde.* Leiden: E.J. Brill, 1970.
Shatzmiller, Maya. "The Crusades and Islamic Warfare: A Re-evaluation." *Der Islam* 59 (1992), 247–88.
Vernet, J. *Ce que la Culture Doit aux Arabes d'Espagne*, transl. G. Martinez-Gros. Paris: Sindbad, 1985.
Lo Que Europa Debe al Islam de España. Barcelona: El Acantilado, 1999.

HIRABA, OR BRIGANDAGE

Hiraba or *qat' al-sabil* (brigandage; highway robbery) is one of a handful of crimes known in Islamic law as *hudud* (sing. *hadd*); its distinguishing legal feature is the mandatory nature of the penalties that are attached to these crimes. The Qur'anic origin of the crime of brigandage is found in verse 5:34–5 (*Al-Ma'ida*) where the Qur'an states that "the recompense for those who wage war against God and His messenger and spread disorder throughout the land is either that they are killed, crucified, amputation of their limbs on alternating sides or banishment from the land, unless they repent before they fall under your control, in which case God is Forgiving, Merciful."

Qur'anic commentary reveals an interesting body of disagreement regarding the circumstances in which this verse was revealed. Although the majority of interpreters concluded that it dealt with an incident involving a group of Arabs that at least outwardly professed Islam, others believed that this verse dealt with an incident involving pagans or a group from the ahl al-kitab who violated the terms of their peace treaty with the Prophet Muhammad. All commentators agreed that, regardless of the circumstances involved in the revelation of 5:34–5, the substance of the verses applied to Muslims. Jurists were also of the view that the crime of brigandage applied not only to Muslims but also to non-Muslims who were permanently residing in an Islamic state as a protected group *(ahl al-dhimma)*.

According to the majority of commentators, a group of persons came to the Prophet in Medina and professed Islam. While in Medina, they grew ill (a condition that occurred frequently among Bedouins who visited Medina) and complained to the Prophet. In response to their complaints, the Prophet provided them with camels and shepherds and instructed them to depart to the outskirts of the city while they recuperated. When they recovered, however, they murdered the shepherds and made off with the camels. Historians reported that the culprits, in addition to killing the shepherds, also amputated their limbs and blinded them. The Muslims, however, were able to track them down and capture them before they returned to their home territory. Upon their return to Medina, the Prophet ordered their execution, which involved a combination of amputating their limbs on alternating sides, blinding them, and abandoning them in the lava plains outside of Medina until they died. The Prophet's treatment of the criminals raised many questions in the eyes of the commentators, including whether 5:34–5, as well as the Prophetic statement prohibiting mutilation, subsequently abrogated the Prophet's action in this case. Those who argued in favor of abrogation assumed that the verses in question were revealed after the aforementioned incident and represented divine reproach *('itab)*. Others, however, argued that the Prophet's actions went beyond the text of the verse and represented retaliation in kind *(qisas)* for the injuries inflicted by the culprits on the shepherds and

that, accordingly, the verses did not abrogate the Prophet's actions.

Finally, commentators also point out that the verse includes an elided noun—friends *(awliya')* or servants *('ibad)* of God—because it is impossible for anyone to wage war against God in a literal sense.

Although the circumstances that were the occasion of 5:34–5 involved an element of treachery, jurists did not include treachery or deception (ghila) as an element of the substantive crime of brigandage. Instead, they focused on the effect of the crime on the security of the public. Accordingly, the brigand who was subject to the mandatory penalties for brigandage was defined by the Shafi'is, for example, as "an adult Muslim interdicting the public highways who relies on force to overpower [a victim in circumstances where the victim is] distant from succor [of the government], even if in a town, or who enters at night into a home and openly takes property and prevents [its residents] from seeking succor of the government." Later jurists also included other crimes of violence (e.g., rape) as instances of brigandage.

Despite the fact that the apparent sense of the verse seems to leave open the possibility for the exercise of discretion in the punishment of a brigand, Muslim jurists—with the exception of the Malikis, who preserved the state's discretion in all circumstances—obliged the government to enforce a particular penalty depending on the substantive conduct of the defendant. The Hanafis, for example, held that, if a defendant brigand took property but did not murder, he was subject only to the amputation of his hand and foot; if he murdered and did not take property, he was to be executed; if he murdered and took property, the government could either amputate him and then execute him or simply execute him (this latter was the position of Muhammad al-Shaybani and Abu Yusuf, the two leading students of Abu Hanifa); and, if he terrorized the public without taking property or killing, he was to be banished.

The law of brigandage, although nominally considered a species of hudud, functioned as public law. For example, considerations of status (e.g., religion, freedom) were irrelevant to the application of the law of brigandage; this is in contrast with the private law of retaliation. Accordingly, if a free Muslim brigand killed a protected non-Muslim person or a slave as part of his brigandage, he would be subject to execution, although he would not have been subject to retaliation (according to most Muslim jurists) had he killed a slave or a non-Muslim protected person in the context of a private dispute. Similarly, although in principle hudud penalties were not generally applicable to non-Muslim protected persons, the law against brigandage applied to any person who "had undertaken to obey the law *(al-multazim bi-fal-ahkam),*" regardless of religion. On the other hand, non-Muslims from hostile states *(harbi)* could not be charged with brigandage; they would simply be treated as prisoners of war.

The public aspect of the law of brigandage makes it similar to the law governing murder by treachery or deception *(ghila)*. Because the defendant in both crimes is believed to threaten the public's security (as opposed to the security of a particular member of the public), the government's responsibility to protect the right of the public to safety trumps whatever private rights the victim or the victim's heirs may have. Accordingly, the government, in each of these two crimes, continues to have power to punish the defendant, even if the victim or his or her family has forgiven the perpetrator or otherwise reached a settlement with him.

MOHAMMAD H. FADEL

Further Reading

El Fadl, Khaled Abou. *Rebellion and Violence in Islamic Law.* Cambridge, UK: Cambridge University Press, 2001.

HORTICULTURE

Gardens in the Arabo-Islamic world resulted from the association of a broad range of heterogeneous components. The *janna,* defined as a garden as opposed to the desert, was associated with the Persian concept of closed royal parks (*pairidaeza; paradeisos* in Greek) that are known, for example, through the Greek Xenophon (428/427–354 BC), and also with the Greco-Roman garden for the cultivation of flowers and vegetables. Gardens constituted an important component of Arabo-Islamic culture, first as a symbolic echo of paradise. Although rooted in the Persian tradition of parks for pleasure, the Arabo-Islamic garden was also influenced by Byzantine horticulture, particularly the gardens of Nestorian monasteries in Iraq. In most of the Arabo-Muslim world, the garden was essentially a response to terrain and climatic conditions, which were characterized by dryness and heat. Water was always an important element: in royal gardens, it was normally flowing from the highest point toward the entrance so that visitors faced it on arrival.

The 'Abbasid caliphs built gardens first in Baghdad (762 CE) and later in Samarra (835), with magnificent architectural structures, ponds, lakes, pools, courts decorated with flowers, playgrounds, parks for wild and domesticated animals (zoos with animal houses), rivers (natural and manmade), basins, channels, and harbors for boats. However, the most important

centers for Arabic horticulture were in Al-Andalus. Gardens—particularly those belonging to princes—were transformed into horticultural stations where experiments were made to acclimatize non-native species of oriental and tropical origin coming from the East and as far as the Near East (India and China). Such specialization of Andalusian horticulture dates back to the first Andalusian emir 'Abd al-Rahmân I (756–788), who built the ar-Rusâfa garden near Cordoba on the model of his grandfather's residence in Syria. Closed to the north by a wood, it was bordered on its western side by a river. At the center, there was the palace and the vegetable gardens, where non-native species imported from Syria were acclimatized. At Medina Azahara, which was also close to Cordova, another garden with a similar vocation was built by the Caliph 'Abd al-Rahmân III (912–961). Both gardens were destroyed in the attack on Cordoba in 1010. In the Taifa kingdoms, rulers had gardens built mainly in Toledo and Almeria but also in Sevilla. The Toledo garden (Bustân al-Nâ'ûra; The Orchard of the Waterwheel) was made under the direction of Ibn Wâfid (d. 1075) from Toledo working in collaboration with Ibn Bassâl, who reported his horticultural experiments in his *Book on Agriculture.* In Almeria, the Sumadihyya garden was built under al-Mu'tasim (1052–1091) and had the twofold purpose of food production and experimental station. In Sevilla, the al-Buhayra was built in 1171 by the Almohad Caliph Abû Ya'qûb Yûsuf (d. 1199), and fruits were brought from Granada and Guadix to be planted. Gardens were also built in Zaragoza, Valencia, and Tortosa and in private properties all over al-Andalus.

The arrangement of these princes' gardens is not known in detail. The species introduced to Spain from the East and acclimatized during the tenth century included eggplant *(Solanum melongea),* henna *(Lawsonia inermis),* cotton *(Gossypium* spp.), rice *(Oryza sativa),* banana *(Musa* sp.), jasmine *(Jasminum officinale),* and perhaps lemon *(Citrus limon),* saffron *(Crocus sativus),* sugar cane *(Saccharum officinarum),* and mulberry *(Morus* spp.). During the eleventh century, acclimatized species included spinach *(Spinacia oleracea),* sorghum *(Sorghum* spp.), lemon *(Citrus limon),* and orange *(Citrus aurantium).*

The eleventh-century *Book on Agriculture* of Ibn Bassâl mentions one hundred and forty different plant names, which probably correspond to a higher number of contemporary species. The most frequently quoted are fig tree, grapevine, almond tree, and olive tree. Next in number of mentions come a dozen different kinds of fruit trees, among which are pomegranate, apple, and plum. Vegetables follow, with eggplant, zucchini, onions, beans, cucumber, and cabbage being mentioned, among others. After such fruit trees as lemon, orange, and palm tree come the legumes and cotton, and, finally, the aromatic herbs, with coriander, sesame, cumin, and saffron being mentioned, as well as some ornamental plants.

Experiments involving horticultural techniques were especially developed in the area of Sevilla in the so-called al-Sharaf *(aljarafe)*. This was an elevated table-land with a surface of approximately one thousand six hundred and fifty square kilometers that was bordered with water. Its soil was made of sand mixed with lime and local layers of clay, and it was highly fertile. The area, which was occupied by an estimated eight hundred to two thousand villages, was cultivated by a dense population working for the wealthy families of Sevilla who hired agronomists and agriculturists to improve cultivation techniques and production. Research relied on such earlier sources as the *Kitâb Filâhat al-Ard (Book of the Culture of Arable Land)*, the *Kitâb al-Filâha ar-Rûmiyya (Byzantine Book of Agriculture)*, and the *Kitâb al-Filâha an-Nabatiyya (Book of Nabatean Agriculture)*. According to such agricultural works as the books by Ibn Hajjâj (eleventh century) and Ibn al-'Awwâm (twelfth century) that reported local experiments, research dealt with such topics as the quality of earth, fertilizers, vegetable production, growing of flowers, improving the production of the olive tree, grapevine pruning, and viticulture.

The tradition of Arabic gardens and horticulture was perpetuated in the Ottoman world, including in the mosque gardens.

ALAIN TOUWAIDE

See also Botany; Gardens

Primary Sources

López y López, Angel C. *Kitâb fî Tartîb Awqât al-Girâsa wa-l-Magrûsât. Un Tratado Agrícola Andalusí Anónimo. Edición, Traducción y Estudio con Glosario.* Madrid: Consejo Superior de Investigaciones Científicas, Escuela de Estudios Árabes, 1990.

Millás Vallicrosa, J.M., and M. Aziman. *Ibn Bassâl, Libro de Agricultura.* Tetuán: Instituto Muley el-Hasan, 1955.

Further Reading

Alemi, Mahvash. "Il Giardino Persiano: Tipi e Modelli." In *Il Giardino Islamico: Architettura, Natura, Paesaggio*, ed. A. Petrucci, 39–62. Milan: Electa, 1994.

Atasoy, Nurhan. *A Garden for the Sultan: Gardens and Flowers in the Ottoman Culture.* Istanbul: AYGAZ, 2002.

Aubaille-Sallenave, Françoise. "La Greffe Chez les Agronomes Andalous." In *Ciencias de la Naturaleza en al-Andalus. Textos y Estudios. III*, ed. E. García Sánchez, 11–41. Madrid: Consejo Superior de Investigaciones Científicas, 1994.

Carabaza Bravo, Julia Ma. "El Olivo en los Tratados Agronómicos Clásicos y Andalusíes." In *Ciencias de la Naturaleza en al-Andalus. Textos y Estudios. IV*, ed. C. Alvarez de Morales, 11–39. Madrid: Consejo Superior de Investigaciones Científicas, 1996.

Carabaza Bravo, Julia Ma., Expiración García Sánchez, J. Esteban Hernández Bermejo, and Alfonso Jiménez Ramírez. "Arboles y Arbustos en los Textos Agrícolas Andalusíes I." In *Ciencias de la Naturaleza en al-Andalus. Textos y Estudios. V*, ed. C. Alvarez de Morales, 269–307. Madrid: Consejo Superior de Investigaciones Científicas, 1998.

———. "Arboles y Arbustos en los Textos Agrícolas Andalusíes II." In *Ciencias de la Naturaleza en al-Andalus. Textos y Estudios. VI*, ed. C. Alvarez de Morales, 157–222. Madrid: Consejo Superior de Investigaciones Científicas, 2001.

Dickie, J. "The Islamic Garden in Spain." In *The Islamic Garden*, eds. Elisabeth B. MacDougall and Richard Etthinghausen, 89–105. Washington: Dumbarton Oaks, 1976.

El Faiz, Mohammed. "L'Aljarafe of Sevilla: An Experimental Garden for the Agronomists of Muslim Spain." In *The Authentic Garden*, eds. L. Tjon Sie Fat and E. de Jong, 139–152. Leiden: Clusius Foundation, 1991.

Fahd, Toufic. "Botany and Agriculture". In *Encyclopedia of the History of Arabic Science*, 3rd ed., ed. R. Rashed., 813–852. London and New York: Routledge, 1996.

Fahd, Toufic. "L'Agriculture Nabatéenne en Andalousie." In *Ciencias de la Naturaleza en al-Andalus. Textos y Estudios. IV*, ed. C. Alvarez de Morales, 41–52. Madrid: Consejo Superior de Investigaciones Científicas, 1996.

García Sánchez, Expiración, and Angel López y López. "The Botanic Gardens in Muslim Spain." In *The Authentic Garden*, eds. L. Tjon Sie Fat and E. de Jong, 165–176. Leiden: Clusius Foundation, 1991.

Hernandez Bermejo, J. Esteban. "Dificultades en la Identificación e Intrepretación de las Especies Vegetales Citadas por los Autores Hispanoarabes. Applicación a la Obra de Ibn Bassâl." In *Ciencias de la Naturaleza en al-Andalus. Textos y Estudios. I*, ed. E. García Sánchez, 241–61. Madrid: Consejo Superior de Investigaciones Científicas, 1990.

Ilhan, Nevzat. "The Culture of Gardens and Flowers in the Ottoman Empire." In *The Authentic Garden*, eds. L. Tjon Sie Fat and E. de Jong. Leiden: Clusius Foundation, 1991.

Lagardère, Vincent. "Canne à Sucre et Sucreries en al-Andalus au Moyen Age (VIII-XVième s.)." In *Ciencias de la Naturaleza en al-Andalus. Textos y Estudios, III*, ed. E. García Sánchez, 337–59. Madrid: Consejo Superior de Investigaciones Científicas, 1994.

Montoro, M.C. "El Cultivo de los Cítricos en la España Musulmana." In *Ciencias de la Naturaleza en al-Andalus. Textos y Estudios, I*, ed. E. García Sánchez, 263–315. Madrid: Consejo Superior de Investigaciones Científicas, 1990.

Rubiera y Mata, Maria Jesús. "Il Giardino Islamico Como Metafora del Paradiso." In *Il Giardino Islamico. Architettura, Natura, Paesaggio*, ed. A. Petrucci, 13–24. Milan: Electa, 1994.

Ruggles, D. Fairchild. *Gardens, Landscape, & Vision in the Palaces of Islamic Spain.* University Park, Penn: The Pennsylvania State University Press, 2003.

Sáez Fernández, Pedro. "Fuentes Grecolatinas del Tratado Agrícola Andalusí Anónimo." In *Ciencias de la Naturaleza en al-Andalus. Textos y Estudios, III*, ed. E. García Sánchez, 237–93. Madrid: Consejo Superior de Investigaciones Científicas, 1994.

Al-Samarrai, Qasim. "The 'Abbâsid gardens in Baghdad and Sâmarrâ (7–12th century)." In *The Authentic Garden*, eds. L. Tjon Sie Fat and E. de Jong, 115–122. Leiden: Clusius Foundation, 1991.

Samsó, Julio. *Las Ciencias de los Antiguos en Al-Andalus.* Madrid: Fundación MAPFRE, 1992.

Sezgin, Fuat. *Geschichte des Arabischen Schrifttums. 4. Alchimie, Chemie, Botanik, Agrikultur bis ca. 430 H.* Leiden: E.J. Brill, 1971.

Ullmann, Manfred. *Die Natur—Und Gegeimwissenschaften in Islam.* Leiden and Cologne: E.J. Brill, 1972.

HOUSES

Two words are commonly used in Arabic for a house: *dār*, derived from *dāra* (to surround, an enclosure), which is used to describe larger houses up to the palace of the caliph (*Dār al-Khilāfa*: House of the Caliphate), and *bayt*, derived from *bāta* (to spend the night), which is used for a small house or apartment or even a single room.

Evidently, the range of housing across the Islamic world is vast and cannot be characterized by brief generalizations. The form of the house is stylistically dictated by environmental conditions and the wealth of the occupants in addition to local culture. In terms of environmental conditions, the area stretches from the cold, green, and mountainous Anatolia and the Caucasus in the north to the hot deserts of Saudi Arabia and Saharan Africa in the south and from the Mediterranean coasts of Andalusia in the west to the monsoon-touched tropics of Bangladesh and Indonesia in the east. The climate and locally available materials dictated the format: wood and stone in the mountains of Anatolia and the Caucasus, unfired earth brick in many drier areas. The variety of environmental conditions also extends from the constricted urban dwelling within a walled city to the more extensive village complex and further to the open spaces of the desert edge dwelling of the seminomad. With regard to range of wealth, the poor commonly occupied one or two rooms, whereas the mansion of the wealthy of Samarra in the third/ninth century could well be two hundred meters long and contain one hundred fifty rooms. The House of the Caliphate in Samarra is one thousand three hundred meters long and covers one hundred twenty-five hectares.

In theory, the Muslim house was centered around a courtyard with a blank wall to the outside, a reception room at the entrance for outside visitors, and a reserved area for family life in the interior to preserve the segregation of women. In reality, practical reasons meant that only the very largest houses conformed to this ideal: for example, Topkapi Saray, the palace of Mehmed II in Istanbul (1482 CE), met these standards. In this palace, there is an outer public courtyard, an inner men's courtyard with reception room (the audience hall of Ahmet III), and the harem for the women and family life on the north side. Nevertheless, the courtyard surrounded by rooms, although by no means original to Islam, played an important role. Only the mountain houses of Anatolia (because of the climate) and the desert edge houses (where there was no pressure of land) lacked courtyards, although today the western model of a house has invaded nearly all of the Middle East.

The first Muslim house was that of the Prophet in Medina, which was at once the mosque of the nascent Islamic community and the residence of its leader. According to the *Sīra* (the biography of the Prophet), as the house existed at the time of the Prophet's death in the year AH 11/632 CE, there was a square courtyard of unfired earth that was one hundred cubits (c. fifty m) in length per side; three entrances; a covered area to the south with palm trunks supporting a roof of palm leaves to protect the faithful at prayer from the sun; four apartments (bayt) for the Prophet's wives, which were described as having partitions dividing them into several rooms; and about five other apartments for dependent women. The Prophet did not possess his own apartment but rather lived in public, preaching and receiving visitors in the courtyard while sleeping each night with a different wife.

This familial pattern was continued under the Umayyad caliphate (41/661–132/750), according to the archaeological evidence. Starting with the mosque of Kūfa, probably dating in its present form to the reconstruction by Ziyād b. Abī Sufyān in 50/670, the Dār al-Imāra (government house) was placed adjacent to the mosque until the beginning of the third/ninth century, when a separation became evident. The Umayyad Desert Castles (e.g., Qaṣr Kharāna, before 92/710) are characterized by a reception hall and a subdivision of the plan into a series of familial apartments, each having a reception room and four small chambers; these were called, by Creswell, "Syrian bayts." The smaller houses of the Umayyad period that were excavated at the Amman Citadel, 'Anjar, and elsewhere, have a Syrian bayt accompanied by rooms around a courtyard. The specialized room functions typical of Late Roman houses are no longer visible.

The basic house in early 'Abbasid architecture is made up of seven rooms on two sides of a courtyard. The palaces and great houses at Raqqa and Samarra employ this unit as an apartment, whereas reception rooms often employ the īwān (vaulted reception room open to the courtyard) and are fronted by a portico to make a T-īwān. The īwān, which is commonly found in symmetrical four-īwān plans around a courtyard, first originated in Parthian second-century Iraq; it then became standard in palaces and large houses in Iraq and Iran, and it was later transferred to mosques and madrasas. The T-īwān version is found in early Islamic Fusṭāṭ (Old Cairo) in the third/ninth century, and from there it was transferred to Western architecture at Sabra/Mansūriyya in Tunisia (935) and Madīnat al-Zahrā' in Spain (936), although the form there is modified into a basilical hall.

Outside of the state-sponsored sector of the great capitals, fewer medieval houses have been excavated. Merchants' houses of the third/ninth and fourth/tenth centuries have been excavated at Sīrāf on the Iranian coast of the Gulf; these consist of four to eight rooms around a courtyard, probably supporting living rooms on a second story. The same plan is found again in Ayyubid Syria (seventh/thirteenth century) at Bālis/Meskene and Mayadine. At Bālis, smaller houses were again found, with one or two īwāns on a courtyard and few other rooms. The same constraints of urban space are found in the dense warren of earth construction of fourth-/tenth-century through fifth-/eleventh-century Nishapur in eastern Iran, reflecting earlier Central Asian construction of the eighth century at Pianjikent in Tajikistan.

By the eighth/fourteenth century, there were standing buildings in Mamluk Cairo. There the reception room *(qā'a)* is placed in the upper story, and, for the first time, the mashrabiyya is found; this is the wooden-grilled projecting window that permitted inhabitants—particularly women—to see out without being seen. From the ninth/fifteenth century in Cairo, there are examples of 'imārāt (multi-storied buildings with regularly planned apartments). One study of traditional houses of Baghdad has concluded that occupation of the courtyard house was not organized by specialized function of the rooms but by seasonal occupation of the cooler and warmer parts of the house. In the hot zones (e.g., southern Iran, the Gulf, Baghdad, Cairo), subterranean rooms (Persian: *sardāb*) are common, with wind towers (Persian: *bādgīr*) to direct airflow into the rooms. Only in the most extremist Islamic societies, such as the Wahhābī-influenced Saʿūdī traditional palaces of Riyadh, is there found architectural evidence of female separation via harem bridges crossing public streets; however, tunnels crossing public areas are already known in third/ninth century 'Abbasid Samarra, but it is not certain that these are intended for women.

ALASTAIR NORTHEDGE

Further Reading

Bazzana, A. *Maisons d'Al-Andalus: Habitat Médiéval et Structures du Peuplement dans L'Espagne Oriental*, 2 vols. Madrid: Casa de Velásquez, 1992.

Chehab, H. "Al-Quṣūr al-Umawiyya fī 'Anjar bi-Lubnān." *Sumer* 34 (1978): 172–80.

Creswell, K.A.C. *A Short Account of Early Muslim Architecture*. Aldershot, 1989.

Hillenbrand, R. *Islamic Architecture*, Ch. VII. Edinburgh: The Palace, 1994.

Insoll, T. *The Archaeology of Islam*, Ch. III., "The Domestic Environment." Oxford: Blackwell, 1999.

Keall, E.J. "Some Thoughts on the Early Eyvan." In *Near Eastern Numismatics, Iconography, Epigraphy and History*, ed. D.K. Kouymjian, 122–36. Beirut, 1974.

L'Habitat Traditionnel dans les Pays Musulmans Autour de la Méditerranée. Actes du Rencontre d'Aix 6–8 Juin 1984. Le Caire: Institut Français D'Archéologie Orientale, 1988

Northedge, A. *Studies on Roman and Islamic Amman, Vol. 1, History, Site and Architecture*. British Academy Monographs in Archaeology no. 3. British Academy/OUP, 1993.

———. *The Historical Topography of Samarra*. Samarra Studies 1. British Academy Monographs in Archaeology/British School of Archaeology in Iraq.

Raymond, A., and J.-L. Paillet. *Balis II: Histoire de Balis et Fouilles des Ilots I et II*. Damascus, 1995.

Revault, J., and B. Maury. *Palais et Maisons du Caire du XIVe au XVIIIe Siècle*. Cairo, 1977.

Warren, J., and I. Fethi. *Traditional Houses in Baghdad*. Horsham, 1982.

Whitehouse, D. "Excavations at Siraf: Third Interim Report." *Iran* 8 (1970): 1–18.

Wilkinson, C.K. *Nishapur: Some Early Islamic Buildings and Their Decoration*. New York, 1986.

HUMANISM

That humanism is not incompatible with a revealed religion is clear from the existence of humanism in all its varieties within Christianity. The same is true for medieval Islam, which shared with Christianity not only its monotheism but also its high degree of urbanization, its well-developed educational system, and its sophisticated court life, all of which are essential for the emergence of humanism. Islam showed itself to be no less open than Christianity to humanistic tendencies; indeed, the encounter with classical Greek culture, which is generally seen as the defining quality of humanism in the West, took place in the Arab world some centuries before the European Renaissance.

In the secondary literature, seven different kinds of humanism have been mentioned, which will be dealt with here in the following order: (1) tribal humanism, (2) steppe humanism, (3) legal humanism, (4) philosophical humanism, (5) religious humanism, (6) literary humanism, and (7) intellectual humanism. The understanding of the term *humanism* varies in each of these, ranging from absolute secularism to the deepest empathy with humankind in all its diversity.

Tribal humanism refers to a pre-Islamic secularism among the pagan Arabs, which was partly absorbed and redirected by the mission of Muhammad (e.g., the equation of fate *[dahr]* with Allah). This is of great importance for the evolution of an Arab-Islamic literary aesthetic, through which pre-Islamic poetry gradually acquired its "classical" status despite its heathen origins, rather like the Christianization of Latin and Greek literature. There is, as a result, a literary fiction of the desert Arab as a laconic and fatalistic nomad who at best combines eloquence with naive cunning and at worst is a simpleton to be treated with derision by the refined town dweller.

Steppe humanism is a marginal variety that may be considered as a subset of tribal humanism, because the term was applied to the world of the Mughul court as depicted in the autobiography of Babur (see Timurids), which portrays the society of that time as highly secularized and materialistic, with obvious similarities to the Renaissance courts of Europe.

A latent humanism has also been perceived in the vast corpus of legal literature. Here the humanism lies in the earthy pragmatism of Islamic law, which acknowledges and indeed seems to approve of (although this aspect is seldom emphasized) the complexity and unpredictability of human nature. The theory frankly admits the ad hoc quality of human judgment, and the case law abundantly documents the irrepressible ingenuity of ordinary Muslims. It has been claimed that the law represents the very essence of Islamic learning, and it is true that the institutions of higher education (see Madrasa) were principally devoted to the training of jurists and practitioners of the religious sciences. Hence it is reasonable to suppose that the textual and exegetical challenge of applying the holy texts to the events of everyday life would lead to a perception of man that can deservedly be considered humanistic.

Philosophical humanism (i.e., the purely Hellenistic type of humanism) appeared in Islam almost as soon as the translators had created an accessible corpus of Greek philosophical, ethical, and scientific literature in Arabic. By the tenth century, this classically derived intellectual mode was well enough established to allow the Arab philosophers a public role, and they attended the rulers at court, holding forth on the duties of princes and the way to achieve happiness. They found their inspiration in the writings of Plato and Aristotle and their Hellenistic commentators, but they also imparted a tradition of political and ethical theory that had come to them from the Persians. From this fusion of Greek and Persian culture emerged a uniquely Muslim perspective that has been labeled *philosophical humanism,* with Miskawayhi (d. 1030) as perhaps the most consistent adherent—in practice as well as theory—of the Greek ideal of virtue through education in an Islamic context.

Not every Muslim scholar felt the same admiration for Greek philosophy as it radiates from the works of Miskawayhi and his predecessor al-Farabi (the latter displaying the greatest commitment to the Platonic ideal of the philosopher as the indispensable moral guide of the monarch; see Al-Farabi [d. 950]). There was an unbridgeable gulf between the way of thought that regarded virtue, happiness, and truth as the inevitable consequences of correct reasoning and the deeply pious belief that all knowledge of the good and true was contained in revelation. However, those Muslims who rejected the universalism of (Greek) logic in favor of the particularity of the (Arabic) Qur'an did not at the same time abandon the use of their intellectual powers; instead, they applied their acumen to the study of Arabic, the history of the Arabs, and the preservation of Islamic values, with a mentality that has been labeled *religious humanism* and that is characterized as a complete acceptance of this and the next world in Islamic terms. The category is somewhat vague, and it would be difficult to single out individual Muslim representatives, but it may best be compared with the Christian scholars who saw themselves as members of a "textual community" with the responsibility of serving as guardians of the language (Latin, Arabic) and the faith articulated by and embodied in it (Christianity, Islam).

Literary humanism is the form that has the most similarities to its European counterpart and is usually understood when humanism is mentioned without qualification, except in a philosophical context, although the two are very closely related. What separates them is the degree of loyalty to the foreign sources (Greek, Persian) and the supremacy of the discipline of philosophy on the one hand as compared with the much broader basis of Arab culture and aesthetics and Islamic morality that underlies literary humanism on the other hand. They have in common the presumption that virtue can be acquired by training (or, even better, innate virtue enhanced by education), for which they share the term *adab,* loosely translated as "upbringing, discipline" (for other senses, especially literature, see Adab). This training corresponds closely with the Greek ideal of *paideia,* and the product of adab is a refined and well-educated individual, usually a courtier or scholar, who is a member of what Arkoun has called "an aristocracy of the mind."

The adib (one so educated) was not only acquainted with a broad curriculum of religious and secular literature but was also adept in the composition of such works, in addition to which the adib was expected to display perfect manners both at court and in society at large. Indeed it is "manners" above all that are implied in the term *adab*, and books were written to prescribe the correct professional behavior of doctors, lawyers, ministers, judges, academics, and others. The founders (so to speak) of the largely secular Arabic literature that resulted are Ibn al-Muqaffa' (d. 758 CE) and al-Jahiz (d. ca. 868), who set the pattern for the prose style and the range of themes that together expressed the Islamic humanist ideal. Its inclusiveness, which sets literary humanism apart from the philosophical type, is seen in the works of writers such as Ibn Durayd (d. ca. 914), in which Greek, Persian, Christian, Muslim, and pre-Islamic pagan Arab sources are all mingled.

The term *intellectual humanism* is not widely recognized in the secondary literature, but it was proposed (Carter, 1997) to accommodate a form of humanism that seems to lie outside—or, rather, across from—those outlined above. Traditional adab, by definition, does not favor the outsider or the eccentric any more than orthodoxy does, but there were Muslim scholars who preferred to allow their curiosity to roam beyond the limits of conformity, exploiting the freedom of thought available to them in their day at the price of being labeled misfits or heretics. Their dissent did not lead to persecution, however, because it was recognized that by testing the boundaries of faith they might (as they in fact did) contribute to the reinforcement of its dogmatic integrity. The name Mu'tazilite, meaning "one who stands apart," covers most of these individuals.

The most striking figure in this category is Abu Hayyan al-Tawhidi (d. 1023), who is frequently labeled a humanist, although his manners fell far short of the standards of an adib; indeed, he despised the patronized subordination of the courtly litterateur. However, it was he who most succinctly expressed the humanist ideal: "Man is a problem for man." Ibn Jinni (d. 1002) is another such individualist: a free-thinking rationalist, boundlessly inquisitive about the workings of language, he reveals more than any other grammarian a deep sensitivity to the vagaries and illogicalities of human speech. An earlier contemporary, al-Rummani (d. 994), went the other way; true to his Mu'tazilite position, he analyzed language as if it were totally rational and all its inconsistencies fully explicable.

These people might fit into the category of the literary or religious humanists (their works certainly range over the same fields), but their individualism justifies giving them a separate label. Medieval Muslims inhabited a fluid and adventurous environment; although an iron orthodoxy was being forged at the time, there was nevertheless a degree of intellectual liberty and experimentalism that gave free rein to the exercise of the powers of reason. This is, after all, the explicit duty of all thinking Muslims.

MICHAEL G. CARTER

See also Aristotle and Aristotelianism; Ethics; Mirrors for Princes; Political Theory; Scholarship

Further Reading

Arkoun, Muhammad. "L'Humanisme Arabe D'Après le *Kitâb al-Hawâmil wa-'l-«Awâmil'*." *Studia Islamica* 14 (1961): 73–108. (Reprinted in *Essais sur la Pensée Islamique*. Paris: Maisonneuve et Larose, 1984.

Arkoun, Muhammad. *L'Humanisme Arabe au IVe/IXe Siècle, Miskawayh, Philosophe et Historien*, 2nd ed. Paris: Vrin, 1982.

Bergé, Maurice. *Pour un Humanisme Vécu: Abu Hayyan al-Tawhidi*. Damascus: Institut Français de Damas, 1979.

Carter, Michael G. "Humanism and the Language Sciences in Mediaeval Islam." In *Humanism, Culture and Language in the Near East, Studies in Honor of Georg Krotkoff*, eds. A. Afsaruddin and A.H.M. Zahneiser, 27–38. Winona Lake: Eisenbrauns, 1997.

Dale, S.F. "Steppe Humanism: The Autobiography of Zahir al-Din Muhammad Babur (1483–1530)." *International Journal of Middle East Studies* 22 (1990): 37–58.

Gabrieli, Francesco. "Literary Tendencies." In *Unity and Variety in Muslim Civilization*, ed. G.E. von Grunebaum, 87–106. Chicago: Chicago University Press, 1955.

Goodman, Lenn E. *Islamic Humanism*. Oxford, UK: Oxford University Press, 2003.

Kraemer, Joel L. "Humanism in the Renaissance of Islam, a Preliminary Study." *Journal of the American Oriental Society* 104 (1984): 135–164.

———. *Humanism in the Renaissance of Islam, the Cultural Revival During the Buyid Age*. Leiden: Brill, 1986.

Makdisi, George. *The Rise of Humanism in Classical Islam and the Christian West, with Special Reference to Scholasticism*. Edinburgh: Edinburgh University Press, 1990.

Watt, William Montgomery. *Muhammad at Mecca*, 24f. Oxford: Clarendon Press, 1953.

HUMAYUN

Nasir ad-Din Humayun, the second ruler of the Mughal dynasty, was born in 1508 CE in Kabul, a few years after his father, Zahir ad-Din Babur, who had been displaced from the Timurid stronghold in Transoxiana, conquered the city. A favorite son, Humayun spent his early career assisting his father with the administration of Kabul and Badakhshan. He joined his father in his invasions of India, participating in the momentous battle of Panipat in 1526 at which Babur defeated the Afghan ruler, Ibrahim Lodi, and established his family's rule in India. Babur died four years later in 1530, leaving Humayun to succeed him as the ruler of a small but shaky state.

Shah Tahmasp receiving the Moghul Emperor Humayun (detail). Period of Abbas II. Sufarid mural in main hall, 1660s. Credit: SEF / Art Resource, NY. Chihil Sutun (Pavilion of Forty Columns), Isfahan, Iran.

Humayun spent the first decade of his rule trying to maintain control over the territories he had inherited from his father. On the one hand, he had to contend with challenges from his brothers who, at various times, rebelled against his authority and threatened to establish their own independence. His brother Kamran, in particular, betrayed him several times, although Humayun, as a forgiving elder brother, refused to have him executed. More threatening to his rule were the challenges he faced from two external forces that were gradually encroaching on his territory: Sultan Bahadur of Gujarat from the southwest and the Pathan leader Sher Khan Suri from the east. The threat from Sultan Bahadur disappeared when he was killed by the Portuguese. The threat from Sher Khan, however, turned out to be so serious that, after a series of defeats (starting with the battle in Bengal in 1539) Humayun had to flee north India, while Sher Khan, then known as Sher Shah, declared himself ruler. Humayun first sought refuge in Sind (ruled at that time by the Arghuns), where he was joined by Bairam Khan, a loyal friend of his father's who would eventually help him recapture the territory he had lost. It was in Sind that Humayun's son,

Akbar, who would turn out to be one of the greatest of Mughal emperors, was born in 1542. From Sind, Humayun eventually went to Iran, where he sought help for his cause from the Safawid Shah Tahmasp. Shah Tahmasp was happy to provide him with military support as long as Humayun pledged allegiance to Shi'i Islam, which had been introduced as the state religion of the Safavid Empire.

In 1545, with the help of Persian forces, Humayun wrested control over both Kandahar and Kabul from his brothers. He spent several years consolidating his authority over his family resources in Afghanistan before finally turning his attention to territories in north India. Squabbles among the descendants of Sher Shah made it possible for Humayun's armies, under the able command of Bairam Khan, to recapture Punjab. In July 1555, he was able to defeat Sikandar Shah Suri and remount his father's throne in Delhi. The last year of his reign was relatively stable, allowing him to pursue his favorite hobbies, primarily poetry and painting. During his sojourn in Iran, he had met several outstanding miniature painters such as Mir Sayyid Ali, Dost Muhammad, and Abdussamad. Having regained control of Delhi, he invited them to his court, where they were responsible for training Indian artists and for the eventual development of the Mughal style of painting.

Throughout his life, Humayun showed an interest in astrology and astronomy to the point that he has often been characterized as being superstitious. At one time, he had even unsuccessfully attempted to organize his empire along astrological lines. On January 24, 1556, he climbed onto the roof of his library to observe the rising of the planet Venus when he heard the call to prayer. As he bent down to kneel out of respect, he slipped and fell down the steep staircase; he died three days later as a result of his injuries.

ALI ASANI

Further Reading

Gascoigne, Bamber. *The Great Moghuls*. London: Constable, 1998.

HUMOR

The concept of humor is derived from the ancient Greek theory of the body fluids determining a person's character and temperament, and humor has often been defined as a quintessential human characteristic. Although humor, to a certain extent, denotes a mental disposition, its tangible effects are most evident in humorous behavior, itself resulting in the articulation of jocular verbal expression. Modern theory understands humor as a way of coping with the conflicts of human existence, aiming to solve the experienced incongruities through the application of humorous verbal aggression and eventually leading to their dissolution in laughter.

The medieval Islamic attitude toward humor and laughter has to a major extent been determined by both the Qur'an and the Prophet Muhammad's normative example. The Qur'an (53:43), on the one hand, mentions God as the one "who makes humans laugh or cry." Because this passage considers laughter as being created and intended by God, it falls within the range of legitimate human behavior. On the other hand, the Qur'an (49:11) unambiguously condemns satire and ridicule as acts that risk jeopardizing the unity of the true believers. The Prophet Muhammad's attitude toward humor is documented in some fifty traditions (hadith). It is well known that Muhammad liked to laugh, although his laughter was rarely of an aggressive kind; rather, he would smile benevolently, giggle understandingly, or laugh as an act of relief. At the same time, the sources do not fail to tell us about a few practical jokes on the

part of the Prophet, such as when he addressed one of the *sahaba* (Companions) as "the one with the two ears" (although all human beings normally have two ears) and when he told an old woman that she would not enter paradise (although all women in paradise, by definition, are huris). Moreover, Muhammad is known to have laughed at times "until one could see his molar teeth." Hence, the Prophet's behavior is understood as legitimizing a humorous approach to life, including its practical consequences of joking and jesting. Alternatively, Muhammad is also quoted as having characterized people who enjoy a ringing laugh as "those who shorten the prayer and eat all kinds of food;" true believers, by contrast, should smile rather than laugh. This rule of intensity implies a degree of moderation, such as had been introduced by the Arabic translation of Aristotle's *Ethics* in the ninth century. An additional rule of frequency has Muhammad say that "frequent (or intensive) laughter kills the heart"; critical research has, however, proven that this rule is a later attribution, because the maxim had originally been uttered by the ascetic Hasan al-Basri (d. 728 CE).

Against the backdrop of the dual norms of the Qur'an and the sunna, later discussions within the Islamic community have mostly focused on two positions. On the one hand, ascetics, mistrusting human vanity, would not accept humor in the face of life's transitoriness and the imminent threat of judgment day; the best they permitted was laughter as an expression of happiness or of wondering about the marvels of God's creation. Pious opponents of the prohibition of laughter would, on the other hand, quote the example of prominent characters of Islamic tradition, such as the learned Ibn Sirin (d. 728), who is said to have laughed until his eyes became wet and saliva dropped from his mouth.

Notwithstanding the ambiguous attitude of learned Islam, joking and jesting have been the topics of authors of Arabic literature ever since its beginning. Early authors, such as al-Jahiz (d. 868), argued for a balance between the two aspects of *al-jidd* (seriousness) and *al-hazl* (humor): serious matters should be discussed as long as the readers or listeners could focus their attention; the subsequent presentation of humorous narratives was permissible so as to liven up serious discourse and serve as a relaxing interlude before the discourse would again return to serious topics. It was not long before this attitude resulted in the separate publication of jocular material, the presentation of which only superficially pretended to submit to the stricter standard. Although the traditional ambiguity is notably felt in the anecdotal compilations of Ibn al-Jawzi (d. 1201), already al-Abi

(d. 1030) had compiled a veritable encyclopedia of anecdotes and jokes that included several thousand items. Although his work starts with anecdotes about the basic Islamic tenets and about the early caliphs, already at the end of the second volume al-Abi treats the jocular types of *tufayli* (sponger) and greedy persons. The third volume, in addition to popular jesters, contains jokes about crazy and stingy people; the fifth volume has chapters about transvestites and homosexuals; and the seventh and final volume treats various professions, including stupid weavers and sweepers, preachers, thieves, and fanatics.

As a jocular monument of Arabic literature in the classical period, al-Abi's encyclopedia also implicitly documents a considerable degree of tolerance in terms of a humorous approach to the contradictions of social life. In addition to the mentioned works, a survey of humorous literature in the Islamic world would probably have to start from invective poetry (practiced since pre-Islamic times), and it would have to mention, above all, the *Maqamat* of Badi' al-Zaman al-Hamadani (d. 1007) and the pointed satire in the works of the Persian poet 'Ubayd-i Zakani (d. ca. 1371). Popular protagonists of jocular narratives in medieval times—in addition to numerous characters whose names are all but forgotten—include Juh, who, over the centuries, became the quintessential jester of Islamic tradition; Ash'ab, the stereotypical greedy person whose greed made him even believe his own lies; and Buhlul, the wise fool who would admonish the contemporary Caliph Harun al-Rashid in a manner similar to that of the European court jester. Numerous medieval jocular narratives lived on after the introduction of printing to the Islamic world, and numerous chapbooks of the late nineteenth and early twentieth centuries continued to exploit the traditional sources.

The topics of medieval Islamic humor, as much as anywhere else, exhibit two contrasting tendencies: on the one hand, a tolerant approach to the exigencies of human existence and to human foibles is regarded as exemplary; on the other hand, a moderate attitude is recommended so that the vanity implied in human nature should not gain the upper hand against the respect for God's omnipotence.

ULRICH MARZOLPH

See also Al-Jahiz; Companions of the Prophet; Hasan al-Basri; Ibn al-Jawzi; Maqama

Further Reading

Ammann, Ludwig. *Vorbild und Vernunft: Die Regelung von Lachen und Scherzen im Mittelalterlichen Islam.* Hildesheim and others: Olms, 1993.
Marzolph, Ulrich. Arabia Ridens: *Die Humoristische Kurzprosa der Frühen Adab-Literatur im Internationalen Traditionsgeflecht*, 2 vols. Frankfurt am Main: Klostermann, 1992.
Rosenthal, Franz. *Humor in Early Islam.* Leiden: Brill, 1956.

HUNAYN IBN ISHAQ (809–873 OR 877 CE)

A gifted translator, philosopher, and physician, Hunayn Ibn Ishaq came from the suburbs of Kufa to the center of ninth-century Baghdad's intellectual life. Hunayn's entire career must be understood within the context of the Translation Movement, which flourished during the Baghdad-based 'Abbasid caliphate (750–1258 CE). The Islamic conquest of the Near East during the seventh century brought under Muslim control areas with Christian scholars, such as Hunayn, who were capable of translating texts from Greek into Arabic. The earliest impetus for the Translation Movement was the Umayyad Caliph 'Abd al-Malik's (d. 705) order for the imperial record books (Arabic *diwan*, pl. *dawawin*) to be translated from Greek and Persian into Arabic. Because native Arabic speakers would now be able to become viziers, there was a need for information, in Arabic, about geometry, arithmetic, and so on. Moreover, viziers could enhance their social status by patronizing translators, philosophers, and physicians such as Hunayn.

The nascent Translation Movement, with its socioeconomic origins, intensified during the 'Abbasid caliphate, because the 'Abbasid caliphs cultivated a mythical connection with the kings of the earlier Sasanian Empire as an appeal to Persian populist sentiments *(shu'ubiyya)*. A key component of this mythology was the inclusion of Hellenistic Greek philosophy and science within the Sasanian intellectual heritage. Recovering this heritage became a priority to the viziers who patronized Hunayn, and they paid a full-time translator as much as 24 thousand dollars per month. Analysis of Hunayn's autobiography has demonstrated that Hunayn's success aroused envy and jealously that in turn led to his temporary downfall.

Although medieval accounts of Hunayn's career method attributed his success in translating to his attention to the contextual meaning of a word or sentence rather than its literal meaning, recent scholarship has shown that he combined the literal and contextual techniques even within the same text. Additionally, sometimes he translated into Arabic directly from the Greek, and other times he first created a Syriac version for his own use or for a cotranslator. Hunayn's fame and the cooperative nature of translation make a precise determination of his oeuvre impossible. By his own account, he translated more than a hundred texts from Galen alone, and these translations should be understood as creative acts in and of themselves.

As a philosopher and scientist, Hunayn's writings pioneered a technical vocabulary for medical literature and natural philosophy that became a foundation for future work. His writings about optics combined a knowledge of ocular anatomy with a theory of vision that was based on Aristotle's. Hunayn held that light is not a body but rather a state of a transparent medium, such as air, that makes that body receptive to color. In medicine, Hunayn's translations of Galen defended the value of both empirical and theoretical medical knowledge, and Hunayn's own compositions (e.g., *Questions on Medicine*) were thorough and thoughtfully organized. Accounts of his service as physician to the caliph attributed his prowess to both his adab (an awareness of how to behave at court) and his medical acumen.

ROBERT MORRISON

See also Translation: Pre-Islamic Learning into Arabic; Medical Literature, Arabic; Medical Literature, Syriac; Materia Medica; Medicine; Ophthalmology; Physicians; Aristotle and Aristotelianism

Further Reading

Anawati, Georges C., and Albert Z. Iskandar. "Hunayn ibn Ishaq al-'Ibadi." In *Dictionary of Scientific Biography*, eds. C.C. Gillispie et al, Supplement 1, 230–49. New York.
Bergsträsser, Gotthelf. "Hunain ibn Ishaq über die Syrischen und Arabischen Galen-Übersetzungen." *Abhandlungen für die Kunde des Morgenlandes* XVII (1925). Leipzig.
Gutas, Dimitri. *Greek Thought, Arabic Culture.* London: Routledge, 1998.
Morrison, Robert. "Hunayn ibn Ishaq." In *Dictionary of Literary Biography*.

HUNTING

The hunting exercised by the ancient Arabs was essential subsistence hunting or defense from wild animals in the Arabian desert. The Qur'an (in particular verse 3:4) and the traditions of the Prophet imposed laws on hunting in cases in which the meat is not lawful (i.e., cats, dogs, mammals with canine teeth, birds with claws, and animals without ritual killing). With the blooming of the Umayyad and 'Abbasid dynasties, a type of hunting done for fun and sport for the monarchs was developed using the example of the traditions of adjacent nations. This led to a specific vocabulary of falconry that was used in the Umayyad age (e.g., *bazi*, meaning "goshawk," a common name for falcons and hawks). Hunting was practiced with horses, arcs and arrows, swords, nozzles, and nets, and it was aided by trained hawks, dogs, and cheetahs. The main Arabic works depicting hunting range from the eighth to the fourteenth century.

Influences were noted in the hunting handbook of medieval Europe (*The First Book of Falconry* of Emperor Federico II, which was later translated into *The Book of Moamin*). The most ancient form of hunting, predating falconry, was practiced around 780 CE by al-Ghitrib ibn Qudama al-Ghassani, the master of hunting of the Umayyad monarchs, by the order of Caliph al-Mahdi. It was based on the acquaintances of Adham ibn Muhriz, on sources from Sasanian times, a Turkish handbook, and a Byzantine handbook received as a gift from al-Mahdi. These sources brought back the history of the origin of falconry, a description of the four types of birds used in falconry (hawk, peregrine, saker, and eagle), a classification based on the black or yellow colors of their eyes, training methods, and cures for diseases. A treaty about hunting and its many aspects was created by the poet al-Kushajim (ca. 961), author of the *Kitab al-Masayid as-l-Matarid (Book of the Traps and Hunting Spears)*, in which literary aspects prevailed.

Decades later, the falconer of the Fatimid Caliph al-'Aziz Bi-llah wrote for the monarch a treaty about falconry, *al-Bayzara*, which contained two clearly distinguished parts. First, the author exposed technical matters, with descriptions of the fauna of the Egyptian Delta; in the second part, poems traced the work of al-Kushajim. A true summation of the falconry knowledge of the Muslims of the Middle Ages, it was entitled *al-Jamhara f 'Ilm al-Bayzara (Collection on the Science of Falconry)*, and it was compiled by Isa al-Asadi (thirteenth century). This volume was not limited to birds but also described other animals, several hunting techniques, the various legal schools, specific vocabulary, hunting dogs, hunting with leopards, and the medical usefulness of specific animal parts. The Turk Ibn al-Mangli (fourteenth century) was an expert in the military arms that serviced the monarch slaves of al-Malik al-Ashraf; immense synthesis of the *Jamhara* of al-Asani was compiled, with the title *Uns al-Mala' bi-Wahsh al-Fala (Entertainment of the Audience [Speaking About] the Wild Animals of the Desert)*. According to the author, hunting is above all suited to the king and his dignitaries, and it involves ten merits: among these, it constitutes the best training for horses and physical exercise for the knights; it helps one acquire courage and distance from suffering and worries; and it removes vain thoughts and develops sharper sight.

Thirteenth century CE. Plate showing a knight with a falcon. Persian, Saljuq dynasty. Ceramic with polychrome point, unglazed. Photo: Herve Lewandowski. Credit: Réunion des Musées Nationaun/Art Resource, NY. Louvre, Paris, France.

The slaves preferred a form of hunting that involved pursuit by horses, with the participants forming a great circle *(halqa)* that locked on the prey. The preferred targets were gazelle, lions, panthers, ostriches, and cranes. Every animal demanded particular hunting techniques, which were meticulously described in the handbook (although sometimes the techniques were decidedly improbable). The Syrian nobleman Usama ibn Munqidh (thirteenth century) described his memories of falconry among noblemen and of capturing aquatic birds, gazelle, and wild donkeys. The products gained from hunting were then used for commerce in all areas of the Muslim world, and they also increased the desire of caliphs to possess exotic animals. Many citations of hunting poems are found in geographic works; in the zoology of al-Jahiz, al-Qazwini, for the Damiri; and in literary anthologies.

Preparation for hunting contained great meaning in that the Muslim hunter must undergo a purification ritual and invoke the name of God on the hawk and the prey. Dogs trained to obey—despite the impurity that Islam attributes to this animal and the curse on those from the black mantle—are used in hunting on the basis of verse four of the Qur'an. It is noted that the hunter was the saluki (a tall, slender

dog): according to Arabic tradition, the name derives from Saluq, which is located in Yemen. South Arabia also deserves note, because hunting wild goats introduced a peculiar ritual that lasted from the pre-Islamic age. Even if medieval testimonies are insufficient, the traditions have maintained many elements of continuity. One form of hunting involved a great number of hunters with various tasks, such as pushing the animal and killing it. The hunting concluded with a procession of dances and songs and with the exhibition of the bodies of the wild goats, which were later placed on walls of edifices in proportional scope.

Scenes of hunting are frequent in ceramics, bas relief in wood and stucco, ivory and metal objects, and miniatures from the tenth to the fifteenth century. The most common type consists of the reconfiguration of falconry, on foot or by horse; it is represented in action or when a member of a court holding a hawk presents it as a reparation to the monarch (the Turk-Iranian). Other reconfigurations show a hawk in action to assault the prey. In manuscripts of the Shahnama, hunting scenes appear in illustrations in the text (e.g., Bahram Gur hunting the wild donkey) but without particular differences from those that describe the activity of the principals. Hunting by monarchs is represented in the art of Turkish minia-tures, the Saravidi, and the Moghuls during the sixteenth through eighteenth centuries.

GIOVANNI CANOVA

See also Hippology; Usama ibn Munqidh; Veterinary Medicine; al-Jahiz; al-Qazwini

Further Reading

Ahsan, Muhammad M. *Social Life under the Abbasids.* London and New York: Longman, 1979.

Al-Ġitrif ibn Qudama al-Ġassani. *Die Beizvögel*, transl. D. Möller and F. Viré. Hildesheim: G. Olms, 1988.

Grube, E.J. "Caccia. Islam." In *Enciclopedia Dell'Arte Med-ievale*, vol. IV, 33–7. Roma: Istituto Dell'Enciclopedia Italiana, 1993.

Ibn Manglî. *De la chasse*, transl. F. Viré. Paris: Sindbad, 1984.

Ibn al-Marzubān. *The Superiority of Dogs over Many of Those Who Wear Clothes*, transl. G.R. Smith and M.A. S. Abdel Haleem. Warminster: Aris & Phillips, 1978.

Lombard, M. "La Chasse et les Produits de la Chasse dans le Monde Musulman (VIIIe–XIe Siècle)." *Annales Économies Sociétés Civilisations* 24 (1969): 572–93.

Mercier, Louis. *La Chasse et les Sports Chez les Arabes.* Paris: M. Rivière, 1927.

Serjeant, R.B. *South Arabian Hunt.* London: Luzac, 1976.

Viré, François "Le Traité de L'Art de Volerie *(K. al-Bay-zara)*." *Arabica* 12 (1965): 1–26, 113–39, 262–96; 13 (1966): 39–76.

HUSAYN IBN 'ALI

Husayn ibn 'Ali was the grandson of the Prophet Muhammad and the son of Ali and the Prophet's daughter Fatima. He is regarded as one of the early imams of the Shi'is, and his defiance of the Umayyad Caliph Yazid, which led to his death and the massacre of his family and supporters at Karbala in 680 CE, has immortalized him in the Muslim—and particular-ly Shi'i—imagination as one of the great martyr fig-ures of Islam.

Husayn was born in Medina in 626 and as a child is believed to have been held in great affection by the Prophet. As a young man, he participated in the work of his father, Ali, including in his military campaigns. After the death of his father in 661 and the accession to power of Muawiyah, Husayn maintained a low profile and, although dismissive of the usurpation of power by Muawiyah, did not seek to foment open rebellion. However, when Muawiyah sought to impose his son Yazid as successor and thereby to institutionalize the rule of the Umayyad dynasty, Husayn declined to offer allegiance *(baya)*. He was approached by the people of Kufa to oppose Yazid and accept the mantle of leadership, which they believed was his right. In response to their call, Husayn—together with a small band of followers and members of his family—left Mecca for Kufa. On his way, he learned of the execu-tions of some of his closest supporters by the Umayyads and decided to urge those from his group who were not willing to put their lives at risk to volun-tarily depart. He continued on his way to Kufa with the rest of the group, and he camped at a place called Karbala. In the meantime, a contingent from Yazid's army of about four thousand members arrived at the scene and ordered the small band to acknowledge Yazid's authority while also cutting off their access to the river for water.

The final confrontation as recorded by Muslim historians is the tragic account of the encirclement and massacre of Husayn and his small army, which was said to number seventy-two men. They fought gallantly, but they were soon overpowered, and Husayn, his brother, and some of his closest relatives were slaughtered. Husayn's head was taken to Damascus to be displayed before Yazid and his court.

The events of Karbala and the death of Husayn catalyzed opposition to the Umayyad dynasty and rallied support around the family of Husayn and the general cause of the Alids. Husayn's son, Ali, who was spared in the battle, assumed the role of leader and imam of Husayn's followers, thus crystallizing further a distinctive Shi'i identity.

Although there are differing accounts regarding where Husayn's remains were taken, it is generally believed that he was buried at Karbala, where, in time, a mausoleum was built to honor his memory. The mausoleum at Karbala is the most visited pil-grimage center in Shi'i Islam after the Ka'ba. It is the center of prayers, devotions, and rituals asso-ciated with Husayn's memory and death, which is commemorated in particular and with great religious fervor and intensity during the first ten days of Muharram, known as Ashura.

The devotions during Ashura have evolved to rep-resent two major ritual expressions. The first, known as *rawzeh-khani*, involves preaching that is based on the Karbala narrative, and, over the ten-day period, a formal recounting of the events is made in the context of the Shi'i interpretation of Muslim history, with a special focus on notions of persecution, suffering, resistance, and martyrdom. Another major ritual ex-pression developed much later in history and is known as *taziyeh*, a form of passion play that reenacts the events of Karbala. During these rituals, some participants express their internal grief through acts of chest beating and flagellation. Taziyed processions can be highly stylized and may include structures representing Husayn's bier and a riderless horse.

Husayn's life and death are also evoked in special poems of remembrance that have been composed to highlight key themes such as justice, devotion, and courage in the face of oppression. Recitations of these poems, accompanied by music, have also developed into a special genre. Although a significant part of the focus of these expressions is found in Shi'i literature and cultural life, Husayn's example has pervaded all periods of Muslim history, thought, and culture, and it transcends geographic and ethnic differences. Shrines, mosques, and places of remembrance are found throughout the Muslim world. Among the Shi'is, special structures called *Husayniyah* are built to commemorate Ashura and to hold sessions of remembrance for other imams and martyred figures.

In situations of historical conflict and warfare, Husayn's example is often invoked to gain support for particular political and religious causes. This is illustrated in the appropriation of the Karbala narrative, for example, during the Iranian revolution in 1979 and during the conflicts in Iraq in the 1990s and 2000s. However, the more enduring aspects of Husayn's life are the ones that continue to inspire Muslims: selfless leadership, commitment to justice, courage in the face of oppression, and, above all, devotion to God and the cause of Islam.

AZIM NANJI

Further Reading

Ahmad, Fazl. *Husayn, the Great Martyr*. Lahore: Muhammad Ashraf, 1969.

Ayoub, M. *Redemptive Suffering in Islam: A Study of the Devotional Aspects of Ashura in Twelver Shiism*. The Hague: Mouton, 1978.

Momen, Moojan. *An Introduction to Shii Islam*. New Haven: Yale University Press, 1985.

Sobhani, Jafar. *Doctrines of Shii Islam*. London: Institute of Ismaili Studies and I.B. Tauris, 2001.

I

IBADIS

Ibadis (whites) were a moderate *madhhab* (school) of the Kharijite sect who had survived the defeat of the more extreme 'Azraqite' Kharijite sect in Iraq in 699 CE. The Kharijite center in Basra, Iraq, then became the center of an extensive network of Ibadite propagandists—*hamalat al-'ilm* (transmitters of learning). As with other Kharijite-inspired sects, Ibadites made headway only on the fringes of the caliphal lands where the sect's leadership and common goal often helped coalesce otherwise fissiparous "tribal identities." In the later eighth century until the end of the ninth century, Ibadites maintained an independent *imamate* in 'Uman (Oman). There was a brief 'Umani Ibadite resurgence in the eleventh century and the development of an Ibadi *madhhab* (theological school), and 'Umani activity in Indian Ocean trade led to the establishment of Ibadi colonies on the East African coast. During the seventeenth century, Ibadite Omanis became a considerable force in the Indian Ocean.

However, it was in the Maghrib where Ibadis were to have their most significant impact. Kharijite emissaries from Basra, both Sufrite (yellow) and Ibadite (white) Kharijites, are reputed to have appeared in Qayrawan in Ifriqiyya circa 719. Kharijite doctrine provided the ideological leadership for the great Berber Kharijite revolt in North Africa that began in Tangier in 740.

In North Africa, Ibadites were first strongest in Tripolitania, and following the collapse of the Umayyad caliphate and prior to 'Abbasid consolidation, an Ibadite imamate was proclaimed—probably also in reaction to the rival Kharijite Sufrite sect's conquest of Qayrawan in 756. The Ibadites then briefly conquered Qayrawan in 758 and installed the (Iranian) Ibadite missionary *Imam* Ibn Rustman. However, the new 'Abbasid caliphate forced Ibadite tribes to move westward. Although the new 'Abbasid caliphate managed to wrest back power over Ifriqiyya in the Maghrib proper, the unity of Islam had been destroyed. *Imam* Ibn Rustman, forced from Qayrawan, founded an Ibadite confederacy of Berber tribes with a capital at Tahart (ca. 761–762). Tahert became the de facto imamate and capital of Ibadite Berber tribes across North Africa.

Trade was vital to the Kharijite success in the Maghrib, and the dynamic of conquest and rebellion reified old trade routes and connections between communities in North Africa dormant since the Arab conquest. Pushed to the fringes of caliphal power, Kharijite communities survived at the oases that were important to the growing trans-Saharan trade. Merchants were prominent members of the original Ibadite community, perhaps accounting for its moderate and pragmatic stance in comparison with other Kharijite sects. Many Ibadite emissaries or missionaries were also merchants, and in the ninth century the persecution of the Ibadite community in the 'Abbasid east forced more of them westward. By the ninth and tenth centuries, merchants from Basra, Kufa, and Khurasan from the old Kharijite strongholds were present in the new Kharijite centers of Tahert, Zawila, and Sijilmasa. Trade routes from Tahert reached the rich Sudanic kingdoms of Gao and Ghana.

The Fatimids brought an end to the Ibadite imamate of Tahert in 909, but Ibadite communities maintained their strong role in trans-Saharan trade and dominated the commercial towns along the route, such as Zawila, Tadmekka, and Awdaghust. Ibadite merchants and missionaries converted some of the first sub-Saharan Africans to Islam, and one community elected a "black slave" as their *Imam*.

CEDRIC BARNES

Further Reading

Brett, M. *Ibn Khaldun and the Medieval Maghrib.* Aldershot, 1999.
———. "The Arab Conquest and the Rise of Islam in North Africa." In *The Cambridge History of Africa, vol 2., from c. 500 BC to AD 1050*, edited by J.D. Fage. Cambridge, 1978.
Levtzion, N. "The Sahara and Sudan from the Arab Conquest of the Maghrib to the Rise of the Almoravids." In *The Cambridge History of Africa, vol 2., from c. 500 BC to AD 1050*, edited by J.D. Fage. Cambridge, 1978.
Lewicki, Tadeuz. "The Ibadites in Arabia and Africa." *Journal of World History* XIII, no. 1 (1971).
Trimingham, J.S. *Islam in East Africa.* Oxford, 1964.
Wilkinson, John C. *The Imamate Tradition of Oman.* Cambridge, 1987.

IBN AL-'ADIM, KAMAL AL-DIN ABU HAFS 'UMAR B. AHMAD

Ibn al-'Adim was a prominent religious, political, and literary figure of the North Syrian city of Aleppo. He was born in Aleppo in AH 588/1193 CE into a family celebrated for supplying *qadis* (Islamic judges) to the city over generations. Ibn al-'Adim was trained in *fiqh* (Islamic jurisprudence) and became director of one of Aleppo's principal Islamic schools, the Madrasah al-Hallawiyya. Successive Ayyubid rulers of Aleppo entrusted him with a number of diplomatic missions. The last of these was in AH 658/1260 CE, in which he went to Egypt to seek help against the Mongols, shortly before they took Aleppo. He died in exile in Cairo two years later.

Ibn al-'Adim wrote a number of works, not all of which have survived. They include a treatise on handwriting, a thesis on the preparation of perfumes, and an address to a ruler of Aleppo on the birth of his son. But he is best known to modern scholarship for his chronicle of Aleppo and northern Syria, the *Zubdat al-halab fi ta'rikh Halab (The Cream of the Milk as Regards the History of Aleppo)*. This is the principal source for events in the area during the author's lifetime.

In his own day, however, Ibn al-'Adim was celebrated for his *Bughyat al-talab fi ta'rikh Halab (What Is Desirable in the Pursuit for the History of Aleppo)*. A characteristic production of the medieval *adab* (belles-lettres) tradition, the *Bughyat al-talab* is a biographical dictionary of notable people associated with Aleppo, from remotest antiquity to the compiler's own times. In addition to factual information, an entry often contains examples of the subject's verse, or transmission of *hadith* (Prophetic tradition). The original work, of which only a quarter survives, apparently filled forty volumes containing seventeen thousand pages of twenty lines each, and is believed to have been penned by Ibn al-'Adim himself during the last two years of his life.

DAVID MORRAY

See also Adab; Aleppo; Ayyubid; Biography and Biographical Works; Madrasa

Primary Sources

Ibn al-'Adim. *Zubdat al-halab fi ta'rikh Halab.* 3 vols. Edited by Sami al-Dahhan. Damascus: Institut Français de Damas, 1951–1968.
———. *Bughyat al-talab fi ta'rikh Halab.* 11 vols. Edited by Suhayl Zakkar. Damascus: Dar al-Ba'th, 1988.

Further Reading

Morray, David W. *An Ayyubid Notable and His World: Ibn al-'Adim and Aleppo as Portrayed in His Biographical Dictionary of People Associated with the City.* Leiden: E. J. Brill, 1994.

IBN AL-ATHIR, 'ALI ABU 'L HASAN 'IZZ AL-DIN

Ibn al-Athir was a scholar (1160–1232 CE) who spent most of his life in Mosul (present-day northern Iraq), with short spells in Syria. Details of his life are hardly known because he rarely referred to himself in his writings. He was the scion of a notable Mosulian family that had acquired some wealth by engaging in trade and owned real estates. His father and two of his brothers played an active role in political life by serving Zankid and Ayyubid rulers in northern Iraq and Syria. It is not clear whether Ibn al-Athir himself had official positions, but he enjoyed at least the patronage of members of the Zankid dynasty and their high officials and served as the dynasty's envoy to Baghdad.

Ibn al-Athir's fame has rested with his universal history *al-Kamil fi al-ta'rikh (The Perfect History)*, which reports events from the creation of the world until shortly before the author's death. The scope of this voluminous work was unusual for its period because most chronicles tended to be local histories that concentrated on the immediate past (such as those by Abu Shama, Ibn al-'Adim, and Ibn Wasil). The *Kamil* was regarded by its contemporaries and following generations as an outstanding achievement in the field of history for several reasons. The coherent account focuses on the main events by artfully integrating a variety of sources. At the same time Ibn al-Athir strove to treat also events in neighboring regions of the Islamic world, such as Egypt and Persia. Although the chronicle followed the period's dominant annalistic scheme of organizing the material, Ibn al-Athir transgressed this rigid framework when necessary. He drew together elements of events, which stretched over several years, under one heading in order to avoid the continuous interruption of the narrative. Finally, as the author eschewed explicit partisanship to political or sectarian causes he was able to reach a broad readership.

Shortcomings of his work, for example, that he hardly covered more distant areas such as the Maghrib, did not alter its popularity. However, from a modern perspective the chronicle poses several problems, chief among them the author's method of omitting his sources to avoid interrupting the narrative. Consequently, the bulk of his work prior to his own lifetime, while retaining its literary value, can hardly be used for historical purposes. The parts contemporary to him are of greater historical value, but the implicit support of the Zankid dynasty has to be kept in mind when reading the text.

The Crusades play no particular role in the *Kamil*'s narrative because they hardly altered the chain of events as laid out by Ibn al-Athir. However, in a famous passage the author linked the advent of the First Crusade in the late eleventh-century Middle East to the Christian advances into Muslim territories in Andalus/Spain and Sicily, an insight of historical broadness rarely found among his contemporaries.

Ibn al-Athir composed another chronicle, *al-Ta'rikh al-bahir (The Splendid History)*, on the Zankid dynasty of his hometown of Mosul, which due to its limited geographical and chronological focus, as well as its more explicit partisanship for the Zankids, did not reach the reputation of the *Kamil*. Ibn al-Athir's fame in history did not only rest on his chronicle but also on biographical works, especially his account of the Companions of the Prophet. This work's virtues, again, were its coherent account and its focus on main issues.

KONRAD HIRSCHLER

See also Historical Writing; Biography and Biographical Works

Primary Sources

Ibn al-Athir. *al-Kamil fi al-ta'rikh*. 13 vols. Edited by Carolus J. Tornberg. Beirut: Dar al-Fikr, 1965–1967 (eprint of 1851–1871 edition with corrections and new pagination).

Further Reading

Ahmad, M. H. M. "Some Notes on Arabic Historiography during the Zengid and Ayyubid Periods (521/1127–648/1250)." In *Historians of the Middle East*, edited by Bernard Lewis and Peter M. Holt, 79–97. Oxford: Oxford University Press, 1962.
Robinson, Chase F. *Islamic Historiography*. Cambridge: Cambridge University Press, 2003.
Rosenthal, Franz. *A History of Muslim Historiography*. Leiden: Brill, 1968.

IBN AL-FURAT

Nasir al-Din b. 'Abd al-Rahim b. 'Ali b. al-Furat al-Misri al-Hanafi (d. 1404–1405), was the Mamluk-era author of a universal history titled *Ta'rikh al-Duwal wa-l-Muluk*. The work has proved valuable for modern historians, particularly for its coverage of the **Ayyubid** and **Mamluk** periods—including details of the late Crusade period—although there are gaps in the surviving manuscripts. The *Ta'rikh al-Duwal wa-l-Muluk* was subsequently used by later Mamluk-era historians, notably **al-Maqrizi** (d. 1442). An analysis of portions of his work reveals Ibn al-Furat to have been interested primarily in the recording of significant political and economic events and the associated activities of the ruling elite.

WARREN C. SCHULTZ

See also Ayyubids; Mamluks; al-Maqrizi

Primary Sources

Ayyubids, Mamluks and Crusaders: Selections from the Tarikh al-Duwal wa'l-Muluk of Ibn al-Furat. Text and Translation by U. and M.C. Lyons. Historical Introduction by J. S. C. Riley-Smith. 2 vols. Cambridge: W. Heffer and Sons, 1971.

Further Reading

Cahen. Cl. "Ibn al-Furat." *Encyclopaedia of Islam*. 2d ed., vol. 3.2, 768–769.
Little, D.P. *An Introduction to Mamluk Historiography*. Wiesbaden: Franz Steiner Verlag, 1970.

IBN AL-HAYTHAM, OR ALHAZEN

The polymath Abu 'Ali al-Hasan ibn al-Haytham (ca. 965–1039 CE), known in Latin as Alhazen, was born in Basra, Iraq. After completing his studies in Iraq, he

343

settled in Egypt, wherein he was commissioned to design a dam on the Nile. The failure of this project led him to feign madness until the death of his erratic patron, the Fatimid caliph al-Hakim (1021 CE). Although his prolific contributions covered a variety of disciplines in mathematics, astronomy, and mechanics, his impact was greatest in the field of optics. His chef-d'œuvre *Kitab al-Manazir (The Optics*, ca. 1027 CE*)*, which was translated into Latin as *De aspectibus* (ca. 1270 CE), decisively shaped the emerging theory of perspective in medieval and Renaissance science and art. His influence is noticeable in medieval scholars such as Roger Bacon, John Peckham, and Witelo and in Renaissance theorists such as Leon Battista Alberti and Lorenzo Ghiberti. In medieval science in Islam, Kamal al-Din al-Farisi's *Tanqih al-Manazir (The Revision of the Optics)* advanced the most substantive critical interpretation of Ibn al-Haytham. His theory of vision constituted an outstanding achievement in optics in the period between Claudius Ptolemy and Johannes Kepler. He resolved the ancient Greek dispute over the nature and causation of vision, which had either been derived, in physical terms, from the intromission of the form of a visible object into the eye or from the mathematical model of the extromission of a cone of light from the eye. Following physicists like Aristotle, Ibn al-Haytham argued that vision occurs by intromission of the luminous form of the visible object into the eye. However, in elucidating this process he employed the model of the cone of vision as formulated by mathematicians such as Euclid and Ptolemy. He thus demonstrated that vision results from the intromission of a luminous form by way of the rectilinear propagation of light through a transparent medium; there is a virtual cone whose vertex is in the center of the eye and whose base is on the surface of the visible entity. He also held that visual perception is not a mere sensation but is primarily an inferential act of discernment and judgment. Moreover, he supplemented his *Optics* with *Treatise on Light (Risala fi l-Daw')*, which further investigated the essence and comportment of luminosity and its radiant dispersion through various transparent and translucent media. His ocular observations were founded on anatomical examinations of the structure of the eye, as well as being supported by experimental installations devised to detect errors and illusions in visual perception and to explore phenomena like the *camera obscura* (the darkroom principle behind the pinhole camera). Ibn al-Haytham also investigated meteorological aspects related to the rainbow and to the density of the atmosphere, as well as inquiring about the nature of celestial phenomena such as the eclipse, the twilight, and moonlight. In this endeavor,

he relied on his accounts of refraction and on catoptrical experimentations with spherical and parabolic mirrors and magnifying lenses. He also presented a thorough critique of the conception of place *(topos)* as set in Aristotle's *Physics*, wherein it was stated that the place of something is the two-dimensional boundary of the containing body that is at rest and is in contact with what it contains. In contrast with this definition, Ibn al-Haytham rather attempted to demonstrate in his *Risala fi'l-makan (Treatise on Place)* that place *(al-makan)* is the imagined three-dimensional void between the inner surfaces of the containing body. Consequently, he showed that place was akin to space in a manner that prefigures Descartes's *extensio*. Building on the legacy of Euclid, and partly informed by the works of the mathematician Thabit ibn Qurra (d. 901 CE), Ibn al-Haytham further systematized the arts of analytical geometry (linking algebra to geometry), infinitesimal mathematics, conics, and number theory. In addition, he studied the mechanics of the first law of motion according to which it is held that a body moves perpetually unless prevented from doing so by an external force that arrests it or alters its direction. In examining the attraction between masses he also seems to have been tangentially aware of the magnitude of acceleration due to a principle akin to the force of gravity. Pioneer in his pursuits, he also strived to develop rigorous experimental methods of controlled scientific testing in view of verifying theoretical hypotheses and substantiating inductive conjectures.

NADER EL-BIZRI

See also Algebra; Aristotle and Aristotelianism; Astronomy; Geometry; Mathematics; Meteorology; Optics; Ptolemy; Thabit ibn Qurra

Primary Sources

Ibn al-Haytham. *Kitab al-manazir*. Edited by Abdelhamid I. Sabra. Kuwait: National Council for Culture, Arts and Letters, 1983.
———. *The Optics of Ibn al-Haytham, Books I-III, On Direct Vision*. Translated by Abdelhamid I. Sabra. London: The Warburg Institute, University of London, 1989.
———. *Majmu' al-rasa'il*. Haydar Abad: Da'irat al-Ma'arif al-'Uthmaniyya, 1937.

Further Reading

Beshara, Saleh O. *Ibn al-Haytham's Optics: A Study of the Origins of Experimental Science*. Minneapolis: Bibliotheca Islamica, 1977.
Nazif, Mustafa. *al-Hasan bin al-Haytham*. 2 vols. Cairo: *Matba'at al-nuri*, 1942–1943.

Rashed, Roshdi. *Les mathématiques infinitésimales du IXe au XIe siècle: Ibn al-Haytham,* Volumes II–IV. London: al-Furqan Islamic Heritage Foundation, 1993–2002.

Sabra, Abdelhamid I. "The Physical and the Mathematical in Ibn al-Haytham's Theory of Light and Vision." In *The Commemoration Volume of Biruni International Congress in Tehran.* Vol. 38. Tehran: High Council of Culture and Arts, 1976.

———. "Sensation and Inference in Alhazen's Theory of Visual Perception." In *Studies in Perception: Interrelations in the History of Philosophy and Science.* Edited by Peter K. Machamer and Robert G. Turnbull. Ohio: Ohio State University Press, 1978.

IBN AL-JAWZI

Ibn al-Jawzi, 'Abd al-Rahman b. 'Ali b. Muhammad Abu 'l-Faraj, a legal scholar, theologian, preacher, and historian, was one of the most prominent figures of twelfth-century Baghdad. Born around 1126 CE to a fairly wealthy family, he lived in the city a life of great intellectual, religious, and political activity. His life, which lasted to the end of the twelfth century, illustrates major characteristics of the political and religious milieu of Baghdad during the so-called Sunni Revival. In particular, his career and activities as a Hanbali master and preacher reflect the significant role played by Hanbali popular preachers of this period in shaping the city's public sphere. Seen in the broader perspective of the medieval Islamic civilization, the century during which he lived was a particularly productive and significant period in the history of Islamic preaching, comparable to the twelfth century in the history of preaching in the Latin West.

By the twelfth century, Baghdad had become a major scene in the development of the madrasa and the crystallization of the Sunni schools of jurisprudence. Ibn al-Jawzi's teaching career began as an assistant to his master in his two madrasas and culminated in the directorship of five prestigious madrasas erected in the city for adherents to the Hanbali school. His prominence in Baghdad's official and public spheres was due to his preaching as to his teaching activity at the Hanbali law colleges. Not only did he deliver the official sermons of the Palace mosque but he also preached many popular sermons to very large and enthusiastic crowds. His sermons vigorously defended the Sunna against all those whom he considered to be schismatic and criticized those Sunni scholars who, in his view, did not fully adhere to the uncompromising demand of Hanbali scholars for conformity and uniformity among the "people of the Sunna" in accordance with the perfect integrity of the simple original faith. At the same time, he called for the restoration of the caliphate—an institution commonly perceived as the symbol of legitimate government and unity among Muslims. For many years he was closely associated with the 'Abbasids who supported and encouraged his teaching and preaching activities in Baghdad's public arena. However, toward the end of his life, he was exiled and put under house arrest by decree of the caliph al-Nasir, whose policy he had refuted. Soon after his triumphant return to Baghdad, Ibn al-Jawzi died in 1200.

Ibn al-Jawzi was clearly one of the most prolific and versatile authors of medieval Arabic literature. Several medieval authors place the number of his writings at nearly a thousand. While this is probably an exaggerated figure, enough information is available to indicate that the extent of his literary corpus is very considerable indeed. A glance at the titles of his works that are extant indicates that they range across the entire spectrum of the great Islamic and literary disciplines.

His outstanding work, *al-Muntazam,* is a universal history, relating the history of the world in chronological order from its beginnings to the year 1179. Following each year entry, he provides richly documented biographies of all prominent people who died during that particular year: caliphs, viziers, judges, high officials, scholars, and pious men. His two other major historical works belong to the biographical genre, one of the most productive genres of the Islamic literary tradition. His *Sifat al-safwa* is a collection of biographies of those whom he considered to be true Sufis, that is, the ascetic worshipers who followed faithfully the teaching of the Prophet and his Companions. His *Manaqib* is a collection of panegyric biographies of the historic figures he regarded as models of proper Islamic creed and conduct.

Ibn al-Jawzi's zeal as a defender of true faith appears with particular fervor in his *Talbis iblis,* one of the major works of Hanbali polemic. In this work he launched an attack not only on the various heretical sects but also on all those whom he considered responsible for introducing *bid'a* (negative innovations) into Sunnism, and of these, particularly, the Muslim mystics. His views and tenets are no more clearly expressed than in his collections of homilies consisting of the four subgenres that make up the medieval Arabic homily: the *khutba* (hymn of praise), the *qissa* (pious story), the *wa'z* (admonition), and the *khawatim* (concluding verses of poetry). Furthermore, the collection of sermons he left reflects his prominence in the society within which he was embedded and his significant contribution to the evolution of the Islamic art of sermon composition and preaching.

DAPHNA EPHRAT

See also Sunni Revival

Further Reading

Ibn al-Jawzi, 'Abd al-Rahman ibn 'Ali. *Kitab al-Lutf fi'l-wa'z*. Beirut: Dar al-Kutub al-'Ilmiyya, 1984.
———. *Kitab al-qussas wa'l-mudhakkirin*. Edited and translated by Merlin Swartz. Beirut: Dar al-Machreq, 1984.
———. *Al-Muntazam fi ta'rikh al-muluk wa'l-umam*. 5 vols. [=Vols. V–X]. Hyderabad, Deccan: Dairat el-Maaref Osmania, 1938–1940.
———. *Sifat al-safwa*. Hyderabad, Deccan: Dairat el-Maaref Osmania, 1936–1938.
———. *Talbis iblis*. Beirut: Dar al-Kutub al-'Ilmiyya, n.d.
Hartmann, A. "Les ambivalences d'un sermonnaire hanbalite." *Annales Islamologiques* 22 (1986), 52 ff.
———. "La predication islamique au moyen age: Ibn al-Jawzi et des sermons (fin du 6ᵉ/12ᵉ siècle)." *Quadrani di studi arabi*. 5–6 (1987–1988): 337–346.
Laoust, H. "Les Agitations Religieuses à Baghdad aux IVᵉ et Vᵉ siècles de l'Hégire." In *Islamic Civilization 950–1150*, edited by D.S. Richards. Oxford: Cassirer, 1973.
Leder, S. *Ibn al-Gauzi und seine Kompilation wider die Leidenschaft*. Beirut: In Kommission bei Franz Steiner Verlag, 1984.
Swartz, Merlin. "The Rules of Popular Preaching in Twelfth-Century Baghdad According to Ibn al-Jawzi". In *Preaching and Propaganda in the Middle Ages*, edited by G. Makdisi et al, 223–239. Islam, Byzantium, Latin West. Paris: Presses Universitaires de France, 1983.
———. "Arabic Rhetoric and the Art of Homily in Medieval Islam." In *Religion and Culture in Medieval Islam*, edited by Richard G. Hovannisian and George Sabagh. Cambridge, United Kingdom: Cambridge University Press, 1999.

IBN AL-MUQAFFA'

Ibn al-Muqaffa' (c. 723–759 CE) was a prolific translator and the author of original works on ethics and statecraft. He was born in Fars (Southwest Persia, today Iran) to a family of local notables. In the course of his education he mastered the various scripts used to write Pahlavi, an archaic written form of Persian. He was thus able to read the epic histories, works of advice to kings, and other genres of wisdom literature left behind by the Sasanian Empire that had once ruled Southwest Asia.

After studying in the southern Iraqi city of Basra to perfect his knowledge of Arabic, Ibn al-Muqaffa' held a series of secretarial posts under the Umayyad governors of Shapur and Kirman. Unlike many of his colleagues, he escaped persecution when the 'Abbasid revolution (750) overthrew the Umayyad dynasty. Returning to Basra, he served as a secretary to the brothers of the reigning caliph al-Mansur. When one of the brothers made an abortive bid for the throne, Ibn al-Muqaffa' was asked to draft a letter asking the caliph not to retaliate against his rebellious relative. The terms of the letter angered the caliph, who expressed the wish that someone might rid him of this troublesome secretary. Taking the hint, the governor of Basra had Ibn al-Muqaffa' executed, reportedly by being chopped to pieces.

In the course of his short career, Ibn al-Muqaffa' translated numerous works of Sasanian literature from Pahlavi into Arabic. The most famous of these is *Kalila and Dimna*, a collection of fables that had been translated from Sanskrit into Pahlavi. The stories, which feature both human and animal characters, show how foresight, self-restraint, and trickery can be used to one's advantage. The book's preface, which claims to be the autobiography of the Persian physician who translated the book from the original Sanskrit, contains a searching critique of institutionalized religion. The work inspired at least seven direct translations from the Arabic into other languages. The most influential was the second Hebrew translation, which was made around 1270. It inspired versions in German, Spanish, and Italian, the last of which served as the basis of the first English rendering (1570).

In addition to *Kalila and Dimna*, Ibn al-Muqaffa' translated Pahlavi works on history, statecraft, and ethics. None of his translations survives in its entirety, although one (*The Letter of Tansar*) is known through a later rendering into New Persian. The rest are widely quoted by classical Arabic authors, and even in this fragmentary form constitute an important source of information on pre-Islamic Iran. He has also been credited with a translation of an Aristotelian work on logic, but the attribution is erroneous.

Of the works he himself wrote in Arabic, the most famous is his work on *adab*. *Adab* means "the right way of doing something," and his book offers advice on how to win friends, prosper in one's career, and avoid incurring the wrath of one's superiors. Due to the influence of this work (as well as an imitation of it commonly misattributed to him), *adab* came to mean not only "social skills" but also "books about social skills," and eventually "secular literature," which, along with "good manners," is the meaning of the term in modern Arabic.

Ibn al-Muqaffa' is also famous for his letter of advice to the Abbasid caliph al-Mansur (AH 136–158/754–775 CE) recommending that the latter promulgate an official statement of the Islamic creed, adopt a uniform code of law, and pay the army regularly. The recommendations were not adopted, but the diagnosis of the state of the empire proved strikingly prescient.

To Ibn al-Muqaffa' also are ascribed a defense of Manichean dualism and a few lines of prose written in imitation of the Qur'an. Authentic or not, these texts contributed to his posthumous reputation as a heretic, which clung to him despite his conversion from Zoroastrianism to Islam.

Industrious, unsentimental, and often irreverent, Ibn al-Muqaffa' deserves much of the credit for preserving the literary legacy of the Sasanian empire and, in the process, creating a precedent for the use of Arabic as a vehicle for secular prose literature.

MICHAEL COOPERSON

See also 'Abbasids; Adab; Aristotle and Aristotelianism; Basra; Sasanians, Islamic Traditions; Umayyads

Primary Sources

Al-adab al-kabir wa al-adab al-saghir. Edited by In'am Fawwal. Beirut: Dar al-Kitab al-'Arabi, 1994.

Kalila wa Dimna li 'Abd Allah Ibn al-Muqaffa'. Edited by 'Abd al-Wahhab 'Azzam et al. Beirut: Dar al-Shuruq, 1973. English translation (based on other sources) in *Kalilah and Dimnah. An English Version of Bidpai's Fables Based upon Ancient Arabic and Spanish Manuscripts.* Translated by Thomas Ballantine Irving. Newark, DE: Juan de la Cuesta, 1980.

La Lotta tra l'Islam e il Manicheismo: un libro di Ibn al-Muqaffa' contro il Corano confutato da al-Qasim b. Ibrahim. Edited and translated by Michaelangelo Guidi. Rome: Accademia Nazionale dei Lincei, 1927 (contains passages from the Manichean tract with Italian translation).

Pellat, Charles. *Ibn al-Muqaffa', mort vers 140/757, "conseilleur" du caliphe.* Paris: Maisonneuve, 1976 (contains the letter to al-Mansur).

The Letter of Tansar. Translated by Mary Boyce. Rome: Istituto Italiano per il Medio ed Estremo Oriente, 1968.

Further Reading

de Blois, François. *Burzoy's Voyage to India and the Origin of the Book of Kalilah wa Dimnah.* London: Royal Asiatic Society, 1990 (with extensive further bibliography).

Latham, J.D. "Ibn al-Muqaffa' and Early 'Abbasid Prose." In *'Abbasid Belles-Lettres,* edited by Julia Ashtiany et al. Cambridge: Cambridge University Press, 1990.

van Ess, Josef. "Some Fragments of the *Mu'aradat al-Qur'an* Attributed to Ibn al-Muqaffa'." [the passages in imitation of the Qur'an] In *Studia Arabica et Islamica, Festschrift for Ihsan 'Abbas,* edited by Wadad al-Qadi. Beirut: American University in Beirut, 1981.

IBN AL-NAFIS

'Ala' al-Din 'Ali ibn Abi l'Haram al-Qurasi, commonly known as Ibn al-Nafis, was a renowned physician and an author of and commentator on medical works. He also wrote about the fields of grammar, rhetoric, logic, religious sciences, and, famously, of religious philosophy. Ibn al-Nafis was born probably in the second decade of the thirteenth century and grew up and was educated in Damascus. At some point, he moved to Cairo, where he practiced and taught at a hospital of unknown identity, perhaps the Bimaristan al-Nasiri, and eventually attained the post of chief of physicians *(ray'is al-aibba)* of Egypt and the influential honor of being personal physician to the Mamluk sultan, probably al-Zahir Baybars (r. 1260–1277). One of his contemporary and compatriot students was the surgeon Ibn al-Quff (1233–1286). Ibn al-Nafis may have crossed paths with Ibn abi Usaybi'a (d. 1270) in Cairo, but it does not figure in the latter's biographical collection of Arabic medicine. Toward the end of his life, Ibn al-Nafis bequeathed his house and library to the Mansuri hospital, founded by the sultan al-Mansur Qallwun (r. 1279–1290) in 1284. He died in Cairo on Dec. 17, 1288.

Ibn al-Nafis was extolled by his admiring biographers and colleagues as a "second Avicenna"; his prominent position in the scholarly heritage of the Arabs until today is reflected in the fact that many hospitals in the Arab world are named after him. In fact, the breadth of his scholarship, his ability for synthesis, and his independent judgment, an indicator of which is the scarcity of his literal references to preceding scholarly literature, are remarkable. More decisive is the fact that Ibn al-Nafis, with his treatment of Avicenna's *Qanun,* inaugurated a long series of commentaries and supercommentaries to this medical encyclopedia and helped to establish its dominant position for some centuries to come. Of his extant commentaries on medical writings a number deal with the *Corpus Hippocraticum*: the *Aphorisms,* the *Prognostics,* the *Epidemics* (for which cf. the essay by P. Bachmann), and *De natura hominis*; the writings of Galen do not seem to have attracted Ibn al-Nafis' solicitude, because, according to his biographer, al-Safadi, and contrary to his Damascene teacher, Muhaddib al-Din al-Dahwar (d. 1230), "he loathed the style of Galen and described it as weak and profuse with nothing in it." Apart from a commentary on the famous medical catechism *al-Masa'il fi l-Ôibb* by Hunayn b. Ishaq (d. 873 or 877), he dealt markedly with Avicenna's *Qanun,* first in the form of an epitome, *Mujiz,* treating all parts of medicine as they are dealt with in the *Qanun,* except for anatomy and physiology; and second, a commentary, *Sarh al-Qanun.* The *Mujiz* gave rise to a host of commentaries, and one Hebrew and two Turkish translations are known. Among the commentators, the most widely read authors are Sadíd al-Din al-Kazaruni (d. 1357); Gamal al-Din al-Aqsara'i (d. 1378); Nafis b. 'Iwad al-Kirmani (wrote in 1437), whose commentary in turn was repeatedly commented on into the nineteenth century; and Ibn al-Amsati (d. 1496). Ibn al-Nafis' *Sarh al-Qanun,* as well as at least one of his manuscripts, written before 1242 and bearing the separate title *Sarh tasrih al-Qanun,* contain the earliest account of the pulmonary blood circulation, which contradicts both common theories of a visible passage and the Galenic assumption of an invisible passage of the blood between the two cavities of the heart and which antedates the publication, in 1553, of the pertinent account by Michael Servetus, possibly through the communication of Ibn al-Nafis' ideas by the translator Andrea Alpago (d. 1520), by three centuries. The anatomical observation that the cardiac wall is impermeable leads Ibn al-Nafis to the logical postulation that "when the blood [in the *right* cavity] has become thin, it is passed through the arterial vein into the lung, in order to be dispersed within the substance of the lung and to mix with the air, whereupon the finest parts of the blood are refined and, after mixing with the air and becoming fit for the generation of *pneuma*, are passed through the venous artery into the *left* cavity" (cf. Iskandar 1970–1980: 603, and Ullmann 1970: 173–176; for the recent discussion of Ibn al-Nafis' theory, cf. Iskandar 1970–1980: 605 f.). Ibn al-Nafis' construction of the pulmonary blood circulation was received scarcely, if at all, by later scholars of Islamic medicine. Equally small was the visible reception of his comprehensive handbook on ophthalmology, *K. al-Muhaddab fi l-kuhl al-mugarrab*. Of his medical *Summa*, the *K. al-Samil fi l-sina al-tibbiyya*, projected to consist of three hundred volumes, only eighty were completed, and a number of manuscripts are extant, some of them autographs of the author.

In his *Muhtasar fi 'ilm uÈÚl al-hadir*, Ibn al-Nafis gives a short summary (some twenty-four folia) of the principles of the science of Tradition, "a reminder for the advanced student and an auxiliary manual for the beginner," which is informed by the school of al-Safr'i and makes extensive use of al-Harib al-Bagdadi's *Kifaya* and, particularly, al-Gazali's *Mustasfa*.

Certainly the most original of Ibn al-Nafis' works is his *Risala al-kamiliyya fi l-sira al-nabawiyya*. The two predecessors of this philosophical allegory are Avicenna's *Risalat Hayy b. Yaqzan* and a work with the same title (but different intention) by the Andalusian physician and philosopher Ibn Tufayl (d. 1185). While Avicenna's tale, with its programmatic title hero who comes into being by spontaneous generation, grows up on an island without fellow human beings, and, by his own observation and reasoning, attains the natural, philosophical, and theological truths, clearly is the inspiration for both Ibn Tufayl's and Ibn al-Nafis' accounts, the relationship between these two latter authors vis-à-vis Avicenna is much closer. This shows in the similar treatment of the hero's anatomical observations, which proceed toward a study of the plants, the meteorological phenomena, the celestial bodies, the Creator and His attributes, and a number of other

parallels, as the hermeneutical issue of why the Divine Law is mediated to the common people in the form of allegories. In turn, Ibn al-Nafis' account deviates significantly from that of Ibn Tufayl insofar as his hero, Kamil, "the Perfect," deduces not only the rules of the religious law, the duties of man in worship and social relations—hence the editors' title of the edition of Ibn al-Nafis' text, *Theologus Autodidactus*—but also the historical events from the Prophet Muhammad down into the author's lifetime, not from information given by visitors to the island from outside, as Ibn Tufayl had related a hundred years before, but by his own reasoning. Ibn al-Nafis links his theological and historical ideas by the concept that the divine providence is bound to produce a course of history that is *asiah* for the community, "that which is best and most proper," a concept that is informed both by Mu'tazilite thought and Galen's anatomical ideas, as famously represented in his *De usu partium*.

HANS HINRICH BIESTERFELDT

Primary Sources

Amarat, Hasan (Ed). *Ibn an-Nafis. Kompendium über die Wissenschaft von den Grundlagen des Hadit. Edition und kommentierte Übersetzung.* Hildesheim, Zürich, New York: Georg Olms Verlag, 1986 (Arabistische Texte und Studien. Band 1).

Meyerhof, Max, and Joseph Schacht (Eds). *The Theologus Autodidactus of Ibn al-Nafis.* Oxford: Oxford University Press, 1968.

Qataya, Salman (Ed). *K. Sarh tasrih al-Qanun li-Abi l-Hasan [...] Ibn al-Nafis.* Al-Qahira: al-Maglis al-A'la li-l-taqhfa, al-Hay'a al-misriyya, 1988.

al-Wafa'i, Muhammad Zafir and Muhammad Rawwas Qal'agi (Eds). *Al-Muhaddab fi l-kuhl al-mugarrab li-'Ali b. a. l-Hazm [...] Ibn al-Nafis.* Casablanca: Malba'at an-Nagah al-gadida, 1408/1988.

Zaydan, Yusuf (Ed). *Sarh Fusul Abuqral li-'Alai al-Din 'Ali [...] Ibn al-Nafis.* Al-Qahira: al-Dar al-misriyya al-lubnaniyya, 1411/1991.

Zaydan, Yusuf (Ed). *Al-Muhtar min al-aydiya, ma'a dirasa li-nazariyyat al-tadawi bi-l-gida' li- [...] Ibn al-Nafis.* Al-Qahira: al-Dar al-misriyya al-lubnaniyya, 1412/1992.

Further Reading

Bachmann, Peter. "Quelques remarques sur le commentaire du premier livre des Épidémies par Ibn an-Nafis." In *Actas do IV Congresso de Estudos árabes e islâmicos.* Coimbra–Lisboa 1 a 8 setembro de 1968. Leiden: E.J. Brill, 1971, 301–309.

Heer, Nicholas, "Talafat mugalladat min Kitab as-Samil li-Ibn an-Nafis." In *Revue de l'Institut des Manuscripts Arabes.* 6 (1960): 203–210.

Iskandar, Albert Z. "Ibn al-Nafis." In *Dictionary of Scientific Biography*, 14 vols, edited by Charles C. Gillespie, 602–606. Vol 9. New York, 1970–1980.

Iskandar, Albert Z. "Comprehensive book on the art of medicine by Ibn al-Nafis." In: *www.islamset.com/isc/nafis/iskandar.html* (accessed online on 9/20/2004).

Kruk, Remke. "History and Apocalypse: Ibn al-Nafis' Justification of Mamluk rule." *Der Islam* 72 (1995): 324–337.

Meyerhof, Max, and Joseph Schacht. "Ibn al-Nafis." In *The Encyclopaedia of Islam*. New edition. 11 vols, edited by B. Lewis et al. Leiden, 1954–2002. Vol. 3: 897–898.

Savage-Smith, Emilie. "Ibn al-Nafis's *Perfected Book on Ophthalmology* and his Treatment of Trachoma and Its Sequelae." *Journal for the History of Arabic Science.* 4 (1980): 147–187 [with an edition of parts of *K. al-Muhaddab fi tibb al-ḥayn*: *namat* 2, *gumla* 2, *bab* 1, *fasl* 20: *fi l-garab*; *gumla* 3, *bab* 1, *fasl* 8: *fi s-sabal*; *fasl* 9: *fi z-zafara*, 31–49 (Arabic pagination)].

Ullmann, Manfred. *Die Medizin im Islam.* Handbuch der Orientalistik. Erste Abteilung. Ergänzungsband 6, Erster Abschnitt. Leiden and Köln: E.J. Brill, 1970, 172–176.

IBN AL-RAWANDI, ABU 'L HUSAYN AHMAD IBN YAHYA

Perhaps the most notorious freethinker of medieval Islam, Ibn al-Rawandi was born in Khurasan around 815 CE. He started out as a respected Mu'tazilite theologian but later became estranged from his former colleagues, perhaps due to the association with his mentor, the Manichaean Abu 'Isa al-Warraq. From that point on Ibn al-Rawandi is depicted by most (though not all) of our sources as a heretic who maliciously scoffs at all religions, particularly Islam... He left Baghdad, apparently to escape persecution by the authorities, and died in 860 (or, according to other sources, in 912).

Although one can see this image as a distorted picture composed by his opponents (as suggested by Josef van Ess), the accumulated information provided by the texts suggests that the image had a firm base in reality, and that Ibn al-Rawandi had indeed outstepped the boundaries of Islam. He is said to have written numerous books, none of which is extant. Extensive quotations in later Muslim sources, however, allow us to reconstruct many of his arguments. In his *Book of the Emerald* he argued that the human intellect makes revelation superfluous. God has provided humanity with the intellect. This intellect, which is part of the definition of humanity, is given equally to all human beings and is sufficient to guide them. The pretenders to prophecy are thus nothing but impostors and charlatans who exploit their knowledge of natural phenomena in order to manipulate and delude simple people. In this book, those who serve as Ibn al-Rawandi's mouthpiece and who present his antiprophetic lore are the so-called Brahmans: Indian polemicists who uphold the intellectual and spiritual equality of all humans. This literary device may reflect actual contacts with Indian philosophy, but it may also have been conceived to ward off accusations of heresy, and as a protective device against persecution.

Apart from a strong skeptical tenor, it is difficult to attribute to Ibn al-Rawandi any identifiable positive belief. He spared no religion, but his most severe criticism was directed against Islam. His sharp, sarcastic censure of the Qur'an is characterized by mocking and irreverent style. He pointed out apparent inconsistencies in the text, as well as to its illogical, immoral concept of a vengeful God who acts arbitrarily. He was preoccupied by questions of theodicy, to which he dedicated one of his books.

Ibn al-Rawandi's mastery of the art of dialectical disputation is recognized by his fiercest opponents. They claim, however, that he put this talent to ill use. His image of an *enfant terrible* is enhanced by lists of his books, from which it appears that he cultivated a habit of writing books on various topics, and then writing refutations of the same books. Muslim heresiographers and polemicists are baffled by this practice, which they see as the mark of senseless nihilism. Thus, they depict Ibn al-Rawandi as motivated by mercenary malice alone. But the quotations from his books transpire with genuine existential anxiety, which must have driven him to his rebellious ideas.

SARAH STROUMSA

See also Freethinkers; Heresy and Heretics; Mu'tazilites; Al-Razi (Rhazes)

Further Reading

Stroumsa, Sarah. *Freethinkers of Medieval Islam: Ibn al-Rawandi, Abu Bakr al-Razi, and Their Impact on Islamic Thought.* Leiden: Brill, 1999.

van Ess, Josef. "Ibn ar-Rewandi, or the Making of an Image." *Al-Abhath* 27 (1978–1979): 5–26.

IBN 'ARAB

Muhyi al-Din Muhammad (1165–1240 CE) was born in Murcia (present-day Spain) and spent his formative years in Seville. After receiving an excellent religious and secular education, he embraced Sufism and traveled widely in search of authoritative Sufi masters in both Andalus and North Africa. In 1201, Ibn 'Arabi set out on a pilgrimage to Mecca, never to come back. Although Ibn 'Arabi spent the first half of his life in al-Andalus and North Africa, his talents came to full bloom in the East—the Hijaz, Anatolia, and Syria. There he composed the bulk of his works—including his controversial masterpieces, *Bezels of Wisdom (Fusus al-hikam)* and *Meccan Revelations (al-Futuhat al-makkiyya)*—and trained his foremost disciple, Sadr al-Din al-Qunawi (1207–1274), who spread his ideas among the scholars of Anatolia, Egypt, and beyond. Ibn 'Arabi died and was buried in Damascus, where his tomb is still in evidence. Although he occasionally counseled rulers on religious matters, Ibn 'Arabi generally eschewed close contacts with secular authorities and amassed no fortune. His written legacy consists, in his own estimation, of some 250–300 works. Nowhere in this vast corpus of writings did Ibn 'Arabi provide a succinct and unequivocal account of his basic tenets. On the contrary, he was deliberately elusive in presenting his ideas and prone to offset them with numerous disclaimers. In conveying to the reader his personal mystical insights, Ibn 'Arabi made skillful use of "symbolic images that evoke emergent associations rather than fixed propositions." Although familiar with the syllogistic methods of reasoning of Muslim philosophers and theologians, he always emphasized that they fell short of capturing the dizzying dynamic of oneness/plurality that characterizes the relationship between God and his creation. To capture this subtle dynamic, Ibn 'Arabi availed himself of shocking antinomies and breathtaking paradoxes meant to awaken his readers to what he regarded as the real condition of the universe, namely, the underlying oneness and identity of all its elements. The intuitive, supersensory awareness of this oneness constituted for Ibn 'Arabi the essence of mystical gnosis *(ma'rifa)*, which he restricted to the perfected Sufi "gnostics," or "saints." His mystical teachings strike us as a mishmash of seemingly disparate themes, images, and motifs borrowed from scriptural exegesis, love poetry, mythology, jurisprudence, and speculative theology. Ibn 'Arabi explored such controversial issues as the status of prophecy vis-à-vis sainthood (the latter, in his view, being more encompassing), the concept of the perfect man (identified as the supreme Sufi "gnostic" of the epoch), the parallelism between the human "microcosm" and its cosmic counterpart—the universe, the ever-changing self-manifestation of the Divine in the events and phenomena of the empirical universe, the different modes and realms of the divine will (namely, the existential as opposed to the normative), and the allegoric aspects of the Muslim scripture. He addressed these issues in ways that were "never really repeated or adequately imitated by any subsequent Islamic author." The goal of this deliberately devious and polyvalent discourse was to "carry the reader outside the work itself into the life and cosmos which it is attempting to interpret." His writings thus function "as a sort of spiritual mirror, reflecting and revealing the inner intentions, assumptions and predilections of each reader... with profound clarity." It is hardly surprising that each Islamic century produced new interpretations of Ibn 'Arabi's ideas and works, especially his controversial *Bezels of Wisdom,* resulting in an entire "industry" of commentaries aimed at bringing out and elucidating the true teaching of the "Greatest Master," as he came to be known among his numerous followers across the Muslim world. Given Ibn 'Arabi's deliberately elusive style it is very difficult to summarize his complex metaphysical ideas. Suffice it to say that he viewed the universe as a product of God's self-reflection that urged his unique and indivisible essence to reveal itself in the things and phenomena of the material universe as in a giant mirror. All divine perfections that are dispersed in the universe are brought together in the persona of the "perfect man" *(al-insan al-kamil)*, who thus serves as their epitome and allows God to contemplate himself in his full beauty and glory. This idea scandalized many medieval Muslim divines who accused Ibn 'Arabi of admitting the substantial identity of God and world—a concept that contravened the doctrine of divine transcendence, which was so central to mainstream Islamic theology. In Ibn 'Arabi's teaching, God's absolute otherworldliness and inscrutability is postulated, paradoxically, alongside the notion of his imminent and immediate presence in the empirical world. His identity/nonidentity with the latter is just a matter of perspective, which should reflect the constant changes in the fluid modes of divine existence. Ibn 'Arabi's complex synthesis of Sufi moral and ethical teaching, Neoplatonic metaphysics, gnosticism, and mainstream Sunni theology (Ash'arism) and legal theory aptly capture the astounding diversity of post-classical Sufism. This diversity allowed it to effectively meet the intellectual and spiritual needs of a broad variety of potential constituencies—from a pious merchant or craftsman in the marketplace to a refined scholar at the ruler's court. Contrary to a commonly held assumption, his philosophical and metaphysical system was not a "foreign implant" grafted onto the pristine body of "traditional" Sufism. Rather, it was a natural development of certain tendencies inherent in Sufism from its very inception. With Ibn 'Arabi these tendencies evolved—probably under the influence of Ibn Sina and al-Ghazali—into a vision of God not just as the only agent but also the only essence possessing real and unconditional existence. This vision, which may loosely be defined as "monistic," was rebuffed by the great Hanbali scholar Ibn Taymiyya (1263–1328), who condemned its followers as heretical "unificationists" *(al-ittihadiyya)* bent on undermining divine transcendence and blurring the all-important borderline between God and his creatures. A fierce polemic between the champions of Ibn 'Arabi and his detractors ensued that has not quite abated down to the present. It has divided Muslim intellectuals into two warring factions, one of which has declared Ibn 'Arabi to be the greatest "saint" *(wali)* and divine "gnostic" *('arif)* of all time, while the other has condemned him as a dangerous heretic who undermined the very foundations of Islamic doctrine and communal life.

ALEXANDER KNYSH

See also Andalus; Ash'aris; al-Ghazali; Gnosis; Ibn Sina; Ibn Taymiyya; Plato and Neoplatonism; Saints/ Sainthood; Theology

Further Reading

Addas, Claude. *Quest for the Red Sulphur.* Cambridge: Islamic Texts Society, 1993.
Chittick, William. *The Sufi Path of Knowledge.* Albany: SUNY Press, 1989.
———. *The Self-Disclosure of God.* Albany: SUNY Press, 1998.
———. "Ibn 'Arabi and His School." In *Islamic Spirituality: Manifestations,* edited by S.H. Nasr.
Chodkiewicz, Michel. *An Ocean Without Shore.* Albany: SUNY Press, 1993.
Corbin, Henry. *Creative Imagination in the Sufism of Ibn 'Arabi.* Princeton: Princeton University Press,1969.
Hirtenstein, Stephen. *The Unlimited Mercifier.* Ashland, OR: Anqa Press and White Cloud Publishing, 1999.
Hodgson, Marshall G.S. *The Venture of Islam.* Vol. 2. Chicago: University of Chicago Press, 1974.
Ibn al-'Arabi. *The Bezels of Wisdom.* Translated by Ralph Austin. New York: Paulist Press, 1980.
Knysh, Alexander. *Ibn 'Arabi in the Later Islamic Tradition.* Albany: SUNY Press, 1999.
Morris, James W. "How to Study the *Futuhat.*" In *Muhyiddin Ibn 'Arabi: A Commemorative Volume,* Edited by Stephn Hirtenstein and Michael Tiernan. Brisbane: Element, 1993.
Nettler, Ronald. *Sufi Metaphysics and Qur'anic Prophets,* Cambridge: Islamic Texts Society, 2003.

IBN 'ASAKIR

Abu al-Qasim 'Ali ibn al-Hasan ibn 'Asakir is the most notable figure of the 'Asakir family, whose members occupied prestigious positions as judges and scholars of the Shafi'i school of Sunni law in Damascus for almost two centuries (AH 470–660/ 1077–1261 CE). Ibn 'Asakir was born in 499/1105 and died in 571/1176. He started his pursuit of religious education at a very young age (six years old), accompanying his father and elder brother to the teaching circles of several renowned Damascene scholars. Between 520/1126 and 535/1141, Ibn 'Asakir embarked on two ambitious educational journeys that took him to the most influential learning centers in the Islamic world, from Egypt and the Hijaz (Mecca and Medina) to Iran and Central Asia (Khurasan and

Transoxiana); he wrote a three-volume work, *Mu'jam al-shuyukh,* in which he mentioned some fourteen hundred teachers whom he met and studied with, including approximately eighty women. The enormous knowledge that he acquired, especially of *hadith,* law, and scriptural exegesis, earned him the title of *Hafiz* (great memorizer), and he became the most learned and renowned scholar of his day.

Shortly after Ibn 'Asakir returned from his travels to settle in his hometown of Damascus, Nur al-Din occupied the city (549/1154). Nur al-Din's political and religious ambition had two focuses: first, on the unification of Syria and Egypt under the banner of Sunni Islam and on putting an end to the Fatimid Shi'i dynasty; second, on mounting an effective military campaign against the Crusaders. Nur al-Din found in Ibn 'Asakir the perfect scholar who could help him achieve his goals: an ardent defender of Sunni Islam, in particular the Ash'ari branch. He ordered that a *madrasa* be built for Ibn 'Asakir, known as *Dar al-Hadith* (School of Hadith). Also under Nur al-Din's patronage, Ibn 'Asakir composed several books, among them the largest work of history ever produced by a medieval Muslim scholar: *Ta'rikh madinat Dimashq (The History of Damascus and Its Environs),* which he started in 529/1134. The *History of Damascus* is primarily a biographical dictionary—now published in a partially complete edition in seventy five volumes plus indices—that celebrates the holiness of Syria, with Damascus as its center, by documenting the lives and achievements of the scholars who lived in it or passed by it. It is one of the treasures of medieval Islamic historiography, in that it preserves extensive excerpts from hundreds of now-lost works authored by historians and religious scholars before the time of Ibn 'Asakir. The first two chapters of the *History of Damascus* focus on the sanctity of the city and its environs and list the sites and events that make it holy. Ibn 'Asakir did not restrict his work to Muslim figures. He included biblical prophets and figures as well: Abraham, Sarah, Hagar, David, Jesus, Mary, and John the Baptist, to name a few. This is the only Muslim biographical dictionary that features substantial biographical notices for pre-Islamic figures.

In addition to the *History of Damascus,* Ibn 'Asakir authored several other politically motivated works. With respect to theology, he authored two books in defense of the theologian al-Ash'ari and his school *(see* Ash'aris*),* which was under attack by rival Sunni groups in Damascus, especially the Hanbalites (see Ibn Hanbal). The two works are *Manaqib ash'ariyya (Ash'arite Virtues)* and *Tabyin kadhib al-muftari 'ala Abi al-Hasan al-Ash'ari (Exposing the Slanderer's Mendacity against Abu al-Hasan* *al-Ash'ari).* Ibn 'Asakir also composed two other works on the virtue of *jihad: Arba'in fi al-ijtihad fi iqamat al-jihad,* which is a collection of forty *hadiths* attributed to the Prophet Muhammad, which emphasize the duty and obligation to wage *jihad;* and *Fadl 'Asqalan (The Merits of Ascalon),* which was written in reaction to the fall of Ascalon to the Crusaders in 548/1153 and as an appeal for the Muslims to recapture it. Ibn 'Asakir obviously used religion to serve the political agenda of his patron, Nur al-Din, and used politics to promote his religious conviction. Exalting the holiness of Syria (Damascus, Jerusalem, Ascalon) and urging the Muslims to wage *jihad* against the Crusaders are, therefore, to be seen as his contributions as a scholar to the success of Nur al-Din's campaign and, subsequently, to the triumph of Sunni Islam in Syria and Egypt.

Ibn 'Asakir's eldest son, al-Qasim (d. 600/1203), followed in his father's footsteps. He composed a continuation of the *History of Damascus* and authored a treatise on the merits of Jerusalem, titled *al-Jami' al-mustaqsa fi fada'il al-masjid al-aqsa (The Verified Compendium on the Merits of the Aqsa Mosque).* The works of Ibn 'Asakir, especially the *History of Damascus,* inspired later Syrian scholars to follow his lead, like Ibn al-'Adim (d. 660/1262), who composed a biographical dictionary of the notables of Aleppo and its environs, and a chronological history of the city. They were also heavily used by scholars such as al-Dhahabi (d. 748/1348).

SULEIMAN A. MOURAD

See also Ash'aris; Ibn al-'Adim; Ibn Hanbal; Jihad; Madrasa; Nur al-Din

Further Reading

Lindsay, James E. (Ed). *Ibn 'Asakir and Early Islamic History.* Princeton: The Darwin Press, 2002. (This edited volume comprises five studies on Ibn 'Asakir's *History of Damascus,* his methodology and agenda for the reconstruction of Syria's past.)

IBN BABAWAYH, MUHAMMAD IBN 'ALI AL-QUMMI, AL-SHAYKH AL-SADUQ

Ibn Babawayh (d. AH 381/991–992 CE) was a Twelver Shi'i compiler of *Man la Yahdaruhu al-Faqih (He Who Has No Jurisprudence with Him),* which was later considered the second great collection of Twelver Shi'i *hadith,* after Kulayni's *al-Kafi,* and numerous other collections of the Imams' traditions. Ibn Babawayh collected many traditions from his father, a contemporary of al-Kulayni, but he also traveled

throughout the region collecting traditions. His *'Uyun Akhbar al-Rida (Sources of the Traditions of al-Rida),* was the product of a sojourn to Khurasan in search of the traditions of the eighth Imam 'Ali al-Rida (d. 202/818).

ANDREW J. NEWMAN

See also al-Kulayni; al-Tusi, Muhammad ibn al-Hasan

Further Reading

Newman, Andrew. *The Formative Period of Twelver Shi'ism: Hadith as Discourse between Qum and Baghdad.* Routledge Curzon, 2000.

IBN BATTUTA

Muhammad ibn 'Abd Allāh al-Lawātī, known as Ibn Battuta (1304–1368 or 1369 CE), was born in Tangier, Morocco. In 1325, at the age of twenty-one, Ibn Battuta embarked on his first journey to perform the Muslim pilgrimage *(Hajj)* in Arabia. This voyage would end up lasting almost twenty-four years (1325–1349) and would take him to lands on three continents: Africa, Asia, and Europe. He returned to his native Morocco in 1349 and within a year decided to cross the Strait of Gibraltar for a visit to Granada, Spain (1350). Three years later, he joined a caravan crossing the Sahara Desert and arrived in West Africa. By 1354, he settled in Morocco, where news of his travels reached the Marīnid ruler Abū 'Inān Fāris (r. 1348–1359), who entrusted Ibn Juzayy (d. ca. 1358), a native of Granada at his employ, with the composition of Ibn Battuta's account of his travels. The result was a work titled *Tuhfat al-Nuzzār fī Ghara-a'ib al-Amsār wa-'Ajā'ib al-Asfār,* commonly known as the *Rihla* (journey or travel narrative) of Ibn Battuta. Not much is known of Ibn Battuta's life after he settled down in his native Morocco, other than that he held a judgeship in "some town" and that he died around AH 720/1368–1369 CE. Ibn Battuta's account was received with skepticism and incredulity by his contemporaries, as stated by the Tunisian-born Ibn Khaldūn (d. 1406).

Ibn Battuta traveled from Morocco, through North Africa, to the Middle East, Anatolia and Constantinople, the Indian subcontinent and Southwest Asia, several islands in South Asia, China, Transoxiana, and areas north of the Black Sea. After returning to Morocco he took two additional trips to Spain and West Africa. His longest continuous stay (almost nine years) was in India, where he was appointed a Malikite judge by the sultan of Delhi, Muhammad Tughluq Shāh (r. 1325–1351). In his travels, Ibn Battuta pursued the medieval Muslim learning tradition of joining the lecture circles of several teachers and collecting certificates *(ijāzāt)* from them to serve as scholarly credentials or as qualifications for future employment, especially in the legal profession. He took advantage of the existence of the *Akhī* and *Futuwwa* networks in Anatolia and of the 'ūfī brotherhoods elsewhere to secure lodging and, at times, material help. In 1348, he witnessed the effects of the Black Death while in Aleppo, Syria.

The degree of reliability of Ibn Battuta's *Rihla* is open to argument. This travel narrative is the product of a joint effort: Ibn Battuta as the source of information and Ibn Juzayy as the ghostwriter. It has been long assumed that Ibn Battuta dictated the content from memory and that the inconsistencies, factual errors, and confusing chronology are due to the failings of his memory. This assumption originated with the first complete edition of the text, which emphasized, based on a misinterpretation of a passage, that the entire *Rihla* was dictated from memory. However, this view is now losing ground and recent studies tend to show, through internal evidence, the existence of written notes of unequal quality in Ibn Battuta's possession and that the *Rihla* is therefore the combination of his recollections, written notes, and occasional exaggeration, if not outright boasting, on the one hand, and the finishing touches of Ibn Juzayy on the other.

The first complete edition of the *Rihla* was made by C. Defrémery and B. R. Sanguinetti and published with a French translation in four volumes between 1853 and 1858, under the auspices of the Société Asiatique. In 1866, the Hakluyt Society published Sir Henry Yule's abridged English translation of the section on Bengal and China. Between 1958 and 1971, the same Hakluyt Society published H. A. R. Gibb's English translation in three volumes. This English translation was completed by C. F. Beckingham (vol. 4, published in 1994) and followed by an index compiled by A. D. H. Bivar (vol. 5, published in 2000).

In 1953, Mahdi Husain published an English translation of the section on India, the Maldive Islands, and Sri Lanka. Finally, the part on West Africa, translated by Said Hamdun and Noël King, was published in 1994.

ADEL ALLOUCHE

Primary Sources

Cathay and the Way Thither. 4 vols. Translated and edited by Sir Henry Yule. New edition revised in light of recent discoveries by Henri Cordier. London: The Hakluyt Society, 1913–1916.

Husain, Mahdi. *The Rehla of Ibn Battuta.* Baroda, India: The Oriental Institute, 1953.

Ibn Battuta in Black Africa. Translated by Said Hamdun and Noël King, forward by Ross E. Dunn. Princeton, NJ: Markus Wiener Publishers, 1994.

Ibn Jubayr, Muhammad ibn Ahmad. *The Travels of Ibn Jubayr.* Translated by R. J. C. Broadhurst. London: J. Cape, 1952.

Ibn Khaldūn. *The Muqaddimah. An Introduction to History.* 3 vols. Translated by Franz Rosenthal. 2d ed. Princeton, NJ: Princeton University Press, 1967.

The Travels of Ibn Battuta, A.D. 1325–1354. 5 vols. Translated by H. A. R. Gibb and C. F. Beckingham. London: The Hakluyt Society, 1958–2000.

Voyages d'Ibn Batoûtah: Texte arabe accompagné d'une traduction. 4 vols. Arabic text with a French translation by C. Defrémery and B. R. Sanguinetti. Paris: Imprimerie Impériale, 1853–1858.

Further Reading

Allouche, Adel. "A Study of Ibn Battutah's Account of His 726/1326 Journey through Syria and Arabia." *Journal of Semitic Studies* 35, no. 2 (autumn 1990): 283–299.

Dunn, Ross E. *The Adventures of Ibn Battuta: A Muslim Traveler of the 14th Century.* Berkeley and Los Angeles: The University of California Press, 1986.

Hrbek, Ivan. "The Chronology of Ibn Battuta's Travels." *Archiv Orientální* 30 (1962): 409–486.

"Ibn Battuta, 1304–1369." *Classical and Medieval Literature Criticism* 57 (2003): 1–75 (a collection of essays).

Netton, Ian Richardson. "Myth, Miracle, and Magic in the Rihla of Ibn Battuta." *Journal of Semitic Studies* 29, no. 1 (spring 1984): 131–140.

IBN EZRA, ABRAHAM (1089–1164 CE)

Ibn Ezra's life was divided among many areas: poet, grammarian, biblical commentator, philosopher, and physician. Born in Tudela, Spain, Ibn Ezra had two very different periods in his life. The first period began in Spain, from where he seems to have traveled through North Africa, seeking the company of scholars in the present-day lands of Morocco, Algeria, and Tunisia. He had a specifically close relationship with the scholar Judah Halevi, and legend even says that Ibn Ezra married Halevi's daughter. Although five of Ibn Ezra's sons are mentioned, only one of them is known, whereas the others may have died young.

The second period of Ibn Ezra's life was from 1140 until his death in 1164. Regarding that period, he stated that he had left Spain for Rome in restless wandering, supposedly "in a troubled spirit" because of the real, or alleged, conversion (ca. 1143) of his only surviving son, Issac, who had lived in Egypt and Baghdad. Most of his work was done in the latter part of his life, partly in Rome, where he wrote a poem that expressed his bitterness against the Jewish community there. He went on to Lucca and from there to Mantua. Then he left Italy for Provence, and later on traveled to northern France, where he wrote a great deal. According to one writer, Ibn Ezra is said to have written no fewer than 108 books. From Spain to the north and east, Ibn Ezra introduced some very needed important works on Hebrew grammar, which most scholars there had never learned previously.

As a poet he wrote both secular and religious poems, introducing them to eastern and northern European scholars. He did so both in the Spanish poetic school, as well as in the Arabic of Jewish poets who therefore tried to write poems in the Spanish meter and imitate its school of structure, form, and style. As a commentator on the Bible, he also began this activity in Rome in 1140, but a number of his books there are not extant.

Although he did not create any new or original grammatical systems for newer generations, he was considered one of the fathers of Hebrew grammar, both because he collected the conclusions of the eastern philologists and those of Spain, and because he wrote in Hebrew, unlike earlier grammarians. Only two of Ibn Ezra's works on mathematics and astronomy are available; the latter was only discovered and published in the twentieth century. His philosophical areas were essentially Neoplatonic, strongly influenced by Solomon Ibn Gabirol, with views, for example, that like God, the intelligible world is eternal, while the terrestrial world was created in time from preexistent matter. The universe was in three "worlds": the "upper world" of intelligibility or angels; the "intermediate world" of the celestial spheres, and the "lower, sublunar world" that was created in time.

WILLIAM M. BRINNER

Further Reading

Center for Jewish Studies. *Rabbi Abraham Ibn Ezra: Studies in Writings of a Twelfth-Century Polymath.* Cambridge, England, 1993.

Ibn Ezra, Abraham ben Meir. *Twilight of a Golden Age: Selected Poems of Abraham Ibn Ezra.* University of Alabama Press, 1997.

Lancaster, Irene. *Deconstructing the Bible: Abraham Ibn Ezra's Introduction to the Torah.* London, 2003.

Levi, R. *The Astrological Works of Abraham Ibn Ezra.* 1927.

Sela, Shlomo. *Abraham Ibn Ezra and the Rise of Medieval Hebrew Science.* Leiden, 2003.

IBN EZRA, MOSES BEN JACOB (CA. 1055 TO AFTER 1135 CE)

Moses Ibn Ezra (also known as Abu Harun), a Spanish Hebrew poet and philosopher born in Granada, appears to have held an honored position.

Moses Ibn Ezra encouraged Judah Halevi in his early poetic efforts, supporting him and forming a lasting friendship. A very decisive change took place in his life in 1090, when the Almoravids captured Granada, its Jewish community was destroyed, and the members of the Ibn Ezra family were dispersed. For some reason he remained in Granada for a while, but only after much effort and suffering was he able to flee to Christian Spain in the North. He was, however, unable to return to his native city for which he yearned the rest of his life. His later years were full of misfortune and disappointments, wandering through Christian Spain and seeking the aid of patrons for whom he had to sing and write their praise. Unable to adapt himself to the manners of the northern Jewish population in its low cultural standards in Christian Spain, he could not adapt himself to all those ways and died far from his native city. Moses Ibn Ezra was one of the most prolific poets of the Spanish school, and the rhetoric of his poetry was seen for many years as a model of perfection that greatly appealed to many. Some modern writers have seen him as having an exaggerated desire for a beautiful poetic form, replete with ornamentation, restricting the flow of free poetic expression. However, many of his poems are perfect in every aspect, with their main themes belonging to love, wine, and nature, and served as a model for medieval poets.

One of his earliest works on Hebrew poetics is found in his treatise on rhetoric and poetry, one of the earliest works on Hebrew poetical literature. This eight-chapter work was written in his old age in an answer to questions on Hebrew poetry posed by a friend. It was published in more modern times: first in a small part of the Arabic original in 1895, then translated into Hebrew in 1924. This was a valuable historical source for Spanish Hebrew poetry and relates to the poet and his environment. Using many metaphors from the Bible, Moses Ibn Ezra showed an appreciation for literary charm and beauty but neglected Jewish writers until recently. Although some seemed perfect, his poetic images and linguistic patterns are so intricate that only other poets can unravel their complexity. Some themes deal with rural life, infidelity in friendship, old age, vicissitudes in luck, death, trust in God, and the beauty of poetry. In his old age, though bitter and dejected, his mood neither impeded his poetic sense nor undermined his joyful poetry. In his great corpus of poems, the *Selihot* (penitential prayers) are so impressive that he was called *Ha-Sallah* (the writer of prayers). Some of his sacred poetry shows signs of ideas, images, and idioms from his secular verse, directly influenced and interwoven with Arabic literature. Many of his poems are scattered in the prayer books of different rites of Judaism.

WILLIAM M. BRINNER

Further Reading

Brody, H., and S. De Solis Cohen (Eds and Trans). *Selected Poems of Moses Ibn Ezra.* 1934.

IBN GABIROL, SOLOMON

Solomon ben Judah ibn Gabirol (ca. 1021–1058 CE), known as Abu Ayyub Sulayman ibn Yahya ibn Jabirul in Arabic, was one of the most important Jewish literary and religious intellectuals of eleventh-century al-Andalus. Scant biographical details of Ibn Gabirol's life survive in brief reports from Ibn Sa'id al-Andalusi, a contemporary Muslim intellectual of Toledo, and from the late eleventh to twelfth century Andalusi Jewish scholar Moses ibn Ezra. Following the collapse of the Umayyad caliphate, Ibn Gabirol's family made its way from Málaga to Saragossa. There the young Solomon established himself in the social and intellectual circle of the Jewish courtier Abu Ishaq Yequti'el b. Isaac ibn Hasan. Yequti'el met an untimely death by execution in 1039, but Solomon also found patronage and developed a relationship, sometimes strained, with the leading Andalusi Jewish sociopolitical and intellectual figure of the period, Samuel ibn Naghrela (Samuel the Nagid) of Granada. Despite his associations with Andalusi Jewish notables Ibn Gabirol seems to have been reclusive and socially alienated and was certainly so preoccupied with the advanced study of philosophy that he expressed considerable disdain for mundane social concerns. According to the testimony of his poetry, Solomon suffered from a serious skin ailment. He died in Valencia in 1058.

Ibn Gabirol's literary production includes highly original devotional and social poetry he composed in Hebrew and philosophical works written in Arabic, some of which are no longer extant in the original. A treatise on ethics, *Islah al-akhlaq (Improvement of the Moral Qualities)*, includes citations from the Hebrew Bible, Greek philosophers, and Arabic poetry. An Arabic metaphysical work on cosmology, *The Source of Life*, survived only in Latin translation *(Fons Vitae)* and in a few Hebrew fragments. The Cairo Genizah also yielded fragments of a collection of Arabic aphorisms attributed to Ibn Gabirol. Entitled *Mukhtar al-jawahir (Choice of Pearls)*, the full compilation survived only in Hebrew translation. Ibn Gabirol's philosophical writings addressed the general rather than specifically Jewish concerns of a Neoplatonic intellectual during the classical age of Islam. In particular Ibn Gabirol seems to have been a reader of the classical encyclopedia *Rasa'il ikhwan al-safa (Epistles of the Brethren of Purity)* that arrived in al-Andalus from the Muslim East during the eleventh century. At the same time, the philosophical vocabulary and speculative orientation of his Arabic prose works inform the language and conceptual framework of Ibn Gabirol's idiosyncratic and enigmatic occasional Hebrew poetry that celebrates his quest for wisdom. An Arabo-Islamic literary and intellectual background is equally apparent in Ibn Gabirol's verse written specifically for recitation in the synagogue about the soul's craving to be restored to its sublime source. Studies of Ibn Gabirol's liturgical verse have also shown the Hebrew poet to be a devotee of contemporary Sufi poetry. A masterful synthesis of Ibn Gabirol's intellectual and literary creativity is the Hebrew philosophical poem *Keter malkhut (Kingdom's Crown)*.

ROSS BRANN

See also Samuel ibn Naghrela; Neoplatonic; Epistles of the Brethren of Purity

Further Reading

Cole, Peter. *Selected Poems of Solomon ibn Gabirol.* Princeton: Princeton University Press, 2001.
Loewe, Raphael. *Ibn Gabirol.* London: Peter Halban, 1989.
Schlanger, Jacques. *La philosophie de Salomon ibn Gabirol. Études d'un néoplatonisme.* Leiden: E.J. Brill, 1968.

IBN HAMDIS

Abd al-Jabbar Ibn Hamdıs, the most notable and prolific of Arab Sicilian poets, was born in Syracuse in 1055 CE to a noble family of the Azd tribe. He spent his childhood between the privileged life of landed gentry and the first rumblings of the Norman Conquest of Sicily. He chose self-imposed exile in 1078, seeking fame and fortune as a court poet and panegyrist.

His thirteen-year sojourn at the 'Abbasid Court in Seville (1078–1091) gave him the security of royal patronage and exposure to wider spheres of poetic experimentation that shaped his literary sensibilities and talents. His praise poems and celebratory odes to al-Mu'tamid on his victory at the Battle of al-Zallaqa in 1086 against Alfonse VI illustrate the perils of life in frontier areas ravaged by civil unrest and threats of the Christian Reconquest, as well as on the diction, themes, and motifs the poet chose to poeticize his life experiences.

The Almoravid invasion of Seville and the expulsion of his patron forced Ibn Hamdis to flee again, this time along the North African littoral where he settled in the province of Ifriqiyya. He spent the second half of his long life shuffling to and from the Zīrid court at al-Mahdiyya (modern Tunisia), singing the praises of new patrons and lamenting the loss of his beloved homeland, themes that often collapse into a single poem.

Ibn Hamdis bequeathed to Arabic literature an anthology *(Diwan)* containing 370 poems, from two lines short to eighty lines long. The multiple genres of panegyric, elegy, love poem, devotional poem, wine song, description, and celebratory ode underscore his artistic versatility. The preponderance of the panegyric, from his earlier to his twilight years, calls attention to a career financially and professionally dependent on the political whims and winds of his time.

Ibn Hamdis's poetics is intricately connected to the neoclassicism of the later 'Abbasid period, one that revamped old forms to convey new meanings. His reworking of the stock phrases, imagery, themes, and motifs of the poetic canons, his conscious tampering with the early tripartite and later bipartite structure of the qasida, and his playful manipulation of the rhetorical devices of the new poetry *(al-badi')*, that is, of punning and antithesis, disclose influences by poets such as Abu Tammam and al-Mutannabi.

Ibn Hamdis is best known for his verses celebrating the life of and lamenting the loss of his beloved Sicily. Themes of nostalgia for the homeland, lost youth, the vicissitudes of time, and Islam's struggle against the infidel enemy coalesce around imagery of a paradise lost.

> I remember Sicily as agony stirs in my soul memories of her.
> An abode for the pleasures of my youth, now vacant, once inhabited by the noblest of people.
> I have been banished from Paradise and I long to tell you her story.
> Were it not for the saltiness of my tears, I would imagine them to be her rivers.
> I laughed at twenty years old out of youthful passion. Now I cry at sixty for her crimes.

WILLIAM GRANARA

Further Reading

'Abbas, Ihsan. *al-'Arab fi Siqilliya*. Cairo: Dar al-M'arif, 1959.
Amari, Michele. *Storia dei Musulmani di Sicilia*. 2d ed. Edited by C.A. Nallino. Catania: Romeo Prampolini, 1933.
Borruso, Andrea. "La nostalgia della Sicilia nel diwan di Ibn Hamdis." *Bollettino del Centro di studi filologici e linguistici siciliani* XII (1073): 38–54.
Gabrieli, Francesco. "Sicilia e Spagna nella vita e nella poesia di Ibn Hamdis." In *Dal Mondo dell'Islam*. Naples: Riccardo Ricciardi Editore, 1954, 109–126.
Granara, William. "Remaking Muslim Sicily: Ibn Hamdis and the Poetics of Exile." *Edebiyat* 9, no. 2 (1998): 167–198.
Ibn Hamdis, 'Abd al-Jabbar. *Diwan*. Edited by Ihsan 'Abbas. Beirut: Dar Sadir, 1960.

IBN HANBAL

Ibn Hanbal, Abu 'Abd Allah Ahmad ibn Muhammad, a hadith collector, critic, jurisprudent, and dogmatist, was born in Baghdad circa 780 and died in Baghdad in 855.

Ibn Hanbal's father, who died when Ibn Hanbal was three years old, was a military officer in Khurasan. An uncle apparently oversaw Ibn Hanbal's early education in Baghdad. At age fifteen, he chose not to become a bureaucrat but rather devoted himself to hadith. He first studied in Baghdad, then traveled to Kufa, Basra, Mecca, Yemen, and Syria. He finally settled down in Baghdad again after 820. His first and second wives each bore one son and predeceased Ibn Hanbal. A concubine then bore him one daughter and four sons. They all lived together in a large house, supported mainly by urban rents.

Ibn Hanbal famously suffered in the Inquisition that the caliph al-Ma'mun instituted in 833, requiring men of religion to testify that the Qur'an was created. The caliph's point seems to have been that he was the arbiter of Islamic orthodoxy. Ibn Hanbal was one of the few to refuse the orders. He was imprisoned, then tried probably two years later before al-Ma'mun's successor, al-Mu'tasim (r. 833–842). He was finally flogged and released. Mu'tazili sources assert that he first testified as bidden, but Hanbali sources state that he lost consciousness (and so could not have been responsible for anything he said).

At the accession of al-Wathiq (r. 842–847), Ibn Hanbal briefly emerged from his house to teach hadith again. He was threatened by the caliph's agents and stayed out of sight until the accession of al-Mutawakkil (r. 847–861), who dismantled the Inquisition over the next five years. Near the end of this period, al-Mutawakkil summoned Ibn Hanbal to Samarra to teach; however, he was unhappy to have anything to do with the ruler, refused to eat, and was finally sent home. There ensued many bitter quarrels with his oldest sons, who were willing to accept the caliph's gifts in spite of their father's objections.

Ibn Hanbal's greatest literary monument is by far *Musnad*, a collection of almost twenty-eight thousand hadith reports (about 80% repeats with variant chains of transmitters; compare the *Sahih* of Bukhari with 7400 hadith reports, about 60% repeats). He generally evaluated hadith reports by comparing variant chains of transmitters. If someone's transmissions were too often uncorroborated by parallels from contemporaries, Ibn Hanbal considered the transmitter unreliable.

Various followers transmitted Ibn Hanbal's legal opinions. He strongly preferred to infer rules from hadith, from the Prophet if possible and from Companions if necessary. Confronted with two contradictory hadith reports, he tested their chains of transmitters to see which was more reliable. If they seemed equally good, he would simply state the alternatives without presuming to impose his own opinion.

Also extant are several collections of his comments on hadith transmitters and two sayings he transmitted concerning the pious life, mainly by early renunciants. In theology he rejected almost all speculation that went beyond what was expressly stated in the Qur'an and hadith. He recognized 'Ali as the legitimate fourth caliph but staunchly rejected Shi'i assertions that some of the Companions had been unrighteous.

CHRISTOPHER MELCHERT

See also Hadith; al-Ma'mun

Further Reading

Cooperson, Michael. *Classical Arabic Biography: The Heirs of the Prophets in the Age of al-Ma'mun.* Cambridge Studies in Islamic Civilization. Cambridge: University Press, 2000.
Hurvitz, Nimrod. *The Formation of Hanbalism: Piety into Power. Culture and Civilisation in the Middle East.* London: Routledge Curzon, 2002.
Patton, Walter Melville. *Ahmed ibn Hanbal and the Mihna.* Leiden: E.J. Brill, 1897.
Spectorsky, Susan A. "Ahmad Ibn Hanbal's *Fiqh.*" *Journal of the American Oriental Society*, 102 (1982): 461–465.

IBN ISHAQ

The traditionalist and historiographer Muhammad b. Ishaq b. Yasar is one of the main authorities in the biography of the Prophet. He was born in Medina ca. AH 85/704 CE, and died in Baghdad in ca. 150/767. Like other authors of this genre, he sprang from a family of manumitted slaves *(mawali)*. His grandfather, probably a Christian Arab, was, at the taking of 'Ayn Tamr in Iraq in 12/633, sent with other prisoners to Medina. Ibn Ishaq collected most of his material in Medina and Egypt. He was accused of having Shi'i tendencies and of being a Qadarite (that is, professing free will and not absolute predestination).

The great work of Ibn Ishaq on the life of Muhammad, related historical, pseudohistorical, and legendary topics, pertains to the historical and hagiographical genre *(historia sacra,* or salvation history*)*. It bears the title *The Book of the Military Campaigns [of the Prophet] (Kitab al-Maghazi).* The most known recension of this work is the rescript/abridgment *(tahdhib)* of ['Abd al-Malik] Ibn Hisham (d. ca. 218/833), known as *The Life of the Prophet* (al-Sira al-nabawiyya), who wrote it on the basis of the transmission of one of Ibn Ishaq's immediate students, al-Bakka'i (d. 183/799). Ibn Hisham undertook omissions in order to reduce the volume of the work. Therefore, he left out the biblical history from Adam to Abraham, and also named of the progeny of Ismael only those who are supposed to have been direct ancestors of Muhammad. Further on, "he has left out some tales recorded by Ibn Ishaq in which the Prophet is not mentioned, to which there are no allusions in the Qur'an." He made in it sundry emendations and additions of manifold and genealogical and lexical import. He has also discarded "such poems as were known to no connoisseur of poetry questioned by him; besides allegations whereof the mention was malicious, or likely to be disagreable to certain people" (Foreword of Ibn Hisham, according to Horovitz).

Ibn Ishaq's work was originally divided into three main sections:

1. The beginning *(al-Mubtada')*: a pre-Islamic history of Revelation. It was divided into four parts:
   a. The pre-Islamic Revelation from the creation of the world till Jesus
   b. The history of Yemen in pre-Islamic times
   c. Arabian tribes and their idol worship
   d. The immediate ancestors of Muhammad and the Meccan cult
2. The sending *(al-Mab'ath)*: the youth of Muhammad and his activity in Mecca.
3. The military campaigns: the Medinan period.

It has been often said that the "complete book" of Ibn Ishaq is no more extant. The problem is that he never wrote or published such a "complete" book, as it has been shown by the Iraqi scholar Sadun Mahmud Al-Samuk for whom: "There never existed a unified text for the traditions of Ibn Ishaq to which the transmitters and later authors could have referred," because Ibn Ishaq has delivered them, often orally, at different times and occasions. It is for this reason that we find different traditions according to the transmitters. Besides al-Bakka'i's recension used by Ibn Hisham, there was that of Salama b. al-Fadl al-Razi (d. 191/806) to which Tabari (d. 3010/923) had access both in his *Annals* and his Qur'anic commentary, and that of Yunus b. Bukayr (d. 199/815), and so on.

As for the sources of Ibn Ishaq, his weightiest teacher was the traditionalist and jurist Ibn Shihab al-Zuhri (d. 124/742), who is credited with a book on the Campaigns of the Prophet. He also received information from several adherents of the house of al-Zubayr. Of course, he quotes the Qur'an, Islamic connoisseurs of Hadith, Qur'anic exegesis, and poetry and poets. He turns also to non-Islamic learned men concerning Jewish, Christian, and Parsi traditions, a thing for which he has been criticized. Apart from Wahb b. Munabbih (d. 110/728 or 114/732), he appears to be the oldest Arabic author who gives passages of the Old and New Testament in literal translation, sometimes in the so-called Palestinian–Christian translation.

CLAUDE GILLIOT

Further Reading

Primary

Guillaume, Alfred. *The Life of Muhammad.* A translation of Ibn Ishaq's Sirat Rasul Allah. Lahore. Pakistan Branch of the Oxford University Press, 1955; reprint, Karachi, 1978.
The History of al-Tabari. Translated by Franz Rosenthal et al. Vols. I–IX (the whole 39 vols.). Albany: SUNY, 1987–1999.

Secondary

Al-Samuk, Sadun Mahmoud. "Die historischen Überlieferungen nach Ibn Ishaq. Eine synoptische Rekonstruktion." Inaugural-Dissertation. Frankfurt am Main: Johann Wolfgang Goethe-Universität, 1978.
Horovitz, Josef. *The Earliest Biographies of the Prophet and Their authors.* Edited by Lawrence I. Conrad. Princeton, NJ: The Darwin Press, 2002, 74–90.
Jones, J.M.B. "Ibn Ishak." *EI* III, 811.
Watt, William Montgomery "Ibn Hisham." *EI* III, 800–801.

IBN JUBAYR, ABU'L-HUSAYN MUHAMMAD B. AHMAD

Ibn Jubayr was an Andalusian traveler, author, and *muhaddith* (recounter of Prophetic tradition). He was born in Balansiya (Valencia) in AH 540/1145 CE, in the last days of Almoravid rule in Sharq al-Andalus (eastern Andalusia), into an Arab family that had settled in Spain soon after the Muslim conquest. He was educated in the religious sciences and *adab* (belles-lettres) at Shatiba (modern Xàtiva south of Valencia), where his father worked as an official during the

unsettled period between Almoravid and Almohad rule. Ibn Jubayr himself was a *katib* (chancery secretary) in Sabta (modern Ceuta on the northern Morocco coast) and Granada for 'Uthman Abu Sa'id, brother of the second Almohad ruler, Abu Ya'qub Yusuf I, and governor of Granada.

In AH Shawwal 578/February 1183 CE Ibn Jubayr left Granada on the first of three journeys that he was to make in the course of his life. It is the only one that he wrote about, or at least the only one of which the account survives. He first went to Egypt, traveling by sea from Ceuta via Sardinia, Sicily, and Crete. After landing at Alexandria, he went south to Cairo, and thence, after crossing the Red Sea, to Jedda. He stayed in Mecca for nine months, and performed the *hajj* (pilgrimage). He then made the desert crossing to Kufa in western Iraq. From there he went north to Baghdad and Mosul, and crossed the Jazira (northern Mesopotamia) to Aleppo in Syria. He next turned south to Damascus, from where he made for Acre on the coast of Palestine. He returned to Spain by sea via Sicily, arriving in Granada in AH Muharram 581/April 1185 CE.

Ibn Jubayr is supposed to have made the pilgrimage to Mecca to expiate the sin of drinking wine. This, perhaps, accounts for the emphasis on the rigors of travel in the account of his first journey, titled *Rihla (Journey)*. At the same time, Ibn Jubayr gives a vivid picture of the eastern Mediterranean and beyond in the late twelfth century. His book is an abundant source of information about religious practices, social customs, commercial life, modes of travel by land and sea, and the principal monuments of the towns and cities that he visited. From Ibn Jubayr we learn, for example, about the formalities to which arrivals by sea at Alexandria were subjected and about the details of the pilgrimage to Mecca. His description of Damascus, meanwhile, is the fullest contemporary account that we have of the medieval city. He also offers a firsthand (Muslim) view of Frankish Palestine: among the places in Frankish hands when Ibn Jubayr visited them were Acre and Tyre.

Encouraged by the news of Saladin's capture of Jerusalem in AH 583/1187 CE, Ibn Jubayr set out on his second journey to the east in AH 585/1189 CE, returning to Granada two years later. He lived successively there and at Malaga, Ceuta, and Fez, devoting himself to the study of *hadith* (prophetic tradition) and *tasawwuf* (Sufism). After the death of his wife in AH 614/1217 CE, he left Spain on his third journey to the east, dying at Alexandria in the same year.

DAVID MORRAY

See also Andalus; Autobiographical Writings; Hajj; Muslim–Crusader Relations; Travel

Primary Sources

Ibn al-Khatib. *al-Ihata fi akhbar Gharnata*. Cairo, 1973.

Further Reading

Ibn Jubayr. *Rihlat Ibn Jubayr*. Translated by R.J.C. Broadhurst as *The Travels of Ibn Jubayr*. London, 1952.

IBN KHALDUN

The jurist and historian Abu Zayd 'Abd al-Rahman Wali al-Din al-Hadrami, known as Ibn Khaldun, was born in 1332 in Tunis. He is best known as the author of *Muqaddima (Introduction)*, the first part of his universal history titled *Kitab al-'Ibar*. This introduction serves as prolegomena to the study of history, in which Ibn Khaldun developed the concepts he felt were necessary to comprehend human civilization. While his universal history is generally considered not to have met the standards detailed in the introduction, his work *Muqaddima* is commonly regarded as one of the most significant works of medieval Muslim civilization.

Ibn Khaldun was concerned with the history of civilization (*'umran*) in all its complexity, and *Muqaddima* outlines the importance of social, economic, and natural factors, as well as political and religious factors. (Ibn Khaldun is thus labeled by some modern scholars as a founder of "scientific history," as well as of sociology.) A major theme of *Muqaddima* is the rise and fall of states, or dynasties (he used the word *dawla* for both). States, as explained by Ibn Khaldun, rose and fell in a cycle similar to human life: birth, maturity, decline, and death. Central to Ibn Khaldun's discussion of the life cycles of states was the concept of *'asabiyya*, variously translated as solidarity, group feeling, or group consciousness. A group with strong *'asabiyya* (established through means such as blood relation, religious solidarity, or other means) would be able to achieve supremacy over other groups and establish a state. However, once predominance was achieved, *'asabiyya* would eventually fade, leading to the overthrow of that *dawla* and the establishment of a new one.

It is likely that Ibn Khaldun's views were shaped in part by the events he witnessed in his own life. Born in **Hafsid** Tunis, his early career as scholar and public official involved him in the politics and struggles between the Hafsids of Tunis, the **Marinids** of Fez, and the Nasrids of Granada. He left public life for a four-year sojourn in Tunis (1378–1382), which he devoted to scholarship. (Details of his career are known primarily through his autobiography, *Ta'rif bi-Ibn Khaldun*.) It was in this period that he completed his first versions of both the *Muqaddima* and the *'Ibar*, although he continued to revise these texts for the remainder of his life. In 1382, he moved to Cairo, the capital of the **Mamluk** Sultanate, where he had a second career in education and as the occasional state official. He was an acquaintance of the Mamluk sultan Barquq (r. 1382–1389 and 1390–1399). While in the service of Barquq's son Faraj (r. 1399–1412 with a brief interregnum), Ibn Khaldun traveled to Damascus as part of an expedition to counter the invasion of **Tamerlane (Timur)**. Ibn Khaldun met with Timur after the latter had taken Damascus, and subsequently wrote a detailed account of his interview, which is preserved in the *Ta'rif*. Ibn Khaldun returned to Cairo where he died in 1406, shortly after his sixth appointment as chief Maliki *qadi*.

WARREN C. SCHULTZ

See also Mamluks

Primary Sources

Fischel, Walter J. *Ibn Khaldun and Tamerlane: Their Historic Meeting in Damascus, 1401 AD (803 AH): A Study Based on Arabic Manuscripts of Ibn Khaldun's "Autobiography," with a translation into English, and a commentary*. Berkeley: University of California Press, 1952.
Ibn Khaldun. *The Muqaddimah: An Introduction to History*. Translated by Franz Rosenthal. Edited and abridged by N.J. Dawood. Princeton: Princeton University Press, 1967.

Further Reading

The scholarship devoted to Ibn Khaldun is abundant. A search of his name in the Mamluk online bibliography (*www.lib.uchicago.edu/e/su/mideast/mamluk/*) maintained by the University of Chicago's Middle East Documentation Center, for example, yields almost six hundred titles. Useful starting points include the following:
Fischel, Walter J. *Ibn Khaldun in Egypt: His Public Functions and His Historical Research (1382–1406); A Study in Islamic Historiography*. Berkeley and Los Angeles: University of California, 1967.
Mahdi, Muhsin. *Ibn Khaldûn's Philosophy of History: A Study in the Philosophic Foundation of the Science of Culture*. London: George Allen and Unwin Ltd., 1957.

IBN KHURRADADHBIH

Abu 'l-Qasim Ubaydallah ibn Abdallah is the author of, among other works, the influential geographical treatise *Kitab al-masālik wa-l-mamālik (The Book of Routes and Kingdoms)*. Little is known of his life, and even the most basic biographical details have eluded scholars. He has been referred to as Ubaydallah or Abdallah, ibn Abdallah or Ahmad, and Ibn Khurradadhbih or Khurdad(h)bih—a name of uncertain meaning, presumably of Persian, Zoroastrian origin. The son of a former governor of Tabaristan, Ibn Khurradadhbih was born either in 820 or 825 CE in Khurasan and grew up in Baghdad, where he received a thorough education in a wide range of subjects. He served as chief of the *Barid* postal service in the Jibal region and, according to some authors, subsequently in Samarra and Baghdad. Importantly, Ibn Khurradadhbih also served as a *nadim* (boon-companion) and close confidante of the caliph al-Mu'tamid (r. 870–82 CE). Hence, the bibliographer Ibn al-Nadim includes him in his chapter on boon-companions and courtiers, rather than in the chapter on state secretaries and administrators (where such "geographers" as Qudama ibn Ja'far, Abu Zayd al-Balkhi, and al-Jayhani are featured). Ibn Khurradadhbih died in 912 CE.

The breadth of his interests and knowledge is reflected in the nine works attributed to him. These include expositions on the etiquette of listening to music, Persian genealogy, cooking, drinking, astral patterns, boon-companions, world history, music and musical instruments, and descriptive geography. Only the latter two have been published; the former *(Kitab al-lahw wa-l-malahi)* is a slim volume on the history of musical instruments, especially in the pre-Islamic period; the latter will be the focus of what follows.

Ibn Khurradadhbih is known primarily for his work *Book of Routes and Kingdoms*, composed in its original version during the reign of the caliph al-Wathiq (r. 842–847 CE) and continuously revised until the reign of al-Mu'tamid. The work is among the earliest extant books on descriptive geography composed in Arabic; a man named Ja'far ibn Ahmad al-Marwazi (d. 888 CE) is said to have embarked on a similarly titled work at an earlier date, but his work remained incomplete at the time of his death. Having few, if any, prototypes with which to work, Ibn Khurradadhbih drew heavily on foreign sources in his description of the world. Claudius Ptolemy (d. 170 CE) is named as an influence both by modern scholars and by the author himself, and there is internal textual evidence that Greek geographical notions shaped Ibn Khurradadhbih's understanding of the universe. However, Ptolemy's mathematical approach manifests itself more obviously in the Arabic works of, for example, Musa ibn Ahmad al-Khwarizmi (d. 847 CE) than it does in *Book of Routes and Kingdoms*. Furthermore, the frequent use of Persian administrative terms, the attention given to pre-Islamic Iranian history, and the division of the world according to Iranian cosmological divisions point to the existence of Iranian sources at the core of the work.

Aside from the pioneering nature of Ibn Khurradadhbih's project, the book is of unique importance for a number of reasons. First, the work contains exhaustive itineraries of the caliphal road system, as well as descriptions of the routes, both overland and maritime, to foreign lands. Such information was of practical use for couriers, armies, pilgrims, merchants, and other geographical writers, some who openly admit to having taken a copy of the work on their travels. Second, the author includes detailed information on the revenue yielded by the various tax regions of the caliphate, information that has been invaluable to historians of the social and economic conditions of the period. Third, the work treats non-Muslim lands in great detail, providing descriptions of China, Byzantium, and the Indian Ocean region atypical of comparable Arabic works that were often limited to the lands of Islam or those aspects of non-Muslim countries that were of direct relevance to rulers and administrators at the time. Finally, Ibn Khurradadhbih provides miscellaneous data for which he is the only—or at least the original—source, including, most famously, passages on an official expedition to the fabled wall of Gog and Magog, and the activities of the Rus merchants and the Radhanite Jews. The passage on the Rus has played a pivotal role in the Normanist debate, while that on the Radhanites has provoked controversy and extensive commentary.

Ibn Khurradadhbih's *Book of Routes and Kingdoms* had a perceptible influence on later writers; some quote the author directly, whereas others preferred to pass off entire passages as their own work. The genre of "Routes and Kingdoms" matured in subsequent centuries, but the content of these later works was often Islamo-centric and laconic on details of the non-Muslim world.

ADAM SILVERSTEIN

See also Human Geography; Mathematical Geography; Merchants, Jewish; Road Networks

Primary Sources

Barbier de Maynard, C. *Le livre des routes et des provinces par Ibn Khordadbeh.* Paris: Journal Asiatique, V (1865).
Ibn Khurradadhbih. *Kitab al-lahw wa l-malahi.* Edited by I.A. Khalifa. Beirut, 1964.
———. *Kitab al-masalik wa l-mamalik.* Edited by M.J. de Geoje. Leiden, 1889.
Maqbul Ahmad, Syed (Trans). *Arabic Classical Accounts of India and China.* Shimla, 1989.

Further Reading

Bosworth, C. Edmund. "Ibn Kordadbeh." *EIr* 8: 37–38.
Hadj-Sadok, Muhammad. "Ibn Khurradadhbih." *EI2* 3: 839–840.

Heck, Paul. *The Construction of Knowledge in Islamic Civilization: Qudāma b. Ja'far and his "Kitāb al-Kharaj wa Sina'at al-Kitabah."* Leiden, 2001 (Ch. II: Geography).

Maqbul Ahmad, Syed *A History of Arab-Islamic Geography (9th–16th Century AD)*. Amman, 1995.

Miquel, André. "Geography." *The Encyclopedia of the History of Arabic Science: Volume 3 Technology, Alchemy and Life Sciences*, edited by R. Rashed, 796–812. London: Routledge, 1996–1998.

Montgomery, James E. "Serendipity, Resistance, and Multivalency: Ibn Khurradādhbih and his *Kitab al-Masalik wa-l-Mamalik.*" *Adab and Fiction in Medieval Arabic Literature*, edited by P.F. Kennedy. Harrasowitz, Wiesbaden, (forthcoming).

IBN NAGHRELA, SAMUEL

Samuel ibn Naghrela (993–1056), known in Andalusi–Arabic historiography as Isma'il ibn Naghrila and in Jewish history as Samuel the Nagid, was a rabbinic scholar, Hebrew poet and grammarian, and a Jewish communal leader in eleventh-century Muslim Granada. He assumed the role of the unofficial head *(Nagid* or prince*)* of the Jews of Granada around 1027. Thereafter, Ibn Naghrela cultivated extensive contacts with the leaders of various Jewish communities under Islam as far as the Muslim East, and he became a patron of other Jewish literary and religious intellectuals and the communal institutions supporting their activities. Because he was also an ambitious and opportunistic Arabic court secretary who rose through the ranks of the state bureaucracy to prominence as vizier in the service of the Zirid Berbers of Granada, Ibn Naghrela arguably came to be the most eminent Jew in Andalusi social and political history. Reliance on non-Muslim administrators such as Ibn Naghrela was not uncommon throughout the lands of classical Islam, but it seems to have been especially pronounced during this period in Andalusi political history. Indeed, Samuel was succeeded by his son Joseph in the office of vizier, as well as in his role as Nagid of the Jews of Granada.

Ibn Naghrela's position in the affairs of the Muslim state as the highest fiscal and administrative official of Granada, from 1038 until his death in 1056, is discussed in important Andalusi sources such as Ibn Hayyan al-Qurtubi, as preserved in Ibn al-Khatib's history of Granada and in *The Tibyan*, a political memoir by 'Abd Allah b. Buluggin, the last Zirid king to rule Granada. The famous and unconventional Muslim polymath Ibn Hazm also reports having come into contact with Samuel when they were young men and engaging him in polemical debate on matters of religion. Both Arabic and Jewish sources credit Ibn Naghrela's rise to position and influence to his legendary mastery of Arabic language and learning, and it is on account of this accomplishment that the figure of Ibn Naghrela became typological among Jews and Muslims. According to his Hebrew poetry, Samuel served Granada in some unspecified military capacity, although recent research raises serious questions about the nature and even likelihood of such service.

Ibn Naghrela was probably the most significant Jewish cultural mediator of eleventh-century al-Andalus, in part because his social and political status among Andalusi Jews and Muslims conferred legitimacy on his production of and support for Judeo-Arabic culture and its fusion of Jewish and Arabo-Islamic elements. His many intellectual endeavors included two works that survive only in fragments: an Arabic treatise on biblical Hebrew grammar, and an Aramaic rabbinical compendium on Jewish law. However, in terms of literary production Ibn Naghrela is remembered principally for his three collections of Arabic-style Hebrew poetry that were edited by his sons. The first highly accomplished poet of the "Golden Age" of Jewish culture in al-Andalus, Ibn Naghrela established the new style of Hebrew verse by drawing fully and creatively upon the prosodic forms, genre conventions, and rhetorical style of Arabic poetry, applying them to biblical Hebrew with all of its important textual associations and allusions. A twelfth-century Hebrew historiography acknowledged Ibn Naghrela's unique position in the history of Hebrew poetry in al-Andalus, by noting that during the two generations before him "the bards began to twitter, and in the days of R. Samuel the Nagid they burst into song."

Ibn Naghrela's distinctive style and range opened Hebrew verse to all of the major genres prominent in Arabic poetry: love lyrics and wine songs, many of which are exercises on a theme, panegyric in the form of epistolary poems of friendship, laments, boasts, satire and invective, gnomic poetry, reflective verse on the vicissitudes of life and human mortality, and "war poems" devoted to Samuel's involvement in the affairs of state. In particular, Ibn Naghrela stands out as a poet for the ways in which he used many of these genres to reflect poetically on his experiences, aspirations and concerns, his achievements and frustrations, and to publicize his claims to unique status and authority among the Jews and to display his grandiose sense of destiny.

Ross Brann

Further Reading

Brann, Ross. *Power in the Portrayal: Representations of Jews and Muslims in Eleventh- and Twelfth-Century Muslim Spain*. Princeton: Princeton University Press, 2002.

Cole, Peter. *Selected Poems of Shmuel HaNagid.* Princeton: Princeton University Press, 1996.
Wasserstein, David J. "Samuel ibn Naghrila ha-Nagid and Islamic Historiography in al-Andalus." *Al-Qantara* xiv (1993): 109–125.

IBN QĀDĪ SHUHBA

Taqī al-Dīn Abū Bakr b. Aḥmad b. Muḥammad b. 'Umar (d. 851/1448) is, for modern historians, the most prominent member of the Ibn Qāḍī Shuhba family. This family, known for its religious scholars, resided in Mamluk Damascus. The name derives from an ancestor who had been a qāḍī in the village of Shuhba in the Ḥawran district of southern Syria. Abū Bakr b. Aḥmad, most widely known by the appellation Ibn Qāḍī Shuhba, was a noted jurist (he was chief Qadi of Damascus for most of AH 842–844/1438–1440 CE) and author. Of his works, he is best known today for his biographical dictionary, *al-Tabaqāt al-shāfi'iyya,* and a work of history, *Ta'rīkh ibn qāḍī shuhba.* The published edition of this work covers the years 741–800/1340–1397, although a manuscript (Chester Beatty 5527) subsequently found extends to 810/1407. The work is an important source for the decades following the death of the Mamluk sultan al-Nāṣir Muḥammad b. Qalāwūn (whose third reign ended with his death in 741/1340), years marked by intense struggle for political power within the sultanate and by the appearance of bubonic plague in Mamluk lands, to name just two significant developments.

The historical work *Ta'rīkh ibn qāḍī shuhba* is considered as part of the so-called Syrian School of Mamluk historiography. This loose designation refers to the tendency of Mamluk-era Syrian historians to place more emphasis on the biographies of the ulama than the more court-centered histories of the "Egyptian School." Ibn Qāḍī Shuhba's work is also part of the *dhayl* (continuation) genre of medieval Muslim historiography, in which the historian envisioned the work as continuing (and frequently modifying) a history written by an earlier author. In this case, Ibn Qāḍī Shuhba built upon a historical work by Ibn Hijjī (d. 816/1413), one of his teachers. While he maintained Ibn Hijjī's annalistic structure of yearly coverage, with each year divided into months, and a list of biographies (in alphabetical order) attached at the end of each year, Ibn Qāḍī Shuhba extensively reworked Ibn Hijjī's text with additional material, and subsequently abridged his version at least twice.

WARREN C. SCHULTZ

See also History, Mamluks

Primary Sources

Ibn Qāḍī Šuhba. *Tārīh Ibn Qāḍī Šuhba.* Edited by Adnan Darwich. 3 vols. Damascus: IFAO, 1977–1994.

Further Reading

Reisman, David C. "A Holograph MS of Ibn Qāḍī Shuhbah's *Dhayl.*" *Mamluk Studies Review* 2 (1998): 19–49.
Schacht, Josef. "Ibn Ḳāḍī Shuhba." *Encyclopaedia of Islam.* 2d ed, vol III, 814.

IBN QAYYIM AL-JAWZIYYA, SHAMS AL-SHAMS AL-DĪN ABŪ BAKR MUHAMMAD IBN ABĪ BAKR AL-ZAR'Ī (AH 691–751/1292–1350 CE)

A prolific writer and a much-appreciated Hanbali scholar, Ibn Qayyim al-Jawziyya is mostly known as the devoted disciple and exegete of the salient Hanbali theologian and jurist, Ibn Taymiyya. His nickname, Ibn Qayyim al-Jawziyya, which may be rendered approximately as "the son of the superintendent of *al-Jawziyya,*" indicates his father's occupation and social status. *Al-Jawziyya* was a *madrasa* (religious school) and court in Damascus.

Biographical details on Ibn Qayyim al-Jawziyya can be found in the works of Ibn Kathīr (d. 774/1373) and Ibn Rajab (d. 795/1397), two prominent scholars who were also his closest students. However, their description of their teacher, although favorable and admiring, is scanty. It seems that ever since Ibn Qayyim al-Jawziyya first met Ibn Taymiyya, at the age of twenty-one, until the latter's death in the year AH 728/1328 CE, their lives were interwoven. The major events of Ibn Qayyim al-Jawziyya's life are connected to the turbulent religious polemics that Ibn Taymiyya conducted with his rivals. The rationale of these polemics lies in Ibn Taymiyya's overall view, which demands an utterly devout adherence to the precepts and exact wording of the Qur'an and *hadith* (the traditions related to the Prophet and his Companions), as well as to the *ijmā'* (consensus) and the teachings of the *salaf* (ancestors, that is, the followers of the Prophet in the first two centuries of Islam), along with a laborious effort to integrate them with some of the doctrines of *kalām* (speculative theology). However, Ibn Taymiyya was most hostile to the methods, theses, and convictions of the traditionalist Ash'ari *kalām*, widely implemented by most of the religious senior officials of the Mamlūk state. By publicly demonstrating the ignorance of his opponents in the content of religious literature, Ibn Taymiyya gained a lot of enemies within the highest ranks of the religious traditionalist establishment of Damascus and Cairo. He also condemned the extreme form of Sufism, embodied in the *Ittihadiyya*, namely the followers of the Sūfī Ibn al-'Arabī (d. 637/1240).

Ibn Qayyim al-Jawziyya, who shared his master's extreme views, although not his zealous style, also shared his fate of persecutions. In the year 726/1326, he was imprisoned in the citadel of Damascus with Ibn Taymiyya, after the latter was accused by his rivals of holding anthropomorphist views.

Ibn Qayyim al-Jawziyya was arrested at least twice after his master's death for defending Ibn Taymiyya's teachings and *fatāwā* (formal legal opinions given by a muftī) and refusing to recognize *al-Khalīl* (Hebron) as a site for Muslim pilgrimage.

During his imprisonments Ibn Qayyim al-Jawziyya deepened his interest in the mystic theories and practices of Sufism. While Ibn Taymiyya tended toward a moderate form of Sufism as a part of his efforts to combine all doctrines of Islam into one, Ibn Qayyim al-Jawziyya was extensively preoccupied with Sufism. He also wrote one of the most important commentaries to al-Ansārī al-Harawī's (d. 482/1089) Sufi manual, *Manāzil al-sā'irīn (The Stations of the Travelers)*. His commentary, titled *Madārij al-sālikīn (The Roads of the Travelers)* combines not only Ibn Qayyim al-Jawziyya's own mystic concepts but also a meticulous theological analysis. Nevertheless, following his master's footsteps, in this work Ibn Qayyim al-Jawziyya does not hesitate to attack several aspects of al-Ansārī's Sufi doctrine, which seem to him extreme and even wrong.

Ibn Qayyim al-Jawziyya wrote works in almost every branch of the Islamic sciences. In the field of theology his works are an elaborated arrangement of his master's work. For example, an extensive part of his theological treatise, *Shifā' al-'alīl fi masā'il al-qadā' wa-l-qadar wa-l-hikma wa-l-ta'līl (Healing the Person with Wrong Concepts about Predetermination and Causality)*, cites freely from Ibn Taymiyya's fatwas and epistles, although it is clear that he has succeeded in developing an original thought. In most cases, he uses Ibn Taymiyya's assertions and ideas as a platform to introduce his own ideas, even though they are hard to trace between the heavily ornamented phrases he inserts, which are the trademark of his eloquent writing.

In the field of jurisprudence, his *Ahkām ahl al-dhimma*, which deals with laws regarding Jewish, Christian, and Sabaean subjects of the Muslim state, is a frequently cited work. His interest in medicine is reflected in *al-ibb al-nabawī,* which deals with remedies for mental and physical illnesses mentioned in *hadith* literature.

LIVNAT HOLTZMAN

See also Ash'aris; Ibn 'Arabi; Ibn Hanbal; Ibn Taymiyya; Mu'tazilites; Sufism and Sufis

Primary Sources

Ibn Kathīr, Abū al-Fidā' Ismā'īl Ibn 'Umar. *Al-Bidāya wa'l-nihāya*. Beirut: Dār al-Kutub al-'Ilmiyya, 1421/2001.

Ibn Qayyim al-Jawziyya, Muhammad Ibn Abī Bakr al-Zar'ī. *Ahkām ahl al-dhimma*. Beirut: Dār al-Kutub al-'Ilmiyya, 1415/1995.

———. *Madārij al-sālikīn bayna manāzil 'iyyāka na'budu wa-'iyyāka nasta'īn*. Beirut: Dār al-Jīl, 1412/1991.

———. *Shifā' al-'alīl fi masā'il al-qadā' wa-l-hikma wa-l-ta'līl*. Cairo: al-Matba'a al-Husayniyya, 1323/1903.

———. *Al-Tibb al-nabawī*. Beirut: Dār al-Ma'rifa, 1417/1996.

Ibn Rajab, Zayn al-Dīn Abū al-Faraj. *Al-Dhayl 'alā tabaqāt al-hanābila*. Cairo: Matba'at al-Sunna al-Muhammadiyya, 1372/1953.

Further Reading

Abrahamov, Binyamin. "Ibn Taymiyya on the Agreement of Reason with Tradition." *The Muslim World* 82, no. 3–4 (1992). 256–272.

Bell, Joseph Norment *Love Theory in Later Hanbalite Islam*. Albany: State University of New York Press, 1979.

Laoust, Henri. *Essai sur les doctrines sociales et politiques de Taki-d-Din Ahmad b. Taimiya*. le Caire: Imprimerie de l'institut français d'archéologie orientale, 1939.

———. *La Profession de foi d'Ibn Taymiyya- La Wasitiyya*. Paris: Geuthner, 1986.

———. "Ibn Kayyim al-*Djawziyya*." *Encyclopedia of Islam* (new edition and CD-ROM version). Vol 3. Leiden: Brill, 2001, 821–822.

Makdisi, George. "Hanbalite Islam." In *Studies on Islam*, edited by Merlin L. Swartz, 115–126. New York: Oxford University Press, 1981.

———. "The Hanbali School and Sufism." In *Religion, Law and Learning in Classical Islam*, edited by G. Maksis, 118–129. Hampshire: Variorum, 1991.

Meier, Fritz. "The Cleanest about Predestination: A Bit of Ibn Taymiyya." In *Essays on Islamic Piety and Mysticism*, edited by Fritz Meier 309–334. Leiden: Brill, 1999.

van Ess, Josef. "Sufism and Its Opponents—Reflections on Topoi, Tribulations and Transformations." In *Islamic Mysticism Contested*, edited by Frederick De Jong and Bernd Radtke, 22–44. Leiden: Brill, 1999.

IBN QUTAYBA

Ibn Qutayba (828–889 CE) wrote books in a wide range of fields but was prized by later generations primarily as a scholar of language and literature. Ibn Qutayba pursued a lifelong scholarly interest in Arabic language and literature, an interest that grew out of and remained closely tied to his early study of religious texts, above all the Qur'an and Hadith.

The close connection between language study and the study of religious texts emerges very clearly in Ibn Qutayba's early writings, which concern problems in the language of the Qur'an and Hadith. It was a book that he wrote around the year 851, however, that secured him 'Abbasid court patronage in the form of a judgeship, a posting that took him from his native Iraq to Iran. That book, the *Adab al-katib (The Chancery Secretary's Handbook)*, furnishes 'Abbasid chancery secretaries, or those who aspired to be secretaries, with a broad range of information about correct Arabic usage, including general matters of style and vocabulary, technical terms in official correspondence, penmanship and orthography, appropriate diction in official correspondence, and the semantic implications of Arabic morphology. The *Adab al-katib* also likely sought to redirect the cultural interests of Persophile bureaucrats back to the intricacies of Arabic as a worthy vehicle of cultural sophistication and appropriate idiom of imperial splendor. The work came to be considered fundamental for the study of Arabic literature *(adab)* by later writers, such as Ibn Khaldun (d. 1406).

The *Adab al-katib* also marked an intellectual turning point in Ibn Qutayba's writings, which thereafter take up a broader range of topics, including traditional Arab astronomy and other pre-Islamic Arab customs, dream interpretation, history, and literary anthologies. One such anthology is the *Kitab al-shi'r wa-l-shu'ara' (The Book of Poetry and Poets),* which collects Arabic poetry up through the early ninth century and also contains an important contribution to Arabic poetics, in its introduction. Another is the *'Uyun al-akhbar (The Jewel-like Anecdotes),* which collects prose anecdotes, stories, and other literary excerpts under topic headings that range from politics to asceticism to food.

A final group of writings, composed after Ibn Qutayba's retirement from the judiciary (ca. 870), directly addresses matters of theological dogma. In these works, and consistent with his earliest writings on the language of religious texts, Ibn Qutayba declares himself against speculative theology *(kalam),* analogical reasoning *(qiyas),* and the doctrine of the createdness of the Qur'an.

Later writings of Ibn Qutayba never achieved the stature of his works on language, literature, and culture. Perhaps his discussion of theological matters was not sufficiently nuanced or rigorous for those preoccupied exclusively with such questions. On the other hand, in these and in his other works, Ibn Qutayba made a variety of topics accessible to a newly emerging class of private readers, a trait that has led some to refer to him as a popularizer. For all that he insisted on grounding the high culture of his time in the Arabic and Arabian heritages, Ibn Qutayba's wide-ranging interests and inclusive view of literature inaugurate the characteristic universalism and humanism of classical Islamic civilization.

JOSEPH E. LOWRY

See also Archives and Chanceries; Education; Grammar and Grammarians; Historical Writing; Intellectual History; Judges; Scholars; Scriptural Exegesis, Islamic; Stories and Storytelling; Theologians

Primary Sources

Ibn Qutayba. *Adab al-katib.* Edited by M.M. 'Abd al-Hamid. Cairo: Maktabat al-Sa'ada, 1963.
———. *Kitab al-shi'r wa'l-shu'ara'.* Edited by A.M. Shakir. 2 vols. Cairo: Dar al-Ma'arif, 1945–1950.
———. *al-Ma'arif.* Edited by Tharwat 'Ukasha. Cairo: Dar al-Ma'arif, 1960.
———. *'Uyun al-akhbar.* Edited by Ahmad Zaki al-'Adwi. 4 vols. Cairo: Dar al-Kutub, 1925–1930.

Further Reading

Bray, Julia. "Lists and Memory: Ibn Qutayba and Muhammad b. Habib." In *Culture and Memory in Medieval Islam,* edited by F. Daftary and J.W. Meri. London: I. B. Tauris, 2002.
Ibn Qutayba. *Introduction au Livre de la Poésie et des Poètes.* Translated by M. Gaudefroy-Demombynes. Paris: Les Belles Lettres, 1947.
———. *Le Traité des divergences du hadith d'Ibn Qutayba.* Translated by G. Lecomte. Damascus: Institut Français de Damas, 1962.
———. "Ibn Quteiba's 'Uyun al-Akhbar" (translated into English). *Islamic Culture* 4 (1930): 171–198, 331–362, 487–530; and 4 (1931): 1–27 (translated by Josef Horowitz).
Lecomte, Gerard. "Ibn Kutayba." In *Encyclopaedia of Islam.* New Ed. Leiden: E.J. Brill, 1954–2002.
———. *Ibn Qutayba: l'homme, son oeuvre, ses idées.* Damascus: Institut Français de Damas, 1965.

IBN QUZMAN, ABU BAKR IBN 'ABD AL-MALIK

Despite the fact, or perhaps because he defied the norms of classical Arabic poetry, Ibn Quzman has come to embody the essence of Hispano-Arabic poetry. Indeed, he has become for modern scholarship the best-known literary figure from the entire 780-year Arabo-Muslim presence on the Iberian Peninsula (modern Spain and Portugal). Ibn Quzman, whose full name was Abu Bakr ibn 'Abd al-Malik, was born in the Andalusian city of Cordoba in AH 470–472/1078–1080 CE, where he also died in 555/1160.

Little of Ibn Quzman's biography has been documented. However, as is the case with many premodern literary figures, much biographical information, reliable or unreliable, has been extrapolated from Ibn Guzman's poetry.

Before Ibn Quzman's time, the traditional means of livelihood for professional poets in both the East and West was the composition of panegyrics in praise of contemporary rulers. On the Iberian Peninsula this situation changed abruptly with the arrival of the Almoravids, led by Yusuf bin Tashfin (489/1096). The Almoravids' conquest and occupation of territories previously held by the fragmented "factional kings" *(muluk al-tawa'if)* led to the displacement of professional court poets employed by the Almoravids' predecessors. Because the Berber-speaking Almoravids had little appreciation for the encomia composed in classical Arabic, poets were compelled to earn a living by composing praise poetry for the lesser aristocracy, or to redirect their efforts into nonpanegyric forms of poetry. Although Ibn Quzman was not the first to compose *zajals* (Ibn Bajja [d. 533/1138] was the most probable originator), he is considered the genre's foremost practitioner. In the context of a volatile social and cultural environment, Ibn Quzman interjected and popularized the *zajal*, a genre of poetry very different from the classical praise poetry that preceded it.

Ibn Quzman's *zajals* represent a radical departure from the seriousness of the classical panegyric that had been the standard poetic form in both the East and West of the Arabic-speaking world. Instead of the formalized, ritualized praise of rulers common in the encomia, Ibn Quzman's *zajals* constitute a highly ironic countergenre to established norms. Ibn Guzman's *zajal* substitutes the bombastic, florid praise of the panegyric with parodic, tongue-in-cheek, faint praise of individuals who in earlier times never would have been the object of serious poetry. This emphasis on the popular, lower strata of society is also apparent in Ibn Quzman's depiction of popular events, such as carnivals, jugglers' entertainment, marketplaces, and foods. Transgressive elements, such as drunkenness, seduction, fornication, adultery, divorce, and slapstick violence are prominent features of his *zajals*.

The *zajal*, as practiced by Ibn Quzman, not only dealt with subject matter alien to classical poetry, but also, the *zajal's* form and language differed significantly from those found in the classical variety. In its structure the *zajal* resembles its counterpart, the classical *muwashshaha*, a form consisting of five to seven strophes with a complicated rhyme scheme. However, the *zajal* differs from the *muwashshaha* in the use of an introductory strophe rather than a concluding envoi. The most striking feature of the *zajal*

is its language. In contrast to the highly formal diction of all classical poetry, the *zajal* subverts the classical norm by introducing often-lengthy passages of the written representation of colloquial speech of Ibn Quzman's time and locale. Ibn Quzman's *zajals*, therefore, not only constitute an innovation on poetic language but also his representations of colloquial speech serve as valuable documentation of Hispano-Arabic, a dialect that often incorporated words and structures from the Romance dialect that coexisted with Arabic in the Iberian Peninsula.

DOUGLAS C. YOUNG

See also Adultery; Alcohol; Almoravids; Andalus; Cordoba; Decadence; Divorce; Gender and Sexuality; Markets; Nawrus; Popular Literature; Romance, Iberian; Shadow Plays; Wine

Primary Sources

de Gunzburg, David (Ed and Trans). *Le Divan d'Ibn Guzman: Texte, Traduction, Commentaire*. Berlin: S. Calvary & Co., 1896.

Further Reading

Lewis, B., V. L. Ménage, C. Pellat, and J. Schacht (Eds). *The Encyclopaedia of Islam*. New Ed. Leiden: E.J. Brill, 1971, 3:849–852.
Monroe, James T. *Hispano-Arabic Poetry: A Student Anthology*. Berkeley: University of California Press, 1974.

IBN RUSHD, OR AVERROES

Born in 1126 in Cordoba to a family of distinguished jurists, Abû al-Wahîd Muhammad Ibn Ahmad Ibn Muhammad Ibn Rushd served as Qadi at Seville and Cordoba and studied deeply works of Sharî'ah (religious law), Kalâm (theological discourse), Aristotelian philosophy, and medicine until his death in 1198. In dialectical religious writings he upheld natural causality in the face of Ash'arite occasionalist assertions of absolute divine power, denied that the Qur'an teaches creation ex nihilo, argued that Divine knowledge is prior to all forms of universal or particular knowledge, and asserted that the Qur'an commands the study of philosophy as obligatory for those capable. In understanding different human beings to be swayed to assent by rhetoric, dialectic, or demonstration, he was able to deny that there can be any "double truth," one of religion and another of philosophy and science, by arguing for the unity of truth. In his *fatwa*-like *Decisive Treatise* on religious law and philosophy, Ibn Rushd insisted that philosophical demonstration, with its necessary character, can be the ultimate arbiter of the meaning of religious statements and even of Qur'anic passages, saying "Truth does not contradict truth but rather is consistent with it and bears witness to it," a surreptitious quotation of Aristotle (*Prior Analytics* 1.32, 47a8–9). That confidence in philosophical method is even more prominent in his work *Incoherence of the Incoherence*, a detailed commentary on *Incoherence of the Philosophers* by Abu Hamid al-Ghazali, arguably Islam's greatest theologian. Working to refute many of al-Ghazali's attacks on the philosophers, Ibn Rushd also pointed out the non-Aristotelian excesses of al-Farabi and Ibn Sina (Avicenna). In his work *Kashf al-Mahanij* and other dialectical writings he appears to reflect the rationalism of the religious reformer al-M͵dî Ibn Tûmart (d. ca. 1129–1130), who held for the essential rationality of the Qur'an and the ability of human rationality to apprehend the created nature of the world.

While in some early philosophical works Ibn Rushd followed the Neoplatonic teachings of his famous predecessors, al-Fârâbî and Ibn Sina, in his mature works he rejected emanationism and vigorously defended many teachings that he held to be geniunely those of Aristotle, such as the eternity of the world, the transcendent and separate nature of the human material and agent intellects, the mortal nature of individual human existence, and the final causality of God as Unmoved Mover subtly argued to be appropriately called "Creator." Although he wrote many valuable short treatises, his philosophical thought is predominantly found in his commentaries on works of Aristotle. Medieval Jewish philosophical thought was powerfully influenced by the dialectical works, a number of his early synthetic *Short Commentaries* and his paraphrasing *Middle Commentaries*, as well as his detailed *Long Commentaries* on the *Posterior Analytics* and *Physics*. In contrast, the Latin translations of the thirteenth century were, for the most part, of *Long Commentaries*, with those on natural philosophy, psychology, and metaphysics prominent; none of his dialectical religious writings were translated. In these commentaries the Latin West discovered the power of philosophical reasoning apart from religious belief, something that scandalized some Christian thinkers, led others to uphold the value of independent reason, and generally compelled a rethinking of the relation of faith and reason. Though he taught a controversial theory of the unity of human material intellect, Ibn Rushd had many Western admirers and some followers through the period of the Renaissance, when additional works translated from Hebrew became available in Latin.

Toward the end of his life, he was condemned, his books were burned, and he was sent into a brief exile. After his death, philosophy was suppressed in Andalusia, and in Islamic lands no school developed following his Aristotelian approach. After a nineteenth-century revival of interest in his dialectical thought, various social and educational reformers in the Arabic-reading world have drawn on his work to provide a way for the conciliation of Islamic religion and the methods of scientific reasoning prominent in the West.

RICHARD C. TAYLOR

Further Reading

Aertsen, Jan A., and Gerhard Endress (Eds). *Averroes and the Aristotelian Tradition: Sources, Constitution and Reception of the Philosophy of Ibn Rushd (1126–1198)*. Leiden: Brill, 1999.

Averroes database: www.uni-koeln.de/phil-fak/thomasinst/averroes/index.htm. Thomas-Institut, Cologne, 2004.

Ibn Rushd. *Averroes. On the Harmony of Religion and Philosophy*. Translated by George F. Hourani. London: Luzac & Co., 1961.

———. *Averroes' Tahafut al-Tahafut (The Incoherence of the Incoherence)*. Translated by Simon Van Den Bergh. London: Luzac & Co., 1969.

———. *Faith and Reason in Islam. Averroes' Exposition of Religious Arguments*. Translated by Ibrahim Y. Najjar. Oxford: Oneworld, 2001. *(Kashf al-Mahanij)* Najjar, Fauzi M. "Ibn Rushd (Averroes) and the Egyptian Englightenment Movement." *British Journal of Middle Eastern Studies* 31 (Nov 2004): 195–213.

IBN SA'D

Ibn Sa'd (784–845) was among the pioneers of biographical writings in Arabic. He was born in Basra and studied Hadith before moving to Baghdad. Unusual for a Hadith scholar, he was also familiar with Arab genealogy, pre-Islamic tribal lore, and Jewish and Christian narrative traditions. In Baghdad, he apprenticed himself to al-Waqidi (d. 823), a collector of reports on the early history of the Muslim community. After al-Waqidi's death, Ibn Sa'd devoted the rest of his life to arranging his teacher's notes and his own into a book. The result was the *Tabaqat (Generations)*, the earliest biographical and historical compilation to be preserved in its entirety.

Before Ibn Sa'd's time, Arabic biographical writing had consisted largely of name-lists or collections of anecdotes about notable personalities. The only work that resembled a proper biography, at least by later standards, was the *Life of the Prophet* by Ibn Ishaq (d. 767). The remaining biographical material at Ibn Sa'd's disposal consisted of historical legends, name-lists, and reports on the Prophet's contemporaries and their successors. By putting all of this material together, Ibn Sa'd's *Generations* became one of the earliest Arabic works to present a coherent (if implicit) vision of universal history.

The work begins with a brief history of the prophets from Adam to Muhammad, intended to establish the latter's descent from the founders of monotheism. It then offers biographies of Muhammad's ancestors, who are represented as devout and courageous men despite being pagans. The biography of Muhammad himself, which takes up approximately one-fourth of the book, follows his career from birth to death. It includes accounts of his childhood and marriage, his reception of the Qur'an, his preaching in Mecca, his emigration to Medina, his negotiations with the tribes of Arabia, his military campaigns, and his final illness. There are also sections (with no parallels in Ibn Ishaq) on the Prophet's appearance, habits, clothing, diet, and personal possessions.

As a biographer of the Prophet, Ibn Sa'd follows the convention of citing first-person reports rather than narrating in his own voice, although he occasionally admits to having combined several reports into a single account. He seems to have been scrupulous in reporting everything he was told, including mutually contradictory reports of the same event. He has no hesitation about miracle stories, which appear in profusion. For these reasons his biography of the Prophet is hardly reliable as a source of documentary evidence. However, it is an indispensable source of information on early Islamic history as it was remembered or imagined in the mid-ninth century.

Unlike Ibn Ishaq, whose work ends with the death of Muhammad, Ibn Sa'd continued his account with biographies of the Prophet's successors, that is, the men and women who took part in the transmission of Hadith. These biographies, which number more than four thousand, are arranged in sections and subsections according to generation, tribal affiliation, and place of residence, with all the women appearing together in a section of their own at the end. Some of the entries, such as those on the first four caliphs, are quite long. The majority, however, consist of short notices giving the names of the subject's teachers and students (that is, the persons from whom and to whom he or she transmitted Hadith), as well as a date of death, if known.

Modern scholarship has tended to assume that *Generations* was used as a work of reference. Given its content, the book could certainly have served as a basis for the validation of *isnads* (the lists of transmitters that precede a Hadith report). Nevertheless, it also contains a good deal of anecdotal information with little evident relevance to Hadith transmission. Clearly, then, Ibn Sa'd was not simply a recordkeeper working for the benefit of Hadith scholars. Rather, he seems to have been a historian whose vision of history happens to give pride of place to the transmission of Hadith.

Ibn Sa'd's *Generations* exerted a formative influence on Arabic historical writing. The arrangements he used for organizing entries were adopted and modified by the authors of subsequent biographical works, many of which were arranged by generation or by place of residence. (The only system of organization Ibn Sa'd did not use was the alphabetical one, which was developed independently at approximately the same time.) Most important, perhaps, *Generations* offered a vision of history writing that was based on the collection of individual life stories. This understanding of historiography remained dominant, or at least influential, until the beginning of the modern period.

In 833, Ibn Sa'd was summoned to affirm the createdness of the Qur'an. This controversial opinion had been raised to the status of official state doctrine by the caliph al-Ma'mun (813–833), who sought to rein in the power of the religious scholars by forcing them to proclaim assent to it. Ibn Sa'd gave his assent, although it is likely that he did so under duress. Thereafter, he seems to have been left in peace until his death in Baghdad at the age of sixty-two.

MICHAEL COOPERSON

See also Biography and Biographical Works

Primary Sources

Ibn Sa'd. *Al-Tabaqat al-kubra.* 9 vols. Edited by Ihsan 'Abbas. Beirut: Dar Bayrut and Dar Sadir, 1957.
———. *Al-Tabaqat al-kubra.* 8 parts in 4. Edited by Riyad 'Abd Allah 'Abd al-Hadi. Beirut: Dar Ihya al-Turath al-'Arabi, 1996 (contains passages unpublished in earlier editions). Partial translations in *The women of Madina.* Translated by Aisha Bewley. London: Ta Ha, 1995.
The Men of Madina. Translated by Aisha Bewley. London: Ta-Ha, 1997–2000.
The Men of Madina II. Translated by Aisha Bewley. London: Ta-Ha, 2000.

Further Reading

Loth, Otto. "Ursprung und Bedeutung der Tabaqat." *Zeitschrift der Deutschen Morgenländischen Gesellschaft* 23 (1869): 593–614.
al-Qadi, Wadad. "Biographical Dictionaries: Inner Structure and Cultural Significance." In *The Book in the Islamic World: The Written Word and Communication in the Middle East,* edited by George N. Atiyeh. Albany: State University of New York Press, 1995.
Roded, Ruth. *Women in Islamic Biographical Collections: From Ibn Sa'd to Who's Who.* Boulder: Lynne Rienner, 1994.

IBN SHADDAD

Baha' al-Din Abu'l-Mahasin Yusuf b. Rafi'

Baha' al-Din Abu'l-Mahasin Yusuf b. Rafi', a leading scholar, writer, and official of the Jazira and Syria, was born in the northern Mesopotamian city of Mosul in AH 439/1145 CE. After a period in Baghdad as *mu'id* (assistant teacher) at the *madrasa* (Islamic school), the celebrated Madrasa al-Nizamiyya, founded by the Seljuk vizier Nizam al-Mulk, he was made *mudarris* (professor) in one of his native city's *madrasas*.

During this period Baha' al-Din was appointed by the Zankid rulers of Mosul to several diplomatic missions, including two embassies to Saladin. In AH 584/1188 CE, on his return home from the pilgrimage, he was received by Saladin, who was besieging the northern Syrian stronghold of Krak des Chevaliers. The judicious presentation to the sultan by Baha' al-Din of a treatise he had written, titled *Fada'il al-Jihad (The Virtues of Holy War)*, resulted soon after in Baha' al-Din's appointment as Saladin's *qadi al-'askar* (Islamic judge of the army). He was later given judicial and administrative responsibilities in Jerusalem. Baha' al-Din became a close companion and confidant of the sultan, remaining so until Saladin's death at Damascus in AH 589/1193 CE. He then played an important part in negotiating the division of power among Saladin's heirs.

After two years in the service of Saladin's eldest son al-Malik al-Afdal 'Ali, ruler of Damascus, in AH 591/1195 CE, Baha' al-Din moved to Aleppo. There he was appointed *qadi* (Islamic judge) of the city by its ruler, al-Malik al-Zahir Ghazi, who was another of Saladin's sons. In AH 601/1204 CE, he founded his own religious school in Aleppo, the Madrasa al-Sahibiyya, adding to it a *dar al-hadith* (school for the study of prophetic tradition). Linking the two foundations was a mausoleum that he prepared for himself.

Meanwhile, Baha' al-Din's diplomatic skills proved useful to the ruler of Aleppo: He made several visits to Cairo on behalf of al-Malik al-Zahir in an effort to resolve disputes among the Ayyubids. He continued to serve al-Zahir's heir, al-Malik al-'Aziz. In AH 629/1232 CE, he headed the delegation that went to Cairo to bring the daughter of the Ayyubid ruler of Egypt back to Aleppo to marry al-Malik al-'Aziz. Baha' al-Din died at Aleppo in AH 632/1235 CE, at nearly ninety years of age.

Baha' al-Din's most important work is his biography of Saladin, *Sirat Salah al-Din*, also called *al-Nawadir al-sultaniyyah wa-l-mahasin al-Yusufiyyah (The Sultan's Rare Qualities and the Excellences of Yusuf [that is, Saladin])*. It combines elements of hagiography, propaganda, history, and autobiography. The first part of the work describes the sultan's accomplishments and moral excellence. Throughout the work Saladin is presented as exhorting the Muslims not to slacken their efforts against the Crusaders. The second part of the book is an account of Saladin's career from AH 558/1163 CE, when he accompanied his Uncle Shirkuh's expedition to Egypt, until his death in AH 589/1193 CE. For events after the summer of AH 584/1188 CE, when Baha' al-Din joined the service of the sultan, the narrative becomes the eyewitness account of someone in Saladin's inner circle, and a commensurately valuable source for the events of the Third Crusade.

DAVID MORRAY

See also Biography and Biographical Works; Diplomacy; Excellences Literature; Historical Writing; Madrasa

Further Reading

Ahmad, M. Hilmy M. "Some Notes on Arabic Historiography during the Zengid and Ayyubid Periods (521/1127–648/1250)." In *Historians of the Middle East*, edited by B. Lewis and P.M. Holt. Oxford: Oxford University Press, 1962.

Cahen, C. *La Syrie du Nord à l'époque des Croisades*. Paris, 1940.

Ibn Shaddad, Baha' al-Din. *al-Nawadir al-Sultaniyya wa'l-mahasin al-Yusufiyya*. Translated by D.S. Richards as *The Rare and Excellent History of Saladin*. Aldershot: Ashgate, 2001.

IBN SHAHIN, NISSIM BEN JACOB (C. 990–1062)

Nissim was a Talmudic scholar of Qayrawan who studied under his father, Rabbi Jacob ben Nissim, and Rabbi Hushiel, an illustrious scholar of Italian origin. Nissim was supported financially by the famed poet and patron of Jewish learning, Samuel Ibn Naghrela. The latter composed a poem of consolation upon the death of Nissim's young and only son and married his son Joseph to Nissim's daughter. Several works (some fragmentary) by Nissim survive in addition to commentaries on tracts of the Talmud and a compilation of legal rulings. Composed in Judeo-Arabic, his *A Key to the Locks of the Talmud* is a reference work of quotations found in the Talmud, and his *Revelation of Mysteries* is a topical treatment of subjects such as biblical exegesis, religious polemics, responsa, and explications of sections of the Talmud and Midrash. These works exhibit tendencies toward systemization and had profound effects on Jewish intellectuals in the Islamic and Christian domains. The Judeo-Arabic collection of rabbinic tales titled *Kitab al-faraj ba'd al-shidda (Book of Relief after Adversity)* is addressed to console a relative called Dunash who had requested a book to relieve him following the death of a son. Dunash had mentioned that the "heretics" (that is, Muslims) possessed such a book on the subject of relief after adversity, possibly referring to al-Tanukhi's *Kitab al-faraj ba'd al-shidda* or a similar work. Al-Tanukhi's work is an *adab* collection on various species of relief (foretold in omens, realized through dreams, freedom from prison or execution, and so on) and aphorisms concerning relief from Qur'an, hadith, and poetry. Ibn Shahin's book is an anthology of stories, mostly gleaned from rabbinic sources, that assures the reader of God's justice (despite its mysteries) and discusses the qualities of scholars, virtuous and perfidious women, the wickedness of hypocrites, and the duty to pursue kindness and charity while abstaining from evil. The book also draws on apocryphal Jewish books (such as *Ben Sira*) and, in all likelihood, stories from Islamic literature; the book bears some earmarks of Arabic storytelling techniques. It enjoyed great popularity in the medieval period (as testified by Geniza letters) and had direct influence on later Jewish works, such as Joseph Ibn Zabarah's *Book of Delights* and Moses de Leon's *Zohar*.

JONATHAN P. DECTER

See also Adab; Judeo-Arabic; Ibn Naghrela, Samuel; Qayrawan; al-Tanukhi

Further Reading

Abramson, Shraga. *Rab Nissim Ga'on, Hamishah Sefarim.* Jerusalem: Mekitzei Nirdamim, 1965.

Ibn Shahin, Nissim Ben Jacob. *The Arabic Original of Ibn Shahin's Book of Comfort Known as the Hibbur Yaphe of R. Nissim B. Ya'aqobh.* Edited by Julian Obermann. New Haven: Yale University Press, 1933.

———. *An Elegant Composition Concerning Relief after Adversity.* Translated with introduction and notes by William M. Brinner. New Haven and London: Yale University Press, 1977.

Scholem, Gershom. "The Paradisiac Garb of Souls and the Origin of the Concept of *Haluka de-Rabbanan.*" *Tarbis* 24 (1956): 290–306.

IBN SINA, OR AVICENNA

Abu 'Ali al-Hasan Ibn Sina (ca. 980–1037 CE), known in Latin as Avicenna, was a physician, natural philosopher, mathematician, poetic mystic, and princely minister. Of Persian descent, he was born in Afshana in the province of Bukhara. His philosophical chief work, *Kitab al-shifa' (Book of Healing),* which was known in Latin as *Liber Sufficientia,* together with its condensed revision, *Kitab al-najat (Book of Deliverance),* led many to regard him as being the authoritative Neoplatonist integrator of the Aristotelian corpus. However, his intellectual acumen elevates his station beyond that of a commentator and lets him stand as an insightful thinker in his own right. His philosophical investigations covered mathematics, music, logic, physical and psychical sciences, as well as metaphysics and theology. In geometry, he critically examined Euclid's *Elements* and attempted to prove its fifth postulate. In his Aristotelian intromission conception of vision, he showed that the velocity of light had a finite magnitude. Partly influenced by Porphyry's *Isagoge,* Aristotle's *Organon,* and Galen's logical investigations, he eventually developed intricate forms of propositional logic. Furthermore, he founded a prototheory of meaning that was partially embodied in his work *Kitab al-hudud (Book of Definitions),* wherein he arrived at definitions by way of a rigorous distinction among concepts while, unlike most Platonists, he celebrated the merits of the art of persuasion and rhetoric. In astronomy he endeavored to systematize his observations that were grounded by Ptolemy's *Almagest,* and in mechanics he built on the theories of Heron of Alexandria while also seeking to improve the precision of instrumental readings. In his physical inquiries he studied different forms of energy, heat, and force, while presenting a more coherent account of the interconnection between time and motion than what is habitually associated with Aristotle's *Physics.* One of his important achievements in natural philosophy is attested to in his account of the soul in *Kitab al-nafs (Treatise on the Soul),* which was preserved in his *al-Shifa* and *al-Najat,* and was translated into Latin under the title *De Anima.* Therein, he presented an affirmation of the existence of the soul that rested on a radical mind-body dualism in an argument that is customarily referred to as "the flying person argument," which anticipates Descartes's "*cogito ergo sum.*" He also elucidated the notion of "intentionality" in the workings of the internal sense of the faculty of estimation *(wahm)* and its pragmatic entailments. Ranking among the most influential of metaphysicians in the history of philosophy, Ibn Sina offered an original elucidation of the question of "being" *(al-wujud)* that was mediated by a methodical distinction between essence and existence and oriented by an ontological consideration of the modalities of necessity, contingency, and impossibility. Taking the contingent to be a mere potentiality of being, whose existence or nonexistence did not entail a contradiction, Ibn Sina construed all creatures in actuality as being necessary existents due to something other than themselves. Consequently, any contingent had its essence distinct from its existence while being existentially dependent on causes that are external to it, which lead back to the One Necessary Existent due to Itself Whose Essence is none other than Its Existence. In this, Ibn Sina eschewed Aristotle's reduction of "being" into the Greek conception of *ousia* (substance or essence), and he conceived the Deity as being the *metaphysical* First Cause of existence rather than being the *physical* Unmoved Cause of motion. Although his consideration of Divine creation was primarily mediated by an attempt to found a synthesis between Aristotle's *naturalism* and monotheistic *creationism*, his ontology remained more akin to Neoplatonist *emanationism*, which took the One Necessary Existent to be the Source of all existential effusion. In this processional hierarchical participation in "being," the Active Intellect played a necessary role in the genesis of human knowledge. Following Plato, Ibn Sina held that knowledge, which consisted of grasping the intelligible, did ultimately determine the fate of the rational soul in the hereafter. Believing that the universality of our ideas was attributed to the mind itself, he additionally held that our passive individual intellects are in a state of potency with regard to knowledge, unlike the Active impersonal and separate Intellect that is in a state of actual perennial thinking. Consequently, our passive intellect *qua* mind acquires ideas by being in contact with the Active Intellect without compromising its own independent substantiality or immortality. In a mystical tone that becomes most pronounced in *Kitab al-isharat wa-l-tanbihat (Book of Hints and Pointers)*, Ibn Sina also maintained that certain elect souls are capable of realizing a union with the Universal Active Intellect, thereby attaining the station of prophecy. His philosophical views were debated by Averroes and Maimonides, criticized by al-Ghazali, and integrated by intellectual authorities in medieval Europe, such as Thomas Aquinas, Duns Scotus, and Roger Bacon. His thinking also impacted the course of development of the ontotheological systems of prominent Muslim scholars such as Suhrawardi, Tusi, and Mulla Sadra. In all of this, his philosophical wisdom did not outshine his celebrated reputation as a physician, and his classic *Kitab al-qanun fi'l-tibb (The Canon in Medicine)*, which was translated into Latin in the twelfth century CE *(Liber Canonis)*, commanded an authority that almost surpassed that of Hippocrates and Galen and acted as the decisive compendium of the Greco-Roman-Arabic scientific medicine, and as the reference *Materia Medica*, throughout the medieval period and up to the Renaissance.

NADER EL-BIZRI

See also Aristotle and Aristotelianism; Astronomy; al-Farabi (Alfarabius or Avennasar); al-Ghazali; Ibn Rushd (Averroes); Illuminationism; Maimonides; Materia Medica; Medical Literature, Arabic; Medicine; Meteorology; Mulla Sadra; Mysticism; Optics; Physicians; Plato and Neoplatonism; Ptolemy; al-Suhrawardi, Shihab al-Din 'Umar; Theology

Primary Sources

Ibn Sina. *Kitab al-shifa', al-ilahiyyat*. Edited by Ibrahim Madkour, George Anawati, and Said Zayed. Cairo: al-Hay'a al-misriyya al-'amma lil-kitab, 1975.
———. *Kitab al-shifa', Kitab al-nafs*. Edited by Fazlur Rahman. Oxford: Oxford University Press, 1960.
———. *Kitab al-najat*. Edited by Majid Fakhry. Beirut: Dar al-afaq al-jadida, 1985.
———. *Kitab al-hudud (Livre des définitions)*. Edited and translated by A.-M. Goichon. Cairo: Institut français d'archéologie orientale du Caire, 1963.
———. *Kitab al-'isharat wa'l-tanbihat (Le livre des directives et remarques)*. Edited and translated by A.-M. Goichon. Paris: J. Vrin, 1999.

Further Reading

Afnan, Soheil. *Avicenna: His Life and His Works*. London: Allen and Unwin, 1958.
Corbin, Henry. *Avicenne et le récit visionnaire*. Tehran: Société des monuments nationaux de l'Iran, 1954.
Gardet, Louis. *La connaissance mystique chez Ibn Sina et ses presupposés philosophiques*. Cairo: Institut français d'archéologie orientale du Caire, 1952.
Goichon, A.-M. *Léxique de la langue philosophique d'Ibn Sina*. Paris: Desclée de Brouwer, 1938.
———. "Ibn Sina." In *The Encyclopaedia of Islam*. Vol. III. Leiden: E. J. Brill, 1960.
———. *La philosophie d'Avicenne et son influence en Europe médiévale*. Paris: Librairie d'Amérique et d'Orient, 1971.
Goodman, Lenn E. *Avicenna*. London: Routledge, 1992.
Gutas, Dimitri. *Avicenna and the Aristotelian Tradition*. Leiden: E. J. Brill, 1988.
Hasse, Dag Nikolaus. *Avicenna's De Anima in the Latin West*. London: The Warburg Institute, University of London, 2000.
Janssens, Jules, and Daniel De Smet (Eds). *Avicenna and His Heritage*. Leuven: Leuven University Press, 2002.

IBN TAGHRI BIRDI, ABU 'L-MAHASIN YUSUF (C. 1410–1470 CE)

Ibn Taghri Birdi was a historian of the Mamluk Sultanate of Egypt and Syria (1250–1517) known for his close ties to the Mamluk elite. His father, Taghri Birdi, was a mamluk *amir* (holder of military rank)

who rose through the ranks during the reigns of the Mamluk sultans Barquq (r. 1382–1399) and Faraj (r. 1399–1412), achieving the position of Viceroy in Damascus prior to his death in 1412. Ibn Taghri Birdi's eldest sister was married to Faraj, and Ibn Taghri Birdi was a close companion of a son of sultan Jaqmaq (r. 1438–1453). Ibn Taghri Birdi received a grant of land revenues from Sultan al-Mu'ayyad Shaykh (r. 1412–1421) and accompanied Sultan Barsbay (r. 1422–1437) on a military campaign in Syria. He also knew Turkish quite well and was familiar with court life in Mamluk Cairo. These and other connections served him well during his career as religious stipendiary, scholar, and author.

Ibn Taghri Birdi wrote several works, but he is best known today for his biographical dictionary and two historical chronicles. The dictionary, *Al-Manhal al-Safi wa al-Mustawfi ba'd al-Wafi,* written in early adulthood, provides biographies of rulers, scholars, and amirs for the period 1248–1451, with scattered additions dating as late as 1458. His chronicle *Al-Nujum al-Zahira fi Muluk Misr wa-al-Qahira* surveys Egyptian history from the Muslim conquest in 641 up to 1468, although the sections post-1441 are mainly summaries taken from his second major chronicle, *Al-Hawadith al-Duhur fi Mada al-Ayyam wa-al-Shuhur*, a detailed account of Mamluk history covering the period 1441–1469. Ibn Taghri Birdi considered this second work a continuation of al-Maqrizi's important history, *Kitab al-Suluk li-Ma'rifat Duwal wa-al-Muluk.*

Ibn Taghri Birdi's chronicles are focused on the elite segments of Mamluk-era society. As a *walad al-nass* (Arabic "son of the people," meaning literally a son of those who mattered, that is, the Mamluks), it is perhaps not surprising that comparative studies of his work have indicated a tendency by Ibn Taghri Birdi to defend the actions and policies of the Mamluk rulers who were frequently criticized by other observers such as al-Maqrizi. That said, his work also contains frank and critical comments about specific officials both living and dead, for which it is possible that Ibn Taghri Birdi suffered both verbal and physical attacks.

WARREN C. SCHULTZ

See also Historical Writing

Primary Sources

Ibn Taghri Birdi, Abu 'l-Mahasin Yusuf. *History of Egypt (845–854 A. H., A. D. 1441–1450): An Extract from Abû l-Mahâsin ibn Taghrî Birdî's Chronicle Entitled Hawâdith ad-Duhûr fî Madâ l-Ayyâm wash-Shuhûr.* Translated by William Popper. New Haven: American Oriental Society, 1967. American Oriental Series, Essays, 5.
————. *History of Egypt, 1382–1469 AD, Translated from the Arabic Annals of Abu l-Mahâsin ibn Taghrî Birdî.* Translated by William Popper. 8 vols. Berkeley and Los Angeles: University of California Press, 1954–1963. University of California Publications in Semitic Philology, vols. 13–14, 17–19, 22–24.
————. *al-Manhal al-Safi wa-al-Mustawfá ba'da al-Wafi.* Edited by Ahmad Yusuf Najati. Vol. 1. Cairo: Matba'at Dar al-Kutub, 1956.
————. *al-Manhal al-Safi wa-al-Mustawfá ba'da al-Wafi.* Edited by Muhammad Muhammad Amin. Vols. 2–7. Cairo: al-Hay'ah al-Misriyah al-'Ammah lil-Kitab, 1984–1993.

Further Reading.

Darraj, Ahmad. "La vie d'Abu'l-Mahasin Ibn Tagri Birdi et son oeuvre." *Annales islamologiques* 11 (1972): 163–181.
Perho, Irmeli. "Al-Maqrizi and Ibn Taghri Birdi as Historians of Contemporary Events." *The Historiography of Islamic Egypt (c. 950–1800).* Edited by Hugh Kennedy, 107–120. Leiden: Brill, 2001.
Popper, William. *Egypt and Syria under the Circassian Sultans 1382–1486 AD: Systematic Notes to Ibn Taghrî Birdî's Chronicles of Egypt.* Berkeley and Los Angeles: University of California Press, 1955, 1957. University of California Publications in Semitic Philology, 15–16.

IBN TAYMIYYA

Taqi al-Din Ahmad Ibn Taymiyya (1263–1328) has been called both the most important figure from the Mamluk Sultanate of Egypt and Syria (1250–1517) and the most significant Hanbali *'alim* after Ahmad b. Hanbal himself. The author of numerous fatawa and many longer works, he was also imprisoned by the Mamluk state six times for a cumulative period of more than six years between 1294 and 1328, including the last two years of his life.

Ibn Taymiyya's family moved to Damascus when he was a boy, fleeing from Mongol advances in upper Mesopotamia. Ibn Taymiyya was educated within the Hanbali madhhab and by 1284 was teaching in a major madrasa in Damascus. His subsequent career was marked by several brushes with state power, the rivalry and admiration of other jurists, and significant popularity among the Damascene population. His public life was marked by zealous devotion to the principals he held dear and the courage to face those whom his statements disturbed, even if that meant imprisonment. It has also been argued that his popularity with the populace disturbed the Mamluk rulers who found it threatening, and this may have contributed to his frequent imprisonment. His contemporary biographers, most of them àlso jurists, write of his personal piety, devotion to justice, and defiance of authority. There is a suggestion, however, particularly in the writings of al-Dhahabi (d. 1339), that Ibn Taymiyya had a difficult personality.

Known first as a Hadith scholar, Ibn Taymiyya's written output ranges far and wide. He wrote about and preached the importance of jihad against enemies of the Muslim world, in particular against the Mongols. (When Il-Khan Ghazan invaded Syria in 1300, Ibn Taymiyya was a spokesperson of the resistance in Damascus.) He stressed the important example of the pious ancestors *(al-salaf al-salih)* and condemned what he saw as the excesses of some Sufi practices. In one of his major works, *al-Siyasa al-Shar'iyya,* Ibn Taymiyya argued that since state and religion were inseparable, the temporal power and the revenues of the state must be harnessed to the path of God. A primary goal of the state was to ensure the centrality of the shari'a, and this required the maintenance of order. Central to the state's mission to maintain order was its ability to use coercive power to enforce the Qur'anic injunction "to command the good and forbid the wrong."

After his death, Ibn Taymiyya's ideas were further disseminated by his chief pupil Ibn Qayyim al-Jawziyya (d. 1350), an individual who also shared in some of his teacher's punishment. Many of Ibn Taymiyya's ideas remain influential today, notably as refracted through the writings of the eighteenth-century founder of Wahhabism, Muhammad b. 'Abd al-Wahhab.

WARREN C. SCHULTZ

See also Hanbali; Mamluks; Mongols

Primary Sources

Peters, Rudolph. *Jihad in Classical and Modern Islam.* (Chapter 5 translates an excerpt from Ibn Taymiyya's *al-Siyasa al-Shar'iyya.*) Princeton: Markus Wiener Publishers, 1996.

Further Reading

Laoust, H. *Essai sur les doctrines socials et politiques de Taki-d-Din Ahmad b. Taimiya.* Cairo: Institute Français d'Archeologe Orientale, 1939.
Little, D. P. "The Historical and Historiographical Significance of the Detention of Ibn Taymiyya." *International Journal of Middle Eastern Studies* 4 (1973): 313–320.
Makdisi, George. "Ibn Taymiya: A Sufi of the Qadiriya Order." *American Journal of Arabic Studies* 1 (1973): 118–129.

IBN TUFAYL

Muhammad Ibn 'Abd al-Malik Abu Bakr Ibn Tufayl was born in Guadix, not far from Granada, in 1110. Reputed for his learning in philosophy,

jurisprudence, theology, and logic, as well as natural science, he gained the favor of the Almohad ruler, Abu Ya'qub Yusuf, whom he served for many years as a political advisor and physician. Apart from his philosophical novel, *Hayy Ibn Yaqzan (Living the Son of Awakened)*—the only writing of his that has survived—Ibn Tufayl is known for the important role he played in presenting Averroes to Abu Ya'qub as the person most capable of commenting on the works of Aristotle, this being a task Ibn Tufayl considered beyond his own reach. He died in Marrakesh in 1185.

Ibn Tufayl focused on the relationship between the rational acquisition of knowledge and the path to it pursued by those who favor mysticism or Sufism in the philosophical introduction to *Hayy Ibn Yaqzan*. The work consists of three major parts. In the introduction, Ibn Tufayl explains his reasons for writing a book such as this and provides a general critique of philosophy, theology, and mysticism within the Arab world during his time. It is followed by the story of Hayy and by a formal conclusion in which Ibn Tufayl returns to the main theme of the work.

As he explains in the introduction, the tale of Hayy ibn Yaqzan comes as a response to a request from a friend that he unfold what he knows "of the secrets of the Oriental wisdom mentioned by the master, the chief, Abu 'Ali Ibn Sina." The question, he says, moved him to a strange state and caused him to discern a world beyond the present; it also caused him to discern the difficulty of speaking intelligently and circumspectly about this state. To prove the latter point, Ibn Tufayl passes in review what mystics and philosophers have said about it. Desirous of avoiding their foolishness, he speaks about the state only to the extent necessary, all the while pointing out the errors of his predecessors. He insists it is to be reached by "speculative knowledge" and "deliberative inquiry" and intimates that at least one philosopher—Ibn Bajja—reached that rank or perhaps even managed to go beyond it.

Ibn Bajja did not describe this state in a book; nor has any other philosopher—either because they had no awareness of it or because it is too difficult to explain in a book. Ibn Tufayl dismisses as useless this task that has come down from Aristotle, Alfarabi, Avicenna, and all Andalusians prior to Ibn Bajja. Even Ibn Bajja, capable as he was of providing an account, failed to do so.

To meet his friend's request, Ibn Tufayl promises to expose the truth and knowledge he has learned from Alghazali and Avicenna, plus what he has gained from the philosophically inclined people of his time via study and reflection. Even so, he hesitates to give the results of what he has witnessed without also providing the principles, lest his interlocutor be content with a lower degree of insight. To arouse his interlocutor's longing and encourage him to move along the path, Ibn Tufayl offers the tale of Hayy ibn Yaqzan. In other words, to leave us short of the end, it will indicate what the path is like.

Hayy is either self-generated from a lump of clay or comes into being as do all humans but is then put into the sea in a basket because his mother, the sister of a very proud monarch, has wedded beneath her status in secret and fears for the fruit of this union should her brother learn of Hayy's existence. However generated, Hayy grows up on a deserted island, nursed by a doe until he can fend for himself. During seven periods of seven years each, he discovers his natural surroundings and the way they interact, ascending by a series of inductions to embrace physics and its many divisions, as well as mathematics and its parts. He also gains insight into the nature of the heavenly bodies and into the character of the creator, as well as of his messenger and prophet, Muhammad.

Hayy's education is all the more wondrous, for his enforced solitude deprives him of language. Only when he encounters Asal, the inhabitant of a neighboring island who is discontent with the way his fellow citizens practice religion, does Hayy learn to speak. They return to Asal's island intent upon showing people the correct path, but they fail miserably. Only Salaman, a friend of Asal's who discerns that most people cannot appreciate the truths Hayy wishes them to grasp and who is content to let them flounder, understands the limits of human reason. He is also too complacent for Hayy and Asal, not to mention most of Ibn Tufayl's readers.

The tale ends with Hayy and Asal deciding to return to the desert island to spend their remaining days meditating about divine matters. The people on the mainland are left without a solution to the problems that plague them, just as Ibn Tufayl's interlocutor is left without a clear answer to his quest. We readers, having been enticed by this story, must now figure out for ourselves what it can possibly mean for us.

CHARLES E. BUTTERWORTH

Further Reading

Fradkin, Hillel. "The Political Thought of Ibn Tufayl." In *The Political Aspects of Islamic Philosophy, Essays in Honor of Muhsin S. Mahdi*, edited by Charles E. Butterworth, 234–261. Cambridge: Harvard University Press, 1992.

Hayy ibn Yaqzan. Translated by Lenn Evan Goodman. New York: Gee Tee Bee, 1995.

Mallet, Dominique. "Les livres de Hayy." *Arabica*. 44, no. 1 (1997): 1–34.

IBN TULUN

Ibn Tulun, also Ahmad b. Tulun, was the founder of the Tulunid dynasty that ruled Egypt and Syria during the late ninth and early tenth centuries CE. Following the example of the Tahirids in Khurasan and the Aghlabids in North Africa, Ibn Tulun exploited his position in Egypt, establishing a semiautonomous state a secure distance from the 'Abbasid capital in Baghdad while the caliphs battled rebellions and independence movements in the East.

Ibn Tulun's father, Tulun, entered the caliphate's service as a Turkish slave, reportedly sent to the caliph al-Ma'mun from Bukhara. He formed part of a large cadre of Turks who served in important military and administrative positions during his time. He eventually rose to become chief of al-Ma'mun's personal guard.

Ibn Tulun received training in military affairs and distinguished himself for his bravery. His widowed mother's marriage to the Turkish general Bakbak gave him new opportunities for advancement. The caliph al-Mu'tamid appointed Bakbak over Egypt in 868. Ibn Tulun became his stepfather's lieutenant.

Ibn Tulun increased his power through scheming, marriage, and fortuitous circumstances. He cultivated good relations with the caliph al-Mu'tamid. After having the infamous controller of finances, Ibn al-Mudabbir, removed, he assumed primary responsibility for Egypt's treasury, especially payments of tribute to Baghdad. When Ibn Tulun's stepfather was assassinated, the new governor, Yarjukh, to whom he was related by marriage, kept him as lieutenant governor. The revolt of the governor of Palestine shortly afterward offered him a pretext to purchase military slaves, though he did not actually put down the revolt. These slaves were fiercely loyal to him and formed the core of his army. He soon gained control of the financial administration of Syria, as well as Egypt.

The appointment of the caliph's son, Ja'far, over Egypt and other Western provinces in 872 CE led to Ibn Tulun's bid for autonomy. Ja'far was a minor so Ibn Tulun exercised nearly independent authority. The caliph's brother, al-Muwaffaq, who controlled the East and held most of the caliphate's effective power, was preoccupied with repelling Turkish incursions and quelling independence movements. When Ibn Tulun failed to send a satisfactory sum of tribute, al-Muwaffaq dispatched an expedition to remove him. The expedition, however, returned without achieving its purpose. The ongoing rebellion of the Zanj in southern Iraq prevented al-Muwaffaq from pressing the matter further.

Ibn Tulun consolidated his power in the years afterwards. He occupied Syria following al-Muwaffaq's failed expedition and led raids against the Byzantines in Anatolia. These raids enhanced his stature as a leader of holy war against the infidel. He later inscribed his name on his coinage, in addition to that of the Ja'far. He never openly opposed the authority of the caliph. The prosperity of Egypt and Syria under his rule owes in part to his skill as an administrator. He showed restraint in his taxation. He kept, in addition, most revenues in these provinces rather than remitting them to Baghdad. Upon his death in 884, rule went to one of his sons, Khumarawayh.

STUART SEARS

See also Tulinids

Primary Sources

al-Balawî. *Sîrat Aìmad b. Øulûn.* Edited by Kurd 'Alî. Cairo, n.d.

Ibn Sa'îd al-Andalusî. *Kitâb al-Mughrib fî ìulâ al-Maghrib.* Edited by K.L. Tallquist. Leiden, 1899.

———. *al-Mukâfa'a.* Cairo, 1941.

Further Reading

Hassan, Z.M. *Les Tulunides.* Paris, 1937.

———. "Ahmad b. Tulun." In *Encyclopedia of Islam.* 2d ed, vol. I. Leiden: E.J. Brill, 1960 (504 words, S.D. Sears, Roger Williams University).

Kennedy, H. *The Prophet and the Age of the Caliphates.* London and New York, 1986, 309–313.

IBN TUMART

The founder of the al-Muwahhidun confederation, Abu Abdillah Muhammad b. Abdillah b. Tumart, a Masmudian Berber, was born (AH 471/1078 CE or AH 474/1081 CE) in the city of Sus, located in Morocco's Anti-Atlas Mountains. We do not have much information about his youth. Observing negative developments such as moral and social decadence, the abandonment of religious principles, and the spread of the anthropomorphist conception of God under the al-Murabitun dynasty, Ibn Tumart was convinced of the necessity of social reform. He went to Cordoba to study theological sciences (499/1106). After taking lessons for about a year from Abu Abdillah Muhammed b. Ali b. Hamdin, Kadhi of Cordoba, he traveled to Mahdiya in Tunisia; there he participated in theological congregations of Abu Abdillah al-Mazeri. Studying with Ibn Abu Rendeka et-Turtushi in Alexandria, Kiyâ el-Herrâs in Baghdad, Abu Bakir Muhammed b. Ahmed al-Shashi, and Mubarek b. Abdilcabbar, Ibn Tumart also read

Imam Malik's *al-Muvatta'* with Abu Abdillah Muhammed b. Mansur al-Hadhrami. He traveled back to Maghreb from Alexandria in 510–511/1116. He also served his duty of pilgrimage to Mecca in this traveling period of eleven years. Traveling first to Bougie, and then to Beni Mallal, he met his first disciple and future successor Abdulmu'min al-Kûmî. His courageous personality caused him to be expelled from Vansharîs, Tlemcem, Shubat Enlil, and Fez; so he went to Marrakech, the capital of the al-Murabitun dynasty, but his activities there also caused him to be expelled to Aghmat. He then went on to Tin Mal and continued his "common knowledge and forbid from denied" *(al-amr bi'l-ma'rûf wa al-nahy an al-munkar)* activities. Rejecting Ali b. Yusuf b. Tashfin's invitation to return to Marrakech, he retreated to a cave, the Ghar al-muqaddas, and in Maghreb he began to spread the idea that Mahdi's appearance was near (515/1121).

That same year, his disciple Abdulmu'min and nine other men declared that Ibn Tumart was the Mahdi and that they would be loyal to him for all their lives. Ibn Tumart then started a violent rebellion in the command of Abdulmu'min el-Kumi ve Abu Muhammed al-Bashir against al-Murabitun, claiming that they supported an anthropomorphist conception of God, that they were unjust and causing the corruption of society, they had designs upon people's lives and properties, and that they had thus given up the Islamic faith. There were many battles in the Anti-Atlas region and the city of Sus for the next two years. Against al-Murabitun's efforts to build up their strength, Ibn Tumart moved to Tin Mal to have a stronger defense (517/1123).

Ibn Tumart began a large campaign in the command of Abu Muhammed al-Bashir to acquire Marrakech in 524 AH/1130. However, al-Muwahhidun could not gain hold of the city after a siege of six weeks and was defeated in the battle of Buhayra; five members of the council of ten were lost in this battle. Ibn Tumart passed away several months after this defeat in 14 Ramadhan 524/August 21, 1130. His successor, Abdulmu'min, and close friends concealed his death for about three years.

His works include: (1) *Kitâbu Aazzi mâ yutlab* (edited by Ignaz Goldziher) Algeria 1903 and AmmAr ÙAlibi (Algeria, 1985); (2) *al-Murshida* (published by Goldziher with a French translation *(ZDMG, XLl, 72–73; XL1V, 168–170)*; (3) *al-Aqide.* In addition to the Egypt edition (Cairo, 1328), another edition is also available in French, translated by Henri Masse (Paris, 1928); (4) *Muhâzzi'l-Muwaùùa'* (Hizânatu'l-Karawiyyin, no. 40/181; Rabat el-Hizânetul-èAmma, no. 840c, 1222c; published by Goldziher as *Muwatta'u'l-Imâm al-Mahdî* (Algeria,

1905). (5) *Mukhtasaru Sahihi Muslim* (Ibn Yûsuf Library, Marakesh, no. 403).

Thinking himself a religious reformist, Ibn Tumart emphasized the notion of unity and doctrine of the imamate in his theory of faith. He defines knowledge, which he takes as the only basis for faith, as "the divine radiance in the heart which allows us to make a distinction between facts and qualities," thus suggesting that only the qualities of objects and events can be known, not their essences. Because of Ibn Tumart's emphasis on the unity of God, his followers were known as al-Muwahhidun (that is, Unitarians). God's existence was known from intelligence; however, this knowledge was not innate, but deductive. Ibn Tumart ascribed some negative and demonstrative attributes to Allah. However, he gave intelligence no function in his definition of the relationship between the individual and his attributes. Therefore, his approach to this problem cannot be taken as the suspension of all attributes but a distinctive approach that avoided comparison and solidification. According to Ibn Tumart, predicative attributes in the dogmas must be believed, without trying to look for analogies.

Ibn Tumart considered the imamate as a religious obligation and maintained that Imam was innocent *(maèsum)*, therefore, we can assert that Ibn Tumart was influenced by Shi'i doctrine. However, he considered only the first three caliphs as legitimate Imams. Ibn Tumart received the acknowledgment of fealty through his disciples, who acknowledged him as the Mahdi, and he named only those who obeyed him as al-Muwahhidun; all others were regarded as infidels. He accepted the idea that the only creator is Allah and believed that the power of acting in a good or bad way was given by Allah to mankind; thus empowerment is the act in the place of the power of the human being.

According to Ibn Tumart, all canonical judgements originated only from the Qur'an and Sunnah, all convictions and conventions reached by syllogisms were not primary, but supplementary; intelligence had no law-making authority. Ibn Tumart accepted ideas of several religious sects on some matters: He was more like an Ash'ari in subjects concerning faith, a Maliki in subjects of fiqh, and also followed Ibn Hazm's zahiri-salafi thought on some matters. However, the movement initiated by him can be regarded as a political movement to put an end to Al-Murabit's confederation more than being a movement of religion and faith.

HÜSEYIN SARIOGLU

Further Reading

Abdulmacid an-Naccar. *al-Mahdi b. Tumart*. Beyrouth, 1983, 24–30, 73–83, 116–117, 145–158, 449–450.

Abu an-Nasr, J.M. *A History of the Maghrib in the Islamic Period*. Cambridge, 1987, 90.

Ammâr at-Talibi, "Ibn Tumart." *Mawsu'atu'l-hadareti'l-Islamiyya*. Amman, 1993.

Aytekin, A. "Ibn Tûmert." *Islâm Ansiklopedisi* Istanbul, 1999, XX.

Basset, R. "Ibn Tumert." *IA* Vol. 2, s. 831–833.

Cornell, V.J. "Understanding is the Mother of Ability: Responsibility and Action in the Doctrine of ibn Tumart." *Sudia Islamica* Paris LXVI, (1987): 71–103.

Ibnu'l-Athir. *al-KAmil fi't-tAriò*. Edited by C.J. Tornberg. Leiden, 1851–1876/Beyrouth, 1979, X, 569–578.

Ibn Khaldun, *al-IIbar wa diwanu'l-mubtada' wa'l-khabar*. Vols. I–VII. Bulaq, 1284/1979, VI, 225–229.

Ibn Khallikan, *Wafayatu'l-Ayan wa abna'u abna'i'z-zaman*. Edited by I. Abbas. Vols. I–VIII/Beyrouth, 1968–1972.

Salinger, G. "A Christian Muhammad Legend and a Muslim ibn Tumart Legend in the 13th Century." In *Zeitschrift der Deutschen Morgenlandichen Gesellchaft*. Leibzig/Wiesbaden 1967, CXVII, 318–328.

SelAwi. *al-lstiqsa li akhbari'd-duwali'l-maaribi'l-aqsA*. Edited by C. an-Nasiri-M. An-Nasiri. Vols I–IX. Daru'l-Beyza, 1954–1956.

Ebû Bekir b. Ali es-Sanhaci. *Akhbâru'l-Mahdi b. Tumart wa bidAyatu dawlati'l-Muwahhidin*. Rabat, 1971.

IBN WASIL, MUHAMMAD B. SALIM JAMAL AL-DIN

Ibn Wasil (1208–1298) was a Syrian scholar most renowned for his chronicle *Mufarrij al-kurub fi akhbar bani Ayyub (The Dissipater of Anxieties on the Reports of the Ayyubids)*, which covers, in detail, historical events of the twelfth and the first half of the thirteenth century. This work has drawn modern interest because it presents succinctly the main Crusading campaigns from a Middle Eastern point of view. Although Ibn Wasil relied on an array of earlier sources for the earlier parts of his work, some of which has been lost since then, he based his account of thirteenth-century events (such as the Crusade of Louis IX, King of France, to Egypt in 1249–1250) on eyewitnesses or his own experiences.

Ibn Wasil was well placed to observe the political developments and military events in the Middle East during his lifetime, as he was widely traveled and closely linked to the ruling echelons of society. Originating from Hama in northern Syria, he visited or dwelled in the main urban centers such as Baghdad, Cairo, and Damascus. Although descending from a family of relatively low prominence, he forged close relationships with prominent administrators and military commanders, as well as with Ayyubid and Mamluk rulers. In his sixties he returned to his hometown, where he led a low-profile life as the town's chief judge.

His educational and professional specialization was law, but no writings of his in this field are traceable. Rather, his extant oeuvre focuses on history, poetry, logic, and astronomy, all of which were of profit to him at various courts. For example, in 1261, while staying in southern Italy at the court of Manfred, the Staufer ruler of Sicily and son of Frederick II, as ambassador of the Mamluk ruler Baybars I, his knowledge of logic gained him the ruler's praise. It is the immersion into these fields of knowledge that allowed him throughout his life close contacts with non-Muslim scholars. Consequently, one finds in his aforementioned chronicle passages where he discusses, for example, the conflict between the emperor and the papacy in thirteenth-century Europe, which is rarely found in other medieval chronicles by Muslim authors.

Ibn Wasil's chronicle did not enjoy wider popularity in the following centuries and was only "rediscovered" in the late nineteenth century with the rising interest in Crusading history.

KONRAD HIRSCHLER

See also Historical Writing

Primary Sources

Ibn Wasil. *Mufarrij al-kurub fi akhbar bani Ayyub.* 5 vols. Edited by J. al-Shayyal, H. al-Rabi', and S. 'Ashur. Cairo, 1953 (final sixth volume not published yet).
Short extracts of Ibn Wasil's chronicle are translated in *Arab Historians of the Crusades. Selected and Translated from the Arabic Sources.* Edited by Francesco Gabrieli. Translated from the Italian by E.J. Costello. New York: Dorset Press, 1989.

Further Reading

Hillenbrand, Carole. *The Crusades. Islamic Perspectives.* New York: Routledge, 1999.
Robinson, Chase F. *Islamic Historiography.* Cambridge: Cambridge University Press, 2003.
el-Shayyal, Gamal el-Din. "Ibn Wasil." In *Encyclopaedia of Islam. New Ed.* 11 vols. Prepared by a number of leading orientalists. Leiden: Brill, 1960–2002.

IBN YÛNUS, 'ALÎ IBN 'ABD AL-RAHMÂN, D. FUSTAT, EGYPT

Ibn Yûnus was the leading astronomer of medieval Egypt and perhaps the most important of the entire Muslim world. He was a careful observer, a highly competent mathematician and calculator, and proposed much that was original. He was also the principal initiator of a tradition of astronomical time-keeping (*'ilm al-mîqât*) in Islamic society, which is of prime importance because it included the regulation of the times of prayer. He compiled a monumental *zîj*, or astronomical handbook with tables, some four times the size of that of his predecessor al-Battânî

(q.v.). This was called *al-Zîj al-Hâkimî* because it was dedicated to the Fatimid ruler al-Hâkim (q.v.). One of its most remarkable features is a record of more than one hundred observations of planetary conjunctions and solar and lunar eclipses, made by his predecessors in ninth- and tenth-century Baghdad and by himself. His solar, lunar, and planetary tables were much appreciated in later Egypt and the Yemen, but some of them were also adopted in a modified form in Iran. It was Ibn Yûnus who compiled the first batch of the tables for timekeeping by the sun and regulating the times of Muslim prayer that later became part of the Cairo corpus of nearly two hundred pages of tables. These tables were used there until the nineteenth century. The medieval tables of this kind for such centers of astronomical activity as Damascus, Jerusalem, Aleppo, Istanbul, Tunis, and Taiz were inspired by the Cairo corpus.

DAVID A. KING

See also Astronomy

Further Reading

Caussin de Perceval, A.P. Le livre de la grande table Hakémite. *Notices et extraits des manuscrits de la Bibliothèque nationale* 7 (An XII [=1804]), 16–240, with separate pagination in the separatum. [Contains the observation reports.]
King, David A. *The Astronomical Works of Ibn Yûnus.* Doctoral dissertation. Yale University, 1972. [Deals only with spherical astronomy.]
———. "Ibn Yûnus.: In *Dictionary of Scientific Biography.* Vol XIV. New York: Charles Scribner's Sons, 1976, 574–580.
———. *In Synchrony with the Heavens....* Vol. 1: *The Call of the Muezzin....* Leiden: Brill, 2004. [Detailed discussion of the Cairo corpus.]

IBN ZUR'A, ABU 'ALI 'ISA ISHAQ

The philosopher Ibn Zur'a (AH 331–398/943–1008 CE) was born and died in Baghdad. Shortly after his death, the dominance of the Baghdad school of philosophy, with its close adherence to the Platonizing commentary tradition and involvement in translation, yielded to other centers of power and learning. Typical for the Baghdad school, Ibn Zur'a was a Jacobite (Syrian Orthodox) Christian who associated on equal terms with Muslim and Jewish intellectuals.

Ibn Zur'a's character and way of life can be seen from three viewpoints. Most significantly, there are contemporary references in his eight short treatises of Christian apologetics. Second, Ibn Zur'a was known to the writer Abu Hayyan at-Tawhidi, whose books record discussions that took place, often under the patronage of powerful Buyid viziers. Finally, the medical biographer Ibn Abi Usaybi'a gives "case notes" regarding the treatment of Ibn Zur'a's last illness, including mention of aspects of the philospher's apparently stressful lifestyle.

Ibn Zur'a earned his living as a merchant, and traded with Byzantium. As a philosopher he was the devoted pupil and close friend of the leading logician Yahya ibn 'Adi (d. 974 CE). The Ibn 'Adi circle, including Ibn al-Khammar, Ibn al-Samh, Miskawayh, and 'Isa ibn 'Ali, attended the salons *(majalis)* of the vizier and patron Ibn Sa'dan. Abu Hayyan was also there, although he was scornful of Ibn Zur'a's "vaunting of Aristotle, Plato, Socrates and Hippocrates."

We know from bibliographies, such as those of Ibn Zur'a's associate Ibn an-Nadim, of works such as *On the Intellect, On the Reason for the Luminosity of the Planets,* and *On the Immortality of the Soul.* These did not survive, although a short *Defense of Logicians and Philosophers against the Charge of Irreligion* is known. To later generations of Arab philosophers, Ibn Zur'a was probably best known as a translator. Ibn Sina (Avicenna) used Ibn Zur'a's translation of Aristotle's *Sophistici elenchi,* and Ibn Rushd may have used his translation of the *Compendia of Nicolaus of Damascus.* Among other translations, it is notable that part of a lost commentary by John Philoponus on Galen's *On the Uses of the Parts of the Body* appears to survive in Ibn Zur'a's version. Ibn Zur'a translated from Syriac into Arabic, and he probably did not know Greek. The importance of Syriac in the transmission of Greek philosophy to the Arabs is well known. Ibn Zur'a played a role in making philosophy available to a wider audience, which demanded introductions and translations in idiomatic Arabic. Some of Ibn Zur'a's introductions to Aristotle's logic have been published.

In 979 CE, Ibn Zur'a saw his late teacher, Yahya ibn 'Adi, in a dream commanding him to write a treatise solving a problem with Ibn 'Adi's definition of God the Father as intellect *('aql).* Ibn Zur'a was then asked to write an account of this vision by an unnamed "lord and brother." This work, *On the Composite Intellect,* is the earliest of his dated treatises of Christian apologetics, which were generally not written for philosophers but at the request of a friend or in response to an opponent. At least twice the request for treatises came from Muslim friends, and often, addressees were high-ranking. One treatise is a refutation of the rationalist theologian *(mutakallim)* Abu 'l-Qasim al-Balkhi. The letter to Bishr ibn Finhas, written to a Jewish friend, is typical of the way Ibn Zur'a combines rationalistic arguments with references to contemporary debates in these apologetic treatises. The work begins by setting out three different categories of law before concluding that the

Mosaic law has been superseded. Then Ibn Zur'a describes Plato's tripartite division of the soul and argues that only Christianity teaches the virtues of the rational faculty to the highest degree. Ibn Zur'a sets out the definition of the Trinity as Intellect, Active Intellect, and the Intellected *('aql, 'aqil, ma'qul),* which he learned from Ibn 'Adi. In addition to such arguments, Ibn Zur'a includes a discussion of proof texts, referring in passing to a group of Jews who expected the Messiah in 970–971 CE. At the end of the treatise Ibn Zur'a gives an account of two problems concerning the resurrection, which he discussed with Jews.

The account we have of Ibn Zur'a's death is tragic. One of the physicians who treated him relates that business opponents from the Syriac community "took him many times to the ruler, money was confiscated, and he was overtaken by many disasters." The physician adds that other reasons for Ibn Zur'a's collapse were his hot temperament, and the pressure of writing a treatise on the immortality of the soul.

PETER STARR

See also Abu Hayyan al-Tawhidi; Buyids; Ibn Rushd, or Averroes; Ibn Sina, or Avicenna

Primary Sources

Gihami, Gérard, and Rafiq al-'Ajam (Eds). *Mantiq Ibn Zur'a.* Beirut: Dar al-Fikr al-Lubnani, 1994.
Rescher, Nicolas (Ed). "A Tenth-Century Arab-Christian Apologia for Logic." In *Islamic Studies.* Vol. 2. Islamabad: Islamic Reseach Institute, 1963. The translation was republished in Nicolas Rescher, *Studies in Arabic Philosophy.* Pittsburgh: University of Pittsburgh Press, 1967.
Sbath, Paul (Ed). *Vingt traités philosophiques et apologétiques d'auteurs arabes chrétiens du IXe au XIVe siècle.* Cairo: Friedrich and Co., 1929.

Further Reading

Haddad, Cyrille. *'Isa ibn Zur'a, philosophe arabe et apologiste chrétien.* Beirut: Dar al-Kalima, 1971.
Kraemer, Joel L. *Philosophy in the Renaissance of Islam.* Leiden: Brill, 1986.
Pines, Shlomo. "La Loi naturelle et la société: La doctrine politico-théologique d'Ibn Zur'a, philosophe chrétien de Baghdad." In *Studies in Islamic History and Civilization,* edited by U. Heyd. Jerusalem: Magnes Press, 1961.
Starr, Peter. "The Epistle to Bishr ibn Finhas." Ph.D. dissertation. United Kingdom: University of Cambridge, 2000.

IDOLATRY

In the tradition of Middle Eastern monotheism, idolatry (literally, the worship of an image of a false god) is one of the greatest sins. Only God may be an object of worship, and some versions of monotheism prohibit any representation, even of God, for a number of reasons, including the fear that the representation will become an object of worship in itself. In religious contexts Muslims, like Jews, have tended to reject the figural representation of God or of any moving being, and some Muslims have extended that rejection more widely.

Although there are words and expressions in Arabic that are semantically equivalent to the English "idolatry," in premodern Islamic culture the concept was more frequently conveyed by *shirk*, a word that at a basic level gives the idea of sharing or associating with something. *Shirk* comes to denote idolatry because it refers to the sin of associating with God, as worthy of worship, other beings or things—divine, human, or superhuman. Although frequently translated as "idolatry" because it is not semantically equivalent to that word, *shirk* may also be rendered by related concepts such as "polytheism" (the recognition of a plurality of gods).

Both idolatry and polytheism are frequently relative and subjective accusations, denied by those accused of them. They are frequently words used in a polemical way to attack opponents. Nobody is likely to refer to his own religion as a form of idolatry, and the distinction between monotheism and polytheism is often in the eye of the beholder. From an Islamic perspective, traditional African religion or Hinduism, for example, might be described as *shirk* with some degree of objectivity, but just as often Muslims have applied the word to other forms of monotheism (notably Christianity) and to other Muslims, accused of failing to respect the unity and uniqueness of God *(tawhid*, requiring on the part of the believer an attitude of complete devotion, *ikhlas)*.

In the AH first/seventh CE century, some of his opponents are reported to have accused the caliph 'Ali of *shirk* when he agreed to put his dispute with Mu'awiya to human arbiters. They claimed that in doing so he was giving mere humans a share in a decision that should have been left to God, an idea expressed in the slogan of the Kharijite movement, "judgment belongs to God alone" *(la hukma illa lillah)*. In the third/ninth century the rationalist Mu'tazili theologians accused their traditionalist opponents of *shirk* for insisting that God's attributes, such as speech, were real and eternal while distinct from the divine essence. In the Muslim west in the fifth/eleventh century the Mu'tazili critique was echoed by the Almohad followers of Ibn Tumart in their attacks on the scholars of the Maliki school of Islam. The accusation has frequently been a part of the arguments between Sufis and their legalist Muslim opponents. Some Sufis are reported as having qualms about reciting the second part of the Muslim credal formula ("there is no god but God, and Muhammad is the Messenger of God") since, they said, by including the Prophet alongside God they were in danger of lapsing into *shirk*.

Another group prone to accuse its Muslim opponents (Sunni and Shi'i) of *shirk* are the neo-Hanbali followers of Ibn Taymiyya, especially the Wahhabis whose school of Islam is the official one of Saudi Arabia. Prominent among what the Wahhabis identify as the errors of other Muslims that reduce them, in effect, to the status of idolaters is their excessive veneration of other human beings (holy men, scholars, Imams, and even the Prophet Muhammad himself). According to the Wahhabis, their veneration, often associated with visits to and prayers at their tombs, necessarily detracted from the veneration and worship of God.

In the Qur'an, there are numerous accusations of *shirk* against opponents whose identity is often not clear. Generally the relevant passages of the Qur'an give the impression that those opponents had an understanding that God (Allah) is the creator and controller of the universe, but in their day-to-day life they took little account of that fact and instead devoted their worship to those whom they "associated" with God.

In traditional accounts of the setting within which the Qur'an was revealed, those opponents are identified as pagan Arabs, in Mecca and elsewhere in Arabia. They were idolaters in a literal sense: people who believed in a multiplicity of gods and worshiped them in the form of representations made out of wood or stone, or as trees, rocks, and other such natural features. Commentaries on the Qur'an, lives of Muhammad, and other types of traditional literature provide us with a relative wealth of detail about this pre-Islamic Arab idolatry—the names of sanctuaries and idols, tribes and families associated with them, geographical locations, stories about the destruction of sanctuaries and idols with the coming of Islam, and other such details. Individual works, such as the *Book of Idols* of Ibn Kalbi (d. 206/820), were devoted to accounts of that idolatry.

According to the tradition the idolatry of the Arabs had come about by the gradual corruption of the pure monotheistic religion that at one time had been brought to Arabia by Abraham (Ibrahim), the father of monotheism. He had built the Ka'ba in Mecca on God's command and established the worship of the one true God there. For some generations the Arabs followed that true monotheism but then gradually fell away from it—partly as a result of human error, partly of satanic intervention. By the time of Muhammad they had lapsed into a gross idolatry. It was Muhammad's task to rescue them from their corrupt religion and restore them to the pure Abrahamic monotheism identical with Islam.

Most academic scholarship has accepted the image of Arab idolatry that the tradition conveys and agreed that the Qur'anic attacks on *shirk* were directed against the idolatrous Arabs. In place of the account of the corruption of Abrahamic religion in Arabia, many academic scholars have substituted an evolutionary theory of Arab religion to explain the mixture of polytheism and monotheism that the Qur'an and the traditional literature, in different ways, attribute to the Arab contemporaries of Muhammad. According to that theory, the Arabs were evolving out of their ancestral paganism into a monotheistic stage of religion but were still in a process of transition. The coming of Islam marked the completion of the process. It was because of its origins in such a milieu that Islam has constantly been so concerned with the dangers of idolatry and the need to stress absolute monotheism.

However, the author of this entry questions the traditional accounts of pre-Islamic Arab idolatry and the academic. The author regards it as likely that the Qur'an's accusation of *shirk* against its opponents is part of a polemic against other monotheists, and not directed at people who were idolaters in any literal sense. The author suggests that Islam's recurrent concern with the problem of *shirk* reflects the tendency within monotheism to extend the notion of idolatry to the critique of monotheist opponents.

GERALD R. HAWTING

Primary Sources

Ibn al-Kalbi. *Kitab Al-Asnam (The Book of Idols)*. English translation by N.A. Faris, Princeton: Princeton University Press, 1952.

Ibn Hisham, *Sira*. English translation by A. Guillaume, *The Life of Muhammad. A Translation of Ibn Ishaq's Sirat Rasul Allah*, Oxford: Oxford University Press, 1955.

Further Reading

Halbertal, Moshe, and Avishai Marghalit. *Idolatry*. English translation. Cambridge, MA, and London: Harvard University Press, 1992

Hawting, G.R. *The Idea of Idolatry and the Emergence of Islam. From Polemic to History*. Cambridge: Cambridge University Press, 1999.

Nöldeke, Theodor. "Arabs (Ancient)." in *Encyclopaedia of Religion and Ethics*, edited by James Hastings, 13 vols. Edinburgh, 1908–1926.

Wellhausen, Julius. *Reste arabischen Heidentums*. 2d ed. Berlin: Georg Reimer, 1897.

IDRISI

Abu 'Abd Allah Muhammad ibn Muhammad ibn 'Abd Allah ibn Idris al-'Ala bi-Amr Allah (ca. AH 493–560/1100–1165 CE) was the greatest medieval

geographer. As a descendant of the Prophet Muhammad, this Muslim Arab scholar was titled al-Sharif al-Idrisi, but in the West he was known for a long time as *Geographus Nubiensis*, the Nubian Geographer. Born in Morocco and educated in Cordoba, he worked in Palermo at the court of the Norman king Roger II. The most important book he produced is a world geography in 1154, *Nuzhat al-mushtaq fi ikhtiraq al-afaq (Entertainment for One Desiring to Travel Far)*; it is also called *Kitab Rujjar (Book of Roger)*. He later wrote a shorter geography, known under a variety of Arabic titles and usually referred to as "The Little Idrisi." Both are extensively illustrated with maps; the maps in *Nuzhat al-mushtaq* are oriented to the South, the maps in the latter book are smaller and often oriented to the east.

Al-Idrisi traveled in Asia Minor, Europe, and North Africa, and in Sicily he was able to consult both European and Islamic sources procured from books and travel reports. Thus his *Geography* is a synthesis of information and cartographic traditions from both Islamic and European cultures; it is unsurpassed in narrative geography and maps of the Middle Ages. Because the work is a compilation and the data occasionally anachronistic, al-Idrisi's work sometimes has been judged unoriginal. However, he introduced a new type of map that strongly impacted later cosmographers and thinkers, such as Ibn Khaldun, and used a projection that remains unexplained. Al-Idrisi produced more regional maps of the world than any other medieval cartographer, and his description of certain regions, such as the Balkans or northern Europe, is remarkably precise. The parts dealing with Africa remained an important source for Islamic and European cosmographers into the seventeenth century. Al-Idrisi's distinctive cartography and narrative method make it possible to identify later imitations as works in "The Idrisi School." Medieval European Mediterranean cartographers may have had some knowledge of his maps. The book *Nuzhat al-mushtaq* became the first secular Arabic work printed in Europe (Rome, 1592); a Latin translation was published in Paris in 1619.

Al-Idrisi credited his patron Roger with the construction of a large world map, but the work was done by al-Idrisi. The text is a detailed description of the map, engraved on a silver disk and based on the Arabic version of Marinus's map reportedly created under the caliph al-Ma'mun (813–833). The silver prototype was lost, but the book contains a round, schematic map of the world and seventy rectangular maps of the seventy parts into which al-Idrisi had divided the world. Ten manuscripts of

Nuzhat al-mushtaq survive, eight of them with maps; there is no complete good translation.

The system developed by al-Idrisi used the Ptolemaic foundation adopted by the early Islamic scholars, whereby the round earth is divided into quarters and only the Inhabited Quarter is described. It is astronomically divided into seven latitudinal belts ("climates"), leaving off the extreme north and equatorial south. Although familiar with coordinates, al-Idrisi did not use them; in addition to the parallel boundaries of the climates, he introduced, instead of meridians, ten longitudinal divisions. Thus the map and the narrative became divided into seventy sections. The numbering of climates is from south to north, the numbers of sections go west to east, again showing Greek influence. The text follows this arrangement after a brief general introduction, describing important geographical features of each section: cities, mountains, rivers, seas, islands, and so on, progressing eastward. Al-Idrisi names the most toponyms since Ptolemy, expanding and updating the medieval Arabic geographical inventory. He is academically unbiased, and all locations get more or less equal attention; he describes many identifiable

locations for the first time in the geographical literature. Only ten of al-Idrisi's sources are named, and contemporary information gets indiscriminately mixed with data compiled from the Greek, Latin, and earlier Islamic sources.

The narrative follows itineraries, connected by travel distances expressed in miles *(mil)*, units *(farsakh)* (three miles), caravan stages *(marhala)*, day marches, or days of sailing. The earth is depicted as surrounded by the Encircling Sea, *al-Bahr al-Muhit* (the Greek Ocean). Africa is extended eastward to form the southern coast of the Indian ocean, which, however, remains open in the Far East. The southern limit of the inhabited world is north of the equator in *Nuzhat al-mushtaq*, but south of the equator in The Little Idrisi. The southern portion of the round world map is filled with the African landmass, not shown on sectional maps. The western limit is the prime meridian drawn through the westernmost part of Africa, but the Fortunate Isles in the Atlantic are included. The easternmost country is *Sila* (Korea), supposedly at 180°E. The northern limit is at the Polar Circle (64°N.). The color-coded maps demonstrate a thoughtful and somewhat artistic approach, but

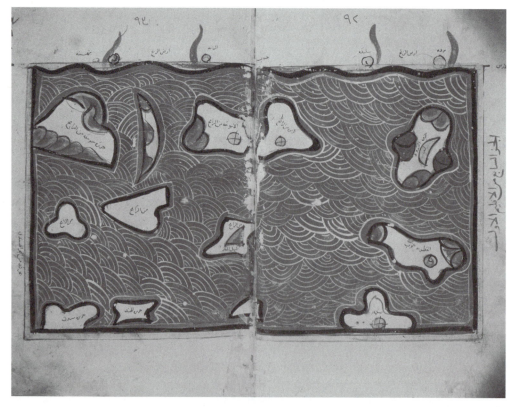

Al-Idrisi (twelfth century). Geographic Atlas of the Indian Ocean. Eleventh to twelfth century. Credit: Bridgeman-Giraudon/ Art Resource, NY. National Library (Dar-al-Kutub), Cairo, Egypt.

neither the degrees nor itineraries are drawn on them, and their practical value is doubtful. A pieced-together Latin version of this map was produced in Paris by Petrus Bertius in the 1620s.

MARINA A. TOLMACHEVA

Primary Sources

Al-Idrisi, Abu 'Abdallah Muhammad. *Opus geographicum; sive, "Liber ad eorum delectationem qui terras peragrare studeant."* 9 vols. Edited by Enrico Cerulli a.o. Naples: Istituto Universitario Orientale di Napoli and Rome: Istituto Italiano per il Medio ed Estremo Oriente, 1970–1984.
———. *Uns al-muhaj wa-rawd al-furaj.* Edited by Fuat Sezgin. Frankfurt: Institut für Geschichte der arabisch-islamischen Wissenschaften, 1984.
Al-Idrisi, al-Sharif. *Kitab nuzhat al-mushtaq.* Reprint of the 1592 Rome edition. Frankfurt: Institut für Geschichte der arabisch-islamischen Wissenschaften, 1992.
Miller, Konrad. *Mappae Arabicae. Arabische Welt- und Landkarten* 6 vols. Stuttgart: Miller, 1926–1927, vol. I, part 2 and vol. VI. Reprint: Frankfurt: Institut für Geschichte der arabisch-islamischen Wissenschaften, 1994.

Further Reading

Ahmad, S. Maqbul. "Cartography of al-Sharif al-Idrisi." In *The History of Cartography*, vol. 2, book 1: *Cartography in the Traditional Islamic and South Asian Societies*, edited by J.B. Harley and David Woodward, 156–174. Chicago: University of Chicago Press, 1992.
Drecoll, Carsten. *Idrisí aus Sizilien: der Einfluss einers arabischen Wissenschaftlers auf die Entwicklung der europäischen Geographie.* Egelsbach; New York: Hänsel-Hohenhausen, 2000.
Khuri, Ibrahim. *Al-Sharif al-Idrisi: Nuzhat al-mushtaq fi ikhtiraq al-afaq.* Al-'Ayn: Markaz Zaydi lil-Turath wa-al-Ta'rikh, 2000.
Tolmacheva, Marina. "The Medieval Arabic Geographers and the Beginnings of Modern Orientalism." *International Journal of Middle East Studies* 27/2 (1995): 141–156.
———. "Bertius and al-Idrisi: An Experiment in Orientalist Cartography." *Terrae Incognitae* 28 (1996): 49–59.
Vernay-Nouri, Annie, Aleksandra Sarrabezolles, and Jean-Paul Saint-Aubin. *La géographie d'Idrisi: un atlas du monde au XIIe siècle.* CD-ROM. Paris: Bibliothèque nationale de France; Montparnasse multimédia, 2000.

IDRISIDS

The Idrisids, a local dynasty of Arab origin, emerged out of the shifting Berber tribal groupings of Islamic northwestern Africa *(al-Maghrib)* in the late eighth century CE. Surviving, often tenuously for some two centuries, the dynasty is notable for having founded the city of Fez *(Fas)*, which was their capital, and for establishing Arabo-Islamic religious and political culture in this area.

In 789, the leader of a powerful Berber tribal group, the Awraba, determined to politically and religiously legitimize his dominion, invited a local *sharif*, Idris ibn 'Abd Allah, a descendant of 'Ali b. Abu Talib, to serve as the regime's *imam*, or spiritual leader. After *imam* Idris was assassinated in 791, a period of political unrest followed, after which one of his young sons was named *imam* as Idris II (808–828). Idris II gained the political initiative from his Berber sponsors in 809 by founding a new capital city, Fez, and inviting Arabs from al-Andalus and the Aghlabid territories to settle there. Fez soon became the capital of the most powerful and dynamic state in the Maghrib, Idrisid power having expanded to include most of modern Morocco. Idris II was succeeded by his brother Muhammad (828–836), who passed the throne on to his son 'Ali (836–859), who was then followed by his brother Yahya (859–863). This was the period of greatest stability for the Idrisids, and Fez continued to be a favored destination of refugees and immigrants from al-Andalus and Ifriqiyya.

The reign of the weak Yahya II (863–866) ushered in the decline of the dynasty, which was beset by internal rivalries and degenerated into a state of civil war. This was aggravated in the early tenth century by the rise of the Fatimids, who made them tributaries in 917. Eventually expelled from their capital by Miknasa Berbers, the Idrisids were driven into an alliance with the Umayyads of Cordoba, who allowed the dynasty to reconstitute itself, this time in the RÔf mountains in the 930s, where their capital was the fortress of Hajar al-Nasr. For the following half century the Idrisids survived in semiautonomy by playing off the Umayyads and Fatimids, all the while beset by a host of tribal enemies. Following a defeat of the Umayyads in 958, the family recognized the authority of the Fatimids. In 972, the Umayyads rallied, defeated the Fatimid forces, and took members of the Idrisid family as prisoners to Cordoba, formally deposing al-Hasan b. al-Qasim Gannun in 974. Eventually al-Hasan made his way to Egypt and was reinstalled by the Fatimids in 985. That same year, al-Mansur, ruler of Umayyad al-Andalus, dispatched an army to depose al-Hasan, who was taken prisoner and executed.

Fez is the Idrisid's greatest legacy. The two great mosques, al-Qarawiyyin and al-Andalusiyyin, founded by refugees from Tunisia and al-Andalus, became centers of a vibrant religious culture, further stimulated by the dynasty's connection to the family of 'Ali. The city remained the cultural capital of the Maghrib until the dawn of the colonial period.

BRIAN A. CATLOS

Further Reading

Cressier, Patrice. "Hagar al-Nasr, capitale idreisside du Maroc septentrional: archéologie et historiore (IVe H./Xe ap. J.C.)."In *Genèse de la villa islamique en al-Andalus et au Mghreb occidental*, edited by P. Cressier and M. García-Arenal, 305–334. Madrid: Casa de Velázques, 1998.

Manzano Moreno, Eduardo and Mercedes García-Arenal. "Légitimité et villes idrissides." In *Genèse de la villa islamique en al-Andalus et au Mghreb occidental*, edited by P. Cressier and M. García-Arenal, 257–284. Madrid: Casa de Velázques, 1998.

Taha, 'Abdulwahid Dhan n. The Muslim Conquest and Settlement of North Africa and Spain. London: Routledge, 1989.

IKHSHIDIDS

The Ikhshidids were a short-lived Turkish dynasty that ruled Egypt and Syria from 935 to 966. The dynasty originally claimed power as the representatives of the 'Abbasid caliph, much like the Tulunids before them. However, with the occupation of Baghdad by the Shi'i Buyids in 945, they styled themselves as independent Sunni rulers.

The founder of this dynasty, Muhammad b. Tughj b. Juff al-Ikhshid, belonged to a military family that served the caliphal government over three generations and was sometimes embroiled in its internecine conflicts. Muhammad grew up in Tulunid Syria and was briefly jailed, along with his father and brother, after the 'Abbasid reconquest. He later received appointment as governor of Egypt. After turning back a Fatimid invasion at Alexandria in 936, he repelled the forces of the 'Abbasids' chief general *(amir l-umara)*, Ibn Ra'iq, in Syria, who wished to check his growing power.

The caliph al-Radi invested Muhammad with the title of al-Ikhshid at the latter's request in 939. This marked a significant concession by the caliph. The title derives from a word for king or ruler in Old Persian and was originally claimed by pre-Islamic rulers of Soghdia and Ferghana.

Muhammad's success relied on his military prowess and practical nature. In addition to the Fatimids and Ibn Ra'iq, he defeated the Hamdanids in Syria in 942 and 945. He did not, however, exploit these victories to his full advantage. He preferred to negotiate settlements in their aftermath to secure the peace.

Political interests tempered Muhammad's profession of support for the 'Abbasids. During his conflict with Ibn Ra'iq, he considered recognizing the Fatimid imam in the Friday prayer and marrying his daughter to the imam's son. Although he offered sanctuary to the caliph al-Muttaqi in 944, he presumably intended to use his presence to bolster his legitimacy. The caliph declined his invitation.

Muhammad sought to ensure the succession of his family, which proved a difficult task. His authority rested on his personal prestige. He and his family did not have an ethnic or religious following. The deterioration of 'Abbasid fortunes, however, aided his plans. During a campaign to Damascus in 942, he had his troops swear fealty to his son Abu 'l-Qasim Unujur. In 944, he secured a thirty-year claim to govern Egypt and Syria from the caliph al-Muttaqqi for himself and his descendants while this caliph fended off dire threats from the East.

Although succeeded by his son Unujur, Muhammad's principal military commander and black eunuch, Kafur, assumed effective control after his death in 946. Kafur had been purchased from Nubia and enjoyed Muhammad's confidence. He participated in important military engagements such as the campaign against the Hamdanids in 945. He was also entrusted with the education of Muhammad's two sons.

Kafur earned distinction as a capable chief minister and later ruler in his own right despite facing numerous crises. He guaranteed the succession of Unujur in 946 and 'Ali in 961. He finally declared himself ruler upon 'Ali's death in 966. 'Ali's son Ahmad was a minor and therefore ineligible to succeed. The 'Abbasid caliph granted Kafur a diploma of investiture, though he seems to have refrained from inscribing his name on his coinage. Kafur guided Egypt and Syria through recurrent famine, a destructive fire in Fustat, and an earthquake, in addition to revolts and external military threats from the Fatimids and Hamdanids. He built palaces, mosques, a hospital, and the capital's Kafuriyya gardens, but no trace of these monuments survives.

The Ikhshidids presented a Sunni bulwark against a rising tide of Shi'i domination in the Near East. The occupation of Baghdad by the Buyids in 945 left them as nearly the only significant Sunni power. Their demise allowed the Fatimids to conquer Egypt and Syria.

STUART D. SEARS

Primary Sources

Ibn Sa'îd al-Andalusî. *Kitâb al-Mughrib fî iulâ al-Maghrib.* Edited by K. L. Tallquist. Leiden, 1899.

Ibn al-'Adîm. *Zubdat al-ialab min târîkh Ìalab.* Edited by Sâmî Dahhân. Damascus, 1951.

Taghrîbirdî. *al-Nujûm al-œâhira fî mulûk Miœr wa-l-Qâhira.* Cairo, Dâr al-Kutub, n.d.

Further Reading

Bacharach, Jere L. Tughj. "The Career of al-Ikhshîd, a Tenth Century Governor of Egypt." *Speculum* 1 (1975), 86–612.

———. "Muìammad b. Tughj al-Ikhshîd." In *The Encyclopedia of Islam*. 2d ed,. vol. VII. Leiden: E.J. Brill, 1991, 411.

Ehrenkreutz, Andrew S. "Kâfûr." In *The Encyclopedia of Islam*. 2d ed, vol. IV. Leiden: E. J. Brill, 1974, 418–419.

Kâshif, S.I. *Miær fî 'aær al-Ikhshîdîyîn*. Cairo, 1970.

ILKHANIDS (1258–1335)

Bowing to the request and entreaties of an envoy from the northern Persian city of Qazvin, the Great Khan Möngke (1251–1259), grandson of Genghis Khan, assigned his brother, Hülegü Khan, to march westward toward the Islamic heartlands. The Iranian Qadi (chief justice) had been explicit in his audience with Möngke Khan. Mongol military rule in Iran was corrupt, brutal, and inefficient. The Assassins or Ismailis, considered heretics and terrorists by most Iranians, were undermining the social fabric of Persian society and terrorizing its citizens and indeed had probably even infiltrated the court of the Great Khan himself. The Iranians wanted the Great Khan to extend his justice and rule into the west and end the anarchy that prevailed there. When Möngke discovered that Ismaili assassins had indeed infiltrated his court, he instructed Hülegü to march on Iran, rid the country of the "heretical" Ismailis, seek the submission of the caliph of Baghdad, and extend the rule of his justice and glory from the banks of the Oxus to the sands of Egypt.

Hülegü razed Alamut, the headquarters of the Ismaili Assassins, to the ground in 1256. For Juwayni, the historian and Hülegü's governor of Baghdad, the annihilation of Alamut justified and explained God's purpose in sending the Mongols to the lands of Islam. In 1258, the caliph of Islam, heeding the self-serving intrigues at his court, foolishly rebuffed Hülegü's calls to peacefully submit and defied the gathering Mongol forces. Advised by his Muslim aides and assisted by local armies of Muslim, Armenian, Kurdish, and Turkish troops, Hülegü destroyed Baghdad, though many including Shi'is, clerics, and Christians were given safe conduct from the city. After the battle the caliph was executed, and it is probable that the libraries and treasures of the city found their way to the first Ilkhanid capital, Maragheh (Azerbaijan, northwestern Iran) where Hülegü built an observatory and university for his court favorite, Shaykh Nassir al-Din Tusi.

Both Hülegü (d. 1265) and his son, Abaqa (r. 1265–1282), the first Ilkhans of Iran, were renowned for their wisdom and justice, and Iran experienced for the first time in many decades a period of security, peace, and prosperity. Maragheh, and later Tabriz, became prosperous hubs of international commerce and cultural exchange. Italian traders, Armenian merchants, Uighur middlemen, Persian poets, Chinese astrologers, Arab mathematicians, and intellectuals, scientists, agronomists, and scholars from east and west mingled in the halls and chambers and crowded bazaars of the Ilkhanid capitals. The city–states of Yazd, Kirman, Shiraz, and Herat all pledged allegiance to the Ilkhan and thrived under Mongol rule.

Ghazan Khan (1295–1304) converted to Islam probably more from political astuteness than from conviction, and Islam became the official religion of the state. However, ties with the Yuan dynasty of China continued to strengthen in all spheres bolstered by the personal ties between the "renaissance men," Bolad Chinksank, a Mongol, and Rashid al-Dīn, the Persian wazir. Both Iran and China thrived economically, culturally, and socially under the relatively enlightened administration of their Mongol rulers and there was mutual benefit from the close ties they maintained. The Ilkhanate did not decline but simply disappeared. The last Ilkhan, Abu Sa'id (r. 1316–1335), died without an heir, and it was at its peak that the Ilkhanate ceased. In its wake it left a state roughly corresponding to the modern state of Iran, and its legacy was a rebirth of the Iranian sense of statehood and national identity.

GEORGE LANE

See also Assassins; Ismailis

Further Reading

Allsen, Thomas. *Mongol Imperialism: The Policies of the Grand Qan Mongke 1251–1259*. Los Angeles: University of California Press, 1987.

———. "Mongolian Princes and Their Merchant Partners 1200–1260." *Asia Major*. 3rd series. Vol. II. Part 2. Princeton, NJ: Princeton University Press, 1989.

———. *Commodity and Exchange in the Mongol Empire. A Cultural History of Islamic Textiles*. Cambridge, UK: Cambridge University Press, 1997.

———. *Culture and Conquest in Mongol Eurasia*. Cambridge, UK: Cambridge University Press, 2001.

Amitai-Preiss, R. *Mongols and Mamluks*. CUP, 1995

———. "The Conversion of Tegüder Ilkhan to Islam." *Jerusalem Studies in Arabic and Islam* 25 (2001): 15–43.

———. "Sufis and Shamans: Some Remarks on the Islamisation of the Mongols of the Ilkhanate." *JESHO* 17, no. 1, 1999.

Browne, E.G. *Literary History of Persia*. Vol. III. New Delhi: Munshiram Manoharlal, 1997.

Komaroff, Linda, and Stefano Carboni (Eds). *The Legacy of Genghis Khan: Courtly Art and Culture in Western Asia 1256–1353*. New York: Metropolitan Museum of Art.,2002.

Lambton, A.K.S. *Continuity and Change in Medieval Persia. Aspects of Administrative,Economic, Social History in 11th–14th Century Persia*. London: I. B. Taurus. 1988.

Lane, George, *Early Mongol Rule in 13th Century Iran*. London: RoutledgeCurzon, 2003.

———. *Genghis Khan and Mongol Rule*. Westport, CT: Greenwood Press, 2004.

———. *Daily Life in the Mongol Empire*. Westport, CT: Greenwood Press, 2005. [forthcoming]

———. "Arghun Aqa: Mongol Bureaucrat?" *Iranian Studies* 32, no.4, 2000.

———. "An Account of Bar Hebraeus Abu al-Faraj and His Relations with the Mongols of Persia." *Hugoye: Journal of Syriac Studies* 2, no. 2, July 1999.

Lewis, Bernard. *The Assassins. A Radical Sect in Islam*. New York: Oxford University Press, 1968.

Lewis, Franklin. *Rumi: Past and Present, East and West*. Oxford: Oneworld, 2000.

Melville, Charles. "Padishah-i-Islam: The Conversion of Sultan Mahmud Ghazan Khan." *Pembroke Papers I*, 1990.

Morgan, David. *The Mongols*. Oxford: Blackwell, 1986.

———. *Medieval Persia, 1040–1797*. London and New York: Longman. 1988.

———. "Rashīd al-Dīn and Gazan Khan." *Bibliotheque Iranienne* 45, 1998.

Rashiduddin Fazlullah. *Jami'u't-Tawarikh: Compendium of Chronicles, a History of the Mongols*. Translated by Wheeler Thackston. 3 vols. Harvard University, 1999.

ILLUMINATIONISM

Derived from "illumination," a conventional translation of the Arabic term *ishraq* (lit. radiance, shining of the rising sun), "illuminationism" refers to the doctrine of the *Ishraqiyyun*, a school of philosophical and mystical thought of various Graeco-Oriental roots whose principles were propounded as an ancient "science of lights" (*'ilm al-anwar*) by Shihab al-Din Yaþya al-Suhrawardi in his *Kitab hikmat al-ishraq*, a fundamental work completed in AH 582/1186 CE. The author—not to be confused with the well-known Sufi Shaykh Shihab al-Dõn 'Umar al-Suhrawardi (d. 632/1234)—was an original thinker in the tradition of Avicenna and, like the latter, a prolific writer of Arabic and Persian philosophical treatises, as well as a number of tales of a more mystical and allusive nature. Born probably around 550/1155 in Suhraward, a village near Zanjan (Iranian Azerbayjan), he is said to have studied philosophy and Shafi'i law in Maragha, according to some accounts also in Isfahan. Some time later, he must have moved for an extended period within the upper Mesopotamian region of Mardin, Diyarbakir, and Kharput, where the Artuqid prince 'Imad al-Din Abu Bakr b. Qara Arslan (r. AH 581–600/1185–1204 CE) became his patron. It was to this 'Imad al-Din that he dedicated one of his characteristic writings, *Al-Alwah al-'Imadiyya*, a work of mixed philosophical and Sufi content ending up with a fervent glorification of the mythical Iranian kings Faridun and Kay Khusraw. He finally settled in Aleppo, where his ideas evidently met with the displeasure of the established religious authorities.

He was executed on charges of heresy in 587/1191 or thereabouts by order of the famous sultan Saladin (hence his byname *al-maqtul*, "executed one").

Skeptical of the formalized structures of Avicennian metaphysics and epistemology in which he himself had been raised, Suhrawardi made an attempt to work out an alternative approach to reality. Based on visionary experience and the recognition of a separate world of images, he envisioned a dynamic world of multiple irradiations originating with the distant "light of lights" (*nur al-anwar*, the *ishraqi* equivalent of the Avicennian "necessary of existence," that is, God) and falling in various ways and degrees of intensity on obscure matter. In technical language his approach came to be known later as the doctrine of the primary reality of quiddities (*asalat alm mahiyya*), as opposed to the primary reality of existence (*asalat al-wujud*). According to Suhrawardi, the human soul is a luminous substance, namely, the "regent light" (*al-nur al-mudabbir* or *al-nur al-isfahbud* in *ishraqi* terminology—perhaps a reminiscence of the Stoic *hegemonikon*), knows whatever it does really know through a direct encounter with the illumined object (*muqabalat al-mustanir*) rather than by way of abstraction in terms of Aristotelian species and genera. The discovery of this type of knowledge, called presential knowledge (*al-'ilm al-huduri*), is regarded as one of Suhrawardi's lasting contributions in the history of Islamic thought.

There can be no doubt that Suhrawardi was intimately familiar with Sufi traditions and spiritual practices such as *dhikr* (remembering or memorizing God) and *sama'* (listening to music), but he does not seem to have been part of the established Sufi organizations of his time, which generally rather enjoyed the favors of Saladin. In his "tales of initiation," the luminous guiding principle is frequently encountered as a cosmic Intellect, a figure of angelic or otherwise mythical qualities (such as the bird Simurgh), sometimes with the attributes of a Sufi Shaykh, or simply as the "Teacher." Suhrawardi makes it clear that he considered classical Sufi saints rather than the *falasifa* as the true philosophers of the present (Islamic) era, and also hints that the ancient wisdom had reached him through mysterious Sufi channels, but he associates his science of lights principally with the names of Plato, Hermes, Empedokles, Pythagoras, and the "Oriental principle (*qa'idat al-sharq*) concerning light and darkness" of the Sages of ancient Iran. In effect, he created a new school of Neoplatonic thought of a distinctly Iranian flavor, which to some extent paralleled earlier developments in Fatimid Ismaili thought. This, together with his ambiguous allusions to the "time deprived of divine administration," when the "powers of darkness take over" and the rightful "representative of God" (khalifat Allah) or "divinely inspired leader" (al-imam al-muta'allih) is hidden, may well have been enough to provoke his enemies among the 'ulama' and to eventually lead to his execution.

His ideas were nevertheless taken up and elaborated one or two generations later by philosophers such as Ibn Kamm.na (d. 683/1284), Shams al-Din Muhammad al-Shahrazuri (d. after 687/1288), and Qutb al-Din al-Shirazi (d. 710/1311 or 716/1316), and were at that time well-known among philosophical Sufis (such as 'Abd al-Razzaq al-Qashani, d. 736/1335) as a distinct *ishraqi* tradition. They continued to exercise considerable influence on later intellectual developments in Persia, especially in the philosophical schools of Shiraz (fifteenth and sixteenth centuries) and Isfahan (seventeenth century) with Mir Damad and Mulla Sadra. They were also influential in Moghul India (notably in mixed Sufi and Zoroastrian milieux at the court of the emperor Akbar) and in Ottoman Turkey, where they appear to have found their way into more orthodox Sufi circles (for example, Isma'il Ankaravi, d. 1041/1631). However, it should be noted that the occurrence of the term *ishraq* in Sufi texts does not necessarily indicate an influence of illuminationism as understood by Suhrawardi. The North African Sufi treatise titled *Qawanin hikam al-ishraq* by Abu l-Mawahib al-Tunisi al-Shadhili (d. 882/1477) and published in English as *Illumination in Islamic Mysticism* (translated by E.J. Jurji, Princeton, 1938) has little more in common with Suhrawardi's principal work than a similar title.

On the other hand, Suhrawardi's *Ishraqiyyun* were by no means unknown in fourteenth-century Muslim Spain, as is evident from the excellent summary of "the views of the followers of [the doctrine of] the lights among the Ancients" given by Lisan al-Din Ibn al-Khatib al-Gharnati (d. 776/1374) in his *Rawdat al ta'rif bi l-hubb al-sharif* (edited by M. al-Kattani, Beirut, 1970, II, 564–574); and it is worth noting that this author clearly distinguishes them from "the views of the philosophers naturalized among the Muslims" on one hand, that is, the Aristotelian tradition ending up with Averroes, and from Sufism on the other.

HERMANN LANDOLT

See also Isma'ili Thought; Mir Damad; Mulla Sadra; Al-Suhrawardi, Shihab al-Din; Saladin

Primary Sources

Kitab hikmat al-ishraq: Shihabiddub Yahya Sohravardi Shaykh al-Ishraq, Le Livre de la sagesse orientale [Annotated French translation of part II of *Kitab hikmat al-ishraq* plus commentaries by Q. Shirazi and Mulla Sadra

by Henry Corbin], edited and intro. by Christian Jambet. Lagrasse: Verdier, 1986.

Shihaboddin Yahya Sohravardi Shaykh al-Ishraq. *L'Archange empourpre: Quinze traites et recits mystiques* [annotated French translation of 15 treatises and mystical tales by Henry Corbin]. Paris: Fayard, 1976.

Shihabuddin Yahya Suhrawardi. *The Philosophical Allegories and Mystical Treatises*. A parallel Persian–English text edited and translated with an introduction by Wheeler McIntosh Thackston. Costa Mesa, CA: Mazda Publishers, 1999.

Sohravardi. *The Book of Radiance*. A parallel English–Persian text edited and translated, with an introduction by Hossein Ziai. Costa Mesa, CA: Mazda Publishers, 1998.

Suhrawardi. *The Philosophy of Illumination*. A new critical edition of the text of *Hikmat al-Ishraq*, with English translation, notes, commentary and introduction by John Walbridge and Hossein Ziai. Provo, UT: Brigham Young University Press, 1999.

Suhrawardi. *Hayakil al-nur* [see entry by B. Kuspinar].

Further Reading

Aminrazavi, M. *Suhrawardi and the School of Illumination*. London: Curzon, 1996.

Corbin, H. *En Islam iranien Sohravardi et les platoniciens de Perse*. 4 vols, vol. 2.Paris: Gallimard, 1971.

Kuspinar, B. *Isma'il Ankaravi on the Illuminative Philosophy*. Kuala Lumpur: Istac, 1996 [contains English trans. of Suhrawardi's *Hayakil al-nur*].

Landolt, H. "Suhrawardi's 'Tales of Initiation.'" Review article. *Journal of the American Oriental Society* 107.3 (1987): 475–486.

Marcotte, R. *Suhrawardi (d. 1191) and His Interpretation of Avicenna's (d. 1037) Philosophical Anthropology*. Ph.D. thesis. McGill University, 2000 (accessible online at: www.collectionscanada.ca).

Pourjavady [Purjawadi], N. *Ishraq wa 'irfan* [important collection of articles, text editions, and reviews, in Persian]. Tehran: University Press, 1380/2001–2002.

Schmidtke, S. "The Doctrine of the Transmigration of the Soul According to Shihab al-Din al-Suhrawardi (Killed 587/1191) and His Followers." *Studia Iranica* 28.2 (1999): 237–254.

Walbridge, J. *The Leaven of the Ancients: Suhrawardi and the Heritage of the Greeks*. Albany: SUNYP, 2000.

———. *The Wisdom of the Mystic East: Suhrawardi and Platonic Orientalism*. Albany: SUNYP, 2001.

Ziai, H. "Shihab al-Din Suhrawardi: Founder of the Illuminationist School." In *History of Islamic Philosophy*, edited by S.H. Nasr and O. Leaman, 434–464. London: Routledge, 1996.

———. "The Illuminationist Tradition." In *History of Islamic Philosophy*, edited by S. H. Nasr and O. Leaman, part I, 465–496. London: Routledge, 1996.

IMAM

The word *imam* (lit., leader, guide) has different connotations in Sunnism and Shi'ism. In Sunnism the word bears no specific doctrinal importance; it may refer to a political/religious leader, a religious scholar, or the person who leads a collective prayer. In Shi'ism, however, the word carries an important semantic and doctrinal significance. To understand its full extent, one must know that the person of the imam is the true hub around which revolves the entire Shi'i faith. The function and the nature of the imam, both concentrated in the central concept of the *walâya* (friendship or divine covenant), constitute the esoteric front of the prophecy *(nubuwwa)*.

In Shi'ism's fundamental vision of the world, any reality is made up of a manifest aspect *(zâhir)* and a secret aspect *(bâtin)*, the latter being hidden under the former. One of the many consequences of this basic doctrine is that the Divine Word, the Revelation at the root of the religion, also has an apparent aspect (that is, an exoteric dimension, a letter) and a hidden aspect (that is, esoteric, a spirit).

In this dialectic, the Prophet is the messenger of the letter of the Revelation. He is always accompanied in his mission by one or more imams who are the guides to the spirit of the Revelation. Moreover, in theology, Shi'ism represents the historical imam as the apparent front of a metaphysical, cosmic, archetypal Imam, who is in turn the revealed face of God, a theophanic vehicle of the Divine Names and Attributes.

These fundamental facts make it possible in Shi'ism to distinguish three separate but complementary meanings to the word "imam," from an exoteric level to more esoteric dimensions:

1. Imam as a religious scholar, teaching exoteric aspects of law, theology, exegesis, cosmology, and so on to an audience of mixed pupils, both Shi'is and non-Shi'is.
2. Imam as initiating master and thaumaturge, who holds the secret knowledge of the mysteries of God, of man, and of the universe and who possesses supranormal and miraculous powers. At this level the imam is the divine guide who teaches the esoteric level of the teachings only to Shi'i disciples. He thus transmits his knowledge and powers to those he has initiated.
3. Lastly, imam as the Face of God, perfect Man in which the divine attributes are manifested. This image of the deified man constitutes the "esoteric of the esoteric" of the imam's person and can be considered as The Secret of all secrets in the Shi'i doctrinal teachings. It is illustrated in several traditions going back to the historical imams, whose daring tone recalls the mystics' paradoxical words *(shatahât)*: "We are (we, imams) the Most Beautiful Names of God; we are the Face of God, His Hand, His Tongue"; "I am the First and the Last; I am the Apparent and the Hidden; I am the Merciful and the Compassionate."

One can thus measure the impact of this sacrosanct title held by political leaders, such as Mûsâ al-Sadr in Lebanon and Khomeyni in Iran, for the first time in Shi'ism after the historical imams, having recourse to the many meanings of the word, as well as to the ambiguity of its connotations.

MOHAMMAD ALI AMIR-MOEZZI

See also Shi'i Thought; Shi'ism; Titles

Further Reading

Amir-Moezzi, M.A. *Le Guide Divin dans le Shi'isme original.* Paris, 1992 [English translation: *The Divine Guide in Early Shi'ism.* Albany, NY, 1994].
———. "Remarques sur la divinité de l'Imam (Aspects de l'imamologie duodécimaine I)." *Studia Iranica* 25.2 (1996): 193–216.
———. "Notes à propos de la *walâya* imamite (Aspects de l'imamologie duodécimaine X)." *Journal of the American Oriental Society* 122.4 (2002): 722–741.
Kohlberg, E. "Imam and Community in the Pre-Ghayba Period." In *Authority and Political Culture in Shi'ism*, edited by Said Amir Arjomand, 25–53. Albany, NY, 1988.

INDIA

The earliest Muslims came to the Indian subcontinent to earn a living, to conquer, to teach religion, and to seek refuge. The first immigrants were Arab traders who, as early as the eighth century, settled in many of the seaports along the western and southern coasts of India. Later, their descendants moved to major cities inland, as well as farther south to Sri Lanka. In 711, a small Arab expedition, under the command of a seventeen-year-old general, Muhammad ibn Qasim, was sent to subjugate pirates who had been pillaging Arab ships. The expedition conquered parts of Sind and, with the assistance of local allies, founded a state that survived for nearly three centuries. These early Arab mercantile and political connections laid the basis for the strong affinity of later Muslim communities in southern and southwestern India with the Arab world and Arabian culture. In contrast, in northern and northwestern regions of the subcontinent, the first immigrants were from Central Asia, mostly consisting of Turks and Afghans who had been culturally Persianized. As a result of political turmoil in Central Asia in the tenth century, these groups crossed the Himalayas and entered India. Initially they were interested in acquiring booty rather than settling in the region. The most prominent of these invaders was Mahmud (d. 1030), ruler of the kingdom of Ghazna (now in Afghanistan) who, from 1000 CE onward, invaded India seventeen times. His looting of a famous temple in Somnath in Kathiawar in 1026 has earned him a reputation of the quintessential Muslim archenemy among Hindu nationalistic circles in contemporary India. The most remarkable legacy of Mahmud's invasions is the *Kitab al-Hind*, the earliest Arabic account of the life, thought, and culture of India, written by al-Biruni, a scholar of Central Asian origin attached to Mahmud's court.

After Mahmud's death, the Ghaznavid empire expanded into India, with the city of Lahore becoming its capital. Over the next several centuries, dynasties such as the "Slave Kings" established a state centered at Delhi, while other Afghans and Central Asians established kingdoms in Bengal, the Deccan, and western India. The most famous of these Central Asian dynasties were the Mughals, founded in 1526 by the emperor Babur. With the support of local Hindu allies such as the Rajputs, the Mughals consolidated control over a vast portion of India, creating an empire under whose auspices there was a veritable renaissance in Indo-Muslim culture.

The growth of sultanates resulted in an influx of Central Asian Turks, Iranians, and Afghans into India. Some sought administrative positions in the state bureaucracies. Poets and artists came in search of royal patronage while religious scholars *(ulama)* and Sufi *shaykhs* looked for new opportunities. Although immigrants were significant to the establishment of a Muslim presence in India, they eventually constituted a minority within the total Muslim population. Ethnically, the vast majority of Muslims in the region are of indigenous origin. We are only now beginning to understand the complex processes by which they became Muslim.

ALI ASANI

Further Reading

Schimmel, Annemarie. *Islam in the Indian Subcontinent.* Leiden-Koln: E.J. Brill, 1980.

INHERITANCE

Inheritance *(ilm al-fara'id, mirath)* pertains to the rules for the division of wealth among the heirs of a deceased Muslim man or woman.

Traditional Islamic Perspective

The intergenerational transmission of property, by means of a last will and testament *(wasiyya)*, was reportedly a common procedure prior to the rise of Islam and during the Meccan period.

In 622, the hijra to Medina necessitated changes in the existing inheritance rules. The Emigrants cut themselves off from their nonbelieving relatives in Mecca, and, for this reason, Muhammad instituted a pact of brotherhood between the Emigrants and the Helpers: Emigrants might no longer inherit from their relatives in Mecca, but they could inherit from Helpers in Medina, and vice versa (Q 8:72). This arrangement was subsequently abrogated by Q 8:75 and Q 33:6.

In the early Medinan period, six verses that regulate testamentary succession were revealed to Muhammad. Q 2:180 enjoins a person contemplating death to leave a bequest for parents and relatives; Q 2:181 holds accountable to God anyone who alters a last will and testament; Q 2:182 encourages the reconciliation of parties who disagree about the provisions of a will; Q 2:240 permits a testator to stipulate that his widow is entitled to a maximum of one year's maintenance, on the condition that she remain in her deceased husband's home; and Q 5:105–106 establish that a last will and testament should be drawn up or dictated in the presence of two witnesses. Under this regime, a person contemplating death continued to enjoy substantial freedom to determine who his or her heirs would be and what they would inherit (hereinafter, Q 2:180 and 2:240 will be referred to as "the bequest verses").

Following the Battle of Uhud in 625, Muhammad received a second series of revelations that appear to establish compulsory rules for the division of property: Q 4:8 affirms the inheritance rights of men *and* women, while Q 4:11–12 and 4:176 specify the exact fractional shares to which daughter(s), parent(s), sibling(s), and a spouse are entitled. Known as "the inheritance verses," Q 4:11, 4:12, and 4:176 form the core of what would become "science of the shares," a system that imposes compulsory rules for the division of property and is justly renowned for its mathematical complexity.

Almost immediately, the Muslim community identified certain redundancies in, and apparent inconsistencies between, the bequest verses and the inheritance verses. Some of these inconsistencies were reportedly resolved by Muhammad. Following the conquest of Mecca in 630, the Prophet stipulated that "a bequest may not exceed 1/3," a pronouncement that strikes a balance between the compulsory and voluntary aspects of the science of the shares: a minimum of two-thirds of any estate is distributed among the heirs in accordance with the inheritance verses; a maximum of one-third may be used, at the discretion of a person contemplating death, for bequests. May a close relative receive a bequest of up to a third of the estate in addition to the fractional share specified in the inheritance verses? No, because Muhammad is reported to have said on the occasion of his Farewell Pilgrimage in 632, "No bequest to an heir," that is, a person contemplating death may not leave a bequest for anyone who will receive a fractional share of the estate as specified in the inheritance verses. Since the time of al-Shafi'i (d. 820), Muslim jurists have regarded this prophetic dictum as an indicator that the inheritance verses abrogated the bequest verses.

Other problems were identified and resolved during the first century AH. Oddly, Q 4:12b awards siblings a maximum of one-third of the estate, whereas Q 4:176 awards siblings anywhere from 50% to 100% of the estate. The apparent contradiction was harmonized by Qur'an commentators who taught that *uterine* siblings are intended in Q 4:12b, whereas *consanguine* and/or *germane siblings* are intended in Q 4:176. This explanation requires that the revelation of Q. 4:12b precede that of Q 4:176. To this end the tradition teaches that Q 4:176 was the last verse revealed to Muhammad.

The mechanical operation of the Qur'anic rules created further problems. For example, Q 4:11 specifies that "a male is entitled to a share of two females," a phrase that the scholars understood as a general principle applying to all males and females of the same class and degree of relationship to the deceased (for example, sons and daughters, brothers and sisters, mothers and fathers). This principle is contradicted, however, in the case of a childless man who dies, leaving his wife and both parents: Q 4:11 assigns one-third of the estate to the mother; and Q 4:12 assigns one-fourth to the widow, leaving five-twelfths for the father, who inherits as the closest surviving agnate. Clearly, the father's share is not twice as large as that of the mother. The principle is also violated if a childless woman dies, leaving her husband and both parents, in which case the Qur'an assigns half to the widower, one-third to the mother, and one-sixth to the father, a solution that inverts the M = 2F "principle."

The solution to this problem is attributed to the second caliph, Umar b. al-Khattab (r. 634–644). Asked about a childless man who died, leaving a wife and both parents, Umar replied, "The wife is entitled to 1/4, the mother is entitled to 1/3 *of what remains* [viz., 1/4], and the father is entitled to whatever is left [viz., 1/2]." Here, Umar preserves the M = 2F principle (the father inherits half, the mother one-fourth) by interpolating the Qur'anic phrase that awards a share of the estate to the mother as if

it reads "one-third of what remains." But the principle was saved at the expense of the Qur'anic specification that the mother should inherit "one-third" of the estate. The solution to the case in which a woman dies, leaving her husband and both parents, was reportedly resolved in a similar manner by Ali (d. 661), al-Harith al-A'war (d. 684), or Zayd b. Thabit (d. 665).

A different problem arises when a person dies and leaves a particular constellation of heirs, all of whom are sharers, and yet, the sum of their Qur'anic fractional shares exceeds 100% of the estate. Suppose that a man dies and leaves two daughters, both parents, and a wife. All six persons qualify as sharers, but the sum of the shares specified in the Qur'an (two-thirds for the daughters, one-sixth for the father, one-sixth for the mother, and one-eighth for the wife) equals 27/24. The solution to this problem is attributed to the caliph Umar, Zayd b. Thabit, and/or Ali: By reducing the share of each heir on a pro rata basis (a procedure known as *awl*), the sum total of the shares is reduced to one. In the present case the shares become 16/27 (for the two daughters), 4/27 (father), 4/27 (mother) and 3/27 (wife), with a total of 100% (27/27). Although this procedure solved a mathematical problem, it created a further hermeneutical and theological complication, for the result of this procedure is that no heir receives the exact share specified in the Qur'an.

The general features of the science of the shares were clearly established by the middle of the second century AH, as reflected in the earliest extant treatise on the topic, written by Sufyan al-Thawri (d. 161/ 778): There are two classes of heirs—sharers and agnates. The sharers are those persons for whom the Qur'an specifies a fractional share of the estate (daughter[s], father, mother, spouse, and, in the absence of children, sibling[s]). The agnates are persons related to the deceased exclusively through male links, arranged in a series of hierarchical classes, with a member of a higher class, excluding all members of a lower class from entering the inheritance; within each class, a person nearer in degree of relationship to the deceased excludes all others in a more remote degree, for example, a son excludes a grandson. In the absence of a blood relative, the *mawla,* or patron, of the deceased inherits.

The division of an estate proceeds in three stages: (1) any debts and/or bequests are paid; (2) the sharers take their Qur'anic entitlements; and (3) the closest surviving agnate inherits whatever remains. For example, if a man dies, leaving a wife, son, and two brothers, the wife inherits one-eighth as a sharer and the son inherits the remaining seven-eighths as the closest surviving agnate, totally excluding the brothers as heirs. If the deceased also leaves a daughter, she is transformed into a residuary heir by her brother: he inherits 7/12 and she inherits 7/24, after the wife takes her 1/8 share. In theory, the person contemplating death is powerless to affect the relative entitlement of the heirs; he or she may not, for example, stipulate that the estate will pass to one heir to the exclusion of the others, that is, the deceased does not have the power to disinherit his close relatives.

The Imami Shi'is reject the systematic residuary entitlement of the agnates. Instead of a principle of male agnatic succession, they rely on a criterion of nearness of relationship that applies equally to males and females and to both agnatic and uterine relations of the deceased. Their system gives priority in inheritance to an inner family consisting of the children, parents, and siblings of the deceased, together with the spouse. These close relatives are regarded as the "roots" through whom are linked to the deceased the "branches" of the outer family, who stand next in priority in inheritance. No branch is excluded on the grounds of nonagnatic relationship to the deceased; every root is capable of transmitting its right of inheritance to its "branch."

Western Perspectives

Islamic sources indicate that the Muslim community's understanding of the Qur'anic inheritance verses was the subject of controversy during the lifetime of Muhammad and in the years immediately following his death.

At the center of this controversy stand Umar b. al-Khattab and the word *kalala*, which occurs twice in the Qur'an, once in Q 4:12b and again in 4:176. The commentators define *kalala* as "a person who dies leaving neither parent nor child." The sources, however, preserve a series of vivid reports that point to early confusion over the meaning of this word and the "reading" *(qira'a)* of Q 4:12b: On one occasion Umar said that he would rather know the meaning of *al-kalala* than possess the equivalent of the poll-tax of the fortresses of Byzantium. After he became caliph, Umar announced his intention to issue a decree about this word but was dissuaded from doing so by the appearance of a snake. Shortly before his demise, Umar said, "If I live, I will issue a decree about [*al-kalala*] so that no one who recites the Quran will disagree about it." On his deathbed, Umar destroyed a document that he had written about *al-kalala* (al-Tabari, Jami', 6:43–44).

Taking these narratives as his starting point, D. Powers has proposed three significant departures from the traditional understanding of the Qur'anic inheritance verses. First, he has suggested an alternative "reading" of Q. 4:12b according to which this subverse refers to the possibility of designating a testamentary heir; understood in this manner, the verse then clarifies the situation in which the deceased disinherits a brother or sister in favor of a wife or daughter-in-law. Second, he argues that the fractional share awarded to a surviving spouse in Q 4:12a was originally intended to apply only in the exceptional case of a wife who had received no dower, and that the exception was transformed into a rule during the generation following the death of the Prophet. Third, he argues that the bequest verses remained in force for at least twenty-five years after Muhammad's death, at which time a shift in the understanding of Q 4:12 made it appear as if the bequest verses were incompatible with the inheritance verses. Muslim scholars harmonized the relationship between the bequest and inheritance verses by invoking the doctrine of abrogation, ostensibly a sign of a change in the divine will, in reality a sign of changed perceptions of the meaning of the divine word. One advantage of the thesis proposed by Powers is that it eliminates the apparent contradictions and mathematical complexities associated with the science of the shares.

Islamic Inheritance System

As the conquests unfolded, Muslims living in the Near East and beyond found themselves subject to the science of the shares, which, to the extent that it was applied, resulted in the progressive fragmentation of wealth and capital. It is not surprising that proprietors found numerous ways to circumvent the inheritance rules or that they received important assistance in this regard from Muslim jurists who, distinguishing between postmortem and inter vivos transactions, taught that the inheritance rules take effect only on property owned by the deceased at the moment that he or she enters his or her deathbed illness and that proprietors are free, for the most part, to dispose of their property in any way they wish prior to that moment. Thus a proprietor may shift assets to his desired heir or heirs by means of a gift, acknowledgment of a debt, sale, or creation of a family endowment, on the condition that these legal actions conform to the requisite formalities. Thus, to understand how property passed from one generation to the next in Muslim societies, it is important to consider not only the science of the shares but also the wider and more comprehensive Islamic inheritance system.

DAVID STEPHAN POWERS

Primary Sources

al-Baydawi. *Anwar al-tanzil wa-asrar al-ta'wil*, 2 vols. Edited by H.O. Flesicher. 1846–1848; repr. Osnabrück, 1968.

al-Bayhaqi. *al-Sunan al-kubra*. 10 vols. Hayderabad, AH 1344–1357; repr. Beirut, 1968.

Bukhari. *Sahih*. 4 vols. Edited by M. Ludolf Krehl and Th. W. Juynboll. Leiden, 1862–1898.

Ibn Ishaq. *Kitab sirat rasul allah* (recension of 'Abd al-Malik b. Hisham). 2 vols in 3. Edited by F. Wüstenfeld. Göttingen, 1858–1860.

Ibn Shubah. *Kitab al-Sunan*. Edited by Habib 'Abd al-Rahman al-A'zami. Dabhil, 1967.

Muslim b. al-Hajjaj al-Qushayri. *Sahih*. 5 vols. Edited by Muhammad Fu'ad 'Abd al-Baqi. Cairo, 1375/1955.

al-Qurtubi. *al-Jami' li-ahkam al-qur'an*. 20 vols. Cairo, 1387/1967.

al-Shafi'i. *al-Risala*. Edited by Muhammad Sayyid Kaylani. Cairo 1388/1969.

al-Tabari. *Jami' al-bayan 'an ta'wil ay al-qur'an*. 3rd ed., 30 vols. in 12. Cairo 1954–1968.

al-Wahidi. *Asbab nuzul al-qur'an*. Edited by Ahmad Saqr. Cairo, 1389/1969.

al-Zamakhshari. *al-Kashshaf 'an haqa'iq ghawamid al-tanzil*. 4 vols. Beirut, 1947.

Further Reading

Chaumont, Eric. "Legs et succession dans le droit musulman." In *La Transmission du Patrimoine: Byzance etl'aire méditerranéenne*, edited by J. Beaucamp and G. Dagron, 35–51. Paris, 1998.

Cilardo, Agostino. *Diritto Ereditario Islamico delle Scuole Giuridiche Sunnite (Hanafita, Malikita, 'afi'ita e Hanbalita) e Delle Scuole Giuridiche Zaydita, Zahirita e Ibadita*. Napoli, 1994.

Coulson, Noel J. *Succession in the Muslim Family*. Cambridge, 1971.

Crone, Patricia. *Roman, Provincial and Islamic Law:The Origins of the Islamic Patronate*. Cambridge, 1987.

Kimber, Richard. "The Qur'anic Law of Inheritance." *Islamic Law and Society* 5 (1998): 291–325.

Mundy, Martha. "The Family, Inheritance, and Islam: A Re-Examination of the Sociology of Fara'id Law." In *Islamic Law: Social and Historical Contexts*, edited by Aziz Al-Azmeh, 1–123. London and New York, 1988.

Powers, David S. *Studies in Qur'an and Hadith: The Formation of the Islamic Law of Inheritance*. Berkeley, 1986.

———. "On Bequests in Early Islam." *Journal of Near Eastern Studies* 48 (1989): 185–200.

———. "Islamic Inheritance Law: A Socio-Historical Approach." In *Islamic Family Law and the State*, edited by Chibli Mallat and Jane Conners, 11–29. London, 1990.

Raddatz, H.-P. "Früislamisches Erbrecht nach dem *Kitab al-Fara'id* des Sufyan at-Tauri." *Welt des Islams* 13 (1971): 26–78.

Yanagihashi, Hiroyuki. "The Doctrinal Development of *Marad al-Mawt* in the Formative Period of Islamic Law." *Islamic Law and Society* 5 (1998): 326–358.

INTELLECTUAL HISTORY

Definition

Islamic intellectual history, like that of other movements, is the story of the longitudinal effort to assist it in surviving, and to implement its ideology in practice. One should bear in mind that the following is a rather schematic survey of positions whose boundaries in reality were far less clear cut.

Age of Ideology

Islam, as a total system, was the solution offered to the basically local practical problem of social justice in Mecca, as reflected in the Meccan suras of the Qur'an. In the seventh century the intellectual context of that society was, according to Islamic historiography, pagan fatalism mixed with harsh capitalism, although some modern scholars question this view.

Viewed from a scholarly point of view, Muhammad's Islam is an Arabic version of earlier monotheistic beliefs of Judaism and Christianity. As many ideologies tend to be puristic, viewed from a believer's point of view, Islam is a renewal of the original monotheistic religion that was sent to the Prophet Muhammad directly from its eternal source, with no foreign contribution whatsoever.

Both ideology and measures were more or less sufficient for the needs of the time of the Prophet and perhaps somewhat into the era of the four righteous caliphs.

Practicality Problems

Already during their reign difficult practical problems arose that threatened ideology:

1. Firstly, Islam as a tool for the solution of a specific problem turned into an end in itself, that is, a universal solution for any problem. Inevitably, with the spreading of the original

faith thinly on new Muslims, the gap between ideology and practicality widened. Perhaps the principal question became how to translate ideology into practicality in running an empire rather than a town.

2. Secondly, class strife, such as the Medinan aristocracy's attempt to preserve power, did little to bridge the widening gap between ideology and practicality. Personal conflicts over claim to justice and power turned ideological: 'Alid's, Shi'a came to occupy a position of guardians of the ideological against what seemed to them unjustified deviation toward the practical.

3. Thirdly, after the death of the Prophet Muhammad, the authoritative fountain-head for ideology ceased to provide, leaving ever-created new questions unanswered. Attempts to solve the problems were made on both the personal and the general levels by assassination and military steps (the first and second civil wars of the old Medinan aristocracy against the Prophet's cousin and son in law 'Ali ibn Abi Talib), neither providing any real remedy.

As the ideological approach was seen to fall short of addressing all the above difficulties, a shift toward the practical was made on more than one level:

Leadership ceased to be granted to individually elected leaders on a basis of equality in Islam. In addition, the Umayyads, replacing it by a dynastic system, were faced with a major problem of ideological justification.

Among the salient problems that resulted was inequality of both the internal Arabs, and also such perceived as directed against the new non-Arab Muslims. Another was the fact that the Qur'an did not suffice for addressing all the contemporary practical needs. Foreign input and connection therefore needed to be sought. As part of the openness toward the exterior, the capital was moved to Damascus, closer to Byzantium and centers of Christianity.

Preference was given to political leaning over religious purist policy. In addition, and perhaps more menacingly, along with a rationalistic view to problem solving, a more humanistic, skeptical, and philosophical direction infiltrated Islam, especially in the form of the Qadariyya and the beginnings of the Muhtazilah.

As a result, the Umayyads were perceived as leaders who were inclined too heavily toward the practical (and also to what might be called secular) at the expense of the ideological.

The reaction was an open conflict between 'ulama' and the court, with strong political opposition that culminated in the Abbasid revolution of 750 CE.

Return to Ideology

The 'Abbasids, belonging to the family of the Prophet Muhammad, claimed to constitute a return to ideology and condemned their predecessors on religious grounds. They, in turn, moved the capital to Al+s basis of power, Baghdad. As on principle the tension between ideology and practicality cannot be undone, not only did it remain during their five centuries of reign, but also it became more acute, spreading over the entire intellectual range.

In the earlier part of the period it took the form of division between the sciences of the Arabs, such as Qur'anic interpretation (ideology), as well as artistic means (poetry), those of the Ancients, such as medicine (practicality), which were translated systematically during the ninth and tenth centuries, and a range of disciplines to bridge the two (for example, kalÁm).

The sciences of the Ancients were all imported, but other disciplines were imported as well, such as literary genres *(adab)*, politics, and some poetic themes from Persia, and philosophies (such as Indian atomism). Furthermore, even within the ideological camp the views ranged; for example, the institution of legal schools *(madhÁhib)*, the existence of the discipline of legal stratagems (Ýilm al-hiyal), or the wide range of Qur'anic interpretation (starting with bilÁ kaifa, and ending with allegorical ones). On the other hand, ideology had to defend itself against opposition from within too (Sufism), where the conflict sometimes took a bloody turn. By contrast, that between practicality and ideology at the time of al-Mamkn created the MiÎnah, the Islamic form of inquisition. Its most illustrious victim was Ibn Hanbal (d. 855 CE), whose redefinition of the ideological holds to date.

Non-Arab Muslims, especially Persians, reacted to Arab Islam puristic attitude with the Shu'ubiyya movement that on the one hand stressed equality in Islam, but on the other hand stressed their special side. This movement produced some of the most outstanding Muslim thinkers in all intellectual domains, thus responding to Islam's practical and growing need for external fertilization.

On the political level, one of the discrepancies between ideology and practicality had to do with the proliferation of Islamic dynasties. It was solved in such a way as to allow their existence (practicality) while maintaining the institution of the caliph (ideology) and justifying reality as the manifestation of God's will. In spite, or perhaps because of, this competition between ideology and practicality, the tenth century was the richest in Islamic history in all domains and contributed the most to world culture.

The shift toward the closed ideological grew stronger especially after al-Ghazali (d. 1111). On the one hand, he declared amnesty to Sufism and incorporated it into official Islam, but on the other hand he revived religious studies (ideological) and attacked philosophy. This very discipline was an issue of reciprocal influence with other cultures, and an important criterion for our controversy: Although import of ideas existed already in the time of the Prophet, it was presented as anything but import.

Ideologically, Islam could, and had to, export its religious message only by inclusion of nonbelievers. Starting in the tenth century CE it exported other ideas that were theological, philosophical, scientific, and medical, without gaining new believers as a result. The Crusades served as yet another, unwelcome, catalyst for this mutual exchange.

Although the fall of the caliphate (1286) to the Mongols put an end to the political representation of the Islamic ideological position, in other domains the latter seems to have gained the upper hand. This was especially manifest in Ibn Taymiyya (d. 1328 AD), who, more than anyone else, has represented the ideological, not the least thanks to his fierce opposition to foreign intellectual import *(Against the Logicians)*.

With the exception of Ibn Khaldun's (d. 1406) unique contribution to the practical, it would seem as though the ideological had the upper hand toward the end of the period.

In conclusion it would seem that it was practical openness to reciprocity with other cultures, rather than exclusive ideology, that helped Islam survive and prosper.

ILAI ALON

See also 'Abbasids; Adab; al-Mamkn; Caliph; Civil Wars; Crusades; Fatalism; Ghazali; Ibn Hanbal; Ibn Khaldun; Ibn Taymiyya; Minah; Mutazilah; Philosophy; Qadariyya; Umayyads

Further Reading

Kraemer, Joel L. *Humanism In The Renaissance Of Islam: The Cultural Revival during The Buyid Age.* Leiden and New York: E.J. Brill, 1992.

Lewis, Bernard. *Islam in History: Ideas, People, and Events in the Middle East.* Chicago: Open Court, 1993.

Nasr, Seyyed Hossein. *Islam: Religion, History, And Civilization.* San Francisco: Harper SanFrancisco, 2003.

Rosenthal, Franz. *Four Essays on Art and Literature in Islam.* Leiden: Brill, 1971.

Von Grunebaum, Gustave E. *Islam; Essays in the Nature and Growth of a Cultural Tradition.* London, Routledge & Kegan Paul, 1961.

INTERFAITH RELATIONS

It would be anachronistic to think of interfaith relations in the Islamic world during the Middle Ages in contemporary postenlightenment terms. The modern virtues of social, religious, and political equality would have been incomprehensible to anyone living in the three great medieval cultural zones west of India—the Dar al-Islam (domain of Islam), Byzantium, and Latin Christendom. Muslims, Christians, and Jews all believed that they had been granted the most perfect of Divine dispensations, and whether they had been given temporal power over others or were themselves subjects to nonbelievers, they would be justified in the next world, if not in this one. A medieval person's true citizenship was not within a political state but within a religious polity, and adherents of other religions were, in a very real sense, aliens although not necessarily enemies. Contact between individuals from the different religious communities took place on many levels (economic, administrative, intellectual, even social) and, depending on time and circumstance, could be more or less cordial, but the overarching framework of interfaith relations was always subject to the parameters imposed by religious identity.

Early Theological, Legal, and Social Setting

Jews, Christians, and Zoroastrians, who were deemed by Islam to have valid, albeit imperfect, scriptural religions, were accorded freedom of religion within certain discreet boundaries, freedom of economic endeavor with some minor disadvantages, and the protection of the state in exchange for accepting the Islamic rule, a measure of social inferiority, and the paying of the *jizya*, or poll tax. They had their own communal officials, courts, schools, and welfare institutions. Under the so-called Pact of 'Umar, they were proteges *(dhimmis)* of the Muslim community. The dominance of Muslims and the subordinance of *dhimmis* was at all times and in all places an underlying subtext to all interconfessional intercourse.

The Qur'an specifically enjoins Muslims not to form friendships with members of the tolerated faiths: "O you who believe! Take not the Jews and the Christians as friends. They are friends to one another. Whoever of you befriends them is one of them. Allah does not guide the people who do evil" (Sura 5:51). In the earliest years following the establishment of the Dar al-Islam, this injunction probably was strictly adhered to, except with regard to the Christian–Arab tribesmen of Taghlib who took part in the wars of conquest and were not considered *dhimmis*.

The ruling Arab Muslims who concentrated at first in their own military camp towns (the *amsar*) constituted a small military elite governing an enormous empire, the inhabitants of which not only belonged to other faiths but spoke other languages as well. However, with the conversion of large numbers of the native population to Islam, the progressive Arabization, urbanization, and prosperity of the empire in the two centuries following the conquests, Muslims and non-Muslims increasingly came into daily face-to-face contact with one another. Although much of this contact was in the commercial sphere of the marketplace or the administrative sphere of the bureaucracy in which many *dhimmis* were employed, there were social and intellectual exchanges even before the period of the Hellenistic renaissance of the ninth through twelfth centuries.

Interfaith Relations on the Intellectual Level

During the Umayyad period (661–750 CE), Syria was one of the few provinces where Muslims and non-Muslims lived side by side in mixed urban communities, and many Arabs had lived there well before the advent of Islam. From the polemical writings of John of Damascus (ca. 675–750) and Theodore Abu Qurra (ca. 740–820), it is clear that Syrian Christian intellectuals were well informed of Islamic beliefs and intra-Islamic theological debates probably from firsthand contact with Muslims. Even if Damascene's *Dialogue between a Saracen and a Christian* is a fictional account, it reflects the kinds of interfaith discussions, both amicable and controversial, that were beginning to take place in the Levant. These discussions centered around such issues as the unity of God and the question of free will versus predestination. Representatives of the *dhimmi* communities sometimes were drawn into religious discussions at the ruler's court. Even when the dialogue was friendly, the inequality of status required the non-Muslim to be defensive and, no less important, inoffensive. The Nestorian Catholicos Timothy I records such a discussion that he had with the 'Abbasid caliph al-Mahdi in Baghdad around 781 in a work appropriately titled *Apology for the Christian Faith*. The Shi'i traditionalist Ibn Babawayh records a theological discussion between a Jewish exilarch and the twelfth 'Alid imam, 'Ali Rida, at the court of the caliph al-Ma'mun, which took place probably sometime between 816 and 818. The Andalusian literary scholar, Ibn 'Abd Rabbih, describes Jews and Christians discussing allegorical scriptural exegesis (*ta'wil*) also in front of al-Ma'mun.

During the period of the Hellenistic revival in the medieval Muslim world, which Adam Mez has dubbed "the Renaissance of Islam," there was considerable contact and even intellectual cooperation that crossed confessional lines. This was particularly true among men of science, medicine, and philosophy. Muslim, Christian, and Jewish physicians served alongside one another not only at the ruler's court but also in the public hospital *(bimaristan)*, and it was not at all unusual for a medical student of one faith to study with a notable teacher of another religion. For example, Ibn al-Jazzar, a well-known Muslim physician, was the pupil of Isaac Israeli (ca. 850–950), a Jew and one of the greatest figures in medieval medicine. Neither was it at all extraordinary for a doctor to have a non-coreligionist as a patient. Several generations of the Christian Bukhtishu' family served as physicians to the early 'Abbasids, and the Jewish physician and philosopher Moses Maimonides, was not only the personal doctor of the qadi al-Fadil and later the Sultan al-Malik al-Afdal in twelfth-century Cairo, but he also was lauded in verses by the Muslim poet Ibn Sana' al-Mulk. Biographical dictionaries of physicians, such as Ibn Abi Usaybi'a's *Tabaqat al-Atibba' (The Classes of the Physicians)* include respectful and complimentary entries on Christian and Jewish doctors.

But in no realm was interfaith cooperation more salient during the height of the Islamic Hellenic renaissance than in the realm of philosophy *(falsafa)* and rational theology *(kalam)*. The Muslim philosopher al-Farabi (d. 950) received his philosophical training in Baghdad from the Nestorian Yuhanna b. Haylan, and later al-Farabi himself took on at least one Christian student. A tenth-century visitor from the Islamic West, Ahmad ibn Sa'di, mentions that at an assembly of theologians in Baghdad, he found not only Muslims, "but unbelievers, Magians, materialists, atheists, Jews and Christians, in short, unbelievers of all kinds." He reports that debates were carried on exclusively on the basis of rational arguments without resort to citing scripture. Disturbed by what he saw, Ibn Sa'di sought out another such gathering but found the same thing, which he described in his own words as "calamity." Even legal scholars of different faiths cooperated with one another on occasion. Although the practice was strongly discouraged by Christian and Jewish authorities, members of their flock sometimes had recourse to the Islamic courts, and cases sometimes went back and forth between the latter and the *dhimmi* courts. Sometimes, the non-Muslim authorities themselves turned to the qadi for government backing when their own rulings had been challenged by recalcitrant members of their community. As Goitein has noted based on the evidence of the Cairo Geniza, professional contacts between members of the Jewish and Muslim judiciary could even develop into personal friendships.

Although it was not a common practice, students of one confessional community sometimes studied in the school of another. The decree of the 'Abbasid caliph al-Mutawakkil issued in 850, reiterating and reenforcing the Pact of 'Umar, specifically prohibits *dhimmi* children from studying in Muslim schools and bans Muslims from acting as their tutors. The inclusion of such prohibitions that are not stipulated in the original Pact would indicate that in ninth-century Iraq, non-Muslim pupils were to be found studying in Muslim schools or at least with Muslim teachers. Hai Gaon (939–1038), the head of the Pumbedita yeshiva and the highest Jewish authority of his day, writes in a responsum that while it is preferable to dissuade non-Jews from attending Jewish schools (which were normally attached to the synagogue, just as Muslim schools were part of the mosque complex and Christian schools were in the church or monastery), it was permissible for the sake of maintaining good relations. However, he rules that they should only be admitted to classes in secular subjects such as arithmetic and mathematics. Muslim scholars voiced similar opinions at the time. The latter occasionally also raised objections to *dhimmis* being taught Arabic language and grammar from Muslim teachers, the primary reason being that such instruction invariably included quotations from the Qur'an, and Qur'anic study was specifically forbidden to non-Muslims by the Pact of 'Umar. Nevertheless, non-Muslims did sometimes pursue Arabic studies with Muslim teachers. The Andalusian poet and anthologist Ibn Bassam (d. 1147) mentions an outstanding Jewish student in the literary study circle of the poet and belle-lettrist Ibn Shuhayd (992–1035) without the slightest indication that this was something unusual.

Interfaith Relations on the Ordinary, Daily Level

The aforementioned interfaith relations took place for the most part on a highly rarefied level between members of a very small social and intellectual elite with the sole, widespread exception of the physician of one faith and his patient of another. However, there were also daily face-to-face contacts between members of the different confessional communities in the cities and towns throughout the length and breadth of the medieval Islamic world. Although there were no enforced ghettos during the first five centuries of Islamic history, *dhimmis* generally preferred concentrating in particular neighborhoods. Some cities in Iraq, Syria, and Spain had Christian and Jewish quarters. In Baghdad, some of these quarters had actually been pre-existing Christian and Jewish villages that were incorporated into the newly founded 'Abbasid capital. However, the documents of the Cairo Geniza indicate that in Fustat in Egypt, and in Qayrawan in Ifriqiyya, both of which were founded as *amsar*, there were no Jewish quarters as such, only neighborhoods with a highly concentrated Jewish population, but with Muslim and Christian residents as well. *Dhimmis* clustered in neighborhoods not only for convenient access to their communal institutions but also for practical security reasons. Because of the stipulations of the Pact of 'Umar, it was advisable not to have a church or synagogue near a large concentration of Muslims. It was also preferable to have a route of access to the Christian or Jewish cemetery that did not go through a predominantly Muslim neighborhood. *Dhimmi* funeral processions were the object of occasional harassment—sometimes minor, sometimes serious—from medieval to modern times.

Living in close proximity to one another and sharing the same market space, members of the different religious communities might maintain cordial, neighborly relations. Muslim and non-Muslim neighbors and business associates exchanged good wishes on each others' holidays despite religious injunctions in each of the different faiths against such practices. However, there were serious impediments to more intimate conviviality. Muslim dietary rules precluded eating meat in Christian homes, and Jewish dietary restrictions kept Jews from eating any prepared food in Muslim or Christian homes. Nor would the vast majority of ordinary Muslims drink wine, the standard beverage of Christian and Jewish hospitality. (The laws of kashrut also strictly forbade Jews from drinking wine produced—and indeed even touched—by gentiles.) Still, there were always exceptions. When Muslims joined Jewish drinking parties, an observant host might add honey to the wine, thus desacralizing it, eliminating the problem of it being rendered unkosher by the touch of a gentile, and at the same time avoiding giving any offense to the Muslim guests.

Perhaps nowhere was more conducive to interconfessional conviviality than the public bath *(hammam)*. As in Roman times the bath was a place for socializing, as well as hygiene. Because all outer signs of status were shed with one's clothing, there were periodic attempts to impose upon non-Muslims some sort of distinguishing mark, even in the bath where one normally wore only a loincloth. An early example of this was the mad Fatimid caliph al-Hakim's decree, issued in 1009, commanding Christians and Jews to wear, respectively, a cross and a bell around their necks when bathing. These measures fell into desuetude with the disappearance of the caliph a few years later, and similar restrictions were not imposed for several more centuries when interfaith relations had seriously eroded throughout the Muslim world.

The commercial sphere also provided for interfaith contact and cooperation. Although business partnerships were preferred among family and coreligionists, it is clear from the evidence of the Cairo Geniza documents that business contracts, joint ventures, and partnerships among members of different faiths were not at all extraordinary. In such cases, it was Islamic commercial law that prevailed. Artisans of different faiths who owned an atelier in common, each took off their own weekly day of rest.

Interfaith Participation in Popular Religious Practices

It may seem paradoxical that in a society in which individual and group identities, state administration, and law were defined first and foremost by religion, that one important domain of interfaith contact among the common folk was within a religious context. This was not the realm of formal, orthodox religion, but of noncanonical popular religious practice. Unlike Christianity with its officially sanctioned cult of saints, normative Islam and Judaism looked askance at the veneration of holy men and making shrines of their tombs. Nevertheless, the graves of biblical figures, rabbinical sages, companions of the Prophet Muhammad, martyrs, and wonder workers not only attracted the faithful from one religious community but not infrequently from others as well. In Iraq, Muslims and Jews visited the shrines of Ezra and Ezekiel, both of which were maintained by the Jewish authorities, and members of all three faiths visited Daniel's tomb in Persia. Likewise the synagogue of Dammuh in Egypt, which supposedly was founded by Moses prior to the exodus, attracted Muslims alongside the Jewish pilgrims. In Damascus, Christians, Jews, and even Zoroastrians brought votive offerings to the tomb of the Muslim saint Shaykh Arslan. The Hanbali theologian Ibn Taymiyya (1263–1328), who rejected all such popular cults as heretical innovation (bid'a), is particularly contemptuous of "ignorant Muslims" who make votive offerings at Christian shrines and "seek blessings from priests, monks and the like." In Islamic Spain and Fatimid Egypt where Christians made up a significant proportion of the population, some Christian festivals were occasions for celebration by the general public despite periodic objections raised by Islamic authorities.

Deterioration of Interfaith Relations in the Late Middle Ages

The spiritual, social, and economic climate of the Islamic world underwent a profound transformation during the course of the thirteenth century due to both internal and external pressures: the Crusades, the Reconquista, the Mongol invasions, the debasement of the currency, and plague. The secular and humanistic tendencies of the Hellenistic renaissance declined and were replaced by a less tolerant and more institutionalized Islam. The number of non-Muslims steadily declined (in the Maghrib, indigenous Christians disappeared in the wake of the Almohads), and they became ever more marginalized in Islamic society. This had a corrosive effect on interfaith relations. The laws of differentiation (ghiyar) came to be enforced with new stringency and vigor. Anti-dhimmi riots erupted periodically— in Baghdad in 1284 and throughout the Il-Khanid empire in 1291, in Cairo in 1301 and 1354, and in Fez in 1438 and 1465. The intellectual common ground that had allowed for interfaith debates in earlier centuries, even at the caliphal court, disappeared. In 1419, the Coptic patriarch was summoned by the Mamluk sultan al-Malik al-Mu'ayyad and was compelled to remain standing before him while Muslim scholars delivered lengthy anti-Christian diatribes. So too, the secular domain of the sciences was no longer congenial to interfaith contact and cooperation. Although there had always been some pious opposition to dhimmis practicing medicine on Muslims, it was never taken seriously. However, in 1448, Sultan Jaqmaq promulgated a decree forbidding Christian and Jewish doctors from treating Muslim patients. During the preceding two centuries, polemical treatises such as al-Jawbari's Kashf al-Asrar (Unveiled Secrets) and al-Wasiti's Radd 'ala Ahl al-Dhimma (Refutation of the People of the Pact) contained horror stories concerning dhimmi physicians and Muslim patients, and legal handbooks such as Ibn al-Hajj's Madkhal al-Shar' al-Sharif (Introduction to the Noble Religious Law) stated outright that such interconfessional doctor–patient relationships are forbidden. The spirit of the times and the general decline in education made attendance by members of one faith at the school of another even rarer than in the past. The implacable Ibn al-Hajj states that Muslim parents should not send their children to Christian schools even to learn arithmetic and geometry and that such conduct is an insult to Islam. Islamic institutions of higher education reflect the hardening attitudes. A deed of endowment for a madrasa stipulates that "no Jew, Christian, Hanbali, or literalist *(hashwi)*" should be admitted.

Members of the different faiths still came face to face in the marketplace. However, even here the scope of interfaith contact was lessened. The economy of the Muslim world began closing in on itself in many places within trade guilds and state monopolies. One area in which *dhimmis* found for themselves an increasingly important niche was as middlemen between European merchants and the local economy. By early modern times this role would only further highlight their otherness.

Domestic living patterns also made for reduced interfaith contact. Non-Muslims increasingly clustered within their own separate quarters by custom or law. The *mellah* of Fez, established in 1438, became the prototype of such ghettolike quarters in Morocco and the rest of the Maghrib in the following centuries. Physical separation reinforced social isolation. In late medieval Yemen and Persia the rise of Shi'i states added an additional impediment to socialization and conviviality because, according to Shi'i doctrine, *dhimmis* were considered *najs* (ritually impure).

Despite the increased barriers standing in the way of interfaith relations at the end of the Middle Ages, the members of different religions still interacted at popular religious shrines and in the recourse to seers and dispensers of folk medicines and amulets.

NORMAN A. STILLMAN

See also Cairo Geniza; Christians; Copts; Hospitals; Ibn Babawayh; Ibn Taymiyya; Al-Jahiz; Jews; Maimonides; Al-Ma'mun; Pilgrimage; Polemics and Disputation; Popular Religion; Zoroastrianism

Further Reading

Goitein, S.D. *A Mediterranean Society*. 6 vols. Berkeley and Los Angeles: University of California Press, 1967–1993.
Lewis, Bernard. *The Jews of Islam*. Princeton: Princeton University Press, 1984.
Meri, Josef. *The Cult of Saints Among Muslims and Jews in Medieval Syria*. Oxford: Oxford University Press, 2002.
Powers, J.F. "Frontier Municipal Baths and Social Interaction in Thirteenth-Century Spain." *American Historical Review* 84 (1979): 649–667.
Stillman, Norman A. *The Jews of Arab Lands: A History and Source Book*. Philadelphia: Jewish Publication Society, 1979.
———. "Subordinance and Dominance: Non-Muslim Minorities and the Traditional Islamic State as Perceived from Above and Below." In *A Way Prepared: Essays on Islamic Culture in Honor of Richard Bayly Winder*, edited by Farhad Kazemi and R.D. McChesney. New York and London: New York University Press, 1988.
Tritton, A.S. *Materials on Muslim Education in the Middle Ages*. London: Luzac, 1957.

IRANIAN LANGUAGES

Iranian languages is the name given to a large grouping of languages, ancient and modern, within the Indo-Iranian branch of the Indo-European language family. Iranian languages and dialects are classified as Old, Middle, or New, and by region of origin, especially "western" and "eastern," and sometimes also "northern" and "southern." The oldest stage of linguistic development is represented by Old Persian (the language of the Achaemenids, 559–330 BCE) and the language of the Avesta; the middle stage by Middle Persian, Parthian, Soghdian, and Khvarazmian, all written in the Aramaic script, Bactrian, written in the Greek alphabet, and Khotanese, most writings in which appeared after the fall of the Sasanians (226–651 CE); and the latest stage by (New) Persian (Parsi, Farsi) and its close relatives Dari (spoken in parts of present-day Afghanistan) and Tajiki (spoken in present-day Tajikistan and adjoining areas), together with other languages of the western group, such as Kurdish, Gurani and Zaza, Baluchi, Tati, Taleshi, Azari, Gilaki, Mazandarani, Luri, Laristani, and Bakhtiyari, as well as the eastern Iranian languages of Pashto, Ossetic, Yaghnobi, the Shughni group, Wakhi, Munji and Yidgha, Parachi, and Ormuri, among others. The "eastern" or "western" origin of an Iranian language does not always coincide with the region where it came to be spoken; for example, Ossetic, a language belonging to the eastern branch, is spoken in the Caucasus, whereas Baluchi, a member of the western branch, is spoken in modern-day Baluchistan, in southern Pakistan.

Among the most authoritative sources of information regarding the linguistic geography of late Sasanian and early Islamic Iran is the *Fihrist* of Ibn al-Nadim, who records a notice from Ibn al-Muqaffa' (d. ca. 759), the Persian man of letters noted for his translations from Middle Persian into Arabic, as well as for his erudition in the latter language. According to Ibn al-Muqaffa', the "languages of Persian" *(lughat al-farisiyya)* were five: Pahlavi, Dari, Parsi (Ar. *farisiyya*, Farsi), Khuzi, and Suryani (Ibn al-Nadim, *Fihrist*, Cairo, 1991, I: 23). Of these five languages the first three are Iranian, and the shifting uses and connotations of Pahlavi, Dari, and Parsi, as Gilbert Lazard has demonstrated, reflect important linguistic and cultural developments in the early centuries of the Islamic period. Pahlavi referred to the Middle Iranian language of Parthian and to the dialects that grew out of that language. Parthian had originated in the eastern regions of Iran but was also adopted as an imperial language, written in the Aramaic script, in the west when the Arsacids (247 BCE–224 CE) made their capital there. Parsi, or literary Middle Persian, also written in Aramaic, was the imperial language of the Sasanians who succeeded the Arsacids, and of the Zoroastrian religious tradition. At the beginning of the Sasanian era, two imperial languages, both written in Aramaic, were in use; however, Parsi eventually displaced Pahlavi, and by the close of the Sasanian era, Parsi was the sole official and written language. Dari was the name given to the vernacular language derived from literary Middle Persian. By the end of the Sasanian period, Dari was spoken not only at the court, from which its name derived (P. *dar*, door, gate, or court), but also probably in much of the empire, and certainly in Khurasan. It seems that in the course of the Sasanian period the vernacular had diverged from the written language to a considerable degree, and had thus acquired a distinct name.

The meanings of Pahlavi, Parsi, and Dari underwent considerable change both during the Sasanian period and after the beginning of the Islamic era in Iran. While the usage of "Parsi" to designate literary Middle Persian is attested to in the works of Ibn al-Muqaffa' and other writers in Arabic, with the advent of Islamic rule it became customary to refer to literary Middle Persian as "Pahlavi." This development reflects the changing context for the use of Iranian languages. Following the conquests, the most striking linguistic contrast was no longer that between Parsi (Middle Persian) and Pahlavi (Parthian), but that between Arabic and any form of Persian, that is, any language or dialect spoken by the Persians *(al-Furs)*. Accordingly, the term *Parsi* or (in Arabic) *Farsi* came increasingly to denote both the common spoken vernacular and the literary language of Islamic Iran. As Parsi acquired this broader use, it became synonymous with Dari, which name, rendered superfluous, gradually fell out of use in most regions. In the Islamic period, Middle Persian continued to be used among Zoroastrians. Indeed, most of the extant literature was committed to writing by priests in the AH third/ninth CE century; it was also used by Manichaeans in Central Asia until the seventh/thirteenth century. Over time, however, the language fell into disuse, such that by the second half of the fourth/tenth century, the script was little known even among Zoroastrians (it is striking that the Zoroastrian Kayka'us, writing in Rayy before 978, composed his *Zaratushtnama* not in Middle Persian but in New Persian).

The major developments in the use of Iranian languages during the early and medieval periods of Islamic history are (1) the gradual spread of one Iranian language, known as Dari or Parsi (Persian), as a spoken language throughout the eastern Islamic world, often at the expense of other Iranian languages, which in turn influenced the various forms of Persian that developed in different regions; (2) the related emergence of literary New Persian, which would develop into a second official and cultural language alongside Arabic, and as such would extend the range of Persian and Perso-Islamic culture well beyond the areas in which Iranian languages were used in daily communication; and (3) the survival and cultivation of other Iranian languages and dialects (the distinction is not always easily drawn) long after the ascendancy of Persian as a literary and official lingua franca.

Spread of Dari as a Spoken Language

In the early centuries of the Islamic period, the use of Dari as a spoken language gradually decreased in Iraq, but elsewhere, especially in the east, it spread considerably. In Khurasan, Dari had largely superceded Parthian during the Sasanian period, and it continued its eastward expansion as Transoxiana and the present-day Afghanistan became integrated into the Islamic world. While numerous languages and dialects remained in use, Persian served as a means of verbal communication among members of different linguistic groups, including Arabs who had settled in the eastern regions. Thus long before the emergence of literary New Persian in Transoxiana and Khurasan, Dari, or Persian, had come to constitute the common language in these regions. The spread of Islam facilitated the linguistic integration of much of the Iranian world in a process similar to that associated with the spread of Arabic in the Western territories.

The variety within Dari is evident from prose works written in the fourth/tenth and fifth/eleventh centuries. The Dari used in the Southwest, known in particular through a number of Judeo-Persian texts, remained relatively close to Middle Persian, which had itself originated in the southwestern regions of Fars and Khuzistan; by contrast, the Dari spoken in Khurasan had diverged much further from its Middle Persian forebear and was characterized by elements found in other Iranian languages and dialects, especially Parthian. It was this latter form of Dari that spread into the neighboring regions of Afghanistan and Transoxiana, where it also acquired a number of

Soghdian words and evolved into the languages known today as Dari and Tajiki. At the same time, the southwestern form of Persian spread across the South as far as Sistan, as attested by a translation of the Qur'an produced in that region in the eleventh century or perhaps even later.

Emergence of Literary New Persian

Given the predominance of Dari as the lingua franca of the eastern regions of Iran and Transoxiana, it is more readily understandable that it was there, under the Samanids (819–1005) or perhaps the Saffarids (861–1003), that the language subsequently known as Farsi or (New) Persian would first find literary form. While the phonetic and grammatical shifts from Middle to New Persian are relatively slight, the new language, sometimes referred to as *parsi-yi dari*, marks a significant break with the past in its adoption of the Arabic script and, as previously noted, in its assimilation of vocabulary from Parthian, Soghdian, and, increasingly, from Arabic. Literary New Persian first appears as a medium for poetic expression, the earliest samples of which date from the middle of the third/ninth century; the earliest surviving prose texts date from a century later. Literary composition in Persian gradually spread to the west, and, in the course of the fifth/eleventh century, Persian emerged as the primary literary language throughout Iran, although several authors continued to write in Arabic as well, especially in the religious sciences.

Additionally, Persian replaced Arabic in official contexts in many of the eastern regions. After the advent of Islamic rule, Middle Persian continued to be used for administrative purposes in western Iran until 78/697–698 and in Khurasan until 124/741–742, when it was replaced by Arabic. In the fourth/tenth century, Arabic gradually ceded its role as the principal official language to Persian, which would become the administrative language of states not only in Iran and present-day Afghanistan but also in Central Asia, Anatolia, and India, most notably under the Mughals (1526–1858); furthermore, courts in these regions often provided generous patronage for Persian poetry and literature.

Continuance of Regional Languages and Dialects

Just as in Sasanian times, local dialects had coexisted with Middle Persian and with Dari, numerous (non-Persian) Iranian languages and dialects, several of which have persisted to the present day and have, like Persian, assumed written form, are recorded by the geographers and historians of the early and medieval Islamic periods. Al-Mas'udi (d. 956) mentions Azari alongside Dari and Pahlavi; in the Caspian regions a number of languages persisted, including Daylami and Tabari, the latter of which also emerged as a literary language in about the fourth/tenth century; Khvarazmian, written in a modified Arabic script, is found from the fifth/eleventh to the eighth/fourteenth centuries. Several regions, including Kirman, Makran, Ushrusana, Gharjistan, and Ghur, were characterized by distinctive dialects, and according to al-Muqaddasi, who wrote in the second half of the fourth/tenth century, the spoken idiom in almost every Khurasanian town differed from the common language, Dari. Pahlavi also survived, especially in its oral literature. It gave its name to the quatrains and other poems in dialect known as the *fahlaviyyat*; indeed, as knowledge of both Middle Persian and Parthian receded, the term *Pahlavi* was occasionally used to describe poetry in other dialects, as long as they were distinct from poetry in Persian. Kurdish flourished as a spoken language with several dialects and a rich oral literature; it was written in the Arabic and in other scripts. Pashto was similarly distinguished by many dialects and a written literature.

LOUSIE MARLOW

See also Persian

Further Reading

Lazard, Gilbert. "*Pahlavi, Pârsi, Dari*: les langues de l'Iran d'après Ibn al-Muqaffa'." In *Iran and Islam. In Memory of the Late V. Minorsky*, edited by C.E. Bosworth. Edinburgh, 1971.

———. "*Pârsi* et *dari*; nouvelles remarques." In *Bulletin of the Asia Institute*, New Series, 4, *Aspects of Iranian Culture. In Honor of R. N. Frye*. 1990, 239–244.

———. "Lumières nouvelles sur la formation de la langue persane: une traduction du Coran en persan dialectal et ses affinités avec le judéo-persan." *Irano-Judaica* II (1990): 184–198.

Schmitt, Rüdiger (Ed). *Compendium Linguarum Iranicarum*. Wiesbaden: Reichert Verlag, 1989.

———. *Die iranischen Sprachen in Geschichte und Gegenwart.*Wiesbaden: Reichert Verlag, 2000.

Tafazzoli, A."Fahlaviyat." In *Encyclopaedia Iranica* IX (1999): 158–162.

ISFAHAN

Situated at the geographical center of modern Iran, the founding of the city of Isfahan dates to well before the arrival of Muslims in the seventh century.

Its origins rest in twin cities of Yahudiyya and Jayy, at a short distance from one another on the plain north of the Zayanda River. The Jewish town of Yahudiyya, traced by one tradition to Nebuchadnezzar's time, flourished in the first centuries of Islam to become the hub of Isfahan. According to another tradition, Yahudiyya was founded on the request of the Jewish wife of the Sasanian king Yazdgird (r. 459–483 CE), who also established Jayy to the southeast of Yahudiyya as an administrative center, a function that it continued to serve well into the medieval period. Early Arab geographers and travelers referred to these as *madinatayn*, the twin cities of Isfahan.

Since the merging of the twin cities and their satellite villages into the early Islamic metropolis, Isfahan by virtue of its geographical location, temperate climate, and fertile soil has occupied a prominent place in the history of Islamic Iran. Twice it has served as the political and cultural center of the Persianate world: during the reign of the Seljuks (1038–1194) and that of the Safavids (1501–1722). It has also been subjected to the vicissitudes and vagaries of conquest and expansion by nearly every conqueror and ruler whose net has been cast over these lands.

In its early Islamic history, Isfahan changed hands from the Umayyad governors of Basra to a rebel devotee of 'Ali to the 'Abbasid governors in the eighth and ninth centuries. During this early period, urban development seems to have largely focused around the Yahudiyya quarter where the 'Abbasid constructions merged Yahudiyya and its satellite villages, initiated the city's first congregational mosque, the nucleus of the famed Seljuk Masjid-i Jum'a, and its marketplace in the vicinity of the mosque.

With the rise to military power in 945 CE of the Iraq branch of the Persian Buyids, under whose tutelage the 'Abbasid caliphs were placed for more than a century, Isfahan received considerable attention leading to further expansions and its flourishing. Buyid emirs and their viziers oversaw the building of a defensive wall with twelve gates that encased the urban growth around the congregational mosque and the marketplace. They also constructed a citadel, Qal'a Tabarak, in the newly walled city. Although the knowledge of the pre-Buyid city depends entirely on descriptions by geographers and travelers, some of the arterial patterns of the Buyid city remain traceable in modern Isfahan, along with a few remnants of their expansion of the congregational mosque and an elaborately carved doorway from the Buyid Jurjir mosque.

Medieval Isfahan gained its lustre and world renown during the reign of the Great Seljuks. Tughril,

the founder of the dynasty, is recorded to have been so fond of the city that he moved his seat of rule to Isfahan. Under the patronage of the Seljuk Malik-shah (r. 1072–1092) and his viziers, Nizam al-Mulk and Taj al-Mulk, Isfahan grew, according to Nasir-i Khosraw and other travelers, into one of the most populous and prosperous cities in the medieval world, becoming famous for its fine crafts and industries. The Masjid-i Jum'a, already twice enlarged, was completely redesigned into the Persianate mosque type that is associated with this central region of Iran and the Seljuk period. The Arab hypostyle (a covered sanctuary roof atop rows of pillars and an adjacent courtyard) was transformed, between the 1070s and 1120s, into a four-*iwan* (vaulted space open to one side), courtyard-centered mosque with a domed *mihrab* (prayer niche) chamber. Two domed chambers—a massive one over the *mihrab* sponsored by Nizam al-Mulk, the other on the opposite, north side of the mosque sponsored by the rival vizier Taj al-Mulk—vaulted roofs of the sanctuary spaces on all four sides of the vast courtyard, and the four massive *iwans* on each side of the courtyard; these Seljuk architectural interventions represent Isfahan's Masjid-i Jum'a as the blueprint for all aspects of design, as well as technologies and materials for building and decorating in Persian architecture of the medieval period.

Some of its architectural features, namely the placement of a domed chamber on the north side opposite the *mihrab* chamber, are unique to Isfahan's mosque both in terms of its very inclusion and, more important, of its superb mastery of design and execution in plain brick. This little building's fame derives from the complex mathematics of its geometric patterns in the inner face of the dome and the way in which architectural and decorative forms are manipulated to create exciting visual transitions from the sidewalls into the dome. It has been suggested that the mathematician, astronomer, and poet 'Umar Khayyam may have had a hand in the conception of this masterpiece. He is recorded to have played a leading role in the Seljuk reformation of the Persian calendar and in the construction of an observatory in Isfahan.

The centrality of the Masjid-i Jum'a in the urban life of Seljuk Isfahan is attested to by the fact that a major public square known as *Maydan-i Kuhna*, bazaars, and the royal residence and administrative quarters were all further developed in the vicinity of this venerable mosque. Indeed, the mosque continued to serve as the site for royal patronage throughout its subsequent history when rulers and conquerors left traces of their dominion through such architectural marks as the magnificent carved stucco *mihrab* in the

Masjid-i Shah (now Masjid-i Imam), Northwest Iwan, Isfahan, Iran, Safavid period (seventeenth century). Photo courtesy of Judith Lerner.

winter prayer hall (by the Ilkhanid Öljeitü), or the gorgeously tiled facades of the courtyard and its four *iwans* (by the Safavid Shah Tahmasb and later).

Mongol invasions reached Isfahan when, in 1240–1241, the city was delivered by some of its own denizens into the hands of the Mongols whose heavy taxation led to the city's decline. In 1387, Tamerlane (Timur) besieged the city and was provoked into massacring some seventy thousand of its inhabitants, thus laying Isfahan to waste and making her vulnerable to further plunders for another century to come. The sixteenth-century phase of the Safavids did not substantially alter the peripheral role of Isfahan in comparison to the capitals of Tabriz and Qazvin.

In the course of the closing years of the sixteenth century, the Safavid Shah 'Abbas (r. 1588–1629) embarked on a vast reconstruction of the urban environment in anticipation of the official transfer of his capital from Qazvin to Isfahan in 1598. The transfer of the capital also signaled Shah 'Abbas's success in the Safavid quest for centralization of the imperial enterprise and the promulgation of Shi'ism in Iran, of which the Safavids were the most powerful exponents in Iranian history. Thus the new urban center was conceived on a level of architectural complexity

and scale more appropriately early modern than medieval in its representation of the increasingly centralized and sedentarized Safavids.

During this last decade of the century the architectural armature of the new capital city was established in the form of two urban foci: a vast public square, the Maydan-i Naqsh-i Jahan (Image of the World), measuring 510 meters by 165 meters and located to the southwest of the Seljuk urban hub; and a tree-lined promenade, the Chahar Bagh (Four Gardens) of more than one and a half kilometers long that ran on a north–south axis linking through a bridge the Safavid capital to new suburbs south of the Zayanda River. The completion of nearly all the constituent parts of this grand urban plan fell in the seventeenth century.

The Maydan, with double rows of shops lining its peripheral walls, and with the strategic and symbolic positioning of a ceremonial palace and administrative building on its western side, a private royal chapel on the eastern flank, a large congregational mosque on the south, and the royal bazaar entrance on its north side was conceived as the new commercial, political, and religious center of the Safavid capital. This new Maydan was connected through a complex intertwining of bazaar arteries to the Maydan-i Kuhna and the Masjid-i Jum'a, rivaling the medieval city and in time succeeding in shifting the urban hub to the new imperial city.

SUSSAN BABAIE

See also Iran; Malikshah; Nasir-I Khosraw; Nizam al-Mulk; Seljuks; Shah 'Abbas; Safavids; Tamerlane (Timur)

Further Reading

Frye, R.N. (Ed). *The Cambridge History of Iran.* 7 volumes. *The Period from the Arab Invasion to the Seljuqs.* Vol. 4. Cambridge: Cambridge University Press, 1975.
Golombek, Lisa. "Urban Patterns in Pre-Safavid Isfahan." In *Studies on Isfahan* [Proceedings of the Isfahan Colloquium], *Iranian Studies* VII, Pt. I, 18–44.
Grabar, Oleg. *The Great Mosque of Isfahan.* New York: New York University Press, 1990.
Holod, Renata (Ed). *Studies on Isfahan* [Proceedings of the Isfahan Colloquium], *Iranian Studies* VII, Pts. I and II.
Jackson, Peter, and Laurence Lockhart (Eds). *The Cambridge History of Iran.* 7 vols. *The Timurid and Safavid Periods.* Vol. 6. Cambridge, London, and New York: Cambridge University Press, 1986.

ISFAHANI, AL-, ABU NU'AYM

Al-Isfahani Abu Nu'aym Ahmad b. 'Abdallah, was born in Isfahan in around AH 336/948 CE. Although he wrote exclusively in Arabic, he was of Persian origin. His second/eighth century ancestor, Mihran, appears to have been the first to have converted to Islam. His most famous ancestor was his maternal grandfather, Muhammad ibn Yusuf ibn Ma'dan al-Banna' (d. 365/976), who was the leader of a school of Sufism in Isfahan, which was still flourishing in Abu Nu'aym's lifetime.

Abu Nu'aym's three major works, all of which have been published, are: (1) his *magnum opus,* the *Hilyat al-awliya' wa-tabaqat al-asfiya',* which is a voluminous collection of biographies of Sufis and other early Muslim religious leaders; (2) *Dhikr akhbar Isfahan,* a biographical dictionary of the prominent scholars of his native Isfahan; and (3) *Dala'il al-nubuwwa,* a biography of the Prophet Muhammad, which focuses in particular on the evident signs of his status. These three works demonstrate Abu Nu'aym's interest in collecting and compiling hadiths and biographical reports about important religious leaders. Like other such traditionist historians preoccupied with seeking knowledge, he would have traveled widely to collect his material. Abu Nu'aym makes specific reference to travels for this purpose to the Hijaz, Iraq, Syria, and Khurasan. In turn, Abu Nu'aym himself attracted traditionists from distant origins who

wished to hear his material, the most famous of whom was probably al-Khatib al-Baghdadi, the compiler of *Ta'rikh Baghdad.*

Abu Nu'aym's most influential work by far, his *Hilyat al-awliya' (The Ornament of the Saints),* consists of 689 biographies in ten volumes (amounting to approximately four thousand pages of twenty-five lines each in the printed edition). He cast a wide net in his selection of religious figures to represent in this work. They include, in roughly chronological order: the first generations of the Prophet's religious successors according to Sunnism *(al-salaf al-salih),* the first six individual successors of the Prophet, or Imams, according to Shi'ism, the eponymous founders of three of the four major Sunni schools of jurisprudence (see later in the paragraph in regard to the notable omission), scholastic theologians, ascetics, pietists, and mystics. However, in spite of its broad sweep the *Hilyat al-awliya'* is certainly not all-inclusive; Abu Nu'aym appears to have deliberately omitted a number of individuals for polemical reasons, including most conspicuously: Abu Hanifa, the eponym of the Hanafite legal school; and al-Hallaj, the outspoken mystic whose execution in Baghdad in 922 is traditionally seen as a major turning point in the history of Sufism.

Like many other such vast works written in the same period, the *Hilyat al-awliya'* shows signs that it was not under the control of a single author. While its colophon gives the date of completion of the work as AH 422 (1030 CE), and its list of biographies ends with his own contemporaries from among the successors of Ibn Ma'dan al-Banna', a number of the chains of transmission, or *isnad*s, within the text include Abu Nu'aym himself, and not simply as the immediate source. Like many other works of Islamic scholarship in the early centuries, the *Hilyat al-awliya'* appears to have been compiled by the students of the author to whom it is attributed, probably for the most part under his direction. The history of the text of the *Hilyat al-awliya'* explains why its biographies appear to have been ordered in various parts according to a number of competing principles (such as chronology, geography, affiliation, alphabetically by name), as well as why certain biographies have been repeated.

Abu Nu'aym's fame rests primarily on the *Hilyat al-awliya',* which has been used as a vast mine of biographical data by later Muslim historians, as well as some modern academics. The fact that its biographies are invariably much longer than those found in comparable biographical dictionaries of the period has made it especially attractive for this purpose. Abu Nu'aym is rarely recalled as a Sufi authority in Sufi biography collections. He is celebrated as a past hero in the later biographical dictionaries of the

Shafi'i school of jurisprudence more than any other, where he is depicted as a staunch defender of this school during disputes with the rival Hanbali school of jurisprudence in Isfahan at the turn of the eleventh century, as a result of which he was expelled from the city. Some Hanbali sources also include Abu Nu'aym among their number. Due to the fact that the prominent Safavid al-Majlisi family considered themselves to have been his descendants, Abu Nu'aym is also portrayed in late medieval Shi'i literature as a sympathizer, and sometimes even as a crypto-Shi'i.

JAWID MOJADDEDI

See also Biography and Biographical Works; Saints and Sainthood; Sufism and Sufis

Further Reading

al-Isfahani, Abu Nu'aym. *Geschichte Isbahans*. Translated by S. Dedering. Leiden: E.J. Brill, 1931–1934.
———. *Hilyat al-awliya*. 10 vols Cairo, 1032–1038.
———. *Dala'il al-nubuwwa*. Hyderabad, 1950.

Studies

Khoury, R.G. "Importance et authenticité de textes de *Hilyat al-awliya'*." *Studia Islamica*, 46 (1977): 73–113.
Mojaddedi, Jawid. *The Biographical Tradition in Sufism: The Tabaqat Genre from al-Sulami to Jami*. Richmond: Routledge Curzon, 2001.

ISHAQ IBN IBRAHIM

A member of the Tahirid family, Ishaq ibn Ibrahim al-Mus'abi held a prominent place serving the 'Abbasids. After a long career he died in 850 CE. All that is known of his early background is that he was a cousin of Abdallah ibn Tahir and that he was possibly born in 793. He first appears in 821, when he was appointed by Abdallah as the chief of police in Baghdad. For the next twenty-nine years he served as the caliphal enforcer of policy, mostly in Baghdad. Given this information, it is striking that we know so little about him. We are forced to infer based on the record in the chronicles of his activities. In 829 or 830, he served as governor of Aleppo, 'Awasim, and the Thughur. In 830, al-Ma'mun (r. 813–833) made him his deputy in Baghdad while he was on campaign against the Byzantines. In 831, al-Ma'mun ordered him to make the soldiers in Baghdad say the *takbir* (Allah Akbar, God is most great) as part of their prayers. Al-Ma'mun began the Mihna (the Inquisition of 833–848 or 851) with a series of letters to Ishaq, instructing him to question all of the judges and hadith transmitters about their position on the createdness of the Qur'an. He was to inform them that the caliph held that it was created. He was the

primary questioner of Ibn Hanbal, a role that he reprised in many cases as the caliphal enforcer of the Mihna in Baghdad. When al-Ma'mun died, his will advised al-Mu'tasim (r. 833–842) to take him into his confidence. He was responsible for bringing the Khurramiyya to heel in 833 on the orders of al-Mu'tasim. He is mentioned, among the most powerful figures in the caliphate, as one of the few witnesses to the trial of the disgraced general al-Afshin in 841. When al-Mu'tasim died, Ishaq was responsible for administering in Baghdad the oath of loyalty to the next caliph, al-Wathiq (r. 842–847). Al-Wathiq relied on him to deliberate the cases against the secretaries in 844. Interestingly, he was not part of the group that placed al-Mutawakkil (r. 847–861) upon the throne. However, he was one of the primary individuals that al-Mutawakkil relied on to strengthen his hold on power. In 850, on al-Mutawakkil's order, he arrested the Turkish general, Itakh, who had been lured to Baghdad by an elaborate ruse. Al-Tabari states quite explicitly that this took place in Baghdad because Itakh was too powerful to be accosted in Samarra. Itakh was killed in Ishaq's house. What becomes clear from this account of his activities is that he served a pivotal role for the post-Ma'mun caliphs. He was their enforcer in Baghdad. The continuity of his position in what still was the most important city in the caliphate economically and culturally argues for his power and influence. It also highlights his surprising loyalty to the office of caliph. He does not make a bid for independence or independent power. He was seemingly content with serving at the will of the sitting caliph.

JOHN P. TURNER

See also Aleppo; Ibn Hanbal; al-Ma'mun; Samarra; al-Tabari

Further Reading

Ka'bi, al-Munji. *Les Tahirides : Etude historico-littéraire de la dynastie des Banu Tahir b. al-Husayn au Hurasan et en Iraq au IIIème s. de l'Hégire/IXème s. J.-C.* Paris: Université de Paris-Sorbonne, Faculté des lettres et sciences humaines, 1983.

Primary Sources

Tabari, Abu Ja'far. *The Crisis of the 'Abbasid Caliphate*. Translated by G. Saliba. Vol. 35. Albany: State University of New York Press, 1985.
———. *The Reunification of the 'Abbasid Caliphate*. Translated by C.E. Bosworth. Vol. 32. Albany: SUNY Press, 1987.
———. *Incipient Decline*. Translated by J. L. Kraemer. Vol. 34. Albany: SUNY Press, 1989.

———. *Storm and Stress along the Northern Frontiers of the 'Abbasid Caliphate*. Translated by C.E. Bosworth. Vol. 33. Albany: SUNY Press, 1991.

ISLAM

Islam is the religious faith that has its origins in the heart of the Arabian peninsula and whose core teachings enshrine not only a firm and uncompromising monotheism but also a detailed system of law and ritual practice. The Arabic term *Islam* technically denotes the act of submission; it is used in the religious context to signify obedience to the will of God. The Prophet Muhammad serves as the figure with whom the Islamic faith emerged in the mid-seventh century in the city of Mecca. The faith appears as an inspired challenge to the cult of polytheistic and animistic rituals that had developed in and around the shrine at Mecca, the *Ka'ba*. This setting provides the background for the promulgation of a return to monotheism preached by the Prophet Muhammad, whom Islam proclaims as being God's final messenger and the recipient of His ultimate book of revelation the Qur'an. The Islamic faith promotes not only a distinct revival of the Abrahamic tradition disseminated by biblical Prophets, with whom it shares a common spiritual heritage, but also a distinctive brand of devotional rituals fused with legal and moral dictates. These dictates covered a wide spectrum of issues ranging from the intricacies of political theory and commerce, extending to family law, dietary code, and personal piety.

The teachings of Islam are decisively derived from two sources: the Qur'an, which encompasses theological, juristic, and ethical imperatives while also serving as a devotional text; and the Prophetic *sunna* (custom), which theoretically forms the sum and substance of the Prophet's words, deeds, and silent affirmations as enshrined in the Prophetic *hadith* (traditions), serving as a normative model for Muslims to emulate. *Qiyas* (analogical reasoning) and *ijma'* (consensus of the community) also play a key role in the formulation of Islamic law. The primary creed of Islam is the belief that there is no deity save God and that Muhammad is His messenger. This pillar of faith is followed by four essential religious obligations: the performance of five daily prayers *(salat)*; the payment of alms *(zakat)*; the observance of fasting during the month of Ramadan *(sawm)*; and the pilgrimage to Mecca *(hajj)*, once in a lifetime for those able to do so. Islam also teaches that a Muslim must believe in all God's Prophets, hence the revered status it grants to biblical figures such as Abraham, David, Moses, and Jesus together with their Divine revelation and scripture. However, Islamic scripture offered critical distinctions regarding the lives and roles of these biblical Prophets. Islam defined an array of eschatological dogmas, including the belief in angels and the reality of the Day of Judgment. Theological doctrines were also refined on issues such as predestination and the infallibility of Prophets. The adherents of Islam are divided into two main denominations: Sunnis, who represent 85% of the faith's followers; and Shi'is, who constitute the remaining 15%, although further, finer subdivisions of these denominations do exist. The religion proclaimed by Muhammad became the predominant creed of the Arabian Peninsula and beyond.

MUSTAFA SHAH

See also Angels; Arabic; Caliphate and Imamate; Charity; Circumcision; Commanding Good and Forbidding Evil; Crime and Punishment; Eschatology; Ethics; Festivals and Celebrations; Food and Diet; God; Hadith; Imam; Law and Jurisprudence; Jesus; Jews; Jihad; Ka'ba; Mecca; Medina; Mosques; Pilgrimage; Political Theory; Predestination; Qur'an; Usury and Interest; Shari'a; Shi'ism; Sufism and Sufis

Further Reading

Berkey, Johnathan. *The Formation of Islam, Religion Society in the Near East 600-1800*. Cambridge: Cambridge University Press, 2003.
Brown, Daniel. *Islam: A New Introduction*. Oxford: Blackwell Publishing, 2004.
Endress, Gerhard. *An Introduction to Islam*. Edinburgh: Edinburgh University Press, 2001.
Watt, Montgomerry. *Islam: A Short History*. Oxford: Oneworld, 1999.

ISMAILIS

The second most important Shi'i community after the Ithna'asharis or Twelvers, Ismailis have subdivided into a number of major branches and minor groups in the course of their long and complex history dating back to the middle of the AH second/eighth CE century.

Early and Fatimid Periods until 487/1094

In 148/765, on the death of Ja'far al-Sadiq, who had consolidated Imami Shi'ism, the majority of his followers recognized his son Musa al-Kazim as their new imam. However, other Imami Shi'i groups acknowledged the imamate of Musa's older half-brother, Isma'il, the eponym of the Isma'iliyya, or Isma'il's son Muhammad. Little is known about the life and career of Muhammad ibn Isma'il, who went into hiding, marking the initiation of the *dawr al-satr*, or period of concealment, in early Ismailism which lasted until the foundation of the Fatimid state when the Ismaili imams emerged openly as Fatimid caliphs.

On the death of Muhammad ibn Isma'il, not long after 179/795, his followers, who were at the time evidently known as Mubarakiyya, split into two groups. A majority refused to accept his death; they recognized him as their seventh and last imam and awaited his return as the Mahdi, the restorer of justice and true Islam. A second, smaller group acknowledged Muhammad's death and traced the imamate in his progeny. Almost nothing is known about the subsequent history of these earliest Ismaili groups until shortly after the middle of the third/ninth century.

It is certain that for almost a century after Muhammad ibn Isma'il, a group of his descendants worked secretly for the creation of a revolutionary movement against the 'Abbasids. The aim of this religiopolitical movement was to install the Ismaili imam belonging to the Prophet Muhammad's family *(ahl al-bayt)* to a new caliphate ruling over the entire Muslim community; and the message of the movement was disseminated by a network of *da'is*, summoners or religiopolitical propagandists. Observing *taqiyya,* or precautionary dissimulation, these central leaders concealed their true identities in order to escape 'Abbasid persecution. 'Abdullah, the first of these leaders, had organized his *da'wa* (mission) around the doctrine of the majority of the earliest Ismailis, namely, the Mahdiship of Muhammad ibn Isma'il. 'Abdullah eventually settled in Salamiyya, central Syria, which served as the secret headquarters of the Ismaili *da'wa* for some time. The efforts of 'Abdullah and his successors bore results in the 260s/870s, when numerous *da'is* appeared in southern Iraq and adjacent regions under the leadership of Hamdan Qarmat and his chief assistant 'Abdan. The Ismailis now referred to their movement simply as *al-da'wa,* the mission, or *al-da'wa al-hadiya,* the rightly guiding mission. Soon, the Ismaili *da'wa* appeared in numerous other regions, notably Yaman, where Ibn Hawshab Mansur al-Yaman (d. 302/914) acted as the chief *da'i*, Egypt, Bahrayn, Persia, Transoxiana, and Sind, as well as remoter regions in North Africa.

By the early 280s/890s, a unified Ismaili movement had replaced the earlier splinter groups. However, in 286/899, soon after 'Abdullah al-Mahdi, the future Fatimid caliph, had succeeded to leadership in Salamiyya, Ismailism was rent by a major schism. 'Abdullah claimed the Ismaili imamate openly for himself and his ancestors who had organized the early Ismaili *da'wa*, also explaining the various forms of guises adopted by the earlier central Ismaili leaders who had preferred to assume the rank of *hujja* (proof or full representative) of the hidden Imam Muhammad ibn Isma'il. The doctrinal reform of 'Abdullah al-Mahdi split the Ismaili movement into two rival factions. A loyalist faction, comprised mainly of the Ismailis of Yaman, Egypt, North Africa, and Sind, did recognize continuity in the imamate, acknowledging 'Abdullah and his 'Alid ancestors as their imams. On the other hand, a dissident faction, originally led by Hamdan Qarmat, retained their original belief in the Mahdiship of Muhammad ibn Isma'il. Henceforth, the term *Qarmati* came to be applied specifically to the dissidents who did not acknowledge 'Abdullah al-Mahdi, as well as his predecessors and successors to the Fatimid caliphate, as their imams. The dissident Qarmatis acquired their most important stronghold in the Qarmati state of Bahrayn, founded in 286/899 by the *da'i* Abu Sa'id al-Jannabi. The Qarmati state of Bahrayn eventually collapsed in 470/1077.

The early Ismailis elaborated a distinctive gnostic system of religious thought, which was further developed or modified in the Fatimid period. Central to this system was a fundamental distinction between the exoteric *(zahir)* and esoteric *(batin)* aspects of the sacred scriptures, as well as religious commandments and prohibitions. They further held that the religious laws, representing the *zahir* of religion, enunciated by prophets, underwent periodical changes while the *batin,* containing the spiritual truths *(haqa'iq)* remained immutable and unchanged. These truths, forming a gnostic system of thought, were explained through *ta'wil,* esoteric exegesis, which became the hallmark of Ismaili thought. The two main components of this system were a cyclical history of revelations and a cosmological doctrine.

The early success of the Ismaili movement culminated in the foundation of the Fatimid caliphate in North Africa, where the *da'i* Abu 'Abdullah al-Shi'i (d. 298/911) had spread the *da'wa* among the Berbers of the Maghrib. The new dynasty, established in 297/909, was named Fatimid (Fatimiyyun) after the Prophet Muhammad's daughter Fatima, to whom the Fatimid caliphs traced their 'Alid ancestry. 'Abdullah al-Mahdi (d. 322/934), the first Fatimid caliph–imam, and his successors ruled over an important state that soon grew into an empire stretching from North Africa to Egypt, Palestine, and Syria. The Fatimid period was also the "golden age" of Ismailism when Ismaili thought and literature and *da'wa* activities attained their summit and Ismailis made important contributions to Islamic civilization, especially after the seat of the Fatimid caliphate was transferred to Cairo, itself founded in 358/969 by the Fatimids.

The Ismaili *da'wa* of the Fatimid times achieved its greatest successes, however, outside the Fatimid dominions, especially in Yaman, where the Ismaili Sulayhids ruled as vassals of the Fatimids, Persia, and Central Asia. The *da'is* of the Iranian lands, such as Abu Ya'qub al-Sijistani, Hamid al-Din al-Kirmani, and Nasir-i Khusraw, also elaborated complex metaphysical systems of thought with a distinct emanational cosmology. The Fatimid *da'wa* was particularly concerned with educating the new converts in Ismaili doctrine, known as the *hikma* (wisdom); and a variety of lectures, generally designated as sessions of wisdom *(majalis al-hikma)*, were organized for this purpose. Ismaili law was also codified mainly through the efforts of al-Qadi al-Nu'man (d. 363/974), the foremost jurist of the Fatimid period. Ismaili law accorded special importance to the Shi'i doctrine of the imamate.

The Isma'ilis experienced a major schism in 487/1094, on the death of al-Mustansir, the eighth Fatimid caliph and the eighteenth Ismaili imam. Al-Mustansir's succession was disputed by his sons—Nizar, the original heir designate, and al-Musta'li, who was installed to the Fatimid caliphate by the all-powerful vizier al-Afdal. As a result, the unified Ismaili *da'wa* and community were split into rival branches, designated later as Nizari and Musta'li (or Musta'-lawi). The *da'wa* organization in Cairo, as well as the Ismaili communities of Egypt, Yaman, and western India, also recognized al-Musta'li as his father's successor to the imamate. On the other hand, the Ismailis of Persia and adjacent lands supported the succession right of Nizar and recognized his imamate. Nizar himself revolted against al-Musta'li (d. 495/1101), but he was defeated and killed in 488/1095. Henceforth, the Ismaili imamate was handed down in two parallel lines among the descendants of al-Mustansir.

Musta'li Ismailis

On the death of al-Musta'li's son and successor al-Amir in 524/1130, the Musta'li Ismailis split into Hafizi and Tayyibi branches. The Musta'li *da'wa* headquarters in Cairo endorsed the imamate of al-Amir's cousin and successor to the Fatimid throne, al-Hafiz. As a result, his imamate was also acknowledged by the Musta'li Ismailis of Egypt and Syria, as well as a portion of the Musta'lis of Yaman. These Ismailis, who recognized al-Hafiz (d. 544/1149) and the later Fatimid caliphs as their imams, became

known as Hafizis. The Musta'li Ismailis of the Sulayhid state in Yaman, as well as those of Gujarat, recognized the imamate of al-Amir's son, al-Tayyib, and they became known as Tayyibis. Hafizi Ismailism disappeared completely soon after the collapse of the Fatimid dynasty in 567/1171. Thereafter, Musta'li Ismailism survived only in its Tayyibi form with permanent strongholds in Yaman.

The Tayyibi imams have remained in concealment since the time of al-Tayyib himself, who disappeared under mysterious circumstances. In the absence of their imams, the affairs of the Tayyibi *da'wa* and community have been administered by *da'i mutlaqs*, that is, supreme *da'is* with full authority. In the doctrinal field, the Tayyibis maintained the Fatimid traditions and preserved a substantial portion of the Ismaili texts of the Fatimid period. Building particularly on Hamid al-Din al-Kirmani's metaphysical system, they elaborated their own esoteric system of religious thought with its distinctive eschatological themes. The Tayyibi *da'wa* spread successfully in the Haraz region of Yaman, as well as in Gujarat. By the end of the tenth/sixteenth century, the Tayyibi Ismailis split into Da'udi and Sulaymani branches over the question of the succession to their twenty-sixth *da'i mutlaq*, Da'ud ibn 'Ajabshah (d. 997/1589). By that time the Tayyibis of India, known locally as Bohras, greatly outnumbered their Yamani coreligionists. Henceforth, the Da'udi and Sulaymani Tayyibis, concentrated in South Asia and Yaman, respectively, followed different lines of *da'is*. Da'udi Bohras have subdivided into several groupings, with the largest numbering around eight hundred thousand. Since the 1920s, Bombay has served as the permanent administrative seat of the Da'udi *da'i mutlaq*. The leadership of the Sulaymani Tayyibis has remained hereditary in the Makrami family with their headquarters in Najran, in northeastern Yaman. At present the Sulaymani Tayyibis number around seventy thousand in Yaman, with an additional few thousand in India.

Nizari Ismailis

In al-Mustansir's time, the *da'i* Hasan-i Sabbah succeeded 'Abd al-Malik ibn 'Attash as the leader of the Isma'ili *da'wa* within the Saljuq dominions in Persia. His seizure of the fortress of Alamut in 483/1090 had, in fact, marked the effective foundation of what became the Nizari Ismaili state of Persia with a subsidiary in Syria. In al-Mustansir's succession dispute, Hasan supported Nizar's cause and severed his relations with the *da'wa* headquarters in Cairo. By this decision, Hasan-i Sabbah also founded the Nizari *da'wa* independently of the Fatimid regime. The Nizaris acquired political prominence under Hasan-i Sabbah (d. 518/1124) and his seven successors at Alamut. Hasan's armed revolt against the Saljuq Turks, whose alien rule was detested by the Persians, did not succeed; and the Saljuqs, despite their superior military power, failed to destroy the Nizari fortress communities. In effect, a stalemate developed between the Nizaris and their various enemies until their state in Persia was destroyed by the Mongols in 654/1256. The Nizaris of Syria, who had numerous encounters with the Crusaders and reached the peak of their fame under the *da'i* Rashid al-Din al-Sinan (d. 589/1193), were eventually subdued by the Mamluks. The Nizaris elaborated their own teachings, initially revolving around the Shi'i doctrine of *ta'lim* or authoritative guidance by the imam of the time. The Nizari imams, who had remained in hiding since Nizar, emerged openly at Alamut in 559/1164.

Disorganized and deprived of any central leadership, the Nizari Ismailis survived the Mongol destruction of their state. For about two centuries, while the imams remained inaccessible, various Nizari communities developed independently, also adopting Sunni and Sufi guises to safeguard themselves against persecution. By the middle of the ninth/fifteenth century, the Nizari imams emerged in the village of Anjudan, in central Persia, initiating a revival in the *da'wa* and literary activities of their community. The Nizari *da'wa* became particularly successful in Central Asia and India, where the Hindu converts were known as Khojas. The Nizari Khojas developed an indigenous religious tradition designated as Satpanth or the "true path," as well as a devotional literature known as the *ginan*s. With the advent of the Safavids, who adopted Twelver Shi'ism as the religion of their state in 907/1501, the Nizaris of Persia also practiced *taqiyya* as Twelvers. The Nizaris of Badakhshan, now divided between Tajikistan and Afghanistan, have preserved numerous Persian Ismaili texts of the Alamut and later periods. The Nizari Khojas, together with the Tayyibi Bohras, were among the earliest Asian communities to settle during the nineteenth century in East Africa. In the 1970s, the bulk of the East African Ismailis were obliged to immigrate to the west. Under the leadership of their last two imams, Sultan Muhammad Shah Aga Khan III (1885–1957) and his grandson, Prince Karim Aga Khan IV, the current forty-ninth imam, the Nizari Ismailis have emerged as a progressive Muslim minority with high standards of education and well-being. Numbering several millions, they are scattered in more than twenty-five countries of Asia, the Middle East, Africa, Europe, and North America.

FARHAD DAFTARY

Further Reading

Corbin, Henry. *Cyclical Time and Ismaili Gnosis* Translated by R. Manheim and J.W. Morris. London, 1983.
Daftary, F. *The Isma'ilis: Their History and Doctrines.* Cambridge, 1990 (with full references to the sources).
———. *A Short History of the Ismailis.* Edinburgh, 1998.
———. *Ismaili Literature: A Bibliography of Sources and Studies.* London, 2004.
Halm, Heinz. *The Fatimids and Their Traditions of Learning.* London, 1997.
Hodgson, Marshall G.S. *The Order of Assassins.* The Hague, 1955.
Madelung, Wilferd. "Das Imamat in der frühen ismailitischen Lehre." *Der Islam,* 37(1961): 43–135.
Walker, Paul E. *Early Philosophical Shiism: The Ismaili Neoplatonism of Abu Ya'qub al- Sijistani.* Cambridge, 1993.

ISTANBUL

For almost sixteen centuries, İstanbul enjoyed a unique status as the capital city of two great civilizations: the Byzantine empire and the Ottoman empire.

The first settlements in the peninsula date from the late third or early second millennium BCE. In 330 CE, Constantine moved the seat of the Roman empire to Byzantium and created a new state. Its name eventually became "Constantinople," meaning the city of Constantine. The name had currency among even the Turks, whose documents and coins frequently referred to the capital as "Konstantiniye" for centuries. In addition, it was used alternately with "İstanbul" in official documents. Constantinople gained some of its most famous architectural landmarks under Justinian (527–565). The Roman construction ingenuity meshed with the Hellenistic design legacy to produce a new synthesis in Justinian's buildings. Aya Sophia (532–537) is the culmination of this synthesis.

Through the ages, the city had seen several sieges of Arabs and a dramatic Latin invasion (1204). On May 30, 1453, Mehmed II made his ceremonial entry into Constantinople and declared it to be his capital. He then inaugurated a new era of building activity aimed at making the city the economic, administrative, cultural, and religious center of the empire. In creating a Muslim city, the process started with the conversion of Aya Sophia into the Great Mosque and seventeen other churches. After the conquest, at the eastern end of the peninsula, almost the entire structure of the Topkapı Palace had been built. The Topkapı Palace remained the official imperial residence until the construction of the Dolmabahçe Palace across the Golden Horn in 1856.

The sixteenth century was a time of great building activity. During the reign of Süleyman (1520–1566), İstanbul was endowed with many monuments, and it was the work of the great architect Sinan (1490–1588). Sinan's *külliyes* brought the ultimate Islamic and Ottoman definition to İstanbul's urban form.

During the seventeenth and eighteenth centuries İstanbul continued to develop, but the scale of the building activity was by no means comparable to that of previous centuries due largely to the gradual decline in the economic power of the empire. The population continued to escalate between seven hundred thousand and eight hundred thousand. This was almost twice the size of the population in 1535. The seventeenth century contributed two monuments to the capital: the *külliye* of Ahmed I and the Valide mosque. The eighteenth century brought no significant monuments to İstanbul but nonetheless marked an important first step toward embracing European architectural fashions. Many foreign architects and artists were invited to İstanbul. The architectural language they introduced to İstanbul developed into the "Ottoman Baroque." Western influences began to be apparent from the early eighteenth century, new forms and dynamic profiles of the Nuruosmaniye and Laleli mosques attesting to the influence of the French and Italian Baroque and Rococo on traditional Ottoman building types. However, the nineteenth century saw an unparalleled stylistic eclecticism, as well as the introduction of a great diversity of new building types: banks, office buildings, theaters, department stores, hotels, and multistory apartment buildings.

SUAT ALP

See also Aya Sophia; Sinan; Süleymaniye Mosque; Ottoman Empire

Further Reading

And, M. *İstanbul in the 16th Century, The City, The Palace, Daily Life.* İstanbul, 1994.

Bator, Robert. *Daily Life in Ancient and Modern Istanbul.* Minneapolis: Runestone Press, 2000.

Celik, Zeynep. *The Remaking of Istanbul: Portrait of an Ottoman City in the Nineteenth Century.* Seattle: University of Washington, 1986.

Freely, John. *Istanbul: The Imperial City.* London: Penguin Books, 1998.

Goodwin, G. *A History of Ottoman Architecture.* London, 1971.

İnalcik, H. "İstanbul: An Islamic City." *Journal of Islamic Studies* I (1990): 1–23.

Kuban, Dogan. *Istanbul, bir kent tarihi: Bizantion, Konstantinopolis, Istanbul.* Istanbul: Turkiye Ekonomik ve Toplumsal Tarih Vakfi, 2000.

Lewis, Bernard. *Istanbul and the Civilization of the Ottoman Empire.* University of Oklahoma, 1963.

Runciman, Steven. *The Fall of Constantinople, 1453.* Cambridge: Cambridge University, 1990.

'IZZ AL-DIN ABU 'ABD ALLAH MUHAMMAD B. 'ALI

'Izz al-Din Abu 'Abd Allah Muhammad b. 'Ali (sometimes confused with Baha' al-Din Abu 'l-Mahasin Yusuf b. Rafi') was a Syrian administrator and author of topographical and historical works. He was born in Aleppo in AH 613/1217 CE, and subsequently served in the government of the city. After an unsuccessful attempt to negotiate an agreement between the Mongols and the ruler of Aleppo in AH 657/1259 CE, he fled to Egypt where he prospered in the service of the Mamluk ruler Baybars I and the latter's successors. 'Izz al-Din died in Cairo in AH 684/1285 CE.

'Izz al-Din wrote a historical topography of greater Syria, Palestine, and the Jazira called *al-A'laq al-khatira fi dhikr umara' al-Sham wa-l-Jazira (Precious Things of Moment in the Account of the Princes of Syria and the Jazira)*, as well as a life of Baybars I al-Bunduqdari.

DAVID MORRAY

See also Archives and Chanceries; Bureaucrats; Muslim–Mongol Diplomacy

Primary Sources

al-A'laq al-khatira fi dhikr umara' al-Sham wa'l-Jazira. (a) Bk. 1, pt. 1 (Aleppo). Edited by D. Sourdel. Beirut, 1953. (b) *Ta'rikh madinat Dimashq.* Edited by Sami al-Dahhan. Damascus, 1956. (c) *Ta'rikh Lubnan wa'l-Urdunn wa-Filastin.* Edited by Sami al-Dahhan. Damascus, 1963. (d) *Ta'rikh al-Jazira.* 2 vols. Edited by Yahya 'Abbara. Damascus, 1977–1978.

Die Geschichte des Sultan Baibars. Edited by Ahmad Hutait. Wiesbaden: Franz Steiner Verlag, 1983.

Further Reading

Ibn Shaddad, 'Izz al-Din. *al-A'laq al-khatira fi dhikr umara' al-Sham wa'l-Jazira.* Translated by Anne-Marie Eddé-Terrasse as *Description de la Syrie du Nord de 'Izz al-Din ibn Saddad.* Damascus, 1984.

J

JA'FAR AL-SADIQ (D. AH 148/765 CE)

Ja'far al-Sadiq was born in Medina in 80/699 or 83/703 and became one of the foremost exponents of the teachings from the Prophet's family. He is the most frequently cited authority on points of law and tradition, transmitting his family's wisdom to Muslims of diverse backgrounds and advocates of other religions, theosophists as well as gnostics who frequented his house in quest of knowledge.

Ja'far al-Sadiq is a central figure in Shi'i tradition, and he is the last common imam recognized by both the Ithna'asharis and the Isma'ilis. His contribution and influence, however, are far wider than his Shi'a. He is cited in a wide range of historical sources, including al-Tabari, al-Ya'qubi, and al-Masudi. Sunni, Sufi' and Shi'i sources all give testimony to his influence. Al-Dhahabi recognizes his contribution to Sunni tradition, whereas Abu Nu'aym and Farid al-Din Attar see him at the head of the Sufi line of saints and mystics. Ithna'ashari writers like al-Kulayni and Isma'ili scholars such as al-Qadi al-Nu'man record his monumental contribution to their respective Shi'i traditions.

Ja'far al-Sadiq inherited his position as a Shi'i imam from his father, al-Baqir. His versatile personality is, however, beyond classification, and his family perhaps saw him as a last attempt for reconciling the diverse groups of Muslims, since he was the great-great-grandson of 'Ali on one side and of Abu Bakr on the other. He remained distant in the power struggle that ensued from extremist Shi'is, with the Zaydiyya and the 'Abbasid movement of the Hashimiyya unfolding from the Kaysaniyya. He faced doctrinal difficulties from individuals who exaggerated his position, who were later known in history as the *ghulat*. Like his father before him, he repudiated them. Ja'far's detachment from politics gave him more time for scholarly activities, holding sessions at home as well as following his family's practice.

Law and Thought

Following the foundations laid by his father, al-Sadiq developed an extensive system of law and theology so that the Shi'i community had its own distinct ritual and religious doctrine. His traditions represent a range of subjects involving the 'ibadat and the mu'amalat, incorporating themes such as faith, devotion, alms, fasting, pilgrimage, and faith *(jihad)* as well as food, drink, social and business transactions, marriage and divorce, inheritance, criminal punishments, and a number of issues dealing with practically all aspects of life. Law in Islam, as is well known, is an all-embracing body of commands and prohibitions consisting of ordinances governing worship and ritual in addition to a proper legal system. Ja'far al-Sadiq is the most frequently quoted authority in Shi'i tradition. The Ithna 'ashari legal school is called the Ja'fari madhhab after him. Ismaili fiqh *(jurisprudence)* as codified by al-Qadi al-Nu'man is also primarily based on al-Sadiq's traditions and those of his father, al-Baqir. Besides guiding his own followers, he was widely regarded as a central reference point for many who sought his advice.

Amidst the theological issues of his day, such as those beliefs held by the Murji'a, the Qadariyya, the Jahmiyya and the Mu'tazila, Ja'far had his own distinct position. For example, he taught a middle position on the question of determinism and followed his father's views, which portrayed human responsibility but preserved God's autocracy. Knowledge was a central theme in his teaching, a duty for all Muslims to acquire through 'aql (intellect), a supreme faculty through which God is worshipped and the knowledge of good and evil acquired. Thus, his views on the imamate as well as those on 'aql, 'ilm, a'mal, and iman were geared toward self-actualization. The personal ethics, morality, and individual communion with God that are discussed in his teachings are used to obtain receptivity in the heart and mind, which he refers to, at times, as ma'rifa (this is not to be confused with the later usage of that word).

Imam and Teacher

In addition to disseminating knowledge of Shi'i law and theology, Ja'far al-Sadiq played the role of a spiritual guide; he was imam and teacher for his Shi'a, initiating them into the inner wisdom that could be experienced in their hearts. The search for haqiqa in the revelation is thus an important aspect of Ja'far's thought. The imam undertakes the amana (trust) from God, rendering him a guarantor (hujja) and a link (sabab) with the celestial world for those who accept his authority. This is part of the universal history, beginning with the pre-creation covenant (yawm al-mithaq) and manifested through the prophets and the imams.

The imam's task is therefore, man's purification, preparing receptacles for the haqiqa (truth), which is the raison d'être of history: restoring man to his original home. This was his role as an imam: to help others achieve ma'rifa qalbiyya (cognition of the heart), channeled through the imam to his followers. The vision of men's hearts perceiving realities of faith does not delegitimize the authority of the intellect or that of the community. In fact, self-sufficiency, which is a serious sin in the Qur'an, can easily become intellectual pride; consequently, man's 'ilm is subordinated to God's gift of ma'rifa, according to Ja'far. It is the prophets and the imams who form the point of contact between man and God, and it is in this respect, perhaps, that Ja'far refers to the sirr (secret) that is discovered through transconscience and for

which he possibly advocated taqiyya (precautionary dissimulation) as a principle.

Ja'far's ideas also became pervasive in the development of Sufi thought, where identical issues were raised, although in a more individualistic manner. His theology was especially significant in that it made use of experience as a hermeneutical principle. Paul Nywia (1970) emphasizes this contribution of Ja'far al-Sadiq, referring to his esoteric interpretation of the Qur'an collected by al-Sulami (d. 412/1021). He emphasised that Muslim conscience is not to be found in the world of imagination but rather in the experience of life itself and that the external symbols have to be transformed by experience to become the truth. It is therefore important to internalize the letters or symbols of the Qur'an through experience. Ja'far thus read the Qur'an discerning a merger between the inner and the outer meanings, and he presented a new exegesis that involved no longer a reading of the Qur'an but revisiting the experience in a new interpretation of it (ta'wil).

Ja'far al-Sadiq is linked to other disciplines as well: divination, including alchemy; the science of jafr, which includes letter–number correspondences; the occult arts, including pulmonancy (divination from body pulses); and hemerology (the study of calendars of auspicious and inauspicious days). These were popular among the Turks and Persians and have been reported in works known as falnamas. In the Indian subcontinent, these also played an important role in the popular life of Muslims and Hindus; evidence of this is found in Sindhi pothis (private religious manuscripts). In South Asia, Ja'far al-Sadiq is credited with writing khab-namas (interpretations of dreams), which are sometimes known as risala or bayan in Sindhi literature.

The plurality of Ja'far's teachings, his magnetic personality, and his spirituality have influenced subsequent generations in more ways than one. His influential contributions to Shi'i thought provided a momentum for the development of law, theology, and mysticism that is apparent in the impressive literature preserved in his name.

ARZINA R. LALANI

Further Reading

Amir-Moezzi, M.A. *The Divine Guide in Early Shi'ism*, transl. David Streight. Albany, NY, 1994.
Attar, Farid al-Din. *Tadhkirat al-Awliya'*, part 1, ed. Nicholson. London, 1905.
Al-Dhahabi. *Tadhkirat al-Hufaz*, vol. 1. Hyderabad, 1375/ 1955.
Ebeid, R.Y., and M.J.L. Young. "A Treatise on Hemerology Ascribed to Ga'far al-Sadiq." *Arabica* 23/3 (1976): 296–307.

Fahd, T. "Ga'far as-Sadiq et la Tradition Scientifique Arabe." In *Le Shi'isme Imamite Colloque de Strasbourg.* Paris, 1970.

Al-Isfahani, Abu Nu'aym. *Hilyat al-Awliya',* vol. 3. Cairo, 1352/1933.

Al-Kulayní, Muhammad b. Ya'qub. *Al-Usul min al-Kafi.* Tehran, 1388/1968.

Lalani, Arzina R. "Ja'far al-Sadiq." In *Encyclopaedia of Religion,* 2nd ed., 4760–2. Detroit, 2005.

Nywia, Paul. *Exegese Coranique et le Language Mystique.* Beirut, 1970.

Al-Qåãí al-Nu'man, Abu Hanifa. *Da'a'im al-Islåm,* 2 vols., ed. A.A.A. Fyzee. Cairo, 1950 and 1960. (See also Ismail K. Poonawala's revised translation of the first volume, *The Pillars of Islam.* Oxford, 2002.)

Sells, Michael A. "Early Sufi Qur'an Interpretation." In *Early Islamic Mysticism,* 75–89. New York, 1996.

Al-Tabari, Abu Ja'far Muhammad b. Jarír. *Ta'rikh al-Rusul wa al-Muluk. Annales,* ed. M.J. de Goeje. Leiden, 1879–1901

Taylor, John B. "Ja'far al-Sadiq, Spiritual Forebear of the Sufis." *Islamic Culture* 40/2 (1966): 97–113.

———. "Man's Knowledge of God in the Thought of Ja'far al-Sadiq." *Islamic Culture* October (1966): 195–206.

Al-Ya'qubi, Ahmad b. Ibn Wadih. *Ta'rikh,* vol. 2. Beirut.

JAHIZ, AL-

Abu 'Uthman 'Amr ibn Bahr ibn Mahbub al-Kinani al-Fuqaymi al-Basri al-Jahiz ("Goggle-Eyes") was a ninth-century intellectual *(mutakallim)* of conceptual subtlety who composed some 200 works (of which sixty are at least partially extant) dealing with the major religious, political, and theological issues of his day. These works have later been understood as prime examples of the belletrist and encyclopedic style *(adab),* and they are universally prized for their command of the 'Arabiyya (the Arabic of the Qur'an). For his immediate contemporaries, al-Jahiz's works were examples of dialectically informed theological speculation *(kalam)* in the tradition of the Mu'tazilite school of thought.

Born in Basra into an obscure family (possibly of Abyssinian origin) of vassals of the Kinana tribe around 776 CE, he received but scant formal education, attending the elementary Qur'an school and perhaps at one time earning a living selling fish. Through frequenting the congregational mosque of Basra and the caravan stop, the Mirbad, where philologists quizzed the Bedouins on the Arabic language, he was exposed to significant trends in contemporary thought and developed his mastery of the Arabic language. Several works on the imamate earned him the favor of the Caliph al-Ma'mun (r. 813–833), who had him brought to Baghdad. Little is known of his employment thereafter, apart from brief spells in the chancellery as a bureaucrat *(katib)* and later, fleetingly, as tutor to Caliph al-Mutawakkil (r. 847–861). His most prominent patrons included the following: the vizier and master architect of the Mihna (the caliphal "inquisition" designed by al-Ma'mun to establish the caliph's sole right to religious leadership of the community), Muhammad ibn 'Abd al-Malik al-Zayyat, (d. 847) to whom he dedicated the first version of *The Treatise of Living Creatures (Kitab al-Hayawan,* an early Islamic investigation of the "argument from design")*;* the Hanafite Chief Qadi Ahmad ibn Abi Da'ud (d. ca. 854), the dedicatee of his distinctive theory of communication *(bayan), The Treatise on Clarity and Clarification (al-Bayan wa-l-Tabyin,* a survey of Arabic rhetoric and an inquiry into the nature of language, set against the controversial doctrine of the createdness of the Qur'an*)* and of an early exercise in legal reasoning, *The Treatise on Legal Verdicts,* and for whose son, Muhammad (d. 854), al-Jahiz had written some works of ethical instruction (such as *The Treatise on the Here and the Hereafter: On Aphorisms, Managing People and Ways of Dealing with Them);* and al-Fath ibn Khaqan, al-Mutawakkil's vizier (d. 247/861), at whose request he revised his work *On the Virtues of the Turks* for the caliph (Turks having become a significant component of the caliphal army). For most of his mature career, al-Jahiz was engaged in the harmonization of the speculations of his master in speculative theology (kalam), Ibrahim ibn Sayyar al-Nazzam (d. between 835 and 845), and the natural philosophy *(falsafa)* of the Greco-Arabic translation movement in an attempt to synthesize a theologically, religiously, emotionally, and intellectually satisfying system of thought that remained faithful to the tenets of the Qur'an. He died in 868 or 869 in Basra, a hemiplegic who was crushed, according to one authority, by a pile of books. Because of their length and difficulty, al-Jahiz's two main works, *Living Creatures* and *Clarity and Clarification,* have not been translated, but there are translations of some of the shorter essays and of two satirical works, the *Book of Misers* and the *Epistle on Singing-Girls.*

JAMES E. MONTGOMERY

See also 'Abbasids; Adab; Arabic; Basra; Law and Jurisprudence; al-Ma'mun; Theology; Translation

Further Reading

Al-Jahiz. *Abu 'Uthman ibn Bahr al-Jahiz. The Book of Misers. A Translation of al-Bukhala',* trans. R.B. Serjeant. Reading, 1997.

———. *The Epistle on Singing-Girls of Jahiz,* trans. A.F.L. Beeston. Warminster, 1980.

Montgomery, J.E. "Of Models and Amanuenses: The Remarks on the *Qasida* in Ibn Qutayba's *Kitab al-shi'r wa-l-shu'ara'.*" In *Islamic Reflections, Arabic Musings: Studies in Honour of Professor Alan Jones,* eds. R.G. Hoyland and P.F. Kennedy, 1–49. Oxford, UK, 2004.

———. "Al-Jahiz's *Kitab al-Bayan wa-l-Tabyin*." In *Writing and Representation in Medieval Islam: Muslim Horizons*, ed. J. Bray. London and New York, forthcoming.

———. "Al-Jahiz." In *The Dictionary of Literary Biography Volume 311: Arabic Literary Culture, 500–925*, eds. M. Cooperson and S.M. Toorawa. Columbia, SC, forthcoming.

———. "'Every Man Speaks in Accordance with his Nature and Ethical Disposition': Al-Jahiz, *Bayan* 2.175–207." In *Arabic Theology, Arabic Philosophy. From the Many to the One: Essays in Celebration of Richard M. Frank*, ed. J.E. Montgomery. Leuven, forthcoming.

———. "Al-Jahiz's *Kitab al-Tarbi' wa-l-Tadwir* and the Reception of Greek *Falsafa*." In *The Libraries of the Neoplatonists*, ed. C. D'Ancona. Leiden, forthcoming.

Pellat, Ch. "Al-Djahiz." In *The Encyclopaedia of Islam, New Edition*, vol. ii, 385a.

———. *The Life and Works of al-Jahiz, Translation of Selected Texts*, transl. D.M. Hawke. London, 1969.

———. "Al-Jahiz." In *The Cambridge History of Arabic Literature: 'Abbasid Belles-Lettres*, ed. J. Ashtiany, 78–95. Cambridge, UK, 1990.

JAMI

Nur al-Din 'Abd al-Rahman Jami was born in Jam (in Khorasan) in 1414 CE, and died in 1492 in Herat, where he had spent much of his life as a valued dependent of the local Timurid court. He was honored in his own lifetime as a poet, a Nakshbandi Sufi, and a prose writer. His conscious attempt to surpass his poetic predecessors, his enormous facility as a writer of both didactic and lyrical verse, and the fact that, with the accession of the Shi'i Safavid dynasty to power in 1501, the cultural life of Iran changed radically within a few years of his death, have together led to his work being traditionally seen as the culmination of the "classic" period of Persian verse.

His major work in verse is the *Haft Ourang (Seven Thrones)*, a collection of seven masnavis (long poems in couplets) that was written in emulation of Nezami's five masnavis (his *Khamseh*). The best known of the seven are *Yusof o Zuleikha* and *Salaman o Absal*; both use stories of carnal desire as allegories for the necessity for the soul to reject the world of the flesh and aspire to the divine. His most famous prose work, the *Baharistan (The Garden in Spring)*, a collection of didactic tales interspersed with gnomic verses, was written in imitation of Sa'di's *Golestan*; predictably, Jami claims his work is superior to Sa'di's. As compared with his predecessors' productions, Jami's works undoubtedly "smell of the lamp," but his immense rhetorical mastery is never in doubt and has ensured their survival.

RICHARD DAVIS

Further Reading

Burgel, J.C. "The Romance." In *Persian Literature*, ed. E. Yarshater. New York, 1988.

Safa, Zabihollah. *Tarikh-e Adabiyat dar Iran (The History of Literature in Iran)*, 5 vols. Tehran, 1366/1987.

JAVA

Unlike the more westerly, trade-oriented Malay lands, largely agricultural Java appears to have attracted little direct interest from Muslim shippers until the late twelfth century CE, when its states began to play a more assertive role in the region politically and as a corollary to increased dealings with the southern Song dynasty of China.

Java has been the site of several major kingdoms, reflecting its diverse terrain and three major ethnic groups: the Sundanese in the west, the Javanese majority, and the people of the neighboring island of Madura, many of whom live in East Java. The most famous of Java's early kingdoms was ruled by the Śailendra dynasty, which was active in central Java until the middle of the ninth century and to which the great Buddhist stupa of Borobudur is attributed. There is also evidence that this dynasty was linked to that of Śrivijaya in Sumatra. After the ejection of the Śailendras, most of the successive rulers in the east and central plains were Śaivite, including the thirteenth-century kings of Singasari, who raided and claimed suzerainty over the ports of Sumatra and the Malay Peninsula. Singasari collapsed as Mongol forces, sent to Java on a punitive mission by Qubilai in late 1292, took sides with the rival court of Majapahit, which emerged victorious in 1293 and took Singasari's place as regional hegemon, reaching its apogee under Rajasanagara (Hayam Wuruk) (r. 1350–1389).

Over the course of the fourteenth century, Islam planted strong roots in the western part of the archipelago. By the fifteenth century, it was represented in some of Java's coastal ports, starting with Demak, Gresik, and Jepara, where it appears to have been introduced by local strongmen, who were recorded in the indigenous literature as being of mixed Chinese and Javanese blood.

Writing from Malacca between 1512 and 1515, the Portuguese apothecary Tomé Pires observed that, although coastal Java had been Islamicized, the major kingdom at its heart remained non-Muslim. However, there was already a Muslim presence at this court. In addition, although Demak is known to have been the first Muslim kingdom on Java, the first hard evidence of Islam on the island is to be found in fourteenth-century gravestones from near the site of Majapahit at Trawulan and Tralaya, which suggests a Muslim presence at court there, perhaps even among the royal family.

According to some Javanese traditions, the Majapahit capital was sacked in 1478 by a force from Demak, with the hero of these raids later founding his own capital at Kudus (named after Jerusalem [al-Quds]). Although the actual course of events linking the rise of Islam to the fall of Majapahit and the foundation in its place of the Sultanate of Mataram is still unclear (1527 is the more likely date for the Demak attack), Java certainly became a more noticeably Muslim island over the course of the coming centuries. By the seventeenth century, the related sultanates of Banten and Cirebon (said to have been Islamized by a saint from the Sumatran kingdom of Pasai) had emerged and played a role in maritime trade with the Atlantic powers. Banten in particular had excellent access to holdings of pepper and maintained close links with the court of Aceh in northern Sumatra. In addition, as they were in Aceh, links were cultivated with the wider Muslim world. The Bantenese king, Pangeran Ratu (r. 1596–1651), sent a mission to Mecca in 1638 to obtain the title of Sultan, reigning thereafter as Mahmud Abd al-Qadir Abu 'l-Mafakhir.

The teachings of the mystical orders associated with the courts—particularly the Shattariyya and Qadiriyya orders—were also fostered. The cult of 'Abd al-Qadir al-Jilani was particularly prominent, and Javanese, Sundanese, and Malay literature contain adaptations of the stories of his life, especially those compiled by the Yemen-born hagiographer 'Abd Allah b. As'ad al-Yafi'i (1298–1367). Furthermore, these stories appear to have been seminal to the very transmission of Islam. Some of his miracles are paralleled in some of the conversion stories found in the wider region. In addition, as G.W.J. Drewes once suggested, Sultan Mahmud Abd al-Qadir Abu 'l-Mafakhir of Banten even appears to have chosen a regal title in 1638 that harmonized with that of a work of al-Yafi'i (Asna al-Mafakhir fi Manaqib 'Abd al-Qadir) and his favorite saint al-Jilani, who is still seen as the primary intercessor for southeast Asian Sufis.

MICHAEL LAFFAN

See also 'Abd al-Qadir al-Jilani; Sufism and Sufis; Sumatra and the Malay Peninsula

Further Reading

Jones, Russell. "Ten Conversion Myths from Indonesia." In Conversion to Islam, ed. Nehemia Levtzion, 129–58. London: Methuen.
Prapañca, Mpu. Deśawarnana (Nâgarakrtâgama), ed. Stuart Robson. Leiden: KITLV Press, 1995.
Pigeaud, Theodore G. Th., and H.J. de Graaf. Islamic States in Java, 1500–1700. The Hague, Martinus Nijhoff, 1976.
Ricklefs, M.C. A History of Modern Indonesia Since c.1200. London: Palgrave, 2001.
The Suma Oriental of Tomé Pires (...) and the Book of Fransisco Rodriguez (...), Cortesão, Armando, trans. and ed., second series no. 89. London: The Hakluyt Society, 1944.

JERUSALEM

Jerusalem in medieval Arabic literature is known as Ilya (from the Latin Aelia Capitolina), Bayt al-Maqdis, al-Bayt al-Muqaddas, or, simply, al-Quds. The latter three names all derive from the pure Arabic roots b.y.t. and q.d.s., meaning "home" and "holy"; hence, "The Holy House." The form of the appellation, however, is an exact Arabization of the Hebrew Beyt HaMiqdash, the common Jewish designation for the ancient Israelite at Temple Jerusalem. The particular Hebrew locution, Beyt HaMiqdash, is not biblical, but it first appears in the Mishnah (c. 200 CE).

The sanctity of Jerusalem predates even ancient Israel; it was a Jebusite (and probably a pre-Jebusite) holy site, the tribal or ethnic name of which has been lost (Genesis 14:18–20). However, as Oleg Grabar has observed, memories can be released from the spaces they occupy, and new memories can fill them. Associated with the great Israelite kings David and Solomon, the Jerusalem Temple on the eastern hill of the city was destroyed by the Romans in 70, a symbolic act that ended any semblance of Jewish political and religious hegemony. Jerusalem would not become a national center again until the twentieth century, but it would nevertheless play an occasional role in the politics of nation and empire.

The city was largely destroyed and then rebuilt under the Roman Hadrian (mid-second century), and its biblical memories were replaced with the standard pagan imperial themes associated with Roman monumental structures. Only after the Christianization of the city under Constantine and his successors (fourth century onward) was Jerusalem refilled with monotheistic sanctity. However, this sanctity was Christian rather than Jewish, and its center of gravity moved westward to the Holy Sepulchre Church, in which the memories of the Crucifixion and Resurrection were linked. The eastern hill, upon which the Temple once stood, was left in ruins as a sign of God's abandonment of the Jews for the new dispensation of Christianity.

Not only did historical and pious memories infuse the city, but there were also "memories" of the future:

Temple of Jerusalem. Spanish miniature, from a mozarabic Bible, fol. 50r. Tenth century CE. Credit: Bridgeman-Giraudon/
Art Resource, NY. S. Isidro el Real, Leon, Spain.

the eschaton or end time, when humanity will be finally judged. Jerusalem became the "gateway to heaven," and the pious made their way there in pilgrimage or burial in hope of resurrection and eternal life. This infused the city with a psychological quality of expectation and hope, but it also suggested that its political control might improve one's merit for salvation. Individuals made their way to Jerusalem to die and be buried there, and Crusades and counter-Crusades would radically increase the number of the holy dead.

When Jerusalem was conquered by the Arabs in 637 or 638, the center of holiness returned to the Temple Mount, now called the Sacred Precinct (Haram al-Sharif). At this early period of Arab conquest, the religion of Islam was in its infancy, and it is not clear how "Islamic" the conquest led by the forces of the second caliph, 'Umar Ibn al-Khattab, actually was. This may account for the ambivalence reflected by the sources regarding the sanctity of Jerusalem in relation to the holy cities of Mecca and Medina. In any case, tradition credits 'Umar with constructing a simple mosque on the Haram. On the same raised earthworks but further to the north, where the Solomonic Temple once stood, the Umayyad caliph 'Abd al-Malik constructed the oldest surviving Islamic monumental structure (ca. 691), the Qubbat al-Sakhra (the Dome of the Rock). Within a few decades, he or his son Walid built the mosque called Al-Aqsa ("the distant mosque"), which became associated with the night journey of Muhammad from Mecca to Jerusalem.

Unlike Christian Jerusalem, which preserved the memory of prior religions only as archaic ruins, Islamic Jerusalem allowed for Christians to maintain their religious monuments and shrines, and Jews were allowed their synagogues. Only occasionally, such as during the reign of the Fatimid Caliph Hakim during the early eleventh century, were churches and synagogues sacked and destroyed.

Medieval Islamic Jerusalem reflected the "memories" of both the past and the future Day of Judgment. In these memories, the new Dome of the Rock represents the Solomonic Temple and the gateway to heaven of past sacrifice and future salvation. At the end time, the rock under the dome will be the stronghold of Muslims against al-Dajjal (the Antichrist) and the place to which the Mahdi (the Messiah) will come in triumph to restore justice to earth. Both Mecca and Medina will be brought to Jerusalem on the Day of Judgment.

However, the primary memory of Islamic Jerusalem is the *isra* (night journey) of the Prophet Muhammad to Jerusalem and his *mi'raj* (ascension) from the *al-sakhra* (rock) to heaven. In heaven, beyond the Lotus tree, he meets God and receives the wisdom that guides him and forms the authority for his leadership and pious behavior. The Prophet's behaviors and aphorisms make up the sunna, and the sunna forms the most sacred religious literature of Islam after the Qur'an. The authority for the sunna derives from Muhammad's infallibility, and that infallibility derives from his journey through the gateway to Heaven in Jerusalem to meet the Creator.

REUVEN FIRESTONE

Further Reading

Asali, K.J., ed. *Jerusalem in History*. Essex: Scorpion, 1989.

Canaan, Tewfik. "Mohammedan Saints and Sanctuaries in Palestine." *Journal of the Palestine Oriental Society* (1927).

Levine, Lee, ed. *The Jerusalem Cathedral*, vols. 2 and 3. Jerusalem: Ben Zvi Institute, 1982 and 1983.

———, ed. *Jerusalem: Its Sanctity and Centrality to Judaism, Christianity and Islam*. New York: Continuum, 1999.

Al-Wasiti, Abu Makr Muhammad b. Ahmad. *Fada'il al-Bayt al-Muqaddas*, ed. Isaac Hasson. Jerusalem: Hebrew University, 1978.

JESUS

Islam celebrates Jesus as a prophet who is superior to all other prophets except Muhammad. Two particular issues in the Islamic dogma led to this recognition: (1) Jesus proclaimed the coming of Muhammad, and (2) Islam will achieve ultimate triumph with Jesus' second coming at the End of Times. The stories about Jesus in the Qur'an and Islamic literature, including the *Tales of the Prophets* genre, relate to his birth, life, career, and miracles. Most of these stories have close parallels in canonical and apocryphal Christian texts. In this respect, one can say that Jesus is a figure who is claimed simultaneously by two religions (Christianity and Islam). However, it is the nature of Jesus where these two religions differ.

Jesus is a legitimizer of Islam. According to Qur'an (61:6), one of the duties of Jesus was to proclaim the coming of Ahmad, which Muslim exegetes identify with Muhammad and relate to one of Jesus' sayings in the Gospel of John (15:26) about the coming of the Paraclete. The eminent relation between the two prophets is emphasized in the hadith; one in particular features Muhammad assuring that adding Jesus' name to the Shahada earns the believer unconditional admission to Paradise (Bukhari, *Sahih*, III, 1267, no. 3252).

The Islamic belief about the second coming of Jesus revolves around the Qur'anic assertion that he did not die but instead was taken from the world by God (4:158). Jesus shall return at the End of Time to bring about the triumph of Islam and then die like every human, thus concluding his prophetic mission. The elaboration of this doctrine is in the hadith; the Qur'an only refers to it vaguely by nicknaming Jesus *'alamun li-l-sa'a* (sign/condition of the coming of the hour) (43:61). At first, the Mahdi of Islam came to be identified with Jesus, but this became a less-popular view after the Mahdi was determined to be a descendant of Muhammad. In Shi'i theology in particular, Jesus becomes the lieutenant of the Mahdi; his second coming will usher in the return of the Mahdi from his *ghayba* (occultation).

Islamic theology, including the Qur'an, was partly concerned with "correcting" the wrong Christian perceptions about Jesus, in particular his divinity (i.e., whether he should be considered to be God, the son of God, or part of the Trinity). This has to be understood in the context of the Islamic obsession with the concept of the oneness of God *(al-Tawhid)* and the outright rejection of any hint of divine associates. The Qur'anic denial of the crucifixion (4:157) is not addressed to the Christians, but it became an accepted discourse in Islamic theology to challenge the Christian belief about the reality of the crucifixion. However, Islam accepts particular Christian concepts about the nature of Jesus, especially Jesus as the Word of God and a Spirit from God (Qur'an 4:171).

Jesus has also been implicated in several religious and political controversies in Islam. His sayings were quoted, for instance, in support of the Murji'a's view of abstaining from judging other Muslims and referring the judging to God (see Khalidi, nos. 1 and 3), and also in support of the predestination creed that God determines everything (Khalidi, no. 69). As for Islamic asceticism and mysticism (Sufism), Jesus features as a patron saint, and his perceived lifestyle became a model to imitate, especially his celibacy, unconcern for property and wealth, and struggle against Satan. His miracles were constantly highlighted, and they were explained as resulting from the divine empowerment because of his total devotion to and reliance on God.

SULEIMAN A. MOURAD

See also Qur'an and Christians; Prophets, Tales of; Messianism; Shi'ism

Further Reading

Ayyoub, Mahmoud. "Towards an Islamic Christology, 2: The Death of Jesus—Reality or Illusion?" *The Muslim World* 70 (1980): 91–121.
Khalidi, Tarif. *The Muslim Jesus: Sayings and Stories in Islamic Literature.* Cambridge, Mass: Harvard University Press, 2001.
Khalidi, Tarif. "The Role of Jesus in Intra-Muslim Polemics of the First Two Islamic Centuries." In *Christian Arabic Apologetics during the Abbasid Period,* 750–1258, eds. S.K. Samir and J. S. Nielsen, 146–56. Leiden: Brill, 1994.
Leirvik, Oddbjorn. *Images of Jesus Christ in Islam: Introduction, Survey of Research, Issues of Dialogue.* Uppsala: Swedish Institute of Missionary Research, 1998.
Mourad, Suleiman. "From Hellenism to Christianity and Islam: The Origin of the Palm-tree Story Concerning Mary and Jesus in the Gospel of Pseudo-Matthew and the Qur'an." *Oriens Christianus* 85 (2002).
———. "On the Qur'anic Stories About Mary and Jesus." *Bulletin of the Royal Institute for Inter-Faith Studies* 1.2 (1999): 13–24.
———. "Jesus According to Ibn 'Asakir." In *Ibn 'Asakir and Early Islamic History*, ed. James E. Lindsay, 24–43. Princeton: The Darwin Press, 2001.
O'Shaughnessy, Thomas. *The Koranic Concept of the Word of God.* Rome: Pontificio Istituto Biblico, 1940.
Robinson, Neal. *Christ in Islam and Christianity.* Houndmills: Macmillian, 1991.

JEWELRY

In the Qur'an, the use of jewelry is not specifically encouraged or prohibited. However, its material value, aesthetic qualities, and ornamental function are definitely acknowledged through several mentions of precious sartorial accessories constituting rewards given to true believers in Paradise. For example, the faithful will be adorned with "bracelets of gold" in Surah 18:31 and "bracelets of silver" in Surah 76:21. Surahs 22:23 and 35:33 state similar promises of adding pearls to bracelets. Belonging to the category of jewelry, pearls, corals, and precious stones are especially considered in the Qur'an, because they are wonders to be found in nature, God's creation (Surah 55:22). In depicting Paradise, Surah 55:58 mentions rubies and pearls as paradigms of beauty and perfection, whereas Surah 76:19 compares heavenly creatures to pearls. By thus including jewels in the depiction of Paradise, the Qur'an attributes a great value to this branch of metalwork; however, it remains mute concerning sumptuary laws in the framework of earthly life.

One has to consult the hadith to find elements of an ethical approach to the custom of using jewels in the Muslim society. Many passages recommend the use of silver instead of gold. However, men are strictly forbidden to wear gold jewelry, although they may use silver rings in reference to the one that Muhammad possessed. With regard to women, the prescriptions appear to be less well defined. Some excerpts allow the use of gold whereas others do not, although there is a demonstrated predominance against it and a negative attitude toward goldsmiths as well. An early hadith (that was later revoked) says: "The Prophet said: 'O Ye women, bedeck yourselves in silver but any woman who adorns herself with gold and displays it

Gold necklace decorated with tiny floral designs in filigree; on the center pendant inscription "da'im" (everlasting prosperity). Naskki script. Mamluk dynasty, thirteenth CE. Credit: Erich Lessing/Art Resource, NY. Museum of Islamic Art, Cairo, Egypt.

openly shall be punished.'" A few traditions report that Muhammad and after him men of wisdom compared gold to fire, obviously alluding to Hell. However, in another hadith, the Prophet also stated that "gold and silk are permitted to women of my congregation and forbidden to the men." In contrast with the ambiguous connotation of gold jewelry, silver adornments clearly constitute licit jewelry according to the Prophetic tradition.

There are numerous references to jewelry in Islamic historical and literary sources. Jewelry was a controlled commodity, subject to taxation *(zakat)*. Both the commerce and making of jewels were supervised by an inspector *(muhtasib)* in a specific office *(Dar al-'Iyar)*. The Hisba literature provides many details about the profession of muhtasib. Inventories and chronicles describe quantities of precious objects that princes of the great medieval dynasties amassed in their treasuries, like the famous one of the Fatimids. Symbols of power and social status, jewels constituted honorific and diplomatic gifts exchanged among rulers and members of the royal family or offered to court subjects and representatives of the state during official ceremonies. Together with descriptive texts, pieces preserved in the worldly museums and private collections attest to the variety of techniques and stylistic influences that shaped the art of Islamic jewelry in the Middle Ages. Goldsmiths adapted the old Oriental Persian–Sasanian and Mediterranean Greco-Roman traditions to the taste and needs of Islamic culture, thereby at once creating new forms and perpetuating the native lore of lands conquered by the Muslims.

VALERIE GONZALEZ

See also Amulets; Artisans; Beauty and Aesthetics; Clothing and Costume; Court Dress; Fatimids; Gender and Sexuality; Gifts and Gift Giving; Guilds, Professional; Hadith; Marvels and Wonders; Metalwork; Mythology and Mythical Beings; Precious Metal; Qur'an; Qur'an and Arabic Literature; Roman Empire, Islamic Traditions; Sasanians, Islamic Traditions; Talismans and Talismanic Objects; Tax and Taxation

Primary Sources

Al-Bukhari, Abu 'Abd Allah Muhammad Ibn Isma'il al-Ju'fi. *Sahih.*
Ibn al-Athir. *Jami' al-Usul min Ahadith al-Rasul*, vol. 5, 408–10. Cairo, 1955.

Ibn Bassam al-Muhtasib. *Nihayyat al Rutba fi Talab al Hisba.* Baghdad, 1968.

Ibn al-Salam 'Abd al-Qasim. *Kitab al-Amwal,* 441, 443–4, 448. Cairo, 1934.

Ibn Majah. *Al-Sunan,* vol. 2, 156–57, 728. Cairo, 1902.

Al-Maqrizi, Ahmad Ibn 'Ali. *Al Mawa'iz Wal I'Tibar bi-Dhikr al Khitat Wa'l Athar,* vol. 2, 72. Cairo, 1856.

Al-Nasa'i. *Sunan, Sharh Hafiz Jalal al-Din al-Suyuti,* vol. 5, 160–1, 165, 172. Cairo, 1930.

Further Reading

Ackerman, P. "Jewellery in the Islamic Period." In *A Survey of Persian Art,* vol. III, 2664–72. Oxford, UK, A.U. Pope, 1938–1939.

Allan, James W. *Islamic Metalwork: The Nuhad Es-Said Collection.* London: Sotheby Publications, 1982.

"Djawhar." In *Encyclopédie de l'Islam, Supplément,* 250–62. 1982.

Gonzalez, Valérie. *Emaux d'Al-Andalus et du Maghreb.* Aix-en-Provence, France: Edisud, 1994.

Hasson, Rachel. *Early Islamic Jewellery.* Jerusalem: L.A. Mayer Memorial Institute For Islamic Art, 1987.

Al Hijjawi al-Qaddumi, Ghada. *Book of Gifts and Rarities, (Kitab al-Hadaya wa al-Tuhaf).* Cambridge, Mass: Harvard University Press, 1996.

Jenkins, M., and M. Keene. *Islamic Jewelry in the Metropolitan Museum of Art.* New York. 1983.

Jewelry and Goldsmithing in the Islamic World. International Symposium. Jerusalem: The Israel Museum, 1987.

JEWS

The word *Jew* can be traced back to the Hebrew *Yehudi,* a word that comes originally from the tribe of Judah (Yehudah), named for the fourth son of the patriarch Jacof (Ya'aqov). After King Solomon died and the kingdom of Judah was split into two kingdoms, the northern kingdom was called Israel and the southern Judah. From the period of the biblical figure Ezra, the name Israel (Yisra'el) is used in all Hebrew literature, with a few exceptions during the time of the Maccabees. In the Christian Gospels, the Jews are recorded as having mocked Jesus by calling him "King of Israel," whereas Pilate the Roman and his soldiers refer to him as "King of the Jews." For early Christians, the figure of Judas Iscariot was early conflated with the gospel story about him as being linked with the devil (Luke 22:3), and there became an evil triangle of "devil—Jew—Judas"; the word *Judaeus* helped to establish the pejorative meaning of *Jew* in popular usage.

The Pentateuch became sacred scripture no later than the fifth century BCE, whereas the later works of the kings, prophets, and other important figures were finally part of the Jewish Bible, or *TaNaKH,* the letters of which stand for its three sections:

Torah (Pentateuch), Nevi'im (Prophets), and Ketuvim (Hagiographia). By the second century CE important civilizations of the East (Persians, Greeks, Zoroastrians, and Romans) influenced several Jewish usages and beliefs.

From early usage in Aramaic and Persian names, there came the Greek name *Ioudaios* and the Latin *Judaeus.* These later developed into early English, and the word can be found from about the year 1000 C.E. in various forms, such as *Iudea, Gyu, Iuw, and Iew,* which developed into *Jew.*

During the nineteenth century, to avoid the unpleasant association and connotation of the word *Jew* as mentioned above, among many Jewish organizations it became usual to use the terms *Hebrews* and *Israelites.* However, these new names quickly became as pejorative as the usage of "Jews" in many nineteenth-century novels and other written works. More recently, in the twentieth century (especially during the years before the Nazi period and more so during World War II), many millions of Jews—even thousands of those who had left Judaism—suffered from the efforts to rid Europe and other parts of the world of all the Jews.

WILLIAM M. BRINNER

Further Reading

Grabbe, Lester L. *A History of the Jews and Judaism in the Second Temple Period.* London, 2004.

Peters, F.E. *The Children of Abraham: Judaism, Christianity, Islam.* Princeton, 2004.

Trachtenberg, Joshua. *The Devil and the Jews: The Medieval Conception of the Jew and its Relation to Modern Anti-semitism.* Philadelphia, 1993.

JIHAD

Jihad is the term most often used in Islamic sources to denote war that is authorized by God. Because the ultimate authority for this category of war is the divinity, it most closely approximates what Western languages refer to as "holy war."

The actual meaning of the term, however, has nothing to do with warring or aggression. It means, rather, "striving," and it is commonly used in the Qur'an and elsewhere in the idiomatic expression "striving in the path of God" *(al-jihad fi sabil Allah).* This is striving to do the divine will and to fulfill one's religious obligation. Such religious obligation, in the Islamic context, includes protecting the religion from both outside aggressors who would dominate it and from internal sedition or subversion away from what is perceived to be the straight path established by God and His Prophet.

In the Qur'an

Although some Qur'anic contexts in which "striving in the path of God" occurs do not convey a sense of stress or physical defense (2:218; 9:64; 49:15), most do (4:95; 8:72, 74; 5:54; 9:16, 19, 41; 31:15; 60:1; 61:11), and some quite clearly refer to engaging in war on behalf of a beleaguered young Muslim community. The more common Qur'anic term, however, is *qital*, and this word means, literally, "warring" (2:190, 244, 246; 3:13, 167; 4:74–76, 84; 9:111; 21:4; 73:20). Like jihad, qital also occurs in the idiomatic expression "in the path of God"; qital thus conveys a sense of religious war more consistently than does jihad. A third term, *harb,* also refers to wars, but this term does not occur in the idiom, "in the path of God," and is distinguished by designating only aggression and wars that are not legitimized by religious authority.

The Qur'an acknowledges that conflict between peoples, religions, and individuals is a part of life (22:40: "If God did not push off [some] people by means of others, then monasteries and churches and synagogues and mosques in which the name of God is often cited would have been destroyed." 5:8, 48; 16:93; 34:24–26; 49:10–13, 109). Other means of resolving religious disputes, such as argument or discussion, are also found in the Qur'an (16:125; 29:46).

In the Hadith

Various activities subsumed under jihad are said by Muhammad to distinguish true believers who are loyal to God's Prophet: "Every prophet sent by God to a nation *(umma)* before me has had disciples and followers who followed his ways *(sunna)* and obeyed his commands. But after them came successors who preached what they did not practice and practiced what they were not commanded. Whoever strives *(jahada)* against them with one's hand is a believer, whoever strives against them with one's tongue is a believer, whoever strives against them with one's heart is a believer. There is nothing greater than [the size of] a mustard seed beyond that in the way of faith" (Muslim, *Sahih,* Cairo; *K. al-Iman* 20.80, 1:69-70). Muhammad is also credited with saying: "The best *jihad* is [speaking] a word of justice to a tyrannical ruler" (Abu Dawud, *Sunan,* Cairo, 1988/1408; *K. al-Malahim* 4344, 4:122).

There are, thus, various subcategories of jihad found in the hadith literature, such as jihad of the heart, the tongue, and the hand, all of which are said to promote God's kingdom on earth by behaving ethically, by speaking without causing harm to others, and by defending Islam and propagating the faith, respectively. Jihad as religiously grounded warfare—sometimes referred to as *jihad of the sword (jihad al-sayf)*—is subsumed under the last two categories of defending Islam and propagating the faith, although these need not be accomplished only through war. When the term *jihad* is used without qualifiers such as "of the heart," or "of the tongue," it is universally understood as war on behalf of Islam (equivalent to "jihad of the sword"), and the merits of engaging in such jihad are described plentifully in the most-respected religious works.

Nevertheless, Muslim thinkers (and particularly ascetics and mystics) often differentiate between the greater jihad *(al-jihad al-akbar)* and the lesser jihad *(al-jihad al-asghar)*, with the former representing the struggle against the self, and only the lesser jihad referring to warring in the path of God. It should be noted that this is not a sound tradition and cannot be found in any of the canonical Sunni hadith collections.

Even within its range of meaning as war on behalf of Islam, the term is often used in relation to conflicts between Muslims. Such examples of jihad include wars fought against groups of apostates rebelling against proper Islamic authority *(murtaddun)*, dissenting groups denouncing legitimate Muslim leadership *(baghi)*, highway robbers and other violent people, and deviant or un-Islamic leadership. The determination of when Muslim leaders may call for jihad and the requisite demands that such a call makes upon the Muslim populace are developed in the legal literature.

In Islamic Law

Muslim jurists developed a highly sophisticated legal doctrine of war, and Averroes (Muhammad ibn Rushd) makes several general points. First, it is a collective legal obligation for healthy, adult, free men who have the means at their disposal to go to war. All polytheists should be fought (Jews and Christians are included in this group). Second, the aim of warfare against Peoples of the Book is either conversion to Islam or payment of the *jizya* (a poll tax) signaling subjugation to Islam. Generally, collection of the jizya is only accepted from Jews, Christians, and Zoroastrians, although some scholars allow it for "any polytheist other than Arabs" (which would include Hindus). Otherwise, conversion to Islam is required of non-monotheists. Third, damage inflicted on the enemy may consist of damage to his property, injury to his person, or violation of his personal liberty (slavery). Such damage may be directed against men, women, and children, but some scholars omit monks. Captives may be pardoned, enslaved, killed, or released either on ransom or as dhimmi (protected Peoples of the Book), who must then pay the jizya to the Muslim head of state. Some scholars forbid the killing of captives. Fourth, certain individuals among the enemy may receive status of aman (safe conduct) to conduct political or economic activities that benefit the state. Finally, in times of war, all adult, able-bodied, unbelieving males may be slain, but noncombatant women and children may not be.

The juridical literature contains discussions of rules of engagement, the use of weapons of mass destruction such as fire, how much damage may be inflicted on the property of the enemy, and so on. Truce is permitted, but there is much discussion about who has the authority to call for it and under what conditions it may be called.

In History

The earliest references to jihad are Qur'anic, but Islamic doctrine was formulated later, during the classical period, when Islam dominated from Western Europe to the Indian subcontinent. Perpetual war against the non-Muslim world seemed natural at the time until victory, but, as with all empires, perpetual conquest could not be sustained. Reversals were considered temporary, however, so until the modern period little new thought was given by Muslim scholars to Islamic military doctrines in either the legal or moral spheres.

A renewed interest in other forms of conflict resolution has appeared recently (Salmi, 1998; Said, 2001), and less aggressive Qur'anic references are beginning to be revisited. The attacks against the U.S. World Trade Center and Pentagon in 2001 and the response of the United States by invading Afghanistan and Iraq has shocked the Muslim world and has encouraged additional reevaluation.

REUVEN FIRESTONE

Primary Sources

Qur'an
Sunan Abi Daud. Cairo.
Sahih Muslim. Cairo, 1988/1408.
Rushd, Muhammad b. *Al-Bidaya wal-Nihaya.* In R. Peters (below).

Further Reading

Abdul Aziz Said, Nathan Funk, and Ayse Kadayifci, eds. *Peace and Conflict Resolution in Islam.* Lanham, MD: University Press of America, 2001.
Cook, David. "Muslim Apocalyptic and *Jihad.*"
Firestone, Reuven. *Jihad: The Origin of Holy War in Islam.* New York: Oxford University Press, 1999.
Johnson, James Turner, and John Kelsay, eds. *Cross, Crescent, and Sword: The Justification and Limitation of War in Western and Islamic Tradition.* New York: Greenwood Press, 1990.
Kelsay, John, and James Turner Johnson, eds. *Just War and Jihad: Historical and Theoretical Perspectives on War and Peace in Western and Islamic Traditions.* New York: Greenwood Press, 1991.
Kelsay, John. *Islam and War: A Study in Comparative Ethics.* Westminster: John Knox, 1993.
Kramer, Joel. "Apostates, Rebels, Brigands." *Israel Oriental Studies* X (1980): 34–73.
Morabia, Alfred. *Le Gihad dans li'Islam Medieval.* Paris: Albin Michel, 1975.
Peters, Rudolf. *Jihad in Classical and Modern Islam.* Princeton, NJ: Marcus Weiner, 1996.
Ralph Salmi, Cesar Adib Majul, and George K. Tanham, eds. *Islam and Conflict Resolution.* Lanham, Md: University Press of America, 1998.

JINN

The Arabic term *jinn* means "invisible beings." The jinn are sentient beings who are composed from a subtle matter. Before Islam, they were worshiped as gods, as tutelary deities, or as spiritual protectors not only in the Arabian Peninsula but also in neighboring areas, such as the ancient Syrian city of Palmyra. Islam incorporated them into the new religion and changed their status from gods to supernatural beings that could be either good or evil. In fact, Islam is the only one of the three monotheistic religions to address its message to both human beings and jinn. Muslims accept the existence of the jinn as part of their faith.

The most important source for understanding the concept of the jinn in Islam is the Qur'an, which strongly condemns the worship of the jinn by the Arabs before Islam and their search for protection from them (72:6). In Qur'an verses 15:26-7 and 55:14-5, there is mention that they are created from "scorching winds" and "a smokeless fire," and it is also said that they are like humans in that they are rational beings formed of nations (7:38). In fact, the jinn are always addressed in the plural. The Holy Book points out also that both jinn and humans are called to worship God (51:56).

In verse 6:130, it is said that God sent messengers to both jinn and humans. Muslim sources differ regarding whether these messengers were from the side of the jinn, or if they were from the human side alone. However, if the messengers were indeed from the human side alone, how did the jinn learn about these messages? The Qur'an says that the jinn have their own communication channel that allows them to receive the Word of God. In one instance, they listened to a recitation of the Qur'an and then went to inform their fellow jinn about Islam (72:1–5).

Islam considers the jinn to be responsible for their deeds. Both humans and jinn are described as free and fully capable of making choices that will determine their abode in Paradise or Hell, and the jinn and humankind are closely associated in the afterlife as well. Both confront the same destiny (6:128; 55:39), both will be judged simultaneously by God, and both will be rewarded or punished in accordance with their deeds (7:179; 55:56).

To understand the concept of jinn in Islam, emphasis must be placed on the repetition of the striking phrase, "Lord of the worlds," that Muslims use in their daily prayers and that is mentioned at the beginning of each chapter of the Qur'an. The use of the plural implies the existence of other worlds that are inhabited by numerous kinds of intelligences, all of which are outside humankind's perception. The world of the jinn is only one of many of such realms.

In many chapters, the Qur'an reminds humankind and jinn of the impossibility of physically coming close to God (55:33). However, this incapability before God is not only physical, it also includes the mental and creative limitations that are shared by jinn and humans alike. God sets a challenge for both species (17:90).

However, the numerous instances of the association of jinn and humans do not imply that these two species are equal. God says in the Qur'an that humans alone are the inheritors of the earth. The first man and prophet, Adam, is considered God's vicegerent on earth; this honor does not go to the jinn who share the earth with humankind nor even to the angels who worship God in the heavens by day and by night (17:70). Even the basic elements from which human beings and jinn are composed give humans greater distinction over the jinn. Although the jinn generally boast about their superiority because they are made of air and smokeless fire, the element of water, which gives life to everything, and from which human beings themselves are created, bestows upon them actual superiority over the jinn. The supremacy of human beings above all other creatures derives from the fact that they are a combination of elements from lower compounds (the same as animals and plants) as well as higher compounds (angelic entities). Only human beings are constituted from both realms.

The association of humans and jinn is not limited to the Qur'an. It is also found in classical Arabic literature, Sufi texts, folklore, and even modern narratives. These diverse texts unravel the belief of a large population of the Arab Muslim world in an abiding relationship between the jinn and humans. Popular culture, even today, abounds with stories of jinn carrying off humans, of marriages between the

two species, and of people possessed by jinn, in which case the jinn are internalized within the human psyche. These lasting beliefs insinuate that, where there are human beings, there are almost always jinn nearby who interfere in their existence and who are subject to the same set of laws and beliefs.

AMIRA EL-ZEIN

Primary Sources

fiAbdu l-?akîm, Shawqî. *Madkhal ilâ Dirâsat al-Fûlklûr wa l-Asâ†îr al-Fiarabiyyah.* Beirut: Dâr Ibn Khaldûn, 1983.
Ajînah, Muhammad. *Mawsûfiat Asâ îr al-Fiarab,* 2 vols. Beirut: Dâr Al-Farâbî, 1994.
Arberry, A.J., transl. *The Koran Interpreted.* Simon & Schuster, 1996.
Ibn Al-Kalbî, Hishâm. *Al-Aβnâm,* transl. Nabîh Fâris. Princeton, NJ: Princeton University Press, 1952.
Ibn Shuhayd, fiAbdu al-Malik. *Risâlat at-Tawâbifi wa l-Zawâbfi.* Beirut: Dâr βadir, 1967.
Shqar, fiUmar al-. *fiÂlam al-Jinn wa l-Shayâ†în.* Cairo: Dâr al-Kutub al-Salafiyyah, 1985.

Further Reading

Crapanzano, Vincent. *The Hamadsha: A Study in Moroccan Ethnopsychiatry.* Berkeley, CA: University of California Press, 1973.
Drijvers, H.J.W. *The Religion of Palmyra.* Leiden: E.J. Brill, 1976.
Goodman, Lenn Evan, transl. *The Case of the Animals Versus Man Before the King of the Jinn: A Tenth–Century Ecological Fable of the Pure Brethren of Basra.* Boston: Twayne Publishers, 1978.

JUDAH HA-LEVI

The poet and religious philosopher Judah (Abu'l-Hasan) ben Samuel Halevi (c. 1075–1141) was one of the outstanding figures among Andalusian Jewry during the first half of the twelfth century. Hailing from Tudela or Toledo, he came to Cordoba at the invitation of the poet Moses Ibn Ezra. Although Halevi was a practicing physician, he also engaged in commerce and was apparently quite prosperous. His fame, however, derived from his Hebrew verse. According to Judah al-Harizi (c. 1165–1225), Halevi was the most versatile of Hebrew writers, a virtuoso in every genre of secular and sacred poetry and rhymed prose. He pioneered the Hebrew girdle song *(muwashshah)* and also produced Hebrew renderings of Arabic verse. The superscriptions to his poems indicate warm relationships with other members of the Jewish elite. Much of his verse was gathered posthumously into a *diwan* (collected poems), which has survived in two recensions. Many of his liturgical compositions are preserved in the rites of Sephardic and oriental Jewish communities.

Deeply immersed in Greco-Arabic culture, Halevi commanded a fine Arabic prose style and was thoroughly conversant with Islamic philosophy. Shi'i and Sufi influences have also been detected in his writings. However, he came to repudiate the truth claims of speculative knowledge while adopting a conservative, particularist conception of Judaism. He expounded his views in *The Book of the Khazar (Kitab al-Khazari)*, a platonic dialogue between a rabbi and a pagan king seeking religious enlightenment. The work draws upon the etiological legend of the conversion of the Khazar kingdom (located in southern Russia between the Black and Caspian Seas) to Judaism during the eighth and ninth centuries. The book's alternate title, *The Book of Argument and Proof for the Despised Faith,* aptly expresses its apologetic character. The rabbi argues for the intrinsic superiority of the Jewish religious tradition, the Jewish people, and the land of Israel while rejecting the claims of other religions (Islam and Christianity), other intellectual systems (Greek and Islamic philosophy), and heresies (Karaite Judaism). Because of its engaging form and powerful, positive message, the *Book of the Khazar* was soon translated into Hebrew by Judah Ibn Tibbon (Provence, 1167); *Sefer ha-Kuzari* became one of the classic works of Jewish thought.

Toward the conclusion of the *Khazari,* the rabbi asserts that he must leave the diaspora for the land of Israel, which is the noblest place on earth. In fact, as an old man, Halevi himself finally abandoned his comfortable life in Andalusia and traveled east to the Holy Land. This journey is documented in a remarkable series of poems that describe his longing for Zion, his planned pilgrimage, his parting from family and friends in Andalusia, and his voyage. This final chapter of Halevi's life has been illuminated by documents from the Cairo Geniza relating to his stay in Egypt (1140–1141) before his final departure for the Holy Land. He died in August 1141, apparently after reaching his destination.

DANIEL FRANK

See also Judeo-Arabic; Pilgrimage; Poetry, Hebrew; Translation, Arabic to Hebrew

Primary Sources

Brody, Heinrich, and Nina Salaman. *Selected Poems of Jehudah Halevi*. Philadelphia: JPSA, 1924.
Halevi, Judah. *The Kuzari: An Argument for the Faith of Israel*, transl. Hartwig Hirschfeld. New York: Schocken, 1964.

Further Reading

Goitein, S.D. *A Mediterranean Society*, vol. 5, 448–68. Berkeley, CA: University of California Press, 1988.
Lobel, Diana. *Between Mysticism and Philosophy: Sufi Language of Religious Experience in Judah Ha-Levi's Kuzari*. Albany, NY: State University of New York Press, 2000.
Silman, Yochanan. *Philosopher and Prophet: Judah Halevi, the Kuzari, and the Evolution of His Thought*. Albany, NY: State University of New York Press, 1995.
Tanenbaum, Adena. *The Contemplative Soul: Hebrew Poetry and Philosophical Theory in Medieval Spain*, 174–94. Leiden: Brill, 2002.

JUDEO-ARABIC

Since antiquity, Jewish communities have adopted local vernaculars as well as literary languages. German and Spanish, for example, have Jewish forms known respectively as Yiddish and Judezmo (sometimes Ladino). Written in Hebrew characters, they possess a traditional Hebrew and Aramaic vocabulary, which varies in size and scope according to situation and speaker/writer. Judeo-Arabic conforms to this pattern. As far back as the seventh century CE, Jews in the Arabian Peninsula spoke a dialect of Arabic called *al-yahudiya* in the hadith (tradition) literature. With the Islamic conquests, Jews throughout the Near East, North Africa, and the Iberian Peninsula began to acquire Arabic, the new *lingua franca;* by the late tenth century, it had largely replaced Aramaic as the language of Jews in Islamic lands. For the most part, they reserved Hebrew for sacred and secular poetry. Judeo-Arabic was their primary language of communication and technical writing in all disciplines, including the religious sciences (biblical exegesis, Hebrew grammar and lexicography, homiletics, law, theology, and philosophy) as well as astronomy and medicine. Sa'adyah's *Kitab al-Amanat*, Moses Ibn Ezra's book on Hebrew poetics, Maimonides' *Guide*, and the great Karaite Bible commentaries were all written in Judeo-Arabic.

Judeo-Arabic is a variety of Middle Arabic, a stage of the language that often deviates from classical usage and includes vernacular, "neo-Arabic" features. The Middle Arabic corpus includes Christian religious writings, Muslim literary works (e.g., *The Thousand and One Nights*), and Jewish texts of many different types. Aside from its Hebrew and Aramaic lexical component, Judeo-Arabic preserves all of the typical Middle Arabic features found in Christian and Muslim texts. These include the following: (1) the disappearance of case endings; (2) the replacement of the ending *-una* with *-u* in the imperfect indicative tense of verbs; (3) the interchange of certain consonants, such as *sin* and *sad;* (4) the interchange of verbal themes, such as I for IV and vice versa; (5) the use of *ma* to negate the imperfect; and (6) asyndetic syntax. Most characteristic are the numerous "pseudocorrections," or failed attempts at classical usage that result in incorrect or even nonexistent forms (e.g., *akhyar*, "better/best"; Classical Arabic: *khayr*).

With the exception of some Karaites who preferred to use Arabic script even for Hebrew texts, most Jews wrote Arabic in the Hebrew alphabet, which all Jewish children learned. This loyalty to Hebrew characters had two important consequences. First, Muslims and Christians could not read Jewish writings of any kind unless they had been specially copied in Arabic letters. The Hebrew alphabet, therefore, constituted a boundary between religious communities in Islamic lands. Second, because the Jewish veneration for the divine name precludes the intentional destruction of any text upon which it may be written, Jews discarded all unwanted documents by placing them in special repositories, such as the Cairo Geniza. This trove of manuscripts contains Judeo-Arabic texts in a range of linguistic registers and in many different genres, from theological treatises to legal documents and personal letters. It attests to the great richness of Jewish scholarship in the lands of medieval Islam.

DANIEL FRANK

See also Education, Jewish; Hebrew; Judah Halevi; Poetry, Hebrew; Nissim Ibn Shahin; Scriptural Exegesis, Jewish; Solomon Ibn Gabirol; Translation, Arabic to Hebrew

Further Reading

Blau, Joshua. *The Emergence and Linguistic Background of Judaeo-Arabic.* London: Oxford University Press, 1965. (Revised edition, Jerusalem: Ben-Zvi Institute, 1981.)
———. *Studies in Middle Arabic.* Jerusalem: Magnes Press, 1988.
———. *A Handbook of Early Middle Arabic.* Jerusalem: Hebrew University of Jerusalem, 2002.
Fenton, P.B. "Judaeo-Arabic Literature." In *Religion, Learning and Science in the 'Abbasid Period*, ed. M.J.L. Young et al., 461–76. Cambridge, UK: Cambridge University Press, 1990.
Halkin, A.S. "Judaeo-Arabic Literature." In *Great Ages and Ideas of the Jewish People*, ed. L.W. Schwarz. New York, 1956.

JUDGES

The *qadi* (judge) has been a key figure in Muslim societies for more than fourteen hundred years. Sometimes a trained scholar, sometimes not, the qadi performs judicial, administrative, and symbolic functions. To him belongs the domain of resolving legal disputes by hearing complaints, applying rules of procedure, soliciting and assessing witness testimony, and issuing and enforcing binding judgments. In many Muslim communities, the qadi also serves as an administrator and an intermediary between the state and its subjects, executing the ruler's decrees and collecting his taxes. The qadi is frequently a revered figure whose office is a symbol of divine justice. He is responsible for the general welfare of Muslims and non-Muslims, the safety and security of travel, ensuring that people are accorded their rights, and promoting respect for Islam and its adherents.

Early History

The early Umayyad caliphs held their own courts but also appointed the first qadis, who were subject to their authority. Recruited from the ranks of pre-Islamic arbitrators, the earliest qadis lacked formal training. Their duties included the resolution of disputes among the conquering tribesmen in the garrison towns based on their understanding of the regulations contained in the Qur'an and the example of the Prophet Muhammad. In the absence of Qur'anic stipulations or prophetic precedent, they exercised personal discretion and relied on ad hoc reasoning. For most of the first century AH, the jurisdiction of the qadis was limited to the garrison towns and to the resolution of disputes among the Arab tribesmen and their families; it did not yet extend to the surrounding countryside or to the towns and cities inhabited by Christians, Zoroastrians, Jews, and others.

Upon his accession to the caliphate, Mu'awiya (r. 661–680 CE) delegated his authority to qadis and other agents in the garrison towns. In addition to resolving disputes, these qadis served as governors, tax collectors, military commanders, leaders of prayer, and supervisors of the public treasury and the land tax. The qadi al-jund exercised authority over the Muslim soldiers who were organized according to military units in the garrison towns, distributing stipends to soldiers among the members of their respective tribes, and guarding the interests of orphans within a particular tribe. Under the Umayyads, the functions of criminal enforcement and the judgeship were often united in the hands of a single individual.

By the turn of the first century AH, the judicial apparatus had expanded outward from the garrison towns and embraced major towns in which Muslims were as yet only a minority of the population. The rapid expansion of the Arab empire and the growing complexity and sophistication of the state apparatus led to the development of the judgeship as a professional office. During the last decade of the first century AH, the functions of the qadi came to be limited to the resolution of legal disputes and the administration of the emerging judicial apparatus. Beginning with

Sulayman b. 'Abd al-Malik (r. 715–717), judges were appointed directly by the caliphs from the capital in Damascus.

The Umayyads used the qadiship as a form of patronage, appointing important and influential religious figures as qadis and using them to disseminate their ideology and to promote the popularity of the regime. Although there was no lack of qualified candidates to fill these posts, many potential candidates either refused to accept such appointments or had to be cajoled to do so, presumably because they were reluctant to associate themselves with a state regarded as unjust or impious.

The early qadis issued their judgments on the basis of their understanding of the Qur'an *(sunna)* and local custom, supplemented by *ra'y* (personal discretion), thereby contributing to the formation of nascent legal doctrine and laying the foundation for what would become the mature legal doctrine of the law schools *(madhhabs)*.

After 750 CE

In Umayyad and early 'Abbasid times, the jurisdiction of the qadi was limited to the town over which he was appointed. At first, the qadi was usually a local representative of the inhabitants of a town who was familiar with many of the residents and responsive to public opinion. Candidates for the office were invited to appear before the caliph or governor, who attached great importance to popular sentiment when making a decision to appoint—or dismiss—a qadi.

The 'Abbasid caliph al-Mahdi (r. 775–785) initiated the regular hearing of petitions and complaints in the forum that came to be known as the *mazalim* (courts of complaint). This was the institution by means of which the state assumed direct responsibility for dispensing justice and responding to complaints regarding administrative and judicial abuses.

A key step in the consolidation of state control over judges was taken by Harun al-Rashid (r. 786–809), who created the office of *qadi al-qudat* (chief qadi), appointing Abu Yusuf (d. 798) as its first incumbent. The chief qadi was empowered to appoint, supervise, and dismiss qadis and other judicial officials throughout the empire. Eventually, it became customary for the chief qadi to nominate the main provincial judge who, in turn, delegated his judicial powers to one or more local agents. Some of these agents were empowered to hear specific types of disputes, whereas others had jurisdiction in all fields in a limited geographical district.

The caliph retained the power to adjudicate cases even though, in practice, he generally assigned this power to qadis who acted as his agents. In most Muslim polities, the caliph (later, the sultan) and executive officials exercised general—albeit not exclusive—jurisdiction over criminal cases. This type of justice is called *siyasa* (literally discipline), a term that signifies both state policy and the right of the ruler and his agents to impose discretionary punishments.

With the failure of the Inquisition *(Mihna)* in 849, the caliph no longer attempted to impose religious uniformity, and, as a consequence, the status of the chief qadiship declined. By the time of al-Mu'tadid (r. 892–902), the vizier had replaced the chief qadi as second-in-command to the caliph, and henceforth it was the vizier who appointed the chief qadi and, on occasion, provincial qadis as well.

By the middle of the ninth century, the men who received appointments as qadis increasingly were people of high standing at the 'Abbasid court who were loyal to the caliph and ready to implement his policies. These men often had no ties to and did not reside in the towns over which they were appointed, and they were appointed from Baghdad rather than by local governors. The jurisdiction of a single qadi now might include as many as three or four towns and their surrounding districts, although the range of legal issues over which he exercised control became more limited. The qadi had become a state functionary whose authority emanated from and was dependent upon his nomination by the caliph.

The qadi carried out his judicial activities in his court *(mahkama)*, where he applied the fully developed legal doctrine of a specific law school. In theory, the qadi's jurisdiction was general and included both civil and criminal cases; in practice, most criminal cases were handled by the police and military governors. Qadis also administered charitable endowments, supervised funds earmarked for orphans, and, especially during later periods, collected the alms tax and poll tax.

Legal doctrine recommends that a qadi should consult with other jurists, and he may ask legal experts to sit with him in the court. Qadis worked closely with *muftis* (jurisprudents), from whom they solicited fatwas (expert legal opinions); in the Islamic West, qadi courts usually included a council of jurisprudents known as a *shura*. Indeed, a proper appreciation of the nature of Islamic justice requires a consideration of the complementary roles of the qadi and the mufti. A mufti's opinion is not binding, however, and a qadi is expected to issue his judgment on the strength of what he himself determines to be the truth of a matter. He must abide by the consensus of the jurists, and he should exercise independent reasoning *(ijtihad)* only on matters with respect to which no consensus has emerged. If he is qualified to exercise independent reasoning, he is bound by it, and he should not follow the recommendation of his advisors, even if their juristic qualifications are better than his.

The classical position of the law schools holds that a judge's decision, when based on the proper legal texts and fulfilling the necessary procedural conditions of judgment, is binding and may not be reversed. However, this formulation leaves open the possibility of reversing a decision that fails to meet these conditions. In fact, a judgment may be reversed in two circumstances: (1) if the pronouncing judge was not legally competent to pass judgment; and (2) if a judge who was legally competent nevertheless engaged in the improper use of ijtihad—that is, if his judgment contradicts a Qur'anic text (the plain meaning of which there is universal agreement on), a widely transmitted hadith, or the consensus of Muslim jurists. Thus, if a judge is not legally competent or if a legally competent judge engages in the improper use of independent reasoning, his judgment may be nullified by another judge. Conversely, a judgment issued by a competent judge that is based on sound ijtihad may not be reversed under any circumstances. Islamic law developed a system of successor review that regulates how a succeeding judge should treat judgments issued by his predecessor.

In those areas of the Muslim world that were independent of central control, local rulers introduced variations on the above-mentioned patterns of judicial administration. In Cordoba, the Umayyad Caliph 'Abd al-Rahman (r. 756–788) manifested his independence from the 'Abbasids by designating his military judge as *qadi al-jama'a*, a term that came to be used throughout al-Andalus and the Maghrib. After conquering Egypt in 969, the Fatimids (909–1171) established a chief qadi in Cairo, and the holder of this office exercised his authority in the name of the imam. Under the Fatimids and Mamluks (1250–1517), there were two chief qadis, one in Baghdad and the other in Cairo. Under the Mamluks, the chief qadi of Cairo delegated his authority to chief qadis in the major cities of the empire so that several chief qadis operated throughout the realm. The Mamluks also appointed a chief qadi for each of the four madhhabs.

The qadi system developed by the 'Abbasids continued to operate under the Mughals in India (1526–1858), the Safavids in Iran (1501–1722), and the Ottomans in the Middle East (1512–1918). The Ottomans, however, transformed the structure of the judiciary. In an effort to exercise greater control over the provinces, Selim I (r. 1512–1520) and Suleiman the Magnificent (r. 1520–1560) created a hierarchical judicial structure headed by the *qadi 'askar* (military qadi) and the *Shaykh al-Islam* (state mufti). Below them were the qadis of the major towns and cities, and then came local qadis, whose jurisdiction was restricted to a district or subdistrict.

Ottoman qadis played a key role in the administration of the empire, serving as conduits between local individuals or groups and the central government. They also performed important administrative duties, such as supervising guilds, recommending the suitability of buildings, securing the availability of foodstuffs, and enforcing economic regulations. The jurisdiction of qadis and of local officials was defined by legislation *(qanun)*. The local qadi monitored the lawfulness of the acts of officials involved in siyasa justice, thereby ensuring the proper conduct of criminal proceedings, including the interrogation and custody of people accused of a crime. The conduct and behavior of the qadi was, in theory, the responsibility of the sultan, although in practice he delegated this responsibility to the local governor, who was empowered to open an investigation into a qadi's actions and, if necessary, to dismiss and/or imprison him.

The Ottomans designated the Hanafi madhhab as the official law school of the empire and instructed qadis to follow the most authoritative opinion within the Hanafi school, although exceptions were allowed for political reasons or expediency. Any judgment issued that was contrary to these instructions was null and void and would not be enforced by the executive authorities.

Beginning during the early nineteenth century, the institutional framework within which qadis operated underwent major changes that have dramatically transformed the nature of the office.

DAVID STEPHAN POWERS

See also Caliphate and Imamate; Consultation; Courts; Crime and Punishment; Law and Jurisprudence; Prisons; Schools of Jurisprudence

Further Reading

Azad, Ghulam Murtaza. *Judicial System of Islam.* Islamabad: Islamic Research Institute, International Islamic University, 1987.

Bligh-Abramski, Irit. "The Judiciary *(Qadis)* as a Governmental-Administrative Tool in Early Islam." *Journal of the Economic and Social History of the Orient* 35 (1992): 40–71.

Dannhauer, Paul Gerhard. *Untersuchungen zur Frühen Geschichte des Qadi-Amtes.* Bonn Inaugural-Dissertation zur Erlangung der Doktowürde der Philosophischen. Bonn: Fakultät der Rheinischen Friedrich-Wilhelms-Universität, 1975.

Hallaq, Wael B. *The Origins and Evolution of Islamic Law.* Cambridge, UK: Cambridge University Press, 2004.

Johansen, Baber. "Wahrheit und Geltungsanspruch: Zur Begründung und Begrenzung der Autorität des Qadi-Urteils im Islamischen Recht." In *La Giustizia Nell'Alto Medioevo (Secoli IX–XI)*, 975–1074. Spoleto: Presso la Sede del Centro, 1997.

Masud, Muhammad Khalid, Brinkley Messick, and David S. Powers, eds. *Islamic Legal Interpretation: Muftis and Their Fatwas*. Cambridge, MA: Harvard University Press, 1996.

Al-Mawardi. *The Ordinances of Government: al-Ahkam al-Sultaniyya wa'l-Wilayat al-Diniyya,* transl. Wafaa H. Wahba. Reading: Garnet, 1996.

Müller, Christian. *Gerichtspraxis im Stadtstaat Córdoba: Zum Recht der Gesellschaft in Einer Malikitisch-Islamischen Rechtstradition des 5.11. Jahrhunderts.* Leiden: E.J. Brill, 1999.

———. "Judging with God's Law on Earth: Judicial Powers of the *Qadi al-jama'a* of Cordoba in the Fifth/Eleventh Century." *Islamic Law and Society* 7 (2000): 159–86.

Nielsen, J.S. "Mazalim." In *Encyclopaedia of Islam*, 2nd ed. Leiden: E.J. Brill, 1991.

Powers, David S. *Law, Society, and Culture in the Maghrib, 1300–1500.* Cambridge, UK: Cambridge University Press, 2002.

Schneider, Irene. *Das Bild des Richters in der "Adab al-Qadi" Literatur.* Frankfurt: Peter Lang, 1990.

Serrano, Delfina. "Legal Practice in an Andalusi-Maghribi Source From the Twelfth Century CE: The *Madhahib al-Hukkam fi Nawazil al-Ahkam.*" *Islamic Law and Society* 7 (2000): 187–234.

Tsafrir, Nurit. *The History of an Islamic School of Law: The Early Spread of Hanafism.* Cambridge, MA: Islamic Legal Studies Program, Harvard Law School, 2004.

Tyan, Emile. *Histoire de L'Organisation Judiciaire en Pays d'Islam*, 2nd rev. ed. Leiden: E.J. Brill, 1960.

———. "Judicial Organization." In *Law in the Middle East*, eds. Majid Khadduri and Herbert J. Liebesny, 236–78. Washington, DC: The Middle East Institute, 1955.

JUHA

Juha, a pseudohistorical character, is the most prominent protagonist of jocular prose narratives in the entire Islamic world. The first securely datable anecdote about Juha is narrated in both al-Jahiz's (d. ca. 255 AH/869 CE) *al-Qawl fi l-Bighal (Remarks About Mules)* and his *Rasa'il (Epistles)*. Substantial anecdotal material about Juha is available in the large adab compilations of the tenth and eleventh centuries, such as the works of al-Tawhidi (d. 414/1023) and al-Abi (d. 421/1030). By the eleventh century, Juha had already been firmly established as a "focusee" of a cycle of jocular prose narratives, and a booklet devoted to these narratives is listed in Ibn al-Nadîm's *Fihrist (The Index;* a late tenth-century Baghdad bookseller's bibliography of works he knew or believed to be extant). During the following centuries, the character attracted ever more material. The only monograph collection of his tales surviving from premodern Arabic literature, a booklet called *Irshad*

Man Naha ila Nawadir Juha (The Guidance of Those Who Feel Inclined to the Stories of Juha), was compiled by Yusuf ibn al-Wakil al-Milawi in the seventeenth century and contains a total of seventy-four tales. The modern image of Juha was shaped by nineteenth-century print tradition. Printed editions of Juha's tales present an amalgam of traditional Arabic material about him, together with tales that had originally been attributed to the Turkish jester Nasreddin Hodja and anecdotes derived from traditional Arabic literature.

Similar to the expansion of the narrative repertoire attributed to him, the depiction of Juha's character has also undergone considerable development. The traditional repertoire presents him mostly as an adolescent with a certain preference for sexual, scatological and otherwise "obscene" matters. Even so, the early anecdotes already imply some of the more charming traits of character, such as when he buries his money in the desert and remembers the position of a specific cloud so as to locate the place later. These traits were elaborated by later compilers, who established Juha in modern tradition as a naive philosopher and social critic.

ULRICH MARZOLPH

See also Books

Further Reading

Farraj, 'Abd al-Sattar Ahmad. *Akhbar Juha*. Cairo.

Marzolph, Ulrich. *Nasreddin Hodscha*. Munich, 1996.

Marzolph, Ulrich, and Inge Baldauf. "Hodscha Nasreddin." In *Enzyklopädie des Märchens*, vol. 6, cols. 1127–51. Berlin and New York: de Gruyter, 1990.

JURJANI, AL-

Abu Bakr 'Abd al-Qahir ibn 'Abd al-Rahman ibn Muhammad al-Jurjani (d. 1078 or 1081 CE) was born, raised and educated in Jurjan and was known during his lifetime primarily as a grammarian. Although his additional identities as Shaf'ite jurisconsult and Ash'arite theologian precluded any great official recognition or support, al-Jurjani's scholarship was sufficiently well known for him to attract a steady flow of students and disciples to his home town. He is best known for his two seminal works on Arabic rhetoric, *Dala'il i'Jaz al-Qur'an (Indications of the Inimitability of the Qur'an)* and *Asrar al-Balagha (The Mysteries of Rhetoric)*.

Indications is first and foremost a work of stylistics, in which al-Jurjani elaborates on ideas that are implicit in the work of earlier philologists and provides them a philosophical foundation that is consistent with his theological views. In the centuries-old debate as to whether eloquence derives from the *lafz* (wording) or the *ma'na* (meaning), al-Jurjani champions the supremacy of meaning and, in particular, the thinking with which it is associated. This, he claims, is the source of excellence in discourse, and, to appreciate it, we must look at how the meanings are connected with each other. The vehicle of these relationships among the individual *ma'ani* (meanings) is the various features of grammar, which reflect the way things are ordered or constructed in the mind of the speaker or writer. Word order, for example, takes on new rhetorical significance for al-Jurjani, who examines the various possible combinations and what they imply about the intention of the speaker and the context of the discourse. Al-Jurjani thus amplifies the notion of *nazm* (ordering, construction), which was mentioned by earlier grammarians and scholars of Qur'anic style such as Abu Sulayman al-Khattabi (d. 996 or 998). Rejecting the simplistic understanding of meaning that had traditionally permitted the facile accusation of plagiarism, al-Jurjani emphasizes the individual nature of the conception or intellectual prototype *(sura)* that discourse is based on. Manipulation of the subtleties of syntax and of figurative language result in a change in the meaning and form (sura) of the discourse. A poet who in this way adds nuances to a hackneyed poetic conceit cannot be said to have plagiarized another poet's ma'na, for he has thus created a new one with its own particularities that make it distinct from the original.

Al-Jurjani's emphasis on the intimate connection between the intellectual processes at the origin of discourse and the linguistic entity itself—especially his notion of sura (form, shape)—derives from his attempt to reconcile Mu'tazilite epistemology with Ash'ari theological views of the Qur'an. His frequent quotations from and responses to the work of the later Mu'tazilite theologian Abd al-Jabbar al-Asadabadi (d. 1024) provide clear indication of this interconfessional debate. Through his emphasis on the abstract intellectual form (sura) of a particular discourse, which in turn is reflected in the way the linguistic system is put into play, al-Jurjani is able, when treating the text of the Qur'an, to remain faithful to the Ash'ari concept of God's ineffable kalam nafsi (internal speech) as distinguished from its external expression in sounds and letters while preserving, in good Mu'tazilite fashion, a means of appreciating the text as text.

In similar fashion, it is al-Jurjani's concern with important theological issues (e.g., the debate surrounding human agency [championed by the Mu'tazilities] versus determinism [as argued by the Ash'aris]; the debate about the attributes of God) that is at the heart of his distinction between two types of *majaz* (figurative expression) - majaz 'aqli (figurative expression that is intellectually based) and *majaz lughawi* (figurative expression that is linguistically based). It is noteworthy that *isti'ara* (metaphorical borrowing) does not fall under the rubric of majaz for al-Jurjani. The rationale for this is once again theological in origin: because the Qur'an, the ultimate source of knowledge, is replete with metaphors, metaphor must be, in every sense, *haqiqa* (truth). Intent on so distinguishing between metaphorical discourse that is ontologically true and that which is imaginative, al-Jurjani establishes a distinction between *ma'ani 'aqliyya* (intellectually verifiable conceits) and *ma'ani takhyiliyya* (imaginative conceits), thus also finding a way to accommodate the kind of figures found in badi' (new style) poetry, which is renowned for its abundance of rhetorical features. Al-Jurjani's two works on i'jaz greatly influenced later generations' discussions of stylistics and rhetoric. Both Jar Allah al-Zamakhshari (d. 1144) and Fakhr al-Din al-Razi (d. 1209) made extensive use of al-Jurjani's texts, and the works of Jalal al-Din Abu 'Abd Allah al-Qazwini (d. 1338) and Siraj al-Din al-Sakkaki (d. 1229), who were responsible for the tripartite division of rhetoric that has dominated up until the present day, relied primarily on the works of 'Abd al-Qahir al-Jurjani.

MARGARET LARKIN

See also Rhetoric; Qur'an and Arabic Literature

Primary Sources

Al-Jurjani, 'Abd al-Qahir. *Asrar al-Balagha The Mysteries of Rhetoric)*, ed. Hellmut Ritter. Istanbul: Government Press (Matba'at Wizarat al-Ma'arif), 1954.
———. *Die Geheimnisse (Asrar al-Balaga) des 'Abdalqahir al-Curcani*, trans. Hellmut Ritter. Wiesbaden: Bibliotheca Islamica, Band 19, 1959.
———. *Dala'il i'Jaz al-Qur'an (Indications of the Inimitability of the Qur'an)*, ed. Mahmud Muhammad Shakir. Cairo: Maktabat al-Khanji, ca. 1984.

Further Reading

Abu Deeb, Kamal. *Al-Jurjani's Theory of Poetic Imagery*. England: Aris & Phillips, Ltd., 1979.
Abu Zayd, Nasr Hamid. "Mafhum al-Nazm 'Inda 'Abd al-Qahir al-Jurjani: Qira'a fi Daw' al-Uslubiyya." (The Concept of "Nazm" according to 'Abd al-Qahir al-Jurjani: A Reading From the Perspective of Stylistics.") *Fusul* 5 (1984): 11–24.
Cantarino, Vicente. *Arabic Poetics in the Golden Age*. Leiden: Brill, 1975.
Larkin, Margaret. "The Inimitability of the Qur'an: Two Perspectives," *Religion and Literature* 20.1 (1988): 31–47.
———. *The Theology of Meaning: 'Abd al-Qahir al-Jurjani's Theory of Discourse*. New Haven, CT: American Oriental Society, 1995.

JUWAYNI (AH 419/1028 CE–478/1085)

An Ash'arite theologian and a Shaf'ite jurist, Abu'l-Ma'ali Rukn al-Din Abd al-Malik b. Abdullah al-Juwayni was born in Nishapur in northern Persia. Also known as Imam al-Haramayn, he received his primary education from his father. He later studied under Al-Bayhaqi, Al-Iskafi, and Abu Nu'aym al-Isfahani, the well-known scholars of the region, and he became a teacher *(mudarris)* in his twenties after the death of his father. He had to leave Nishapur in 450/1058 and stay in Mecca and Medina for four years as a result of the discriminations of the Seljuki Vizier al-Kunduri against the Ash'arites. Soon after his return to his hometown, he was appointed the head of the Nizamiyya Madrasa, a higher educational institution built by the new grand vizier Nizam al-Mulk. Among his many students at Nizamiyya were famous Islamic scholars such as Al-Ghazzali, Kiya al-Harrasi, and Ali b. Muhammad al-Tabari. He died in Nishapur in his fifties.

Most of Juwayni's works address theological and legal theories; his *al-Shamil, al-Irshad,* and *al-Burhan* are major source books in these fields. He also wrote books about governance, dialectics, and inter religious polemics. Because he did not necessarily follow his own school of thought in all theological and legal issues, he represents the period of transition between the early Ash'arite theology and the post-Ghazzalian synthesis with logic and philosophy. Contrary to the previous Ash'arite thinker al-Baqillani, for instance, Juwayni did not hesitate to include philosophical terminology and use logical premises in his theological arguments. He also tends to partly accommodate the Mu'tazilite theory of *ahwal* (modes) with regard to the relationship between divine essence and attributes within the Ash'arite system. Although he supports the possibility of *ta'wil* (rational interpretations) of certain verses in the Qur'an when the literal meaning of the text raises difficulties, he considers it to be applicable only when necessary. The sources of religious knowledge, according to Juwayni, are primarily scriptural; therefore, God's will and authority identify good and bad. Regarding the question of divine justice, he rejects the Mu'tazilite theory of the intrinsic nature of the moral act, instead defending the Ash'arite idea of subjectivity.

Juwayni was also interested in and wrote about Islamic political thought. Under the patronage of Nizam al-Mulk, he dealt with the principles of governance in his book *al-Ghiyasi.* According to al-Juwayni, some of the qualities required for governing are essential, whereas the others are advisory only and could be ignored depending on time or conditions. For example, the capability for the leadership and full control of authority are always necessary; however, characteristics such as belonging to a certain family (i.e., Kuraysh) or being a *mujtahid* (scholar) or a pious person are not to be weighted as heavily. Because the main responsibility of the governing body is the protection and public service of society, Juwayni thinks that, to avoid a potential problem, the head of state and other important officials should excuse themselves from, for example, the performance of hajj (pilgrimage to Mecca) for the sake of unity and stability. Hajj is an individual duty, whereas public interest is a collective obligation and should therefore be given priority.

MEHMET SAIT ÖZERVARLI

Further Reading

Al-Juwayni, Imam al Haramayn. *A Guide to the Conclusive Proofs for the Principles of Belief: Kitab al Irshad ila Qawati 'al-Adilla fi Usul al I'tiqad,* transl. Paul Walker. Reading: Garnet Publishing, 2001.

Allard, Michel. *Textes Apologetiques de Guwaini.* Beirut: Dar al-Mashriq, 1968.

Bernand, M. "Abu-l-Ma'ali al-Guwayni: al-Giyati," *Bulletin Critique des Annales Islamologique* 3 (1986): 46–7.

Dib, Abd al-Azim. *Fiqh Imam al-Haramayn.* Cairo: Dar al-Wafa, 1988.

Gilliot, Claude. "Quand la Théologie S'Allie a L'Histoire: Triomphe et Échec du Rationalisme Musulman a Travers L'Oeuvre d'al-Guwayni." *Arabica* 39 (1992): 241–60.

Harfush, Ashraf. *Falsafat al-Kalam Inda Imam al-Haramayn el-Juawayni.* Damascus: al-Hikma li-al-Tiba'a wa'l-Nashr, 1994.

Hourani, George F. "Juwayni's Criticisms of Mu'tazilite Ethics." *The Muslim World* 65/3 (1975): 161–73.

Jah, Omar. "Preliminary Remarks on De Facto Government and the Problem of its Legitimacy: Imam al-Juwayni's Theory of al-Shawka." *al-Shajarah* 6/2 (2001): 229–51.

Nagel, Tilman. "Al-Guwaini's Kitab al-Burhan un die Theologische Begrundung der Scharia." In *Actas del XII. Congreso de l'Union Europeenne des Arabisants et Islamisants,* 647–56. Madrid: UEAI, 1986.

Saflo, Mohammad Moslem Adel. *al-Juwayni's Thought and Methodology with a Translation and Commentary on Luma' al-Adillah.* Berlin: Klaus Schwarz, 2000.

K

KA'BA, OR KAABA

The structure and its immediate precincts in Mecca that also house a large mosque are referred to in the Qur'an and subsequently in Muslim tradition as the House of God *(bayt Allah)* and the sacred Mosque *(masjid al hayam)*. The Ka'ba is the point of orientation for Muslims when they pray, and it is also the focal point of the Pilgrimage *(Hajj)* as well as the *umra* (minor pilgrimage). The Hajj takes place over a fixed period in the prescribed month, whereas the umra may be undertaken at any other time.

During pre-Islamic times, the Ka'ba served as a shrine and a sacred space *(haram)*. Arab tribes and others made annual pilgrimages to the site and visited it to honor tribal and ancestral deities that included several goddesses. Representatives of these deities were kept in the Ka'ba, and the ritual visits were often accompanied by music, dance, and the recitation of poetry.

The Prophet Muhammad was forced to leave Mecca as a result of the opposition he encountered because of his preaching, his activities against many tribal practices and values, and his claim to be the messenger of a new revelation. He migrated to Medina in 622 CE, but he subsequently negotiated to undertake the pilgrimage to Mecca with his followers. In 629, Mecca submitted to him, and he was able to enter the town peacefully and purge the Ka'ba of its idols, restoring it to its original role as the symbol of a monotheistic faith and affirming its place as the site of the Hajj, which became established as a major pilgrimage practice of the new faith of Islam. He also linked the Ka'ba to Abraham, who, with his wife Hagar and son Ismail (Ishmael), is also believed to have established a place of worship there. According to Muslim tradition, it is also the location of the first-ever place of worship. The formalized practices for the Hajj were also instituted by the Prophet, thereby linking the Ka'ba to other nearby centers to constitute the totality of pilgrimage rituals. An irregular cube-like structure, the Ka'ba itself measures approximately fifteen meters in height, ten meters in length and twelve meters in width. Its four corners are generally aligned with the four points of the compass. On one of the corners, set in a silver bezel, is the Black Stone *(al hajar al aswad)*, which is believed to be of miraculous and ancient origin. Pilgrims customarily kiss or touch it, and they also begin the circling *(tawaf)* of the Ka'ba during the pilgrimage from this point.

The Ka'ba is generally covered with a black silk covering embroidered with Qur'anic verses which is replaced annually, a practice that originated during medieval Muslim history. It has one entrance and the interior is empty, but it is customarily cleansed and swept in a ritual that precedes the Hajj.

The *maqam* (station) of Abraham is located just outside of the Ka'ba. Muslim tradition records that God instructed Abraham to establish the Ka'ba as a place of worship. In the vicinity, just east of the Ka'ba, is also found the Well of Zamzam, which carries forward the linkage with the Abrahamic traditions in which the well sprang forth by God's grace in response to the fervent prayers of Hagar. Its water is

Muslim pilgrims before the Kaaba in Mecca. Miniature, 1577. Inv.: Ding A, fol.3/fol.46a. (Pertscn Nr. 1016) Photo: Ruth Schacht. Oriental Division. Credit: Bildarchiv preussischer Kulturbestiz/Art Resource, NY. Staatsbibliothek Zu Berlin, Berlin, Germany.

now circulated through a modern system of pipes and made available to pilgrims as is ancient Muslim custom.

The symbolism and significance of the Ka'ba are evoked in Muslim mystical tradition, in which it plays a cosmic role as the center of the earth. Although the Ka'ba serves as the *qibla* (direction for prayer), Muslims also traditionally bury the dead facing the Ka'ba.

AZIM NANJI

Further Reading

Bianchi, Robert. *Events of God: Pilgrimage and Politics in the Islamic World.* Oxford, UK: Oxford University Press, 2004.

Crone, Patricia. *Meccan Trade and the Rise of Islam.* Princeton, NJ: Princeton University Press, 1987.

Kamal, Ahmad. *The Sacred Journey: The Pilgrimage to Mecca.* New York: Duell, Sloan & Pearce, 1961.

KABBALA

Derived from the root *qbl*, which is a cognate to the Arabic, the term *qabbâlâh* (reception, initiation) designates the Jewish esoteric tradition, but it is not synonymous with all of Jewish mysticism. It is specifically based on the system of the ten sefîrot (powers) through which the Divine Being progressively manifests itself in the existential realm. There existed pre-Qabbalistic forms of Jewish esotericism, some of which—like many of the later major developments of Qabbalah itself—flourished in an Islamic environment. Several points of contact and similarity (not only external) exist between Islamic mysticism and Qabbalah, although they are far from being variations of an identical doctrine, as early comparatists suggested. The ten sefîrot of the Qabbalistic system have no immediate equivalent in Sufism. Despite their independent developments, significant parallels exist between them. Certain Qabbalists distinguish three levels of the sefirotic world: the highest and most recondite aspect of the Divinity is called *keter* (crown); the intermediate level extends until the lowest sefîrah and is called *malkhuth* (kingship), which is the interface (much like the Sufi notion of barzakh) between the metaphysical and the lowest level, which is the phenomenal world. These three levels roughly correspond with the Sufi designations of *'alam al-jabarut, 'alam al-malakut,* and *'alam al-mulk.* Some scholars assign a post-Islamic date to the two great classics of Qabbalistic literature, the *Book of Creation (Sefer Yesirah)* and the *Book of Splendor (Sefer ha-Bahir).*

The Provençal Qabbalists and even the Ashkenazi pietists saw as their spiritual forebears the sages of the Ge'onic period in Baghdad, whose mystical speculations form the ancient strata of Qabbalistic literature. Their early writings, such as the contemplation of the Heavenly chariot (Òôfey ha-Merkâbâh), bear a striking resemblance to the Ôûfî accounts of spiritual ascension, such as that of al-Bistâmî. Sufis also see Baghdad as their spiritual cradle, and it is there that Sufism's formative period evolved in the shadow of the great Eastern wellsprings of Jewish spirituality. Although recognized in early studies of comparative religion, the connections between Jewish and Islamic mysticism in Spain are still unclear. Both were imbued with prophetic and messianic aspirations, which were later transported to Egypt, a land where the two mysticisms developed into institutionalized brotherhoods. R. Abraham Maimonides' (d. 1237 CE) attempt to legitimize his Sufi-type Jewish pietism parallels Sufism's efforts to shed itself of the suspicion of heresy by espousing strictly orthodox norms, as exemplified in the works of al-Ghazzâlî (d. 1111).

Just as Sufism integrated philosophical elements from the Neoplatonist and Aristotelian systems, so too the thirteenth- and fourteenth-century Spanish Qabbalists in particular undertook to reconcile the doctrines of Qabbalah and philosophy. Some, such as Judah Ibn Malka and Joseph Ibn Waqâr, composed their esoteric writings in Arabic. The "science of letters" plays a central role in the speculative and contemplative methods of many Sufis, such as at-Tustarî and Ibn 'Arabî (d. 1240), just as its Hebrew equivalent permeated the works of Qabbalists, such as R. Abraham Abû l-'Afiyah (d. ca. 1291). Indeed, the latter's "balance of letters" and his meditative technique known as hazkârâh recall both by their names and methods the doctrine of Jâbir ibn Hazyyân and the Sufi dhikr ritual. The speculative and cosmological system embodied in Muhyî d-Dîn Ibn 'Arabî's Mekkan *Revelations (al-Futûhât al-Makkiya)* completely revolutionized Islamic mysticism, as did the teachings of R. Isaac Lurya (d. 1574), which reached maturity in the Muslim East. Just as all previous Sufi theory was reinterpreted through the prism of Ibn 'Arabî's system, so too in Judaism was the Spanish Qabbâlâh; even its crowning work, the Zôhar, was reconstructed in the light of Luryanism.

Analogies can also be observed in the literary domain. The listing and clarification of istilâhât (technical terms) used by Sufis are essential components of their manuals, as are the technical lexicons (kinnûyîm) that are found in Qabbalistic textbooks. The formation of Sufi brotherhoods around their shaykhs affords yet again an instructive analogy to the various Qabbalistic groups centered around the charismatic saddîq.

Finally, the modern politicization of Sufi fraternities and the involvement of their spiritual leaders in the public areas of politics and academia (e.g., the Khalwatis in Egypt) parallels the activities in prewar Poland and contemporary Israel of Hasidic dynasties, whose ranks have furnished not a few public figures and academic scholars. The most significant influences of Sufism on the development of the Qabbala came in the period of the latter's expansion at the time of Isaac Lurya, who lived in Safed. Safed was a center of Muslim mysticism, and several practices were adopted by the Qabbalists, such as the visitation of tombs. Influence was felt too in the musical domain, where Qabbalists and Sufis often shared the same melodies and developed spiritual concerts known as *baqashh-shot* that were based on the structure of the Sufi samas. At the time of the pseudo-messiah, Sabbatay Zebi, close relations were established between the Bekatshis and his disciples, some of whom, as doenme (converts), became Mevlevi shaykhs.

Paul B. Fenton

See also Mysticism, Jewish

Further Reading

Cohen, G. "The Soteriology of Abraham Maimuni." *Proceedings of the American Academy for Jewish Research* 35 (1967): 75–98; 36 (1968): 33–56.

Fenton, P.B. "Some Judaeo-Arabic Fragments by Rabbi Abraham he-Hasid, the Jewish Sufî." *Journal of Semitic Studies* 26 (1981): 47–72.

———. *The Treatise of the Pool, al-Maqâla al-Îawdiyya by 'Obadyah Maimonides*. London, 1981.

———. "The Literary Legacy of David II Maimuni." *Jewish Quarterly Review* 74 (1984): 1–56.

———. *Deux Traités de Mystique Juive*. Lagrasse, 1987.

———. "La Hitbôdedût Chez les Premiers Qabbalistes d'Orient et Chez les Soufis." In *Priere, Mystique et Judaïsme*, ed. R. Goetschel, 133–58. Paris, 1987.

———. "Shabbatay Sebi and the Muslim Mystic Muhammad an-Niyâzi." *Approaches to Judaism in Medieval Times* 3 (1988): 81–88.

Goitein, S.D. "A Jewish Addict to Sufism in the Time of Nagid David II Maimonides." *Jewish Quarterly Review* 44 (1953–1954): 37–49.

———. "A Treatise in Defence of the Pietists." *Journal of Jewish Studies* 16 (1965): 105–14.

———. "Abraham Maimonides and his Pietist Circle." In *Jewish Medieval and Renaissance Studies*, ed. A. Altmann, 145–64. Cambridge, Mass, 1967.

Goldziher, I. "Ibn Hud, the Muhammadan Mystic, and the Jews of Damascus." *Jewish Quarterly Review* 6 (1893): 218–20.

Idel, M. *Abraham Abulafia and the Mystical Experience*. New York, 1988.

Maimonides, David. *Al-Murshid ila t-Tafarrud*, ed. P.B. Fenton. Jerusalem,1987.

Rosenblatt, S., ed. *The High Ways to Perfection of Abraham Maimonides*. New York and Baltimore, 1927–1938.

KALILA WA DIMNA

There once lived a lion who terrorized the animals of the jungle by hunting them, until one day they agreed to supply him daily with an animal as long as he stopped his cruelty. The animals continued to cast their lots every day until one day it was the hare's turn. The crafty hare arrived late to the hungry and angry lion and explained to him, "I was bringing another hare for your lunch, but on our way here another lion snatched the hare from me, proclaiming that he is the true king of the jungle." The furious lion wished to confront his adversary, and so he followed the hare to a deep well full of clear water. "Look here, my king!" said the hare, perched over the well. The lion saw his reflection and, thinking it was the other lion, leaped in and drowned. Thereafter, the animals lived happily ever after.

This is just one of the many "nested" stories from the tales of *Kalila wa Dimna*, adapted and translated into Arabic from the Pahlavi in the eighth century by Ibn al-Muqaffa' (d. c. 757 CE). The ultimate source of the *Kalila wa Dimna* can be traced to an original Sanskrit "mirror for princes" that was compiled by an unknown author around 300 and entitled the *Pañcatantra (Five Books* or *Five Cases of Cleverness)*. The Sanskrit tales were translated in the sixth century into Middle Persian (Pahlavi) by the physician Burzuya (or Burzoy) at the behest of the Sasanian King Khusraw Anushirwan (r. 531–579). In addition to the tales of the *Pañcatantra*, Burzuya incorporated various other stories into his corpus, principally from the *Mahabharata* epic and other Hindu and Buddhist sources. Burzuya's Pahlavi title, *Karirak ud Damanak*, was derived from the names of two jackals, Karataka and Damanaka, the principal characters in the first book of the *Pañcatantra*. Ibn al-Muqaffa's *Kalila wa Dimna* is therefore an Arabic recension of Burzuya's now lost *Karirak ud Damanak*, although the Arab author also inserted a number of additions into his final work.

The earliest surviving manuscripts of the *Kalila wa Dimna* date from the thirteenth and fourteenth centuries, and the widespread popularity of this work is clearly attested to by references to it in other medieval literary works, including the *Shahnama* of Firdawsi. However, the *Kalila wa Dimna* was never seen as a fixed corpus of stories, and later authors and editors felt free to add to, subtract from, and otherwise alter its contents. Scholars from the nineteenth century onward have attempted to trace the complex history and origins of the *Kalila wa Dimna* through both literary and art historical analysis. The tradition of illustrating the tales of the *Kalila wa Dimna* is probably based on older, well-established traditions of illustrating the animal fables of the *Pañcatantra*. Eighth-century frescoes found at Panjikent, near Samarkand, that include depictions of the *Pañcatantra* tales attest to a well-established iconographic tradition that was later absorbed and adapted in the Muslim Near East.

Ibn al-Muqaffa' states in his introduction the four-fold purpose of the *Kalila wa Dimna*: (1) to engage the youth through the vehicle of animal fables; (2) to delight the hearts of princes through richly illustrated depictions of the tales; (3) to entice kings and common folk everywhere to acquire their own copies and benefit the painters and scribes; and (4) to engage the philosophers in the wisdom of its tales. Were he alive today, Ibn al-Muqaffa' would not have been disappointed in the least. Throughout the ages, the *Kalila wa Dimna* has been reworked and translated, as both prose and poetic verse, into Persian, Mongol, Malay, Ethiopian, Hebrew, Greek, Latin, Spanish, Italian, French, German, and several Slavonic languages. The most famous Persian recension from the Timurid period is the *Anvar-i Suhayli*, which was later translated into Ottoman rhymed prose as the *Humayunnama* for Sultan Suleiman the Magnificent. A new version of the Timurid work entitled *Iyar-i Danish* was commissioned by the Mughal emperor Akbar.

FAHMIDA SULEMAN

See also Adab; Akbar; Arabic; Books; Firdawsi; Frescoes; Hindus; Ibn al-Muqaffa'; Manuscripts; Mirrors for Princes; Mughals; Painting, Miniature; Painting, Monumental and Frescoes; Persian; Poets; Popular Literature; Scribes; Shahnama; Stories and Storytelling; Suleiman the Magnificent; Timurids; Translation, Arabic to Persian; Turkish and Turkic Languages

Further Reading

Atil, Esin. *Kalila wa Dimna: Fables from a Fourteenth-Century Arabic Manuscript*. Washington, DC: Smithsonian Institution Press, 1981.

Brockelmann, C. "Kalila wa-Dimna." In *Encyclopaedia of Islam, New Edition*, vol. 4, 503–6. Leiden: E.J. Brill.

De Blois, François. *Burzôy's Voyage to India and the Origin of the Book of Kalîlah wa Dimnah*. London: Royal Asiatic Society, 1990.

Grube, Ernst J., ed. *A Mirror for Princes from India: Illustrated Versions of the* Kalilah wa Dimnah, Anvar-i Suhayli, Iyar-i Danish, *and* Humayun Nameh. Bombay: Marg Publications, 1991.

O'Kane, Bernard. *Early Persian Painting: Kalila and Dimna Manuscripts of the Late Fourteenth Century*. London and New York: I.B. Tauris, 2003.

Raby, Julian. "The Earliest Illustrations to *Kalila wa Dimna*." In *A Mirror for Princes from India*, ed. Ernst J. Grube, 16–31.

Walzer, Sofie. "An Illustrated Leaf from a Lost Mamluk Kalilah wa-Dimnah Manuscript." *Ars Orientalis* 2 (1957): 503–5.

KARAITES

A Jewish sect, the Karaites emerged in the Islamic East during the eighth and ninth centuries CE. The Hebrew name *qara'im* (Arabic *qara'iyun*) probably derives from *miqra*, or "scripture," because the Karaites are scripturalists who deny the authority of the rabbinic tradition embodied in talmudic and midrashic literature, depending instead directly on the Bible, which they interpret rationally. Although the sect's origins remain obscure, medieval sources connect its rise with a certain Anan ben David (active in Iraq during the middle of the eighth century). During the late ninth century, Karaite ideology crystallized around three principal ideas: (1) opposition to rabbinic teachings and leadership; (2) an apocalyptic worldview; and (3) the physical return to Zion. Daniel al-Qumisi of Damaghan argued that the Jews' suffering in exile was divine punishment for their having instituted rabbinic legislation of human origin. Reading scripture prognostically, he referred prophecies to contemporary times, identifying biblical names, places, people, and images with the world he knew. Assuming a central role in the unfolding eschatological drama, his followers called themselves "Mourners for Zion" (Isa. 61:3). Settling in Jerusalem, they studied and recited scripture, observed vigils, and fasted.

The Karaites elicited firm opposition from rabbinic leaders, notably Sa'adyah Gaon. Polemics between Rabbanites (adherents of rabbinic Judaism) and Karaites were harsh, but competition between the two groups undoubtedly contributed to the intellectual flowering of eastern Jewry. During the tenth century, Karaite scholars stood at the forefront of Jewish learning. Like Sa'adyah, they wrote extensively in Arabic on a range of subjects, including law, biblical exegesis, grammar, lexicography, and theology. Most of the leading figures hailed from Iran and Iraq, but, with the notable exception of the exegete and codifier Ya'qub al-Qirqisani (d. c. 938), they migrated to the Holy Land.

During the tenth and eleventh centuries, Jerusalem became the Karaites' intellectual center. Among the foremost scholars of the city were the commentator Japheth ben Eli, the grammarian Abu'l-Faraj Harun, and the theologian and jurist Yusuf al-Basir. Writing mostly in Arabic, they adapted Mu'tazilite theology, Islamic legal theory, Qur'anic hermeneutics, and Arabic grammatical terminology to their own sectarian needs.

Meanwhile, new Karaite centers developed in Egypt, Byzantium, and Andalusia. In Egypt, where members of the Karaite Tustari family served the Fatimid caliphs, Rabbanite and Karaite Jews maintained cordial relations, even intermarrying. With the extinction of the Jerusalem community (late eleventh century), the Egyptian center became the most important in the Islamic lands, surviving until the end of the twentieth century. In Spain, Ibn Hazm documented the presence of Karaites during the mid-eleventh century. Andalusian Rabbanites, such as Judah Halevi, Abraham Ibn Daud, and Maimonides, sharply condemned Karaite teachings, and they recorded efforts to suppress the sect. In Byzantium, the sectarians translated a large body of scholarship from Arabic to Hebrew, adapting Karaite teachings and practices to a new Christian environment. The communities that later developed in the Crimea, Poland, and Lithuania originally looked to Constantinople for spiritual guidance. Today, there are perhaps twenty-five thousand Karaites in the world; most are of Egyptian extraction and reside in Israel.

DANIEL FRANK

See also Hebrew; Judah Halevi; Judeo-Arabic; Kalam; Polemics and Disputation; Sa'adyah Gaon; Scriptural Exegesis, Jewish; Translation, Arabic to Hebrew

Primary Sources

Nemoy, Leon. *Karaite Anthology*. New Haven, CT: Yale University Press, 1952.

Further Reading

Ankori, Zvi. *Karaites in Byzantium: The Formative Years, 970–1100*. New York: Columbia University Press, 1959.
Baron, Salo W. *A Social and Religious History of the Jews*, 2nd ed. 18 vols., vol. 5, 209–85. New York: Columbia University Press; Philadelphia: The Jewish Publication Society of America, 1952–1983.
Frank, Daniel. *Search Scripture Well: Karaite Exegetes and the Origins of the Jewish Bible Commentary in the Islamic East*. Leiden: Brill Academic Publishers, 2004.
Polliack, Meira, ed. *Karaite Judaism: A Guide to Its History and Literary Sources*. Leiden: Brill Academic Publishers, 2003.

KARBALA

Karbala is the site of one of the earliest tragedies in Muslim history, where Husayn (grandson of the Prophet Muhammad) and several members of his family and supporters were killed in 680 CE. It became in time a place of pilgrimage for the Shi'is and other devotees and the location of the mausoleum of Husayn. At present, it is one of the largest towns in southern Iraq, located some sixty miles southwest of Baghdad, and it has grown to become one of the most important pilgrimage centers for Shi'i Muslims.

More recently, after the fall of Saddam Hussein and his regime in 2003, Karbala became the scene of battles and conflict for control by various Shi'i groups and others, but it has also regained its significance as a pilgrimage site for the global Shi'i community after a long period of the suppression of devotional practices associated with its historical significance. Its many seminaries attract Twelver Shi'i students for study and training as religious teachers and leaders.

In 680 CE, after the death of Muawiyah, who had forcibly assumed the role of caliph and established his rule based in Damascus, Yazid, his son, whom he had nominated as his successor, faced opposition from several quarters. Many Muslims saw an opportunity to restore just and legitimate rule though Husayn, whose accession to power they supported. He set out from Medina to Kufa to build further support and to challenge Yazid. However, he and his band of followers and family members were intercepted by Yazid's troops and forced to camp at Karbala. The battle—or, more appropriately, the massacre—that ensued at the hands of Yazid's army is recorded by Muslim historians as an event of tragic proportions and as an act of brave defiance, leading to the martyrdom of Husayn. The event and the site became reference points for commemorating the tragedy and elaborating a set of ritual acts and remembrances that reflect themes of suffering, persecution, oppression, and martyrdom that have since dominated Shi'i writings and rituals.

Husayn and his brother Abbas, as well as others killed in the battle, were buried in Karbala, and soon members of his family and followers visited Karbala for prayers and remembrance. Over the course of Muslim history, several rulers opposed to its significance as a pilgrimage site either attempted to destroy the site or to restrict access to it, and the tomb was also destroyed by fire. The great fourteenth-century traveler Ibn Battuta describes his visit to Karbala and the site of the tomb as well as the presence of a mosque and madrasa. Over the course of subsequent history, Safavid rulers from Iran and the Ottoman sultan visited the site to pay homage and to endow improvements and enhancement of the shrines of Imam Husayn and his brother Abbas. The present gold covering of the dome of the mausoleum was donated by the Iranian Qajar ruler toward the end of the eighteenth century.

In 1801, Karbala was taken by the new Wahhabis from Arabia, who destroyed and looted the shrine, sacking the town in the process. However, the shrine was restored in due course through donations from the devout, and it has undergone continuous refurbishment and expansion since that time. During the regime of Saddam Hussein (1979–2003), the Shi'is of Karbala and other groups who were opposed to Hussein were severely persecuted, and heavy restrictions were placed on visits to the shrine as well as on scholarly activity in Karbala. Karbala is surrounded by a number of cemeteries, reflecting the wish of many devout Shi'is to be buried near Imam Husayn and other martyrs. It is also the seat of several places of learning, and, after its recent turbulent history, Karbala is struggling to revive its traditional role as a pilgrimage city and a seat of religious learning and scholarship.

AZIM NANJI

Further Reading

Ayoub, M. *Redemptive Suffering in Islam: A Study of the Devotional Aspects of Ashura in Twelver Shiism*. The Hague: Mouton, 1978.
Cole, Juan. *Sacred Space and Holy War*. London: I.B. Tauris, 2002.
Jafri, S.M. *The Origins and Early Development of Shia Islam*. London and New York: Longman, 1979.
Litvak, Meir. *Shii Scholars of Nineteenth Century Iraq: The Ulama of Najaf and Karbala*. Cambridge, UK: Cambridge University Press, 1998.
Pinault, D. *Horse of Karbala: Muslim Devotional Life in India*. New York: Palgrave, 2001.

KHALID IBN AL-WALID

Khalid ibn al-Walid was the most famous military commander of early Islamic times. He was a member of the powerful Makhzum tribe, who converted to Islam after the hijra. He fought against Muhammad at Uhud in AH 3/625 CE, where his tactical brilliance played a significant role in Muhammad's first military defeat. After his conversion, Khalid assisted Muhammad in taking Mecca in 9/630. He then subdued the Hawazin and the Thaqafis, who continued to defy Muhammad after his success at Mecca. During the ridda wars, Khalid aided Abu Bakr in preserving the community by defeating the false prophet Musaylima at Akraba in 12/633.

Khalid is most famous for his leadership of campaigns against the Byzantines and Sasanians to the north. Abu Bakr sent a force under Khalid's command to Iraq in 12/633. There, Khalid subdued al-Hira and other important cities along the Euphrates. In 13/634, he was ordered to turn his forces to the west to reinforce the Muslim armies fighting the Byzantines in Syria. His six-day march through the waterless Syrian desert is one of the most daring and celebrated exploits of the Muslim conquests. After successfully crossing the desert, he led Muslim forces at Bostra and Yarmuk, and he then negotiated the surrender of Damascus in 14/635. 'Umar ibn al-Khattab dismissed

him from his command soon thereafter. Khalid continued to campaign on the Byzantine frontier until his death in 21/642.

Like 'Amr ibn al-'As and others, Khalid was an elite Meccan who joined Muhammad's movement rather late but rose to prominence despite his earlier opposition to Muhammad. The historical sources display a certain ambivalence about him, reflecting the distrust many of the ansar held for the Meccan latecomers who supplanted them in leadership positions. Consequently, his tactical brilliance and martial valor were tainted by suspicions about his morality and the sincerity of his faith. His moral shortcomings were apparently sufficient to persuade 'Umar ibn al-Khattab to dismiss his most successful general.

There is also some debate among scholars about details of Khalid's famous journey across the Syrian desert. It is impossible to reconcile contradictions in his itinerary, which has him taking either a northern or a southern route through the desert. However, details of his route are less important than the evidence of the centralized command presented in the stories. The caliph's orders to his army in Iraq to reinforce his army in Syria suggest a high degree of coordination of forces under the command of the caliph. Khalid's willingness to submit to the command of other generals in Syria and to accept the caliph's dismissal also suggest that the command structure of the conquering armies was more sophisticated and hierarchical than is sometimes suggested.

STEVEN C. JUDD

Primary Sources

Al-Baladhuri, Amad ibn Yahya. *Futuh al-Buldan*, ed. M.J. de Goeje. Leiden, 1866.
Al-Tabari, Muhammad ibn Jarir. *Ta'rikh al-Rusul wa-l-Muluk*, ed. M.J. de Goeje. Leiden, 1879–1901.

Further Reading

Donner, Fred. *The Early Islamic Conquests*. Princeton, NJ: Princeton University Press, 1981.
Kennedy, Hugh. *The Prophet and the Age of the Caliphates*. London: Longman, 1986.

KHARIJIS (768 CE)

The Khariji "seceders" or "those who go out" (khawarij) were a sect that arose at the time of the first Rashidun (Rightly Guided) Caliphate and during the struggles over succession between the companions of the Prophet. Kharijis who had initially supported 'Ali's (656–661) accession to the caliphate found that his compromises with Arab interests after the battle of Siffin (in 657) against Mu'awiya after the murder of 'Uthman were a violation of religious principles. Kharijis rose against 'Ali at Nahrawan in 658 and were defeated, but a Khariji later assassinated 'Ali in 661, indirectly leading to the Arab succession of Mu'awiya and the Umayyad dynasty.

The Khariji opposition centered on the political leadership of Islam and the rejection of the worldly authority of the (initially) Umayyad caliphal regime. They maintained that there was no precedence in Islam except for virtue (the fulfillment of all laws and duties incumbent on Muslims as individuals), and, by committing a sin, sinners had apostatized, renounced their faith, and—some extreme Kharijis said—thus incurred the penalty of death. The Kharijis thus rejected the hereditary succession to the caliphate and the restriction of it to Arabs; rather, Kharijis held that the head of the Islamic community was the imam elected on the basis of religious learning and piety. Ultimately, the Kharijis contributed to the emergence of a self-conscious Islamic identity.

With such an uncompromising stance, especially toward the incumbent caliphal regime, the Kharijis became a disparate and persecuted group with rebellious and fanatical inclinations, and they often found refuge in the peripheral regions of the empire. Initially based in Basra, the Kharijis inspired numerous rebellions against Umayyad rule in the Arab east (Mashriq) from the 660s. In Iraq, Kharijis led by Ibn al-Azraq (known later as Azariqa) gained the support of non-Arab Persian Muslims and propagated the most extreme form of Khariji doctrine. However, from 675 to 684, the Umayyad Governor 'Ubayd Allah ibn Ziyad undertook a bloody campaign against the Kharijis, supplying numerous martyrs to the sect. From their ideological epicenter in Basra, the Kharijis gradually divided into three distinct groups named after their eponymous leaders: the extremist Azariqa ("blues"), the radical Sufriya ("yellow"), and the moderate Ibadiya ("whites"). In the Arab peninsula, Najda ibn Amir in particular used Kharijism as a banner for rebellion in the empire, and the Najdites controlled large territories in eastern Arabia, Yemen, and the Hadramawt until they were finally defeated by 'Abbasid power. Later in the ninth century, Khariji doctrine inspired a revolt of African slaves (the Zanj) in southern Iraq. At times and places in which the caliphate was weak, Khariji leadership filled the void.

Khariji Islam had its most profound influence in North African Maghrib. Political fugitives from the Arab east (Mashriq) brought the Khariji teachings and found a receptive audience in the independently minded Berber populations in the Maghrib. Khariji missionaries (both Sufrite and Ibadite Khariji) are reputed to have appeared in Qayrawan (Ifriqiya) at around 719. Sufrite Khariji influence in the Maghrib is attributed to a Berber missionary, 'Ikrima. Berbers used the Khariji doctrine against the remote and sometimes oppressive rule of their Arab conquerors, denouncing caliphal rule as having departed from the true Islamic path. At issue were the demands that the Arab conquerors of the Maghreb made on the Berber populations, who, as well as the usual—and Islamic—principles of *jizya* (poll tax) and *kharaj* (land tax), also bore the unlawful levying of human tribute, especially of slave girls. Moreover, as non-Arab converts to Islam (mawali; clients of Arab tribes), Muslim Berber recruits to the Muslim army were given a status that was inferior to Arabs.

The Berbers, who were initially under the leadership of the Sufrite Maysara, a "water carrier from Qayrawan" who was influenced by 'Ikrima, rebelled against caliphal rule in 739 and 740 in Tangier. In 741, they destroyed a large Umayyad army in North Africa, but they were prevented from taking Qayrawan. Only in 756 did the Sufrite Kharijis (and the Warfajuma Berbers who dominated the ranks) conquer Qayrawan. Ibadi Kharijis then briefly conquered Qayrawan in 758 and installed the (Iranian) Imam Ibn Rustman, who was forced westward by the consolidation of the new 'Abbasid dynasty over the empire.

Resistance and recalcitrance continued, which brought about the foundation of small sectarian Khariji states in Algeria and Morocco. The western Maghrib became a stronghold for independent Khariji Berber leaders. Berber-Khariji states were founded at Tlemsen (under the Sufrite leadership of Abu Qurra), Tahert (Ibadite Rustamids), and Sijilmassa (Sufrite Midrarids). The Berber Kharijis also founded small trading oases, and they developed trade routes with the Sudanic African kingdoms and were among the first carriers of Islam into Sudanic Africa.

CEDRIC BARNES

Further Reading

Abun-Nasr, Jamil M. *A History of the Maghrib in the Islamic Period*. Princeton, NJ: 1987.

Berkey, Jonathan P. *The Formation of Islam: Religion and Society in the Near East 600–1800*. Cambridge, 2003.

Brett, M. "The Arab Conquest and the Rise of Islam in North Africa." In *The Cambridge History of Africa, Vol. 2., From c. 500 BC to AD 1050*, ed. J.D. Fage. Cambridge, 1978.

Hourani, Albert. *A History of the Arab Peoples*. London, 1991.

Lapidus, Ira M. *A History of Islamic Societies*. Cambridge, 2002.

Lewicki, Tadeuz. "The Ibadites in Arabia and Africa." *Journal of World History* Vol. XIII (1971).

KHATIB AL-BAGHDADI, AL-

Al-Khatib al-Baghdadi, Abu Bakr Ahmad ibn 'Ali ibn Thabit ibn Ahmad ibn Mahdi al-Shafi'i, the "Preacher of Baghdad" and the "Traditionalist of the East," was born in 1002 CE in a village in the vicinity of Baghdad, and he died in the city in 1071. Beginning his studies very early with his father and other local sheikhs, he soon immersed himself in the science of the prophetic traditions (hadith), which remained the focus of his intellectual pursuits thereafter. His keen interest in the hadith led him to undertake long journeys to several centers of learning, reaching as far as Nishapur in search of knowledge. He sought to hear Islamic traditions directly from the lips of various authorities and, through them, become a link in the chain of transmission extending back to the Prophet. During the years after his first return to Baghdad in 1028, he became a great authority on hadith, and his fame spread far beyond the city's walls.

Al-Khatib's life belonged to a particularly crucial period in the history of Baghdad and the eastern part of the 'Abbasid caliphate as a whole, a period marked by the expansion of Shi'ism under the Buyids and the restoration of Sunnism under the Seljuks. During the "Shi'i century" as well as the period immediately after, Ibn al-Hanbal's pupils, who were numerous and powerful in Baghdad, not only took it upon themselves to persecute the Shi'is, but they were also occupied in fighting rationalism of all types. At first a Hanbali like his father, al-Khatib later followed the Shafi'i school of jurisprudence and adopted the Ash'ari opinions, thereby entering upon the clashes between the Hanbalis and the "masters of opinion" over the status of rational investigation. The religious and political turmoil in Baghdad at his time further encouraged him to embark on long journeys to several Syrian towns and on a pilgrimage and long sojourn to Mecca. Finally, in 1059, he returned to his native city after the Seljuks restored order there.

Al-Khatib's magnum opus is *Ta'rikh Baghdad,* an immense biographical dictionary containing more than 7800 entries about scholarly, pious, and famous men and women connected with Baghdad from the earliest times. Prefaced by a substantial topographical introduction, the *History of Baghdad* was intended by its author to convey the imperial splendor of the city's physical image and the intellectual climate created by its thousands of noted scholars and pious individuals. In the view of the famous preacher, Baghdad was the geographical center of the Islamic empire and the most important center of Islamic thought. At the same time, his monumental work set the model for the genre of local history, one of the most productive genres of Arabic and Persian historiography during the Middle Periods (950–1500).

For all its value as a local history and for furthering the evolution of this genre, *Ta'rikh Baghdad* should not be regarded merely as a panegyric of local intellect. The accuracy with which al-Khatib reconstructed the chains of transmission over the generations and the judicious care with which he recorded and narrated the transmitters' lives and activities resulted in a comprehensive work of scholarship and the product of a renowned traditionalist. His extensive work on hadith demonstrated his profound erudition in this science and established his authority as one of the greatest critical experts of hadith methodology throughout the Islamic medieval period.

DAPHNA EPHRAT

Further Reading

Al-Khatib al-Baghdadi, Abu Bakr Ahmad ibn 'Ali ibn Thabit ibn Ahmad ibn Mahdi. *Ta'rikh Baghdad aw Madinat al-Salam*, 14 vols. Cairo: Maktabat al-Khanji, 1931.
———. *Ta'rikh Baghdad*. (Topographical introduction.)
  a) Arabic text: Vol. 1 of 1931 Cairo Edition.
  b) Translated by G. Salmon as *L'Introduction Topographique à L'Histoire d'Abou Bakr Ahmad ibn Thabit al-Khatib al-Baghdadi*. Paris: Bouillon, 1904.
  c) Translated by Jacob Lassner as *Topography of Baghdad in the Early Middle Ages: Texts and Studies*. Detroit, Mich: Wayne State University Press, 1970.
Ahmed, Munir ud-Din. *Muslim Education and the Scholars' Social Status up to the 5th Century Muslim Era (11th Century Christian Era) in Light of Ta'rikh Baghdad*. Zurich: Verlag "Der Islam," 1968.
Cahen, Claude. "L'Historiographie Arabe: Des Origins au VIIᵉ S. H." *Arabica* 33 (1986): 150–198.
Humphreys, R. Stephen, "Historiography, Islamic." *Dictionary of the Middle Ages*, 13 vols., ed. Joseph R. Strayer, vol. vi, 249–55. New York: Charles Scribner & Sons, 1982–1989.
Sellheim, R. *Arabische Handschriften, Materialien zur Arabischen Literaturgeschichte*. Wiesbaden: Steiner, 1974.

KHURASAN

One of the most important cradles of the Iranian civilization, the province of Khurasan (also called Khorasan) has been a crossroads of cultures since antiquity. The cultures of Iran during the pre-Islamic, Islamic and Pahlavi (ca. 1925–1979 CE) periods, the cultures of Central Asia up to China, and the cultures of India encountered each other constantly. The name is probably a contraction of *Khur* and *istan*, literally the "place of the sun."

The province's borders have blurred and changed with time. One can, however, roughly delineate them during the classical and medieval eras from the southeast of the Caspian Sea to the center of modern Afghanistan and from the upper Oxus River in Central Asia up to the north of Sistan.

During the Middle Ages and up to the Mongol invasion at the beginning of the AH seventh/thirteenth century CE, the city of Marw and the capital city of Nishapur were two of the biggest metropolises of the Islamic empire. Both were almost entirely destroyed by the Mongol troops, and even if historians have possibly exaggerated, it seems that about 1.5 million people were massacred there. The devastation of Khurasan would last for more than a century, and it would not be until the arrival of the Timurids in the mid-eighth/fourteenth century that both great cities—and others, such as Herat and Bayhaq—would gradually recover their former prosperity.

What was once the village of Sanabad became the city of Mashhad ("place of martyrdom"), which was built around the mausoleum of the Twelvers' eighth imam 'Ali al-Rida; the mausoleum was already richly decorated by the time of Ilkhanid Iran. Mashhad began to grow more and more, starting with the Safavid era (tenth/sixteenth century) and the proclamation of Shi'ism as the state religion in Iran. To this day, Mashhad remains the capital city of Khurasan, with more than two million inhabitants.

The population of Khurasan has always been mixed. The Iranian substratum has of course always been its main component. After the Arab conquest, however, under the reign of the third caliph 'Uthman, expatriates from Yemen's Qaysite and Azdite tribes settled there permanently. In addition, Turkmens, Kurds, Baluches, Hazaras, and Central Asian nomads contributed to make the population a rich ethnic melting pot.

Around 130/748, Khurasan became the center of the 'Abbasid revolution, and the Khurasanian troops of the famous Abu Muslim were its main participants. Al-Ma'mun acceded to the caliphate from Marw in 193/813. This explains, at least in part, the great influence of the Iranians under the first 'Abbasid rulers.

During the Islamic era, Khurasan was indeed the heart of what could be called "Iranity." The Samanids from Khurasan, succeeding two other Iranian dynasties, the Tahirid and Safavid, started in the third/ninth century the great movement to preserve Persian culture and language. Thus, Persian became the second language of Islam, after Arabic.

To illustrate this Irano-Islamic Renaissance, one need only recall the great numbers of scholars, learned persons, and intellectuals that came from Khurasan: Bukhari, Muslim, Ibn Sina (Avicenna), Ghazali, Bayhaqi, Nasir-i Khusraw, the authors of the great classics of Sufism (Sarraj, Kalabadhi, Qushayri, Ansari, and Jami), and the founders of Persian mystical poetry (Abu Sa'id Abu 'l-Khayr, Sana'i, and 'Attar).

MOHAMMAD ALI AMIR-MOEZZI

See also Nishapur

Further Reading

Cambridge History of Iran, vol. I, ed. W.B. Fischer. Cambridge, 1968. vol. IV, ed. CE Bosworth. Cambridge, 1975.
Bosworth, C.E. "Khurâsân." In *EI2*, vol. V, 57–61.
Herzfeld, E. " Khorasan: Denkmalsgeographische Studien zur Kulturgeschichte des Islams in Iran." *Der Islam* 11 (1921): 107–194.
Shaban, A. "Khurasan at the Time of the Arab Conquest." In *Iran and Islam. In Memory of the Late Vladimir Minorsky*, ed. C.E. Bosworth, 479–90. Edinburgh, 1971.

KHUZA'I, AHMAD IBN NASR

Ahmad ibn Nasr al-Khuza'i died in 846 CE at the hands of the Caliph al-Wathiq. Of the different versions of this story, al-Tabari presents the most complete account. Ahmad's execution is usually pointed to as being the result of a steadfast refusal to acquiesce during the Mihna (the Inquisition of 833 through 848 or 851); however, when his activities are considered in context, this assessment seems to be less certain. The basic outline of events is that, in 846, Ahmad, at the prodding of a group of prominent hadith (tradition) scholars, proclaimed his vehement opposition to the createdness of the Qur'an, and followers quickly gathered around him. Al-Tabari, in an aside, tells us that Ahmad was one of the members of the "vigilante" movement in Baghdad from 813 to 819; however, he does not mention this in his recounting of those troubles. One suspects that this information was added to enhance Ahmad's prestige as one who had a long history of commanding good and forbidding evil.

Ahmad gathered followers and prepared for a revolt. There is disagreement about the particulars, but his attempt to rebel was discovered, and the plotters were rounded up. Evidence was found to implicate some of them, but not Ahmad. He and five other conspirators were sent off to Samarra to face trial in front of the caliph. At this point, the narrative turns to focus on Ahmad exclusively. The Caliph al-Wathiq (r. 842–847) tried Ahmad himself. Asked twice about his position on the createdness of the Qur'an, Ahmad responded twice saying that it is "the word of God" and refused to go any further.

Next, Ahmad was questioned about the beatific vision—that is, whether one would be able to see God on the Day of Judgment. His response did not mollify the caliph. The caliph then turned and asked those around him for their verdict. Ahmad's blood was declared forfeit, and the caliph moved to enforce the verdict. However, it is made clear that the caliph was in charge the entire time. Al-Wathiq called for his sword and proceeded to implement the sentence. It took a series of blows, but the job was eventually done. This, however, leaves the central question unanswered: for what was Ahmad convicted that incurred the death penalty? There were many others tried during the Mihna, but very few were actually executed. In all versions of the narrative, Ahmad's body was then gibbeted next to the notorious rebel Babak. His head was sent to Baghdad to be put on display, with a description of his crime hung on his ear. This gives us some clues as to what al-Tabari perceived to be his crime. He was clearly tried and convicted as a rebel against the community of believers as embodied in the caliph. His association with rebellion established a case against him, and his refusal to answer the caliph correctly under questioning defined and proved his rebellion. Some sources characterize him as a steadfast defender of the faith in the same vein as Ibn Hanbal; other versions characterize him as a rebel worthy of his punishment. Al-Tabari includes the removal of Ahmad's body from the gibbet in 851 as part of his notation that al-Mutawakkil forbade any debate about the createdness or uncreatedness of the Qur'an, thus indicating that the Mihna had come to an end.

JOHN P. TURNER

See also Commanding Good and Forbidding Evil; Ibn Hanbal; al-Ma'mun; al-Tabari

Primary Sources

Al-Khatib al-Baghdadi. *Ta'rikh Baghdad*, vol. 5. Cairo: Maktabat al-Khanji, 1931.
Al-Tabari, Abu Ja'far. *Incipient Decline*, transl. J.L. Kraemer, vol. 34. Albany: State University of New York Press, 1989.
Al-Ya'qubi, Ahmad ibn Abi Ya'qub. *Ta'rikh al-Ya'qubi*, ed. 'Abd al-Amir Muhanna. Beirut: Mu'assasa al-'Ulami li'l-Matbu'at, 1993.

KILWA (KILWA KISIWANI)

Kilwa is an island off the coast of southern Tanzania. The urban settlement located there and known by the same name (also known as Kilwa Kisiwani; "Kilwa on the island") was one of the earliest Swahili trading towns. From approximately the tenth century CE, stone structures were erected, as were sea barriers. Iron was used, and it was also an important trade item. During the following centuries, because of its safe harbor and good fresh water supply, Kilwa rose to become the foremost entrepôt of East African

Kilwa, East African trading town. The ruins of the great mosque which was founded in the thirteenth c. and much extended in the fifteenth c. by Sultan Muhamed. Islamic. Credit: Werner Forman/Art Resource, NY. Kilwa, Tanzania.

coast goods such as gold, slaves, and ivory from the interior. Imported goods included cloth, beads, furnishings, and pottery, mainly of Asian origin. Chinese pottery and Persian earthenware have been excavated from the early Kilwa settlements.

Like many of the Swahili cities, Kilwa mythological origins are recorded in a chronicle. The oldest recorded version of the Kilwa chronicle was recorded by the Portuguese de Barros during the sixteenth century. This was called the *Cronica dos Reyes de Quiloa,* and it referred to the arrival of kings from Shiraz, Persia, who set up kingdoms in Kilwa, as well as other places. Later research has interpreted the chronicle as the arrival of social and political hierarchical structures related to the emergence of Kilwa as a Muslim society as well as the transition from hunting and fishing to trade.

Archaeological evidence has demonstrated that the minting of coins took place at Kilwa and in the northern islands of Pemba, Zanzibar, and Mafia in the period from about 1000 to 1150. There is also architectural evidence of a uniform layout of mosques and prayer rooms. On this basis, Horton and Middleton have suggested that a closely related Muslim dynasty may have lived on these islands during the period before 1200, thus adding some substance to the mythical origins related in the chronicle. There exists also a corresponding Arab foundation myth, which is also found in the chronicles. Here, the newcomers arrive from Arabia (most likely Yemen or al-Hasa near

Bahrain), and they are Zaydis. Here, too, archaeological and historical evidence suggest some truth to the myth, revealing information about ruling houses of Arab origin that ruled from approximately 1300 to 1600.

By the time the Moroccan traveler Ibn Battuta visited Kilwa in 1331, it was a well-established city with one- or two-story houses and a Friday mosque that was first constructed during the eleventh century and expanded during the 1300s. Between about 1100 and 1500, Kilwa remained one of the principal ports for Indian Ocean trade.

Starting in the late fifteenth century, Kilwa went into a decline. This was marked by the arrival of the Portuguese on the coast and later by the rise of the northern cities of Mombasa, Lamu, and—finally, during the nineteenth century, under Omani rule—Zanzibar. After a brief period of revival based on slave trade, Kilwa, by the late eighteenth century, had become an outpost of the Omani empire. By the mid-nineteenth century, it was abandoned. In 1981, the ruins of Kilwa Kisiwani were named a UNESCO World Heritage Site.

ANNE K. BANG

Further Reading

Freeman-Grenville, G.S.P. *The East African Coast: Select Documents from the First to the Earlier Nineteenth Century.* London, 1962.

Chittick, H.N. *Kilwa: An Islamic Trading City on the East African Coast,* 2 vols., memo 5. Nairobi: British Institute in Eastern Africa, 1974.

Hamdun, S., and N. King. *Ibn Battuta in Black Africa.* Princeton, NJ: Marcus Wiener Publications, 1998. (First edition: 1975.)

Horton, Mark, and John Middleton. *The Swahili.* Blackwell Publishers, 2000.

KINDI, AL-,

Al-Kindi was a tenth-century Arab–Muslim historian of Egypt who died in 961 CE. There is little available information on the life of Abu 'Umar Muhammad ibn Yusuf al-Kindi apart from that transmitted by a contemporary, the historian Abu Muhammad 'Abd Allah ibn Ahmad al-Farghani (d. 973). The latter's writings, in turn, are known only from quotations in later Arab-Islamic sources, most notably the *Kitab al-Muqaffa al-Kabir* of al-Maqrizi (d. 1441), which contains a short biographical note about al-Kindi with material from al-Farghani. A small amount of information can also be culled from al-Kindi's two surviving works (see below). Born in Egypt in 897, al-Kindi was of Arab descent. He received a classical education that consisted mainly of Qur'anic exegesis, study and transmission of hadith (tradition), and the law. Al-Maqrizi identifies him as an historian *(mu'arrikh)* and legal scholar *(faqih)* and adds that he belonged to the Hanafi legal school. Among those from whom al-Kindi learned hadith were the prominent scholar and author of one of the canonical Sunni collections of hadith, Abu 'Abd al-Rahhman al-Nasa'i (d. 915). Another teacher, 'Ali ibn al-Hasan ibn Qudayd (d. 925), was a key historical informant judging from the frequent citations of his name in al-Kindi's writings.

Al-Kindi is credited with at least eight works, only two of which appear to have survived. These two works, preserved in a British Museum manuscript, are *Tasmiyat Wulat Misr* (The Enumeration of the Rulers of Egypt), usually called *Umara' Misr* (The Governors of Egypt), and *al-Qudat* (The Judges). These were edited and published in 1912 by Rhuvon Guest. Both works are used extensively by later writers, most notably al-Maqrizi who, in many instances, is content to do so without acknowledgment.

The Governors, in its extant form, covers the period from the Arab-Islamic conquest of Egypt (641) to the end of the reign of Muhammad ibn Tughj (d. 946), the first of the Ikshidid rulers of Egypt. A later unknown writer added material to the manuscript that brings the work up to the arrival of the Fatimids (969). The book, arranged chronologically, is divided into sections that are each devoted to a particular governor or ruler. It consists largely of political and administrative history, although it provides valuable details about the lives of the officials themselves. It is often cited as a key example of provincial histories from the early Islamic period that provide counterweight to the sources generated in Iraq, most notably al-Tabari's *Ta'rikh (History)*. Among the sections of greatest value are those devoted to al-Sari ibn al-Hakam (d. 820), an early 'Abbasid governor, and to Ahmad ibn Tulun (d. 884), head of the Tulunids (868–905), the first autonomous dynasty in Egypt. Al-Kindi's lost works apparently included a biography of Sari ibn al-Hakam.

The second work, *The Judges,* concludes around 861 (with the appointment of a certain Bakkar ibn Qutayba) and is similarly supplemented by two continuations, one attributed to an Ahmad ibn Burd and the second by an anonymous author, that bring the work into the eleventh century; it is organized chronologically as well. Information, often given in anecdotal form, sheds valuable light on the judicial and legal history of Egypt during the early Islamic period.

MATTHEW S. GORDON

Further Reading

Guest, Rhuvon. "Introduction." In al-Kindi, Muhammad ibn Yusuf. *The Governors and Judges of Egypt*, ed. R. Guest. Leiden: E.J. Brill, 1912

Rosenthal, Franz. "Al-Kindi, Abu 'Umar Muhammad." In *The Encyclopedia of Islam*, 2nd ed.

KINDI, AL-, PHILOSOPHER

Al-Kindi, Abū-Yūsuf Ya'qūb ibn-Ishāq ibn-al-Sabbāh (d. ca. AH 252/865 CE), was a scientist and philosopher. Coming from a distinguished family of the Kinda Arabs, he was connected with the caliphal court of Baghdad until the political changes of the mid-century. He was tutor to the 'Abbasid Prince Ahmad ibn al-Mu'tasim (son of the Caliph al-Mu'tasim, r. 833–842). Both as a scientist and as a literary figure, he reflected the practical and intellectual interests of the autocratic aristocracy and its administrative elite. His enormous oeuvre encompasses the whole range of the Hellenistic sciences, which were made accessible during his lifetime through translations from Greek and Syriac, where al-Kindi appears to have been directing his own circle of translators. His activity marks the taking over—after the predominantly Iranian bias of the early 'Abbasid administration—of Hellenism (allied with Arabism in literary erudition [adab]) during the formative period of classical Islamic culture; this earned him the byname of "Philosopher of the Arabs" *(Faylasūf al-'Arab)*.

In astronomy, his writings attended the final success of Ptolemy's Almagest (e.g., his *Book on the Great Art* [*k. fī –Sinā'a al-'Uzmā;* dependent on Theon's commentary]), and descriptions of observational instruments. In astrology, while applying the Iranian "world year" model, he used it for predicting the continuance of the Arab caliphate *(Epistle on the Kingdom of the Arabs and Its Duration [Risāla fī Mulk al-'Arab wa-Kammiyyatihī])*. In optics, he contributed to the Euclidian geometry of vision and perspective in his *Revision of Euclid's Book on Optics (Islāh al-Manāzir)*. In musical theory, he presented the Greek doctrine of harmonic proportions (e.g., in his *Risāla fī Khubr ta'līf al-Alhān*). In pharmacology, he applied Galen's doctrine of the forces of the simplicia to develop a theory of the action of composite drugs (*K. fī Ma'rifat Quwā l-Adwiya al-Murakkaba* and other works on pharmacy and perfumes). His works on magic and the occult (e.g., *De Radiis,* which is extant in a Latin version) and also his doctrine of the immortal soul and its return to the "world of intellect" are based on a system of cosmic sympathy in which the gnostic and hermetic tendencies of late Neoplatonism survive in a religion for intellectuals.

His philosophy is based on the physics and metaphysics of Aristotle as well as on the Neoplatonic sources transmitted under Aristotle's name, all of which were translated in his circle. In his treatise *On the First Philosophy,* which was dedicated to the caliph al-Mutasim *(K. ilā l-Mu'tasim bi-Llāh fī l-Falsafa al-ūlā)*, he demonstrated that the First Cause—the cause of being and the highest object of knowledge—must, by necessity, be one. With this, he legitimized the rational sciences by exposing their consistency with the Islamic creed, the unity of God *(tawhīd Allāh)*. Employing the creationist Neoplatonism of his sources, he built a philosophical ideology that was in harmony with Islam and in which the revelation to the Arabic Prophet serves as a necessary mediator of absolute knowledge to all of mankind.

GERHARD ENDRESS

Further Reading

EI² s.n.; Sezgin, *GAS*, iii: 244 –7, 375–6 (medicine); v: 117, 255–9 (optics, mathematics), vi: 151–5 (astronomy), vii: 130–4 (astrology).

d'Alverny, M.-Th., and F. Hudry. "al-Kindi: De Radiis." *Archives d'Histoire Doctrinale et Littéraire du Moyen Âge* 41 (1975): 139–267.

Endress, G. "Die Wissenschaftliche Literatur." In *Grundriss der Arabischen Philologie*, vol. iii, 3–152. Wiesbaden, 1992.

Endress, G. "Al-Kindī Über die Wiedererinnerung der Seele." *Oriens* 34 (1994): 174 –221.

Farmer, H. G. *The Sources of Arabian Music*, 45–56. Leiden, 1965.

Ivry, A.L. *Al-Kindî's Metaphysics*. Albany, 1974.

Jolivet, J. *L'Intellect Selon Kindî*. Leiden, 1971.

Jolivet, J., and Roshdi Rashed, eds. *Œuvres Philosophiques et Scientifiques d'al-Kindī*. Leiden, 1997–1998.

Lindberg, D.C. "Alkindi's Critique of Euclid's Theory of Vision." *Isis* 62 (1971): 469–89.

Loth, O. "Al-Kindî als Astrolog." In *Morgenländische Forschungen*, 261–309. Leipzig, 1875.

Rescher, N. *Al-Kindî: An Annotated Bibliography.* Pittsburgh, 1964.

Rosenthal, V.F. "Al-Kindî and Ptolemy." In *Studi Orientalistici in Onore di G. Levi Della Vida*, vol. ii, 436–56. Rome, 1956.

Ullmann, M. *Die Medizin im Islam*, 123, 301f, 314. Leiden, 1970.

———. *Die Natur- und Geheimwissenschaften im Islam*, 313f. Leiden, 1972.

Walzer, R. *Greek into Arabic*, 172–205. Oxford, UK, 1962.

KIRMANI, AL-, HAMID AL-DIN

Hamid al-Din al-Kirmani was a major Islamic theologian–philosopher who was the most prominent voice of the intellectual tradition among the Ismailis at the time of the Fatimid Caliph al-Hakim (r. 996–1021). A substantial number of his writings survive, although—typically—almost no information about his life and career is available. In fact, all of the details available now derive from chance comments made by him in his own books and treatises. They indicate that he was originally active in Iraq and that later he visited Egypt and taught there before ultimately returning eastward again. The only dates known for him range from 1007 CE, when the earliest of his works was written, to 1021, the year of his last known work; all carry an explicit dedication to al-Hakim.

In his exposition of Ismaili doctrine, al-Kirmani followed his predecessors in that movement except with regard to the exceptional rigor that he himself brought to the explanation of it. In matters of philosophy, by contrast, he tended to steer away from the Neoplatonism of the earlier Ismaili writers, such as al-Sijistani and al-Nasafi, and instead to favor of a more Aristotelian approach. In doing so he was evidently influenced by the famous philosopher Abu Nasr al-Farabi, many of whose ideas were reinterpreted by al-Kirmani to create an Ismaili version of them. In his adoption of such elements from the thought of al-Farabi, he resembles his contemporary Abu 'Ali Ibn Sina (Avicenna).

His most important teachings include the following: a radically austere concept of God's absolute, unqualified unity that excludes the supreme deity from any form of intellectual apprehension; a scheme of ten angelic intellects that correspond with the heavenly spheres that together govern the physical realm; a doctrine of human soul that has it commence its existence as the first perfection of the natural body, then be devoid of knowledge but able thereafter both to learn and to perform worthy acts, if properly guided, and finally to achieve a second perfection when it survives the death of its body; and a doctrine of prophecy that considers the prophets to be the intermediaries between the higher intellects and the human community, making of them those who are responsible for conveying the enduring reality of the world of intellect to mankind and thus lead the latter to salvation and ultimate bliss.

His major works are The Comfort of Reason (Rahat al-'Aql); The Golden Sayings (al-Aqwal al-Dhahabiyya); The Meadow (al-Riyad); The Exhortation to the Guiders and the Guided (Tanbih al-Hadi wa'l-Mustahdi); The Pure Treatise Concerning the Hallmarks of Religion (al-Risala al-Wadi'a fi ma'A-lim al-Din); The Protecting Links to Guidance and the Validation of the Superiority of 'Ali Over the Companions (Ma'asim al-Huda wa'l-Isaba fi Tafdil 'Ali 'ala al-Sahaba); and Lights to Illuminate the Proof of the Imamate (Masabih fi Ithbat al-Imama).

All of these survive, although several have not been published; others exist in unreliable editions. A number of his minor treatises are also important, but to date none have been translated.

Although a towering figure in his own time, al-Kirmani's subsequent influence during the era of Fatimid rule was not as remarkable. Among the later Tayyibi Ismailis of the Yemen and India, however, he and his works rose once again to the highest levels.

PAUL E. WALKER

Further Reading

De Bruijn, M.T.P. "al-Kirmani." In *Encyclopaedia of Islam, New Edition.*

De Smet, Daniel. *La Quiétude de L'Intellect: Néoplatonisme et Gnose Ismaélienne dans L'Oeuvre de Hamíd ad-Dín al-Kirmání (Xᵉ/XIᵉ s.).* Leuven: Peters, 1995.

———. "Perfectio Prima—Perfectio Secunda, ou les Vicissitudes D'Une Notion, de S. Thomas aux Ismaéliens Tayyibites du Yémen." *Recherches de Théologies et de Philosophie Médiévales* 66 (1999): 254–88.

Walker, Paul E. *Hamid al-Din al-Kirmani: Ismaili Thought in the Age of al-Hakim.* London, 1999.

KONYA

The modern town of Konya in Turkey is dominated by the green cupola of the shrine marking the torbat (grave) of its most illustrious son, Jalāl al-Dīn Rūmī, Maulānā. Today Rūmī is big business, and the Rūmī industry pervades the town as once the spirit of the Mevlevi dervish order did Konya's mosques and bazaars. Although Konya, which was named Iconium in Roman times, has a long history, it was the Seljuk sultans of Rum that saw the city in its heyday, and it was the Seljuk sultans under Mongol domination that nurtured the creative and vibrant milieu in which Rūmī and the ethnically and culturally diverse citizens of Konya thrived.

The apogee of the Seljuk state in Anatolia with its capital in Konya occurred during the thirteenth century. Under the reign of Kay Khosrow I (1205–1211 CE) through to that of his grandson Kay Khosrow II (1237–1246), the city blossomed. The battle of Köse Dag in 1243 saw the Mongols defeat the heterogeneous Seljuk armies. Using classic Mongol maneuvers of feigned retreats, Baiju Noyen, the Mongol commander, achieved so overwhelming a victory that he felt he could afford to be gracious in his triumph, and he allowed negotiations to decide the fate of Anatolia. Batu Khan of the Golden Horde, the kingmaker of the Mongol Empire, recognized the Seljuk sultans and endorsed their continued rule from Konya as Mongol vassals. Real power, however, was exercised by the Mongols through their own appointee, the pervāne: Mu'īn al-Dīn Suleymān, governor of the province.

Medieval Konya reflected the cultural, religious, and ethnic diversity that made up the Anatolian peninsula during the thirteenth and fourteenth centuries. Turcomans, Mongols, and other nomadic elements usually kept to the mountains and hills outside of the city. In the city, Greeks, Turks, Arabs, Persians, Jews, Europeans, and the Mongol elite each had their own quarters. Émigrés, refugees, religious exiles, wandering dervishes, qalandars (antinomian heterodox dervishes), poets, and Sufis all found a home in this spiritually and culturally vibrant city. The Mongol–appointed pervāne maintained the delicate balance between representing the interests of the citizens and satisfying the mainly monetary demands of the Il-Khans (the Mongol dynasty ruling greater Iran from 1256 to 1335) in their capital, Tabriz. His moral dilemma is recounted by Rūmī in the poet's book *Discourses*.

Medieval Konya acted as a beacon of hope and a symbol of enlightenment in what was often a chaotic and violent period in western Asia. By being in but not of the Mongol Empire, the Seljuk Sultanate of Rum with its capital of Konya gained all of the advantages of inclusion in the greatest contiguous land empire ever while retaining enough independence to fully exploit the cultural and economic benefits that the empire bestowed on those it encompassed.

GEORGE LANE

Further Reading

Cahen, Claude. *The Formation of Turkey: The Seljukid Sultanate of Rum; 11th to 14th Century*, transl. P.M. Holt. Harlow: Longman, 2001.

Lewis, Franklin D. *Rumi: Past and Present, East and West*. Oxford, UK: Oneworld, 2000.

Holt, P.M. *The Age of the Crusades: The Near East from the 11th Century to 1517*. Harlow: Longman, 1986

KUFA

After the defeat of the Iranian Sasanian dynasty in 637–638 CE, the conquering Muslim army occupied Iraq and established on the banks of the Euphrates a garrison town called Kufa. The new province would henceforth be ruled from this newly founded settlement. In time, it grew into a major administrative capital that had a mosque, a governor's palace, markets, and accommodation for a growing population of soldiers and immigrants.

As the diverse population of Kufa that included various Arab groups as well as converts of Iranian origin increased, it also grew as a center of learning, attracting scholars and also becoming a commercial center for trade and agriculture. The expansion of the economy of the growing Muslim state and the rise of a cosmopolitan Muslim community were largely under the control and direction of the caliph in Medina. Under Caliph Uthman (r. 644–656), growing differences and an increasing pattern of decentralization of authority often caused conflicts with regard to official appointments and the distribution of land and wealth, mirroring emerging tensions within the Muslim community based in Medina.

Opposition to Uthman's policies, emanating from Kufa, erupted into conflict and resulted in his assassination, throwing the young Muslim community into turmoil. Ali, the prophet's cousin and son-in-law, whom many regarded as the originally designated successor to the Prophet, received majority support and became the new caliph. He shifted his headquarters to Kufa, effectively making it the new center of authority. He was opposed by several leaders in Medina but supported by the Prophet's wife Aisha. He was forced to put down the revolt, but he faced a more serious challenge from the governor of Syria, Muawiyah, an appointee as well as a close relative of Uthman who was putting pressure on Ali to execute those he held to be responsible for the murder. These divisive events are recorded by Muslim historians as *fitna* (civil disorder), and Ali eventually found himself having to confront Muawiyah in battle as the governor's larger ambitions for power became apparent.

After attempts were made to prevent bloodshed, hostilities were ended, and arbitration was agreed upon. However, emotions ran high on the part of some of Ali's followers who were adamantly opposed to Muawiyah and to arbitration, and the group seceded, turning its wrath on both armies. One of the secessionist murdered Ali while he was at prayer in the mosque in Kufa in 661.

After Ali's death, Muawiyah succeeded in gaining power and eventually control of many of the new Muslim dominions, and he imposed his authority in all regions. He appointed a new governor for the region that included Kufa, who was ordered to institute public cursing of Ali's name during the Friday prayers in the mosque of Kufa and to brutally suppress all partisan support in favor of Ali. During the Ummayad period to 751 and later under the 'Abbasids, Kufa had evolved into a major city, particularly as the, 'Abbasids made it their headquarters while awaiting the construction of Baghdad, their new capital.

As other towns and cities developed and the focus of trade and political power shifted to other regions, Kufa declined in importance. However, as a center of Shi'i influence and scholarship and as the city closest to Najaf, where a mausoleum was erected over Ali's grave, Kufa continued to be influential as a center of learning and Shi'i activity throughout the period of later Muslim history. In particular, Kufa became well known as a center for Arabic literature, language, and grammar. It gave birth to a new Arabic script called Kufic, and it continued to attract important scholars, jurists, historians, and poets. In addition, it remains to this day a major site for visits and remembrance, including to the grave of Muslim b. Aqil, a cousin of Husayn who was executed by the Ummayads for supporting the Ali cause. In modern times, Kufa has continued to be a cultural and religious center and a home to various scholars and centers of Shi'i learning and scholarship.

AZIM NANJI

Further Reading

Djait, Hickem. *Kufa, Naissance de la Ville Islamique*. Paris: Maissoneuve, 1986.

Morony, Michael G. *Iraq After the Muslim Conquest*. Princeton, NJ: Princeton University Press, 1984.

Zaman, Muhammad Qasim. *Religion and Politics Under the Early Abbasids*. Leiden: E.J. Brill, 1997.

KULAYNI, AL-

Muhammad b. Ya'qub al-Kulayni (d. AH 329/941 CE) was a Twelver Shi'i compiler of *al-Kafi fi 'Ilm al-Din (What is Sufficient in the Knowledge of the Faith)*, a collection of more than sixteen thousand hadith (traditions) attributed to the Shi'i imams of whom the twelfth had disappeared in 260/873–874. A native of Kulayn, near the Iranian city of Rayy, al-Kulayni resided in Qum for some years before relocating to Baghdad, where he assembled *al-Kafi*.

Although the bulk of *al-Kafi*'s traditions come from a handful of members of Qum's Ash'ari tribal elite, the collection speaks to an effort to strike a balance between conflicting tendencies within the contemporary Shi'i community.

Traditions circulating in Qum, the region's only Shi'i city-state that had withstood repeated challenges from Sunni Baghdad, presented the imams as possessing near-miraculous knowledge and powers and depicted the twelfth imam's return as imminent. In Baghdad, the Shi'i minority, facing rising Sunni traditionism (typified by the appearance of such great Sunni hadith collections as the *Sahih* of al-Bukhari [d. 256/870]) and hostility to Shi'i messianism, were disavowing the imams' traditions as the source of knowledge and inspiration in favor of rationalist and politically quiescent discourse.

Al-Kafi's traditions downplayed the separatist and messianic tendencies of the previous century, rejected the anti-traditionist tendencies of Baghdadi Shi'is, and countered rising Sunni traditionism with a collection of texts that at once addressed both theological issues and, on a par with contemporary Sunni collections, practical issues.

ANDREW J. NEWMAN

See also Ibn Babawayh; Al-Tusi, Muhammad ibn al-Hasan

Further Reading

Newman. AJN. 2000.

KURDISH

In general, the term *Kurdish* applies to a range of languages and dialects belonging to the Iranian language family spoken in the Kurdish areas, from eastern Anatolia via northern Iraq and northern Syria to western Iran and by significant groups in Georgia and Armenia (see also Kurds). From a perspective of historical linguistics, however, these languages can be divided into Kurdish proper on the one hand and Gurani and Zazaki on the other. The latter two languages derive from a different Old Iranian dialect than does Kurdish. The oft-heard assertion that Kurdish derives from ancient Median is not borne out by the available data.

Kurdish proper can be divided into three groups of dialects: Northern, Central, and Southern Kurdish. Northern Kurdish, which is also known as Kurmanji, is now spoken in Turkey, northern Syria, northwestern Iraq, northwestern Iran, Georgia, and Armenia. Central Kurdish, or Sorani, is spoken in northeastern Iraq and the adjoining regions in Iran. Southern Kurdish dialects, such as Lakki, are spoken in Iran in the provinces Ilam, Kermanshah, and Lorestan. Southern dialects do not have a standard written form and have not yet been adequately studied. Zazaki is spoken in eastern Anatolia in the triangle formed by Diyarbakir, Sivas, and Erzurum. Gurani or Hawrami, once an important literary language in the region, is now spoken by a relatively small number of people in the Iranian province of Kermanshah.

There is no evidence that a significant written literature existed in any of these languages before the late sixteenth century CE. The textual traditions of religious groups such as the Yazidis and Ahl-i Haqq were composed during the medieval period; these were mainly transmitted orally, but writing may have played a role in their genesis. For most forms of written communication, however, Kurds used the dominant language of their region—Arabic, Persian, or Turkish—so that no literary standard languages evolved until later. The existence of a standard language often counteracts a tendency for dialects and subdialects to diverge rapidly.

Their absence in the Kurdish sphere during the medieval period may account in part for the profound differences that developed between, for example, Northern and Central Kurdish. Although the former dialect still has case endings and gender, the latter does not; contacts with Gurani, it seems, caused Central Kurdish to adopt a number of grammatical features of that language, which are unknown in Kurmanji. Therefore, from a grammatical point of view, these dialects are very different from each other. Even subdialects belonging to the same dialect group can show considerable differences. Given the use of languages other than Kurdish for purposes of writing and the considerable similarities in vocabulary, it seems unlikely that dialectal or linguistic differences were perceived as markers of separate linguistic identities during the Middle Ages.

PHILIP G. KREYENBROEK

Further Reading

Kreyenbroek, Philip G., and Stefan Sperl, eds. *The Kurds: A Contemporary Overview*. London and New York, Routledge, 1992.

Kreyenbroek, Philip G., and Christine Allison, eds. *Kurdish Culture and Identity*. London and New Jersey: ZED Books, 1996.

MacKenzie, D.N. *Kurdish Dialect Studies*, 2 vols. London, Oxford University Press, 1961–1962.

KURDS

The word *Kurd* is generally used for an ethnic and linguistic group living in a more or less continuous area from the eastern part of Anatolia, via northern Iraq and northern Syria, to the central western regions of modern Iran. During the medieval period, some Kurdish groups lived in Transcaucasia. An account of Kurdish society and history during the period from the mid-seventh to the sixteenth centuries CE can at best be tentative, owing to the scarcity of reliable data. A contributory factor to these uncertainties is that the word *Kurd* was not necessarily used in medieval sources in the sense it has today. In pre-Islamic, Sasanian Iran, it is thought, the word denoted the largely tribal populations of the mountainous areas to the west of the Iranian heartland, so certain non-Iranian tribes in those areas may have been referred to as *Kurd,* whereas sedentary people speaking an early form of Kurdish may not. Because a significant part of the population in question spoke Iranian languages, however, the word eventually came to be used particularly for speakers of these languages. Except in discussions of historical linguistics, speakers of the Gurani and Zazaki languages are generally regarded as Kurds.

During the period under discussion, Kurdish society was strongly tribal in character, with tribal confederations, (semi-)nomadic tribes, and subtribes and a sedentary population at the bottom of the social structure. Tensions usually existed between the Kurds' aspirations to autonomy and the desire of surrounding states to control them. During the early centuries of Islam, the Kurds were a force to be reckoned with. They are known to have revolted several times against the Umayyads. They supported the 'Abbasid al-Ma'mun against his brother al-Amin in the 810s CE, and they rebelled repeatedly when 'Abbasid power grew weaker during the second half of the ninth century. On the other hand, Kurdish troops, with their reputation for military prowess, were often recruited into the 'Abbasid—and later into the Seljuq—army. Saladin (Salah al-Din, born in 1138 of Kurdish parentage), who defeated the Crusaders and founded the Ayyubid dynasty that ruled in Egypt, Syria, and Iraq, is the best known of many Kurds who achieved fame as military leaders in the Islamic army. Among the Kurdish tribes in the heartlands, Islamization was a slow process, and large tribal groups were still said to be Magians (adherents of a non-Islamic Iranian faith) during the early thirteenth century.

As 'Abbasid power waned, several Kurdish dynasties emerged for a time, most notably the Shaddadids (955–1075) in Transcaucasia, the Marwanids (984–1083) in the region from Diyarbakir in the north to the Jazira area in the south, and the Hasanwayhids (959–1095) in the Zagros region. None of these dynasties seem to have been very influential, and they were quickly defeated when the Seljuqs and others reasserted their authority over the region. The Kurdish areas suffered greatly under the Mongols from 1231 to 1258 and later again under Tamerlane in 1393 and 1401. With the new balance of power between the surrounding Safavid and Ottoman states during the sixteenth century, the Kurds entered a new phase in their history.

PHILIP G. KREYENBROEK

See also Kurdish

Further Reading

Van Bruinessen, Martin. *Agha, Shaikh and State: The Social and Political Structures of Kurdistan*. London and New Jersey: ZED Books, 1992.

Kreyenbroek, Philip G., and Stefan Sperl, eds. *The Kurds: A Contemporary Overview*. London and New York, Routledge, 1992.

Kreyenbroek, Philip G., and Christine Allison, eds. *Kurdish Culture and Identity*. London and New Jersey: ZED Books, 1996.

McDowall, David. *A Modern History of the Kurds*. London and New York: I.B. Tauris, 1996.

INDEX

INDEX

INDEX

INDEX

INDEX

INDEX

INDEX

INDEX

INDEX